D1605617

Jimmy and Rosalynn Carter

Jimmy and Rosalynn
Carter

POWER AND HUMAN RIGHTS, 1975–2020

E. Stanly Godbold, Jr.

OXFORD
UNIVERSITY PRESS

OXFORD
UNIVERSITY PRESS

Oxford University Press is a department of the University of Oxford. It furthers
the University's objective of excellence in research, scholarship, and education
by publishing worldwide. Oxford is a registered trade mark of Oxford University
Press in the UK and certain other countries.

Published in the United States of America by Oxford University Press
198 Madison Avenue, New York, NY 10016, United States of America.

CIP data is on file at the Library of Congress

ISBN 978–0–19–758156–8

DOI: 10.1093/oso/9780197581568.001.0001

1 3 5 7 9 8 6 4 2

Printed by Sheridan Books, Inc., United States of America

TO JEANNIE

IN MEMORY OF MARTIN I. ELZY

FOR MY FATHER AND MY SON

Contents

Acknowledgments

My family comes first. When Jeannie married me on that rainy day in Starkville, Mississippi, December 30, 1988, neither she nor I imagined the life we had ahead. Eighteen months later I was spending long days, weeks, and months in the Carter Library in Atlanta. She helped with the research, made many a trip to Atlanta, kept the rest of our lives afloat, and always believed that we could do it. My stepdaughter Heidi, during her high school years, helped process the voluminous number of photocopies I brought home from the Carter Library. My son Kran, a scholar himself, gave help, encouragement, and plenty of advice. In time, they gave the most precious gift of all in the persons of four beautiful grandchildren: Samuel, Thomas, Maya, and Neha. My parents, Ed and Louise Godbold, would have moved mountains, and almost did, to make certain I would not be tied forever to that cotton farm in Sumter County, South Carolina. At both Duke University and Southern Methodist University, I was fortunate to have excellent professors and intelligent fellow students who stimulated my interest in learning and writing. My mentor at Duke, Robert H. Woody, became a close companion and co-author on one of my earlier books.

Many people, famous and less so, kindly granted me interviews. Their names are listed in the bibliography, but special credit should go to Tip O'Neill, Edmund Muskie, Cyrus Vance, and Stansfield Turner, all of whom granted me extensive amounts of time under what must have been difficult circumstances for them. Steven Hochman, a highly accomplished historian who is a special assistant to Jimmy Carter, had many conversations with me and helped arrange my interviews with the Carters. He read many of the chapters in the final draft and offered excellent corrections and suggstions. Jimmy and Rosalynn Carter granted me interviews, access to papers and photographs, and respected the distance I tried to maintain in order to create a detached work of scholarship. Nevertheless, they deserve the credit for living such incredible and productive lives, creating and preserving the evidence that will serve many generations, and despite human foibles, being both servant and beacon for humankind.

Because this project has spanned more than three decades, to acknowledge properly all the people, institutions, and pets who helped is a task at which this account falls short. Since this volume is a sequel to my *Jimmy & Rosalynn Carter: The Georgia Years, 1924*-1974 (2010), those people and institutions acknowledged in that earlier volume deserve equal credit for their contributions to this one. At the Jimmy Carter Presidential Library in Atlanta, my home away from home for many years, the following administrators and archivists served me patiently and brilliantly: Don Schewe, Martin Elzy, David Alsobrook, Jay Hakes, Robert Bohannan, Susan Ament, Bettie Joe Brown, Betty Egwinike, Gary Foulk, Jim Herring, Yolanda Logan, Shelia Mayo, Ceri McCarron, Mary Anne McSweeney, Sylvia Naguib, Bert Nason, Sonia Robinson, Keith Shuler, Sara Saunders Mitchell, David Stanhope, Chuck Stokely, Jim Yancey, Polly Nodine, and others. Sara Mitchell was particularly helpful in acquiring and processing much of the art work. The staffs of the Georgia Department of Archives and History and the Woodruff Library at Emory University helped in many important ways.

The Gerald Ford Foundation awarded me a grant to research in the Gerald R. Ford Library. The staffs of the presidential libraries of John F. Kennedy, Ronald R. Reagan, George H. W. Bush, and George W. Bush welcomed me and guided my research in their collections. Other libraries where I found collections and able assistance include: Library of Congress, the Oral History Collection at Columbia University, the James Earl Carter Library at Southwestern State University, Lake Blackshear Regional Library, and the Lander University Library.

My home university, Mississippi State, supported me with a job, sabbatical leaves, and occasional research assistance. The staff of Mitchell Memorial Library, especially reference librarian Amanda Clay Powers, guided me through baffling technology as well as assisting with collections, interlibrary loans, and fast responses to my numerous "ask a librarian" questions. The John C. Stennis Oral History Project assisted with my interviews and travel budget. Former students who worked as research assistants include: David Gleeson, Richard Haydel, Kevin Hall, Qiming Han, Todd Herring, David Hirsch, Todd Holden, Tony Iacono, Craig Piper, John Selman, Ryan Semmes, Tommy Upchurch, Kenneth Vickers, and others. Kenneth Vickers and Tommy Upchurch read and critiqued many of the chapters in the first volume, and much of their research contributed to this volume. Non-student volunteer helpers include George Robson, Scott McMurry, Russell Motter, Louise Godbold, John Glass, and Susan Wansbrough.

Two special colleagues who shared many hours in the Carter Library, lunches, visits with families, meetings at professional meetings, lengthy discussions, and exchanges of information deserve my great appreciation. They are Carl Biven of Georgia Tech University and Leo Ribuffo of George Washington University.

Although I worked from primary sources as thoroughly as possible, this book is built upon those of many others who have written about the Carters. They include the excellent studies by the scholars, journalists, biographers, and memoirists whose works are cited in the notes and bibliography. Special thanks go to the distinguished television journalist Mary Beth Durkin of Yellowbrickroad Productions, who jumpstarted my work on Rosalynn Carter and brought me into conversation with others who were helpful, namely, Peter Bourne, Scott Kaufman, Allida Black, and Susan Hartman.

Scholars and friends who read all or parts of the current volume include Martin Elzy, Richard McMurry, Fred Smith, Phil Chase, Kranti Dugar, and Jeannie Godbold. Martin Elzy, the retired assistant director of the Carter Library, gave bibliographical advice as well as suggestions for corrections in the first two chapters. Fred Smith, an accomplished and well-published scholar of twentieth-century America, gave much of his retirement time to helping correct factual errors and put this manuscript into good English and proper scholarly form. Richard McMurry, a much-published and prize-winning Civil War historian, as well as friend for many years, was the kind of sharp, quick, and detailed critic I needed. Kranti Dugar, my son and a fine scholar in his own right, helped with both research and technology questions. Jeri Weiser, a high-tech specialist, solved technical problems quickly and speeded the manuscript to conclusion.

Special thanks go to Phil Chase, editor emeritus of the papers of George Washington and associate professor of history emeritus at the University of Virginia. One of the renowned documentary editors in the country, Phil contributed many days of his time and the advantage of his skill and experience to reading the entire manuscript, making suggestions and corrections, adding research, and editing it. He brought his talent and experience as an historian to discovering and correcting numerous errors that might have otherwise been overlooked. My debt to him is very great. His wife, Jeanne, an enthusiastic cheering squad of one, lifted my spirits when I often needed it, and I believe she is the most positive and optimistic human being I have ever known.

My wife Jeannie was there from start to finish, reading the final manuscript as if it were a book that might be appropriate for her book club and commenting accordingly. All remaining errors remain the sole responsibility of the author.

During the making of this book, a group of wonderful pets gave unconditional love and support and staged frequent interruptions. Most of them were our cats—Baby Mange, Maurice, Houdini, and Tommicat. A couple of fine dogs, Sparkplug and Misty, did their bit to help.

Susan Ferber, executive editor at Oxford University Press, knows how to deal with a wide variety of authors. She has the ability to size up each individual author and give him exactly the right amount of space, advice, and push that is necessary to complete the book. She became a good friend. As an editor she was kind, patient, efficient, and extraordinarily skilled. I would place her a few levels above Maxwell Perkins and suggest that she deserves a biography of her own. I am particularly grateful to her and her colleagues for bringing this book into being.

Coming full circle back to Jeannie, when she made outrageous promises on that chilly, rainy day in 1988, she never dreamed what a wild ride a girl from Chicago, a preschool teacher, was about to take across the South and into the exciting world of research and biography. Always smiling, she is a tower of strength whose dedication helped bring this project to completion. She deserves so much more than a mere dedication.

Introduction

When Rosalynn Carter told a reporter in 1975 that "it's going to happen," she meant that her husband Jimmy would get the Democratic nomination for president in 1976 and that he would win the election. Born three years and three miles apart, theirs is a story of hard work, good luck, and incredible personal and political drama that ultimately sent them to the White House in 1977.

Jimmy Carter grew up on a prosperous farm in Archery, Georgia, where his playmates, nanny, and most of his neighbors were African American. The oldest of four children, his father nicknamed him "Hotshot" and expected him to excel in all that he did. His mother, who became the nation's beloved "Miss Lillian," was a nurse who openly practiced kindness to both blacks and whites and instilled in her son a sense of caring for others. Jimmy's father, "Mr. Earl," became the more formative parent, the model and teacher for Jimmy, whose concern and help for needy neighbors he kept secret. Both parents practiced Christianity, although Mr. Earl took it more seriously. Financially successful, despite the Great Depression, they expected Jimmy and his siblings to become well educated and to make their way in the world.

Rosalynn, also the oldest of four children, was the daughter of a schoolteacher and a bus driver. Petite, pretty, inquisitive, and very intelligent, her childhood changed with the death of her father when she was only fourteen, and her mother had to work at the post office to support herself and four children. Imbued with the missionary spirit typical of Methodists, Rosalynn grew up to be the valedictorian of her class at Plains High School and to attend a junior college in nearby Americus, Georgia. She was still in her teens when Jimmy saw her on the steps of the Methodist Church, fell in love with her immediately, and asked her to marry him. By then, he was a midshipman at the United States Naval Academy, handsome, she thought, in his dress white uniform, and possibly a ticket out of Plains. They were married on July 7, 1946, in a simple ceremony at that Methodist Church. As a young Navy wife, she had to manage the household finances and care for three young sons who were born to her and Jimmy during the early years of their marriage. She traveled from one coast to the other, spent time in Hawaii, met people from all over the country and the world, and generally enjoyed that lifestyle. An honors graduate of the Naval Academy, Jimmy had joined Admiral Hyman Rickover's elite atomic submarine group and had risen rapidly through the ranks until he was ready to command his own submarine.

When Mr. Earl died of pancreatic cancer in 1953, and Miss Lillian told Jimmy that he must come home to run the family business, Rosalynn balked at the idea of moving back to Plains and threatened divorce. She went, however, with her husband, and soon she became his successful business partner in their tiny hometown. When he entered state politics in 1962, Rosalynn discovered that she could be a good campaigner and politician. Helping him to negotiate the labyrinth of changing race relations in the South during the Civil Rights Era, she was as crushed as he in 1966 when he lost the governorship to segregationist Lester Maddox. After adding a daughter, Amy, to their middle-aged lives, and developing their farms and warehouse into a lucrative agribusiness, they vowed never to be defeated again. When, with Rosalynn's help, Carter won the Georgia governorship in 1970, he announced that the time for racial discrimination in Georgia was over, shocking some people who had voted for him but attracting national attention. He and Rosalynn took an unusual interest in international trade and foreign policy, traveled extensively, and set their sights on the presidency. Jimmy had developed a governing style that he would carry to the White House with him, and Rosalynn emerged as a woman with a mind of her own who could plan strategy and grasp complex economic and political issues as well as sew and cook. They believed that they could make a difference in the world and that the best way for them to do it would be through the power of the presidency.

In both their private and public worlds, Jimmy and Rosalynn Carter lived a life of conflict and resolution, triumph and defeat, sickness and health, fame and disgrace, power and helplessness. Married almost thirty years by the time he ran for president, they had reared three sons and were the parents of a nine-year-old daughter. Jimmy was strict and demanding like his father, practicing the tough love that the younger generation did not always understand. Rosalynn was forgiving, kind, helpful, and nonjudgmental, while often balancing domestic life with her public career. Their relationships with siblings, especially Jimmy's brother Billy, and in-laws, especially the powerful Miss Lillian, were often challenging and even maddening. They sometimes disagreed about whether to be Baptists or Methodists and often found themselves too liberal to be completely at ease in their church, but they both remained steadfastly grounded in the Christian faith. In business, beginning with a large inheritance of property, they worked together to become so financially successful that by 1975 they could afford to devote themselves full time to campaigning for the presidency. As the primary business manager, Rosalynn kept the books and often served sandwiches to the clients. Jimmy excelled at marketing and public relations. Although caring for the family, developing their business, involving themselves in church and missionary activities, and enjoying fishing and other outdoor activities dominated their lives, both Carters remained firmly grounded in humanitarian concerns and advancing their knowledge of the humanities. They studied Spanish, read novels and poetry, and became well versed in the commonality of humanity as well as its diversity.

The world stage the Carters proposed to occupy and shape was crowded with problems and challenges. The United States was reeling from the economic and social problems related to the ending of the Vietnam War, the longest in its history at that time. The Watergate scandal in the executive office of the government had forced the first resignation ever of a president, in order for him to escape impeachment, and placed an unelected president in office. The people seemed to have lost faith in their government and to have concluded that all politicians were liars. A major energy crisis caused in large part by US dependency upon foreign oil affected practically every household. The arms race between the United States and the Soviet Union had caused both superpowers to amass huge nuclear arsenals capable of destroying the planet. Emerging nations, if they wished to survive and prosper, were forced to choose one side or the other. Civil wars and political and religious revolutions raged—especially in Iran; persecuted Jews in the Soviet Union, Palestinians in Israel, impoverished blacks in apartheid African countries, and women almost everywhere cried out for help. Rich, comfortable, powerful world citizens as well as religious and government leaders often showed little interest in those who were hungry, homeless, diseased, illiterate, and deprived of basic human rights by tyrants and dictators or governments that placed power and wealth ahead of human needs.

When Jimmy Carter had announced formally on December 12, 1974, that he was a candidate for president of the United States, he believed that he and Rosalynn could bring stability and peace to their country and to the world. As governor and first lady of Georgia, the largest state east of the

Mississippi River, they had weathered many a political and personal battle as they practiced what they hoped to accomplish for the country and the world. Ambitious to create "a more caring society," as Rosalynn put it, they were starry-eyed and determined to succeed as they packed up to leave the Georgia governor's mansion in January 1975 and aim for the White House.

ONE

Candidate from the South, 1975

Two men loaded a truck parked behind the Georgia governor's mansion in Atlanta. Casually dressed in blue jeans and flannel shirts, and wearing gloves for protection against the December chill and their rough work, they could have passed for hired helpers. The younger one, Billy, was stout, jovial, and eager to help his older brother. Taller, leaner, and thirteen years older than Billy, Jimmy was in impeccable physical condition at age fifty, grinning, hurried, happy, determined. He was so confident that within two years' time he would be elected president of the United States that, in Washington, DC, on December 12, 1974, he had declared, "I will be the next President."[1]

No ordinary workers, the Carter brothers were well known in Georgia and beyond, because Jimmy was completing his term as governor. What the public did not know, however, was that Jimmy and Rosalynn Carter, with the help of their closest allies, had been campaigning for the Democratic nomination for the presidency since the fall of 1972. They had invited the leading Democratic candidates for the nomination one by one, to the Georgia governor's mansion and, over drinks, secretly studied them. Some of their drink preferences, especially Edmund Muskie's Scotch and milk, amazed Carter. After meeting his potential rivals, Carter concluded that he was better than any of them. Meeting with the Carters at the governor's mansion, Hamilton "Ham" Jordan, Carter's political adviser since 1966, had outlined a detailed seventy-page plan for victory. Carter had begun to follow it to the letter as early as 1972.

If Carter won the White House, however, it would not be by accident or luck. He and Rosalynn had been executing Jordan's plan subtly for almost two years. Extremely intelligent and willing to work hard, Carter had shrewdly volunteered to be the Democrats' national leader for the off-year elections in 1974, thus quietly placing them in his debt when they won. Rosalynn's political skills and ability to size up candidates had already emerged, perhaps to the amazement of both of them.[2]

In the wake of the Watergate scandal and President Nixon's resignation in August 1974, Carter wisely promised never to tell a lie, to operate an open government in touch with the people, and to deliver fair and compassionate treatment for all Americans. He presented himself as an honest father and husband, businessman and politician, whose experience in the military and in government qualified him for national office. In preparation, as governor he had made trips to Latin America, the Middle East, and Europe. Using the offices of the internationally active Coca-Cola Company, he had created a shadow state department. Running for president, he later said, was his "best way to be myself." He expected to win, but he intended to run if he "only got my vote and Rosalynn's vote."[3] Hamilton Jordan said that "All you ever had to do for Jimmy Carter was to tell him something was impossible and he would usually do it."[4]

Carter labored under the last politically acceptable prejudice, that against Southern White men, but he had already proved that he was an exceptional member of his class. The outgoing governor of Georgia, he had won that office in a tough trek through the tangled web of changing racial relations in the South and the miasma of Georgia politics. On the day of his inauguration, January 12, 1971, he had stunned the audience with his announcement that the day for racial discrimination in Georgia was over, and he had used the power of his office to try to make it so.

An honors graduate of the United States Naval Academy, Carter had worked with the tough-minded and controversial Admiral Hyman G. Rickover, the father of the nuclear navy, who demanded perfection from his juniors and insisted upon intense education for all who would enter the navy. Carter's career in the post–World War II navy ended abruptly in 1953 at the moment when he was ready to assume command of his own submarine, because his father in Plains was terminally ill. After Mr. Earl's death, Jimmy was surprised to learn about his father's charitable nature. He took upon himself Mr. Earl's mantle of social consciousness, business success, and political involvement. As his father lay dying, however, Jimmy yearned to hear his father's approval and feel his embrace, a need that would be a driving force for the rest of his life.

As Jimmy and Billy loaded the truck in late December 1974, Rosalynn Carter cheerfully packed the family's personal belongings inside the governor's mansion for their return to Plains. Her mood was precisely the opposite of what it had been in 1953 when she had vigorously protested her husband's dragging her back to that remote South Georgia town. She had overcome her shyness, learned to give public speeches, and emerged as a quiet but determined feminist. She relished her role as the mother of three grown sons and an eight-year-old daughter. She had learned to manage the staff of a mansion, converse with celebrities of all kinds, deal with the press and security guards, and champion the cause of care for the mentally ill. The skills that she had acquired as a businesswoman who had helped transform the family's farms and warehouse into a multi-million-dollar agribusiness she now applied to her and her husband's expanding political ambition. Much to her amazement, she discovered that she loved being a politician, planning strategy, organizing rallies, and advising her husband on policy statements and the wording of his speeches. Motivated by a strong sense of social justice, intensely devoted to her husband's success, she immersed herself in the campaign.

Those days before and after Christmas 1974 were filled with hope, anticipation, and image-making. The railroad depot in Plains would provide a homey and attractive setting for a presidential campaign, but the serious work would be done in Atlanta, where a large motel at 1795 Peachtree Street NE provided the space and communication facilities necessary for such an enormous campaign. The heart and soul of the campaign, however, were on Woodland Drive in Plains, where the family gathered for Christmas and on many weekends thereafter to plan political strategy. Since they hoped to give as many voters as possible personal contact with an immediate Carter family member, Rosalynn, the three sons and their wives—Jack and Judy, Chip and Caron, Jeff and Annette—would campaign separately from Jimmy and from each other. Lillian Carter's sister, Aunt Sissy Dolvin, and Jimmy's sisters, Ruth and Gloria, promised to help. Jimmy's mother, "Miss Lillian," attracted more attention that the others with her humor and homespun wisdom, and she also took care of Amy when she did not feel like traveling. Brother Billy remained in Plains where he granted colorful, country-boy interviews and operated the family business while the others scoured the nation for votes.[5]

The Carters had promised incoming governor George S. Busbee and his wife that they would vacate the mansion early in order to give the state's new first family time to settle in before the official inauguration. Busbee, who as a member of the assembly had supported Governor Carter, had defeated both Carter's best friend Bert Lance and worst enemy Lester Maddox to win the Democratic nomination and the governorship. Carter liked Busbee, and he and Rosalynn had no regrets about decamping before the end of his term. Rosalynn returned to Plains to unpack boxes and enroll Amy in the second grade. Carter moved into a hotel in Atlanta where he completed his responsibilities to the state while continuing to pursue the presidency as vigorously as a lame-duck governor could.[6]

From the time Carter formally announced his run for the presidency on December 12, 1974, until he left the governorship on January 13, 1975, his days were filled with media attention and frenzied activities that he hoped would catapult him into the White House. Using letterhead paper that announced "Jimmy Carter Presidential Campaign for America's Third Century, Why Not the Best?," he spelled out his gubernatorial accomplishments that had brought positive social, political, economic, and judicial changes, as well as international attention and investment, to Georgia. Two days after his big announcement, with Rosalynn at his side, Carter gave a short humorous speech to some of the nation's most prestigious journalists at the annual Gridiron Club dinner in Washington's Statler Hilton Hotel. He poked fun at the media that had ignored him and at members of Congress who also might want to run for president.[7]

That same day, Patrick Anderson, writing for the *New York Times Magazine*, declared Carter to be "a peanut farmer," who "cheerfully put the knife to his Southern archrival" George Wallace. Carter, Anderson reported, was "a deceptively mild-looking man," whose aides described as being "aloof" and enjoying "neither giving nor receiving compliments." He was, his intimates said, a "cool, self-critical and very private politician."[8]

Carter was no ordinary peanut farmer, but it was a political image he cultivated. He was a wealthy agribusiness man who had made more money in the cotton industry than peanuts, but peanuts recalled the image of the African-American scientist George Washington Carver, whereas cotton reminded one of slavery. Although he, and especially Miss Lillian, did not deny the family's wealth, for purposes of the campaign, he downplayed it.[9]

Private Carter was, but to win the office he sought, he had to create an extroverted public persona. Two days after he joked with journalists at the Gridiron Club, he appeared on the television program *Meet the Press*, watched by seven million viewers and listened to by two and a half million more on the radio. Carter portrayed himself as a liberal on civil rights and environmental issues and conservative on government management. He believed that the government should not waste taxpayer money and that it should be run like a well-organized business. He attacked two of his rivals, Senator Lloyd Bentsen of Texas and Henry M. Jackson of Washington, for their attempts to collect campaign contributions before the law restricting such gifts to a maximum of one thousand dollars went into effect.[10]

Zbigniew Brzezinski, an academic expert on international affairs, wrote Carter that he had done "extremely well" on *Meet the Press* and offered to continue helping with foreign policy, an area where he thought Carter was weak. "I do think that a serious discussion of foreign policy alternatives to present foreign policy is increasingly needed," Brzezinski continued, knowing that he would strike a sympathetic chord with the candidate. Brzezinski had co-founded the Trilateral Commission with David Rockefeller, to study economies in Europe, North America, and Japan, and invited Governor Carter to join it in 1974. Through this group, Carter had met the leading liberal international and national leaders of the day. Brzezinski had been sending Carter position papers during his unannounced campaign. Once Carter's campaign was open and heated, the two men formed a close personal and professional alliance. Jimmy began to address him affectionately by his nickname "Zbig."[11]

Former Secretary of State Dean Rusk, who had grown up in Cherokee County, Georgia, and South Georgia native and prominent Jewish scholar Morris Abram also offered to help. Rusk's suggestions mostly encouraged the Carter team, but Morris Abram, who had become president of Brandeis University, wanted a position in a presidential administration and volunteered to help with the campaign.[12]

Before Christmas, Carter dashed off to San Francisco to give a speech to the North American Congress on Alcohol and Drug Problems, an area where as governor he had created a model for the nation with the help of psychiatrist Peter Bourne. Back in Atlanta a few days later, he taught Sunday School at the Northside Drive Baptist Church, and with Rosalynn he hosted a Christmas Open House at the governor's mansion. After spending Christmas in Plains, he returned to Atlanta and wrote notes to many who had complimented him on his job as governor, saying repeatedly that he cherished the comments that compared him to John Kennedy and that he was proudest of his achievements in race relations. He thanked the top officials in his state government and wished them well.[13]

Media coverage of Carter's candidacy routinely mentioned that he was from the South. Many journalists seemed incredulous that a president might come from a region that had not sent a native and contemporary resident of the South to the nation's top office since 1848. Others speculated that the South had changed and might indeed send a Southerner to the White House. Carl Rowan, in the *Chicago Daily News*, noted that Carter might win over black voters in the South as well as liberal whites, a phenomenon that would be good for both the South and the Democrats. A Republican newspaper in

Minnesota conceded that Carter's belief in racial integration and high ethical standards made him an attractive candidate.[14]

Praise for his integrity and success in streamlining the government of Georgia became a common theme, and even the *New York Times* granted that his "high personal quality and authentic liberal credentials" might surmount the disadvantages of being from the South. On the West Coast, the *Los Angeles Times* with its syndicate of 175 papers found the reputed humble peanut farmer to be an intellectual and sophisticated man, sincerely committed to the elimination of nuclear weapons and convinced that the impossible dream of a stable world could become a reality. Columnist Garry Wills of the Universal Press Syndicate begrudgingly conceded that Carter had a quick mind, considerable wealth, a love of the longshot, and a resemblance to John F. Kennedy that, despite his being "a loner," enhanced his chances to leap from Plains to the White House.[15]

The political climate in early 1975 favored Carter's run for the Democratic nomination, and he had positioned himself well to take full advantage of it. When Nixon resigned the presidency in August 1974 to escape impeachment, and the unelected Gerald Ford ascended to the office and pardoned Nixon, the Republicans unwillingly gave a major gift to any candidate the Democrats might choose. Carter's work as campaign chairman for the election or reelection of all Democrats running in 1974 had given him national exposure and subtle influence within the party. Edward (Ted) Kennedy's withdrawal from the race in September 1974, resulting in the proliferation of possible liberal candidates, could only benefit Carter. Carter's military career and native son status would help him in the South, while his liberal stand on race relations and other social issues would bolster his appeal elsewhere. Carter learned quickly, read widely, and absorbed complicated information that he could use in his speeches. Although he had several good advisers in addition to Rosalynn, he basically had a brain trust of two. Stuart Eizenstat, a savvy attorney who understood domestic policy and economics like few others, gave him practical, political, and substantive advice. Brzezinski, an astute student of foreign policy with hawkish tendencies and a burning ambition for a top spot in a presidential administration, sent Carter some of his recent writings about specific policies.[16]

So confident was Carter that he would win that he informed the majority leader of the House of Representatives, Massachusetts Congressman Thomas P. (Tip) O'Neill, that he would be the 1976 nominee of the Democratic Party. O'Neill, a devout party man almost certain to become the next Speaker of the House in 1976, was shocked that an upstart peanut farmer from Georgia could even entertain such an idea. No Southerner had risen to the presidency during O'Neill's lifetime, and he never thought any would. The popular cliché about Carter being just a rustic peanut farmer obscured the fact that he was a prosperous businessman, had had a distinguished military career, and as governor had acquired extensive knowledge and skills in domestic and international politics.[17]

Although Carter reached out to large contributors who sometimes helped, money remained a problem. In mid-January, Carter and Jody Powell, his press secretary and close friend, began a low-budget trip across the nation to win votes and acquire funds. Wherever they went, Jody handed out flyers and collected names of those who showed interest. They accepted invitations from families to stay or rented cheap motel rooms. From Georgia, they flew to Louisiana, Texas, New Mexico, and California, states where they might face competition from Democrats George Wallace and Henry "Scoop" Jackson and Republican Ronald Reagan. Carter resisted organizing a large paid staff. Since he had limited funds, he collected volunteers and sought to make appearances that would not cost him anything. In San Francisco, for example, he held a news conference and declared that liberals need not be prejudiced against a candidate from the South. A short time later, at the state Democratic convention in Sacramento, he made the same argument, but the audience ignored him.

After that speech, however, Carter walked the aisles of the convention hall greeting delegates who would surely remember his unusual approach. From the convention hall, he took his campaign to the people. He walked the rows of crops in rural areas, presenting himself as a fellow farmer and hard worker. The next day, he flew to Washington, DC, where again he emphasized his liberal credentials at a meeting of the Wildlife Management Institute. He took a stand in favor of conservation, which piqued the interest of a nearby liberal think tank, the Brookings Institute.[18]

Carter returned home to Plains to attend a fundraiser dinner but soon headed to Nebraska, Iowa, and New Mexico, states where he thought he could win early victories and collect volunteers who could help him in the Midwest. He addressed high school assemblies, legislatures, and laborers' luncheons. His national name recognition skyrocketed from 7% to 50% in seven months. His message that he would reduce atomic weapons, create a simple and fair tax structure, decline to punish draft dodgers, and give the nation an adequate defense system attracted good press coverage. Addressing a nation facing an energy shortage, he told them that he had written to President Ford and Congress urging the conservation of fuel by imposing import quotas and standby rationing. Always emphasizing the personal touch, he told them that he was a good Christian family man who would keep the country free and strong.[19]

The campaign was moving so rapidly that Carter had to hire a larger paid staff for research and scheduling. He became adept at handling people, fundraising, and presenting himself as a savvy but honest politician. Wherever appropriate, he reminded his audiences that he had visited that state in 1974 to help their Democratic candidates win elections. Despite his special appeal for African-American voters, many of them did not trust him; Georgia civil rights leader Hosea Williams doubted Carter's avowed commitment to help Blacks, for he had not participated in the civil rights movement. Likewise, many doubtful Jews and Catholics struggled to understand a born-again Baptist whose rural Georgia background seemed very strange to them. Jewish friends, especially prominent members of the Atlanta Jewish community, defended him against charges of anti-Semitism as they attempted to convince Northern voters that Jimmy was really "a good guy."[20]

The Carter campaign's first significant success came in Iowa, but only after many months of hard work in overcoming the voter apathy that it initially encountered there. In February 1975, almost a year before the state's first-in-nation presidential caucuses, Jimmy and Jody Powell drove into a small town near Sioux City, Iowa, where Carter was to give a speech to a group of local Democrats gathered to honor the retiring recorder of Plymouth County. Only a few people came to listen. Unfazed, Carter graciously accepted the proffered remuneration of a free pizza, a movie ticket, and a car wash. He circulated through the small crowd, shaking hands, memorizing names, and directing Jody to record names and contact information. Upon leaving, he had no more money for his campaign coffers than when he arrived, but he had a list of people who would remember him when Rosalynn and others in his campaign contacted them. He also had perfected a person-to-person contact technique that would help him to become known and trusted. Practicing the tenacity he had learned from his father, Carter would return to Iowa again and again in the coming months until he eventually carried the caucuses.[21]

That same month, February 1975, as Carter's name became more familiar to grassroots America, the better known Senator Scoop Jackson of Washington State officially announced his candidacy. An experienced insider with a conservative reputation, especially his past support of the war in Vietnam, Jackson had the potential to become a formidable contestant. Likewise, Senator Lloyd Bentsen of Texas declared his candidacy on February 17, 1975. Bentsen had served four years in the Senate and six in the House. Wealthy from his career in the insurance business, he had defeated Ralph Yarborough in the Democratic primary and George H. W. Bush in the 1970 general election. Like Carter, Bentsen cast himself as a successful businessman who could solve the nation's problems, but Carter's social and economic agenda would likely have a greater appeal than Bentsen's more conservative proposals.[22]

During their life on the road, Jimmy and Jody Powell got plenty of support from helpers back in Atlanta. Tim Kraft, Ham Jordan, and Rosalynn helped plan their schedule, and they provided lists of people to ask for financial contributions. Brzezinski sent Carter speeches about the dangers of military intervention and importance of nonpartisanship in foreign policy, as well as numerous notes about the importance of a Middle East settlement. He included an article by former United Nations Ambassador Charles W. Yost on how quiet diplomacy would promote détente with the Soviet Union and benefit Jewish emigration.[23]

When Carter talked about balancing the budget, Democratic traditions, and making government work more efficiently, members of the crowd sometimes booed him as an "unrealistic" liberal. It was, however, a message, Ham Jordan thought, "in tune with what the American people wanted."[24]

In late January 1975, Carter addressed an audience at Princeton University where he shifted his focus to serious foreign policy issues. He declared that the nation's foreign policy goals should be coordinated with its defense policy and that foreign policy should mirror domestic goals. The cost of defense needed to be reduced, the white elephant B-1 bomber scrapped in favor of a more efficient aircraft, the Soviet Union boldly confronted to reduce nuclear arsenals, and US troops withdrawn from South Korea.[25]

Carter had the ability to incorporate vast amounts of facts and ideas into his speeches, which he often wrote himself. But he also understood that his personal touch might be more important than what he said. After every stop, he wrote letters thanking those who had greeted, helped, or just casually met him. By so doing, he gave them his name written in his own hand to help them remember his face and hopefully vote for him. He wrote to top Democratic Party officials, leading politicians, religious leaders, academic administrators, and others in leadership positions who might keep his name before the public. He mined his Baptist connections, accepted honors from prestigious academic institutions, and even courted "Ann Landers," an extremely popular syndicated personal advice columnist. In real life, Ann Landers was Eppie Lederer, a wealthy, active Democrat who had supported Hubert Humphrey. After visiting with her in Chicago, Carter wrote for her "advice & active political & financial support." Their friendship gave him exposure to the millions who read her daily advice column, Jewish voters, women, and liberal members of his party.[26]

Those aides who worked closely with him in the campaign quickly learned that the public Carter was quite different from the man who was their boss. He was a highly intelligent, self-disciplined, Spartan man who kept his problems to himself, but he drove himself and his staff mercilessly. He quoted time and again Admiral Hyman Rickover, who had once asked him "Why not the best?" Having worked on his campaigns in twenty-one states by the first of March, one staffer complained, "we're all getting to hate Rickover. Jimmy thinks he's Rickover but none of us think we're Jimmy Carter."[27]

At a fundraising dinner in Baltimore on April 2, 1975, Carter declared that since the presidency of the United States was the most important job in the world, he was fortunate to be able to take time from his business in order to campaign full time. He knew that Americans wanted a person of integrity and competence who would not lie to them. He seemed a bit ill at ease when discussing the war in Vietnam, which was a thorny issue for him, because he had earlier supported US involvement. By 1975 he evaded the controversial issue and attempted to correct his earlier unpopular stand by saying he favored withdrawal because the United States was losing. Later that month, the government of South Vietnam collapsed.[28]

More than a week later at a news conference in Little Rock, Arkansas, Carter confronted head-on the question of whether a Southern governor could be elected president. He declared that the South had solved its race issue and removed that millstone from around its neck. "I honestly have not detected any prejudice against me because I am a Southerner," he said. "I've always been liberal on the race issue, on environmental questions and on human justice, but I consider myself to be a tough conservative on the management of government." He declared that he would enter every Democratic primary, defeat Arkansas Governor Dale Bumpers if he decided to run, and not settle for the vice presidency.[29]

Rosalynn had been working quietly at home in Plains with schedules, thank-you notes, and campaign strategy. On April 14, 1975, she became an active campaigner. With the help and company of her friend Edna Langford, whose husband was a Georgia state senator, she set out for Florida in Rosalynn's green Chevrolet, rather than Edna's Cadillac. They knocked on doors, visited television and radio stations, and met people in their gardens or on the streets. Rosalynn introduced herself as "Mrs. Jimmy Carter" and suggested that radio and television emcees interview her. When they did not know what questions to ask, she gave them the questions, told them Jimmy's story, and asked for the listeners' support. Rosalynn and Edna, two middle-aged women traveling alone, reinforced the cause of women's rights that was getting nationwide public attention. After two weeks of physically grueling activity, they returned to Plains where Rosalynn beamed with self-confidence. "I know we can do it," she told Jimmy.[30]

After resting for a week at home with Amy, Rosalynn went to Iowa for the first of many trips, where she visited 105 communities. Following a carefully planned itinerary, she returned to Florida, then went on to New Hampshire and more New England and Midwestern states. She stopped in Mississippi and often spent her evenings learning about other candidates, issues, and how to raise money. Having worked in the Carter warehouse, she could easily discuss the price of fertilizer and the impact Nixon and Ford's embargo on grain had on Midwestern farmers. She gathered information and names to take back to campaign headquarters in Atlanta.[31]

Jimmy went to Washington in May to meet with Admiral Rickover and others who might help him. He stayed overnight with Peter Bourne and his wife Mary King, who introduced him to a few members of Congress. From there, he went to Boston to meet with Harvard professors. He addressed businessmen of all faiths in Concord, New Hampshire, gave radio interviews in Massachusetts, worked the crowds in Buffalo and New York City, gave a speech in Atlanta, and then joined Andrew Young to receive an honorary degree from Morehouse College. After seven grueling days, he arrived home to learn from Jody Powell that a *Christian Science Monitor* poll showed him ahead of his competitors. He invited Pat Caddell, the pollster for George McGovern in 1972, to join the campaign. A twenty-six-year-old Harvard University graduate and South Carolina native, Caddell had attached himself to liberal political candidates and promoted the idea that the path to victory was paved by the alienated voter, a notion that appealed to the Carters.[32]

Jimmy and Rosalynn welcomed the competition from more Democrats who entered the race, because multiple candidates would divide votes among themselves and make Carter appear a more attractive candidate. It would be difficult for new entrants to compete with someone who had been running since 1972. Duke University President and former North Carolina Governor Terry Sanford declared his intention to run in May. The following month, Governor Milton Shapp of Pennsylvania declared at a National Governors' Conference in New Orleans. Sargent Shriver, a brother-in-law to Ted Kennedy, picked up the Kennedy mantle and surprised no one with his announcement on July 15. Senator Birch Bayh of Indiana was more reticent, partly because his wife was battling cancer and had a career of her own that would not be compatible with the campaign lifestyle, but he ventured into the fray in October. Although some of these candidates were more liberal than Carter and possibly even better known, Carter, by virtue of his work in the 1974 Democratic reelection campaigns, had attained a strong position in the party.[33]

All eyes remained on the feisty former governor of Alabama. Confined to his wheelchair since an assassination attempt in May 1972, George Wallace remained a formidable opponent. Although he did not announce his candidacy until November 12, 1975, it seemed clear that he had not abandoned his dream of becoming president. The famed segregationist governor had a conservative following in the South, the Midwest, and even in New England. Although New Hampshire, according to a Wallace spokesman, was "a stronghold of Wallace support," Wallace did not enter that primary because he wanted to concentrate on Florida. When opening his campaign headquarters however on May 14, in Concord, New Hampshire, "a stronghold of Wallace support," Carter leveled a major attack against his fellow Southerner. "When George Wallace was standing in the school house door," he said, "playing games with the lives of the people of Alabama, I was in Georgia trying to put my business back together, following a boycott initiated because I was the only businessman in my hometown to refuse to join the White Citizen's Council." Carter acknowledged that many of Wallace's supporters had voted for him because of their frustration with inefficient government, but "the vote that Wallace received because of racial prejudice . . . he can keep."[34]

Appealing to conservative, patriotic voters who might have supported Wallace, Carter strongly supported President Gerald Ford's use of force to rescue the crew of the *Mayaguez*, a merchant ship with a crew of forty that had been seized by the Khmer Rouge in Cambodia. Despite the fact that more American lives were lost than saved, and the international community was horrified by President Ford's shocking display of machismo, the electrifying news made Jerry Ford a patriotic hero. By endorsing Ford's action, Carter hoped to win the votes of some conservatives.[35]

Leaving the campaign trail briefly, Carter attended a Trilateral Commission meeting in Japan. Following a greeting by Japanese hosts who had opened a zipper company near Macon, Georgia, when he was governor, Carter had planned to address a meeting of foreign correspondents. Since that group had engaged another speaker, he had to settle for a poorly attended luncheon quickly arranged by Peter Bourne, the psychiatrist and friend from Georgia who now worked as his political adviser, and the American Chamber of Commerce. Despite the small audience, on May 29 Carter delivered a major foreign policy address. Written largely by Zbigniew Brzezinski and Richard N. Gardner, both Trilateral Commission members and academic experts on foreign policy at Columbia University, the speech outlined his foreign policy for Asia.

Although few voters seemed to be interested in it, Carter's speech gave a clear summary of his goals for Asia. The United States would honor its commitments to Asian countries, he said, and move toward normalization of relations with China. He would withdraw US troops from South Korea and press for human rights in North Korea. The security of Japan, he promised, was also the security of the United States. The goals of US foreign policy, he contended, should be national security, "peacefully" promoting democracy, and cultural exchanges. Reassuring his Japanese hosts, he remarked that he was aware that the Arabs had the oil that many other countries, especially Japan, needed. Since the availability of that fuel might depend upon peace in the Middle East, Carter attempted to explain his country's relationship with Israel. Israel did not expect US military intervention in its behalf, he said, but Israel wanted the military capacity to defend itself, moral support, and reconciliation of differences among all parties that the United States could provide.[36]

Carter understood the world, the place of the United States in it, and the awesome power of the presidency. He told a group of US businessmen in Tokyo that the Ford, Nixon, and Johnson administrations had erred with excessive secrecy in foreign affairs, and he argued that the United States could keep its treaty obligations with South Korea without supporting "a particular leader," referring to Park Chung-hee whom the United States considered repressive. His speech attracted virtually no attention back home, but it endeared him to his fellow Trilateral Commissioners. Responding to the speech, Richard Holbrooke, managing editor of *Foreign Policy*, offered to help with the campaign.[37]

The day that Jimmy addressed the businessmen in Tokyo, Rosalynn helped the citizens of Salem, New Hampshire, celebrate their 225th anniversary. After thanking the organizers for the invitation, she talked about the history of their town, compared it to Plains, and indicated that she and Jimmy were just ordinary people. "We live in a great country. I love it, and I know that it can be—and will be in the future—even greater," she said.[38]

Despite her disclaimer, Jimmy and Rosalynn were no ordinary people, and they soon discovered that the summer of 1975 was no time for a vacation. Jimmy sped away to Alaska with Peter Bourne, thanking all he met there with notes claiming meeting them had been the "greatest day" in his life. In Chattanooga he attacked Secretary of State Henry Kissinger verbally for being "too inclined to get militarily involved in other nations," and he pored over Senator Sam Nunn's Judicial Commission study for ideas on how to reform the federal judiciary. He kept in touch with Ham Jordan, who advised him on the financing of the campaign and the need for federal matching funds. At the headquarters on Peachtree Street, Madeline F. McBean, Rosalynn's special assistant, wrote the president of Southwestern Bank & Trust Company in Oklahoma City that the campaign "is going extremely well all over the country, and things are wildly hectic here at the national headquarters."[39]

At the Washington Press Club on July 11, 1975, Carter delivered the first of many speeches about energy. The country was in a severe energy crisis, he warned, caused by the skyrocketing cost of imported oil from Organization of the Petroleum Exporting Countries (OPEC) countries. He deplored the fact that the Ford administration had no energy policy and allowed the country to be blackmailed by Arab nations. He called for a bold plan to make the nation energy self-sufficient by using nuclear power more effectively. The government should control the importation of oil, enforce anti-trust laws, monitor electric power companies that charged too much, reduce waste, and promote the use of coal, solar energy, wind turbines, and heavy-water breeder reactors. It should also initiate an international conference on energy. "We need strong leadership, and we need it now!," he declared in a letter to an admirer.[40]

Carter promised to deliver that leadership. He welcomed the law limiting campaign contributions to one thousand dollars per contributor; by the middle of July he had raised $350,663. He hoped that his success outside Georgia would prove to citizens of his home state that he was a viable candidate who could defeat Alabama's Wallace, who had not officially announced yet, and President Ford, the likely Republican nominee. He made a plan to attack Wallace on his failures in Alabama and Ford for his nonexistent energy policy and dependence on Henry Kissinger in foreign affairs.[41]

The structure of the Carter campaign, well hidden from the public, became larger, tighter, and better constructed as the weeks passed. Congressional legislation that limited contributions to $1,000 and required candidates to raise a minimum of $5,000 in multiple amounts of $250, or less, reinforced the campaign's calculated appeal to the "little people." Furthermore, candidates who received 15% or more of the popular vote in every state could get a proportional number of the delegates. The 3,071 delegates to the national convention would be chosen in the state primaries and caucuses. Seeking those delegates, the Carter team raised money in a variety of ways, ranging from cutting costs to active outreach to every member of the campaign. Chip Carter asked people in the streets for $10 to help his Daddy win. Fundraisers planned dinners, concerts, and a telethon. Carter's long-time political adviser Charles Kirbo asked Morris Dees, a noted civil rights lawyer and political activist, to head a national finance campaign. Dees had done it for the George McGovern presidential campaign in 1972 and was highly praised by Colorado Senator Gary Hart, the author of *Right from the Start: A Chronicle of the McGovern Campaign* that was virtually the bible for the Carter campaign.[42]

Rosalynn stepped up her effort to get her husband's name and accomplishments before the public. Petite, and possessing boundless energy and a sweet, lilting Georgia accent, she gave Carter a boost that no other candidate's spouse could replicate. She told 350 women at a $25 per plate luncheon that by the time the election of 1976 rolled around, everyone would know about Jimmy Carter because she was going to tell them, and the ladies listening to her were going to help. She said their campaign had already qualified in eleven of the twenty states needed to receive federal funds. She must work harder, she said, because her son Jack and his wife Judy would soon have a baby and thus be less available to campaign, an announcement that no doubt thrilled the ladies. Jimmy and Rosalynn were thrilled themselves when their first grandson, Jason, was born on August 7, 1975. But Rosalynn did not miss a beat on the campaign trail. When Jimmy returned home from his own campaigning, she took intense interest in where he had been, the size of the crowds, and the amount of money he had raised. Ham Jordan told a campaign speech writer that Rosalynn "wants to be first lady as bad as he wants to be president." "Hell," he added, laughing, "She wants it worse than he does."[43]

Throughout the summer and fall Rosalynn hardly rested. In Dallas she listened to bad jokes about peanuts and attempted to slice an atrociously baked and decorated "peanut cake" that had supposedly been made from her own recipe. She had to care for her wardrobe and make sure she had a wig ready when she needed it. In Washington Rosalynn made her debut on the stage at Constitution Hall in July 1975 when, with knees shaking, she narrated Aaron Copland's *A Lincoln Portrait* as part of a performance by Leonard Bernstein's orchestra to celebrate the Fourth of July. Two thousand guests were in the hall, and Rosalynn had not had time to rehearse. Gaining confidence, she sometimes gave five or six speeches a day and handed out leaflets before dawn at factory gates. Overcoming her natural shyness, Rosalynn telephoned hundreds of potential donors to ask for money, and she monitored the travels of her three sons. Meanwhile, Jimmy focused on foreign policy, beefing up his promises when Brzezinski sent him more facts about US-USSR détente and the need to negotiate with clear US *"political objectives."*[44]

Although Carter allowed the *Atlanta Constitution* to publish a picture of him barefooted and relaxed in Plains, he peppered the accompanying interview with his plan to give the nation a guaranteed minimum income, a national health plan, a balanced budget, a streamlined government, and a way to "cool off our coziness with the Soviet Union." He said that he welcomed the hard campaign road ahead. In no way was he surprised when Gerald Ford, the only unelected president in US history, announced on July 8 that he would be a candidate for the Republican nomination.[45]

Unsuspectingly, Ford gave Carter a lucky break. When he announced that he had chosen Georgian Howard (Bo) Callaway, an old Carter adversary, to manage his campaign, there was a roar of applause in the Carter campaign headquarters. Carter had attempted to win the governorship in 1966 partly because he wanted to defeat his archrival Callaway. Although Lester Maddox had defeated both of them, Carter had proven that he could defeat the wealthy Republican at home. Slyly, Carter said, "I was well-pleased to know that Bo will be campaign manager for him. I think that all of us are familiar with Bo's strengths and weaknesses . . . as I am sure he is familiar with ours."[46]

The revelry was short-lived. Tim Kraft, the New Mexican in charge of the Plains states, insisted that the campaign must concentrate on Iowa. He convinced Ham that although allocation of time and funds to all fifty states was a good idea, much more should be given to the states that had the earliest caucuses and primaries: Iowa, Oklahoma, New Hampshire, and Florida. Those states would attract the most media attention and thus raise the national profile of the campaign.[47] Complaining that Carter's son Jeff was "not doing [his] job [paying bills] right," he requested that Ham allocate $18,125 from their low budget operation to Iowa because a victory there would be critical to winning the nomination. When Rosalynn planned to visit the state in early September, he gave her a detailed itinerary. Although she wanted to make her trip solo, Kraft planned to drop in on her a couple of times. Rosalynn, however, did not need supervision. In Iowa, she charmingly won the confidence of undecided steering committee members and their wives and soon had them committed to her husband.[48]

Carter, with seemingly boundless energy and an equal amount of determination, did not become discouraged by small turnouts. In state after state, he presented his message that he wanted to cut the federal income tax in half, treat the rich and poor the same, and double the current tax on capital gains. He criticized President Ford for being unwilling to stand up to the big oil companies and not working out a program for reduced consumption and alternative forms of energy. Yet, he reacted positively when Ford's secretary of state, Henry Kissinger, announced on September 1, 1975, that he had communicated to Israel promises that Egypt would cease acts of hostility, an unexpected development that Carter hoped might be a first step toward easing tension in the Middle East.[49]

Carter's many friends helped with the campaign. Bert Lance loaned him his new plane, which Carter said allowed him to visit and hold his infant grandson Jason for the first time and facilitated his fundraising. Charlie Kirbo asked people across the country for money, and he personally sent a check for $1,000. His wife gave $965. Atlanta attorney Bob Lipshutz and his wife Betty each contributed. To his sister-in-law Sybil Carter, Jimmy wrote, "yours is the greatest contribution, taking care of things in Plains while I'm gone! Love, J."[50]

In September and October, Carter and his family campaigned from New Hampshire to Florida. In early September, the Carter family blanketed New Hampshire in an intensive five days of seeking votes. Jimmy visited ten towns, Rosalynn five, Jack and Judy four, Chip and Caron three, before they all converged on Manchester. In nearby Springfield, Massachusetts, Carter told people that he favored revenue-sharing funds going directly to local governments instead of being channeled through states. At the University of Massachusetts in Amherst, he informed students that racial integration was the best thing that had ever happened to Southern schools. In October, at Bethune-Cookman College, a traditionally African-American school in Daytona Beach, Florida, he maintained that Martin Luther King Jr., had liberated Whites as well as Blacks and that African Americans needed to be incorporated into the national decision-making process.[51]

Although the Carter campaign had not been slowed by it, the team was jolted on September 22, 1975, when a mentally deranged woman in San Francisco attempted to assassinate President Ford, the second attempt on his life that month. Rosalynn reacted immediately, hoping that Ford and other presidential candidates would reduce their public appearances in order to discourage copycats. She doubted that any of them, including Jimmy, would do it and hoped that the government would step up security for all of them. Her husband was not receiving Secret Service protection because he had not yet qualified for federal campaign funds, but only a week later when Carter qualified as a major candidate, the agents arrived in Plains. Relieved, Rosalynn kept to herself whatever fears she might have had for Jimmy's safety.[52]

A homebody, Rosalynn cherished those times that the campaign brought the family together in Plains to plan their next moves. When they won, she told Jimmy, the Little White House would be in Plains.[53] In the meantime, she planned the schedule for family members and traveled alone giving speeches that gave a human touch to her husband's promises.

As he worked through the last days of October, Carter adjusted his speeches to his audiences. He promised attendees at an American Federation of Labor and Congress of Industrial Organizations (AFL-CIO) convention in Savannah that jobs for Americans would be the key to balancing the budget. In Oxford, Mississippi, he labeled George Wallace "a perennial loser" and President Ford "lazy." He told that Southern crowd that the nation should not have to help New York City out of its financial difficulty. A straw poll in Iowa showed Carter at the head of the pack, and Sumter County raised funds for him to campaign in New Hampshire. Carter himself declared that "running for President has not been an ordeal for me." Despite spending twenty-four or twenty-five days a month outside Georgia, he contended, "I feel mentally and physically more relaxed and more confident than I did at the beginning." By the end of October 1975, major newspapers were declaring Carter to be the front runner.[54]

Since the first test would be in Iowa caucuses little more than three months away, Kraft and the Carters continued to target that state. A Jefferson-Jackson

Day fundraising gala at Iowa State University gave them the perfect opportunity. Carter's friends streamed into Ames and scattered around the arena where all the Democratic candidates would speak. Numerous journalists dotted the large audience. Rosalynn handed out Carter buttons to those in the front row of the balcony, where they would be easily seen by the television cameras. Many US newspapers reported that Carter was strong in Iowa.

In Iowa, Carter demonstrated his ability to appear to be on both sides of a political issue when Catholics demanded to know his stand on abortion. Carter said he opposed abortion personally, but he would support the Supreme Court decision, *Roe v. Wade*, which made it legal. The ambiguity of his answer made it seem to the pro-life faction that he agreed with them, but those who favored the Court decision also thought he was on their side.[55]

Shaping his life story into a fashion that would win votes, Carter published his campaign autobiography, *Why Not the Best?*, on October 30 with Broadman Press in Nashville, Tennessee, the publisher for the Southern Baptist Convention. Cast in such a way that it might have passed for inspirational literature, the book took its title from Jimmy's famous interview with Admiral Hyman Rickover in 1949. In the book, Carter told his own story, couched in positive and optimistic terms, emphasizing his values and discussing his military career. He did not comment on his alleged "born again" experience, or any other details of his life that might have made him a questionable candidate. Carter had written the book in bits and pieces in airports between flights or on the back seats of automobiles. Using quotations from Reinhold Niebuhr, Bob Dylan, and Dylan Thomas, he criticized current pop culture and urged public officials to be trustworthy. An enthusiastic local Georgia reviewer declared the book would help readers and voters understand what made Jimmy tick, a man equally at home with kings or on the family farm. The book would also help them to understand why Jimmy Carter was the best person to be president.[56]

Jimmy dedicated his book to his mother and his wife, but he spent notable space discussing his father and his Southern heritage. He remembered Mr. Earl as "an extremely competent farmer and businessman," a good tennis player, a party goer with a sense of humor, and a dedicated public servant. But his father was also "a stern disciplinarian" who punished Jimmy "severely" when he misbehaved. Carter remembered six whippings, with no chance to defend himself, when his sister Gloria accused him of wrong doing. The father expected his eldest son to work long hours on the farm with little or no reward for his labors, a trait that Jimmy himself already mimicked in his relationships with his sons and closest staff members.

Despite some good times fishing and hunting with his father, Jimmy always felt that he did not measure up and must be on guard for criticism or punishment that would surely come if he made a misstep. Such a life on a prosperous farm in the Deep South might build character and inspire ambition, but Carter was apprehensive that his home in Plains might be an impediment to his drive for the presidency. Hence, he asserted repeatedly that Plains was a microcosm of the nation and proof that people of all races and types could work together in harmony.[57]

The people of Plains swelled with pride for their hometown boy. On Saturday night, November 8, Jimmy told a cheering crowd of 300 of them that "It could only have happened . . . in Plains, because this is where the man grew up . . . met his wife, raised his family, and most of all came to love his fellowman more than his own self." Jimmy used the word "love" freely in conversation, speeches, and letters, a word choice not typical of other politicians. Since Plains had so few voters, Carter did not stay long but went to Iowa and Colorado, where he promised to reduce the waste in the Pentagon and vigorously criticized the Central Intelligence Agency (CIA) for its violations of human rights. These themes did not go unnoticed by the US military or those who served in the CIA.[58]

Even as he traveled nationally, Carter began to get support in the South from liberals, African-American leaders, and many women for his determined campaign against George Wallace. So popular did he appear to be in the South that his rivals Wallace, Jackson, Bentsen, and Sanford skipped a regional meeting in Atlanta because they surmised that it would not gain them any delegates. Not only in the South, but also in New England and Iowa, the Carter dark horse picked up speed.[59]

Carter had come to realize that as a Southerner and a Baptist, he would have to work to win the Jewish vote. Growing up in rural Georgia, he had known only a few Jewish merchants in Americus; his knowledge of Jewish culture came mostly from his study of the Old Testament. In the governor's mansion, however, he had won the support and respect of such men as Stuart Eizenstat and Robert Lipshutz, as well as other prominent regional Jewish leaders. Among them, Morris Abram, president of Brandeis University and a native of Fitzgerald, Georgia, had noted the "quiet eloquence" of Carter's speeches. Thinking Abram might be of help to them, Jimmy and Rosalynn had invited him to the mansion for breakfast, whereupon Jimmy told him that he did not know many Jews outside Georgia and asked for his help. Morris had arranged for him to address the Einstein College of Medicine in Palm Beach, Florida, in February 1975. When Rose Kennedy heard his speech, she remarked that his looks reminded her of her son Jack. Abram thought it strange that since he and Jimmy shared a common background, he had heard so little about him during Carter's public career in Georgia. Nevertheless, he supported him and defended him as a liberal who should not be denigrated because of his religion or Southern heritage. Abram criticized Carter's "provincial staff," however, notably Hamilton Jordan and Jody Powell, who he cynically described as mere "carriers of his sedan chair."[60]

Carter disagreed vehemently with Abram's criticism of Jordan. "Hamilton," he later said, "had an incredibly developed ability to take a whole complicated, morass of issues and items and ideas and put them in a cohesive and understandable form." Although Hamilton got a lot of credit for putting together the 1976 campaign plan, in reality, according to Carter, Hamilton based it on "a number of sessions at the Governor's Mansion when we planned the campaign collectively." Consolidating remarks by Jimmy, Rosalynn, Don Carter, Peter Bourne, Jody Powell, and Charles Kirbo, Hamilton produced the famous plan for victory in secret long before Carter announced his candidacy.[61]

Carter and his inner circle never warmed up to Abram, who had long ago left the South for England, Chicago, and New York City. Their childhood ties to the same South Georgia soil had not bonded the Baptist politician and businessman with the Jewish lawyer and scholar. Since Abram had originally supported Scoop Jackson, Carter may not have trusted him, but he doubted that Abram could contribute significantly to his campaign and turned to a few Jewish attorneys in Atlanta whom he had met during his gubernatorial years. Although Carter had made earlier campaign references to the Jewish vote, he began to seek it seriously in November 1975. When the United Nations declared that Zionism was racist, Carter argued that it was "a ghastly and reprehensible mistake." The Jewish people had fought for their identity for over two thousand years, he said, and the UN would surely lose support by labeling them racist. He noted, not so subtly, Jewish promotion of human rights in the United States and globally.[62]

Human rights, especially in its anti-Soviet manifestations, appealed to the Polish émigré Zbigniew Brzezinski, who saw an advantage in connecting his own career to Carter's. Ambitious to become an insider in a presidential administration, he sent the man from Plains information about foreign affairs, a campaign contribution check from his wife, and a memorandum from

Henry Kissinger about China. Kissinger and Brzezinski believed that the United States should try to block a China/Soviet reconciliation by offering significant aid to China. In addition to the advice, Zbig flattered Jimmy: "I am delighted to see a key member of our Trilateral Commission doing so well."[63]

During the last two months of 1975, the Carters' pace did not slacken. Campaigning had become a way of life for them and their message and their style were well established. In her interactions with individuals and groups, Rosalyn offered a soft human touch, showing she cared about them and promising that her husband would make their lives better. Carter made promises and presented himself as one of the people, but he also had solid factual information to criticize the current administration and build a platform. His promises were so vast that most people could not remember them, but they did note that he seemed to be honest, promised not to tell a lie, and offered a breath of fresh air after the Nixon scandals.

Doubling his efforts, Carter had his assistants write thank you notes to small contributors, sought friendships with rock musicians, and generated more posters displaying his image. The Allman Brothers, a popular Southern country blues and rock band, gave a fundraising concert in Georgia that netted $64,051 for the campaign. Carter hired a professional photographer who advised him to look at the camera and avoid his tendency to "slight the wife unless she's pretty." Jimmy laughed and promised to look at the camera and "at ugly women."[64]

Joking aside, Rosalynn knew how to use a makeup rag and look at the camera. She also had an effective strategy to raise money. She would go into a state first, attend teas and coffees, ask for volunteers, and then her sons would follow to ask for money. "Mom does a wonderful job of firing people up," Chip said as he followed up on one of her appearances in New Hampshire. In Jackson, Mississippi, Rosalynn called the state Democratic Party chairman just to tell her she was thinking of her. Rosalynn was forty-eight, but looked younger. Her striking appearance, intriguing soft accent, and personal touch, reaped huge benefits in money and votes.[65]

Jimmy carried a more sophisticated substantive message. In blunt terms, he laid out his policies. He demanded that the CIA be reformed; its role in the assassination of foreign leaders and other illegal activities had been exposed under Ford's leadership. Likewise, Kissinger's "Lone Ranger" diplomacy must be ended, he said, and economic stability and judicial reform should guarantee justice for all and a "government as good as the people."[66]

He favored strict registration of handguns, and he often emphasized the vital importance of peacemaking and developing a viable energy policy. He saw issues concerning the Middle East, the State of Israel, and energy as interrelated, and he increasingly used the term "human rights" in his speeches.

By the end of 1975, human rights had emerged as the central theme of his campaign. Carter's advisers believed this focus to be a pragmatic way to win votes. Stuart Eizenstat, the campaign's director of issues, pressed Carter to verbalize his abhorrence of Soviet discrimination against Jews and demand that they be allowed to emigrate to Israel and elsewhere. Eizenstat's concern for Jewish refugees meshed with Carter's own experience in Georgia regarding the discrimination against African Americans, his and Rosalynn's religious dispositions, and political expediency. All fell under the umbrella of human rights.[67]

In December 1975, one full year since Carter had formally announced and three years since he had begun quietly campaigning, he assessed his situation. He had collected information from experts in such areas as nuclear armaments, Korea, laws of the sea, foreign policy, loss of confidence in government, human welfare, and national defense. He had learned to finesse questions he could not answer. Sizing up the opposition, he had studied the platforms of every other presidential candidate. He thought that if, as a Southerner, he could trounce Wallace, he would easily move to the head of the pack of Democratic candidates. He expected the incumbent president Gerald Ford to win the Republican nomination, although his staff kept a wary eye on Ronald Reagan, the former governor of California, who had announced his candidacy on November 20 and appeared to be a strong challenger to Ford. Early in 1976, Carter announced proudly that "There is no evidence of sectional prejudice, and being a Southerner running for the presidency is no handicap."[68]

"It's Going to Happen"

"I just assume it's going to happen," Rosalynn proclaimed early in 1976. Before any votes were cast in state caucuses or primaries, she believed that Jimmy would win the Democratic nomination. For more than three years, they had been working diligently to gain control of the party and boost Carter's image as an honest outsider who would bring justice to Washington and peace to the world. Despite her vigorous protest of her husband's unilateral 1953 decision to return to Plains, the past two decades had convinced her that he had made the right choice. "I was wrong," she said. "I love being home." Expecting to become First Lady, she continued that "if I could build the White House anywhere, it would be right here [in Plains]."[1]

Neither Jimmy nor Rosalynn, however, dared take anything for granted. The Carters believed that the man Jimmy had to beat was Senator Henry "Scoop" Jackson, an ardent anti-Soviet, social liberal who believed that the Vietnam War was necessary. To defeat him and other rivals, the Carter campaign created the image of Carter as a man who would not lie, was compassionate, progressive, patriotic, and a family man in tune with the will of the people. His sweet, intelligent, hard-working, and ambitious wife planned to leave no stone unturned in their quest for the White House. The Carters planned to enter every state primary and caucus to procure delegates and to attract media attention. They gave numerous interviews, and he managed to get his photograph on the covers of both *Time* and *Newsweek*.[2] They posed as ordinary people, and they planned to have as many personal contacts with as many voters as possible.

Concentrating on Iowa, the Carters had made multiple trips there in 1975. Rosalynn asked people about themselves and Jimmy postured as a farmer no different from those whose votes he sought.[3] Avoiding any hint of wealth for both political and economic necessity, he often shared a hotel room with Jody Powell. Jody, when scheduling Jimmy's Iowa appearances, tricked him into appearing on a local Iowa television channel wearing a chef's hat while explaining to the audience how to fry fish.[4]

Iowans may not have questioned the candidate's ability to fry fish, but they did question his position on abortion and women's rights. Carter explained that he supported the Supreme Court decision in *Roe vs. Wade* that upheld a woman's right to decide, but he and Rosalynn personally opposed abortion. Both of them supported ratification of the Equal Rights Amendment (ERA) to the Constitution, which would guarantee gender equality. On January 19, 1976, Iowa Democrats gave him 27.6% of the votes cast in their caucuses, whereas Birch Bayh got 13%, Fred Harris 10, Morris Udall 5, Sargent Shriver 3, and Scoop Jackson only 1.[5]

The abortion issue revealed Carter's ability to compromise, to be politically evasive, and to win votes on both sides of an issue; he offered some thing to those who favored a woman's right to choose as well as those who categorically opposed abortion. His being "hazy" or "ambiguous" on the issues attracted the attention of major journalists and indicated that he and his advisors had studied "the inner workings of the press." His well-planned videos and meetings with grassroots voters captured the attention of "elite political reporters" who would boost his national image and name recognition.[6]

The Iowa results also reflected Rosalynn's hard work planning and executing strategy as well as advising Jimmy about issues and tactics. She rarely campaigned with Jimmy in the same place at the same time. Carter was in New York City on the night of the Iowa caucuses when Jody Powell called to tell him the news. From Plains, Rosalynn happily reported that Iowa put him "on the political map."[7]

As Carter's prominence as a candidate grew, the press and the public took more interest in his criticism of the CIA. President Ford had issued an order prohibiting the assassination of heads of state, which was believed to have happened during the Kennedy, Nixon, and Johnson presidencies. Working with the Carter campaign, Stuart Eizenstat recommended that the CIA should not be allowed to do domestic intelligence gathering, should not track US citizens abroad, should not become involved in the change of government in a foreign country, and should be subject to civilian oversight. The agency's director, Eizenstat argued, should resist political pressure, because the current director, George H. W. Bush, had served President Nixon better than he had served the nation. The CIA, he believed, should be a high-level channel through which the National Security Council could advise the president and recommend action he might take.[8]

In Mississippi, a state where Carter's plan to reform the CIA would not have been warmly received, he lost badly to George Wallace, whose state rights position had a great appeal there. Carter was little known in the Magnolia State, although he had campaigned at Mississippi State University and very small gatherings elsewhere. The state Democratic Party was divided into the Regulars—mostly white, traditional Democrats—and the Loyalists—a new faction known as the Mississippi Freedom Democratic Party that had sprung up before the 1964 presidential election. The latter achieved fame in 1968 when delegate Fannie Lou Hamer had threatened to nominate Edward Kennedy for the presidency. Pat Derien and her husband Hodding Carter III, who published the liberal *Delta-Democrat Times* in Greenville, bankrolled the Freedom Democrats and endorsed Carter in 1976. Carter thus allegedly healed "a nasty split between the warring white and black factions," according to journalist Bill Minor, but he collected only 28% of the Democratic votes cast to Wallace's 42%.[9]

Other caucuses gave the Carters necessary victories. In Oklahoma, where native son Senator Fred R. Harris was not very popular, a large Baptist population seemed primarily interested in oil, agriculture, and welfare reform. Carter promised them most of what they wanted: opposition to deregulation of "old Oil" but limited deregulation of natural gas; promoting the export of farm products; and restructuring the welfare system to prevent fraud. Sensing an opportunity, both Jimmy and Rosalynn spent hours on the telephone; Rosalynn called twenty people in Tulsa on Election Day, February 7, who in turn bragged to their friends that they had received her calls. Carter walked away with a win in Oklahoma, leaving Harris, Wallace, and Bentsen to consider if they should even remain in the race.[10]

With Oklahoma already in their fold, the Carters next welcomed Alaska and Maine. On February 10, his Alaska supporters who were elected as uncommitted delegates gave him a hidden victory. In Maine, Carter had made friends with Governor Kenneth Curtis and used his love of the outdoors to appeal to that rural state. Carter had been there himself, and his Aunt Sissy Dolvin had braved the frigid climate, knocked on doors, given interviews, and waited there until the last vote was counted. He won the state easily, thus retaining his position as the Democratic front runner.[11]

On the eve of the crucial February 24 New Hampshire primary, Carter went on *Face the Nation* and brought his case to a national television audience. Money spent on health, education, and welfare projects provided jobs, he said, but money spent on atomic bombs did not. The Civil Rights Acts were good for the South and liberated both Blacks and Whites, but mandatory busing did not work. Détente with the Soviet Union might work if it was openly negotiated. With the US president's top priority being to "guarantee the security of this country," Carter pledged to remove troops from Korea, reduce their numbers in Europe, and curb the "bloated bureaucracy in the Defense Department." Carter reassured his listeners that he had never been close to Wallace and would run against him as though he were just another candidate.[12]

The next day Democrats went to the polls in New Hampshire, the nation's earliest primary. Carter had first campaigned there on February 11, 1975, and since then the family and the Peanut Brigade, first called "Georgians for Carter," had made gargantuan efforts to win the state. Members of the Brigade, ranging in age from eighteen to eighty and intoxicated with success in Maine, had arrived in early January 1976 aboard a chartered jet from Atlanta. Carter met the plane to thank the approximately forty campaigners and advise them to divide into two groups. One group went to Manchester and the other to Nashua, the two cities where most of the state's Democrats lived. Rosalynn, Hamilton Jordan, Tim Kraft, and Peter Bourne all had helped plan the strategy. Chip and Caron had moved to Manchester in May 1975 and remained there for eight months.

Other volunteers from Georgia lived in a dilapidated house in Concord nicknamed "Camp Carter." Traipsing through deep snow, braving extremely cold weather, the determined Peanut Brigaders went door to door, telling personal stories about Jimmy and his family and asking for votes. Amazed New Englanders often invited them to come into their homes and out of the cold. Many decided to vote for Carter.[13]

The Carters and their posse of followers had redoubled their efforts during the final two weeks before the New Hampshire vote. Although Scoop Jackson and Mo Udall continued to attack Carter, neither could equal the Carter effort. On Valentine's Day, Morris Dees, chief counsel for the Southern Poverty Law Center, staged a telethon that raised $250,000 and made the candidate eligible for $150,000 more in matching federal funds. Martin Luther King, Sr., better known as "Daddy King," sports figures, and rock stars who liked the candidate's promise to decriminalize marijuana, all declared their loyalty. The Allman Brothers grossed $50,000 for him at a spring concert in Providence, Rhode Island.[14]

Making a spectacle of himself, former Georgia governor Lester Maddox showed up in New Hampshire to campaign viciously against his perennial enemy, blasting Carter as a liar, a radical liberal, and a completely dishonest person. Jody Powell retorted that "Being called a liar by Lester Maddox is like being called ugly by a frog," and it was Jody, not Lester, who got the positive press coverage. The more sophisticated Stu Eizenstat suggested that Jimmy simply say, "Indeed, the measure of a great leader is whether Lester Maddox dislikes him."[15]

More troubling were attacks by two respected journalists. In the March issue of *Harper's Magazine*, released before the New Hampshire primary, Steven Brill published an article titled "Jimmy Carter's Pathetic Lies" that reviewed Carter's 1970 election as governor. Brill implied that Carter had been duplicitous in wooing the Maddox and Wallace voters and that he had made deliberately misleading comments about race. Jody Powell issued an impassioned rebuttal. Jimmy was livid, thus bringing more attention to the article. Carter had declared emphatically during the 1970 campaign, and he had subsequently proved as governor, that he favored equality of the races. Carter labeled the article "a collection of lies, distortions and half-truths."[16]

Following Brill's piece, Reg Murphy, the former editor of the *Atlanta Constitution*, published an article in the February 14 issue of the *New Republic* titled "The New Jimmy Carter." It offered a blistering attack on Carter as a "good old boy" who could not get African-American votes in his home state and alleged that his presidential "mythmakers" had turned him into an extraordinary manager and populist, which he was not. Murphy contended that Maddox was correct, because there were two Carters—the "charming Populist reformer with an impeccable reputation" and the one who had run for governor of Georgia in 1970.[17]

The next month, one of Carter's disillusioned speechwriters, Robert Shrum, continued the assault on the candidate's integrity. Shrum had resigned from the campaign after only nine days because he thought Carter was lying and contradicting himself. Shrum, a former speech writer for the ill-fated presidential campaigns of both Edmund Muskie and George McGovern, liked to work for liberal Democrats and thought he had found a winner in Carter. Carter had hired Shrum because he thought he might be a bridge to the liberal Northern Democrats, many of whom did not trust Carter. The match did not work, and soon the disillusioned Shrum complained that Carter was a "liar and a deceiver."[18]

Angrily, Shrum explained why he hated Carter. He believed that what Carter said in private on almost every topic did not square with what he said on the stump. He cringed when he heard Carter tell Eizenstat that Maynard Jackson, the first African-American Mayor of Atlanta, "can kiss my ass and you can tell him that." Jackson, because of Carter's "ethnic purity" remark, had dragged his feet before endorsing him. Likewise, Carter privately conceded that he could not win Jewish votes. He told his speechwriters not to make any more statements on the Middle East. "[Scoop] Jackson has all the Jews anyway. It doesn't matter how far I go. I don't get over four percent of the Jewish vote anyway, so forget it. We get the Christians." Shrum did not think Carter anti-Semitic, but he did not think he was an enthusiastic supporter of Israel. Shrum thought Carter, when out of the public eye, was a pragmatic, humorless, cold-hearted taskmaster.[19]

On April 27 Shrum published a scathing attack on Carter in *New Times.* Carter at first declined to comment, then became flustered and angry, and finally ended the episode with his declaration, "I'm not a liar. I don't make a statement in private contrary to what I make in public." Shrum's complaints vanished from the public stage after Carter won the Pennsylvania primary, Jackson conceded, and Senator Hubert Humphry did not enter the race. But Shrum remained an enemy in the wings who would work for Carter's opponents.[20]

Despite Brill, Maddox, Murphy, and Shrum, Jimmy's critics seemed to vaporize once the Carters reached the New Hampshire primary. On election night, Jimmy and Rosalynn were together with their sons and daughters-in-law, as well as Jody Powell and Pat Caddell. When the news came that they had won, the Manchester headquarters erupted into pandemonium as the staff and supporters danced, hugged, and screamed while awaiting the arrival of Jimmy and Rosalynn. Jimmy flashed his big smile and a victory sign. Rosalynn quickly told him not to do the latter because it conjured up the image of the disgraced Republican Richard Nixon. She triumphantly declared, "We're on the way to the White House."[21]

Although the path to the Democratic nomination in the wake of the New Hampshire victory remained long and potentially full of potholes, the Carter campaign was confident and practical. Looking ahead to the general election, it kept an eye on the Republican presidential campaign, assuming that incumbent President Jerry Ford would win the nomination, even though Governor Ronald Reagan of California seemed to be a strong opponent. Ford beat Reagan in New Hampshire, but a poll taken the month before that election showed that Carter had a 38% approval rating to Reagan's 45%, should Reagan become the nominee. One wise observer warned Carter not to take a Reagan defeat for granted. The Democrats, he urged, should start a file on him, because "Reagan is simplistic but far from a fool." Scarcely "the boob we thought he was going to be," the citizen wrote, Reagan was an efficient governor of California, albeit a man without compassion.[22]

Those isolated warnings about Reagan fell through the cracks, because victory in New Hampshire drew attention to Carter's Democratic rivals. The other liberal candidates—Harris, Shriver, Bayh—dropped out of the race. Udall alone among the liberals complained that he had almost won and tried to deny that tiny New Hampshire would be decisive for the 1976 election. Carter had received only 23,000 of 80,000 votes cast, but one journalist thought he was "cocky and confident." Rosalynn, however, looked ahead to the primaries in South Carolina, Vermont, and Massachusetts, fearing that she and Jimmy had not spent enough time working in those states.[23]

The Vermont primary on March 2 was an easy win, but the Wallace challenge in South Carolina was more than Carter could best. Because Wallace had strong support from former governor John West and state party chairman Don Fowler, Carter decided not to spend much of his meager resources in that state. Wallace wanted to remove the glow from Carter's New Hampshire win, pick up a Southern state, and strengthen his position as he headed into the Florida contest. Intensive battles between the two Southerners, many of them aired on African-American radio stations, did not save Carter. Wallace took the Palmetto State with 27.6% to Carter's 22.9%.[24]

Ignoring that defeat, Carter beamed into Boston and convinced himself that he could knock out Massachusetts on his way to Florida, where he and Rosalynn had already invested so much time. But when Massachusetts moved its primary to March 2, they did not have time to canvass the state properly. Evan and Kit Dobell, the Republican mayor of Pittsfield and his wife, changed parties to work for Carter, and Governor Michael Dukakis provided some help, but there was a strong anti-Southern sentiment in Kennedy country. Carter made a strategic mistake by declaring that he opposed busing of children to schools to achieve racial balance, creating an opportunity for his opponents to accuse him of being a Southern racist. Jackson came in first, followed by Udall, Wallace, and finally the "hot shot from Georgia."[25]

Rosalynn was campaigning in Pensacola, Florida, when Caddell phoned to tell her, "My God, it's snowing like hell. This is not what we needed." Blame it on the snow, or the *Boston Globe*, as he did, a very shaken Carter "stuttered" as he spoke to reporters. He was "stunned and disappointed," "unhappy," and "off-balance," according to those who were with him. Rosalynn and others in the family were devastated, but instead of tucking tail and running back to Georgia, they became even more determined to defeat Wallace in Florida. Gerald Rafshoon slyly asked a brunette lady in Orlando if she thought Carter could defeat Wallace. Her quick and sincere response was, "Lord, it's about time *somebody* beat Wallace, isn't it?"[26]

The contest with George Wallace in Florida would not be easy. And Scoop Jackson, who had beaten Carter in Massachusetts, hoped to do the same in Florida. For weeks, the Carter group in Florida had done heavy door-to-door canvassing and intensive media advertising. Jimmy and Rosalynn rode Greyhound buses, separately, from town to town through the middle of the state, stopping at each town to ask for votes. Taking a controversial position that he hoped would help win liberal votes in the state, Carter announced that, if elected president, he would pardon, but not grant amnesty to, those who had left the country to avoid being drafted to serve in Vietnam. Pardon, he said, meant forgiveness, whereas amnesty suggested that what they did was not wrong. Furthermore, he promised Jewish residents that he would not recognize Palestinian interests until Palestinians recognized the state of Israel.[27]

As the March 9 vote approached, press stories contended that Wallace's mind had been affected adversely by his life in a wheelchair. Wallace complained that the Democratic Party had turned against him, denounced Carter as "a newly-turned liberal," and suspected that other candidates were staying out of the Florida primary, hoping that Carter would "knock off Wallace because they are afraid to try."[28]

Scoop Jackson, who had greater appeal for Jews and Catholics than Carter or Wallace, attacked Carter mercilessly. The barbs became quite nasty as each of the candidates called the other a racist and argued over tax reform. Carter lost his patience and cut new tapes for television ads in which he distorted Jackson's positions, underscored Jackson's long ties with Washington, and finally said that, after thirty-five years in Congress, Jackson was not dishonest or bad, "but he wants to be President so bad he's departed from his normal truthfulness."[29]

Fearing that an exhausted Carter would become testy and destroy his nice guy image, his top staffers convinced him to go home to Plains and rest for a day. He did so, attending church and Sunday School on May 7, but he got very little rest before he returned to Florida. While the voters cast their ballots in Florida on March 9, Carter flew to North Carolina to prepare for the primary there. When Jody Powell called to tell him that exit polls showed him winning in Florida, he returned to Orlando. He sat with Rosalynn and Amy in their suite at the Carlton House showing more emotion than usual. When favorable returns came in from Tallahassee, he triumphantly looked at his wife and shouted, "Hey, Rosie!" Carter led with 34%, Wallace had 31%, and Jackson trailed with 24%. Carter spoke kindly of Wallace in his post-election interviews, taking care not to alienate him, for he knew he might need the Alabamian's help against Jackson later in the campaign.[30]

The campaign in Florida took a toll on Carter. Sleep deprived, fatigued, and suffering from a cold, he became ill tempered with his aide Barry Jagoda, who had committed Carter to a television appearance without consulting him. Livid, Carter dressed Jagoda down for scheduling him to fly to New York City for an appearance on *Face the Nation* when he wanted to go home to Plains, rest, and attend church. But to New York he went, and the show was a success.[31]

So popular had Carter become after the Florida primary that the press and others had to fight to get interviews with him. Kandy Stroud, a prominent sympathetic journalist who, after the election wrote a perceptive account of his campaign, called Powell dozens of times but did not get an answer. Finally, she took matters into her own hands. After consulting with Peter Bourne, she acted upon his advice to fall in with an NBC crew filming in Plains. She called Carter first and found him in a testy mood. "I don't know anything about any television interviews," he told her. And he continued that, if Jody "has set up an interview on my day off, I'll fire his ass." Kandy told him that it was Bourne who had suggested she go to Plains. "If Peter Bourne suggested that, I'll fire his ass too," Carter retorted. When she began to cry, Carter relented and gave her the interview.[32]

By the middle of March, Carter had laid out the most important tenets of his campaign: reform of the CIA, establish a code of ethics promising an open government, public financing of elections, the appointment of judges and diplomats based on merit, and the protection of the personal privacy of citizens. His aides created a "Campaign Issue Reference Book" that included his ethics code and much more. Carter promised racial justice, pardon for Vietnam War draft evaders, women's rights and human rights for all both at home and abroad, a reduced military budget while maintaining a tough and muscular military, and the "preservation of rights of Jewish people in Israel and throughout the world." Some voters and analysts were confused because Carter promised so much that they could hardly decipher where he actually stood, other than the fact that he wanted to be president.[33] Carter clearly had genuine principles, but he was also a practicing politician, and in both his gubernatorial and presidential campaigns, he came across as a skillful chameleon who never let himself be pigeonholed.

After the Florida primary, the Carters rushed to Illinois where they hoped to win more delegates in that state's March 16 primary. On the flight Carter fine-tuned a major address he was to deliver to the Chicago Council on Foreign Relations on March 15. Carter emphasized what he had been saying for months, namely that "the prime responsibility of any president is to guarantee the security of our nation, with a tough, muscular, well-organized and effective fighting force. . . ." Such a force was necessary for peace, he said. He condemned Secretary of State Henry Kissinger for conducting foreign policy in such a way as to erode public trust in détente. Carter called for a reevaluation of US support of the United Nations, not to weaken that institution but to insist that other countries share more responsibility for it. It was a theme he would apply to NATO as well. The only hope for a "stable world order," he said, would be for nations to cooperate to end "mass starvation." And finally, Carter declared that "the foreign policy spokesman of our country should be the President, and not the Secretary of State." Not only was he criticizing Kissinger, he was also giving an unmistakable indication of how he would deal with his own secretary of state.[34]

Without exerting much effort, Carter won an astounding victory in Illinois, claiming 48% of the vote and fifty-five of the state's convention delegates. He had befriended Chicago's powerful mayor Richard Daley, whom he had been courting since 1972, and had benefitted from the good work of James Wall, a Methodist minister from Georgia who had chaired George McGovern's Illinois campaign. Illinois was Carter's first victory in a Northern industrial state.[35]

Euphoric from his victories in Florida and Illinois, Carter went to North Carolina for its March 23 primary, in which he had to confront Wallace again and two new entrants, Governor Jerry Brown of California and Senator Frank Church of Idaho. Carter had asked Brown not to enter the race, but Brown did so anyway, hoping for a brokered convention. Church also hoped to win enough delegates to force the party into a brokered convention. Carter feared a brokered convention, because major party leaders such as Bob Strauss, Scoop Jackson, and Hubert Humphrey might control it and determine the outcome of the election.

In the meantime, in North Carolina, Wallace savaged Carter as a liar, an opportunist who coyly won African-American votes by hanging the portrait of Martin Luther King, Jr., in the Georgia State Capitol, and a phony conservative who had misrepresented himself in the 1970 governor's race. Carter tolerated him, for the image of Wallace himself made Carter glow in contrast as a Southern progressive. Ham Jordan told Jimmy, "For the first time ever, I find myself feeling sorry for George Wallace, the man. He is pathetic in defeat, sitting in his wheelchair filled with hate and disappointment."[36]

The real thorn in the North Carolina primary was not Wallace; it was religion. Hamilton Jordan called it "the weirdo factor," and it remained an albatross for the remainder of the campaign. North Carolina was the home state of Carter's sister Ruth Carter Stapleton, an evangelist who had been writing letters to her huge network of religious friends across the state asking them to support her brother. She made references to his personal commitment to Jesus Christ, being born again, and spiritual commitment. Carter declared in Kenosha, Wisconsin, that "The most important thing in my life is Jesus Christ," but he did not want to mix religion with politics.[37]

Many people had no idea what it meant to be born again and wondered if it were a sign of mental instability. Sally Quinn, who had spent some of her youth in Savannah, Georgia, wrote in the *Washington Post* that Carter was not weird: "Relax, Eastern Establishment, Jimmy Carter's OK. He's not crazy. He's just Southern."[38] Most North Carolina voters accepted that explanation, and Carter took 54% of the vote to Wallace's 35, collecting thirty-six more delegates to give him a total of almost 200. The discussion of Jimmy's religion, however, had become a permanent part of his political life.[39]

The favorable outcome of the North Carolina primary helped both Jimmy and Jody Powell forget an episode that often typified their relationship. Carter had become outraged when he showed up at the airport in Winston-Salem to meet Jody Powell and two busloads of reporters. Jody phoned sheepishly to tell him that he and his reporters were at the wrong airport. Carter ended up having to fly by private plane to the Greensboro airport where Jody and his busload of journalists waited. Sally Quinn of the *Washington Post* boarded the plane first, taking the seat next to Carter. Carter told her that Jody would be the last one to board, thus delaying as long as possible facing his boss. When Jody boarded, Carter told him that he should thank Sally Quinn, whose calming presence, diverted Carter from giving Powell a good tongue lashing.[40]

After leaving North Carolina, Jimmy and Rosalynn took advantage of a break in the primary schedule and went home to Plains for almost three weeks. The media's interminable questions about their marriage elicited the same answers he had given many times before. Jimmy declared that

Rosalynn was "the only woman I've ever loved." He confessed that "Rosie and I are both naturally shy." They divided domestic responsibilities at home, he said, which gave him the chance to cook the Southern foods he liked. Out on the trail, Rosalynn spoke for him, commented on issues, and defended him against all criticism. When questioned about his stand on the Vietnam War, she said that Jimmy had never been for it, but he just "thought foreign policy should not be a divisive issue." She declared to one interviewer that the "wives of presidents should be informed and if things are important to them, they should speak out. And I intend to do that."[41]

Even on vacation, Jimmy and Rosalynn prepared for the next primaries. Both Carter and Mo Udall were soon campaigning hard against one another in Wisconsin. In a state where beer and cheese were like holy sacraments, Phil Wise and his staff, accompanied by beer-drinking Billy Carter, hoped to woo both the liberal and the blue collar voters. New York, with a large Jewish population, would be choosing delegates the same day as Wisconsin: April 6. Carter won Wisconsin by only 7,449 votes out of 740,528 cast. The contest was so close that the *Milwaukee Sentinel*, which went to press before the votes were all counted, announced "Carter Upset by Udall." Carter gleefully held the paper high, recalling 1948 when President Truman stood grinning beneath the "Dewey Beats Truman" headline. Udall grumbled that everywhere he went Carter had already been there. "But damn," Udall continued, he is "shaking hands with everybody in the nation. . . . The sonofabitch is as ubiquitous as the sunshine."[42]

In New York, Rosalynn drew huge crowds in Albany and New York City. From the steps of the capitol in Albany, she addressed a sea of people. In New York City, she stood on a chair to address crowds in front of the Tavern on the Green Restaurant, and eager crowds later filled Madison Square Garden and a hotel ballroom for the chance to see and hear her.[43]

Scoop Jackson also campaigned tirelessly in New York, thinking the state would give him the big break he needed. The fact that he was not from the South, had extensive experience in Washington, and was compatible with Catholics and Jews would work in his favor. He won a majority of votes and delegates, 38% to Carter's 12.8%. Carter had given Jackson an unintended boost. During an interview on Friday, April 2, four days before the New York and Wisconsin primaries, Carter said he would do nothing to encourage the deterioration of family neighborhoods. He saw nothing wrong with "ethnic purity" being maintained. He would not force racial integration on a neighborhood, nor would he tolerate discrimination against a family that chose to move into an integrated neighborhood. Carter repeatedly used the shocking phrase "ethnic purity" in subsequent interviews, arguing that it was quite natural for people to want to have neighbors like themselves. His contorted explanations of what he meant made matters worse, and finally he grew agitated with the questioning. That issue and Carter's stubborn defense of his language hurt him in New York and undoubtedly would be a significant problem for him in Pennsylvania.[44]

Although the Carters had poured considerable time and money into the Pennsylvania campaign, the "ethnic purity" comment would not go away. ABC television correspondent Sam Donaldson, who had a talent for going directly for the jugular, asked Carter if his statement was "almost Hitlerian?" In the minds of many the phrase recalled the thinking that led to the Holocaust. Trying to disguise his anger, Carter said that he was not a racist. Congressman Andrew Young of Georgia, who had been prominent in the Civil Rights Movement, joined sixteen other members of the Congressional Black Caucus to denounce the offensive words. Both Young and Vernon Jordan told Carter that he must apologize, and Charles Kirbo drawled that further clarifications would only muddy the issue more.

Rosalynn called Jimmy and told him in no uncertain terms that he must apologize. The next day, in Philadelphia, he issued a statement: "I do want to apologize to all those who have been concerned about the unfortunate use of the term *ethnic purity*."[45] An apology was a small price to pay for the chance to defeat Jackson. "If we beat Jackson in Pennsylvania, and I know we can," Rosalynn said, "we can beat him in Indiana too. Then I don't think anybody can stop Jimmy."[46]

Following their weekend visit to Plains, Jimmy and Rosalynn returned to Philadelphia, where they were relieved to learn that he carried Pennsylvania with 37% of the vote to Jackson's 25%. With this victory guaranteeing the nomination, Jimmy and Rosalynn made a grand entrance while descending the circular stairs of the Sheraton Hotel into the ballroom where dozens of tearful supporters cheered them.[47]

The "ethnic purity" issue, however, left lingering doubts in the minds of African Americans about whether they could trust Carter. Andrew Young dismissed the episode as an honest error caused by Carter's Southern heritage, but Julian Bond and other African Americans wondered if Carter had deliberately appealed to conservative voters. Hosea Williams denounced Carter as a racist who had done less for blacks in Georgia than Lester Maddox had, and he asked Daddy King and Andrew Young to renounce their endorsement of him. Carter attempted to rise above the fray, declaring in St. Louis that he wanted a nation "as good, and honest, and decent, and truthful . . . as filled with love as are the American people."[48]

Carter moved ahead after the April primaries. He discounted Jackson and Udall and practically dared Hubert Humphrey to enter the race. He expected to have at least 1,000 of the 1,505 delegates needed for the nomination by the time the convention began on July 12. Humphrey, the quintessential liberal Washington insider, resented Carter's or anyone else's criticism of Washington. He took it as an attack on the legislation that he and his boss Lyndon Johnson had gotten through Congress to bring about racial equality and social and economic justice for poor and rich alike. Carter denied that he opposed those reforms but leveled his complaints against the recent Republican administrations, a corrupt CIA, and an imperial government that had lost touch with the people.

Humphrey never quite trusted Carter. Humphrey's wife Muriel, who did not like Carter, urged Hubert to run. She, along with many of their friends in the Democratic Party, believed that he could take the presidency for himself. But Humphrey realized that it was too late for him to enter the race, and he carried too much baggage from his public career as vice president and his defeat as a presidential candidate in 1968. There were also legitimate fears that he was not healthy enough to serve. When he announced that he would not enter the New Jersey primary, he enabled Carter to enter with a certain chance to win it and the nomination.[49]

THREE

Mini-Juggernaut

The remainder of the Carters' sail through the primaries to the Democratic convention in July was anti-climactic. Carter galloped through Texas, Indiana, Georgia, and the District of Columbia. Lloyd Bentsen's favorite son status in Texas did not stop Carter from getting ninety-two of the ninety-eight available delegates on May 1. He got all fifty delegates from Georgia three days later, where he survived a taunt from Wallace that he was just a "warmed over McGovern." Most of the Georgia politicos who had not supported Carter for governor in 1970 did not change their minds about him six years later. A major exception was Senator Eugene Holley, who had managed Carl Sanders's campaign but switched his support to Carter.[1]

Forty-five percent of the voters in the District of Columbia voted for Carter on May 4. Late challenges from Jerry Brown of California and Frank Church of Idaho, as well as Mo Udall's stubborn refusal to surrender, slowed Carter in the West but could not stop his momentum. Church took Nebraska on May 11, a result that Jimmy treated as only a "fleabite." Carter decided not to enter the primary held that same day in West Virginia where the powerful Senator Robert Byrd was the favorite son candidate. A week later, Jerry Brown humbled Carter, winning 49% of California's vote to Carter's 37%. Carter barely won Michigan with 44% to the indefatigable Udall's 43. On May 25, Kentucky, Tennessee, and Arkansas moved into the Carter column, while Idaho remained Church's. Church took Oregon, too, collecting 35% of the vote to Carter's 28. Yet, from those states Carter gleaned enough delegates to bring his count up to a solid seven hundred.[2]

Rosalynn, who was less confident than her husband, and traveling alone or with Edna Langford, called Jimmy every night. He would encourage her to count the delegates, not the lost primaries, and she would report what she was learning on the trail. She urged him to come to Rhode Island and South Dakota where people wanted to see him. He did so, on June 1, cutting his loss to Brown in Rhode Island and winning South Dakota. Virtually ignored a few days later when he spoke to the California senate, he quickly moved on to an outdoor rally in Reno, Nevada, where he connected perfectly with a young crowd intent upon hearing what he would do about draft dodgers. They liked what he said: "To me amnesty means that what you did was right and you are to be congratulated for it. Pardon means that what you did, whether it was right or wrong, is forgiven. So I'm going to declare a pardon and forget the Vietnamese war and let those young people come home."[3]

Carter continued to be neither liberal nor conservative, difficult to predict, and, some said, evasive. Nevertheless, he delivered one of his most eloquent and liberal speeches at the dedication of the Martin Luther King, Jr., Hospital in Los Angeles on June 1, 1976. Written by speechwriter Patrick Anderson, the address celebrated the life of King in short, crisp, dramatic sentences. In conclusion, Carter said that King's dream made it possible "for a Southerner to stand before you this evening as a serious candidate for President of the United States." Repeating King's phrase "I see an America," Carter set forth his own promises. King's dream, he concluded, is "our national dream." Carter promised that, with the help of his audience, he would make that dream come true. The speech, as stirring as it was, did not change the minds of California voters, for the polls showed Brown led by 51% to 20% of the vote over the second-place Carter.[4]

It now seemed obvious to most Democrats that Carter could win the presidency for them in the fall election. By courting blacks who sought racial justice, blue collar workers who had supported Wallace, and whites who favored the liberalization of the South, as well as using his regional favorite son status, he had brought the South back into the Democratic fold. More than that, he forced the rest of the United States to look at the South very differently, as a land of change and promise.[5]

Dean Rusk, who had served President John Kennedy as secretary of state before returning to Georgia, publicly said that Carter was the man to be president. Privately, Rusk offered Carter advice on how to choose a cabinet and how to govern. He recommended cabinet colleagues who "fly on four engines" in their relations with the president, Congress, other departments, the press, and the public. He reminded Carter that Dean Acheson, a renowned former secretary of state under Truman, "once remarked that in the relations between a President and a Secretary of State it was of the utmost importance that both of them understand at all times which one is President." He advised Carter to appoint only those people who were personally loyal to him, and he averred that, if he were loyal to the millions of civil servants, they would be loyal to him.[6]

Stu Eizenstat worried about Carter's religious views and the Jewish voters. A liberal Southern Jewish attorney himself, Eizenstat feared that Carter's religion might "hurt among liberals and *particularly Jews*."[7] Carter, who believed in the separation of church and state, could distinguish the Israeli government from Jewish faith, but Judaism was a culture that in the minds of many adherents did not separate their faith from their state.

Carter got more opportunities than he wanted to try to explain his religion to the American public. On May 6, highly respected journalist Bill Moyers interviewed him on the Public Broadcasting Service (PBS). Moyers, educated in a Baptist seminary and a veteran of the administrations of John Kennedy and Lyndon Johnson, was a sympathetic interviewer. Appearing uneasy when discussing religion, Carter said he had "only one life to live" and wanted it to be "meaningful." He prayed frequently, but he "never asked God to let him win," only "to let me do what's right." He did not think he was better than anyone else, and he found it "embarrassing . . . because it's personal" to talk about "my relationship with Christ and with God." He did not "look on the presidency with religious connotations." He wanted "power in order to change things," not for the sake of being powerful. He emphatically stated that he believed in the separation of church and state, which was as much a sincere statement of his faith as it was a political comment.[8]

Carter had no doubts about his faith, but he was too much a thinker and reader, and a politician, to be a fundamentalist. Paul Tillich, perhaps the most liberal theologian of the twentieth century, influenced Carter's thought more than any other. Quoting Tillich in *Why Not the Best?*, Jimmy agreed that "religion is the search for truth about man's existence and his relationship to God," and that "when we think we know it all and are satisfied with what we have accomplished in the eyes of God, we are already far from God."[9]

Early in his career, Carter had quoted Tillich more often than Niebuhr and once explained to a Baptist audience that Tillich was "too liberal for a Southern Baptist like me," but the theologian's writings stretched his mind. Reinhold Niebuhr enabled him to understand how a man could be both Christian and a politician, for no man or nation was perfect, and the search for justice and equality was ongoing.[10]

Carter believed that Muslims and Jews worshipped the same God that he did. According to historian Leo Ribuffo, Jimmy "not only acknowledged American religious diversity but explicitly identified with early Baptists like Roger Williams and John Leland, who had championed freedom of conscience." Neither narrow-minded nor judgmental, Carter put his belief into practice when as a state senator, he voted "to permit eighteen-year-olds to drink alcohol, and later ended regular religious services at the governor's mansion."[11] Furthermore, he did not favor compulsory prayer in public schools, did not impose his ethics upon people working for him, and did not intend to use the White House as a pulpit. Citizens of any religion, or no religion, could trust him.

Questions persisted, however, and Rosalynn often had to explain Jimmy's religion. She defended it as being perfectly normal and not unusual for a Southern Baptist. Those who agreed with Jimmy did not question his faith, and Rosalynn tried to convince others that they should not be intimidated by it. Jimmy would win, Rosalynn thought, because he had "taken his campaign directly to the people." With "no political machines backing him," she said, his "kind of campaign" would be "historic."[12]

In the weeks leading up to the convention, Carter began to prepare to run as the Democratic presidential nominee. The major labor unions, including AFL-CIO, United Auto Workers and the National Maritime Union Workers, endorsed him, believing that he would provide more jobs and justice for workers. Anticipating that foreign policy would play a major role in the fall election, Carter invited Richard Holbrooke, a diplomat with extensive experience in the foreign service, to join his task force. He welcomed Holbrooke's observation that a candidate runs as commander in chief, not just as a party man.[13]

On May 13, Carter, acting like a commander in chief, addressed the United Nations on nuclear energy and world order. He asked the United States to keep its dependence on nuclear energy at a minimum and for international action to limit the spread of nuclear weapons. "The nuclear age, which brings both sword and plowshare from the same source, demands unusual self-discipline of all nations," he said, directing his remarks primarily at the Soviet Union.[14] A few days after he delivered the speech, Bantam Books reissued his 1975 campaign autobiography, *Why Not the Best?* Basking in the publicity, Carter said that he had a vision of America, in Bob Dylan's words, "Busy being born—not dying."[15]

So successful did Carter appear to be by late spring that the Ford presidential campaign, even though neither Ford nor Carter had yet been nominated, launched a major effort to stop him from getting the Democratic nomination. Ford accused him of having a personality similar to Richard Nixon's, of flip flopping on the issues like McGovern had done, and of being a full-time, lying politician who claimed that he was a non-politician.[16]

Carter ignored the Republican slurs and proceeded to take his vision of an America being born anew to Jewish voters in New Jersey. At a rally in Elizabeth he assured his audience that a basic tenet of his Baptist faith was "an absolute and total separation of church and state." Harry Truman had been a Baptist, he reminded them, and also the president who had facilitated the reestablishment of the nation of Israel. Pledging absolute assurance for Israel's survival, Carter had supported UN Resolution 242, which established principles to negotiate an Arab-Israeli peace settlement, and he promised full financial and military aid to Israel. Declaring it not an impossible dream, he said that as president he would "make our nation an agent of peace in the Middle East."[17]

Getting Jewish Northerners to understand Southern Baptists continued to be an uphill battle. Carter had a well-publicized private meeting with Israeli Prime Minister Golda Meir at the Waldorf Astoria Hotel in New York City. Jewish Mayor Abraham Beame reluctantly endorsed him but only after Carter sent some of his Southern Jewish supporters north to endorse Beame in his bid for reelection in 1977. Help for Carter came from Jewish Senator Abraham Ribicoff of Connecticut who addressed the Senate on June 7, 1976: "I have been deeply disturbed during the past months by those who would deny a man the presidency solely because he was a Southerner. . . . A Georgia Baptist is entitled to the same rights and opportunities as a Massachusetts Catholic or a Connecticut Jew." Ribicoff had never met Carter, but he was convinced of his character, integrity, and ability to be president. After returning to Atlanta, Carter went to the Jewish Education Center on June 8 and explained that Jews and Baptists worshipped the same God. In what many in his audience thought to be a silly gesture, Carter donned a yarmulke. According to journalist Meg Greenfield, it made him look like one of the Three Musketeers and came off like "grits at a *seder*."[18]

While declaring loyalty to and support for Israel, Carter also gathered information on the Arab point of view. Charles W. Yost, former United States ambassador to the UN, provided him with an extensive study of Arab views on the Arab-Israeli conflict. The Arabs, Yost said, thought the establishment of Israel by "naked force" took part of the homeland they had claimed for 1,300 years. Israel started the wars of 1956 and 1967, but the Arabs attacked in 1973 only to free their territories that had been occupied for six years. In 1973 President Anwar Sadat of Egypt had declared that he was prepared to make peace in exchange for Israeli withdrawal from those territories occupied since 1967. Saudi Arabia would recognize Israel provided that the Arab

Holy Places in Jerusalem would be restored to Arabs. The Palestinians who had lived in squalid camps since the establishment of Israel had organized themselves into the Palestinian Liberation Organization (PLO) under the leadership of Yasser Arafat. They wanted a secular state in which Arabs and Jews lived together peacefully, but the Israelis would not allow it. Therefore, they would settle for a Palestinian state confined to the West Bank and Gaza.[19] Carter did not use that information in his campaign, for it would not help him win Jewish votes in New Jersey and New York.

Moving westward into Ohio and Illinois, Carter counted upon Mayor Richard Daley of Chicago for help, calling him three or more times a month to keep him informed about the campaign. On the morning of Election Day, June 8, Carter told Daley that he would lose California and New Jersey but he would win Ohio. Daley, who intended to be on the winning side, hung up the telephone and called a press conference. "This man, Carter," he announced, "if he wins in Ohio, he'll walk in under his own power." Daley said he admired his courage, his "religious tone," and his "true values." Daley's influence paid off. Despite Jerry Brown's victory by 59–21 in California and 42–28 in New Jersey, Carter's victory in Ohio, plus the delegates he won in the other states, gave him an additional 218 for the day.[20]

Jimmy and Rosalynn flew individually to Atlanta on June 8, where they met and boarded a Greyhound bus together to go to Plains. Arriving there after midnight, Jimmy looked "confident and happy" as he greeted the cheering crowd waiting at the depot. Rosalynn was touched because the welcome was at the place to which they "always returned." Carter received a note from his mother telling him to call George Wallace no matter how late the hour. He phoned the former Alabama governor at 2:15 a.m. and could hardly believe it when Wallace promised to support him because he wanted a Southerner in the White House. He said he would ask nothing in return but for Jimmy "to make all the people of this country one of the finest Presidents we've ever had."[21]

Scoop Jackson, Mayor Daley, and Senator Adlai Stevenson followed in releasing their delegates and backing Carter. Hamilton Jordan gleefully announced to the staff that "historians will write that Jimmy Carter won the Democratic nomination on June 9th." Reveling in their success and relieved to be together at home again, the entire Carter family escaped to Sea Island, Georgia, for a few days of rest and recuperation.[22]

There was little rest for Rosalynn, however, as the press tried to learn everything about her. She told the *New York Times* that the past grueling fourteen months had been like "being in a tunnel—I don't know any of the new books, I don't know any of the new movies, I don't know anything." Most interviewers were fascinated by her petite size, poise, and intelligence. She was forty-eight years old and had been married to Jimmy for almost thirty of those years. He called her his best friend. Hamilton Jordan said Rosalynn was a tough lady, and Miss Lillian said she was "very ambitious." Rosalynn confessed that she sat in on strategy meetings, and sometimes she yelled and said "damn" and got angry with Jimmy. Rosalynn contended that they never disagreed in public. They respected each other's judgment and worked together as partners. Rosalynn had quietly rededicated her life to Jesus, she confessed, when they lived in the governor's mansion. She opposed abortion and premarital sex because she thought the Bible said they were wrong. As First Lady, she would not want to vacation in a San Clemente or a Vail, exotic resorts where Nixon and Ford had relaxed; she would only want to go home to Plains where she could read Carson McCullers and Shakespeare.[23]

Plains was undergoing a metamorphosis from a sleepy little remote town into one of the most famous in the world. Amy set up a lemonade stand in front of their house on Woodland Avenue, replaced a cardboard stand with a wooden one, and declined to offer discounts to members of the press who were on expense accounts. Jimmy promised his high-school class that they would have their thirty-seventh reunion in the White House if he were elected. He had hosted the thirtieth at the Governor's Mansion. The Best Western Motel in Americus became the home away from home for most of the press, and the site where Jimmy liked to joke that he was semi-retired and his family was in the lemonade business.

But Plains would never again be the same. At least three tour companies served the hordes of tourists who came to the town, and since there were not enough public restrooms to accommodate so many people, they had to go in the bushes. The six-man police force had to call for help from the state, and Billy Carter did such a booming business selling beer from his service station that the town collected more money in beer taxes than property taxes. The three major networks were there ready to report anything the Carters did from selling lemonade to making major foreign policy statements.[24]

At staff meetings secluded from the press in their home, they developed a platform.[25] At those meetings, Charles Kirbo, with his inscrutable, sleepy-eyed look and his distinctive white hair, reigned as Carter's most respected adviser. An accomplished attorney, Kirbo understood the law and the Constitution much better than Jimmy did, and he understood Jimmy. Professionally, Kirbo was closer to Jimmy than either Mr. Earl or Admiral Rickover, both of whom demanded strict discipline and absolute perfection. Kirbo was the loving, helpful, tight-lipped older man whose advice Jimmy needed.

As the Democratic convention drew near, the Carters-—coached by Kirbo—developed a platform that would reflect the concerns of the Democratic Party and the promises they had made on the campaign trail. Carter assigned the task of writing a draft to Stuart Eizenstat, who likely knew more about the issues than any other member of the campaign. Eizenstat created a noncontroversial document that pleased almost every group in the Democratic constituency. Labor, African Americans, women, and Vietnam veterans were offered half a loaf in the form of limited health insurance, moderate welfare reform, silence on the school busing issue, a promise to work for passage of the ERA, and individual presidential pardons for draft evaders. Labelling the document "A New Beginning: July 16, 1976," Carter revised and presented it to the Platform Committee.

Carter's goals, he wrote in the revised document, were openness, compassion, efficiency, and the protection of human rights at home and abroad. Rather than treating developing countries as "pawns in a big power chess game," he wanted his country's international aid to be directed to meet "*human needs of the greatest number of people.*" The focus of his administration would be on food, jobs, housing, education, public health, and world peace. The prerequisite for peace and the security of our nation, he said, was "a well-organized and effective fighting force." He wanted practical weapons, not exotic ones, and hard bargaining with the country's leading enemy, the Soviet Union. He wanted a major reduction in nuclear weapons and policies that would favor both nations, not just the Soviet Union.[26]

There was no time to be idle in the month before the convention. Carter studied a memorandum from Brzezinski on the crisis in Cyprus where two US allies, Greece and Turkey, were at war with each other. Both nations were important in the troubled Middle East, and both were helpful to the United States. To further his message Carter delivered an address in June to the Foreign Policy Association in New York on "Relations between the World's Democracies." He condemned the Ford-Kissinger Lone Ranger approach and secrecy in favor of a foreign policy that reflected "the decency and generosity and common sense of our people." Carter wanted to strengthen alliances and create "a community of the free." Back home in Plains he posed for campaign videos, wrote thank you notes, hosted a fish fry for Secret Service agents, and consulted Charlie Kirbo on final campaign issues.[27]

Although victory was in sight "by conquest rather than love," as Jody Powell put it, Carter thought that the national Democrats still would not accept him. Having learned to govern without being loved in Georgia, he expected to conduct his presidency like a business. He planned to continue the same type of management style, perhaps naively thinking that Washington would simply be Atlanta writ large. His staff would be in a support role, for Carter himself would make the decisions. Although no one dared say it, they all knew that the person closest to the president would be the First Lady.[28]

The final act of Carter's campaign for the Democratic nomination was the execution of his thoroughly researched plan to choose his running mate. He had talked about the kind of person he wanted for vice president, but he had not suggested any names. He sought someone who was qualified to be president, politically and personally compatible with him and Rosalynn, and not necessarily from the South. Hamilton Jordan compiled a list of Democratic Senators, Congressmen, governors, mayors, and prominent party leaders, then rated them according to their interest in the position, integrity, and ability. The five senators were Alan Cranston of California, Abraham Ribicoff of Connecticut, Philip Hart of Michigan, Walter "Fritz" Mondale of Minnesota, and Mike Mansfield of Montana. Some on the list were more cosmetic than serious choices, since Carter had decided that he needed a senator with a sustained liberal record to counter the criticism that he was inexperienced and a Southerner. The vetting had begun inconspicuously in May when Charlie Kirbo could be seen wandering in and out of senatorial offices on Capitol Hill.[29]

Kirbo had become Carter's kitchen cabinet of one, for the two men communicated frequently and usually without leaving a written record. Kirbo had grown up, in his own words, "hungry and pore [sic] as hell," but he had risen to the top of the legal profession in Atlanta, counting some of the largest corporations in the state as his clients. He had introduced Robert Strauss to Carter, understood human nature, and, like Carter, was "a duck hunter and a church goer."[30]

When Carter gave Kirbo the names of the seven men he wanted to interview personally, Kirbo met with them first, in the week before the convention. Gleaned from Jordan's long list, Senators Edmund Muskie, Walter Mondale, John Glenn, Scoop Jackson, Adlai Stevenson, and Congressmen Peter Rodino and Brock Adams comprised that short list. Kirbo and his law partner Griffin Bell, a relative of Rosalynn and a judge with a liberal record by Georgia standards, began the process of vetting the finalists. They asked the men to submit information about marital partners, campaign contributions, psychiatric treatment, health records, tax returns, complete financial records, and anything of a personal or financial nature that could potentially become a source of embarrassment. Carter was unique among presidential finalists. Obligated to no one, he had such early success in the polls that he had time to identify and evaluate choices for a running mate.[31]

Jimmy and Rosalynn invited three of the finalists and their wives to Plains. Edmund Muskie and his wife Jane arrived first. Carter liked Muskie's independence and willingness to campaign, but thought he lacked the energy and organizational skills for the job.

When the Mondales arrived in their twin-engine Cessna that landed on a grass air strip near Plains, they must have felt like they were entering a foreign country. While Jimmy spent time with Fritz, Rosalynn got to know Joan. Mondale had done his homework well. He had read Jimmy's campaign autobiography and everything else he could find about him. Furthermore, Mondale had speculated that the office of vice president could be powerful in the development of foreign and domestic policy, especially if the president lacked Washington experience. He was quietly Christian, the son on a Methodist minister, happily married to an intelligent woman, and by all accounts a devoted husband and father. Carter also discovered that he was strong on defense, favored a balanced budget, and was less liberal than his reputation suggested. Likewise, Rosalynn liked Joan, shared her interest in art, and found that she too was close to her family.

Later the same day, John Glenn and his wife appeared in Plains, an invitation that Carter must have issued for political reasons rather than serious consideration. Despite Carter's claim of compatibility with the popular former astronaut during the Ohio primary campaign, perhaps intended to appease the voters in the Buckeye state, Carter was nonplussed by Glenn's lack of knowledge of the Carter family and found little common ground with him. Carter met the other four finalists in New York during the first days of the convention, but he delayed announcing his decision until the last hour.[32]

FOUR

The Carters Take New York

The Carter family arrived in New York City on Saturday, July 10, 1976, two days before the Democratic National Convention was to begin. It was a triumphant entry by the man who hoped to be the next president of the United States. The Secret Service rose to the challenge of keeping him alive, insisting that he wear a bullet proof vest. Carter had emerged from the primaries with 1,117 delegates of the 1,505 needed for the nomination. As other candidates released their delegates, he would be assured victory on the first ballot. The atmosphere in the city was particularly festive, not just because of the convention, but also because of the bicentennial celebrations held the previous week. The tall ships from around the world had barely left the harbor, and even the cab drivers and policemen were unusually cordial.[1]

Patriotism was in the air, and many citizens were ready to welcome a fresh, energetic family into the White House. The Carters, with their Southern accents, public religion, eccentric relatives, recent national publicity, and ferocious independence might fill that bill. Despite Carter's attempt to channel John F. Kennedy, however, his campaign was grounded in a real world that had little resemblance to Camelot.

The Carters and their closest advisers occupied the entire twenty-first floor of the Americana Hotel. The spacious windows of the penthouse were blacked out by heavy curtains, and the balconies sealed off to ensure that no sharpshooter perched on a nearby skyscraper could get a shot at them. Emerging from their secure quarters, Jimmy and Rosalynn attended services at the Fifth Avenue Presbyterian Church the next morning. For the remainder of the day, they gave speeches and interviews and attended receptions and parties. Rosalynn addressed the Women's Caucus at the Metropolitan Opera House.[2]

Ignoring demands from party leaders to meet the nation's most powerful newspaper editors, Jimmy and Rosalynn hosted a rural Georgia–style party for all 5,000 delegates. Staged at the Hudson River's Pier 88, the picnic featured fried chicken, coleslaw, peanuts, and beer. As he greeted guests,

Carter remembered the names of many of the men and women he had met throughout the campaign. He apologized to one African-American woman from North Carolina, "Mazie," who stood in line to greet him, because when they last met in the earlier days of the campaign, she had not had to stand in line to shake his hand.[3]

In New York during the short time she had before the convention, Rosalynn discovered that she dare not go to a department store to shop, and when she took daughter Amy and grandson Jason to the Central Park Zoo, the press photographers descended upon them. Edna Langford, who accompanied her, commented that we suddenly realized "we were the zoo." The park was also crowded with ten thousand protesters marching toward Madison Square Garden, some carrying signs that read "Carter Backs Baby Murder," trying to persuade Carter and the Democratic National Convention to oppose abortion.[4]

On the convention's opening day, crowds of delegates milled about Madison Square Garden, paying little attention to Senator John Glenn's uninspiring keynote address. But they stopped and listened when Representative Barbara Jordan of Texas took the podium. Party Chairman Bob Strauss had chosen the African-American Congresswoman to be the second keynote speaker after her impassioned defense of the United States Constitution in 1974 that facilitated the impeachment and resignation of President Richard Nixon. Nevertheless, Strauss had great reservations about his choice, questioning whether Jordan would be a much-needed unifying force.

Jordan refused to allow Strauss to approve her speech in advance and insisted upon delivering it her way. Strauss sweated it out knowing that the unity and success of the party depended on someone whose message he had no control over. He advised Jordan to quiet the crowd if she could, but if she couldn't, "just ignore the bastards" and speak to the television cameras. Jordan, disgusted with his patronizing and crippled by a bad knee, snapped at him, "Bob, if you can get me up the damn steps, *I* can make the damn *speech*." When the lights went down to show an introductory film, the Dallas millionaire practically carried her up the steps.

When the lights came up, Jordan captured the attention of the cheering crowd. The first African-American woman to give a keynote address at a Democratic Party convention, Barbara Jordan brought down the house with words of wisdom delivered in a Black evangelical style. Adapting the words of Abraham Lincoln, she ended her speech by reminding her audience that "the concept of a national community . . . in which I would not be a slave, so

I would not be a master" rested upon "my idea of democracy . . . in which every last one of us participates." The wild cheers of the crowd forced her to pause before delivering the last lines. Hubert Humphrey, seated next to Rosalynn Carter, jumped to his feet in applause. Others followed suit, and for a shining moment Barbara Jordan owned the hall and unified the party.

She returned to the floor and stood beside Strauss. Both from Texas, one the wealthy son of a Jewish Dallas businessman, the other the daughter of a poor Houston Black preacher, they symbolized the range of voters Carter hoped to reach. He was peppered with telegrams telling him to choose her as his running mate.[5] Carter, however, kept his own counsel as the rumors escalated about who he would choose.

Meanwhile, the raucous convention proceeded apace. Hubert Humphrey received wild cheers for his impassioned pleas for party unity. On Tuesday night, George McGovern, a victim of a divided party only four years earlier, urged the delegates to unite around their candidate and retake the White House. On Wednesday night, July 14, Congressman Peter Rodino, an Italian Catholic from New Jersey who had gained prominence through the Watergate investigation, placed Carter's name in nomination. He delivered a rousing speech, proclaiming that Carter had brought the South back into mainstream America and "America back to a position of respect and esteem in the eyes of the world." Midge Costanza, a feminist from New York who served on the National Democratic Committee, declared Carter to be a "sensitive" person and "a decent human being." Andrew Young spoke of how Carter's Southern heritage made him put aside the yoke of racism and become sensitive to needs of poor people. Furthermore, Carter's military career taught him how to build a strong nation without squandering all of its wealth on weapons. Those laudatory statements were prophetic, but that exciting night they stirred the delegates and millions of television viewers to pin their hopes on the man from Plains.[6]

Drifting about the convention like a hungry ghost, however, Senator Edward Kennedy looked for a chance to disrupt Carter's drive for the nomination and hopefully find some loophole to claim the prize for himself. The intense rivalry and muted bad blood between the two men had escalated six weeks earlier, when, speaking about Kennedy, Carter had repeated to a reporter in New York that he was "glad I don't have to kiss his ass" to become president.[7] Knowing how popular Kennedy was, Carter had deliberately given him a bit part in the convention, the chance to read the healthcare section in the platform. Kennedy declined, perhaps insulted because he had not been offered a larger role.

Working behind the scene, however, Kennedy visited the CBS anchor booth manned by Walter Cronkite. Cronkite, the most celebrated news man in the country, probed the senator for his thoughts. Kennedy denied being interested in the presidency, but only interested in retaining his Senate seat. He wished Carter well, he said, but he would be too busy campaigning for his own reelection in 1976 to assist him.[8]

Perhaps hoping to help her brother-in-law, Jackie Kennedy Onassis, John F. Kennedy's widow, appeared briefly for a well-guarded and unrecorded meeting with party Chairman Robert Strauss. When she took a seat in the VIP section of the hall, however, virtually everyone present turned in her direction. She slipped quietly out of the hall, and Ted faded into the background, thus removing the threatening shadow of the Kennedys from the Carters' celebration.

Waiting confidently with family, friends, and speechwriters in his hotel suite, Carter revised draft after draft of his acceptance speech. Although he received suggestions from his chief speechwriter Patrick Anderson, his campaign issues director Stuart Eizenstat, his pollster Pat Cadell, and Adam Walinsky, formerly an attorney for Robert Kennedy, who insisted that he knew everything the Southerners did not, Carter wrote the speech himself, by hand. Rosalynn helped with the final draft.[9]

Carter watched the events at Madison Square Garden on television. He hugged Miss Lillian, held Amy and his grandson Jason on his lap, and smiled when Rosalynn appeared on camera. She sat in the balcony with Muriel Humphrey, Bob and Helen Strauss, and the Carter sons and their wives. When California was called, Jerry Brown himself announced that his state was voting unanimously for Carter. Ohio's votes gave him the 1,505 he needed. Peter Duchin's orchestra struck up "Happy Days are Here Again," the song Franklin Roosevelt had used when he had promised to lift the nation out of the Great Depression. Mazie Woodruff, in the North Carolina delegation, jumped to her feet and waved a sign reading, "Peanut Butter Is Love. Spread Some Around Today." Miss Lillian placed her hand on her son's cheek as Congresswoman Lindy Boggs announced that the chair would appoint a committee to ask Carter if he would accept the nomination. Rosalynn told a reporter to tell Jimmy, "We won!"[10]

Two Georgians, Bert Lance and Lester Maddox, diverged in their reactions to Carter's nomination. Lance swelled with emotion that night as he wrote

Jimmy a note of thanks for "Showing me what dedication, commitment, and integrity are all about." He continued, "I love you greatly and consider myself fortunate to be your friend." Lester Maddox, however, remembering bitterly his lieutenant governorship under Carter, wrote: "Whoever the vice president is, he'll do what Jimmy Carter tells him. And if he doesn't, I expect Carter will exile him to Siberia." Maddox continued that Carter was "Forceful, dynamic, hardworking, hardheaded, cold, cunning, brilliant, ambitious, and dishonest."[11]

Carter used his time at the hotel to settle on his choice of a running mate. At 8:26 the next morning, shortly after telling Rosalynn of his plan, he called Senator Walter Mondale and asked if he would run with him. "Honored and thrilled," Mondale and his wife Joan soon joined Jimmy and Rosalynn on the stage to make the formal announcement. They smiled and joined hands as camera flashes went off. The two wives made their own statements, but Rosalynn, who wanted to make sure that everyone understood that she was in charge, stepped to the microphone and tactfully commented that she was certain that Mrs. Mondale "would be very capable of helping me with anything I try to do."[12]

Mondale, addressing the convention, declared that "we reject . . . the idea that this nation must sit by passively while terrorists maim and murder innocent men, women and children." After the roar of applause subsided, he went on to praise Israel's "bold and brave mission" in rescuing 103 hostages from the Entebbe Airport in Uganda. The New York Board of Rabbis sent Carter a congratulatory telegram on July 16, but William Safire, Jewish journalist and former Nixon speech writer, began to search for any episodes petty or significant that he might use to criticize the Democrats.[13]

On the last night of the convention, July 15, all attention turned to the Georgia peanut farmer who in a matter of weeks might become the most powerful man on the globe. Sitting in a trailer deep within the bowels of Madison Square Garden before going to the platform to give his speech, Carter was nervous. Only Rod Goodwin, his director of media production, and his Secret Service guards were with him. Goodwin, who had been with Jimmy and Rosalynn recording political advertisements on numerous occasions, knew that Jimmy did not want to be disturbed. During their work together, Goodwin had frequently solicited Rosalynn's help to get Jimmy to turn toward the camera and limit his verbiage. She sometimes grabbed the makeup rag herself to apply some color to Jimmy's fair skin. But Rosalynn, at this important moment, waited on the platform for the arrival of her husband. Jimmy told Rod that the tray of fruit in the room was making him nauseous and asked him to remove it. When the word finally came down through a chain of Secret Service agents that it was time for Carter to begin his walk to the platform, he left the trailer, according to Goodwin, "as if going to a fight, or a football player headed for the field."[14]

The "field" had been carefully prepared for his arrival. The Secret Service had calculated the time it would take him to walk to the hall. As Rosalynn and the delegates eagerly awaited Jimmy's arrival, the operators showed a film revealing the serious and humorous moments in Jimmy's rise to glory. The cartoon of teeth glowing in the dark, with Rosalynn commenting, "Jimmy, cut it out and go to sleep," thrilled the Democrats. Finally, Robert Strauss introduced "the next President of the United States."[15]

Sitting in the "Honored Guest" section immediately above the path Carter took to the podium was a civics teacher from Vienna, Georgia: Mrs. Joseph Powell, the mother of Jody Powell, had never been to a convention or flown on an airplane. Tears streaked her cheeks as she looked not at Carter, but at her thirty-two-year old son, who for ten years had worked to bring Carter, and his mother, to this exhilarating moment.[16]

Striding into the hall with a smile large enough to disguise his nervousness, Carter passed through throngs of cheering delegates, shaking hands on all sides, and promising that he would always be just one of the people. At the podium, he accepted the party's presidential nomination, saying that he had been humbled by the experience of campaigning for and winning it. Carter told the crowd that he was pleased that he had won not by the actions of power brokers but by the power of the people.

Quoting Reinhold Niebuhr, he said, "I have spoken many times about love, but love must be aggressively translated into justice." He praised earlier Democratic presidents from Franklin Roosevelt through Lyndon Johnson, the latter of whom, he said, did "more than any other President in this century to advance the cause of human rights." He spoke about the generations of immigrants who had built the party and the country. "It is time for America to move . . . with a quiet strength . . . in world affairs not merely on the size of an arsenal but on the nobility of ideas—and govern at home not by confusion and crisis but with grace and imagination and common sense." Freedom at home meant that US freedom should be the fate of all peoples everywhere. Barriers of race, region, and religion must give way to equality, productivity, and a "new spirit" for a country whose citizens could be proud of their government.[17]

As the crowd roared its approval, Rosalynn and the rest of the family gathered around Carter at the podium, while Strauss motioned for party leaders to come to the stage. Helen Strauss led the way, but soon Scoop Jackson, George Wallace, Abe Beame, Hubert Humphrey, and dozens more began to crowd around the Carters. Strauss took the microphone and announced that Daddy King would give the benediction. Father of the martyred Martin Luther King, Jr., King had emerged as a symbol of justice, forgiveness, Christian love, perseverance, and hope. With his thunderous voice and the cadence of African-American evangelism, King silenced the noisy hall by preaching to the delegates. He asked for no words to be heard unless they were "uttered to God." Some listeners pierced the silence with loud "Amens." "Surely the Lord sent Jimmy Carter to come on out and bring America back where she belongs," he shouted. He prayed, hugged his daughter-in-law Coretta Scott King, Jimmy, and Rosalynn. People on the stage and in the audience joined hands and sang, "We Shall Overcome."[18]

ABC correspondent Sam Donaldson pushed his way up to the crowded platform and asked Carter if he had ever had a "finer night than this?" Jimmy replied that it was the best of his life, "Perhaps with the possible exception of that night when I married my wife 30 years ago." Rosalynn smiled but remained unchanged by her new role as wife of the Democratic presidential candidate. When, on their return to the Americana, an assistant manager of the hotel delivered three bottles of imported champagne to their door, she declined it on the grounds that it cost $33 per bottle. After he explained that it was on the house, she graciously accepted, took a small glass for herself, another for Jimmy, then passed it around the room.[19]

The celebrants were reminded that the nomination was not the presidency and that there remained another tough campaign ahead. Although the Republican candidate had not yet been officially nominated, President Ford telephoned to say, "Good luck Jimmy, I look forward to a fair contest next fall." Reagan, however, expressed doubt that the Democratic team could succeed, because "liberalism is pretty much out of fashion."[20]

The Carters, focusing on the contest with their Republican opponent, did not linger in New York City. Traveling overnight by private plane, they returned to Plains, where at 5:30 a.m., hundreds of friends met them at the depot. Happy to be home, Jimmy and Rosalynn were not swept away by the euphoria of becoming celebrities. Confident of victory in November, they fine-tuned their strategy and made plans for their presidency. All who knew Carter knew he would put up a tough fight. Jimmy's mother had said at the beginning of the year that "he is like a beautiful cat with sharp claws." Charles Kirbo, in a rare revelation, told a reporter that "Jimmy is tough. He'll cut your throat if you get in his way." And the journalist Rick Allen, who observed him at work in Georgia, said, if angered, "He'll cut your dick off."[21]

Rosalynn remained demurely in the shadows, where her gentle, lady-like nature masked the ambition of a brilliant, politically experienced woman who stood ready to work tirelessly to assure that she and her husband would win the White House.

The immediate obstacle in their path would be the Republican candidate, who would be chosen at that party's national convention in August. The leading contenders were the incumbent President Gerald Ford and the former governor of California, Ronald Reagan. Although the press expected Ford to get the nomination, Reagan was a charming former actor with a large following and a winning personality. His wife Nancy, a former movie starlet, elegantly dressed and sharp-tongued, knew how to attract crowds wherever she campaigned. The former first couple of California and the former first couple of Georgia had little else in common, except that both aspired to become President and First Lady of the United States.

The incumbent First Lady Betty Ford was a down to earth, trim, former dancer whose candid interviews about how she reared her four children and combatted breast cancer had won the hearts of the American people. Her husband, who had become president under such difficult and unusual circumstances, was a long-time Congressman and dedicated public servant. His strategists and advisers were not comparable to those who worked for the Reagans and the Carters, and he had been saddled with the image—not entirely accurate—of being clumsy, an unpersuasive speaker, and a bit dense. The Carter camp calculated that Ford would be easier to defeat than Reagan.

Since Reagan had never promised not to tell a lie, he was free to do so, and he did it on a grand scale. Focused on the sound of his words, he promised, while stump-speaking in New Hampshire, to reduce the size of the federal government without first conducting any responsible study of its practicality or how it might affect millions of citizens. A lackadaisical speech writer, who had carelessly revised an old speech, and a relaxed candidate who did not read it through before he delivered it made Reagan appear vulnerable and unprepared. His promise to cut $90 billion from the federal budget seemed incredible, and when it appeared certain that most of that reduction would be in social services so much in demand in New Hampshire and elsewhere, the Ford camp attacked him.

From the sidelines, Carter mumbled "ridiculous," but Reagan poured on the charm and the catchy one-liners to try to squirm his way out of it. Carter himself campaigned before a large, enthusiastic outdoor audience in Manchester, New Hampshire. His emphasis on the family and honoring one's father and mother brought cheers, establishing him as the candidate of the people. He promised that government efficiency would provide the social services that the people of New Hampshire and the rest of the nation needed.[22]

The Reagan campaign rolled ahead with Hollywood glitter and dramatic statements that thrilled some and horrified others—especially retired folks in Florida who gasped on hearing that he wanted to reduce social security benefits. When he talked about how small businessmen and farmers had to fill out thousands of pages of documents per year, and how welfare recipients in Chicago were "welfare queens," his good looks and seductive language charmed well-to-do conservatives but raised major doubts in the minds of the less well off. They looked to the government for help and justice, not condemnation.

The Ford campaign rallied, but it was poorly managed by Howard "Bo" Callaway, Carter's former, unsuccessful, gubernatorial adversary from Georgia. Shortly before the Illinois Republican primary, Callaway had been accused of having used his earlier position as secretary of the army to acquire federal land in Colorado upon which he built his Crested Butte Mountain Resort. Forced to resign from the campaign, he was replaced temporarily by Stu Spencer and permanently by Rogers Morton, both Republican strategists who hoped that differences between Reagan and Ford might be resolved for the benefit of the party. But Reagan, eager to defeat the limpid Ford, would have none of it. He pounded Ford time and again for clinging to his unpopular secretary of state, Henry Kissinger, and using the power of the presidency to maintain himself in office.[23]

Ignoring history, Reagan announced that he would pursue "Morality in Foreign Policy" and railed against giving away the Panama Canal, which endeared him to many Americans who were not well versed in history. Tension between the United States and Panama had flared since the early 1960s as Panama threatened to stage a coup and seize the US-controlled canal. The United States under the leadership of President Theodore Roosevelt had supported a Panamanian revolution against Colombia, recognized the new nation of Panama in 1903, and signed a treaty in perpetuity to build and operate the canal. Never legally the property of the United States, the canal had been built and operated by it on land leased from Panama. Reagan accused Ford of secret negotiations to surrender the "path between the seas" to the disgruntled Panamanians, an issue that caught fire in the 1976 Republican contest and thereafter became a hallmark of Reagan's political career.

The Reagans and the Fords were quite a contrast as they crisscrossed the nation seeking delegates. They were Hollywood and Mid-America, disarmingly humorous and whimsically clumsy. They battled for votes in Jimmy Carter's native South, where, since the Eisenhower era, the Republicans had steadily gained strength. The warring Republicans converged at the Kansas City convention early in August to choose their leader with neither Ford nor Reagan having enough delegates to secure the nomination.[24]

No delegates wanted to surrender their votes, and there were occasional tussles and epithets, most of which were directed at the president. Nancy Reagan was elegant, gorgeously dressed, defensive of her Ronnie, and, despite her best efforts to disguise it, haughty and out of touch with the common people. Betty Ford was exactly the opposite, sometimes inebriated and opaque but always friendly, frank, and exuding the approachability of an ordinary person. The night before the nomination, as the crowd cheered, Nancy arose to the applause, the epitome of stylish beauty. Betty, a former dancer, petite and vivacious, stood in her place in the gallery and danced with Tony Orlando as the band played "Tie a Yellow Ribbon 'Round the Old Oak Tree." The wives, however, had little effect on the nomination, for most die-hard Reagan and Ford delegates had come to Kansas City with their minds firmly set. When the voting began on August 18, the uncommitted delegates broke for Ford. When West Virginia, represented by Governor Arch Moore, cast twenty votes for the president, Ford became the party's nominee. He chose Senator Bob Dole of Kansas as his running mate. Dole was a hard campaigner, a conservative Republican, a quick-witted speaker, and a war hero. Reagan had made it clear that he would not accept the number two spot on the ticket, and as the wary Democrats no doubt surmised, he saw his loss that night only as a pause in his journey to the White House.[25]

While the Republican show went on in Kansas City, Jimmy and Rosalynn rested in Plains, preparing for the next stage in their long run for the presidency. Facing a national race against an incumbent president, they kept their lives grounded in Plains and retained their trusted Georgia advisers. Charles Kirbo was never more than a whisper away, and Jerry Rafshoon, who had advised Carter on his public image since he had run for governor, transformed him from the peanut farmer with a populist image into a man of experience in government who was ready to take on the nation's top job. Peter Bourne and his wife Mary King, who had moved from Atlanta to Washington, provided useful information about the nation's capital, campaign issues, and political contacts.

Jody Powell had grown in wisdom and experience as a press secretary; he was ferociously loyal to Carter and possessed a quick wit and sense of humor that disguised his impatience with a Yankee press uninformed and often prejudiced about the South. Atlanta attorney Robert Lipshutz managed the campaign's treasury, and Richard Harden, an accountant from Atlanta who had headed Georgia's controversial Department of Human Resources, lent his skill as a budget director. The adult Carter children, in-laws, other relatives, and the veterans of the Peanut Brigade stood ready to swing into action.[26]

None could rival Hamilton Jordan's dedication to Jimmy and Rosalynn and skill as campaign manager. Ham embraced the image of the indolent and dense country boy who embodied all that was negative about the South. The man himself, however, was the antithesis of that image. Born in Charlotte, North Carolina, in 1944, William Hamilton McWhorter Jordan grew up in a traditional, middle-class Southern family in Albany, Georgia. Immersed in history, politics, and the civil rights movement throughout his childhood and youth, Ham acquired the model training for his public career at the knee of his maternal grandfather, Hamilton "Hamp" McWhorter, who served as president of the state senate. During the summer of 1961 Ham witnessed the march for justice and the subsequent trial of Martin Luther King, Jr., in his hometown of Albany. Ham secretly visited his Uncle Clarence Jordan and Aunt Florence, founders of the interracial and socialistic Koinonia community near Americus, and he campaigned for the progressive governor Carl Sanders in 1962. At the end of his freshman year at the University of Georgia he went to Washington to serve as an intern for the powerful Senator Richard Russell, where he got passing glimpses of President John F. Kennedy and his gruff and profane Vice President Lyndon Johnson, and learned the ways of the Senate.

During the summer of 1966, before his senior year, Ham heard Carter, then a state senator, deliver a speech in Albany that resonated with his own interest in using political power to achieve racial and social justice. He accepted a position in Carter's ill-fated 1966 campaign for governor, and a year later he went to Vietnam for ten months. Since his flat feet kept him out of the military, he volunteered with the International Voluntary Services that provided agricultural and community assistance to the Vietnamese peasants. Back in Georgia, Ham managed Carter's successful 1970 gubernatorial campaign and served him as executive secretary during his governorship. His lengthy 1972 memorandum became the blueprint for Carter's presidential campaign. Carter knew that in Jordan he had a brilliant strategist and adviser who could lead the team to victory in 1976.[27]

Since, with the help of Jordan and the others on his team, Carter had been campaigning for the presidency since 1972, he made very few changes after he won the Democratic nomination. Most important, Walter and Joan Mondale and Mondale's staff significantly strengthened their chance for victory. Mondale's staff understood the workings of Washington, and the Mondales were politically savvy and dedicated to the same ideals that drove the Carters.[28]

After his nomination and before his general election campaign began in early September, Carter prepared for his anticipated presidency. On July 22, only a few days after he had won the nomination, he invited experts in defense and national security, economics, and foreign policy to visit him and Rosalynn. They had to pay their own way to the Atlanta airport, where a chartered bus picked them up for the three-hour ride to Plains. Distinguished men and women, potential cabinet members and advisers, most of them had never ridden a bus before or seen a town like Plains. As their bus rumbled through the tiny town, then turned onto a dusty red clay road to Miss Lillian's Pond House, an isolated retreat her sons had built for her, some of them must have wondered what price they had to pay for the uncertain chance in a Carter administration. Upon arrival, Jimmy, Rosalynn, and Mondale warmly welcomed them. They dined on cold sandwiches, held substantive but short conversations with their hosts, and then boarded the bus back to Atlanta.[29]

Experts on defense arrived the first day. Carter studied the group intently, frequently displayed his deep knowledge of defense matters, and served notice to those gathered and those watching him from afar that, despite his geographical location, he was no ignorant country hick. Carter allowed Paul Nitze, a well-known hawk who acted as if he expected a nuclear attack by the Soviet Union at any moment, to dominate the discussion. The more dovish Cyrus Vance, Paul Warnke, and Harold Brown, whose opinions would be more congenial with Carter's, mostly kept silent despite their impeccable credentials. Harold Brown had been secretary of the air force, and Cyrus Vance and Paul Nitze had served as secretary of defense and deputy secretary of defense, respectively. Warnke, a seasoned diplomat who favored arms control, did not believe that the Soviets would attack the United States or that if they were foolish enough to do so that they could win. A few researchers from the Brookings Institution and Columbia University provided Carter with the results of their latest research on international diplomacy. He asked tough questions about the Soviet Union, took notes, and reported what he wanted to the press, but he evaluated the advisors and their information in terms of how he might use them in his administration.[30]

The next day, Carter entertained economists who came from the University of Pennsylvania, Yale University, and the Massachusetts Institute of Technology by bus, as usual, from Atlanta. Among them, Alfred E. Kahn and Charles L. Schultze impressed Carter, but he showed particular interest in a report sent by Carolyn Shaw Bell, a professor at Wellesley College in Massachusetts, who argued that unemployment could be reduced without causing inflation. As potentially the first president since the end of the war in Vietnam, Carter faced the prospect of dealing with runaway post-war inflation, and full employment was not only humane but politically expedient.

The economists bored Carter, who thought he learned virtually nothing of value from them, but the next day when experts on foreign policy arrived by bus from Atlanta, Carter was eager to learn from them. Zbigniew Brzezinski reigned supreme, since he had actively sent position papers to Carter during his primary campaign. Carter invited Cyrus Vance, who had not participated in the campaign, for the second time. A man of considerable experience who believed that diplomacy could prevent war, he and his ideas appealed to Jimmy. Brzezinski and Vance appeared to be the leading contenders for secretary of state. Others who had served previous Democratic presidents, or had distinguished records in universities or government agencies or think tanks, included Richard Gardner, Tony Lake, Michael Blumenthal, Milton Katz, Robert Pastor, and Richard Holbrooke. Carter listened to all of them and imagined how they might serve in his administration. He left Mondale at Pond House to entertain the visitors, while he retreated to his home to relax and confer with long time aides Jody Powell, Greg Schneider, and Pat Anderson over dinner. Later he entertained the avid consumer advocate Ralph Nader and his young associate Jim Fallows.[31]

Once the others were gone, George H. W. Bush, the director of the CIA, arrived. Unlike others, who had a long journey to Plains, Bush arrived aboard an army helicopter, which set down on Peterson's field, a farm on the outskirts of town. For more than five hours, he and his team briefed Carter. So intensely interested was Carter that he asked Bush to return later for a second briefing. On this subsequent occasion Rosalynn got the chance to know the CIA director. She chatted with Bush and his team members and served them sandwiches for lunch and snacks when they took breaks. Miss Lillian, in her inimitable way, had told some reporters that her son would "clean house" at the CIA once he was inaugurated. Bush had heard her comment, and he had prepared a courteous and professional letter of resignation to be presented to Carter at the proper time. In the meantime, Carter learned from him about the Soviet Union, China, South Africa, and North Korea.[32]

No presidential candidate or president-elect had ever before asked so many questions about the CIA, nor had a beleaguered director worked so hard to answer them. Despite Carter's calm, inquisitive approach, Bush sensed correctly that Carter "harbored a deep antipathy to the CIA."[33] Mondale, who had served on the Senate's Church Committee that had recently investigated the spying agency, was, like Carter, as interested in protecting the civil liberties of US citizens as collecting useful foreign intelligence. Carter and Mondale depended upon the CIA for foreign intelligence, but they demanded an end to what they saw as its domestic abuses and violations of human rights.

The CIA, which had become the bête noire of restless liberals who had opposed the war in Vietnam and demonstrated for civil rights, had come under heavy criticism since the Nixon years. Nixon and Kennedy had used the intelligence agency to spy on US citizens and plan assassinations of certain foreign heads of state, including Fidel Castro of Cuba. President Ford had fired William Colby as director of the CIA and replaced him with George H. W. Bush, then the ambassador to the People's Republic of China. Ford issued Executive Order 11905 setting up a completely new structure for control of intelligence, including an Intelligence Oversight Board (IOB) made up of three private citizens to whom all agencies must report quarterly. Since the public furor had hinged on revealed assassination plots, Ford's order specifically stated that "no employee of the United States government shall engage in, or conspire to engage in, political assassinations."[34] The role of the CIA and how to use it was one of the toughest challenges Carter would face.

In dealing with the Soviet Union, Carter could use intelligence gathered by the CIA, but he also looked to the Helsinki Accords, signed by both the United States and the Soviet Union in Finland on August 1, 1975. The Soviet Union, under heavy criticism from the West for its abuse of Jewish dissidents who wished to emigrate, wanted to improve its relationship with the United States and its allies. Hence, its representatives joined Ford and thirty-three other leaders in Finland to sign the accords. Although all parties committed to guaranteeing human rights, the accords did not have the status of a treaty and therefore could not be enforced. The Soviets freely violated the agreement.

Hoping to stop those violations, both Carter's issues adviser and a prominent Jewish dissident living in Russia looked to Carter for help. Stuart Eizenstat abhorred Russian persecution of Jews, an argument that he used to reinforce Carter's stand on human rights and elevate it to a major goal of his foreign policy. Anatoly Shcharansky joined seventy-two other dissidents in sending a message to President Ford and candidate Jimmy Carter, urging them as US leaders to compel the Soviet Union to honor its commitment to the Helsinki Accords.[35] Carter, who was fully aware of the emigration problem, discussed it and many other issues with his advisers, concluding with no firm policy statements but only Reinhold Niebuhr's statement that "The sad duty of politics is to establish justice in a sinful world."[36]

Before he could formulate policy, Carter first had to win the election. Jordan fine-tuned his master plan of 1972, filtered in Mondale and his staff, eyed the budget, and calculated a strategy for Carter to campaign in every state. Tim Kraft vetted hundreds of persons to work as organizers in each of the states, and Stuart Eizenstat wrote issue papers. Meanwhile, members of the press flooded into southwestern Georgia. They could still only find lodging at the Best Western Motel in Americus, which was scarcely equipped to provide the space and comforts so many of them desired. Many of them were mystified by the strange politician from Plains.[37]

A man with a mission, Carter took his campaign westward into areas where he thought he needed to defeat Ford. Ham Jordan urged him to stop referring to "the Nixon-Ford administration," because so many Americans sympathized with Ford, a decent man whose quiet demeanor obscured his strengths and who had been handed a thankless task after Nixon's scandalous resignation. Attacking him personally would not win votes for Carter, who did remove Ford's name from his heated rhetoric about Nixon's "unsavory" character.[38]

On August 22 in Los Angeles, Carter delivered a mundane talk about tax shelters to a group of mostly Hollywood executives. The evening proved more exciting after a limousine whisked him away to actor Warren Beatty's suite at the Beverly Wilshire Hotel. Jerry Brown, the governor of California and a former rival, showed up, as did actors Faye Dunaway, Diana Ross, Tony Randall, Sidney Poitier, *Playboy* magnate Hugh Hefner, and other Hollywood stars. Without regard for how it might sound to his wealthy audience, Carter declared that "public servants like me and Jerry Brown . . . have a special re-sponsibility to bypass the big shots, including you and people like you, and make a concerted effort to understand people who are poor, black, speak a foreign language, who are not well educated." The government should be run, he said, so that "those services that are so badly needed can be delivered."[39] Many of those present agreed with him, and Carter departed believing that he might count on their help.

Moving northward and eastward on his trek back to Plains, often con-fusing his audiences by saying some things they wanted to hear and some that they did not, Jimmy got the attention of many Americans. Joining the Republican vice-presidential nominee Bob Dole at an American Legion con-vention in Seattle in late August, he cited a long list of ways he would im-prove the Veterans Administration. Then he dropped a bombshell by stating frankly that he did not favor amnesty for the Vietnam War draft dodgers, but he would give them a "blanket pardon." The legionnaires stood up and booed him. Bob Dole, decorated hero of World War II, followed him to the stand and received a rousing welcome. Moving on, in Des Moines, Iowa, Carter told the farmers that he would not impose a grain embargo unless there was a national emergency. Since that comment did not seem to square with what he had said in non-farming states, Dole and Ford immediately accused him of flip-flopping and being unpredictable.[40]

Prominent African-American leaders also worried about Carter's sin-cerity. Jesse Jackson in Chicago had endorsed Carter for the presidency, but he remained skeptical after he got the nomination. He urged Blacks to keep pres-sure on Carter because "once a politician moves from his roots to the fruits, he may forget his roots." Julian Bond maintained his view that Carter could not be trusted on the race issue. Carter rebutted by planning appearances in urban areas around the country; he reassured African Americans during a speech in Los Angeles, explaining that "the granting of equal opportunities to our black people" was "the best thing that has happened to the South." He served as Honorary Chairman of the United Negro College Fund Capital Resources Development Program, and he welcomed Daddy King's remark that "Jimmy Carter has been with black people when it wasn't easy for him."[41]

Carter also needed Jewish votes in the general election. He had chosen human rights in part as his theme to win over those voters. He first expressed it explicitly at a B'nai B'rith meeting in late August.[42] Later in the fall, Jewish intellectual Morris Abram, who grew up in Fitzgerald, Georgia, about eighty miles from Plains, defended Carter against Jewish criticism: "We were both poor; I was an outsider because I was a Jew and he because he was an integrationist Southern Baptist." Abram believed that Carter was a person of character and competence, but many listeners in largely Jewish audiences responded that "Carter still has an uphill fight in our community."[43]

Jewish citizens, the majority of whom were Democrats, debated over support for the mysterious Southern Baptist. Rabbi Mayer Abramowitz, quoting Moshe Gilboa, former consul general of Israel in Atlanta, argued that Carter had great intellectual ability and made many positive remarks about Israel.[44] Journalist Meg Greenfield contended that Carter's religion was private and no threat to minorities who might disagree with him, but perhaps he should cut back on the use of the word Christian.[45] Hyman Bookbinder, the executive director of the American Jewish Committee, believed that the concern of Jews about Carter was exaggerated because he found "very little personal anti-Carter attitudes in the Jewish community."[46]

From New York to Los Angeles, Carter played the human rights card. Speaking to the New York Board of Rabbis on August 31, he praised the "tremendous commitment that Jewish citizens . . . have made to humanitarian issues." There was no difference between Jews and Baptists, Carter said, for they believed in the same god. President Truman, who had recognized the nation of Israel in 1948, was a Baptist. Some Jewish Americans believed that Carter might be the person to resolve the crisis in the Middle East. The "very essence of my faith is the very essence of the Jewish faith," he declared, for "we both believe in a fair and just legal order and the principles of ethics and morality."[47]

When Carter spoke to the B'nai B'rith Convention in the nation's capital on September 8, he emphasized that he was "proud to meet with a group of men and women with whom I share a total commitment to the preservation of human rights." A strong military defense, he said, was essential to the preservation of human rights. "We should quit being timid and join Israel and other nations in moving to stamp out international terrorism!"[48] Carter frequently referred to the Helsinki Accords and its support for international human rights, including the rights of private citizens to exercise freedom of speech and religion.[49]

Despite Carter's effort to appeal to all ethnic groups, he tried to avoid becoming the candidate of any special interests. Shortly after the Democratic convention, he had reminded his friend Bert Lance that he "really want[ed] to keep a lonely candidate image as much as possible."[50]

In parallel with her husband's travels, Rosalynn conducted her own campaign. She traveled to many states on a chartered jet accompanied by her secretary Madeleine McBean and her press secretary Mary Hoyt. Mary Hoyt, who had once worked for Eleanor McGovern during the 1972 presidential campaign, knew the Washington scene, and was especially capable of helping a politician deal with the press. Following a carefully planned itinerary—sometimes stopping in six states in a single day—Rosalynn attracted more attention than the candidate himself. Sometimes she got tired and irritable: she told one hostile crowd, "If you feel better with Gerald Ford, vote for him!"[51] But she soon recovered her calm demeanor, looking forward to returning to Plains where she drew strength from the place and its people, and from Jimmy.

Carter nearly derailed all of their good work, however, with an infamous interview he gave to *Playboy Magazine*. In meetings that had been set up by Powell and Jordan earlier in July, Carter had spoken with the editors of *Playboy* about giving them an interview. When two writers arrived at Carter's home in Plains, they found him sewing a rip in his jacket; he mumbled in answer to their question that he always did his own sewing. Carter gave his visitors a good summary of his campaign promises, but he was preoccupied and bored. He wanted Robert Scheer, a freelance writer, and Barry Golson, an editor of the magazine, to leave. They asked him another question about his religion, which irritated him. Unbeknown to him, they kept their tape recorder running as he ushered them to the door. Carter defended his Christian belief and need for forgiveness angrily, using salty language that was atypical of his public image. Unaware that his outburst had been recorded, Carter moved on from the interview as quickly as he showed his guests to the door. When Jody Powell was given the opportunity to review the piece before it was published, he declined because he had no idea it would be anything other than a routine interview.[52]

The day after Carter gave the *Playboy* interview, he did another with the *Washington Post* in which he expressed an innocent belief that what he had said to Sheer and Golson would not be controversial. "I had an interview yesterday with *Playboy Magazine*," he said. "Their article is going to come out in October and I would guess that the major point they are covering is my religious beliefs." He suspected that people who did not know him had a "normal concern" about "what the evangelical churches believe." Carter explained that "there is nothing distinctive about the Southern mind," including its religion, and that the South had made such progress in race relations and reducing poverty that it was little different than the rest of the nation.[53]

Carter's religious beliefs were already well known, for both he and Rosalynn had been compelled to answer many questions about his born-again status. During the campaign, when in Plains, Carter continued to teach his Sunday School class. Shortly after his nomination in July, he had explained to his class that he had once participated in a foot-washing ceremony and found it to be "one of the most moving experiences" he had had in church. A Christian could not be a hermit, and churches should not be organizations of elites, for "Christ dealt with simple people . . . prostitutes . . . tax collectors . . . dark-skinned people, and lepers."[54]

Less than a month before the general election, a Gallup poll showed that Carter's born-again status helped him with 19% of the voters and hurt him with 9%, whereas 68% did not care.[55] Still concerned about Catholic and Jewish voters, Carter did more outreach to both groups. He addressed a meeting of the National Conference of Catholic Charities, telling his listeners that "the basic beliefs and concerns that unite us . . . are more important than the issues that divide us." A friendly rabbi in Atlanta, Emanuel Feldman, traveled to eastern cities during the fall campaign, giving speeches and benedictions, and gleaning information about Jewish concerns for Stuart Eizenstat. Billy Graham, the renowned Southern Baptist evangelist who had virtually been the private pastor for Richard Nixon, did not leap on to the Carter bandwagon, nor was he invited. Nevertheless, he promised to remain neutral, pray for Jimmy, and support him should he become president.[56]

Carter won endorsements from the best known Jewish newspaper columnist in the country and academe's most renowned Catholic humanitarian: Eppie Lederer. Better known as syndicated advice columnist Ann Landers, she liked Carter and Miss Lillian so much that she supported his candidacy and helped with other contacts. When Carter's phone calls did not get through to Father Ted Hesburgh, president of Notre Dame University, Eppie sent Carter his private number and the details of a conversation she had had with Hesburgh. Referring to "Ted" as "the most highly respected and influential Catholic in the USA," she explained that Carter's acceptance speech had convinced him that Carter was the man the country needed. The two men began a friendship that would serve each of them well.[57]

Convincing Jewish voters to support him became a daily task. With Mondale at his side in Plains, Carter explained to a reporter that Israel should withdraw from major portions of territory captured in the 1967 war, relinquish control of the Golan Heights to Syria, and recognize Palestine. Knowing that those words would not be well received in Jewish circles, he repeated his "unequivocal" commitment to Israel. He believed that the Bible taught that Israel must exist as a Jewish State.[58]

Prominent Democratic leaders were easier to convince. Tip O'Neill, who anticipated becoming Speaker of the House after the election, assured Carter, that he, current Speaker Carl Albert, and the other Democrats in the House would work for his election.[59] They found Carter hard to get to know, but they liked his comments about arms control, improvements in agriculture and education, and protection of the environment.[60] The Carters appeared to have won the support of most members of their party as they moved toward Election Day.

FIVE

Jimmy, and Rosalynn, Won!

On Labor Day 1976 members of the Peanut Brigade stood shoulder to shoulder to form a wedge through which Carter could walk to approach the podium on the front porch of President Franklin Delano Roosevelt's "Little White House" in Warm Springs, Georgia, seventy miles northwest of Plains. The crowd was small, but Carter had rejected the Democratic tradition of kicking off the campaign in Cadillac Square in Detroit, Michigan, to attract the labor vote, since it was in the home state of Jerry Ford. Carter proudly drew the eyes of the world to his own home state and to the sainted Democratic President Franklin Roosevelt. Carter wanted to take upon himself the mantle of Roosevelt's New Deal and creation of the United Nations as an international peace keeping institution.[1]

Carter's campaign managers played the Roosevelt theme to the hilt. The lectern sported a famous picture of Roosevelt, and two of his sons stood on the platform. An African-American accordion player, Graham Jackson, who had been a favorite of Roosevelt's, played "Happy Days are Here Again." Patients in wheelchairs who were receiving treatment at the Roosevelt Institute for Rehabilitation occupied the front rows. The crowd applauded when Carter declared his aspiration to become the first person from the Deep South to be elected president since Zachary Taylor in 1848. He proudly proclaimed that he owed nothing to special interests and everything to the people. His promises to head a government that elevated work above welfare and to never tell a lie, captivated his audience.[2]

It was the Roosevelts' venue, but the atmosphere on that Labor Day in Warm Springs was charged with enthusiasm, hope, and great expectations for the extraordinary folks from Plains. The short ceremony ended, and Carter hit the campaign trail as soon as the television lights were turned off. Campaigning in South Carolina, Virginia, and New York City, he defended himself against Ford's charge that he was "flip-flop Jimmy," once again attempting to clarify his position on abortion, justice for African Americans, and the importance of education. He praised the courage of Southerners for

JIMMY, AND ROSALYNN, WON! 73

liberating themselves from "the long preoccupation with the racial issue" and argued that Southern politicians should not be stigmatized because of their stand on race in a bygone era.[3] Philanthropist John D. Rockefeller III, who liked Carter's commitment to social justice as well as business success, wrote him: "I find so much that is refreshing and encouraging in your outlook on our society today."[4]

Bob Jones, the president of Bob Jones University in Greenville, South Carolina, however, did not find Carter refreshing or encouraging. The extremely conservative, fundamentalist academic condemned Carter as a phony. He judged the Baptist candidate to be an imposter posing as a Christian who would "ride the gospel train into the White House by deceiving gullible Christians with his talk about being born again." He condemned Carter's stand on the rock music culture, abortion, women's liberation, and gay rights.[5]

The Carters' views did not hew to conservative religious positions about homosexuality, and they were openly supportive of the rights of gay people, who supported Carter for his liberal, humanitarian point of view. Some of them worked in the campaign, and the *Advocate*, the newspaper of the gay community, ran a full page advertisement showing Rosalynn talking to two gay leaders, one of them a minister, the other a medical doctor. Carter said the topic made him "nervous" because he had no "personal knowledge" about it but thought it should be handled like "any other sexual acts outside marriage." He would be president of all the people, he said.[6]

Carter returned to Plains feeling confident that he had satisfactorily defused Republican and evangelical attacks, but when the November issue of *Playboy* hit the stands, there was no escape for Jimmy or Rosalynn or Jody Powell or anyone who might now be called upon to explain Jimmy Carter to the voters. Governor George Busbee of Georgia thought that Carter's *Playboy* interview was a "refreshing change" from the "computerized politician," and that his openness and honesty erased stereotypes about Southern politicians. Others were not so kind. The national media immediately saw how they could profit by exploiting the gaffe, and others speculated that, if Carter won the presidency, the lingering, high-profile, salacious interview would contribute to his being a one-term president.[7]

Both Jody Powell and Hamilton Jordan had recommended that Carter give the interview, thinking it would be innocuous because readers would likely support him. Neither expected it would stir so much controversy, let alone damage the campaign. Powell read the interview shortly after his arrival in

New York City; later, he dryly remarked, "I figured we were going to catch some shit." Catch it they did. For the most part, the interview was another account of what Carter had said about himself and his platform many times before, but then he proceeded to explain to the interviewers the relationship between his religion and his public life. According to his understanding of the Bible, Carter said, "hate . . . sexual intercourse outside marriage . . . homosexual activities . . . steal[ing] . . . l[ying] . . . are sins." But, he believed that while all Christians are sinful, they should not judge others. He would not appoint judges according to their cultural positions, he said, but based upon their "judgment and integrity."

Becoming extremely angry with the persistent questions about how his religion might affect his politics, Carter declared that his faith did not condemn or persecute others. With increasing ire, he said that he did not run around as governor "breaking down people's doors to see if they were fornicating." According to Patrick Anderson, his speechwriter turned memoirist, "the Berkeley radical [Scheer] and the Southern Baptist moderate" considered each other "a freak," and Carter's outburst "can best be understood as a rebuke to Scheer and an attempt to have the last word."[8] Jews, however, who were skeptical of Carter's proselytizing ways, may have noticed that he was attempting to persuade the Jewish interviewers of the merits of Christianity.[9]

Scheer, a self-styled radical who had been educated at the University of California at Berkeley and had little understanding of Protestant beliefs, pushed Carter to emphasize once again that as a Baptist he believed in absolute separation of church and state. Carter quoted theologian Paul Tillich that religion is a continuing search for the truth and for an understanding of man's relationship to God and his fellow man. Carter wanted to emphasize, however, that he was human, tempted to sin like any man, and that he had violated Christ's impossible standard by committing adultery simply by looking upon a woman with lust in his heart. "I've looked on a lot of women with lust. I've committed adultery in my heart many times," he continued. God forgave him, he said, and he added that the fact that he was a sinner did not give him license to judge the guy who "leaves his wife and shacks up with someone else," or the one "who screws a whole bunch of women." Carter later said he did not know the tape recorder was still running and thought he was only talking to two men whom he could trust. Golson, however, countered that Carter knew the tape was running when he made his angry outburst and thought perhaps Carter was being quizzed about his religion and his "goody-two-shoes" image.[10]

Hoping to make clear how his religion would affect his public life, Carter clenched his fist while declaring that "I don't think I would *ever* take on the same frame of mind that Nixon or Johnson did, lying, cheating, and distorting the truth." Although the piece was in the November issue and was scheduled for release on October 14, the editors decided to release it on September 10, hoping to boost sales and perhaps influence the outcome of the presidential debates that were scheduled to begin on September 23. As reporter after reporter attempted to question Carter and Jody Powell about the article, Powell reprinted parts of the interview, drawing attention to the theology and ignoring the allegedly dirty words. Powell insisted that the interview revealed Carter as a "human being" coming to terms with the intersection of "his religious faith and his public policies."[11] Both Carter and Powell took a nonchalant attitude toward the bombshell review.

Some thought Carter wanted to deny the notion that he was narrow-minded, self-righteous, and a fundamentalist. Others thought he might be remembering the story he told about the time he found himself sitting across the table from actress Elizabeth Taylor. She directed a question to him, which he did not answer until she said, "Well, Mr. Carter?" Embarrassed, he quickly answered, "I'm sorry Ms. Taylor. I'm sure you were talking to me, but I didn't hear a word you said." When a female reporter asked Jimmy if Rosalynn knew that he lusted in his heart, he grinned broadly and said, "She knows!" But Carter was plenty worried about how that interview might affect his campaign. In his role as Carter's principal spin master, Jody hammed it up, declaring that the real shock would come when readers discovered that he was the centerfold. Furthermore, he joked: "Who knows, by putting spiritual quotes in *Playboy*, we may even get more people to read the Scriptures."[12]

The timing could not have been worse, for as Carter prepared to debate President Ford, Baptists and others became more and more vocal in condemning Carter for what he had said in the interview. Reverend W. A. Criswell of Dallas, the country's leading fundamentalist pastor, led the attack. Rosalynn dismissed it as of no consequence, but Carter's own pastor said he wished his parishioner would have chosen "other words." A former president of the pastors' conference of the Southern Baptist Convention wondered why Carter would give *Playboy* an interview at all and doubted that he was in "the evangelical Christian camp."[13]

In a lighter vein, members of the press traveling with Carter greeted him on his fifty-second birthday with a humorous song: "Lust in my heart, that's my theology . . . I'm a Christian eager-beaver; As *Playboy* said, I've got lust in my heart." Carter guffawed with delight when he heard it, but the notoriety was no laughing matter because it shook the very foundation of his run for the presidency. Privately, Carter was furious with Jody and the press for giving it so much attention, but he blamed only himself for the stupid mistake.[14]

Carter got some friendly advice too. Jack Valenti, the Hollywood mogul who had been an adviser to President Johnson, recommended not responding to questions about *Playboy* but to invite Lady Bird Johnson to meet him at the airport in Austin and campaign with him in Texas. Norman Vincent Peale suggested that Carter make no further mention of his religion. And an incensed Rosalynn went on the attack against the Republican advertisements about the interview and suggested that it would work against them, not Jimmy. "We have not brought up Watergate; we have not brought up the pardon," she said, bringing them up.[15]

Peppered with questions about the interview, Rosalynn said she never doubted Jimmy's faithfulness to her, but she was angry with the magazine for tricking her husband. She came up with various short answers: "Jimmy talks too much, but at least people know he's honest and doesn't mind answering questions." When a television reporter in Louisiana asked if she had ever committed adultery, she snapped, "If I had, I wouldn't tell you!" When the radical feminist Betty Friedan pushed a microphone in her face and asked "Can women lust?," Rosalynn coolly answered, "I think men and women have equal rights." Wasting little time on such questions, she worried about how the interview caused their whopping ten-point drop in the polls. Instead she told reporters that she preferred to discuss the issues of mental health, elderly care, and ratification of the ERA.[16] In the real world of politics, however, the titillating topic of lust lingered in the minds of the public more than the important policy matters Rosalynn emphasized.

From September 6 through November 1, the day before Election Day, Rosalynn journeyed coast to coast, visiting more than one hundred cities, carrying her message that the country needed Jimmy Carter. She was a powerful influence on the campaign, often urging Jimmy to move on from talking to one prominent man to the next one, telling her son Chip to put out a cigarette, moving Joan Mondale out of the limelight, and sometimes overruling political strategists. She avoided personal comments about Ford, read and studied history and politics while on the road, talked about her family, and worried if Amy would have trouble adjusting to life in the White House. Rosalynn saw no conflict in "being a good Christian and in being a good public servant." The press, not her husband, had interjected religion into the campaign. Despite her hesitancy and shyness when Jimmy first ran for office, she had come to enjoy campaigning, did it well, and treated it as hard work that must be done.[17]

From Michigan to California to Virginia, in a series of speeches during late August and September, Rosalynn fought hard to help Jimmy win the presidency. In Detroit, Michigan, she reported that the Republican Party was trying to escape its past, whereas the Democratic Party would build on its past to renew the United States. "And I can promise you this about Jimmy and me—we are going to do our best to make it so." On another occasion, as the contest intensified during the final days before the election, she told a crowd in Virginia that "We won this nomination—Jimmy did, I helped—with no strings attached." Although few, if any, commentators may have realized it at the time, she was campaigning for a dual presidency for herself and her husband. She declared her love for country music in Opryland, praised former First Lady Eleanor Roosevelt in Los Angeles, and called for government assistance to promote mental health legislation in Bakersfield, California.[18]

Jimmy frequently announced that as his equal partner, Rosalynn would assume responsibilities and activities equal to those of the president. He would send her, he said, on diplomatic missions to Mexico, South America, and Africa to "let them know we care about them" and to bring back information that could "correct a mistake or strengthen an alliance or friendship." His sons and their wives would help in similar ways. He agreed with one suggestion that "Rosalynn would be an excellent vice presidential running mate . . . , but . . . she is also held in my highest regard as my wife and my partner."[19] Hamilton Jordan told the press that Rosalynn was smart, tough, and would be more involved in the presidency than a traditional First Lady. Rosalynn did not "try to compare" herself "with anybody else," for she had learned that she could help Jimmy with anything.[20]

Rosalynn said that Jimmy never asked her or their sons to campaign, but they naturally did so because that was the way their family had always worked. Her life, she said, had never been "submerged in Jimmy's," for she had "always had her identity" and expected that would continue to be true in the White House. Time and again, she told admiring crowds that the First Lady should know the needs of the country, do something about them, and speak out on important matters. "I intend to do that," she promised.[21]

Ignoring Rosalynn, the Ford camp stepped up its attacks on Jimmy. It put out a series of newsletters filled with Carter quotes and Ford rebuttals.

On September 22, the day before the first debate, the Manchester, New Hampshire, *Union Leader* reprinted an editorial by former governor Marvin Griffin of Georgia. Griffin, who despised Carter's stand on race relations, accused Carter of doing an about face after he was elected governor, of "political perfidy," and of being a man whose "word is no good." "When I hear him telling my countrymen 'I will not tell you a lie,' it makes me sick in my stomach," Griffin declared. To have another of Carter's fellow former governors, other than Maddox, call him a liar, might, the Ford people hoped, help convince US voters not to trust him.[22]

Carter had his own plan to win the public's trust. He expected to use the debates to regain his lead in the polls and convince voters that he was the better person for the job. He thought that if he confronted Ford man to man without the White House and Rose Garden ambience, he could prove his superior intelligence and worthiness to be president to an anticipated television audience of one hundred million people. Taking some risk, Carter declined practice debate sessions, but he studied briefing books on all issues of domestic and foreign policy. The day before the first debate on September 23, he visited the site for the debate, the old Walnut Street Theater in Philadelphia, and checked to see how the blue suit he intended to wear would look under the lights there. On the day of the debate, he spent the final three hours alone with Rosalynn, later explaining that nothing was healthier for him psychologically than to be with her.[23]

What advice Rosalynn might have given him during their private time went unrecorded, but Carter got plenty of suggestions from his advisers and staff members. Speechwriter Pat Anderson recommended brevity, no sweating, being at ease, answering the question you want even if it is not asked, and appearing very certain of your answers. Jack Valenti told him to be accurate with details, keep cool, avoid the abortion issue, and keep Ford on the defensive. The editor of *US News and World Report* sent Carter a copy of the magazine's recent interviews with him and Ford, hoping they might help him predict what Ford would say. Ted Sorensen, John Kennedy's former presidential speechwriter, sent him a three-minute closing statement, recommending that his last words be "Ford and I see the country through very different eyes."[24]

Carter arrived at the debate site first. He stood quietly behind a lectern while an aide plugged an audio wire into an outlet taped to the heel of his shoe. He was fitted with another wire that extended from his shoe along the outside of his pants leg, around his waist, under his coat, up to his chest where it was secreted behind his tie. His lectern resembled the presidential podium but without the seal, and it was designed to lessen the appearance that he was much shorter than Ford. When Ford, who had carefully rehearsed for the event, arrived, he shook hands with Carter as they exchanged smiles, then moved to his lectern and had his microphone connected. The sponsoring League of Women Voters had attended to every detail, including carefully selecting the news persons who would ask the questions. Elizabeth Drew of the *New Yorker*, Frank Reynolds of ABC News, and James Gannon of the *Wall Street Journal* were seasoned political researchers and commentators who understood that the eyes of the country would be on them as well as on the candidates.

Carter drew the first question, and Frank Reynolds of ABC News asked him how he would deal with unemployment. In a lengthy and stilted response, Carter said he would call upon the government and private sectors to cooperate, increase production, and shift the tax burden to wealthier people. Ford pounced, accusing him of having no specific answers to any problems, and proclaimed again that the Republican solution would be to cut taxes and offer incentives to the private sector.[25]

No sooner had Carter begun to improve his performance than a technological error cut him short in mid-sentence. As he deplored the excesses of the CIA and FBI, the sound system malfunctioned leaving both men standing like frozen statues for twenty-seven minutes while technicians repaired it. The cameras remained on them most of that time as they mopped their brows. Carter sat down briefly. Once the sound was restored, Carter proved he understood domestic issues and the goals of his party, but it did him no good. He dropped in the polls from a 54–36 lead to 50–42. The first debate proved nothing, but Carter's concluding condemnation of the CIA for spying on American citizens prompted Tip O'Neill to say that Carter had "creamed" Ford.[26]

The morning after the debate, Carter left for campaign stops in Dallas and Houston before moving on to California. In Texas, Carter found himself in hot water because in the *Playboy* interview he had accused native son Lyndon Johnson of being a liar. Carter had phoned Lady Bird Johnson and apologized for having linked her husband's name with Nixon's. Bob Strauss, national chairman of the Democratic Party, and a Texan, met Jimmy at the plane in Houston and told him bluntly that his comment could lose Texas for the Democrats and would be exploited by the Texas Republican John Connally. Carter hastily held a press conference in which he said he was "truly sorry" for any embarrassment he had caused Lady Bird. When pressed by Sam Donaldson of ABC news and Robert Scheer, Carter confessed that he had made the pejorative remark about Johnson. By coming clean, he escaped further drilling and completed his Texas tour uneventfully.[27]

The Johnson family attempted to be gracious, but Lady Bird said she was confused and hurt by Carter's *Playboy* comment. She forgave him, however, and promised to vote for the party in the November election. Lady Bird welcomed Rosalynn to Austin and gave her a tour of the Lyndon B. Johnson Library. Rosalynn told her that the comment had been taken out of context, for Jimmy had only respect for Johnson.[28] Lady Bird dropped the topic, but her son-in-law Charles Robb, a Democratic politician in Virginia, sent Carter a long letter protesting the remark and reminding the upstart Carter of the importance of his family to the Democratic Party. Jimmy apologized again and assured Robb that he had not intended to malign former President Johnson in any way.[29]

Carter attempted to keep the issues, not personal controversies, before the public. The country, he said, should cease dependence upon foreign oil, conserve energy, and reduce nuclear weapons in all countries to zero. Détente with the Soviet Union meant peaceful competition, not US surrender of military strength or abandoning commitments to its allies. If China would recognize the independence of Taiwan, the United States should normalize relations with her. NATO needed more support from member nations, and no one should expect the United States to support it alone. Morality, which emphasized diplomacy over war and human rights for all people, should be imposed upon foreign policy. Following the example of Father Ted Hesburgh, Carter wanted the United States to lead the battle for human rights around the world. Religious persecution and corporate bribery of foreign officials should be stopped. US volunteers should take pride in improving their country, and the government should protect the environment and national parks. The United States need not be a melting pot, Carter thought, but a beautiful mosaic and a beacon of light to the world.[30]

Both Ford and Carter survived petty arguments about campaign contributions and questionable minor political favors from large corporations as they headed into the second debate. The candidates met on October 7 at San Francisco's Palace of the Fine Arts on a set almost identical to the one in Philadelphia, but this time the topic was foreign policy. Nevertheless, Ford seemed rattled by lingering questions about his campaign financing as a Congressman, and he resented questions that impugned his integrity. Carter's preparation for the debate at the hands of Hamilton Jordan, Jerry Rafshoon, Zbigniew Brzezinski, and others was short but thorough. Carter attacked the Republican administration as being style without substance, lacking character, and having a failed foreign policy partly because it allowed Henry Kissinger to be the "President of this country." Ford counterattacked, charging that Carter's economic policy would weaken the nation's defense and limit its negotiating position.

For more than an hour, back and forth they went, attacking and denying, until Max Frankel, former Moscow correspondent for the *New York Times*, asked Ford a tough question implying that he had been soft on the Soviet Union. Referring to the Helsinki Accords of 1975, signed by thirty-five nations including the Vatican, Frankel baited the president, one of the signers, by saying it recognized that "the Russians have dominance in Eastern Europe." Ford shocked the panel, Carter, and the nation with a firm declaration that "there is no Soviet domination of Eastern Europe, and there never will be under a Ford administration." Incredulous, Frankel repeated the question, thinking Ford had simply not understood and had misspoken, but Ford gave the same response. When Ford repeated his incredibly stupid remark, his national security adviser Brent Scowcroft turned white, but the Democrats were beside themselves with glee. Carter may have gained more votes from Ford's gaffe and the implication that he, Carter, would be tough on the Soviet Union than he did from all his moralizing and work to win Jewish votes.[31]

No one could believe that the president of the United States could have made such an incorrect statement. After investigation, Frankel discovered that Ford's answer came from a Kissinger briefing paper, but one which he had not understood. Ford later explained that peoples in Eastern Europe did not consider themselves under Soviet rule even though their governments were controlled by the Soviets. Ford's aides fielded questions trying to cover and explain his terrible mistake, and Ford himself made ineffectual attempts to clarify what he had meant. Carter took the offensive during the debate with dramatic overkill, urging Ford to tell the truth about how he had overdrawn his personal bank account to repay money he had taken from a political account to pay for the family's ski vacation. Ford admitted that he had lied about supporting legislation that would penalize US companies who cooperated with an Arab boycott of corporations that employed Jews and dealt with Israel. After the debate, Ford finally apologized for the "misunderstanding" about Soviet domination of Eastern Europe and did his best to woo

Polish American voters. Five days after the debate, back in the Oval Office, Ford conceded that he had made a serious mistake; the damage had stopped his campaign dead in its tracks. A poll showed that Carter had won the debate by a whopping 45%, emerging with a lead of 48–42% over Ford, though this was a 2% drop from his previous lead.[32]

The second debate had scarcely ended before Carter collected congratulations and advice. He was bombarded with information about how to condemn Ford's foreign policy on Vietnam, the Middle East, Cyprus, and Angola. One Columbia University professor told him that he "took charge from the beginning, put the President on the defensive, and showed an extraordinary grasp of the issues . . . ." Andy Young urged him not to go on the "defensive and answer ridiculous charges." Let "'Miz Lillian's Boy' show through," his African-American friend advised. Share the "deep and abiding hopes that you have for people." "Keep Faith," he said, "and know that there is an inner spiritual reserve which will never let you down. Love, Andy."[33]

The best advice came from Rod Goodwin, the image specialist and camera man who had come to know Jimmy and Rosalynn quite well. He had quickly realized that Rosalynn knew how to turn to the camera, use a makeup rag, and gently guide Jimmy and others in a photograph; she also understood the importance of brevity.[34] Goodwin also wanted Jimmy and Rosalynn to win. He sent Jimmy some "random thoughts," the most important of which was that "Rosalynn's probably the best advisor you have." Be more aggressive, keep calm, don't listen to too many people other than Rosalynn, give simple answers, and promise that there will not be a tax increase, he said. He reported that "our boys are working their tails off," and "we don't intend to lose." "Hope to see you victory night in Georgia," he concluded.[35] Jimmy and Rosalynn did not intend to lose, and Jimmy would admit, although she would deny it, that Rosalynn was his best adviser. And Rod would be with them on victory night.

In the meantime, the vice-presidential candidates Walter Mondale and Bob Dole held a debate. Dole accused the Democrats of being responsible for all the wars of the twentieth century. Mondale retorted that he wondered if Dole, a wounded hero of World War II, believed there had been a partisan effort to defeat Nazi Germany. Mondale gave serious answers to questions about Democratic policies and added a three-point increase to the ticket. Carter and his camp were thrilled, and Carter called Mondale to congratulate him on proving he was capable of being president. The campaign prepared literature to emphasize Mondale's partnership with Carter, which it would distribute everywhere except in the South where Mondale was not popular.[36]

In the meantime, Carter and Ford attempted to outdo each other in making negative remarks. Carter said Ford was even "worse than his predecessor," Nixon, in managing the nation's economy, and Ford accused Carter of being willing to do anything to become president. Their final debate took place in Williamsburg, Virginia, at the College of William and Mary on October 22. Barbara Walters moderated, and Carter's friend Jack Nelson of the *Los Angeles Times* sat among the inquisitors, who included Joseph Kraft and Robert Maynard. Under Nelson's intense questioning, Ford was unable to deny convincingly that he had not conspired with the Nixon White House to pardon the former president. Carter, speaking about the low level of the campaign, admitted that his *Playboy* interview had been a bad mistake and a poor forum in which to express his Christian faith. He hoped that both candidates could admit their mistakes and leave the mudslinging behind them. Ford pledged to conduct the final ten days of the campaign on a high plane, but as the combatants left the hall that fall day, the bored voters probably anticipated very few changes before Election Day.[37]

It was not the candidates themselves, but Rosalynn who gave an "electrifying performance" in Alexandria, Virginia, the day after the debate. Fueled by passion, anxiety, and hope for a satisfactory end to a grueling campaign, she told her audience that "Jimmy knows human beings." She assured them that she and her husband had won the nomination with no strings attached and that Jimmy would be "a great President." Supported by her own campaign team located at 100 Colony Square in Atlanta, she went to New York, Michigan, Indiana, and Tennessee, among other places. At the Washington Press Club, only a block from the White House, she declared "Jimmy and I don't believe in mediocrity in government." On a Public Broadcast Service (PBS) broadcast, she talked about Southern women, family values, and having roots.[38]

Rosalynn, Jimmy, and Ford all virtually ignored the independent candidacy of Eugene McCarthy. An ultra-liberal from Minnesota who had attempted twice before to win the presidency, he thought he might have a chance again in 1976. He despised Carter and Mondale, calling Carter a demagogue, a religious phony, and "a pet redneck." He drew liberal votes away from Carter, which prompted the Carter campaign to urge voters not to waste their votes on McCarthy, who picked up twenty electoral votes in Oregon, Maine, and Iowa. In New York, where Carter was vulnerable, the

Democrats spent $50,000 in legal fees to prevent McCarthy's name from getting on the ballot. McCarthy's biographer thought that had he succeeded getting on the ballot in New York, he would have drawn enough liberal voters and delegates to make Ford the winner. But it didn't happen that way, and McCarthy faded from the national political scene.[39]

Thinking the race almost won, Carter was faced with a new crisis in Plains. On October 31, the last Sunday before Election Day, an African-American minister, Reverend Clennon King of the Divine Mission Church in Albany, Georgia, accompanied by two black women and a child, was turned away from the door of Plains Baptist Church. The church's minister, Reverend Bruce Edwards, would have admitted King, but his hands were tied by the Board of Deacons who had voted the previous Tuesday not to let him in, because he was neither a Baptist nor a resident of Plains. King had written Edwards in advance, and sent a copy of his letter to Carter, saying he planned to present himself for membership on October 31 because he believed "that my prayerful choice to seek your direct fellowship will greatly please our Celebrated Brother James Earl Carter and his family."[40]

The "Celebrated Brother" was not pleased and notably shaken by this unexpected challenge to his veracity. When the deacons contacted him by phone, Carter strongly favored admitting King. The deacons, however, would not relent. Some of them suspected that the maverick King was put up to taking that action by Republicans who wanted to embarrass Carter. The incident may have cost Carter some Black votes, although Andrew Young, Hamilton Jordan, Jesse Jackson, and Daddy King rushed to rally support for him. In California, Carter hastily gave a speech deploring discrimination in his church and said he would admit anyone who lived in the community. King, however, did not live in the community, and he may have been a plant by Republican operatives. The President Ford Committee for Reelection sent messages to hundreds of Black ministers, signed by his campaign manager Jim Baker, arguing that if Carter could not influence his own church, how could he be expected to influence Congress.[41]

On Election Day, November 2, the Carter family voted in Plains. The polling place, a small cinder block building, looked more like the storage facility it actually was than a voting place. Rosalynn voted first, followed by Chip and Caron, then Jimmy. Emerging from the unpretentious tiny building, he smiled and announced that he had voted for Walter Mondale and his running mate. Then, the Carters all departed immediately for Atlanta, where they would await the results in the posh Capitol Suite of the Omni

International Hotel. Their children, Rosalynn's sister, and Jimmy's sister Ruth were already there. They laughed, talked, and prayed. Miss Lillian remained in Plains where she joined Rosalynn's mother at the railroad depot to await the results of the election. Others in the Atlanta suite and rooms below included Edna Langford and her husband state Senator Beverly Langford, Hamilton Jordan, Jody Powell, Charles Kirbo, Jerry Rafshoon, Pat Cadell, Madeline McBean, Mary Hoyt, Rod Goodwin, and more close friends.[42]

By two o'clock in the morning, the Carters still needed a few more electoral votes to win. They held hands, fell silent, and waited for the good news that was sure to come. Downstairs in the hotel ballroom, more than 3,000 supporters and workers awaited the votes from Hawaii and Mississippi. Jody Powell took the podium and told them to be patient, for "We have waited more than a hundred years for this moment. We can wait a few minutes more." A Carter victory would mark the return of the South to the presidency after more than a century in exile. Governor Cliff Finch of Mississippi called Jimmy at 3:30 a.m. to tell him that he had won Mississippi just as John Chancellor made the announcement on NBC news.[43]

Carter took 297 electoral votes to Ford's 241 and squeaked in with 51.05% of the national popular vote. Carter carried the South, except for Virginia, and won by narrow margins in New York, Ohio, and Pennsylvania. He won most of the Democratic, independent, and liberal votes. An overwhelming majority of Blacks and Hispanics voted for him, but only 47% of whites. Ford got a majority of the Protestant vote, but Carter's work to win Catholic and Jewish voters paid off when he won 54% of Catholic and 64% of Jewish voters. On the dawn of Election Day, the vote had been too close to call, but by 3:30 the next morning, Carter had been elected thirty-ninth president of the United States.[44] One group that remained skeptical of Carter, and whose goodwill he would need but was not likely to get, was the media. Since their rise to prominence, Jimmy and Rosalynn were difficult for the elite media to fathom, and Carter saw himself in combat with them, an unfortunate relationship for a president who depended upon the media for a complete and accurate presentation of what he might accomplish in office.[45]

Carter immediately called Tip O'Neill, "I just want you to know that I will be able to work with you and the members of Congress, and we'll get along great together." After thanking labor leaders, mayors, and senators, Carter announced to the room "We won," and all there cheered, cried, and embraced. Ushering Rosalynn and their children into a bedroom for a private conference, he told them that he could not have done it without them, and with them he could accomplish the huge task ahead. Carter thanked the jubilant crowd at the Omni, traveled home with Rosalynn, and arrived at the old railroad depot in Plains just as the sun rose.[46]

Miss Lillian, weary from the long wait, smiled broadly at the news and proudly spread wide her arms to reveal a sweat shirt declaring "Jimmy Won!" At a 7 a.m. rally, Jimmy thanked his friends and neighbors. Claiming humility, he told them that he and Rosalynn never felt "we were better than anyone else." Each individual must help to make the country great, he said, and he hoped he could "be the kind of leader to tap the greatness in the people." Paraphrasing the famous comment Benjamin Franklin had uttered at the conclusion of the Constitutional Convention almost two hundred years earlier, he noted that "The sun's rising on a beautiful new day . . . a beautiful new spirit . . . a beautiful new commitment to the future." Rosalynn simply said, "Thank you. I'm glad to be home. Thanks every one of you."[47]

As the rising sun cast its first rays on that dazzling gathering in such a remote place, Jimmy and Rosalynn glanced at each other as the tears streamed down their cheeks. Rosalynn had never felt so proud of her husband, she said, as a "new beginning both for us and for our country" dawned.[48]

At the White House, First Lady Betty Ford whispered to her daughter: "He doesn't know what he's gotten into."[49]

SIX

The Shadow Presidency

Following their rally in Plains, the Carters returned to Atlanta where he delivered his official victory statement at the World Congress Center. President Ford had conceded the night before, promising "whole-hearted support" and a smooth transition. Carter, the first Georgian ever and the first Southerner in over a century to be elected president, promised to unify a proud nation, put people back to work, correct mistakes of the past, and make the nation as great as its people.[1] Then he and Rosalynn returned to Plains to rest and to prepare for his first press conference the next day.

On November 5, President-elect Carter held his first press conference at the Plains railroad depot. The few hundred of his friends and neighbors who gathered in the chill could hardly believe that their neighbor and friend would soon be the most powerful person in the world and that their little town would be the site of the Southern White House. Carter made clear, however, that Jerry Ford would be president until January 20, that Mondale would represent the incoming administration in Washington, and that he himself would spend a few days each week there during the transition. Mondale and Carter made an unusual team. Never before had a president and vice president had such a close relationship. Carter treated Mondale with respect and appreciation and intended for his role in their administration to be more than merely ceremonial.[2]

On November 6, Jimmy and Rosalynn left to vacation at Musgrove Plantation on St. Simon's Island off the Georgia coast. The family trip was a time for rest and recreation punctuated by work. Rosalynn, Jimmy, their three sons and their wives, nine-year-old Amy, and their Secret Service agents boarded an Air Force 707 jet to travel to the estate owned by the grandson of tobacco tycoon R. J. Reynolds. Jimmy himself paid for their use of the property.[3] He and Rosalynn used some of their time there to respond to the avalanche of correspondence they were receiving, often writing by hand dozens of personal letters.[4]

Among their correspondents, the Shah of Iran sent a friendly and professional congratulations note. According to the shah's closest adviser, however,
the elevation of Carter to the presidency meant that the relationship between
Iran and the United States was heading for an upheaval. Mincing no words
and showing no respect, Asadollah Alam, the shah's minister of court, had
written after the Democratic convention that, if Carter became president,
"who knows what sort of calamity he may unleash on the world. He's no more
than an ignorant peasant boy." On November 26, 1976, Alam told US journalist Joseph Kraft that, unless the stubborn shah moved quickly to change
the new president's mind, the Carter administration would turn against Iran
because Carter did not want a further military build-up in the Middle East
and he blamed Iran for the rise in oil prices. Alam also predicted that Carter
would attack the shah's record on human rights.[5]

Carter was caught in a bind between the politics and economics of US support of the shah and his commitment to human rights, as well as his responsibility for solving the energy crisis. Furthermore, Carter was involved in a
complicated triangular relationship with the shah and John D. Rockefeller
III that few, if any, knew anything about. Rockefeller's brother David had
organized the Trilateral Commission and had tapped Carter to serve on it,
which had provided him with important contacts, incentives, and support
in his bid for the White House. From 30 Rockefeller Plaza in New York City,
where David presided over the operations of Chase Manhattan Bank, the re-
pository for much of the shah's wealth, John and David sent their individual
congratulations to Carter. John wrote that he welcomed Carter's call "for
unity" and the "exciting opportunity to lift our country and to move it forward." Republican David Rockefeller promised "full cooperation," but it was
not clear what he meant by that.[6]

The oil industry, through which the Rockefeller family had made millions
of dollars, viewed Carter's victory with alarm. Since the nation was in an
energy crisis, at the heart of which was the skyrocketing cost of imported
oil, the president would inevitably be involved in plans to solve it. Some oil
executives feared that a humanitarian, reportedly hostile to big business,
would make decisions that would limit their profits, control consumption,
reduce demand with alternative sources of energy, upset international trade,
and possibly revolutionize their industry.[7]

Many Jewish Americans and Israelis also remained in a quandary. Despite Carter's promises of support, and a detailed knowledge
of their history and the Old Testament, his born-again Christian status

disturbed them. Carter asked Paul Zuckerman, his campaign adviser on Jewish affairs and chief executive officer (CEO) of the Velvet O'Donnell Corporation, famous for his development and marketing of homogenized peanut butter, to go to Israel and make his case for him. Zuckerman had worked for both Nixon and Ford but disliked them both and had attached himself to Carter during the campaign. In defense of Jimmy, Zuckerman gave an interview to the *Jerusalem Post* in which he argued that the president-elect "Feels that Israel is America all over again, only two hundred years later—a small country of farmers and idealists— outgunned and outmanned by its enemies, but determined to survive and grow . . . contributing more than its share to the welfare of all people—all over the world."[8] Unconvinced, Jewish Americans watched and waited to see what Carter would do. Carter's humanitarian sympathies were deeply stirred, however, by the plight of Jewish dissidents who suffered persecution in the Soviet Union. Touched by a telegram from Andrei Sakharov, the best known Soviet dissident, Carter decided to intervene. A physicist who had joined the Soviet research group on atomic weapons, Sakharov had become one of the best known researchers and scientific writers in the world. In 1953, aged thirty-two and only three years older than Jimmy, he had become the youngest person ever elected to the Soviet Academy of Sciences. By the late 1950s, Sakharov, increasingly aware of the great dangers of nuclear testing, had begun to urge Soviet leaders to cease such testing and abandon the arms race.

By 1970, Sakharov was militantly pressing for civil liberties in the Soviet Union. He condemned his country's 1968 invasion of Czechoslovakia and published a powerful essay urging cooperation between the Soviet Union and the United States. Banned from scientific circles and the Soviet press, he escaped arrest because of his fame as a scientist. His wife Elena Bonner supported and encouraged him, and in 1975 he received the Nobel Peace Prize.[9]

The day after Carter was elected president, Sakharov sent him a telegram saying: "I welcome your election. Your decisive, unambiguous statements in defense of the rights of man throughout the world have a deep significance and raise new hopes." Fearlessly, he continued, flattering the United States for its "courage and decisiveness," "democratic and moral traditions," and powerful "economic and military relationships" that made it "the leading nation of the West."[10] Carter, waiting in the wings to assume the power of the presidency, embraced Sakharov's challenge.

In the meantime, the newly elected president was bombarded with advice. Jack Valenti, who had been very close to Lyndon Johnson, knew that much of Johnson's success came from his close relationship with Congress, but as he and others studied Carter's career, they realized that the Georgian's soft spot was his tortured relationship with the state assembly when he had been governor. On the day of Carter's victory, Valenti gave him unsolicited advice on how to get along with Congress: answer phone calls the same day, instruct staff to reply to trivial requests, give Congressional receptions at the White House, and choose his congressional liaison wisely. That advice fell on deaf ears, as did that of another friendly critic who told him that he was being insulated by his senior staff and ignoring the people who had worked hard to see him elected.[11]

Too busy creating a shadow presidency to consider advice that might have helped them, Jimmy and Rosalynn proceeded to set up the administration that they would transfer to Washington after his inauguration. A month before his nomination, Carter had asked Jack Watson, an attorney who worked with Kirbo, to establish a Transition Planning Group. He told Watson to ask for any help he needed, and "all the John Gardners of the world, the McGeorge Bundys, the Clark Cliffords, and anybody you call will help." Throughout the summer and fall, Watson had done as instructed, collecting a group of experts who produced briefing books for Carter to study. Watson set up a computerized Talent Inventory Program to analyze the resumes of potential presidential appointees and held discussions with former cabinet members, White House Staffers, and academics, providing the president-elect with the opportunity to choose a highly qualified staff. Watson objected to Carter's choice of Frank Moore, who had served as Congressional liaison during the campaign, as liaison with Congress. Many members of Congress agreed with Watson, but Carter stubbornly insisted that Moore was the man for that job.[12]

Carter became the first modern president who chose not to have a chief of staff. He did not want an "interim boss" between himself and a dozen or so people who would have direct access to him, nor did he care if those advisors disagreed with each other. Carter wanted to function more like the center of a wheel with spokes going out in every direction.[13] He accepted responsibility for the buck to stop with him and him alone.

While deeply involved in the important business of setting up his administration, Carter was distracted again by Reverend Clennon King, who again attempted to attend the Plains Baptist Church and was again turned away.

A week later Jimmy and Rosalynn attended a church meeting at which it dropped its racial barrier, chose a committee to screen new members to determine if they were sincere, and voted to retain Bruce Edwards as its pastor. The deacons realized that the world was looking at Plains. Clennon King did not try to attend a service but rejoiced in the decision. The next time Jimmy attended, it was a night service at which he was accompanied by a Black Secret Service agent.[14]

For the remainder of November, Carter granted interviews and issued memoranda in which he spelled out what he intended to do with foreign relations. He promised to meet with Brzezinski and key members of Congress to plan a policy that would create "world order" by attempting "to establish peace." Taking up the challenge of the Cold War, he said he would treat developing nations not as a bloc but as individual sovereign states that should make their own decisions about whether to support the Soviet Union, the United States, or neither. He expected to use members of his family as unofficial emissaries. Carter spent many hours reading memoranda from advisers on foreign policy issues involving nuclear proliferation, the Soviet Union, Israel, China, Panama, Japan, and others. He called for the CIA to brief him frequently about its operations.[15]

Rosalynn, who was not intimidated by the impending move into the White House, faced a media blitz. She would welcome her sons Chip and Jeff and their wives as permanent residents in the White House, she said. Jeff would attend a local university while Chip and her daughters-in-law worked unofficially for the president. Rosalynn expected her mother and mother-in-law to be frequent guests, and she planned to schedule quality time with Amy and direct her education. Rosalynn had studied the history of the White House, selected a new wardrobe, begun to organize her staff of eighteen, and planned to set up a presidential commission on mental health. She expected her husband to confide in her about most issues that were not top secret. She had become used to media criticism and insisted that "I'll just be me—Rosalynn."[16]

One interviewer found Rosalynn to be cool, calm, with the "ability to handle whatever comes up, or to turn it aside," and a "woman of real feeling, of vigor and health and character."[17] Nor would Rosalynn be intimidated by her husband's role as president, but she would reserve private time for recreation, travel, and enjoying life with him.

As First-Lady-in-waiting, Rosalynn was an extraordinarily unpretentious hostess to the hundreds of people, whether eminent or undistinguished, who came to Plains. At a potluck fundraiser for the national Democratic Party staged at the Pond House, she had proved right before the election that her egalitarianism was genuine. Although the guests paid $5,000 a plate and arrived in limousines and Lear jets that landed at Peterson Field, she greeted them the same way she did her neighbors. They were provided with name tags written on pieces of torn brown bags, seats in rickety chairs at picnic tables, and entertainment by a band named "Gritz" while Amy did a clog dance. Eighty local women each cooked enough food for ten people at their own expense, and the champagne was donated. Because the guests had paid enough for the opportunity to relax and enjoy themselves, Rosalynn barred the press. It was a party unlike any that most of the important people had ever attended, and Rosalynn pulled it off, raising $1.3 million with zero overhead.[18]

Rosalynn had already negotiated several life transitions: from shy school girl to competent Navy wife; from business manager to political strategist and First Lady of Georgia. She intended to support Jimmy's projects in the White House, and she knew that he would enable hers. Jimmy valued her judgment of people, and one observer of the process of making cabinet appointments said, "If Rosalynn okays you, you're in. If she doesn't, you're dead."[19] Jimmy often listened to her, but, she said matter-of-factly, "Nobody controls Jimmy, and nobody ever will."[20]

Carter, traveling back and forth between Washington and Plains, continued to welcome advice from a wide variety of people other than Rosalynn. One among them, wrote that his "heart bleeds" when he thought of the "unfortunate youngsters" who were dragged into the Vietnam War while the more affluent escaped, a sentiment shared by Carter. Father Hesburgh, who agreed with the letter writer and worked with draft dodgers, met Carter for the first time at Blair House in November. The two men bonded quickly, and Hesburgh shared his voluminous information about the draft dodgers of the Vietnam War with Carter.[21]

Carter, who had promised to pardon the draft dodges, also had to answer more questions about his religion. He and Charlie Kirbo tried to reassure liberals, conservatives, and those who worried about his religion that they had no need for concern. Wishing to minimize the issue, Carter reminded his secretary, Susan Clough, that when she wrote letters for him, "Do not [insert] 'prayers' unless the incoming letter has it."[22] Kirbo emphasized Carter's business success, not his religious viewpoint. Speaking at a private luncheon for business people in Cincinnati, Ohio, in late November, he declared: "I like to make money, Jimmy likes to make money, you like to make money, we're all going to get along fine." He asked "liberals in the audience" to spread that word.[23]

Carter was more interested in making peace in the Middle East. Israeli Prime Minister Yitzhak Rabin sent him a message on November 30, saying that the impending 1977 elections in Israel would not hinder peace efforts and that he wanted to visit the United States early in 1977 to meet with Carter.[24] Carter had already collected information on the Middle East, some of it from Senator Abraham Ribicoff who had recently visited Israel and Egypt and had talked to both Rabin and Egyptian President Anwar Sadat. According to Ribicoff, the United States would be the key to a settlement, relied upon by all parties to work out a formula for peace. Since Egypt had broken with the Soviet Union, President Sadat and Foreign Minister Ismail Fahmy were willing to recognize the right of Israel to exist, ignore the PLO, and restore territories taken in the Yom Kippur War of October 1973. Since Sadat was the only Arab leader ready to sign a peace agreement providing security for Israel, he wanted the United States, the United Nations, or another body to guarantee that Egypt would have the same protection. Carter, Ribicoff said, might be able to control Egyptian moderates at a rare moment when they were ready to talk peace.[25]

Fully briefed on the Middle East and most other issues that would drive his presidency, Carter met with Mondale at a retreat in Hilton Head Island, South Carolina, to discuss their relationship. Responding to the invitation to be honest and open, Mondale was forthright in what he wanted as vice president, namely to share the power of the presidency. Carter agreed. He would give Mondale an office in the West Wing, accept his chief of staff Dick Moe as a senior member of the president's staff, and instruct his staff to treat orders from Mondale as if they came from the president. Carter also agreed to appoint two of Mondale's friends to the cabinet: Bob Bergland as secretary of agriculture and Joe Califano as secretary of health, education, and welfare.[26]

A man of his word, Carter instructed Stuart Eizenstat to prepare a book organizing and listing all of his campaign promises. The finished project ran to one hundred pages divided into categories of Economy, Natural Resources, Human and Urban Needs, Justice, General Government, Special Groups, Technological Resources, Foreign Policy, East-West Issues (including the Panama Canal, the United Nations, and Foreign Aid), and Defense Policy. In the last category, Carter had promised to reduce spending by $5–7 billion a year, engage in long range planning, and evaluate the effectiveness of volunteer military recruitment. He wanted to reduce arms sales, work with the

Soviet Union for a quick freeze on atomic missiles and warheads, and call upon all nations to stop the sale of nuclear materials.[27]

On November 21, Jimmy and Rosalynn departed Plains to meet the Fords for the first time, tour the White House, and make preliminary plans for Amy's schooling. The two men planned to meet in the Oval Office while Rosalynn toured the mansion with Betty.[28] The Fords were cordial, but the visit did not go quite as planned. Betty's aide called Rosalynn at the Blair House to tell her that Betty was not feeling well enough to see her. The Ford White House did not want to publicize the fact that the First Lady was dealing with alcohol abuse. Betty rallied, however, and gave Rosalynn a superficial tour of the family's private living areas. The Fords and the Carters posed for a photograph, and the public knew nothing of the personal drama that had taken place away from the camera's eye.[29]

Back in Plains, Jimmy and Rosalynn gave the nation a rare glimpse of their personal home and lives in a short television interview with ABC journalist Barbara Walters, watched by fifteen million viewers, in mid-December. The Carters spoke about their personal closeness, love of home and family, and their church, but they said no more than they had already revealed during the campaign. After attending church with Jimmy and Amy, Barbara left town convinced that the country would be "led by a wise and good man and woman."[30]

During the month that began with Barbara Walters's interview, the Carters got a preview of what their future life would be like. Rosalynn accepted a private invitation to attend the inauguration of President Jose Lopez Portillo in Mexico along with other US guests. After the inauguration ceremony, she attended dinner at the home of the new president and his wife. Although the guests included President Ford's son Jack, Lady Bird Johnson, and Henry Kissinger and his wife Nancy, Rosalynn was the one toward whom all eyes turned. She delivered a message of "strong friendship" from Jimmy and endeared herself to the group by speaking in Spanish.[31]

More interested in how she might serve in the White House than international publicity, Rosalynn prepared to make mental health her primary project. Peter Bourne, a psychiatrist who had been the Carters' friend and adviser since they had lived in the governor's mansion, assured Rosalynn that a presidential commission on mental health would have a large professional staff to support her plan to look at all aspects of mental health. It would be a new world for Rosalynn, where others would stand at the ready to do her bidding and where experts and aides would research and execute her plans.[32]

The national media could not believe that a petite, pretty woman with such a soft voice could be so tough and accomplished. One journalist snipped that Washington would have to adjust to "flowers that aren't quite right and square dancing in the White House."[33] Jimmy encouraged Rosalynn to rise above such clumsy stereotyping of Southerners. They chuckled at a cartoon portraying them as country hicks who placed an outhouse on the White House lawn. It stuck in their craws, nevertheless, for, despite Carter's determination to reconcile the South and the nation, they were not allowed to forget that they were from Georgia and outsiders in the White House.[34]

Rosalynn had excellent manners and appreciated classical music, fine art, and great literature. She dressed properly for every occasion, and she could greet both the mighty and the ordinary with disarming warmth and charm. For the balls following the inauguration, she planned to wear the same starlight blue chiffon gown she had worn on the similar occasion when Carter had been inaugurated governor of Georgia. It was for "sentimental reasons," she said, but it also bespoke of "Jeffersonian" simplicity and economy. Reinforcing her intention to remain unchanged, she said she intended to shop at the same stores in Americus that she had always patronized, including Jason Cohens, and the Tog Shop. What she did not say in advance is that she would wear a designer dress for the pre-inauguration gala at the Kennedy Center.[35]

But in the time leading up to the inauguration, Rosalynn devoted more attention to non-sartorial matters. She participated in meetings at the Pond House where Carter prepared for their transition to the White House. There he met in a closed session with the Senate Foreign Relations Committee to discuss defense pacts with Greece and Turkey and their dispute over Cyprus. The same day, he welcomed economists, businessmen, and former Deputy Secretary of Defense Cyrus Vance to discuss inflation, stimulus packages, and international trade. The stony-faced sixteen economic experts wore business suits and generally predicted a gloomy economy, but Carter dressed casually in grey pants, a blue sports shirt, a beige cardigan sweater, and remained smilingly confident about the future.[36]

Savvy, organized, and tireless, Carter set up an elaborate procedure for choosing talented people to serve in his administration. He announced that Jody Powell would be his press secretary and Hamilton Jordan would supervise the Talent Inventory Process designed to identify persons competent to serve in the administration in areas of natural resources, human resources, economics, foreign affairs and defense, business and labor, and independent regulatory agencies. Jordan especially collected the names of women and African Americans who might be qualified to serve. After identifying the top three in each category, Jordan gave their names to Carter who selected the one he wanted. That work done, Carter, on November 20, released the names of his advisers: Ted Hesburgh, Lane Kirkland, Vernon Jordan, Irving Shapiro, Robert Strauss, Lucy W. Benson, Carol Foreman, Marian Wright Edelman, Hank Lacayo, Owen Cooper, and Patricia Harris. They represented the elite from the worlds of academics, business, labor, entertainment, religion, economics, and politics. Charlie Kirbo would investigate each person's financial records and other potentially embarrassing personal background information before the final appointments were made.[37]

Since Carter had campaigned against the CIA, he had no intention of accepting George H. W. Bush's offer to remain as director until a smooth transition could occur. To replace Bush immediately after inauguration day, Carter selected a former speechwriter of President John Kennedy, Theodore Sorensen, whom he believed to be a person of integrity, with attitudes toward the CIA similar to his own. Upon investigation it was learned that in 1946 Sorensen had registered for the draft as a conscientious objector, and some accused him of taking classified documents from the White House to use when he wrote his biography of Kennedy. Many Democrats, led by Senator Robert Byrd of West Virginia, were appalled. Joined by leaders of the AFL-CIO, they protested the choice of a man who was a pacifist and conscientious objector and whom they feared was too liberal for the job. On January 17, three days before the inauguration, Sorensen withdrew his name, leaving Carter with the prospect that, when he assumed the presidency, Bush's deputy would head the massive spy agency.[38]

Among Carter's inner circle, Ham Jordan got a bit cocky and assumed that he had more influence over the president's selections than he did. He told *Playboy* in late December that "If Cyrus Vance were named Secretary of State and Zbigniew Brzezinski head of National Security . . . I would quit," but he felt confident that would not happen.[39] It happened, Jordan did not quit, and Jimmy predictably did things his way.

When Carter introduced Juanita Kreps, a vice president at Duke University, as his choice for secretary of commerce, she gratefully accepted but rebuked him for his lack of knowledge about qualified women. Grateful, but outspoken, she said that she was Carter's second choice and that he was wrong when he said there were not a great many qualified women. Carter, standing nearby, smiled gentlemanly and stuck with his appointment.[40]

African-American candidates for major government positions were scarce. Patricia Roberts Harris, who had had a distinguished academic career at Howard University and later served as President Johnson's ambassador to Luxembourg, accepted the appointment to head the Department of Housing and Urban Development. Carter's friend Andrew Young, the well-known civil rights leader, agreed to represent the United States in the United Nations. Young might help the United States achieve rapport with African countries and rescue them from the Soviet fold, but he had no diplomatic experience and his civil-rights-era rhetoric and penchant for speaking his mind even when critical of the United States cast overshadowed his good deeds.[41]

Congresswoman Barbara Jordan wanted to be attorney general. When Carter invited her to Blair House to discuss a possible appointment, the meeting was disastrous. Hamilton Jordan and Walter Mondale were present. She took an instant dislike to Ham who teased her about how she pronounced her last name differently from the way he pronounced his. When she told Carter bluntly that she would like to be attorney general, Ham blurted "no, that's Griffin Bell." Barbara left the meeting disappointed and angry. Carter's later appointment of her good friend Azie Taylor Morton as the first African-American treasurer of the United States did not appease her. Carter missed his chance to place one of the best known African-American female politicians in high office.[42]

Griffin Bell, a slow-talking south Georgian, a relative of Rosalynn, a federal judge, and a former law partner of Charles Kirbo, was Carter's choice for attorney general. Bell was virtually unknown to the public and to the Senate, and his conservative lifestyle raised questions about whether he would be confirmed. Carter asked conservative Strom Thurmond, the ranking Republican on the Judiciary Committee, if he would support Bell. Thurmond's affirmative answer almost guaranteed his confirmation.[43]

Likewise, Carter's friendship and business relationship with banker Bert Lance assured him the position of director of the Office of Management and Budget. Closely allied philosophically and politically, Lance had loaned Carter money for the operation of his warehouse, and the two men shared a deep religious faith. Older than Carter, much wealthier, and extroverted, he was in a unique position to advise the president, although he lacked the political skills needed for such a high-level federal job.[44]

Many of Carter's other appointments were governors he had known or colleagues on the Trilateral Commission. Despite Jordan's boast, Carter chose Cyrus Vance for secretary of state. Although Carter had had limited association with Vance through the Trilateral Commission, Vance was recommended by Brzezinski, Henry Kissinger, and others. Selfless in his devotion to the country, Vance favored negotiation rather than war and shared Carter's strong interest in human rights. He had begun the negotiations that led to a temporary cease-fire in Vietnam during the Johnson administration, and he had served as deputy secretary of defense during the critical years of the Vietnam War and the civil rights disturbances. A protégé of former ambassador to the Soviet Union Averell Harriman, Vance impressed Carter with his quiet demeanor and negotiating skills. Like Carter, he wanted to resolve tension between Greece and Turkey, end the arms race with the Soviet Union, and achieve a comprehensive peace in the Middle East. Vance and his wife Gay were active in the Episcopal Church and soon became close friends with the Carters.[45]

For the most part, Carter selected candidates like Vance because he thought them best qualified for the positions, not because they had supported him or because he knew them well. He announced that Michael Blumenthal, CEO of Bendix Corporation, a major manufacturing and engineering company, would become secretary of the treasury, and Washington State Representative Brock Adams, a native of Georgia, would be secretary of transportation. Throughout December, Carter announced his other nominations: Governor Cecil D. Andrus of Idaho for secretary of the interior, Charles Schultze to chair the Council of Economic Advisors, and Zbigniew Brzezinski as special assistant to the president for national security. Bob Bergland of Minnesota, who had risen from poverty as a farmer to become a Congressman, seemed right for agriculture, and F. Ray Marshall, an economics professor from Texas, could manage labor.[46]

Brzezinski, who had written most of Carter's foreign policy position papers during the campaign and was well liked and respected by both Jimmy and Rosalynn, was an inevitable choice for one of the top positions in the administration. Zbig had admired Carter's work with the Trilateral Commission. He had listened carefully to Carter's campaign speeches about peace between Arabs and Israel, which often contained material he had submitted, and decided that it was "nice to hear a Democratic candidate for president with guts." When Carter named him national security adviser in mid-December, Brzezinski confessed that the position was precisely what he had always wanted. A native of Poland and professor at Columbia University, Brzezinski was a scholar of the Soviet Union and Eastern Europe with an increasing interest in China and Africa. Aggressive and ambitious, Zbig found himself in a position to get close to the seat of power. However, he was not liked by many others in the administration, including the secretary of state.[47]

When Bob Bergland went to Plains to meet Carter, Jimmy got straight to his point. "You know my family is in the peanut business," he said. When asked how he would he deal with peanut matters, Bergland replied that he knew nothing about peanuts but would hire someone who did. "Would you ask me for advice?," Jimmy asked. "Respectfully, no sir," came the response. "Good," Carter said. "I don't want to be involved in this business."[48] Although Carter continued to receive income from the peanut business, he and Rosalynn left its operation to his brother Billy.

A former naval officer, the president-elect gave special attention to selecting his secretary of defense. A physicist who had worked to discontinue nuclear tests, president of the California Institute of Technology, and former secretary of the air force under Johnson, Harold Brown had the experience and principles for the job. With a PhD from Columbia University, earned at age twenty-one, he had experience managing large budgets and strongly favored tightening purse strings, eliminating wasteful spending, and running a streamlined department. Ironically, Brown's Jewish faith was never mentioned in an administration often engulfed with Jewish affairs.

Brown thought like Carter thought, wrote tight and clear memoranda, understood weapons systems and world politics, and perfectly fit the role of secretary of defense. He readily accepted Carter's terms that he accept Charles Duncan, Jr., former president of the Coca-Cola Company, as his deputy. Brown and Duncan went to work immediately, much to Carter's approval, exchanging memoranda with McGeorge Bundy, who had been national defense adviser during the Vietnam War, and Ted Hesburgh about Vietnam war draft resisters, a controversial issue that Carter promised to address immediately after his inauguration. Loved by the military and respected by the public, Brown polled as the best of Carter's cabinet appointments.[49]

On Christmas Eve, Carter completed his cabinet nominees by naming Joe Califano for secretary of health, education, and welfare, as already agreed with Mondale. Califano had served Johnson well as his top domestic aide, enjoyed a lavish lifestyle, and may have expected the Carter presidency to be like Johnson's.

The reasons Carter chose James R. Schlesinger, a Republican, to advise him on energy and later to head the new Department of Energy may have been because Schlesinger possessed strong credentials in defense and other government positions. Ignoring Schlesinger's reputation for abrasive-ness and insubordination and his dismissal by President Ford from his po-sition as secretary of defense in November 1975, Carter took a chance that Schlesinger's experience and knowledge might override the negatives. Carter gave Schlesinger and his other cabinet appointees a free hand to choose their own staffs, but he instructed them to prioritize appointing women and minorities to top positions at every level of the federal government.[50]

Carter attempted to establish a cordial relationship with Congress be-fore his inauguration. His initial meeting with Democratic congressional leaders at Talmadge Farm in Georgia on November 17, 1976, went well. Georgia's senior senator Herman Talmadge hosted Mike Mansfield, Robert Byrd, Hubert Humphrey, Ed Muskie, Gaylord Nelson, Alan Cranston, Floyd Haskell, Russell Long, and House Speaker Tip O'Neill. Carter had wanted to include a few Republicans in the guest list, but O'Neill vigorously opposed this, warning the president-elect that they would play the role of obstructionists. The Speaker disagreed with the president-elect on dealing with Congress, the budget, and a stimulus package for the economy. Following that gath-ering in Georgia, Carter went to Washington several times to meet with the House and the Senate Foreign Relations Committees, Republican leaders, and Senate committee chairs. He learned that all Democrats would not rou-tinely support him, some Republicans would work with him, and that the rocky road he had tread in Georgia would likely be replicated with Congress in Washington.

Tip O'Neill, the incoming Speaker of the House, was appalled to discover that Carter intended to treat the United States Congress like the Georgia leg-islature. Destiny had cast the two men, who had almost nothing common, together as two of the most powerful men in US politics, the success and failures of each depending in part upon those of the other. Carter had never met anyone quite like Tip O'Neill. An Irish Catholic from Boston, an ex-quisite political manager, who placed domestic affairs involving the needs of the people above all else, O'Neill was plain spoken. His dislike for Carter's Georgian aides and incredulity about Southern culture became legendary, but he was prepared to educate the new president about the power of the Speaker and of the Congress. A man of iron will himself, Carter declined to relinquish any of the power of the presidency as he learned how to work with O'Neill to get his proposed legislation enacted into law. O'Neill's infa-mous account of how chief aide Hamilton Jordan had insulted him with a gift of inferior tickets to a gala at the Kennedy Center may well have been embellished to dramatize how he would not allow the power of the Congress to be diminished by the president. He nicknamed poor Ham "Hannibal Jerkin" and thereafter refused to deal with the president's de facto chief of staff. Ham denied the ticket story, but O'Neill repeatedly recounted it and continued his name calling. With the exception of Jody Powell, Carter's team never did get along well with the Congressional leadership. Tip O'Neill supported the Democratic president, but he never quite understood the intellectual, driven, sometimes arrogant Carter and usually did not like dealing with him.[51]

Endeavoring to remain the plain man from Plains, Carter took a breather from his presidential preparations to celebrate Christmas at home with his family. For the family's Christmas tree, he chose a scraggly pine from his woods, which was decorated with ornaments that had been homemade by the Carter children. On Christmas morning, Amy read the Christmas story from the Bible, the family exchanged gifts, and then they had breakfast with Miss Lillian. Dress was casual when they departed for dinner, the noon meal in Plains, at Miss Allie's home. Jimmy passed some of his time on Christmas Day writing letters and making phone calls to relatives and friends.[52]

The holiday over, Jimmy convened his first cabinet meeting at Musgrove Plantation, on Sea Island, Georgia, on December 28. Ostensibly a get-acquainted session, Carter was too much like his father and Admiral Rickover to waste time that might be used for productive work. He gave his new cabinet the bad news that his plan for frugality in the federal government meant that he would reduce the White House staff by 30%, including not choosing a chief of staff or providing limousines for cabinet members.[53] As *Time Magazine*'s writer showcased him in its man of the year piece, Carter emerged as a mystery and enigma, a man unlike any other president, a man with the "potential for greatness—or the possibility of disaster."[54]

Carter himself confidently expected to achieve greatness. He wanted his inaugural address to set the tone for his administration. After studying Woodrow Wilson's call for national repentance in his 1913 inaugural address, Carter decided that he too would use an appropriate Bible verse in his own speech. Beginning in early January, he went through multiple drafts and listened to several advisers, including his speechwriter Patrick Anderson and Rosalynn, before settling upon a passage from the prophet Micah: "what doth the Lord require of thee, but to do justly and to love mercy, and to walk humbly with thy God." Carter hand wrote his first drafts on a legal pad, and later typed drafts are peppered with his changes and corrections.[55]

In the final days leading up to the inauguration on January 21, 1977, the Carters sent thank you notes to many who had congratulated them, from Bobby Seale of the Black Panthers to Pope Paul VI. When Billy Graham, the conservative evangelist who was practically the personal pastor to Richard Nixon, could not accept the invitation to attend the inauguration because of illness, Carter replied that "We will miss you." Graham had signed his letter "with warmest Christian affection," but Jimmy closed with a simple "sincerely." Chief Rabbi of Israel Shlomo Goren wrote that he prayed for Carter's support to "achieve peace based on the Democratic institutions so sacred to us." To the rabbi and separately to Mother Teresa's blessing, "May the Light of Jesus always be with you," Jimmy responded that he looked "forward to the opportunity of working toward these goals we share in common."[56]

Perhaps with Mother Teresa's blessing in mind, Carter dictated a tough ethics code for members of Congress. They should divest themselves of holdings that might conflict with their official duties and reveal details of their personal wealth. After their terms ended, they should wait at least two years before taking a private sector job that might cause them to deal with anyone executing their former governmental duties. Many congressmen may not have appreciated such a lecture from the president-elect; and his code of ethics might be interpreted as Carter's contempt for or misunderstanding of the constitutional separation of powers.[57] None were bound by it. On Sunday, January 17, 1977, the Carters said farewell to the members of the Plains Baptist Church. Jimmy told them that he hoped his performance as president would "make his friends proud" and be satisfactory "in the eyes of God." The congregation sang "Amazing Grace" and "America the Beautiful" and wished them "Godspeed."[58]

The next day, the excitement surrounding a native son who was less than forty-eight hours away from becoming president of the United States swelled in Plains. Rosalynn could scarcely keep her feet on the ground, but Jimmy steadied himself repairing a water pipe that had burst as a result the previous night's freeze. A chartered passenger train, dubbed the Peanut Special, pulled in beside the tiny historic depot that had been the Carters' symbolic campaign headquarters. Excited members of the Peanut Brigade and others, some 350 strong, piled aboard and anxiously waited for Jimmy and Rosalynn to join them. As the hour for departure neared, Plains resident Maxine Reese, who had actively participated in the campaign, called the president-elect, and said, "Jimmy, you and Rosalynn better get on down here because it is time to leave." Upon hanging up, she thought about her neighbor and friend in startling new terms, "Oh my God, I just told the President of the United States not to be late."[59]

But Carter was never late. After the train arrived at Union Station, the Carters made a grand entry into Washington and took up residency at the Blair House, the official guest residence, across the street from the White House. All eyes were on them the evening of January 19 when they attended a pre-inaugural gala at the Kennedy Center. Rosalynn was splendidly dressed in a black designer outfit with tiny rhinestone buttons down the front, a wide skirt, and a red sash around her waist. Miss Lillian and Amy, as well as several cabinet members, joined the celebration. During intermission, Brzezinski, stealthily securing his power, presented Carter with a presidential directive, which he signed. It would shock those in the departments of state, defense, and intelligence to learn that Brzezinski would approve and edit all documents that went to the president.[60] After a post-gala reception, Jimmy and Rosalynn returned to Blair House for their last night as private citizens.[61]

On the other side of Pennsylvania Avenue, the Fords prepared for their final night as President and First Lady. The White House was undergoing the controlled chaos that characterizes the changing of the presidency. Boxes were packed and ready to be loaded, staffers were saying their farewells, and the Fords prepared to leave the home they had inherited by accident and failed to keep. Earlier in the day, Betty Ford had walked over to the West Wing to express her own thanks and say goodbye to the president's staff. As she passed the empty Cabinet Room with the White House photographer, David Hume Kennerly, she said, "You know, I've always wanted to dance on the Cabinet Room table." Kennerly, young and funny and close to the Fords, said, "Well, there is no one around." While the Secret Service agent stood stone faced outside the door, Betty took off her shoes, hopped up on the table, gracefully did a step or two, struck a final pose, and threw a kiss. "It was a wonderful and whimsical ending to the magical time I spent as the first lady," she recalled many years later.[62]

SEVEN

A Different Presidency

"Let the spirit of heaven guide the new spirit of Washington," Reverend Nelson L. Price advised the president-elect and his family at a private service the morning of the inauguration. Visiting from Marietta, Georgia, where he was pastor of the Roswell Street Baptist Church, Price had accepted Carter's request that he occupy the pulpit of the First Baptist Church in Washington on that cold January morning. His audience of twenty consisted of Jimmy, Rosalynn, Amy, Miss Lillian, Walter and Joan Mondale, some cabinet members, and a handful of others. Quoting the nation's second president, John Adams, Price admonished those about to embrace power, "May none but wise and honest men ever rule under this [the White House] roof."[1]

Just before noon, two honest and decent men, Jerry Ford and Jimmy Carter, ambitious political rivals aligned in their respect for the nation and its civic rituals, rode together, accompanied by Speaker Tip O'Neill, in the presidential limousine from the White House to the Capitol. Carter was quiet, commenting only on the size of the crowd. Rosalynn, Betty Ford, and Millie O'Neill followed in a separate limousine. Joined by families and dignitaries in the Capitol Building, those departing and those arriving descended the stairs to the bunting-draped platform where Jimmy Carter would take the oath of office as the thirty-ninth president of the United States.

At precisely noon, Jimmy Carter stood on the platform at the East Front of the Capitol, scanning the crowd before turning to face Rosalynn. Cool and intense, she held a Bible upon which he placed his right hand and solemnly swore to uphold the Constitution of the United States. Miss Lillian had given him that Bible several years earlier, but the Bible that George Washington had used in 1789 lay nearby. Chief Justice of the Supreme Court Warren E. Burger administered the oath.[2]

Smiling, gazing over the huge crowd of people who had defied the morning's icy chill to witness the ceremony, Carter prepared to deliver to them a carefully prepared, inspirational, yet brief speech. Jimmy promised them a new commitment, a new spirit, a new America. Opening on a note of gratitude and unity, he said, "I want to thank my predecessor for all he has done to heal our land." Celebrating the "inner and spiritual strength of our nation," Carter praised his high-school teacher, Miss Julia Coleman, who had taught him that "we must adjust to changing times and still hold to unchanging principles." Setting the tone for his presidency, he quoted the prophet Micah (6:8), the verse that he and Rosalynn had chosen together: "He hath showed thee, O man, what is good; and what doth the Lord require of thee, but to do justly, and to love mercy, and to walk humbly with thy God." Carter wanted a government "both competent and compassionate," strong abroad and at home. "Our commitment to human rights must be absolute, our laws fair, our national beauty preserved."

Rising to the challenge of being a world leader, Carter continued: "Because we are free, we can never be indifferent to the fate of freedom elsewhere." He enumerated his goals: protection of the weak, preservation of human dignity, and "the elimination of all nuclear weapons from this earth." He believed that both he and the American people could achieve those goals. Within the American people he saw, he said, "a serious and purposeful rekindling of confidence."

When his time in the White House was done, Carter said, he hoped his legacy would be justice, equality, peace, prosperity, and pride in the government. His accent was Georgian, his voice strong and passionate, and the eight-minute speech a roaring success.[3]

After the ceremony, Jimmy and Rosalynn retreated into the Capitol for a simple lunch with Walter and Joan Mondale and their families. Carter had ordered the traditional elaborate lunch to be cancelled. Before eating, Carter signed his nominations for eleven cabinet positions and sent them to the Senate for approval in order to get the executive branch of the government in full operation as soon as possible. After lunch, he, Rosalynn, and Amy entered the armored presidential limousine that would take them from the Capitol to the White House.

Security was minimal, and Pennsylvania Avenue was lined on both sides with thousands of cheering citizens who hoped to get a glimpse of their new President and First Lady. Shortly after leaving the Capitol, the presidential limousine suddenly stopped, and the crowd fell silent, fearing what might have happened. The doors of the vehicle swung open, and the president and First Lady stepped out energetically and began an historic walk, hand in hand, down Pennsylvania Avenue. The crowd roared their approval. Secret Service agents, who knew of the planned walk and that Carter wore a bullet

proof vest under his shirt, scoured the largest ever crowd to attend an inauguration, and there were no artificial barriers separating the First Family
from the people. Rosalynn was clad in a teal-colored, cloth coat and warm
boots. Jimmy wore a dark-colored top coat that might have hung in the closet
of any middle-class man. Their children fell into step behind them, young
Amy sometimes clasping each parent by the hand. The Carters smiled and
waved to the cheering crowd. Walking, they believed, was good for one's
health, saved expensive fuel, and symbolized kinship with those millions of
Americans who walked to work. Their walk recalled that other "farmer" president, Thomas Jefferson, who loved the environment and the benefits of fresh
air and exercise, and who, in 1801, had walked from his boarding house to the
Capitol to become the first president to be inaugurated in Washington, DC.[4]

Jimmy and Rosalynn had invited 300,000 people to come to Washington
for their inauguration, many of whom they had met during the campaign.
Although most events were free, participants had to have admission tickets
and be acceptably dressed if they wished to attend the concerts, fireworks,
and other events. Some events did have small admission fees, but the Carters
intended their inauguration to be available to as many people as possible, regardless of wealth or class. For his swearing in and stroll along Pennsylvania
Avenue, Carter wore a business suit that he had purchased in Americus for
$175. Eschewing an expensive designer outfit, Rosalynn dressed profession-
ally in a yellow suit that she had also purchased in Georgia. They wanted to
appear no different than the people who had elected them.[5]

When the Carters reached the small reviewing stand at the North Portico
of the White House, they took their places in it to view the parade. Heated
with solar energy as Carter had directed, the stand sheltered the group there
from the twenty-eight degree Fahrenheit temperature they had experienced
during the ceremony and their walk. Looking pensive, Rosalynn waved and
smiled at the bands and parades that passed below. One unusual float displayed huge letters spelling USA composed of a material that reflected the
faces of the people observing it. It symbolized the Carters' idea that this day
belonged to the people, not just the Carters. Inevitably, there was a large
peanut-shaped float honoring the Carter family's association with the peanut
industry.

From the viewing stand, the Carters were ushered into the White House.
Their personal belongings were already in place, and a staff and security
force stood ready to introduce them to their new home. Rosalynn smiled ap-
provingly when she noted that seven rooms were bedecked with flowers and

greenery, transported and arranged by the women of the Plains Garden Club. Jimmy was seeing the living area on the second floor for the first time, but Rosalynn had returned the previous December when the Fords were away for their Christmas holiday, and Chief Usher Rex Scouten had given her a thorough guided tour of the residence. For the new residents, exploring all 162 rooms in the White House complex would require more than the short amount of time they had that afternoon before dinner and that evening's inaugural balls.[6]

Jimmy lingered only briefly upstairs before going in search of the Oval Office. Uncertain how to find it, he casually told the security man that he was going to the office. Jimmy followed him down the ground level corridor, out onto the south arcade, and to the entrance of the Oval Office. Standing inside alone, he was awed by the most historic and famous office in the United States that now was his. He noted the new oval yellow carpet that Ford had ordered, pulled back the drapes to observe the beautiful grounds, and sat at the desk. He had requested the same desk that John F. Kennedy had used, but since the desk that had been placed there was not the correct one, he planned to have it changed when he began work there the next day. Upon it there rested his schedule for the afternoon of January 21, the first entry into a Presidential Daily Diary that would become a detailed historical record of his every move.[7]

While Jimmy acclimated himself to the Oval Office, Rosalynn explored other parts of their new home. During her visit to the White House kitchen, she informed the cooks that her family preferred healthy meals that were not always traditionally Southern.[8] Moving quickly about the second and third floors, accompanied by her grown children and Amy, she traversed the long hall that stretched across the second floor. Art masterpieces hung on the walls, and there were cozy sitting areas and rows of shelves laden with books. From the second floor, a secret staircase led to the third. Taking it, the Carters found bedrooms and a solarium with a magnificent view of the Washington Monument and easy access to the roof.

Rosalynn assigned Miss Lillian to the Queen's Bedroom, her mother to the Lincoln Bedroom, and Jeff and Chip and their wives to third floor bedrooms. A nursery was ready for Chip and Caron's unborn baby. Jack and Judy planned to remain in Calhoun, Georgia, where he had a law practice. Amy's room on the second floor was close to her parents. The entertainment and public areas that Rosalynn saw included a bowling alley, a movie theater, a map room, and a Diplomatic Reception Room.

Keeping to a tight schedule that first afternoon, Rosalynn and the children walked over to the West Wing and entered the Oval Office where they stood breathless at the sight of Jimmy sitting behind the president's desk.[9] The family next gathered in their private dining room, where the wallpaper had scenes depicting the early history of the country and staff served their food on historic china.

After the meal, Jimmy, Rosalynn, and Amy dressed to attend eleven dances scheduled in seven venues. Carter called them "People's Inauguration Parties," not inaugural balls. Rosalynn was resplendent in the same blue chiffon gown she had worn for the Georgia inaugural ball. Considered by many to be quite beautiful, others condemned it as an "old inaugural dress." Jimmy, at every stop, jokingly asked people if they liked his wife's "old dress" and chuckled at the resounding "yes." Jimmy dressed in a traditional tuxedo, and Amy donned a blue gown and cape. She wore glasses and had a book tucked under her arm. At each venue, Jimmy and Rosalynn danced a quick waltz and, before departing, Jimmy told the crowd, "I love every one of you." More than 35,000 people attended the People's Parties, and many of them would be in line the next day to greet the President and First Lady personally at the White House.[10]

On Friday morning, January 21, the Carters prepared to receive thousands of supporters at the White House. Unlike President Andrew Jackson's White House reception, where hundreds of muddy and unkempt people crowded into the mansion and made a mess on the carpets and furniture, the crowd was controlled by admission tickets, security precautions, and informal dress and behavior codes. Those receptions for family, friends, Democratic dignitaries, military personnel, and citizen supporters tested Rosalynn's endurance to shake thousands of hands. When her feet got tired, she removed her shoes and greeted visitors in her stocking feet. Unlike any previous First Lady, she had a "Whispering Aide" standing behind her to tell her names and other pertinent information. Since the president had his own "Whispering Aide," this small addition to the receiving line signaled to the White House Staff that this First Lady would be active and powerful.[11]

After the guests left and the First Family had lunch, Carter went to the Oval Office to get to work. As his first act as president, Carter issued Presidential Proclamation 4483 to fulfill his promise to pardon the Vietnam War draft evaders. The witnesses in the Oval Office were disabled veteran Max Cleland, Griffin Bell, Charles Kirbo, Bob Lipshutz, and Zbigniew Brzezinski. Cleland, whom Carter had named to head the Veterans Administration, warned

Carter that there was growing opposition in the Senate. Carter, who said he would do it even if all one hundred Senators opposed, claimed it was "a deed that was made possible through the goodness of God."[12] Republican Senator Barry Goldwater thought the pardon was more likely the work of the devil, and he immediately led the negative response. Soon, however, the crisis passed and Carter had proved that he would be a man of his word.[13]

Unbeknown to Carter, Miss Lillian visited the Oval Office before he went to work there the next morning. She had placed a brief note on his desk: "Dear Hot—I like your office . . .—Good bye! ILYTG Ma."[14] Her closing, "I Love You The Goodest," had become a family tradition many years earlier.

Rosalynn, who did not want any help from her mother-in-law, assumed management of the White House highly qualified and experienced staff. She liked the idea that Jimmy would work at home. Since she had always had her own work space in Plains and during the campaign, she looked forward to occupying her own "modest" office in the East Wing. With both of them having home offices, the Carters expected to have more time with nine-year-old Amy and frequently take her with them wherever they went.

Chip and Jeff, and their wives, could live at the White House as long as they paid their own expenses, or their parents paid for them. Two months after settling in, Chip's wife Caron delivered their son at the Bethesda Naval Hospital. Named James Earl Carter IV, the infant grandson received Secret Service protection from the moment of his birth. The baby brought the family count up to seven Carters living at 1600 Pennsylvania Avenue. They soon added a nanny for Amy.[15]

Mary Fitzpatrick, the African-American woman who had cared for Amy at the Georgia governor's mansion, went to the White House to continue the same role there. Before being chosen by Jimmy and Rosalynn to care for their child, she had been falsely accused of murder and was serving a life sentence in prison. Because of her good behavior, and selection of her to work at the Governor's mansion, the parole board had released her from the life sentence and allowed her to work for the Carters. She and Amy bonded, the Carters trusted her, and all of them wanted her to move to the White House with them. Because she was still on parole, Jimmy had negotiated a three-day pass for her to attend the inauguration, and a month later he secured a reprieve that would allow her to move to the White House permanently. Although the Secret Service did not like the idea of giving a convicted felon unguarded access to the first family, the Carters got their way. The State of Georgia eventually pardoned her, and she became a proud voting citizen.[16]

Carter left the task of settling the family into their new home to Rosalynn while he moved quickly on his first full day in the Oval Office to give his national security adviser, Brzezinski, unprecedented power. On January 19, the night before he was inaugurated, he had signed the Presidential Directive that reorganized the National Security Council into a policy review committee and a special coordinating committee. The special coordinating committee, chaired by the national security adviser, gave Brzezinski authority to control virtually all security information that reached the president. Active, aggressive, engaged, Brzezinski was the kind of advisor Carter respected. Carter gave him cabinet rank, an unprecedented move that entitled him to attend cabinet meetings to present his policy views.[17]

At his first cabinet meeting, on January 24, 1977, Carter, perhaps subconsciously remembering all those memoranda that his mother had left for him as a child, told the gathered secretaries that he preferred to communicate with them by correctly written memoranda. He expected, he said, to see women, African Americans, Hispanics, Native Americans, Asian Americans, and other ethnic minorities prominently represented in their appointments. Since he believed that, as a farmer, farmers were affected by the weather as much as by government policy, he asked Secretary of Agriculture Bob Bergland to check with the CIA for weather forecasts. To conserve energy, he announced that he had ordered thermostats in all federal buildings to be lowered to 65 degrees during the day and 55 degrees at night. He appointed E. H. Knoche, deputy director of the CIA under President Ford, as acting director until he could choose a permanent director.[18]

Unlike other cabinet members, Brzezinski stuck close by the president. On January 23, Brzezinski had sent Carter a secret communication informing him that the Soviet Union's reaction to his inauguration was "heartening." The Soviets, he wrote, thought that Carter would work toward improving "the international political climate," negotiating a Strategic Arms Limitation Treaty, and resolving the Middle East situation.[19]

Although others in the administration disliked Brzezinski, Carter did not. Speaking of Carter, Zbig said later that "in a way I think we were both kind of strange birds, he was Georgian and very conscious of the fact that he was a Georgian, and he was the first Southern President in a long time." Carter, Zbig continued, sensed the "hostility of others toward him as a Southerner and Georgian." Zbig once gave Jimmy a page from *Sophie's Choice* by William Styron, a novel about a Polish refugee girl in New York City who chose a Jewish man over a reticent displaced Southern boy. The passage described the similarities between Polish history and that of the South. Both shared a sense of tragedy, of defeat, and a curious "cult of male chivalry." Zbig felt that he was the only peer Carter had in the White House.[20]

Like Brzezinski, Vice President Walter Mondale assumed an unusually powerful position in the Carter White House. Carter made clear that in his absence the vice president could speak with the president's authority. Wishing to reassure allies and friends in Europe and Japan, as well as send a message to potential adversaries, Carter sent Mondale on a goodwill tour on January 22, the second full day he was in office, to collect facts and information from European and Asian allies that would facilitate economic and political cooperation. Carter himself settled into a routine of going to work by 7:00 a.m., soon moving from the Oval Office into the smaller, more private adjacent office, and listening to classical music as he read and annotated memos and talked to key advisers.[21]

The Senate had moved quickly to confirm Carter's nominations for cabinet posts. Only two African Americans—Patricia Harris and Andrew Young, and two females—Harris and Juanita Kreps—were in the group. Although James Schlesinger had been selected as secretary of energy, he could not assume the job until that department was created. Therefore, Carter designated Schlesinger as his personal representative to coordinate all energy-related initiatives, one of which would be to create a cabinet-level Department of Energy. Schlesinger presented the proposal to Congress, and Carter received the necessary cooperation to win its approval without delay.[22] Carter insisted that it, as well as all departments, should conserve energy and cut costs.

Trying to practice what they preached, the Carters modeled their personal lives after the egalitarian and frugal style they recommended for the government. They chose a local public school for nine-year-old Amy. No presidential child had attended one since Theodore Roosevelt's children had lived in the White House some seventy years earlier. The Carters selected a school near the White House, Thaddeus Stevens Elementary School, which was located in a predominantly African-American neighborhood. About 10% of the students were white and the 30% who were foreign born were mostly children of embassy employees. Arriving with her mother on her first day at that school, Amy was grim faced as she navigated through the gang of reporters and television cameramen and tolerated her Secret Service guards. Her fourth-grade teacher, Veronia Meeder, attempted to make Amy comfortable in the small class of twenty-one students. Soon, Amy found a best friend in a girl from Chile, the daughter of a cook.[23]

With Amy settled in at school, Carter established the pattern that would be typical of how he managed his week. He, Rosalynn, and Amy attended the First Baptist Church on Sunday mornings, and after lunch, he went to his office to work. Carter wanted Congress to approve an economic stimulus package, an immediate $4 billion for emergency public works, and he needed a director of the CIA. That first full week in office was filled with so many memos, speeches, orders, and other activities that it amazed both Congress and the public. Speaker of the House Tip O'Neill must have been shocked too, but he appreciated Carter's remark that he hoped they could work together to streamline the government.[24]

Carter wanted talking points to deal with Korea and Asia, selection commissions to nominate federal judges, the abolition of as many other commissions as legally possible, integration of state department activities with the United Nations, and an entirely new treaty with Panama concerning the canal. His projects ranged from zero based budgeting to normalization of relations with Cuba, a list so long and impractical that Senator Robert Byrd, majority leader of the Senate, grumbled that Carter did not look to him for advice when he should have.[25]

What Byrd and many others soon learned, however, was that Carter's changes had scarcely begun. He ordered Brzezinski to prepare weekly briefings for Rosalynn and his senior staff members.[26] His speechwriters complained that they did not have adequate access to him, and he accused them of giving him poor material. He bawled out his young, chief speechwriter Jim Fallows for sending him inferior material for a speech he planned to deliver at the DC Press Club. "At the last minute, I had to write my own," he said. Later, he called them a pain "in the neck" and griped that "they could not understand that I was the President and they weren't."[27]

The favoritism that Carter showed to Rosalynn should not have surprised those who had come to know him. Jimmy scheduled weekly lunches with her in the Oval Office when they discussed matters of state, not personal issues. She was also a wife, a mother, and a companion who skillfully transformed a mansion into a home. Her complaint that the White House was too cold for her fell upon deaf ears, but she swam and jogged with her husband and enjoyed the amenities of the White House. She welcomed Jimmy home from his travels and reveled in looking over his and Amy's designs for a tree house that he directed the White House carpenters to build.[28]

At work, with a staff of eighteen, Rosalynn created the Office of First Lady in the East Wing and selected an experienced staff. She hired Mary Hoyt, who had helped her during the campaign, to be her press secretary. In Gretchen Poston, a friend of Joan Mondale, Rosalynn found a social secretary who could plan and execute social events exactly as Rosalynn wanted them. Next to Hoyt, Kathy Cade, who headed special projects, became her most valued aide. A Yale graduate, Cade assisted with Rosalynn's plans to help the mentally ill and challenged, women who needed the protection of the ERA, young children, and the elderly. She hired Kit Dobelle at an annual salary of $56,000, the same amount paid to Hamilton Jordan at the West Wing, to manage her office. Rosalynn did not think that she herself should be paid, for Jimmy's annual salary of $200,000 was sufficient for both of them, and they received income from the family's agricultural business in Georgia. A demanding boss, Rosalynn was also kind and earned the affection and respect of her staff. She insisted they call her Rosalynn.[29] The East Wing was never quite equal to the West Wing, but the Office of First Lady became a powerful part of the executive branch of government.

Rosalynn studied the regular briefings from the national security adviser. Brzezinski, or another member of his staff, informed her on protocol for visiting heads of state, their religious and dietary restrictions, appropriate floral arrangements, and any other information she might want. Choosing entertainers suitable for the nationalities and interests of foreign guests, Rosalynn planned sophisticated cultural performances. One of the first groups she invited was Los Tiempos Passados, a classical and folk musical ensemble consisting of doctors, professors, language teachers, and an engineer, whom she had seen perform at the inauguration of President Lopez Portillo in Mexico in December. Since Portillo would be honored at Carter's first state dinner, she would surprise him with his own choice of entertainment.[30]

Rosalynn fulfilled her role as hostess with grace and charm, but she was also involved in the affairs of state and comfortable with her independence. Jimmy, always ready to tease her, noted that ten days into office he still hadn't seen the East Wing of the White House. Finally, he quipped, he was "getting permission to go."[31]

Rosalynn could hardly keep up with her husband's plans for his presidency. She monitored all he said and did on the issue of national security. Carter set up regular weekly meetings with his national security adviser, the secretary of defense, and the acting director of the CIA. As commander-in-chief of the military, he delegated authority to his secretary of defense and involved the joint chiefs of staff in his decisions. He announced a plan to withdraw all ground troops from South Korea within four or five years, a decision with which the joint chiefs disagreed. Within the boundaries of the Constitution and the law, he issued a Presidential Directive to continue certain electronic surveillance in Berlin that he considered vital to national security. Carter frustrated the joint chiefs with his insistence upon cutting the budget, his own knowledge about weapons systems, and his insistence that he was the man to give the orders. The military chiefs were not accustomed to having a president who knew so much about the military.[32]

Carter planned to visit other NATO members early in his tenure and re-assure allies that his drive for a SALT II nuclear arms control treaty with the Soviet Union would not jeopardize their security but make it stronger in Europe. Like his predecessors, he hoped to get other member nations to shoulder more of the cost and responsibilities of that organization.[33] Carter asked Secretary of State Vance to set up a Geneva-type conference on the Middle East and Brzezinski to initiate correspondence about nuclear arms reduction with key foreign leaders, including Indira Gandhi of India, Helmut Schmidt of Germany, and Leonid Brezhnev of the Soviet Union.[34]

Preferring work to ceremony, Carter wanted to avoid the image of Richard Nixon's "imperial presidency." He reduced the White House staff by one-third, and he asked his staff and cabinet members to do likewise. Rosalynn alone was allowed to keep a large staff and even expand it.[35] Carter dispensed with chauffeur-driven limousines for most staff members and demanded that they not use their government positions for personal financial gain. Only Brzezinski as national security advisor retained a car service. Carter eliminated several of the presidential limousines and sold the presidential yacht *Sequoia*, which was rarely used and cost the government $800,000 per year. He requested that "Hail to the Chief" not be played when he entered a room, and he carried his own suitcases when traveling. Carter once joked that he wished one of the wax figures of himself, commissioned by Madame Tussaud's Wax Museum in London, might be sent to diplomatic banquets in his place.[36]

Carter's closest advisers, next to Rosalynn and Brzezinski, were Hamilton Jordan and Jody Powell. Jordan, according to Carter, was at ease with the other staff members. He was "quiet," "not forceful," "a natural leader," whose judgment they trusted. Powell had worked comfortably with Carter since 1966 as a campaigner and press secretary. Carter also brought his personal secretary Susan Clough and his legislative liaisons Frank Moore and Dan Tate from Georgia to Washington. If his Georgia friends Andrew Young, Griffin Bell, and Bert Lance did not make good impressions on Congress,

Carter did not care, for he felt no particular loyalty to any of the long-serving Democrats, not even those from his home state, with the exception of Sam Nunn.[37]

Carter's relationship with Congress got off to a rocky start. Many of the Congressmen were newly elected, most of them as a result of Carter's own service to the Democratic Party in 1974. Before the inauguration, Carter went to Washington to meet with key members, especially Senator Abraham Ribicoff and Congressman Jack Brooks, who chaired their respective government operations committees. Both men supported his plan to reorganize the federal government, just as he had done in Georgia. Carter invited all Democratic members of Congress to meet with him at Blair House, but he soon discovered that they were more competitive than cooperative with the White House. Despite the fact that his party controlled the House 292–143 and the Senate 61–38, he could not count on their automatic approval of his legislation. Carter, according to his friend Bert Lance, "didn't like to fool with them . . . didn't enjoy it, didn't respect them," and he didn't want to deal with their petty egos.[38]

Nevertheless, Carter was a pragmatic, power politician, who could compromise if necessary to win his point, but he did not think he needed to get along personally with Congress. Despite a popular criticism that he micromanaged, he did not lose sight of the larger picture. He used Frank Moore as his Congressional liaison. Moore had served Carter well in Atlanta, but he was less effective in Washington. Many members of Congress, especially O'Neill, despised Moore, accused him of being a liar, and loathed Carter's preferred government by memo in lieu of old-fashioned backslapping and horse trading. One journalist complained that Frank Moore was loyal only to Carter, and Carter did not respect Congress as an equal arm of the government.[39] Dan Tate, Carter's liaison with the Senate, fared somewhat better, but Carter was doomed to have a majority leader of the Senate and a Speaker of the House who never quite understood or warmed up him.

Senate majority leader Robert Byrd of West Virginia had been a rival candidate for the Democratic nomination himself and was antagonistic from the beginning. Byrd was disappointed when Carter withdrew his nomination of Ted Sorensen as CIA director three days before his inauguration, since Byrd had looked forward to defeating the confirmation "to teach Carter a lesson." Carter, for his part, found Byrd to be single-minded, unduly demanding of respect, and a "formidable ally or opponent."[40] Likewise, Scoop Jackson, who had been another bitter rival for the Democratic presidential nomination, attempted to undermine Carter's legislative program any way that he could. The reason, Charlie Kirbo thought, was "jealousy, sheer jealousy."[41]

Despite Carter's effort to build a strong tie with Tip O'Neill before the in-auguration, the seasoned old Democrat from New England never became comfortable with the strange man from Georgia who had become the titular head of the Democratic Party. While Carter eventually came to understand and appreciate O'Neill, O'Neill never fully comprehended Carter or his pe-culiar Southern ways. Nevertheless, the Speaker was loyal to his party and thus to the president who headed it. He did fight, often successfully, to get Carter's legislation through the House.[42]

Undaunted by his difficulties in dealing with Congress, Carter welcomed an initiative spearheaded by senators Jacob Javits and Alan Cranston to de-criminalize possession of small amounts of marijuana, even though they were unsuccessful. Carter's sons were known users, and Carter had promised during the campaign that he would try to reduce marijuana possession to a civil crime punishable by a small fine.[43]

Less than two weeks after taking office, Carter focused on a key issue that would define his presidency. His hope to bring peace to the Middle East con-vinced him of "the urgency of an American Initiative."[44] Carter planned to ask Congress for a $285 million increase in aid to Israel to counter the per-ception of some Senators and journalists that his administration was filled with individuals who were prejudiced against that nation. William Safire's pro-Israel articles in the *New York Times* fueled Jewish suspicion of Carter, who ignored all such criticisms as he sought an initiative to bring peace be-tween Israel and Egypt based on ideas from both sides.[45]

When William Quandt, the administration's expert on the Middle East, presented Carter with a detailed plan, complete with maps, Carter responded that "this probably asks too much of Israel. Let's stick to our specific items = a) '67 borders & minor adjustments; b) real peace; c) Palestine homeland; ref-ugee problems resolved; d) no specifics re Jerusalem; no PLO contact ab-sent UN 242 endorsement, etc."[46] Impressed by Egyptian President Anwar Sadat, who had "demonstrated a good attitude" toward Israel, Carter favored strengthening him. Egyptians needed food, which he would gladly send to them. Sadat, he thought, had the same goals that the United States did, such as reduced spending on weapons and a worldwide reduction in arms transfers.[47]

Carter's faith in Sadat encouraged him to pursue an "aggressive foreign policy" that would bring peace to the Middle East. Written by Tony Lake, his director of policy planning, "A Human Rights Strategy for the United States" became the blueprint Carter had requested. Lake, who had impeccable liberal credentials, had served in the State Department for a decade. In his "Strategy," Lake wrote that there would be moral, legal, and political advantages to pursuing a human rights policy. In Latin America, Africa, the Soviet bloc, East Asia, the Near East, and South Asia, the United States could help individual victims, raise human rights standards, and disassociate itself from repressive regimes. Quiet diplomacy, symbolic acts, financial pressure, and multilateral approaches would be the most effective means to achieve those goals. The United States must put its own house in order and prepare to deal with criticisms of inconsistencies. Lake attached the 1948 United Nations Declaration of Human Rights and a Memorandum for All Assistant Secretaries of Human Rights from Secretary of State Cyrus Vance. Vance made clear to his assistants that the State Department must help implement the president's human rights policy.[48]

Carter's appeal for Jewish votes during the campaign and Stuart Eizenstat's urging that he should help dissidents who were being persecuted in the Soviet Union fueled his choice of human rights as the central theme of his administration. Politically, Carter's human rights advocacy not only appealed to Jewish voters, but also attracted pre-existing interest groups, both conservative and liberal. It also set a standard not easy to maintain, for the reality of domestic and international politics and national security often contradicted it.[49]

Carter's personal commitment to human rights came primarily from three sources. First, his Christian faith instructed him that all people were equal, were children of God, and were entitled to decent lifestyles, which included justice and equality. Second, Carter believed that Jewish citizens shared that view, but without the same theological basis. Taking such a strong stand for human rights could win Jewish votes, which he badly needed and had difficulty obtaining. Third, he had spent his youth in a racially segregated society and witnessed the civil rights movement that had exposed and challenged injustices heaped upon people with dark skin. His introduction to apartheid in South Africa only deepened his commitment to human rights.

Andrew Young had not intended to support Carter for president. He changed his mind suddenly when, on the campaign trail, a student in California had asked Carter about his policy toward Zimbabwe. Carter knew nothing about that country, which Black nationalists called Zimbabwe as they battled the White rulers who called it Rhodesia. Carter asked Young, then a Georgia Congressman, for advice. Young gave him the extensive information about the abuses of white colonialism in Africa that had been collected by the National Council of Churches and the United Church of Christ. That information convinced Carter that human rights must become part of his foreign policy toward Africa, the Soviet Union, and the rest of the world.[50]

Carter and his advisers were not naïve about the challenge of making human rights the central pillar of the nation's foreign policy. Unanticipated crises and national defense would be inevitable impediments. The Soviet Union would not likely revise its tough attitude toward the United States and Soviet Jews simply because of a US human rights policy and might not even understand it. In emerging countries, where the United States had economic power, however, it could be successful. Encouraged by recent reforms of the CIA, the 1975 Helsinki Accords, détente with the Soviet Union, and the restlessness of emerging nations that did not want to be identified with either of the superpowers, Carter saw the chance for his central theme to work. He legitimized human rights as a tool in US foreign policy, a legitimacy that would last far beyond his administration.[51]

At the personal level, Carter attempted to respect the basic human needs of his White House staff. A taskmaster who demanded perfection but rarely complimented or rewarded excellent work, Carter sent a memorandum to his top staff members on February 2: "I am concerned about the family lives of all of you. I want you to spend an adequate amount of time with your husbands/wives & children, and also to involve them as much as possible in our White House life. We are going to be here a long time, and all of you will be more valuable to me & the country with rest and a stable home life. In emergencies we'll all work full time."

EIGHT

One Hundred Days

On the evening of February 2, 1977, when Carter donned a beige cardigan sweater and sat beside a blazing fire in the library at the White House to address the nation about the energy shortage, he may have thought he would get the same response that President Franklin Delano Roosevelt (FDR) had received almost fifty years earlier during the Great Depression. He did not, because his speech lacked the soothing tones, the elegant words, and the dire national crisis that had made FDR's talks so riveting. Carter's energy crisis, as severe as it was, fell short of the suffering and panic caused by the Great Depression. Very few of Carter's viewers were inspired by his fussy emphasis on strict conservation measures and the search for alternative forms of energy. Both Rosalynn and White House communications director Jerry Rafshoon observed that the "chat" did not stir the public to want to hear more of the same. Less polite media critics carped that "even the fire fell asleep."[1]

Although Carter did not go on national television to discuss his religion, it very often was the subject the media chose to focus on. Carter prayed often, read the Bible with Rosalynn, presided at prayer breakfasts, and was never shy about stating what he believed. When Amy was baptized in the First Baptist Church in Washington, DC, on February 6, many in the non-Baptist world were amazed by the full-immersion ritual. The baptism of Mary Fitzpatrick there a few months later did not prove that Carter's church believed in racial equality.[2]

Neither Carter's personal religion nor his public fireside chats attracted the attention that his cutting of budgets and issuing of personal conduct edicts did. He questioned the pay for the White House barber shop staff, reduced the size of the staff at Blair House, cancelled excessive newspaper subscriptions, and searched for other ways to reduce costs. He thought twenty-three presidential cars and other armored vehicles were enough and banned further additions. He issued a dictum to the White House staff that they were not to waste the president's time, would be fired if they made personal attacks on their colleagues, and should understand that the vice president spoke for the president.[3]

Kinder in deed than in the wording of his memos, Carter broke precedent by not restricting the use of the White House swimming pool and tennis courts to the First Family. Responding to a request, he announced that staff members, cabinet officers, and their families could use those facilities provided they requested permission from him and scheduled through his secretary. Because his secretary knew the First Family's schedule, Carter's personal role in the process was minimal. Nevertheless, he soon received a barrage of criticism for micromanaging.[4] The charge was off base, because it was not true that he paid less attention to essential issues because of his close attention to daily details.

Frugal with his time, Carter thought state dinners were a waste of it. Rosalynn disagreed. She enjoyed learning about the likes and dislikes of visiting heads of state, as well as planning the décor and menu to honor them. The first state dinner was easy, because she already knew President José López Portillo of Mexico and his wife Carmen. When the Portillos arrived at the White House on February 14, 1977, Jimmy and Rosalynn greeted them like personal friends. The after-dinner toasts were long and flattering, but Portillo enchanted the group with his remark that Carter "is not only a statesman but a man of solid moral principles who . . . loves his wife."[5]

Rosalynn had planned her first state dinner carefully. The tables were decorated with a Valentine's Day theme, set with President Truman's green and gold china, and adorned with engraved menus and place cards. The bill of fare encompassed three courses of all-American food, including dessert, each accompanied by an appropriate American wine. Banks of potted tulips lined the platform upon which rested a Steinway grand piano that would be used for the after-dinner entertainment.

The president in his tuxedo and the First Lady in her formal gown paused at the top of the grand stairway ready to make their hailed entry. Downplaying pomp and frills, the Carters had banned the traditional color guard and trumpets. The Marine Band announced their presence, military aides saluted, guests and journalists stood in respect.

At that moment, Misty Malarky Ying-Yang, Amy's Siamese cat, darted in front of the First Couple, scampered down the entire stair case, and claimed the distinction as the First Feline to make a grand entrance at a state dinner. Rosalynn later laughed that she didn't know who was "more surprised, the guests, the press, me, or Misty." The laughter marked the beginning of a relaxed evening. During the dinner, Amy sat between her parents and read a book, but Misty was secured someplace out of sight.

After dinner, there was no hard liquor or dancing, but Rosalynn had planned a concert. Since she knew that Mrs. Portillo had once been a concert pianist, she invited Rudolf Serkin to entertain them. At the conclusion of his concert, Mrs. Portillo walked onto the stage and "played two Chopin pieces—and brought the house down."[6]

Carter enjoyed the classical music, but he preferred to discuss business and problems of mutual interest with Portillo and other international leaders. A few days later, Canadian Prime Minister Pierre Trudeau came for a visit, and on March 10 he welcomed Prime Minister James Callaghan of the United Kingdom and his wife Audrey as "our closest allies and friends." Callaghan did not get the usual nineteen-gun salute, however, because twelve Hanafi Muslim terrorists were holding 134 hostages a few blocks from the White House, and law enforcement officers feared that the salute might cause them to panic. The terrorists released the hostages during the night, and Carter explained to Callaghan why he did not get his salute. When Prime Minister Takeo Fukuda of Japan visited on March 21, he received a proper military salute, followed by Carter's hailing him as "one of the great leaders of one of the greatest nations on Earth." During all three visits, the crisis of an energy shortage and how these nations might cooperate dominated their conversations.[7]

From the beginning of Carter's presidency, trouble was brewing with Iran. Carter sent the shah a letter on February 7, in which he said that "our approaches to these problems may naturally differ," but it would be a difference between old friends. The shah responded in a similar tone, but Gary Sick, the State Department's expert on Iran, noted in a February 12 memorandum to Brzezinski that tension with the shah "is the price we pay if we intend to pursue an independent policy on such issues as oil prices, human rights, and arms transfers."[8]

Since tension with the Soviet Union was a pressing matter, Carter needed a CIA director and someone to lead US participation in the SALT discussions. Acting Director E. Henry "Hank" Knoche had met with Carter and Brzezinski at the White House at 3:20 p.m. on his first full day in office. Only a few hours before Carter's inauguration, the CIA had received the first images from the KH-11 satellite, a revolutionary new intelligence tool that could transmit digital satellite images to the White House less than an hour after they were taken. Knoche could hardly contain his excitement when he explained to the president and the national security adviser how useful the new satellite would be in the SALT II negotiations with the Soviet Union. For a successful treaty to be negotiated, verification that the Soviets kept their word would be essential.[9]

Despite Knoche's experience, Carter passed over him when he chose a permanent intelligence chief on February 2, 1977. By creating the new position of director of central intelligence, Carter brought all fifteen national intelligence agencies, including the CIA, under the same umbrella. To fill the position, he asked Admiral Stansfield Turner, his former classmate at the naval academy, currently stationed in Naples as Commander in Chief of NATO forces in southern Europe, to take the job. Turner, who had hardly known Carter at Annapolis, accepted, but he was miffed when he learned that all CIA briefings would first go to Brzezinski, who would then take them to the president. Turner, nevertheless, did have direct access to the president when he requested it. Turner's aggressive and moralistic style, which impressed Carter, made him unpopular with many people in the agencies.[10] A Christian Scientist who drank hot water with a lemon slice for breakfast, Turner was intellectually curious and tough.

A good match with Carter, Turner was pleased to work for a "president who's got high morals and high ethical standards and certainly stands for doing things legally."[11] Turner placed technology above human intelligence. Bucking controversy, he eliminated 820 positions within two years and forced 147 immediate retirements in what he later called the Halloween Massacre.[12]

With a trusted director of central intelligence and a new spying tool, the United States was in a stronger position to proceed to discussions with the Soviet Union about SALT II. The SALT I treaty was due to expire in October 1977, and both sides seemed ready to put a new one in place. Carter chose Paul Warnke to direct the Arms Control Disarmament agency and become the chief negotiator for the SALT discussions with the Russians. Warnke was no hawk; he had helped persuade Lyndon Johnson to initiate peace talks in an effort to end the war in Vietnam, and he had long protested the high cost of defense. A graduate of Columbia University Law School, he had served in the Coast Guard and had advised Carter during the campaign. When Warnke was sworn in on March 15, he said that he was optimistic about a new arms control treaty and did not think that disagreement with the Russians on human rights would prevent it. Jody Powell's telephone call to Tom Wicker of the *New York Times* resulted in an article praising Carter's selection. Pleased with himself for that small victory, Jody sent a handwritten note to Carter urging him to "pick up the phone and call any of these jokers [journalists]—day or nite. They love it!"[13]

The State Department's secret analysis of human rights violations in the Soviet Union might discourage the US negotiators from making generous concessions to the Soviets. The West Germans, who felt their security was at stake, wanted to be consulted on SALT II. Zbig warned the president that, in whatever they endeavored to achieve in foreign policy, the road would be "rocky." He knew that the words "defeat" and "surrender" were not in Carter's vocabulary, and the president would fearlessly attempt whatever and however many policies he believed to be right. Carter thought it was right to establish diplomatic relations with Vietnam, and he lifted the ban on travel to Cuba. Fully aware that Cuba remained under Soviet influence and had sent thousands of troops to Angola, he hoped to open channels of communication with the United States' close island neighbor.[14]

When making foreign policy decisions, Carter did things his way and quickly. He sent Clark Clifford as his personal emissary to Greece, Turkey, and Cyprus, where he hoped to end the dispute over the division of the island. Clifford had served presidents Truman, Kennedy, and Nixon and thus had the knowledge and diplomatic skills Carter thought necessary to resolve a long-standing dispute in an area of vital interest to the United States. He named Governor Reubin Askew of Florida to chair an advisory board on ambassadorial appointments, which was part of his plan to select ambassadors for their qualifications rather than their political connections. To negotiate new treaties with Panama regarding control and operation of the canal, he chose Sol N. Linowitz and Ellsworth Bunker. Linowitz, a prominent attorney and businessman, had represented the United States in the Organization of American States (OAS) and Bunker, an ambassador at large, was an expert in Latin American affairs.[15]

India presented a greater challenge than Latin America, because Carter hoped to loosen its ties with the Soviet Union.[16] When Indian President Sarvepalli Radhakrishnan died in early February, Miss Lillian and Chip attended the funeral. Although Miss Lillian had a cordial meeting with Prime Minister Indira Gandhi, Brzezinski warned Carter that India's ruling Congress Party still had major problems with the United States, citing its unmet demand for nuclear fuel, need for government loans, and desire to get CIA cells out of the country. When the Congress Party lost the election on March 24, Carter, diplomatically disguising the fact that he was glad that

Gandhi had lost, wrote to her on March 30: "I fully share your belief that winning or losing an election is not the purpose of political life."[17]

With the Janata Party in power in India, Brzezinski thought that democracy and human rights would be fully restored, that India would be less favorably disposed toward the Soviet Union, and that its expectations of the United States might be greater than they could meet. Nevertheless, he believed that India could not entirely reject the Soviet Union as long as it felt threatened by China. If the United States wanted a better relationship with India, he recommended that Carter would also have to improve his country's relationship with China.[18]

Improving relations with India and China would take time, and in the meantime, Carter tried to honor his campaign promise to help US women in their battle for justice and equality. He sent a message to his senior staff members in late February asking for a tally of the number of women and minorities they had working with them. Carter had already named two women to his cabinet; he had placed Mary King on his transition staff, had put Esther Peterson in charge of consumer affairs, and he had named Eleanor Holmes Norton to be the first black woman to head the Equal Employment Opportunity Commission. He planned to appoint a woman to the Supreme Court if a vacancy should occur during his tenure. He asked Attorney General Griffin Bell to remove sex discrimination from the "laws and policies of the United States." Meanwhile, Rosalynn reigned as the most powerful woman in the administration, a model for others, an advocate for the appointment of women, and a trusted adviser to the president.[19]

Acting on another campaign promise, Carter proposed a $19.4 billion budget increase to help the needy, stimulate the economy, provide greater support for education, and put a ceiling on hospital costs, which he intended to be the first step toward instituting universal health insurance coverage.[20] Carter thought he could provide better government service and reduce the federal budget by making internal cuts. On March 1 he ordered heads of executive departments and agencies to hold federal employment down to the lowest adequate level. The next day, after receiving a report from Defense Secretary Harold Brown about the inflated number of officers in the military, as well as "ten times as many super grades GS 16, 17, 18, in government as fifteen years ago," Carter drafted a blistering memorandum to cabinet level officers that "now is the time" to reverse that trend. He later cooled down and sent a more temperate memorandum with the same message.[21]

Looking for more ways to end government waste, Carter planned to study the possibility of selling Camp David, the private, wooded presidential retreat in Maryland about 62 miles northwest of Washington. When he visited there, however, Camp David instantly became his "Shangri-La," as it had been called by President Franklin Roosevelt, before President Eisenhower renamed it for his father and grandson. Carter asked his budget director Bert Lance to please not tell him how much it cost to operate Camp David and to make whatever repairs were needed. Jimmy and Rosalynn loved the place. They also made Camp David available to cabinet and staff members upon request, imposing a limit of two families at a time in the guest houses. Guests, who were relatives or friends of the cabinet and staff members, were billed for their food and transportation, a rule Rosalynn attempted in vain to change.[22]

Rosalynn was privy to all that happened in the government. Carter welcomed her, as well as other advisers and visitors, to the cabinet meetings, sometimes attended by as many as seventeen people other than cabinet members. On one occasion Jimmy's Aunt Sissie Dolvin and his sister Ruth Stapleton came. The guests, including Rosalynn, sat in chairs around the walls where they listened but did not participate. Carter commended Secretary of Commerce Juanita Kreps for including some of her sub-cabinet staffers, and he said he would like to invite cabinet members and their wives to briefings by experts. He even wanted to open cabinet meetings to the press, but he dropped that idea when he learned that the secretaries were unanimously opposed.[23]

Carter's brother Billy did not attend cabinet meetings, but he attracted extensive media attention to his family and to the South. Before the election, Billy had titillated reporters by claiming that he was the only sane one in the family. His mother, Billy noted accurately, had joined the Peace Corps at age 68; one sister was "a holy roller preacher"; his other sister "wears a helmet and rides a motorcycle"; and his brother "thinks he's going to be President." Billy spared no one. He openly insulted television reporters as people who could not read and write, and he freely expressed his opinion that there were a "bunch of damned hypocrites down there in that [Plains] Baptist church."[24]

Although he had responsibility for managing the peanut business while his brother was in Washington, Billy was frustrated because he thought he would have been the son to take over the family business while his brother continued a career in the Navy. Billy suffered from disappointments, severe sibling rivalry, and alcoholism. Despite their differences, the Carter brothers loved each other, and Jimmy never attempted to suppress or berate Billy in public. In fact, Jimmy would often use jokes that Billy had told about him. Before the Gridiron Club in March 1977 he quoted Billy as saying that the president's smile reminded him of "a fox lapping sorghum syrup from a live light socket."[25] Rosalynn did not find Billy to be quite so funny.

Despite humorous references to Billy, Jimmy kept busy with the serious business of government. He asked the Department of Defense and the National Security Council (NSC) for a comprehensive examination of the overall United States national defense strategy and military capabilities. He wanted a review of fifty funding projects for dams that had been authorized by the previous administration, and he wanted the Special Coordination Committee of the NSC to review the interrelationships among all intelligence agencies. Learning as much and as quickly as he could, Carter collected talking points on the Middle East, reviewed energy legislation sent to him by James Schlesinger, conversed with UN Secretary General Kurt Waldheim about Vietnam, Cyprus, and the two Koreas, and made plans to address the UN. He paid particular attention to correspondence with Chairman Leonid Brezhnev of the Soviet Union, still the major enemy of the United States.[26]

In a lighter vein, Carter enjoyed some of the public relations aspects of his job, especially opportunities to demonstrate that he was still one of the people. He remembered John Shanklin, the first person whom he had asked for his vote for president. Nine hours before he made his formal announcement of his candidacy in December 1974, Carter had walked through the lobby of the Sheraton-Carlton hotel in Washington, approached the first person he saw, shook hands with him, and said, "I'm Jimmy Carter of Georgia. I'm running for president, and I would appreciate your vote." "Mr. Carter, you can count on me," the building engineer, a native of South Carolina and graduate of the University of Georgia, had replied. Carter invited him to the White House for breakfast on March 11, 1977.[27] Carter used his first two press conferences, on February 8 and 23, as congenial affairs to talk about human rights and arms reduction agreements with the Soviet Union.

On February 25, he and Rosalynn went home to Plains for the first time since the inauguration. Air Force One landed at Warner-Robbins Air Force Base near Macon, about seventy-six miles northeast of Plains. Thinking he would save taxpayers money by traveling by motorcade from Macon to Plains, he quickly learned that it would not work. The large number of Georgia Highway patrolmen, as well as the federal Secret Service detail, proved to be more expensive than taking a helicopter. Thereafter, he used the helicopter.

Jimmy and Rosalynn reveled in being home. He walked down the main street and chatted with the storekeepers while ignoring the press that was always at his heels. And Rosalynn rested in her own home for the first time since she had become First Lady.

After a short stay in South Georgia, the Carters returned to the White House. Their visitors ranged from Senator Sam Nunn to folk singer John Denver. Carter marveled at how easily Rosalynn made each of them feel comfortable and at home. After everyone had gone, the Carters retired to their private bedroom and read a passage from the Bible in Spanish. On Sundays they took speed reading courses and attended the nearby First Baptist Church. Jimmy sometimes taught Sunday School there.[28]

With his unique style of governing, Carter pushed ahead relentlessly, sometimes recklessly taking political risks, to contain the cost of government. Before the end of his first one hundred days in office, Carter axed all but nineteen of 320 water projects that had been approved by former President Ford. Secretary of the Interior Cecil Andrus suggested that Carter use a "scalpel" to remove several really bad water projects that would save the taxpayers millions. Instead, Carter listened to environmentalist groups who opposed dam construction for ecological reasons and cancelled 301 of the 320 water projects. Carter defended his action, arguing that Congressmen with seniority got their requests approved automatically. "The Corps of Engineers would deliberately falsify the cost versus benefit," of the projects in order to justify them, he argued. "I do not think I could have done differently."[29]

The wrath of Congress descended upon him, for Carter had mistakenly assumed that members of his own party, the entire Congress, and the public would rejoice that he had saved $5.1 billion. On March 10 he had a tough meeting with thirty-five members of Congress. Senate majority leader Robert Byrd, the master of pork-barrel legislation, told him that "The road can be smooth or the road can be rough." Carter had taken the rough route. Strong criticism from fellow Democrats reminded him that he was still an outsider in his own party. Senate Finance Chair Russell Long, House Majority leader Jim Wright, House Interior Committee Chair Morris Udall, Senate Armed Services Chair John Stennis, and Senator Edmund Muskie all condemned his budget reduction. Many of the projects were in their states and were meant to fulfill promises they had made to their constituents. Speaker Tip O'Neill worked out the compromise plan that left nineteen projects intact, but Carter never recovered from the self-inflicted political damage.[30]

At every turn, Carter seemed to sink deeper and deeper into the morass that was his tortured relationship with Congress. He opposed building a memorial for the sainted President Franklin D. Roosevelt on the grounds that "it will destroy some beautiful open space and directly violate FDR's request" that any monument honoring him be no larger than the size of his desk and placed in front of the National Archives.[31] Complaining that Congress did not monitor foreign economic aid to insure that it reached its proper destination, he urged members to reduce aid to countries that violated human rights and give it only to those that defended such rights or at least improved their records in that area.[32]

On March 17, 1977, Carter appeared before the UN General Assembly, where he expressed "my own support and the continuing support of my country for the ideals of the United Nations." He asked US allies and other nations to help the United States shoulder the burden of the UN's international peace keeping. He touched upon problems of global poverty and injustice, focusing on the Middle East, Africa, and the Soviet Union. Peace without justice, he said, would be a hollow victory. The four basic priorities of the United States, Carter declared, should be peace in troubled parts of the globe, arms control, international economic progress, and "dedication to the dignity and well-being of people throughout the world."[33]

After delivering his speech, Carter shook hands with a number of delegates, including representatives of the Palestinian Liberation Organization (PLO), but he did not talk to the Palestinians. The PLO and Israel both praised Carter's speech and welcomed his remarks about human rights. The Palestinians were pleased that Carter supported their need for a homeland, but the Israelis seemed anxious about just what Carter planned to do for the Palestinians.[34]

Rosalynn supported Carter's sympathy for the Palestinians, because she played a tough political game as much as she soothed and encouraged her husband. Sympathetic with the needs of women, she comforted the wife of Russian dissident Anatoly Shcharansky, supported her husband's attempt to get more women in the administration, approved his appointment of Joan Mondale to the Council on the Arts and Humanities, and helped seek ratification of the ERA.[35] She devoted much of her time to working for better mental health care, improved government policies, and the removal of the stigma associated with the retarded and mentally ill.

By executive order on February 17, Carter established the President's Commission on Mental Health to recommend policies to overcome deficiencies in the national mental health system. At a ceremony in the East Room, he and Rosalynn jointly made the announcement. She declared that it was "a great day for me," and then she introduced Thomas E. Bryant, who would serve as executive director of the commission, with Rosalynn as honorary chair. Bryant had worked with the Johnson Administration on policies related to medicine and the law. As president of the national Drug Abuse Council, he had become friends with Peter Bourne, who had served the Carter governorship in a similar capacity. A nepotism law prevented Rosalynn from being the chair, but she became an active honorary chair.

Rosalynn outlined the commission's goals when she opened their first meeting before turning the session over to Bryant. The term "mental health," she said, would include mental illness, retardation, and substance addiction. In all of those areas, the commission promoted research for treatment and ways to counter the stigma so often attached to the mentally ill. The president gave the commission one year to accomplish its work. It had twenty members, thirty-two study groups, and 13,400 volunteers scattered across the country. With a budget of $850,000, $100,000 of which came from the president's Unanticipated Needs Fund and the rest from the Department of Health, Education, and Welfare, it was generously funded. Access to mental health care, the Carters believed, should be a basic human right.[36]

Human rights was also an integral part of Carter's foreign policy, including negotiations with the Soviet Union. Only five days into office, Carter sent Brezhnev the first of a series of letters that he hoped would bring the two nations together to end the Cold War. Carter noted the areas of recent progress in the SALT II arms control discussions, preventing troubled regions such as the Middle East and Southern Africa from exploding, and bilateral economic relations. He wanted, and he believed that the Soviets also wanted, a world "More peaceful, just and humane." Brezhnev's response of February 4 claimed that the Soviet Union wanted "fundamental principles of equality, . . . non-interference in internal affairs, . . . disarmament, . . . [and] lasting peace in the Middle East." Both men knew that tough areas of disagreement, possible threats, and months of negotiation lay ahead.[37]

Throughout February and March, Carter and Brezhnev exchanged letters that became increasingly serious and distrustful. On February 25, Brezhnev wrote bluntly that the Soviet Union did not "intend to impose upon your country or upon other countries our rules," but neither would it accept any interference with its own country, including "pseudo-humanitarian slogans" that might test "our patience." Carter responded on March 4 with an urgent telegram protesting the harsh tone of that letter and reminding the chairman that no final agreement had been reached at the meeting in Vladivostok in November 1974 when Brezhnev and former President Ford had agreed that their two countries would restrict themselves to an equal number of weapons, including nuclear delivery vehicles. Carter included a long list of items to discuss at the SALT II conference. "I hope," Carter concluded, "you will not predicate your future correspondence on the erroneous assumption that we lack sincerity, integrity, or the will to make rapid progress toward mutually advantageous agreements." Neither Brezhnev nor Carter would budge.[38]

Knowing that he could not trust the Soviets, Carter initiated new covert actions to spy on them. Egged on by Brzezinski, and aggravated by the Soviets' recent arrests of human rights activists Yuri Orlov and Anatoly Shcharansky, who had been founders of the Helsinki Watch Group, Carter reinforced his support of the dissidents and sought ways to attack the very legitimacy of the Soviet government. The Helsinki Watch Group was composed of prominent Jewish dissidents who intended to hold the Soviets to the 1975 Helsinki Final Act agreement with the United States and thirty-three other nations. That non-binding agreement said the Soviets would accept the status quo after World War II and respect the human rights and fundamental freedom of all people, which included Jewish dissidents. By arresting Orlov and Shcharansky, the Soviets plainly were not keeping their word. Carter thus approved clandestine propaganda, the secret distribution of books and periodicals written by Soviet critics, and the broadcast of interviews and writings of the dissidents back into the Soviet Union. Thus, according to a later director of the CIA, Carter changed the rules of the Cold War with his "challenge directly" to "the legitimacy of the Soviet government in the eyes of its own people."[39]

Carter's public correspondence with Andrei Sakharov during the first month of his presidency served notice to the Soviet Union in particular, and the world in general, that he was serious about his promotion of human rights. Sakharov, the elite Russian scientist and principal developer of the Soviet hydrogen bomb, had become disillusioned with the Soviet regime and published a popular essay decrying its anti-Semitism and calling for the democratization of his country. A US attorney and assistant director of the American Civil Liberties Union went to Sakharov's apartment in Moscow and asked for a message to take back to the new US president. Sakharov drafted a letter to Carter listing the names of sixteen political prisoners and suggesting that the intelligence and internal-security agency, popularly

known as the secret police or KGB, was attempting to snuff out the dissident movement. A week after Carter received the letter, he released it to the
New York Times, which gave it front page publicity. By doing that, Carter
coyly supported Sakharov's appeal for help.[40]

In the middle of February, Carter sent his response to Sakharov in care of
the US embassy in Moscow. When Sakharov read it, he was shocked to learn
that the president of the United States had assured the Soviets' most famous
dissident that "we shall use our good offices to seek the release of prisoners
of conscience" and build a world in which "nations of differing cultures and
histories can live side by side in peace and justice." The US government, he
promised, would monitor and protest any trials, arrests, or persecutions of
Russian Jewish dissidents. Since the tone of his letter offered more sympathy
than help, Sakharov could expect a long imprisonment.[41]

What Carter could accomplish in the Soviet Union was limited, but he
meant business. He appointed Patricia M. Derian of Mississippi to head the
Bureau of Human Rights and Humanitarian Affairs, a position he soon elevated to undersecretary of state for human rights. Pat Derian and her husband Hodding Carter III had been active in the Civil Rights movement in
Mississippi, had supported the Kennedys, and had worked on Carter's campaign. Hodding became spokesperson for the State Department, but his wife
had the more difficult job. At first uneasy about it, she relaxed when she decided it was "just like Mississippi politics." Derian often challenged the president to keep his word. Realizing that Carter would not jeopardize national
security for human rights, she targeted Latin American and African countries where national security was not an issue, especially Argentina, Chile,
El Salvador, Uruguay, and Ethiopia, where she was able to make significant
inroads.[42]

To further his goal of bringing peace to the Middle East and defending
the rights of suffering people there, Carter invited the leaders of Israel and
Egypt to Washington early in his term. Israeli Prime Minister Yitzhak Rabin
came in March, but he did not get along with Carter. He became enraged
when Carter referred to the "Palestinian homeland." He did not want Carter
to reconvene the 1973 Geneva peace conference, in which many Arab nations would participate. Carter thought Rabin was "timid, stubborn," and
distrustful of the United States. Rudely, he declined to listen to Amy play the
piano, and, worse, he butted out a cigarette on a White House carpet. What
Rabin knew at the time, and Carter did not, was that Rabin was under severe
stress. It would soon become public knowledge that he and his wife Leah had

improper financial accounts in the United States. He also faced a tough battle for reelection in Israel.[43]

As stubborn as the prime minister, five days later at a town hall meeting in Clinton, Massachusetts, Carter called for "a homeland for Palestinian refugees." The negative response from Jewish Americans and his adviser Ken Stein, an expert on Middle Eastern history at Emory University, signaled a rocky road ahead for the peace effort in the Middle East and for winning Jewish votes at home. In Massachusetts, Carter attempted to first ignore and then defuse the controversy. He stayed at the home of a blue collar family, mixed easily with the people at the town meeting, and polished his image of being one of them. But all was not well. In the heart of Kennedy country, Senator Ted Kennedy carefully watched the intruder from the South in action, but kept his thoughts to himself. Israelis and Jewish Americans also observed the president closely, because it appeared to them that Carter was turning away from Israel.[44]

Carter's turn toward Egypt reinforced the fears of skeptical Jewish observers. Egyptian president Anwar Sadat planned to find a way "to give President Carter the cards to move forward on the Middle East peace effort." He asked Carter for military equipment that would not upset the balance of power in the region but that would keep the military loyal to him. Sadat also stated flatly that Egypt would never agree to a peace settlement that did not refer to a "Palestinian 'homeland,'" nor address the problem of Israeli settlements in lands claimed by Arabs.[45]

On April 4, late in the evening, Jimmy and Rosalynn welcomed Anwar and Jehan Sadat to the White House. Carter met privately with Sadat the next morning, agreed to his modest request for military aid, and praised the Egyptian's historic gesture toward making peace with Israel.[46] It had been a very long journey from Sadat's childhood until that day he arrived in Washington for the purpose of making peace with Israel. The grandson of African slaves who had been liberated by the British and born into an excruciatingly poor Nubian family, Anwar escaped poverty by entering the Royal Military Academy in Cairo in 1938. A beneficiary of the British system, he nevertheless hated the British. In the army he met Gamal Abdel Nasser, and they, along with others, formed the secret Free Officers Society that sought Hitler's help at the beginning of World War II. The British captured him and sent him to a minimum security prison.

After his release, Sadat met and married Jehan Safwat Raouf, fifteen years his junior. Theirs was a whirlwind romance not unlike that of Jimmy and

Rosalynn. Jehan, who idolized Sadat as an Egyptian hero, met him at her fifteenth birthday party in 1948. Fascinated with her, Anwar could not believe that she was only fifteen. Jehan's parents, an Egyptian surgeon married to a British woman, did not want their daughter of privilege to marry an older man with no prospects of earning a decent living. Jehan persuaded them that she was in love and did not need money. Sadat divorced his wife, by whom he had three children, in order to marry Jehan on May 29, 1949. Like the Carters, they became parents of four children and formed a close partnership that helped Jehan progress educationally through a doctoral degree. She also emerged as a humanitarian, activist, and advocate for peace, like her friend Rosalynn Carter.[47]

Jehan shared her husband's rise through the political process from his role in many radical movements, including the Free Officers who launched the Egyptian Revolution of 1952 that overthrew King Farouk. After Gamal Abdel Nasser's death in 1970, Sadat became Egypt's president. A strong leader, he encouraged an Islamist movement, made overtures of peace toward Israel, dismissed ministers with close ties to the Soviet Union, and expelled the Soviet military from his country.[48]

Israel had ignored Sadat's gestures of friendship and still held territory it had seized in the 1967 Six Day War with Egypt. By controlling the Sinai Peninsula and the Gaza Strip, Israel's borders reached to the Suez Canal and the Red Sea. Israel took the West Bank from Jordan and the Golan Heights from Syria, creating thousands of Palestinian refugees who congregated in the West Bank and the Gaza Strip. The UN Security Council passed UN Resolution 242 on November 22, 1967, calling for the Israelis to return those territories and suggesting that Israel allow the Palestinians to determine their own future. It had gone unheeded.

Sadat turned from the Soviet Union to the United States in the early 1970s and endorsed a UN proposal for peace with Israel if Israel would return the occupied territories. Neither Israel nor the United States accepted the proposal, but Sadat did not give up. With increased confidence that he might win a war against Israel, he joined with President Hafez al-Assad of Syria to launch the Yom Kippur War on October 6, 1973. After initial Egyptian successes, the Israeli troops rallied with such force that the situation frightened the superpowers into imposing a ceasefire on October 25, 1973. Despite their superior strength, the Israelis signed agreements to disengage their forces, but they continued to control the occupied territories.[49] Sadat, in 1977, hoped to get help from the United States.

Jimmy and Rosalynn had done their homework and knew the history of their Egyptian guests. During the day after their April 4 arrival, the two couples got to know each other on a personal level. To honor the first lady of Egypt, Rosalynn skipped the traditional tea and small talk in favor of a seminar with experts on problems common to the United States and Egypt. The participants discussed topics ranging from domestic violence to the King Tutankhamen exhibit, which was then on display at Washington's National Gallery of Art. When one speaker raised the issue of battered women, Jehan commented that the resulting emotional problems were often worse than the beatings.

Jehan wanted to cooperate with Rosalynn in their work for human rights. Jehan explained that she worked with the disabled in her home country and suggested to Rosalynn that they should plan exchange visits for handicapped people of Egypt and the United States. According to Jehan, the two women wanted their husbands to achieve peace in the Middle East. Jimmy dropped by the meeting in the Blue Room, held hands with Rosalynn and listened to a young woman play the piano. Joan Mondale, who was present, noted how Rosalynn transformed a social occasion with a like-minded first lady into a plan to promote caring and human rights among peoples of diverse nations.[50]

At the state dinner on April 5, Carter toasted Sadat, commenting that he and the Egyptian leader shared a background of "a small village" and "an unswerving religious commitment." Sadat was a man of courage, a man of his word, a man who wanted peace, and a man who believes in "the God who organizes our lives," Carter continued. The US president believed that his "charming and frank" guest might hold the key to peace in the Middle East.[51]

In further conversations with Sadat, Carter revealed his hope of reviving the 1973 Geneva peace talks by following his meeting with Sadat with similar communications with King Hussein of Jordan, Crown Prince Fahd of Saudi Arabia, and President Hafez al-Assad of Syria. Carter's plan envisioned persuading the Israelis to withdraw from Egyptian territories they had seized and held since 1967 and self-determination for the Palestinians if they recognized Israel's right to exist. Sadat knew that selling the idea to other Arabs would be difficult, and Carter knew that convincing the Israelis bordered on the impossible and would surely cost him politically.[52] Nevertheless, as the Sadats left the country, both first couples believed that peace in the Middle East was possible.

NINE

Governing Carter Style

During the very days that the Carters were entertaining the Sadats and dreaming of an unprecedented peace in the Middle East, Secretary of State Cyrus Vance handed Carter a hopeful letter from Leonid Brezhnev. Apparently the aged and possibly ill Brezhnev felt an urgent need to come to terms with the new president of the United States. Carter's commitment to human rights had placed the Soviet leaders on the defensive, for, according to Brzezinski, they understood that Carter's idealism not only strengthened the United States, but also generated "pressure from within their own system." Continuing negotiations for SALT II might weaken the tired old Russian bear, and the growing strength of China and India could upset the balance of power between the United States and the Soviet Union. More ominous for the Soviets, as both the Soviet and US leaders knew, but apparently the press did not, was Carter's secret plan to rebuild the US war-ravaged military machine into the most powerful and technologically efficient ever assembled.[1]

The weakened Brezhnev found himself facing an unusual enemy. The untimid Jimmy Carter, exuding excellent health and physical stamina, stood ready with formidable military might to pressure the Soviets into a peace agreement. Preferring peace to war, Carter seeded an internal Soviet revolution with his offer of hope to the Soviet Union's persecuted political dissidents. At the beginning of the century, President Teddy Roosevelt had elevated the United States to a global power, but near the end of the century Carter and his immediate successors transformed it into the only world power. Unwilling to cede dominance to the United States, however, Brezhnev, in his letter of April 4, stressed that Soviet policy in relation to the United States was "equal security and non-interference in internal affairs."[2]

The next month when Cy Vance went to Moscow to resume talks about arms limitation, he found the Russians in a bad mood. Although Vance refrained from mentioning human rights, the angry Soviet delegates refused to accept any plan the US presented, and talks collapsed. As Carter received news of the failure via telephone, his face turned red, he coughed, and he tried to hide his anger. He would not back down from his emphasis on human rights. He wrote Brezhnev that "our two countries should soon undertake cooperative efforts in dealing with the global challenges confronting all of mankind: poverty, nutrition, health, and economic development." Such an agreement, Carter said, would not only help many people, but it would also be "a positive step toward peace."[3]

Although peace with the Soviet Union remained uncertain, Carter hoped for peace in the Middle East. His meeting with Sadat at the White House on April 4 and 5 had encouraged him to involve other Arab nations in the peace process. He scheduled a White House meeting with King Hussein of Jordan. Prior to his visit, Hussein served notice in an April 23 interview that the Arab world did not like the fact that Israel was developing "its armed forces to a level never before achieved." Israel, the King said, was a threat to moderate Arab leaders, and anyone who thought that peace might be established in 1977 was mistaken.[4]

Carter welcomed Hussein to the White House two days later and felt sorry for him when he broke down in tears talking about the recent death of his third wife, Queen Alia Toukan, in a helicopter crash. Postponing business, Carter set up a week's vacation for Hussein on the Georgia coast, where he swam and fished, but he did not change his mind about peace between Israel and her Arab neighbors. Carter hoped for a Middle East peace conference in Geneva, but Hussein said it would not occur unless Israel first gave up territories she had conquered from Egypt, Syria, and Jordan in the 1967 war and a PLO delegate was included among the Arab delegates. The news from Jerusalem that acting Prime Minister Shimon Peres had said that there were too many obstacles to a peace conference and approved a new settlement at Mes'ha on the West Bank caused Carter to conclude that the Israelis were less interested in peace than the Arabs were.[5]

Carter failed to win the confidence of Jewish Americans and Israelis. He stirred a hornet's nest of Jewish complaints when he thoughtlessly mentioned in his Sunday School lesson at the First Baptist Church the typical Southern Baptist teaching that the Jews had crucified Jesus Christ. Quickly, he backtracked and explained that he understood "that Jesus forgave the human instruments of his death" and that the Jewish people were "falsely charged" and as a result "persecuted terribly" for many centuries. The crucifixion of Jesus, he said, was preordained and required a human instrument, hence the Jews bore no "collective responsibility" for it.[6] He reaffirmed his approval "with all my heart" of a four-year-old statement that the Southern Baptist

Convention condemned anti-Semitism.[7] The majority of polled Israelis were not convinced; 61% of them opposed Carter's plan to have Israel return to its pre-1967 borders.[8]

On the home front, where Carter had more authority, advocacy for human rights took many forms. Esther Peterson, the aging consumer advocate from the Lyndon Johnson administration, accepted the same post with Carter. Rosalynn led a White House roundtable discussion on aging, set aside a day to welcome senior citizens to the White House, and toured local nursing homes. The federal government supported minority banks, just as Carter had coerced the Georgia state government into doing when he was governor. Carter supported public works that gave people jobs and citizens a better life and signed a bill that appropriated $4 billion for that purpose. He also wanted welfare reform and hospital cost containment legislation.[9]

Reaching beyond his administration, Carter opened a meeting of the OAS in the United States on April 14, Pan-American Day, with a resounding commitment to the sovereignty of individual nations and a reminder that freedom and human rights went hand in hand. When, a month later, Brzezinski showed him an account of the changes he had helped to bring about, he learned that more than two dozen nations reported improvements in human rights. Argentina, Brazil, Chile, Colombia, and Haiti had released twenty-one political prisoners, Honduras and Jamaica a total of fifty-three, Paraguay ninety-two, and Peru had granted amnesty to 314 political and criminal prisoners. Iran pardoned 653 prisoners, and others in eastern and western Europe, Asia and Africa, went free. Russia allowed exit visas for at least three Jewish dissidents, and Bangladesh and India also freed some political prisoners. Several other countries made constitutional changes regarding human rights and lifted bans on newspapers.[10]

Freedom and human rights, Carter said, rested in part upon the United States and other nations having an adequate energy supply. Since his first fireside chat on February 1 and his town hall meeting in Massachusetts on March 16, he had pushed for legislation and public awareness of the need for major action to solve the energy crisis. His plea for Americans to lower their thermostats and wear sweaters and thermal underwear fell on deaf ears. His plan for conservation, the use of nuclear power, insulation of homes, alternative sources of energy such as solar power, and reduced dependence on foreign oil all made good sense, but to persuade the public to cooperate and get legislation through the Congress was an uphill battle. When he consulted with former Republican presidents Nixon and Ford, they gave him good advice and promised to ask Republican Congressmen to support needed legislation. Impatiently, Carter's commented that the country was "the most wasteful nation on earth," a remark that offended more citizens than it inspired. Finally, on April 18 he declared on national television that the energy crisis was "the moral equivalent of war."[11] Carter's call for citizens to make sacrifices to deal with the energy shortage did not strike the House Speaker as the way to go about solving a serious problem.[12]

As Carter prepared to deliver a major address to a joint session of Congress on April 20, asking for a comprehensive energy plan, he became outraged with some of the information his speechwriters sent him. For the basis of his argument, he studied a declassified CIA report on international energy outlook, but he was disgusted with the contents. "This is bureaucratic b.s.," he said. "All I asked for were estimates of reserves" and the number of "barrels in a cubic mile."[13] In a speech he wrote himself, Carter presented a huge energy package to Congress. Speaker O'Neill, shocked by the magnitude of the package and the challenge it would present him to get House approval, nevertheless supported the president. James Schlesinger, Carter's representative for energy matters, thought that his staff could break down the huge energy package of proposed legislation into smaller bills that would be easier to get through both houses of Congress. Carter agreed, and drawing upon the loyalty of his fellow Democrats, and with the help of Tip O'Neill, he got House approval.

When the House Omnibus Energy Bill reached the Senate, however, Senator Robert Byrd immediately opposed it because, Frank Moore thought, Byrd's pride was wounded because the House had passed the bill before the Senate. Neither Scoop Jackson, chair of the Energy and Natural Resources Committee, nor Senator Russell Long, chair of the Finance Committee, wanted to help Carter. Jackson still simmered from being defeated by him, and Long thought the bill would be detrimental to the oil industry in his state of Louisiana.[14]

Carter, in typical fashion, took his argument to the public by publishing a detailed open letter on the national energy plan. He proposed that an excise tax be levied on automobiles that were not fuel efficient and that the price of newly discovered oil be allowed to rise over a three-year period to the 1977 world price. New natural gas would be subject to the price limitation at the BTU equivalent of coal and nuclear energy. Long and complicated, Carter's letter went unread by most of the public.[15] Producers, consumers, and Congressmen all seemed confused, but the producers feared a government tax that was confiscatory. Carter would not give up. When Rosalynn asked him how his energy program was progressing, he replied: "It's a bitch! I know why no other President was willing to tackle it."[16]

Another tough problem, which former presidents had failed to solve, was the negotiation of new treaties with Panama about ownership of the canal. Carter was almost defiant in his determination early in his presidency to settle the Panama Canal issue rapidly and justly. It would be difficult to get the Senate's approval, and every adviser, especially Rosalynn, asked him to wait until a second term. Uncertain of reelection, Carter risked failure and rejected this advice. He ordered the relevant cabinet secretaries and advisers to begin the negotiations only three months into his first term. He viewed them, according to Deputy National Security Adviser David Aaron, "as a statement about human rights, a statement about equality . . . a statement about justice . . . a statement about the end of colonialism and racism."[17] Knowing that he would need bipartisan support to win the Panama Canal debate, which he thought "vital to our nation's security and well-being," he attempted to build a strong relationship with Congress.[18]

Nor did Carter think he needed advice from Congress or the army brass when on May 5 he issued Presidential Directive/NSC-12 announcing that he would gradually withdraw US ground troops from South Korea because they were no longer needed there and their deployment was an unnecessary expense. When the press reported that Major General John K. Singlaub criticized his plan, Carter summoned the general to the White House, listened to his denials, felt sorry for him, but relieved him of his position. Without consulting the Pentagon, Carter vetoed the neutron bomb and canceled production of the B-1 bomber, weapons he thought were inhumane or not needed to guarantee US military superiority. Tip O'Neill congratulated him for being a president who could make vital military decisions without Pentagon approval, but some key senators, who were motivated more by politics than balancing the budget, became embittered toward their country's aggressive commander in chief.[19]

Carter made a better first impression upon the international community than he did upon the US Congress. His trip to an economic summit in London on May 6 raised his and his country's standing in the eyes of the world. A meeting of the seven industrialized nations, the G-7, it became the first in a series of annual conferences. Enjoying himself, Carter first went to Newcastle-Upon-Tyne where tens of thousands of people lined the highways to see him, and he thanked "my good friend, Jim Callaghan," for arranging the visit. "There is no way that I can express the sense of friendship and common heritage, common commitment to the future that I feel with the people of Great Britain," he said, before attending a dinner hosted by Prime Minister Callaghan. There Carter learned that the Germans liked his human rights speeches, for they had quietly assisted many Eastern Europeans to reach freedom in the West. The next morning at breakfast he met with West Germany's Helmut Schmidt and thought they had worked out their minor differences, but in reality they had not. He became acquainted with the presidents of France and Italy and ascertained what the other attendees thought of his human rights position. The Canadians and French agreed that the western world should lead the way, but the British and Germans feared antagonizing the Russians. The Japanese and Italians had little to say about it.[20]

On the evening of May 7, the peanut farmer from Georgia dined with Queen Elizabeth at Buckingham Palace. He had seen the palace before, but only as a tourist peering through the fence. Before dinner he had made a faux pas that irritated the queen. When introduced to the Queen Mother, he stepped close to her, as he would have with any older woman in Georgia, and planted a kiss on her lips. She recoiled, but the offense could not be erased.[21]

Reportedly miffed by the improper kiss, Queen Elizabeth maintained perfect decorum at the state dinner where the president of the United States sat between her and Princess Margaret and across the table from Prince Charles and Prince Philip. Carter told Queen Elizabeth how much the American people appreciated her coming to the United States the past year to help celebrate the country's independence bicentennial. After telling Carter that she had appreciated the warm US reception, Queen Elizabeth made small talk with him. She had to watch her waistline, she said, and make certain that she fit into the seven tunics she wore on certain ceremonial occasions. Together they solved the problem by joking that waist dimensions should be measured in inches while everything else in centimeters. Carter was impressed, too, with the Queen's knowledge of world affairs and politics, although she was reticent to express an opinion on anything more than just the need for world peace.[22]

The next day, Archdeacon Edward Knapp-Fisher gave Carter and others a VIP tour of Westminster Abbey. Although a Baptist, Carter participated in an Anglican Eucharist service, saw the room where thirty-two scholars translated the King James Version of the Bible, and finally reached Poets' Corner where he told the archdeacon that it was time they honored his favorite poet, Dylan Thomas. The archdeacon politely reminded the president that the Welshman was a drunkard, but Carter argued that others honored in Poets' Corner had many personal failings of their own. Callaghan tried to get Carter to mind his own business, but Carter persisted. Four years later a plaque for Thomas could be found at Poets' Corner in the abbey.[23]

While enjoying the extracurricular activities, Carter never forgot why he was there. He was meticulously prepared to deal with any economic or other issue that came up at the G-7 meeting. Some delegates, who thought that Carter would behave like a preacher, were surprised to find him an unpretentious, modest man with an open mind and willingness to listen to others. Carter found himself in a position to be more influential among international allies than with lawmakers at home. Discussions about the Middle East, however, remained vague, and West Germany would not back down from its plans to sell nuclear processing equipment to Brazil. The Germans would soon learn, however, that Carter's easy-going demeanor merely disguised the tough leader who would stand up to friend and foe alike, and expect, as his father had taught him, every man, and woman, and nation to carry a fair share of responsibility. At NATO meetings, he repeated his insistence that the United States should not be the principal supporter of the alliance, but that all members should be equally involved.[24]

On May 9, Carter took a short side trip to Geneva, the beautiful Swiss city that served so often as the site for peace conferences. Wanting to confer with additional Middle Eastern heads of state other than those who had been to Washington, he met with President Hafiz al-Assad of Syria, who agreed to offer what Carter labelled "guidance and advice" on how to procure peace for his part of the world. Assad did not give him much hope that the Arab nations would soften their attitudes toward Israel. The Syrian spoke in friendly terms but made it clear that, before progress could be made, Israel would have to surrender all of the territories it had taken in 1967 and recognize the legitimacy of Palestine. The two heads of state were able, however, to solve the dilemma of several hundred young male Syrian Jews who had migrated to the United States. Since they could not find wives in the United States, the Syrian government sent over five hundred young female Syrian Jews. The men chose their mates, and the remainder of the women returned to Syria.[25]

Rosalynn and Mondale met Jimmy and Vance when they returned home from London late on May 10. Following one day of rest and relaxation, Carter and Vance briefed Congressional leaders and national defense officials who were pleased to learn about their hopeful meetings. Carter had come to know other heads of state, to move easily among them, and to realize his power and responsibility to influence international events.[26] After his trip to London and Geneva, he was emboldened to pursue peace between Israel and her Arab neighbors.

Committed to dealing evenhandedly with both sides in the Arab-Israel dispute, Carter approved the sale of airborne warning and control systems (AWACS) to Iran, a long-time US ally. Shah Mohammad Pahlavi said his country, which was representative of Arab nations that feared Israeli's military power, needed the planes for protection against developments in Africa and on the Indian sub-continent. Carter, by assuaging the fears of Jewish American and Israelis, gained Senate approval for an arms package that assured Israel of privileged access to US military technology, and also provided weapons to Egypt and Saudi Arabia.[27]

In Israel a turn of events that was a greater threat than the AWACS to Carter's peace plan sale occurred on May 17 when voters chose right-wing Likud Party leader Menachem Begin as prime minister. A notorious arch nationalist who had commanded the Irgun Zva'i Leumi terrorists during the establishment of Israel in the 1940s, the sixty-three-year old Begin pledged to open peace talks with Egypt. Carter and his advisers, however, thought Begin's election would demolish their hope for peace.[28]

The election of Begin stirred a reaction from both Carter and Jewish Americans. In June, Hamilton Jordan advised Carter that his team did not understand the strength of the Jewish lobby because "that was not a part of our Georgia and Southern political experience." Members of the American-Israel Public Affairs Committee, Jordan said, were nervous because Carter was not well known to Jewish leaders who thought that he did not give priority to the welfare of the state of Israel. Carter's special adviser for Jewish affairs, Mark Siegel, published in the *New York Times* on June 1 a long article in which he explained that Jews believed that they could only count on their own people. The existence of Israel, he wrote, was key to their psychic liberation. His job, if he could do it, was to help the administration understand the Jewish-American mind.[29]

While the hope for Middle East peace rested upon precarious events with a future that could not be predicted, Carter turned his attention to another unpopular issue: the Panama Canal. Against Rosalynn's advice, he attempted to settle that controversy quickly. The dispute over US control of the canal had dogged every president since Eisenhower, and Ronald Reagan had made it a hot issue in the 1976 presidential campaign. The canal's history was a shady one. In 1903 the opportunistic and diplomatically artful President

Teddy Roosevelt, determined to make the United States a world-class naval power, had bought the rights to build and operate the canal from a French company that had begun construction. Roosevelt supported a revolution against Colombia that resulted in the creation of Panama as an independent nation, and then he quickly signed a treaty with its provisional government giving the United States the exclusive right in perpetuity to build and operate a canal across the Panamanian isthmus.

Although the legality of that treaty remained untested, the United States opened the canal in 1914. Thereafter, it steadily raised the annual fee it paid Panama from the original $250,000 to almost $2 million in 1955, when political unrest in Panama challenged the US presence. For the next eight years, Panamanian riots, in which three US soldiers and twenty-one Panamanians had died, forced the United States to hire more Panamanians to operate the canal, fly the Panamanian flag alongside the US flag, and commence negotiations for new treaties. Both Presidents Johnson and Nixon had attempted to negotiate with Panama, but without results. Nixon's Secretary of State Henry Kissinger had signed an agreement to discuss a new treaty with Panamanian Foreign Minister Juan Antonio Tack before Carter was elected. Acting on that agreement, Carter opened discussions with Panama. He chose two career diplomats, Ellsworth Bunker and Sol Linowitz, along with Secretary of State Cyrus Vance and Secretary of Defense Harold Brown, to investigate the US relationship with Panama and the canal.[30]

Before those negotiations were launched, Carter proved that he would not buckle under pressure from Congressional disagreements and demands. When the Senate proposed an aid package for Pakistan designed to discourage it from developing a nuclear fuel reprocessing plant, Carter rejected it. "I'm not inclined to bribe" the Pakistani president, he said. Carter agreed with his National Security Advisor Brzezinski that selling excessive military equipment to Pakistan would jeopardize the US relationship with the new Indian government, which seemed to be reaching out to the United States as well as the Soviet Union.[31]

Neither was Carter willing to compromise on human rights. He wrote an open letter to abusers, especially Argentina, threatening economic pressure, which allegedly resulted in more than two thousand prisoners going free. He planned to use the power of US foreign aid to support, monitor, and publish whatever progress the affected countries were making. Countries that needed US economic and military support or feared US power were served notice that they must respect the rights of their citizens. Rabbi March Tanenbaum of New York declared that Jimmy Carter will be a "great, if not the greatest," president in history if he continues his strong stand on human rights.[32]

When Father Ted Hesburgh invited Carter to give the commencement address at Notre Dame University, Carter used the occasion to deliver a major speech about human rights.[33] The trip to South Bend brought Carter and Tip O'Neill together in an informal way. Since O'Neill was to receive an honorary degree at the ceremony, Carter invited the Speaker to fly with him on Air Force One. O'Neill was flattered to be invited to travel with the president, and the two men enjoyed an informal visit.[34]

On May 22, Carter told his Notre Dame audience that the best way to counter Communism was to make human rights fundamental to foreign policy. Human rights would win, he promised. The war in Vietnam had failed, and the United States must transcend the "crimes" of her "Cold War past." It would be impossible to apply human rights concerns with rigid uniformity because there were different levels of oppression, and traditional foreign policy concerns also had to be addressed, he said. To end the Cold War when the Russians and the Americans could push other nations around, he would stop the arms race, address the disparity between the rich and the poor, and recognize the needs and hopes of developing nations.[35]

Drawing on his words at Notre Dame, Carter began to lace every memorandum and comment about his administration with some reference to human rights. When he welcomed Crown Prince Fahd of Saudi Arabia to Washington on May 24, he remarked that their two countries shared "deep religious convictions" and a long friendship. He hoped they could work together toward peace, but realistically he knew that the resolution to the energy crisis and chaos in the Middle East would require more than friendly rhetoric.[36]

Turning his attention to Africa, which had been ravaged by the Cold War, and whose people suffered from poverty, disease, and war, Carter hoped, with the help of the UN, to launch major reforms. The United States, he said, should respect the integrity of those countries, rendering humanitarian aid, and end the tug of war for control of them between the superpowers. UN Ambassador Andrew Young and Vice President Mondale hoped to win the trust of Black African leaders, and the United States refused to supply arms to either side in the civil wars that ravaged the Horn of Africa. In the Ethiopian-Somalia confrontation, however, Russia sent aid to both sides, and there were Cuban troops in Ethiopia.

The United States faced an extraordinary challenge in trying to remain neutral when Russia and Cuba refused to do so. Ambassador Young built trust with African nations, but his modus operandi damaged public support for the Carter presidency. Young's effort to insulate the struggle in Africa from the Cold War by encouraging an end to apartheid wherever it existed, improvements in the economy, and the rise of democracy was exactly what Carter wanted. However, when Young remarked that many in the United States were unnecessarily afraid of communism, Cuban troops in Angola were a stabilizing force, and there were political prisoners in the United States, the gains he made in Africa were offset by domestic political fallout.[37]

Carter wanted to assist South Africa in becoming a progressive society without racial conflict. After talks with Prime Minister John Vorster in early May, he told Mondale "it's best to assume better intentions than Vorster probably has and also to give them a way NOT to acknowledge past mistakes."[38]

Unwilling to shy away from any topic, no matter how thorny, Carter pursued his hope of controlling the CIA. Brzezinski asked Robert M. Gates, a Georgetown University historian who had earned a PhD in Russian history and Soviet studies, to become his special assistant. Gates, who had been coordinating all CIA research on the Soviet Union, was well positioned to give Brzezinski the information about the Soviet threat that he sought.[39]

Although he welcomed advice from Brzezinski, Carter remained actively involved with the CIA. Following the lead of former President Ford, he believed that Congressional oversight of the intelligence community was essential. Carter met with a Senate committee chaired by Daniel Inouye of Hawaii to discuss cooperation between the White House and Congress to produce legislation that subjected the CIA to congressional scrutiny. Since the Watergate scandal, Congress had not wanted to give any president a free hand to use those agencies as he saw fit. Carter wanted Congressional oversight, but he also wanted to make certain that such oversight would adequately serve his need to know. The aggressive approach of Carter and Stansfield Turner fueled the declining morale in the agency, but at the same time underscored the interdependence of the CIA and the presidency. Despite lingering bureaucratic and murky areas within the spying agency, enough change did take place for the CIA to serve the demanding president well during his tenure.[40]

Increased surveillance of the CIA was only one of the many things Carter attempted during his first months in office. On April 26 Stuart Eizenstat sent him a memorandum listing all the domestic accomplishments, both

completed and in progress, of his first one hundred days. The list was so long
that Carter had trouble reading all of it. The range of items, from reorgani-
zation to welfare reform to ethics in government, was impressive. Almost no
topic that interested Carter was omitted. The $50 tax rebate that had been
rescinded because he thought it inflationary, the arts, the environment, civil
service reform, and budget cutting all made the list. Many of those items
won him praise, but others, like the reverse tax rebate, cost him politically.
Nevertheless, according to the polls, 80% of the people approved of his performance.[41] The remark of a Swiss newspaper editor that the United States is
"returning to innovation and regeneration" pleased Carter so much that he
quipped, "give this to Jody or give him Jody's job."[42]

During that spring of 1977, the Carters settled into a comfortable lifestyle
in the White House. Southerners to the core, they were relaxed, smart, ambitious, committed to the welfare of humanity, and tough enough to withstand
criticisms and the rigors of the office. Their musical interests ranged from
country music to classical piano, and they had learned to feel comfortable in
the homes of ordinary people or the palaces of kings. They held their families and friends close, cherished and learned from their heritage, argued with
and loved each other. Their faith was unshakeable, but they did not impose
it upon others. They did not have a summer home or expensive retirement
property. When they went home to Plains, Rosalynn usually did the laundry
and cooking herself.[43]

As further evidence that they did not move far from their roots, Jimmy
identified country music star Willie Nelson as his favorite entertainer. Two
days after Nelson was released from jail on a drug charge in the Bahamas, he
was performing in the Rose Garden at the White House. Jimmy introduced
him with a wink and a smile as he told Willie that he was glad all went well
in the Bahamas. After dinner, they talked farming, peanuts, and pigs. The
Nelson daughters slept in the Martha Washington bedroom, while Willie
and his wife retired to the Lincoln bedroom. As he lay awake thinking that
two days earlier he was in the "pokey," a knock came on his door. It was Chip
Carter, who told him about a back staircase that would lead to the roof and
a stunning view of the city. Once there, Chip pulled out a joint, and the two
of them got stoned, prompting Willie to meditate about how he and Jimmy
had gotten there. Carter had moved from farming to politics and had found
a way "to help out the average Joe," whereas Willie had learned to entertain
the average Joe. So together both under and on the roof of the White House,

they bonded in a friendship that would anchor Carter's presidency in his Southern heritage.[44]

Jimmy was Mr. Earl's son. One moment Earl could be strict, demanding, and unforgiving, and the next minute show love and concern, although qualified by the tough, practical side of his personality. Jimmy was like him, except Jimmy always wanted the hug, the forgiveness, the recognition that he had lived up to his father's expectation that he be the "Hot" of his nickname. He never got it. Success came to him, but at the cost of loneliness.[45] When with Rosalynn, however, he was never alone. Aside from defending and caring for him, she also helped him shoulder the awesome responsibility of the presidency.

Rosalynn's increasing involvement in the government was revealed in the presidential memoranda that occasionally mentioned Carter's plan to make her an ambassador. When he learned that President Morales of Peru, responding to United States pressure, planned to announce a general amnesty for political prisoners in May, Jimmy commented, "Maybe he'll do it while Rosalynn's there."[46] When the president of Brazil, Carlos Marchi, criticized Carter for his position on nuclear proliferation and human rights, Carter responded, "Let Rosalynn's trip proceed regardless of the government attitude in Brazil."[47]

Despite numerous references to Rosalynn's participation in the affairs of state, the press and the public had been slow to understand that the First Lady would be a key player in the Carter presidency. The stage had been set, however, for her to shock the country and the world, especially the macho world of Latin America, when she stepped alone into the limelight, embodying the power of the presidency.

Rosalynn Steps Out

When Rosalynn walked down Pennsylvania Avenue on January 20, 1977, hand in hand with her husband, waving to the adoring crowds, and dressed like any middle-class woman on a cold day, she was going to work. Work for her meant, as it had since she was a teenaged bride, managing family and business affairs, political campaigning, and having the freedom to choose her own ventures. As First Lady, she would have a staff and resources that would enable her to do more than she could have imagined only a few years earlier. She knew how to manage a mansion, greet heads of state, and work easily with a large staff. She had entered the White House with a canvas satchel full of projects she intended to pursue.[1]

Rosalynn quickly learned that the media and the public would know every word she said or action she took, which gave her power that she could manipulate. She could deliver speeches, make phone calls, plan state dinners, travel to exotic places, and take care of Amy and her other family members. Jimmy was always there to help, or to argue, and aides and experts of all kinds were available at a moment's notice.[2]

Rosalynn learned that life in the White House would be a mixed blessing. She and Jimmy unlocked all the doors between the floors, and she created comfortable areas where the family could gather. When Jimmy turned all the thermostats down to 65 degrees, she cried, and Jimmy brought her a sweater. When she attended a cabinet meeting on February 28, 1977, the media made it into a major event. However, she only took notes and said nothing until she was in private with Jimmy. Brzezinski sent her national security briefings, which she read carefully, and she was in her office by 9:30 a.m. every work day.[3]

Rosalynn created the Office of First Lady with a professional staff. Her intent to devote time to getting the ERA ratified before the March 22, 1979, deadline posed a unique challenge because she had so little in common with the leading feminists of the day. They judged her as no more than a mouthpiece for her husband, and they rarely recognized her intelligence, independence, and ability to be both a traditional wife and a feminist. Rosalynn wanted to maintain her own identify, to be, she said, "my own person" and get "close to the people."[4] Her press secretary, Mary Hoyt, commented, "Rosalynn Carter is unpackageable."[5]

Turning the mansion into a home, Rosalynn had fun with Amy sharing the bowling alley, movie theater, pool, and enjoying the treats prepared by the pastry chef. Rosalynn and a maid draped white sheets over themselves one Halloween, so that when Amy and a friend went to the Lincoln bedroom they got to see the "famous" ghosts. Amy's enjoyment of her tree house and companionship with her cat Misty Malarky Ying Yang pleased Rosalynn as much as her opportunity to pose with children in a spelling bee or preside over a major presidential commission. Making a political statement as well as entertaining her daughter, Rosalynn took Amy to the National Zoo to accept Sri Lanka's gift of a baby elephant named "Shanti," the Sanskrit word for peace. She also liked to make the mansion a home for Jimmy and particularly enjoyed choosing famous paintings with him, according to their tastes, from the extensive White House collection to display in their residence area.[6]

The media pelted Rosalynn with questions that she thought were mindless. What aggravated her most were the questions about her clothing. She thought there were "so many more important things to talk about." Sometimes she was tempted to ask the inquisitor if he would ask such questions of her husband. Her projects, Rosalynn said, should be the focus of her publicity.[7]

Nevertheless, Rosalynn patiently answered those questions, many of which bordered on gossip. She thought unwed couples should not live together, her decision not to serve liquor in the White House was only to save the taxpayers money, and she would get psychiatric help for her children if they needed it. Although Chip and possibly her other sons were known marijuana users, she said that she did not want them or their friends to smoke weed—and she especially did not want anyone to light up a joint at the White House. Amy attended state dinners because Rosalynn and Jimmy wanted her with them, and the book that Amy read at the table not only kept her from fidgeting but was part of the Carter family lifestyle in Plains. A political wife, she revealed that she would give Jimmy advice on political matters whether he asked for it or not.[8]

Expecting good service from the West Wing as well as the East, Rosalynn was irked by a memo from speechwriter Jim Fallows complaining about the difficulty that he had in finding time to write a human rights speech she wanted because, as he said, of "all the messages to Congress your husband has loaded on us." He soon mended his ways, however, and sent her a draft incorporating the Carters' major themes about human rights and foreign policy. Fallows learned, as did other aides to the president, that the First Lady had access to any of the president's advisers whose assistance she might require.[9]

Working with a president who demanded that his administration accomplish more with less, Rosalynn fought hard to get the financing her commission on mental health needed. She persuaded Jimmy to give her $100,000 from the president's emergency fund to begin work immediately. He braced for the fallout from "coming into office and giving his wife $100,000 for her pet project," but he gave it to her anyway. Knowing that she needed more time to persuade Congress to provide additional funds, as well as raise money from other sources, Jimmy reluctantly promised the seed money from his emergency fund, but like his father, he qualified it with an order directing the commission to give him a preliminary report by September 1, 1977, and a final one by the first of April 1978. Intending to meet that deadline, Rosalynn appealed to the public for additional funds and volunteers. Organizations and individuals sent money, and 450 people volunteered to help. Despite Secretary Joseph A. Califano's reticence, his Department of Health Education and Welfare provided staffers for Rosalynn's commission and paid their salaries in the amount of $750,000. Califano, however, grumbled that mental health should be under his jurisdiction. Rebuffing him, Rosalynn and Director Thomas Bryant fought for their commission's independence, a battle they won with the president's support.[10]

Rosalynn believed that "it was not that Jimmy got elected, . . . it was that we all did." Jody Powell, who knew Rosalynn well, said, "She may be soft-spoken, but people tend to underestimate her. If you've ever been on the opposite side in a dispute, you've made a very serious mistake."[11] Rosalynn's strength, she said, came from her mother, her husband, her experience, and her faith. According to her close friend Mary King, Rosalynn thought "the Lord had put her in a unique situation where she could get things done."[12]

On March 29, Rosalynn presided at the first meeting of the twenty mental health commissioners at the White House. Each had been briefed on a variety of issues related to mental health, and they came together in a seminar to exchange their concerns and ideas. They decided to concentrate on the needs of those with serious mental illnesses and to enlist the help of professionals, volunteers, consumers, and ordinary citizens in every part of the country. One of their first reports dealt with the problems of delivering services to people of color, who sometimes bore the brunt of the stigma attached to those who were mentally ill. Rarely referred to as ill, Rosalynn remembered, they were called "crazy" or "not right" and usually were locked up in an institution where they received little or no effective treatment. She became as passionate about destigmatizing mental illness as she was about research, treatment, and insurance payments for it. She insisted that mental health care was not only for "them—but for all of us."[13]

Throughout April, when Jimmy was working for international peace and a domestic energy policy, Rosalynn interspersed serious work on the mental health commission with her other responsibilities. On separate occasions she addressed the National Council on Aging and the President's Committee on Retardation. To the first group, she announced that she would host a First Lady's Roundtable Discussion on Aging at the White House on May 10 and host special tours for the elderly. Many senior citizens had sent her letters about their unemployment, loneliness, and poverty, issues which she hoped to address. She emphasized that recommendations to help those suffering from intellectual disabilities should be translated into policy "that will significantly improve the quality" of their lives. She listened to what the committee members said, took notes, and promised to take their concerns to the President. Califano, who was wary of her power, commented that the best thing that had happened for the nation's retarded people was not only "the direct election of Jimmy Carter but the indirect election of Rosalynn."[14]

On April 19 and 20, Rosalynn attended a three-hour meeting of her Mental Health Commission in Chicago. She spoke briefly about mental retardation and listened to numerous papers dealing with definition, research, financing, and public communication. After a luncheon she visited the Community Mental Health Center at Northwestern Memorial Hospital. About one hundred medical students who were picketing outside the hospital to protest tuition fees, paused to cheer for her. Inside the center, she met patients who had been drug addicts and teenagers who wanted to know about life in the White House. When they asked about the decriminalization of marijuana, which her husband's administration supported, she replied that she knew of a twelve-year-old boy who had experimented with marijuana and wound up in jail for months. "That's very bad," she warned the students. She thought that it was more urgent to provide inexpensive medical care for the twenty-six million people suffering from mental illness.[15]

Working much in the same style as the Goals for Georgia program of the governor's years, Rosalynn and Bryant planned to stage four one-day public meetings in different sections of the country to hear ideas and concerns about mental health from ordinary citizens. Each speaker was allotted eight minutes, and those too shy to speak could submit written presentations. Rosalynn attended all four, the first two in Philadelphia on May 24 and the remaining in Nashville the next day. She explained that she opposed placing mentally ill persons in institutions, but favored community programs and group-living environments that would stimulate improved mental health and help the residents become useful citizens. It was exactly the program that she had begun in Georgia so successfully.

On June 20 and 21, Rosalynn and the other commissioners journeyed to Tucson and San Francisco where they again listened to the mental health concerns of minorities and elderly citizens. They flinched at horror stories about lack of doctors, unattended children, cultural superstitions, sexual abuse, and fear of the public stigma typically associated with mental illness. Peter Bourne coordinated the commission's final report, but before it could be assembled, hundreds more pages of reports by various task forces had to be collected and analyzed.[16]

In early May, Rosalynn set the toils of the mental health committee aside in order to prepare to visit seven Latin American countries in June. She would go not as an ambassador or First Lady but with the full responsibility and authority of the president himself. Accompanied by expert state department and national security advisers, she would be going to familiar territory but never before with the authority to conduct substantial talks with heads of state. Although Jimmy justified her trip by arguing that he, Vice President Mondale, and Secretary of State Vance all were occupied with other international matters, both Jimmy and Rosalynn intended for her diplomatic trip to make a statement about her elevated position in the White House.[17]

Rosalynn prepared for her diplomatic journey by attending speed reading classes, studying Spanish, and reading in the history and culture of Latin America. The State Department and National Security Adviser Brzezinski funneled information to her. A good student, she took notes on the briefings, and she studied the speeches Carter had given at the UN, the Organization of America States, and Notre Dame University.[18]

The seven nations Rosalynn would visit had been carefully selected because they were either democracies or military dictatorships that leaned toward becoming democracies. By including those countries and excluding the most repressive regimes in South America, the Carters sent a clear message that US policy would favor those nations that treated their citizens decently and reject those that did not.[19]

Interjecting a personal request into official business, as was typical for him, Carter gave Rosalynn information about a Peace Corps volunteer who had been kidnapped in Colombia, and reassured the man's anxious mother that both the Colombian government and the US State Department were working on it. "I have asked my wife, who is about to visit Colombia during her Latin American trip," he continued, "to pass on to Colombian authorities my personal concern for your son's welfare."[20]

Latin American leaders watched the US First Lady and president with jaundiced eyes. Many State Department officials, members of Congress, and Latin American diplomats were aghast. Some did not want to surrender their power over diplomatic affairs to the White House, and others feared that sending a woman to macho countries could only spell disaster.

Four days before Rosalynn's departure, Carter declared Latin America the world's first nuclear-weapons-free zone, and on June 1 he signed the American Convention on Human Rights. Many Latin American countries saw Carter's action as interference in their domestic affairs, which raised a red flag that Rosalynn might not always be welcomed at every stop on her twelve-day, grueling journey. Controversy in Latin America and at home also swirled over the issue of a woman conducting presidential diplomatic business that had always been done by men. Rosalynn became a leading advocate of women's rights on the world stage in the highest political circles.

She assembled an entourage of nineteen advisors and aides, plus twenty-seven members of the press and her Secret Service detail. Robert Pastor, the National Security Adviser for Latin American affairs, and Terry Todman, the Assistant Secretary of State for Inter-American Affairs, served her as top advisers. The presence of Todman, the first African American to achieve such a high diplomatic post, may have coincidentally been a silent human rights statement, but he was chosen because of his experience and skills. Robert Strauss, whom Carter had recently named the United States trade representative, could guide her on trade matters if she needed it. From the East Wing, Mary Hoyt, her press secretary, Madeleine McBean, her personal assistant, and Kit Dobelle, her chief of protocol, joined the group. Both Hoyt and McBean were also close friends with the First Lady. Rosalynn also included her hair dresser, a person to manage her wardrobe, and Gay Vance, the wife of the secretary of state.[21]

The inclusion of Mrs. Vance was both a matter of protocol and friendship, since the Vances and the Carters had many interests and attitudes in common. But Rosalynn rarely mentioned Gay during the trip and subtly relegated her to the background, making sure that everyone understood that it was Rosalynn, not Gay Vance, who was in charge.

On May 26 Rosalynn's East Wing press office announced that the purpose of her trip would be to discuss human rights, arms control, and economic assistance with the South American leaders. Rosalynn thought that she could "talk to them about Jimmy and develop a personal relationship with the heads of other states and our family." Rosalynn also intended to rub shoulders with the people she met in the streets and in the cane fields and to find human solutions to human problems.[22]

Despite talk about human rights and the personal touch, the fact remained that the military and economic power of the United States was central to all negotiations. As a witness to it, on May 27 Rosalynn joined Jimmy and Amy on a visit to Cape Canaveral, Florida, where Admiral Rickover gave them a personal tour of the submarine USS *Los Angeles*. The Carters spent nine hours on the nuclear attack submarine, learning every aspect of its operation. Rosalynn steered the vessel, taking it up and down. Rickover later said, Jimmy joked, that "she did a lot better steering job than I did."[23]

Rickover was all business, however. He used the occasion to tell the president that "it would be one of the greatest things that could happen" to have all nuclear weapons removed from the earth. Carter agreed and made a note to himself that he would keep the seventy-seven-year-old admiral on active duty for at least two more years. After the submarine's dive and safe re-emergence, Carter declared that Rickover's nuclear submarines were "the finest exhibition of superb engineering ever created by man." He and Rosalynn came away even more impressed by their country's military power.[24]

From Cape Canaveral, the Carters went to Musgrove Plantation, near Brunswick, Georgia, where they rested and prepared for Rosalynn's departure. On May 30, a solemn but admiring Jimmy watched as Rosalynn gave her departing remarks to the press in Brunswick, Georgia. Declaring that she understood Jimmy's foreign policy, she said she wanted her journey "to be more than just a good will trip;" she wanted it "to be valuable to the countries" that she would visit. Amy stood close to her parents, but she stepped back with her father when her mother walked up the stairs of the Air Force C-137 Boeing Stratoliner that would lift her and her entourage away to Kingston, Jamaica, the first stop on her historic Latin American tour.[25]

During the flight, Rosalynn studied her itinerary—Jamaica, Costa Rica, Ecuador, Peru, Brazil, Columbia, and Venezuela—six of which she had visited within the past five years, and all states with which the United States was trying to develop better relationships. She would report daily by telephone and written memo to the president and secretary of state. Rosalynn kept cards with talking points in her purse should she need them on informal occasions. In her formal talks with heads of state she would reiterate the US commitment to human rights, the urgency of arms control, and the value of democratic government.

After landing at Jamaica in the rain, Rosalynn was welcomed by the prime minister and his wife. Once the ceremonies and pomp ended, Rosalynn talked privately with Prime Minister Michael Norman Manley about finances, Cuban interference in Africa, the Panama Canal controversy, human rights, and Jamaica's desperate need for rain. Since she knew the country was in a serious financial crisis because it had to buy expensive foreign oil and its unemployment rate was 25%, she told him that Jimmy had requested $10 million from Congress to assist Jamaica. According to the *Jamaica Daily News*, Rosalynn's visit established "mutual understanding" between two heads of state, which would help the United States work more effectively "with developing nations." Manley was polite but restrained throughout their discussions, because, as Rosalynn knew, he had a close relationship with Cuba's Fidel Castro and feared that there might be a western attempt to overthrow him.[26]

When a reporter asked Rosalynn why she thought she should discuss foreign policy with heads of state since she had not been elected or confirmed by the Senate, she replied: "I am the person closest to the President of the United States, and if I can help him to understand the problems of the world, that's what I intend to do." Having been warned that everywhere she went, rooms would likely be bugged, Rosalynn was careful about what she said. She dared not tell Mary Hoyt and Madeleine McBean aloud what Manley had told her in their first meeting, so she sent them notes on matchbook covers when all three went to the ladies room.[27]

Sometimes tense, often relaxed, always professional and diplomatic, Rosalynn journeyed from country to country. At her second stop in Costa Rica, both President Daniel Oduber and his wife Marjorie Elliott de Oduber greeted her at the airport. Rosalynn addressed them in Spanish and asked substantive questions that soon caused President Oduber to realize that she meant business. Seeking to please the Costa Ricans, she announced that the next day Jimmy would sign the American Convention on Human Rights, the negotiations for which had begun in their country twelve years earlier. Costa

Rica, Rosalynn learned, wanted increased commercial preference and security of coffee prices more than lectures about human rights.[28]

Avoiding controversy, Rosalynn declined commenting on Costa Rica's contested presidential race, in which the central issue was Robert Vesco, a criminal US financier wanted in the United States for defrauding the Investors Overseas Service mutual fund of $224 million. Rosalynn's two-day stay in Costa Rica ended on an encouraging note, when the country's leading newspaper, the *La Republica* praised President Carter's "emphasis on the dignity of man" by sending "a lady who combines personal attractiveness with a well proved sensitivity that unites all those who suffer, struggle and hope—in whatever latitude they live."[29]

When Rosalynn deplaned in Quito, Ecuador, on June 2, she received a military welcome suitable for a head of state, except there was no head of state to greet her. Only the wives of the three-man ruling junta—or Supreme Council as they styled themselves—and US Ambassador Richard J. Bloomfield met her at the airport. Conscious that no high-ranking US official had been in Ecuador since 1958 when Vice President Nixon's motorcade had been bombarded with eggs, Rosalynn patiently reviewed an honor guard as a military band played both the US and Ecuadorean national anthems. When she finally met the junta at the National Palace, Rosalynn found herself and her four aides sitting on one side of a long table facing the three military rulers and seventeen more officials, all dressed in uniform and looking unfriendly. Calmly addressing them she expressed US support for Ecuador's drift toward democracy and apologized for Congress's inadvertent removal of Ecuador from the US system of trade preferences in 1974, when it was mistakenly thought that Ecuador had participated in an OPEC oil embargo the previous year. Rosalynn sympathized with Ecuador's concern about a possible attack by Peru and promised to discuss that threat when she reached Peru.[30]

Rosalynn, however, had not come to Quito simply to placate the military junta. She bluntly told her hosts: "The people are one hundred percent for Jimmy's view on human rights." That statement did not upset the junta, because the next day, the Quito newspaper *El Tiempo* said that human rights was fine, but it was not the whole of US foreign policy. What the junta did not want to hear was the news Rosalynn conveyed that the United States would not permit Israel to sell Ecuador its KFIR jet fighter, powered by a US engine, because President Carter did not want to introduce sophisticated weapons into countries that did not already have them. The junta members strongly disagreed with her, but Rosalynn held her ground, and her husband's blocking of the sale remained in effect. Jimmy was not swayed by a protest in Israel, but he did give the Israelis an additional $285 million to compensate for their loss of the sale to Ecuador.[31]

During her stay in Quito, Rosalynn got her first opportunity to meet the people when she visited the Working Boys' Center. The staff and residents there greeted her warmly, but unbeknown to Rosalynn, while she was speaking to the junta inside the National Palace, about two hundred student demonstrators outside hurled stones and bricks at the military police and press, set fire to police barricades, and shouted "Go home, bloody Rosalynn." The group, calling themselves Revolutionary Democratic Students, shouted: "Yankees want to reinforce their imperialism . . . exploit the people, the workers, the farmers." The riot police dispersed them, and the demonstrators probably never knew what she was discussing with their three military leaders.[32]

Safely in the air journeying from Quito to Lima, Peru, Rosalynn gave journalist Judy Woodruff an interview, in which she was serious, humorous, and relaxed. The hardest part of her trip, Rosalynn said, was deciding what to say to foreign officials, because she wanted to say meaningful things that would be "of value to our country" and hopefully be successful enough for Jimmy and the State Department to ask her to go on other such trips in the future. Rosalynn laughed as she told Judy that when she had met the chief justice of the Ecuador Supreme Court, they had both inadvertently leaned into each other before sitting down and "just cracked our heads." The press did not get a photograph of the incident, and she and the judge just pretended it never happened. By the time she had reached Ecuador, Rosalynn told Judy, she was really tired, perhaps the impact of the high altitude. Someone told her that if she and others in her party would sniff a little oxygen, it would make them feel better. She did it, three sniffs, and it picked her up immediately.[33]

After her arrival in Peru on June 4, Rosalynn rested in a luxurious country inn before visiting a nearby agricultural research center. She needed the rest, because the ensuing entertainment and tense discussions would test the skill and stamina of even an experienced diplomat. Once rested, Rosalynn passed three hours at the government's headquarters with Peru's president, General Francisco Morales Bermudez, who had seized power twenty-one months earlier in a bloodless coup that had ousted a leftist military regime. Rosalynn maintained that the United States was absolutely committed to human rights. Since Peru was buying weapons from the Soviet Union, with no belligerent intentions, they said, she brought up the subject of arms control. She urged the Peruvians to limit arms purchases and return to civilian rule by 1980. Bermudez replied that he needed the arms for self-defense and planned to continue the buildup. Although her hosts did not like what Rosalynn said, they entertained her with an evening of music, dance, folklore, and food. Despite lack of progress in her talks, Rosalynn departed, promising to tell Jimmy that the ties of friendship with Peru were strong, but in reality they remained less than satisfactory.[34]

According to a Latin American expert, Rosalynn was staging "a diplomatic spectacular exceeding anything Henry Kissinger ever did."[35] The acid test awaited at her next stop, Brazil. One journalist described her as "enchanting and ravishing" when she appeared "at the top of the stairway of the plane." A "fresh breeze of goodness" and "a frail and small lady of high purpose," he said, she embodied everything that was simple, kind, and sweet.[36]

In truth, however, Rosalynn got a low key welcome to Brazil on June 6 when she arrived at the Brasilia airport. Jimmy thought the lack of pomp and circumstance was because its leaders wanted to show that they are "equal with us and will not be dominated, which of course suits me fine."[37]

The US focus on human rights irritated Brazilian government officials. In fact, they were so angry about a State Department report to Congress on the poor condition of human rights in Brazil that they rejected a $50 million credit for military purchases and canceled a twenty-five- year-old military assistance pact with the United States. The Brazilians also were infuriated by President Carter's attempt to have West Germany void a $5 billion deal to sell Brazil nuclear processing technology, an action that did not please the West Germans either. Carter argued that the sale would violate the Nuclear Nonproliferation Treaty and possibly give Brazil the capacity to build an atomic bomb, an outcome he hoped to prevent at any cost. In an effort to come to a better understanding with the United States, President Ernesto Giesel scheduled more time for talks with Rosalynn than he usually did with foreign leaders. Giesel gave not an inch in their discussions, how-ever, arguing that he needed the nuclear plant to produce energy. Rosalynn did not yield either. Although the Brazilians were impressed by her know-ledge of the issues, she would depart the country having made no significant breakthroughs.[38]

Rosalynn's arrival in Brazil had coincided with student uprisings against the government. Hundreds of young people were arrested, and the govern-ment closed the federal university in Brasilia for the duration of Rosalynn's visit. The students handed her a letter saying that they had lived under repressive regimes since 1964. She glanced at it briefly and said that she would take it to Jimmy, who would be pleased "to receive the perspective on human rights of the students." On June 7, Rosalynn addressed the Brazilian national congress, explaining that hers was not just a goodwill trip but an exploration of how the United States could be helpful in Latin America. After a seventy-five-minute talk with President Giesel in his office, she later attended a formal dinner at his residence with twenty-four US and Brazilian officials and their wives.[39]

The next day Rosalynn went to the coastal city of Recife to visit the family she had lived with for ten days in 1973 as part of the exchange program Friendship Force. Two Americans there, Catholic missionary Father Lawrence Rosebaugh, aged forty-two, and a Mennonite missionary Thomas Capuano, twenty-four, had been arrested for participating in a program of direct assistance to the poor and were subsequently stripped, beaten, and held for three days before they were allowed to call the US Consulate and be released. Rosalynn met and sympathized with them, and she promised to take their story back to her husband. Then she posed for photographs standing between the two bearded men dressed in work clothes. As stubborn and determined as Jimmy, Rosalynn protested the mistreatment of her fellow citizens. Government officials in Brasilia were frustrated and embarrassed, and Rosalynn, as Jody Powell said she always did, won her argument. The governor of Pernambuco, the state in which Recife lay, immediately cabled Washington with an apology for the mistreatment of the two US missionaries. According to Rosalynn, he "expressed regrets and said he wanted everyone who visited his state to have proper treatment." "Our point about human rights," she noted with pride, "had been made."[40]

The US Embassy in Brasilia thought that Rosalynn's visit to Brazil was successful in presenting the administration's position on human rights, nuclear proliferation, reducing the gap between the rich and the poor, and the interaction of countries in that hemisphere. Presenting did not mean acceptance, but Rosalynn left Brazil with at least the satisfaction of knowing she had done her best.[41]

Although Rosalynn did not visit Panama, Panamanian dictator General Omar Torrijos kept a close eye on her travels in Latin America. Since President Carter was attempting to negotiate new Panama Canal treaties with him, Torrijos had a vested interest in the results of her regional trip. In an unprecedented action, he secretly notified the US Embassy in his country that Mrs. Carter's visit impressed him and that he found her activities to be "stupendous." Thus, Rosalynn's visit to Latin America may have indirectly eased the way for the later successful negotiation of the Panama Canal treaties.[42]

In Colombia, the sixth country on Rosalynn's itinerary, there were no welcoming remarks, no honor guard, and no reception for a head of state, when she arrived in Bogotá on June 9. She was treated only with the courtesy given to the wife of a chief of state. President Alfonso Lopez-Michelson, resentful that neither the US president nor secretary of state had come themselves, sent his stepsister to greet Rosalynn. Rosalynn smiled, shook hands with her, and noted "we're wearing the same dress." The dresses were not the same color, but Rosalynn told her hostess, "It looks nice on you." After hearing about the receptions that Mrs. Carter had received in the other five countries she had visited, the Colombian Foreign Minister decided to greet this most unusual ambassador from the United States more formally.

When Rosalynn met President Michelson and gave him a copy of *Why Not the Best?*, she discovered that he already had one. Michelson agreed to extensive talks about human rights, nuclear non-proliferation, bilateral relations with Cuba, and narcotics control. At that time there were about sixty US citizens in Colombian jails on drug charges, the result of previous efforts to disrupt the extensive narcotics traffic from Colombia to the United States. After confronting Michelson with evidence that there was drug-related corruption in the highest ranks of his government, Rosalynn convinced him to accept a two-man US team to discuss curbing the illegal drug trade. She left that job up to Peter Bourne and Mathea Falco, a special narcotics adviser from the State Department.[43]

Before leaving Colombia on June 11, Rosalynn brought up the case of Richard Starr, a Peace Corps volunteer who had been kidnapped by leftist guerrillas in Colombia the previous February. Sending troops to search for him might endanger his life, Michelson told her, but he assured her that the Colombian legal system would get to his case soon. Finding that Michelson's "soon" was not very soon, Rosalynn again interceded in 1980, successfully won his release, and welcomed him to the White House.[44]

On June 11, Rosalynn reached Caracas, Venezuela, her final stop, where she was greeted by an official welcoming committee. President Carlos Andrés Pérez, who was scheduled to visit the United States a few weeks later, said she was an "extraordinary woman." A friendly, energetic man, he approved of Carter's human rights and nonproliferation goals. He liked Rosalynn and thought she represented the new "style of diplomacy, frankness, no half-truths." She ingratiated herself with the crowd who welcomed her arrival by saying that the United States and Venezuela shared "common ideals of democracy and freedom and human dignity and equality under the law." Then she was taken to the tomb of Simón Bolívar, the famed liberator of South America, where she placed a wreath on behalf of the American people. During her two-day stay in Venezuela, Rosalynn talked to women's groups about social issues and educational programs, met labor union leaders, held news conferences, and greeted US embassy personnel.

Pérez nevertheless made clear to Rosalynn that he was miffed by her husband's decision to suspend US preferential trade agreements with Venezuela because it was part of the OPEC cartel. Nor was Pérez able to give Rosalynn much help in learning the location of US citizen William Neihous, the head of Venezuela operations for Owens-Illinois glass bottlemaker, who had been kidnapped the year before. Despite these setbacks, and being sick on one of the two days she was in the country, Rosalynn received favorable stories in the Venezuelan newspapers.[45]

On June 12, en route home, Rosalynn received a message that "The President of the United States requests the honor of your presence for dinner tonight at 8:30 at Aspen Lodge," their favorite dining cabin at Camp David. When her plane touched down at Andrews Air Force Base, she was greeted with the dignity and fanfare accorded to a diplomat, an ambassador, a head of state, and a wife and mother. Jimmy, Amy, Fritz and Joan Mondale, Brzezinski, Cy Vance, and the press were there. "I bring you the best wishes of the people of Latin America and the Caribbean," Rosalynn said in a brief speech, diplomatically concluding that she had "found friendship and good will" everywhere she had visited. Then she traveled with her husband and daughter to Camp David. Jimmy said that the twelve days of Rosalynn's trip might have been the longest time they had ever been apart since he left the Navy, "and twelve days is just too long."[46]

A week after her return, Rosalynn reported on the facts, findings, and results of her trip to the president and the Senate. The Senate unanimously congratulated her, and a poll gave her a 74% approval rating as an ambassador. Moreover, 72% of those polled said that they thought that she was better than the State Department in gathering diplomatic information for the president. When Jimmy saw the poll, before it was sent on to her, he scribbled in the margin, "Rosalynn—don't run against your husband! J."[47]

Jimmy loved his wife's popularity. Rosalynn could look over papers on the president's desk in the Oval Office, hold hands with him in public, read the Bible in Spanish with him in private, and jitterbug with him at informal dinners. "Rosie, what think," he often wrote on the margins of memoranda, and he would listen to what she said. Brzezinski believed that Rosalynn's sympathy for him and his hawkish approach to foreign affairs strengthened his position with the president. Rosalynn, he wrote, was tough, charming, "politically shrewd," and "had a knack for getting to the guts of a problem."[48]

Carter also liked the way that Rosalynn, like himself, would quickly plunge back into her routine work. Continuing her work with the mental health commission and other unfolding events, Rosalynn had achieved something no other First Lady had ever done: she was an equal partner with the president.

ELEVEN

Religion, Race, and Politics

Rosalynn embarked in July on a week-long trip to the West, attending public mental health hearings in Tucson, San Francisco, San Jose, and Honolulu. At each stop, she talked about the president's hope that Latin America would remain free of nuclear weapons, but she concentrated on mental health issues.[1] Distinguishing between mental health and mental illness, she bemoaned the existing shortcomings in financial support and medical care delivery services for those in need. She contended that underprivileged and minority groups were especially vulnerable, and she was moved by heartbreaking stories from women who were sexually abused, college students who feared being labelled "crazy," and others who were misdiagnosed and given incorrect treatments.[2]

Six thousand miles away, Empress Farah of Iran attempted, like Rosalynn, to bring compassionate mental health care to suffering Iranians. When private institutions in the United States invited the empress to the country in July to honor her for her work, Rosalynn hosted a low-key luncheon for her at the White House. Thousands of demonstrators outside the fence shouted, "Death to the Shah!" Rosalynn tried to shield her guest from the demonstrators, but the empress assured her that she was accustomed to such displays. The guests that pleasant day included members of the Harp Renaissance Society who entertained the group with pieces by Ravel. Rosalynn maintained a friendly, professional, businesslike demeanor, carefully avoiding any suggestion that her relationship with the Shia Islamic empress might be interpreted as being anti-Semitic.[3]

Both Rosalynn and the president found themselves in the unhappy position of having to fight a growing perception that they were anti-Semitic. Tirelessly trying to counter that impression, Carter, on June 16, issued a proclamation establishing a Jewish Chapel at the United States Military Academy.[4] He met privately with Mondale, Brzezinski, and Senators Abe Ribicoff, Ed Muskie, and Hubert Humphrey, and asked them to help alleviate concerns within the Jewish community. He needed Jewish-American support, he said, to convince Prime Minister Menachem Begin that the Arabs were willing to make major concessions for peace and that, in exchange, the Israelis must relinquish their occupied territories and allow the creation of a Palestinian state tied to Jordan. A month later on July 6, Carter "approached with trepidation" a meeting with fifty leaders of the Jewish American community. He conceded that a separate Palestinian nation could be a threat to peace in the Middle East, but he reassured them of his commitment to Israel as a "peaceful and sovereign" nation. He explained, however, that he must be fair to both sides to resolve the Arab-Israeli conflict.[5]

Both Jewish Americans and Israelis remained skeptical of Carter's sincerity. Israeli Prime Minister Begin and Foreign Minister Moshe Dayan vigorously opposed withdrawal to the pre-1967 boundaries and the establishment of a separate state of Palestine. The Israeli press condemned Middle East peace speeches by Carter and Mondale, declaring emphatically that the US president was anti-Israel.[6] Stuart Eizenstat, whose Judaism was well known in the administration, took personal and professional offense at the anti-Semitic charge and became "livid" at accusations that the administration was anti-Israel and tried to prove on many occasions that "nothing could be further from the truth."[7]

To prove that, and with peace and votes on their minds, Jimmy and Rosalynn prepared for Prime Minister Menachem and Aliza Begin's July visit. Carter had invited Begin for a private meeting in order to get to know him and anticipate how he might react to a peace conference with the Arabs. Responding, Begin had sent Carter a secret telegram, laying out his own plan for peace. Carter was shocked to learn that Begin offered to negotiate on everything.[8] Begin also requested a full kosher meal, and Rosalynn thought it "would be a gracious gesture to give it to him." Carter, coached by US Ambassador to Israel Samuel Lewis, planned to flatter the prime minister with ceremonies that appealed to his ego.[9]

The Carters knew that the Begins had experienced a difficult personal and political life that would explain how challenging it might be to entertain and negotiate with them. A slightly built man, unimposing in stature, Begin had been born in 1913 to Polish Jewish parents in the Russian Empire. His father sent him to Polish rather than Jewish schools because they were free and because he thought his son would get a better education there. The father's influence upon him was as powerful as that of Mr. Earl upon Jimmy. Emblazoned in Begin's memory was the time his father was walking with a rabbi when a Polish police sergeant, an anti-Semitic bully, attempted to cut off the rabbi's beard. Begin's father struck the policeman's hand sharply with his cane, which provoked the police sergeant into giving the rabbi and the father a severe beating. When recounting the story to his son and family at home, the badly beaten father happily told them that he had "defended the honor of the Jewish people and the honor of the rabbi."[10]

Following in his father's footsteps, Begin became a passionate Zionist. He had received a solid legal education at the University of Warsaw where he fought back against those who bullied him and organized other Jewish students into Zionist groups to defend themselves against anti-Semitic harassment on campus. A poor student, he boarded in private homes where he met Aliza Arnold, whom he married in May 1939.[11] Life bore down hard on the young couple. The Depression, the rise of the Nazis, the Holocaust, the advent of World War II, and the fierce determination of Zionists to retake the Holy Land from the Palestinians became the world in which they operated.

On September 20, 1940, a little more than a year after their marriage, the Russians arrested Menachem for being an "agent of British imperialism." His captors tortured him and sentenced him to eight years in a labor camp in the northern part of Russia. His young bride managed to make her way to Palestine. After Nazi Germany attacked Russia, Begin won his freedom as a Polish citizen. He joined the Polish Armed Forces in the East, popularly known as Anders' Army after its commander and went with it to Palestine, arriving there in May 1942, where he and Aliza were reunited. Both of Begin's parents and his older brother died in the Holocaust. Menachem and Aliza remained in Palestine, where they became the parents of three children and fought for the establishment of a Jewish state. Protected by his wife when living undercover, Begin led many of the attacks that caused the British to abandon Palestine in November 1947.

After the State of Israel was formed in 1948, Begin emerged from underground and organized the Herut Freedom Party, the forerunner of the Likud Party. Elected to parliament, Begin became an Israeli hero, and in a shocking landslide victory for his right-wing Likud Party, he became prime minister in 1977.[12]

At the appointed hour on the morning of July 19, 1977, the Carters welcomed Menachem and Aliza Begin with an elaborate ceremony on the South Lawn of the White House. The Americans escorted their guests to a platform where they stood for a nineteen-gun salute. The two men then reviewed the troops, returned to the platform, and each made a few remarks lavishing praise on the other. The ceremony concluded with the colorful Army Old

Guard Fife and Drum Corps, dressed in the white livery of the Revolutionary War, parading in front of them.

Retiring inside the White House to the Diplomatic Reception Room, the Carters and Begins became better acquainted, but there was no instant magical chemistry between them as there had been with the Sadats. Initially reticent and skeptical of each other, the Georgian and the Israeli seemed to share little more than a love for the Old Testament. However, Aliza smiled as Carter quoted the Old Testament prophet Isaiah: "And the work of righteousness shall be peace, quietness & assurance forever." Carter thought that the presence of the leaders' wives created a more relaxed atmosphere, and Aliza's presence may have worked as he hoped. Taking the prime minister into his small private office for a short personal conversation, Carter found Begin to be surprisingly "congenial, dedicated, sincere, and deeply religious."[13] Begin recounted the story of his father and the rabbi, because he wanted Carter to know, Begin later told his secretary, "what kind of a Jew he was dealing with."[14]

The subsequent two-hour discussion among the two heads of state and their advisers in the Cabinet Room was amiable and emotional. The Americans included Cyrus Vance, Zbigniew Brzezinski, and William Quandt from the NSC. Begin had the assistance of the Israeli ambassador to the United States Sincha Dinitz, his special adviser Yehuda Avner, and others, so each had a total of six. The group talked about a possible Geneva conference, Soviets in the Horn of Africa, Palestinians and Arabs, common concerns, and hope for peace. Carter summarized the US position, saying that he wanted a comprehensive peace based upon UN Resolutions 242 and 338, requiring Israeli withdrawal from *all* occupied territory since 1967 and the creation of a Palestinian "entity." Begin rejected the latter categorically but seemed willing to discuss the other points, including the possibility of withdrawing from *some* of the occupied lands.[15]

Then, after a moment of silent staring at each other, Begin spoke at some length, emphasizing that Judea, Samaria, and the Gaza Strip would not be relinquished. Vance became agitated, and an angry Carter managed to hold his temper only by clenching his jaw as his steel blue eyes glazed over. Exasperated, almost shouting, Carter finally told Begin that, if he insisted upon a permanent military occupation of those conquered territories, there would be no hope for negotiations.

With a quivering voice, Begin replied, "Ours is an almost biblical generation of suffering and courage." "Ours is the generation that rose up from the bottomless pit of Hell." Firmly facing "the iron cast Carter," he insisted that the disputed territories were not only historically and biblically Israel's but also a matter of vital security. Showing the Americans the map of Israel that he had brought with him, Begin pointed to the mountains above Samaria and declared that "whosoever sits in these mountains holds the jugular vein of Israel in his hands." "There is no going back," he said, for "no nation in our merciless and unforgiving neighborhood can be rendered so vulnerable and survive." Breaking down, Begin fought back tears, clenched his fist, and bowed his head. The others in the room looked away, perhaps to give him privacy. A stunned Carter suggested a recess, but Begin recovered his composure and said that he had made his point, "explaining Samaria to the American."[16]

The meeting ended soon afterward, and the Begins went to Blair House for an afternoon of rest and privacy. Carter attended his other business of that day, played tennis, and got a haircut.[17]

In the evening, Rosalynn entertained Aliza Begin at a performance of George Gershwin's penny opera "Porgy and Bess" at the Kennedy Center. Despite the spectacular music and the dramatic saga of love gone wrong among poor African Americans who lived on Catfish Row in Charleston, South Carolina, Aliza, exhausted by her long flight from Israel and the White House ceremonies, slept through the entire performance.[18]

There was no sleeping at the White House where Jimmy hosted a working dinner for his enigmatic visitor. The president and the prime minister were joined by approximately fifty guests, including their personal advisers, top cabinet officers, and representatives from Congress. After a kosher meal in the state dining room, the two heads of state exchanged lengthy toasts. Flattering Begin to the extreme, Carter referred to their earlier talks, with his characteristic hyperbole, as "the most gratifying and stimulating discussions that I have had since I have been President." His guest, Carter said, was a man of "deep convictions . . . of truth and quiet dignity," and they agreed that courage and urgency were needed for a "real, permanent peace in the Middle East." Carter reassured the Israelis that, when he had met with Arab leaders, "the basic premise on which we approached a possible Middle East discussion leading toward progress and peace was our commitment to Israel." Since a "common religion" as well as economic, cultural, and blood relationships bound the two nations, Carter believed that they had a strong base upon which to deal with difficult challenges. Begin praised Carter in return as "the leader and defender of the free world."[19]

When the Begins left town the next day, the two men had laid the foundation for mutual respect, but they had not developed personal and political
ties that might make their work easier. The two women remained distant and
professional. For the media, Carter put on a happy face, declaring that, despite obvious differences, he felt that they would have a peace conference in
Geneva in October. Cyrus Vance, who had handled most of the preliminary
negotiations with Israel, found Begin to be "a combination of Old Testament
prophet and courtly European." He would be a tough, but not impossible,
negotiator.[20]

In a private conversation with Rosalynn after the Begins left, Jimmy said
that at the Cabinet Room meeting the previous day, Begin wept so hard that
he could not talk as he pointed on his map to vulnerable borders "where we
couldn't even save our wives & children." Moved by the sincerity and passion of the prime minister, as well as the history of Israel, Carter thought
Begin's toast at the working dinner was so moving that the men and women
attending were "transfixed" and "looked like a tableaux of the last supper."[21]

Begin appeared to trust Carter more than Carter trusted him, for Begin
had left the country holding his host in "high regard" and feeling a strong
"personal rapport" with him. They had made no progress toward solving
the Middle East dilemma, but they had opened the possibility for future
dialogue.[22]

Carter faced a more immediate dilemma precipitated by UN Ambassador
Andrew Young. The former US Civil Rights leader reported to Carter in early
June that African countries welcomed the involvement of the United States
in their struggles for justice and equality. He warned, however, that a race war
in Africa, would ignite one in the United States. Whites in America would
panic and start attacking Blacks, he predicted. Young's comments, published
in *Playboy* magazine, elicited a barrage of criticism. A Congressman from
Rhode Island wrote President Carter complaining that Young's statements
were "appalling" and expressing amazement that Carter had not called him
to account for them. Carter's loyalty to Young, and vice versa, remained intact, even though Young had accused the last four presidents, the Russians,
and Abraham Lincoln of being racists. When journalists asked him about
his remarks, Young denied them, arguing that such fake publicity was a
Republican conspiracy. The presidential mail, however, overwhelmingly
called for Young's resignation.[23]

Joining those who criticized Young, the Ku Klux Klan demanded that
Young be fired and Carter censored. On a hot, mid-July night, dozens of

its members converged on Plains dressed in the full regalia of white sheets and hoods that disguised their identities. They carried torches as they congregated beneath the water tower where they burned a cross that they said symbolized their Christian faith. The imperial wizard argued that the cross was a symbol of Christ's love, a love they apparently did not extend to Black people or politicians who favored racial equality. One intoxicated participant rammed his Jaguar into the podium, injuring twenty-nine and causing others to flee for safety. There were no deaths, but a gunshot, alleged to have been accidental, created panic among the crowd of onlookers. Miss Lillian, a curious spectator, escaped injury.[24]

Young did, in time, backtrack when he realized that he was harming Carter and that his role on the international stage was quite different from what it had been during the Civil Rights movement. Young had once called Cuban troops in Africa a "stabilizing force," but by the end of 1977 he had become convinced that their continued presence on that continent contributed to "destruction and chaos." Labeling it a "kind of new colonialism," he realized that his enthusiasm for progress in Africa would not be served by the invasion of a new colonial power.

Carter found himself in a bind. He sent Young about fifty copies of a poll that showed how strongly public opinion condemned him.[25] A close personal friend, Young was a political ally who had helped him win the election. As the US ambassador to the UN who happened to be Black, he was well suited to facilitate the United States' dramatically changed policy toward Africa. On the other hand, Young's language was often undiplomatic, and he was a serious impediment to Carter's attempt to build bridges to Jewish Americans. Cy Vance called Young a liar.[26]

Hoping to rise above the furor about Young, Carter left the White House to barnstorm across the South for his most important legislation. On one occasion he stood in the rain before a crowd of thousands in Jackson, Mississippi, and promised the soaked crowd that the future would be better than the past if Congress would approve a new Panama Canal treaty. His predecessor, Gerald Ford, during his battle with Ronald Reagan for the 1976 Republican presidential nomination, had promised Panamanian leader General Omar Torrijos Herrera that he would settle the canal issue after the election, but it turned out to be Carter who had to settle it. It was a task that fit nicely with his theme of human rights, and he hoped to achieve it within six months.[27]

Jumping from topic to topic in his stump speeches and an interview in Washington, Carter shocked some in his audiences by declaring that he would use nuclear weapons to protect US allies if necessary. The United States would never fall behind the Russians, he promised. Carter thanked Speaker O'Neill for supporting the sale of the AWACS to Iran, a move Carter thought would stabilize the Middle East. The shah, however, was not pleased when he learned that there would be a month's delay before the systems could be delivered. Carter maintained his public composure but angrily recorded in his diary that he did not "care whether he [the shah] buys them from us or not." Nor would Carter knuckle under to pressure from Congressmen for pork barrel legislation. When Pennsylvania Congressmen threatened to vote against the administration's legislation if Carter did not make an appointment they wanted, Carter "told them in a nice way to go to hell." They voted against him.[28]

The US need for energy, more than placating the shah or pleasing a few disgruntled Congressmen, drove Carter to sign the legislation to create the Department of Energy on August 4. As anticipated, he appointed James Schlesinger as secretary. By creating a cabinet level Department of Energy, Carter emphasized the importance of the energy crisis and drew public support that he needed. His ratings in the August polls rose to 78% approval, and Rosalynn discovered that hers jumped from 56% to 76%. Schlesinger, nominally a Republican who would help get bipartisan support for Carter's energy plan, had a history of public service that might have helped the ratings. A contrarian, Schlesinger had many supporters among the hawkish anti-Soviet wing of the Democratic Party, and he privately briefed Carter on defense and foreign policy as well as energy.[29]

A plethora of issues, many of them unpopular, dominated the looming dog days of summer. Jimmy seemed happiest when classical music filled his small private West Wing office and he faced an array of decisions that might beleaguer any other occupant. Israel remained intransigent, continuing to build settlements on the West Bank. Vance reported from the Middle East that the Arabs wanted peace but Israel did not. The mail continued to run one hundred percent against Andrew Young.[30]

Meanwhile, a historical matter raised its head. The family of Dr. Samuel A. Mudd, whose reputation had been sullied by the accusation that his treatment of the wounded John Wilkes Booth, the man who had killed Abraham Lincoln, made him a co-conspirator in the 1865 assassination, pressed to have their ancestor's name cleared. After a thorough investigation, Carter discovered that a complete exoneration was legally impossible, but he expressed his opinion that Samuel Mudd had had a minimal involvement in the assassination, a decision that won him thanks from Mudd's grandson and 389 other descendants. Not only wanting to be just in that ancient case, the man from Georgia residing in the White House also wanted to lay to rest forever a thorny vestige from the Civil War.[31]

Carter attempted to replicate the aid and comfort he gave to the Mudd family on a global scale. He instructed his ambassadors to inform him personally, or his Undersecretary of State Pat Derien, of human rights abuses in their countries. He scanned Congressional correspondence and CIA reports for information about human rights. He wanted to know about any progress made in protecting them that was related to US policy or the fulfillment of the UN Charter and Declaration of Human Rights. The brain child of former First Lady Eleanor Roosevelt, that charter guaranteed individuals freedom from government violations of their integrity, economic and social well-being, and all kinds of civil and political liberties. There could be no better statement of the great moral ideal that Jimmy and Rosalynn had chosen to make the cornerstone of their presidency.[32]

Carter's first human rights achievement came in Chile. During the presidential campaign debates, Carter had raised the issue of Chilean dictator General Augusto Pinochet's violation of the rights of his people. Consequently, even before he was inaugurated, Carter had a greater impact on human rights in Chile than had Henry Kissinger or any previous secretary of state, for as soon as Carter had been elected, Pinochet released 323 political prisoners, hoping to curry favor with the new US president. News of Carter's moral victory in Chile did not become commonly known until seven months into his presidency. It was, nevertheless, the beginning of a human rights record upon which Jimmy and Rosalynn could stand tall and continue the battle for freedom and justice.[33]

Needing rest and rejuvenation, in August Jimmy and Rosalynn went home to Plains to attend the wedding of Rosalynn's brother Murray in the Methodist church where they had been married thirty-one years earlier. The day before the wedding, when Air Force One landed near Macon, the scattered farm houses and parched fields might have reminded Jimmy of his childhood, but the dozens of reporters, state patrolmen, Secret Service agents, and the military helicopter that would take him and Rosalynn to Plains had no resemblance to his previous trips back there. When Jimmy stepped off the helicopter at Petersen Field near Plains, he scooped up his grandson James Earl Carter IV and headed to the bulletproof blue Lincoln Imperial limousine, with its presidential flags drooping from its fenders in the stifling, breezeless

Georgia heat. Rosalynn, Amy, Chip, Jeff, and Annette completed the heavily guarded presidential party.

The family relaxed at the Carters' home before Jimmy, accompanied by his Secret Service agents, walked the short distance along Main Street to the Methodist church. His route was lined by a cheering crowd shouting, "We love you, Mr. President." After he entered the church and joined Rosalynn and other family members in the front row, they attracted more attention than the bride and groom did. Their security while in their tiny home town cost taxpayers nearly $20,000.[34]

For relaxation while in Plains, Jimmy walked around his property, attended church, and played softball. He introduced the entourage that accompanied him to the pleasures of life in a small Southern town. His softball team, composed of advisers and Secret Service men, lost to the press team. Miss Lillian welcomed her son home with motherly advice and solace. He and Rosalynn searched for arrowheads and went fishing together. They discovered that two dozen or more members of their Baptist Church who had supported their position to admit Black members had formed a new church. Called Maranatha, or "God with us," it appealed to the Carters, but they decided to remain neutral.[35]

Upon returning to Washington on August 10, 1977, Carter lifted the ban on travel to Cuba and hoped to restore relations with Castro. Castro, who refused to reciprocate by releasing political prisoners, promised to meet Carter at the UN in the fall. Carter did not trust Castro when the Cuban dictator told him that the Soviets wanted peace with the United States.[36]

Carter wanted peace with the Soviets badly enough that he risked détente and perhaps even SALT II by pressing the Soviets to release Jewish dissidents who were in Russian gulags. He also intended for that pressure on the Soviets to send a goodwill message to those Jewish citizens at home who doubted him. Since Jewish Americans and Israelis needed more proof of his support, Carter yielded to pressure from Congresswoman Elizabeth Holtzman of New York and other powerful Jewish leaders to build a Holocaust Museum on the National Mall in Washington.[37] That venture would take time and be fraught with controversy, but Carter relegated it to committee members and politicians while he worked for the negotiation and ratification of new Panama Canal treaties.

TWELVE

Quests for Justice
Panama, Israel, Iran

After reviewing the Hay-Bunau-Varilla Treaty of November 3, 1903, which had allowed the United States to build the Panama Canal, Carter said that he found it unjust. Indeed, that treaty was Yankee imperialism at its worst. When Panama rebelled against Colombia, President Teddy Roosevelt had placed US warships on either side of the Isthmus of Panama, blocking Colombia's access to the area. Free of Colombia, and virtually under the control of Philippe Bunau-Varilla, the French engineer who had attempted to build a canal, Panama quickly signed the treaty with the US Secretary of State John Hay. For $10 million and an annual fee of $250,000, the United States received a lease on a ten-mile-wide strip of land across the isthmus and the right to build, operate, and defend a canal. The greatest human engineering feat accomplishment of that era, the canal was completed just in time to become a part of the US defense network during World War I. After the war, US presence in the Canal Zone symbolized the power and dominance of the United States in Latin America. The money the United States paid to Panama, although negligible to the United States, was an important source of income for the Panamanians.[1]

History passed the canal by. During World War II, aircraft carriers and some other warships were too large to use it, and a modern air force rendered the path between the seas less important, although the Canal Zone did provide a convenient air force base. After World War II, Latin American nations entered a new era in which they were caught in the middle of the contest between the two superpowers for allies and control. The Russians were determined to spread their hegemony to the western world, and the Americans were equally determined to prevent them from doing so. Many Americans feared that the establishment of Soviet power in their backyard would be a major threat to their own national defense. Panamanians benefitted from the annual fee, but they wished to be independent of US domination.

Anti-US riots began in 1964, which initiated the first discussions with President Lyndon Johnson about a new canal treaty. Successive presidents continued the discussions, and in 1974 the two nations agreed upon a set of principles that might guide the negotiation of a new treaty.[2]

In 1976, however, when Governor Ronald Reagan attempted to wrest the Republican presidential nomination from President Ford, he derailed any progress that had been made with his repeated mantra: we bought it, we built it, and we should keep it at all costs. Hoping to return to the progress of 1974, and, despite Reagan, proceed to negotiating a new treaty, Carter planned to settle the canal issue once and for all. Rendering justice to the Panamanians, Carter believed, would demonstrate good faith to all of Latin America, buttress his human rights efforts, and inject morality into US foreign policy.[3]

Determined and fearless—Rosalynn said reckless—Carter plunged into the Canal controversy, until finally on September 7, 1977, he emerged wounded and scarred but triumphant. Knowing that ratification of a new treaty by the Senate would be an uphill battle, the president attempted to establish a more flexible relationship with Congress. Working the Panama side, Hamilton Jordan developed a close relationship with Panamanian leader General Omar Torrijos Herrera and opened a direct line of communication between the two national leaders. Ellsworth Bunker, who had served as canal negotiator for the previous fourteen years, was joined by Carter's choice, Sol Linowitz, the energetic, highly respected chair of the Commission on US-Latin American affairs.

Carter laid the groundwork for the canal negotiations in a speech at the April 14, 1977, meeting of the OAS. He shocked the delegates by eschewing the traditional US claim to hegemony in the area in favor of a new policy of respect for the sovereignty of every Latin American nation. The speech was effective, for the US and Panamanian negotiators agreed upon two treaties. The first would transfer the control of the canal to Panama after December 31, 1999. The second guaranteed the permanent neutrality of the canal but gave the United States the right to defend it militarily if necessary. Until the year 2000, US employees in the Canal Zone would keep their jobs, and Panama would receive a share of the canal tolls and an annuity of $10 million. Furthermore, the United States committed to giving Panama military and financial aid worth about $150 million over the next ten years.[4]

Carter, with Rosalynn's help, went to work trying to convince senators from both parties to approve the unpopular treaties. He counted on Senator Howard Baker, leader of the Senate Republicans, for his assistance. A native of

Tennessee, married to the daughter of powerful Republican Senator Everett Dirksen of Illinois, Baker remained open-minded, even though approval of the treaties was not in his own self-interest. By reaching across the aisle to Baker, Carter shrewdly turned ratification into a nonpartisan issue. Jimmy and Rosalynn made telephone calls to several other important senators such as Republican Barry Goldwater and Democrat Robert Byrd. Rosalynn called the wives of Democratic Senators Paul Hatfield of Montana and Edward Zorinsky of Nebraska to ask them to sway their husbands to favor the treaties. Carter enlisted the support of Governor Averell Harriman of New York. Republican former President Gerald Ford and Democratic former First Lady Bird Johnson, pitched in to support Carter's nonpartisan effort.

Senator Fritz Hollings, a Democrat from South Carolina, helpfully declared that the treaties were not giving the canal away but, to the contrary, would help protect it for US use.[5] Brzezinski agreed. Failure to ratify the treaties, he thought, would lead to a serious deterioration in relations with Latin America. An explosion of political turmoil in Panama, he predicted, would necessitate sending US troops there and open the possibility of the country and the canal falling to the Cubans.[6]

Prior to the Senate's vote on the treaties, Carter and Torrijos Herrera planned to sign them formally at the Washington headquarters of the OAS.[7] On September 6, 1977, Carter greeted the heads of Latin American states one by one as they arrived at the Oval Office before the signing the next day. Immediately before the ceremony in the OAS Hall of the Americas, Carter and Torrijos Herrera met privately in a small room. The Panamanian general burst into tears of joy, sobbing so violently that his wife had to steady him. Regaining control, he went out with Carter to the signing ceremony. Afterward, Torrijos told Carter that "more than a million Panamanians wept this evening during the ceremonies." Eighteen heads of state, half of them dictators and human rights abusers, listened quietly as Carter said that "fairness, and not force" would be the new United States way of dealing with Latin America. Carter had won a victory for human rights, but he knew that in the real world of US politics, a treaty once negotiated still needed to be ratified by two-thirds of the Senate.[8]

Carter intended for the signing ceremony to be an elaborate display of not only solidarity with all of the American countries, but also political unity in the United States. Gerald Ford and Lady Bird Johnson joined the Carters in the Hall of the Americas. More than 850 guests, including prominent US political and military leaders and numerous Latin American officials, attended.

Later in the evening, the Carters hosted a state dinner at the White House for the Latin American heads of state and their wives. Lady Bird Johnson, who declared it to be a "glittering success," hoped that the Senate would ratify the treaties.[9]

Knowing that large majorities in both the Senate and the public forum shared Ronald Reagan's simplistic views about the canal, Carter plotted his strategy to win public support as well as the Senate's approval. One poll showed that 78% of the people did not favor giving up the canal, a statistic that influenced senators who hoped to be reelected. Carter sent telegrams to every senator asking each not to speak against ratification until learning the details of the treaties. He knew that some of them might be persuaded to support him once they found that the second treaty gave the United States the right to defend the canal. Many moderate Republicans, including former President Ford, former Secretary of State Henry Kissinger, and Senate Majority Leader Howard Baker began to work for ratification. Others remained open-minded, except for, in Carter's words, a "few nuts like Strom Thurmond and Jesse Helms." Taking no chances, Jimmy and Rosalynn invited Senator Robert Byrd and his wife to a private dinner at the White House, where the Carters flattered the Byrds with conversation about how much the president depended upon the senator.[10]

Carter also worked hard to try to change public opinion about the new canal treaties. During the weeks before and after signing them, he organized a nationwide campaign to take the issue to as many people as possible. He drew in people from all walks of life, from labor union leaders to editors to religious leaders. He brought them to the White House, discussed the treaties with them and sought to educate them on the history and contemporary worth of the canal. They were to spread the word back home, but when they did so, they found that a majority of their fellow citizens stubbornly continued to view the canal treaties as Reagan did. The mail and polls showed 55% or more Americans still opposed the treaties.[11]

Determined to change that, Jimmy, Rosalynn, and key members of the administration went to work. Many of the senators whom Carter telephoned, however, refused to support ratification despite his effort to convince them that the treaty would guarantee the neutrality of the canal, security of its employees, and US use of it for United States defense if necessary.[12] Carter's fireside chat defending the canal treaties, supplemented with speeches by Secretary of Defense Harold Brown and Secretary of State Cyrus Vance, may have influenced a few more senators, but the public remained unconvinced.

Deputy Secretary of State Warren Christopher made speeches supporting the treaties, and Carter held candid talks with leading senators. Rosalynn incorporated into her speeches a comment that the treaties would end the United States' imperial image. David McCullough, the historian whose work had informed Carter about the history of the canal, wrote that, were Teddy Roosevelt alive, he would approve the treaties and that they would give us "a humane and more stable world."[13]

Prominent among the senators who remained opposed to the canal treaties was the chairman of the powerful Armed Services Committee, Senator John Stennis of Mississippi, an unrelenting segregationist and defense hawk who was also known for his ability to garner bountiful shares of federal monies for his home state. Wanting his influence and vote for the treaties, Carter allowed Stennis to keep a massive and much disputed water project that would connect the Tennessee River with the port of Mobile via a series of locks and dams on Mississippi's and Alabama's Tombigbee River. In addition to the canal ratification debate, Carter had other controversial items on his agenda, such as canceling the building of the B-1 bomber and prohibiting building a neutron bomb, all of which would require Stennis's help. When Secretary of Defense Harold Brown informed Carter that Stennis wanted a new ammunition plant in Mississippi, a facility that could be justified on need and common practice with all NATO countries, Carter responded, "we need him on Panama."[14]

In Panama, the enthusiastic Torrijos tried to do his part to sway United States senators. Acting unlike a dictator, he sent telegrams to six doubting senators promising to relax his military rule and be more generous in allowing freedom of assembly and fair trials if the canal treaties were ratified.[15] The anxious dictator and the president who would not accept defeat could only hang in limbo, working and waiting for the six months it would take the slow, indecisive Senate to act.

That six months of suspense about the fate of the Panama Canal treaties was packed with so many other issues, great and trivial, that the president had to spread his time in dozens of different ways. In September he became excessively irritated by the mice in his office who resisted all human efforts to get rid of them. After two or three months of asking the custodians to exterminate them, Jimmy exploded, "I am determined either to fire somebody or get the mice cleared out—or both."[16]

The same day that Carter went after the hapless rodents, the Bakke case tested his commitment to affirmative action. Allan Bakke, a White man, had applied in 1973 for admission to medical school at the University of California at Davis. Claiming to be the victim of reverse discrimination because several minority students with lesser credentials had been admitted, he sued and won his case in the California Supreme Court. When the case reached the US Supreme Court, the Carter administration prepared an amicus curiae brief that was supposed to reflect Carter's stated belief that there was a clear "distinction between flexible affirmative action programs using goals and inflexible racial quotas."[17]

Carter found himself in a bind. Secretary of Health, Education, and Welfare Joseph Califano adamantly favored a quota system based upon race. Every African American in the administration, from Andrew Young to Eleanor Holmes Norton and the numerous judges Carter had appointed, agreed with Califano. So did Vice President Mondale. Jewish groups, whose support Carter struggled to win, vigorously opposed a quota system, because they had been victimized by it by elite Ivy League universities. Hamilton Jordan, who wished the administration could not be involved at all was overridden by Stuart Eizenstat and Vice President Mondale who thought it an important issue on which they should take a stand. Carter did not want to endorse a system of quotas for any group, and his Justice Department filed a brief solidly supporting affirmative action, but without saying that the administration opposed rigid quotas based on race. The Supreme Court turned the case back to California, which resolved it in favor of Bakke but without condemning quotas or disallowing affirmative action.[18]

More damaging to Carter than the mice or the Bakke case was the Lance Affair. A long-time friend and protégé of Carter's, Bert Lance relished his work as director of the Office of Management and Budget. A jovial politician-at-large for the president, Lance reached out to business groups, members of Congress, and the general public with a Southern folksiness that did not always sit well with the media and some national politicians. Carter maintained a close tie with him, once declaring that only Bert and "Rosalynn will know the whole picture in any particular situation."[19]

Lance and his wife LaBelle had amassed great wealth through their control of the National Bank of Georgia. When Lance became director of the Office of Management and Budget, they had placed their stock in that bank in a blind trust which was supposed to sell the stock by the end of 1977. Since the stock went down in value, however, Carter wrote Senator Abraham Ribicoff, Chairman of the Senate Government Operations Committee, requesting indefinite postponement. Ribicoff, a strong supporter of Carter on most issues including Israeli affairs, was not sympathetic toward Lance, who he thought was an impediment to the administration and its increasingly successful record for getting its legislation passed. Ribicoff was perturbed, however, when William Safire, who routinely skewered Carter for his Middle East policy, began doing a "hatchet job" on Lance in his widely syndicated columns, accusing the budget director of peddling influence and improper banking practices.[20]

Carter defended Lance in public and in private. As the controversy in the media mushroomed, he met with his friend every morning to read Scripture and pray. Clark Clifford, the politically influential Washington lawyer who served as an unofficial adviser to four Democratic presidents from Truman through Carter, gave more worldly help by proposing that Lance be given the chance to defend himself before Ribicoff's committee. It was arranged for him to do so on September 16. On that morning before Lance left for Capitol Hill to testify, Brzezinski found it "touching" to discover him and the president on their knees in Carter's small office praying. As it turned out, Lance performed very well before the committee.

A month later, on August 18, John Heimann, comptroller of the currency, released a lengthy report revealing the results of his investigation of Lance's banking practices. The report exonerated Lance of any legal wrong doing, but it did suggest that he had indulged in some unsound actions.

Nevertheless, all the negative publicity surrounding Lance unleashed a continuing barrage of media criticism of him. Depressed by the deteriorating situation, Carter complained to Jody Powell that the *Washington Post* appeared to have a vendetta against Lance, publishing numerous damning articles accusing him of being a virtual criminal with great influence upon the president. James Reston, a fair-minded journalist with the *New York Times*, contended that the president risked his prestige because of his personal friendship with Lance and general stubbornness. As the Senate and journalists continued to investigate, many White House staff members gloomily assumed that Lance would resign and feared that the damage done to the president would be "irreparable."[21] Finally, Mondale, Powell, Jordan, and Kirbo, all of whom understood Carter's personal crisis, convinced him that Lance must resign. Lance yielded to the pressure, but LaBelle met with Carter on September 21 and accused him of betraying her husband. Later that day, with a "film of tears in his eyes," Carter announced at a news conference that he deeply regretted Lance's resignation and still strongly believed in his friend's integrity and innocence.[22]

The Lance Affair inflicted lasting damage on the young presidency. Carter stubbornly refused to admit that his friend had done anything wrong, and the press, led by Safire, equally insisted that the Lance affair was similar to Watergate. There was no comparison to Watergate, for neither Lance nor Carter had committed any impropriety in office. The fact, however, that Lance may have been guilty of improper, if not illegal, banking practices ran counter to Carter's promise to set a high ethical standard for his top officials. Stuart Eizenstat thought the harm that the controversy did to the Carter administration was "as damaging as it was to Bert himself." Speaker Tip O'Neill later said of Lance that "history may show that his departure was a major step on Jimmy Carter's road to defeat in 1980."[23]

With no time to grieve the loss of Lance, the president continued to wage the Cold War with the Soviet Union. During a three-hour conversation with Soviet Foreign Minister Andrei A. Gromyko in late September, Carter tried to convince him that the United States wanted a good relationship with the Soviet Union. Their conversation ended in a draw, for Gromyko rebutted everything that Carter said. Carter denied that the US interest in human rights, particularly the cases of imprisoned Russian Jewish dissidents, was intended to embarrass or interfere with the Soviet Union's internal policy. Gromyko replied that no one in the Soviet Union had heard of Anatoly Shcharansky, but he believed that US views on human rights were an attack on the Soviet Union. Furthermore, Gromyko insisted that the Russians would continue to defend the presence of Cuban troops in Angola. He refused to believe Carter when he promised that the United States' relationship with China would not be used to harm the Soviet Union. There seemed to be some agreement that arms control was essential, that peace in the Middle East was a common goal, and that both nations wanted peace and successful SALT negotiations. Still, Carter doubted Gromyko's veracity as much as Gromyko doubted his.[24]

Despite Gromyko's complaint, Carter continued to vigorously defend Russian Jewish dissidents both on humanitarian grounds and to convince doubting Jewish Americans that he was not anti-Semitic. Shcharansky's case aroused his ire. The Russians had accused Shcharansky of being a CIA agent, a charge that Carter investigated and determined to be false. When Shcharansky's wife Natasha came to the United States to solicit support for her husband, Carter held a news conference to help her defend her husband.

The Russians did not back down. A year later the unfortunate Shcharansky was sentenced to thirteen years in a prison camp, where he remained until six years after the Carters left the White House. Carter rarely linked his defense of dissidents with diplomatic negotiations, but the Russians routinely did so. They used their Jewish citizens as pawns, granting more exit visas when they had something to gain and fewer when it was no advantage to them.[25]

In addition to his presidential job, Jimmy was distracted by family business matters. Although his brother Billy's alcoholic antics, comical television appearances, and outrageous remarks irritated him, he would not rebuke his brother publicly. However, when Carter learned from Charlie Kirbo that Billy was not giving sufficient attention to managing the Carter warehouse in Plains, he became concerned. Kirbo subsequently took charge of the business, leased it to Gold Kist, and placed it in a blind trust for as long as Carter was president.[26]

Meanwhile, Rosalynn kept busy with her own agenda, traveling the country to promote mental health and women's rights, and standing in for Jimmy wherever he needed her. Addressing the World Federation for Mental Health in Vancouver, British Columbia, on August 25, 1977, she gave a definitive statement of the need for "a more caring society." She declared that "our value as individuals, our success as a society, can be measured by our compassion for the vulnerable." Stigma and lack of medical treatment, she said, inhibited the creation of an environment for proper mental health care. It was a global issue, she insisted.[27] As First Lady, Rosalynn worked closely with the president, the Department of Health Education and Welfare, and Congress to pass new laws and raise funds for research. A week after her Vancouver speech, Thomas E. Bryant presented the Preliminary Report of the President's Commission on Mental Health to Carter.[28]

For his birthday on October 1, both Jimmy and Rosalynn went to Camp David with Amy. Rosalynn gave him tennis shorts, a matching shirt, and a book to identify trees of North America. Amy gave him a pencil holder made from a jar covered with bits of masking tape and painted with liquid brown shoe polish. The Navy chef in charge of the Camp David kitchen prepared for him a pistachio cake and a pepper steak dinner. A few days later, a routine analysis of Senate and House votes on key issues may have been his best gift of all. Except for weak support in the Southeast, he received more than 40% approval from those representing the rest of the country, including 91% from Senator Edward Kennedy.[29]

In a relaxed mood at Camp David, Carter gave a long interview to Trude Feldman, a friendly journalist, for a publication to be released during the upcoming Jewish High Holidays. Carter pointedly praised the Jewish people as "representative of one's relationship to God and one's responsibility to mankind." That awareness of dual responsibility, Carter said, was "the foundation of our own country's Human Rights policy." Aware that his kind words about Israel would not have the desired impact, Carter had attempted in late September to pressure Prime Minister Begin into making the concessions needed to open discussions with the Arabs; Carter privately threatened to halt further military deliveries if Israel continued its own military activity in the West Bank.[30]

In the tough ongoing conversations leading up to what Carter hoped would be a general peace conference in Geneva, he made no progress. The *New York Times* was filled with stories critical of Carter's push to get Israeli leaders to talk to the PLO and arguments that his efforts were counterproductive. Puzzled and provoked, Carter did not understand the "Jewish uproar," which he first read about on October 3. He had spelled out the general principles of a Middle East Geneva conference compatible with what the United States and the Soviet Union had previously agreed upon, and he was surprised that his Jewish critics did not approve them.[31]

The next day, October 4, Carter journeyed to New York City for a two-day visit to the UN where he would deliver a speech and meet with attending foreign ambassadors and heads of state. Rosalynn joined him in time to hear his speech about peace, disarmament, and nonproliferation of nuclear weapons. After the speech, they met with the Egyptian foreign minister Ismail Fahmy at the Plaza Hotel. Fahmy brought Carter a letter from Sadat urging him not to agree to anything that might prevent a peace conference between Egypt and Israel with Carter serving as mediator. At a luncheon the Carters hosted for forty-five or fifty African nations, they attempted to get the Israeli delegates in attendance to understand that it was in their country's self-interest to accept Carter's willingness to mediate a conference between Israel and Egypt. Refusing to be discouraged, Carter held a private meeting with UN Secretary General Kurt Waldheim after which he signed the International Covenants of Human Rights. The United States then issued a joint statement with Israel agreeing that the resumption of the Geneva Peace Conference should be based upon Security Council Resolutions 242 and 338, which had mandated that Israel withdraw from the occupied territories it had acquired in 1967.[32]

Back at the White House the following day, Carter met with the House Jewish caucus and explained to them the difficulty of dealing with the complex Middle East question. He told them that he was trusted by the Arabs, Israelis, and Soviets, and "asked the same degree of trust from the Congress." He explained that it would be damaging to Israel if it became isolated from the United States. Later in the day, Carter met with key Senators who favored standing strong with Israel: Robert Byrd, Alan Cranston, Clifford Case, Frank Church, Jacob Javits, Henry Jackson, Danial Patrick Moynihan, Abraham Ribicoff, and Richard Stone. The president assured the senators that the administration was in close consultation with Israel concerning the resumption of the Geneva Peace Conference. He would not impose a settlement on Israel, nor would he insist on a Palestinian state on Israel's border. Although he held firm to his belief that Palestinian rights should be protected, Carter said that he hoped that the Russians might influence the Palestinians to be more flexible. Concluding, Carter emphatically declared that "I'd rather commit political suicide than hurt Israel."[33] Then he went back to Camp David to rest.

Despite his efforts, the Jewish response to Carter's pleading remained mixed. Brzezinski reported to him that they thought the administration was back-peddling on human rights. Others disagreed, and one Jewish citizen wrote Carter that "I want to reassure you that the Jewish people understand and welcome your sincere effort to bring a just peace in the Middle East." An editorial in the New York Times warned Jewish Americans that Carter genuinely sought peace and, if they were too outspoken, they might jeopardize the process.[34] When Rowland Evans and Robert Novak published a piece condemning his Israeli policy, Carter publicly called them liars and scheduled briefings with more Jewish leaders.[35]

Carter's preoccupation with the Arab-Israeli peace effort, as well as the Cold War, dwarfed other ominous issues involving terrorism. The threat of terrorist attacks in the United States and against US citizens abroad had become frequent enough by 1977 that Carter attempted to develop a plan to deal with terrorism. He recognized that both the Germans and Israelis had extensive experience in that area and had made progress in devising countermeasures. In a handwritten note to Secretary of Defense Harold Brown and National Security Adviser Zbigniew Brzezinski, Carter instructed them to "ask Schmidt (& perhaps Begin) for a thorough briefing on handling terrorists. Develop similar U.S. capability."[36] No one, however, could have predicted the unique act of terrorism that would soon engulf the administration.

The same day that Carter had asked Brown and Brzezinski to develop a plan to counter terrorism, he received a long letter from Paris, dated October 18, with implications about terrorism of which he had never dreamed. Prince M. Firouz, a former Vice Prime Minister of Iran, appealed to the US president to apply his human rights policy to Iran. Firouz represented a group of anti-shah exiles who had abandoned hope during the "Nixon-Kissinger-Helms era," but who now saw Carter as "a ray of light and hope." Firouz contended that the shah's regime was propped up by the CIA and that the shah's secret police and intelligence organization SAVAK was systematically violating the human rights of the Iranian people. He begged Carter to warn the shah that, unless he restored the rights of the people, the United States would terminate friendly relations with him. There is no indication Carter answered the letter, since he was attempting to maintain the traditional, cordial US relationship with Iran.[37]

As trouble with Iran brewed, the US system of intelligence gathering was increasingly called into question. Director of Central Intelligence Stansfield Turner relied more on electronic advances than human involvement, and the analyses he forwarded to the National Security Advisor did not satisfy Brzezinski. Brzezinski wanted more facts that he told Turner could be gathered better by human intelligence.[38] Carter trusted Turner, but he stayed personally involved in intelligence gathering. Under normal circumstances, he said, the government should not spy on US citizens, but on one occasion he was flexible. He and Attorney General Griffin B. Bell authorized warrantless electronic surveillance to convict two men of spying for Vietnam. Truong Dinh Hung and Ronald Louis Humphrey appealed their case, but they lost. The US Court of Appeals for the Fourth Circuit decided that the chief executive had "inherent authority" to wiretap enemies, such as terrorists, without warrants when such surveillance was for "foreign intelligence reasons."[39] Although Carter demanded that he know daily if there were any threats against the country, he instructed the CIA that it should conduct no surveillance against US citizens and emphasized that "no person employed by or acting on behalf of the United States shall engage in assassination."[40]

While Carter dealt with spying issues, Rosalynn went to Toccoa Falls, Georgia, to express the administration's concern for flood victims there. A dam above the Toccoa Falls Bible Institute had given away and drowned about forty people in a fast-moving flood. Rosalynn rushed there to comfort the victims by touching the arms of survivors, promising to pray for them—and to lobby Congress for funds to build safe dams.[41]

In Washington, Carter faced a different type of crisis when he met with Golda Meir, former prime minister of Israel, who was paying a private visit to the United States. At a meal attended by Cy Vance and Walter Mondale, she was "obnoxious," but later when she met with Carter, she was "deferential" and friendly. Meir was even tougher than Begin on the Palestinian issue and had "a deep feeling of hatred" for those who had wronged her people. Carter restrained himself from declaring his strong disapproval of Israel's recent attack on Lebanon, killing 120 people, in retaliation against a minor PLO firing of "a few mortar rounds into a little village on the coast."[42]

To break the tension, Carter welcomed a humorous report from his mother. She was visiting Ireland and said that, if she could stay another month, she could resolve the problem between the Catholics and the Protestants. For further relaxation, on November 12 he attended the Georgia Tech–Navy game, pardoned the midshipmen who had demerits, and enjoyed Navy's victory.[43]

By the middle of the month, however, the Carters had their first direct encounter with the difficulties they would face in dealing with the shah and empress of Iran. At the welcoming ceremony on November 15 for Mohammed Reza Pahlavi and Farah Pahlavi, demonstrators outside the White House fence created such a disturbance that Park Service Police fired tear gas into the crowd. The pungent vapor floated across the South Lawn and into the nostrils of the dignitaries, reducing them to tears and forcing them to reach for handkerchiefs.[44]

Once safely inside the White House, the shah expressed his admiration for Egyptian President Sadat's courage in planning to go to Israel to seek peace, but he feared that Arab militants wanted an empire in Syria and Iraq that would become a haven for terrorists and a threat to Sadat and to Iran. Over supper, the shah and empress relaxed and enjoyed the hospitality of the White House. The shah joked with Rosalynn that he had attended more state dinners at the White House than she had. The guests and their hosts enjoyed a jazz concert featuring Dizzy Gillespie and Sarah Vaughn, but the empress concluded privately that, for the security of Iran, the wrong person had been elected president of the United States.

The shah agreed with his wife when Carter confronted him privately about his country's disregard for human rights. Embarrassed, the shah defended himself and blamed the abuses on the law that made it illegal to be a Communist. He dismissed the demonstrations against him as "little more than a nuisance." Carter, who had been briefed by the Secret Service, knew that the anti-shah demonstrations were far more serious.[45]

Iranians interpreted the demonstrations quite differently. Followers of the Ayatollah Khomeini, a Shiite Muslim cleric living in exile in Paris while awaiting his opportunity to return to Iran as the leader of the anti-shah forces, rejoiced that the demonstrations had disrupted the welcoming ceremony. Khomeini's group assumed that Carter had deliberately staged the protests to embarrass his guests who were a liability to his human-rights administration. From his Paris exile, Khomeini issued an edict against the shah, which directed the faithful not to obey his laws. When the shah saw it a week later, he became enraged and asked why such "vermin" were allowed "to continue to crawl." He also declared that Khomeini's edict was "a consequence of Jimmy Carter's election and the triumph of 'liberal circles in Washington.'"[46]

Carter was not to be duped. Assistant Secretary of State for Human Rights Patricia Derian and Carter knew that Pahlavi used his secret police to persecute his political opponents. Carter, however, could not sidestep the pressures to prop up the regime of a long-time ally leading an oil rich nation. Furthermore, he needed the radar stations on the Soviet border, and he thought that negotiating SALT II with the Soviet Union and brokering a peace agreement in the Middle East took precedence over the revolution in Iran. Derian, who had worked on the Civil Rights movement in Mississippi, was inexperienced in foreign policy and often resented that her recommendations for humanitarian action were subject to compromise if the president thought they endangered the nation's security.[47]

Playing his oil card, the shah was blunt with Speaker Tip O'Neill when he went to Capitol Hill and marched into O'Neill's office. Bedecked in his uniform and medals, and acting like "a cocky little guy," he outright criticized O'Neill and the United States for selfishly using 35% of the world's energy and driving up the price of oil. He threatened to reduce Iran's shipment to the United States from four to one million barrels per day.[48] Whether Carter knew of that exchange or not, he would have agreed that the United States needed to use less Iranian oil, but, like O'Neill, would not be intimidated by the pretentious Persian. The shah may have been trying to use O'Neill to put pressure on Carter. If so, the ploy did not work.

Once the shah and Empress Farah had left town, the Carters hosted more congenial guests at the White House. On November 17 they held a reception for the American Film Institute (AFI). Producers, directors, actors, and composers milled about the historic rooms, and Carter met some of his favorites, including Lillian Gish, Olivia de Havilland, Henry Mancini, and Henry Fonda. He was particularly pleased that AFI had declared "Gone With the Wind," the incredibly popular Civil War era epic story that was set in Georgia, to be the best movie of the past seventy-five years. After the guests left, Jimmy spent time on the balcony with Rosalynn before going to the roof with his son Jeff to look at the galaxies through Jeff's telescope. The flights of ducks and geese over the White House, illuminated by the city lights, gave him one of his most "pleasant evenings."[49]

Meanwhile in Cairo, Sadat, who did not believe that a Geneva conference involving the Russians would work, decided to take matters in his own hands and go to Jerusalem alone.[50]

THIRTEEN

The Revolutionaries

In November 1977, Egyptian president Anwar Sadat launched one of the most dramatic diplomatic efforts ever attempted in the Middle East when he visited Jerusalem to offer an olive branch to Israel. Sadat made his decision alone, but Carter had encouraged him by praising his "uncommon statesmanship," "commitment to peace," and "determination not to be deterred or delayed by petty differences over procedure." Carter also promised to work "hand in hand" with Sadat "for the peace that we both seek."[1] On the eve of Sadat's journey, Israeli Prime Minister Menachem Begin wrote Carter: "I believe, Mr. President, that without your contribution these events could not and would not have been set in motion. . . . You have created it, Mr. President, and I express to you my deepest heartfelt thanks."[2] Sadat was a courageous, revolutionary statesman acting alone. No other Arab nation supported him, and Carter feared that Sadat's life might be in danger from Islamic extremists in his own country. Carter asked Israel to show some signs of reconciliation in order to prove to Sadat's Egyptian enemies that his mission might succeed.[3]

On November 19, Carter watched Sadat's televised arrival in Israel. Tense and fearful, Carter stared at the screen as Sadat, the former drama student, descended the stairs from his plane and found himself face to face with one of Israel's political icons, former Prime Minister Golda Meir. She appeared dazed, perhaps thinking of all the young Jews who had died in Israel's battles against him and his fellow Arabs. Sadat told her that he had wanted to meet her, and now he was here. Jehan Sadat had urged him not to treat her like a man, but he greeted Meir saying that, in his country, she was called "the strongest man in Israel." Meir was delighted, but in Cairo, Jehan winced and feared for her husband's safety. Sadat moved down the line of Israeli greeters, sometimes joking with incredulous former enemies, but as one of them observed, his eyes were asking for reciprocity to end their generations of enmity.[4]

The traditional Arab rejection of Israel had been shattered, and Carter had been thrust into the center of the quest for peace between the two countries. Begin telephoned Carter later that day and told him that "there would be no more war between Israel and Egypt."[5]

On November 20, the morning Sadat addressed the Israeli Knesset in Jerusalem, Carter led a prayer session at the First Baptist Church, but he hurried back to the White House to listen to Sadat. Carter thought his Egyptian friend made a "great speech, spelling out in very blunt terms the Arab requirements for any peace settlement." A blanket of silence spread across the Knesset when Sadat told his old adversaries that he had come there not to sign a treaty, but to demolish "the barriers of suspicion, fear, illusion, and misrepresentation" that had prevented any talk about peace.[6]

Sadat became the principal player in what Carter called one of "the most dramatic events in modern history." Sadat's speech was sincere, Carter thought, but Begin's response was disappointing. Nevertheless, Sadat, no longer alone, had succeeded in drawing the Israelis into a radically new approach to bringing peace to the Middle East.[7]

A month later, after meeting with Begin, who welcomed Sadat's outreach for peace but was unwilling to accept his blunt terms, Carter changed his own approach to Middle East peace. "I came to believe," he said, "that I could have a fruitful meeting involving just Begin, Sadat, and me." And thus the idea for a Camp David summit was born.[8]

First, however, Carter had to deal with the Russians, who did not want to be left out. Distrust reigned on both sides as the correspondence and media reports passed back and forth. Brezhnev insisted on linking arms reductions with a Middle East settlement. Carter wanted a reduction in arms, a comprehensive ban on all nuclear testing, an end to Russia's space tests of anti-satellite devices, and a safer US embassy in Moscow. But he realized that any hopeful approach to peace between Israel and Egypt could not include the Soviet Union. Brezhnev protested Carter's plan to deal alone with Israel and Egypt; he wanted to convene a conference in Geneva where the Russians would participate in working out a comprehensive agreement.[9]

"I want to cooperate with the Soviets," Jimmy wrote in his diary, "but if they take a negative attitude we will have to pursue a Middle East settlement unilaterally."[10] It had become clear to Carter that, for the Egyptian and Israeli leaders, the issue of war and peace between them could be resolved only by them—and by Jimmy Carter. Carter risked the ire of Jewish voters at home and the intransigence of Soviet negotiators at the SALT II conference where both countries were attempting to reduce nuclear armaments. At the time he accepted that risk, an agreement between the Israelis and Arabs seemed far off and even impossible.

For Carter, diplomacy and resolving conflicts was based on education, facts, and knowing as much as possible about the history and cultures of every country or person involved. He blended his long-standing goal of improving education with his approach to diplomacy and military strength and set about improving the curricula in the military service academies by incorporating more history, math, and political science courses. With the help of Admiral Rickover, who enthusiastically helped design the new curricula, Carter also raised standards for the existing engineering courses.[11]

Although Jimmy and Rosalynn allegedly left matters of domestic education up to Secretary Joseph Califano, they did not trust him. When Califano notified Carter late in the year that school districts often failed to experiment with a variety of new approaches, Jimmy, a product of Plains High School, curtly replied, "Some do too much experimenting & not enough teaching."[12] Rosalynn, through her public appearances and interviews, made her own contribution to advancing education. During the fall, she addressed the Washington Press Club on the topic of mental health, and, at the White House, she met with Margaret Mead, the distinguished cultural anthropologist. At working lunches with Jimmy in the Oval Office, she discussed education and other government business, and she occasionally wrote an op-ed piece for the *New York Times*.[13]

Rosalynn wielded power in Washington, but she inevitably became entangled in the robust feminist movement of the 1970s. A passionate advocate for ratification of the ERA since she had entered public life in Georgia, Rosalynn had mixed feelings about the range of feminist activities. She did not favor burning bras, massive protests, or outrageous declarations, such as those Gloria Steinem and more radical leaders of the movement were in the habit of making. Often identifying herself as "a Southern feminist," she acted the part of the liberated woman. It would be smarter, she thought, for her and others to work behind closed doors for passage of the amendment, rather than protesting in the streets as so many Northern women did.[14] She hoped that all women could experience the freedom and independence she enjoyed. Rosalynn "pretty much did what she wanted to do," noted Kathy Cade, one of her senior assistants.[15]

Sometimes Rosalynn's official duties required her to do something she did not want to do. When her husband yielded to pressure from outspoken New York Congresswoman Bella Abzug and leading feminist Gloria Steinem to fund a women's conference, Rosalynn felt that she must attend. Carter, who would create a National Advisory Committee on Women headed by Abzug, joked that he would rather deal with Abzug and Steinem than with Prime Minister Begin. Abzug's commission sponsored the National Women's Conference, which convened in Houston, Texas, November 18–21, 1977. Bitter controversy preceded the meeting. Phyllis Schlafly, leader of the anti-feminist movement, vigorously opposed such conferences as destructive of the family and Christian values.

Rosalynn Carter disagreed with Schlafly and solicited the help of former first ladies Betty Ford and Lady Bird Johnson to contest Schlafly's position at the conference. More than 22,000 women attended, and most were eager to hear what the first ladies would say. Rosalynn told them that "our message should be—that women can live and work and learn as they choose. . . . [I am] proud to be a woman and proud to be the wife of a very special person who shares my desire for the ratification of the ERA."[16]

At the end of the conference, Rosalynn and the others had accomplished two of their goals: the following year President Carter established the National Advisory Committee for Women, and the Senate granted a three-year extension for states to ratify the ERA.[17]

With a much easier assignment, early in December Rosalynn went home to South Georgia to dedicate the Plains Welcome Center. Standing in a chilling wind, holding her hat in place with one hand, she said, "Jimmy and I never dreamed that Plains would become the attraction it is." Stability comes from having roots, a sense of belonging, she told her audience. She belonged to Plains, to her family, and to the Americus Business and Professional Woman's Association. On December 7, the latter group, meeting at the Americus Country Club, presented her with their Woman of the Year Award. Thanking them, she said that she had told people all over the United States that she was proud to be a professional woman in the South, for she was an ambassador of goodwill for the South as well as the nation. Hers was a triumphant return to the country club that had expelled her and Jimmy for their liberal views many years earlier. She ended her remarks cheerfully, "I have to leave now to fly back to Washington. Goodbye, and I love you all."[18]

Back at the White House, Rosalynn learned about the unfolding crisis with the nation's farmers. They had announced on December 1, 1977, that they rejected the government's farm program because it did not guarantee them the parity prices for their products that had been promised under the Agricultural Adjustment Act of 1938. If enforced, that act meant that whenever the price of farm products declined from the previous ten-year average, the government would buy farmers' products at at a price equal to the cost of producing the commodity and sufficient to provide them a decent livilhood. Traditionally, a financial depression for farmers signaled a broader economic decline that might affect the entire nation. The farmers planned a massive protest in Washington and other locations nationwide. Jimmy confronted a unique dilemma as a former farmer who had to explain and enforce the federal programs the farmers protested. He confessed that when he was a farmer he didn't understand the government's program either, but as president he had to maintain domestic tranquility and find a resolution.[19]

But that didn't mean his family back in Georgia had to agree with him. Jimmy's sister Gloria boarded her tractor on December 10 and rode in a "tractorcade" bound for Atlanta to demand 100% parity for their crops. "I've never been so proud of farmers," she declared, as she denied any conflict between herself and her brother.[20]

As the tractors rumbled along the highway toward Atlanta, Carter studied the farm issue and prepared to address the protesters. He asked Bob Bergland, his secretary of agriculture, and Jody Powell to prepare a brief summary of legislation and farm prices related to the previous year. He wanted it in the form of a simple letter to individual farmers, so that when he addressed the Georgia farmers and others during the Christmas holiday he could tell them what he had done.[21]

As Christmas 1977 approached, Jimmy and Rosalynn began to see positive results from the administration's human rights policy. The president of Bolivia released five US citizens being held on narcotics-related charges, began to process more for release, and provided medical care for others in Bolivian jails.[22] The president of Freedom House, an independent watchdog organization that analyzed the expansion of freedom and democracy globally, contended that Carter's human rights "initiatives abroad" were effective. He reported that at least seventeen more countries were free of dictatorships, whereas eight were partly free. A dozen more were not, but other nations in Africa and South America were planning to hold free elections. Notably, Carter's emphasis on the Helsinki agreements on human rights raised new hope for dissidents in the Soviet Union and Eastern Europe.[23]

Encouraged by the progress he had made in reducing human suffering, Carter wrapped up his first year in Washington by making notes for a speech that would emphasize the Christian's Prince of Peace when he lit the Christmas tree on the White House lawn.[24]

The festivities of the Christmas season, and their firm faith in the Prince of Peace, could not remove all the irritants Jimmy and Rosalynn had in their private lives. Their relationship with the Southern Baptist Convention came into question when its president, Jimmy R. Allen, condemned Carter's decision to send an emissary to the Vatican. Carter responded with kindness, and Rosalynn sent Allen a check for $350 for the Mission Service Corps. But the Carters had become too liberal to be accepted by their traditional conservative religious group.[25]

Like any parents who suffered if their children suffered, the Carters were grieved by the marital troubles of their son Chip and his wife Caron. Since Billy had vacated his position managing the warehouse, there was space for Chip to assume that job. He left Washington alone, but soon Caron and their young son joined him at his parents' home in Plains. Perhaps they thought that once free of the hothouse of the White House they might be able to salvage their marriage, but the change of venue did not solve their problems. They later divorced, casting a gloom over the family that Rosalynn tried to hide from the public.[26]

Before leaving the capitol for the Christmas and New Year holidays in Plains, Carter cataloged his accomplishments during his first year in office. The impressive list that his staff and Cabinet members provided to him revealed that he had accomplished more in his first year in office than any president since Franklin Roosevelt.[27] Unwilling to completely accept such a positive report, ABC reporter Sam Donaldson whined that Carter worked too much, too fast, and talked down to members of Congress.[28]

Carter looked upon his first year as a learning process in which he dealt with Congress and achieved nonpartisan support for key legislation such as the proposed Panama Canal treaties. Despite his dislike for socializing and for humoring members of Congress, he did enough of it to achieve a 75% success rate in 1977. Like presidents before and since, Carter deplored unfair and inaccurate media coverage, but he took pride in involving the public as much as possible in his vision for the country. At the same time, he understood that the public was often confused by so many agenda items and too few quick solutions. Carter implied that his most important accomplishments were still works in progress that would head his agenda in 1978.[29]

Looking ahead, Carter asked Ham Jordan for a memorandum spelling out the coming year's political challenges. In more than a hundred pages, Ham presented a scenario that called for studying and catering to the needs of multiple ethnic and economic groups. Knowing that Rosalynn would be Carter's closest adviser, Ham added: "Rosalynn might have different and/or better ideas about how to deal logistically with these various groups."[30]

On December 20, the night before they planned to leave for Plains, Jimmy and Rosalynn hosted a reception and dance at the White House for about 1,200 members of the White House press and their wives. Jimmy danced with "about one hundred of the wives, a brief time each. They just lined up to break in on me, and I really enjoyed it," he wrote in his diary.[31] The next day, December 21, Jimmy, Rosalynn, Jeff and Annette, and Amy happily returned to Plains for the Christmas holiday. At home and comfortable in dungarees, Carter went quail hunting with friends, walked in the fields, and strolled down Main Street, casually greeting neighbors.

The serenity of his vacation was shattered, however, when angry farmers came to his doorstep to protest his administration's agricultural policies. From Georgia, Florida, and Alabama, the unhappy farmers, driving hundreds of tractors and pickup trucks, blocked the tiny town's main street. The governor sent state troops to disperse them, but they stubbornly refused to leave.[32] Carter agreed to meet with them at his home at 8 a.m. on December 23. Dressed like a farmer in blue jeans and a flannel shirt, and joined by his son Chip, he expressed sympathy and explained that he would submit a plan to Congress that included increased crop loan levels and target prices, farmer-owned grain reserves, emergency drought relief funds, and an effective energy policy. He urged the disgruntled farmers, who had threatened not to plant new crops, to plant their crops the next year but not to expect 100% parity prices because that would prevent the United States from competing internationally. After about thirty-five minutes, the farmers' representatives left. The demonstrators disbanded but they were not satisfied with Carter's promises.[33]

On Christmas morning, Jimmy and Rosalynn walked down Main Street to Miss Lillian's house, then to Miss Allie's, before attending worship services and Sunday School at the Baptist church. Christmas dinner was always at Rosalynn's mother's place. Back at home, Carter called to wish season's greetings to Anwar Sadat, Menachem Begin, Speaker Tip O'Neill, Daddy King, labor leader George Meany, Senator Hubert Humphrey, and others. The Carter home was so crowded with relatives, with presents, and clothes piled on the floor, that Jimmy gave a huge sigh of relief later that day when he and Rosalynn returned to the White House with their immediate family and "walked into a spacious mansion practically alone."[34]

The Carters had little time, however, to rest and reflect as 1977 came to an end, because they had to prepare to embark on a nine-day, six-nation multi-purpose tour that would begin in Poland and end in France with stops in Iran, India, Saudi Arabia, and Belgium. Leaving from Andrews Air Force Base on December 29, they took Amy and a host of diplomatic staff members with them.[35]

In Warsaw that evening, his first visit to a communist country, Carter delivered a moving speech commending the Poles for their long struggle for freedom. Carter's mind, however, was preoccupied with a secret communique that he had received from the White House during the flight, informing him that Egyptian President Anwar Sadat would welcome Carter to Aswan if he would come, a rendezvous on which Brzezinski had been working. Sadat needed public support from the United States, as he feared the Saudis might cut off his economic aid because of his peaceful gesture toward Israel. More ominously, internal enemies in Egypt might pose a serious threat to his life. The communique also reported that Israel's foreign minister Moshe Dayan had met secretly with the shah of Iran in Tehran to discuss Soviet arms shipments to Iraq.[36]

In addition to the disconcerting communique from the White House, the welcoming ceremony at the airport was seriously marred by the incompetence of the president's translator. When Carter referred to the Poles' "desires for the future," the interpreter translated his words as "your lusts for the future." It got worse, for when Carter said "when I left the United States," the interpreter said "when I abandoned the United States." The downhill slide could not be stopped, and what at first was amusing to the audience became embarrassing. The inadequate translator lost his job.[37]

In Warsaw, a city filled with monuments to Polish heroes, Jimmy and Rosalynn braved a snow storm the day after their arrival to stand in awe before the statue of Nike, the Greek goddess of victory, which commemorated all the World War II heroes and heroines of Warsaw. Carter doubted, he said, that any nation had suffered the ravages of war more than Poland had. The Nazis had slaughtered 800,000 mostly non-Jewish Poles in Warsaw alone, and six million nationwide. Jimmy, wrapped in warm clothing and with hair tousled, appeared transfixed as he looked up at the monument. At his side, Rosalynn stood, gracefully dressed in a warm cape and gloves, looking serene, moved and respectful, and incredibly beautiful. Moving on to the monument erected for Polish Jews who had been forced into the Warsaw ghetto, resisted the Nazis, and lost their lives, the Carters showed their respect there too.[38]

As the Polish émigré Zbig Brzezinski had argued, Carter, as a Southerner, shared common experiences with the Poles. They, like American white Southerners, had been defeated and become outcasts in their homeland, but were nevertheless patriotic and hopeful to lead their nation into forgiving and tranquil times. Human rights, and respect for all people no matter where they were from or their individual circumstances, never seemed so important.

The foul weather did not disrupt the Carters' schedule. Rosalynn had planned activities deemed suitable for a First Lady. As she toured Warsaw's Old Town in a downpour, she was surrounded by a crush of people, applauding and waving. Later, she attended a private luncheon at a children's health center that was hosted by Mrs. Edward Gierek, the wife of the Polish leader. After a discussion of care for the mentally ill and retarded, Rosalynn presented two hundred coloring books entitled "Poland" to the children who resided there.[39]

Rosalynn represented her country well at such traditional First Lady events, but she yearned to be more involved in politics and serious affairs of state. Getting her way, she soon joined Brzezinski for a spontaneous visit to Cardinal Wyszynski, the head of the Roman Catholic Church in Poland. She spent an hour and a half with the two men discussing moral and social issues, but she also brought up a sensitive political matter, prodding the Cardinal into commenting upon his relationship to the Communist regime. Wyszynski diplomatically replied that it had fluctuated, only recently becoming friendly. The Cardinal had been interned by the Communist regime in the 1950s, but he had remained patriotic and a fighter for church rights. He had met the current Communist Polish leader Edward Gierek only two months earlier when, some said, Gierek needed the support of the church in Poland's economic crisis.[40]

Gierek also needed aid from the United States. Knowing that, Carter discussed with Gierek the need for restraining arms sales and the reduction of nuclear weapons by the United States and the Soviet Union, hoping that the Soviet satellite would influence the Russians to move toward compromise. The Poles, however, needed food, grain, and meat more than a heavy dose of international politics. Taking advantage of the Polish first secretary's weakened position, Carter boldly suggested that he should visit the Cardinal more often and learn about the Christian's Prince of Peace. Taken aback, Gierek quickly explained that as a Communist he served only his fellow human beings. Carter persisted, telling him that it was never too late to believe in Jesus Christ, but he failed to make a convert.[41]

Since a majority of the Polish people were Catholic, and the Communist regime had loosened its grip on the country since the mid-1950s, the Carters "scored a considerable personal success with the public," according to the US embassy's analysis. The people of Poland yearned to be free. For the president of the United States to include Poland, a member of the Communist bloc, on his itinerary was revolutionary. The gesture was not lost on the Polish people, who gave the Carters a tumultuous welcome as they traveled in an open limousine through the streets of Warsaw. Many people in Poland and in the Carter administration, especially Brzezinski, must have been pleased with the easing of the Cold War tensions and the increasing liberalization of the economy and society in one of the least oppressive of Soviet satellites.[42] That success might have lessened Jimmy's disappointment at having to leave the country without making a Christian convert.

On the last day of the year, the Carters flew to Iran, with its much warmer climate. Arriving in Tehran on New Year's Eve with celebrations and greetings like none before given to a head of state or a king, Jimmy and Rosalynn embarked upon their visit with the shah and the empress. After an elaborate exchange of greetings at the airport, their motorcade passed a monument, several years old, which the shah explained had been built to commemorate 2,500 years of the Iranian nation. Thousands of school children and other friendly Iranians waved to them as they proceeded to their guest quarters at the royal family's summer home, Saadabad Palace, which was one of the world's most elegant residences. The imposing palace, "nestled below the white capped Alborz Mountain Range," according to a cynical pool reporter, "beats Stone Mountain in Atlanta."[43]

In a country where the female partner to the ruler often shared the spotlight, Rosalynn attracted the attention of the people and their media. In an extensive interview, she told her hosts the details of her daily life, her work for ratification of the ERA, and her involvement in promoting legislation and more enlightened public opinion about mental health. As for the president, she was his "sounding board," his goodwill ambassador, and his political partner. Like her husband, she believed that personal relations with foreign leaders, such as their hosts, made "a lot of difference in the relationships of the countries."[44]

Speaking for himself at the royal couple's Niavaran Palace, Carter met with the shah, discussed the Middle East, nuclear nonproliferation, and the threat of Soviet troops in Ethiopia. On every issue, Carter said, it was "hard for us to find differences between ourselves." King Hussein of Jordan, who had been visiting the shah, joined them briefly before they adjourned for an elegant banquet followed by New Year's Eve celebrations. They "offered toasts, drank champagne, exchanged kisses, and danced," the ebullient president of the United States recalled. Raising his glass in a toast that would become infamous, Carter said: "Iran, because of the great leadership of the shah, is an island of stability in one of the more troubled areas of the world." The British ambassador groaned that Carter's toast was "mawkish," but the shah was pleased with the "flattering terms," and the empress thought Carter's visit a good omen for the future.[45]

Returning to serious business on New Year's Day, Carter and his advisers had a short conversation with King Hussein. Carter briefed Hussein on what he thought Begin and Sadat might agree upon. He thought that for any agreement to work, it might not have to be acceptable to Syria and Iran as long as it was agreeable to the Jordanian king. After comments by Vance and Brzezinski, Carter noted that "Israel is conceding that both Jordan and Israel have claims to the West Bank." Hussein thanked Carter for the briefing and promised to do all he could to support Sadat. Carter warned Hussein, however, that there would be no easy dealing with Begin, and he would be challenged by Jewish Americans. "When U. S. Jews are roused about danger to Israel, they prevail in the media," he said.[46]

The meeting with Hussein ended abruptly when the shah arrived from Niavaran Palace, driving his own Rolls Royce with the empress "riding shotgun." Guards followed, and soon the shah was bidding farewell to the US visitors. Two hundred US citizens greeted the Carters at the airport, and one young man begged Carter, "Take me home with you." Carter replied that he was not going home, "I'm going to India." The youth, anxious to get out of Iran, said, "well, take me there," reflecting complaints from others in the crowd. As Air Force One took off, about two hundred anti-shah Iranian students picketed the White House.[47]

What none of the heads of state or diplomats knew was that the shah was dying of cancer, and already in the streets of Tehran and Paris, the forces were gathering that would overthrow him and pose an insurmountable challenge to Carter's presidency. The shah kept his fatal illness secret as he subtly tried to prepare his country internally and diplomatically for his son to inherit the throne.[48]

When the Carters arrived in New Delhi, India's prime minister M. R. Desai gave them a warm welcome. The next day, January 2, Carter addressed the Indian parliament, with a lengthy review of the relationship between the two nations, much of it tainted by the Cold War in which India leaned toward the Soviet Union. Carter drilled home once again his favorite themes: the need for nuclear disarmament and the importance of human rights. "We share many common problems. But we also share an obligation to advance human rights," he told the lawmakers of a nation where millions scarcely had basic necessities.[49]

An Indian journalist asked Rosalynn tough questions. Retaining her composure, Rosalynn answered that she believed the world was making progress in human rights, and she hoped to see more women in the US Senate and one as president. She argued that her husband had rectified past abuses by the CIA, and she praised the Indian people and reminded them of the time when Miss Lillian had served in their country as a Peace Corps volunteer. Rosalynn hoped her visit would bridge the gap of what the reporter called Americans' "colossal ignorance about India."[50]

Rosalynn joined her husband and Prime Minister Desai for a stroll through Daulatpur-Nasirabad, a village outside New Delhi. Desai insisted that such a personal visit represented the heritage of Nehru and Gandhi. Sealed off for security reasons and prepared for a festive visit, the village was ready for the fleet of black limousines that arrived in a cloud of dust in the town that had no roads. The Indian greeters presented a traditional dress to Rosalynn, which she wore as she and her husband walked among untouchables and viewed the thatched huts that were the homes of the impoverished families who cultivated mustard and barley. Horrified by the poverty she witnessed, Rosalynn felt helpless and frustrated at not being able to offer a solution. Carter and Desai discussed the local method of fermenting cow dung and water into methane gas for energy.

Desai told Carter that they would rename the village Carter Poori, or Carter Place, and Carter asked if he could adopt the village and upgrade it into a modern place. The prime minister declined, promising that the Indian government would take care of the people there. More than thirty years later, however, the village remained unchanged, although some residents did occasionally get letters from their famous guests. Carter, sometimes recalling the visit, contemplated the *Bhagavad Gita*, memories of his mother, the beauty of India, common national interests of freedom and peace, and poets and philosophers that transcended the grinding poverty and corruption that also existed there.[51]

Before leaving India on January 3, Carter and Prime Minister Morarji Desai signed the Delhi Declaration, which expressed their faith in democratic government, their hope to create "a more equitable international economic order" to "secure world peace," and their belief that "nations, like individuals are morally responsible for their actions."[52] Tension between the two democracies remained however. Determined to make his nation into a nuclear power, Desai disagreed sharply with the United States over the use of nuclear fuel for peaceful purposes only. In fact, Desai was adamant that such a restriction violated India's sovereignty and that only after all nations, including the United States and the Soviet Union, ceased producing nuclear weapons would he accept it.[53]

At their fourth stop, in Riyadh, Saudi Arabia, where the Carters arrived on January 4, Rosalynn complied with the Islamic traditions that relegated women to secondary roles. There was no place for her on the welcoming platform at the airport, and she walked a respectful six feet behind her husband on the red carpet that had been rolled out for him. During an opulent banquet for the men, Rosalynn dined in a different wing of the palace with the wife of King Khalid and the widow of King Faisal and about forty Arabian women, some of whom were professionals or students in elite US universities. Back home, Gloria Steinem and the National Organization of Women criticized Rosalynn for taking such a public subordinate position. Her press secretary defended her, noting that it was typical in many Arab nations for heads of state to walk in front of their spouses and for a host first lady to entertain visiting first ladies separately from their husbands. Rosalynn herself did not know there was any controversy until she returned home and read about it in the newspapers. With no political or social business to attend to in Saudi Arabia, she had fun visiting a museum, staying in the late King Faisal's ornate palace, experiencing the local culture, and tasting such native foods as camel's milk and local truffles.[54]

By contrast, Jimmy entered an Arab man's world where King Khalid was eager to tell him about how he governed. The king held an open court each day, allowed common men to dine at his table, and set aside time each evening for women to seek his advice. He traveled around the desert with a portable hospital that could accommodate up to one hundred patients. Khalid's half-brother, Crown Prince Fahd, who served as de facto prime minister, had more serious conversations with Carter about the Horn of Africa, the Middle East, and the oil trade. Although the Saudis' support for Sadat and his peace initiative seemed sincere, they would not make it public for fear of alienating those in the Arab world who disliked the Egyptian president.[55]

After leaving Saudi Arabia, on January 4, the Carters squeezed in a brief stop at Aswan, Egypt, to meet with President Sadat. On the ground barely an hour, Jimmy saw Sadat for the first time since his groundbreaking trip to Jerusalem and discovered that there were no differences between them on the issue of Middle East peace. Sadat was convinced that they were headed toward "permanent peace." Carter concluded that he and Sadat had a "common commitment" and would, "with God's help, make 1978 the year for permanent peace in the Middle East."[56] While their husbands talked, a driver in an armored vehicle took Rosalynn and Jehan to speed along the top of the 364-foot-tall Aswan High Dam at eighty miles per hour.[57]

Later that day, the president and his entourage landed at Orly Airport in Paris. Carter delivered an arrival speech repeating his usual concerns about the international economy, energy, arms control with the Soviet Union, peace in the Middle East, "and continuing the struggle for basic human rights, which our two nations proclaimed 200 years ago." President Valery Giscard d'Estaing gave him and Rosalynn a welcome as grand as any a Napoleon, a Lafayette, or a Woodrow Wilson might have received. Thousands waved and cheered as their motorcade passed along the Champs Elysees to the Arc de Triomphe where the two heads of state placed a wreath at the tomb of the unknown World War I soldier who represented the bravery of the French people. Afterward, the US president addressed members of various business, civic, and cultural societies at the Palais des Congres. He included a message for Western Europe that Chancellor Helmut Schmidt of West Germany did not want to hear, namely that the United States could not defend and solve the world's problems alone; it must have more cooperation and help from those North Atlantic Treaty Organization countries who had bonded together to defeat their enemies in World War II.[58]

From Paris, Carter traveled to the beaches of Normandy. There he paid an emotional visit to the site of the D-Day landings where many of the bravest of his own generation had given their lives in the final push to free Europe from the grip of Hitler's tyranny. Riding in a car with the French president, he toured the area much as Allied military and political leaders had done at the end of the war. In a speech at the Bayeux town hall, Carter reviewed

in moving detail the military and cultural ties that had bound the two nations together from their revolutions of 1776 and 1789 through two centuries of history and two major world wars. Snapping back into the present,
the two leaders boarded a fast train for Paris. During the journey, Carter informed the French president about the support among Arabs for Sadat, and
they discussed other issues as contemporary as their mode of transportation.
Past and present met again that evening at a state dinner and reception at the
Chateau de Versailles.

Rather than go to Normandy, Rosalynn, dressed in the latest Paris fashions
but striving to be more productive than pretty, spent about an hour with
Health Minister Simone Veil. She wanted to learn how France dealt with physical and mental health issues. Rosalynn was impressed also by the significant
role that the French government took in caring for the country's elderly.[59]

The next morning, January 6, after a final meeting with Giscard d'Estaing
at the Élysée Palace, the Carters departed for a day trip to Brussels, Belgium
where they attended a state luncheon, and Carter gave five speeches at various
venues. The seat of the European Communities and headquarters of NATO,
Brussels gave Carter a perfect opportunity to emphasize his country's bond
with those nations of Europe. He assured the Commission of the European
Communities that he hoped to continue with the plans they had made at
the earlier summit in London, namely to promote economic growth and
trade, work creatively with "the developing nations," and make peaceful use
of nuclear technology without the threat of nuclear proliferation. At NATO
headquarters he urged the members to become a peacekeeping institution of
equal partners.

By the end of that long day they were home, in Washington, where Jimmy
thanked Walter Mondale sincerely for managing the home front while he
and Rosalynn toured much of the world. Tip O'Neill welcomed the president
with exuberant praise. He said that Carter was "a beautiful man," who had
been "greatly misrepresented by the press." The Speaker thanked Carter for
his support in getting "an economic-stabilization act, a tax bill, minimum
wage, CETA [Comprehensive Employment and Training Act], an energy bill
in the House, and ethics legislation" passed.[60]

The year 1977 ended on a high note for the Carters, because despite unfinished key business and seething political turmoil, they were not only loved by
majorities at home and abroad, they had also met sixty-eight foreign heads
of state, had achieved 68.2% support in the House and 72.9% support in the
Senate.[61] More important, their teamwork had resulted in a remarkable new

style of presidency. Rosalynn had assumed "an awesome responsibility" to manage a staff, visit foreign countries, hold press conferences, and host state dinners. According to one reporter, she had assumed "a workload and status approaching that of head of state."[62]

Jimmy gave Rosalynn credit for being his co-head of state. At a White House reception for Polish Americans a month after they got back home, Carter said that Rosalynn's visit with Cardinal Wyszynski was the first time any First Family members from the Western nations had met with him. He joked about his attempt to convert First Secretary Gierek to Christianity and the goofs that his own translator had made. But on a serious note, he talked about the history of Warsaw "and the heroism of the people there and the courage in rebuilding that beautiful city." Ever the politician, Carter bragged about the millions of Polish Americans, the leaders of whom were assembled before him. "Dr. Brzezinski . . . is very close to me," he said with pride and a hint of emotion, "and the man who's had the most effect on my life, other than my own father [and] Admiral Rickover . . . is also from Poland."[63]

Their travels together, as well as life in the White House, tightened the bond, both personally and professionally, between Jimmy and Rosalynn. "I've been with Rosalynn more than I have in many years. We work in harmony. We're partners . . . in almost every respect," he told a reporter in early January 1978. Rosalynn thought that the presidency had not changed Jimmy. "But then I didn't expect that it would," she said in the same interview. "He is still the same strong, kind human being I fell in love with."[64]

Rosalynn, too, remained the same strong woman she had always been. Her last day in Europe must have been bittersweet. Despite the adulation she and Jimmy received in Belgium, her mind wandered to Budapest where a ceremony was taking place that she herself had hoped to lead. But it was Secretary of State Cyrus Vance and his wife Gay who led an entourage of distinguished Americans in an elaborate ceremony returning the Holy Crown of St. Stephen to Hungary. Fraught with political controversy, but charged with religious and humanitarian symbols, it was emblematic of much of what she and Jimmy, and their administration, stood for. Although both of them had wanted to be in Budapest for that occasion, neither of them was, and others would get credit for what they had done. Jimmy and Rosalynn had argued vigorously with Cy Vance to have Rosalynn lead the delegation, but ultimately, she accepted invitations from the Queen of Belgium to social events on the same day. The Hungarians who had dismissed Rosalynn as "a mere President's wife," underestimated her.[65]

FOURTEEN

The Perils of Political Courage

For months, Carter had been using the debate about the Holy Crown of St. Stephen to appeal to the people of Hungary over the heads of the Communist government. The crown had been in the custody of the United States since the end of World War II because previous presidents did not want to surrender it to a Communist dictator. By deciding to give it to the Hungarian people instead of the Communist government, Carter hoped to weaken Soviet control of Hungary.

Tradition had it that the crown had been a gift from Pope Sylvester II to King Stephen I of Hungary, later canonized as St. Stephen, when he assumed the throne in 1000 AD. It had been used in the coronation ceremonies for all the kings, except two, until the monarchy ended in 1916. Symbolic of the unity and nationhood of Hungary, the crown was an intricate creation in enamel and gold embedded with precious jewels and topped with a leaning cross. It was revered by the Hungarian people. The last freely elected Hungarian ruler, Ferenc Nagy, certain that his nation would fall under Soviet domination, asked the United States government to keep the crown safe for the Hungarian people.[1]

President Dwight D. Eisenhower ordered the crown to be placed for safe keeping at Fort Knox, Kentucky, and to be held there until Hungary was again free. Failed Hungarian revolutions in 1956 and 1966 sent thousands of Hungarian and other Eastern European refugees to the United States. They achieved citizenship and became numerous enough to form a voting bloc, and they voted for Carter in 1976. Every president from Eisenhower to Nixon, distrusting the regime in Hungary and yielding to pressure from the Eastern European voters in the United States, refused to return the crown.

The election of Carter gave new hope to those in Hungary and elsewhere who wanted the crown to go home. Secretary of State Cyrus Vance favored returning it as did two recent Hungarian defectors who held prominent academic posts in the United States—Professor Janos Radvanyi of Mississippi State University and Istvan Deak of Columbia University. Many Eastern

European immigrants and their descendants however—including Zbigniew Brzezinski—did not want the Crown to go back to their Communist-dominated homeland.

More troubling, Hamilton Jordan produced a study that proved to Carter that the Eastern Europeans who voted for him in 1976 had been vital to his election. If he did not win their votes again in 1980, he might not be reelected. More than 3,000 Hungarian immigrants, representing eighty different organizations, marched on the White House to protest the return of the crown.[2] After analyzing the reports and the evidence, Carter reasoned that relations with Hungary had improved and that returning the crown would help loosen Hungary's ties with the Soviet Union. Carter made it clear that he was giving the crown directly to the people of Hungary, not their repressive government, and he insisted that it be displayed in the state museum where it could be seen by all citizens of that nation.[3]

The transfer ceremony took place in the landmark Hungarian Parliament Building in Budapest on January 6, 1978.[4] Because Rosalynn had a meeting in Belgium that day, she was disappointed not to be able to lead the US delegation. Secretary of State Cyrus Vance, Mrs. Gay Vance, and their entourage were greeted by the Cardinal of Hungary, the Chief Rabbi, Protestant bishops, leaders of academic, scientific and cultural communities, and only a few representatives of the Hungarian state. The historic occasion marked the beginning of Hungary's departure from the Soviet orbit.[5]

The political courage that Carter exhibited when he returned the crown also served him well in various events of his professional and personal life. Carter's life was unlike that of an ordinary citizen, for in the course of a day, he might confront global issues of war and peace, chat with his son about the ratification of the Panama Canal treaties, consult with a candidate for director of the FBI, and attend a movie in the White House with Amy and her friends. Even so, the "juxtaposition of global issues and the mundane," are present in every life, Carter said, trying to prove his ordinariness.[6]

The Carter family tried to maintain normalcy by gathering in the evenings in the family dining room located in their private quarters. But it was still the White House, very unlike a private home. Murals depicted the history of the country; the meal was cooked and served by servants; and the family ate from china that had once belonged to former presidents. In fact, Rosalynn often used the china to give the family history lessons by asking questions about the president who had once used it and speculating about the tastes of that former first family. She did not add a set of Carter china to the collection, for she discovered that the set that had once belonged to Woodrow Wilson was large enough to accommodate her entertainment needs. The group around the table usually consisted of Jimmy, Rosalynn, and Amy, but sometimes Miss Lillian, Miss Allie, Chip and Caron, Jeff and Annette, and a few of Amy's young friends joined them.[7]

Personal tragedies sometimes disrupted the image of an ideal family household. With the pain of Chip and Caron's divorce still fresh, the Carters learned in January 1978 that Ham and Nancy Jordan, who were as close to them as their own children, planned to divorce. Ham's father died a month later, adding to Ham's grief and depression. Sympathetic and caring, Carter supported his young chief of staff as much as possible.[8]

The death of Senator Hubert Humphrey on January 13, 1978, inevitably carried political consequences for the president. A major ally of both Mondale and Carter, Humphrey was one of their most reliable supporters in the Senate. On January 15, Carter attended a Senate reception before the memorial service. There, he and Rosalynn found Lady Bird Johnson, Gerald Ford, Nelson Rockefeller, Henry Kissinger, and Richard Nixon, all of whom seemed a bit ill at ease until Ford broke the ice with friendly small talk. Carter greeted his old adversaries cordially but remained aloof. At the memorial service, however, he praised Humphrey gratefully: "In a time of impending social crisis, 30 years ago, his was the first voice I ever heard, a lone voice, persistently demanding basic human rights for all Americans."

The next day the Carters flew to Minneapolis to attend the funeral at Hope Presbyterian Church, and later Carter honored Humphrey by asking Congress to create the Humphrey Fellowship Program, which invited mid-career professionals from dozens of countries to study in US universities.[9]

Far less admirable than the life of Hubert Humphrey was the conduct of Billy Carter, who had begun wading into international politics in a way that further embarrassed his brother. Using gross language, he condemned the Jewish bias of the media, and worse, he planned to host a delegation of Libyan politicians and oil men. Although there was little anyone could do about this irresponsible exercise of his freedom of speech, the State Department announced in January that, if Billy were being paid as a tour guide for the Libyans, he must register as a foreign agent. Jimmy tried to ignore his brother's antics, laughing them off when possible, but he publicly dissociated himself from Billy's dealings with the Libyans.[10]

More difficult than Billy, Senator Ted Kennedy defied "strong advice" from Carter and Brzezinski about dealing with China. On a goodwill mission to

Beijing in December 1977, Kennedy had "plunged headlong into a discussion of normalization" with the Chinese foreign secretary Huang Hua and emerging leader Deng Xiaoping. The results, in Brzezinski's view, were "discouraging" in that they had frozen the Chinese into their intransigent position, risked more publicity than the administration wanted, and raised the "problems of Congressmen playing diplomatic roles." Kennedy's action undercut and weakened Carter's secret negotiations to normalize relations with that emerging superpower, a controversial maneuver that would abrogate a long-standing treaty with Taiwan but create a balance of power among the United States, the Soviet Union, and China as an impediment to nuclear war.

It became apparent that, whatever his other motives may have been, Kennedy had a secret agenda to weaken Carter however possible. Senator Joe Biden of Delaware, who had supported Carter in the campaign, later told Carter, on January 30, 1978, that there were three things he needed to know: Ted Kennedy would challenge him for the presidency in 1980; the Jewish community deeply distrusted him because he was a Baptist; and Hamilton Jordan needed a better relationship with Congress. The Jewish distrust was also based on international politics and the security of Israel as well as Carter's personal religion, but Biden knew whereof he spoke about Kennedy and Ham Jordan.[11]

Against this challenging political backdrop, Carter delivered his first State of the Union Address to Congress on January 19. The usual work of speechwriters and recommendations from cabinet members and senior staffers were eclipsed by Jimmy's own handwritten draft on a legal yellow pad and Rosalynn's annotations. Rosalynn recommended that Jimmy open his speech on a high note: "we are a strong country," followed by statistics proving they had reached their goal of reducing unemployment and inflation rates. Referring to a line where Jimmy said that we have "failed the American people" by not solving the energy crisis, she wrote "I question this," and added: "I want you to associate with success—you've done more than your share to get a good energy program. Say 'we now have an Energy Department. I've called on you, the people & Congress for help and a bill, etc.' Don't talk about failure." Rosalynn added that he should not be "too positive" either. Carter took her advice, collected that of others, and polished his speech. The advice he gave to himself on the final draft was "talk to people—acknowledge gov't limits—preach—inspire."[12]

Carter's arrival at the Capitol on January 19 proved eventful. While the members of Congress, the Supreme Court, and the cabinet, and other government officials gathered inside to hear the president speak, 2,500 farmers and others stood in the snow outside to remind Carter that they needed help.

The demonstration contrasted starkly with the pomp and ceremony of Carter's arrival in the House chamber and walk to the podium, where he delivered the speech that he and Rosalynn and others had carefully prepared. Carter laid out his top priorities for the new year: a strong energy bill, a co-ordinated economic program, approval of the Panama Canal treaties, a $25 billion tax cut, the creation of a Department of Education, and reform of the civil service system.

Remembering the people outside in the snow, Carter departed from his prepared text to recognize their plight. "What's best for farmers and their families in the long run is best for American consumers," he said. He conceded that the price of fertilizer was too high and that farmers needed the government to grant them some relief. More comfortably, Carter noted the progress of the past year in getting political prisoners released as a result of his human rights policy. The country, he also reported, was holding its own in "areas of peaceful competition with the Soviet Union," but he was pressing hard for a strategic arms limitation agreement and world peace. Senator Ted Kennedy may have winced when Carter declared his plan to submit to Congress a national health insurance plan because it was very different from one that Kennedy planned to propose.[13]

On January 20, the day after the state of union speech, which was well received by the public and the media, the Carters went home to Georgia. First, they attended a fundraiser for the Democratic Party in Atlanta organized by Bert Lance. Addressing the crowd of well-heeled fellow Georgians, Carter reminisced about growing up in Plains and joked about how as a Southerner, he sometimes felt that he needed an interpreter in Washington. Referring to the two great men of the South who were born in January, he said that one of them, Martin Luther King, Jr., "gave his life that the South and the people he loved, both black and white, might reach our full potential." The other one, Robert E. Lee, in Carter's 1978 view, was "a man who understood the values of the region," including love, humility, courage, and "duty to the high standards spoken to us by God."[14] Later that same day, Jimmy and Rosalynn traveled on to Musgrove Plantation on the Georgia coast to spend the night. Commenting that he was "about as tired as I've ever been," nevertheless, the next morning, he and Rosalynn went to Plains to attend "Uncle Buddy's funeral." Alton Carter, Mr. Earl's brother, had been like a father to Jimmy ever since Mr. Earl had died in 1953.[15]

With little time to rest or grieve, Jimmy and Rosalynn returned to Washington, where in February, Carter faced a full agenda of important matters. As was his practice, he evaluated almost every issue that came across his desk in the context of national security. Defending the United States against the Soviet Union demanded his vigilant attention. His correspondence with Secretary Brezhnev during the first two months of 1978 followed a rising curve in which the Soviet leader tried to convince Carter that his country meant no harm to the United States or its own East European satellites. Carter's polite responses became increasingly forceful until he became convinced that the Soviet Union was not to be trusted. The best hope for preventing a nuclear holocaust, Carter thought, was a strategic arms limitation agreement.

Brezhnev condemned Carter's rumored plans for a neutron bomb and placement of nuclear weapons in Western Europe. He assured the US leader that the recently launched Soviet reconnaissance satellite Kosmos 954 was for research purposes only, and he denied that the border conflict between the Cambodian state of Kampuchea and the Socialist Republic of Vietnam was "a proxy war between China and the Soviet Union." Brezhnev claimed that the Soviet Union only wanted to restore justice and peace in the Horn of Africa by helping Ethiopia, which suffered from Somalian aggression. Moreover, Brezhnev complained, in his letter of February 27, that the United States had broken its agreement of October 1, 1977, by omitting Soviet involvement in negotiations between Egypt and Israel.[16]

In his replies, Carter argued the opposite. He informed the Russian leader that the US public feared that its government was making too many concessions to the Soviets. He denied that the United States was supporting separate deals in the Middle East; he wanted a comprehensive settlement in a Geneva framework. The United States, Carter said, was not supplying weapons to either side in the African Horn dispute but was deeply troubled by Soviet and Cuban involvement. His nation, Carter said, only wanted a peaceful settlement, with all foreign military personnel removed from both Ethiopia and Somalia.[17]

While tense relations with the Soviet Union simmered, Carter achieved a major political victory at home. Leaving no stone unturned, Carter, his family, his staff, his cabinet, and key members of Congress had spent months trying to get the Senate to ratify the Panama Canal treaties. Cyrus Vance,

Ellsworth Bunker, Sol M. Linowitz, and other State Department officials made more than two hundred appearances in more than a dozen states, explaining the treaties to doubtful crowds. On the day of Hubert Humphrey's funeral, Carter himself had telephoned Aubrey K. Lucas, president of the University of Southern Mississippi, and their conversation about the need for the treaties was amplified to several hundred citizens attending a town hall meeting there.[18]

Knowing that he would need Republican votes, Carter had met with Republican Senators Barry Goldwater and Howard Baker on January 18. Goldwater had gone to Panama to talk with Torrijos and had been impressed by him, but still would not commit to the new treaties. Baker, however, was willing to cross party lines to vote for a treaty he thought necessary. Carter found him to be a "shrewd politician and sly," but one whose bipartisan cooperation did not often not serve his own self-interest.[19]

Carter prepared a statement for release early in February in which he explained the treaties to the public. Irked by a draft from his speechwriter, Jim Fallows, Carter angrily wrote the speech himself, emphasizing "we cannot give back land we have never owned." There were two treaties, he said, one dealing with the present to the end of the century, and the other guaranteeing the openness and neutrality of the canal after 1999 and giving the United States the permanent right to defend the canal. The United States, Carter emphasized, wanted a partnership, not a military confrontation, with Panama.[20]

Carter continued his efforts to try to persuade two-thirds of senators to vote for the treaties. Former President Ford helped by calling nine Republican senators: John Heinz, William Roth, Richard Schweiker, Robert Dole, Barry Goldwater, Ted Stevens, Milton Young, Robert Griffin, and Richard Lugar. Carter called fifteen Republicans himself and asked Henry Kissinger and Nelson Rockefeller to do the same, but they failed to get any new commitments.[21]

During the crucial month of February, Carter brushed aside all other important business such as the balance of power among the United States, the Soviet Union, and China to focus on the treaties. "Later—post-Panama," he told Brzezinski as he went to work on key senators.[22] Uncertain of Southern senators in his own party, he sent a handwritten note to Senator Kaneaster Hodges of Arkansas, a Democrat, asking for his vote on this "bipartisan issue." The treaties, Carter told Hodges, were supported by the Joint Chiefs of Staff, some of whom had been appointed by Republican presidents, and they had been negotiated in accord with principles established by former Secretary of State Henry Kissinger.[23] Senator Russell B. Long of Louisiana agreed with Carter and issued a strong statement in favor of the treaties.[24]

In March, two days before the Senate was to vote on the first canal treaty, Carter again went after the biggest fish of all. Not only was Senator John Stennis of Mississippi Chairman of the Senate Armed Forces Committee but he could influence his colleagues. The president promised the senator, whose home state contained one of the nation's largest ship building industries, that he would meet with him and others to discuss a five-year shipbuilding program.[25] "I understand your long-standing position on the Panama treaties," he wrote Stennis on March 14, "but as has been the case with several of your respected colleagues I hope that the prospective amendments will make it possible for you to help me."[26] Stennis kept Carter in the dark about how he might vote.

At 3 p.m. on March 16, the Senate galleries filled with anxious observers who had come to hear the contentious debate on the less controversial of the two treaties, the one that would simply guarantee the canal's neutrality. The wives of at least two dozen senators joined the chief treaty negotiators—Ellsworth Bunker and Sol M. Linowitz—in the crowded gallery. Ten members of the House, unable to find seats, had to stand. Millions of Americans listened in from their homes and offices to what was the first-ever live radio broadcast of a Senate floor debate. Among those listeners was the president in his private White House office.

Senator James B. Allen, a Democrat from Alabama who opposed both treaties, called the debate an "interesting study in human character, human frailty and human strength." Senators Baker and Church declared the treaty to be good for the nation, but Republican Strom Thurmond from South Carolina thundered that it was "the big giveaway of the century." His colleague Bob Dole of Kansas mourned that the "American people have lost." Vice President Mondale, who was presiding, announced only twenty minutes into the voice vote on the neutrality treaty, that "two-thirds of the Senate having voted in the affirmative, the resolution of ratification is agreed to." Visibly relieved, Carter still needed to get the second treaty approved.[27]

Despite Carter's attempt to win Stennis's vote, the Mississippian voted "no." The Democratic Majority Leader Robert C. Byrd of West Virginia cast the sixty-eighth and final vote in favor of the treaty, an honor bestowed upon him because he along with Republican minority leader Howard Baker had been principally responsible for shepherding the canal treaties through the daunting ratification process that he had called his personal "trial by fire." Although Byrd voted "aye," he repeated an earlier warning that no senator would find "any political mileage in voting for these treaties." His fellow West Virginia Democratic Senator Jennings Randolph agreed with him and voted "no."

The heroes of the hour were the fifteen Republican Senators who followed the lead of their Minority Leader Howard Baker, Jr., and in a show of nonpartisanship voted for the treaty. Eighteen other Republicans voted against it, for a final tally of 68–32, a two-thirds majority by only one vote. Most of the opposition came from the South and West, and Baker's vote seriously jeopardized his future political ambitions.

In a subsequent vote, 75–23, a larger number of Senators agreed to a reservation that United States troops could be used in Panama to forestall any threat to the canal's operation after the year 2000. Carter agreed to the reservation, thus improving the chances that the Senate would ratify the second treaty.

Carter declared that this extraordinary victory was a "new and promising step" toward better relations with Latin America, and that all US citizens owed "thanks to the Senate for its courageous action." He quickly wrote personal thank you notes to the senators who had supported the treaty. Among them, a small group of Southern Democrats had wrestled with their consciences and political careers before voting with the president. Senator Herman Talmadge of Georgia knew that if the Panamanians could not gain control of the canal by treaty, a small group of nationalist guerrillas might take over a tiny section of it and stop all traffic. Since that was one of the arguments the Carter people had used to justify the treaties, Talmadge latched onto it as his reason for supporting them. He also admitted that, since the president was from his state, he reluctantly supported the native son even though his constituents would not approve of his vote.[28]

Carter's thank you notes to Senators Talmadge, Russell Long, Sam Nunn, Edmund Muskie, Thomas McIntyre, Ernest Hollings, Paul Hatfield, S. I. Hayakawa, John Chafee, and others were well deserved, for, as Byrd said, their votes earned them no political advantage. Not only had they enabled Carter to achieve a nonpartisan triumph, but they had also undermined what Senator Edward Zorinsky of Nebraska called the "media's lack of integrity in trying to drive a wedge between the members of the Senate and the Administration."[29]

The second treaty, which returned control of the canal to Panama, faced the same opposition as the first. On April 18, the day the Senate was to vote, Carter worked hard to get the votes of wavering Senators S. I. Hayakawa of California, Howard Cannon of Utah, and James Abourezk of South Dakota. Carter had stayed up most of the previous night reading Hayakawa's book, *Language in Thought and Action*. Hayakawa, a semanticist and former president of San Francisco State University, was flattered the next morning when the president invited him to the White House to discuss his book and later voted for the treaty. Carter called local news editors in Salt Lake City and Mormon church leaders to help get Cannon's support. Abourezk angrily hung up on Carter when the president refused to grant his questionable requests. A strong defender of Native Americans, Abourezk apparently had a serious interest in energy legislation that diverged from the president's. Later in the day, Prince Sultan in Saudi Arabia called the president of the United States to tell him that Abourezk would support the treaty.

In the meantime, the United States and Panama prepared for massive violence in Panama if the Senate did not ratify the second treaty. Based upon CIA reports and Torrijos's warnings, Carter was convinced that the passage of the treaties was necessary to prevent a serious military engagement with Panama that would ruin "our efforts in the Middle East and Africa, SALT, and our relationship with the developing world."[30]

Both heads of state were able to breathe sighs of relief when Carter notified Torrijos that the Senate had ratified the second treaty. In a public statement, Carter declared that it was a day "of which Americans can always feel proud, for now we have reminded the world and ourselves of the things that we stand for as a nation." The country reached a decision, he said, "in the best interest of our Nation."[31] The Senate's ratification of the Panama Canal treaties, for which Carter had worked so diligently for so long, gave him one of his finest presidential moments. Carter called it "the most courageous vote ever taken by the United States Congress in the history of our country." But courage came at a price, because five Democratic and two Republican Senators failed to be reelected. One of them, Herman Talmadge of Georgia, had voted for the treaty only because he wished to support the native son president.[32] Thinking that he was getting rid of outdated colonialism, Carter had defied public opinion polls to transform his "deep conviction" into legislative success.[33]

No spouse could have been more involved, more anxious, and more helpful in winning the Senate's approval of the Panama Canal treaties than

Rosalynn. In Latin America, she had asked the heads of state she met to be prepared to approve any treaty between the United States and Panama. She had made telephone calls, had worried about the political consequences, and had collected detailed information about the treaties from Jimmy and others. Every chance she got she argued the case in favor of ratification. She had hosted a luncheon for influential people who might persuade senators to vote for the treaty, and she had persuaded the wife of Senator Thomas J. McIntyre, a Democrat from New Hampshire, to convince her husband to vote for ratification.[34]

Apart from working for ratification of the canal treaties, Rosalynn's involvement touched virtually every aspect of her husband's presidency. She solicited help from nongovernment groups to improve the quality of life in cities, raised money for and perceptions of Washington's public schools, and used her bully pulpit as First Lady to improve the quality of care at St. Elizabeth's Mental Hospital in the nation's capital.[35]

In a major speech that Rosalynn gave to the Sumter County, Georgia, Chamber of Commerce on February 4, she was candid about her life as First Lady. Referring to her attendance at the tenth anniversary celebration of the restoration of Ford's theatre, she said: "Well, there I was in the front row of Ford's Theatre with the President of the United States—looking at Abraham Lincoln's box and a picture of George Washington which had been there when Abraham Lincoln was wounded—and I said to myself, 'and God only knows how I find myself in this position!'" Despite her privileged life, Rosalynn worried about whether the people were getting the facts about energy, the economy, mental health, and other social problems. She believed, however, that Jimmy had developed a spirt of partnership between the American people and their governments. On a personal level, she told the guests at the Chamber of Commerce that day, she no longer worried about her image but cared about people. She still found time to take tennis lessons and violin lessons with Amy, and she assured her local Georgia audience that "no matter where we go we will always come back home" to Plains.[36]

Rosalynn also made time to improve life for her family in the well-lighted private section of the White House. She hired Wayne Dean of Americus to redecorate the solarium, place a small kitchen in an alcove, and brighten an inclined hallway to the solarium. She added a billiard room and transformed the hallway into an art gallery. It was a place for the family to be out of the public eye, a home within the people's house. Those spending time in the quarters included Miss Lillian, who always attracted attention for her colorful personality and deadpan remarks, but she too needed to escape the public glare. The world knew her as Miss Lillian, but Jimmy called her "Mama." On January 28, he had sent her a leather-bound copy of his inaugural address with the inscription, "Mama, thank you for helping to make this possible. Jimmy."[37]

Despite Rosalynn's down-to-earth, homebody image, as one journalist observed, Eleanor Roosevelt's highly regarded work as First Lady "cannot match that of Rosalynn." Always in close touch with her husband, she once asked him and her staff what she should do at a fundraiser for the ERA in Florida if the largest contributor asked her for a dance. The staff was divided, but Jimmy told her, with a laugh, that she should accept because "it will keep you from being a wallflower." No wallflower, Rosalynn wowed the audience at the March 1978 Gridiron dinner at Washington's Capitol Hilton by jitter-bugging with her husband to the tune of "Sweet Georgia Brown."[38]

Even when she was out of town on business, Rosalynn kept a finger on the pulse of Washington. She gave her speech to the Sumter County Chamber of Commerce the day Anwar Sadat arrived in Washington and then hurried home to the White House where she asked Jimmy for every detail about Sadat's visit. On another occasion, when passing Jimmy in the White House, Rosalynn stopped him to inquire about the latest developments, for she wanted to be able to answer questions from the public and the press accurately. To conserve time, Jimmy told her to come to the cabinet meetings and collect the information for herself. Although she had received criticism for attending one meeting a year earlier, she went again on March 13, 1978. Unintimidated by the ensuing criticism that such involvement was not appropriate for a First Lady, she defended herself: "I just sat in the back of the Cabinet Room around the edges, with Max Cleland and others who were not Cabinet level." There could be no doubt, however, that of all present at the cabinet meeting, the one who had the most and the closest access to the president was Rosalynn.[39]

With the Panama Canal issue settled, despite lingering accusations that Carter was weak on defense, Carter proved his critics wrong with a powerful speech at Wake Forest University in North Carolina. He made it clear to the Soviet Union and to the rest of the world that he intended to be tough. On that very day, a CIA satellite revealed a massive Soviet airlift of arms to the Marxist regime in Ethiopia to assist in its war against Somalia, proving that the Soviets were up to no good. In his speech Carter refuted the assertions that the United States was retreating from protecting its interests and that of its friends around the world. He emphasized that the United States would "not allow any other nation to gain military superiority over us." Strong ties with NATO, a SALT II treaty with the Soviet Union, a "superb submarine fleet," and deployment of the Trident 1 submarine missile and the M-X intercontinental ballistic missile would, he promised, make the country invulnerable to Soviet attack. The United States would use its power for peace, but Carter understood that "those who would destroy liberty are restrained less by their respect for freedom itself than by their knowledge that those of us who cherish freedom are strong."[40]

At Wake Forest, Carter also noted the relevance of the South's unique perspective on war. "Southerners," he said, "whose ancestors a hundred years ago knew the horrors of a home land devastated by war, are particularly determined that war shall never come to us again." Not only Southerners, he added, but "all Americans" understand "that we need to be resolute and able to protect ourselves, to prevent threats and domination by others." He may have irritated some in the audience by underscoring his commitment to removing entirely any "remnants of discrimination against black people." Moments after his speech, Carter departed to visit the crew aboard a "nuclear-powered aircraft carrier" in the Atlantic Ocean, where he repeated the conclusion of his speech: "we will always maintain the strength which, God willing, we shall never need to use."[41]

Juxtaposed with the controversial Panama Canal treaties, Carter's speech at Wake Forest University proved again that his emphasis on human rights would never undercut national defense. Without national defense, there could be no human rights. The rest of the world, especially the Soviet Union and China, paid attention to Carter's speech. China sent a subtle signal that it wanted a "broadened relationship" with the United States.[42]

Defense, its cost, and its utilitarian value drove many of Carter's presidential decisions. With his ability to analyze and understand weapons and weapons system, Carter was in an optimal position to use the analyses and information brought to him to make a wise decision. For example, after extensive study, and with the approval of Secretary of Defense Harold Brown, Carter announced that he would not produce the neutron bomb. Immediately accused of being soft on defense, his critics spoke in ignorance. They did not know that the United States was secretly building the stealth bomber that would make the neutron bomb unnecessary. Publicly, Carter said that he hoped the Soviets would not build a neutron bomb either and that they would cooperate on a new strategic arms limitation treaty. German

Chancellor Helmut Schmidt assured Carter that Brezhnev wanted to conclude a SALT II agreement, but Schmidt remained critical of what he perceived as the US president's inadequate defense of Europe.[43]

Unable to satisfy Schmidt, Carter directed his attention to South America and Africa. He and Rosalynn planned a seven-day trip to Venezuela, Brazil, Nigeria, and Liberia between March 28 and April 3. The issues they planned to discuss included nuclear nonproliferation, foreign oil, and the Cold War. Carter had welcomed General Olusegun Obasanjo, the president of Nigeria, to the White House the previous October, and he intended to use his visit to ask Nigeria's help in discouraging Soviet and Cuban influence in Africa. He was mindful, too, that 20% of US oil imports came from Nigeria and that the United States needed a more positive image in Black Africa. The negative image and reception that US diplomats had received in earlier visits to Venezuela and Nigeria's refusal to allow Secretary of State Henry Kissinger into their country meant that, if the Carters were successful, they would bring about a dramatic change in the US relationship to those parts of the world.[44]

Upon their arrival at Simón Bolívar International Airport in Caracas on March 28, Venezuela's president Carlos Andrés Pérez treated them to a red-carpet welcome. The Carter entourage included Secretary of State Cyrus Vance and Mrs. Vance, Zbigniew Brzezinski, Assistant Secretary of State for Inter-American Affairs Terence A. Todman, and Director of Policy Planning for the Department of State W. Anthony Lake. That gracious welcome they received was very different from the violent protests Nixon and Kissinger had faced in previous years.

From the airport, the Carters and their hosts traveled to Pantheon Plaza, where Carter delivered a short, eloquent speech in Spanish at a wreath laying ceremony at the tomb of Simón Bolívar. Declaring that he felt "the generous friendship of this great democracy," Carter said that the dream of Bolívar, the liberator of South America, was also the dream of George Washington and of "all of those who struggle today for human liberty." Meeting with former President Rómulo Betancourt, Carter welcomed the opinion that Betancourt and Pérez shared that US human rights policy was the best thing that had happened for Latin America in many years.[45]

During the remainder of their time in Caracas, the Carters attended a state dinner, he addressed the Venezuelan Congress, and he had intensive conversations with President Pérez. Rosalynn attended the official functions, where she often heard herself praised for her previous diplomatic trip to

Latin America. The two presidents found almost nothing about which to disagree. At the end of their visit, Carter and Pérez issued a joint communiqué
reaffirming their commitment to strengthening democracy, security for
the Caribbean basin, the peaceful use of nuclear energy, and cooperation in solving energy needs. Pérez promised to continue oil exports to the
United States and its allies. Before parting company, the two men signed a
Memorandum of Understanding on Narcotics and agreed to conduct future
negotiations when needed.[46]

In Brazil, where tension existed over the human rights program and US
disapproval of that country's installation of a nuclear processing plant, Carter
defused the issues with friendly speeches and long meetings with religious
and media figures. He was pleased to learn that the number of political
prisoners had declined by 90%. Although he probably had little influence on
President Ernesto Geisel, he made his point about human rights and nuclear
nonproliferation. Geisel understood that Carter took seriously the Nuclear
Non-Proliferation Act of 1978, which he had recently signed, and which he
expected countries that wished to deal with the United States to observe.
Carter glossed over disagreements with Brazil that had emerged during
his presidency, especially with regard to Israel's use and sale of US-made
weapons. In their parting statement, the presidents and first ladies politely
listed the topics of mutual concern that they had discussed and ambiguously
declared that their exchanges on wide-ranging issues had been beneficial.[47]

As the Carters were the first president and First Lady of the United States
to visit sub-Saharan Africa, much less deliver a major policy speech there,
their visit to Nigeria stirred excitement on both continents. An Australian
journalist burbled with enthusiasm that Black Africa would be seeing and
hearing "that hell-fire and damnation Baptist human rights loving gent, who
is taking steps that others before him never dared to take, because they lacked
the visionary call."[48]

After flying from Brazil to Lagos on March 31, Air Force One hung low
in the sky as it approached its landing runway in a photograph that dominated the front page of the leading Nigerian newspaper. Thousands of
cheering Nigerians, most of whom had never seen such a magnificent airplane or imagined they would get a glimpse of a US president, lined the path
Jimmy and Rosalynn would take. Ambassador Andrew Young had reversed
the image of the United States in the minds of Black Africans and paved the
way for the visit. He had brought African-American artists to Nigeria and
had confirmed Carter's commitment to Black majority rule in Rhodesia and

THE PERILS OF POLITICAL COURAGE   219

to ending apartheid in South Africa. Carter, Young thought, offered more hope for independence and justice to Black Africans than any Western leader had ever done.[49]

Although the hour was late, when Air Force One taxied to a stop at Lagos's Murtala Muhammed Airport, it was, according to the *Nigerian Tribune*, "a vivacious Jimmy Carter and his wife, Rosalynn," and daughter Amy, who stepped off the plane into "water tight security" to begin their historic "royal visit." The Nigerian army greeted them with a twenty-one gun salute, and Carter later thanked the hundreds of Nigerians who stood along the roadway to welcome him and his family. He and President Olusegun Obasanjo exchanged complimentary greetings before proceeding to the State House Marina, where the Carters and their diplomatic entourage were greeted by the US ambassador to Nigeria, Donald B. Easum, and members of the US community. After an hour, Jimmy, Rosalynn, and Amy retired to an elegant suite.[50]

On the morning of April 1, Carter and Obasanjo reviewed Nigerian troops, conferred with both US and Nigerian officials, made remarks to the press that suggested a close friendship, and placed a wreath at memorials for Nigerian soldiers who died in both world wars and the Nigerian civil war. In the afternoon Carter delivered a major policy address at the National Arts Theatre. Rejecting the "past aloofness," of the United States, he declared that his country and Nigeria now shared a future. With words never before heard in Africa from a Western leader, the White Georgian proclaimed, "We share with you a commitment to majority rule and individual human rights . . . economic growth . . . a commitment to an Africa that is at peace, free from colonialism, free from racism, free from military interference by outside nations, and free from the inevitable conflicts that can come when the integrity of national boundaries is not respected."[51]

Carter rejected the idea that the United States and the Soviet Union were in a contest for influence in Africa; he condemned Soviet and Cuban military intrusions on the continent, and demanded an end to apartheid in Rhodesia and South Africa. His public message grew out of a private meeting with Obasanjo in which they had discussed Rhodesia. Both feared that a civil war might drag the United States and the Soviet Union into military conflict with each other.[52] Later in the evening, the US visitors relaxed at a performance by the Nigerian Army dance troupe.

The next day, Sunday, April 2, began with the US and Nigerian leaders attending a Baptist church service. President Obasanjo read the Scripture, and Carter gave a prayer and led the congregation in a responsive reading. Carter thought that if all Christians could get together "with an enlightened pope," they could have a profound impact on "human rights throughout the world." The music reminded the Carters of their beloved Black gospel songs back in Georgia. As they left, one journalist noted that the First Lady's hips swayed gently back and forth in rhythm with the music.[53]

In the afternoon the presidential parties boarded *Maris III*, a cruise ship that took them to Tin Can Island where they enjoyed more entertainment, viewed the harbor, and boarded a visiting US Navy ship. The day ended with a state dinner and the two heads of state signing a joint communiqué underscoring their mutual commitment to "the principles of the United Nations Charter, particularly those concerning the importance of human rights in all societies."[54]

Both US and Nigerian journalists understood the significance of that trip. The United States needed Nigeria, a current member of the UN Security Council, to mediate African disputes, especially the one between Ethiopia and Somalia. More important, Nigeria, one of the OPEC nations, was the second largest supplier of foreign oil to the United States. Because the oil-rich Arab nations were threatening to impose an oil embargo on the United States and its allies, Carter wanted to keep Nigerian oil available in case he needed it. He also used his trip to Nigeria as a bully pulpit in an African country to denounce apartheid and white racism in South Africa and to criticize the Soviet Union for its effort to control African countries. Carter also wanted to honor Africa's expectations from the "leading democratic state and the most powerful nation on earth."[55]

Back home, Blacks and other US voters remained unimpressed. On April 3, Carter's hometown newspaper ran an article by Reverend Joseph Lowery, the president of the Southern Christian Leadership Committee, who contended that Carter's efforts to help Blacks were feeble.[56] The Soviets condemned Carter's trip as a complete failure, and a cynical anonymous writer in the Nigerian political magazine *Afriscope* said that Carter would "tell them anything as long as the oil keeps flowing."[57]

During the Carters' short visit to Liberia, their final stop on their tour, President William Tolbert declared a national holiday in their honor. Founded by former slaves from the United States, Liberia had a special meaning for the US visitors. In addition, Tolbert was a Baptist preacher and the first Black to head the World Baptist Alliance. The Carters felt at home in a Christian nation with a democratic government and many descendants of Black Americans. At a welcoming ceremony, Carter spoke of the countries' long friendship. "Liberia was born out of mankind's eternal desire for freedom," he said. "The free black people who came from America to this beautiful coast" joined with others "to form the first independent republic in Africa."

The first US president to visit Monrovia, the capital of Liberia, Carter declared that his country believed in "economic justice," "respect for human rights," and "a search for peace." President Tolbert, after saying that Carter's visit "brightens the horizon of our hopes," invited his guests "to rise and raise your glasses with me and drink lustily" to the president of the United States and lasting cooperation between the two nations.

Although some might have drunk lustily, Jimmy and Rosalynn did not. A sober president praised the leadership of Tolbert and thanked "the wonderful people of the great nation of Liberia" before he, Rosalynn, Amy, and the others in their entourage boarded Air Force One for home.[58]

FIFTEEN

The Tightrope to Peace

After returning to the United States, Jimmy and Rosalynn resumed the battle they had begun earlier in the year to keep Israel on track for peace with Egypt and to garner Jewish support at home. Carter's distrust of Begin and the volatile controversy over the Palestinian question haunted him. Israel attempted to avoid the Palestinian question, but when Carter opposed creation of a separate Palestinian state, his support in the Jewish community rose dramatically. It dropped again, however, because of speculation that Carter might sell F-15 fighter planes to Saudi Arabia and Egypt. Israel's participation in a peace conference seemed to hang in the balance, based on how much that tiny nation could trust Carter to keep it stronger than its enemies.[1]

Rosalynn helped to win Jewish-American votes: her combination of feminine softness, a strong will, and political toughness appealed to Jewish women. Addressing a reception for the National Council of Jewish Women in the East Room of the White House on January 17, 1978, she had told them that she and they had much in common—the same problems, the same elders, families, mental health concerns, and the need to reform cities. "I support your efforts," she had said, "and I hope that you will support mine," in a thinly veiled appeal for votes and endorsement of the president's effort to bring peace to the Middle East.[2]

A week later Rosalynn spoke to 425 Americans going to Israel under the auspices of the Friendship Force, a nonprofit cultural organization that she had helped organize. They would live and work with Israeli families, learn from each other, and develop emotional ties. Likewise, she spoke to the 425 Israelis coming to the United States under the same program. "The Friendship Force," she said, "can contribute to understanding and peace in the world."[3]

Food, Carter thought, like friendship, was essential for peace. He tackled the problem of world hunger by appointing a Presidential Commission to study it and make policy recommendations. Chaired by Panama negotiator Sol M. Linowitz, it included famous actress Shirley MacLaine, his mother and Peace Corps veteran Lillian Carter, and Norman Borlaug, the recipient of the 1970 Nobel Peace Prize who had devoted his life to improving agricultural production. Other commission members included D. W. Brooks, Carter's friend from Georgia who led Gold Kist, Incorporated, which assisted farmers and operated on Brooks's premise that ending hunger would bring international peace; Republican Senator Robert Dole from the farm state of Kansas; and Carter intimate Peter Bourne. Access to sufficient food, Carter thought, was a basic human right, and without human rights there could be no peace.[4]

It was not food but warplanes that riled the Jewish-American community who questioned the president's approach to peace with Arab countries. On January 26, the Jewish Community Council of Washington notified Carter that it categorically disapproved of his intention to sell sixty F-15 fighter-bombers to Saudi Arabia.[5] Brzezinski warned the president that the sale would impede the peace process and there was no guarantee that the Saudis would never use the planes against Israel. Carter explained that the sale would not weaken the Israeli military, which was at an all-time high level of combat readiness. Both Republican Senator Howard Baker, who had rendered vital assistance with the Panama Canal treaties, and new Democratic Senator Muriel Humphrey promised to support the Saudi arms bill.[6]

Leaving the arms sale debate for more analysis, Carter planned meetings with both Sadat and Begin. Anwar and Jehan Sadat came to Camp David on February 3, 1978, but, exhausted after their long trip from Egypt, via Morocco and Washington, they retired after supper. The next day, Carter, Mondale, and Sadat had a lengthy discussion about the status of peace talks. Sadat said that the president of Romania, Nicolae Ceausescu, had told him that Begin desired genuine peace and was strong enough to implement it. Sadat was convinced that the Israelis wanted to negotiate directly with Arab leaders, to be recognized as a permanent state, and to live in peace, all of which he was willing to give them. However, if Begin raised the issue of Israeli settlements in the Sinai and a proposal for self-rule quite different from what Carter and Sadat had expected, Sadat said he would announce his withdrawal from further discussions.

Carter and Mondale persuaded Sadat to be more positive and continue discussions if Israel would abide by UN Resolution 242 and give up her illegal settlements. Sadat, however, made it clear that he favored joint sovereignty over the one-mile-square area that contained the various holy sites in Jerusalem, an issue that could derail the peace talks. After their long and intense conversations, Carter felt that he better understood why Sadat wanted the peace process to move forward quickly, something that Carter too desired. They did not know it at the time, but Begin favored it as well. As a gesture of understanding and friendship, Sadat told Carter that he wanted to help him to get "the U.S. Jew lobby (as he refers to it) off my shoulders."[7]

The Carters and the Sadats spent five days together engaging in recreational activities as well as political discussions. "May God protect you," Sadat said in farewell. "May God protect my dear friend, President Carter, Rosalynn, and his family." Rarely, if ever, had two presidents and two First Ladies, one couple Christian and the other Muslim, bonded so tightly, both personally and professionally.[8]

That friendship might have made it easier for Carter to decide about an arms sale to an Arab nation. Senator Abraham Ribicoff of Connecticut, who supported Carter, met with the Senate behind closed doors and explained that it was important to sell the planes to Saudi Arabia because the United States needed its oil. He told those at the secret meeting that Carter had promised that air superiority would always remain with the Israelis and that the planes that went to Saudi Arabia would not have sufficient range to reach Israel. Ribicoff's fellow Senators applauded his speech; they knew that it required courage for a Jewish Senator to speak frankly in support of the sale of warplanes to an Arab country.[9]

Carter announced that he would make the sale and ask for Senate approval. The political fallout was immediate. He declared he was still committed to Israel's security, and Brzezinski met with Jewish officials to try to convince them that US foreign policy was in the best interest of both the United States and Israel. Mark Siegel, the administration's liaison with the Jewish community, was appalled by the decision to sell the planes to the Arabs; when he occasionally delivered a speech trying to explain the administration's policy, he was hissed at and booed by Jewish audiences.[10]

Despite Israeli disapproval of the sale, Carter hoped that Begin might be more flexible when he came to Washington in about two weeks. In the meantime, Israeli Defense Minister Ezer Weizman arrived for preliminary discussions. Weizman, Carter noted, was "level headed" and better informed about Egypt and the outside world than the prime minister. Carter assured him that he had no intention of pressuring Begin, a strong person and leader of an independent nation, into a decision about the Palestinians. Carter saw his role only as mediator. "We do not and never have favored an independent

Palestinian nation," he declared, knowing that such a position would appeal to the Israeli prime minister.[11]

Carter's difficulties in pursuing Middle East peace deepened, however, on March 11, when a radical faction within the PLO, intent on derailing any peace talks, attacked an Israeli coastal road. Leaving from the port of Tyre in Lebanon, the PLO terrorists killed US photographer Gail Rubin, a niece of Senator Abraham Ribicoff, and then hijacked a bus, killing thirty-five Israeli civilians and wounding seventy-one more. Three days after the highway massacre, Israel, against Carter's wishes, retaliated by attacking PLO bases in southern Lebanon. According to Carter, the Israelis destroyed "hundreds of villages, killing many people, and making two hundred thousand Lebanese homeless." Carter informed the Israelis that the United States would introduce a resolution in the UN calling for their withdrawal and for UN forces to keep the peace in Lebanon. He was particularly irked because Israel was using US equipment to invade a foreign country. Six weeks after the Israeli raid, Carter planted a Cedar of Lebanon on the White House grounds and mourned the suffering Lebanon had endured.[12]

The US condemnation of Israel's raid on Lebanon hung like a dark cloud over Washington when Begin arrived for his scheduled visit. During a ninety-minute meeting with Begin on March 21, with large groups of advisers on both sides, Carter referred to their ties of blood, history, and the pursuit of justice. But he warned Begin that "Israel's determination to keep political control over the West Bank and Gaza" was an obstacle to peace. He explained to Begin that Sadat was not calling for full withdrawal from those areas or for a Palestinian state. Carter secretly noted that he was discouraged by the "hardening of positions" that he saw in Begin.[13] Their talks were characterized by harsh exchanges, causing Carter to believe that peace "seems far away." As Begin delivered a public, falsely optimistic speech in Washington, a very glum Carter stood politely at his shoulder.[14]

While the Begin debacle puzzled Carter, he also had to deal with Senator Ted Kennedy about national health insurance. Both Kennedy and Carter wanted it, but Kennedy and Carter's secretary of health, education, and welfare did not agree on how to bring it about. The divisive issue between Califano, as Carter's spokesperson, and Kennedy was how to fund such a massive federal health program and the question of whether they could get Congressional approval. On April 6, 1978, Carter and Califano had "a heated meeting" with Kennedy, Douglas A. Fraser, head of the United Auto Workers, George Meany, head of the AFL-CIO, and other labor representatives, all of whom pressured Carter for a healthcare package that he thought would be impossible to deliver. Carter told the others to "let us" work it out and in May he would present principles for which he himself, and no one else in the administration, would be responsible. Aware of Kennedy's plan to campaign against him for the Democratic nomination in 1980, he noted in his private diary, "I believe Kennedy was posturing before the labor leaders."[15]

The bickering between Carter and Kennedy about national healthcare continued into the summer. Carter told the senator that he wanted a comprehensive health program, but because of the cost, it would take years to accomplish. Kennedy disagreed and wanted a bill before the fall elections. When Kennedy held his own press conference to blast the administration, it backfired, making Kennedy look like an irresponsible liberal who favored an expensive system, Carter said, and Carter's plan seem practical.[16]

Oblivious to the growing tension between Kennedy and Carter, some Jewish-American leaders tried to persuade Begin to be flexible and to get the so-called American "Jewish lobby" to relent with its attacks on the president. White House Counsel Robert Lipshutz, Domestic Policy Adviser Stuart Eizenstat, and others delivered numerous speeches to largely Jewish audiences urging Begin to moderate his demands and consider Carter's peace effort. Lipshutz made a particularly impassioned peace appeal on April 8 at The Temple in Atlanta, the place of worship on Peachtree Street for those Jewish Georgians who went to Washington with Carter.[17]

As stubborn as the Israelis, Carter proceeded with the arms sale to the Arabs. During an Oval Office visit on April 20, David Rockefeller told Carter that the Saudis attached the utmost importance to buying the F-15s. Carter asked him to pass that information on to key senators whose help he would need to approve the sale.[18] Since the powerful Chairman of the Board of the Chase Manhattan Bank had been instrumental in smoothing the path for his Democratic nomination and ultimate victory in 1976, Carter would not ignore him.

Brotherly love, more than power, cemented the relationship between Carter and Sadat. In a handwritten note dated April 24, Sadat addressed Carter as "brother" and promised to help the United States assume "a pivotal role in bringing a peaceful settlement in the Middle East." He believed that the strength of "Brother Carter's" faith and soundness of judgment would enable him to overcome all obstacles. "I pray to God almighty," Sadat wrote, "to give you the strength and support you are entitled to in the discharge of your awesome responsibilities."[19] Sadat, who favored scuttling plans for a Geneva conference that involved several Middle Eastern nations and the Soviet Union, realized that peace between Israel and Egypt would depend upon the skill of Carter as mediator. For a peace conference to work, it would have to be Carter's party.[20]

Both sides might call upon their god, but Begin remained unconvinced of Carter's judgment. Jewish Americans, too, were disillusioned and angry with Carter. Some of them thought he openly favored the Arabs and had been grossly rude to Begin.[21]

Rosalynn trusted her husband's judgment, but she avoided public comment on Jimmy's dilemma and engaged in mental health and women's issues. The President's Commission on Mental Health presented its report on April 1, 1978, the culmination of several drafts on which Rosalynn had made numerous annotations. Carter liked its recommendations for a federal grant program, supplements to existing services, community efforts, the reduction of numbers of state-operated large mental hospitals, federal investments in research, and the inclusion of mental health coverage in all health insurance programs, including Medicaid and Medicare. He particularly liked the fact that it called for only a modest increase in funding and did not recommend new programs. Carter directed Secretary of Health Education and Welfare Joseph Califano to draft a law that would implement the commission's recommendations.[22]

Rosalynn, who was pleased with the results of the committee's work and its immediate impact, did not always agree with all of Jimmy's appointments. She particularly disagreed with his choice of Congresswoman Bella Abzug to co-chair the National Advisory Committee on Women. Carter was acting upon the advice of his special assistant Midge Costanza when he named the controversial and outspoken Representative from New York to that position. Rosalynn reluctantly accepted the appointment once she was convinced Bella could help them win reelection in 1980. Carter then sent a cryptic note to Costanza saying that it was okay with him for the committee to consist of about forty members, including "Bella & Lesbians."[23]

Rosalynn, whose interests encompassed more than women's rights, attended her third Cabinet meeting on April 24, 1978, joining twenty-four others in the back of the room who were there as advisers or assistants to Cabinet members. She was pleased to learn that her husband was ready for a tough fight with Congress over the Middle East arms sales package and that he planned to lift the arms embargo on Turkey, strengthen NATO, and slow down the rate of troop withdrawal from South Korea.[24]

Carter also reviewed the status of the Marshall Islands in the Micronesia area of the Pacific Ocean. The United States had occupied and administered the islands since World War II, but many of the people who lived there were getting restless and asking for home rule. Carter directed that the people who lived there be allowed to "freely determine the nature of their future association with the U.S." and terminate the trusteeship agreement by 1981. The United States would retain the use of the Kwajalein Missile Range for purposes of its security interests. Although negotiation of the agreement dragged on and it was not signed before the end of his presidency, the attention and detail Carter gave to this little-known issue reveals in microcosm how much he understood and how all such events were placed in his master plan for governing the country and setting it up as an example for the world.[25]

Pro-Israel demonstrators, however, did not think that Carter treated Israel with the same fairness he afforded the Marshall Islands. They picketed the White House, carrying signs that read "Aid to Israel! Best Investment for America," and "Hell No to the PLO!" When he had announced that he would sell warplanes to an Arab nation he had lost more of the Jewish vote. Many of those voters, including some among the 75% who had voted for him in 1976, thought Carter was betraying them with his criticism of settlements on the West Bank and his plan to sell war planes to Egypt and Saudi Arabia.[26]

Carter fought back. Grudgingly, he met with Begin privately for thirty minutes at the White House on the first day of May. Carter guessed that Begin, "a small man with limited vision," would agree to conditions that could bring peace to Israel. Carter planned to bring the maximum pressure possible to bear upon the Jewish leader. To mark the thirtieth anniversary of Israel's founding, Carter hosted a White House reception for Begin and 1,200 rabbis, a thousand of whom had not been invited. The Baptist president and the Jewish prime minister gave short, emotional speeches and shook hands with each rabbi. Carter announced that he was forming a commission to establish a memorial to the victims of the Holocaust. He appointed Elie Wiesel, the great humanitarian and survivor of that horror, to chair the thirty-four member commission.[27] Also, to appease Begin, Carter removed discussion of Jerusalem from the peace negotiations, because he feared the disputants would never agree on whether to divide or share the city that was holy to Christians, Jews, and Muslims.[28]

Meanwhile, the Israelis and Jewish-American lobby waited to learn how the Senate would vote on the arms sale. When the Senate approved the sale on May 15, the White House was bombarded with both condemnations and approvals. Averell Harriman, the mentor of Cyrus Vance and former ambassador to the Soviet Union, was delirious with excitement. He wrote to Carter congratulating him on his "historic victory in the Senate." He added, with emphasis, that the "*Israeli lobby was defeated for the first time to my knowledge. This is not only in the interest of the United States but of Israel as well.*"[29] Many Jewish Americans disagreed, and they, and their sympathizers, filled Hamilton Jordan's mail with hate letters.[30] Sadat sent messages to senators thanking them for the aircraft sale, but Begin declared that the Senate vote was a blow to Israel's security and undermined its special relationship with the United States.[31]

Carter thanked Senator Abraham Ribicoff for his courageous leadership and great speech supporting the sale. "The Republicans really came through," Carter wrote, and he was pleased that the aftermath was not as bad as he had feared. He thought the sale was interpreted not as a wedge between Begin and himself, but as "a defeat for the Israeli lobby." In letters to other members of Congress, Carter argued that the sale was in the best interest of Israel because it would facilitate the peace process and that, since it was essential for the defense needs of a "firm Friend," Saudi Arabia, it contributed to the national security of the United States.[32]

In another controversial decision that he hoped would enhance peace in the Middle East and give the United States another important ally, Carter announced that he would lift the arms embargo on Turkey. He telephoned Prime Minister Bulent Ecevit on May 31, 1978, to tell him that Turkey was crucial to the security of the United States, and that he would remove the arms embargo and reopen normal relations. Carter's action was a direct response to the Soviet threat, but he also intended it as support for a friendly country where Jews and Arabs might peacefully co-exist. Lifting that embargo made German Chancellor Helmut Schmidt nervous, however, for he did not trust a well-armed Turkey and he also did not think that Carter was giving adequate support to Western Europe.[33]

During the month of May, Rosalynn was making history too. Prepared to answer questions and defend her husband wherever she went, she accepted the Eleanor Roosevelt Award from a group in Kansas City as the woman who most exemplified the values of women in the United States. She went to Austin, Texas, to meet Lady Bird Johnson and tour the LBJ Library, and she addressed the Hogg Foundation for Mental Health at the University of Texas about their shared commitment to improving care for the mentally ill.[34]

Carter gave Rosalynn plenty to talk about. That spring he finalized two farm programs, which set aside 10% of feed grain for future sale and increased federal storage payments for the farmer-owner grain reserve program. He also resolved a coal miners' strike in Ohio that had been going on for three months: after he threatened to invoke the Taft-Hartley Act to require miners to return to work, they ended their strike and thus alleviated the energy crisis in a small way.[35] Although coal remained a vital component in the country's energy needs, Carter continued to look for better sources. In Golden, Colorado, on May 4, 1978, he announced that he would set aside $100 million for solar research during the following year.[36]

Celebrating spring with social events, as well as progressive presidential edicts, Jimmy and Rosalynn threw a White House lawn party in late April for the members of Congress and their spouses. More than 1,000 people attended the picnic and listened to a piano concert by Andre Kostelanetz, the Russian-born pianist who blended popular and classical music in style and presentation; his final piece, Tchaikovsky's *1812 Overture*, was timed with a huge fireworks display. The following month, the Carters hosted the White House Jazz Festival, a celebration of jazz that had begun during the Kennedy administration. More than fifty musicians, including Dizzy Gillespie, Stan Getz, and John Lewis entertained the Carters, the vice president, and members of the Cabinet. For the final number, Dizzy Gillespie invited Jimmy to the stage to join him in singing "Salt Peanuts." The Carters' love of music, virtually all kinds but especially classical, provided them with relaxation and demonstrated to the country that they were educated, sophisticated people.[37]

The calming influence of music helped Jimmy deal with the rigors of his job. The CIA report on human rights for June 1978 painted a bleak picture. The Soviet Union had denied the wife of prominent Russian scientist and human rights activist Yuri Orlov permission to visit her husband in prison; on May 15 he had been convicted for chairing the Moscow Helsinki Group, which for the past two years had been documenting Soviet infractions of the human rights clause in the Helsinki Accords. Both Carters thought that he was not only a political prisoner, but also a victim of his attempt to promote human rights in Russia. The CIA also reported that in Ukraine two daughters of imprisoned Baptist leader Georgiy Vins were refused permission to emigrate to Canada. After Carter had confronted Soviet Ambassador Gromyko in a three-hour meeting, he concluded that Gromyko had only told him "outright lies" based on whatever Soviet policy was at the time.[38] Elsewhere in

Eastern Europe, Latin America, Pakistan, and South Africa, small numbers of political and religious dissidents were being arrested, flogged, and sometimes mutilated and executed.[39]

Carter thought that his ability to deal with such gross human rights abuses, as well as other major foreign policy issues, was enhanced by the information and advice he received from both National Security Advisor Brzezinski and Secretary of State Vance. The press, however, made a major issue of the disagreements between Vance and Brzezinski and used it to assault Carter for being weak and indecisive. Vance, who was disturbed by the news stories and what he thought was Brzezinski's excessive power, approached Carter "in a very friendly way" on June 1 to discuss the "fact that we had too many voices speaking on foreign policy." Carter agreed and promised to "put a clamp on so many diverse voices."[40] Carter, as the final arbiter, saw the different opinions of Brzezinski and Vance as helpful, and Brzezinski ignored the stories about his conflicts with the secretary of state. Rosalynn stayed out of the fray, but she leaned more toward the hawkish Brzezinski.

The difference between Vance and Brzezinski was more one of style than substance, a clashing of egos, and, as one scholar wrote, expressive of "the philosophical schizophrenia of the president." With his engineer's mind and pragmatic approach to politics, Carter analyzed issues one by one. Dovish in his commitment to peace and human rights, he could also be hawkish in his equal commitment to military superiority and the use of both economic and military power for national security. Since he made the decisions himself, sometimes more in alignment with the more dovish Vance, sometimes with the more hawkish Brzezinski, he saw no reason that the two men should be in conflict with each other. Vance saw it differently. He believed that Brzezinski took advantage of his closeness to the president to infringe upon the duties of the State Department.[41] Since Carter thought that neither Vance nor Brzezinski had any authority independent of the president, any real or imagined dispute between the two of them would not affect his final foreign policy decisions.

Carter turned to both Vance and Brzezinski for advice about Iran and Afghanistan. Soviet activity in Afghanistan frightened the shah of Iran, whose borders were at stake. Uneasy about the faithfulness of the United States, the shah asked Carter frankly if Iran could count on him. "Let me assure you," Carter replied on June 2, "of the firm United States commitment to the defense of our friends and allies all over the world from aggression in any quarter."[42]

Backing up his promise with action, Carter prepared a major policy speech on United States-Soviet relations that he intended to deliver at the Naval Academy's commencement a few days later. As was his practice, he wrote the first draft of his speech in longhand on a yellow legal tablet before he sought advice from Vance and Brzezinski, as well as Harold Brown, Ham Jordan, Walter Mondale, Andrew Young, Stansfield Turner, and Rosalynn. All of them, except Rosalynn, agreed with only minor edits to what he had written. Rosalynn's handwritten notes revealed her hawkish ire with the Soviet Union, and Carter included some of her ideas in the final draft.

When Carter delivered his speech at his old alma mater's one hundred and twenty-eighth commencement on June 7 in the Naval-Marine Corps Memorial Stadium, he took his toughest stand yet with the United States' powerful Cold War enemy. He told the Soviets that they must choose between cooperation and confrontation and that the United States would meet them on either field they chose. But he reminded his military audience, US citizens, and Soviet leaders that the United States was stronger militarily, politically, economically, and socially because it stood for justice and freedom.[43]

On that warm summer day in Annapolis, Carter joked with his audience that thirty-two years ago he was thinking more about marriage than world events, and he did not remember anything that Admiral Chester Nimitz said at his own graduation. Nor did he dream then that someday he would come back as president of the United States. After the ceremony, he and Rosalynn went to the room he had occupied as a First Classman in Bancroft Hall, a coveted corner room on the third floor, number 2315. They visited the chapel where he had taught Sunday School, then viewed the crypt of navy hero John Paul Jones. "I felt at home," Carter sighed.[44]

As Carter was giving the commencement address at the Naval Academy extolling the virtues of the military power and goodwill of the United States, the famous Russian dissident writer Alexander Solzhenitsyn was painting a very different picture at Harvard University's commencement. An estimated crowd of more than 20,000 listened to him proclaim that the human soul longed for a higher, spiritual existence than that of the decadent West. Solzhenitsyn had received the Nobel Prize for literature in 1970 and become renowned for his exposure of the cruelties in Russian society. After his country expelled him in 1974, he had settled in Vermont, where conservative politicians and religious evangelicals, who mistakenly thought he was one of them, welcomed him. In *The Gulag Archipelago* (1973) he criticized the Communist government and exposed the Soviet Union's forced labor camp system. Although he enjoyed personal and publishing freedom in the United States, he excoriated its decadence that dampened the human spirit.

Speaking at Harvard, Solzhenitsyn explained that the West did not understand the Russia that was in Communist captivity. The Western world, he said, had lost its "civil courage," was legalistic, and dominated by a press that wielded more power than the government. On the other hand, Russia, because of its intense suffering, had achieved an ethereal development superior to the "spiritual exhaustion" of the United States. People in the West had become materialistic and intellectually blind to the crimes of Communism. If his comments about the West and his host nation were taken literally, they invited a rebuttal.[45]

Solzhenitsyn's speech stuck in the craw of the very aggressive First Lady. Along with her husband and millions of other Americans, Rosalynn Carter was working to make sure the United States was not the spiritual and political weakling the distinguished Russian alleged it was. Outraged by the Russian novelist's allegations, Rosalynn began to look for an opportunity to refute his arguments.

Other business pushed to the forefront as Rosalynn bided her time. Jimmy hosted a working dinner on June 13 with the prime minister of India, and he signed legislation that changed oil entitlement regulations to the satisfaction of the governor and oil workers of California. He probably smiled mischievously when his feisty "Rosie" graciously accepted *The Ladies Home Journal* Woman of the Year Award on June 15.[46]

Rosalynn got her chance to settle the score with Solzhenitsyn on June 20 when she addressed the National Press Club in Washington. The heart of her country's strength was for people to serve one another, she said. "The spaciousness of mind and spirit which exists in America is unique," she declared, in a veiled response to the Russian writer. "I've noticed a great deal of commentary about the commencement speech of a Soviet intellectual who takes the point of view that we have grown weak, cowardly, and spiritually exhausted," she said, but "I reject these observations." In her distinctively quiet but firm way, she fired back: "Solzhenitsyn says that he can feel the pressures of evil across our land. Well, I don't sense that pressure of evil. Edmund Burke once observed that the only thing necessary for evil to triumph is for enough good men to do nothing."

"It simply cannot be said," Rosalynn asserted to the delight of the journalists who had gathered to hear her, "that good men and women are doing nothing in our country today. There is a pervasive desire among Americans to lead a useful life, to correct the defects of our society, and to make our nation even greater than it already is." "I know this," she told her audience; "fifty millions of us are volunteering. . . to fill a broad range of human and social needs." "This is not the sign of a society that's lost its spirit." Rosalynn noted that her country had given billions of dollars in foreign aid to those in need, and it was always there when a natural disaster struck any place in the world. Such generous actions were not a sign of "unchecked materialism," she argued. Furthermore, private individuals, corporations, and foundations gave more than $35 billion a year to charitable organizations. Finite government resources could not meet unlimited needs, she declared, but "people in our country want to contribute."

In a question and answer session following her speech, Rosalynn had fun sparring with her audience of journalists and communications professionals. She insisted that, despite reports to the contrary, she got along well with Jimmy's mother and admired Bella Abzug. If Amy married a Republican, Amy would still be her daughter, she said. As Jimmy's closest advisor, she laughed as she confessed that *she* had solved all of the country's domestic problems, and that she had done her job as chief foreign policy adviser so well that Jimmy could fire Vance, Brzezinski, and Young. Making certain that her audience understood that she was joking, she continued that Jimmy ought to appoint "brother Billy" to replace them.[47] Her joke brought down the house and capped her memorable answer to Solzhenitsyn.

Jimmy, listening at his office in the White House, recorded in his diary that Rosalynn "did very well and got excellent publicity because she answered [Alexander] Solzhenitsyn's attack on the quality of Americans." One reporter observed that Rosalynn, sitting at the head table, elegant and delicate, did not look like the top adviser to the president. Her soft Georgia accent and feminine appearance belied her power, knowledge, and wisdom. Liz Carpenter, the former press secretary for Lady Bird Johnson, told the president, "Jimmy, Please unleash Rosalynn. She has a great grasp, an ability to humanize and she can bring attention to a program."[48]

Rosalynn had never been leashed, nor was there much chance that she could be. After the National Press Club luncheon she went back to her office in the East Wing of the White House and responded to a letter from Aliza Begin. Aliza wanted her to help a Russian Jewish dissident, Ida Nudal, who had actively defied Communist authorities and launched numerous efforts to help Soviet Jews. Forcibly separated from her family and charged with "malicious hooliganism," Nudal faced a rigged trial in Moscow. Rosalynn told Aliza that the United States was very concerned about Ida and that her name would be raised by Secretary Vance and any US official representatives who could "demonstrate American concern and our continuing support for those who wish to exercise their just rights under the Helsinki Final Act."[49]

Rosalynn wielded more clout in the White House than she did in the Soviet Union. When she targeted Joseph Califano, he was doomed. She recommended people she admired for appointment to his committees, but Califano politely ignored her.[50] Rosalynn's chief ally in this battle, as in all battles, was her husband, the president. After visiting the Secretary, Carter wrote in his diary that "What has existed in HEW is nauseating—lack of enforcement of the law and no administration of very costly programs." He cited the example of how Califano never asked students to repay their loans, which at some colleges amounted to 80% default rates. Since Califano seemed to agree with Kennedy about national health insurance, Carter had another reason to dislike him.[51]

Carter had more reason not to trust his brash, young speechwriter, James Fallows. On June 21 Fallows resigned because, he said, he did not have adequate access to the president, and he was disappointed that Carter was not the liberal he had envisioned. In his polite resignation letter, he did not mention his grievances but simply said that he wanted to be his own journalist.[52]

Shortly before Fallows resigned, Carter had just returned from Fort Hood, Texas, where he had been treated to a firepower demonstration. He wrote to the general in charge that he personally appreciated "our fine troops." "They made me proud," he continued.[53] Carter refrained from using those troops in battle, however, because he favored first exhausting all alternatives to war. Developing events in Afghanistan nevertheless made him appreciate his country's military capability.

In April 1978 the communist People's Democratic Party of Afghanistan had seized power in a bloody coup d'état against President Mohammed Daoud Khan, and established Nur Muhammad Taraki as general secretary. As head of the Russian puppet government, Taraki ordered rebel *mujahideen* soldiers who had surrendered to be executed, and then he ruled the country by decree. Unwilling to break diplomatic relations with Afghanistan, Carter sought an ambassador who might understand that troubled country. On June 27, 1978, he appointed a career diplomat who had extensive experience in Russian, Near Eastern, and South Asian affairs. Adolph Dubs, was fifty-eight years old, a Navy veteran, and a man of distinction in the foreign service, the perfect choice to bridge the cultural divide between the United States and an Islamic country turned Soviet satellite.[54]

Ever attentive to his waning reputation with Jewish voters, who were continuously apprehensive that Carter might make international decisions that would disfavor Israel, in June Carter established the Office of Special Investigation within the Justice Department. It was supposed to locate and prosecute Nazi war criminals who had sought refuge in the United States. Scott McMurry, an expert on German history and language, and others in that small office masterminded the capture and prosecution of several notorious Nazis who had persecuted and executed Jews in Germany.[55] Their work did not help Carter's standing in the polls with Jewish voters.

More troubling to Carter, negotiations for SALT II with the Soviet Union were not going as smoothly in 1978 as he had hoped. On September 2, he wrote to Brezhnev that he was distressed that relations had not developed well. "I do not believe either of us can afford to forget how much responsibility is in our hands for issues vital to the peace and well-being of hundreds of millions of our fellow human beings," he told Brezhnev. Brezhnev agreed, but neither nation trusted the other. The Russian ruler urged Carter to stop promulgating the "myth" that the Soviet Union posed a military threat to the United States. However, he added, if events forced his country to build up its military force, "we will have no other alternative."[56]

SIXTEEN

Quiet Path to Camp David

Rosalynn brooded about the deadlock between Sadat and Begin and how she and Jimmy might resolve it during the summer of 1978. She jotted down random observations about Camp David, noting that it was "far removed from the pressures and controversies of Washington."[1] About mid-July, during one of their walks along a wooded path at the secluded Camp David, she turned to Jimmy and said, "Jimmy, if we could only get Prime Minister Begin and President Sadat up here on this mountain for a few days, I believe they might consider how they could prevent another war between their countries."[2] Carter doubted that Begin would agree, but he asked her if she was serious. She told him that if he did not try, he would not succeed. Failure was not in his vocabulary. He would try.[3]

Carter discovered that the political atmosphere of the hot months of July and August were not conducive to convening the peace conference between Egypt and Israel that he and Rosalynn envisioned. The struggle for Jewish votes, staff problems, international apathy, trouble with Congress, and uncertainties about what to expect from Israel not only demanded the president's time but seemed to indicate that the time was not right for a conference.

Vice President Mondale, who had just returned from leading a group of twenty-eight Americans, most of them Jewish, on a goodwill trip to Israel did not bring back a positive report. His group was shocked to discover the tension in Israel over Carter's speeches and policies, a tension Mondale knew would cost the Democratic Party Jewish votes and financial contributions. Mondale's report, as well as meetings involving Carter, Jordan, Eizenstat, Brown, and others, hinted that chances for failure were greater than for peace, because so many Jewish leaders claimed to see the administration's "erosion of the commitment to Israel."[4]

The chance of failing to negotiate SALT II became evident too, partly because of a warning from Senator Stennis that the time was not right to send such a treaty to the Senate, as too many senators remained skeptical of the intent of the Soviet Union and might not vote in favor of ratification. The

Soviets continued to violate human rights and rejected Carter's appeal to release Jewish dissident Anatole Shcharansky, whom they had convicted of spying for the United States and sentenced to thirteen years hard labor. Andrew Young irritated some of the senators, as well as Carter and much of the public, when he told a French newspaper that there were "hundreds— perhaps even thousands" of political prisoners in US jails. A veteran of the Civil Rights movement, Young had witnessed the incarceration of African-American demonstrators. He told "an embarrassing truth at a particularly awkward time," according to one journalist, but the fallout from senators and others who demanded that Young be fired did not affect Jimmy's continued support of his friend—nor did it bode well for Senate approval of SALT II.[5]

Preparing to attend an economic summit in Bonn, Germany, Carter telephoned German Chancellor Helmut Schmidt, who questioned whether Carter, who wanted NATO partners to assume more responsibility for their defense, could be counted upon for Western European security. Despite their disagreements, they apparently planned an amiable meeting. Schmidt insisted that he speak with the president in English, but he was not accustomed to a Georgia accent, which made it difficult to be certain how much they understood each other. They ended on a cordial note: "Thank you very much, Jimmy. Thank you, Helmut. Good-bye."[6]

Rosalynn and Amy accompanied Jimmy on the trip to Germany, July 13– 17. Schmidt met the Carter family informally at the airport on the evening of July 13. He jokingly said that "being chancellor would be very enjoyable without the Bundestag and without the press," a sentiment with which Carter could identify. The next day Mrs. Schmidt took Rosalynn and Amy on a tour of the Ludwig van Beethoven House and to a concert. That evening at the state dinner for all of the leaders attending the summit, Carter noted in his remarks how pleased he was to make his first trip as president to the Federal Republic of Germany and to be in the city that "nurtured Beethoven—a symbol not only of German culture but also of the indomitable spirit of a free people."[7]

At the summit working sessions, Carter found the heads of state from Canada, France, Germany, Italy, Japan, and the United Kingdom to be warm and trusting. They agreed with each other about events in Africa, the Middle East, Pakistan, Afghanistan, and the Soviets' concern about the People's Republic of China. Carter felt comfortable knowing that his country's traditional allies remained in place. "We feel like members of a fraternity," he wrote in his diary; "we share problems and political analyses" and a "mutual admiration and respect."

However, Carter disagreed with British Prime Minister Jim Callaghan, a dove who thought they could "divide up our influence in Africa" with the Soviets. Carter was not willing to accept any Soviet presence in Africa "that was superior to our own in any country." But he agreed with the others that they would combat terrorism by ceasing all flights to and from a country "that did not return hijacked planes or the hijackers to the country in which the crime was committed." Five nations, all enemies of Israel, had announced that they would allow hijackers of commercial airplanes to enter their country. Libya, the worst offender, immediately ceased the practice after its leader Muammar Gaddafi received letters from each of the attendees at Bonn that he could expect no more flights in or out of his country if he did not conform to their demands.[8]

Carter took advantage of his time in Europe to compliment General George S. Blanchard, commander of the US Army in Europe, for his service to the security of NATO. Carter promised him and the commander of the US Air Force in Europe that he would seek increased pay for US servicemen. At the Wiesbaden-Erbenheim Air Base, Carter thanked the troops for their work, courage, and patriotism. "God bless all of you," he told them.[9]

The next day, Carter flew to the Rein-Mein Air Base in Frankfurt to meet Schmidt. The two leaders addressed several thousand German and US troops, and Carter learned from his hosts that the German Leopard tank and a personnel carrier were superior to those of the United States. He and Schmidt discussed the possibility of standardizing German and US military equipment. In West Berlin later the same day, he participated in a wreath laying ceremony at the Airlift Memorial, commemorating the breaking of the Soviet embargo of West Berlin thirty years before, and he gave a rousing talk at a town meeting designed to inform those Berliners on the eastern side of the wall how much better life was in the West. The German East Berliners were intensely interested in his opposition to their Soviet occupiers. After farewell remarks, the Carter family returned home on Air Force One, fast asleep, concluding what Carter thought was a very successful summit.[10]

Almost as soon as he awakened the next day, Carter received bad news about his drug czar and friend, Peter Bourne. A professional psychiatrist, Bourne had written a prescription for Quaalude, a sedative, for his assistant, Ellen Metsky, using the fictitious name Sarah Brown to avoid negative publicity. The scheme backfired. Metsky was arrested when she attempted to get it filled, and Bourne resigned, explaining to Carter that he had written the prescription in good faith for a troubled person and that he did not wish to cause anyone harm. Carter declined to answer questions about the incident, but he defended Bourne "as a close friend" and "able and dedicated public servant." The loss of Bourne as an adviser hurt, but it hurt more because Bourne had been a key person in his governorship and the campaign.[11]

Arguing among his fellow Democrats aggravated Carter. At a meeting with the Democratic members of the Ninety-Fourth Congress on July 27, he found them loyal but restless. One Republican Congressman, Robin Beard of Tennessee, who also attended the meeting because he wanted to speak to Carter in the presence of some Democrats, confronted the president for causing him problems with his constituency. Carter's approach to the Middle East, Panama, Rhodesia, and the Turkey arms embargo did not play well in Beard's district, nor did it in some of the Democratic districts either. That Congressman and others told Carter that, if he did not help them more, he might not get reelected. Carter responded bluntly that he "was sympathetic, but reelection was not the most important thing in my life."[12]

More annoying for Carter was a nasty exchange at breakfast with Speaker Tip O'Neill. O'Neill wanted his friend Bob Griffin to remain as Jay Solomon's deputy at the General Services Administration, but Carter, who had fired Griffin for causing personnel problems, refused. O'Neill angrily replied with "extremely abusive" language "in the most personal way," Carter wrote in his diary. O'Neill warned the president that his Congressional liaison Frank Moore would be barred from his office permanently. Time healed the damage, and soon the president and the Speaker were cooperating again. Carter thought they had "a natural affinity" for each other, but there is no evidence that O'Neill felt the same. According to Senator Edmund Muskie, Carter came to respect O'Neill and to understand that he was no longer dealing with the Georgia legislature.[13]

In general, Carter did not waste time listening to his critics or mourning losses. In the Middle East he had promises to keep. He approved a huge arms sale to Iran, which included thirty-one phantom jet fighters, a dangerous maneuver with a faltering ally. He proposed legislation to lift the arms embargo on Turkey, a nation whose alliance would be "in the national interest of the United States." That legislation, he thought, would help resolve the long-standing Cyprus dispute and would strengthen NATO. After the bill passed the House and went to the Senate, Senator George McGovern led the fight for its passage there. McGovern, a former political rival, gave an impassioned speech in which he extolled the accomplishments of the president in his first year: no Vietnam, no Bay of Pigs, no Watergate, no battles anywhere, international justice for Panama, cancelation of the expensive and unnecessary B-1 bomber, an even-handed policy toward the Arab-Israeli dispute, promoting self-determination for Africa, starting limited diplomatic relations with Cuba, pushing for Vietnam participation in the UN, reducing ground forces in South Korea, and pressing the Soviet Union on SALT II. And now, McGovern concluded, he is calling upon us to remove the "diabolic and self-defeating embargo against Turkey" that is "exacerbating relations involving Greece, Turkey, and Cyprus." In conclusion, the erudite senator whose advanced study of history sometimes served him well, quoted historians Charles and Mary Beard: "Sometimes it gets the darkest just before the stars come out."[14]

Fifty-seven senators, including several Republicans, voted for the bill on July 25, giving Carter a major victory. Carter sent thank you notes to all fifty-seven, including Abraham Ribicoff, who supported him on most Middle East matters. When McGovern sent Carter a copy of his remarks, he genuinely thanked him for his "sensitive appraisal of my policies and actions."[15]

At the White House, however, Carter found it more difficult to make peace with some of his female advisers. On August 2, Public Liaison Officer Midge Costanza resigned amid controversy that she did not conform to the administration's political style. She thought that the lobbying in the South for passage of the ERA, which avoided identifying the president with feminists, might have been handled differently, and she openly expressed the president's belief that gays had the rights and responsibilities of any other citizens. Jody Powell accused Costanza of saying negative things about the administration, and Gerald Rafshoon asked her not to appear on a news program where she might be led into making negative comments about the use of marijuana in the White House. Miss Lillian had never liked Costanza and once told her that she did not understand why her son thought her "a beautiful woman." Although Rosalynn thought Costanza served the administration well as a liaison to more liberal Democrats, she always appeared uneasy in Costanza's presence.[16]

Jimmy and Rosalynn had more serious matters on their minds than Costanza's resignation as they pondered inviting Begin and Sadat to Camp David. Knowing that Begin might be difficult to convince, on August 3, 1978, Carter sent the letter of invitation to him as a secret, flattering, urgent note arguing that the leaders and their people wanted peace. "The boldness and leadership qualities exhibited by you and President Sadat have contributed to a new and better relationship between Israel and Egypt which was not anticipated by the rest of the world," he wrote. He thought it "imperative that every effort be made . . . while those of us who presently serve as leaders of our respective nations . . . have such a chance to advance the cause of peace in the Middle East." Casually noting that he had no preference about the location of the meeting, he added, "Camp David is available." He asked Begin to keep the invitation as quiet as possible.[17]

While waiting anxiously for Begin's response, Carter enjoyed his role as commander in chief of the armed forces. On August 4, Rosalynn went with him for an unannounced visit to a Marine barracks in Washington and attended the evening parade. After applauding the parade, he signed the guest book: "The Marines were at their best. Superb! It made me even prouder of our great country and its fighting men."[18]

The next day Carter attended the commissioning of USS Mississippi at the navy base in Norfolk, Virginia. Since, as a young officer, he had served on an earlier Mississippi, he enjoyed visiting the base in the town where he and Rosalynn had lived as newlyweds. When he spoke, he emphasized the fact that the United States maintained "the greatest arsenal on earth, to protect and preserve our freedom and liberty." Continuing, he praised "the finest servicemen and women in the world" and "pledged as President—and as a Navy man—that the United States will maintain military . . . and Naval . . . forces second to none." Surely the Soviet Union and any pundits and politicians who thought him weak because of his interest in human rights should have gotten that message.[19]

The speakers at the commissioning ceremony included Admiral Rickover who remarked that the office of the presidency "is the most difficult one in our history." Effusively praising his former student, Rickover asserted that "Deep within President Carter is the knowledge that struggle is the law of growth; character is built in the storm and stress of the world; and a man reaches his full height only through . . . responsibilities, and suffering. With the winds of circumstances blowing in so many directions, he knows that the only sure way is to act on principle . . . ."[20]

Rosalynn, regardless of which way the winds blew, often followed her own instincts. On one awkwardly humorous occasion, Carter kept his cool when the First Lady arrived forty minutes late to the cabinet meeting and, finding no vacant seats along the wall or at the table, except the vice president's chair next to the president, hastily slipped into it. Protocol required that that seat be left vacant if the vice president was absent. As usual, Rosalynn said nothing during the meeting while she took notes. Having confessed that his administration had room for improvement, Carter concluded that he expected everybody to work together. Rosalynn returned to her office "high" with the excitement of having sat in the vice president's chair. If there was any private discussion about her tardiness and her improper seating, it did not get recorded.[21]

In reality, Rosalynn was closer to the president than the vice president was. After Pope Paul VI died on August 6, Jimmy attended a memorial service at St. Matthew's Catholic Cathedral in Washington, but he asked Rosalynn to attend the funeral in Rome. When journalists questioned why the president or vice president did not go, Jimmy gave his usual response that Rosalynn was his "closest representative." She headed a group of five dignitaries, including Senator Ted Kennedy and New York Governor Hugh Carey, but she attracted more attention than the others.[22]

Upon arrival at the Vatican, Rosalynn said that the world had lost a wise and beloved symbol of the goodness of mankind. The Pope's concern for the poor and sense of social justice made him, in Jimmy's words, a "spiritual beacon" who would be missed. Because of security, Rosalynn was not permitted extensive exposure to the public, but she spoke a few words to all she met, posed for photographs with men and women from all walks of life, and represented the country, as one journalist reported, with "grace and dignity."[23]

On August 6, the same day the Pope had died, Carter received Begin's response to his invitation. Begin had "responded enthusiastically, almost emotionally," Carter wrote in his diary, "in favor of the summit meeting at Camp David." Sadat had already agreed to meet, but without so much emotion. A few days later, Carter, while Rosalynn was in Rome, had briefed former President Ford and Congressional leaders about his Camp David plans. All, including Ford, had responded positively, except Howard Baker who wanted to keep his options open, and Scoop Jackson, who disapproved of the plan.[24]

After Carter told Rosalynn, Brzezinski sent a secret telegram to Samuel Lewis, the United States ambassador to Israel at the Tel Aviv Embassy telling him that the president would announce that Sadat and Begin had accepted his invitation to come to Camp David on September 5.[25] Carter made the official announcement on August 8, that President Sadat and Prime Minister Begin would meet with him "to seek a framework for peace in the Middle East."[26]

In the meantime, avoiding publicity about the upcoming peace conference and uncertain about whether Begin might yet impose some impediment to the conference, Jimmy and Rosalynn worked together to improve
Jimmy's standing with the media and with the CIA. Rosalynn joined him
for a political trip to Missouri and later hosted media executives at a small
White House dinner on August 15, hoping to establish good relations with
the press.[27] Carter went to the CIA headquarters in Langley, Virginia, on
August 16 and assured everyone "that there is no truth to allegations that
CIA conclusions are tailored to fit the fashion of the administration's objectives. . . . I have found that the CIA tells me what I need to know, not what
I want to hear." He urged the agency to continue to do so, "for the objectivity
and the independency of the CIA are its most vital assets." He hoped that security leaks could be stopped and that the CIA could achieve improved relations with Congress. The conflict between "openness" and "security," he said,
could be resolved only by "sound judgment." He praised the thirty-five agents
honored on the memorial wall for giving their lives in the line of service and
he complimented the agency for its "high professionalism, training, education, [and] experience."[28]

The US public knew very little about Carter's relationship with the CIA,
but listened when he spoke about the Soviet Union. His approval rating for
condemning the Soviet Union's treatment of dissidents Anatoly Shcharansky,
Alexander Ginsberg, and others reached 67%.[29] The majority of Americans
thought he should cancel the sale and shipment of technology equipment to
the Soviet Union, but the question of US participation in the 1980 Summer
Olympics in Moscow was especially controversial. In the summer of 1978,
68% of Americans thought that US athletes should compete in Moscow, but
that still left a sizable opposition.[30]

Consideration of that issue and other controversies was postponed during
the last two weeks of August as the Carters took some much-needed vacation time in South Georgia and the Central Rockies. They arrived in Plains
on August 18, Rosalynn's birthday, and had a private celebration at the Pond
House with their two mothers, Amy, and Carter's siblings. Billy arranged a
party for the family at the Best Western motel in Americus. Three days of
fishing, walking the streets of Plains, attending a worship service, and playing
tennis gave them a welcome change from Washington.[31]

From Plains, Jimmy and Rosalynn, accompanied by their sons Chip and
Jack, as well as the usual entourage who advised and protected them from
all harm, flew to Idaho. For three days they rafted down the Middle Fork of

the Salmon River, camping overnight at the Lower Grouse Creek campsite, observing beautiful scenery and wildlife, fishing for trout, and enjoying almost "complete isolation from the press." It was, Jimmy said, "among the best three days of my life."[32]

They moved on to Jackson Hole, Wyoming, where they met Mary Fitzpatrick, who had arrived there with Amy. They went sailing, fished, rode horses, and attended a rodeo. After a day in Yellowstone, they returned to Jackson Hole and attended the Chapel of the Transfiguration.

On the last day of August, Jimmy and Rosalynn returned to Washington. While on vacation, they had planned their roles in the fall midterm election campaigns for Democratic candidates. Rosalynn would go to Texas early in September and reserve blocks of time for other places later in October.[33] Jimmy, leaving much of the campaigning to Rosalynn, stayed in Washington tending to some of the policy items on his agenda. He sent identical letters to all one hundred senators asking for their support for a natural gas conference. He contemplated a strategy for non-military competition with the Soviet Union that would involve Western Europe, Saudi Arabia, Iran, China, Japan, and South Korea. He ordered a study of the US military presence abroad from the standpoint of how to maintain and enhance the US "political and military position" relative to that of the Soviets. It seemed like a dull, low-key end of the summer in the nation's capital. But something was in the air.[34]

For most of August, whether the Carters were in Washington, Georgia, or the West, the looming prospect of the upcoming Egyptian-Israel peace conference was on their minds. Jimmy had used some of his vacation quiet time to prepare himself. He had consulted senators occasionally on the telephone, but he passed most of his time studying the psychological profiles of Sadat and Begin that the CIA had prepared for him. Armed with massive amounts of information from the State and Defense Departments, Carter seemed most interested in the psychological profiles. If he were to succeed as the catalyst to bringing about a miraculous peace agreement at Camp David, he would do it in his own way, namely on a personal level.[35]

SEVENTEEN

Miracle at Camp David

"Rosalynn and I," Jimmy said on the third day of September, 1978, "are pleased to extend warmest good wishes to our fellow citizens of the Muslim faith who will be celebrating *Id al-Fitr.*" It was a joyous occasion for the millions of Muslims in the United States and around the world who broke the fast at the end of their holy month of Ramadan. Usually they gathered in large convention halls or expansive outdoor spaces to greet each other, exchange gifts, and offer prayers. To his fellow Americans of that faith, Carter continued: "You can take great pride in the constructive influence you have on American life by your devotion to the moral and spiritual values of your faith." He and his family, Jimmy concluded, join "in your prayer that we will see continued progress toward the goal of peace and a greater realization of your very deep belief in the dignity and worth of every individual."[1]

Islam was but one faith Carter had on his mind that day. He was thinking of Begin's Judaism and his own Christianity because he was ready to take on "the most vexatious dispute on earth," the long-standing Arab-Israeli conflict.[2] For decades there had been no resolution, but Carter thought that he might be able to help the Egyptians and Israelis come to an agreement. His and Rosalynn's own prayer was that when three leaders who embodied the beliefs and virtues of Islam, Judaism, and Christianity, came together in the tranquility of Camp David, there would be a chance at finally making peace in that troubled region.

Carter had given careful thought to his negotiating strategy; he had drafted a written agreement for peace between Egypt and Israel with specific details about how to implement it. Carter packed maps, briefing books, notes on previous discussions, and his "annotated Bible." He took along his son Chip to run errands and help protect his privacy. He wanted Rosalynn, he said, "for personal support and advice."[3]

The next day, September 4, he delivered a farewell remark from the White House lawn, stating that his, Begin's, and Sadat's search for peace in the Middle East would help "ensure peace in the future throughout the world."

He would not predict how the conference would proceed or end. While he was away, he promised to push Congress to deal with "very important issues, including the evolution of an energy policy for our Nation." The Arab-Israeli conflict directly influenced the energy crisis in the United States, and the United States and its allies' need for Middle Eastern oil might have a negative effect on US-Israeli relations.[4]

Carter wanted the leaders at Camp David and their teams to work in isolation from the press. They could then, he thought, be candid, blunt, and emotional, and thereby avoid "political posturing" and pursue "personal interchange" that might range from stubborn, suspicious, and angry to friendly and trusting. The press set up its headquarters in nearby Thurmont, Maryland, at the Rambler Motel where, according to famed Voice of America journalist Philomena Jurey, they awaited "dribs and drabs" of information from Jody Powell.[5]

Seldom had three heads of state, and their spouses, appeared to be more different, but underneath their public images they held values and experiences in common. Anwar Sadat, renowned for his stunning trip to Jerusalem the previous November, was a courageous Arab leader. When he and Jehan were in Alexandria, Egypt, during the Ramadan celebration, he told her that Cyrus Vance had invited him to attend a summit in the United States with Begin. Since he believed that the United States might apply pressure on Israel to be reasonable, he intended to go. When Jehan reminded him that his son Gamal would be getting married on September 24, he assured her that he would be back by then.[6]

The Carters went to Camp David early to prepare for the arrival of the Sadats and the Begins. Jimmy went on September 4 and Rosalynn joined him the next day ahead of the other dignitaries. She intended to remain at Jimmy's side, but occasionally travel back and forth to Washington to supervise activities at the White House. Carter hoped to get the negotiations done quickly because he did not like to take too much time away from other presidential responsibilities.

Through secret channels, Carter knew what was transpiring in Cairo and Jerusalem on the eve of the conference. He understood that Sadat had many enemies among Islamic fundamentalists and that there was a chance that an assassin might be planted in the Egyptian entourage. He instructed his own security team to redouble their efforts to protect the Egyptian. Informants in Cairo also told him that Sadat had publicly told a group of Egyptian military and civil officials that Camp David represented a turning point in relations with Israel and that failure might mean unending conflict. From Jerusalem, Carter learned that many Israelis, both within and outside his government, were urging Begin to be more flexible, a stance it might be very difficult for him to take.[7]

Carter's team included Rosalynn, Cyrus Vance, Zbigniew Brzezinski, and Vice President Mondale. William Quandt, who served on the NSC and had been an expert on Middle Eastern Affairs for more than a decade, was an excellent resource and adviser. Assistant secretaries of state Alfred Atherton and Harold Saunders, joined by ambassadors Hermann Eilts to Egypt and Samuel Lewis to Israel, Jody Powell, and Hamilton Jordan completed the team.

Although Carter claimed that he would be only a mediator at the discussions, he had with him his detailed handwritten "Framework for a Settlement in Sinai" that laid out the terms for Israel to return that peninsula to the Egyptians. He also brought his extensive notes on the demilitarization of the West Bank, the cessation of the construction of more new settlements there, strict adherence to UN Resolution 242, and a proposal for Jerusalem to become a united city-borough type town that would accommodate all three major religions. Carter did not recommend an independent Palestinian state because he knew that such a recommendation would be so unacceptable to Begin that it might kill any chance for a successful peace conference. Carter planned to pressure Israel into agreeing to his terms by offering it advanced technology, military sales, a mutual defense pact, and military support if the treaty were broken.[8]

Sadat arrived first on the afternoon of Tuesday, September 5. When Jimmy and Rosalynn moved quickly to greet him as he emerged from his helicopter, Sadat opened wide his arms to give Jimmy a tight embrace, then kissed Rosalynn on each cheek. Jehan had remained behind in Paris with a sick grandchild. Rosalynn was disappointed that her friend was not there, and Jimmy had hoped that the presence of the three wives would enhance discussions and make agreements easier. Sadat was alone in another sense too, because the team of eight officials accompanying him was almost entirely opposed to the summit. Two foreign ministers had resigned in protest of his earlier trip to Jerusalem. Mohamed Ibrahim Kamel, who had recently become minister of foreign affairs, came to Camp David, but he thought that even talking to Israelis was an act of treason. Sadat's only support within his delegation came from Boutros Boutros-Ghali, minister of state for foreign affairs, who thought Kamel's opinions had little relation to reality. He also thought that Sadat's astrologer, who believed that God would slaughter the Jews, "was mad."

Sadat had assured his skeptical crew that Egypt would lose nothing from the meeting, because if Israel yielded to them, it would be a great victory. If not, then Egypt would benefit from a closer relationship with the United States. Clearly, however, Sadat would stand virtually alone in the meetings that followed.[9]

Jimmy and Rosalynn escorted Sadat to his quarters in Dogwood Lodge. Two hours later, Begin arrived, also without his wife. The president and prime minister embraced, and Begin kissed Rosalynn on her cheek, before the Carters took him to his quarters in Birch Lodge. While Begin rested, Sadat walked the short distance to the Carters' Aspen Lodge to meet privately with Carter. Sadat assured Carter that he was prepared to agree to a comprehensive peace agreement, but he would accept nothing less than Israeli withdrawal from all occupied Arab lands. The next day, Begin and Sadat had a chance meeting during their noon walks, and they exchanged pleasantries that would not characterize the formal meetings to follow.[10]

Aliza Begin arrived separately from her husband. She thought she had a "relaxed, informal relationship" with Rosalynn, but Rosalynn did not find their relationship particularly relaxed. Jimmy reminded Rosalynn that when the Begins said "Judea and Samaria," they meant what the others called the West Bank, and "Palestinian Arabs" to them were simply Palestinians to the Americans. After her arrival at Camp David, Aliza Begin paid little attention to the Americans and spent as much time as possible at her husband's side.[11]

Begin brought with him a more sophisticated and helpful team than Sadat had, but they were divided among themselves. Most of the Israeli delegation expected a short meeting with no results. There were two notable exceptions, however. Foreign Minister Moshe Dayan was rational and prepared to help the Americans deal with the tough Israeli leader. Defense Minister Ezer Weizman, the father of the Israeli air force, who respected both Sadat and Carter, wanted a peace treaty. The Carter team understood that they might have to use Dayan and Weizman to influence Begin. The rest of the Israeli team, consisting of Attorney General Aharon Barak, Ambassador to the United States Simcha Dinitz, and four more legal and military advisers would be of no help.[12]

On the evening of his arrival, Begin had a private talk with Carter at Carter's lodge that Carter found discouraging. Carter reminded the prime minister that he and Sadat had already committed to no more war, security for Israel, honoring UN Resolution 242, and no independent Palestinian state. Begin asked Carter to send a message to President Hafez al-Assad which put the blame on the Lebanese for the hostile military confrontation between the two countries following the bloody PLO attack on Israeli civilians in March. Carter sent the message as requested, even though he thought the Israelis were more at fault for that carnage. While Carter talked with Begin, Vance met with Defense Minister Weisman to discuss differences of views within the Israeli delegation.[13]

With the three principals and their security teams and entourages settled in, Camp David looked more like a well-maintained national park than the serene mountain retreat that Jimmy and Rosalynn loved. The Carters, Sadat, and the Begins occupied private cabins within a hundred yards of each other. Other cabins, and at least one barracks, housed the staffs, secretaries, cooks, doctors, security people, helicopter pilots and crews, and any others needed to make the camp comfortable, secure, and ready to serve the needs of people from three different nations. A well-guarded gate and the security fence surrounding the complex would hopefully keep all the attendees safe. It was packed with people beyond its normal capacity, but journalists were noticeably absent.[14]

Rosalynn suggested that the entire group's first meeting on September 5 open with a prayer and asked several interfaith groups in Washington to write one for her. Sadat accepted the text, but Begin insisted upon modifying it. Finally, they all prayed: "after four wars, . . . the Holy Land does not yet enjoy the blessings of peace." "Gathered to bring peace to the Holy Land," they continued: "we place our trust in the God of our fathers, from whom we seek wisdom and guidance. . . . We ask people of all faiths to pray with us that peace and justice may result from these deliberations." The prayer did not unify the attendees, however, for during the opening days of the conference they did not agree on anything.[15]

At the end of the first day, Sadat telephoned his wife in Paris. He reported that Begin was difficult, complicated, and discouraging. "It is exhausting to have to fight so hard for peace," he told her. "I'm praying for you and know that God will help you," she responded. Likewise, at the end of the day, Jimmy informed Rosalynn about everything that had happened, confiding to her that he doubted Begin would go through with a peace treaty. Knowing that Rosalynn shared his frustration, Jimmy moved his lips silently to tell her that Sadat and Begin needed to "stop assing around."[16]

Whatever prayers anyone might offer were sorely needed. On the second day, Carter met individually with Sadat and Begin in their respective cabins in the morning and jointly with them in mid-afternoon. In their private meeting, Sadat presented Carter with a harsh proposal that would never be accepted by Israel. But he also gave Carter a three-page memorandum outlining concessions that Egypt might make, which he urged Carter to keep secret, and suggested that Carter use it as a US proposal at some appropriate time. The afternoon meeting went as expected, with Begin listening stony-faced to Sadat's reading of his harsh proposal. Carter broke the ice by turning to Begin and joking that he could save all of them a lot of time by just signing the document as Sadat had presented it. The remark produced guffaws from all three men, and Begin and Sadat patted each other on the back as they departed.[17]

Whatever camaraderie they created on the second day quickly evaporated on the third. During an acrimonious confrontation, Sadat criticized Begin for wanting territory more than he wanted peace. Sadat tried to discuss the principles of UN Resolutions 242 and 338. Begin quickly interjected that he would return the Sinai only under certain conditions. Sadat, changing the subject, accused Israel of causing the recent armed confrontation in Lebanon. The discussion became increasingly bitter, with Sadat sometimes pounding his fists on the table, Begin refusing to budge, and both men threatening to terminate the meeting. Rosalynn, in a different room, overheard the personal insults they shouted at each other, and Jimmy later told her the meeting was mean and brutal.

Carter stood in the door to prevent both men from leaving. He produced a list he had compiled of remaining problems, and he persuaded them to stay to discuss those issues. The day ended with Sadat reluctantly agreeing to give Carter a chance to influence the negotiations. Begin also agreed, suggesting not only that he trusted Carter but also that he wanted peace with Egypt. When Carter realized that Begin and Sadat could not deal with each other face to face, he became the messenger who passed comments and revisions, many of which were his own, back and forth between their respective cabins.[18]

At the State Department level, Vance supplemented Carter's tenacity by creating a good rapport with Weizmann and others who might influence Begin. Mondale met with Dayan for a walk in the Camp David woods that he hoped would be helpful in dealing with the stubborn prime minister. Carter had no intention of giving up.[19]

Rosalynn entertained Aliza by riding with her over the pristine grounds in a golf cart before serving lunch on the patio of the Carter cabin. Neither woman mentioned the intense meetings involving their husbands or their anxiety about what might be transpiring. When Jimmy told Rosalynn later that night how brutally insulting Begin and Sadat were to each other, she was glad to be there to give her husband the "personal support and advice" he needed. Though, she was relieved when a telephone call from Amy changed the topic to Amy's first day in her racially mixed sixth-grade class at the Rose Hardy Middle School in Washington.[20]

On Friday evening, Jimmy and Rosalynn accepted Aliza's invitation to join the Begins and other Israelis for their traditional Shabbat dinner. A moving and humbling experience, that dinner helped the Carters better appreciate emotionally the history and faith of Judaism. The ceremony included the story of the Exodus when the Jews miraculously escaped from Egyptian captivity. While offering prayers of thanks to God for His deliverance of them from the ancient Egyptians, the participants must have given somber thought to their current effort to come to peaceful terms with the Egyptians of the twentieth century.

The Carters sat at the head table on either side of the prime minister, Jimmy between him and Aliza and Rosalynn between Begin and Dayan. Begin reminded Rosalynn that they were supposed to worship God with gladness, and he sang a traditional Shabbat song about the hope of his people to be free in the land God had promised them. After the song, he chatted with Rosalynn about his grandchildren. Aliza smiled, relaxed, and appeared to be unusually calm. Jimmy and Cy Vance, wearing skullcaps that matched those of the Israeli men, sat on either side of her, but it was Cy who paid Aliza the most attention. Jimmy was stone-faced and ill at ease.

Carter remained preoccupied with the negotiations and the hope that the Israelis would become more flexible.[21] Earlier in the day, Vance had met with Defense Minister Weizman, who worried about Begin's rigidity and fretted that the tripartite meeting the previous day might have pushed the strained relationship between the Egyptian and the Israeli to a breaking point. Vance hinted that a US proposal was almost complete, news that would likely be welcomed by both parties.

Saturday, the Jewish Sabbath, became a day of rest and recreation for those who wished it. The Carter camp, acting on a request by Menachem Begin, planned to give Sadat and the Begins a tour of the Gettysburg, Pennsylvania, Civil War battlefield,[22] which Begin, a student of the US Civil War, wanted to see. Sadat, a military man schooled in the history of warfare, welcomed the opportunity to visit the site, which symbolized the horrors and residual grief warfare could bring to a country. The United States, like both Israel and Egypt, still had deep scars from previous wars.

During the short ride to Gettysburg, Carter sat between Begin and Sadat in one seat of the presidential limousine, and Rosalynn and Aliza sat together in another seat. Carter banned any discussion of the peace issues. Since Begin and Sadat were both military men, they were familiar with the 1863 battle in which General Robert E. Lee had led an invading Confederate States Army into a battle against Union forces under Major General George Meade. As many as 50,000 soldiers, from both sides, were killed, wounded, or captured in three days. That battle was a "sober reminder" of the tragedy and futility of a fratricidal war in which diplomacy had failed and stubborn resistance to surrender dragged out the carnage and chaos longer than needed to end the conflict.[23]

Begin fell strangely silent and separated himself a short distance from the others. When he reached the spot where Lincoln had delivered the Gettysburg address, he slowly began to recite it, like a prayer, not missing a single word, while the others watched, mesmerized. How Begin related those famous words about history, freedom, justice, the will of God, and the hope for the future to the history of Israel and the historic peace mission he had set himself upon remained unspoken. Lincoln's address proclaimed that redemption was possible and necessary for combatants to recover from war. Like Begin, Carter and Sadat kept whatever private thoughts they had to themselves, but all three knew what war and defeat meant for their countries.[24]

The trip to Gettysburg and subsequent discussions with the Israelis about the necessity of agreeing with UN Resolution 242, which condemned the acquisition of territory by war, brought hope. Early on Sunday morning, Carter walked with Dayan and asked for his help in convincing Begin to be reasonable. It was before daylight, and Dayan, who had lost an eye in World War II, crashed into a tree. Carter helped him back to the main path, and later they joined Sadat, Vance, and others for exhausting meetings that ended with some small hope that Begin might make concessions.

For three more days, Carter shuttled back and forth between Sadat's and Begin's cabins presenting revision after revision, but he could not get them to agree. Carter felt an increasing urgency to reach a solution, for the political situation in Afghanistan was deteriorating to the point that he thought he might need to leave Camp David to deal with a more urgent national security challenge.[25]

Carter was also plainly worried about security for Sadat. One evening shortly after they had returned from Gettysburg, he saw Sadat engaged in a heated argument with his advisers on the porch of his cabin, after which the lights went out in Sadat's cabin earlier than usual. Carter called and asked to see him, but was told he had gone to bed. Carter himself went to bed, but he woke up in the middle of the night, remembering the unusual appearance of Sadat's cabin. Terrified that something had happened to him, he told Rosalynn that he had an uneasy feeling about a threat to Sadat's life. He called Zbig, who came over in his pajamas, accompanied by the head of the Secret Service detail who could do no more than increase security around Sadat's cabin.

Carter was relieved the next morning when Sadat emerged for his usual morning walk and rushed out to walk with him. Sadat told him that, since Gettysburg, he realized that his Southern host understood the ravages of war, the "spirit of a defeated people" in their civil war, and the "psychic wounds" of the US war in Vietnam. He wondered aloud if people in the Middle East, even if they agreed to a peace treaty, would ever recover from their wars. Encouraged by that conversation, Jimmy reported to Rosalynn that he thought it was "all coming together now."[26]

News from the outside world, however, was not good. The Soviet press continued to attack the Camp David talks and accuse Carter of attempting to divide the Arab countries and encourage conflict in the region.[27] In Iran, the Ayatollah Khomeini, the radical Islamic cleric who planned to take control of the country away from the shah, called for a general strike, the effectiveness of which might reveal the strength of the religious opposition to the shah. Carter's sale of arms to the shah's repressive regime tarnished the image of the United States as the champion of human rights.[28] Both Carter and his advisers were wary of any activities by the Soviet Union, but none of them realized the magnitude of the upheaval about to overtake Iran.

The intense meetings at Camp David, however, captured Carter's attention more than events elsewhere in the world. The Carters seemed to be forgiving of Sadat's past, especially his admiration of Hitler during World War II and his country's Cold War association with the Soviet Union, but they also learned that they could take nothing for granted with the Egyptian leader. By the eleventh day of the talks, Carter, in spite of his earlier optimism, was ready to concede that he could not bring Sadat and Begin to an agreement.[29]

Carter's most terrifying moment dealing with Sadat occurred on Friday morning, September 15. Vance, ghostly pale, walked into Carter's cabin to tell him that Sadat was leaving. He had called for a helicopter to take him to the airport in Washington. Carter, trying to control his anger, kneeled beside his bed and prayed, then dressed formally in a suit and tie before rushing over to Sadat's cabin. Carter convinced the angry Sadat that if he ended negotiations it would "damage severely the relationship between the United States and Egypt and between him and me." It would, Carter emphasized, "violate his word of honor." Sadat agreed to stay.[30]

Unbeknown to Carter, Sadat had already changed his mind by the time Carter arrived at his cabin. A short time earlier when Sadat had called Jehan to say that he was leaving Camp David, she had urged him not to quit. When he told her there was no hope, she replied, "But, Anwar, then there will be no chance for peace." She implored him to be patient and stay a few more days. She reminded him of his commitment to Carter, "a man of morals and principles." She reminded him that he too was a man of principles, and he could not go back on his word to Carter. "All right," Sadat told her, and he stayed.[31]

Time was running out, however, and if the three men did not reach an agreement soon, they probably never would. On September 15, Carter sent a handwritten letter to both Begin and Sadat in which he asked for their "most constructive recommendations." He suggested that they spend the next day, Saturday, drafting an agreement and "conclude the meeting at Camp David at some time during the following day." If they agreed, then the three of them would issue a joint statement to the press on Monday.[32] In the meantime, to keep Sadat in their good graces, Carter, Mondale, and Vance joined him that evening to watch the televised Muhammed Ali-Spinks boxing match. Sadat was a great fan of Ali's and delighted when he won the match. He called to congratulate his fellow Muslim but was fast asleep by the time Ali returned the call.[33]

Saturday, instead of being a day of rest or the traditional Jewish Sabbath for Begin, became a marathon of drafting and redrafting, separate meetings with Sadat and Begin and their advisers, and nail-biting moments for the others when Begin responded unpredictably. Carter and Vance concentrated on discussions with Dayan and Weizman, because they agreed with the terms of the proposed peace agreement and might be able to persuade Begin to accept it. Sadat said he would assent to the agreement if Israel committed in advance to withdrawing its settlements from the Sinai. Carter promised Sadat that he would work to get the same peace agreement with Palestinians and to freeze Israeli settlements in Palestinian lands.

The final draft, complicated and lengthy, declared that Israel would accept UN Resolution 242 and ensure that Egypt would regain full sovereignty over the Sinai. There were to be no new settlements in the West Bank, and there would be a permanent solution to Palestinian self-government within five years. When Carter personally presented the draft to Begin, the prime minister became angry and emotional about withdrawing Israeli settlements from Sinai. Carter calmed him by suggesting that the Knesset should decide the issue of the settlements. Carter and Vance planned to use their influence in the Jewish-American community, Congress, and Israel to get the Knesset to act favorably. If it did so, Carter could then declare that Camp David was a complete success.[34]

Sadat agreed fully with Carter. In an almost jovial mood, he phoned Jehan in Paris on Saturday night, telling her that there was a good chance that Carter would soon bring the conference to an honorable conclusion. He joked with his grandson on the phone, then accepted a handwritten note from Carter, delivered by an aide, which he thought meant that success was at hand.[35]

The key to that success still rested with Begin. Before approaching him with trepidation on Sunday morning, Carter discussed the final draft with Sadat. Sadat was generally pleased with the documents, but he wanted there to be no mention of Jerusalem and a chance for Palestinians to participate in future negotiations for an Israeli-Jordanian peace treaty. On the Israeli side, Dayan told Carter that he did not believe that the Knesset would vote to withdraw the settlers from the Sinai before a peace treaty was signed, but Weizman promised to fight for it. Prompted by Carter, Weizman reminded a very angry Begin that evacuation of the settlements on the Sinai would be essential to an agreement with the Americans and Egyptians.

When Carter finally confronted Begin later than morning, he went armed with photographs of himself, Begin, and Sadat that Begin wanted signed for his grandchildren. Sadat had already signed them, and when Carter signed, he personalized them with the names of each of Begin's grandchildren. With tears in his eyes, Begin talked about each grandchild. He promised to call Carter at his cabin later. He did so, promising to allow the Knesset to decide the fate of the settlements.

Rosalynn, who had returned to the White House to supervise matters there, slipped out of a Sunday afternoon concert in the East Room to call Jimmy. Aliza and she were listening to a classical music performance by

Rostropovich and his daughter, but Rosalynn's mind was at Camp David. Jimmy told Rosalynn to stay there, for if there was a formal signing it would be in the White House.

A subsequent meeting between Begin and Sadat, their first since the Gettysburg trip and without Carter present, and some minor changes in wording concluded the Camp David meeting. Sadat and Begin then met Carter in front of his cabin where they embraced each other "enthusiastically." Carter subtly disrupted their embrace, still fearful that hostility might override their enthusiasm.[36]

Jimmy promptly called Rosalynn to tell her that he was coming home. She broke down and wept at the news that she had worked so hard for and waited so long to hear. Sadat almost simultaneously called Jehan to tell her that they had reached a solution. Israel would withdraw from the Sinai, not approve any further settlements on the West Bank, and set a timetable to negotiate Palestinian autonomy. He warned her, however, that the agreement would only be initialed, not signed. Begin restrained his excitement until he could tell Aliza in person. Rosalynn urged Jimmy to get the documents signed right away before either Begin or Sadat could change his mind. Jimmy reassured her that they would be initialed and there would be no turning back.[37]

Carter quickly planned a formal ceremony for later that night at the White House, where the principals would officially initial the documents. After telephoning former President Gerald Ford with the good news, he called key politicians from both parties to invite them to the ceremony. Rosalynn, Kit Dobelle, Mary Hoyt, and Jody Powell called cabinet members, Congressmen, and the staffs at the Egyptian and Israeli embassies, asking them to attend. The White House chefs quickly put together leftovers from earlier events that day for a reception, including orange juice for the Arabs who did not drink alcohol and white wine and champagne for guests who did. The White House staff readied the East Room for the event, while Secret Service agents and crews at Camp David prepared the helicopters that would fly the leaders and their staffs to the South Lawn.

A hail storm swept over Camp David and briefly delayed their departure. Carter, Begin, and Sadat rode in the same helicopter. It was an eerie flight in the dark that Sunday night for the exhausted travelers. Having been cut off from the media for so long, it may have seemed to them that they had been forgotten by the world. Sadat must have felt particularly isolated. Mohamed Kamel, the Egyptian foreign minister, had resigned in protest, leaving him with no foreign secretary and dubious members of his team.

When the three leaders emerged from their helicopter on the brightly lit South Lawn, they were surprised by the tumultuous welcome from employees of the Egyptian and Israeli embassies—and from Rosalynn and Aliza. Rosalynn, her cheeks still damp with tears, maintained the decorum of the First Lady. Begin, given to unpredictable emotional outbursts, rushed to Aliza, shouting, "Mama, we'll go down in the history books!" The wives seemed to be as happy that the long conference was finally over as they were about the agreement. The weary statesmen revealed little more to the eager press than the fact that an agreement had been reached.[38]

At the hastily arranged late-night ceremony, Carter sat between the Israeli and the Egyptian, who with his help had managed to accomplish the most sweeping achievement in Middle East peacemaking in modern history. Seated shoulder to shoulder at a small desk in the East Room, they simultaneously initialed multiple copies of the two documents, "Framework for Peace in the Middle East" and "Framework for the Conclusion of a Peace Treaty between Egypt and Israel." It was 10:15 at night, but each man wore a fresh suit and an expression that revealed his mood. Carter smiled seriously, not with his usual grin, as he penned his initials. Begin had the trace of a smile and the appearance of a man who believed that he was doing something important. Sadat showed no emotion as he placed his initials on the documents; there were empty chairs where his foreign secretary and some other members of his delegation should have been sitting.

Carter spoke first and at some length, explaining the documents. "Framework for Peace in the Middle East," he said, dealt with the Palestinian problem and the Israeli occupation of the West Bank and Gaza. After a five-year transitional period, the Palestinians were to determine their own future based on UN Resolution 242. By delaying the Palestinian issue for five years, Carter took a pragmatic approach to concluding the conference and getting the second document signed. That document, "Framework for the Conclusion of a Peace Treaty between Egypt and Israel," restored Egyptian sovereignty over the Sinai Peninsula and established peaceful, diplomatic relations between the two countries. Together, Carter declared, the "two Camp David agreements" would establish "the basis for progress and peace throughout the Middle East." According to Brzezinski, Carter looked tired, "with a wistful smile on his face, but not particularly elated." Carter had not gotten all that he wanted, because the Palestinian question remained unresolved and he knew that most of the Arab world did not approve of Sadat's action.[39]

Sadat and Begin spoke more briefly. Sadat praised Carter for having the courage to convene the peace conference. Carefully choosing his words, he read from a text he had prepared in advance. "Let us pledge to make the spirit of Camp David a new chapter in the history of our nations," he declared firmly but with the knowledge that more hard work would need to be done. Despite his public optimism, he was despondent about his many critics in the Arab world and the fact that there was no agreement about the Israeli settlements in Gaza and the West Bank. Nor was there any mention in the agreements of Lebanon, Syria, or the Israeli occupation of the Golan Heights.[40]

Begin appeared a bit manic in his unrehearsed comments. He declared that the Camp David Conference should be renamed "the Jimmy Carter Conference." Effusive and exhausted he cleverly referenced the ancient Egyptian captivity and enslavement of the Jews. Begin thought Carter had worked harder "than our forefathers did in Egypt building the pyramids." He had hoped, Begin said, changing his tune from thirteen days earlier, that from every corner of the world they could hear shouts that peace had come. But that could not occur until he and Sadat signed a formal peace treaty between their nations as they had just pledged to do within three months' time. Turning toward a quizzical Sadat and bemused Carter, Begin asked Sadat to sign the treaty sooner. Sadat smiled and agreed. After the ceremony, Begin "told a friend, 'I have just signed the greatest document in Jewish history!'"[41]

The next day, the three national leaders announced to the world that they had reached an agreement. That evening Carter addressed a joint session of Congress about the new Camp David Accords. He wrote much of his speech while riding to the Capitol in his limousine with Begin and Sadat. Upon arrival, Begin and Sadat took seats in the balcony of the House chamber and listened while Carter delivered his address. Televised and broadcast on radio, the speech attracted a large audience. For the first time in more than two thousand years, Carter said, if the "present expectations are realized," there would be peace between Egypt and a free Jewish nation. Paying tribute to Sadat and Begin as "the two men who have made this impossible dream now become a real possibility," he declared that such a peace would be vital not only to their two nations "but to all the people of the Middle East—to all the people of the United States—indeed, to the rest of the world as well." Carter concluded by quoting Psalm 85, verse 8: "God the Lord will speak . . . peace unto His people, and, to His saints. But let them not turn again to folly." Then, looking up at the Muslim and the Jew in the balcony, he added, "As a Christian, I would like to repeat to my two friends the words of Jesus: 'Blessed are the peacemakers, for they shall be called the children of God.' "[42]

The Biblical admonition "not to turn again to folly," might have been better heeded by Begin, who, according to Carter, made "an ass of himself with his public statements . . . until he finally left the United States."[43] In public speeches before largely Jewish audiences in New York City, Begin retreated from the terms of the framework. He disparaged Carter for having put so much pressure on Israel, and he reassured his audiences that Israel would continue to build settlements and maintain a permanent military presence in Gaza and the West Bank. Carter, dismayed by those comments, urged Jewish-American leaders to restrain Begin from behaving in such an irresponsible way. Carter warned Begin in a private note on September 27 that his remarks would make it impossible for other Arab leaders to participate in the peace process.

Begin refused to yield to pressure from Carter on the issue of the Gaza and West Bank settlements. When he returned to Israel at the end of September, he honored his promise to submit the agreement to the Knesset for a vote. The Knesset overwhelmingly endorsed it, and soon afterward Israeli forces withdrew from the Sinai. Gaza and the West Bank were different matters, however. When some members of Begin's party accused him of being a traitor, he told the Knesset that he had had to surrender the Sinai settlements to make peace with Egypt and satisfy the United States, but Israel would never surrender its sovereignty over "Judea, Samaria, and Gaza."

Carter was privately outraged by Begin's denial of the agreement to discuss Palestinian autonomy and the cessation of settlements in the West Bank and Gaza. Whatever rapport Carter had mustered with Begin evaporated, but Carter refused to give up until the treaties were actually signed the following spring. Begin's influence in Israel and in the United States was difficult to measure, but it seemed apparent that both Carter and Begin would welcome the other's dismissal from power.[44]

Unlike Begin, Sadat liked the terms of the agreements. Before departing for home, he told Vice President Mondale that, as soon as the Israelis moved from the Sinai, he would return the Egyptian flag to Mount Sinai and build a church, a mosque, and a synagogue there. It would be a place where he,

Carter, and Begin could pray.[45] Sadat then flew to Morocco to meet Jehan; from there they returned home to Cairo for the wedding of their son a few days later. Sadat danced and smiled happily, the first and only time Jehan ever saw him dance. White doves were released at the wedding, but the Arab reaction to the returning hero would not be so peaceful.[46]

For a few days after the Camp David summit, Carter enjoyed being "on the side of the angels." It was a label Secretary of the Interior Cecil Andrus had given him in a different context, but the agreement he had brokered at Camp David seemed like a miracle to many people.[47] The New Republic, which had recently referred to Carter as "blubber lips," announced, "Jimmy Parts the Red Sea."[48] Miss Lillian called her son from Little Rock, Arkansas, bursting with emotion and excitement. The ultimate accolade came from former Secretary of State Henry Kissinger, who had tried but failed to bring peace to the Middle East: "I hate to say 'You've not only done as well as I could have—but better.' "[49]

Carter's successful personal diplomacy at Camp David became a permanent milestone in his foreign policy career. His rating in the polls shot up dramatically, but the bump did not last for long and he did not receive an outpouring of public praise for this triumph. To the contrary, Carter's political rivals, many Arabs, many Israelis, and many Jewish Americans criticized him harshly for investing so much time and effort in the Camp David summit. Many Israelis and Jewish Americans were particularly offended by his friendship with the Arabs and his defense of the Palestinians. In truth, although the increased financial and military support that both Israel and Egypt would receive from the United States might contribute to their stability and the continued success of their peace treaty, the Middle East would remain a troubled and potentially dangerous part of the world. Nevertheless, Carter, with the help of Cyrus Vance and others on his team, as well as Begin and Sadat, had accomplished something that no one else had succeeded in doing for over two thousand years.[50]

After performing at the White House, celebrated Russian conductor and cellist Mstislav Rostropovich wrote the president and First Lady a moving letter. He thought that the agreements at Camp David had happened because Sadat and Begin believed in Carter "as a human being," not as a President, but as "a man of honesty, integrity and goodness."[51]

The ultimate compliments came from Israel and the UN. Israeli Foreign Minister Moshe Dayan and Defense Minister Ezer Weizman wrote to one of Carter's aides for Jewish affairs that "all of us, to a man" admired the way

Carter had handled the conference and the huge amount of work he invested in it. "Were it not for him, there would have been" no agreement, they said. Kurt Waldheim, UN secretary general, told Carter: "Mr. President, how much I have admired your courage and skill in conducting these unprecedented and intensive negotiations."[52]

EIGHTEEN

"A Great and Beautiful Job"

When Tip O'Neill exclaimed, unexpectedly, that Carter was doing "a great and beautiful job," he was referring to the Democratic Party's success at the polls and in the halls of Congress, not the hopeful result of Camp David. The euphoria that the exhausted Carters felt when the three heroes of Camp David initialed those two cumbersome documents at the White House did not captivate the rest of the country or the world. The signing of a treaty was set for a future date, and there was a real possibility for international events to spin out of control in the meantime.

A month after the Camp David summit, the Nobel Peace Prize Committee insulted Carter by awarding the prize to Sadat and Begin, but not to Carter. Jimmy privately recorded in his diary that Sadat deserved it, implying that Begin did not. Sadat did not think that Begin deserved it either; he refused to travel to Oslo to accept the prize, but sent a representative in his place. He did not want to confront Begin personally, nor did he want to participate in a ceremony that did not include his American friend. Many years later, the chairman of the prize committee admitted that in 1978 Carter deserved to receive the prize along with Begin and Sadat, but the essential role of Carter at Camp David became lost in the politics and international crises of the day.[1]

Many Egyptian Arabs deplored Sadat's work at Camp David because he did not win all the concessions they wanted from Israel.[2] Both Iran and the Soviet Union also refused to support the Camp David agreement: the Soviet Union because it had been prohibited from participating in the summit; and Iran because it saw the agreement as too generous to Israel. Israeli intelligence warned Carter that the shah had little chance to survive the revolution against him and that the leader of the Iranian opposition, Khomeini, hated Jews and denied Israel's right to exist.[3] Setting aside the complaint, Carter tried to persuade Brezhnev to support the Camp David accords and to encourage the Syrians and Palestinians to do likewise. Brezhnev refused, calling upon Carter to abandon the Camp David agreement himself and revert to convening a Geneva conference that would include the Soviet Union.[4]

When a revolution broke out against the shah of Iran in October, Brezhnev notified Carter that any military interference by the United States in the affairs of a country that bordered the Soviet Union would affect its security. Carter replied that the United States would firmly support the shah and remain committed "to the independence and integrity of Iran," but it would not interfere with the internal affairs of any country. If the Soviet Union chose to interfere in Iran, the United States would consider it "a matter of utmost gravity to us."[5]

Carter took all that disheartening information, as well as the unwelcome news that his brother Billy and a Georgia delegation would make a private visit to Libya, in stride as just part of another day's work. He told his cabinet that he would continue dialogue with the Arab leaders to resolve the remaining issues of the future of the West Bank and Jerusalem, as well as the fate of the Palestinians. At the same time, he would work on major domestic issues, such as airline deregulation, a tax bill, hospital cost containment, the appointment of new federal judges, and especially an Alaska lands bill pending in the Senate.[6]

Carter scored legislative victory after legislative victory. Since the passage of the Omnibus Judgeship Act of 1978 on October 20, he could now appoint 152 new judges, which gave him not only the opportunity to name more federal judges than any other president in history but also influence over the federal judicial system for many years beyond his tenure in office. Within a year, Carter nominated 75 White men, 16 White women, 4 Black women, 10 Black men, and 4 Hispanic men to serve as federal judges. Despite the relatively low numbers of nonwhites, they still comprised a larger number than ever before in the nation's history.[7]

Congress also passed his Civil Service Reform Act, a major item of legislation that Carter had proposed to try to bring honesty and financial stability to the government. At his signing of it on October 13, 1978, he called the act "momentous." It created the Office of Personnel Management, replacing the Civil Service Commission, and it required political appointees to be approved by a centralized agency controlled by the White House. Also in October, he signed airline deregulation and energy legislation, the latter of which mandated about 60% of the energy savings he wanted. Carter continued work on the Alaska lands bill and signed legislation to extend the time for passage of the ERA to June 20, 1982. At the close of the legislative session on October 15, 1978, Senator Robert Byrd told him that in his twenty-seven years of service in Congress he had "never seen such tremendous legislative achievement, nor such harmony between the Congress and a president."[8] Speaker Tip O'Neill, traveling in Georgia in late October, conceded that Carter had done a "great and beautiful job."[9]

O'Neill and Byrd were pleased too when the president joined other Carter family members to campaign for Democratic candidates in the 1978 mid-term elections. On Tuesday, September 19, 1978, the day after the Camp David Accords were officially proclaimed before Congress, Rosalynn left for Florida and Texas to campaign for Democratic candidates.[10] She reminded her audiences that she had fought hard for the ERA. She did acknowledge some conflict, however, between winning Southern votes for her party and fear that pushing too hard for the amendment in Southern states might be a political disadvantage. She told one reporter that she was concerned about getting Democratic legislators elected in South Carolina, North Carolina, and Florida, "where we need votes," and that she feared they might lose if she pressed too strongly for the ERA in those states. That comment led some feminists to accuse her of not working as hard as possible for passage of the ERA, an accusation that both she and Jimmy denied.[11]

Rosalynn's campaigning paid off. Despite small losses in the House and the Senate, the Democrats maintained majorities of 58 to 41 in the Senate and 277 to 158 in the House.[12]

Backed by Democratic majorities in both houses, Carter attacked the issues of inflation and intelligence gathering. He appointed Alfred E. Kahn to advise him on inflation and to chair the Council on Wage and Price Stability. Carter welcomed the Foreign Intelligence Surveillance Act of 1978, which attempted to strike a balance between "adequate intelligence to guarantee the Nation's security" and "the preservation of basic human rights." The act required a judicial warrant for electronic surveillance of US citizens, but the president could make exceptions. The act, Carter thought, was the first step toward establishing "statutory charters for our intelligence agencies."[13]

In addition, Carter signed the Ethics in Government Act, the Full Employment Acts, the Public Rangelands Improvement Act, legislation for student assistance, energy and food import bills, an act designating national monuments in Alaska, and many more. They would help the United States and its people in the realms of national security, human rights, protection of the environment, the conservation of natural resources, and aid for cities and individuals.[14] Despite earlier criticisms at the beginning of his presidency that he was attempting too much, Carter had, against the odds, achieved many of his goals by mid-term and had others moving toward success.

Having grown accustomed to criticism, Jimmy and Rosalynn enjoyed their work and life in the White House. On one occasion they particularly enjoyed hearing the African-American diva, Leontyne Price, a Metropolitan Opera star from Laurel, Mississippi, sing the Lord's Prayer, and at another time the popular actor and dancer John Travolta performed for them and their guests. The Carters usually included Amy at the entertainment as well as the state dinners. On October 1, 1978, she flew to Florida with her parents to help her dad celebrate his fifty-fourth birthday. At the Kennedy Space Center, she and her parents met Alan Shepard, the first American in space; John Glenn, the first to circle the earth; and Neil Armstrong, the first to walk on the moon. For his birthday gift, the astronauts presented Carter with a photograph of the Sinai Peninsula that had been taken from space.[15]

While in Florida, Carter delivered a passionate speech to the International Chamber of Commerce at Disney World. When preparing it, he had said he wanted it to be bold, brief, global, and "hit hard on what these fat cats ought to do." Toning down his rhetoric for the actual speech, he told his affluent audience that he wanted peace, increased trade with China and the Soviet Union, and above all, national security. Strong nations should not exploit poor ones, he said, and all should attempt to understand the "individualism and diversity of the world's people." Eastern and Western nations should be brought together under the same economic structure in order to deal with energy problems, control terrorism, and "stabilize food supplies."[16]

Carter was also disturbed because his brother Billy, aspiring to become one of the "fat cats," seemed to be undertaking illegal international activities. Billy had departed for Libya on a private visit, with unidentified companions. The good news was that Billy could not drink alcoholic beverages in an Islamic nation, but the State Department alerted the US embassy in Tripoli that the delegation did not know the sensitive nature of relations between Libya and the United States. Billy did not have a reputation for diplomatic sensitivity in any situation. His public use of terms like "bastardized Jew" and "Polack" offended many Americans who thought the president's brother should be chastised.[17]

Whereas Billy usually tarnished the first family's reputation, Miss Lillian added humor, charm, and wisdom to the family lore. Saying exactly what she pleased, in a November interview for the Louisville, Kentucky, *Courier Journal*, she talked about a fact-finding trip she had made the previous August for the President's Commission on World Hunger. She had gone to Africa by way of France and Italy, including a stop at the Vatican. During her audience with Pope Paul VI, coincidentally shortly before he died on August 6, she asked him to pray for the United States, for human rights, and for rain in Africa. His prayers were efficacious, she claimed, for everywhere she went in Africa, it rained. Reinforcing the gist of Jimmy's speech in Florida, she cocked her head slightly when revealing that she was bothered by seeing "some people so very rich and others so poor." Empathizing with poor and hungry people, she recalled that she had been hungry when she served with the Peace Corps in India in the mid-1960s. When quizzed about the rights of gay people, Lillian stated forthrightly: "I think every human has the right to do what he wants."[18]

Miss Lillian's audience with the Pope in August was the first of several episodes in the summer and fall of 1978 during which the Carter family interacted with popes. After Paul VI died in August, his successor, John Paul I, lived for only eight weeks. His successor, John Paul II, the first Polish Pope, gave Carter the opportunity to praise Polish Americans and possibly improve his reputation among US Catholics. By asking Millie O'Neill, wife of the quietly Catholic Speaker Tip O'Neill, to attend the funeral of John Paul I, Carter improved his relationship with the Speaker as well as US Catholics. Speaking publicly, Carter welcomed the "new hope" that John Paul II brought to the world. As a native of Poland, the new Pope, Carter continued, understood "the struggle for faith, for freedom, for life itself."[19]

But there was little time to celebrate Polish Americans and popes, as Carter confronted more demanding diplomatic challenges. Begin threatened to subvert the Camp David Accords; Brezhnev wanted SALT II to be concluded early; and the shah's control of Iran steadily weakened. On November 18, an unexpected crisis broke out in Guyana when Congressman Leo Ryan of California and five other US citizens were murdered by Reverend Jim Jones. Jones then led hundreds of his followers to commit suicide at their remote jungle encampment in that South American country. Golda Meir died the following month, but Jimmy's show of respect in sending his mother to attend her funeral did not improve his standing among Jewish Americans. Meanwhile, issues involving Cuba, Nicaragua, and China also remained unsettled.[20]

The president's focus, however, pivoted back to Iran, a country about which Carter had too little reliable information and to which he was too tightly bound by previous administrations. As religiously motivated demonstrations against the shah increased, the shah attempted to stifle them by placing their leaders under house arrest for "corruption." The seventy-eight-year-old Ayatollah Khomeini remained safely exiled in Paris where he called for a "holy war against the Shah." He hoped that immediate strikes and demonstrations would be sufficient to depose the shah, he said on public television, but he would not rule out the need for violence. The US embassy in Tehran, incredulous that Khomeini could wield so much power, nevertheless warned US citizens living in Iran to exercise caution in their daily lives.[21]

Intensified anti-US feelings, however, soon caused frightened Americans to flee the country. During the last three months of 1978, 38,000 of them left, leaving only about 7,000 still in Iran. Fearing that the Soviets might take advantage of the chaos in Iran to extend their influence in the region, Carter warned them to stay out of it. On Christmas Eve, 1978, an Iranian mob attempted to storm the US embassy in Tehran, but US marine guards lobbed a tear gas grenade into the crowd, forcing it to disperse.[22]

Frustrated by the poor intelligence about Iran that he received from the CIA, Carter looked to Brzezinski for advice. The National Security Advisor also complained about the "inept and vague" CIA "comments on the crisis in Iran." Under Stansfield Turner's leadership, the CIA increasingly depended upon electronic surveillance, but Carter and Brzezinski thought they needed more human intelligence. When the US ambassador in Tehran, William Sullivan, cabled Washington in late November 1978 that the shah might be forced to abdicate, Carter sent a stern note to "Cy, Zbig, Stan," saying "I am not satisfied with the quality of our political intelligence." Turner, embarrassed by being reprimanded by the president, attempted to improve his intelligence gathering from Iran, and within a few days he gave Carter a briefing that was, according to Carter, "more political & strategic, & less technical." Carter, Brzezinski, and Ham Jordan were satisfied with the material, but it did not help them understand Khomeini, who seemed to be in control of Iran.[23]

The shah, ill and desperate to stop the revolution, appointed a moderate politician, Shapour Bakhtiar, to lead a civilian government. The chance that Bakhtiar might prevail against the religious revolutionaries who wanted to rid the country of the shah and to establish an Islamic state seemed remote. Ignoring the magnitude of the revolution against Pahlavi, the United States stubbornly continued to support him. In a meeting with Iranian ambassador Zahedi on November 21, Carter reassured him that he would stand by the shah and that he would inform the Soviets of his intention to do so.[24]

In truth, the shah's days were numbered. The British thought he would soon be out of power. Khomeini continued to urge violent demonstrations against the "satanic ruler and his parasitic henchmen." With help from the State Department, more US citizens joined other foreigners fleeing from the crumbling country.[25]

Tending to domestic political issues, as well as foreign developments, Carter went to Memphis, Tennessee, on December 8 to address the midterm Democratic Congress. He tried to "inspire the convention" and "restore faith and confidence" in the Party by spelling out a future agenda for "peace—health—human rights—justice . . . strength . . . democracy." His speech writers gave him what he wanted, but White House communications director Jerry Rafshoon could not resist the urge to joke with him through private memos. Rafshoon advised that, when *Sports Illustrated* asked him about his "tennis ability and athletic prowess," he should "break policy and LIE." Enjoying the joke, Jimmy quickly replied, "This would not deviate from policy."[26]

In a very different mood, a few days earlier in a televised speech from the East Room, Carter had celebrated the thirtieth anniversary of the adoption of the Universal Declaration of Human Rights. "As long as I am President," he solemnly vowed, "the government of the United States will continue throughout the world to enhance human rights." All peoples, Carter boldly declared, should be free of "arbitrary violence . . . whether from governments, from terrorists, from criminals, or from self-appointed messiahs, operating under the cover of politics or religion."[27] From his Christian perspective, his message not only served notice to the perpetrators of human abuses, but also gave hope to the victims.

The joy and relief that Jimmy and Rosalynn felt as the Christmas season approached was diminished by Jimmy's personal ailment. He suffered with a severe case of hemorrhoids, an ailment that had plagued him from his youth. On December 22 he underwent corrective surgery, signing over the powers of the presidency to the vice president for the time he would be under anesthesia. On December 23, the day after his surgery, Jimmy and Rosalynn went home to Plains for the holiday, leaving behind Chinese Nationalists, American Indians, and disgruntled farmers who demonstrated in Washington.[28]

Casually dressed, Jimmy enjoyed Christmas Day with his family at Miss Allie's home. While the Georgia Christians thanked God for sending them the Prince of Peace, Islamic Egyptians, who had heard about Carter's surgery, asked Allah to bless and cure him. Carter recovered quickly, more likely because of the skill of his doctors than diverse intercessional prayers. After contemplating thanking the Egyptians, he decided that enough had already been said about his "rear end."[29]

NINETEEN

Carter's Coup: China

On December 14, 1978, Carter dropped a bombshell on the unsuspecting Soviets. "I want to inform you," he wrote Brezhnev, "that on Friday, December 15, at 9 p.m. Washington time, I will announce the normalization of relations between the Government of the United States and the People's Republic of China (PRC). This is an historic moment [with] . . . no other purpose but to promote the cause of world peace."[1] Prior to the announcement, Brzezinski invited Soviet Ambassador Anatoly Dobrynin to his office. The ambassador "looked stunned" when Zbig told him that the United States would soon announce the initiation of full-scale relations with China.[2]

Historic it was, and for what purpose the Soviets could only guess, but it raised the possibility, even the fear on their part, that the United States might enter into an alliance with China against the Kremlin. Whatever the new diplomatic initiative might mean for the future relationship between the United States and China, Carter intended for it to put pressure on the Soviet Union to pursue an arms limitation agreement with the United States.

Although the news may have struck Russia like a bolt from the blue, Carter had been planning for it from the very beginning of his administration. In 1972, former President Richard Nixon had made his famous visit to China, opening up a new era in US-Chinese relations, but Nixon did little more than orchestrate some feel-good cultural exchanges and receive a commitment from China, known as the Shanghai communiqué, that the two countries would continue to talk in the future. Deng Xiaoping assumed leadership of China after the death of Chairman Mao in 1976 and shortly before Carter became president. For economic reasons, Deng was eager to advance science, technology, and business in his country. He looked to the United States for help, but Carter, engulfed in matters related to the Panama Canal and the Middle East hardly realized it until July 1978 when his science adviser Frank Press visited China. Press was shocked when Deng requested permission to send many more faculty and students to the United States than Press had been authorized to accept.

Press called Carter, who instantly approved Deng's request. Although there was little Carter could do about the Communist government's human rights violations in China, he agreed to science and technology exchanges, including medical and agricultural personnel whose work could contribute to ending hunger and disease epidemics in the PRC. The plan fit neatly into Jimmy and Rosalynn's belief that helping the people at the level where they actually lived would trickle up to pressuring the government into formulating more democratic and humane policies.

Quite unexpectedly, Carter and Deng found themselves with a good working relationship that would facilitate the normalization of relations between their countries. Carter discovered that Deng, unlike Soviet leaders, had the ability to get directly to the heart of important matters. Theirs was a relationship that worked so long as Carter did not press human rights and Deng ignored the continuing friendship and defense treaty between the United States and Taiwan.[3]

Carter, Vance, and Brzezinski moved quickly to take advantage of Deng's desire for a better relationship with the United States. Apart from political issues, the primary obstacles were the American Mutual Defense Treaty of 1954 with Taiwan and Carter's determination to normalize relations with Vietnam, an action that Deng categorically condemned because he believed Vietnam to be a Soviet satellite. Brzezinski had received a secret memorandum from the US embassy in Taiwan reporting that Taiwan was "resilient enough" for the United States to accomplish normalization with the mainland without destabilizing the island. Brzezinski wanted a closer relationship with China to check the power of the Kremlin and to disprove the perception that the United States was soft on the Soviet Union. Vance thought that normalization of relations with China would block any reconciliation between China and Russia. On July 30, Carter, who wanted to defuse the Cold War, told Vance "to go for it," but he wanted little publicity or serious negotiations until after the Panama Canal treaties had been ratified.[4]

Vance prepared a thirteen-page memorandum briefing Carter about Deng and his expectations. Vance sized Deng up as "impatient," "direct," "forceful," and "clever." The Chinese leader's future plans included making an official visit to the United States to help Carter sell normalization to Congress and the US public, urge the United States to resist increasing Soviet expansion, and nudge it toward hostility, not Carter's proposed friendship, with Vietnam. Vance concluded that, if successful, normalization would have a major impact on Asia and the world.[5]

The events that led to the normalization of relations with China began in May 1978, two months before Frank Press's visit and Vance's July 10 memorandum, when Brzezinski had made a secret visit to Peking. Carter gave him carte blanche to go as far as possible with Deng in outlining the terms of an agreement but warning him not to make any final commitment.[6] Zbig, his wife Muska, and their ten advisers had arrived in Peking on May 20. The advisers, a blue ribbon team indicating the importance Carter attached to the mission, included Samuel Huntington of the NSC, Mort Abramowitz of the Defense Department's military intelligence, Richard Holrooke from the State Department, Ben Huberman from Frank Press's science group, and Michel Oksenberg from Brzezinski's national security staff.[7]

Wasting no time, Deng met with Brzezinski for two hours in the afternoon, later over dinner, and again in the evening. He pressed Brzezinski on issues involving Taiwan, Vietnam, the sale of high tech equipment to China, whether Carter seriously wanted normalization, and an invitation to the White House. Deng became openly angry when Brzezinski could not commit to the United States abandoning Taiwan or refraining from pushing for normalizing relations with Vietnam. Deng questioned why the US would sign an arms limitation treaty with the Soviets, but Brzezinski cleverly and convincingly won that point when he explained to the vice premier how much he distrusted the Soviet Union. Making his argument personal, Zbig added, "I would be willing to make a little bet with you as to who is less popular in the Soviet Union--you or me."[8]

Deng calmed down, and Zbig reassured him that the United States, despite the SALT II negotiations in Vienna, would not form any kind of alliance against China. Deng dropped the topics of Taiwan and Vietnam and seemed satisfied when Zbig told him that "the President personally is prepared to resolve this question [of normalization] as rapidly as it proves practical." Furthermore, Brzezinski continued, Carter would be guided "by the principle that there is only one China, and that the resolution of the issue of Taiwan is your problem."[9] Brzezinski departed China on May 21, placing continuing negotiations in the care of US Ambassador Leonard Woodcock, who would communicate directly with Brzezinski or the White House and the State Department.

Upon Brzezinski's arrival back in Washington, Deputy Secretary of State Warren Christopher greeted him in a symbolic show of solidarity with the State Department. When Zbig visited Carter in his private office, Carter leaped from his chair to give Zbig a vigorous handshake and a bear hug. After giving the president a condensed verbal recap of the conversations, Zbig wrote up a much longer report the next day, which he hoped that "Rosalynn will also read."[10]

Brzezinski appeared on *Meet the Press*, which turned into a fiasco. The questions he received virtually ignored his trip to China and focused on the Soviet Union. Brzezinski's answers revealed his hawkish attitude toward the Soviets and strong condemnation of Brezhnev's alleged aggression in the Middle East, Africa, and the Indian Ocean. Cy Vance was chagrined that Brzezinski had, in a major public forum, usurped the work of the State Department. Carter angrily warned Zbig that he went too far with his comments about the Soviets, which threatened détente and possibly the SALT II talks. But Carter calmed down and moved the talks with the Soviets in Vienna forward while secretly continuing the dialogue with Deng. On May 26, he jokingly recorded in his diary that he thought Zbig had been "seduced" in China.[11]

Through the summer and fall, Ambassador Woodcock continued serious discussions with Deng's government, and Carter occasionally met with Chai Zemin, the head of the Chinese Liaison Office in Washington. Both Brzezinski and Vance remained in the loop, keeping Carter informed. Carter decided to make the two concessions that Deng had requested: he would abrogate the 1954 defense treaty with Taiwan but retain the right to defend the island, and he would postpone normalization of relations with Vietnam. In a telegram to Brzezinski on December 13, Deng accepted the offer. Carter shook Zbig's hand "warmly" and gave him credit for being "the driving force behind the whole effort." The White House began to prepare for Deng's visit, when he and Carter would officially sign the normalization agreement.[12]

Carter had managed the negotiations with China, while at the same time working for the SALT II treaty with the Soviet Union, without the Soviets knowing about the China discussions. The result was a diplomatic coup in which Carter concluded important game-changing treaties with both countries within a few months of each other, restoring the balance of power among the three superpowers and striking a damaging blow to the Soviets in the Cold War.

Inadvertently, Carter also struck a damaging blow to the relationship between Vance and Brzezinski. After giving Vance the initial go-ahead to begin normalization talks with the Chinese, he had allowed Brzezinski to gain control of the final negotiations and thus receive the lion's share of public credit for the ultimate success of the talks. From the early days of the administration,

Carter had become closer to Zbig, who had helped him and Rosalynn during the campaign and, in his official capacity, saw him every day. Brimming with ideas, Zbig advised the president on both foreign policy and domestic politics. Being on good terms with Rosalynn, Brzezinski later conceded, placed him on good terms with the president.[13]

Vance worked in a quieter, more diplomatic, less aggressive way, but he understood foreign policy and defense quite well. He and his wife Gay, enjoyed a good rapport with the Carters and shared social occasions with them, but he was not the aggressive political campaigner Jimmy and Rosalynn would have liked him to be. With Carter's blessing, Vance had met with Deng at China's Treaty Hall in August to try to convince him that the United States needed to maintain a connection with Taiwan. Vance was more focused, however, on negotiating the SALT II treaty with the Soviets, which was also of particular interest to the Chinese, who thought that, if the United States won its Cold War with the Soviets, it would be to China's advantage to form a better relationship with the United States. Neither Carter nor Brzezinski shared Vance's cautious advice that SALT II should be completed before normalization with China. Brzezinski, with Carter's acquiescence, had wrested the process of normalization from the State Department, and when Deng's acceptance of Carter's terms landed on Carter's desk on December 13, Brzezinski walked away with more credit than he deserved for the improved relationship with China. The negotiating that Vance had done to make this possible was forgotten in the ensuing swell of public approval.[14]

In preparation for full diplomatic relations with the Communist PRC, Carter terminated the mutual defense treaty with the Republic of China (Taiwan). Since Congress was out of session when he did it, a group of outraged conservative senators, led by Barry Goldwater of Arizona, brought a suit against him and fought it through the federal district court, the court of appeals, and the Supreme Court. The latter dismissed it, thus handing Carter the victory on June 6, 1979, after which Carter dryly commented that the decision "restores some of my confidence in the judicial system." Former Presidents Ford and Nixon approved the agreements as farsighted diplomacy that transcended partisan politics.[15]

The treaty gave Carter the right to assure Congress and the American people that the United States would continue to provide security assistance to Taiwan. It also enabled the two countries to have increased cultural and scientific exchanges, Chinese access to US universities, and trade agreements for the 1979–1980 fiscal year. Deng got his long-held hope for an invitation to the White House for the signing, but he did not win US support for his plan to punish Vietnam for its invasion of Cambodia.

Carter's hope for a safer world prepared him to accept the domestic political consequences of abandoning the defense treaty with Taiwan. His justification for his action was based upon the Shanghai Communique of 1972, a joint statement issued by Nixon and Mao that each nation would periodically re-examine their positions. The president of the fundamentalist Bob Jones University in Greenville, South Carolina, however, would not accept Carter's justification. He questioned Carter's Christianity and openly wondered "how a Christian" could do that to "the 17 million souls in Taiwan." He, and others with his mindset, began to work against Carter's reelection.[16]

On December 20, 1978, Nixon wrote Carter a letter advising him to do what he had already done: act with secrecy, maintain security for Taiwan, and consider the impact of Chinese normalization on other foreign policy initiatives. "From a purely partisan political standpoint," the old Republican wrote, "I would hope you would not take my advice. But I feel that the stakes for America and the world are too high for partisanship as usual." Writing as a sage senior statesman, Nixon continued: "You have a supreme opportunity to lead the nation and the world into a new era of prosperity, peace and justice. . . . what is good for you is good for America, and if it results in many happy returns for you in 1980, you will deserve it." Two days later, Carter thanked Nixon for his "excellent letter," promised to ask his advice on SALT II, and invited him to the White House for the banquet and signing with Deng.[17]

With normalization of relations with China assured, Carter announced that he would continue to withdraw troops from South Korea, a proposal he had put forth two years earlier. It had not sat well with the public or the Joint Chiefs of Staff, who argued that the troops might be needed for the security of South Korea. Carter reasoned that China, as a stronger presence on North Korea's border, would lessen the need for US troops in South Korea to guarantee its defense against possible North Korean aggression. US recognition of China had the potential to upset the stability in North Korea, Vietnam, and Cambodia, for those countries feared what an emboldened China might do. Likewise, a nervous Taiwan lobby in the United States succeeded in getting Congress to pass the Taiwan Relations Act, which Carter signed on April 10, 1979, and which promised that the United States would continue to provide weapons and equipment for Taiwan's self-defense.[18]

In preparation for the arrival of Deng on January 28, 1979, Brzezinski told Carter that the US-Chinese-Soviet triangle would be fragile because neither the Russians nor the Chinese desired the balanced relationship among the three nations that the United States sought. Partially driven by his own intense dislike of the Soviet Union, Brzezinski explained that the Chinese were frightened by recent Soviet advances in Africa, Afghanistan, and Vietnam. They supported the shah of Iran and had invested heavily in Pakistan, and they feared being surrounded by Soviet-dominated countries. The Carter administration shared those concerns, thus finding common ground with their Chinese visitors.[19]

On January 28 after their eighteen-hour flight from Peking to Washington, Brzezinski, not Carter, met the Chinese delegation at Dulles International Airport and took them into his nearby home in Northern Virginia for a roast beef dinner. The Brzezinskis knew that Deng enjoyed beef, which they served cut into small portions to make easier to pick up with chop sticks. Since they also knew he liked folk singers Joan Baez and Bob Dylan, Zbig entertained them by playing their music on a stereo.[20] After dinner, the US hosts escorted Deng and his wife to Blair House to spend their first night in the United States.

The next day, January 29, at 10:12 a.m., the Carters formally welcomed the Dengs to the White House with full military honors. After effusive words of thanks, praise, and expectations, Carter and Deng retreated to the first of two meetings in the Oval Office that they would have during the day.[21] Carter found Deng to be "tough, intelligent, frank, courageous," and a pleasant person with whom to negotiate. Carter outlined five basic factors that motivated his administration: enhancing US power was for the benefit of US citizens and the rest of the world; that people throughout the world wanted freedom and a better quality of life; power was shifting from a few nations such as the United States and the Soviet Union to emerging nations; and the security of the United States was tied to good relations with the emerging nations. Deng responded that the world was "untranquil" and that the United States should join with the emerging nations "to oppose the Soviet Union." He said that the PRC recognized the right of Israel to exist but there was no possibility that his country would open a path of communication with Israel. He predicted that problems in the Middle East would spread to Saudi Arabia, Iran, and other countries, whose animosity toward Israel would impact Israel's allies.[22]

At a late afternoon conference in the Oval Office shortly before the state dinner, Carter, joined by Mondale, Vance, and Brzezinski, talked with Deng and three other top Chinese officials about the touchy subject of Vietnam. The Chinese were preparing to mount a limited short-term military invasion of their southern neighbor to restrain what they perceived as reckless Vietnamese ambitions. "We find," Deng told Carter, "that Vietnam had become totally Soviet controlled, and the fact of its flagrant invasion of Cambodia, its plot to establish an Indochinese Federation under Vietnamese control is more grave than you think. . . . Vietnam is playing the role of Cuba. Of course, the Soviet Union will make use of Vietnam to harass China. Vietnam is also an important factor in the Soviet 'Asian collective security system' . . . . If we do not punish them, their violent actions will continue on a greater scale. They will expand their activities also on China's borders."

Carter replied: "I do not need to know the punitive action being contemplated, but it could result in escalation of violence and a change in the world posture from being against Vietnam to partial support for Vietnam . . . . We have joined in the condemnation of Vietnam, but invasion of Vietnam would be a very serious destabilizing action." He concluded the forty-minute meeting by telling Deng: "I would like to talk to you tomorrow—privately. In the meantime, I would like to assess American reactions, of my own people. The situation is serious. I understand you cannot allow Vietnam to pursue aggression with impunity."[23] The meeting ended cordially, and both leaders returned to their living quarters to prepare for the state banquet and evening of gala entertainment that Rosalynn had orchestrated.

The formally dressed heads of state and their wives made the traditional grand entry down red-carpeted stairs as trumpets announced their entrance. Although Jimmy and Rosalynn were relatively short by US standards, they towered above their diminutive Chinese guests as they processed to their elegantly set table decorated with camellia blossoms, believed to have originated in China, which Rosalynn ordered from Georgia. The menu included Timbale of Seafood, Roast Stuffed Loin of Veal, endive and watercress salad, chestnut mousse, and chocolate truffles, with each course accompanied by the appropriate wine. Strolling violinists performed while the guests nibbled on the mousse and truffles. The meal ended, stewards served Hans Kornell Extra Dry Champagne in preparation for the after-dinner toasts.[24]

The laudatory after-dinner remarks and subsequent toasts seemed to have a more serious tone than usual, for all present knew they were players in a dramatic historical event. Jovial during the toasts, Deng raised his glass of Californian champagne to Ambassador Leonard Woodcock and to the new Sino-US relationship.[25] Among the 140 carefully selected guests were former President Richard Nixon, on his first visit to the White House since his resignation in 1974.[26] Actress Shirley MacLaine sat next to the vice premier and enthusiastically thanked him for the gracious reception she had received during a visit to China in the early 1970s. He smiled, though scarcely disguising his toughness and authoritarianism with his response: "The people who were your hosts then are in jail now." Life for him, as for nearly everyone in his country, he noted, was a constant struggle.

Speaking more softly to Carter, who was seated at his other side, Deng thanked him for what he had helped the Chinese people to achieve and asked if there was something that China could do for Carter. Carter responded that Deng could let his people worship freely, own Bibles, and allow US missionaries back into China. Deng later granted the first two but declined to allow missionaries to return.[27]

Following the dinner, the two first couples went to the Kennedy Center for the evening entertainment. A program entitled "An Evening for the Performance of American Arts" featured the Joffrey Ballet, folk singer John Denver, and Deng's dinner companion Shirley MacLaine.[28] Deng smiled broadly, obviously enjoying the celebrations, and he, Madame Zhou Lin, Rosalynn, and Amy went up onto the stage after the performance. Deng placed his arms around some of the small children who had sung a Chinese song and kissed them.[29]

At the private meeting between the two leaders in the Oval Office the next morning, January 30, Carter again condemned the Chinese plan to invade Vietnam. Defending his position, Deng argued that "China must still teach Vietnam a lesson . . . . If Vietnam thought the PRC soft, the situation will get worse . . . . The action will be quick, lasting 10–20 days, to be followed by withdrawal . . . . This matter has been thoroughly vetted at the top of the Chinese government."[30] Carter responded politely but emphatically that such an attack would not be successful. Furthermore, it would bring down world-wide condemnation on the PRC and make it very difficult for the United States to settle the Taiwan issue. He urged Deng to avoid military conflict and to instead seek help through the UN.[31]

Later that day, Deng met with both houses of Congress, which were discussing whether to grant China most favored nation status. Deng was trying to learn how the US system of government worked, and he cleverly defused criticism of his immigration policy. He said that China had no relationship with the Soviet Union, which had a very restrictive emigration policy. Since the Jackson-Vanik Amendment required Communist countries to allow free emigration if they wished to trade with the United States, some Congressmen asked him about his emigration policy. Deng quickly replied, "How many do you want? Ten million? Fifteen million?" Carter interjected a bit of humor by offering to exchange 10,000 journalists for ten million Chinese. Deng quickly rejected that proposal, and everyone laughed. The doubting Congressmen dropped that topic and granted China most favored nation status.[32]

On January 31, Carter and Deng met for the last time and signed the multiple agreements associated with normalization.[33] The foreign secretaries for both nations also signed the agreements, formally beginning a new era in the histories of the United States, China, and Russia. The United States and the PRC agreed to cooperate on science, technology, exploration of space, and cultural exchanges. The United States would sell a communications satellite system to China and open consulates in Canton and Shanghai; the Chinese would establish their own in San Francisco and Houston. After the signing, Carter praised the agreement for bringing tangible benefits to both nations. He knew Deng would find Americans hospitable as he traveled from one end of the country to the other. Deng, after thanking the president, extended Carter's statement, contending that the agreement the United States and China had reached would not only benefit their countries but all the peoples of the world. Before leaving on his tour of the United States, he invited the Carters to visit China in the near future.[34]

Despite his friendly departure from Washington on January 31, Deng had not agreed to what Carter had asked him to do about Vietnam. Shortly after returning to China, he ordered his army into Vietnam. Carter quickly sent a telegram to Brezhnev asking for Russia's cooperation in maintaining independent states in Asia. Brezhnev replied that Russia could not be indifferent to "Chinese Aggression," but he did not say what action he might take.[35] In the end, he did nothing.

The agreements between China and the United States hastened China's emergence as a powerful nation with which the United States and others would have to deal in the next century. Reflecting upon them in 1994, shortly after the death of Deng, Jimmy and Rosalynn shared their recollections about him. Carter thought that he was honest, a "great leader" for China, and one who was establishing a free enterprise system. Rosalynn was less certain and reminded her husband that Deng was not politically perfect, especially because of his willingness to violate human rights in his country. The official attitude toward Deng's use of his visit to the United States to condemn Moscow was silence.[36]

TWENTY

Khomeini, Bella, and Rosalynn

While Carter entertained Deng, the shah of Iran lost control of his country. In early January when US citizens began leaving Iran in large numbers, Carter sent Air Force Lieutenant General Robert Huyser, deputy commander in chief of the US European Command, to Tehran to persuade the Iranian military to support a stable government that would maintain close ties with the United States. Both Huyser and Vance advised Carter to also send an emissary to Paris to talk with Ayatollah Khomeini, who had been living in exile there and waiting for his chance to return to Iran and reestablish it as an Islamic nation free of Western influence. When Brzezinski went further and tried to get Carter to approve a covert military coup to disperse Khomeini's supporters, Carter lost his temper, refused to do it, and said that he found it "morally troublesome" to deal secretly with the shah's enemy. He promised his advisers, however, to discuss the problem with French President Giscard d'Estaing, at an upcoming conference.[1]

Both Vance and Huyser were disturbed by Carter's refusal to dispatch an envoy to Paris. The communique that Vance received from Ambassador William H. Sullivan on January 2 was more urgent than he had reported to the president. The ambassador informed the secretary that both he and General Huyser agreed that the president had made a "GROSS and perhaps IRRETRIEVABLE MISTAKE by failing to send an emissary to Paris to see Khomeini." Huyser had asked Defense Secretary Brown to persuade Carter to change his mind. If he did not, Huyser argued, the relationship between Iran and the United States would be "permanently" damaged.[2]

Carter did not change his mind. He was preoccupied with Deng's upcoming trip and the conference of Western leaders in Guadeloupe scheduled for January 4–9. Spending time at the conference on a relaxing tropical island, with Rosalynn and Amy, offered Carter a brief respite from his ongoing domestic political worries. Senator Ted Kennedy routinely dropped hints that he would challenge him for the nomination.[3] Jewish public opinion ran strongly against the peace treaty with Egypt because it did not adequately protect Israel's security.[4] Increasing numbers of Iranians gathered outside the White House and in large cities across the country to demonstrate against the shah. A majority of Americans opposed the treaty with China and Carter's plan to terminate the Mutual Defense Treaty with Taiwan.[5]

With those issues, and more, pending, on January 4, Jimmy, Rosalynn, and Amy arrived at Pointe-a-Pitre airport, where they soon met French president Giscard d'Estaing, West German chancellor Helmut Schmidt, and British prime minister James Callaghan. While the three European leaders and their wives took a helicopter to the conference resort hotel on the eastern end of the main island, Jimmy, Rosalynn, and Amy drove the twenty miles there in order to do a bit of sightseeing. "The Presidential motorcade," the New York Times reported, "Followed a two lane road through poor villages of tin-roofed shacks and past the luxury hotels that line the island's southern coast. Cattle and goats grazed beside the road, and every few miles French policemen stood guard." That evening, the leaders and their wives relaxed and got acquainted over dinner in an outdoor cabana.[6]

The next morning the men, overdressed for the tropical venue in business suits, began two days of informal, unpublicized discussions. Despite the distraction of an adjacent topless beach frequented by many young women, the middle-aged leaders agreed that they needed to increase security and reduce tension in the world.[7] While they hoped to resolve any differences they had about military, economic, and foreign policy issues, they were unsure, according to the New York Times, "about each other's intentions and abilities."[8]

The Western leaders were all concerned about the Soviet deployment of new SS-20 intermediate-range ballistic missiles with nuclear warheads aimed at Western Europe. Schmidt wanted Carter to station US intermediate-range missiles on German soil, but Carter favored waiting to see what the Soviets might do and what agreement might come out of the SALT II discussions. Giscard d'Estaing and Callaghan believed that such a step might become necessary, but not yet. Carter found himself in a troubled relationship with Schmidt, because the chancellor thought that Carter was ignorant of the problem of a divided Germany and naïve about the threat of the Soviet Union.[9]

Carter reassured the apprehensive Europeans that any agreement between the United States and the Soviet Union would not jeopardize their security. All of the leaders gathered there agreed that their relationships with Russia and China were improving because of US diplomacy. At their final meeting on January 6, Carter was "quite explicit" in telling the Europeans that they might have to do more to defend themselves than simply depend upon the United States. "Helmut," Carter reported to his diary, "was quite contentious, Jim was cooperative, and Valery minimized French involvement." At their last luncheon together, Callaghan led the light, joking conversation when he "complained strenuously that his back was turned to the beach," where "topless women bathers" casually strolled along in the bright sunshine.[10]

Before departing, the four men held a joint news conference at their hotel. Carter said that the conference had been productive politically and economically for the four allies and a good step toward global peace. The British and French leaders observed that Carter had strengthened the NATO alliance and helped the West to stand united against the weakening Soviet Union. Anything said about the revolution in Iran went unrecorded.[11]

Jimmy, Rosalynn, and Amy remained at Guadeloupe for three extra days of vacation. But the peaceful atmosphere of their seaside bungalow, surrounded by hibiscus and bougainvillea, was disrupted by frequent telephone calls about Iran. Carter and Cy Vance, who was also in Guadeloupe, decided to support the shah and the military, because they thought the military remained loyal to the shah. The other Western leaders seemed unsurprised that the shah's regime was collapsing. They showed no interest in supporting him, believing that a civilian government should be established. Carter meanwhile continued evacuating thousands of US citizens from the troubled country.[12] Pahlavi himself believed that the French, Germans, and British were united with the Americans in favor of his "ouster," a decision he compared to President Franklin Roosevelt's concession to the Russians at Yalta in 1945.[13]

Carter had not cut such a deal with his colleagues at Guadeloupe. Shortly after returning to the White House, he concentrated on building bridges with African-American voters. He and Rosalynn went to Atlanta to celebrate the fiftieth birthday of Martin Luther King, Jr. At Ebenezer Baptist church on January 15, Rosalynn praised King as a "great man of hope, faith, and love." She confirmed to the admiring audience that both she and Jimmy wanted to make King's birthday a national holiday. Carter declared that at a time when tyranny and violence often occurred in the name of religion, it was important to remember how the nonviolence practiced by King triumphed over adversity.[14]

While Carter praised nonviolence in the United States, the often-violent situation in Iran deteriorated rapidly. Prime Minister Shapour Bakhtiar, the sixty-two-year-old leader of the civilian government, asked the Majlis, the

The Train Depot in Plains, Georgia, which served as Jimmy Carter's campaign headquarters for the 1976 presidential campaign.
Source: Library of Congress, LC-DIG highsm – 42764.

Rosalynn Carter shaking hands during the 1976 presidential campaign.
Source: Carter Library.

Jimmy Carter and Walter Mondale, after being nominated for the presidency and vice presidency at the Democratic National Convention, New York, July 15, 1976.

Source: Library of Congress, LC-DIG ppmsca – 09739.

Jimmy Carter and his family at Warm Springs, Georgia, September 1976, making the official announcement of his presidential campaign.

Source: Carter Library.

Amy kissing her Dad on the nose with Misty Malarky Ying Yang in her arms, during the 1976 presidential campaign.
Source: Carter Library.

Jimmy Carter campaigning on the Mississippi State University campus, Fall 1976. 1977 *Reveille* Annual Yearbook.
Source: Mississippi State University Libraries.

Jimmy Carter and Billy Carter (second from left) at Billy's Gas Station, 1976 campaign.
Source: Carter Library.

The Carter family in November 1976.
Source: Carter Library.

Rosalynn Carter's mother, "Miss Allie" Smith, who celebrated her daughter's becoming First Lady of the United States in 1976.

Source: Library of Congress, LC-DG-gtfy- 00830.

The Pond House at the Carter Farm, where Miss Lillian lived and Carter interviewed candidates for positions in his administration.

Source: Library of Congress, HABS GA,131-PLAIN,19—3.

Incoming First Lady Rosalynn Carter and outgoing First Lady Betty Ford before Carter's inauguration, January 20, 1977.

Source: Carter Library.

President Carter and First Lady Rosalynn Carter walk down Pennsylvania Avenue after his inauguration at the Capitol, January 20, 1977.
Source: Carter Library.

Jimmy and Rosalynn wave at an inaugural ball during celebrations for his becoming the Thirty-Ninth President of the United States, January 20, 1977.
Source: Carter Library.

Lillian Carter visits her son after her return from India, February 17, 1977.
Source: Carter Library.

Mary Fitzpatrick and Amy Carter on the White House grounds, February 23, 1977.
Source: Carter Library.

Anwar and Jehan Sadat with Jimmy and Rosalynn Carter at the White House, April 4, 1977.
Source: Carter Library.

President Carter
contemplating his first
one hundred days in
office, April 14, 1977.
Source: Carter Library.

Jimmy and Rosalynn Carter
on the submarine *Los Angeles*,
May 1977.
Source: Carter Library.

First Lady Rosalynn Carter greets children at a child care center in Recife, Brazil, June 8, 1977.
Source: AP Photo.

President Jimmy Carter and Vice President Walter Mondale welcome Rosalynn home from her diplomatic trip to Latin America, June 12, 1977.
Source: Carter Library.

Rosalynn Carter honored at a luncheon with members of the Senate Foreign Relations Committee after she had reported to them on her June 1977 trip to South America.
Source: Carter Library.

Zbigniew Brzezinski (left) and Cyrus Vance (right), architects of the Carter Administration foreign policy, June 10, 1977. *Source:* Carter Library.

President Carter greets Margaret Thatcher at the Oval Office, September 13, 1977, before she became prime minister of the United Kingdom. *Source:* Carter Library.

Rosalynn Carter and Betty Ford with two unidentified women's rights leaders at an ERA Rally in Houston, Texas, November 19, 1977.
Source: Carter Library.

Carter meeting with Edward Gierek, First Secretary of Poland, December 30, 1977.
Source: Carter Library.

President Carter and First Lady Rosalynn Carter in Warsaw viewing the Nike monument honoring Polish heroes, December 30, 1977. Rosalynn is wearing a scarf that was loaned to her by Mary Fitzpatrick.
Source: AP Photo/ Dennis Cook.

Rosalynn Carter and Zbigniew Brzezinski with Cardinal Wyszynski in Warsaw, Poland, December 30, 1977.
Source: Carter Library.

First Lady Rosalynn Carter with
Empress Farah Pahlavi at a New
Year's Eve party, Niavaran Palace,
Tehran, December 31, 1977.
Source: Carter Library.

Jimmy and Rosalynn Carter tour a village in India, January 3, 1978.
Source: Carter Library.

Jimmy Carter and General Olusegun
Obasanjo in Nigeria, April 2, 1978.
Source: Carter Library.

First Lady Rosalynn Carter holds a Nigerian child during her tour with Amy Carter in a Nigerian village, April 2, 1978.
Source: Carter Library.

Rosalynn Carter and Joan Mondale in the Solarium at the White House, August 4, 1978.
Source: Carter Library.

Jimmy and Rosalynn dancing on the *Delta Queen*, August 20, 1978.
Source: Carter Library.

Jimmy Carter vacationing in Grand Tetons, Wyoming, August 26, 1978.
Source: Carter Library.

Jimmy Carter, Rosalynn Carter, Anwar Sadat, and Menachem Begin greeting
each other at Camp David, September 7, 1978.
Source: Carter Library.

Jimmy Carter and Menachem Begin at Camp David, September 1978.
Source: Carter Library.

Jimmy Carter and Anwar Sadat meet at the beginning of the Camp David
Summit, September 6, 1978.
Source: Carter Library.

Rosalynn Carter and Aliza Begin visit Gettysburg with their husbands and
Anwar Sadat during the Camp David Summit, September 10, 1978.
Source: Carter Library.

Jimmy Carter, Anwar Sadat, and Menachem Begin initial the Camp David
Accords at the White House, September 17, 1978.
Source: Carter Library.

Anwar Sadat and Menachem Begin at the Capitol while President Carter
addresses a joint session of Congress about the Camp David Accords,
September 19, 1978.
Source: Carter Library.

Jimmy Carter and Tip O'Neill on Air Force One, December 8, 1978.
Source: Carter Library.

Jimmy Carter and family celebrating Christmas in Plains with Miss Allie,
December 25, 1978.
Source: Carter Library.

Zbigniew Brzezinski hosts a dinner for Chinese Vice Premier Deng Xiaoping, Cyrus Vance, and the Chinese delegation, January 28, 1979.

Source: Carter Library.

President Carter and Chinese Vice Premier Deng Xiaoping waving from the balcony of the White House, January 1979. Their wives are conferring in the background.

Source: Library of Congress, LC-DIG-ppmsca-56538.

Jimmy Carter and Deng Xiaoping signing normalization agreements, White House, January 1979.

Source: Carter Library.

The Ayatollah Khomeini en route from Paris to Tehran, February 1, 1979. *Source:* Library of Congress, LC-DIG-ppmsca-68526.

Billy Carter greets his brother Jimmy Carter at Georgia Tech commencement ceremonies, February 20, 1979. *Source:* Carter Library.

Jimmy and Rosalynn Carter on a train in Cairo, March 1979, making a whirlwind trip to Egypt and Israel to prop up the Camp David Accords.
Source: Carter Library.

Rosalynn Carter testifies for the Presidential Committee on Mental Health before the Senate Sub-Committee on February 3, 1979.
Source: Carter Library.

Jimmy Carter and Leonid Brezhnev converse before signing the SALT II treaty in Vienna, June 18, 1979.
Source: Carter Library.

President Brezhnev kissing Jimmy Carter on the cheek after they signed SALT II in Vienna, June 18, 1979.
Source: AP Photograph 7906180257.

Jimmy and Rosalynn arrive jogging for the Catoctin Mountain 10K race, September 1979.
Source: Carter Library.

President Carter delivering his Crisis of Confidence Speech, often mislabeled as the "malaise" speech, Oval Office, July 15, 1979.
Source: Carter Library.

President Jimmy Carter hugging country music star Dolly Parton before a luncheon at the White House on October 2, 1979. Rosalynn looks on and laughs.
Source: AP Photo/Georges.

Pope John Paul II visits the White House, October 6, 1979.
Source: Carter Library.

Senator Ted Kennedy shaking hands with President Carter after
Carter dedicated the John F. Kennedy Library, October 20, 1979.
Kennedy's wife Joan is watching.
Source: Bill Brett/The Boston Globe via Getty Images.

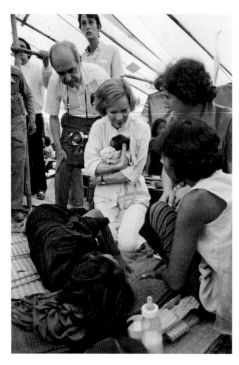

First Lady Rosalynn Carter visits a refugee camp in Sa Kas, Thailand, November 9, 1979.
Source: Carter Library.

President Carter lighting the menorah to honor the Jewish holiday Chanukah, December 17, 1979.
Source: Carter Library.

Senator Ted Kennedy reluctantly shakes hands with President Carter at the Democratic National Convention, Madison Square Garden, New York, August 15, 1980, after Carter won the nomination. Tip O'Neill (next to Carter) and Bob Strauss (next to Kennedy) are distressed by the chaos of the convention.
Source: AP Photo.

The Ku Klux Klan protesting Carter's official announcement for his 1980 campaign for reelection in Tuscumbia, Alabama September 1, 1980.
Source: Carter Library.

Rosalynn Carter, celebrating her last Christmas in the White House, shows her grandchildren Sarah and Jason the tree she had decorated as an "Old Fashioned Christmas," December 15, 1980.
Source: Carter Library.

The hostages inside the US Embassy in Tehran, Christmas 1980.
Source: Library of Congress, LC-DIG-ppmsca-04926.

The Carter family visiting Mr. Earl's grave in the family cemetery plot, January 1, 1981.
Source: Chuck Fishman/Getty Images.

Rosalynn Carter and Nancy Reagan leaving the White House to attend the inauguration ceremony for Ronald Reagan, January 20, 1981.
Source: Reagan Library.

Former President Jimmy Carter congratulates President Ronald Reagan immediately after Reagan's swearing in as his successor, January 20, 1981.
Source: Carter Library.

Rosalynn Carter blows a kiss to well-wishers as she and Jimmy prepare to leave Washington after Reagan's inauguration, January 20, 1981.
Source: Still Picture Branch, National Archives.

Mary Fitzpatrick, Amy Carter holding Misty Malarky Ying Yang and accompanied by her friend, and Secret Service agents rushing toward the plane that will take them back to Georgia, January 20, 1981.
Source: Carter Library.

Jimmy, Rosalynn, and a tearful Amy Carter as they prepare to board the plane that will take them back to Georgia after Reagan's inauguration, January 20, 1981.
Source: Still Picture Branch, National Archives.

Freed hostage Kathryn Koob hugs a baby prior to her departure from the Wiesbaden hospital to the United States, January 21, 1981. She was one of the fifty-two freed hostages who spent a few days in the hospital.
Source: Still Picture Branch, National Archives.

Jimmy Carter toasting with friends on an airplane, celebrating the release of the hostages, January 22, 1981.
Source: Carter Library.

Iranian parliament, for a vote of confidence and promised that he would cease exporting oil to Israel and South Africa, disband SAVAK (the shah's secret police), fire many foreign government workers, free political prisoners, and cooperate with religious leaders. On January 16, the shah and empress flew out of Tehran's Mehrabad Airport ostensibly for a vacation, but in reality it was a journey into exile. Carter said that they would be welcome to come to the United States where wealthy businessman and philanthropist Walter Annenberg had offered them a place to live on his large and secure California estate, but the royal couple chose to go first to Egypt, then to Morocco.[15]

A few days later, when Andrew Young, United States ambassador to the UN, greeted Palestinian leaders at UN headquarters in New York City, the political reaction was swift. Young argued that the Palestinians were decent human beings to whom the Americans should relate. More than a dozen Jewish leaders disagreed, and the American Jewish Congress urged Carter to disown statements by both Young and Billy Carter, who had persistently made gross anti-Jewish statements. The president did neither. He would not condemn his brother in public, and he believed that Young was an excellent spokesman for the administration in Africa.[16]

Carter regretted his appointment of Bella Abzug, however, and on the day the shah and the empress left Iran, Carter fired her. Twenty-six of the forty members of the National Advisory Committee on Women commission resigned in protest. Bella had infuriated the president by issuing a news release critical of his plan to reduce funding for social programs. Furthermore, she had canceled a meeting with him in November because he allotted only fifteen minutes for it. She did not consult her committee members on how to spend the committee's $300,000 budget, and she had attempted to organize a women's walkout at the mid-term Democratic Convention in Memphis in December.

Rosalynn defended Carter's decision to fire Abzug. "We have worked unbelievably hard on equal rights for women," she said, and neither the country nor the administration needed the distractions that Bella caused.[17] Bella responded by warning Carter that he would be in political trouble, but it was a risk that Carter, unintimidated by Bella's threats, was willing to take.[18]

In their discussion of Bella's firing, the Carters cautiously avoided the Jewish issue, but the fact that Abzug was a well-known Jewish Congresswoman from New York could not be denied. The debate about Bella was still making news when Mark Siegel, Carter's deputy assistant for political affairs, quit on January 23. Siegel felt that he could not speak his pro-Jewish mind in administrative meetings, and he thought the administration had taken a pro-Arab bent.[19]

As Carter prepared his upcoming second State of the Union address in January, he included comments on the president's responsibility to treat both Arab and Jew equally and to emphasize the need for unity among all Americans. When Rosalynn read her husband's seventh draft, she went a step further, suggesting that the address needed to be a "call to action" for Americans to assume responsibility for their country. She also thought that people did not want "new Foundations," but that they believed "our country was founded on a sound basis, and want[ed] a return to old values."[20]

On January 23, 1979, Carter delivered the speech before a joint session of Congress. He declared the state of the union to be sound, but the United States must accept the challenge to build a stronger foundation for "a sound economy, for a more effective government, for more political trust, and for a stable peace." For the economy to be sound, he said that the government would have to exercise fiscal restraint. When he called for "real sacrifices . . . to overcome inflation," liberals who favored Kennedy were so outraged that Kennedy pulled ahead in the ensuing polls.[21] The popularity Carter had enjoyed a year earlier was slipping away.

When Carter mentioned foreign policy, however, he faced less opposition. His country did not want to be the world's policeman, but rather its peacemaker, he said. His programs, in place and in progress, would provide that new foundation. Since the ongoing SALT II negotiations loomed larger than other issues, he reminded his audience that when the new treaty was finally signed and implemented, it would not replace skilled diplomacy. Likewise, a strong defense would remain essential to building a world where all peoples were free and lived together in tranquility.[22]

There was no tranquility, however, in Iran, where, on February 1, 1979, the seventy-six-year-old Ayatollah Khomeini returned from fifteen years in exile and made a triumphant entry into Tehran. Millions of his supporters demanded that the shah's provisional prime minister Shapour Bakhtiar resign, and some of the Iranian military declared loyalty to the Ayatollah. Having underestimated the Ayatollah's ability to gain power, the CIA had no psychological profile on him.[23]

Khomeini held a personal grudge against the shah: his son, Mustafa, a brilliant cleric who had joined his father in exile, had died mysteriously in October 1977 after being visited by two "strangers." Khomeini thought that his healthy forty-nine year old son had been assassinated by the SAVAK.

Three months later the shah had published a slanderous letter in the prominent Iranian newspaper *Ettelaat*, accusing the Ayatollah of being homosexual and a British agent. When Khomeini's followers marched in protest the next day, the shah's police opened fire on them, killing twenty. The hatred and grief over the loss of his son festered in Khomeini for more than a year until circumstances in early 1979 made it possible for him to return to Iran and seek his revenge.[24]

Blindsided by an Islamic revolution with antecedents deep in Persian history, US officials attempted to guard US interests in Iran by trying to talk with the new revolutionary government. That effort failed. The Americans had to surrender their electronic communications listening posts at Behshahr and Kakan, which had been significant sources of information about the Soviet Union. On February 11, Khomeini named a pro-democracy scholar Mehdi Bazargan as prime minister of a provisional government and asked him to set up an Islamic Republic.[25]

The US State Department quickly produced a sketch of Khomeini, and the CIA prepared one of Bazargan, but neither account was sufficient to enable the United States deal with what lay ahead. According to the State Department, Ruhollah Khomeini was the charismatic and intransigent leader of the religious opposition to the shah's government. He had spent fifteen years in exile, mostly in neighboring Iraq, where both the shah and the United States assumed that he would die without causing any problem for Iran. His triumphant return, however, placed him in a position of political power that the West had not anticipated. Born in 1901, Khomeini was the grandson of a native of India, who had immigrated to Iran. Living in the Holy City of Qom, Khomeini, in his fifties, had rebelled against the shah and had subsequently been jailed and then exiled. A thin, old man in 1979, he ate very little and prayed often. He was reputed to be an outstanding Persian poet and literary figure. The brief report offered no clue why and how such an unlikely character might exercise so much power in Iran.[26]

Prime Minister Mehdi Bazargan, the CIA reported, was a professor, politician, businessman, and devout Shi'a Muslim with a long history of opposition to the shah and strong support for democracy in his country. He had lauded Carter for his human rights policy and had called upon him to end US support for the shah. When Carter failed to do so, Bazargan had moved into the Ayatollah's camp.[27]

Smarting from the criticism that the CIA did not have adequate intelligence about Iran, Stan Turner assured the president on February 7 that there had been "no failure of intelligence."[28] Nevertheless, he promised to improve political intelligence. In the meantime, Turner found himself in a sticky situation not of his own making. He had taken charge of the CIA at a difficult time when a Congressional investigation had revealed its involvement in assassination plots and international coups during the two previous decades. Falsely accused of gutting the agency in the name of reform, Turner got little credit for the work he undertook to deal with the Iranian crisis or the continuing Cold War. He knew the details of the Ayatollah's life, but he and the entire United States government were duped by information sent to them by the shah and his government. Carter's Republican predecessors had trusted the shah and had simply accepted whatever information the shah and his SAVAK gave them. With virtually no useful information about Iran in the files, and no one in the government who could help, Turner had to gather from scratch the intelligence Carter needed about the crumbling Persian kingdom.[29]

Matters took a serious downward turn on February 14 when US ambassador to Afghanistan Adolph Dubs was kidnapped in Kabul by four unidentified militants and killed in the crossfire between Soviet-backed Afghan forces and the kidnappers. Afghan soldiers killed Dubs's abductors, but the Afghan government denied any responsibility for his death. "Shocked and saddened" by the murder of a friend who was loyal to his administration, Carter moved to reduce military and humanitarian aid to Afghanistan, a country increasingly falling under Soviet domination. He paid tribute to Dubs as a victim of what he called "senseless terrorism." Dubs's murder and the increasingly ominous presence of the Soviets in Afghanistan helped Brzezinski win Carter over to his hardline anti-Soviet views, leaving a frustrated Vance to consider his diminishing role in the administration.[30]

On the same day that Dubs was murdered in Kabul, unruly students roamed the streets around the US embassy in Tehran, hurling epithets and sometimes stones at the building. A barrage of gunfire from all directions sent the diplomats running for cover or hitting the floor. The embassy's nineteen marine guards fired rubber bullets and rounds of tear gas at the attackers but could not turn them back. Within a few hours the ordeal ended, when one of Khomeini's closest followers, Ebrahim Yazdi, organized a few hundred students from Tehran University in a counterattack against the militant, communist-inspired rebels who had stormed and occupied the embassy. Yazdi freed Ambassador William Sullivan and his staff, and Khomeini later apologized and expressed relief that no Americans had been killed.

One marine guard, however, had been wounded and was held in an Islamic Revolutionary Prison for a week. When Carter learned that the marine had been released due to his and Ambassador Sullivan's efforts, he quickly picked up the telephone, eyes moist with relief, and called the man's mother in Pennsylvania to give her the good news.[31]

Ambassador Sullivan ordered improved fortification of the embassy compound, and the Defense Department instructed US citizens to leave Iran as soon as possible. Two Pan American 747s and one Air Force C-141 stood by at the Tehran airport to transport approximately 1,000 Americans out of the country. The Defense Department recommended that others leave by sea or automobile, or any means possible. Carter, since the revolution began, had already reduced the size of the diplomatic staff in Tehran from about 1,100 to less than seventy-five. Although disillusioned with Sullivan, he kept the embassy open, and he maintained secret channels of communication with Mehdi Bazargan, hoping to establish a working relationship with the new Islamic government.[32]

Mexico was not in crisis like Iran, but the president and First Lady received a cool reception there during a three-day state visit beginning on Valentine's Day, April 14, 1979. Despite several earlier visits, and the Carters' ability to speak Spanish, Mexico did not trust the United States. "You and I, Mr. President," President López Portillo said at a luncheon, "have a task of . . . keeping insensitivity, ambition, fear, or self-seeking manipulation" from ruining "a relationship founded on friendship."[33] Jimmy cracked jokes and thanked all the people who had made their visit possible. Rosalynn expressed gratitude to Portillo for "all you do for us." Their comments had an unintentional paternalistic tone that did not escape their hosts, who yearned for equality, not paternalism. Despite reassurances and the signing of a communique in which Carter and Portillo agreed to trade negotiations and cultural exchanges, possibilities for misunderstanding still haunted the long-time neighbors.[34]

That same day, Billy once again embarrassed Jimmy in the national media. At a reception in New York City given on that date by the Libyan delegation to the UN, Billy told an interviewer from the Mutual Broadcasting System that the Jews "can kiss my ass."[35] Carter explained that Billy suffered from alcoholism, and he was relieved a short time later when Billy entered a rehabilitation hospital.[36] Jewish voters demanded that the president denounce his brother, but Carter refused. "He's seriously ill," the president said. "I love him. I have no intention [to make] any condemnation that I don't think is warranted." Rosalynn stood by the president: "I disagree with some of the things [Billy] says, and so does Jimmy. But, I would not publicly criticize him."[37]

Rosalynn garnered more favorable media attention during that February. As honorary chair of the President's Mental Health Commission, she became the first wife of a president wife to testify before Congress since Eleanor Roosevelt thirty-four years earlier.[38] Ironically, Senator Ted Kennedy chaired the Senate Subcommittee on Health and Scientific Research. As one of his sisters lived with mental disabilities, Senator Kennedy had a personal interest in Rosalynn's pet project. Rosalynn accepted his invitation to escort her to the subcommittee hearing, where she boldly made her remarks with passionate, emotional language and illustrations that impressed Kennedy and other members of the committee. Kennedy promised that he would help her get legislation passed, and Carter added $27 million to his proposed national health care plan.[39]

Carter, as fearless as his wife, gave rousing speeches at Georgia Tech in Atlanta on February 20 and at a Democratic fundraising dinner in California a few days later. In California he promised to bring peace to Israel, and in Georgia he warned the Soviets not to interfere with Iran and to complete the SALT II treaty. "Peace is paramount, a strong defense necessary," he told his fellow "Techies." The United States, he declared, is a source of both ideals and power.[40]

Back in Washington the next month, the Carters became embroiled in a controversy focusing on Secretary of Health Education and Welfare Joseph Califano. On March 27, Carter instructed Califano to support legislation to create a separate Department of Education, a proposal that Califano vigorously opposed. Although Carter trusted Califano, many of his senior staff, and Rosalynn, did not. Upon reading in the newspaper about appointments Califano had made in his department, Hamilton Jordan wrote the secretary an angry note on April 10 accusing him of being "completely insensitive" to "modest requests" from the president to clear such appointments with him first.[41]

More ominous for Califano, Rosalynn criticized him severely when she learned that he had hired a private firm to help his staff members quit smoking. "I resent this VERY much," she said. "Why do I, a non-smoking taxpayer, have to pay for Joe's staff to 'kick the habit'?"[42]

More than a month later, Rosalynn's disapproval of Califano reached a boiling point. On May 21, she received a note from her projects director,

Cathy Cade, alleging that Califano had not defended the Mental Health Systems Act well during an appearance before the Senate Subcommittee on Health and Scientific Research. Not only was Califano ill-informed, according to Cade, he also failed to seize opportunities to defend the bill, note accomplishments of the past year, and clarify the bill's provisions for various constituencies. Cade concluded that the secretary's performance "was such a discredit to you and to everyone who worked so hard on the Commission and this legislation" that Rosalynn should know about it. Incensed, Rosalynn immediately forwarded Cade's memorandum to her husband with a handwritten note: "Jimmy, Any suggestions? We had a long meeting Wednesday with representatives of the Mental Health Association and think we had them convinced to support us. Then this from Joe." Jimmy's brief handwritten note to his domestic policy advisor Stuart Eizenstat—"Stu: hold personally J."—suggested that "Joe" might be in hot water. By the end of May, Rosalynn was determined to get rid of Califano. She, like Jordan and others, saw him as "disloyal."[43]

Rosalynn was not shy about expressing her opinions, and although Jimmy sometimes disagreed with her, he always listened. Throughout April and May, she was a whirlwind of activity defending her husband, fighting for her own causes, and trying to strengthen their political position. Outraged because Congress was investigating their peanut warehouse for a possible illegal relationship with Bert Lance, she remained focused on her campaigns for legislation that would contain hospital costs and her efforts to elect or reelect Democrats. However, Rosalynn looked on one Democrat, Ted Kennedy, with a jaundiced eye. She cringed at Kennedy's proposal for a national healthcare system that differed from her husband's primarily in size and cost. Healthcare, Rosalynn knew, pitted Kennedy against her husband; she claimed that she did not know or care if Kennedy would run against Carter for the Democratic nomination.[44]

On several occasions, Rosalynn met with Jimmy and other key advisers to talk about his declining popularity. During intensive discussions over dinner with Rosalynn, scholars Daniel Bell and Christopher Lasch, Reverend Jesse Jackson, John Gardner, Bill Moyers, and others, Carter learned nothing that he found useful. Carter initially dismissed the advice of the professors with the comment that they were "too erudite to be practical."[45]

Rosalynn was practical. With amazing energy, charm, and confidence, she traveled widely during the spring of 1979, from Washington to New York to Georgia, and points in between, delivering the administration's message.

At a luncheon for the New York Women in Communications on April 27, she made an impassioned plea for the ERA and defended what she and her husband had done to try to get it ratified. It was not true, Rosalynn said, that "nice women" did not support the ERA. Controversial statements by Bella Abzug and Gloria Steinem, she contended, had ruined its chances for passage. She had pushed hard to win the extension of time for ratification. She rejected the accusations that she and Jimmy had tiptoed around the ERA in the South, limited their comments in support of it to a few special occasions, called only legislators they knew personally, and sometimes passed the issue off to staff. She also chastised the journalists who were not interested in her work with the mentally ill, the elderly, the poor, and the handicapped, because they did not think they were "sexy" issues for a first lady.[46]

Carter supplemented Rosalynn's work with that of Father Ted Hesburgh. Reminded by Hesburgh that human rights were as important for draft dodgers and illegal immigrants as Jewish dissidents in the Soviet Union and abused African Americans, Carter later appointed the former Notre Dame president to chair the Select Commission on Immigration and Refugee Policy. After eighteen months of intensive study the commission drafted a policy that would help identify the millions of illegal migrants in the United States, allow a larger number of legal ones to come, and provide special consideration for Canada and Mexico. Their proposal failed to win the support of Congress, but Hesburgh remained in the forefront of the battle for human rights.[47] He also remained enamored of the president's humanitarian work; "Jimmy Carter is a saint," he later wrote.[48]

TWENTY ONE

A White House Signing

Although the peace treaty between Israel and Egypt had been successfully negotiated in September 1978, the December 17 deadline for signing
it had passed. Israeli Prime Minister Menahem Begin continued to expand
settlements on the West Bank and threatened to move his office to East
Jerusalem. When Carter protested, Begin replied that he had to appease the
extreme right wing of his party in order to keep their support. Begin's action infuriated the Palestinians and raised a red flag for Arabs who did not
think he could be trusted. A desperate Carter decided to invite both Begin
and Sadat back to Washington, planning for Begin to come first. After vac-
illating over the invitation and worrying about his political base in Israel,
Begin agreed that he and Aliza would make the trip and arrive on March 1.[1]

After landing at Andrews Air Force Base, Begin told the media and the US
diplomats who greeted him that he would not sign an agreement that was "a
mere sham" and worthless document. While Begin and Aliza had lunch and
rested at Blair House, Jimmy and Rosalynn quickly assembled a luncheon
meeting with Vice President Mondale and senior advisers Ed Sanders and
Stuart Eizenstat to discuss the stalemate in the Middle East and their strategy
for dealing with Begin. All present expected Begin to be very difficult, but
Carter typically hoped that Rosalynn might have some influence with Aliza
and through her on Begin. He told the morose group that Begin had gotten
"off the plane" making "some very combative statements."[2] Carter passed the
remainder of the afternoon alone contemplating how he would deal with
Begin, before joining him and their wives for a private supper.

After supper, Carter and Begin met alone for two hours in his small office
adjacent to the Oval Office. Begin appeared to be nervous and demanded
to speak first. Although he had suffered personally from the Camp David
Accords, he said, he was willing to go through with them. The Egyptians were
adding unreasonable demands, he complained, and the Russians, who held
some Jewish dissidents as prisoners and refused to allow others to immigrate
to Israel, were not human. Begin's rambling and negative mood aggravated

Carter, but he controlled his temper and reassured the Israeli leader that both of their countries had many common interests. Israel, he told Begin, would benefit significantly in a global context from the Camp David treaty. Begin ended the meeting on an amiable note, and the two men agreed to meet again the next morning in the Oval Office.[3]

The following day, Carter and Begin, along with their top advisers, met first in the Oval Office and then the Cabinet Room. Begin, Carter recorded in his diary, remained "very strong, negative, apparently confident, making unreasonable demands and adamant statements."[4] Begin offered no solution that would break the alleged deadlock with Sadat; nor did he respond to Carter's urgent request to accept the treaty because it would enable the United States to deliver enhanced security to Israel. After the meeting, Carter despaired that he could not influence Begin; he wrote in his diary that Begin distorted the American position and lied to the news media. Pondering his next move, Carter considered going to Egypt to confer with Sadat first and then traveling to Israel. If that did not work, he was ready to "let the whole thing shift to the UN."[5]

In a separate meeting with Aliza Begin and a group of Israelis who had accompanied her, Rosalynn attempted to convince them that the treaty would be to their benefit. Then she hosted a lunch for Aliza, at which Gay Vance tried to help persuade Aliza to influence her husband. Mrs. Begin stuck with her husband and would not try to change his mind. Afterward, in her thank you note to Gay, Rosalynn revealed her own frustration with the unpredictable Israelis: "I admire you and Cy, and your patience. Maybe something good will yet come from all the efforts toward Middle East peace."[6]

The next day, Saturday, March 3, it appeared to Carter that the peace treaty might never be signed. Begin came to the White House, "moody and sullen," and unwilling to give any assurance that he would sign. Carter bluntly told him that the United States would end negotiations if they could not make any progress. Unbeknown to Carter, Begin could not sleep that night because he feared what might happen to Israel if its relationship with the United States broke down.[7]

On the following day, Carter told his Sunday School class that he and Begin had made no progress. Refusing to give up, he drafted identical letters to both Begin and Sadat telling them that he hoped to resolve their differences "based upon the nuances of our treaty text, and including guarantees of U.S. action in case the agreements were violated."[8] The basic agreements in the treaty, which all three men had initialed at the end of the Camp David conference remained intact. Carter later spent another hour and a half with Begin before the latter departed for Israel. The White House issued a statement that the two men had completed eight hours of "intensive conversations" about the Middle East and "unresolved issues in the negotiations."[9] Sadat wanted to come to Washington to condemn Begin for causing the treaty to fail, but Carter asked him to stay in Egypt and give Carter more time to seek a solution.[10]

Fearful that the United States might cut off all aid to Israel, Begin took a giant step toward resolving those issues on Monday. He consulted with his cabinet, then called Carter to tell him that the Israeli ministers had accepted the treaty. Carter told both Begin and Sadat that he and Rosalynn had decided to travel to Egypt and Israel immediately. Begin promised him a "good reception" in Jerusalem, and Sadat was overjoyed by the news of Carter's visit.[11] The White House announced the president's impending trip at noon on March 5. The president had accepted invitations from Begin and Sadat, the announcement read, traveling first to Egypt, then to Israel, hoping to prevent the prospects for peace from vanishing. "If we do" allow them to vanish, the announcement continued, "the judgment of history and of our children will rightly condemn us."[12]

In preparation for travel on such short notice, Carter sent messages to Saudi Arabia and "a few more reasonable ones" requesting their support for the Middle East peace process. He asked Cy Vance to hold fast to changing the US relationship with Taiwan and the commitment to normalization of relations with China. He welcomed Henry Kissinger's approval of his plan to make the Middle East trip, and he told Vice President Mondale to clear his calendar and be prepared to manage the presidency during his absence.[13]

Three days later, on March 8, Air Force One touched down at Cairo International Airport where President Sadat and his wife Jehan waited to greet their American friends. Traveling in a well-guarded motorcade from the airport to Qubba, where the official welcome would take place, the Carters waved at the millions of Egyptians who lined the streets shouting "welcome, Kartar" and "We believe in God." Rosalynn joked, "Perhaps we should move to Cairo." The Qubba Palace, where Jimmy and Rosalynn would stay during their short visit, was a 166-year-old structure with twenty foot high walls sitting in the middle of two hundred acres of land, a virtual fortress. At the reception there Sadat called Carter his "dear friend and brother," and Carter responded by referring to his host as a man of "extremely great courage," whom he looked upon as a "partner."[14]

Carter and Sadat talked for about thirty minutes the night of their arrival before being joined by both US and Egyptian advisers, focusing on settling unresolved issues with Israel. The next day, the two couples, heavily protected by both US and Egyptian guards, rode an antique train from Cairo to Alexandria, where Rosalynn marveled at the rich land of the Nile Delta, while both Carter and Sadat answered questions informally for US television correspondents. After sharing laudatory toasts at a dinner in Alexandria on March 9, the entourage returned to Cairo.[15]

On March 10, Jehan and Rosalynn rode together to the National Assembly to hear Jimmy address the Egyptian parliament. Carter spoke about peace, drawing examples from the Quran, the Old Testament, and the Sermon on the Mount. "He wanted peace as much as we did," Jehan wrote. "And he was as religious as we were." Ever the peacemaker, Carter defended Begin, arguing that he was courageous, honest, and vilified by many of his old friends. Carter explained that Begin, upon reflection, had decided that he gave too much at Camp David and now regretted it. Sadat agreed, responding, "I don't know how you performed this miracle at Camp David." Trusting his American friend, Sadat gave Carter carte blanche to negotiate with Begin in Jerusalem. After a quick trip to view the Pyramids of Giza, the Carters returned to the Cairo International Airport to fly on to Tel Aviv.[16]

The hostile greeting the Carters received in Israel was the opposite of what they had seen in Egypt. Riding with Begin and President Yitzhak Navon the twenty-eight miles from the Ben Gurion Airport to Jerusalem, they saw angry demonstrators who did not pelt their vehicle with eggs as the Secret Service had feared but hurled epithets and mean gestures at them. Among the numerous negative signs, including "Go Home, Carter," one stood out and particularly tickled the president: "Welcome, Billy's Brother!" Nevertheless, the Carters exchanged laudatory tributes with their hosts. President Navon praised "my dear Rosalynn" for her "heartfelt involvement" in the needs of individuals. Begin told Carter that he deserved the "heartfelt title of servant of peace," and Carter promised to stand by Israel steadfastly.[17]

The meeting with Begin at his residence the next day, however, was hostile, so much so that Carter threatened to leave. Standing almost nose to nose with Carter, Begin confirmed that he wanted a peace treaty, but he was "disgusted" that his American counterpart did not believe him. On March 12, both men addressed the Knesset in what threatened at several moments to disintegrate into a chaotic, undiplomatic session. Carter managed to bring order to the meeting by speaking directly to the 120 members of the Knesset. Although the people "of the two nations" are ready for peace, he said, the "leaders have not yet proven that we are also ready for peace, enough to take a chance." Dispelling Begin's earlier fears, Carter emphasized that "with or without a peace treaty, the United States will always be at Israel's side."[18]

Despite some silence and heckling, the majority of the Knesset, followed by the Israeli cabinet and foreign ministers, rejected Begin's stubborn position. The following day when Carter was about to leave at noon, and the Israeli cabinet had made it clear they wanted a settlement before he left, Begin relented and told Carter that he would go to Washington to sign the treaty. Relieved, before departing Carter also persuaded the Israelis to exchange ambassadors with the Egyptians.[19]

Out of the public spotlight, Rosalynn quietly heeded Israelis who reminded her of the plight of Jewish dissidents in Soviet prisons. She saw people holding up signs asking her to please help Anatoly Shcharansky, the most celebrated of the prisoners. Rosalynn promised to pray for peace, and she planted a cypress tree, her gift to the Mevaseret Zion Absorption Center, where new immigrants were housed and assisted in adjusting to life in Jerusalem.[20]

At the conclusion of their visit on March 13, the lobby of the King David Hotel, where the Carters and Begins had a final meeting before saying farewell, was filled with reporters waiting for the arrival of their elevator. Jimmy and Rosalynn, Menachem and Aliza Begin, and two security agents were in the elevator when it jammed about six feet above the lobby. Hotel employees and the security agents pried the door off with a large crowbar, then placed a ladder for the two first couples to descend in a rather undignified manner into the lobby. Rosalynn kept her sense of humor; Jimmy smiled and refused to tell the journalists what had transpired between him and Begin.[21]

As quickly as possible, the Carters, accompanied by Begin and other top Israeli officials, made their way back to Ben Gurion International Airport. In short farewell speeches, the two leaders praised each other, but Begin gave an unexpectedly upbeat speech in which he proclaimed that his country was grateful for its friendship with the United States, and he "cherished Carter's "personal friendship for Israel."[22]

Jimmy and Rosalynn returned to Egypt for Carter to get Sadat's approval of the concessions he had made to Begin. Those changes were more matters of semantics than substantive changes, but Carter told Begin again that Sinai oil would come to Israel and Sadat would agree to the exchange of ambassadors as soon as Israel withdrew from the Sinai. Begin had promised that Palestinians would be permitted peaceful political activities, reunion with their families, and limited movement within the West Bank and Gaza.[23] Anwar and Jehan, and millions of peace-hungry Egyptians, eagerly awaited their arrival. As soon as he set foot on Egyptian soil, Carter exclaimed, "I feel like I'm coming home." Rosalynn and Jehan held hands and prayed. Carter and Sadat called Begin, then turned to the two women and said they had reached an agreement. "God has answered our prayers," Jehan declared.[24]

Without leaving the airport, the Carters boarded their plane for the flight home. On board, Carter opened a short note from his secretary: "Mr. President—It's from the 'peanut gallery' . . . but a good number of your staff and others, though we have no way to express it, feel strongly much respect, admiration, and love for the truly great man President Sadat is, and the great man you are."[25]

As soon as they were in midair, Carter telephoned Mondale, Senator Robert Byrd, and Speaker Tip O'Neill with the good news. O'Neill, who had already heard it before he received Carter's call, greeted him on the telephone with "Mr. President, you're not just a deacon anymore but a pope."[26]

Aboard the flight, there was an atmosphere of jubilation and almost disbelief, as Carter walked through the aisles of the plane thanking all of his staff members. White House Counsel and special liaison with Jewish voters Robert Lipshutz sipped on his Scotch and reflected on Carter's success with Begin and Sadat. Carter, he thought, had studied and mastered two complex personalities, centuries of history, and intense religious conflict and faced incredible odds with patience and tenacity. More than simply fulfilling the president's constitutional duties, Lipshutz mused, Carter had drawn deeply on his own personal feelings, often held privately, that had driven him to the zenith of his presidency. Jack Watson, who later served as chief of staff, stated it best: "His getting on Air Force One and actually going to Cairo and to Israel . . . was a political risk . . . of the highest order. . . . The man had extraordinary grit—and a profound sense of purpose."[27]

Carter made the hard political compromises and concessions necessary to get the treaty signed. He gave both Israel and Egypt significant economic and military assistance that became the solid foundation for an enduring treaty between the two nations. His task, according to Eizenstat, had been further complicated by his need to compete with the Soviets and cultivate friendship with the oil-rich Saudis and other Arab nations, for whom almost any accommodation with the Israelis was unthinkable.[28]

Tired but happy, the Carters received an exuberant welcome when they landed at Andrews Air Force Base at 1:30 a.m. on March 14. Hundreds of people, including cabinet members, Congressmen, and their families, cheered them as they descended from the plane. Vice President Mondale officially welcomed them home, saying: "You and Rosalynn took with you our love, our prayers, and the hopes of all humanity." Carter thanked everyone sincerely and called for Secretary Vance to come stand with the small group that had gathered around him and Rosalynn. The "pursuit of peace," Carter told the crowd, must be as daring and steadfast as the pursuit of war. "I believe that God has answered our prayers," he said in a rare religious reference on an official occasion.[29] Privately, Carter admitted that the negotiations had taken their toll on him; he penned in his diary, "I resolved to do everything possible to get out of the negotiating business."[30]

There was no rest for the president, however. When CBS news reported that the treaty had been bought at the cost of $10–20 billion, Carter, bristling at what he perceived as Jewish and media prejudices against him, asked Budget Director Jim McIntyre and Secretaries Cyrus Vance and Harold Brown to get an estimate of how much the United States would pay Israel and Egypt. Using their figures, Carter told Congressional leaders that the cost would be about $4 billion in increased economic and military aid to both nations combined over the next three years. Those funds would cover the costs of removing Israeli installations from the Sinai and Egyptian expenses for implementing the treaty. Carter also insisted that the $1.47 billion for both countries not be increased. Apart from defending the financial cost to the United States, Carter feared possible terrorist attacks against Israel, Egypt, and the United States in the few days before the signing. He ordered increased security at the US embassies in Tel Aviv and Cairo.[31]

On March 26, the Carters, Sadats, and Begins made small talk over a casual lunch in the president's dining room before moving out to the White House's North Lawn for the signing ceremony.[32] As the three couples ate, they could hear the sounds of the crowd of more than 6,000 that was gathering outside. Begin remarked that the last time a treaty between Israel and Egypt had been signed was "3,000 years ago" when "King Solomon had made a deal with a Pharaoh." To which Carter quipped, "I bet no one remembers the mediator."[33] At precisely 2:05 p.m. the three men took their places behind the signing table, with Carter seated in the center. To the left of the table, the flags of the three nations fluttered in the breeze. The rarely used North Lawn, separated by Pennsylvania Avenue from Lafayette Park, was a convenient place for observers to gather. More than 1,500 invited guests assembled on the lawn, and thousands more spectators congregated across the street. Microphones and cameras broadcast the ceremony live to the park, to US television and radio stations, and to the world via Voice of America. The Egyptian president and Israeli prime minister signed the documents, and Carter witnessed their signatures.

All three men spoke of peace: "let us now lay aside war" (Carter); "let there be no more wars" (Sadat); "no more war" (Begin). Begin pulled out a black silk yarmulke, placed it upon his head, and recited Psalm 126 in Hebrew. Those who understood the recitation knew that it was a repeat of the Jewish dream to return to the homeland.[34] When he concluded, the three heavily guarded world leaders moved from the signing table to greet the hundreds of people who gathered under a huge tent for a banquet. One of the invited guests was Avital Shcharansky, wife of the imprisoned Jewish dissident Anatoly Shcharansky. Carter greeted her warmly and conveyed his concern for her husband's welfare.[35] Looking over the crowd, Carter smiled broadly at the sight of former enemies welcoming each other. Israeli violinists Itzhak Perlman and Pinchas Zuckerman provided music, and Metropolitan Opera star Leontyne Price sang "The Lord's Prayer."

Breaking precedent for a state banquet, Carter began the meal with a prayer, an act he thought appropriate because of the religious atmosphere. In brokering a conflict resolution between Israel and Egypt, Carter had built upon the work of Nixon, Ford, and Kissinger, and he recognized the seminal work of Secretary of State Cyrus Vance. Without the Israeli and Egyptian acceptance of his mediation, however, it could not have happened. Stability, albeit tenuous, came to the Middle East, but Carter himself gained nothing. In fact, he lost ground in his political base at home.[36]

"Peace has come," Carter said after the signing, but he knew how hard won it had been and how fragile it continued to be. Throughout the day, he cautiously and almost sadly added: "We have no illusions."[37]

Carter had reason to be apprehensive, as many Arabs did not approve of the treaty. There were angry demonstrations against Sadat in Syria, Iran, Lebanon, and Libya. When Begin visited Cairo on April 3, many Egyptians appeared to be indifferent to him, while others politely cheered his arrival.

Despite the polite relationship between Begin and Sadat, there remained the unresolved issues of Jerusalem and the West Bank, unrest in Lebanon, and Palestinian rights.[38]

The treaty led to problems in the United States as well. The Carter administration still struggled to get the peace treaty accepted by Jewish Americans. Representing the president, Ed Sanders traveled widely across the nation, visiting states and organizations with large Jewish populations. He attempted to convince them that Carter was their friend, and he found that more than a few recognized the significance of the Camp David agreement and appreciated Carter's personal contribution. However, most remained tentative and wary, wanting more reassurance that Jerusalem would never be divided and that they would always have free access to its holy places. They did support Carter on SALT II and his energy proposals, but they distrusted his incessant statements that he would defend Israel and were unhappy about his poor relationship with Begin.[39]

In early April, Carter summoned Robert Strauss, the Jewish millionaire from Dallas who had supported him politically, to the White House. Strauss thought that Carter would ask him to run the 1980 campaign, but Carter surprised him: "I've got something far more important in mind than my or anyone else's political future." "I have in mind peace in this world." He asked Strauss to take charge of the next stage of the peace negotiations in the Middle East. Strauss protested that he was a Jew who had never read the Bible. Carter, always the Baptist missionary with a sense of humor, replied that it was not too late to start. Besides, former Secretary of State Henry Kissinger was also a Jew.

Three weeks later, Carter appointed Strauss as ambassador at large to the Middle East. The appointment touched off a squabble in the administration, for Strauss would report directly to the president, not the secretary of state. Vance threatened to resign, but he soon backed down. Strauss accepted the appointment, and Carter explained to Begin, Sadat, and "a few congressmen" that he had chosen Strauss because if "anyone could keep these negotiations on track and *protect me from the Jewish community politically*, it's Bob Strauss." Although Vance felt increasingly removed from essential diplomatic negotiations, he nevertheless graciously praised and thanked Strauss upon the official announcement of his appointment.[40]

The peace treaty between Israel and Egypt became a durable monument to Carter's personal diplomatic skills and willingness to risk his prestige and

presidency for world peace. By placing the burden of continuing the negotiations related to the treaty on another's shoulders, Carter freed himself
for other pressing developments. The White House signing of the Israeli-
Egyptian peace treaty would live on in history, and some said would be
Carter's greatest accomplishment.

TWENTY TWO

Dangerous Rhetoric and a Harmless Rabbit

On Friday, March 30, Carter learned about an accident at the Three Mile Island nuclear power plant on the Susquehanna River near Harrisburg, Pennsylvania. That unprecedented event, not Robert Strauss's appointment as Middle East envoy, captured the morning headlines. A malfunction of the cooling system and partial meltdown of the reactor core were dangerous issues and frightened the public. Carter, a former nuclear engineer, knew that the technical problems could be corrected, but the sensationalist media employed rhetoric that sold newspapers.

After church on Sunday, April 1, Jimmy and Rosalynn boarded a helicopter, which took them from the South Lawn of the White House to the Air National Guard Facility in Middletown, Pennsylvania. Republican Governor Richard L. Thornburg and other dignitaries greeted them there and traveled with them by motorcade to the Three Mile Island Nuclear Power Station. The group then transferred to a bus to complete their journey to the plant's main facility. To reassure the nation, Carter entered the Three Mile Island control room to demonstrate that it was safe. After returning to Middleton, he told the people gathered at the town's City Hall that they had no need to worry about the accident. Demonstrating calm in his life by attending a prayer service at St. Patrick's Episcopal Cathedral with Rosalynn, showing up at Amy's violin recital, and jogging on the White House grounds, he tried to prevent mass hysteria by downplaying the accident. He continued to argue that nuclear power would be a major source of energy in the United States as it already was in Europe.[1]

The accident at Three Mile Island was fresh in the minds of most Americans on April 5 when Carter delivered an address to the nation about energy. The preparation for it was a comedy of errors. When he received the draft from speech writer Rick Hertzberg and publicist Jerry Rafshoon, he grumbled: "This is one of the worst speeches I've ever seen. No one will listen except the Mobil [Oil Company] PR man." He thought that it should be organized, plain, blunt, and "hit hard and early." Nor should it "evade tough issues." He ordered them to meet with him later that day.[2] He corrected a second draft himself, stated facts, and defended nuclear power plants. When he delivered the speech, he stressed the need for the United States to catch up with other Western nations who were using wind or solar energy in place of coal and other fossil fuels.[3]

Carter thought that solar energy could be the answer to the country's energy needs because it was plentiful and could be harnessed inexpensively. In his State of the Union Address, Carter had promised to send legislation to Congress asking for federal money to support research into solar energy and funds to pay for installing solar panels on the roof of the White House. In mid-April, the same month that the accident happened at the Three Mile Island power plant, he ordered thirty-two solar panels to be installed on the roof of the West Wing. He did it, he said, "to move our nation toward true energy security and abundant, readily available energy supplies."[4] Once the panels that were designed to capture the sun's rays and to heat water were installed, the Carters attended a highly publicized ceremony on June 20 on the White House roof. He hoped that the publicity surrounding the White House's use of solar energy would inspire the private sector to follow that example.[5]

Closely related to the energy problem, the question of how to deal with the recently exiled shah of Iran haunted the president. David Rockefeller visited the White House on April 9 to ask Carter to allow the shah into the United States, a request which Carter politely refused because he said he thought it would be best for the shah to stay in another country. Whether Rockefeller knew that Carter had initially invited the shah to come to the United States, and the shah had refused, he did not say. Much of the shah's fortune was in Rockefeller's bank. Kissinger and Brzezinski agreed with Rockefeller, putting additional pressure on Carter. When former President Ford called on April 11 to ask Carter to provide a haven for the shah, Carter explained to him that to do so would provoke kidnappings in Iran of US diplomats and pro-US Iranians. Furthermore, it would prevent the United States from regaining control of its intelligence satellite sites in northern Iran, sites that Carter felt the United States needed to help persuade both Congress and the public that SALT II would work.[6]

The shah had moved from Morocco to the Bahamas before going to Mexico. When Carter received a secret memorandum from Vance on April 20 that Mexico would take the shah and that David Rockefeller's office would facilitate the trip, he wrote "Hooray!"[7]

Completing the SALT II agreement with the Soviet Union, Carter thought, was a much more important issue than the shah's exile. He sent a memorandum to all top administration officials advising them that "No issue facing our administration, our nation or the world is more important than SALT." He attached State Department documents with detailed explanations of the need for the agreement and details of the negotiations. Vance had already reported to him that the Soviets had accepted his proposals and that a summit meeting with Brezhnev seemed imminent.[8]

Many senators still had serious questions about the proposed treaty with the Soviet Union, however. At a function at Groton, Connecticut, Senator John Glenn of Ohio planned to talk about the loss of listening stations on the Soviet border, arguing that this meant that the US would not be able to monitor Soviet compliance with SALT. Rosalynn, who was scheduled to deliver a speech at the same function, received an advance copy of Glenn's proposed speech and gave it to Jimmy. Glenn planned to say that SALT II should include the demand that the Soviets give the United States two days' notice before test firing missiles and allow US planes to fly over those sites during the launches. Carter knew that such a demand would not be accepted by the Soviets and that it would end all negotiations immediately. Carter exploded angrily, told Rosalynn that Glenn was an "ass," and threatened to call Glenn immediately. Rosalynn intervened and urged Jimmy to wait until he had cooled down. The next day, April 7, Carter called Glenn and demanded that he modify his speech. Although Glenn did so, Carter did not trust him or other senators who were skeptical of the new agreement with the Soviet Union. He continued to press hard for the conclusion of the treaty. He defied not only Glenn, but the Joint Chiefs of Staff, who believed that he did not understand the complexity of reducing the US nuclear arsenal.[9]

At Rosalynn's urging, Jimmy took a break from the stress of his job in April for a ten-day vacation in Georgia. He, Rosalynn, and Amy, went to Sapelo Island, Georgia, a state-owned and protected coastal barrier island. They swam, fished, strolled along Nanny Goat Beach, and generally enjoyed being away from Washington. Carter limited his work running the government to about two hours per day. They attended church on Easter Sunday and welcomed visits from Charles Kirbo and others. On April 20 the Carters went to Plains, stayed in their own home, and took a walking tour of the small town, much to the delight of the hundreds of local citizens and tourists who greeted them. They visited relatives, walked through their fields, and went to the Pond House to relax and fish in the Carter Farm Pond.[10]

One day while fishing in the family pond, Carter confronted the alleged "killer rabbit" that hissed as it swam toward his boat. It was a small swamp rabbit that so alarmed the Secret Service guard that he wanted to shoot it. Carter told him that there was no reason and that firing his weapon might upset the boat. A White House photographer standing on the bank got a picture of the rabbit, which Jimmy used a paddle to divert from the boat. No harm was done to the rabbit or to the president. The small creature was scarcely a killer, but the story was magnified with every telling until Jody Powell, the White House Press Secretary, became exasperated by the interminable media questions about the little beast. Finally, when approached in a local tavern, where he had imbibed a bit too much, he told an inquisitor that it was a "killer rabbit" that had attacked the president. That version of the story mushroomed until those fishing for any evidence to demean Carter snidely suggested that he was such a coward and weakling that he was intimidated by an innocent bunny.[11]

On April 22, Jimmy and Rosalynn returned to Washington, where they were confronted with more serious and dangerous issues than a hissing swamp rabbit. Carter wanted to focus on SALT II, but Iran, the Middle East, and Jewish Americans kept intervening. When he raised the number of refugees admitted to the country to about 10,000 per month, he directed that, of the 3,000 people from places other than Southeast Asia, preference should be given to Jews from the Soviet Union. Carter rejected Israel's request for a more lucrative aid package from the United States, but he made a moving statement at a Capitol Rotunda ceremony on April 24 remembering the Holocaust. The keynote speaker, Elie Wiesel, a survivor and chair of the Holocaust Memorial Committee, scolded the United States for remaining silent during that time, a rebuke that Carter thought "was justified." He urged Khomeini not to murder Iranian Jews simply because they were friendly toward Israel, and he denounced any form of discrimination against Jews.[12]

Carter took another tough blow when the May 1979 issue of the *Atlantic Monthly* hit the newsstands. Under the provocative title "The Passionless Presidency: The Trouble with Jimmy Carter's Administration," a former speech writer provided plenty of grist for those eager to criticize the president. Written by James Fallows, it was an odd blend of admiration, frustration, popular analysis, and advice for the president. Following a few paragraphs that praised Carter for being decent, good, stable, mostly truthful, and "usually patient," Fallows proceeded to elaborate more extensively upon the talents Carter lacked.

Carter, according to Fallows, was unsophisticated, ineffective as a leader, fairly naïve in his grasp of historical analysis, and casual in his choice of his closest advisers. Furthermore, in his opinion, the way Carter's mind worked was not what was needed or expected from a president. Carter, Fallows alleged, was a poor speaker who made no effort to improve. He and his fellow Georgians were often so defensive about their Southern heritage that they never learned to play the power game in Washington. Concluding that Carter's only peers were his longtime Georgia mentor Charles Kirbo and "his wife Rosalynn, who has given no sign of thinking that anything her husband might do could be wrong," Fallows must not have realized the powerful role of Rosalynn in the administration, or he resented it.

The fallout was quick, devastating, and possibly more painful for Fallows than Carter. On *Atlantic Monthly* letterhead, Fallows had written Carter on April 4 that he hoped the president would understand that his forthcoming article was intended to be "constructive" and that he respected the president's good qualities so much that he would certainly vote for him in 1980. After the article appeared and Jody Powell dressed him down, Fallows confessed that "I sure as hell haven't enjoyed the last two days," but he defended his piece. Carter had cynically written a note to Jody on Fallows's April 4 letter, "we all have to make a living" and declined any further comment.[13]

James Reston, writing for the *New York Times*, defended Carter. He observed that the accidental personal problems "of a Billy Carter, a Bert Lance, or a Jim Fallows" and their dramatization in the press did not define a president or his administration. Furthermore, Reston noted, Fallows had promised not to write about what he had seen and heard in the White House for at least a year after he left, but he had not kept his word. A better title, according to Reston, might have been, "A compassionate presidency, full of doubts about an ambiguous and difficult world."[14]

The article also touched off a flurry of correspondence between Fallows and Carter's assistant Susan Clough about one of Fallows's sillier criticisms of Carter, namely that he personally scheduled the use of the White House swimming pool. More generous than previous presidents, Carter opened use of the pool to his cabinet members and senior staff. The scheduling was Clough's job, not the president's, because she always knew when the first family used the recreational facilities.[15]

Carter tried to avoid such petty squabbles, for he feared the proliferation of nuclear weapons more than he worried about the power of a former speechwriter's pen. India's relationship with the United States remained tenuous, because as long as the Gandhi family's Congress party ruled, it remained sympathetic to the Soviet Union. Once India acquired nuclear weapons, Carter feared a nuclear arms race between India and Pakistan. To counter that possibility, he agreed to sell Pakistan fighter planes and help the country develop nuclear power plants if the Pakistanis would promise not to produce nuclear weapons. The Indian government assured Carter that it would use nuclear fuel from the United States only for peaceful purposes and handle it properly, but a skeptical Carter hoped that India, and other nations, would accept stronger regulations for the handling and disposal of nuclear fuel and waste. He did not trust either India or Pakistan, but he hoped to bring them into the nuclear nonproliferation fold and especially to disengage India from the Soviet Union.

Carter defended the US construction of nuclear submarines, which appeared to show partiality toward the branch of the service in which he had served. He denied any favoritism, arguing that nuclear submarines were the "single weapons system that has ensured our Nation's integrity and security." They are, he said, "a great insurer of the peace."[16]

Vance thought the Soviets, who cared nothing about Rockefeller or the shah, agreed to a prisoners' exchange to create a positive pre-summit atmosphere for the SALT II talks. The Soviets released four prominent Jewish dissidents and one Baptist missionary from labor camps in exchange for two minor spies held by the United States. When Alexander Ginsberg, a well-known Jewish dissident, and Georgi Vins, a Baptist missionary, arrived at New York's Kennedy airport aboard a Russian aircraft, on April 27, the Russians insisted that the two released spies walk up one ramp into the plane at the same moment that Ginsberg and Vins and the other three dissidents walked down another one. Vins attended Carter's Sunday School class the following Sunday, and later he revealed a photograph of Carter that he had kept hidden under the inner sole of his shoe while in prison. Vins told the president that many prisoners knew of his human rights policy and took hope from it.[17]

In May, while Jimmy studied Cyrus Vance's progress reports on the SALT II discussions in Vienna, Rosalynn focused on other important matters of particular interest to her. On May 3 she met with Jimmy over lunch to discuss yet again how to get the ERA ratified and a few days later she flew to Geneva to address the Medical Society of the World Health Organization. Quoting Margaret Meade, she told its members that the success of any society could only be measured by the compassion it had for its most vulnerable, including the mentally ill.[18]

The May 7 issue of *Time Magazine* carried a feature story declaring Rosalynn to be the "Second Most Powerful Person" in the United States. With a fine "mind for statecraft and politics," the author argued, she had distinguished herself from other First Ladies. She kept regular working hours and had counseled her husband on the Camp David conference and the recent choice of Strauss as ambassador at large for the Middle East. On rare occasions, Jimmy surprised her with decisions, such as the normalization of relations with China, about which she had previously been ignorant. Otherwise, Rosalynn's knowledge, influence, and access within the White House were remarkable. She discussed with Jimmy or his top advisers anything that was not top secret. She had sat in on only five cabinet meetings, but no one in the White House dared criticize her. One aide commented, "The President was nuts about her."[19]

Jimmy often asked his wife, "Well, Rosie, what's on your agenda this week," and she did not hesitate to tell him what was on her mind as well as what was on her schedule. Bob Strauss thought her "judgment is superb." She once got her husband to chew out Joe Califano, Secretary of Health, Education and Welfare, because his public comments countered the administration's position. Carter concluded his upbraiding of the poor chap with a warning that "when Rosalynn gets ahold of you, it's going to be even worse."[20]

Rosalynn was a working First Lady. No sooner had she returned from Geneva than she was off again to Chicago to address the American Psychiatric Association and accept an award for her work on mental health. From there she went to Rome where on May 11 she and Amy had a thirty-minute audience with Pope John Paul II. Rosalynn was disappointed that he was more interested in politics than religion, and she forgot to ask him to endorse Jimmy in 1980. She also met with Italian President Sandro Pertini and other top Italian political officials. Pertini was charmed by her, and Richard Gardner, the US ambassador to Italy, informed Carter that his wife and daughter had "conquered Rome in two days."[21]

After returning to Washington, Rosalynn and Amy joined Jimmy for a brief three-day vacation. They flew to a beautiful, rustic spot at Camp Hoover in Virginia's Shenandoah National Park, where they fished for trout and sighted two black bears. From there they traveled east to meet Secretary of the Interior Cecil Andrus and his wife Carol at Virginia Beach, where they enjoyed deep sea fishing. By May 15 the Carter family was back in the White House where they welcomed country music stars Charlie Pride and Willie Nelson.[22]

The friendly musicians may have briefly diverted Carter's mind from the election of Margaret Thatcher as prime minister of the United Kingdom. Carter had first met her on September 13, 1977, when she had visited him as the leader of Britain's Conservative Party. At that time she told him that she anticipated her party would win the next election and that she would become prime minister. Carter wrote in his diary that he found her to be "overbearing," but not "unattractive." Forewarned by Brzezinski that Thatcher was "wise . . . hard-driving . . . pragmatic [and had] courage," Carter was nevertheless pleased to learn that she would support him on the SALT II negotiations with the Soviet Union.[23]

Encouraged about the SALT II negotiations, Carter took the time to prepare the commencement address for a little known, historically important Black college. He rarely accepted invitations to speak at graduation ceremonies, but he was inspired by the twentieth-fifth anniversary of the Supreme Court's *Brown v. Topeka, Kansas, Board of Education*, in which the Court had declared that racial segregation in public schools was unconstitutional. Cheyney State College, located about twenty-five miles west of Philadelphia, was an ideal place to observe that anniversary because, founded in 1837, it was the nation's oldest African-American college. In his address to the graduating class, Carter reviewed the civil rights era and his efforts to bring racial equality to the White House. "I'm going to tell it to you straight," he said, "because I care about the things you care about, because you and other black Americans are the reason that I am President, and because one of you may someday have my job."[24]

On May 20, 1979, however, Jimmy Carter still had the job of President of the United States, and the most important issue on his desk was concluding the SALT II negotiations with the Soviet Union. It was finally time for him to prepare to go to Vienna and meet with President Leonid Brezhnev.

TWENTY THREE

SALT II, Enemies, and Allies

Carter began in late April to convince the US public that SALT II was essential to prevent confrontation with the Soviet Union. On April 25, 1979, at the Waldorf Astoria Hotel in New York, he poured his heart and soul into a speech he delivered at the American Newspaper Publishers' convention. "We have a common interest in survival, and we share a common recognition that our survival depends, in a real sense, on each other," he told the journalists, knowing that his message would soon ricochet across the country. The world would be imperfect with a SALT agreement, he said, but it would be "imperfect and more dangerous" without it.[1] He was building, he said, upon the legacies of Presidents Truman, Eisenhower, Kennedy, Johnson, Nixon, and Ford. In detail, he explained the need for the treaty, the ability of the United States to support it economically, and how it would guarantee US nuclear power equality with the Soviet Union. The possibility of "mutual annihilation," he emphasized, made "a strategy of peace the only rational choice for both sides." The treaty, he said, would make the United States and its allies stronger, not weaker. It would, he concluded, "reverse a dangerous and a wasteful arms race which neither side can win. This is a path of wisdom. This is a path of peace."[2]

Carter insisted that his negotiators in Vienna not be "timid" in their dealings with the Soviet Union. The Soviets, in his view, with about 2,000 military personnel stationed in Cuba, clearly remained a potential threat to the United States.[3] Peeved by a memorandum from Brzezinski that suggested how they would cover up failure, he responded that the United States should "set the maximum goals and work toward them; at least we would have done our best." He confided to his diary: "I wasn't interested in going to Vienna to the opera."[4]

Vance and his team did exactly as Carter wished. Despite Vance's increasing dissatisfaction with his position in the Carter administration, and rumors that he might resign, he served Carter and the nation well at Vienna.[5] On May 8, he reported to the president that a basic agreement had been reached with the Soviets to limit long-range bombers and missiles and to hold a summit attended by both Carter and Brezhnev in the Austrian capital in mid-June. Although the news was to be kept secret, Rosalynn forgot and told the president of Italy about it during her visit to Rome. Jimmy teased her by telling her that Brezhnev had cancelled the summit on account of the news leak.[6]

Jimmy joked with Rosalynn, but he was filled with emotion when he shared Vance's report at a White House breakfast for the National Retail Federation. "I have only one life to live on this this earth, as you have," Carter told the retailers. "I think the most important single achievement that could possibly take place for our nation during my lifetime is the ratification of the SALT treaty that we have just negotiated with the Soviet Union. Rejection of this treaty, now that [it] has been negotiated, would be a devastating blow to the United States of America and to the Soviet Union. It would harm our nation's security and it would be [a] massive destructive blow to world peace." If the Senate failed to ratify the treaty, he said, "we would be looked upon as a warmonger, not a peace-loving nation, by many other people of the world." Countries like Pakistan, India, Taiwan, South Korea, South Africa, Argentina, and Brazil would ask: "Why should we listen to the voice of the United States encouraging us not to develop nuclear weapons when they themselves will not approve a treaty designed for the same purpose?" He asked the retailers, who, he said, he had helped with his social legislation, to influence Congress and their organizations to understand that peace and human rights benefitted the economic health of the nation.[7]

Most senators, however, were wary of committing themselves in advance to approving the treaty. Senate Majority Leader Robert Byrd asked "two very basic questions . . . . First, what would be the net effect of the treaty on the strategic balance and on United States national security . . . . Secondly, can the agreement be adequately verified?"[8] Although Carter had answered those questions in his April 25 address, Byrd had not been satisfied with those answers. On June 13, Carter met with the Joint Chiefs of Staff, all five of whom thought the treaty was good for the national interest and three of whom believed it would be militarily advantageous to the United States.[9]

The ratification battle lay several weeks ahead. In the meantime, Carter used the month before the summit meeting to gather every bit of information available about the background and personality of the leader he would face in Vienna, Leonid Brezhnev. Although they were frequent correspondents, they had never met in person. Carter read numerous reports about Brezhnev and carefully "studied videotapes of the Soviet leader's behavior and mannerisms on public occasions." The health of the seventy-two-year-old Brezhnev was of particular concern, because there was evidence that it had been steadily deteriorating and that he sometimes experienced notable lapses in memory and alertness. CIA Director Stansfield Turner, however, told Carter that the latest reports indicated that Brezhnev had "regained strength in recent weeks after extensive convalescence."[10]

Eighty-seven-year-old Averell Harriman, who had been United States ambassador to the Soviet Union during World War II, advised Carter that the Soviets respected him and that Brezhnev wanted the summit to be one of his greatest accomplishments. Harriman told Carter to treat Brezhnev as a friend, not to embarrass him, and not to expect him to be well-informed. In addition to Harriman, Carter also talked with former Presidents Nixon and Ford and others who had met the Soviet leader at previous conferences. They reported, according to White House aides, that Brezhnev was "an outgoing, confident man given to bursts of humor and backslapping" camaraderie when he felt well. In order to make his points, he could be expected to single "out a member of the opposite delegation as the butt of gently sarcastic jokes."[11]

The Soviet Union, according to a CIA report, was as intensely devoted to its "liberation" movement in emerging countries as the United States was to its human rights concerns. Furthermore, the Soviets liked the process of negotiating, whereas Carter looked upon it "as an aggravating procedure toward a solution."[12]

Carter, nevertheless, was willing to put up with considerable aggravation to reduce the chances of nuclear war and safeguard human rights for Soviet political prisoners. Edward Sanders, Carter's advisor on Jewish affairs, reminded Carter that his discussions of human rights with Brezhnev must include references to "Anatoly Shcharansky, Ida Nudel, Iosif Mendelevich, Isosif Begun, Vladimir Slept, Josef Goldman, and Lev Tukashensky." Sanders emphasized "the importance of you being able to report after your return that you did, in fact, discuss . . . specific individuals."[13] Carter had no intentions of changing his practice at Vienna of linking human rights to foreign policy.

Standing on the South Lawn of the White House on June 14, Carter delivered an impassioned departure speech. Since "man had unleashed the power of matter itself" thirty-five years ago, he said, "world events have never been the same." The task of every US president since then "has been to avoid nuclear war while maintaining and even enhancing the security of the United

States of America." That was the purpose of his trip to Vienna, he said, and "the only way to have peace . . . is to wage peace constantly from a position of constant and sustained national strength." He hoped that the Soviet Union would agree that "the security of both nations and the stability of the world" depended upon their avoiding a nuclear conflict that no one would win. Carter was thankful that he went to Vienna "representing the greatest, the most powerful, and the most free society on Earth."[14]

During the flight, Carter and his team worked on numerous details with regard to deep arms cuts, verifying that the other party kept its word, a prohibition against building more atomic bombs, and a comprehensive test ban treaty.[15] Somebody mentioned that the weather in Vienna was overcast. Raising the memory of Neville Chamberlain carrying an umbrella when he appeased Hitler at Munich in 1938, a presidential aide, quipped "Would [to] God that it doesn't rain," to which Carter quickly responded, "I'd rather drown than carry an umbrella."[16]

When the president's plane landed outside Vienna on the night of June 14, only a few drops of rain were falling. President Rudolph Kirchschlager and Chancellor Bruno Kreisky of Austria greeted Carter, Rosalynn, Amy, and the rest of the US party. "I have come to meet with President Brezhnev on a mission of peace," he said, "to reduce the dangers of a nuclear war, to move toward a more secure and stable world." The treaty, he said, would not "end all differences between our two nations. But we are confident that it will reduce substantially the dangers of nuclear holocaust." The Carters then went to the US ambassador's residence, where they stayed for the duration of the summit.[17]

The next morning, Brezhnev landed in Vienna. Foregoing a speech, he "walked carefully and slowly along a red carpet to review an Austrian Army honor guard in sunny, fresh weather." A New York Times reporter described him as looking "gray, somewhat uncertain on his feet but spry."[18] Late that afternoon, Carter and Brezhnev met during a courtesy call on the Austrian president. By previous arrangement, Carter arrived a few minutes before Brezhnev at the president's palace, the Hofburg. Brezhnev walked toward Carter "at a steady pace" as hundreds of flash bulbs and television cameras nearly blinded them. Communicating through their interpreters, they agreed that the future safety of their countries and the rest of the world depended upon the success of their conference. Then the mysterious Russian surprised Carter with a "very strange" comment: "If we do not succeed, God will not forgive us."[19]

The leaders of the world's two superpowers walked with President Kirchschlager to his office, where Carter gently reminded Brezhnev that he was to speak first. Brezhnev read a prepared speech directed entirely toward friendship with Austria. Carter remarked that the peaceful environment of Vienna would contribute to the success of their meeting. Then Jimmy joked, in a typically Southern manner, that the Soviets had set such a rigorous schedule that he hoped he "could keep up with the energetic Soviet President." Brezhnev, who did not catch the humor, "did not react." Nevertheless, the Russian put his hand on Carter's shoulder as they left, and Carter "felt close to him."[20]

When Brezhnev and Carter "moved off by ourselves to chat for a few minutes as real people," each discovered that neither wanted to attend the opera that evening. However, since it had been arranged by the Russian delegation, they felt they had to go.[21] Both of them went to the State Opera to see Mozart's "The Abduction from the Seraglio." Jimmy and Rosalynn sat in the same box with Brezhnev, who wore a dark blue suit and maroon necktie. They were joined by Soviet Foreign Minister Andrei Gromyko and Soviet Defense Minister Marshal Dmitry Ustinov, who was wearing his uniform. Both Carter and Brezhnev left at the first intermission, Brezhnev first, followed a few minutes later by Carter.[22] Outside on the street, Brezhnev "was heckled by relatives and friends of Soviet dissidents" who had been demonstrating in the city "for several days in an effort to secure the dissidents' release or emigration."[23]

Early on the morning of June 16, the first official day of the summit, Carter went for a jog around the grounds of the US ambassador's residence before going to the US embassy to welcome Brezhnev and his delegation. An unidentified US official who was present at the sessions reported that the atmosphere was "relaxed" and devoid of "the sharp talk and rancor that characterized the Soviet-American summit conference in Vienna in 1961, when John F. Kennedy met with Nikita S. Khrushchev." It was, as the next day's New York Times headline said, a "Parley in Friendly Discord."[24]

At the first session, which lasted eighty-five minutes, the two delegations sat on opposite sides of a twenty-five-foot-long wooden conference table. Brezhnev "pulled on a pair of rimless reading glasses, [and] drew some typewritten pages from a black folder," while across the table from him, Carter "reached into his breast pocket and pulled out several folded yellow legal pages on which he had summarized in his own hand the remarks he wanted to make."[25] While Brezhnev talked, the US delegates paid close attention to the

Soviet entourage: Foreign Minister Andrei Gromyko, who always remained close to Brezhnev and often spoke up; Dmitry Ustinov, who was highly regarded by US military experts; and Konstantin Chernenko, a Politburo member who never spoke, but whom the Americans speculated might be Brezhnev's successor. Rambling on at length, Brezhnev remarked that both countries were so powerful that they had a special responsibility. It had been a tough path, he said, from cooperating during World War II to their current disagreements. Laughing, he pointed to Cyrus Vance, saying "This man disagrees." As everyone else laughed too, Vance cringed and must have felt even less comfortable about his position in the Carter Administration.[26]

The two leaders sometimes interrupted each other. When Brezhnev contended that the United States had doubled its military outlays, Carter denied it and noted that the Soviet Union had made huge military expenditures during the past decade. Brezhnev proceeded to declare that their two countries should limit weapons and that US leaders should cease referring to the Soviets as "adversaries." He implied that the two countries should be honest with each other, not "carry stones inside your shirt," and have "good and stable relationships as equals."[27]

Carter then inadvertently embarrassed Brezhnev by reminding him of his remark the previous day that if they failed God would not forgive them. But, Gromyko quickly defused the moment by saying, "Yes, God above is looking down at us all." Carter denied that the United States and the Soviet Union had ever been adversaries; he said their differences sprang from lack of understanding and miscommunication. Everyone laughed when he said, in the presence of Vance, that the "meetings between Vance and Gromyko have not always contributed to progress," but he expected his meeting with the Soviet leader to be productive and eventually draw other nations into arms limitations discussions.[28]

After a break for lunch, Brezhnev again spoke first, impressing Carter with his attempts at humor and ability to speak without notes. Animated, Brezhnev denied that the Soviet Union had caused the delays and lack of progress. He would not accept amendments that the United States Senate might propose during the ratification process, but both parties, he said, should abide by the treaty as signed. The Soviets questioned whether the new US MX mobile missile system was consistent with SALT II, while the Americans objected to the Soviets' claim that their Backfire bomber was an intermediate-range weapon and not a long-range one covered by the treaty. Neither side was able to agree upon an immediately effective date. By this time, all participants wanted to adjourn until the next day.[29]

The US group and the Russian group left separately but later reconvened at the US ambassador's residence where the United States delegation hosted a working dinner. Carter offered a brief toast to "our two nations' success . . . to control and to regulate the arms competition."[30] Brezhnev was more interested in the vodka and the dinner than the toast. He called for vodka and impatiently asked for the meal to be served. He made small talk about grandchildren, wine, and the large number of automobiles in the United States. More relaxed, he made many toasts during the meal, and, according to Carter, "bottomed up his glass of vodka each time," and "there never was a time for discussion of issues."[31]

The Soviet delegation hosted the second day of meetings on June 17 at the Soviet Embassy. As the guest, Carter led the discussion by telling the Soviets that the United States was ready to agree to an annual 5% reduction in nuclear weapons. Brezhnev agreed but said that the Soviets and Americans could not go it alone; other nuclear powers should also be discouraged from building up their stockpiles. The two men discussed nothing new but merely repeated their key points, namely that they should "halt production of nuclear weapons and reduce existing stockpiles, retaining the current ratios of weapons so that neither nation would gain an advantage." As they rode together in the elevator they relaxed and for a moment became two very human men who had similar responsibilities and problems that they shared as friends. Anticipating that there would be another SALT conference after they completed the current one, Brezhnev asked Carter for a list of issues they should discuss at a SALT III conference, and Carter gave it to him.[32]

During the afternoon session, Carter raised topics upon which there was little chance the Soviet leader would agree: Cuban military activity in Africa, Soviet expansion into the Arabian Peninsula and Persian Gulf, the Middle East peace process, human rights, and China. Brezhnev had an answer for every question. He was surprised that the Persian Gulf and Arabia were of so much interest to the United States. He wanted an "on-first-use-of-arms treaty between the Warsaw Pact and NATO." He believed that the United States had not kept its promise to involve the Soviet Union in a Middle East peace treaty, and he thought that the Camp David Accords had failed. He disliked having US bases so close to the Soviet Union in Japan, the Philippines, and South Korea.[33] Furthermore, Brezhnev said that China threatened the Soviet Union's neighbors and was a danger to countries with which the Soviets had treaties. He defended the presence of Cuban troops in Angola and Ethiopia on the grounds that they had been invited by the governments of those nations, and he added: "The American leaders should remember that foreign troops fought with George Washington during your own revolution."[34]

Having made no progress, the group retreated to the banquet room of the Soviet embassy, where the Russians had prepared an elaborate feast. According to Carter, who disliked all banquets, the US banquet had been "adequate," but the Russian one was "exquisite." Brezhnev took pride in the fact that the menu was printed in both Russian and English, whereas at the US banquet the night before it had been only in English. Brezhnev offered so many toasts, following each with bottom-upping his vodka glass, that Carter had to ask the waiter for a smaller glass and a milder drink. They relaxed, joked, and shared an enjoyable evening like friends celebrating some triumph or significant holiday. Carter, however, hoped the Soviets had taken seriously his "expressions of concern about their constant impulse to inject military aid into any trouble spot." He hoped also "that they had listened carefully to [his] warning about the Persian Gulf region."[35]

Upon returning to the US ambassador's residence, Jimmy confessed to his diary and likely remarked to Rosalynn how tired he was of speeches and conferences. He dreaded to think about what might transpire during his conversations with Brezhnev and the signing ceremony the next day. He dreaded more the speech he would have to deliver to Congress when he returned home for what he knew would be an uphill battle to get Senate ratification. Rosalynn kept a low profile during the summit, but she reminded Jimmy to create a positive political image, not to appear to be making unnecessary concessions to the Russians, and not to trust the Soviets. Late that night, perhaps after Rosalynn had gone to bed, Jimmy and Amy took flashlights and jogged for two miles around the embassy.[36]

The next morning, June 18, the two men met at the US embassy, where they reviewed the terms of the treaty and continued discussing remaining points of contention. Brezhnev wanted to talk about China. He had no objection to the normalization of relations between the United States and China, but he bluntly declared that he would not take lightly any resulting anti-Soviet attitudes, such as those expressed by Brzezinski. He argued that China wanted the United States "to cover their political rear," because it had "territorial claims against Japan, Vietnam, India, and the Philippines . . . [and] was not bound by any international agreements regarding nuclear weapons," a threat that Brezhnev said was "of double concern." Carter reassured him that the United States was interested in peace among all nations and "would not use our new friendship with China to the detriment of the Soviet Union."

He tried to convince the Russian leader that the US relationship with China was good for all three countries. Brezhnev retorted, but in a friendly tone, "Certainly not good for the Soviet Union!"[37]

Leaving the discussion of China for the more volatile topic of Soviet abuse of human rights, Carter told the Soviet leader: "The subject of human rights is very important to us in shaping our attitude toward your country." After expressing his pleasure that the Soviets had released several political prisoners in recent months, Carter asked that he "release Mr. Shcharansky and other dissidents." Brezhnev responded that Shcharansky had broken the law and had been tried and convicted of espionage. Brezhnev looked at his watch as if it was time to end the discussions and prepare for the formal signing ceremony at 1:00 p.m.[38] Carter again asked Brezhnev to release the Jewish dissidents, but Brezhnev refused, responding that he must obey the law. The two men then moved on to the well-orchestrated signing ceremony.[39]

Seated about six feet apart at a long table in the Imperial Palace, each man was flanked by his advisers. Secretary Cyrus Vance stood at mid-point as if he were separating the two groups from each other, but he kept his eyes on the Russian leader who had insulted him. Interpreters stood nearby as each man signed the documents and then passed them to the other one. After both had signed, they stood up and walked around to the front of the table. Carter reached out to shake Brezhnev's hand, but the aging Russian leaned toward him, clasped him warmly, and laid a cheek tightly against the president's in a European-style embrace. Rosalynn was horrified, for she thought that the Soviet leader's kiss would make Carter look weak on television. Soviet Foreign Minister Gromyko and Defense Minister Ustinov, on the other hand, were "pleasantly surprised . . . when President Carter took the initiative, sealing the treaty with a formal embrace and a kiss." In moments it was over, and both men rushed to catch their flights home.

Carter now faced the task of trying to convince the Senate to ratify the treaty that he and his predecessors had so laboriously negotiated for more than seven years. He already knew that it would be a tougher battle than getting the Panama Canal treaties ratified.[40]

During his flight home, Carter worked on the nationally televised speech that he was to give to a joint session of Congress two hours after landing. Brezhnev had warned Carter that if the Senate tried to amend the treaty, there would be "grave and even dangerous consequences." Carter resolved to rally public support, marshal cabinet members and others to campaign for the treaty, and persuade the required two-thirds of senators to ratify SALT II as it was written.[41]

Standing before Congress on the night of June 18, Carter made his best pitch to a mostly unconvinced audience in the House chamber and a larger but equally doubtful one watching on television. Having acknowledged the gracious introduction by Speaker Tip O'Neill, Carter began: "The truth of the nuclear age is that the United States and the Soviet Union must live in peace or we may not live at all." The new treaty, Carter acknowledged, would not end the arms race, "but it does make that competition safer and more pre-dictable, with clear rules and verifiable limits." "SALT II," he declared, "is not a favor we are doing for the Soviet Union. It's [a] deliberate calculated move that we are making as a matter of self-interest . . . that strengthens both the military position of our own country and the cause of world peace."[42]

In the ensuing days, while the Senate debated the treaty, Carter moved on to deal with the other pressing issues. Rebels in Nicaragua, Menachem Begin, Vietnamese refugees, and more demanded his attention. To make matters worse, he prepared to face head-on a rumored challenge for the Democratic nomination from Ted Kennedy. When a liberal Democratic Congressman asked him at the June 20 White House breakfast for Democrats what he would do if Kennedy ran, Carter quickly replied, "I'll whip his ass."[43]

Shortly after noon on June 23, just five days after returning from Vienna, Jimmy, Rosalynn, and Amy departed on a twelve-day, 17,350-mile journey to Japan for a G7 meeting of the western world's leading democracies. After the conference, they planned to go to South Korea to visit US troops and confer with South Korean leaders.[44] En route, they stopped in Alaska where contro-versy still raged over Carter's executive order to protect fifty million acres of wilderness land in seventeen national monuments. Congress had not passed legislation to protect the land, and many people in Alaska opposed the exec-utive order. Republican governor James Hammond and Republican Senator Ted Stevens avoided political comment when they met the Carters briefly at Anchorage International Airport. Governor Hammond gave Carter a mule whip in case he needed it "to whip somebody's ass."[45]

Upon arrival in Tokyo on the night of June 24, Carter and his party were put under the guard of 26,000 Japanese policemen. Unbeknown to Carter, prior to his arrival, "leftist urban guerrillas," according to the *New York Times*, had attempted to prevent his plane from landing by trying to disrupt communication between the control tower and Air Force One. Furthermore, "about 700 white-helmeted and white-masked leftist activists" had staged demonstrations chanting "'Stop Carter's arrival' and 'Destroy the summit.'" Riot policeman beat them back with wooden sticks, and Carter's security force, which had preceded him, thought it safe for his plane to land on schedule.[46]

The Carters were welcomed much more cordially the next day by Emperor Hirohito at a ceremonial reception in the Akasaka Palace courtyard. Excited to meet the diminutive emperor, Carter was disappointed that he did not talk about politics but instead conversed about air pollution and marine biology. Prime Minister Masayoshi Ohira escorted the Carters to his seafront villa and to the fishing village of Shimoda, where the first US consulate in Japan had been established in 1858. The president and the prime minister discussed official topics such as strategy for conserving oil, protecting Japan's petroleum supplies from the Middle East, and a plan for Japan to take more of the Vietnamese refugees who were adrift in the China Sea, fleeing their country.[47]

Jimmy and Rosalynn relaxed at the formal banquet where Carter sat between the emperor and Crown Princess Michiko and learned that both of them knew his sister Ruth. If there had been "such a U.S.-Japan wise men's group fifty years ago," Carter told them, "the tragic turn of history might have been averted." The emperor agreed and was delighted when Carter gave him copies of Rachel Carson's *Silent Spring* and *The Sea Around Us*.[48]

On June 26, Carter's hosts took him to the same small restaurant where he and journalist Richard Halloran "had eaten four years earlier." The restaurant seated only about twenty or twenty-five guests and specialized in "yakitori" chicken. Jimmy relished the symbolic significance of his being identified as "a man of the people." He "drank a lot of sake," laughed with the other patrons, and gave toasts to "all the Japanese citizens." The next day Carter attended a town meeting in Shimoda, where most of the questions were about his family background, Amy, and whether he would marry a Black woman. Later in the evening he invited G-7 attendees British Prime Minister Margaret Thatcher and Canadian Prime Minister Joe Clark to visit the US embassy. He liked Clark immediately, but he reserved judgment on Thatcher.[49]

When the two-day meeting began the next day, June 28, Carter discovered that the Europeans had ganged up against him. Helmut Schmidt verbally abused him for interference in the Middle East that Schmidt contended had caused Western Europe's problems with its oil supply. Thatcher liked the fact that Rosalynn and Amy were with Carter, but she thought that his analysis of international economics was "badly flawed," and she doubted that he understood the seriousness of the Soviet threat. Before retiring for the night, Carter wrote in his diary that the "first day of the economic summit was one of the worst days of my diplomatic life."[50]

In spite of their personal frictions, the seven world leaders resolved most of their differences by turning their attention to a common enemy, OPEC, which had raised oil prices, resulting in shortages and fears of shortages in industrialized nations. Carter asked his colleagues to stop bidding against each other for OPEC oil and to reduce their imports in 1980. Accepting Carter's plea, at the conclusion of their meeting on June 29, they signed a declaration agreeing to oil import quotas and urging other industrialized nations to do the same. While searching for alternative energy sources, they agreed to use coal and nuclear power.[51]

When the meeting concluded, the Carters flew to South Korea on June 29 to spend the night with US soldiers at Camp Casey, the headquarters of the US Army Second Infantry Division, located about twelve miles south of the Demilitarized Zone separating South and North Korea. Very early the next morning Carter jogged with Brigadier General Bruckner and about 120 soldiers, who chanted in cadence as they ran in formation: "Raise your eyes and what do you see—Mr. President is running with me." When Carter found out that the three mile run was going slower than he liked, he picked up the pace and many of the troops could not keep up. At the end of the twenty-two minute run, Carter shook hands with all of the soldiers as they filed by. They had been ordered to shout "Fit to fight" as they passed him, but he said that half of them were too tired to speak. After changing clothes and going to the parade ground, Carter spoke briefly, paying tribute to the more than 50,000 US soldiers who had died in the Korean War three decades earlier. He did not mention his previously announced intention to withdraw all US forces from Korea, a plan that he was reassessing while 31,000 remained on the Korean Peninsula.[52] He did, however, joke about the run he had shared with them earlier in the day. He promised that "the next time I would run in combat boots and let them wear running shoes—but would not race anyone less than fifty-five years old."[53]

The Carters then traveled forty miles south to Seoul to be formally welcomed by South Korea's authoritarian President Park Chung Hee. As their motorcade passed through the streets of the capital city, they were greeted by thousands of cheering, flag-waving Koreans who government officials had asked to turn out. Upon arrival at the presidential residence, the Blue House, Carter sat down for a two-hour discussion with President Park. He discussed religion, human rights abuses in South Korea, and the level of US troops, but President Park did not promise to make any policy changes. Carter had, as a *Washington Post* correspondent noted, "a delicate diplomatic mission of showing support for the country's security without appearing to embrace [a] government that persistently is at odds with his human rights policy."[54]

Without criticizing President Park or demanding that he restore democracy to South Korea, Carter signed a joint communique with him reaffirming US commitment to defending South Korea. Carter did, however, meet with several political and religious dissenters. One of them, Kim Young Sam, leader of the opposition New Democratic Party, took some solace in the fact that "of all American Presidents to visit South Korea, President Carter praised President Park the least." At his toast before the state dinner on June 30, according to Kim Young Sam, "Carter said the Korean people are great, but never said President Park was great."[55] Carter had chosen his words carefully, and he was ready to go home. He cancelled a stopover in Hawaii and arrived back in Washington on July 1.

TWENTY FOUR

Crisis of Confidence

Carter's foreign policy triumphs of the first half of 1979 did not translate into popular approval or political success. Despite his earlier dismissal of Professor Christopher Lasch's analysis of a US society in "moral crisis" as being "too erudite to be practical," Jimmy and Rosalynn turned back to those same ideas in early July. Relaxing at Camp David after a grueling trip to Asia, they reflected upon Carter's poor standing in the polls.[1]

Rather than enjoying a festive celebration of the nation's independence, the president and First Lady felt discouraged by their falling approval numbers and the drama playing out in US communities, cities, and streets. The energy crisis was creating extraordinary long lines at gasoline and diesel stations across the nation with no obvious solution in sight. Even the cultural commentary was foreboding. Movies such as *The Deer Slayer* reminded Americans of the futile Vietnam quagmire and conveyed a loss of faith in the government. Some doubted that Carter had told them the truth when he promised never to tell a lie and to restore trust in the government. Economic stagnation, a trucker's strike, and Congressional unwillingness to heed the president's call for comprehensive energy legislation made Carter, a born-again Baptist, vulnerable to debilitating self-criticism, crippling guilt, and ill-advised proposals for solutions.

It seemed to the president that whatever had happened in China, Russia, or the Middle East did not matter, if at all, to average Americans. Jimmy and Rosalynn decided that he should cancel his next scheduled speech on energy, seek the advice of experts from a cross-section of US society, and prepare a new speech that would address their perception of the state of the country. Rosalynn won the debate within the administration over the preparation and content for Carter's July 15 speech. During the previous April, Pat Caddell had approached Rosalynn to suggest a way that she and the president might deal with petroleum fuel shortages and Carter's 25% approval rating. At a two-hour breakfast meeting on April 9, Caddell convinced her that there was a crisis of confidence in the country, symbolized by the long lines at gas stations and the unresolved energy crisis. Caddell, the pollster and data specialist who owned Cambridge Survey Research, never joined the White House staff. An admirer of Carter, he took it upon himself to become "a political guru" and spent about a week each month at the White House. The "boy wonder," according to Eizenstat, had endeared himself to Carter during his time as governor by talking Southern politics and revealing his deep family roots in South Carolina.[2]

In a seventy-five page memo, Caddell painted a gloomy picture of the rot that gripped the country, but he also explained that Carter could take advantage of it to emerge as a great president. Rosalynn liked Caddell's argument that Jimmy might become a hero who healed the nation's ills and convinced Jimmy to take the moody Caddell's argument seriously.[3] Both Carters met in the Oval Office with Caddell on Saturday, April 28, to discuss his philosophical, utopian, and impractical plan. Carter's style of leadership, however, was not commensurate with such a nebulous idea that he should be a "transforming president." His style was to speak frankly about any crisis, make a careful analysis, gather informed recommendations, and make a final decision. He was practical, honest, courageous—sometimes to the point of being reckless—but never philosophical.[4]

Walter Mondale thought that twenty-nine-year-old Caddell was too enamored of contemporary sociological analyses of US society, politically naïve, and "crazy." Indeed, Caddell had become fascinated with Christopher Lasch's *The Culture of Narcissism: American Life in an Age of Diminishing Expectations*, as well as similar works by professors Daniel Bell of Harvard and Robert Bellah of Berkeley. All agreed that hedonistic US culture had created a crisis of confidence in the country. To regain their moral footing, citizens needed to be willing to make sacrifices, learn to live in an age of limits, and make commitments to civic virtues and responsibilities. Mondale thought Caddell was selling the Carters a "bunch of crap" from books he might have read in college.[5]

Nevertheless, it was an idea that played directly to Carter's own sense of morality and citizenship. Caddell developed a method of making "end runs to both Carters" that Carter's senior advisers learned about only after the fact. Jerry Rafshoon recalled that, while the senior staff "went home to their wives," Caddell "would be on the phone calling Rosalynn: 'It's all falling apart; you know your husband is in danger; they're not listening to him; this is what he has to do.'" The next day, Carter would tell his staff that he had decided to do what Pat recommended, and he would not allow any discussion about it.[6]

Meanwhile, the daily lives of Americans from coast to coast were beginning to be disrupted by sudden shortages of fuel for operating their motor vehicles and heating their homes, among many other purposes. The revolution in Iran had greatly reduced the amount of that country's oil in the world market. Saudi Arabia, following the Camp David Accords, had led OPEC into restricting oil shipments to the United States and raising prices. Saudi Arabia regarded Carter's agreement with Israel, that seemed to leave the Palestinians and other Arabs in Israel suspended in limbo, with suspicion. Since it was a major source of foreign oil, Carter knew that if he lost the Saudi's oil, the desperate voters in New Hampshire and Massachusetts would not favor his reelection.[7] Uncertain about what to expect from the Saudis, or Iran, the previous April Carter had asked Congress to approve his energy legislation. It called for increased taxes on windfall profits oil companies might make if decontrolled, research on alternative sources of energy, assistance for low income citizens, new public transportation systems, and conservation. On July 10, he issued a proclamation that the country was experiencing a severe energy shortage, a copy of which he sent to Congress with the additional declaration that he would issue a standby energy conservation order if the situation deteriorated to such a level that he thought an order was needed.[8]

Senator Ted Kennedy condemned the president's energy plan as inflationary, politically damaging, and burdensome to middle income families. Ronald Reagan, the rising presidential candidate in the Republican Party, addressed the energy crisis in his home state of California with simplistic reassurance.[9] Fully aware of Reagan's rivalry and the fact that California was a microcosm of the nation's fuel crisis, Carter traveled to Los Angeles on May 5, where he addressed small groups that had gathered for the Cinco de Mayo celebration and possibly escaped death when the Secret Service agents arrested a would-be assassin loitering only fifty feet from the podium. Before leaving the state, Carter visited terminally ill movie star John Wayne in his hospital room.[10]

For the remainder of May, events seemed to conspire against Carter. His address to the Democratic National Committee at the Sheraton Hotel in Washington on May 25, according to the *Washington Post*, sounded like a sermon based on Caddell's ideas. Carter blamed Congress for failure to enact legislation and kowtowing to American selfishness. The energy crisis, he said, could only be solved if the US people faced reality and were willing to make sacrifices. The crowd applauded politely.[11]

Jimmy and Rosalynn's inner circle did not applaud. On July 5, the Carters called Caddell, Jordan, Powell, and Rafshoon to come to Camp David to discuss the president's declining popularity in the polls.[12] Caddell stuck to his guns, but the others, supported afterward by Eizenstat and Mondale, argued vigorously against the moody pollster. Mondale feared that Caddell's naive ideas would destroy Carter's presidency and, with it, his own career. Mondale asked himself and his wife whether he should resign as vice president. He doubted Carter's liberalism and was horrified by the popularity of Ted Kennedy. After delivering a positive commencement address at the University of Wisconsin in late May, a worried vice president departed for a fishing trip.

While canoeing the Boundary Waters of his home state of Minnesota, Mondale further pondered his resignation. Both he and Carter were free of scandal, but he felt alienated from the president who had given him so much power. Joan told him to quit, but he decided to stay and try to avoid the media storm that would weaken the administration even more. Mondale returned to work on June 3, determined to be the liberal stalwart in the administration and, as such, help the president however he could. Jimmy and Rosalynn never knew that Mondale considered resigning, nor did they doubt his loyalty and ability.[13]

Mondale did remain loyal to Carter, whose ratings in the polls plummeted when a right-wing preacher, Jerry Falwell, organized conservative evangelical Christians into what he called "the Moral Majority" that wanted to return the country to "traditional family values." A restless group in Minnesota started a draft Kennedy movement, and the worsening petroleum crisis severely impacted the everyday lives of most Americans. Much of the nation's economic and social infrastructure was dependent on the availability of plentiful and affordable supplies of gasoline and diesel fuel. The gasoline lines that had begun in California spread quickly across the country, sometimes sparking violent confrontations among drivers desperate for fuel. Truckers, who blamed Carter for the fuel shortage, went on strike in some places, refusing to transport goods and forcing plants in Nebraska and Iowa to shut down.[14]

Desperate to find a solution, Carter met with his staff on July 2 to plan his fifth speech on energy. Speechwriters Rick Hertzberg and Gordon Stewart did not think another speech on energy could offer anything new, but they produced a draft. In the meantime, Jimmy and Rosalynn together reread Caddell's analysis of what was wrong with the United States. Convinced that he should follow Caddell's line of thought, Carter suddenly announced on July 4 that he was cancelling his speech scheduled for the next day. Without consulting anyone, he and Rosalynn decided to host a meeting with experts from all walks of life at Camp David. Carter first summoned Jordan, Eizenstat, Mondale, Rafshoon, Powell, and Caddell to Camp David to demand their support for his and Rosalynn's plan to host the experts.[15]

Alarmed by the Carters' plan, Eizenstat and Mondale tried to block it. Mondale thought Carter was "tired and in a funky mood" and was surprised that he had succumbed to Caddell's illogical ideas. Mondale had earlier, according to Eizenstat, become "enraged and even vituperative that a 29-year-old wonder kid was peddling what he considered pop-culture Kool-Aid to the president and First Lady based on pseudo-psychology." Both Rafshoon and Eizenstat thought that cancelling the speech was a bad decision that would make the president appear panicky. Rafshoon said that the country would wonder if he had "cracked up." Jody called Caddell himself to ask him "what the hell have you done?," but it was too late. The outraged vice president and appalled senior advisers joined Jimmy, Rosalynn, and Pat Caddell at Camp David on July 5.[16]

The debate among the Carters and their advisers was lengthy and furious. Sitting around the very same conference table where the Camp David Accords had been negotiated, Mondale and Eizenstat faced Rosalynn, seated between Caddell and Jody Powell. Ham and Rafshoon were next to them, and Jimmy sat at the head. Mondale and Eizenstat adamantly opposed the Carters' plan to invite 130 alleged experts and common citizens from a cross-section of society to Camp David for an informal seminar on what was wrong with the United States. The Carters had called the group together to announce their intentions, not to be dissuaded. Eizenstat thought it preposterous for Carter to make a speech that blamed the people for inflation, the gas lines, and the weakening economy. The people, he said, were not angry at themselves; they were angry at the government. Ham urged Carter to proceed with his energy speech, but Caddell stubbornly pressed for a speech about the crisis of confidence in the country.

Again, Caddell gave advice that no one—except Rosalynn—endorsed. Mondale was emphatic that Caddell's ideas were "silly and sophomoric." He argued that the president should not scold people for being selfish, as Caddell and Lasch recommended, but address the issues of energy, inflation, and unemployment that troubled them. When Caddell became nervous, Rosalynn quietly patted him on the knee. She had read the cancelled speech Jimmy had prepared on energy and declared it to be awful. She thought Jimmy needed the advice of experts and citizens outside the government.[17]

Carter informed the group that he expected them to support the proposed seminar. Mondale alone refused, and after the meeting, Carter invited him for a private talk as they walked around the grounds. Mondale would not be easily consoled, but he stuck with his decision to remain loyal to the president and the administration.

Although Caddell had won his point in the meeting, he was visibly shaken by the angry responses of the inner circle. Rosalynn gave him a ride in a golf cart while she explained that Jimmy had deliberately not told his staff in advance about his plan to cancel the speech, because he wished to demonstrate that the president was in charge. Caddell confided to Rosalynn that it had been a "terrible 36 hours" for him, since he had not expected to land in the middle of such a violent disagreement between the president and his top advisers.[18]

Treating it as a separate issue, Carter discussed with Mondale and others the future of his cabinet members. Carter did not want to dismiss any of them, but everyone else thought it was time for Health, Education, and Welfare Secretary Joe Califano, Treasury Secretary Michael Blumenthal, and Energy Secretary James Schlesinger to be replaced. Califano was often at loggerheads with Rosalynn and generally perceived by Carter's senior staff, especially Ham Jordan, as disloyal.[19] Blumenthal had Carter's respect, but he had not been able to deal with inflation and stagflation.[20] Schlesinger had not succeeded in dealing with the energy crisis, and he behaved arrogantly toward the president and had a condescending attitude to his staff.[21]

Carter appreciated the staff's hard work and was often forgiving of those with moral lapses or intrusive personal problems. He defended them, especially when they, like himself, were underrated by the media and the Washington establishment.[22] In a shocking, private, post-presidential interview, he confessed that "the quickest way" Rosalynn could "aggravate" him would be for her to point out some mistake one of the staff members had made. "It really aggravated me," he emphasized.[23]

The public knew nothing about Carter's private discussions with his staff or the impending cabinet changes, nor was it prepared for the virtual disappearance of the president. For ten days following the unsettling July 5 meeting, the stream of 130 people whom Jimmy and Rosalynn had chosen to advise them came and went at Camp David's Laurel Lodge. The guests visited in separate groups of African Americans, politicians, journalists, economists, governors, and religious leaders. Jody Powell struggled to limit news releases and to refute wild speculations ranging from the president's having left the country to his having had a mental breakdown. It was an unusual, even odd, action for a president to take. For Jimmy, however, it might have seemed normal, since he likely attended retreats for meditation and study as part of his youthful religious experience.[24]

Mondale was noticeably absent from the gatherings, where Carter posed as director of a series of seminars about himself. He sometimes sat on the floor in the middle of a circle of attendees, but he more often sat at a table where he could make eye contact with the participants, who were arranged in a semicircle before him. Sometimes Rosalynn sat beside him, held his hand, and whispered advice. Once, she reluctantly left the seminars long enough to join Mondale at a Democratic campaign rally in Louisville, Kentucky, where she defended her husband's record and reassured the audience that he was fine and working hard. Mondale gave a rousing speech praising the ability of the country to survive previous crises and expressing confidence in the country's resources to conquer the current energy crisis.[25]

The mood back at Laurel Lodge, however, was not so optimistic. Carter stared at wooden walls covered with maps, sometimes clenched his jaw, but usually showed little emotion as his guests let him have it. One told him that "a country already speechless with rage had a leader who said nothing," and others spoke in apocalyptic terms. Carter admitted that it was difficult for him to take criticism, and voluntarily listening to so much of it forced him to make an "intense reassessment" of his presidency.[26]

The first group to join him, eight governors representing both parties and different parts of the country, did not agree with Caddell. They thought that Carter was excessively self-deprecating and was searching for answers in the wrong place. Thirty-two-year-old Bill Clinton of Arkansas told the president that he had come only to try to help him. He advised Carter to tie all jobs possible to energy, and emphasize the positive aspects of the crisis. He warned the president that the country did not appreciate his intelligence and dedication, but it would respond to an upbeat talk about opportunities and hope for the future. Carter tensely responded "very well." Governor Richard Riley of South Carolina bluntly told Carter that he had taken on too many difficult issues and that the people would not like being called upon to make sacrifices.[27]

The next day, Carter sat stoically as he listened to brutally honest remarks from government and civic leaders, including: J. Lane Kirkland, secretary treasurer of the AFL-CIO; Sol Linowitz, who had helped negotiate the

Panama Canal treaties; Jesse Jackson and Vernon Jordan, prominent African-American leaders; Barbara W. Newell, president of Wellesley College; and John Gardner, who had served Lyndon Johnson as Secretary of Health, Education, and Welfare. All told him things that were difficult for Jimmy and Rosalynn to hear. They said his clean campaign image did not translate into effective governing, that his secretary of energy, James Schlesinger, was arrogant and politically worthless, and that Jody Powell and Hamilton Jordan were overworked. The president, some told him, needed to prove that he could govern the country.[28]

When a bipartisan group of Congressional leaders arrived on July 9, they did what Carter expected, namely asked the president for political favors. Speaker O'Neill lit up a cigar inside the room, slapped Jimmy on the back, and told him that his gasoline rationing plan would soon get through the House. Senator Robert Byrd of coal-mining West Virginia urged him to use coal to solve the energy shortage. Senator Ted Stevens of Alaska advised drilling in his state's wilderness areas. Senator J. Bennet Johnston from Louisiana wanted relaxed environmental standards, while Senator Toby Moffett from Connecticut demanded stricter regulation of the oil industry. Despite the pork each wanted for his own state, they all agreed, as the previous group had, that Schlesinger was useless as secretary of energy. Carter learned from them that Congress's lack of consensus remained a major obstacle to enacting a workable energy policy.[29]

The downhill drift of the meetings continued with the economists, businessmen, and labor representatives often wasting more time bickering among themselves than offering constructive criticism. Carter's dislike for the media representatives may have been balanced by his appreciation of the religious leaders. Nicknamed "the God Squad," they included Andrew Young, who believed that the people simply did not know that Carter was a good man and a good leader.

The religious leaders were the last group to arrive at Camp David, and Carter relaxed as he greeted them in "Christian fellowship." Robert Bellah, the University of California sociologist whose belief in civil religion was a hot topic of the day, argued that a revival of the idea of covenant might reverse the self-centered attitude that others railed against. Marc H. Tanenbaum, the "human rights" rabbi in New York City who became known for trying to improve Jewish-Christian relations, envisioned the president as Moses leading the children of America out of the wilderness of consumerism and self-indulgence.

Throughout the session, the smiling president heard the type of religion he held dear, the Reinhold Niebuhr approach, that men and nations might fall into selfish ways but it was the duty of moral men to right the wrongs of immoral society. As Tannenbaum, at Carter's request, closed the meeting with a prayer, Carter felt that he had acquired the information he and Rosalynn needed to finish writing his speech.[30]

During the course of the Camp David seminars, Carter seemed at times more engaged with other matters than the tongue lashing he was receiving from many of his guests. On July 6 he talked to Bob Strauss in Egypt about Sadat's high opinion of Begin, which surprised Strauss. Frustrated because King Hussein of Jordan had not participated in the peace process, Carter told Strauss to "tell Hussein to get off his ass & help us—I'm not going to provide a White House forum for him to blast the Middle East peace effort."[31] Carter also met with Secretary of Energy James Schlesinger to tell him it was time for him to step down, and he thanked Speaker Tip O'Neill for successfully pushing through the House the legislation that established the Department of Education. More distracting and troubling was the unpredictable revolution in Iran, especially since the Carter administration still had not succeeded in finding a working plan to communicate with the new Iranian leaders.[32]

Rosalynn was in and out of the Camp David meetings as she worked on the fast-approaching 1980 presidential campaign by making numerous telephone calls to solicit support and the one speech in Louisville, Kentucky, where she appeared with Mondale.[33] Seriously missing and needing her, Jimmy wrote in his diary that day: "I called Rosalynn on her way to Louisville to tell her that I loved her. She's been a tower of strength and fountain of wisdom throughout this Camp David stay."[34]

Together, Jimmy and Rosalynn moved doggedly toward his July 15 Sunday night address to the nation. Hoping to get the opinions and reactions of ordinary citizens, they visited about twenty of them on July 13 in Martinsburg, West Virginia. They telephoned citizens in Ohio, Pennsylvania, and Florida, trying to capture the mood of the country. The night before the speech, they hosted forty reporters at a buffet of hamburgers and French fries. Rosalynn watched her husband "intently"; Carter seemed defiant and defensive when he told the reporters what he intended to say the next night.[35]

During the two days leading up to Carter's ill-fated speech, Pat Caddell gave him more discouraging information and bad advice. After meeting with journalists and studying his polls, Caddell reported that pessimism racked the country. No one cared about the Middle East peace treaty; Congress was in disarray over the windfall profits tax that Carter wanted to impose on the oil companies; and Jane Byrne, the mayor of Chicago who had recently overthrown the Daley machine that had favored Carter, officially backed Ted Kennedy. Carter was caught at a stressful and vulnerable moment as Caddell underscored the urgency for the president to address the crisis of confidence in the country.[36]

At the same time, Tim Kraft, Hamilton Jordan, John White, and others gave the president exactly the opposite advice. John White, chairman of the Democratic National Convention, joined the chorus of those who wondered why Carter had isolated himself for so long at Camp David. "He's got to come down and prove he's running the goddamned place," he said. Senator Ralph Yarborough of Texas urged Carter not to "kick the people. Brag on the people. Tell them they have done a good job by obeying the speed limit but we have more to do." He urged Carter to speak to the "plain people like Truman and Roosevelt" had done and to "forget about Washington politics." Hamilton Jordan concurred, and there emerged a horse race between Jordan and Caddell to get to Rosalynn, for they knew that she alone might change Jimmy's mind. When Ham realized that Caddell had won, he fell silent, discouraged.[37]

On Saturday Carter kept tinkering with the draft, making some additions in his own handwriting. "Our neck is stretched over the fence, and OPEC has the knife," he wrote, referring to the way country people in Georgia slaughtered chickens in preparation for frying them for Sunday dinner. In a more upbeat tone, Carter noted that the United States was strong, capable of regaining confidence and unity, adding: "We are the generation that dedicated our society to the pursuit of human rights and equality."[38]

As Carter rehearsed his speech, he reluctantly accepted coaching from Rafshoon and Gordon Stewart. Rafshoon repeatedly instructed him: "Speak with your hands. Talk louder. Don't flash your grin all the time." Gordon Stewart, a Yale-trained director of Broadway plays, thought Carter was almost hopeless as a public speaker, but he finally angered him enough by repeatedly telling him to speak up that Jimmy did so, also gesturing with his hands.[39]

Back in Washington, Jimmy and Rosalynn attempted to have a normal Sunday morning. They attended church at First Baptist and had lunch together in the White House family dining room. In the afternoon and early evening, however, either individually or collectively, they had seven contacts with Gerald Rafshoon, their chief image maker. Carter jogged, telephoned

Tip O'Neill and Robert Byrd, and then prepared to address more than one hundred million people for half an hour, beginning at 10:00 p.m.[40]

Carter appeared nervous, stiff, ill at ease, and uncomfortable, making gestures that were not characteristic of his style. "This is not a speech of confidence or reassurance, but it is the truth and it is a warning," Carter said, using language that many Americans may not have wanted to hear. He condemned the hedonistic lifestyle so common in the United States. He referred to the assassinations of the Kennedys and Martin Luther King, Jr., the Vietnam War, and Watergate as causes of the crisis of confidence. He promised to restore the people's belief in the nation. "It is our task to commit ourselves to a reassurance of America," he emphasized, "a rebirth of the American spirit. With a common faith, we cannot fail." Ignoring all advice, he added, "There is simply no way to avoid sacrifice."[41]

Rosalynn sat nearby, watched and listened, her heart in her throat. He did not disappoint her. She thought his speech was "profound and effective" as he appealed to the people to pull together to solve the nation's energy problem.[42] The speech was everything she and Pat Caddell had hoped it would be. Carter later wrote Caddell that his "analysis was a masterpiece," and asked him to "stick with me during the coming weeks." "We will win together. You are a great ally to have in fighting our crisis of confidence.[43]

Carter gave two speeches in one. Following his crisis of confidence comments and call for sacrifice, he listed Mondale's and Stuart Eizenstat's points on how to solve the fuel crisis: setting rigorous import quotas to halve the nation's reliance on foreign oil by the end of the 1980s; making massive investments to find alternative sources of energy; and creating an energy security corporation to lead those efforts. Furthermore, treating the energy crisis with the urgency of winning a war, Carter called for creating an energy mobilization board to expedite the completion of "key energy projects" such as oil refineries and pipelines, taxing petroleum companies' windfall profits, and requiring utility companies to halve their use of oil within the next ten years by switching "to other fuels, especially coal, our most abundant energy source." That board, he said, should be charged with launching a major conservation program, including carpooling, increased use of public transportation, and lowering home thermostats. Solving the problem, he explained, must be a "shared purpose that the nation had to embark upon in order to fight the energy crisis, like a war." In thirty-two minutes it was all over.[44]

When the television lights were out and the cameras gone, Jimmy and Rosalynn met at the Roosevelt Room, then went to their quarters. Before retiring for the night, Jimmy called his son Jack, his mother, Pat Caddell, Vice President Mondale, and Speaker O'Neill. He felt good about his speech, and eventually he and Rosalynn would defend it as one of his best.[45]

Carter was still in a good mood the next day when he spoke at the Annual Convention of the National Association of Counties in Kansas City, Missouri. He referred to his speech of the night before in a serious but jovial manner, but he limited his comments in Missouri to the problems and proposed solutions associated with the energy crisis. Although a good crowd turned out to hear him and many more listened on national radio and television, the media focus was on the crisis of confidence speech he had delivered from the Oval Office.[46]

The first response was overwhelmingly positive. During the next few days, favorable phone calls and letters poured in to the White House. Carter's approval rating shot up seventeen points. Many Americans praised their president as an honest politician whose astute analysis and blunt language promised an end to the long-standing energy crisis.

It was a promise Carter could not keep, because his political antagonists quickly found ways to turn the speech against him and label him as the "malaise" president. The friends and advisors who had urged him to deliver a more positive, upbeat address had been correct. The public wanted a priest, not a prophet, a friendly advocate rather than an admonishing doomsayer.[47]

Ted Kennedy, and later Ronald Reagan, both of whom wanted Carter's job, discovered the word "malaise" in a *Washington Post* interview with Clark Clifford. Clifford, seventy-two years old, had advised all Democratic presidents since Franklin Roosevelt. He thought Carter had made "spectacular, even historic, accomplishments" during his second year in office, but he found it difficult to believe that a president of such high achievement would humiliate himself and denigrate his office with those seminars at Camp David. As a participant on July 8, Clifford said it pained him to see the president sitting on the floor, taking notes on a yellow pad as guests told him what was wrong with him. On the day the seminars ended, Clifford gave Martin Schram an interview in which he said that "the country was in a mood of widespread national malaise." The newspaper used the word in its headline, and it quickly spread across the country.[48]

Although Clifford's use of the word "malaise" had been fairly innocent, Kennedy and Reagan agreed that there was a malaise in the country all right, and Carter was the cause of it. The answer to the nation's problems, they argued, was to get rid of Carter.[49]

Some oil producers in Texas agreed with them. Mayor Oliver Howard of Abilene, Texas, wrote a polite letter to the president on July 17 saying that a windfalls profit tax would not work. It would have very little impact on major oil companies, he said, but it would harm small operators. Holding down the price of "old oil," he wrote, would retard production of "new oil" and lead to increased importation of foreign petroleum, exactly the opposite of what the president desired. Mayor Howard wanted to dissolve the distrust between oil producing and non-oil producing states, so that they could "join hands and do the job together." It may have been the best response Carter received to his request for solutions, but he did not heed it. Many oil producers in Texas and elsewhere became angry voters.[50]

Two days after his "crisis of confidence" speech, in an unusual and dramatic gesture, Carter asked for each of his cabinet members to submit a letter of resignation. Every member had verbally agreed in advance, but some thought it an odd way to approach a presidential decision to fire some of the secretaries. Both Rosalynn and Ham Jordan were insistent that he fire Califano, Blumenthal, and Schlesinger. Carter could accept the resignations of those whom he wished to remove and reject the rest. Carter thought that firing his cabinet members would prove that he had the power and the guts to govern, but Secretary of State Cyrus Vance disagreed. He warned Carter that such an approach was a bad idea, for it would give the public the impression that "the world is coming to an end."[51]

The press proclaimed a crisis in which the president had no confidence in any of his cabinet officers, which was not true. Internally, however, according to Eizenstat, the days after Carter requested the letters of resignation were "like being in hell." Schlesinger, Califano, and Blumenthal all knew that they would be fired. Mondale and Eizenstat defended Califano, for they believed he did his job well and served as a significant link to the liberal faction of the party and the Washington establishment. Carter seemed hesitant, but Califano had two implacable enemies—Rosalynn and Jordan—who persuaded the president to let him go. Blumenthal had not controlled inflation and headed the department that had released the damaging report on Bert Lance's banking practices. The abrasive and arrogant Schlesinger had few, if any, defenders. Tempers flared within the administration, and the administration turned onto a fast track downhill, and, despite notable accomplishments, the slide could not be reversed.[52]

In another dramatic change, Carter appointed Hamilton Jordan as his chief of staff starting July 18. Although Carter had vowed that he needed no such person, Jordan had functioned de facto in that position from the beginning of the administration. Jordan swelled with pride with the official appointment and accepted the "great challenge." He praised the president for his plan to lead, rather than manage, the country. "I will," Jordan promised Carter, "meet regularly with Rosalynn, Pat Caddell, Jim McIntyre, Jody Powell and Jerry Rafshoon to solicit their advice." With his insider's understanding of Rosalynn's power, he continued, "If you and the First Lady will trust me and give me the support and flexibility that I will need, we cannot and will not fail." Charles Kirbo told Jordan, who recently had begun to wear business suits, that he "should start acting like 'the big man'" that he would be.[53]

The very next day, Chief of Staff Jordan ventured to suggest that Carter should reduce the number of his weekly meetings with the First Lady. "Rosalynn spends more time with you than anyone," he noted, referring to the weekly luncheons in the Oval Office. "It seems that these luncheons might take place every other week." It was, Ham admitted, "a suicidal suggestion on my part."[54] Jimmy ignored his advice but maintained a close relationship with him.

In the middle of the turmoil surrounding the cabinet changes, conservative critics questioned Carter's human rights policies. A civil war in Nicaragua reached a climax on July 17, 1979, when the brutal dictator Anastasio Somoza, whom the United States had supported, resigned. When the pro-Communists Sandinistas took power three days later, Carter recognized them as a political and cultural force that might democratize Nicaragua, but Congress refused the aid the president requested for the new regime. Relations with Nicaragua deteriorated, opening the way for conservative critics to argue that Carter's human rights policy had resulted in a Communist takeover of Nicaragua.[55]

Carter denied it, but he was more engulfed at the time in rebuilding his cabinet. Carter handled Califano gingerly, almost apologetically, allowing him to resign on July 19, because firing him would drive a wedge between the administration and the more liberal wing of the Democratic Party that favored Ted Kennedy.[56] Schlesinger left the Energy Department with no apparent regrets, but replacing Blumenthal at Treasury became a fascinating political event. Carter invited David Rockefeller to interview for the job, but when Rockefeller arrived, he acted as if he were interviewing the president. Nonplussed by the powerful banker, Carter dismissed the idea of offering him a cabinet post, despite the political debt he owed him.[57]

Brock Adams vacillated about whether to stay or go as secretary of transportation. Although Carter had asked Adams to stay, he finally told him to go. Adams had resisted efforts to speed up airline deregulation, had complained about the dismissal of some of his aides, and had demanded greater access to the president. Senior staff labeled him as disloyal.[58]

On August 3, Griffin Bell announced he wanted to return home to Georgia and accused Carter of intruding upon the prerogative of the attorney general. Indeed, since Carter and Mondale were more liberal than Bell, they had tried to influence his decisions. In departing, Bell told Carter that he had failed to work with the Washington establishment, trivialized the presidency by attempting to tackle too many problems, and tried to act like one of the boys instead of like the president. Not responding to his criticisms, Carter accepted Bell's resignation, praising him for his service and friendship.[59]

By early August Carter had finished restructuring his cabinet. He elevated Deputy Attorney General Benjamin R. Civiletti to replace Bell at Justice, and he appointed G. William Miller, his Chairman of the Federal Reserve Board, to Treasury. Charles W. Duncan, Jr., Deputy Secretary of Defense and former president of the Coca Cola Company, took over the Energy Department, and Neil Goldschmidt, mayor of Portland, Oregon, became secretary of transportation. Carter asked Patricia Roberts Harris, an African-American lawyer who had served as a diplomat for Lyndon Johnson, to move from her position as secretary of Housing and Urban Development (HUD) to head Health, Education, and Welfare. Moon Landrieu, Mayor of New Orleans, replaced Harris at HUD.

When William Miller moved from the Federal Reserve Board to the cabinet, Carter made one of the most consequential appointments of his presidency by naming Paul Volcker to replace him. A giant of a man at six feet seven inches tall, Volcker had been a vice president of the Chase Manhattan Bank and then an under-secretary of the treasury in the Nixon administration before becoming president of the New York Reserve Bank in 1975. Volcker was surprised, nevertheless, when Carter called asking him to chair the Fed. He would take a 50% cut in salary, but he wanted the job. His wife, who suffered from rheumatoid arthritis, urged him to accept it even though she would have to remain in New York to be near her doctors. He did so, and his confirmation sailed through the Senate. He accepted the job provided that he could operate independently of the president.

During Volcker's brief swearing-in ceremony, Carter appeared to have a long face. Bert Lance had previously sent Carter a message warning that if he appointed Volcker, he would "be mortgaging his reelection to the Federal Reserve." Carter had promised, however, to bring inflation under control, and he sensed that Volcker might be able to accomplish this. True to Carter's expectation, Volcker succeeded in taming inflation by sharply braking the money supply. He was so successful in reducing inflation that he drove interest rates very high and soon brought on a recession that dogged the president until his last day in office.[60]

The co-architect of the administration's massive changes, Rosalynn, traveled about the United States during the last days of July, declaring that the president was "Healthy, happy, and confident about the future of the country." One journalist ranked Rosalynn ahead of the universally acclaimed Eleanor Roosevelt. Rosalynn denied that claim, but she admitted to being an equal political partner with the president. In Los Angeles, she told a reporter that she and Jimmy were surprised when national attention was riveted upon them when he canceled his speech on energy and retreated to Camp David. Neither of them had anticipated the negative response to his "crisis of confidence" speech. Nevertheless, "We realized that we had the attention of the country," she said, and "we decided that we could really talk about the problems of the country."[61]

TWENTY FIVE

Kennedys and Terrorists

Senator Ted Kennedy's absence from the president's July 9 meeting with Congressional leaders at Camp David indicated that he had had enough of Carter. Kennedy had been infuriated by Carter's "crisis of confidence" speech and had cunningly led to its being dubbed the "malaise" speech. He accused Carter of failing to keep his promise to deliver a national healthcare program: their disagreement over the type and urgency of a federal healthcare law, Kennedy said, was the primary reason he had become disillusioned with Carter.[1] Emboldened by the power of the Kennedy name, the notion that he was the rightful heir to the presidency, and the quixotic belief that he could win in a contest with the incumbent president from his own party, he planned to challenge Carter.

Oddly, Carter may have derived some solace from former President Richard Nixon, who wrote him on July 23 that he "had a great deal of empathy for you during this rather difficult period." Nixon admired the "effective way" Carter had presented himself during his "crisis of confidence" speech. He thought Carter had the right to shake up his cabinet and he urged him to go over the heads of the Washington press corps to the people, and ignore those who might "question your emotional stability." As a partisan, Nixon wanted a member of his own party to win in 1980, but as an American, he wrote, "I want to see our President do well, particularly in the international area." He congratulated Carter on his "loyal wife," and he assured him that, win or lose in 1980, "you will know you have given it your best shot." "God bless you—and I know He will," Nixon concluded. Four days later Carter politely thanked him for advice from one of his few "fraternity brothers."[2]

The brevity with which Carter answered Nixon typified the president's determination to put politics aside and concentrate on presidential business. In July 1979, he was concerned about how to get the Senate to ratify SALT II, recently negotiated with the Soviet Union, and discussed it with Sam Nunn, Henry Kissinger, and others who might help influence the Senate vote. He reassured Jewish Senator Abraham Ribicoff that he would use the treaty to pressure Brezhnev to release more political prisoners and step up the rate of Soviet Jewish emigration.[3]

Carter had trouble understanding why his support of Jewish emigration did not make it easier for him to relate to Israel. The answer lay, his senior advisors told him, in the fact that Israel did not want a settlement with the Palestinians. Carter, on the other hand, continuously pushed for that settlement, at the least getting the Palestinians to recognize Israel's right to exist. He complained to Israel's Ambassador Ephraim Evron that Israeli verbal attacks on him and the United States were "unwarranted, false, and unacceptable." Irked and puzzled by the stubbornness of Israel, he wrote to Senator Abraham Ribicoff: "We are their main friend, and when they can't get along with us it leaves them almost isolated."[4]

UN Ambassador Andrew Young complicated Carter's troubles with Israel and the PLO. On July 20, Young met with Zahdi Labib Terzi, a PLO observer at the UN, to try to persuade the PLO to agree to delay a forthcoming UN report favoring an independent Palestinian state. The Israeli national intelligence agency Mossad had learned in advance from a phone tap about the meeting. Rather than protesting to Washington that the meeting would violate the US promise not to deal directly with the PLO without Palestinian recognition of Israel's right to exist, Mossad let the meeting take place, then leaked it to the press hoping to force Young's resignation. That resignation would please Israelis and many Jewish Americans but anger African Americans, who were an important part of Carter's political base.[5] When questioned about it by the State Department, Young lied. Later, when he admitted the truth to the Israelis, they made his lie public despite the fact that he had been trying to help Israel. Seeking help, Young flew to Washington to meet with Secretary of State Cyrus Vance. Vance, a man of impeccable manners and integrity, rebuked Young for the improper meeting with Terzi and would never forgive him for having told a lie.

Vance, Jody, and Ham all told Carter that Young would have to leave. Vance appreciated the "very good job" Andy had done in improving "the relationships between the United States and the Third World countries, particularly in Africa," but "we, as the great nation we are, cannot be in a position where people cannot trust our word." He recommended "that Andy step down," because the "integrity of the government" must be maintained. Ham and Jody concurred with the secretary of state, and, Carter, with tears in his eyes, sadly accepted the recommendations.[6]

Carter, too close to Andy to request his resignation, asked Jesse Hill, their mutual friend, who was president of the Atlanta Life Insurance Company, to do so. Jody wept as he read Young's resignation letter to the press on August 14. In accepting his friend's resignation, Carter praised Young's sensitivity to "the demands for world peace and racial justice." He had brokered the peace agreement that made it possible for the former British colony of Rhodesia to transition in 1980 to the independent Zimbabwe. He also had been instrumental in winning African-American votes for Carter. His loss to Jimmy was as professional as it was emotional, and Carter knew that no one could take his place.[7]

Disappointed, but forgiving, Young promised to work for Carter's reelection in 1980, but the resignation complicated Carter's relationship with Jewish Americans. There was a growing perception among African Americans that Young had fallen victim to the well-known Jewish dislike for Carter. African-American leaders such as Jesse Jackson and Benjamin Hooks blamed their hero's forced departure on pressure from Jews, an allegation that Carter and Vance flatly denied. Nevertheless, major Jewish organizations and some Jewish members of Congress including New York's Republican Senator Jacob K. Javits openly condemned both Young and Carter for Young's communicating with the PLO. Many Jewish voters, already skeptical of the Baptist president, did not return to the Democratic fold, but most African Americans remained loyal to Carter.[8]

Despite the emotional and political pain caused by Young's resignation, Carter had to deal with important economic issues. Fomenting more controversy, Carter decided to bail Chrysler Corporation out of financial difficulty with a $1.5 billion loan guarantee. Chrysler was a major defense contractor and the employer of more than 200,000 people. When the bail out was completed in November 1979, Carter could rightly claim that he was using the power of his office to improve the country's sagging economy, guarantee jobs, and keep the United States militarily strong. He had given similar help to New York City in June 1978, which became the model for the Chrysler decision and the precedent for other such decisions he deemed necessary.[9]

It was also necessary for Carter to deal with Pakistan, no matter how difficult it would be. Because of the United States' odd Cold War alliance with Pakistan, the Pakistani government praised the SALT II agreement with the Soviet Union, whose forces in neighboring Afghanistan posed a serious threat to Pakistan. Pakistani president General Muhammad Zia-ul-Haq wrote Carter on August 9 thanking him for pursuing "this noble objective."

He wished, Zia said, to have a better understanding with the United States regarding the peaceful use of nuclear energy. Since Pakistan also shared a border with its foremost enemy India, which had once been under the influence of the Soviet Union, Zia viewed an improved relationship with the United States as beneficial for his country's national security.[10] Carter, meanwhile, saw Pakistan's peaceful use of nuclear energy as boosting the standard of living for the Pakistani people.

It was easier for the US government to promote human rights in Ecuador than in Pakistan. When Rosalynn attended the inauguration of Ecuador's president Jaime Roldos Aguilera on August 10, 1979, she was greeted with the same fanfare accorded a head of state. She was pleased to learn that the young Ecuadorian president took a firm stand in favor of human rights. He reduced the length of the work week, raised the minimum wage, instituted a National Development Plan, and opposed the military dictatorships that were so common in Latin America. He prided himself upon being the first Ecuadorian leader in almost a decade to come to power as a result of a majority vote of the people rather than a military coup. At his inauguration, Rosalynn felt that she was among friends.[11]

Stepping back into her role as wife and mother, Rosalynn joined Jimmy and Amy on August 17 for a week-long trip aboard the paddle wheel steamboat *Delta Queen*. The trip down the Mississippi River from St. Paul, Minnesota, to St. Louis, Missouri, was supposed to have been a relaxing journey, with only four stops, few speeches, and isolation from the media, but it turned into a media circus. The family had two small cabins at the stern, one of which served as a temporary substitute for the Oval Office. For security, a military helicopter flew low overhead, and Coast Guard vessels accompanied the historic river boat. Instead of dining together, Jimmy and Rosalynn ate at separate tables and changed tables from meal to meal in order to meet as many people as possible.[12]

Life aboard "Steamboat One" was filled with fun, politicking for energy legislation, and casual socializing with other passengers. Stops at locks and towns became full-scale rallies as crowds gathered to greet the president and his family. Journalists and photographers hung from bridges to get pictures and stories. Jimmy and Rosalynn jogged around the ship in the early hours of the morning. When other guests complained that the noise disturbed their sleep, they began to jog along the locks while their ship passed through. Carter read Mark Twain's *Life on the Mississippi* and spent time in the pilot house to learn about operation of the boat. While aboard, word reached him that Hamilton Jordan, Jody Powell, and Tim Kraft were accused of using cocaine in the Studio 54 nightclub in New York City; Carter was disgusted, though charges were eventually dropped or proven unfounded. Near the end of his trip, Carter received more agreeable news that what he considered the ridiculous charge that Bert Lance had an illegal relationship with the Carter peanut warehouse had been proved false.

Aboard the *Delta Queen*, Jimmy and Rosalynn celebrated Rosalynn's fifty-second birthday with "prayers, anthems, and the melodious calliope." They danced to the music of the Riverboat Ramblers while Amy played hide and seek. Jimmy sipped gin and tonic, while Rosalynn had white wine as a rare nightcap. Jimmy attended sessions on riverboat gambling, played the boat's calliope, and at some stops went fishing. He shook hands with thousands, kissed a few ladies on the cheek, and once asked the crowd, "Will you help me to make the greatest nation on earth even greater?" The crowds adored them.[13]

After the vacation, Jimmy and Rosalynn's schedule resumed its usual fever pitch. He appointed Donald McHenry, Andrew Young's deputy and an experienced African-American diplomat, as ambassador to the UN. That appointment further eroded Carter's relationship with the Israelis, who thought McHenry would favor Palestinians as underdogs like himself. In Atlanta, Carter conducted a seminar at Georgia Tech on new developments in energy, and at Emory he delivered a speech on morality and ethics. He and Rosalynn flew to Tampa, Florida, to campaign at a town meeting, and finally they went home to Plains, arriving, exhausted, at midnight on August 30. During the next four days, they rested, walked through the peanut fields together, fished in the Carter pond, jogged, and attended church. Jimmy played softball in the afternoon, pitching for a winning team of inmates from the Sumter County Correctional Institute.[14] After the game, he went with his mother for a private moment visiting Mr. Earl's grave in Lebanon Cemetery.[15]

Back in Washington, Jimmy and Rosalynn worked for his reelection knowing that Ted Kennedy would soon challenge him for the Democratic nomination. Rosalynn traveled to Texas and elsewhere, briefed the Women's National Democratic club in the East Room of the White House, and kept a wary eye on the senator from Massachusetts.[16] Carter consulted his political advisers, helped Rosalynn prepare dozens of campaign speeches for her solo appearances, and remained confident that he would win the nomination and be reelected. He and Rosalynn "felt remarkably at ease" about the Kennedy challenge, he told Mondale, who needed to be reassured. Despite evidence

within the party and reports from other senators that Kennedy was not a serious threat, Carter marveled how some newspapers practically anointed
"Kennedy as the president" and claimed "the 1980 election is already over."[17]

Miss Lillian remarked to a reporter for the *Atlanta Constitution* on
September 9 that, if Kennedy did run, "I hope to goodness nothing happens
to him, I really do." Since two of his three brothers had been assassinated, and
the other one killed in World War II, she claimed that she genuinely cared
about his safety. Rosalynn, whose opinion usually carried more weight with
her husband than any other, told the same journalist that she would not mention Chappaquiddick during the campaign. Having thus mentioned it, she
did not have to do so again.[18]

Tip O'Neill thought that Chappaquiddick would prevent Ted Kennedy
from running for president. So, when Kennedy visited O'Neill at his office on
September 17 to tell him that he would run, the Speaker was flabbergasted.
He bluntly advised the ambitious Kennedy: "Let me tell you something. You
can't measure morals. I said that's an issue you just can't measure. My advice
this year, not to run."[19] Kennedy did not take his advice, nor did he ever find
a believable way to explain the death of Mary Jo Kopechne in his car that July
night in 1969 when he drove off of the bridge on Chappaquiddick Island in
Edgartown, Massachusetts.

In order to deal with Kennedy and his life in general, Carter became an
avid jogger. On September 15, while spending the weekend at Camp David,
the almost fifty-five-year-old president entered a 6.2-mile foot race on
Catoctin Mountain, but he overestimated his ability. As he neared the four-
mile mark, he stumbled and was unable to complete the race. The Marine
One helicopter hovered, ready to airlift the president for emergency medical
care, and an ambulance quickly appeared. Dr. William Lukash, his physician
who had been running with him, decided to take the dangerously exhausted
runner by car to Aspen Lodge. There, with the aid of intravenously administered fluids, Carter recovered within an hour and returned to the race in
time for the awards ceremony. Some cynics compared his performance in the
race to his presidency, but they ignored the fact that he recovered quickly and
planned to continue his running.[20]

After leaving Camp David on September 17, Carter was pleased to learn
that Fidel Castro had freed the last four US citizens being held on political
charges in Cuban jails. Castro, for his own reasons as well as because of pressure from Washington, released the prisoners in response to Carter's having
released four radical Puerto Rican nationalists eleven days earlier. Carter still

hoped to restore friendly relations with Cuba, but for the moment, Brzezinski hailed the event as "another significant human rights accomplishment" for the Carter administration.[21]

Carter also helped thousands of Americans on the Gulf Coast whose homes were destroyed on September 12 by Hurricane Frederic. The death rate was low, but 500,000 people had been evacuated. To deal with such disasters, Carter had created the Federal Emergency Management Agency (FEMA). He brought thirty diverse agencies together into one, appointed a competent administrator, made it directly responsible to the president, and supported it with ample funding. Responding to Hurricane Frederic, it functioned exactly as Carter hoped.[22]

A more serious storm hovered over the Russian troops that had been stationed in Cuba since the 1962 missile crisis. In a bizarre episode, Chairman of the Foreign Relations Committee Frank Church of Idaho, who was fighting to save his Senate seat and to prove that he was not soft on communism, announced on August 30 that there was a Soviet combat brigade in Cuba.[23] Church called for SALT II to be scrapped unless the brigade was promptly removed. In fact, that brigade had been there since the Cuban missile crisis of 1962 and consisted of two to three thousand military advisors, not combat troops. The failure of US intelligence agencies to produce the truth quickly and convey it to the president without political bias created a headache for Carter that should have never occurred.[24]

Carter discussed with his staff the damaging publicity about the Soviet brigade, which he described as "one of the most complicated non-substantive issues we've ever addressed."[25] He asked Clark Clifford to organize a Citizen's Advisory Committee on Cuba, consisting of most of the same "Wise Men" who had advised President Lyndon Johnson about the Vietnam War in 1968. Two former national security advisers—McGeorge Bundy and Brent Scowroft—joined former CIA director John McClone, Ambassador Sol Linowitz, former Republican Deputy of Defense David Packard, and John J. McCloy, who had advised Franklin Roosevelt during World War II and every president since then. After a full day grilling CIA operatives at their headquarters, the group learned that President John F. Kennedy had made an agreement with the Russians to leave the noncombat troops there. During the sixteen years since then, the State Department had lost track of them, and Clifford's committee concluded that Carter's intelligence agencies had blundered. He advised Carter to tell the truth quickly and simply.[26]

But Carter did not want to admit that Brzezinski and his intelligence agencies had blundered. Speaking from the Oval Office on October 1, 1979, he addressed the nation on the Soviet Troops in Cuba and SALT II.[27] His long, cumbersome, confusing speech was anything but the simple statement of the truth that Clifford had recommended. Placing the discovery in historical context from the 1962 missile crisis through the contemporary Soviet-approved presence of Cuban troops in Ethiopia, he calmly explained that the troops were "not a threat to our country or a violation of any Soviet commitment." He did not admit the serious failure of the US intelligence agencies that had caused the crisis, choosing instead to emphasize that the United States and the Soviet Union were on "the threshold of a great advance in the control of nuclear weapons." As agreed in 1963, the US would keep troops and a base at Guantanamo, which he attempted to link to the country's need to verify SALT II, which the Senate had not yet ratified. The Senate's rejection of the treaty, he added, would seriously compromise the peace and security of the United States.[28]

Carter recorded in his diary that he had successfully defused the brigade issue and placed the focus on SALT II. He thought that both the domestic and international reaction to his speech was good, "except in Israel," where his continuing demand for a just settlement of the Palestinian problem remained unpopular.[29] Clark Clifford disagreed. Carter's speech was "almost unintelligible," he wrote, and he had negated his insistence that the brigade was no threat by promising that he would intensify US surveillance of it. Furthermore, Clifford believed the speech ruined Carter's chance to get a quick Senate ratification of SALT II, which meant that subsequent Russian actions would prevent the Senate from ever ratifying it.[30]

Even as he pushed for ratification of SALT II, Carter knew the Russians were not to be trusted. On September 17, Brzezinski had received a secret memorandum from an NSC analyst revealing that the United States did not know what the Russians were up to in Afghanistan. In response, Brzezinski asked Director of Central Intelligence Stansfield Turner to appraise the scale of Soviet military involvement there in order to determine if a major Soviet intervention might be in progress.[31] If the Russians invaded Afghanistan, he wrote, the United States would prevent them from achieving a psychological victory, change the Communist government in Afghanistan, create a "self-sustaining security system in southwest Asia," and provide limited arms sales to Iran, India, and Pakistan.[32]

As any role the United States might play in Afghanistan remained un-known, Carter enjoyed two important legislative victories. On September 27, he had signed the Panama Canal Act of 1979 implementing the 1977 Canal treaties, and on that same day, Congress passed his bill establishing an independent Department of Education. Carter sent Tip O'Neill a thank you note, telling the Speaker how much he appreciated his courageous and difficult speech that had made the legislation possible.[33] By the end of the month Carter asked Shirley Hufstedler, a distinguished judge on the US Court of Appeals Ninth District in California, who had served the cause of education well since the Johnson presidency, to head the new department.[34]

On October 1, 1979, while Jimmy prepared his Russian brigade speech, Rosalynn made a quick roundtrip to Boston with Speaker O'Neill to welcome Pope John Paul II to the United States. Standing in the rain at the Boston airport, she said: "Your holiness, . . . America welcomes you" with love and appreciation for "your compassion for the most vulnerable among us" and "your concern for the enduring values of human life." She thanked John Paul II for his "vision that unites mankind—our Creator's vision of a world of justice and freedom—a world of peace."[35]

When Pope John Paul II visited the White House on October 6, he put his arms around Amy, kissed her, and recalled her visit to him, with her mother, at the Vatican on the occasion of his investiture the previous spring. Standing with the Carters and the Mondales at the North Portico, he addressed a crowd of more than 3,000 that included members of the cabinet, Congress, the Supreme Court, their families and friends, and citizens who had gathered in Lafayette Square across the street. He agreed with Carter that support for international covenants and human rights should be the cornerstones for a nation's policies. Pausing at the top of the stairs leading into the White House, the Pope momentarily stood hand in lifted hand with the president as both smiled broadly.[36]

Inside, the Pope asked to meet alone with the president with no notetaker. Despite the language barrier, the two men talked for an hour in the Oval Office. Admitting that he wrestled with the conflict between attempting to be a humble Christian while being surrounded by the trappings of the presidency, Carter asked the Pope how he dealt with that kind of internal conflict. The Pope replied frankly that he had to spend hours daily praying for humility. More broadly, they discussed the status of Christianity in China, Eastern Europe, and the Americas. When Carter told him about his attempt to convert First Secretary Gierek in Poland in December 1977, the Pope, who was familiar with the Polish ruler of his native country, said that he doubted Gierek's nonbelief but thought his "faith in communism and atheism may be stronger."

Knowing the Pope's commitment to peace, Carter asked the pontiff to visit Jerusalem. Taken aback by such an unexpected request, John Paul questioned why his going there would facilitate peace in the Middle East. Carter, confessing to his loneliness as one of the few world leaders working actively for peace among all religious groups, replied that he needed the Pope's help. A visit from the Pope, he argued, would reassure Christians and Arabs that Jerusalem was not exclusively a Jewish holy site. When the Pope protested that such a visit might cause him embarrassment, Carter determinedly responded that "it would not be a catastrophe for the Pope to be embarrassed if acting in a good cause." Carter persisted, asking the Pope to mention Israel in his speeches. John Paul smiled and promised to mention it "once," but clearly Carter had failed to enlist the Pope's help in bringing peace to the Middle East.[37]

Their discussion reverted to safer topics. Poor people, they agreed, distrusted rich people. The Pope expressed amazement at the reception he had received in the United States, especially by non-Catholics. Jimmy agreed with the Catholic church's position on the right to life, but, as president, it was his responsibility to enforce the law that permitted abortions.[38]

From the privacy of the Oval Office, the Pope and the president moved out to the South Lawn, where more than 6,000 people had assembled. Quoting the Pope, Carter told the attentive audience that all people were masters of their own destiny, and he lauded His Holiness as an extraordinary man of peace, humility, and love. Someone shouted for the Pope to bless the crowd. John Paul turned to Carter to ask if it was okay; Carter told him to go ahead and bless them, an action he normally would not have taken as president. Leontyne Price sang the Lord's Prayer and "America the Beautiful" before the crowd dispersed.[39] After the Pope's visit to the White House, large numbers of Southern Baptists showered the president with hate mail for entertaining the Catholic pontiff.

During the five days before the Pope made his way from Boston to Washington, the Carters had entertained country music stars Dolly Parton, Johnny Cash, Tom T. Hall, Ronnie Millsap, and others at lunch before attending their gala evening concert at Ford's Theatre. When Jimmy hugged buxom Dolly Parton, as Rosalynn smiled at his elbow, she told him to "get a good one now." He joked about forming a country group called "The Carter

Family," or "Just Plain Folk."[40] At Ford's Theatre, Carter remarked, before the show began, that country music encompassed all kinds of experiences with sad songs about wasted lives and the "dirty dog that took advantage of you" and happy songs about "love that lasts for a lifetime and sometimes, I admit, love that lasts just for one good time."[41]

The concert hardly took Carter's mind off politics. During the remainder of 1979 he made campaign speeches and supported Democratic candidates. He and Rosalynn kept a wary eye on Kennedy and were encouraged by the straw polls, call-in radio programs, and Senator Joe Biden's poll of fourteen Democratic Senators, all of which indicated that there was little support for a Kennedy candidacy. The Washington press, however, ignored such favorable reports, and Israeli and Jewish Americans continued to criticize the president.[42] Rosalynn defended her husband in a flattering address to the National Council of Jewish Women at a reception in the East Room of the White House on October 16.[43] Eizenstat urged Carter to be more generous in guaranteeing Israeli access to United States oil in the event of emergencies. He also took Carter to a seder where he could learn more about the Jewish faith.[44]

Ted Kennedy posed a greater threat than the discontented Jewish voters. When the John F. Kennedy Presidential Library was completed in Boston, Carter dedicated it on October 20. Bubbling with excitement, he and Rosalynn arrived at the magnificent edifice perched on the edge of Boston's Dorchester Bay. The last of the dignitaries to approach the outdoor stage, Carter bounded up steps and kissed Ted's wife Joan, Lady Bird Johnson, and Jackie Kennedy Onassis. Jackie turned her face away from Carter and made a spitting motion, which dismissed as being "because of the women's liberation movement or something like that."[45]

During the five days before the event, Carter had carefully written and rehearsed his speech. "In America," Carter said, "the records of a great political leader will not be threatened by succeeding political regimes which might fear them, because we are a nation committed not only to freedom but also to the pursuit of truth." He was proud of the renewal of JFK's global commitment to social, political, and economic justice "and that America once again holds out her hand to the poor, the silenced, and the oppressed of every country in the world." His love and respect for Jack Kennedy had motivated him for decades, Carter declared, and on the day Kennedy was assassinated he "wept openly . . . for the first time since the day my father died."[46]

Carter endeavored to keep the day cordial and respectful. His speech was gracious, humorous, and a tribute to John F. Kennedy.[47] Nevertheless, Carter could not resist including a humorous reference to his political rival Ted Kennedy. Referring to a 1962 press conference given by President Kennedy, Carter reminded the audience of a question that John had been asked: "Mr. President, your brother Ted said recently on television that after seeing the cares of the office on you, he wasn't sure he would ever be interested in being President . . . . I wonder if you could tell us whether . . . whether you can recommend this job to others?" Jack answered, "No. I do not recommend it to others—at least for a while." As the audience laughed, Carter added with a sly grin: "As you can well see, President Kennedy's wit—and also his wisdom—is certainly as relevant today as it was then." The crowd laughed even louder and applauded.

Seriously, Carter praised John F. Kennedy's life and legacy, proclaiming that in the late 1970s Americans still needed "unselfish dedication to the common good."[48] Referring to contemporary social and political challenges, Carter continued: "we face . . . forces of regionalism, forces of ethnicity, of narrow economic interests, [and] of single-issue politics" that test "the resiliency of American pluralism and of our ability to govern. But we can and we will prevail."[49] Pamela Harriman, wife of Averell Harriman and long-time friend of the Kennedys, wrote Carter that his speech was great, "Your wit and eloquence was [sic] very inspiring . . . . It was brilliant."[50]

Ted Kennedy maintained his dignity during the ceremony. Following Carter's speech, he said: "We thank President and Mrs. Carter for being with us today, and for the support and assistance of the administration over the past three years in helping to complete the library and make it part of the fine system of Presidential libraries."[51] Despite the family's efforts to keep the ceremony nonpolitical, however, Joe Kennedy II, age 27, looked Carter in the eye on the stage and accused him of policies that injured the poor. Ted cradled his head in his hands, blushed, and subtly rebuked his nephew, while the Kennedy women sat stony faced.[52]

The battle between Ted Kennedy and the incumbent Carter, both Democrats, both with similar attitudes toward social justice, captured the headlines for most of October. Rosalynn told one interviewer that she and her husband prepared carefully for every race and ran to win. She did not compare herself to Kennedy's troubled wife Joan, and despite her earlier pledge, she no longer denied that the infamous Chappaquiddick incident would be mentioned. The Kennedys would not be "a mountain," she thought, for she was confident that people would easily choose Jimmy over "the alternative."[53]

Assorted country music stars and famed African-American educator Benjamin E. Mayes all supported Rosalynn and Ham Jordan's efforts to reelect Carter. "There are no philosophical differences between me and the Senator," Carter said in a note to Mayes on October 25. "He's just an impatiently ambitious man," Carter wrote, but, with the help of his African-American friends, he expected they would "win together."[54]

Besides campaigning, the Carters filled their October days with the typical business of the presidency. Traveling together or independently, they stumped around the country raising money for Democrats and explaining their accomplishments and worthiness for reelection. They attended a World Series game between the Baltimore Orioles and Pittsburgh Pirates, who won 4–1, in Baltimore. Whether at White House meetings or on the road, they argued the need for the ERA to guarantee women's equality. Carter talked with German Chancellor Helmut Schmidt and Egyptian president Anwar Sadat, both of whose help he needed to support SALT II and continued peace efforts in the Middle East. Although Schmidt and Carter personally disliked each other, they both wanted peace in the Middle East and a strong NATO alliance.

Carter's daily exercise and frequent weekends at Camp David ultimately did not prove restorative, because the gathering storm cloud over the whereabouts of the shah and the crisis in Iran weighed heavily upon him.[55] The itinerant shah was then living in Mexico after having failed to find suitable asylum in Egypt or Morocco. The Mexican government was willing to let him stay, but since his doctors had diagnosed him as seriously ill with cancer, he did not think he could get the care he needed there. In September, a Columbia University Medical School professor examined the shah in Mexico and reported that he needed to be brought to Cornell University Medical Center in New York City for tests and diagnosis. When Vance contacted the US embassy in Tehran, the staff all recommended against admitting the shah to the United States, apprehensive that such an action would prompt the Iranians to seize the embassy. Carter had reduced the staff there from more than 1,100 when the revolution began to less than seventy-five, and he had ordered that the security of the compound be reinforced.[56]

Feeling an urgency to change US leadership in Iran, Carter had become disillusioned with Ambassador William Sullivan, an aging diplomat who he had chosen because of his record of defying dictators, although he did not want the appointment and knew nothing about Iran. Sullivan had insulted Carter by accusing him of having made a gross error by not sending an emissary to Paris to consult with Khomeini before he came to power. Infuriated by the ambassador's criticism, Carter forced his resignation in April. Carter then named the level-headed and loyal Bruce Laingen as chargé d'affaires. Laingen understood Iranian culture and had the potential to help the United States work with the post-Pahlavi rulers.[57]

He and Carter had no easy task, because Ayatollah Khomeini demanded that the shah be returned to Iran for trial and that the revolutionary government confiscate his wealth. The shah and his family had about $6 billion on deposit at various branches of the Chase Manhattan Bank around the world. Carter did not want the shah to be repatriated, but he did not want him in the United States either. David Rockefeller, Henry Kissinger, and Brzezinski had all pressured Carter to grant permanent asylum to the shah since his flight from Iran in January. Carter strongly disagreed with their advice, because he thought it would ruin any chance the United States had to build a relationship with the new Iranian regime. When Kissinger threatened in a telephone conversation that he would not support ratification of SALT II unless the shah was admitted to the United States, Carter reportedly hung up in anger and shouted: "Fuck the Shah! I'm not going to welcome him here when he has other places to go where he'll be safe."[58]

The Iranian nightmare began on the evening of October 20, 1979, after Carter had returned home from dedicating the Kennedy library and gone to Camp David for an extended weekend, where he received an urgent message from Deputy Secretary of State Warren Christopher explaining that the shah could not get the care he needed in Mexico. Although Hamilton Jordan later learned that the shah could have received the necessary treatment in Mexico from French doctors, that information was either deliberately or inadvertently withheld. Brzezinski confirmed the shah's fatal illness for Carter, and Cy Vance, who had allegedly received a call from Rockefeller, reversed his position and said the shah should be allowed to come to New York City for humanitarian reasons.

In addition to humanitarian concerns, Carter was influenced by his long association with David Rockefeller. Before making his final decision, he called Rockefeller, in whose bank the shah had much of his fortune, and Henry Kissinger, Nixon's former secretary of state who believed that the United States should not turn away from a long-time ally. Both repeated their long-standing argument that the shah should be permitted access to the country.

Carter yielded to the pressure. Against his own judgment, he called Brzezinski at the White House and instructed him to grant the shah permission to go to New York for medical treatment on condition that he would not make any political statements while in the United States. Having thus cast the die, Carter asked a small group of his advisers who were with him and Rosalynn at Camp David, including Vice President Mondale, if anyone had the answer to what they would do if their diplomats in Iran were taken hostage. Since no one answered, he said, "I gather not. On that day we will all sit here with long, drawn, white faces and realize we've been had."[59]

Brzezinski promptly informed the US embassy in Tehran of the president's decision. The Iranian foreign minister promised that his government would try to protect the embassy, set in a huge compound, but he feared it might be impossible to control a violent crowd. Bruce Laingen knew that the Iranians would not believe that the shah had gone to the United States for humanitarian reasons; they would assume his visit was for the purpose of being restored to the Peacock throne with the aid of the CIA. Barry Rosen, the embassy's press attaché, could not believe what he was hearing, and he wondered if students would start coming over the wall to shoot him and his colleagues.[60]

When the shah arrived in New York City on October 22, he checked into the renowned Sloan Kettering cancer hospital under the name of David Newsom, a top assistant to Brzezinski. The US embassy in Tehran telegraphed the secretary of state that Abolhassan Bani-Sadr, Iran's finance minister, was not fooled by the pseudonym and had expressed deep bitterness toward the United States for helping the shah. "This man is a criminal," Bani-Sadr said. "He should be extradited." Cy Vance reassured the irate Iranians that the shah would make no political comments and would leave the country as soon as his health improved. The Iranian revolutionaries were not convinced. Bruce Laingen reported that the Iranians thought the shah could have gotten treatment in Mexico or anywhere else in the world, and any hope that Carter had of finding a working relationship with the new regime in Iran vanished.[61]

The same day the shah arrived in New York City, Carter had to deal with a shocking intelligence report that either Israel or South Africa may have tested a nuclear weapon in the South Atlantic Ocean the previous month. Although neither country ever admitted to conducting such a test, both Russian and US intelligence discovered that South Africa had an underground nuclear testing program. There were also indications that the South Africans and the Israelis were cooperating in secret efforts to develop nuclear weapons. The likelihood of a de facto alliance between Israel and South Africa involving nuclear weapons revealed both countries' disdain for the United States.[62]

Despite Iran's increasing hostility toward the United States, Carter was in a relaxed mood on the first day of November when he gave newscaster Howard K. Smith an interview in the Oval Office. His upbeat analysis of the state of the nation contradicted his "crisis of confidence" speech. He quoted Truman, who had said that if the president were controlled by public opinion polls, then he was unworthy of the job. "We are the strongest nation on Earth," Carter asserted, "militarily, economically, politically, and I hope morally and ethically." When asked if there was anyone on his staff who was unafraid to contradict him, he replied: "Rosalynn." He praised her ability to be "out among the people," sensitive to their needs, and a strong voice in their defense. Carter predicted a bright future for the country. "We have never been faced with a challenge that we could not meet."[63]

To help meet one of those challenges, Carter had sent Brzezinski to Algeria to represent him on October 31 at the twenty-fifth anniversary of the Algerian Revolution. Zbig, whom Carter thought was "very, very shrewd," ingratiated himself with his hosts when he asked to see the secluded place where the Algerian revolution had been planned. Brzezinski was charged with the responsibility to tell the Algerians that, although Carter had decided two weeks earlier to provide arms to Algeria's neighbor Morocco, he favored a political solution to the territorial dispute between the two nations over Western Sahara. The primary purpose of Brzezinski's visit, however, was to inform the Algerians that the United States was eager to improve economic and political relations with that country as well as encourage its role in promoting nonaligned nations. "Brzezinski," the New York Times reported, "said his presence was a symbol of President Carter's acceptance of the [nonaligned] movement." Algeria, he said, "was truly independent . . . [and] not a tool of others."[64]

In Algiers, Brzezinski mingled with Raul Castro of Cuba, Muammar Gaddafi of Libya, and Yasser Arafat of the PLO. After shaking hands with Arafat, Brzezinski accepted an invitation to meet both Prime Minister Mehdi Bazargan and Foreign Minister Ebrahim Yazdi of Iran. Both intellectuals, they were not liked by the radical followers of Khomeini, but they warned Zbig that the United States should not grant asylum to the shah. When a photograph of Brzezinski shaking hands with Bazargan appeared on the front pages of Iranian newspapers, the revolutionaries there interpreted it to mean that their civilian government was too friendly with the United States. As Zbig returned home optimistic that relations with Iran would improve, exactly the opposite was happening in Tehran.[65]

On November 2, Ayatollah Khomeini addressed a letter to "Dear Students, pupils and theological students." He asked them "to expand with all their might their attacks against the United States and Israel, so they may force the United States to return the deposed and criminal shah." The letter went unnoticed in the United States.[66]

TWENTY SIX

In the Name of God, Iran!

"The trouble with you Americans is that you are stupid," Iranian theologian and senior Shi'a cleric Ayatollah Mahmud Taleqani wrote in January 1979." You do not understand Shi'a Islam and the way we Iranian Muslims choose our leaders. . . . The books that are published in the West about Islam are mostly about Sunnis and most are blasphemous."[1]

Ten months later, Taleqani's words rang true. Early on Sunday morning November 4, when Jimmy and Rosalynn were at Camp David preparing to attend a worship service, Brzezinski called with disturbing news. Iranian students, Shi'a radicals, had stormed the US embassy in Tehran and captured the Marine guards and the diplomats who were taken by surprise and unable to escape. The Muslim students, devotees of the Ayatollah Khomeini, believed that the CIA, using the embassy as its headquarters, planned to take control of Iran.[2]

Although Carter had feared that such an action might occur, he was not prepared for dealing with a rogue country whose government defied traditional rules of diplomatic courtesy. He expected the Iranian government to take over control of the hostages and release them to resume their work or return to their home country. The Iranian Prime Minister Mehdi Bazargan and Foreign Minister Ebrahim Yazdi had assured Carter that the host country would protect the embassy, but they had underestimated the power of Khomeini. Carter kept his Sunday schedule of attending church and talking with various people involved in his reelection campaign, but he spent more time with Rosalynn and relaxed watching the movie *Sahara* before retiring.[3]

The next day, Brzezinski informed Carter that he had called his Special Coordinating Committee to meet in the Situation Room at the White House. They learned that about four hundred angry students had entered the bottom floor of the main embassy building, but all personnel had moved to the top floor. Eleven people who took refuge in the secure communications vault room established a direct line to the State Department and reported that three Marines and two civilians had been taken hostage without violence. Bruce Laingen, Chargé d'Affaires of the embassy, immediately assumed leadership. Using an open telephone line, he briefed Brzezinski and Gary Sick, the National Security Adviser on Iran. Laingen also asked Foreign Minister Ebrahim Yazdi to tell Khomeini to order the intruders "to cut it out."[4]

Instead, the intruders cut the contact line and forcibly rounded up the unprotected embassy personnel who had been frantically destroying classified information. The jubilant conquerors blindfolded the Americans, tied their hands, and paraded them in the courtyard. The scene horrified US viewers and dramatized the need for Washington to act quickly. The vault room, however, with its frightened occupants, remained secure.[5]

Coincidentally, that same Sunday morning, at Fort Bragg, North Carolina, the United States was staging an inaugural ceremony for Delta Force, a highly trained military organization that could respond swiftly to terrorist attacks. Early in 1978, Colonel Charles Beckwith, formerly of the US Army Special Forces, had begun training a special military force that could be used to rescue hostages. Delta Force had been kept so quiet by the army that Carter and Brzezinski knew very little about it before November 4. Anthony Quainton, who had recently become director of the State Department's Office on Combatting Terrorism, was observing the inauguration of Delta Force when he heard the news of the attack on the embassy in Tehran. Upon his return to Washington, Quainton set up a crisis center in the State Department, although Brzezinski virtually ignored it in favor of working with his Special Coordinating Committee.[6]

Early Monday morning, Jimmy and Rosalynn returned to the White House; within five minutes of landing, Carter was in the Oval Office meeting with Brzezinski and Ham Jordan. Most of their information came from the State Department, which still had telephone contact with parts of the embassy that the students had not yet reached, or from sites nearby. Carter learned that the mob had taken sixty-six US citizens hostage. From the US Cultural Center building, Kathryn Koob made a marathon telephone call to the State Department that lasted more than one day before being taken hostage herself. The Iranians later presented her with a huge bill, which she declined to pay.[7]

Angered because, as he wrote in his diary, "The students are still holding our people with the public approval of the idiot Khomeini," Carter issued an Executive Order immediately freezing Iranian assets in any bank anywhere in the world where the United States had jurisdiction. It effectively prohibited the revolutionary government from accessing any funds owned by any person or agency of the Iranian government.[8]

While trusting the State Department to gather news from Iran, Carter kept up his busy schedule. He discussed synthetic fuels legislation, signed the Emergency Energy Conservation Act of 1979, talked to numerous elected officials ranging from mayors to senators about the upcoming election, and met with Black leaders from Alabama who came to talk about the election. But his most important meeting was with senior staff members, the vice president, Rosalynn, and his press secretary. Responding to desperate conditions in refugee camps, Rosalynn planned to go to Thailand, visit the refugee camps, publicize them, and bring pressure on the United States and the UN to provide help. Since most of the information about Iran, he told the group, came from the State Department, he would let Secretary Vance handle statements about Iran. During the following days, he often spoke with Vance before and for longer than he consulted Brzezinski.[9]

Inside the embassy building in Tehran, the Marine guards, before they were captured, had secured the consulate and the chancery areas behind locked steel doors, but some staff members were in places where they could not be protected. The chanting students, one of them reported, looked like "scruffy kids" with guns, bicycle chains, and sticks. Incredulous, confused, and frightened, some of the first Americans taken could not believe what was happening to them.[10] Carter ordered an aircraft carrier to be sent to the Arabian Sea as a warning to the protesting Iranians.[11]

While chaos reigned in Tehran, Brzezinski's Special Coordinating Committee advised the president. The committee members included Deputy Secretary of State Warren Christopher, Central Intelligence Director Stansfield Turner, Secretary of Defense Harold Brown, Chief of Naval Operations Admiral Thomas B. Hayward, and Gary Sick. Fearing that the ailing shah's private guards might not be able to protect him in the event of an attack, the committee asked for help from the New York City Police and urged Pahlavi to make no incendiary political speeches. The empress slipped out of her secure room next to her husband's in the hospital and went to the East Side apartment of the shah's sister, where her children waited.[12]

The shah sent Carter a message on November 8 via "the Rockefeller group" who had supported his desire and need to come to the United States, that he felt terrible about the taking of the US hostages. He promised to leave the country as soon as his doctors said it was medically safe. When his doctors told the State Department that the shah would need to stay in the New York hospital for three or four weeks, Carter moaned that by then all the hostages could be dead.[13]

Beginning about seven o'clock in the morning on Tuesday, November 6, Carter telephoned numerous people for advice. First, he talked with Cyrus Vance, then Brzezinski, Mondale, and Secretary of Defense Harold Brown. He explored every possible avenue, including preparation for military action, to rescue the diplomats. Later that morning he met with Gary Sick, Charlie Kirbo, and Bob Strauss. He talked to Rosalynn briefly but often, and he welcomed a call from Sadat who gave advice about dealing with Muslim radicals.[14] He elevated Anthony Quainton, Director of the Office of Combatting Terrorism in the State Department, to a more important advisory position.[15]

One of the more urgent telephone calls Carter made that morning was to Canadian prime minister Joe Clark to discuss the status of six US diplomats who were hidden in the Canadian embassy in Tehran, having slipped away from the US embassy. The Canadian ambassador Ken Taylor had notified Prime Minister Joe Clark, and Clark informed Carter. Fearful that they might be discovered by the Iranians, Taylor, Clark, Carter, and the CIA initiated a secret plan to get them out of the country before the Iranians could learn about their whereabouts.[16]

In the afternoon, Carter attended the second meeting of the Special Coordinating Committee in the Situation Room to meet with the most important military and diplomatic members of the administration: Brzezinski, Vance, Brown, Chairman of the Joint Chiefs of Staff General David C. Jones, Turner, and Hamilton Jordan. As Carter listened, they discussed ways to retaliate if the hostages were hurt. Economic pressure, cessation of military supplies, air strikes to destroy Iranian military resources, support for the Kurdish separatists in western Iran, and kidnapping a high Iranian official to hold as a counter hostage were among the more serious options the committee considered. There were also some preposterous ideas ranging from delivering the shah for trial to dropping an atomic bomb on Tehran, the latter of which Rosalynn favored. Carter listened to their suggestions, but he was determined to avoid spilling blood or jeopardizing the lives of the hostages.[17]

Carter returned to the Oval Office to initiate a plan to communicate with Khomeini. When Prime Minister Bazargan and Foreign Secretary Yazdi realized that Khomeini would not stop the students, they resigned, leaving Khomeini and the Council of the Islamic Revolution to dominate Iran. Carter called upon the UN Security Council to demand that the militants free the hostages "without delay." Carter hoped to negotiate with the "idiot Khomeini," as he called him, by sending a personal envoy to Iran. William G. Miller, staff director of the Senate Select Committee on Intelligence, and former Attorney General Ramsey Clark agreed to go. They were to travel to Ankara, Turkey, and, from there, contact the Revolutionary Council in Iran and ask permission to enter the country. Carter also asked Algerians, Syrians, Turks, Pakistanis, Libyans, the PLO, the UN Security Council, and the International Court of Justice for help to deal with "a crazy man," as Carter labelled him. Carter also hoped that the world of Islam would condemn Khomeini if he threatened to murder sixty innocent people.[18]

If Carter hoped for support from Israel, he would be disappointed. Despite its major vested interest in both Iran and the United States, Israel remained aloof. Once the radical students ransacked papers that had not been destroyed, they found and published a secret CIA report entitled "Israel: Foreign Intelligence and Security Services Survey." It revealed to the Arab world many of Israel's intelligence secrets, and it revealed to Carter's world that despite the triumphant Camp David Accords, relations between the United States and Israel would likely continue on a rocky path.[19]

Acting alone without support of allies, Carter returned to the NSC meeting for twenty minutes to inform them about Miller and Clark's mission. After he left, Charlie Kirbo joined him in the residence for a private conversation. Dinner that night was a private family affair with Rosalynn, Amy, Chip, Edna Langford, Ruth Carter Stapleton, and Kirbo. After dinner, Carter jogged on the White House grounds, then worked late into the night telephoning people around the country who played a role in the 1980 election.[20]

Carter arose early the next day not to deal with Iran, but to see Rosalynn off to Thailand. Accompanied by Surgeon General Julius Benjamin Richmond and Mrs. Jean Young, chair of the US National Commission of the International Year of the Child, Rosalynn planned to visit the refugee camps in Kampuchea, where half of the population had died, promise that help would come from the United States and the UN, and recruit international help. The civil war in democratic Kampuchea, formerly Cambodia, had produced thousands of refugees, many of them children, who poured across the Thai border to escape the ruling Khmer Rouge's genocide. By going to Thailand, Rosalynn hoped to call the world's attention to the thousands of desperate and dying people who needed help.[21]

Before her departure from Andrews Air Force Base, Rosalynn said that the United States had already pledged $69 million to assist international relief, but it was not enough, and she vowed to approach private agencies for help. "I pray that we can quickly act to ease the burden of a people who have suffered too much," she concluded. Upon arrival in Bangkok the next day, where Thai prime minister Kriangsak Chomanan met her, she praised the government and people of Thailand for their humanitarian effort and expressed "the profound concern of all Americans for the suffering peoples in this part of the world."[22]

Carter returned to the White House to host a breakfast for Democratic Congressional leaders. He told the group that Rosalynn had just left for Thailand and that the Khmer Rouge genocide in Cambodia was worse than the Holocaust, but he was preoccupied with the situation in Iran. Despite multiple evacuations that had occurred before the fall of the embassy, there were still several thousand US citizens in Iran, many of them permanent residents married to Iranians. Other countries would help them escape, he thought. The PLO sent word from the UN that they would send a delegation to Iran to get the hostages released, and the Pope offered to help as long as he got no publicity for it. Carter urged the Congressional leadership to "be calm and say nothing to incite" the public. This was not a time for "verbal abuse," he warned. When questioned, he said there had been no agreement on admitting the shah to the country, nor did he know what would transpire next for the shah. He had not planned any military action, he said, but the Senate was considering a law that would expel Iranian students in the United States who were loyal to the revolutionary government in Iran.[23]

In Iran, the Ayatollah did not reciprocate Carter's hope for a quick diplomatic settlement, and on November 7, denied Miller and Clark entrance into the country. His Revolutionary Council had taken charge, and he believed that he had the support of the Iranian masses. He and the council were more interested in creating their ideal Islamic Republic than the mechanics of governing. The Ayatollah cared nothing about the traditional courtesy to foreign diplomats in his country; he wanted to prove that the president of the United States was a paper tiger who was too weak to impose his culture upon Iran.[24]

Carter was not weak. The day after Khomeini's rant, November 8, Carter approved the Coordinating Committee's plan to rescue the hostages. Simulating the climate and topographical conditions near Tehran, Delta Force began practicing in the Southwestern desert for a rescue operation that they would deploy in Iran if so ordered by Carter. Carter, however, believed such an operation had a high risk for failure and might result in too many deaths. He still hoped for a diplomatic settlement.[25]

Later that day, in addition to attending the formalities related to a state visit from Prime Minister Jack Lynch of Ireland and his wife, Carter met with key senators and advisors to talk about Iran. He was pleased to learn that Congressmen of both parties were almost unanimous in their demand that the administration stop Iranian student demonstrations, revoke their visas, freeze Iranians assets, and arrest any who did not obey the new law.[26]

On Friday, November 9, Carter resumed discussions about Iran. He met first with Brzezinski and later with Mondale, Vance, and Harold Brown. He reported that he was pursuing every diplomatic avenue possible and that even "radical Islamic nations like Libya and Iraq" condemned Iran's actions.[27]

That meeting was disrupted by a phone call from Rosalynn in Bangkok, who told Carter about the starvation, disease, and suffering she had witnessed as she walked through the recently opened Sa Kaeo refugee camp, forty miles from the Kampuchea border. One little girl, she said in a later interview, "was so weak that she couldn't control her limbs and if you held her then her arms would just hang down, and so I had to take those little arms and lay them across her chest." The girl died shortly after Rosalynn put her down. Accompanied by US Ambassador to Thailand Morton Abramowitz, she made her way among blue refugee tents with no sanitation facilities filled with moaning and dying people. New waves of refugees, she said, would make the situation even more intolerable. Before her scheduled time for departure, she planned to visit the refugee transit center near the US embassy in Bangkok.[28] After an audience with the king and queen of Thailand the next day, she said she would return home.[29]

Before Rosalynn arrived home, a horrifying event took place before daylight on November 10. Bill Odom, Brzezinski's military assistant, awakened him at three o'clock in the morning to tell him that the Soviet Union had launched 220 missiles that were headed toward the United States. One minute before he would have called Carter, Brzezinski received another call from Odom explaining that someone had mistakenly put exercise tapes into the computer system that would simulate an attack and that no such attack was underway. Carter learned about this the next day, but he and the State Department attempted to keep it top secret.[30] The episode leaked to the press anyway, and when two similar events occurred in May of the following year, Carter agreed with Secretary of Defense Harold Brown that the United States must continue to place its confidence in "the human element of our missile attack warning system."[31]

Carter had not anticipated a breakdown in the US missile warning system when he went on November 9 to the State Department, where Cy and Gay

Vance had welcomed about twenty family members of the Iranian hostages, including some children. He joined the Vances in trying to comfort those who suffered from intense anxiety, but they could do little more than reassure the families that the government was doing everything possible to protect and free their loved ones. In a statement that Carter released after that meeting, he said that he shared the "outrage," "frustration," and "deep anger" that many Americans had expressed, but he called upon all Americans "to exercise restraint, and to keep the safety of their countrymen uppermost in their minds and hearts."[32] The next day, November 10, Carter took hope from the report that Khomeini would see the Pope's representative and the news that Syrian and Swiss officials who had seen the hostages found them in good health.[33]

Late that night, Jimmy met Rosalynn at Andrews National Air Force Base. Despite her jet lag and emotional fatigue, Rosalynn poured out the details of what she had seen and her plans to help the refugees. The next day she prepared her report to the president, the people, and the UN. In order to expedite getting help to the desperate refugees, she recommended that the UN choose a single coordinator for relief, a suggestion UN Secretary General Kurt Waldheim quickly acted upon. Carter committed the US government to making a large contribution, and for the remainder of the year, despite the escalating Iranian crisis, Rosalynn became an avid and successful crusader to get help for the wretched people in the Thai refugee camps. International Voluntary Relief agencies, folk singer Joan Baez, and the Council on Foreign Relations all listened to her pleas. Carter granted UNICEF (the United Nations Children's Fund) an additional $2 million, which, combined with other monies, funded immediate assistance. The Peace Corps accelerated its support for UN programs, and Carter appealed to Americans of all faiths to give generously.[34] At the Norton Simon Museum in Pasadena, Rosalynn told the audience of mostly wealthy Hollywood actors that they were communicators whose help she needed to help raise money for Cambodian refugee relief.[35]

Carter needed her help too, because the hostage disaster coincided with Ted Kennedy's announcement on November 7 that he would campaign for the Democratic presidential nomination, challenging the incumbent president in his own party, a decision that was shrouded in ambiguity. On national television that day, he was unable to give an interviewer clear reasons for turning against Carter. Carter thought his tv appearance devastating to Kennedy, for the senator could not answer "a simple question about what he would do if elected or why he should be president." Kennedy apparently thought that polls rating him better than Carter, as well as what he perceived as Carter's inability to get things done, would be in his favor. But he erred in thinking that Carter was not getting things done, and he underestimated Rosalynn's skill as a campaigner.[36]

Taking advantage of the Iran trouble, Kennedy held a press conference to condemn Carter for allowing the shah into the country. He may not have factored in Miss Lillian's entering the fray against him. The day after Kennedy's announcement, she went to Florida, Iowa, Arizona, California, and Chicago, where she thrilled the crowds and collected votes for Jimmy. To help win Jewish votes away from Kennedy, Bob Strauss recommended Philip Klutznick for Secretary of Commerce. Klutznick, Strauss said, had made a fortune in Chicago real estate, was a liberal Democrat, and had "excellent ties to the Jewish community." Eizenstat endorsed Klutznick, and Carter sent his name to the Senate for confirmation.[37]

Responding to Kennedy's news conference, "I relish a fight," Rosalynn proclaimed, as she campaigned in New England and the South, raising money, praising her husband's accomplishments, and sometimes casting doubts upon Kennedy's character. "She's got guts," Governor Hugh Gallen of New Hampshire said, about the energetic First Lady.[38] Before the nation had become distracted by the hostage issue or her humanitarian trip to Thailand, Rosalynn had marched into the Sam Rayburn Office Building to counter whatever Senator Ted Kennedy might say to a group of senior citizens who had gathered there to lobby for better healthcare. She arrived first, and when the senator appeared, greeted him cordially. Asking Congress to support her husband's proposed hospital cost containment bill, she told them that she was "furious how cost containment . . . has been bogged down in Congress." The senator had been out foxed.[39]

News magazines put Rosalynn's picture on their covers, and some began to declare her the most influential First Lady in modern times, a politician superior to her husband, tough, and unforgiving. In private, Rosalynn made no pretense at being cordial toward the Massachusetts senator. She suggested to Jimmy that Mike Royko, a Chicago columnist, and his sons be treated to a ride on Air Force One from Chicago to Washington because he "dislikes K." Royko had written a week earlier that Kennedy was a dummy, royal born, who thought he deserved the presidency, whereas the country boy Jimmy Carter had made it to the White House on his own.[40] The Roykos got their ride.

On another occasion, when Kennedy visited the White House, she left him alone while temporarily tending to something else. In her absence, Amy's cat jumped into his lap. Rosalynn returned to find Kennedy, who was allergic to cats, sitting there looking like he had stuck a finger into an electrical socket. "And I thought that was appropriate," she devilishly remarked many years later.[41] Carter himself avoided any public disparagement of Kennedy, being initially content just to make his case for reelection. Rehearsing all that he had done, he thought his greatest accomplishment was keeping the nation at peace.[42]

As important as the reelection campaign was to Jimmy and Rosalynn, it was Iran that dominated their daily lives. Rosalynn bluntly told Carter to stop buying Iranian oil, but he had already begun to search for a substitute for it by purchasing more oil from Saudi Arabia. Through the State Department's back channels, on November 9, the US Ambassador to Lebanon, John Gunther Dean, secretly contacted Hasib Sabbagh, a wealthy Palestinian businessman who had influence with the Saudis. Two days later, Sabbagh, accompanied by two US citizens of Middle Eastern origin met with Crown Prince Fahd in Saudi Arabia. The details of the deal they cut with him remained secret, but on November 12 Carter announced that the United States would boycott Iranian oil. The Crown Prince called Yasser Arafat and asked him to use his influence with Khomeini to get the captive Americans released. Six days later, Khomeini released five women and eight African-American men, justifying this action with a statement that women had a special place in Islam and Blacks were an oppressed minority. Saudi Arabia increased its oil production in order to compensate for the US boycott of Iranian oil.[43]

To bring the cabinet up to date, Carter called an emergency meeting for the evening of Sunday, November 11. He told them that his first concern was for the hostages and that their families were being helpful. He reemphasized that his freeze on Iranian assets would prevent Khomeini's government from withdrawing funds it needed. In addition to freezing Iranian assets, he ordered the expulsion of undocumented Iranian students, halting the purchase of Iranian oil, and ending all exports and commerce with Iran.[44]

Early on Monday morning, Carter went to his office and began the routine that would characterize his presidency for months to come. The first person he met there was Brzezinski who presented him with the daily CIA brief and any other information he had that was pertinent to the security of the country. After speaking with Vance or any other person who might have information about Iran, he interspersed routine political, family, and state matters, with conversations and meetings about Iran.[45]

On November 13 Carter approved continued sanctions against Zimbabwe-Rhodesia, where a rebellion remained unsettled and all major US allies kept sanctions in place. Closer to home, he shamed Castro into releasing "thousands" of political prisoners, and he invited a few of them to visit the Oval Office.[46] One of them wrote him a grateful letter thanking Carter for the interests he and the United States had shown that had resulted in his release and reunion with his family.[47]

On November 14, realizing that Khomeini would remain intransigent, Carter increased the pressure. After issuing Executive Order 12170 blocking Iranian assets in all US banks and their subsidiaries worldwide, which legalized the action he had announced ten days earlier, he reported to Congress and the US people that he wished to protect any claims US citizens might have against Iran. The order did not affect accounts held by entities other than the government of Iran, implying that the shah's personal fortune remained untouched. Carter asked Vance to check on the status of the shah, who was in a New York hospital, but not to encourage him to leave the United States.[48]

Believing that the Pope's prayers helped, Carter wrote "His Holiness" a personal letter on November 14 thanking him. Signing himself "Yours in Christ," Carter praised John Paul II for giving comfort to the hostages and continuing to support the United States in its pursuit of "every peaceful means to free our people."[49]

Encouraged by the Pope's prayers, and hoping to boost the morale of the US people, Carter took a positive stand. In a speech to the AFL-CIO Convention on November 15, he warned that "No one should underestimate the resolve of the American people . . . [to] refuse to permit the use of terrorism" to enable the terrorists to achieve their demands. Americans had the "character" and the "courage" to face the "difficult test," "I know that we shall not fail." He gave similar speeches elsewhere, often including a pitch for his reelection.[50]

Despite the Pope's prayers and Carter's optimism, the situation in Iran deteriorated daily. When Khomeini threatened on November 17 to execute the hostages as spies if Carter did not return the shah, Carter increased US military presence in the Arabian Sea. He ordered the aircraft carrier *Kitty Hawk*, with five helicopters aboard, and five other Navy warships to join the aircraft carrier already there.[51] Carter hoped that his show of force would persuade the "crazy man" to release all of the hostages. In a secret communiqué,

Sadat told Carter that a US attack on Iran would be followed by one from Egypt.[52]

Unintimidated by Carter's threat of force, huge Iranian crowds marched in front of the US embassy where the students held the hostages. Chanting that America was the enemy, they waved posters with portraits of Khomeini, Carter, and the shah. Many of them, who were ready to become martyrs, wore "white burial shrouds."[53] They would release the hostages, they said, if Carter would return the shah for trial. They promised to give him a fair trial which Carter could attend. Supporting the demonstrators, Khomeini dubbed Carter the "Great Satan" who, "with bayonets bristling . . . is violating all human rights" by sheltering the shah, "a criminal" who "emasculated Iran." His struggle with the United States, the Ayatollah declared, was a contest "between Islam and atheism."[54]

Fired up by the demonstrations in Iran, Muslim terrorists went on rampages in Saudi Arabia and Pakistan. On November 20, armed Muslim zealots seized control of Mecca's Grand Mosque, the most sacred place in Islam, and for more than two weeks they held hundreds of pilgrims hostage while demanding the overthrow of the ruling Saudi family and the embargo of all oil supplies to the United States. The next day in Islamabad, Pakistan, crowds of Islamic terrorists attacked and burned the US embassy, killing two US employees—Chief Warrant Officer Bryan Ellis and US Marine Corporal Steven J. Crowley—and forcing three hundred more to leave the country. Carter, who did not know about the death of Ellis, issued a public statement expressing "heartfelt sympathy to Steven Crowley's family and to the U.S. Marine Corps," but did not hint at military retaliation.[55]

Most US diplomats remained in Pakistan; Pakistani president Zia apologized and offered to pay for the damage. Carter did not trust him but did not want to start a confrontation with a Muslim nation whose help he might need with the Iranian crisis. Jimmy and Rosalynn attended a funeral mass with Crowley's family on November 30 at Fort Myer, Virginia. Saudi security forces in Mecca regained control of the Grand Mosque in early December at the cost of many deaths, both zealots and innocent pilgrims. Khomeini blamed radical "Zionism" and US "imperialism," which provoked anti-US demonstrations across the globe from Turkey to the Philippines. The United States was forced to confront a new global enemy: Islamic terrorism.[56]

Locked in his prison cell in the Tehran embassy, Bruce Laingen knew nothing about what was happening in Washington, Saudi Arabia, or Pakistan. On November 22, he smuggled a telegram out of the occupied embassy to

Cyrus Vance, warning the Secretary of State that the "public atmosphere here is one of dangerous emotional frenzy." He believed that Khomeini might go ahead with trials of some hostages, but he thought trials would humiliate the Iranians more than the Americans. Maintaining his composure under stress, Laingen concluded, "We wish you and all of our colleagues in Washington a very blessed Thanksgiving Day." Laingen also smuggled out a few upbeat letters to his wife and sons, saying he was treated well, but was tired of wearing the same clothes, although their guards allowed them to wash underwear and socks. He was hopeful, he maintained, that the captivity would end soon.[57]

On Thanksgiving Day the thirteen hostages the Ayatollah had freed on November 19 and 20 arrived at Andrews Air Force Base. Cyrus Vance quietly welcomed them, as the Carters warned that their own celebration of the hostages' return might jeopardize those still in captivity.[58] Although in good health, all thirteen declared that they had been bound hand and foot, threatened with death, and denied exercise, visitors, and messages. One of the African Americans accused the administration of being racist for not having made a major public event of their release. Civil Rights leader Vernon Jordan, Chairman of the National Urban League, believed, however, that the freeing of Blacks and females was a cynical ploy to divide Americans. Hamilton Jordan stated flatly that the Iranians were badly mistaken to expect that there would be an uprising of African Americans and women in protest of Carter's Iranian policy.[59]

After informing Carter that UN Secretary General Kurt Waldheim was too weak to assist, Jordan offered to piece together secret contacts who could provide access to the Ayatollah. Carter was desperate enough to approve Ham's cloak and dagger approach.[60] Apparently, help could not come soon enough, because in Iran, both Foreign Minister Bani-Sadr and Director of the Iranian Radio and Television Service Sadeq Gotzbadeh repeated the Khomeini's anti-US rantings. Speaking on Iranian radio, Gotzbadeh promised that the trial of the US hostages "would begin 'soon' if the United States continued to 'play for time' in refusing to extradite the deposed Shah."[61]

Carter refused to meet the Iranian demands, vowing to preserve the integrity of the United States and save the lives of the hostages. On November 23, he pondered how he might punish Khomeini if he harmed any of the hostages. Brainstorming with Walter Mondale, Cyrus Vance, Harold Brown, David Jones, Stan Turner, Jody Powell, Ham Jordan, and Brzezinski, they discussed mining Iranian ports and urging allies to cease shipments to Iran. Carter told Vance to warn Khomeini that, if he put the Americans on trial, the United States would disrupt commerce with Iran and take "direct retaliatory action." Carter also sent his message to Japan, France, Germany, and the United Kingdom, which had maintained their relationships with Iran. He hoped that threatening to disrupt their commerce with the rogue country might encourage America's traditional allies to help the United States.[62]

Meanwhile, David Rockefeller continued to manage the shah's affairs, and both he and Kissinger repeatedly emphasized that the shah had been brought into the United States only for a humanitarian reason. Carter was particularly irked with Kissinger, whom he said had "made a personal crusade of getting the shah to the U.S.," but now was "trying to force" the administration "to ask the shah to leave." After consulting his advisors, Carter wrote in his diary, "We all agreed that Kissinger is irresponsible and must be dealt with in some way."[63] Publicly critical of Carter, Kissinger told a Republican governors' conference in Austin, Texas, on November 20 that "lack of national leadership has allowed the United States to become weak and encouraged the kind of crisis now faced in Iran."[64] Brzezinski, however, was not so critical of Kissinger and agreed with him that power was more important than human rights. Brzezinski spent so much time consulting with Kissinger, a fellow hawk, that Carter thought his National Security Advisor had become disloyal.[65]

Not only Kissinger, but teenage girls on the streets of Washington also expressed their disapproval of the president. An assistant to Brzezinski overheard the following conversation: "I wonder if Jimmy Carter can do anything to protect Americans overseas. I get awfully disgusted with him." "Before long they will be burning down all our embassies around the world." "Carter ought to do something about that, but I don't suppose he will." "I wish somebody would shoot him. Then we could get somebody better as President." "I wonder what will happen if they send our army into Iran. Russia is very close." "The Russians will probably march in too." "That would be a world war, wouldn't it?" "We would have to fight them. We can't let them push us back." The girls then agreed that they would "just have to make the best of it" before discussing their plans for the Thanksgiving weekend.[66]

Cyrus Vance, who would have been appalled by the teenagers' conversation, also increasingly disagreed with how Carter was handling the crisis. He opposed the idea of mining the harbors and imposing commerce restrictions on Iran. When, on November 27, Vance read a ticker tape headline, he interpreted it to mean that Carter had said he would "put our nation's honor above the hostages' release." He angrily visited Carter, and, as Carter recorded in his diary, "threatened to resign [once again]." Carter calmed the secretary of state by explaining that what he had really said was that "we would never apologize to Iran, never deliver the shah to them to be put on trial, and never pay reparations."[67]

As anxious as her husband to find a way to approach the Ayatollah and get the remaining hostages released, Rosalynn had suggested to him that Billy's connection with the Libyans might possibly help. Carter asked Brzezinski to call Billy to the White House to confer and ascertain if that was an option.[68] Billy and the Libyans were happy to try to help. He and a top Libyan diplomat met with Brzezinski first on November 27, then with the president, Rosalynn, and Kirbo. They promised to do anything possible to get the students to release the hostages, but they accomplished little more than softening the US relationship with Libya.[69]

Rosalynn had a better suggestion that she transmitted through an aide to Jimmy on November 28. She recommended that he consult with Catherine Bateson, the daughter of famed anthropologist Margaret Mead. Bateson, a professor at George Mason University, was an Islamic scholar and expert on Iran, where she had lived for seven years. She advised Carter to express sympathy to the world's Muslims, who themselves were sometimes victims of violence. Carter should remind Muslims that as demonstrated at Camp David the Muslims, Christians, and Jews shared a common belief in one God and all were committed to peace. Furthermore, Carter should reassure the Muslim world that he would not allow illegal acts in Iran to work "against our more fundamental kinship and our common concern for world peace."[70]

Brzezinski had no confidence in appeals for religious unity or backdoor attempts to negotiate with Khomeini and told Carter that only military pressure could end the crisis.[71] Khomeini's actions reinforced Brzezinski's view. The Ayatollah dismissed his Foreign Minister Bani-Sadr, on November 28, because he had recently argued that the hostages should not be held indefinitely. In order to escape being tried and executed, Bani-Sadr fled to Paris. Khomeini replaced him with Sadeq Gotzbadeh and announced that the hostages should be released only after the shah was returned to Iran. UN Secretary General Kurt Waldheim called an emergency session of the UN Security Council and appealed to both sides for restraint. Carter asked the International Court of Justice in the Hague to pressure Khomeini into releasing the hostages. In the meantime, his treatment in New York having ended, Mexico refused to allow the shah to return there. Wanting to keep the shah safe while searching for a home for him, Carter ordered him moved to Lackland Air Force Base near San Antonio, Texas.[72]

Coping with a chaotic, crumbling world, Carter, on December 4, officially announced that he was a candidate for reelection.[73] During the campaign, he would have to address the hostage crisis, the economy, the opposition within his own party, and the controversy surrounding his accomplishments. Since he had announced that he would remain secluded in the White House until the hostages were freed, he could not spend time on the campaign trail but would have to depend on surrogates.

Rosalynn rose to the occasion. She made numerous phone calls to politicians and political operatives in key states, kept good notes on the responses, and traveled across the country giving speeches, extolling her husband's accomplishments, and explaining why he had to remain in Washington.[74] Five days before Jimmy formally announced his candidacy, Rosalynn had begun to focus her efforts on the first tests, the Iowa caucuses on January 21 and the New Hampshire primary on February 25. Joan Mondale, Judy Carter, and Miss Lillian joined her, each working independently in order to reach as many voters as possible.[75]

Miss Lillian, outspoken as always, provided comic relief with deadly serious overtones. The first woman ever to speak at the men's club in Bow Lake Village, New Hampshire, she offered to put out a contract on the Ayatollah, pretended that she did not know a gay person from a hole in the ground, and confessed that her sex life had ended with the death of her husband. In that December meeting, she obliquely referred to the major scandal in Ted Kennedy's life: "Don't ask me about Chappaquiddick because I wasn't there."[76]

Despite the campaign's effort to win Jewish voters, many of them remained doubtful about supporting Carter. Despite three Jewish cabinet members—Klutznick, Brown, and Goldschmidt—and several key Jewish advisors—Strauss, Eizenstat, and Linowitz, among others—conservative Jewish communities opposed the president. They did not support Kennedy either, but it seemed ironic that they did not embrace the first president to engineer a peace treaty between Israel and an Arab neighbor, spend billions to back it up, and push for additional agreements. Yet, many Jewish Americans were skeptical of Carter's religion, repulsed by his sale of jets to Arab nations, disgusted with Billy's anti-Semitic remarks, and perceived Brzezinski as hostile toward Israel. Not even Carter's humane treatment of Iranian Jews changed their opinion; he signed Executive Order 12172 giving visitor visas that would only expire when the shah returned to Iran to some 50,000 Iranian Jews. Since they feared for their lives in Iran, many of them credited Carter with saving them, and most of them became US citizens.[77]

Despite the intricacies of a tough reelection campaign, and the pressure of an unprecedented hostage situation with a rogue government, Carter still had to manage the national security of the United States within the context of the Cold War. He knew from history and experience, and contemporary CIA reports, that the Soviets would take advantage of any turmoil to strengthen their position in the world and to antagonize the United States. The US crisis in Iran gave them an opportunity they were ready to seize.

TWENTY SEVEN

The Soviet Union Makes a Move

On December 4, the day that Carter announced his intention to run for reelection, the CIA informed him that the Soviet Union wanted to stabilize the relationship of the United States with Iran. The US threat to use force in Iran had prompted the Soviets to send clandestine broadcasts in the Persian language into Iran calling for the release of the hostages "on humanitarian and political grounds." Clearly "worried about the possibility of U.S. military action against Iran," the Soviets had made a vague offer to help Iran if the United States should attack, but in reality the Soviets did not want a US-Iran war. The Russians knew that the radical Muslims were hostile to Communism and would resist any effort the Soviets made to take over Iran.[1]

Carter did not believe the Soviets. Later the same day, the Soviet ambassador to the United States, Anatoly Dobrynin, issued a statement that the Soviet Union had communicated with the Iranian leadership, asking them to avoid further aggravation of the hostage situation. Disgusted, Carter commented in a note: "This is b.s." "No one knows if they're telling the truth here." Privately, Dobrynin told Carter that he hoped the United States and the Soviet Union could continue negotiations on nuclear arms control. Carter, who seriously wanted the Senate to ratify SALT II, wondered if the intelligence he received from the CIA and the lies he heard from Dobrynin should make him rethink the dangers of making any agreement with the Soviets. Not backing down from SALT II, however, he suggested that the United States might modify it by delaying military cuts until a future SALT III.[2]

The Soviets, who did not want the US quarrel with Iran to escalate into a war between the superpowers, had reason to be apprehensive about what Carter might do in Iran. Ready to consider military options, Carter held a two-hour NSC meeting beginning in the Cabinet Room immediately after his reelection announcement. He told the council members that he thought that US allies were too "timid," and he wanted to put pressure upon them for more help. Continuing to refuse Khomeini's demand for him to return the shah to Iran, Carter said he wanted to find the shah a home outside the

United States and notify the Ayatollah that the United States could blockade Iran, destroy its refineries, and take out its aircraft and airfields. With the support of Brzezinski, but against the advice of Vance, Carter decided to send AWAC (airborne warning and control system) radar planes to Egypt, where Sadat stood ready to help if asked, and to increase substantially US naval forces in the region. He planned to be ready to win a quick victory if he had to launch mining or military action against Iran.[3]

Carter made his decision about how to deal with Iran in part because of the Soviet presence in Afghanistan. After Muslim radicals had murdered US Ambassador to Afghanistan Adolph Dubs in February 1979, Brzezinski had warned the Soviet Union that the United States disapproved of its presence in Afghanistan. Brezhnev had ignored the warning, and Brzezinski had persuaded Carter to start a covert program of providing medical and non-military supplies, as well as communication devices, to the Mujahideen, the Islamic warriors who had rebelled against the repressive pro-Soviet regime in Kabul. By secretly providing Afghan resistance fighters with materials to help them to hold the Soviets at bay, Carter had opened a new chapter in the Cold War which he hoped would stop Soviet expansion into vulnerable countries. Brzezinski, however, had an agenda of his own, namely that secret US aid to Afghanistan might make the resistance there strong enough that the Soviets would invade Afghanistan, become bogged down there, and experience their Vietnam.[4]

On that same day, December 4, Congress, wishing to show solidarity with the president and support for the hostages and their families, passed a resolution praising Carter for his "calm strength" in the face of the crises in Iran and Afghanistan. One distraught citizen urged Carter to "appeal to Mother Teresa of Calcutta . . . to lead all the People in the world in a moment of Prayer, for the release of the American hostages in Iran."[5]

Carter prayed, but he also searched for practical, tough solutions. Meeting with American Muslims, he showed respect for their faith as well as seeking their aid in understanding the crisis in Iran. When dealing with some members of Congress, however, Carter could not understand why they debated and criticized interminably instead of taking action. Losing his temper at a buffet dinner for a select bipartisan group of Congressmen, he exploded: "I don't give a damn whether you like or do not like the Shah. I don't care whether you think he is a thief or not. I don't want to analyze whether SAVAK was better or worse than the American CIA. I don't care whether you think I was wise or not wise or every president since Eisenhower was wise or not wise in accepting the Shah as one of our allies. . . . The issue is the American hostages, 50 of them are being held by kidnappers, radical and irresponsible kidnappers, with the encouragement and support of the Iranian government, contrary to every element of propriety or morality or decency or international law as hostages, trying to blackmail this country."[6]

On December 7, Carter delivered the same message to members of the hostages' families and State Department employees. Omitting the profanity, he reassured the gathering in the State Department building's lobby that he would not take "any military action that would cause bloodshed or arouse the unstable captors" to injure the captives. He planned to be "very moderate, very cautious, guided and supported and advised by Secretary Vance." He and Vance had made a total commitment to getting the hostages home safely. He believed that the families of the hostages and all 220 million Americans joined him in thanking the State Department employees for working with Secretary Vance to ensure the safety of the hostages. "I pray every moment of my life," he added, that we "will be successful in getting our hostages home where they belong."[7]

Accused of "waffling" and unnecessarily using military threats, Carter defended himself by referring to the confusing and contradictory intelligence reports that came to him.[8] The CIA reported on December 6 that Moscow had escalated its anti-US propaganda alleging that the United States was at fault for causing "one of the most serious international conflicts of postwar times." The Soviets demanded that the shah be returned to Iran, and Senator Ted Kennedy and former Ambassador Andrew Young supported "Iranian demands for the Shah's extradition." Kennedy condemned Carter for admitting the shah to the country, and Andrew Young granted an interview to a national television journalist on December 9 in which he said that the United States had been wrong to support the shah who had used SAVAK to torture innocent people.[9]

Right or wrong, the shah languished at Lackland Air Force Base while Carter searched for a new home for him. Dressed in disguise, Hamilton Jordan went to Panama, negotiated with his friend General Omar Torrijos Herrera, and cleared the way for the shah and his family to flee to Panama. Carter telephoned the shah at Lackland early on the morning of December 15 to wish him and his wife well as they departed for Panama.[10]

Three days earlier, on December 12, Carter had greatly reduced diplomatic ties with Iran. The State Department, acting upon Carter's order, had expelled 183 of the 218 Iranian diplomats in the United States. It allowed a skeleton crew of fifteen in Washington and five each in consulates in San Francisco, Chicago, New York, and Houston to remain.[11] Carter requested legislation that would allow him to raise tariffs by as much as 50% on goods from countries, especially Japan, that continued to trade with Iran. Japanese companies stopped buying oil from Iran, and, following the US example, looked for alternate sources. In Tehran, Khomeini ranted against the intrusion of Western culture into Iran, urging Iranians to "look to their own history and traditions and to Islam for their salvation."[12]

Nothing changed in Iran. The International Court at the Hague ordered Iran to free the hostages, but Khomeini would not yield. Carter therefore asked the UN to impose more economic sanctions on Iran. The Iranians remained implacable. Khomeini allowed Christian clergymen to visit the hostages, but he declared that if the UN imposed sanctions, the hostages would be tried as spies. Frustrated by lack of progress, Carter vowed to remain in his "Rose Garden" seclusion until the hostages were released.[13]

Secret meetings in Austria and Israel had not been fruitful, but a glimmer of hope came from Algeria whose new government indicated it would like a closer relationship with the United States. Hopeful, Carter told "Cy, Zbig," in a short handwritten note, "some good ideas and opportunities here."[14] After Algeria, a large North African country, had gained independence from France in 1962, the United States had established good diplomatic relations with it. The relationship was broken by the Arab-Israeli War of 1973, but reestablished in 1974. Chadli Bendjedid, elected prime minister in February, was a pro-Western liberal who avoided foreign entanglements. As a nonaligned Muslim nation, Algeria was uniquely positioned to mediate between the United States and other Islamic countries.

On December 6, Carter received some momentary much-needed relief from dealing with Iran. He and Rosalynn attended Shirley Hufstedler's swearing in ceremony as the first secretary of the Department of Education. Hufstedler had become a close friend as well as a cabinet secretary. A few months earlier, when she had come to Washington to be interviewed for the job, Carter had walked with her in a small garden on the White House grounds and poured out his soul to her about his work for better education and concern for people who were left out. In the months since that meeting, Iran had cast a dark shadow over the entire administration. She was particularly sympathetic with Carter, and he relished her friendship and support.[15]

The gloom of the hostage crisis fell over the Christmas season. On December 13, when Jimmy and Amy together threw the switch to light the national Christmas tree on the White House Lawn, it remained dark except for the star at the top. Carter had ordered that the tree should not be lighted until the hostages were released. Four days later, when British Prime Minister Margaret Thatcher visited Washington for the first time, Carter toasted her at a state dinner, quoting Charles Dickens, "she knows what's what, she does." Cy Vance and others sang Christmas carols for entertainment, but the forced frivolity hardly covered the serious issues on everyone's minds. The season's greetings Carter sent to his cabinet were somber, religious, and hopeful.[16] Carter thanked Mother Teresa in Calcutta for her blessings and prayers, but her intercession did not change Khomeini's Muslim heart.[17]

On Friday, December 21, Jimmy, Rosalynn, and Amy flew by helicopter to Camp David to spend Christmas week together in Aspen Lodge. It was the first time, Jimmy sadly wrote in his diary, that they had not been with their folks at home "since the year my daddy died." On Christmas Day, they exchanged gifts and telephoned family members, including Miss Lillian and the imprisoned renegade nephew William "Tody" Spann. Rosalynn invited the thirty-nine senior staff and Filipino stewards who were at Camp David to join them at dinner, but as much as they loved Camp David and the staff there, it was not Plains.[18] In Tehran, Khomeini allowed three US clergymen and an Algerian Archbishop to conduct Christmas services for small groups of the hostages. En route home to New York, the clergymen reported that they had seen 43 of the captives, leading to a grim debate about what might have happened to the others and to confusion about how many Americans the students still held as prisoners.[19]

Carter had no time to feel nostalgic about his family's traditional Christmas, because on Christmas Eve, large numbers of Soviet airborne troops had begun to fly into Kabul, the capital of Afghanistan. A few days later, KGB commandos stormed the presidential palace, killed President Hafizullah Amin, and installed in his place Babrak Karmal, an exiled Afghan Communist and veteran KGB agent. Brezhnev claimed that the Soviets had been invited into Afghanistan, but they had murdered the man who had supposedly invited them. About 80,000 Soviet soldiers and 1,880 tanks were soon stationed in strategic cities and military bases around the country. Carter declared the invasion the "most serious threat to peace since World War II."[20]

Rosalynn found Jimmy more upset than she had ever seen him when he heard the news that the Soviets had invaded Afghanistan. Almost repeating a secret note from Brzezinski, he told her, "We will help to make sure that

Afghanistan will be their Vietnam."[21] Carter had reason to be dismayed. The threat of nuclear war again hung in the balance, and his work to prevent it by negotiating SALT II had not yet been ratified by the Senate.

In a secret memorandum of December 26, Brzezinski gave Carter further advice in light of the drastically changed circumstances. "We should not," he cautioned, "be too sanguine about Afghanistan becoming a Soviet Vietnam: A. The guerrillas are badly organized and poorly led; B. They have no sanctuary, no organized army, and no central government—all of which North Vietnam had; C. They have limited foreign support."

Brzezinski proposed giving the insurgents "more money as well as arms shipments" and asking Pakistan, China, and Islamic countries for help. He also recommended telling "the Soviets that their actions are placing SALT in jeopardy." The Soviets, he said, should ask themselves "whether such local adventurism is worth the long-term damage to the U.S.-Soviet relationship."[22]

On December 27, Carter was pleased to learn that a federal court had upheld his November 10 order that the Justice Department review all Iranian student visas. Carter insisted that the law be obeyed and that the rights of those Iranians in the United States be respected. By December 20, the Immigration and Naturalization Service had determined that more than 45,000 of the 55,000 students had complied with US laws regarding their visas, about 6,500 were in violation of their status, and the remainder needed to have their documents reviewed.[23]

Early the next day, the Carters returned to the White House, and Carter went directly to meet with the NSC to discuss Brzezinski's suggestions. Afterward, he telephoned the heads of allied states to explain to them how Moscow had "changed a buffer nation into a puppet nation under Soviet direction." He told Margaret Thatcher, Helmut Schmidt, Giscard d'Estaing, and Italy's Francesco Cossiga that he intended to proceed with SALT II, but he hoped some nation, such as "Britain or China," would take the issue to the UN. Thatcher gave him a vague answer about how she would "be about" during the weekend and would welcome a representative from the United States. Schmidt concurred with Carter's commitment to continue with SALT II and agreed to call a meeting of the North Atlantic Council to discuss Afghanistan. Giscard D'Estaing said the allies should make the invasion costly to the Soviets, but he offered no specific answers. The French leader agreed to a meeting of NATO but was not enthusiastic. None of the leaders wanted to confront the Soviets over Afghanistan, except for Italy's Cossiga, who promised to support Carter in whatever he wanted to do.[24]

Carter reconsidered US policy toward Pakistan. With the Russians in Afghanistan and a revolution in Iran, the United States looked to its unlikely ally Pakistan to help stop what the edgy Americans feared might be a Soviet march to the Indian Ocean. Brzezinski argued that US security with regard to Pakistan could no longer be based upon Carter's nonproliferation policy, but the United States should give more guarantees to Pakistan, including weapons. Carter telephoned President Muhammad Zia-ul-Haq to tell him that the United States and Pakistan must strengthen their ties and stand together in "mutual resolve against further Soviet intrusions into Southern Asia." Zia, eager to get more US aid, took advantage of the US fear of Soviet expansion.[25]

Over the next several years, increasingly large amounts of lethal as well as non-lethal US supplies secretly flowed across the Pakistani border to the Mujahideen in Afghanistan. Brzezinski visited the Pakistan border and told Muslim warriors that "God is on your side."[26] Congress approved sending aid to Muslim resistance groups in Pakistan, from where it could be routed to the rebels in Afghanistan.[27] Carter ordered the CIA to render assistance to the Afghan fighters who had no weapons other than Enfield rifles. A month later, Sadat agreed to a secret personal request from Carter to assist the CIA in channeling Soviet-made weapons to the Mujahideen.[28]

The US secret involvement in the Soviet-Afghan War distracted Carter from his reelection campaign. Kennedy was attacking him at every turn, causing Hamilton Jordan, Bob Strauss, Tim Kraft, Stuart Eizenstat, and Jody Powell all to urge Carter to debate Kennedy in Iowa. Carter agreed in principle that a debate with Kennedy would be helpful, but he placed his presidential responsibility above his hope of being reelected. On December 28, he wrote to Jody: "I cannot break away from duties here, which are extraordinary now and ones which only I can fulfill. We will just have to take the adverse political consequences & make the best of it. Right now both Iran & Afghanistan look bad, and will need my constant attention."[29]

What Carter would not do himself, Rosalynn and others did for him. In Iowa, she faced farmers, anti-Carter demonstrators, and pro-Kennedy journalists. The farmers liked her, and with the help of Mondale, Secretary of Agriculture Bob Bergland, and her son Jack, who operated a grain elevator in Georgia, she convinced the farmers that Carter would keep the price of grain high and find new markets other than the Soviet Union. In time, he did so, sending tons of grain to Argentina, and he won Iowa.[30]

Leaving the campaign to others, on December 29, Carter engaged in a heated exchange with Leonid Brezhnev. According to a London newspaper, the Soviet leader was "fat and autocratic and often drunk" when he sent the army into Afghanistan. Using the hot line, Carter told him, "Unless you draw back from your present course of action, this will inevitably jeopardize the course of United States-Soviet relations throughout the world. I urge you to take prompt constructive action to withdraw your forces and cease interference in Afghanistan's internal affairs. Many years of promoting more stable and productive relations between our two countries could well be undermined if this situation is not resolved promptly."[31]

Brezhnev replied with equal sharpness: "the immoderate tone of certain formulations in your message hit us squarely between the eyes. . . . Would it not be better to evaluate the situation more calmly, keeping in mind the supreme interests of the world rather than, ultimately, the mutual relations of our two powers." The old Soviet dictator, increasingly irritated with Carter, told the US president that "we already informed you, and here I repeat again, that as soon as the reasons which prompted the Afghanistani request to the Soviet Union disappear, we fully intend to withdraw the Soviet military contingents from Afghanistani territory." Brezhnev continued that he did not think that if negotiations should break down, it would be the fault of his country. "The Soviet Union," he said, "is an advocate of conducting affairs in . . . the interest of peace, equal cooperation, and international security."[32]

On the last day of the year, with the Soviet occupation of Afghanistan still firmly in place, Carter told journalist Frank Reynolds that he found Brezhnev's remarks to be "completely inadequate and completely misleading." Pressing further, Reynolds asked, "Well, he's lying, isn't he, Mr. President?" Carter responded: "He's not telling the facts accurately, that's correct."[33] Carter elaborated that he thought the Soviets had gone into Afghanistan to impose "atheistic beliefs on a religious people" and to acquire a puppet nation on their border. He believed that their action made it more urgent to ratify SALT II. Carter vowed to keep the United States strong and at peace and to put his political ambition second to the welfare of the nation. He reserved the right, however, to change his mind if circumstances warranted it. Although he had said earlier in his presidency that Iran was an island of stability, he confessed, "I was wrong."[34]

On New Year's Eve, Jimmy and Rosalynn went to a small dinner party hosted by long-time Georgia friends Frank and Nancy Moore. The other guests included only Jody and Nan Powell and two of their friends. Leaving before midnight, Jimmy wrote in his diary, "Rosalynn and I welcomed in the New Year by ourselves, which is the best way for us to do it."[35]

Carter began the new year facing the same problems that had plagued the old one. Although a public opinion poll showed him leading Kennedy 58–38, he and Rosalynn did not take his reelection for granted.[36] The Soviet Union's invasion of Afghanistan greatly lessened the chance that the Senate would ratify SALT II, which necessitated reconsidering trade agreements that had been negotiated along with it. Furthermore, Carter worried that the Soviets might take advantage of the chaos in Iran and move through the five hundred miles to the Indian Ocean, which would give them a substantial presence in the Middle East.[37]

Taking no chances with the Soviet Union, Carter had begun a massive rebuilding of the US military machine. As early as the previous June, he had announced the beginning of construction of the MX intercontinental ballistic missile with the ability to deploy it in a mobile mode. The CIA had given Carter such a disturbing analysis of Soviet military strength that he determined to exceed it. Madeleine Albright, Brzezinski's liaison with Congress, had informed her boss and the president that SALT II would not stabilize arms control nor would it improve US-Soviet relations; therefore, the United States must be prepared to contain Soviet power. Taking her advice seriously, Carter ordered an improvement in nuclear command and intelligence systems that would make it possible, if necessary, for the United States to wage an extended nuclear war. He increased spending for the Trident II nuclear submarine program, and convinced NATO members to allow new US nuclear forces into Western Europe.[38]

By 1980 the United States had deployed 550 Minuteman ICBMS with triple nuclear warheads within its borders and at strategic locations around the world, developed the multi-warhead MX missiles, placed longer range missiles on submarines, and advanced many kinds of weapons research, including on the Stealth bomber that could escape detection by radar. The number of Soviet targets the US was capable of reaching increased from 1,700 in 1970 to 7,000 by the end of 1980. Carter had dropped his cherished goal of balancing the budget, just short of accomplishing it, and had substantially increased spending on defense.[39]

When Carter addressed the nation on January 4, 1980, to explain how he would retaliate against the Soviets for their invasion of Afghanistan, he did not reveal the secret military options he already had in place. The Soviet incursion, he said, was "an extremely serious threat to peace" and "a callous violation of international law." The world, he said, could not stand by and "permit the Soviet Union to commit this act with impunity." Carter ended Soviet fishing privileges in US waters and halted exports to the Soviet Union, including delivery of seventeen million tons of grain that the Soviets had ordered for cattle feed. He reassured Iowa farmers who might be damaged by the grain embargo, and whose votes he needed, that he would find a way to compensate them. Furthermore, Carter said, he would consider withdrawing US athletes from the Olympic Games scheduled for the following summer in Moscow.[40]

Rosalynn, who supported her husband's tough foreign policy decisions, kept up the campaign against Kennedy and supervised cultural events at the White House.[41] On January 3 she invited twenty-one poets, representing all sections of the country, to participate in a seminar at the White House where they would read and discuss their poetry. She set up seven salons in seven different rooms with three poets to a room. Seventy-five other writers and literary critics attended. The presenters included such diverse artists as Maxine Kumin, children's book author; Sterling Brown, a leading African-American poet; Stanley Kunitz, a poet and teacher in New York City; Lucille Clifton, a relatively unknown African-American poet; and James Dickey, a friend of the Carters who had written a poem for Jimmy's inauguration.[42]

After the readings, Rosalynn gave her own commentary to the entire group. Aware of Jimmy's love of poetry, especially that of Dylan Thomas, and cognizant of his ambition to become a poet and writer, she observed that US writers had always reflected the hopes and dreams of society. They revealed emotions about life, both funny and tragic, she said, and they interpreted events that filled the history of the country. Rosalynn recalled how Jimmy had gathered their children by the fire when they were small and read poetry to them. In times of stress, she continued, poetry "can lift our spirits," "bring us together," and "transform a dull existence." "And when we listen to poetry—and what you hear—and what I hear—will not be the same. That's the joy!" More than a comment on poetry, her words revealed her own hope for endurance and better times ahead. Carter briefly attended the reception for the poets, but he seemed preoccupied with Iran and the Soviet Union.[43]

The day after the poetry event, a Gallup poll announced that Rosalynn Carter, Betty Ford, and Mother Teresa were the women most admired by the US public. Miss Lillian came in sixth on that list, proving that the adult Carter women were more popular than he was.[44]

Jimmy liked the idea that his wife was so popular, but he had little time to tease her about it or pretend to be jealous. How to keep a good relationship with Pakistan and get its help to block the Soviets became a touchy problem. If the Soviets moved unchecked into Pakistan, they would gain access to warm-water ports on the Arabian Sea and establish naval stations there. Carter favored sending the Pakistanis weapons to be used to stop the Soviets at the Pakistan border, but Pakistan also wanted tanks and armored personnel carriers that it could use on the plains of the Punjab and Sindh on the Indian border. Yielding to Zia's requests, Carter began to send the materials he requested, but he also ordered that Soviet-made weapons, which were plentiful in Pakistan, be shipped secretly to the Afghan rebels. He could thus disguise the fact that they actually came from the United States. Since the CIA informed him that Moscow was not likely to attack Pakistan if other nations condemned the Soviet invasion of Afghanistan, Carter sought help from the UN and from US allies. The UN Security Council passed a resolution calling for Soviet withdrawal, but the Soviet Union ignored it. Since stronger support from US allies also was not forthcoming, Carter depended upon advice from Secretary of State Cyrus Vance to help him decide how to deal with Pakistan.[45]

Vance warned Carter that President Muhammad Zia-ul-Haq, the four-star general who had staged a military coup in 1977 and become head of the Islamic Republic of Pakistan the next year, had manipulated the United States to get its support and that he could not be trusted. Zia, a British Indian military officer and a Muslim, had opted to live in Pakistan in 1947 when it had been partitioned from India and had become an independent state. Wanting to maintain his country's Islamic identity and promote economic progress, Zia hoped to stop Soviet influence in his country, and, more important, to gain help from the United States against India. The United States, however, expected Zia to work with India, which Zia would not accept. The United States would not endorse Pakistan's nuclear programs, Vance said, but it would give it economic and military aid, and it would show no disfavor to Pakistan's Islamic and non-aligned ties.[46]

In the meantime, pressure built for Carter to boycott the Olympic Games in Moscow and thus drive the wedge deeper between the United States and the Soviet Union. Journalist Mary McGrory, of the *Washington Star*, the reputed "queen of the Washington press corps" and an unapologetic admirer of the Kennedy family, urged the president to keep the US athletes at home. Despite the disappointment of the athletes and fans, McGrory argued that "the grisly alternative would include selling arms to China and Pakistan, dropping rifles on rebellious Afghan tribesmen, tripling our defense budget and drafting our young men." The boycott would cost the Soviets prestige, she said, and "more money than they have ever seen at any one time." They could hide their casualties in Afghanistan but not their empty stadiums. Both Rosalynn and Cy Vance agreed with McCrory that the United States should boycott the games, but Mondale favored moving them to another venue.[47] Saudi Arabia was the first country to withdraw from the Moscow Olympic Games in protest of the Soviet invasion of Afghanistan. Most European nations backed the US grain embargo, but they hesitated to become involved in the thorny issue of boycotting the games.[48]

Farmers in the Midwest, however, protested the grain embargo because they thought it would impact their livelihood. "When I was a farmer," Carter explained in a meeting with his senior staff on January 8, "I couldn't understand all nuances of federal controls [either]." He felt compelled to impose the grain embargo, because, he said, "We must stop the Russians." Even if it caused every farmer to vote against him, he maintained, he would still have taken that action. But he added that there would be a plan to repay the farmers and others, as well as readjust the federal budget to distribute any financial distress evenly across the population of the country. In another staff meeting two days later, however, Carter muttered that he couldn't "give the farmers every damn thing they want."[49] Secretary of Agriculture Bob Bergland thought the entire debate about the embargo was much ado about nothing, because it would not affect the Soviets or the US farmers. The Russians, he said, would simply buy their grain from Argentina, and the United States in turn would acquire Argentina's customers.[50]

In the meantime, Rosalynn, Billy, and others waged the campaign against Ted Kennedy. Billy spent the night of January 8 at the White House, had a long talk with his brother, much of it apparently about his dealings with the Libyans, and reported that he was helping win the support of country and western music stars. Tom T. Hall and about seventy-five others, Billy told Carter, would stage a fundraiser in Nashville that "could be very significant."[51]

Rosalynn, Joan Mondale, Muriel Humphrey, and Ruth Carter Stapleton campaigned in Iowa. Rosalynn delivered the same speech wherever she went, explaining what Jimmy would do about the Soviet invasion of Afghanistan and why he was so much better than Kennedy, adding why he would be good for Iowa. When a poll in Iowa, where she had worked hard, showed that Carter led Kennedy by 2 to 1, she opined that she was surprised that the senator did not do better. She was confused about why Kennedy ran for the nomination, she said, because he almost always agreed with Jimmy on legislation. She was more nervous about the grain embargo, but when she was in Iowa, she had encountered very little opposition to it. One farmer told her that he would rather lose a little money than send his boy off to war. Many Iowan protesters who carried "Embargo Carter" signs lowered them to shake her hand. Most Iowans, she learned, favored moving the Olympic Games away from Moscow, except for one whose son was training for the competition.[52]

Rosalynn also attended an ERA Coalition Fundraiser in Ames, where she impressed the media with her gracious manner and knowledge of the facts. Pamela Harriman, the wife of Averell Harriman and a rising star in the Democratic Party, was so excited by Rosalynn's work that she wrote her that "America is blessed to have such a fine First Lady in the tense and difficult times we live in."[53]

As the Carter camp pushed the campaign forward and the president sought ways to thwart the Soviets in Afghanistan, the US hostages continued to languish as Iranian prisoners. A new late-night television program, first called *America Held Hostage* and later *Nightline*, began relentlessly reminding viewers day after day exactly how many days had elapsed since the crisis had begun. Its sharp-tongued host, Ted Koppel, seemed to pass harsh judgement nightly on the president for not having solved the issue; he ignored the virtues of Carter's attempts to bring the captured Americans home alive and to prevent the outbreak of a major war. It was not the United States that was held hostage, however, but fifty-two citizens whom Carter intended to liberate as soon as possible.

In his search for a traditional diplomatic avenue of communication with the Iranian government, Carter wanted the support of as many nations as possible. When Mexico refused to help, Carter exploded in a January 14 staff meeting: "I think we ought to bust hell out of them." He asked Cy Vance to do more and more to gain support from other nations, but Cy, who did his best and worked long days, failed in his efforts. Carter remarked to his staff that he had almost caused Vance to resign, not from anger but from resistance to an inhuman work load.[54]

Preoccupied though he was with the twin crises in Iran and Afghanistan, Carter still managed to find time in his long, heavily scheduled White House days to try to keep his political fences mended. On many nights in early and mid-January, he made numerous telephone calls one after another to his

Iowa grassroots supporters ahead of the January 21 Iowa caucuses, and he met with several campaign support groups. Nor did Carter neglect his crucial labor and African-American constituencies. On January 14, he and Rosalynn hosted a reception at the White House for approximately 124 members of the United Automobile Workers and the AFL-CIO who supported his reelection. The next morning, Carter joined Muriel Humphrey, widow of Hubert Humphrey, and Vice President Mondale at a requiem mass for longtime AFL-CIO president George Meany at Washington's St. Matthews Cathedral. That afternoon Carter marked the fifty-first anniversary of the birth of Martin Luther King, Jr., by signing an executive order designating February 1980 as "Afro-American History Month." Once again he called for the establishment of King's birthday as a national holiday, an action that Congress did not take until 1983.[55]

Carter was losing his patience and his temper with the Soviets and with Congress. Since SALT II would not be ratified in the immediate future, he told his senior staff at their regular morning meeting on January 16, he was freed from having to "kiss any senators' asses" in order to get it approved. He believed that the majority of the people in the country agreed with him that he should get tough and "bust hell out of [Congress]" to get them to pass viable energy legislation and "quit messing around" with the water projects that he loathed. "What are they gonna do," he asked about his Congressional critics, "put me in jail?" As for the summer Olympic Games, he stated emphatically, "Bottom line is, if the Soviets are not out of Afghanistan, *we are not going.*"[56]

Four days later, during a nationally televised interview on *Meet the Press*, Carter gave the Soviets a dramatic public ultimatum. "Neither I nor the American people," he told the interviewers, "would support the sending of an American team to Moscow with Soviet invasion troops in Afghanistan. I've sent a message today to the United States Olympic Committee spelling out my own position: that unless the Soviets withdraw their troops within a month from Afghanistan, that the Olympic games be moved from Moscow to an alternate site or multiple sites or postponed or canceled. If the Soviets do not withdraw their troops immediately from Afghanistan within a month, I would not support the sending of an American team to the Olympics. It's very important for the world to realize how serious a threat the Soviets' invasion of Afghanistan is."[57]

In the *Meet the Press* interview, Carter defended the military strength of the United States and attempted to explain how he wanted good ties with both Pakistan and India. Asked about allegations that the Soviets had been emboldened to move into Afghanistan because they thought he was weak and wouldn't fight, Carter responded forcefully: "We've not been weak." Referring to the "steady increase in our commitment to the strength of our national defense," Carter said that, if necessary, he would use military force to protect the security of Pakistan against a potential Soviet invasion.[58]

Not wanting to offend India, Carter sent Clark Clifford to Delhi to meet with Prime Minister Indira Gandhi, whom he distrusted because of her country's association with the Soviet Union. Carter wanted to make sure that she understood that the United States' new relationship with Pakistan did not negate its goodwill toward India. He sent a note to her via Clifford in which he assured her that the United States was interested in the safety of *both* India and Pakistan.[59]

Carter planned to take a tough, hawkish stand against Soviet aggression in his State of the Union speech scheduled for January 23. Despite opposition from some key advisers, he wrote the speech his way, calling for a resumption of draft registration but avoiding the thorny issue of registration for women.[60] After Carter had given the speech, Rosalynn, ever the advocate for gender equality, told a reporter that "if we register men, I think we're going to have to register women," but added that she was "not for drafting anyone."[61] Carter maintained that only men should have to register.

In his annual State of the Union address to Congress and to the nation on the night of January 23, Carter acknowledged that the "last few months has not been an easy time for any of us," before outlining the steps that he had taken and was taking to confront the twin challenges of "international terrorism" in Iran and "military aggression" in Afghanistan. "If the American hostages are harmed," he warned the Iranians, a "severe price will be paid." And "the Soviet Union," he said, "must pay a concrete price for their aggression," including economic sanctions and the cancellation of US participation in the Moscow Olympic Games. Carter called for an increase in the defense budget, reestablishment of draft registration, standby gasoline rationing, and a windfall profits tax on petroleum. As if addressing his contest with Ted Kennedy, he emphasized the nation's need for a viable national healthcare program. Fearlessly, he reiterated his deep-rooted commitments to human rights and nuclear arms control. Referring to SALT II, he promised that "the effort to control nuclear weapons will not be abandoned." But he emphasized that while the invasion of Afghanistan continued, it was impossible "to conduct business as usual with the Soviet Union." Then he proclaimed what was to become known as the Carter Doctrine: "Let our position be absolutely clear: An attempt by an outside force to gain control of the Persian Gulf region will be regarded as an assault on the vital interests of the United States of America, and such an assault will be repelled by any means necessary, including military force."[62]

That crucial sentence had been written by Brzezinski who, in a memorandum on January 2, had pointed out the relevance to the current situation in Afghanistan of the 1947 Truman Doctrine. Responding to "the threatened collapse under Soviet pressure" of Greece and Turkey, Truman had "announced that it was the policy of the United States to support free peoples who were resisting attempted subjugation by armed minorities or by outside pressures." "The Soviet intervention in the present case," Brzezinski wrote, "is both more blatant and more brutal than in 1947, and the Gulf is unquestionably more vital to Western interests today than were Greece and Turkey thirty years ago."[63]

Journalists labeled Carter's bold statement the Carter Doctrine. To emphasize that he was quite serious, Carter created the Rapid Deployment Joint Task Force and gained permission from allies in the Persian Gulf area to use bases from which to launch an attack if he thought it was necessary.[64] Many members of Congress and most US allies had more respect for Carter after he issued the Carter Doctrine. The day after his speech, the House of Representatives voted almost unanimously to support the president's Olympic boycott ultimatum, and the Senate did likewise on January 30.[65]

Most European nations, plus Israel, welcomed the Carter Doctrine, thinking it would protect their Middle East oil supplies. The Carter Doctrine demonstrated Carter's firm belief and practice that national security always took precedence over human rights. He believed that a show of US strength would help to maintain peace in the Middle East.[66] The Soviet Union, with plenty of strength of its own, remained in Afghanistan and continued to tout its position as host of the Olympic Games.

Hostages and Politics

The day after his State of the Union speech, working in the Oval Office, Carter answered questions from the press about Billy's dealings with the Libyans and announced that the facts about Billy's case should be fully disclosed.[1] Billy and his wife Sybil, along with country music singer Tom T. Hall and his wife, spent the night of January 24 at the White House, attended a state dinner for Italian prime minister Francesco Cossiga, and again embarrassed his brother. Although Billy was not present at Jimmy's private discussions with the prime minister about relations with Italy, terrorism, the hostage situation, and the Soviet invasion of Afghanistan, Billy made a scene for the media after the dinner and entertainment. Speaking of Afghanistan, "I didn't even know the place existed until the Russians invaded it," he told reporters, but he quickly corrected himself to say, "Well, I did know about it, but I damn sure couldn't pronounce it." Jimmy had conveniently slipped away to have a private conversation with Cossiga and thus escaped having to respond to Billy's comments.[2]

While the media was preoccupied with Billy's shenanigans, Carter secretly watched the CIA's execution of a plan to rescue the six US diplomats who were still hiding with their Canadian counterparts.[3] After November, the diplomats had moved into the homes of Canadian Ambassador Ken Taylor and one of his colleagues. In Ottawa, the Canadian parliament went into secret session to approve a plan to rescue them.[4] In Washington, Carter and Vance called the major news sources to ask them not to publicize the story about the six hidden diplomats.

The CIA asked Tony Mendez, an espionage artist and exfiltration expert who had previously rescued CIA agents in other parts of the world, to help the six diplomats in Tehran. Four of them were two young couples still in their twenties, Mark and Cora Lijek and Joseph and Kathleen Stafford. Robert Anders and Henry Lee Schatz completed the group. As a subterfuge, Mendez worked with a Hollywood makeup artist to create a bogus Canadian film company that proposed to film a movie called *Argo* in Iran. Canadian

Prime Minister Joe Clark promised Carter that he would authorize fake passports for the six, and the CIA forged Iranian visas. Drilled and coached on their fake names, and disguised by the makeup artist, the six prepared to depart Tehran on January 27. Before dawn that day a Canadian embassy van took them and their CIA escorts to Mehrabad International Airport. They escaped detection by customs agents and boarded the plane. After a frightening mechanical delay, during which the diplomats feared being discovered and dragged from the plane, they finally lifted off and soon cleared Iranian airspace. The relieved Americans, with unsuspecting Iranians sitting around them on the plane, raised their glasses of Bloody Marys in celebration.

As soon as the plane entered Turkish air space, the Swiss pilot notified Carter that all six were safely out of Iran. Cloaked in secrecy, unidentified State Department officials met the plane in Switzerland, and CIA personnel drove them to Germany. Fearful for the safety of the fifty-two remaining hostages, as well as the Canadian embassy staff, Carter attempted to black out the news about the escaped Americans, but the story broke in a Montreal newspaper on the January 28. So, instead of being sequestered, the six escaped diplomats, after a short rest at Ramstein Air Base, boarded a US Air Force jet bound for Washington. At Andrews Air Force Base, Secretary of State Cyrus Vance and their families tearfully welcomed them home. An honor guard then escorted them to the Oval Office where a smiling President Carter greeted them. Carter called Prime Minister Joe Clark to thank him, Ambassador Ken Taylor, and Canada for their friendship and help.[5]

The publicity surrounding the homecoming of the six escaped US diplomats did not provoke retaliation from the Iranian militants. The Canadians closed their embassy, and the plight of the other fifty-two hostages remained unchanged. The Oval Office meeting, nevertheless, triggered a question from one of the African-American hostages who had been among the thirteen Blacks and females whom the captors had released earlier. Sergeant James Hughes wrote Carter that although he had welcomed the six to the White House he had not done that for the thirteen released the previous November. "I wonder if it is because they are white and we were mostly black?," he asked. Carter replied on February 26, thanking Sergeant Hughes for his letter and assuring him that his safe return brought "great joy and relief to me personally, and to the entire Nation." Carter promised to welcome him and the other twelve former hostages to the White House after the others were released.[6]

In the meantime, Italian actress Sophia Loren captured the limelight when she visited the Oval Office on January 28. Representing the National Alliance for the Prevention and Treatment of Child Abuse and Maltreatment, Loren asked Carter for a presidential endorsement of her cause. He did so, and, showing her appreciation, she told him that Europeans were looking to him for leadership. She promised to do everything she could to help him win the Italian American vote. Carter thanked her and later he wrote in his diary that "She was even more beautiful than I had expected."[7] Neither distracted by her beauty, however, nor trusting the Europeans, especially since the United Kingdom and others had made only noncommittal responses to the Soviet invasion of Afghanistan, Carter announced in the press that he intended to use military power to stop the Soviet Union if necessary. He asked Congress for a 3.3% increase in military spending, with more increases over the next five years.[8]

Despite his efforts to control inflation and reduce the federal budget, Carter also pledged $5.3 million in immediate aid for the Afghan relief program of the UN High Commissioner for Refugees. In addition, he committed $16 million in food and blankets and sent three people to Pakistan to investigate how the aid was being used and to determine what additional help might be needed.[9] Carter also sent Brzezinski and Deputy Secretary of State Warren Christopher to Pakistan to assure President Zia-ul-Haq that US forces would be deployed there in the event of a massive Soviet strike. Zia, just as apprehensive about the historic threat from India, wanted a substantial increase in the $400 million in economic and military aid over the next two years already promised by the Carter.[10]

The US effort to build a regional coalition against the Soviets in Afghanistan created an odd fragile alliance among Iran, India, Pakistan, and the United States. A strong believer in Islamic unity, Ayatollah Khomeini had condemned the Soviet invasion of Afghanistan and had promised support for Muslim insurgents who hoped to drive the Soviets out of their country. Iran also provided a haven for many Afghan refugees fleeing the Soviet invasion. Carter's January 22 letter to Indira Gandhi had had the desired effect; India would not support the invasion. Indian foreign secretary Ram D. Sathe informed Zia that he would try to persuade Moscow to withdraw its forces from Afghanistan. Knowing that such an alliance would not intimidate the Soviets, the United States prepared to send 25,000 troops into Iran if it were invaded by the Soviet Union.[11]

The Soviets' refusal to leave Afghanistan gave Carter the ammunition he needed to push for US withdrawal from the Moscow Olympic Games. The analytical division of the CIA gave him additional support. It translated a passage from pages 158–71 of the Handbook of Party Activists, published in Moscow in November 1979: "The decision to give the honored right to hold the Olympic Games in the capital of the world's first socialist state has become convincing testimony to the general recognition of the historical importance and the correctness of the foreign political course of our country." The Soviets seemed to be saying that any country that sent athletes to Moscow would be endorsing their political system. Carter used that assertion by the Soviet Union, as well as its invasion of Afghanistan, as a strong reason for the United States to boycott the Olympic Games. Carter told Jody Powell, his press secretary, to read the Soviet statement and "promulgate" it.[12]

The need to withdraw from the games and to reinstate registration for the draft became major themes of the Carter reelection campaign. Rosalynn campaigned against Kennedy from coast to coast and from North to South. She defended Jimmy for taking the "Rose Garden" approach by staying off the campaign trail to show empathy for the fifty-two innocent Americans who were incarcerated, suffering and fearful in their Tehran prisons. Following her husband's advice, Rosalynn noted in every speech that Kennedy's position on the Olympic boycott was the same as the president's. Boycotting the Moscow games, she argued, would wreck the Soviet Union's economy and help end the Cold war. Young people, both men and women, she thought, should be required to register for the draft, but no draft would take place unless there was a national emergency. Carter himself attacked Kennedy in five recorded radio commercials, portraying the senator as a failed leader who voted for a "weaker defense."[13]

When Abolhassan Bani-Sadr was inaugurated as president of Iran on February 4, Carter thought that the end of the crisis might be in sight, which might give him the additional leverage he needed to defeat Kennedy. US intelligence informed Carter, however, that, although Bani-Sadr had criticized the seizing of the embassy and the Soviet invasion of Afghanistan, he could not be trusted.[14] In desperation, Carter hoped that Christian Bourquet and Hector Villalon, two mysterious characters who claimed to have access to the Ayatollah, would help. Bourguet was a French lawyer and Villalon an Argentine businessman who knew Iranians in exile who could contact Khomeini. Calling themselves lawyers for the Iranian Revolution, they planned to present briefs to have the shah extradited to Iran. Carter occasionally sent them messages, which Hamilton Jordan covertly delivered. Ham had met them earlier in Panama, and in January he met them again in

London and Washington. With those messages, Carter attempted to inform the Iranian government that he would consider their terms for release of the hostages. When Bourquet and Villalon consistently failed to deliver useful information, an exasperated Carter angrily wrote Ham a note, "Ham, they are crazy."[15]

Carter thought that some of his critics and opponents at home were also crazy. Many Jewish Americans and Israelis contended that aiding the Muslim country of Pakistan signified that the United States was abandoning Israel. When the *Washington Post* published an article on February 10 claiming that Carter was shifting toward the Arab leaders and away from Israel, he became irate. "This is b.s.," he told Stuart Eizenstat. "We've made no statements to the Arab leaders."[16] Furthermore, Carter thought that Menachem Begin's continuing to establish settlements on the West Bank was intended to irritate him and to prevent "the Palestinians from becoming moderate and cooperative."[17]

Carter was also aggravated by Ted Kennedy. Carter had won decisively over Kennedy in the Iowa and Maine caucuses and led him by a substantial margin in the upcoming New Hampshire primary on February 26. Kennedy was becoming increasingly shrill, stirring up students with references to Vietnam. "I was almost nauseated," Carter told his senior staff after hearing that news. He asked someone in the Carter campaign to "bust hell out of him today" and promised to follow up that night. "The worst thing we can do is" let the Soviet Union be influenced by Kennedy and "think invasion of Afghanistan is unimportant." Kennedy, he said, was the "worst damn example of irresponsibility I've ever seen."[18]

Rosalynn followed up later in February In a televised interview on CBS News, she argued that the Olympic boycott "is devastating to the Soviet Union." It shows the Soviets that "we are strong, very prepared and have stood up to them in the world." Rosalynn declared that there was no longer a "malaise" in the country and that the "Iranian situation has rallied our people together." When she was asked about her and Jimmy's future, her answer was straightforward: "In five years after Jimmy serves his second term we'll go home to Plains." Hoping to comfort the athletes who no longer could travel to Moscow, Carter flew a group of them to the White House for a presidential greeting.[19]

Far more serious than the fallout from the Olympic Games, the Carter administration's relations with Israel took a serious downward turn on March 1 when the United States voted with fourteen other Security Council members in favor of a UN Resolution to restrict Israel from building settlements in the territories, including parts of Jerusalem, captured during the 1967 war. It was the first time the United States cast a vote against Israel since Begin had begun his settlement expansion policy. Carter had approved the vote provided that there would be no mention in the resolution of the highly sensitive issue of Jerusalem. Carter had an understanding with Begin that the issue of Jerusalem and dismantling existing settlements would be resolved by future negotiations. The resolution that was passed, however, referred to Jerusalem at least six times, references which the United States thought had been deleted.

Carter and Vance promptly issued a joint statement that the US vote had been an error, and on March 4, Carter met with leaders of the World Jewish Congress in the White House's Roosevelt Room to reassure them that "Israel's security" and "right to live in peace was a high priority." Brzezinski also addressed the group, arguing that the United States would persist in the Camp David peace process and try to get other Arab nations to be less hostile toward Israel. Carter himself, a week earlier, had made an impassioned plea at a conference for the United Jewish Appeal, emphasizing "in the strongest possible terms" that the close relationship between the United States and Israel was "in the moral and the strategic interest" of the United States.[20]

Vance shouldered most of the blame for an error that had not been his. He, Carter, and Brzezinski, however, believed reversing the UN vote had been the right decision. Addressing a Senate committee on March 21, Vance said that the United States had always opposed Israeli settlements in occupied territories because they were contrary to international law and harmful to the Camp David Accords. Carter privately agreed with him, but he could not publicly say so and risk harming his reelection chances, especially his contest with Kennedy who was favored by many Jewish voters in the northeast.[21]

Rosalynn and others turned the heat up on Kennedy. Tim Kraft, who managed the campaign, told Rosalynn, Ham Jordan, and Bob Strauss on March 3 that they needed to get Kennedy out of the race as soon as possible in order to save money. The Boston Globe had recently quoted Kennedy as saying that the reason he was running was because "my father always told us, 'if it's on the table, eat it.'" "It's time he was told in no uncertain terms that it's not on the goddamned table," Kraft said. Prominent Democrats and Southern governors should tell him that there was no way he could carry a single "Southern state, nor could his kids nor his nephews." Like a cheerleader at a pep rally, Kraft emphasized, "let's go. . . . we ought to try and throw his ass out."[22]

Rosalynn campaigned in Birmingham, Chicago, Richmond, and Atlanta, and elsewhere, telling her audiences what her husband was doing and why and emphasizing the virtues of a united party.[23] Carter's relatively calm public speeches disguised the frustration and anger he felt about Jewish support for Kennedy. At a secret meeting upstairs in the White House with some of his senior advisers, he blurted out that if he got reelected, "I'm going to fuck the Jews." New York City's Jewish Mayor Edward Koch, an avid supporter of Israel, promised to help Carter, but the National Security Agency had intercepted telephone conversations between Koch and Begin's Jerusalem office, in which Begin was heard giving Koch advice on how to defeat the Carter.[24] All the work done by Rosalynn and Jewish members of the senior staff was of no avail.[25] Rabbi Bruce E. Kahn of Richmond, Virginia, however, apologized to Carter in a March 19 letter for "the abuse you have had heaped upon you by my rabbinic colleagues and coreligionists." The Camp David Accords, he thought, should place all "who seek the survival of Israel in your debt for decades to come."[26]

Decision after decision seemed to cost Carter the loyalty of the groups that had elected him. His anti-inflation plan of March 14 and continuing effort to balance the budget, according to Mondale, had a devastating impact on the campaign. Carter proposed slashing $13 billion in 1980 from such programs as the Comprehensive Employment and Training Act, food stamps, child abuse, and some programs for the poor and elderly. Mondale argued that such cuts would not help the budget but would alienate large groups of people who had supported Carter. Jordan agreed, but Carter proceeded to increase amounts for defense because he thought doing so essential for the security of the nation.[27]

As Carter struggled for popular approval, Rosalynn remained the star, not just on the campaign trail but in the administration as well. Widely read journalists Rowland Evans and Robert Novak declared Rosalynn to be "the most powerful First Lady since Abigail Adams." In their opinion, Rosalyn was "tough, resilient, tireless and opinionated." She had done more, they thought, to shape presidential policies, "even on finer points of foreign policy than all the First Ladies" who had preceded her. Evans and Novak recalled how, in the spring of 1978, at the inauguration ceremonies for the president of Ecuador, Rosalynn had stopped the procession to speak privately, in Spanish, to each general of the outgoing military junta to congratulate him on a peaceful transition to democracy. On the campaign trail she was vigorous and fearless. "At this point," she proclaimed in her disarmingly soft accent, "we don't care about the past history of Iran," because the "important thing—is getting the hostages home." She defended the grain embargo, often advised her husband on when to use the veto, and joked that she often had to forgive him when he didn't take her advice.[28]

It seemed that there were three White Houses—one that ran the campaign, one that dealt with Iran and Afghanistan, and one that managed domestic affairs. Carter met frequently with his domestic policy advisors, Congressional leaders from both parties, state and locally elected officers, and labor representatives to discuss inflation and the economy. In Congress, key Democrats worked on an anti-inflation package, and there was good progress on Carter's proposals for trucking deregulation, the windfalls profit tax, fair housing, and registration for the draft.[29] On March 18, Carter signed legislation increasing the number of refugees admitted to the country from 17,500 to 50,000 per year.[30]

The one refugee, namely the shah, who caused Carter the most grief had left the United States but was still the reason that the militants in Tehran held the hostages. When the shah agreed to have a splenectomy at a Panamanian hospital, Cyrus Vance promised to send a team of US doctors, including renowned surgeon Michael DeBakey of Houston, to perform the surgery on March 16. The Panamanians demanded that the shah's surgery be done by Panamanian doctors, which was likely a ruse to cover the more urgent reason the shah suddenly left Panama on March 21: Iranian president Bani-Sadr and Prime Minister Sadeq Gotzbadeh had secretly sent Christian Bourget and Hector Villalon to Panama to arrest the shah. Tipped off about this new threat to his safety, the shah went looking for a new refuge where he could get the medical care he needed. Carter talked to Sadat, who insisted that he wanted the shah to come to Egypt.[31]

After a harrowing flight, the shah and empress arrived in Cairo on March 25. Carter flew Dr. Michael DeBakey and his team to Cairo to perform the operation. Continuing US assistance to the shah, the Iranians said, would make it more difficult to free the hostages. Brzezinski responded with an announcement that the United States no longer had any commitments to the shah, but the Iranians were not convinced.[32]

Rosalynn had little time to think about the shah, because Kennedy handily won the primary in his home state of Massachusetts on March 4 and later in New York and Connecticut. Carter, however, won the eleven other Democratic primaries and caucuses in March, stretching from Vermont south to Florida and Puerto Rico and west to Wyoming and Washington state. Kennedy would have to get 63% of the remaining delegates to win the Democratic nomination, a virtual impossibility.[33] But he had no intention of dropping out of the race. He and Carter presented an odd picture of a liberal fighting a liberal in a political civil war that could only damage their party.[34]

More than Kennedy, Iran loomed as the major obstacle in the course of Carter's reelection. The news from Iran was contradictory, unreliable, and unpredictable. Events there seemed to be driven by the whims of the Ayatollah. When Prime Minister Gotzbadeh visited the embassy to demand that the militants allow visitors to see and speak with the hostages, he was refused and expelled from the compound. Other reports that the hostages would be turned over to the Revolutionary Council proved false, and efforts by the UN were for naught.[35]

Maintaining an atmosphere of normalcy at the White House, Carter issued proclamations, signed bills, gave brief statements, and posed for photographs with departing staff members, politicians endorsing his reelection campaign, and citizens representing a variety of charities and other worthy causes. Between late January and early March, Jimmy and Rosalynn hosted state dinners for three foreign leaders—Italian prime minister Francesco Cossiga, Kenyan president Daniel Arap Moi, and German chancellor Helmut Schmidt—and they entertained the press corps with a Valentine's Day dance and a St. Patrick's Day party. On March 23, the Carters, together with the Egyptian and Israeli ambassadors, celebrated the first anniversary of the Camp David Accords at a reception in the White House's grand entrance hall.

The bittersweet battle over US participation in the Olympic Games continued to plague the administration. When the winter games at Lake Placid, New York, concluded on February 24 with major US victories, the Carters honored the teams with a White House ceremony and luncheon. The euphoria generated by the Lake Placid victories was dampened considerably by the death on March 31 of Jesse Owens, the renowned African-American athlete who, as Carter said in his tribute to him, had triumphed over "tyranny, poverty, and racial bigotry" to become a four-time Olympic gold medalist in Hitler's racially charged Berlin Games of 1936.[36]

Carter had been worried from the beginning about his inability to enforce the boycott of the Moscow games. In early February, he sent Cutler to Ireland to ask the president of the International Olympics Committee, Lord Killanin, to delay or cancel the summer games or move them to an alternative site such as Greece. Killanin flatly refused. "It's Moscow or nothing," he declared.[37] Carter also asked African-American boxing champ Muhammad Ali to tour five African countries as a special envoy for the Olympic boycott. Ali reported back that he had been able to convince only Kenya to join the boycott movement and that it was "tougher to be a politician and a statesman than a boxer."[38]

By early February, seven nations, including Canada, Japan, China, and Egypt as well as Kenya, had announced that they would not send teams to Moscow. France categorically rejected the boycott, while other nations—notably Britain, West Germany, and Canada—began to reconsider their earlier support for it.[39] At the luncheon for the Lake Placid heroes, Carter expressed his regret that the United States would not participate in the summer games."[40] A month later, on March 21, he told a large group of athletes who gathered at the White House to be briefed about the political and international ramifications of US participation in the games, "I can't say at this moment what other nations will not go to the Summer Olympics in Moscow. Ours will not go." Trying to soften the blow, he told the gathered athletes, "I understand how you feel," and how much he hated to tell the fine young Americans and their coaches that it was a decision he felt compelled to make.[41] The US Olympic Committee voted 1,604 to 779 in favor of the boycott.[42]

As spring approached, Carter spent less time publicly defending his decision to boycott the Olympic Games than he did pondering a graver concern. Since it seemed that he was making no progress in his diplomatic efforts to free the hostages, he decided to use army commandos to rescue them. He knew they were centrally located within the embassy compound, because the enemy's Greek cook, who had been released by the Iranians, had given that information to covert CIA agents in Iran. At Camp David on March 22, Carter met for five hours with members of the NSC reviewing with them in detail the rescue operation for which army personnel had been secretly practicing in the Southwest. He ordered the CIA to increase its surveillance in Tehran, and he sent a secret flight into Iran to identify a remote place in the Iranian desert where it would be possible to land the C-130 transport planes and large helicopters that would be essential to the rescue. The plan was to land large helicopters near Tehran, where they would be met by Army Rangers, who would have overpowered the student guards, snatched the hostages, and brought them to the helicopters. The helicopters would transport them all to a nearby airbase where waiting transports could evacuate them from Iran.

In preparation, Carter ordered eight large helicopters to land on the aircraft carrier *Nimitz* in the Indian Ocean and be prepared for a mission in Iran.[43]

Life in the White House for the president and First Lady was more peaceful and calm than all the disturbing news about foreign affairs and domestic politics might indicate. In separate interviews with a *Washington* Post reporter on March 25 both claimed that Jimmy did not miss a night's sleep. He tried to comfort others, especially Rosalynn, who suffered from stress caused by personal and political developments. They read books about the Muslim religion, attended movies in the White House about twice a week, and conversed with visiting friends and relatives. They relaxed with vigorous exercise, trips to Camp David, and reading the Bible daily in Spanish. After reading a biography of his favorite president, Harry Truman, Carter concluded that Truman had much more difficult problems than he did. Despite the fairly idyllic picture the Carters painted of their private lives, close aides noted that Carter read more, slept less, looked tired, and very often was accessible only through Rosalynn.[44]

Carter could not find someone in Iran with the authority and willingness to negotiate in good faith about the fate of the hostages. "I think we've learned," Rosalynn said in her March 25 interview, "that there's no functioning government and there's nobody there to work with."[45] Carter most recently had hoped that the new Iranian president Bani-Sadr might be such a person and agreed not to impose additional sanctions on Iran if the hostages were transferred to the custody of the Iranian government and released. When Bani-Sadr insisted that the agreement must be approved by the new Iranian Parliament when it met on May 28 and that in the meantime Carter must not make "hostile statements," Carter again consented. Then in early April, Khomeini killed the deal; he ruled that the US captives should remain with the militants.[46]

Carter broke all ties with Iran, immediately expelled all remaining Iranian diplomats from the United States, repeated his freezing of Iranian assets, and invalidated all visas issued to Iranian citizens for future entry into the country. He still hoped for a peaceful solution, but the United States would be ready to do whatever was necessary to get its captives safely home. When Iraq began hostilities along its border with Iran and an intelligence report suggested that the Russians might be preparing for a military move into Iran, Carter notified 200,000 army reservists that they would be mobilized in a crisis situation.[47]

At the White House and at Camp David, an eerie façade disguised the fact that the world seemed to be spinning out of control and that the Carters' political fortune teetered in the balance. For relief on Easter Sunday, April 6, Jimmy and Rosalynn attended a sunrise service at Camp David, watched staff hide Easter eggs for their children, played tennis, went fishing, and watched movies in the evening. "It doesn't matter what it is," Rosalynn said of her husband's film preference, "he has no favorite type: It's an escape."[48]

Early the next day, the Carters returned to Washington, where they hosted the annual White House Easter Egg Roll on the South Lawn. In mid-afternoon, Carter announced to the press his decisions about breaking diplomatic relations with Iran and imposing sanctions on all US exports to that nation. Before dinner Jimmy and Rosalynn had a one-hour meeting with Mondale, Ham Jordan, Bob Strauss, and other key campaign staff members. Jimmy insisted that he would continue the Rose Garden approach to the campaign because he thought it more important to remain at the White House to deal with Iran and Afghanistan. Nevertheless, he stayed in close communication with the campaign, continuing to meet often with his advisors and supporters in the White House and talking with them frequently on the telephone.[49]

By early April most of the candidates for the Republican nomination—John Connally, Howard Baker, Bob Dole, and others—had withdrawn from the contest, leaving Ronald Reagan the front runner against George H. W. Bush and John Anderson. On April 7, Reagan delivered a major speech in the nation's capital vehemently attacking Carter's domestic and foreign policies. Among other things, he accused Carter of using Soviet-style coercion to enforce the Olympic boycott.[50] Carter ignored Reagan's accusations, but he tried to reassure US farmers that they would not be injured by the embargo on grain exports to the Soviet Union. He boosted the sale of corn for conversion into ethanol by increasing the amount of that biofuel that could be added to gasoline, and he increased limits on farm product storage loans.[51]

Some Iranians feared that Carter might use his need to be reelected to justify military action against Iran. Shahriar Rouhani, the young radical physicist who had been in charge of the Iranian embassy in Washington since February, was apprehensive enough about the possibility of US military action to lie shamelessly about the condition of the hostages. In an April 7 meeting with Henry Precht, the State Department director of Iranian affairs, Rouhani assured him that the hostages were well cared for and under the protection of the Iranian government. "Bullshit," Precht responded. Rouhani walked out of the meeting and complained to the press about Precht's language. But Precht's boss in the White House completely approved. Carter sent him a letter the next day saying: "One of the elements of good diplomatic language is to combine conciseness, clarity & accuracy. You have mastered this principle."[52]

Let down by some heads of state and thwarted by others, Carter was relieved on April 8 when Anwar and Jehan Sadat visited to reconfirm their commitment to peace and the principles of the Camp David Accords. When they walked into the White House, Carter said there was an "instant feeling of warmth and friendship . . . and love." At the state dinner that evening, Carter praised his friend for his historic 1977 trip to Jerusalem. Sadat toasted the Carters for their commitment to peace and friendship with Egypt. Mindful of Kennedy and Reagan's challenges to Carter's reelection, Sadat assured his US friend that he would do anything he could to help him get reelected. If it would help him win the Jewish-American vote, Sadat gave Carter complete freedom to deal with the Israelis as he thought necessary. Egypt was flourishing with the US aid package and $2 billion in revenue from oil wells that Israel had returned to the Egyptians under the terms of the peace treaty.[53]

Perhaps encouraged by Sadat's offer of support, every evening Jimmy and Rosalynn drew closer to each other as, like many other Americans, they watched the television news programs. As the bound and blindfolded hostages paraded before the cameras, they attempted to count them to make sure all were still there. Jimmy sat in angry silence, repulsed by the sight and disgusted with the reporter's reminder of how many days the United States had been "held hostage."[54]

On April 10, 1980, Carter angrily told a Washington audience of about 1,000 newspaper reporters that he was "disappointed" that the allies did not heed his call for diplomatic and economic sanctions against Iran even though he had made it clear that he was not asking them for an "oil boycott of Iran." Although most European nations, plus Greece and Japan, demanded that the Iranian students release the hostages, no one expected that the students would listen. In the afternoon new border clashes between the Iraqis and the Iranians dragged the United States deeper into the debacle. The Iranians accused the United States of encouraging the Iraqis, and the students announced that they would kill the hostages if the United States made any military move against Iran, including support of Iraqi military action.[55] Carter, who had never recognized Saddam Hussein's government in Iraq and had strongly condemned the Iraqi attacks on Iran because he thought they would worsen the plight of the US hostages, recorded in his diary that the Iranian terrorists were "making all sorts of crazy threats to kill the American hostages" if Iraq invaded Iran.[56]

Since Iranian student pilots who were training at Shepherd Air Force Base in Wichita Falls, Texas, and Columbus Air Force Base, Mississippi, technically belonged to the revolutionary government, Carter ordered them to get out of the country by midnight the next day. Departing from the Dallas-Fort Worth International Airport, thirty-eight of the pilots and their dependents from Shepherd Air Force Base complained about the short notice but said they were pleased to leave the country.[57]

A larger group of seventy-one airmen and fourteen dependents arrived at the Golden Triangle Airport, Mississippi, under tight security. Many of them had had to sell expensive sports cars at low prices, ditch their laptop computers in dumpsters on the Mississippi State University campus where they were part-time students, and bid farewell to weeping girlfriends. Each was presented with a one-way, $1,050 prepaid ticket to Tehran, courtesy of the US Air Force. Those who requested to seek asylum in the United States were allowed to stay until the State Department could consider each individual case. Most of them wanted to go home. A small number of Iranian students from Mississippi State University showed up to say goodbye to their fellow countrymen. When they became an unruly crowd, chanting "Long Live Khomeini," airport police dispersed them, and, since they had valid visas, they returned to their studies at the university.[58] Carter had sent a clear statement to Iran that he could be pushed too far.

Two days later, relaxing on the Truman Balcony, Jimmy took Rosalynn into his confidence about the top-secret rescue plan he had been developing since the day the hostages had been taken. Over the next twelve days, Rosalynn had to conduct White House functions, campaign around the country, listen to criticisms of her husband, and pretend that nothing unusual was happening as she waited for the day of rescue to arrive.[59]

TWENTY NINE

Delta Force

"OK, let's go," Carter said to the rescue plan his elite military personnel had been rehearsing for five months. All of his top military and civilian advisers were at that top-secret luncheon meeting of the NSC on April 10: Vice President Mondale, Deputy Secretary of State Warren Christopher, Defense Secretary Harold Brown, Director of Central Intelligence Stansfield Turner, National Security Adviser Zbig Brzezinski, and Joint Chiefs of Staff Chairman General David Jones. Except for Cyrus Vance, who was on vacation, to a man, they agreed that rescue was the best option, and, because of weather conditions, April 24 would be the optimum date. Carter informed the group that he had talked it over in general terms with Rosalynn, "Ham, Fritz, Jody, and Cy." All except Cy agreed with him that "our national honor is at stake." Carter feared that he might have already damaged the country by waiting too long, and he was ready to "move quickly" with the rescue option.[1] Since Cy Vance had missed the meeting, Carter reconvened the same group on April 15 with Vance present, after having given the others several days to think about it. Although Vance had been involved in planning the rescue mission, he disagreed with the decision to proceed with it. He stated his reasons: "(1) the Red Cross visit has accounted for all hostages and all of them are OK; (2) our allies are beginning to move—on April 21 they will Plan to adopt sanctions." Furthermore, Vance continued in an impassioned plea to get the others to change their minds: "There will be loss of lives (5–15 hostages); risk to other Americans and maybe Europeans; and our allies will not understand this." No one changed his mind, and Carter declared, "I will stick with the decision I made."[2]

Carter insisted that casualties be limited and that there should be no "wanton killing." Brzezinski urged him to avoid the mistake President John F. Kennedy had made at the Bay of Pigs in Cuba, namely "so limiting the military operation that its chances of success were reduced." But since the Iranians had killed nobody, Carter did not want to "kill innocent Iranians." General Jones announced that "The operation will proceed unless the

President disapproves next Thursday," April 17. Vance left the meeting and once again seriously contemplated resigning as secretary of state. Wounded by this threat, Carter privately said that he felt as if Vance had "put a knife in my back" by threatening to leave at such a risky time.[3]

On the same day Carter made his final decision to go with the rescue mission, Begin and his entourage arrived to celebrate the Camp David Accords. As stubborn as ever about unresolved details, in a long afternoon negotiating session in the Cabinet Room, Begin would not budge on anything related to Jerusalem, including giving Palestinian Arabs in East Jerusalem the right to vote. Neither would he yield on the issue of a moratorium on the Israeli settlements in the occupied West Bank of the Jordan River.[4]

At the state dinner that evening, the president and the prime minister were politely and even humorously frank about their differences, while praising one another and each other's nation fulsomely. "I have noticed," Carter joked in his toast, "that when Prime Minister Begin and I agree, we both prosper, not only in public acclaim but also politically; when we don't quite agree, neither one of us benefits substantially . . . . Lately, for instance, my own policies have caused him some trouble, as you may have noticed a month or so ago, on the West Bank of the Jordan. And I might say that our disagreement also caused me some trouble on the east bank of the Hudson River," a reference to his lack of support from Jewish Americans in New York City during the recent New York primary. More seriously, Carter said: "Now we are moving to the next step—how to carry out those detailed, complicated, very carefully negotiated agreements at Camp David; how to define the [Palestinian] self-governing authority; how to set up the procedure for the elections. They are difficult issues; we acknowledge them to be so . . . . But when he [Prime Minister Begin] and I and President Sadat have set our mind to overcoming an obstacle or answering a difficult question, so far—and I knock on wood—we have never failed. It would be a tragedy, having come this far, to fail."

Begin responded with a similar mixture of candor and humor: "Before I came here, there were rumors in the American press and also in the Israeli press, Mr. President, that pressure is going to be exerted on me and my colleagues." But, Begin continued, "we talked for hours on end . . . and no pressure was exerted and no confrontation took place." The Cabinet Room, Begin said, "became a familiar place to me . . . the same Cabinet Room in which all of us felt friendship for each other, understanding for each other. And together we looked for solutions and for formulations. . . . We shall continue negotiating until we reach the agreement which is necessary. We want it with all our heart, and we shall honor it as we do honor the Egyptian-Israeli peace treaty and all its commitments.[5]

Shortly after noon the next day, Carter and Begin went to the South Grounds of the White House for the usual laudatory farewells. Begin departed "in a spirit of faith," reaffirming his "deep friendship for the American people," and wishing "that very soon the hostages" could "come back home . . . and rejoin their families." "All men who believe in liberty," Begin said, yearned for the freedom of those captive Americans.[6]

As he and Begin exchanged farewell remarks on April 16, Carter knew that at the end of that day he would make a secret visit to the Situation Room to learn the details of how the mission would be launched. Colonel Charlie Beckwith, the founder of the elite army counterterrorist unit called Delta Force, was hanging around the Pentagon waiting for his assignment. General James Vaught, who had masterminded the rescue plan, invited him to attend a meeting of the Joint Chiefs of Staff. Surprised when he found out they were going to the White House, he joined generals David Jones, Philip Gast, and James Vaught for the ride there. Never having been in the White House before, Beckwith noted every nook and cranny he passed until he reached a small windowless room. Jody Powell, Ham Jordan, Warren Christopher, Cy Vance, Harold Brown, and Brzezinski, all informally dressed, had assembled there as if they were waiting for something important to happen. Sitting around a conference table, they waited for Vice President Mondale to arrive.

Shortly after Mondale arrived, President Carter walked in wearing a blue blazer and gray slacks, looking healthy and confident. General Jones began the meeting by explaining that he believed they had developed a sound plan for rescuing the hostages, a plan they had been working on since November. Beckwith had been collaborating with the generals to plan every detail of how Delta Force would get to Tehran, free the hostages, and bring them out of the country. When Beckwith was introduced to the group, Ham announced that he was from Schley County, Georgia, a few miles north of Plains. Carter said, "Oh! . . . we must have been neighbors."[7]

General Vaught, the joint task force commander, spoke next, outlining the plan, code named Operation Eagle Claw. Beckwith's Delta Force would first fly on three C-130 transport planes to Desert One, an isolated camp located in central Iran about three hundred air miles southeast of Tehran. Three additional transport planes would bring fuel for eight helicopters that would arrive at Desert One from the aircraft carrier *Nimitz* in the Arabian

Sea. Beckwith and his men would fly on the refueled helicopters from there to Desert Two, fifty-two miles from Tehran. A CIA agent in Tehran, masquerading as an Irish businessman, had purchased and hidden in a warehouse the vehicles that they would use to travel after dark to the embassy. Once at the embassy, the rescue team would snatch the prisoners from their captors and take them by helicopter to the abandoned Manzariyeh Airfield sixty miles southwest of Tehran, where transport planes would be waiting to fly the hostages and their saviors out of the country.[8]

Carter listened intently as Beckwith walked him through every detail of how Delta Force would accomplish the mission. The Colonel had divided his men into three sections, designated Red, White, and Blue. The first two were assault groups of forty men each; Blue was a smaller support group. Camouflaged, and under cover of night, they would hide at Desert Two until sunset the next day, when six Mercedes trucks and two smaller vehicles would transport them to the east wall of the embassy. After climbing over the wall, they would set off an explosion that would blow a hole in it large enough for an eighteen-wheel truck to pass through. The explosion would break windows and throw nearby Iranians into confusion. The assault parties would "neutralize" the guards at the three areas where the hostages were being held and quickly lead the rescued diplomats to an adjacent stadium where helicopters would be standing by to fly them to Manzariyeh where fixed-wing Air Force C-141 Starlifters would be ready to fly them out of Iran. Although all of them could fit into one helicopter and one C-141, there would be backup helicopters and planes in case they were needed. Not knowing how safe they would be for the flight back to Masirah Island, a small, sparsely inhabited island off the coast of Oman, which would be the staging site for Operation Eagle Claw, Beckwith was relieved when Carter promised them air cover until they left enemy air space.

When Carter asked about potential casualties, Beckwith replied that his men would kill the armed guards or any armed person who tried to interfere. He expected most guards would turn and run, but if anyone was so inspired by religious zealotry that he chose not to do so, Delta Force was "prepared to help him reach his maker." Trained marksmen who could hit their targets in the dark, Beckwith's men could place one bullet between the eyes, and a second one, if needed, would dispatch any armed resistance quickly.

The greater problem, according to Beckwith, would be controlling the freed hostages, for there was no way to predict how they might act in such unexpected and confusing circumstances. Some might protect their guards, and others might wrest weapons from the guards and turn on them. Delta Force would assure the hostages that they had come to rescue them and provide the hostages with yellow arm bands, so they could be readily identified during the rescue. Beckworth asked Carter if he could tell them that "The President of the United States has sent us," to reassure the confused prisoners that the invaders were US military men who were there to rescue them and not Iranians who intended to torture them even more. Carter laughed and said he doubted that would mean anything to them, and Beckwith did not bother to explain to him that the purpose of the statement was more significant than simply to flatter the president. But Carter was pleased to hear that Delta Force would not leave the stadium until all hostages were accounted for. When pressed, Beckwith predicted that a few of his men and several hostages might be wounded, but only those guards or others with weapons would be killed.

Carter ordered the mission to go forward. In the quiet atmosphere that followed, he approached Beckwith and asked him for two favors. First, he should tell his men that, if the mission failed, it would be the president's fault, not theirs. Second, should any American die in the process, Beckwith was to bring the body back, if that was possible without jeopardizing the lives of others. Carter agreed that Delta Force would enter Iran on April 24, go over the wall on April 25, and leave Iran early on the morning of April 26. He directed General Jones to keep him and Harold Brown informed about all developments. General Vaught, the task force commander, would be forward based at Qena, Egypt, from which he could report to the president through General Jones and Secretary Brown.[9]

After the meeting broke up at 10:00 p.m., Carter returned to the residence, where he slept soundly, and the next day resumed business as usual. During a nationally televised press conference that afternoon, he patiently answered questions about the economy, the NATO alliance, Middle East peace negotiations, and the responsibilities of the presidency. But Carter began the news conference by announcing several new sanctions against Iran including bans on Iranian imports to the United States and US travel to Iran, warning: "We are beyond the time for gestures. We want our people to be set free. . . . The authorities in Iran should realize . . . that other actions are available to the United States and may become necessary if the Government of Iran refuses to fulfill its solemn international responsibility." Questioned by the reporters about those "other actions," Carter said: "The only next step available that I can see would be some sort of military action."[10]

Carter's trademark toothy grin during the televised press conference seemed more noticeable than usual to his publicity manager, Jerry Rafshoon. "Mr. President," an exasperated Rafshoon wrote in a private note the next day, "you smile too damn much" and often "at the most inappropriate times." Since journalists "don't think you should have much to smile about," Rafshoon continued, your "ridiculous smiling" takes "on an aspect of insincerity, cunning, and a little deviousness." Rafshoon advised: "Smile when it is relevant and when you have something to smile about. Smile when you are interacting with real people. But think before you smile."[11] Rafshoon, however, did not know what lay behind his boss's nervous grin on that day, because the rescue plan remained a closely guarded secret.

Cyrus Vance was not only critical of the impending rescue mission, but also of Carter's new refugee policy. The Refugee Act of 1980, which Carter had signed on March 17 and had taken effect on April 1, provided a more flexible, equitable, and generous system for admitting and resettling refugees in the United States for humanitarian reasons. As required by the act, Vance appeared before the Senate Judiciary Committee on the morning of April 17 to announce that during the current year the US would admit "231,700 refugees, among them 168,000 from Indochina, 38,000 from the Soviet Union and Eastern Europe, 20,500 from Latin America, 1,500 from Africa, and 2,500 from the Middle East." Vance had disagreed with this new policy, because he thought that US diplomatic relations with the countries from whence the refugees came would create a better environment for those countries' citizens at home and lessen their need to emigrate. He knew he was fighting a losing battle, however, because the president and First Lady were compassionate and sensitive human rights advocates, which often took precedence over diplomacy and political expediency.[12]

The Carters' commitment to refugee relief was about to be challenged by the unfriendly nation close to US shores—too close in fact—where Fidel Castro had come to power in 1959. By the spring of 1980, a sagging domestic economy and lack of political freedoms were prompting increasing numbers of Cubans to seek asylum in various South American embassies in Havana. Matters came to a head on April 1 when a bus crashed into the Peruvian Embassy, and its six passengers asked for political asylum. An angry Fidel Castro announced that no one would be prohibited from entering the embassy compound, and soon some 10,000 Cubans who wanted to leave the island occupied every inch of space on the grounds and in and on the buildings. Carter intervened about a week later, noting the hunger of so many people "to escape political deprivation of freedom." At his urging, the president of Costa Rica offered an air link to help the refugees get to his country, but a Russian newspaper cynically observed that it would be shorter to go directly by boat across the Straits of Florida to Key West, a distance of only about ninety miles.

On April 14, Carter announced that the United States would accept 3,500 refugees from the Peruvian embassy. Six days later, Castro opened the flood gates by opening the port of Mariel, west of Havana, to facilitate the departure of anyone from the embassy grounds for any destination they desired, spreading the word that boats would come over from Florida to pick the refugees up. This set the stage for a massive exodus by Cubans to the United States, which would soon challenge Carter's commitment to human rights and create a logistical nightmare for federal, state, and local officials. The political fallout would cost the Carters valuable votes in their drive for reelection. Carter called Secretary of Education Shirley Hufstedler to inform her that 250,000 Cuban refugees would be landing in Florida and to ask her to find teachers to educate them during the summer months, a task she managed to accomplish.[13]

The influx of Cuban refugees caused Carter concern, but there was more ominous news from Iran. On April 18, Carter received secret intelligence that Khomeini had no intention of releasing the hostages, and he had threatened to interfere in the US election to defeat Carter.[14]

Despite Khomeini's threat, the Carters continued the day-to-day operations of the White House. Carter briefed the press, made appointments, and welcomed the King and Queen of Belgium for a state visit. He issued proclamations praising Jewish citizens and other groups on their special holidays, and he awarded the Presidential Medal of Freedom to recipients whom he and Rosalynn had chosen, including Ansel Adams, Beverly Sills, Robert Penn Warren, Eudora Welty, Tennessee Williams, the late John Wayne, Rachel Carson, and ornithologist Roger Tory Peterson. The list also included civil rights heroes Clarence Mitchell, Jr., and Archbishop Iakovos. Carter also honored Hubert Humphry, Lyndon B. Johnson, and Admiral Hyman G. Rickover.[15]

The day that Carter announced his Presidential Medal of Freedom recipients—Monday, April 21—seemed, on the surface, typical. In the morning, he had meetings with his national security and domestic policy teams. He lunched with the executive editor of the New York Times, posed for a photograph with visiting Jaycees, gave an interview to CBS News anchorman Walter Cronkite, and hosted a reception for the Mexican ambassador. After a longer meeting with Brzezinski, Secretary Brown, and General Jones, he went jogging with Rosalynn.[16]

At 6:00 p.m. that same day, Cyrus Vance met Carter in the Map Room and handed the president his letter of resignation as secretary of state. Carter had been trying to convince him not to resign, but Vance had made his decision. More regretful than angry, Vance later said, "with great sorrow, I handed him the letter. He started to put it away. I asked him to read it." Carter did so. It had been a "privilege" and an "honor," Vance wrote, to serve and be a part of such accomplishments as the Panama Canal treaties, the Camp David Accords, the normalization of relations with China, the strengthening of military forces, SALT II, and the opening of Africa to democracy. However, since he could not support the decision to try to rescue the hostages, he could not give the president the public support he needed on such an important issue. Therefore, he must resign.[17]

Carter tried to give the letter back to Vance, but he refused to take it. No matter how the rescue effort went, Vance said he would remain firm in his decision. He agreed to Carter's request not to make his resignation public until after the rescue. For the foreign policy of a nation to run smoothly, he wrote, the president and the secretary of state must work together. Vance did not mention Brzezinski or the numerous times he had felt that he had not had the level of involvement in foreign policy decisions that his office expected. He maintained that he liked Carter, was privileged to work for him, and respected him as the most intellectual of any of the several presidents he had known.[18] "I would not try to talk him out of it," Carter wrote in his diary.[19]

Meanwhile, as the Red Cross was unable to return the hostages, the operation scheduled for April 24 seemed likely. Hundreds of US troops, some of them aboard *Nimitz*, the Delta Force, secret native agents plying the streets of Tehran, and unknowing hostages waited. Much closer to home, thousands of Cubans seeking freedom made their way toward the port at Mariel. They were joined by hundreds more that Castro had released from prison, most of whom were political prisoners, though he included a few hardened criminals.[20]

Carter was well informed about Cuba, but his attention was focused on Masirah Island off the coast of Oman, where preparations for Operation Eagle Claw were underway. Delta Force had flown there from an abandoned Soviet air field in Wadi Kena, Egypt, to await departure for Desert One in

Iran. In the Arabian Sea, the USS *Nimitz*, the largest aircraft carrier in the world at that time, moved closer to the southern Iranian coast to assist in the rescue. Earlier, eight RH-53D Sea Stallion helicopters had landed on its deck and had been hidden below, an unprecedented and unannounced event for the ship's crew, who were disgruntled when they received news that their previously scheduled departure for home would be delayed for undisclosed reasons.[21]

At dusk on April 24, the first of six large MC-130 planes lifted into the air. Three were MC-130 Talons carrying the troops and three were EC-130Es carrying the fuel bladders. The first one to take off carried Colonel Beckwith and his Blue group, Colonel Jim Kyle and his Combat Control Team, and a road-watch team. The five others, carrying Beckwith's Red and Blue assault groups and fuel for the helicopters, followed an hour later, each plane taking a low, "lurching, stomach-tumbling route" to escape the Iranian radar system as they flew into the darkness. As Beckwith worried about the spies on the ground, the trucks that were to meet them at Desert Two, and whether the helicopters would perform properly, he got the good news that all fifty-two imprisoned diplomats were in the same chancery building. More good news reached him when he heard that all eight of the helicopters had lifted off the *Nimitz* and were headed for Desert One.[22]

Carter arrived in the Oval Office at 6:00 a.m., a few hours before Operation Eagle Claw was launched on the far side of the globe. He spent much of the morning and afternoon discussing domestic economic issues and his presidential campaign with various advisors, aides, members of Congress, and special interest groups. In mid-afternoon, Carter talked on the telephone with General Jones for about ten minutes, likely to get an early update about the rescue mission. Then, in late afternoon as more news began coming in from Desert One, Carter met with members of the NSC—Mondale, Brzezinski, Vance, Brown, and Warren Christopher—plus Ham Jordan, Jody Powell, and Lloyd Cutler. Carter continued meeting with that group off and on until shortly after midnight. He also stayed in close contact by phone with General Jones and with Rosalynn, who had been campaigning in Detroit and was on her way to Austin, Texas.[23]

As the evening wore on, the news about the rescue mission grew steadily worse. When the first C-130, carrying Beckwith and his advance party landed at Desert One, they encountered the last thing that they expected to see on an isolated desert road in the middle of the night: a busload of more than forty Iranians apparently on a religious pilgrimage. The Americans stopped the bus, told its occupants that they would not be harmed, and ordered them to lie down on the ground. The question of what to do with them was relayed by satellite back to the White House, where Carter said that they should be flown out on one of the C-130s and returned home after the mission was over. A second security problem occurred when the Americans spotted a fuel truck on the road followed by a pickup truck. Unable to stop either vehicle, one of the US soldiers fired an anti-tank weapon at the fuel truck, which exploded in an enormous ball of fire, lighting up the entire area. The pickup escaped.[24]

Setting aside their fears that the pickup driver might alert Iranian authorities about their presence, Beckwith and his men proceeded with their mission. The remaining C-130s soon arrived, but the helicopters were delayed. Unexpectedly, the Sea Stallions had flown into a *haboob*, a massive cloud of suspended dust that had nearly blinded the pilots for an extended period of time, disorienting them and slowing their progress. Only six of the eight helicopters made it to the Desert One rendezvous. One had been abandoned early in their flight, because of a badly cracked rotor blade, and failing electronic equipment had forced another to return to the *Nimitz*.[25]

The six remaining Sea Stallions was the minimum number needed for the operation. Beckwith wanted to load his men and get to Desert Two before daylight. He was stunned to learn that a hydraulic pump on one of the helicopters was broken and could not be repaired at Desert One. That bad news was relayed to Brzezinski and, through him, to Carter. Carter left the decision of whether to proceed or abort the mission to Beckwith. Unprepared to proceed with only five choppers, Beckwith asked Carter for permission to abort the mission, evacuate the camp, and try again another day. Carter granted it, and Beckwith prepared to evacuate.[26]

At the White House, Brzezinski broke the news to the president, whom he found standing in a corridor. "Damn, damn," Carter mumbled. He then called the whole group of advisors into the Oval Office and explained why Operation Eagle Claw had been aborted. "At least," Carter said, "there were no American casualties and no innocent Iranians hurt."[27]

At Desert One, however, a terrible tragedy was about to happen. As men and equipment were being hastily loaded on the C-130s and the helicopters in the dark, the swirling dust kicked up by the props and rotors caused one helicopter to collide with a C-130 transport plane, setting both aflame and leaving eight servicemen dead in the wreckage. Five more suffered injuries. With their cover blown, the men of Delta Force would not get the opportunity to try again. Back at the staging camp in Egypt, Beckwith ranted and raved, called the Marine helicopter pilots "cowards," and bemoaned how the failure would reflect so badly on both him and the president. When Carter learned of the deaths, he turned ashen, but quickly regained composure and proceeded with preparing to console the families of the dead servicemen.[28]

In the middle of the night, official cars began to arrive at the White House. CIA Director Stansfield Turner urged Carter not to announce the disaster until he was certain that his CIA team in Iran was safe. Tears streamed down Jody's face, and Jimmy called Rosalynn in Austin and asked her to come home. She arrived early the next morning and joined him in the Cabinet Room where he briefed his staff and answered questions. Miss Lillian, who was in Egypt, canceled a press conference and exclaimed, "My poor Jimmy, my poor Jimmy, my poor Jimmy." Henry Kissinger, George H. W. Bush, Howard Baker, and former presidents Richard Nixon and Gerald Ford all quickly gave their support. Kennedy evaded comment on Carter but said that the people were united in their determination to have their diplomats freed. Some Congressmen who had not known about the plan, grumbled about their dislike for the president. The next days, Rosalynn said, were "grim," "like the night my father died."[29]

At 7:00 a.m. the president addressed the nation from the Oval Office: "I ordered this rescue mission prepared in order to safeguard American lives, to protect America's national interests, and to reduce the tensions in the world that have been caused among many nations as this crisis has continued. It was my decision to attempt the rescue operation." He claimed no hostility toward Iran, explained the equipment failure, and expressed admiration for the courage of those who had died or were injured, telling their families of "the sorrow that I feel personally for their sacrifice." He would continue to hold the government of Iran responsible for the safety and release of the hostages, and he promised that he would not give up. He would call upon other nations to seek a resolution of the crisis through diplomatic and peaceful means.[30]

Later that day, Carter met with the Senate and House leadership to brief them about what had happened. Most of them were supportive of the president, although, Carter noted in his diary, "a couple had been acting like asses beforehand: Frank Church the worst, and Scoop Jackson second."[31]

Jimmy and Rosalynn began to call the anxious families of the hostages twice a week, and Congress considered providing aid to the families. No one knew what was happening to the hostages in Iran, but former prisoner Barry Rosen later said they were put in vans, "as if we were pieces of meat," and distributed all over the country. Not until two months later did Rosen learn what had happened in April, from a newspaper he found on the ground. He could read Farsi well enough to realize that Carter had attempted a mission, which he felt good about, but he felt bad that eight men had died.[32]

The confused hostages did not know what was happening with their families in the United States. Sometimes letters, gifts, and visits did get through to them, but they mostly wondered if they would ever see their loved ones again. Scattered around Iran in groups of two or three, the hostages also knew nothing about the fate of their comrades. Sometimes they had good food and adequate sanitation, but nothing was certain. Usually they were left alone. They gave their guards nicknames like "Santa Claus," "Chief Guard," "Four Eyes," and "Hamid the Liar," but rarely did they bond with them as sometimes happens in hostage situations.[33]

With the majority of the hostages dispersed, the chancery seemed like a tomb to the five who remained there. Two women, Katherine Koob and Elizabeth Ann Swift, were carefully separated from the three men, but they were allowed to pass notes back and forth. The men were sixty-six-year old Robert Ode, seriously ill Richard Queen, and an army medic. Referring to themselves as the "Men in the Back Room", they passed notes to "Les Girls." After the Iranians allowed the women to cook, this small group found themselves treated to delicious meals. They had a great view of the mountains, and they passed the time playing Scrabble. Don Hohman, the medic, joked that his patient Richard Queen was superb at the game, but it was easy to catch up with him because, despite having a master's degree in history, "he couldn't spell worth a shit."[34]

The day after the fiery disaster at Desert One, Carter wrote personal letters to the families of each of the eight men who had died there, extending the nation's sympathy. Two were single men who left behind parents; the others were married and left widows. Carter referred to each by name: "Harold, who bravely undertook a humanitarian mission for our country . . . Rosalynn joins me in assuring you of our prayers for your strength at this difficult time." Iran promised to return the US dead to the United States, but before doing so, the Revolutionary Guards, "in a macabre spectacle directed by the Iranian ayatollah, . . . put the Americans' remains on display at the U.S. Embassy in Tehran."[35] Gloating over the failure of Operation Eagle Claw, the jubilant Iranians enjoyed reading the many news articles detailing the mishaps that had doomed the US rescue effort. They accused Carter of being willing to commit any crime to get reelected.[36]

With negative publicity raining down on him, Carter went to church on Sunday morning and that afternoon flew secretly to meet the Delta Force team at Camp Smokey, their secure training site in rural North Carolina. When he and Beckwith met, the two men embraced and wept. "Mr. President, I'm sorry we let you down," Beckwith said. Jimmy noted afterward in his diary that he had "an inspirational and thrilling meeting with the rescue team." Each team member struggled to maintain his composure as he shook the president's hand and apologized for not being able to complete the mission. Carter told them that he appreciated what they had done for their country, and, taking the blame upon himself, confessed to Beckwith: "I have been remiss for not knowing more about Delta Force."[37]

Brzezinski accompanied Carter to Camp Smokey, wearing green rubber boots. Mystified, one of the soldiers who knew Polish asked Zbig why the boots. He responded that when the president called and told him they were going to "The Farm," he thought it was a real farm, not a code name for the secret CIA camp.[38]

During the flight back to Washington, Carter told Harold Brown and Brzezinski about Vance's resignation and asked them to suggest a possible replacement. Both men agreed with Carter that Edmund Muskie was the man for the job. Deputy Secretary Warren Christopher expected to get the appointment, but, when he did not, he agreed to stay and serve the president and Muskie.[39]

On April 28, Cyrus Vance held a State Department press conference to announce his resignation. "I have the greatest admiration for the President," he said, "and I am most grateful for the opportunity which he has given me to serve him and our nation."[40] Many journalists, however, speculated that Vance's action was a sign of deep trouble and confusion within the Carter administration. "The resignation," the *Washington Post* wrote, "is a stunning embarrassment to Mr. Carter and deprives him of a trusted counselor in the middle of his most difficult passage. One wonders at the least why Mr. Vance could not have found another time to leave."[41] At a White House press conference later that day, Jody Powell "denied that Vance had lost a power struggle pitting his advocacy of moderate diplomacy in dealing with the Iran crisis against the tougher line allegedly backed by Brzezinski, the other architect of administration foreign policy. 'It was an honorable difference over principles,' Powell said about Carter and Vance. 'Both men regret it, but the decision was unavoidable.' "[42]

Vance's unhappiness with his position in the administration had been building long before the rescue episode. He had frequently complained that the National Security Advisor usurped powers that rightly belonged to the State Department. He had suffered a major humiliation in March 1979 by taking responsibility for the UN vote involving the word Jerusalem, even though he was entirely innocent.[43] He had disliked Carter's support of Andrew Young and Billy Carter. A man of integrity and honor, he had tried valiantly to give to the president the loyalty Carter demanded from all who served him. Meanwhile, Carter was unhappy that the State Department sometimes acted as if it were independent of the presidency. Brzezinski claimed that differences between himself and Vance were exaggerated, but Vance and the media did not see it that way.[44] Vance's disagreement with the rescue plan gave him the opportunity to do what he had thought he should have done much earlier.

Shortly before Vance made his resignation public, Carter posed for a photograph with him in the Oval Office. He presented Vance a handwritten note, thanking him for his "dedicated and effective service," and "notable accomplishments." "Because you could not support my decision regarding the rescue in Iran," Carter wrote, "you have made the correct decision to resign." Declaring his respect for the secretary's reasons for resigning, Carter continued to thank him for his "close friendship" and being "a source of strength and reassurance to me." Looking forward to Vance's "continuing advice and counsel," he signed it, "Your friend, Jimmy Carter."[45]

Prior to his morning meeting with Vance, Carter had already called Senator Edmund Muskie of Maine, who was eager to become Vance's successor, and arranged to meet with him in the Oval Office that evening.[46] Despite his relative lack of experience in foreign affairs, Muskie was a popular senator who would easily be confirmed by his colleagues. Unlike Vance, he was aggressive and outspoken. Brzezinski was not likely to surrender any of his turf to the new secretary, and they quickly became rivals. But their disagreements tended to be muted by the overwhelming problem with Iran.[47]

Between the early morning meeting with his outgoing secretary of state and his evening meeting with Muskie, Carter took a quick round trip to San Antonio, Texas, to thank and comfort the five men who had been injured in Iran and their families.[48] When Carter departed from the White House, the weather was too poor for the usual helicopter flight to Andrews Air Force Base. Instead, the commander in chief traveled by presidential limousine, US flags flying from the front fenders, and under heavy guard, through the dreary streets of the capital to visit his fallen warriors. Top military officials met Carter and took him to Wilford Hall Medical Center at Lackland Air Force Base, where he visited Airman First Class William Tootle, recoving from a broken leg, and members of his family. From there, Carter went to the burn ward at Brooks Army Medical Center at Fort Sam Houston, where the four burn victims were being treated. Accompanied by Defense Secretary Harold Brown and Congressman James Wright of Texas, the president donned a surgical gown and spoke individually with Army Staff Sergeant Joseph J. Beyers III, Air Force Lieutenant Jeffrey B. Harrison, Marine Major James H. Schaefer, Jr., Marine Major Leslie B. Petty, and their immediate families. Carter gave each of the men an autographed copy of the Bible and told them "we are praying for you. God bless you." In an interview with a journalist, Congressman James Wright declared that he thought it was "a mark of greatness that the Commander in Chief himself would want to go and see them personally." Such a gesture, he added, was "characteristic of Jimmy Carter's entire activities since he's been President."[49]

The next day, at a televised press conference, Carter praised the men who had participated in Operation Eagle Claw. "In troubled times America has strong men to help guide her," he said. "I believe no other country could have contemplated such a mission. But there can be a deeper failure than the failure to succeed—and that is the failure to try. Had we not made the attempt, we could never have forgiven ourselves."[50]

When Carter returned to the White House after visiting the wounded soldiers in San Antonio, Senator Muskie was waiting to accept the appointment as secretary of state. Carter promised to ask the Senate to approve him quickly. He finished the long day by hosting an economic briefing and buffet dinner for Democratic members of Congress.[51]

The next afternoon, April 29, Carter discussed his appointment of Muskie with members of the House and Senate Committees on Foreign Relations before announcing it at a televised press conference. Until Muskie was confirmed by the Senate, he explained, Warren Christopher would be acting secretary and then would continue as deputy secretary. Most senators and cabinet members approved of Carter's choice of Muskie. Democratic Senator Joe Biden of Delaware praised the appointment, and Republican Senator Barry Goldwater of Arizona declared it to be a "hell of a good choice." When asked why he did not give the post to Brzezinski, Carter quickly replied that he needed him in the White House, and he wanted to appoint someone who would be easily confirmed by the Senate. Furthermore, Muskie had been one of Carter's staunchest supporters in the Senate and had no record of hostility with the National Security Advisor. He was prepared to advise the president on foreign policy and to defend Carter's decisions.[52]

Far away in the Arabian Sea, the *Nimitz*, with the surviving helicopter, Bluebeard-5, on board—the one that had turned back because of electronic equipment problems—began her long journey home to Norfolk, Virginia. Accompanied by two other carriers that had been available for backup help if needed and now served as potential convoy decoys, they made their way across the Atlantic Ocean to their home port. When the *Nimitz* arrived there on May 26, the disappointed and tired sailors were eager to go ashore. Then an announcement came that they were to don dress uniforms and go to the flight deck where a VIP would greet them. As the unhappy sailors stood there, President and Mrs. Carter appeared. Carter expressed his pride and gratitude for their performance during their long and arduous cruise. "Our Nation stands for freedom. Our Nation stands for human rights. Our Nation stands for democracy. Our Nation stands for peace," he told them in a speech that most of them must have thought lasted too long. He promised additional compensation for their service to the country and to the captive Americans, and he thanked them again for being a part of the "strong military" that the country must have if it were to preserve peace and freedom.

The stunned crew witnessed an emotional greeting between the president and their captain. Some of them wondered why the president thanked them because they did not get the job done. Nevertheless, after addressing them, Carter spoke to the families waiting for their loved ones to disembark from the *Nimitz*, as well as those aboard USS *Texas* and *California*, which were not very far away. "It's hard for me this afternoon to express adequately my appreciation to the men on those three ships. . . . Like your hearts, my heart was with them when they were on duty protecting the interests of our Nation."[53]

The rescue failure, the beginning of the Mariel boat lift, the continuing Soviet military presence in Afghanistan, and the unrelenting Kennedy political challenge at home might have derailed a man less strong and courageous. Carter fell back on his faith, his wife and family, and his father's admonition never to quit but to find a way around any obstacle in his path. Those close to him, and many members of Congress, marveled at how steady he remained during the crisis that might end his presidency.

THIRTY

Keeping the Faith

"Good Morning, Mr. President," the Reverend Nelson L. Price wrote Jimmy on the first day of the month following the rescue failure. "THANKS for being faithful on behalf of our hostages." The Baptist minister, whose Marietta, Georgia, church, the Carters had often attended when Jimmy was governor, continued to console the president: "Even in this, ALL things work together for good to those who love the Lord. . . . Keep up the good work!" Touched by his friend's encouragement, Carter replied: "Your good words & prayers always come at the right time."[1] Carter loved the Lord, but he was also mired in the global demands of his office and encumbered by the fickle mistress of domestic politics. He empathized with the farmers who were going through a tough time, and he felt the pain of the hostages and of those who had tried to rescue them, but he had to deal with pressing political challenges. Hoping to persuade Kennedy to drop out of the race, Carter offered him the opportunity to have input with the Democratic National Convention's platform committee. Kennedy still declined to end his campaign for the Democratic nomination. One poll showed that 40% of the Democratic Party would never vote for Kennedy. Carter thought that "personal animosity influenced Kennedy's actions."[2] Rosalynn, distraught by Kennedy's refusal to give up, reminded an audience in Kennedy's home state, "My husband is the President of Massachusetts too." What she said in private to Jimmy mercifully escaped the written record, but an aide who overheard their conversation reported that "The leader of the free world took quite a chewing-out from his wife last night." Another aide remembered that when Jimmy called her to find out how things were going on the campaign trail, she responded that it was really rough how people were beating up on him. When Jimmy said he didn't want to hear that, she told him, "you can just go to hell," and hung up.[3]

Rosalynn was equally frustrated by the speed at which Jimmy was operating in getting the hostages freed. She urged him to mine Iran's harbors and take any other serious military action that might be needed to bring them home.[4] Jimmy appeased her with good news from Brzezinski on May 2 that

Algeria was loosening its ties with the Soviet Union. Since the United States had agreed to sell the Algerians L-100 convertible cargo/passenger aircraft, they were taking a "quietly constructive approach to the Iran crisis."[5] Carter hoped Algeria would help him end the hostage crisis.

The death, on May 4, of Marshall Josip Broz Tito, the pragmatic Communist dictator of Yugoslavia for the past thirty-five years, gave Carter a convenient chance to cultivate better relations with the nonaligned bloc of nations, of which Tito had been a principal founder. Although remaining a Communist, Tito had kept Yugoslavia strongly united and independent from the Soviet Union. His state visit to Washington in March 1978 had apparently strengthened the United States in its Cold War competition with the Soviets. Calling Tito "a towering figure on the world stage," Carter promised that the United States would continue "to support the independence, territorial integrity and unity of Yugoslavia." The next day, Carter announced that his mother, the vice president, and the secretary of state would lead the US funeral delegation.[6]

The Yugoslavs were disappointed that Carter, unlike many other world leaders, did not go to Belgrade for Tito's funeral on May 8.[7] Carter thought it was more important to remain at home to honor the hostages who remained in captivity. At the time of Tito's funeral, Carter was leading the United States in an official three-day mourning period for the US servicemen who had died in the line of duty. He left the White House for the short trip across the Potomac River to Arlington National Cemetery to lead a memorial service for the US heroes whose mangled bodies the Iranians had returned. On May 9, when Jimmy and Rosalynn approached the small room where they were to wait for the service to begin, Carter felt anxious that their families might blame him for having sent their loved ones into harm's way. His anxieties were quickly dispelled, however, when the parents, wives, and small children hugged him. Speaking at the cemetery's amphitheater, Carter expressed his and the nation's sympathy and gratitude to the families of the fallen. "Every American," he concluded, "shares your rightful price in the valor & dedication to duty of those who died in the dark desert night. Of such men as yours was our beloved country made, and of them is our beloved country preserved in freedom."[8] Later, he wrote in his diary that the families "were more solicitous about my feelings than about their own sorrow."[9]

The public did not show Carter much sympathy, however, for the way he handled the refugee crisis in South Florida. In addition to the 25,000 Haitians who had already made it to the United States to escape poverty and repression during the past decade, many thousands of Cubans risked their lives in what became known as the Mariel boat lift from mid-April through October 1980; about two thirds of the nearly 125,000 refugees landed in Miami and Key West. A smaller continuing flow of Haitian boat people also looked to the president of the United States for help. After his adviser for Latin American affairs, Robert Pastor, told him that attempting to stop the refugees at sea would result in many deaths, Carter decided to help them.[10]

The scenes on both sides of the Florida Straits were filled with chaos, hope, and fear. Cuban-Americans flocked to Key West and paid cash to small boat captains to go pick up their family members at Mariel Harbor in Cuba and bring them to the United States. Many of the hundreds of vessels were not safe, and twenty-five people died when one sank. In Cuba, most of the refugees fled their homes voluntarily or left from the Peruvian embassy where they had been camped. Others, whom Castro wanted out of his country, were awakened by policemen knocking on their doors and telling them to leave immediately, taking only those possessions they could carry. At Mariel they slept on cots or on the ground, awaiting the boats. Some cried because they did not want to go, and all of them were sometimes pelted with eggs and tomatoes by angry mobs who supported Castro. Within a month Carter, began trying to negotiate with Castro to stop the flow, but not until late October did the Cuban dictator agree to end the chaotic boatlift. By then the political damage that had been done to Carter in Florida and elsewhere in the United States where the Cubans were not welcome could not be reversed.[11]

Carter established a processing center in the Truman Annex at the Key West Naval Air Station. More than half of the arrivals were young males who had little hope of succeeding under Castro's regime; 30% had served prison sentences mostly for political reasons or petty crimes; only about 2% were considered serious criminals. Most were ordinary Cubans who found jobs, finished school, and blended into US society. But the city of Miami would never again be the same.

Those refugees considered dangerous, as well as many others, were sent to military bases in Indiantown Gap, Pennsylvania, Fort Chaffee, Arkansas, Fort McCoy, Wisconsin, Pensacola, Florida, and Puerto Rico. Some went to the federal penitentiary in Atlanta. Many of them were eventually deported, but a group of about 300 escaped from Fort Chaffee, pelted officers with rocks, and had to be subdued by federal troops. Arkansas Governor Bill Clinton, although not responsible, was blamed for the incident and failed to get reelected. Carter directed the Justice Department to expel those refugees who had committed serious crimes in Cuba.[12]

As the Cubans poured into the country, the president dealt with changes in his cabinet, most importantly the new secretary of state. At the swearing in ceremony for Edmund Muskie at the White House on May 8, the day of Tito's funeral, Carter summarized the United States' current foreign policy challenges and then reminded the group that "this is a nation of immigrants . . . a nation of refugees . . . a nation that prevails, that triumphs . . . a nation that has been able to meet every test . . . through unity and the courage of our people." His comments were almost the opposite of what he had said in his infamous "malaise" speech almost a year earlier. "As much as anyone I know," Carter continued, "this national character of which we are all so proud is personified by Ed Muskie, . . . a patriot who is committed to the preservation of our Nation's strength and the enhancement of peace throughout the world." Carter, who believed in the power of couples, gave Muskie, Deputy Secretary Warren Christopher, and their wives time together at Camp David to get better acquainted and plan the organization of the department.[13]

In the following days, Muskie supported Carter's policies in two controversial areas. He denounced the French for attending the Olympic Games that the United States had committed to boycott. He also reported to Carter that the Australian government supported the boycott, but the Italian, Irish, Austrian, and Icelandic teams would go to Moscow. And, on May 20, Muskie directed US Ambassador to the UN, Donald McHenry, to abstain from voting on a UN Security Council resolution calling for Israel to allow deported West Bank officials to return, a political maneuver that allowed the resolution to pass unanimously. The Israelis were greatly displeased, as were many Jewish-American voters.[14]

Counting potential votes, Rosalynn traveled extensively in May, proclaiming the Carter campaign message at numerous venues around the country. At Morehouse College, the alma mater of Martin Luther King, Jr., in Atlanta on May 11, she reminded her audience that her husband was a strong promoter of Black colleges. Even in this "bittersweet time," Rosalynn said, "the president of the United States has dreams of racial equality and justice for the country, and because of the influence of Morehouse, his dreams can come true."[15]

The Carters were less comfortable with Senator Robert Byrd, whom Jimmy thought used his Saturday press conference on May 17 to stab him in the back by making pro-Kennedy statements. Carter swallowed his pride and made every effort to stay in the majority leader's good graces. Rosalynn countered Byrd, telling a crowd in Maryland that Carter needed a second term to complete his work. An extraordinarily effective campaigner, she helped her husband win all of the May primaries, except in the District of Columbia. Carter also came out on top in the Colorado caucus, giving him a total of 1,664 of the 1,666 delegates he needed to secure the Democratic nomination.[16]

The opposition did not go away, however. Hate mail from Jewish-American voters, accusing Carter of being anti-Semitic, piled up in Jordan's office. Referring to a statement that Ham had made about breaking the back of the Israeli lobby in Washington, one correspondent threatened that "the broken Israeli lobby" would send him and his boss back to Plains.[17] More dangerous than Jewish discontent with Carter was a serious financial recession that gripped the country. Stuart Eizenstat warned Carter that no president had ever been reelected during a serious recession that he was blamed for causing.

The economy took another blow when Mount St. Helens erupted in Washington State on May 18. At least fifty-seven people were killed, and thick clouds of light gray ash spread across a wide area, reducing visibility to zero and blanketing highways, fields, and buildings. Carter quickly went to Washington to survey the damage. At a press conference in Portland, Oregon, he announced that FEMA, which he had created, would be primarily responsible for coordinating the rescue and reconstruction effort. He praised the local people and government agencies for having responded in such a way as to minimize deaths, noting that the death rate was higher than it should have been because "curious tourists" would not obey the rules. The explosion, he said, was a natural disaster more deadly than he believed had ever happened before in the nation's recorded history. It was the "equivalent of 10 megatons of nuclear bombs or 10 million tons of TNT that swept across [the land] . . . 12, 15 miles away." The result of such a massive volcanic explosion, he said, was "almost indescribable." In addition to what FEMA would do, he promised that the federal government would help the people who were affected by the eruption.[18]

A week later, on May 29, because his contest with Kennedy had reached a white heat, Carter emerged from the Rose Garden to campaign in Ohio. A few days later, on June 3, his and Rosalynn's hard work paid off: he won the Democratic nomination.[19] Shortly after nine o'clock that evening, they walked from the White House to the nearby "The Buck Stops Here" restaurant to celebrate with a large group of campaign workers. "I have one deep feeling in my heart," Carter told the crowd, of "thanksgiving to all of you who turned what 8 months ago was a prediction of absolute defeat into a wondrous victory tonight." Carter attributed his victory to "two secret weapons: one is all of you out there who worked so hard, and the other one is my wife." But, Carter promised, "I intend to be very active as a campaigner in the fall. And I look forward to meeting the Republican nominee—I presume it will be Governor Reagan—both on the campaign trail and in intense, head-on-head debates to let the American people choose whom they want."[20]

Although Carter had gained more than enough delegates to win the nomination at the convention in August, Kennedy would not concede. "We are determined," the senator told his supporters, "to move on to victory at the convention and in November." Kennedy believed that his five victories on June 3rd gave him an unstoppable political momentum and that his stands on the issues, his eloquence, and his family name would enable him to best the president in debate and grab some of Carter's delegates in an open convention. More concerned about party unity, Speaker O'Neill wanted Carter to give Kennedy a dignified way out by meeting the senator and compromising with him on most platform issues. Kennedy at first declined Carter's invitation for a meeting, then reconsidered, and agreed to meet him at the White House. For fifty minutes on the afternoon of June 5, the two men talked in the Oval Office with no one else present.[21]

At a press briefing half an hour later, Carter told reporters that he had not asked Kennedy to drop out of the race but had "congratulated him on a very forceful campaign." Carter wanted the two of them "to address their differences "through the platform process," but Kennedy continued to demand a public debate and an open convention that would allow delegates to make the final decisions about the party platform and the party's nominee.[22] In his diary, Carter wrote that he felt sorry for the senator, because it was the first time "the Kennedys had been rebuffed by the electorate or by anyone else."[23]

In the meantime, as the warring Democrats remained hopelessly fractured, Ronald Reagan chalked up landslide wins in Republican primaries across the country. Confident that he would defeat Reagan, Carter promised an increase in military pay and pushed for legislation to reinstate the draft. After Congress passed the necessary legislation to reinstate the draft for males only between the ages of 18 and 26, Carter signed a proclamation on July 2 announcing it to the country.[24] Still annoyed by the fact that Kennedy had not dropped out of the race, and concerned about how Reagan might pitch for the Jewish vote, Carter again met with Jewish editors to reaffirm his commitment to Israel, promise to veto any initiative that would alter UN Resolution 242, and explain his concern for Jewish people who were being persecuted in Iran and the Soviet Union. He would not negotiate with the PLO or recognize their status, he said, unless they recognized Israel's right to exist.[25]

To get the help he needed to be reelected, Carter appointed Jack Watson as chief of staff, thus freeing Hamilton Jordan to work as deputy campaign chairman with Bob Strauss.[26] On separate occasions, he and Rosalynn hosted Democratic Party state chairmen and members of the Democratic national platform committee. They attended a private reception to thank members of Congress who had endorsed Carter's reelection, and on another night they appeared at a national ERA rally and dinner at a Washington shopping mall. They also hosted a "Salute to Congress" picnic and dance on the South Lawn. Carter enthusiastically wrote in his diary that that party was one of their "finest" "with food from different regions of the country and different bands and choirs singing."[27]

Continuing stories about Billy and Libya threatened the campaign. When the attorney general advised Carter on June 17 that Billy had registered as an agent for Libya, Carter was surprised to learn that his brother had taken a $220,000 payment from the Libyans to help market their crude oil. He instructed the White House Staff to cooperate fully with the Special Subcommittee of the Senate Judiciary Committee in its investigation of Billy, and he planned a news conference before the Democratic convention to explain Billy's story to the public. The Justice Department's investigations concluded that no members of the administration had engaged in any illegal activity, but Carter still found it difficult to convince the public that he had not known about Billy's dealings with Libya.[28]

Hoping to refute the negatives, Carter made a whirlwind campaign tour around the country in June. On June 1, he went to Fort Wayne, Indiana, to visit National Urban League president Vernon Jordan, who was recovering in a hospital after having been shot by a White racist two days earlier. Four days later, Carter flew to Baltimore to speak at the White House Conference on Families, and on June 9, he went to Miami to address the annual convention of the Opportunities Industrialization Centers, a nonprofit adult education and job training organization. Carter also met with Black, Cuban, and White community and business leaders to discuss Miami's recent racial justice riots before flying to Seattle to address the annual conference of US mayors. On his flight back to Washington, he stopped in Nebraska to inspect extensive tornado damage in the city of Grand Island.[29]

On June 19, Carter, joined by Rosalynn and Amy, set off on his first international trip in almost a year, to attend the G7 Economic Summit in Venice with the leaders of Britain, Germany, France, Italy, Canada, and Japan. The eight-day journey would include Rome, Belgrade, Madrid, and Lisbon for more diplomatic talks and some tourism. Their traveling party included Ed Muskie and his wife Jane, Brzezinski, and Jody Powell as well as various staff members. Carter was on a mission to prove that, despite the failed rescue effort and the domestic political conflict, the United States still stood strong and proud and determined to defend the free world from Soviet aggression.

In Rome, after resting overnight, Carter met with President Alessandro Pertini and Prime Minister Francesco Cossiga and laid a wreath at Italy's Tomb of the Unknown Soldier. Later in the afternoon he, Rosalynn, and Amy toured the Coliseum and the Roman Forum. That evening, Carter exchanged toasts with President Pertini at a state dinner. "I do not accept forecasts of weakness or failure for democracy in the world," he said. "Our societies, our values, our freedoms will decline only if we allow them to do so." He reminded his hosts how well the members of NATO had stood strong against Soviet aggression. "Our faith in human rights—the freedom, the dignity, and the value of every individual—is the most compelling revolutionary concept of our times," he declared.[30]

Early the next morning, June 21, Carter laid a wreath at a memorial for former Italian prime minister Aldo Moro, who had been kidnapped and murdered in 1976 by the far-left terrorist organization known as the Red Brigades. He addressed about 700 members of the diplomatic staff at the US embassy before flying to Vatican City, where he, Rosalynn, and Amy, along with the Muskies, Brzezinski, and other members of the presidential party met Pope John Paul II in his "book-lined study overlooking S. Peter's Square." The *Washington Post* correspondent reported that the Pope shook hands with the president, spoke with him privately, and then exchanged gifts. "The Pope gave the President a leather-bound, illustrated 15th century Bible, remarking, 'it's to read.'" When he opened the Bible and noted that the text was in Latin, he remarked to the Pope, "'It would be easier for you than me.'" In his talk with the Pope, Carter claimed that reconciliation among disputing nations was possible if they would heed "a universal moral and political imperative that the protection of the human rights of each person is the premise and purpose of governments."[31]

From the papal study, the Carters and their party accompanied the Pope to the Clementine Room, where they participated in a ceremony on the occasion of the beatification of Kateri Tekakwitha, a young Mohawk woman who died in 1680. Afterward they toured the famous Vatican Museum, the Sistine and Pauline chapels, and St. Peter's basilica. "The presidential visit to the splendors of the Vatican," according to the *Washington Post* correspondent, provided Carter with "a perfect election year setting" to garner US Catholic votes.[32] It also gave him the chance to ask the Pope personally to pray for the hostages.

Late that afternoon the Carters arrived in Venice for the economic summit. An Italian navy boat carried them from the airport across the lagoon to the luxurious Cipriani Hotel. Soon arrival, Carter, Muskie, and Brzezinski, had a hour-and-a-half preconference meeting with German chancellor Helmut Schmidt. Carter and Schmidt had a difficult exchange about a moratorium on the deployment of certain nuclear weapons in Western Europe. They resolved their difficulty with Schmidt's promise to take a firm message to the Soviets regarding Afghanistan and nuclear weapons if Carter would make a public statement to the press that he had confidence in the belligerent German. Carter did so, but privately he noted that Schmidt was "a strange man" who made a good leader for Germany despite being "constantly critical of the United States."[33]

On their first night in Venice, the Carters enjoyed a boat tour of the city's famous canals, and early on Sunday, they took the boat to the Sant'Eufemia Roman Catholic Church to attend the morning worship service before Jimmy began a long day of meetings. The setting for the G7 talks was the Cini Foundation located in a former monastery on the picturesque Island of San Giorgio Maggiore. There he joined his peers: Chancellor Schmidt, President Valery Giscard d'Estaing, Prime Ministers Francesco Cossiga, Margaret Thatcher, and Pierre Trudeau, and Japanese Foreign Minister Saburo Okita acting in place of Prime Minister Masayoshi Ohira, who had died suddenly ten days earlier. After the day's meetings, Carter talked separately with French president Giscard d'Estaing for an hour. Dinner that night was at Doge's Palace on historic St. Mark's Square.[34]

On June 23, Carter began the day by eating breakfast with twelve Benedictine monks at Giorgio Maggiore. Afterward he had separate meetings with Pierre Trudeau and Margaret Thatcher before participating in the conference's last formal session and a final working lunch with all seven leaders. He urged the other leaders to support the United States on freeing the Iranian hostages, condemning the Soviet invasion of Afghanistan, and recognizing the need for all of them to work together. Despite widespread disagreement in their discussions, they emerged from the summit with public statements of unanimity.[35]

Early on the morning of June 24, the Carters flew to Belgrade, where they were greeted by Cvijetin Mijatovic, president of Yugoslavia's new eight-man presidency that governed "a country made up of six nationalities and a dozen or so smaller minorities." Carter, knowing he needed to make amends for his absence from Tito's funeral several weeks earlier, joined Rosalynn and Amy in a visit to the former president's tomb, where they placed a bouquet of roses and observed a moment of silence. Shortly thereafter, Carter met for two hours with Yugoslavian officials at the Palace of the Federation. They discussed international issues such as Afghanistan, Iran, and the Middle East, but mostly they talked about Yugoslavia's ongoing leadership transition and the country's serious economic problems.[36]

In his toast at the state dinner that evening, Carter paid fulsome tribute to Tito and voiced strong support for the still fragile new Yugoslavian government and its continued independent, nonaligned role in world affairs. He praised "Yugoslavia's concept of nonalignment [as] . . . a bold, creative, imaginative approach to the problems of the world, particularly the problems of the developing nations." He welcomed Yugoslavia's wish "to strengthen this bilateral relationship" with the United States "on the basis of independence, equality, and mutual respect."[37]

After breakfast the next morning, June 25, he, Rosalynn, and Amy flew to Madrid. King Juan Carlos, who had played a key role in Spain's recent democratic development, and his wife, Queen Sophia, greeted them at the airport and hosted a formal luncheon for them in the Royal Palace. At a state diner, the king and the president exchanged lengthy toasts. Speaking in Spanish and noting his "great personal interest" in the Spanish language and culture, Carter made a point of saying: "The growth of Spanish democracy has been a tonic for the entire Western World. . . . So, Spain is a source of hope and inspiration to democrats everywhere."[38]

Following the luncheon, Carter met with the king and other Spanish and United States officials for nearly an hour, toured the Prado Art Museum with Amy and Rosalynn, and then went to the US embassy residence, where they were to spend the night. Carter talked briefly with the leader of the Spanish

Socialist Party, Felipe Gonzalez, who had been to Iran to try to work out a plan for release of the hostages. That evening Carter, Brzezinski, and other US officials spent two hours at Moncloa Palace discussing "a broad range of international issues, including Afghanistan, Iran, and the Middle East" with Spanish prime minister Adolfo Suarez Gonzalez and several of his principal officials. After dinner, Suarez took Carter to the La Estacion de Los Porches Restaurant, where they joined Rosalynn and Mrs. Suarez to see a traditional flamenco show.[39]

In Lisbon, their next stop, the Carters stayed only for a six-hour layover on their way home to the United States. President Antonio Romahlo Eanes and his wife greeted them and escorted them to the Jeronimos Monastery to lay bouquets of flowers at the tomb of Renaissance poet Luis de Camoes and explorer Vasco da Gama. Carter had separate meetings with President Eanes, Socialist Party leader Mario Soares, and Prime Minister Francisco Sa Carneiro, a compulsive talker who was very friendly toward the United States and instrumental in bringing democracy to Portugal.[40] The visit ended with a state luncheon in the Ajuda Palace hosted by President and Mrs. Eanes. In his luncheon toast, Carter expressed his gratitude to Portugal for being a steadfast member of NATO, and, as he had done in Spain, he warmly congratulated the country's leaders for their efforts in "building a strong and permanent democracy."[41]

By 4:00 p.m. Lisbon time, the Carters were flying home. Exhausted by their travels, they went to Camp David for a three-day weekend of fishing and relaxing.[42] An avid angler since childhood, Carter fished the creeks near Camp David on weekends, and more recently had been going to Wayne Harpster's farm on the banks of Spruce Creek in central Pennsylvania. So close had the Carters become to Harpster, his wife Marjorie, their five children, and Harpster's mother, that the Harpsters spent two nights at the White House.[43]

Returning to the White House on Monday morning, June 30, Carter was not surprised to learn that many of the American people did not want him to be reelected. His European trip did not influence US voters who were more concerned about the hostages, energy shortages, inflation, unemployment, and not participating in the Olympic Games than international diplomacy.[44]

THIRTY ONE

An Uphill Battle

Before plunging into the uphill battle to win reelection, on July 3, Jimmy and Rosalynn went home to Plains to rest and to celebrate the Fourth of July holiday.[1] The next three days were idyllic for them. They walked downtown, had lunch with Miss Lillian, and visited friends; Jimmy went fishing and "skinny-dipping in the pond." On Sunday they tactfully attended both of the town's Baptist churches, going to Sunday School at Maranatha Baptist and worship service at First Baptist, and then returning to Maranatha in the evening for Vespers. On Sunday afternoon Jimmy and members of the White House staff played a softball game against Billy and members of the press. Jimmy's team won 13–3. After the game, Jimmy "jogged around a large peanut field and ran home," and the two teams played again the next day with Jimmy's team winning 26–4.[2]

On July 7, Jimmy left Rosalynn in Plains while he flew to Tokyo to attend the memorial service for his friend former Japanese prime minister Ohira. He stopped in Detroit, where the Republican National Convention was to meet the next week, to join Vice President Mondale and meet with representatives of the auto industry. They discussed ways to help the industry transition into making more fuel-efficient cars "The Republicans raised hell," Carter wrote in his diary, "because they said I was trying to steal headlines from them in Detroit." In Tokyo, Carter placed flowers on the funeral alter at the impressive memorial service that was attended by 108 nations, met with Emperor Hirohito, and visited Ohira's widow and her family. On his return flight, Carter stopped over in Alaska and spent a morning fishing in a stream near Clarence Lake. He fried some of his catch for lunch and then flew home to Georgia where he met Rosalynn and Amy on Sapelo Island.[3]

While relaxing on Sapelo Island, Jimmy fished and thought about the issues on which his opponents condemned him—the hostage crisis, inflation, attitudes of allies, and unemployment—all of which, he thought, were out of his control.[4] He also paid close attention to the news from the Republican convention in Detroit. He had been disappointed that Ronald Reagan had locked in his party's nomination to run for president, instead of Gerald Ford. Carter was disappointed again when Reagan did not choose Ford as his running mate, but instead named former CIA Director George H. W. Bush. At about 9:30 a.m. on July 17, in a brief conversation, Jimmy congratulated Reagan and challenged him to a series of debates in the fall, a challenge that Reagan immediately accepted.[5]

Not waiting to hear Reagan's nomination acceptance speech on the night of July 17, Jimmy and Rosalynn shifted into full campaign mode, flying by noon to Jacksonville, Florida. In rapid succession, Carter spoke to a welcoming crowd of approximately 4,000 supporters, attended a fundraising reception for about 150 donors, and participated in a question-and-answer session with about seventy Jacksonville community leaders. The economy was foremost in the minds of many of the community leaders, who, like Carter, were aware of Reagan's recent call for a federal income tax cut as a cure for stagflation. "We will stand firm, hold a steady course on economics," Carter responded to his first questioner. He declined to promise an unrealistic and irresponsible tax cut, as Reagan was doing, until he was sure that he could bring inflation under control. Risking losing voters, he stated, "I see no reason for moving ahead on a tax cut."[6]

From Jacksonville the Carters flew to Hollywood, Florida, for the convention of the International Transport Workers Federation and a fundraising dinner for about 600 guests, who paid $1,000 per couple to attend. He told the audience that he would be running "against a party almost exactly opposite from us, . . . a party with a narrow vision, a party afraid of the future, . . . a party that never has been willing to put its investment in human beings who were below them in the economic and social status." Having "fired the first shots in the fall campaign," the Carters returned to the White House later that night to prepare for the Democratic National Convention in New York City scheduled to begin in three weeks.[7]

Carter felt good about the campaign, because the Republican convention did not mask the previous rivalry among Ford, Bush, and Reagan, and most agreed that Reagan had delivered a very poor acceptance speech.[8] Mondale was also optimistic. On July 10, he had sent a memorandum to Carter suggesting that he needed to make a great acceptance speech at the Democratic Convention and ask Reagan for four or five debates instead of the usual three. Mondale thought the debating rules were "made in heaven" for Carter and that he could win back traditional Democrats. Mondale even thought that "we have a real chance with the Jewish voters in America if we really go to work on it," because Reagan was not doing well with them. Their votes would be necessary to win New York, New Jersey, Massachusetts, Connecticut, and California. It would be necessary too, to appeal to women voters in order to win. Carter scribbled a note in the margin, "Ros info J," and passed it to his wife.[9]

Jimmy and Rosalynn liked Mondale's ideas, but they had their own plan for the speech. He told his speech writers that "First we should build an image of statesmanship & sound progress for ourselves" before launching an all-out attack on Kennedy or anyone else. "I should come across as a sober & concerned President: maybe a little angry," he continued with emphasis. Remembering the success of Martin Luther King's "I Have a Dream" speech, he told them "I'm hoping for a new equivalent to I see an America. . . ." Rosalynn drafted her own version of the speech, proclaiming "we will win in November."[10]

Hamilton Jordan, Jerry Rafshoon, Tim Kraft, Bob Strauss, and Rosalynn produced a 300-page plan for the campaign. They agreed that it would be necessary to repair the damage done by the Kennedy challenge and that Carter must communicate his vision to the public. They must take seriously the possibility that the emergence of a third-party candidate might determine the winner in a close race. They warned that people tended to underestimate Reagan, whose solidly held conservative philosophy many found attractive. He did not work hard, had few close friends in politics, had a nasty temper that he controlled in public, allowed his wife Nancy to have a strong influence on his political decisions, and, "above all, Ronald Reagan is a very effective, 'communicator.'" Debating Reagan would give Carter the chance to emphasize their differences in age, intelligence, and visions for the future. Blaming all of their problems on the press, Rafshoon said, would not work.[11] In the days before the convention, Jimmy and Rosalynn frantically canvassed the country raising money. Carter flew to Kentucky and Texas on July 21 for fundraising events that were technically for the benefit of those states' Democratic parties and the Democratic National Committee, but would actually be used to help get him reelected. In tiny Robards, Kentucky, the home of a wealthy banker who had befriended Carter in 1975, Jimmy sweated profusely as he shook the hands of all 500 fundraiser attendees, each of whom had paid $500 to be there. In Texas, at the farm of Olen and Mertie Helen Range near Fort Worth, Carter declared his sympathy for farmers suffering miserably from the drought. In Dallas he spoke to about 200 guests who had gathered at the home of wealthy Dallas financier Jess Hay. By the time he returned to Washington, Democratic party officials estimated that he had raised more than $800,000 that day alone.[12]

Traveling separately from Jimmy, Rosalynn delivered numerous speeches during the weeks before the convention, trying to make the campaign as human and personal as she could in order to convince voters that the Carters were just ordinary folks. In New York's Chinatown, she was frightened by a three-headed dragon that gyrated toward her, but quickly regained her composure and later gave a major fundraising speech at a banquet. After her speech, she shook hands with every diner and everyone who helped in the kitchen and service. She never needed the ladies' room with its special stall "reserved for the First Lady of the United States." Outside, she slipped through a police barricade and waded into the crowd, causing her angry security men to mutter, "Damn that woman." In Chicago and Baltimore, she kissed Cambodian and Spanish babies, ignored questions she did not want to answer, and denied there was any difference between her and Jimmy's private and public lives. When pressed about what it meant to be born again, she attempted to put it to rest forever by saying she had been born again and all it meant was to live in Christ, put away the past, and to be forgiven.[13]

In Washington, Carter worked on finding a resolution for the hostage crisis. He met Richard Queen, one of the hostages whom the Iranian students released because he suffered from multiple sclerosis. Queen told the president how he and his fellow captives had been held in a "tomb" for weeks without light or fresh air. At times he had endured mock executions. Listening to his story, and watching his weakened and excited manner, Carter ached all the more for those still in captivity and desperately hoped to find a way to set them free. At a later, secret, meeting on August 1, Carter indicated that he was tired of memoranda and wanted more action on the hostage situation. He wanted hostage families and Congressmen to have more frequent contacts with Iranians, and he asked the Algerian government to instruct the Algerian Ambassador in Tehran to launch its own investigation into the dilemma.[14]

While the hostage issue remained in limbo, Carter concentrated on saving the environment, especially the Alaskan wilderness. Fascinated by the complex issue of what to do with large portions of land in that enormous, sparsely populated state, Carter worked with Interior Secretary Cecil Andrus to determine how he might preserve them. Several diverse groups with equally diverse interests—Native Americans, big oil companies, landowners, environmentalists, fishermen, timber companies—and sometimes powerful lobbyists in Washington had a stake in the Alaska lands. Using Teddy Roosevelt's Antiquities Act of 1906 and guided by Andrus, Carter had issued an executive order in December 1978 to designate 56 million acres as national monuments and thus buy time to preserve the "last frontier" in the United States. As Reagan's star rose in the afterglow of the Republican Convention, Carter worked hard to win Congressional support for the Alaska Lands Bill that would permanently protect 157 million acres. Carter thought this "one of the most important decisions that the Congress will ever make" and also "the most important decision on conservation" that century.[15]

July 23 and 24 were banner days for the Carters. On July 23, Carter signed the "River of No Return" wilderness bill that protected over two million acres of wilderness land on the Salmon River in central Idaho, where he and his family had vacationed in August 1978.[16] Rosalynn rejoiced when Congress passed the Mental Health Bill on July 24. Both of them were pleased with Senator Byrd's rebuttal of Reagan's criticism of US policy with China, because Carter thought that his decision "to normalize relations with China was historically one of the most significant and progressive actions of the decade or of our generation."[17]

As the Olympic Games in Moscow got underway in late July, Carter felt that he had been right to boycott them. Eighty nations participated in the games, from July 19 to August 3—the smallest number since 1956—while sixty-six boycotted them. Carter kept his promise to honor the US Summer Olympians by presenting them medals in the nation's capital. Standing on the west steps of the United States Capitol at noon on July 30, along with House Speaker Tip O'Neill and Senate Majority Leader Robert Byrd, he presented specially struck gold-plated congressional medals to more than 450 US athletes who had not been able to compete in Moscow. Later that afternoon, Jimmy, Rosalynn, and Amy hosted the athletes at a reception on the South Lawn, posing for individual photographs with each of them. On August 5, members of the Olympic swimming team, who had missed the Capitol steps ceremony, received their Congressional medals at the White House. Most of the athletes at the ceremonies, however, did not feel the satisfaction that Carter did. "The President and some of his dignitaries said things," one of them remembered forty years later, "but it was, 'Rah-rah, Team USA, this is for the country. We're all in this together.' We didn't buy it. Our dreams were up in smoke."[18]

Carter risked seeing his own dreams go up in smoke if he did not get reelected. Peace in the Middle East, like freedom for the Iranian hostages, remained elusive, because Begin hoped to consolidate Israel's exclusive claim to Jerusalem, an act that would demolish the Camp David Accords. Carter thought Begin was isolating Israel from the rest of the world and losing much of his US support.[19]

Carter also could not rebut the argument that he had weakened the country militarily, because he could not give away security secrets during the campaign. Voters could not know that Carter had rebuilt the US military after its depletion during the long and failed war in Southeast Asia. For more than a year, Carter and Secretary of Defense Harold Brown had been working to develop sophisticated new weapons systems. Precision bombs, missiles that could attack a specific target from a long range, and especially the stealth bomber capable of avoiding detection by radar were all part of their top-secret program. Since thousands of scientists, engineers, workers, and businesses were involved in the massive projects, leaks were inevitable, but still Carter could not use this major accomplishment as part of his campaign. He had, however, been successful with the most important responsibility of his administration, namely to keep the country strong and free.[20]

Doing her part, Rosalynn sometimes stood in for the president at important international affairs, such as the inauguration of the new president of Peru on July 27. The Peruvian President-elect Fernando Belaunde Terry, a sixty-seven-year-old architect, had earned his degree at the University of Texas at Austin and had spent a decade teaching at several US universities. When the Peruvian military dictatorship had collapsed because of economic troubles, he returned home and was elected president in April 1980. Dignitaries from more than one hundred countries attended, but Rosalynn was the only female there representing a head of state. She strengthened US ties with Peru, confronted neighboring Chile about its human rights violations, and had substantive discussions with leaders of Costa Rica, Spain, Colombia, and Venezuela. According to her husband, Rosalynn was "an outstanding diplomat" who could approach subjects "very difficult to raise through an ambassador or the State Department."[21]

On the day of Terry's inauguration, the shah of Iran died in Egypt. Although neither of them would attend his funeral, Rosalynn and Jimmy sent condolences to his widow Farah Pahlavi and her family. Their contact with the grieving and embittered family went through Ambassador Alfred Atherton, whom Carter instructed to attend any official observance of the shah's death. In a personal letter to the empress, Carter wrote: "I have admired your fortitude, courage and dignity through days that have been exceedingly difficult for all," he wrote. "It is my prayer that . . . you will find the strength to rebuild again a fruitful and satisfying life. . . . May God comfort you and your children." Rosalynn added her own sympathy letter. "I pray that peace and strength will be yours in the days ahead," she told the grieving widow.[22]

Farah probably took little comfort in the condolences from the Americans as she walked behind her husband's casket on that broiling day in July. Anwar Sadat had staged a grand funeral at the nineteenth-century el-Rifa'i Mosque in Cairo. The shah's casket, draped in the Iranian flag and placed on a military caisson drawn by eight black Arabian horses, slowly made its solemn journey to the mosque. Thousands of mourners and a few dignitaries followed the family. Sadat, dressed in his blue field marshal's uniform and sweating profusely, led the procession. Empress Farah and Jehan Sadat, walked in step with him. The shah's nineteen-year-old son and sixty-year-old twin sister completed the family group. Only two heads of state, former President Richard Nixon and deposed King Constantine of Greece, attended. Ambassador Alfred Atherton represented the United States. Nixon, who was there as a private citizen, told the press that Carter's treatment of the shah was "shameful."[23]

Unruffled, Carter seemed to relish the problems that arrived at his desk. He welcomed kind words of sympathy and support, often accompanied by Bible verses, from friends and others who mistakenly believed that he was despondent. "A lot of people think I'm a lot more burdened down and discouraged than I actually am," he wrote in his diary. "I have a lot of problems on my shoulders, but strangely enough I feel better as they pile up. My main concern is propping up the people around me who tend to panic."[24]

The domestic political problems that Carter faced in the summer of 1980 centered not only on Ted Kennedy and Ronald Reagan, but also John Anderson, a fifty-eight-year-old Republican Congressman from Illinois, who had announced his campaign for the presidency on June 8 as a liberal independent candidate. "Anderson can hurt Reagan more than it hurts us before it is all over," Ham Jordan had confidently declared at the time, but fears were growing in the Carter camp that Anderson could attract support from enough dissatisfied Democrats in crucial states like New York, Pennsylvania, and Ohio to shift their electoral votes to Reagan.[25] Posing as more liberal than Carter, Anderson favored Ted Kennedy and even said that, if Kennedy got the nomination, he would withdraw from the race. Since Kennedy would not get it, Anderson decided to run as an independent, naively believing that he could beat Carter. Ironically his political philosophy was much closer to that of Carter than Reagan.[26]

Knowing that the nomination was his, Carter relaxed as he moved through the days before the Democratic National Convention in August. In the White House briefing room on July 29, he promised to reveal all that he knew about Billy's dealings with the Libyans, and he reassured reporters that Billy had had no influence upon the administration.[27] Carter worked on a speech explaining and defending Billy, as well as the one accepting the Democratic nomination. He took time to reassure Sadat that Begin's posturing about Jerusalem would not likely change anything except to weaken Begin himself. He welcomed news that Greece and Turkey might come to an agreement that would allow Greece to join NATO, and he listened to the fears of two Jewish members of his cabinet, Klutznick and Goldschmidt, who worried about the Jewish vote but had no solution to suggest. During a quick trip to New York City on August 3 to address the Urban League, Carter gave Mayor Edward Koch "hell for his daily stabbing me in the back." He noted that the Ku Klux Klan had endorsed Reagan, and he observed a growing group of alleged Christians on the extreme far right who were likely to support the Republican candidates.[28]

Carter's own Southern Baptist religion had evolved into an increasingly liberal approach to the Scriptures and society. Carter believed in and practiced the separation of church and state. He thought the radical right wing religious "performers" were a "threat to the Christian faith." Their most outspoken leader, Reverend Jerry Falwell of Lynchburg, Virginia, claimed to have had a conversation with Carter in the Oval Office, which Carter denied. Conservative leaders of his own Southern Baptist Convention began to look askance at the socially liberal Baptist in the White House.[29]

On August 10, the day before the Democratic convention began, Carter and Rosalynn appeared on the television news program *60 Minutes*, during which journalist Dan Rather fired negative questions at them. Asked to grade various aspects of his presidential performance, Carter gave himself a B or C + on foreign policy, an A on energy, a C on the economy, and a B on leadership. Rather questioned the president sharply on several specific topics, including his poll numbers, the reliability of his convention delegates, inflation and taxation, efforts to reduce the number of federal agencies, Iran, and the Soviet threat. After saying that he did not want to spend much time on Billy's problems, Rather proceeded to grill Carter about them at some length.

Carter steadily denied all of Rather's negativism, especially the contention that he was a man "under some kind of siege."

In the same interview, Carter had fun teasing "Rosie" and being cynical about how little the press really knew about her. She makes phone calls to delegates, he said, is a good seamstress, and "takes care of me and Amy and our needs on the sewing machine." He also praised her for being his close friend, his partner, and his sweetheart, who enjoyed fishing and politicking. Rosalynn was less jovial during the interview. She got angry about her husband's being blamed for things that previous administrations had done and accused the press of overplaying the Billy affair. Concerned about the embarrassment the negative publicity about Billy might be causing his wife Sybil, she had Jimmy call Sybil to tell her that "we love you and we're sorry all of this happened."[30]

The Kennedy supporters, however, were unapologetic and continued to cause trouble for the Carters. They threatened to stage a demonstration at the convention in favor of the senator, and the press printed stories about how Kennedy would take over the convention. Carter responded by sending word to the Kennedy campaign through his deputy campaign manager Hamilton Jordan that, if they filibustered, time would be taken away from Kennedy's speech or it would even be delayed until late in the evening, well past TV prime time.

When the convention began in Madison Square Garden on Monday, August 11, the delegates almost immediately faced their most crucial decision: a vote on a rule requiring all delegates on the first ballot to support the candidate to whom they were pledged by their respective state primaries or caucuses. The rule was adopted, ending Ted Kennedy's hope for an open convention. Carter had 1,935 committed delegates, giving him a lead of more than 700 over the senator. That evening Kennedy called to tell Carter that he would withdraw from the race, but he did not promise to endorse Carter and Mondale. On August 12, the second day of the convention, Kennedy gave a rousing speech, written largely by his speechwriter Bob Shrum, that brought down the roof but offered nothing in support of Carter. Distrust and hatred burned beneath the surface, but Kennedy finally did ask Massachusetts to cast its delegates' votes for Carter.[31]

On the evening of August 13, Senator Bob Graham of Florida delivered the nominating speech. Seconding the nomination was Coretta Scott King, who praised Carter as the "champion of rights." She believed that history would record that Jimmy Carter "helped build peace on earth."[32] When Texas cast its votes for him in the roll call, Carter had won the nomination.

When Carter delivered his acceptance speech on Thursday night, he could not see the teleprompter; whether this was a coincidental technical malfunction or sabotage was never determined. He spoke from memory and the heart, occasionally looking down at his notes. With passion and confidence, he thanked the Democrats for again nominating him and Mondale. He mentioned the magical names of previous Democratic presidents—Franklin Delano Roosevelt and Harry Truman—and he praised Kennedy for the speech he had given earlier in the convention. Reminding the cheering crowd that "a President must sometimes ask for sacrifice when his listeners would rather hear the promise of comfort," Carter referred to the reality of an energy crisis and the necessity to be prepared militarily to defend the country. Segueing into the cadence made famous by Martin Luther King, Jr., he proclaimed, "I see a future of economic security," "I see a future of justice," and "I see a future of peace." Carter spoke for about fifty minutes, ending with the words, "I want us to be what the Founders of our Nation meant us to become—the land of freedom, the land of peace, and the land of hope."[33]

Hundreds of delegates jumped to their feet, cheering, shouting, and applauding. Horns blared, music played, balloons cascaded from an overhead net. The first tug did not free the balloons, but after a few seconds that seemed much longer, they gradually came floating down. Although Kennedy still had not arrived in the arena, the Mondales and the Carters remained on the platform waving to relatives, friends, and the crowd. Bob Strauss, who, with Jordan, had been managing the delegates, shouted to the convention chairman Tip O'Neill, "Keep that goddamn music going. Walk around, keep this thing stalled. . . . For Christ's sake, smile a little bit up there. You look like a band of undertakers."[34]

Dignitaries, many of whom O'Neill summoned, began to fill up the stage, but still no Kennedy. The television news commentators took note of Kennedy's absence and of the balloons that did not fall properly. Although Carter had won the nomination and had delivered an impressive acceptance speech, many of the commentators acted as if the convention belonged to Kennedy. When he finally arrived upon the stage, after keeping the crowd waiting almost twenty minutes, he appeared to be emphasizing the division in the party, not offering to unify it.[35]

The Carters, the Mondales, and other party dignitaries welcomed Kennedy to the stage. He towered over Carter as he slowly moved toward him and hesitantly offered to shake his hand. Rosalynn and Tip O'Neill looked on in dismay. O'Neill placed a hand on Kennedy's elbow as if pushing him to shake hands with Carter—or steadying a slightly tipsy man. Carter thought Kennedy had "had a few drinks, which I would have probably done myself." Refusing to raise clasped hands with the winner as was traditional, Kennedy did shake hands with Carter but turned his back to him as he greeted others on the stage. Kennedy later dismissed his failure to raise clasped hands as no "big deal," but the press and the Carters saw it otherwise. Kennedy was on the stage for "two minutes and sixteen seconds," according to his biographer, who also noted that he "milled about among dozens of Democrats, looking as if he did not know what to do." Kennedy had gotten his revenge.[36]

Bert Lance thought it was a bad mistake to allow Kennedy on the stage, but Carter thought that by doing so he would heal the schism in the party. Carter needed the Kennedy supporters to vote for him, not Anderson or Reagan, in November. Cy and Gay Vance, who attended the convention as Carter's special guests, greeted the Carters warmly as they moved through the crowd that gathered around the podium, suggesting that there was no lingering dissension within the party.[37]

Jimmy and Rosalynn may have felt more relief than euphoria as they left the convention to resume the duties of the office and to begin the next level of their campaign. For an incumbent president during peace time, Carter faced extraordinary obstacles. Although he had had major successes in both foreign and domestic policy, they seemed to be ignored in the heat of the campaign. A shaky economy, Billy's escapades, a continuing hostage crisis in Iran, a phony media-made image of weakness that was difficult to refute, angry farmers, the lingering shadow of Kennedy, and the skill and determination of his Republican opponent all, as New York Times columnist Tom Wicker wrote, afflicted a good man most foully at "what should have been his time of triumph."[38]

In the face of such odds, only Jimmy and Rosalynn Carter could have had the confidence, faith, and determination that he would win. Together they practiced the positive thinking that they expected would give them four more years in the White House. Carter also believed, according to one observer, that his Republican opponent was stupid and dangerous. Carter launched his campaign like a moral crusade against Reagan.[39]

Reagan was not stupid. In his campaign notes for August 14, he wrote that in his view there "wasn't a political convention this week in New York—it was a four-day serial featuring weak, incompetent, divisive leadership." He thought Kennedy, not Carter, had won for all intents and purposes, and Carter's record was "a litany of disasters." To exploit those weaknesses, he jotted down ideas that he would use to combat Carter.[40] Reagan kicked off his campaign on August 3 at the Neshoba County Fair near Philadelphia, Mississippi, where the Ku Klux Klan had murdered three civil rights activists in 1964. By making his pitch for Southern white voters who remained conservative on the race issue, and for conservative, right-wing evangelicals, Reagan grabbed two large groups in Carter's native South. Conversely, Reagan drove African Americans deeper into Carter's camp, making them virtually Carter's only secure voters for the uphill campaign.[41]

Speaker Tip O'Neill, who had chaired the convention for Carter, had a different opinion. "I believe we left that Convention a truly united Party," he wrote to his "friend" Carter on August 19, "due in no small part to the fact that you are a very gracious winner. . . . I'm sure we will be successful in November!" In reply, Carter thanked him for his "superb leadership [and] good humor."[42]

In typical fashion, Carter quickly put the convention behind him. What he and Rosalynn wanted first was to rest, then to concentrate hard on campaigning against Reagan. Before the Carters left New York City on August 15, Miss Lillian joined them and Amy at the Museum of Modern Art to view a special retrospective exhibit of paintings by Picasso, an artist whose staggering achievement Jimmy admired. Jimmy and Rosalynn also attended breakfasts for Black delegates and Democratic fundraisers. At midday, they flew to Camp David and then traveled on to Wayne Harpster's cabin on Spruce Creek to fish. But the rigors of the campaign and demands of the presidency remained with them.

When Carter saw the media coverage after the convention, he was incredulous that the *Washington Post* treated him like a combination of "Adolf Hitler and Goofy," "incompetent and untrustworthy." The newspaper, he wrote in his diary on August 17, ignored "the fact that we had beaten Kennedy, won the rules fight, had the nomination, prevailed well on the platform, and that Kennedy had endorsed him." On August 18, Rosalynn's birthday, the Carters received the good news that two polls showed them within seven points of Reagan and that the Senate had passed the Alaska Lands bill by a vote of 78–14. Carter's greatest accomplishment in preserving the environment, the act protected more federal lands than all the previous national parks combined. Since he and Rosalynn liked to fish in Alaska, it was like a birthday present for her. He also gave her a "beautiful little picture frame and put Ecclesiastes

9:9 in Spanish written in the frame as a message from me to her": "Live joy-fully with the wife whom thou lovest all the days . . . which he hath given thee under the sun."[43]

The Alaska Lands Act placed 28% of Alaska off limits to commercial de-velopment. It had been nine years in the making, and it was 446 pages long. Leaving lands already administered by the Bureau of Land Management as they were, it set aside 43.6 million more acres for new national parks, protected 53.8 million acres in new wildlife refuges, and provided wilder-ness protection for 56.7 million acres already a part of various conservation units. It allowed exploration for oil and gas in the western coastal plain, but no drilling. Also included were two national monuments in southeastern Alaska: a 2.3 million acre national monument in the Misty Fjords area and 921,000 acres on Admiralty Island. Carter called the act his "highest environmental priority" and later would consider it one of the greatest accomplishments of his presidency.[44]

Carter's love for the environment stemmed from his youth in Archery, Georgia. From his father, he had learned to appreciate the land, terrace the fields, and protect wildlife. He felt "closer to God" too, he said, when he was in the woods, and it had been a walk in the piney woods of rural Georgia where he had had what he termed his "born again" experience. As president, Carter elevated preservation of the environment to a global issue, and he ac-complished more than any president before, including Theodore Roosevelt, in preserving precious lands and resources while it was still possible.[45]

Neither the Republican nor the Democratic candidate waited until the offi-cial Labor Day start on September 1 to begin his campaign. In a speech at the Charleston, South Carolina, Navy Yard on August 20, Reagan viciously crit-icized Carter for not building up the military, which was a complete misrep-resentation of all that Carter had actually done.[46] Carter responded the next day by addressing the American Legion in Boston about his defense policy. He reaffirmed his commitment to peace through strength, safeguarding allies, the value of MX missiles on land, Trident missiles on submarines, nu-clear arms control, and peacetime registration for the draft. "No potential enemy of the United States," he sternly warned, "should anticipate for one moment a successful use of military power against our vital interest."[47]

The Reagan campaign used surrogates, including prominent politicians such as Senator Charles Percy of Illinois, to deliver bellicose speeches crit-icizing everything Carter said. In charge of the surrogates and much of the campaign, Reagan's special research director and speechwriter Tony Dolan proved to be a highly effective asset. A brilliant journalist, graduate of Yale, and Roman Catholic, he was a super patriot who thought the country needed Reagan. He hated Carter, Democrats, and especially the South, all of which fueled his passion in organizing the surrogate attacks and collecting vast amounts of research on Carter.[48]

Carter continued to run tough and to fight for every vote he could get, particularly among Jewish Americans. On August 21, he thanked his Jewish friend and former White House Counsel Robert Lipshutz for a speech he gave to Jewish veterans in New Orleans, reminding them of all that Carter had done for Israel and for Jewish Americans.[49] Following the advice of his Jewish Domestic Policy adviser, Stu Eizenstat, Carter agreed to give a radio interview for the upcoming Jewish holidays. He stressed his opposition to John Anderson's drive to have the United States declared a Christian nation, and he listed his often overlooked accomplishments that had helped Jewish Americans. He had insisted on Soviet compliance with the Helsinki Accords, defended Russian Jewish dissidents, promoted Soviet Jewish immigration, awarded block grants for Jewish welfare groups, protected Iranian Jews, and opposed recognition of the PLO unless it accepted Israel's right to exist.[50]

Carter remained calm, hardworking, and optimistic. He let Mondale worry about a UN vote regarding Jerusalem, and he explained to Archbishop John R. Quinn that he disagreed with the party's platform that supported a woman's right to have an abortion. Defending his veto of the B-1 bomber, Carter allowed Secretary of Defense Harold Brown to explain that cruise missiles as well as the stealth bomber made the B-1 bomber obsolete. Billy testified before the Senate committee, handled himself well, and received a congratulatory call from his brother. Jimmy discussed with advisers the status of the campaign, considered his public appearances, and did not seem bothered by the liberal Democratic defectors who committed to John Anderson. He kept a sharp eye on a democratic revolution in Poland that seemed destined for success and a major factor in weakening the Soviet Union's grip on Eastern Europe.[51]

Despite the disgruntled Kennedy and the added challenge of third-party candidate John Anderson, Jimmy and Rosalynn were already knee deep in their battle plan against Reagan before the campaign's official kick-off on September 1.

THIRTY TWO

A Surprise in October

Carter kicked off his reelection campaign in Tuscumbia, Alabama, the home of Helen Keller whose conquest of deafness and blindness had inspired millions. It was September 1, 1980, and it brought back memories of the launch of his 1976 campaign at Warm Springs, the west central Georgia home of Franklin Roosevelt. The 1980 election would involve a battle for the South, and Carter hoped to carry his native region again. Ronald Reagan, determined to win on his third attempt to gain the White House, had created a Southern strategy that would take most of the region away from its native son.[1]

The Secret Service had initiated very tight security measures at the Tuscumbia's Spring Park where Jimmy, Rosalynn, and Amy arrived to help the attendees celebrate the Labor Day holiday. Politicians from surrounding states joined those from Alabama to welcome the president. They included some of the South's most conservative old guard, most notably former Mississippi Senator James Eastland and former Alabama governors George C. Wallace and James E. "Big Jim" Folsom. From his wheelchair, Wallace gave Carter a bear hug that was in sharp contrast with the halfhearted handshake that Ted Kennedy had given him at the National Democratic Convention. Representatives of the New South, with whom Carter was more congenial, included Senator Howell Heflin of Alabama and Mississippi Governor William Winter. The 54,400 attendees who came from Alabama, Tennessee, and Mississippi listened to an old-time Gospel group, the Singing Speers Family, and then the country music of Larry Gatlin and the Charlie Daniels Band. One observer noted that the thousands of people filled beautifully landscaped Spring Park and spread out across the golf course, beyond the creek, and down Woodmont Avenue for as far as the eye could see.[2]

By choosing a site in northern Alabama, Carter hoped to attract conservative blue collar workers and farmers who might be influenced by his agrarian, populist politics. Because of its association with Helen Keller, the site also appealed to compassionate humanitarians. Carter wanted to give the impression that he came from a New South, which was not unlike the rest of the nation, where all people, no matter their race or religion, might be treated equally and with dignity. One group, however, defied him. Near the airport on the day he arrived, numerous Ku Klux Klansmen, ceremonially dressed in white sheets, held signs that read "Reagan for President." Some of their signs proclaimed that Carter hired Blacks, fired Whites, and endorsed programs that took jobs away from US citizens. One sign simply said, "Whites have rights, too." Carter had not seen a Ku Klux Klan demonstration since Klansmen had marched around outside the Georgia State Capitol in 1974 as he dedicated a portrait of Martin Luther King, Jr., inside.[3]

Irked by the Klan demonstrators, Carter condemned them soundly in his opening remarks. "As the first man from the Deep South in 140 years to be President of this nation," he declared, "I say that these people in white sheets do not understand our region and what it's been through."[4] It made him angry, he said, to see Klansmen waving a Confederate battle flag, because he remembered Judah P. Benjamin, the secretary of state for the Confederacy who was a Jew, and he remembered that generals Pat Cleburne of Arkansas and P. G. T. Beauregard of Louisiana "who had served under that flag" were Catholics. When he saw a cross raised up, Carter testified, he remembered that the "One who was crucified taught us to have faith, to hope, and not to hate but to love one another." Rejecting the misuse of such symbols, Carter thought that "the South and all of America must move forward." He recalled his experiences growing up on a Georgia farm, and he emphasized his presidential accomplishments as a peacemaker, especially his mediation of the Camp David Accords. Carter strongly believed, he said, that "together we will be victorious, our Nation will be strong, united, and free, and we will have a better life for all Americans."[5]

In a paragraph that attracted almost no attention, Carter said that, while celebrating Labor Day in the United States, he would like to express his "admiration" for workers in Poland, who just the day before had successfully forced the Communist government to recognize their free trade union and Solidarity Movement; they soon brought down the Communist regime there. He did not say how much the Vatican and the United States had given clandestine support to the movement, but he did say: "They have shown the world not just how to win a victory for labor, but that the hunger for human rights is everywhere. And they've accomplished this by themselves, without any interference from anywhere."[6] Although he was appealing to American labor for its vote, he also implied that the freedom he wished for all Americans should not be jeopardized by white supremacists.

In Michigan, on that same day, Republican candidate Ronald Reagan said that Carter had gone to the "home place of the Ku Klux Klan to begin" his campaign, which caused Carter and seven Southern governors to immediately rebuke him. Carter compared the Republican campaign, which had begun in the heart of Klan country at Neshoba County, Mississippi, to "the specter of white sheets." Reagan protested and asked for an apology, but Carter refused.[7]

The next day, September 2, Carter went to Independence, Missouri, where he visited Harry Truman's widow, Bess, before delivering a speech at the Truman Presidential Library and holding a town meeting at the local high school. Carter attempted to keep the question and answer session at the town meeting on a high level. He discussed his record, his economic plan and the energy program, SALT II, tax reform, the right of all Americans of all faiths to pray wherever and whenever they wished, defense spending, and his hope for Palestinian self-determination. Carter's comment that Reagan's stance on nuclear weapons was "contrary to peace" attracted more media attention than his defense of his administration. Carter wrote in his diary that the "press reaction was that Reagan and I were involved in a serious public verbal battle. I'll try to be more presidential, but he [Reagan] genuinely aggravated me with his Klan remark."[8]

The same day that Carter campaigned in Missouri, the Gannett News Service published a detailed account of Carter's presidential record. Arguing that the president's accomplishments were better than many realized, journalist Don Campbell pointed out that under Carter the national unemployment rate had dropped from 7.3% to 6%, money for education had increased, and he was unusually accessible to the public. The framework for peace in the Middle East, SALT II, the normalization of relations with China, and the improved image of the United States in Africa were also significant presidential accomplishments. Carter, Campbell wrote, had succeeded in making the United States and other countries of the world understand and accept his focus on human rights. Campbell did not mention Carter's rebuilding of the military, because most of it was top secret and still in progress. He did note that Carter had appointed more women and Blacks to senior federal positions than any previous president, had reformed both the civil service and welfare, and had deregulated the airline industry. On the negative side, Campbell found that the 13.2% inflation rate, Carter's persistent defenses of Billy, Bert Lance, and Andrew Young, and his lack of success in getting Congress to pass an energy program and a hospital cost containment bill reflected poorly on his presidency.[9]

Each candidate himself, in heated debate through the media, town meetings, and huge rallies, tried to convince the voting public that he was the better man for the job. Accused of "meanness" for his attacks on Reagan, Carter softened his rhetoric but not the content of his message that Reagan would be a disastrous president. Carter again tried to convince Jewish voters that he had served and would serve their interests, and that of Israel, well, but he often received a cool reception. In fact, Morris Abram, his former South Georgia supporter and the president of Brandeis University, published a devastating rejection of Carter in the *New York Times* on September 5. Denying that he was bitter because he did not get an appointment in the Carter administration after campaigning for him in 1976, Abram condemned Carter not for his religion or Southern origin, but for perceived failures in foreign and domestic affairs, the antics of his brother, Andrew Young's anti-Israel comments, and his letting down so many who had expected so much from him.[10]

Carter became mired in the Republican accusation that he was covering up a serious scandal involving his brother that threatened the integrity of the Justice Department and the federal government. Defending himself, Carter allowed the Senate investigators to see his personal notes about Billy, and he disclosed the role Rosalynn had played in trying to transform Billy's association with the Libyans into freeing the hostages. Brzezinski did not want the Senate committee to know that Rosalynn had been involved for fear that the investigation would implicate both Jimmy and Rosalynn in some shady maneuver. White House Counsel Lloyd Cutler, Carter, and Rosalynn, however, thought that revealing Rosalynn's participation would protect them from allegations of wrong doing. Both Jimmy and Rosalynn were unabashedly proud and grateful for the role Rosalynn played in their presidency, and they freely told all to the Senate investigation committee.[11]

William Casey, the prominent New York attorney and former chairman of the Securities and Exchange Commission in the Nixon administration who was managing the Reagan campaign, publicly condemned the president and his brother, but had a more nefarious strategy for helping Reagan get elected. He believed that, if he could block Carter from getting the hostages freed before the election, Reagan would easily win. To accomplish that goal, Casey, who had served during World War II with the Office of Strategic Services, the forerunner of the CIA, began to negotiate with the Iranians. In July and August 1980 he met with Ayatollah Karubi in Madrid and told him that, if he would deliver the hostages to the Reagan people, Khomeini would get his money back, apparently a reference to the Iranian funds Carter had frozen ten days after the hostages had been taken. Casey also promised the Iranians an immediate generous supply of arms, weaponry that Iran sorely needed in its brutal war with Iraq.[12]

While the Republican campaign moved ahead, the president relished one of his most important and unheralded victories. On August 27, he had welcomed Robert Mugabe, the newly elected leader of Zimbabwe, to the White House. Carter later said that he had spent more time working on helping Zimbabwe win its independence from the White minority government that had ruled the country as Rhodesia than he had on the Camp David Accords. The fact that Zimbabwe's independence finally happened during the furor of the 1980 campaign denied Carter the publicity and credit that he deserved, but this event reinforced the success of Carter's vision for a country and a world that could be free and humane. Concurrently with the administration's work for the independence of Zimbabwe, former Secretary of State Cyrus Vance had spearheaded the diplomatic effort to help the nearby nation of Namibia also gain its independence, which it finally won in 1988.[13]

In the meantime, Rosalynn had stepped onto the campaign trail with a vengeance. When Jimmy kicked off his campaign in Tuscumbia, Rosalynn accompanied him at every event on that hot day in Alabama and gave her own short campaign speech. "My husband," she declared to a sympathetic, family-oriented audience, "is a man of compassion and courage who believes government has a basic obligation to the disadvantaged." Over the next several weeks, Rosalynn made her own independent campaign appearances in other cities in Alabama, Illinois, Texas, Louisiana, Mississippi, Florida, and South Carolina, where she flattered local audiences and tried to bring the Southern states back under the national Democratic umbrella. More than five thousand African-American women in Birmingham listened to her explain what her husband had done for them during his first term in office. In Chicago, Eleanor Daley, the widow of former Mayor Richard J. Daley, was so impressed with Rosalynn that she called Jimmy to tell him that his wife "gave the finest and most sincere speech" she had ever heard.[14]

As Rosalynn excelled wherever she went, Congressional Democrats predictably rallied around Carter as the party's standard bearer. Senator Robert C. Byrd wanted a Democratic majority in Congress and a Democratic agenda for the country and for the party.[15] H. Brandt Ayers, a liberal journalist in Birmingham, Alabama, saluted Carter for his patriotism and for putting the good of the country above all else.[16] Hugh Sidey, the White House correspondent for *Time* magazine, sent him a quotation from President Herbert Hoover that Carter, a dedicated fisherman like Hoover, particularly liked: "Fishing is the chance to wash one's soul with pure air . . . and it is discipline in the equality of man—for all men are equal before fish."[17]

Believing that all men are equal, Carter pleaded with African Americans in Atlanta and Jewish voters nationwide to appreciate what he had done for them and to vote for him in 1980. He had worked hard to enforce the civil rights acts of the 1960s by emphasizing justice and equality for African Americans, women, and all minorities in US society. He hoped, he said, that history would record that he had contributed to the security of Israel and a lasting peace in the Middle East.[18] Vigorously attacking Reagan, Carter told audiences, both Black and White, that Reagan's views would mark a return to the racism that had defined and split the country for generations. He reminded them that, despite his disavowals, Reagan had been endorsed by the Ku Klux Klan, and he accused his opponent of being a warmonger who was oblivious to human rights. Reagan, Carter said, was ignorant of Carter's presidential accomplishments, especially the facts that he had maintained peace during his first term, substantially rebuilt the military, and formulated an effective energy policy.[19]

Reagan, in his relaxed Hollywood style, politely chastised the struggling president as if he were a child. The Republican campaign, however, was not nearly so polite. It organized a group of speakers known as the "Truth Squad" to follow Carter around the country. Wherever Carter made a speech, one of them would soon appear to "tell the truth" that the president had evaded. Their official theme was that Carter's was a failed presidency, a trail of broken promises, but Reagan would provide "four years of opportunity and growth." Members of the Truth Squad included senators John Tower of Texas, John Warner of Virginia, and other powerful, well-known politicians. They accused the president of misusing surrogates at government expense—most of Carter's surrogates were cabinet members or advisors who went off the government and onto the Democratic Party payroll when they campaigned. The Reagan team called the Carter team a "group of down-home brawlers" who were "preparing to bite, gouge, and kick."[20]

More deadly than the Truth Squad, Ayatollah Khomeini portrayed the hostage issue as a battle between good and evil, freedom and slavery, while masking the fact that Iran was struggling politically and economically with its war against Iraq. Carter analyzed the Ayatollah's speeches in terms of how they might affect the US hostages and whether they might lead to a Russian invasion of Iran.[21] If the latter happened, the hostages would likely be killed and the United States would be drawn into war with Russia, two events that Carter desperately wanted to prevent.

In addition to Iran and the Soviet Union, Carter also had to deal with Nicaragua, an impoverished Central American country where for many years the United States had supported President Anastasio Somoza DeBayle and his Somoza family predecessors. They had US backing because they were anti-Communist and pro-Israel. Carter changed that policy. As part of his commitment to punish human rights violators, he had blocked a shipment of weapons from Israel to Somoza in 1979. Overthrown by the Sandinista National Liberation Front, on July 17, 1979, Samoza fled to Miami, taking with him most of the Nicaraguan treasury, as well as the caskets of his father and brother. When Carter refused him legal entry into the United States, he went to Paraguay. Before he was assassinated on September 17, 1980, by Argentine activists who were connected with the Sandinistas, Somoza blamed Carter for his downfall. The Israelis, who wanted to continue selling arms to Nicaragua, also resented Carter's actions. In addition, Carter faced a new problem in Nicaragua. The Sandinistas, in control of the government there, had been partly funded in their guerrilla insurgency against Somoza by the Soviets and Cubans. Fearing an increasing Communist presence in Nicaragua that would threaten US national security, Carter approved a CIA plan for covert action to acquire information about Communist aid to the Sandinistas.[22]

In the meantime, the fighting between Iran and Iraq had escalated. Each nation attacked the other's oil refineries, which meant that both—especially Iraq—ceased shipping oil through the Persian Gulf, reducing exports by three million barrels a day. After Iran bombed Iraq's capital city of Baghdad, Carter convened his NSC, which supported his intention to remain strictly neutral in the Iran-Iraq war. Carter hoped, however, that the combatants might agree upon a cease-fire that would induce Iran to free the hostages and improve its relationship with the rest of the world. That did not happen, but Carter used that war in his campaign against Reagan to argue that he was the candidate for peace, whereas Reagan favored gunboat diplomacy.[23]

A conservative religious group calling itself the Moral Majority took Reagan's side on most issues. Extremely right-wing Christians, they joined

the Republican Party ostensibly because they believed it endorsed their condemnation of abortion, homosexuality, and the ERA. Furthermore, they accused Carter of giving away the Panama Canal, being soft on Communism,
and jeopardizing their children's education with the new Department of
Education. They favored prayer in schools, united families, and mothers who
did not work outside the home. When Jimmy and Rosalynn watched a television special about the Moral Majority hosted by the liberal Baptist Bill
Moyers, Carter wrote in his diary that Moyers "gave the religious nuts fifty
minutes of uninterrupted bragging on themselves."[24]

Comfortable with his own faith, Carter celebrated his 56th birthday on
October 1. His publicity director, Jerry Rafshoon, gifted him with the opinion
that Carter would win reelection in 1980 and "go down as one of the great
Presidents and human beings." Secretary of Education Shirley Hufstedler
agreed that Carter would "go down in history as a great President" and, she
added, also as "a gallant, caring man."[25]

At Bishop Airport in Flint, Michigan, where Carter had spent much of his
birthday campaigning, a question about the hostages brought out the famous
Carter temper, although he managed to keep it under control. Reagan, one
of the interviewers said, had recently accused Carter "of using the hostage
issue in the primaries" for political gain and he would "expect an October
surprise." "If you're trailing Reagan in the polls in the last week of October,"
the interviewer continued, "are the hostages coming home before election
day?" Struggling to keep calm, Carter replied: "I would pray that the hostages
would come home at the earliest possible moment regardless of the date of
the election. . . . I've never used the hostage issue for political purposes and
never will. The allegation that I would play with the lives of innocent hostages
for political purposes or delay their coming home to have some good news
just before an election is ridiculous."[26]

Carter had no time to think about a so-called October Surprise, because
he had to keep scheduled campaign stops in Dayton, Ohio, and Philadelphia
before returning to Washington. On October 3, Carter welcomed Pakistani
president General Mohammad Zia-ul-Haq to the White House and learned
that Zia was willing to accommodate refugees from Afghanistan coming into
Pakistan, but at a price. Zia wished to reschedule the repayment of Pakistani
debts to the United States, and he wanted to buy US F-16 fighter planes.
Carter agreed to both demands.[27] After Zia departed, Carter hosted a White
House reception for the National Association of Women Judges, a group
who praised him for having included more women in the federal judiciary.

Shortly after they judges left, Carter flew by helicopter to the Northern Virginia Community College, Loudoun Campus, in Sterling, Virginia, where he addressed approximately 400 guests who had gathered to witness his signing into law education amendments that increased federal funding for secondary and elementary schools, the Head Start program, and for historically Black colleges. At the end of the day, he flew aboard Air Force One to Americus, Georgia, where he joined his siblings Billy, Gloria, and Ruth for a visit and dinner with their mother who was recovering from a broken hip in the Sumter Regional Hospital. Finally, he went home to the White House, and, after a twenty-minute jog around the grounds with Rosalynn, he and Rosalynn went to bed.[28]

The next day, a Saturday, Jimmy joined Rosalynn, Amy, and Amy's friend "Cricket" Keating for a weekend fishing trip to Wayne Harpster's place at Spruce Creek. Primarily entertaining Amy, Harpster took them on "a wild trip through his field." They saw many deer, some raccoons, a fox, and two skunks, which were Amy's favorite. Others in their party had seen five black bears the night before.[29]

Rested and rejuvenated, Carter campaigned in Wisconsin and Illinois on Monday and the next day he joined Rosalynn and Ted Kennedy at the Woodburn Center for Community Mental Health in Annandale, Virginia, to sign the Mental Health Systems Act of 1980. Carter praised the role of Roman Catholics, many of whom were skeptical of his presidency, in its passage. After noting that the act was "designed to provide vital services to the most underserved group in this Nation," he introduced the Honorary Chairperson of the President's Commission on Mental Health, Rosalynn Carter, to make a few remarks. She thanked all involved, including Jimmy and Kennedy, and declared the law to be a great victory for all who had worked so hard to bring it about but especially for "those people who need help and who need care."[30]

To enjoy more such victories, Jimmy and Rosalynn knew that he had to be reelected. Reagan was slightly ahead in the polls, but the Carters refused to be discouraged as they continued campaigning separately. On October 9, Carter attended various rallies and fundraising events in Tennessee and North Carolina before flying on to Tallahassee for another fundraiser. The next morning at the Florida State Capitol, he addressed legislators and special guests and signed the Refugee Education Assistance Act that was important for a state dealing with the thousands of newly arrived refugee children from Cuba and Haiti. Later that day at a town hall meeting with a group of senior citizens in St. Petersburg, Carter attacked Reagan as a racist who would be bad for the country, especially for the Sunshine State's many retired citizens who drew Social Security checks. Campaigning in other parts of Florida, Rosalynn stressed to Jewish residents what the administration had done for Israel.[31]

Wherever the Carters went, they worked the crowds shaking as many hands as possible and creating a challenge for their security details. It was almost impossible to identify a lone would-be assassin. When Carter went to Nashville on October 9 to hold a town meeting at the Grand Ole Opry, he narrowly escaped becoming the victim of John Hinckley, a mentally deranged young man who sought the notoriety of being a presidential assassin. Hinckley stalked him at the Opryland Hotel and elsewhere, but Carter always coincidentally left before Hinckley could get a shot at him. The Nashville police, unaware of Hinckley's intent, arrested him at the airport, found three guns in his suitcase, called the FBI, and took him away to a local jail. After paying a small fine, he was released. In the meantime, Carter had safely left Tennessee.[32]

The Reagan campaign mounted an attack of words. There was no place Carter could go to escape the annihilation by language that Tony Dolan planned for him. Dolan monitored Carter's every action, every use of a member of his administration as a surrogate, and ruthlessly attacked him for abusing his powers as an incumbent president. Dolan gleefully collected cynical accounts of the administration from the pages of the *Washington Post* and the *Wall Street Journal*. Whenever Carter made a speech about tax cuts and defense strength that "played well," Dolan worked with campaign adviser Ed Meese to "turn it on him." Once it was known that Carter and Reagan would engage in their only debate on October 28 in Cleveland, Ohio, Dolan and company began to coach Reagan. A public opinion poll taken in mid-October revealed that 77% of the responders said that the economy and inflation was the number one issue, and 51.3% believed that Carter would win the debate and the election.[33]

Reagan's conservatism in both domestic and foreign matters was in his favor, but the major issue that might swing the election was the plight of the hostages. Being realistic, Carter recorded in his diary on Sunday, October 26: "It was increasingly clear to me and my advisors that if we could not secure the release of the hostages before the election—an unlikely prospect at best—our chances of beating Reagan were slim."[34] Reagan knew that too, and he assigned William Casey, Ed Meese, and George H. W. Bush the task of making certain that the Iranians did not release the hostages before the election.

More loyal to the Democratic Party than to Carter, Ted Kennedy made a few appearances in October 1980 to help the Democratic candidate. On October 15, Kennedy and his wife Joan greeted Carter when he arrived at Logan International Airport, Boston, and later Kennedy introduced him before he addressed about 300 guests at the Christopher Columbus Community Center. After that indoor address, Carter spoke to about 500 more guests at an outdoor rally. Later the same day, at Secaucus, New Jersey, Kennedy introduced the president for the third time that day to a group of 400 guests who had come to hear him at the Meadowlands Hilton Hotel. On October 19, Jimmy and Rosalynn attended a Carter-Kennedy Unity Celebration at the Shoreham Hotel in Washington, where Kennedy again graciously introduced the president. Finally, on October 20, at the end of a long day of campaigning, Carter arrived in New York City. Kennedy was among the dignitaries who accompanied him to the Concord Baptist Church and less than an hour later, introduced Carter to about 1,000 community leaders from the Bedford Stuyvesant area of Brooklyn. After visiting various ethnic groups, Carter arrived at the Regency Hotel, where Kennedy introduced him to New York Jewish leaders and major contributors to the Democratic National Convention.[35] The press paid virtually no attention to the lame attempt to prove that Kennedy and Carter had been reconciled, because the big story was the hostages.

Neither the Republican campaign nor the media would allow Carter to minimize the hostage crisis. CBS anchorman Walter Cronkite continued to sign off his widely watched evening news program every night with a statement of how many days the hostages had been held. Ted Koppel's popular *Nightline* show shouted daily that the United States had been held hostage for yet another day. Commentators frequently reminded their listeners that the impending election day of November 4 would be the first anniversary of the militants having captured the US diplomats. While repeating his standard public statements about his efforts to free the hostages, Carter was also secretly working with Algeria, various individuals and groups within Iran, the International Court of Justice, and the UN to win their release. He thought he had everything in place to gain their freedom before the election.[36]

The Reagan people continued to accuse Carter of planning an October surprise that would benefit his candidacy. So concerned was the Reagan camp that Carter might pull off an unexpected release of the hostages in October that Reagan himself publicly declared that Carter might do it. Carter responded, "It'll be a surprise to me too." He prayed for his imprisoned countrymen every day, he said on October 10 during a television interview in St. Petersburg, Florida, and again on October 17 during a question and answer session with journalists in the Cabinet Room at the White House, but he had no idea when they might be released.[37]

Unbeknown to the Democratic campaign, the Republicans were planning an October surprise of their own. Coaching Reagan for the October 28 debate with Carter, Dolan advised Reagan to call "an October moratorium" on the hostage issue. Reagan could say, Dolan continued, that there are "hopeful signs and some diplomatic movement," but he should not mention it anymore in October.[38] In the meantime, Casey made a generous offer to Ayatollah Khomeini. Meeting secretly with Khomeini's representatives and Israeli agents, in two Paris hotels between October 15 and 20, Republican operatives increased their offer of arms for weapons-hungry Iran if the Iranians would promise to hold the hostages until after the election.[39]

How much Reagan knew about the secret plan is uncertain, but he knew what Carter might say and what tactics he might use during their debate. All thirteen of his advisers had gained access to part of Carter's briefing book and were using it to prepare Reagan for the debate. Allegedly stolen by Donald Gregg, a CIA employee assigned to the NSC with access to the Carter administration's security information, the pilfered pages contained notes from a debate brainstorming session of Carter-Mondale staffers. The unidentified person who delivered them to Edwin Meese, long-time Reagan confidante and attorney in charge of daily activities of the campaign, assured Meese that the notes were "provided by a very reliable source who has intimate connections to a Carter debate staffer."[40]

A Congressional investigation in 1984 revealed that the Carter briefing material had been taken unethically from the White House and delivered to the Republican campaign. The most likely avenue was the NSC, where Donald Gregg would have had access to the documents, but there were other possibilities. Of the thirteen persons interviewed by the Congressional committee who said they had seen or received the material, four were prominent Republicans: James A. Baker II, David R. Gergen, David A. Stockman, and George Will III. When questioned, William J. Casey, manager of the Reagan campaign, admitted that he had seen the material.[41]

More potentially devastating to Carter's reelection than the purloined briefing notes, was the clandestine meeting in Paris between Republican operatives and Iranian officials that sealed the immediate fate of the hostages. After several weeks of secret preparations, the participants began to arrive at the hotel on the night of October 20. This drama in Paris, which many could not believe possible, determined the immediate status of the hostages and may have influenced the outcome of the presidential election.[42]

Witnesses later reported what they had seen. Ari Ben-Menashe, an Israeli military intelligence officer whose knowledge of Farsi qualified him to deal with Iran, recognized Republican aide Robert McFarlane and CIA officers Robert Gates (executive assistant to Stansfield Turner), Donald Gregg, and George Cave (the agency's expert on Iran) when they arrived at the hotel. Mehdi Karrubi, the top foreign policy aide to the Ayatollah, showed up, and soon thereafter, vice presidential candidate George H. W. Bush and Republican campaign manager William Casey arrived. Bush and Casey hurried to the conference room trying to avoid being seen. According to an agreement, the Iranians would release the fifty-two hostages in return for a payment of $52 million, guarantees of arms sales to Iran, and the unfreezing of Iranian assets in US banks. Money and weapons would be sent into Iran via Israeli sources. The date for the release depended on the Americans delivering what they promised but was finally set for Reagan's expected inauguration on January 20, 1981.

The US participants were motivated by a strong wish to prevent Carter's reelection. Although the CIA remained loyal to the United States government, it was a massive organization so secret that it was not possible for the top leadership to know what all of its operatives might be doing. Some disgruntled old officers allegedly resented the fact that Carter had not kept their former chief George H. W. Bush as the agency's head. Carter had campaigned against corruption in the CIA, worked to reform it, and fired a number of unproductive or untrustworthy agents. His appointment of Stansfield Turner as director was not popular with the organization. His use of Brzezinski to edit and present the daily CIA briefings to him did not sit well with Turner and possibly others in the spy agency.[43]

The Israelis had their own reasons for participating in the October Surprise. Some members of Begin's Likud Party did not want Carter to push for a Palestinian state or use his nonproliferation preaching to stop Israel from selling nuclear devices to other countries. Begin was the proud leader of a proud country that owed much of its existence to the United States, but his political position was jeopardized by his shaky friendship with Carter.[44]

In Tehran, where some of the US hostages were held, a strange conversation took place sometime after the Paris meeting. Kathryn Koob, one of the two women still held by the students, asked her captor if he would mail letters she and others had written and left in the mailbox back at the embassy. He smiled and said, "You'll be home before they get there." She latched on to the word home, but she didn't trust him and could only wonder what he knew that she and the other hostages, as well as the US government, did not know.[45]

Meanwhile, in the United States, the public debate between the two candidates raged. The Republicans delighted in a newly published biography of Carter by Betty Glad, a political scientist at the University of Illinois. Entitled *Jimmy Carter: In Search of the Great White House*, it emphasized the negative side of Carter's rise to power in Georgia and generally criticized his presidency. Upon presenting the book to Ed Meese for his use to instruct Reagan, Tony Dolan said, "keep meanness story going."[46] Reagan, somewhat devious himself, was willing to bring international pressure to defeat Carter. On October 11, he wrote a private letter to Chancellor Helmut Schmidt stating that, if elected he would return consistency to foreign policy, keep the United States strong, preserve peace, and negotiate an agreement with the Soviet Union that would be better than SALT II. In a public statement six days later, Reagan, trying to damage Carter's main platform of human rights, contended that Carter had not adequately represented the principles of the country to the Soviet Union and to the world and that he had actually encouraged some of the "evil" rulers in Asia and elsewhere who were major abusers of human rights. George H. W. Bush, on the same day he secretly went to Paris, delivered a strong pro-Israel speech in an attempt to win more Jewish voters to the Republican side.[47]

Carter welcomed a *US News and World Report* story on October 20 that may have helped him win votes. The magazine reported accurately that Carter had put his stamp on the federal courts. He had appointed 264 of the 648 federal judges, which was more than any other president had done. Many of his appointees were women, Blacks, and Hispanics, and 154 of the 264 he appointed served in new judicial seats that Congress had created in 1978. The next day Carter went on the attack again. He ridiculed a speech of Reagan's, in which he claimed that he had "some ideas" on how to deal with the hostage issue, as "horse manure." Reagan may have been puffing smoke, or he may have known what Casey and company were planning.[48]

Rosalynn went toe-to-toe with Nancy Reagan by answering a series of questions posed to both of them by the *Ladies Home Journal*. As First Lady, Rosalynn said that she would continue "to spotlight the projects that can help to create what I call a more caring society." Such projects, she said, were those that dealt with the mentally ill, the elderly, poor, women, and refugees. She intended to use the office of First Lady to be as helpful in those areas as possible. She still hoped for ratification of the ERA, and despite the Supreme Court decision in *Roe v. Wade* she opposed abortion. There was no doubt in her mind that her husband was the best person to lead the country for four more years, and she would continue to give him support and advice. She and Jimmy, she said, would work for preservation of the family, economic security, improved and expanded educational opportunities, justice and equality for all people, and "above all, we want peace."

Nancy Reagan's answers reflected the differences between her husband and Rosalynn's. If she became First Lady, she said she wanted to continue the Foster Grandparent Program, support drug rehabilitation, and pass the ERA as a statute rather than an amendment. She would also, she said, urge the women's movement to settle down. The five people she admired most were the Pope; Dr. Jonas Salk, who had discovered a vaccine for polio; Beverly Sills, the famed opera singer; actor James Cagney; and Russian ballet dancer Mikhail Baryshnikov. She thought "Ronnie" should be president because he was a man of integrity. The five issues that concerned her most were inflation, foreign policy, crime, moral decline, and unemployment, but she gave no specifics about any of them.[49]

Day after day, Carter and Reagan debated the issues more concretely than their wives' interviews in the *Ladies Home Journal*. Reagan claimed he would slash the budget and reverse all that Carter had done in foreign policy. Carter replied that he would not make cuts in indexed programs such as Social Security, but that he would use tax incentives to encourage businesses and support affirmative action. He would always keep the US military combat ready, and he would maintain the honor of the country while trying to free the hostages. Carter intended, as they had agreed at Camp David, for the United States to be a full partner with both Israel and Egypt. He supported an undivided Jerusalem and the emigration of Soviet Jews. He promised to search for, denaturalize, and deport ex-Nazis living in the United States.[50]

Matching the substantial Republican campaign war chest and finding a sufficient number of capable surrogates were major problems for Carter. Connecticut Senator Abraham Ribicoff, seeking to help him win Jewish and Northeastern voters, declared that Carter was not weak but a good president with a sound energy program. He was "a man who believes peace is possible and is willing to take that extra step to achieve it," Ribicoff insisted.[51] Nevertheless, Carter's call for energy austerity and punitive boycotts, when compared with Reagan's promise of unlimited consumption, made Reagan clearly the winner in the minds of many voters. Carter's concerns about energy conservation, nuclear proliferation, and human rights put him ahead of his time, but it did not win the approval of contemporary voters who were unwilling to make sacrifices to achieve those goals.[52]

Usually lightening his speeches with a joke, Carter planned to poke fun at Reagan's cool attitude toward women's liberation and opposition to speed limits in a speech, which he apparently never delivered, at the University of Detroit Law School: "Mr. Reagan is the only candidate I know," he had planned to say only days before their scheduled debate, "who wants to speed up cars and slow down women."[53] Michigan, too, became the site for an hilarious exchange between Carter and former President Ford, who was campaigning for Reagan. Carter had referred to Grand Rapids, Michigan, as "Cedar Rapids," an error that irritated Ford who claimed Grand Rapids as his hometown. Without thinking, he quickly retorted in a newspaper interview that Carter must not even realize that Michigan was "one of the *forty-eight* states"! They must have enjoyed joking about that years later, but the imminent election was no joke.[54]

Carter and surrogates—the primary one being Rosalynn, but most of them from his cabinet or administration—toured the country proclaiming what he had done and would do. Attempting to mute the impact of an inflation rate that had hit 15.7%, Democratic surrogates dropped hints that the hostages might be freed. Carter himself visited fourteen states during the nine days leading up to the October 28 debate, but he scrupulously avoided any reference to the hostages that he did not know to be absolutely true. Rewarding African-American voters who appeared to remain loyal to him, Jimmy and Rosalynn hosted a ceremonial dinner in honor of famous eighty-seven-year-old Benjamin Mays, a pioneer in Black education, and a reception for African-American ministers at the White House. Rosalynn passed more of the days before the debate not hosting dinners, but traveling alone to the South and the West dispensing the message that Jimmy was strong, courageous, and a man of peace who served the best interests of all Americans.[55]

Jimmy and Rosalynn often retreated to Camp David to meet, rest, and plan strategy, just as they had retreated to Plains during the 1976 campaign.

THIRTY THREE

The Agony of Defeat

In the seclusion of Hickory Lodge at Camp David, with Rosalynn intently observing, Carter laboriously rehearsed for his debate with Reagan. To play the role of Reagan, Pat Caddell had chosen his friend Sam Popkin. Popkin, a political science professor from California, set up a podium, lights, and every other detail exactly like they would be in the auditorium where Carter would face Reagan on October 28. Popkin, in his late thirties, rumpled and wearing glasses, did not look like Reagan, but he had studied Reagan carefully and determined that Reagan had no more than twenty or thirty set paragraphs. Popkin did not try to imitate Reagan the genial guy, but he concentrated on what Reagan would say and how he would say it. Privately, Popkin later confessed that it had been emotionally draining to look the president in the eye, tell him he had failed, brought the United States to its knees, and humiliated the country. Nervous not only because Rosalynn was watching, but also because he wondered if the Secret Service guards might hit him "in the knee," Popkin nevertheless led the president through several intense rehearsal sessions.

A good student, Carter improved with practice, but he had a hard time refraining from interrupting, keeping his composure, and not revealing his anger. He mastered the lesson, however, and was prepared to keep calm and focused during the debate. His tutor noted that by the end of the grueling sessions, Carter was "handling things" well, as "you would expect from a man of that intelligence and demeanor." Adept at defending his record, Carter thought he was ready to debate Reagan in Cleveland.[1]

On the eve of the debate, October 25, the polls showed Carter leading Reagan by 45% to 42%, but a third party candidate, John B. Anderson, claimed 8% of those polled.[2] Refusing to leave the race, Anderson organized the independent National Unity Party, chose a Democrat, the popular former Democratic governor of Wisconsin and former ambassador to Mexico Patrick Lucey as his running mate, and developed a platform that favored support for research in universities, environmental protection, ratification of the ERA, and a woman's right to have an abortion. He opposed Carter's reinstatement of the military draft, but he strongly supported US military strength and the NATO alliance against the Soviet Union.[3] The son of an immigrant father who had been willing to make sacrifices in order to give his family a better future, Anderson appealed to moderate "Rockefeller" Republicans and liberal Democrats, especially college students, who had supported Ted Kennedy.

In early September, the League of Women Voters, which determined the eligibility of candidates to participate in debates, decided that Anderson was qualified. Carter refused to debate him, because he found it difficult to take his candidacy seriously. Reagan did debate Anderson in Baltimore on September 21, an event Carter found "really depressing," because Anderson "helped himself with liberals" while Reagan seemed to be "ineffectual."[4] By early October, Anderson's following declined but still remained numerous enough that he might be a spoiler in a tight race between Reagan and Carter.[5]

Former Republican President Richard Nixon, the master of dirty tricks, sent the Reagan campaign a long letter the day before the debate with advice about what to say about Carter. After a discourse on the Carter presidency, Nixon concluded that Reagan should say: "It is time to rip off the mask of self-righteousness & let people see the failed leader he has proved himself to be."[6]

Carter, who was neither self-righteous nor a failure, was well prepared and felt confident when he went to Cleveland on the eve of his only debate with the Californian. Carter had wanted a series of debates in various parts of the country, as with Ford in 1976. Reagan, who had a high profile and often appeared to be in the lead, wanted only one debate in which the image of the two men side by side would very likely favor the experienced actor. Carter was strong on the issues and knowledgeable about specific constituencies, but no coaching could give him the speaking ability to match that of the "Great Communicator."

Before leaving for Cleveland, Jimmy talked with Amy about the debate. No typical thirteen-year-old, Amy had grown up around her parents and world leaders talking "shop." She told her father that she thought the atomic bomb was the issue that was most important, an idea she had no doubt gotten from his frequent references to nuclear proliferation and the need for SALT II. She was also unusually knowledgeable about sizes of atomic bombs, international issues, and the hostage crisis.[7]

On the day before the debate, Rosalynn was campaigning in Philadelphia, making an earnest appeal to Jewish voters. She had accepted an invitation from Avital Shcharansky, wife of imprisoned Jewish dissident Anatoly Shcharansky, to address the National Conference on Soviet Jewry on Monday, October 27. Rosalynn reminded her audience how well her husband served the needs of Jewish Americans and other Jewish people around the world, especially those who desperately wished to emigrate from Russia. "The Carter administration has made human rights one of the cornerstones in American foreign policy," she said. "Around the globe—in Latin America, in Asia, and in the Soviet Union—the name of Jimmy Carter is synonymous with human rights," she emphasized. Quoting statistics that proved that the number of exit permits from the Soviet Union had increased to 50,000 from 14,000 during Carter's administration, she promised that America's fight for Jewish dissidents' freedom would continue. Referring to Avital Shcharansky, Rosalynn commented that the fact "that she is here with us tonight is a testament to the human spirit. I know that she will not rest until her husband is released from a Soviet prison." Shcharansky had been imprisoned in 1977 for monitoring the Helsinki Accords in order to force Soviet compliance, but Carter had not yet been able to win his release.[8] In the evening Rosalynn attended a performance of the Broadway play "Elephant Man," which had been directed by one of Carter's speechwriters, Gordon Stewart. The next day, she flew to Cleveland.[9] Carter was already there and had been to the Cleveland Public Auditorium to check on the sound system and preview the venue.[10]

During the debate, Carter came across as experienced, knowledgeable, compassionate, but obviously smaller in physical stature than Reagan and sometimes ill at ease. Relaxed in front of the audience, Reagan posed as a friendly critic looking down upon the president and casting vague aspersions on the accuracy of his answers. The master of short phrases and gimmicks that would stick in the minds of his listeners, Reagan denied that he was a warmonger, that he would destroy most social programs, or that he would run up enormous debt. Reagan had the advantage of knowing what was in Carter's purloined briefing book, which made it easy for him to guess how Carter would respond to the questions he was asked. After Carter said something profound, Reagan would say, "There you go again," as if he were addressing a child who had repeated some offense.

When Reagan asked the rhetorical question whether citizens were better off now than they had been four years earlier, the specter of gasoline lines, inflation, and long-held hostages might have easily passed through their minds. Serious issues of SALT II, the normalization of relations with China, civil service and welfare reform, mental health, and human rights were not nearly so obvious. When Carter mentioned his conversation with Amy before the debate, he walked directly into Reagan's trap. It sounded as if Carter relied on an adolescent for advice about a most serious matter, whereas Carter was actually saying that nuclear proliferation was such a serious issue that a young person could understand it. Nevertheless, the reference to Amy would subject him to ridicule after the debate ended.

Carter easily won the factual and intellectual debate, but Reagan walked away with the image prize. Carter's standing in the polls began to drop, while Reagan's rose, and continued to do so, despite daily hopeful news from Iran. The media's focus on Iran and on Reagan's verbal jabs highlighted major trends that had emerged in the United States during the past two decades. Carter's tenure in office coincided with the end of a liberal era that had begun with the election of Kennedy and Johnson in the early 1960s, declined under Nixon and Ford, and nearly collapsed during the Carter years. Reagan had the advantage of riding the swelling conservative tide that was sweeping over the nation. It was social, religious, political, international, and held goals the opposite of those Carter had set for the future of the country. The day after the debate, the polls showed Carter trailing Reagan 43% to 44%, with Anderson at 8%.[11]

During the six days between the debate and Election Day, Jimmy and Rosalynn separately blanketed the country, desperately trying to pick up the votes he needed to be reelected. On October 29, Carter campaigned in Cleveland, Pittsburgh, Rochester, Newark, and Philadelphia. The next day, after two more speeches in Philadelphia, Carter spoke at a rally in New York City's Garment District before moving on to Saginaw, Michigan; St. Louis; and finally, Columbia where he stayed overnight as a guest with South Carolina Governor Richard W. Riley and his family at the Executive Mansion. From there, he made whirlwind visits to Florida, Tennessee, Mississippi, and Texas, all Southern states that he hoped to keep in the Democratic fold.[12]

After spending most of Saturday, November 1, campaigning in the Texas cities of Houston, Brownsville, San Antonio, Abilene, and Fort Worth, a tired Jimmy Carter flew to Milwaukee and then to Chicago to end his day. In the middle of the night, Carter was awakened in his Chicago hotel room by a telephone call from the White House switchboard conveying news from Iran that seemed to suggest that the Iranian parliament had offered conditions that could lead to the release of the hostages. He hurriedly conferred in separate telephone calls with Ed Muskie, Warren Christopher, and Rosalynn. Skipping church that Sunday morning and cancelling his campaign schedule for the day, Carter flew back to the White House, arriving around 8 a.m. Over the next several hours, he discussed the hostage situation in long meetings with administration officials and shorter private meetings with Ham Jordan and Charles Kirbo.

Carter had noticed after October 20, the date of the Reagan campaign's secret meeting in Paris about which he knew nothing, that the Iranians either quit talking or began to be less intransigent. Then on November 2, the Iranian parliament unexpectedly announced formal terms for releasing the hostages: unfreezing assets in US and foreign banks, cancelling legal and financial claims against Iran, and recognizing Iran's claim to the Shah's family fortune. Khomeini wanted the militants who held the hostages to become available to fight on the war front against the Iraqis, and he needed money for arms and munitions. Carter thought the offer a positive development, but he remained wary. Reagan did not comment.[13]

The Carters, exhausted from the campaign, found it hard to believe that the Iranian government was suddenly softening on the issue. When the militants agreed to turn the hostages over to the government and use the Algerian president as an intermediary, Carter's response was simply "we do not know what will happen—so let us not speculate." Aboard Air Force One on his way back to Washington, he commented that "We have good relations with Algeria. We provided disaster relief after the earthquake. They also have good relations with Iran." Jody Powell pointed out that an Algerian was co-chairman of the UN commission that went to Tehran to investigate the hostage situation, but neither he nor Carter would predict that the hostages would start coming home that week. At the end of the day on November 2, when it seemed that there was serious hope for the hostages' release, the polls had showed Carter and Reagan almost evenly matched. By the end of the day on November 3, however, when it appeared the release was not imminent, the polls quickly trended in favor of Reagan.[14]

Early on the morning of November 3, Carter had returned to the campaign trail, frantically leapfrogging across the nation from one rally to another in the Midwest and then in the Pacific Northwest, ending up in Seattle late that night. From there, he took a long overnight flight back east to Warner-Robbins Air Force Base, near Macon, Georgia. From there he could get home to cast his election day ballot and await the judgment of the voters.[15]

Rosalynn was already in Plains, having just returned from her own grueling schedule of campaign appearances during the hectic days after the Cleveland debate. Calling Hamilton Jordan from the field on Friday night, October 31, she had reported that the crowds were large and enthusiastic, but she was still "very worried." Ham told her that the race was tight and he had no idea how the hostage crisis might impact it. They encouraged each other, but when he hung up, Ham thought to himself, "hell, I am as worried about the election as she is."[16]

On Sunday, November 2, while Jimmy was flying from Chicago to Washington to deal with the new hostage developments, Rosalynn was at the Veteran's Memorial Center in Martin's Ferry, Ohio, and later in Columbia, Missouri, where she asked those who had come to hear her speak to pray for the hostages and to vote for her husband. "We must have a President who is courageous," she said, but privately she wrote, "damn, damn Khomeini."[17] On Monday, she and Chip made one last desperate appeal for votes in the Midwest. Chip Carter, who had led the first Hartford-Tel Aviv Friendship Flight two and a half years earlier, asked Jewish voters to understand that his father's negotiation of the Camp David Accords had served the best interests of Israel very well.[18] Then they flew home to Plains.

In the wee hours of Election Day, November 4, while flying home, Carter talked on a conference line with his pollster Pat Caddell, his publicist Gerald Rafshoon, and Hamilton Jordan. Caddell gave him the bad news that the polls showed that he could not win. Carter reported to his three senior staffers that the hostages had been supposedly "transferred" from control of the militants to the Iranian government, but there was no confirmation of an actual physical transfer. An Algerian, acceptable to both sides as an intermediary, had not communicated with the Americans, and thus Carter had nothing to announce about the hostages at the dawn of Election Day.[19] The mood aboard Air Force One turned funereal. Stu Eizenstat, who had worked so hard to influence Jewish votes, went into Carter's cabin and burst into tears. Hugging the man from Plains who had taken all of them to the White House, he said, "Mr. President, we have let you down." Emotionless, Carter attempted to console Stu and his other friends, but he could think only of Rosalynn and the grief and pain she would inevitably have to endure. He asked all on board with him not to notify Rosalynn until they reached Georgia.[20]

Rosalynn had already admitted to herself that they would lose, but she did not know whether Jimmy knew it. Her deep, compassionate concern for

Jimmy equaled his for her. She worried about Amy in the White House and the rest of the family who would share the heartbreak. Extremely tired, she slept a few hours until Jimmy arrived.

At 6:40 a.m., Air Force One touched down at Warner-Robbins where a helicopter was waiting to take Jimmy home to Plains. When his helicopter landed at Souter Field an hour later, he immediately spotted Rosalynn waiting to greet him. After a quick emotional embrace, she asked, "How are the polls?" Jimmy turned his thumb down and told her: "They are bad. We just have to accept it." Keeping up a positive public image, Jimmy and Rosalynn rode together to Plains High School to cast their votes. When a reporter asked how he would vote, Carter grinned and said he would vote for the best candidate. He evaded questions about what he already knew, and he stubbornly, like a South Georgia turtle to which he had been frequently compared, held out hope that, if enough of his supporters voted, he might yet win.

After voting, Jimmy and Rosalynn went to the Railroad Depot, which had been their symbolic campaign headquarters four years earlier, to greet the friendly crowd that had gathered there. Jimmy, who had not slept the night before, briefly reviewed the things he had done as president, remarking that he had made decisions in the White House with the memory of his upbringing in Plains always in his mind. He had tried to honor the commitment he had made to his neighbors four years earlier, he said, but his words could not mask the pain and disappointment that he, Rosalynn, and the local people who revered them felt so intensely. In Houston, Texas, a very different scene transpired, as an elated George H. W. Bush told reporters that the Republicans were "in like a burglar."[21] After going home to pick up Jack and Judy, Jimmy and Rosalynn rode to the Sumter County Hospital in Americus to visit Miss Lillian, who was still in the hospital recovering from hip surgery. Despite her tear-stained face, Rosalynn tried to comfort the family who had always banded together during the campaigns and the presidency and who felt the loss almost as deeply as she and Jimmy did. Unable to tarry in Georgia, Jimmy and Rosalynn left at midmorning for the sad trip back to Washington, where a crowd of well-wishers and some members of the press waited at the White House to greet them. Aboard Marine One as they flew to the South Lawn of the White House, Jimmy and Rosalynn looked at each other, and she reached out and touched his face. The Secret Service agent who witnessed it smiled and thought that the healing process had begun. Carter bounded from the helicopter, flashed a grin, and thanked those who had come out in the rain to meet them. Trying to cheer them, he told them that he felt confident of the outcome, and he urged them to vote.[22]

The healing process had in fact begun a few hours earlier. Jimmy and Rosalynn had talked privately in Plains and taken a nap, before appearing "remarkably at ease" when they gathered the family to tell them what to expect by the end of the day. Rosalynn informed the family that they had lost. Jimmy went into a bathroom to change his clothes. Rosalynn followed him, and when he sat on the side of the tub, she sat on his knee, leaned her head on his shoulder and cried. Later, when a friend commented that Jimmy did not seem bitter, she said that she was bitter enough for both of them.[23]

In his private office at the White House, Carter talked again with Pat Caddell, who confirmed the bad news that he could not win, and with Jody Powell. After many telephone calls, and a short jog, Jimmy, accompanied by Rosalynn, Chip, and Charlie and Boo Kirbo, went to the Oval Office at 5:30 p.m. to meet with their key campaign advisors. The exit polls showed they were suffering an overwhelming defeat. Bob Strauss, Pat Caddell, Ham Jordan, Jack Watson, Gerald Rafshoon, Tim Kraft, and Phil Wise had gathered like a group of mourners. Jimmy attempted to comfort them. "We have all done the best that we could," he said, trying to cheer them slightly.

Getting down to business quickly, Carter then asked the "mourners" for suggestions for his concession speech. It was important to him and Rosalynn, he said, that "we be proud and gracious in defeat." As those friends in victory and in defeat filed past the First Couple, Rosalynn kissed each one of them, and Jimmy gripped their arms and gave each a firm handshake. Ham Jordan could not look Jimmy in the eye. He gritted his teeth, shook his hand, and tried to avoid direct eye contact. "I just wanted to get the hell out of there," he later admitted.[24]

After a private dinner with members of the Carter and Kirbo families, Carter placed a two-minute call at 8:35 p.m. to President-elect Reagan to congratulate him upon his victory. He then spoke with his mother in Georgia for another two minutes before preparing to go to the Sheraton Washington Hotel to greet campaign supporters who were gathered there. "It hurts," he told them, but "we must come together as a united and unified people." "I have been blessed," he continued, "to have the opportunity to try to shape the destiny of this nation." He had accepted the "special responsibility" to seek solutions to the world's problems, and "we have had four years of peace," he proudly noted. "God has been good to me and to this country," he said in a kind of re-affirmation of the faith that had always sustained him in difficult times. Despite his disappointment, he would continue to love the country and its people. He would continue to work every day to free the hostages in Iran. Rosalynn, who stood beside him, said it pained her to look out over the crowd who had worked so hard for them, many of whom were crying, but she worried more about how the loss might impact her family. After heartfelt thanks, the Carters returned to the White House.[25]

Before the polls closed in the western part of the country, Carter sent a telegram to Reagan: "It is now apparent that the American people have chosen you as the next President. I congratulate you and I pledge to you our fullest support and cooperation in bringing about an orderly transition of government in the weeks ahead. My best wishes are with you and your family as you undertake the responsibilities that lie before you." At 12:30 a.m. he went to bed and slept until 7:30.[26]

Tip O'Neill thought Carter's loss was "sad" and undeserved, but he and other senior Democrats, especially those from the western states, were outraged that Carter had conceded before the polls closed in California and jeopardized other Democrats' chances for victory. Jody Powell had tried to get Carter to delay until after those polls closed, but Carter wanted to "get it over with." O'Neill told Frank Moore, whom he had always loathed, "You guys came in like a bunch of jerks, and I see you're going out the same way." Representative John Brademas of Indiana, the House Majority Whip, who lost his seat in the election, caustically remarked that the born-again Georgian "had the attitude of a Calvinist white man's burden regarding politics" and moaned that Carter "wasn't a good politician."[27] The good that Jimmy and Rosalynn had accomplished seemed to float down into the dust as their party, as well as much of the public, repudiated them.

When all the votes were counted, Reagan had 51% of the popular vote to Carter's 41%. Anderson got 7%. Carter won only five states: Georgia, Minnesota, Hawaii, West Virginia, and Maryland, plus the District of Columbia. The first president from the Deep South since 1848, he was largely rejected by that region except among the African-American voters who were not numerous enough to impact any state other than Georgia. As the somber crowd at the Plains Deport listened to his televised concession speech, there was not a dry eye among them.

Carter had worked hard to win Jewish voters, who comprised only 4% of the electorate, but he was not surprised that he got only 45% of their votes. Reagan received 39%, and 15% went to Anderson. Carter had won 64% of them in 1976. His policy toward Israel and hope for justice for the Palestinians did not win him favor among Jewish-American voters. Most of them would give him high marks for his human rights efforts, but many rejected his stand on Palestine and disliked his criticism of Israel. Both Jimmy and Rosalynn thought that in the aftermath of the Camp David Accords, as well as other things he had done for Jewish people, that he "deserved and should have had the Jewish support."[28]

The morning after the election, Jimmy and Rosalynn sat at the breakfast table with Charlie Kirbo and confronted the reality of their new lives. Kirbo told them that the peanut warehouse was nearly $1 million in debt. They decided to sell it, for they did not intend to operate it themselves, and the proceeds from the sale might be sufficient to cover their debts.[29]

Later in the morning, Carter sent instructions to his senior staff that they were to behave with class, come up with good transitional ideas, and carry out their duties. He reminded them that "Carter will be President until noon on Jan. 20." Chief of Staff Jack Watson would head the transition team. Jimmy and Rosalynn planned to go to Camp David for about ten days to rest, thank their supporters, and plan their future. Carter told reporters he had invited to the Oval Office that he and Rosalynn "had no hard feelings or bitterness" and that he hoped to make the final two and a half months of his administration the best of the entire four years. The next day, he reemphasized to his staff that he wanted to conduct the best transition ever, but *"full cooperation does not mean sharing responsibility and authority."*[30]

Carter spent much of that morning of November 5 in the Oval Office getting the usual reports from the National Security Adviser, conversing with Cabinet members, and consulting Director of Central Intelligence Stansfield Turner. Secretary of State Edmund Muskie, National Security Advisor Zbigniew Brzezinski, and Deputy Secretary of State Warren Christopher, who had taken a leading role in negotiating with the Iranians, joined him to analyze confusing statements coming from Khomeini. Later, Jimmy talked with Rosalynn, their son Jack, and Charlie Kirbo. He also contacted Ezer Weizman, the former Minister of Defense for Israel with whom Carter had been able to communicate, but the subject of their conversation went unrecorded.[31]

Shortly after noon, Jimmy and Rosalynn departed for Camp David, their place of solace. Jimmy was finding comfort in family, friends, the natural environment, and his religious faith. Unable to accept defeat, he was already thinking about what he might do in the next stage in his life. Rosalynn, however, was seriously depressed.[32]

Close friends tried to cheer them. Brzezinski said it best in a personal note: "Mr. President and Rosalynn—Life is full of mystery, and victory is often followed by defeat and then again by victory. But you have already won the greatest victory of all: You have touched, and improved the lives of thousands and thousands of people—in prisons abroad, underprivileged at home, ignored and slighted or just forgotten. You made love of others into a tool of power, and those who have worked with you have also come to love you. I will always be gratefully and personally better because of you."[33]

In a telegram from Cairo, President Sadat praised his friend profusely: "hail President Carter for . . . the peace process [and] . . . bilateral relations." Carter, he wrote, had "acted as a statesman who honors his word; a statesman who appreciates the standing of the nation he represents and acts accordingly." Sadat appreciated how Carter and the people of the United States stood by Egypt during difficult times. He wished peace upon "our friend Carter when he implements the will of his people and steps down."[34]

Carter dealt with his loss as his mother and father would have done. He retreated into the balm of nature and went fishing. His and Rosalynn's close friends from Georgia, Betty and John Pope, sent them a note saying they looked forward to having them home in Georgia to walk by a mountain brook, climb a mountain, and generally enjoy the outdoors of their native state. Before passing it on to Rosalynn, Jimmy noted in the margin: "Ros— Something to look forward to in the months ahead!"[35] Carter spent a day and a half at Camp David in his carpentry shop, making four "very complicated little fly line drying reels," three of which he would use as gifts for his fishing friends.[36]

On November 7, Jimmy and Rosalynn went to visit their friend Wayne Harpster and their favorite fishing hole in Pennsylvania. Carter had made a trout fishing box for Harpster while at Camp David. The next day, he and Rosalynn fished, and he hunted pheasant and quail. He also signed documents for Warren Christopher to take to Algeria to help the Algerians get the hostages freed. He took care, he wrote in his diary, to make certain that the wording would not be embarrassing to the United States. In the evening they watched the movie *The First Deadly Sin*. The next day, they kept the same relaxed schedule, returning to Camp David.

Carter discussed with Ham his post-presidential plans to stay in Plains and commute to Atlanta. Ham would teach at Emory University, Jody Powell and Frank Moore would remain in Washington, and Phil Wise, Susan Clough, and Madeline McBean would stay with the Carters. Carter promised to find jobs for all of his people, either in business or academe. On Sunday he and Rosalynn attended a worship service conducted by Major Ray Woodall, a US Army chaplain. After telephone conversations with friends and officials, they watched the movie *The Brothers Karamazov* in the evening. On Monday afternoon, November 10, they returned to the White House.[37]

Despite media claims that the Carters were in isolation at Camp David, while there they had had many contacts with sympathizers, friends, and government officials. Robert Woodruff, CEO of the Coca-Cola Company in Atlanta, offered Carter use of the Woodruff Room in the Woodruff Library at Emory University when he returned to Georgia. As a departing president, Carter could anticipate that he would have financial security. He learned that his annual pension would be $69,630, the amount earned by a Supreme Court justice. In addition he would get $150,000 per year for thirty months to hire staff and office help. A few weeks before leaving the White House, he and Rosalynn met with literary agents who explained to them the process of signing book contracts for their memoirs.[38]

Carter created a form letter to thank those who offered their support. "My love for this country," he told them, "has guided my actions." He had faith that the people would "meet the challenges of the future in a manner which reflects our highest principles of freedom, justice and human rights for all." To those of a religious persuasion, such as Jimmy Allen of the Southern Baptist Convention, he would mention a reciprocal prayer arrangement and usually sign his name "in Christ."[39]

The Carters ignored those individuals and groups that did not vote for him, particularly religious conservatives who considered themselves part of the Moral Majority and White male blue collar workers who feared for their jobs under the administration of a president who pushed for civil rights and equal opportunity. Carter had clearly become more liberal and implemented social and foreign policies that ran counter to an increasingly conservative nation. Not only many Jewish Americans, but also other citizens who favored a stronger relationship with Israel, likely voted against him.[40]

Two days after the election, Menachem Begin sent him a coldly professional letter. "The 4th of November 1980," he wrote, "is another example of American democracy and freedom," which was a clever statement that disguised how he might have really felt about the outcome. Begin had actively worked for Carter's defeat, but he thanked Carter for the good he had done for Israel: "thank you Mr. President on behalf of the people and Government of Israel for your friendship, your great contribution to Israel's security and incessant efforts to bring about peace in the Middle East and especially your devoted work to achieve the Peace Treaty between Egypt and Israel." Carter responded in a similar fashion with a thank you more formal than warm.[41]

On November 13, when Begin was in the United States for a private visit, Carter invited him to come to the White House. Begin had become unpopular in Israel; some members of his Cabinet had resigned, forcing him to confront the chance of losing the next election. In the Oval Office, Begin, according to Carter, was at first "ill at ease." Carter tried to help him relax by telling him that he "had accepted the result of the election." Begin seemed surprised, but he became less tense when Carter thanked him for his contribution to the Camp David Accords. Carter nevertheless warned Begin, as he had done many times before, that it would be a detriment to peace if Israel annexed the Golan Heights in defiance of UN Resolution 242 and the commitment he had made in the Camp David Accords. Begin did not respond. He simply thanked Carter again on behalf of the Israeli people for all he had done for Israel. Cagily political, Begin also remarked that Carter had proven the "beauty of Democracy" by graciously accepting the decision of the US people not to reelect him. Carter did not think Begin's promise to help find a way to bring about full autonomy for Palestinian Arabs was sincere. The two men whose political careers had been so intertwined bid each other farewell, and Begin continued with his private visit in the United States.[42]

Carter remained as disgusted with Jewish voters who had contributed to his defeat as he was with Begin. Carter noted that Blacks and Hispanics had given him more than 80% of their votes, but Jewish Americans did not give him a majority. Puzzled why they did not support him in greater numbers, Carter turned to Al Moses, his adviser on Jewish affairs, for an answer. Moses reminded him that Andy Young, Southern Baptists, and the Billy-Libya affair had alienated many Jewish voters who interpreted those issues as anti-Semitic. Writing in his diary, Carter praised Moses as "an outstanding person," and he noted that he recognized the fact that "most of the Jewish leaders supported me but the rank and file didn't." The time and money his campaign had spent trying to get the 45% of Jewish votes that he won, he wrote, was not worth it. He would have been better off if he had simply ignored them.[43] Carter's strong belief in the separation of church and state, which was ingrained in his Baptist religious belief, conflicted with a Jewish nation and faith where religion and politics were intricately intertwined. Carter was not anti-Semitic, but he attempted to deal with Israel as a secular state constrained by the rules and challenges of diplomacy.

Rosalynn, upon her return to the White House from Camp David, was touched by the loyalty of the household staff members who were saddened that the Carters would be leaving the White House in a few months. She wandered through the mansion and out onto the Truman Balcony, visiting the places she had enjoyed so much. She kept her tears private as her press secretary compiled a summary of her accomplishments. Besides her work with the mental health commission and on the ERA, Mary Hoyt listed Rosalynn's meeting the Pope in Boston, her holding Cambodian refugee children in her arms, her testifying on Capitol Hill, and her trips to Latin American countries where she exercised the authority of the president.[44]

On November 15, 1980, just eleven days after the election, a *New York Times* poll found Rosalynn Carter to be the second most influential woman in the country after Katharine Graham, publisher of the *Washington Post*. Rosalynn Carter was a modern First Lady who brought classical music to the White House and shared it with the public on public television, saluted poets and artists, and raised the national conscience about people around the world who were in need. She had reason to be satisfied with all that she had done during the four years she had worked as an equal partner with the president.[45]

Rosalynn, however, like Jimmy, always believed that there was more to do, and she was eager to do it. Her excellent record, and the public and private recognition and congratulations that had come to her, comforted her, but they could not erase the grief and agony she felt about losing the election. She also felt a strong responsibility to help Jimmy and their family with the difficult transition each had to make. She once again found the courage to be strong in face of adversity. She would be First Lady until January 20, 1981, and the hostages were not yet free.

THIRTY FOUR

Welcome Home

The Iranians did not like President-elect Ronald Reagan any more than they liked Carter, but they would have to deal with him unless they let the remaining US captives go free before inauguration day. A spokesman for the office of Prime Minister Mohammad Ali Rahai said that the "two men [Carter and Reagan] are equally bad." Students holding the Americans claimed that Khomeini had known that Carter would not be reelected. Some Iranian officials, however, remarked privately that they would prefer to negotiate with Carter because they believed Reagan was more pro-Israel. Regardless of the upheaval in US politics, faithful Muslims who followed Khomeini believed that Allah was on their side.[1]

Despite the will of Allah and the incoming Reagan administration, Carter still hoped to free the hostages and secure his legacy of peace and human rights during the months he had left. When the State Department held a reception for Cy and Gay Vance on November 18, Jimmy and Rosalynn attended. Carter praised Vance for his service during "a time of crisis and achievement," and he thanked Gay Vance for accompanying Rosalyn on her June 1977 diplomatic trip to Latin America.[2] The next day Carter addressed the Washington meeting of the OAS, emphasizing the achievements of a ban on nuclear weapons in Latin America, the Panama Canal treaties, and progress in human rights."[3] The Latin American country that remained of particular concern for him, because of its ongoing civil war and the dangers of foreign intervention, was Nicaragua. All who "care about freedom," he said, should join with the United States "to help the Nicaraguan people chart a pluralistic course that ends bloodshed, respects human rights, and furthers democracy."[4]

The next day, November 20, Carter smiled politely as he welcomed Chancellor Helmut Schmidt to the White House for a working lunch with Secretary of State Edmund Muskie. Schmidt and Carter had disagreed on strengthening NATO, the small US military presence in Western Europe, SALT II, and anything else that Schmidt thought might not deter the Soviet threat to Europe. Since Schmidt had praised Reagan's victory, Jody Powell and Zbig Brzezinski refused to attend. Carter later confessed in his diary that he was "glad to deliver Schmidt and Begin to Reagan." Walking back to the Oval Office with Muskie after the luncheon, Carter remarked that "Helmut Schmidt can be a pain in the ass."[5]

Only a few minutes after Schmidt left, President-elect and Mrs. Reagan arrived to tour the White House. Carter escorted Reagan to the Oval Office and Rosalynn took Nancy for a tour of the mansion. Carter gave Reagan a comprehensive briefing, and urged him to continue working on the Camp David Accords. Reagan appeared to be oblivious to all that Carter said, and at the end of the two-hour meeting Carter doubted that Reagan cared about any of the information he had given him.[6]

The private tour that Rosalynn gave Nancy of the living quarters ended in disaster. After viewing the family room and part of the third floor, Mrs. Reagan broke away to enter the president's private study without permission and wanted to see other private areas of the residence. Since they had already exceeded the allotted time by fifteen minutes, Rosalynn would not allow her into the dressing rooms and took her to meet Chief Usher Rex Scouten who escorted Mrs. Reagan to the Map Room while Rosalynn went upstairs. After the men had finished their conference, Rosalynn quickly joined the three others for a photograph before the Reagans departed. That night Nancy Reagan told the press that the tour had been too hard for her and that she would need to come back. Jody Powell made a brief public statement: "It was a dismal ending of a dismal day. We found she wanted to redecorate before the Carters leave."[7]

Adding insult to injury, a female journalist, Allison Leland, published an article in which she stated that the Reagan entertainment style was "elegant," but the Carters' style was the opposite. Incensed, Rosalynn scrawled a note to her press secretary, "Mary, she can go to hell! I think [Social Secretary] Gretchen [Poston] ought to talk with Allison to tell her what we did." Mary Hoyt contacted the journalist, who apologized, explained that the newspaper account was incorrect, and assured Hoyt that she admired Rosalynn Carter very much.[8]

After spending a quiet Thanksgiving holiday at Camp David, the Carters returned to the White House where Carter worked as hard as he had always done. On December 2, he signed the Alaska National Interest Lands Conservation Act. The bill protected 157 million acres in Alaska, including national parks, wildlife refuges, and monuments; wild and scenic rivers;

national forests; and recreational areas. It was the biggest expansion of protected lands in US history. The National Park System more than doubled in size. "We cannot let our eagerness for progress and energy out strip our care for our land, water and air and for the plants and animals that share them with us," he said at the signing ceremony.[9]

Carter focused on getting the hostages released.[10] Iranian president Bani-Sadr offered to free them, and Foreign Minister Gotzbadeh expressed his hope that it could happen soon in cooperation with UN Secretary General Kurt Waldheim. Knowing the intense negotiations that Deputy Secretary of State Warren Christopher was secretly conducting with the Iranians through an Algerian intermediary, Carter was more hopeful than usual. On December 17, he wrote to Penne Laingen, the wife of Bruce Laingen, that "We are working hard, and praying a lot that Bruce and our other loved ones will remain safe and will soon be home."[11]

At an NSC meeting, Carter insisted that the United States would never allow a direct Soviet intrusion into Iran, which could precipitate a nuclear war between the two superpowers. He recorded in his diary on December 17 that, if the United States could get along with the Soviets for five or six years, his policies of emphasizing the independence of emerging nations, human rights, arms control, and "economic warfare" would cause the Soviet Union to collapse.[12]

So engrossed was he in standing strong against the Soviet Union and hoping for better news from Iran that Carter had little interest in a retirement gift that his staff planned to give him. When he learned that they were planning to buy him a $10,000 Jeep, he privately told Jack Watson that such a gift would be "excessive." When Watson asked him for suggestions, Carter told him "a television set—which we don't have—or some woodworking equipment for a shop at my house."[13] The gift Carter wanted to give to the nation that Christmas, namely an announcement that the hostages were coming home, he could not deliver. At the national Christmas tree lighting ceremony on December 18, the tree, which stood on the Ellipse south of the White House, was fully lit for only 417 seconds, one second for each day that the hostages had been held captive. Then it was darkened, as it had been the year before, except for a single light at the top. Rosalynn and Amy accompanied Jimmy to the ceremony, where he made comments about peace, faith, and hope and led the crowd in moments of silent prayer.[14]

Because he knew the progress the United States, with the help of Algeria, was making to free the hostages, Carter had reason to be hopeful as he and his family left for Plains two days before Christmas. When the plane landed at Warner-Robbins Air Force Base, a crowd of more than 1,000 gave them a rousing welcome. They celebrated the holiday on Woodland Drive, strolled through Plains, exchanged gifts with family members at home, and visited Miss Lillian and her poodle Perry at the Pond House before going to Miss Allie's for their traditional Christmas dinner. They talked about how they might change their house and grounds when they came back home to stay. "We are very happy to be in a nation that's at peace, Carter told a reporter.[15] Before returning to Washington, he received a report from an Algerian diplomat that the location of all fifty-two hostages was known and that they were well. The report included a film allegedly showing that they were being properly treated.[16]

Instead of returning to the White House on December 26, Jimmy and Rosalynn went to Camp David for the remainder of the year. Carter broke his collar bone while skiing in the nearby Catoctin Mountains, but he did not let that slow his work on his farewell speech. Rosalynn read the first draft and suggested he show more compassion and include more information about how he had protected the quality of the environment. Although he was in considerable pain, he missed very little time from work.[17]

Jimmy and Rosalynn did, however, take the first day of January for a holiday. Accompanied by Amy, Jeff, and his daughter-in-law Annette, they flew to New Orleans to attend the Sugar Bowl football game where the University of Georgia was playing Notre Dame. After Georgia won the game, 17 to 10, Carter called Georgia's coach Vince Dooley to congratulate him and his team upon their victory. Given his injury, Carter attempted to avoid being jostled or shaking too many hands, but the enthusiastic Herschel Walker, Georgia's Heisman Trophy-winning running back, "jerked it pretty hard," leaving Carter "sore all over" for the remainder of the day. By the time they returned to Washington that evening, they were very tired, elated for their home state, and slept soundly.[18]

His vacation over, Carter worked on the hostages' release, said farewell to friends and heads of state, and wrote and rewrote his farewell speech. Early in the year, the Algerian mediator returned to Tehran with a new US offer to unfreeze Iranian assets and remove sanctions against Iran in exchange for release of the captive Americans. Still, nothing happened. Carter braced for the worse scenario, which he said might cause him to have to ask Congress for a declaration of war against Iran, but he continued to hope for a resolution. The Reagan people showed no interest in learning what was happening with the hostages or about the status of the military that Carter had so carefully strengthened and made ready to defend the nation if necessary.[19]

When he said goodbye to his Bible class on Sunday, January 4, Carter talked about how he related earthly power to the teachings of his Christian faith. "The acquisition of power as measured in human terms is not greatness but sin in the eyes of God." Rich people, he said, were often not the happiest. He reassured the receptive group that he and Rosalynn would go to church in Plains, and he reminded them that Jesus taught that "the foundation of greatness is serving others."[20]

Carter urged his staff to practice Christian charity toward members of the Reagan family and others in the Reagan campaign who had sometimes ridiculed them. He told his cabinet and staff not to respond "to the barbs of Mrs. Reagan or Ronald Reagan, Jr." Reagan's son had called Carter a "rat" and said he would not shake hands with him at the inauguration. Nancy continued to press the Carters to move over to nearby Blair House before inauguration day so she could begin redecorating the family quarters. Rosalynn refused to consider the idea, saying that the Carters would move after noon on January 20 when they would fly home to Plains. Carter avoided the debate, but he told his staff that, "in spite of all this gossip among ourselves, it's our duty to help them as much as possible."[21]

The Carters intended to depart Washington with dignity. The city passed a "Rosalynn Carter Appreciation Resolution," praising her work in building a more caring society. Mayor Marion Barry said, "You did more volunteer work than some of our own citizens."[22] The Pope thanked Carter for working "to bring a deeper consciousness of the rights of the human person to the world's quest for peace."[23]

Still hopeful that the hostages might be released any day, Carter welcomed a secret telegram, dated January 9, from Bruce Laingen, who sometimes got information out of Iran with the aid of the Swiss or Spanish embassy. Laingen assumed that the Algerian ambassador had passed along to the State Department news that all of the hostages were back at the US embassy in Tehran. He also reported that they had had contact with the Algerian ambassador, and he was aware of Iran's desire to have Carter release their frozen assets because they urgently needed the money to finance their war against Iraq.[24]

Carter's efforts to free the hostages intensified as inauguration day approached. He sent Deputy Secretary of State Warren Christopher to Algiers to meet with the Algerian mediator, Foreign Minister Mohammed

Benyahia. Benyahia reported to Christopher that the Iranian parliament had met to authorize negotiations through Algeria to end the hostage crisis. Subsequent reports indicated that the hostages would be released within five days, but the Iranian bank and twelve others where assets were frozen needed more time, they said, to transfer $4.8 billion, about half in cash and the rest in gold, to an escrow account that Carter could control and release to the Iranians at the right time. Carter thought "a few greedy bankers" wanted to hold the deposits as long as possible to earn more profits on them, and he still did not trust any news from Iran.[25]

With only one week remaining in office, Carter worked on finishing his farewell address. The day before Carter was to broadcast it from the Oval Office, Mstalav "Slava" Rostropovich, his and Rosalynn's favorite composer and cellist as well as a passionate advocate of human rights, joined the Carters for dinner. Rostropovich, who had performed at the White House as the Camp David Accords were being completed, told the defeated president and First Lady that often the people were wrong. He noted that the masses had rejected Verdi, Puccini, and Beethoven, but history had been kind to them and now they were revered. He predicted that the same would happen for the Carters. His encouragement may have helped Jimmy and Rosalynn complete the farewell address.[26]

Broadcasting from the Oval Office on the night of January 14, Carter assumed his most professional and serious posture. "In a few days," he began, "I will lay down my official responsibilities in this office, to take up once more the only title in our democracy superior to that of President, the title of citizen." He thanked all who had helped him, wished his successor "success, and Godspeed," and promised to support him in his task. After some references to his accomplishments as president, Carter spent more time discussing the challenges ahead. He urged the country to avoid nuclear war, protect the environment, and enhance human rights. He defended the constitutional system of checks and balances, and he asked his fellow citizens to join him in his continuing prayer for freedom for all people.[27]

For the heart of his speech, Carter returned to the theme of his presidency: "The battle for human rights, at home and abroad, is far from over." We should avoid "self-righteousness" and "complacency," he said, for if "we are to serve as a beacon for human rights, we must continue to perfect here at home the rights and the values which we espouse around the world." Those rights, he continued, included education, medical care, an end to all forms of discrimination, job opportunities, and "freedom from injustice and religious intolerance." He would work hard during his last five days as president for the release of the hostages and pray constantly for their well-being and freedom. When he returned "home to the South, where I was born and raised," he expected to "work as a citizen, as I've worked here in this office as President, for the values this Nation was founded to secure."[28]

Rosalynn listened to his speech with staff and cabinet members in the adjacent Roosevelt Room. Reviewing the past four years in her mind, she was "thankful for Jimmy's time in history." She knew he had served with honor, and she knew how much he had enjoyed doing it. She believed he would leave a legacy "for peace and human rights and compassion."[29]

Early the next morning, January 15, Carter resumed work as usual. He sent a budget message to Congress, and he noted the fifty-second anniversary of Martin Luther King, Jr.'s birth, praising King for leaving a legacy "of brotherhood and freedom, peace and love for all people."[30] Carter issued Presidential Directives NSC-62 and 63, entitled "Modifications in US National Strategy" calling for greater military readiness, sharing the burden with allies, arms control, and Persian Gulf Security in accord with the Carter Doctrine of the previous year.[31]

That same day, Carter planned to transfer Iranian gold from an escrow account that he controlled to the Bank of England and to issue an order for the other US banks to transfer unfrozen funds there, where it would become available to the Iranians. White House Counsel Lloyd Cutler advised that the banks were willing to pay the full amount into an escrow account, in what he described as "the most complicated financial transaction that he had ever heard of."[32]

The next day, January 16, in an emotional ceremony, Carter presented the Presidential Medal of Freedom to some members of his cabinet and other close advisers: Secretary of Defense Harold Brown, National Security Advisor Zbigniew Brzezinski, and Deputy Secretary of State Warren Christopher. Cognizant of all that Christopher had done through many crises, including the resignation of Cyrus Vance, and especially his intensive work behind the scenes to gain freedom for the hostages, Carter ranked him first among the public servants who had served him as president. With freedom for the hostages seemingly close at hand, Carter added, "I am indebted to him, and so is the Nation, far beyond what the general public knows." Since Christopher was in Algiers negotiating with the Algerian mediator, Carter presented the medal to "his lovely wife." Carter also honored current Secretary of State Edmund Muskie; Adviser for Consumer Affairs

Esther Peterson; and Andrew Young, whose diplomatic service, Carter said, reflected his lifetime commitment to human rights.[33] Other Medal of Freedom recipients included television anchorman Walter Cronkite, actor Kirk Douglas, Margaret Craig McNamara for creating a fundamental reading program, Karl Memminger for his work in psychiatry, and Gerard C. Smith for his work with the Trilateral Commission and on the first SALT.

The same day, January 16, Carter sent his State of the Union message to Congress. Following the recommendation of his advisers and the precedent of former presidents Hoover, Truman, and Eisenhower, he did not deliver an in-person state of the union message to Congress shortly before the president from the other party was inaugurated.[34] It was a very long, detailed account of all he had done as president, which he wished to become a permanent part of the archives and history of the country. He concluded on a positive note: "We have new support in the world for our purposes of national independence and individual human dignity. We have a new will at home to do what is required to keep us the strongest nation on earth." He urged Congress to "move together . . . with the strength which comes from realization of the dangers before us and from the confidence that together we can overcome them."[35]

The news from Iran and Algeria was tantalizing, virtually promising that the hostages would be free before the inauguration. From Algiers on January 17, Christopher reported that the Algerian airplanes were ready to leave for Tehran on a moment's notice, the accomplishment of a "tough day" of negotiating. The next day, Christopher reported that "everything seemed to be nailed down." The Algerians would announce when they were ready to proceed, and Carter should plan to go to Wiesbaden, Germany, to greet the freed Americans. Carter spoke with Thatcher and Schmidt, and he called Reagan to give him an update. He talked with members of the hostage families and the widow of Captain Harold Lewis, one of the servicemen killed in the rescue effort.[36]

Choosing his words carefully, Carter issued a statement that the United States and Iran had reached an agreement under which the Iranian assets he had frozen would be released and the fifty-two US hostages would be freed. Many had worked and prayed, he said, to bring about this day and "preserve our national honor and vital interests." He thanked those who had risked and given their lives in the rescue effort, the families of the captives, and the concern of his successor. "Our present expectations," he said, "are that our fellow Americans will soon be free." He would speak again, he promised, when they were free and on their way home.[37]

Prime Minister Begin took Carter's announcement as the final word on the release: "I am sure the entire people of Israel join me in this sentiment. For this day we waited and prayed, joining you and the American people in your pain and concern." Sharing the rejoicing, Begin said, "Please accept my heartfelt congratulations on this humanitarian achievement." He ended by again offering his gratitude for the Camp David Accords, inviting the Carters to visit Israel, and saying "God bless you and your family." Carter's private response went unrecorded.[38]

On January 19, after days of round-the-clock negotiations, Warren Christopher and Algerian Foreign Minister Mohammed Benyahia at the Algerian Foreign Ministry signed the Algerian Accords, the document that settled the complicated financial agreement with Iran, clearing the way for release of the hostages.[39]

Later that day, Carter sent a written message to Congress in which he spelled out in great detail the "United States-Iran Agreement on Release of the American Hostages." He directed all banks and other institutions that might hold Iranian frozen assets under his order of November 14, 1979, to transfer those funds to the Federal Reserve Bank of New York. Such transfers were to be completed as soon as possible but no later than the moment Iran released the hostages. He revoked most of the sanctions against Iran, but prohibited claims against the shah's estate. The agreement also included a US commitment not to intervene politically or militarily in Iranian internal affairs.[40]

A final glitch emerged. The Iranians said that until the frozen assets were deposited in an Algerian bank, they would continue to hold the hostages. The US negotiators had added an eleven-page appendix to the agreement, which Iran flatly rejected. Infuriated, Carter quickly amended it to meet the Iranian demands. Further delays involved a one-digit typo in a bank code and the refusal of Ernest Petrikis, the Federal Reserve lawyer, to sign the amended agreement because of technicalities. Communicating through a Treasury Department lawyer, Carter informed Petrikis why the document had to be signed, and he signed it. After more delays caused by communications among the banks, finally at 8:06 a.m. the transfer of almost $8 billion to the Bank of England was completed.[41]

In Tehran, the unruly Iranian guards seemed to know that their captives would soon be released, taunting the hostages with hints but no promises of freedom. On one occasion, Iranian guards took the weary Americans out one at a time to tell each one alone that he or she would soon be free.

Those waiting their turn did not know the reason for the unusual treatment or what might happen to them when escorted away from the group. The captors urged the hostages to report that they had been treated well, and they allowed Algerian doctors to give each captive a physical examination. The guards knew well before Reagan's inauguration that they would be setting the Americans free.[42] Early on the morning of Tuesday, January 20, just hours before Carter had to leave office, Behzad Nabavi, Iran's chief hostage negotiator, announced that "The government of the Islamic Republic of Iran and the United States finally reached agreement on resolving the issue of the hostages today." The Americans were not yet on their way home, however, and Carter was reluctant to announce their release until he was absolutely certain that it was true. Nevertheless, both the United States and Algeria had made preparations to bring the Americans home. A thirty-member hostage recovery team, headed by Cy Vance, had gathered in Washington ready to go to Germany. A team of Algerian doctors had already arrived in Tehran.[43] While awaiting more definite word from Tehran, Carter reviewed the note cards for the speech he intended to give when he departed from the South Lawn to meet the freed hostages. "Moments ago," it read, "I received word that the aircraft carrying the 52 American hostages had departed Tehran on the 1st leg of the journey home. Later today I will leave for Germany and welcome them to Freedom." The country, he said, had accomplished its two objectives: "to secure their safe release, and to preserve our national honor and vital interests." Privately, he remarked that he would not go to Germany if it conflicted with the inauguration.[44]

The prepared speech was not just wishful thinking, for Carter had received a telegrammed intelligence report via Hong Kong telling him that two Algerian Boeing 727 airliners had landed in Turkey en route to Tehran to pick up the fifty-two Americans. At least five other telegrams, with the same date, gave him further information. Some of them contained the news that the planes had arrived in Tehran, the medical exams had been completed, and the hostages were at the airport. Reagan called Carter to tell him that if the hostages did not get out before the inauguration, he would request that Carter travel to Germany on Air Force One to greet them on behalf of the United States. Touched by Reagan's offer, Carter graciously accepted. Reagan fully understood that Carter and his team, led by Warren Christopher, had done the work that induced the Iranians to liberate the captive Americans.[45]

Early in the morning of January 20, the militants inflicted final insults upon the Americans, some of whom had been held in solitary confinement during the final weeks of their captivity. Upon being released, they were allowed to take with them only what they had on their persons, but each hostage could retrieve one pair of his or her own shoes that the captors had piled into a large room. On the buses taking them to the airport, they were blindfolded and ordered to sit without talking. At the airport they were forced to run a gauntlet of militant students shouting "Death to America, Death to Reagan," as they jostled, spat upon, and struck the Americans with sticks or fists. Some of the Americans responded with raised middle fingers and defiant shouts of "Death to Khomeini" as they rushed toward the Algerian aircraft. One of them, Mike Metrinko, was almost killed when he lost his temper with a student who muttered "Goddamned Americans." He shouted back at him, "Shut up yourself, you son of a whore," for which he was dragged aside and beaten severely before being allowed to board the bus.[46]

As the confused Americans, most of them ragged and thin and fearful of what awaited them, ran up the steps of one of the two waiting airliners, bulky guards in strange uniforms with machine guns reached down and pulled them aboard by their arms. The Algerian guards were as eager to get out of Iran as were the Americans. Inside the aircraft, a couple of the Algerians who could speak English told the Americans that they were free. Together as a group for the first time since their capture, the former hostages barely recognized each other after the physical toll that their 444 days in captivity had taken on them. As the plane's doors closed "52 wildly happy Americans, embracing each other," fell into an ecstatic chaos that defied description. The Swiss ambassador, with the Algerian ambassador watching, listed each name, checking and rechecking to make certain all were present. The Americans themselves repeated the count; they wanted to make certain that no one was left behind. The Algerians had planned the trip carefully, refusing to take any food on board from Iran for fear it would be poisoned. Unfortunately, the turkey dinner they had intended to serve had spoiled during the time the planes were on the ground, and the only food available was some cheese.[47]

At the White House, a different tense drama played out. Through the night and the early morning of January 20, Carter waited anxiously in the Oval Office, where he had already been for two days, welcoming every report that events were falling into place. Shortly after 3:00 a.m. Washington time, he learned that the money was moving to London. The Tehran control tower instructed Flight 133, which consisted of three planes—the two 727 Algerian Airliners with the freed hostages on board one of them, the other probably serving as a decoy, and the third aircraft carrying the Algerian medical team back home—to line up in preparation for departure. An Iranian F-4 jet also stood nearby, perhaps to be used as an escort.[48] Three hours later, the Bank of England certified that it held the $7.977 billion, which was the correct amount. At 8:28 a.m., the three planes comprising Flight 133 were at the end of the runway. Since the runway was kept in blackout due to the war with Iraq, the Algerian pilots had to ask the Iranians to turn on the lights long enough for them to take off.[49]

Meanwhile, Rosalynn brought a barber to the Oval Office for Jimmy, and at 10:45 she told him that he had only fifteen minutes to get dressed in his rented formal morning clothes. Jimmy and Rosalynn, following protocol precisely as if nothing else was happening, welcomed the Reagans to the White House, had coffee with them, and rode with the incoming First Couple to their inauguration. Rosalynn attempted to put Nancy at ease and later admitted that she felt a bit smug because she knew the hostages were coming home. Warren Christopher, waiting anxiously in Algiers to greet the freed hostages, noted that his Algerian counterpart, Benyahia, had promised that the planes would leave Tehran before the inauguration of Reagan at noon in Washington. The fact that they did not may not have been so much an insult to Carter as the result of Iranian ineptitude.[50]

During the solemn ride to the Capitol, Carter found Reagan "to be an affable and a decent man," but old in his attitudes and jokes. He and Rosalynn scarcely paid attention to the ceremony, and Rosalynn thought that both her husband and Mondale looked handsome as she recalled the triumphs of their administration. After the swearing-in ceremony, as Carter passed a Secret Service agent, the agent told him that the planes were in the air on their way to the Turkish border. Another agent pushed through the crowd to tell Rosalynn that the first plane had taken off at 12:33 p.m. Washington time and the second one nine minutes later.[51]

Bound for Algeria via Greece, Flight 133 began the first stage in the former hostages' twelve-hour flight to freedom that would end at the US military hospital in Wiesbaden, Germany. Prime Minister Pierre Trudeau of Canada wrote Carter that "you have succeeded in reaching an agreement with Iran which allows all the hostages to return home safe and sound. . . . It must be particularly gratifying to you that this matter could be resolved before you leave office." Carter asked that the national Christmas tree, which had been dark for two Christmases while the hostages remained in captivity, be illuminated as a signal to the world that they were free at last. Rosalynn thought it "despicable" that the Iranians had held the planes until precisely the moment Reagan became president, but she was overcome with "the thrill" that they were free because of Jimmy's negotiations.[52]

Fritz and Joan Mondale joined Jimmy and Rosalynn in the limousine that took them to Andrews Air Force Base where what had been Air Force One waited to take them home to Georgia. They rejoiced in the news that the former hostages were also on their way home. In the crowd of well-wishers along their route, they spotted an African-American woman holding a sign that read, "Thank you, Carter." At Andrews Air Force Base they reviewed an honor guard, received a twenty-one gun salute, and listened to a military chorus sing the "Star Spangled Banner." The telephone rang in the terminal's VIP room they had just vacated. A State Department official asked Lafayette Collins, a Secret Service agent in that room, to "Tell the President that the hostages have just cleared Iranian air space." Forgetting that Carter was no longer president, he did so just as Carter made his way toward the plane. The Carters' departure from the White House was as dramatic as their famous walk down Pennsylvania Avenue from the Capitol to the White House had been when they had arrived in January 1977.

On that January day four years later, Carter stood proud and erect, with his hand over his heart as the band played the national anthem in the style of the commander-in-chief reviewing the troops. The first person Carter met on the tarmac was Mrs. Thomas Schaefer, wife of the senior military officer who had been held by the Iranians. He embraced her and listened to her emotional thanks and hope that he would someday meet her husband. When he told her that he would be with her husband the next day in Wiesbaden, they both broke down and wept. Climbing the stairs to the plane with Rosalynn a step behind him and Amy following her, the Carters turned to wave goodbye. Amy, aged fourteen, crying because she did not want to leave her friends, broke loose from her mother and started back down the steps. Rosalynn descended a few steps to catch her hand and pull her back up.[53]

As the Algerian airliner carrying the freed hostages and the two accompanying planes passed into Turkish air space, they were met by an escort team of US Air Force fighter jets. Cy Vance headed a group already in the air to greet them when they arrived at Wiesbaden. The Carters were also in the air, scheduled to arrive in Plains at 3:43 p.m. At 4:08, the Algerian planes made a refueling stop at a US airbase in Athens, where the US ambassador to Greece, Robert McCloskey, greeted them. At 5:30, with Algerian officials and others now on board with the Americans, the three planes flew another eighty minutes to Algiers, where they were greeted by Deputy Secretary of State Warren Christopher and the Algerian foreign minister.

For eight minutes, from 8:32 to 8:40 p.m., the freed hostages were seen live on US television exiting the plane. Two women, Elizabeth Ann Swift and Kathryn Koob, stepped off first. All were dressed in warm clothing provided by their Algerian rescuers. Cheering crowds lined the airport fences. In Plains, with no television at his house, Jimmy, having arrived home on schedule, slipped into a back room at Billy's house to watch the coverage on television. An hour later, the jubilant Americans boarded two US Air Force Medivac planes, upon which they could begin to get any medical care they might need, en route to the large US Air Force Base in Wiesbaden. They landed there at 12:45 a.m. Wednesday, January 21, 1981. As Carter had requested, the lights were illumined on the nation's Christmas tree while thousands of Americans cheered, wept, shouted, and thanked God. As soon as the planes carrying the Americans left Algiers, Warren Christopher flew home to Andrews Air Force Base, where his wife Marie met him. Thinking they would slip quietly into a neighborhood restaurant on their way home, Christopher was shocked when the crowd inside stood and applauded to give him a hero's welcome.[54]

Earlier that day, Jimmy, Rosalynn, and Amy had been met on their arrival in Plains at the railroad depot by 3,000 people, many of them bringing food for a covered dish supper. There were cheers, hugs, and a kiss from Miss Lillian. A flood of rain could not dampen their spirits. Maxine Reese, who had often organized people in Plains to support the Carters, said it was as if the heavens opened up and cried. The more realistic Carter said the rain would be good for Georgia farmers. He told them that he had received word that every one of the former captives was alive, well, and free. So deeply emotional was the experience Jimmy could not describe how he felt. The Algerians were heroes, he said. Vance would be in Germany to shake the hands of the happy Americans as they disembarked from the planes. Carter would fly to Germany early the next day.

Jimmy could and did describe, however, exactly how he felt about his hometown friends and fellow citizens. "Rosalynn and I, and our family," he told them, "hope forever to honor you with our lives in the years to come."[55] Jimmy recalled his Southern heritage and how it had equipped him to serve the nation and the world. "It is good to be home again," he said, forcing back tears, in front of an audience where there was scarcely a dry eye. The United States looks "at every person as valuable and noble" he made clear before getting more specific about his native South. "We Southerners came face to face with the worst emotions a person can feel," referring to the Civil War and the long struggle for racial equality and justice, he said. "That is why I have done my best to have our country and our government stand up for liberty and human rights, because only if people are free can they too express the best that is within them." He continued: "We in the South—perhaps like no other part of the country—know what war is all about. We learned it at Gettysburg and Chickamauga." A band struck up "Dixie," and, trying to lighten the moment, he and Rosalynn danced at a lively pace on the platform as the crowd cheered. Most of the nation's attention, however, was on the Reagans, who were dancing the night away in Washington.[56]

The Carters were free, the hostages were free, the United States were free, and no longer could Ted Koppel use his "America Held Hostage" headline on his evening news program. Miss Lillian was relieved that Jimmy had lost the election, she said, because her "whole family had been attacked and split wide open from Jimmy being president."[57]

Her exhausted son, the former president, turned his attention to important unfinished business. Thirty minutes after the Medivac planes left Algiers, Carter telegraphed Algerian president Chadli Bendjedid, thanking him for the help his country had given. A Muslim country, independently Communist, it alone had emerged as the nation that could mediate between the United States and Iran. "No threat to the balance of international relations, no quarrel between nations in these past years has become so complex and difficult to resolve as the hostage crisis," Carter told Bendjedid. "We would certainly not have concluded this accord today if we had not had the assistance of your government. The United States will never forget it."

Two and a half hours later, while Jimmy and Rosalynn rested at home, the freed Americans landed safely at the air force base near Frankfurt, Germany. It was well before dawn in Germany, but the streets that their transports would take were lined with hundreds of cheering Americans and Germans. The former hostages were loaded into small vans and escorted convoy style the twenty-five miles to the hospital in Wiesbaden, where US soldiers, patients, and a military band hailed their arrival.[58]

The next morning, the world probably paid little attention to the details of the Algiers Accords that had freed the US hostages. The lead stories in the media focused instead on news of the new US president's first day in office and the old one's first day out of office. Traveling with the authority and blessing of President Reagan, Carter flew by helicopter to Warner-Robbins

Air Force Base, where he had landed so many times as president, to join those who would travel with him to Germany. Reagan had sent "Special Air Mission 26000" to transport the Carter team to Germany. Carter had chosen the members of his administration whom he wanted to travel with him: Walter Mondale, Edmund Muskie, Lloyd Cutler, William Miller, Rick Hertzberg, Mike Cardozo, Peter Constable, Henry Precht, Gary Sick, and his friends Phil Wise, Jody Powell, Hamilton Jordan, and Susan Clough. Rosalynn chose not go.[59]

During the flight, Carter, showing no signs of bitterness over the election, appeared simply happy that the hostages were free. He talked by radio with Warren Christopher; he wrote a detailed account of his negotiations with Iran before the hostages were released; and he studied photographs and other information about each former hostage. When the plane touched down on German soil, he walked down the ramp to thousands of cheering people waving small US flags as flashes from dozens of cameras lit up the night sky.[60]

Cy Vance, Helmut Schmidt, and other German officials met Carter and his party and escorted him to the hospital in Wiesbaden. Crowds of well-wishers greeted him along the way. Dr. Jerome Korcak, who had already met with the former hostages, advised Carter that they had been treated much worse than anyone had known and that some of them might be hostile toward him. The recently-freed Americans watched from a third-floor window as Carter's limousine pulled up to the hospital. Thirty-five of them, "some in blue Air Force pajamas, crowded onto balconies in freezing weather to wave a wel-come to him."[61] Secret service agents jumped from the cars to protect the former president as he strode toward the hospital entrance. Bruce Laingen waited at the top of the stairs on the third floor. Carter embraced him and inquired about his health, as both men fought back tears.[62] Laingen escorted Carter inside a small dining room where the freed Americans stood uneasily in front of their chairs. Dressed in hospital attire, they appeared to be healthy and ready to go home. Carter reached out to greet the first one, but what began as a handshake quickly became an embrace. That pattern continued as Jimmy moved around the room, calling each person by name and revealing how much he knew about them and their families.

Carter abandoned his prepared speech and spoke to the group from his heart. He told them how deeply they had been loved and how committed their country had been to their safety. All humans, including presidents, make mistakes, he said. And if any of them had made mistakes during the ordeal of their incarceration, they were forgiven. They were never alone. "The country is proud of you and grateful for your service," he emphasized. "We owe a debt of gratitude to many people and institutions, foreign leaders and governments, the Vatican, the Red Cross, and brave volunteers," particularly those who had given their lives attempting the rescue. "Welcome to freedom. God bless you."[63]

The majority of the freed Americans responded warmly and gratefully to their former president. Others were more questioning, wanting to know why the government had not done more to protect them, why he had allowed the shah into the United States, and details about the rescue mission. Without apology, Carter explained what he had done, and his relief that they were free was evident in his soft and steady voice. The men and women gathered there, who had remained loyal to their country during their long ordeal, broke into applause when he told them that the United States had not paid a ransom and thus had maintained its honor during the long process of procuring their freedom. Ever the politician, he pulled out two newspapers to show them, one of which displayed headlines about their freedom more prominently than news of Reagan's inauguration.[64]

Kathryn Koob welcomed Carter's warm hug and news about her mother; she thought he was "a caring, compassionate man." One of the men, Barry Rosen, later spoke for the group when he admitted that they owed their lives to Carter's dogged determination to bring them home alive and without sacrificing the honor or peace of the country.[65]

Some of the former hostages later felt a bit hurt because Carter quickly moved on with his own life and work, putting the hostage crisis firmly behind him. On that emotional day in Germany, however, Carter listened intently to their stories of "unbelievable acts of criminal savagery." Each person had had to run a gauntlet of kicks and jeers before leaving Iran. Some had been held in solitary confinement, told falsely that their mothers had died, and blindfolded and lined up before mock firing squads. Carter advised them to stay together for a few days so the weak could benefit from the strong. Colonel Thomas Shaefer, who had endured death threats and solitary confinement, emerged physically and mentally intact; two years later, he praised Carter for his display of "the patience, the maturity and most of all the dignity of the office of the president." Although one former hostage refused to greet Carter and others felt sorry for him, most thanked him. One of the freed Marine guards, who did not like Carter's politics, said, "I won't criticize the man, because my friends and I are alive today."[66]

Aboard Special Air Mission 26000 returning to the United States, Carter penned a handwritten report to President Reagan, the first of many reports on many subjects he would make to his successors. His visit with the "liberated Americans," he wrote, "was one of the most exhilarating experiences of my life, & I thank you for helping to make it possible." Carter had found them to be in "fairly good shape," but they needed to remain in the hospital for a few more days. He was shocked to learn how seriously they had been abused. "This long, official criminal act of terrorism should never be accepted nor forgotten nor forgiven by the civilized world," he wrote. Recalling how he and Rosalynn had used the code name "children" for the hostages, he continued: "I love each one of them like a member of my own family. They have honored our country by their actions & performance." Fearful that some of them might be charged with impropriety or even some crime because of their behavior during their long ordeal, he advised Reagan: "None of them should ever be criticized for anything that happened during their captivity."[67]

Then the celebrations aboard the plane began. Lloyd Cutler provided champagne. Each person was allowed two glasses and the privilege of keeping the Air Force One champagne glass from which he or she drank. Carter later confessed that he was severely sleep deprived at the time he drank the champagne and struggled to stay awake. As his traveling companions joked and reminisced, Carter became serious, raised his champagne glass and toasted, "To freedom!"[68]

After landing in Georgia, Carter paid his final emotional farewells to those who had accompanied him for most of his four-year journey as president. On board the helicopter that would take him home to Plains, he appeared to be sad as he waved goodbye to Mondale and Jordan. As he arrived in Plains before sunrise on January 22, Rosalynn met him and told him that she had watched him on television. Chip moved the woodworking tools that his staff had given him into the garage while Jimmy slept. Mondale called to tell him that he had delivered his letter to Reagan and briefed him minimally on their visit with the freed hostages.[69]

While Jimmy slept, Reagan's staff researched how he had once greeted a US diplomat who had been held hostage in Colombia as they prepared to welcome the freed hostages home from Iran. They also made a careful outline of all that Carter had done to win the freedom of the Americans, a quiet acknowledgment that it was Carter's work for which Reagan might receive the glory.[70]

And then it was over. A photographer caught Jimmy and Rosalynn walking along the sidewalk in front of their home in Plains. A journalist who did not know much about Carter wrote that the former president had returned to a small town in Georgia, his dreams in ashes.

THIRTY FIVE

A Place in the World

Disintegration into ashes had no place in Carter's plan for his and Rosalynn's future. "I don't think anyone has gone out of office as happy and gratified as I did," he told a local journalist the day he returned to Plains from Germany. According to Hamilton Jordan, Carter was at peace with himself and concerned about helping others.[1] Clark Clifford predicted that "history will acknowledge Jimmy Carter's accomplishments as President," Cy Vance identified a multifaceted foreign policy legacy of human rights.[2] Gaddis Smith, a distinguished scholar of US diplomatic history and foreign policy, concluded: "the four years of the Carter Administration were among the most significant in the history of American foreign policy in the twentieth century." Carter, Smith said, quickly discerned that Rosalynn's role in the presidency was truly that of an equal partner. Rosalynn "discussed every problem and decision in detail." Unintimidated by anyone, including Jimmy, she dealt with "domestic political fence-mending," and major diplomatic missions to Latin America and Thailand. "She was intelligent, perceptive, and had firm, quickly formed opinions."[3]

Neither Jimmy nor Rosalynn were changed by leaving the White House. To the contrary, they used the presidency as the foundation for a new career based upon the human rights goal that had always motivated them. When they had walked down Pennsylvania Avenue, hand in hand, on January 20, 1977, they had a vision for the nation and for the world that would be tested and battered by the realities of the economics, politics, and international relations of their era. But no challenge seemed too great, or too small, for them. Self-made, they were a team whose Southern roots, military experience, faith in themselves and in God, and rapid rise to power had emboldened them, like David, to believe that they could slay the giant Goliath. US voters had denied them a second term, but their passage through the halls of power had made a difference to individuals, to groups, to nations, and to the world order. Tip O'Neill told Carter that "History will treat you well."[4]

More motivated than defeated when they went home to Plains, the Carters had made their plans about how to deal with history. They pored over documents and memoirs in search of an understanding of their legacy, which they intended to write about and to defend. They did not attend the White House reception given by President Reagan for the former hostages only one week after the Carters had vacated the mansion. They were no doubt pleased to hear about the "much praise for former President Jimmy Carter" from the hostages, Reagan, and others who were present on that occasion, but they were already looking forward to the next stage of their lives. True to his nature, Carter planned his future, and true to her nature, Rosalynn prepared to continue to be his equal partner. The path ahead became easier when Bantam Books offered Carter a $900,000 advance for his presidential memoir, plus multiple sales opportunities.[5]

Carter slipped more easily than Rosalynn did into the role of common citizen, but both of them went to work improving their immediate environment. They returned to a house that had been semi-abandoned for ten years. Doing most of the work themselves, and sometimes with the help of Chip, they cleaned the grounds, floored the attic, turned the garage into a study for Jimmy, and created a dressing room for Rosalynn. Jimmy drove his pickup truck until the Secret Service told him that they could not guarantee his safety if he continued to do so. Jimmy and Rosalynn joined the Maranatha Baptist Church, whose congregation had separated from the Plains Baptist Church during the controversy over racial equality. The small church on the outer edge of town remained Baptist but it welcomed all people and soon became famous for its First Couple congregants. Jimmy and Rosalynn, like all other members, took their turn at maintaining the building and the grounds. Carter agreed to teach an adult Sunday School class, and Rosalynn sometimes taught a children's class.[6] Rosalynn fought her depression with diet and exercise; she had minor cosmetic surgery to keep her face and especially eyes looking youthful.[7]

In Plains, the Carters dealt with the personal and economic realities of their lives. Carter's elderly mother, Miss Lillian, who had been diagnosed with breast cancer, fell and suffered minor injuries that put her back in the hospital. Jimmy and Rosalynn purchased Billy's interest in the warehouse, which gave them 77% of the operation and Miss Lillian the rest. In early March, Kirbo sold their warehouse for $1.2 million to Archer Daniels Midland of Decatur, Illinois. The proceeds liquidated the business's debt and left the Carters with about a quarter of a million dollars in capital gain. They chose partners to cultivate their farms, and they received good income from 1,800 acres of managed woodlands.[8]

Although Jimmy and Rosalynn attended a mid-March Jefferson-Jackson dinner sponsored by the Georgia Democratic Party in Atlanta, they made no public comments and seemed uneasy among the Georgia Democrats. The Carters were at the beginning of decades of rejection by their own party.[9] When the Egyptian ambassador telephoned to tell the Carters that Jehan Sadat wanted to visit them in Plains, the ambassador asked Carter if he could arrange transportation for her from Warner-Robbins Air Force Base to Plains. Carter quipped that he had a pickup truck. When the ambassador said he was thinking of a helicopter, Carter replied that former presidents did not have helicopters.[10]

At his home on Woodland Avenue, Jimmy plunged into writing his presidential memoir. He announced that he intended to "make it highly personal in nature, not a definitive history." Joking about his writing ability, he said that he hoped the publisher had a good editor for he planned to write it himself. Seeking advice on how to proceed, Carter went to Princeton University to consult with distinguished historian Arthur Link, the editor of the magisterial Woodrow Wilson Papers, and other invited scholars. Link suggested that he hire an historian who could help with research and organization. After considering several candidates who were suggested by Link, Carter chose Steven H. Hochman from the University of Virginai, who had assisted Dumas Malone with three of the six volumes of his Pulitzer Prize–winning biography of Thomas Jefferson, thus adding a professional historian to his staff.[11]

Carter's work schedule remained as it had been for many years. He paid $10,000 for a word processor, which represented the cutting edge of technology at that time, but it was cumbersome as well as expensive. On a typical week day, Carter went to his study at 5:00 a.m. and worked for a couple of hours on his memoir. Then he saw Amy off to school and had coffee with Rosalynn before going back to his writing. When he tired of writing, he passed the remainder of the day either in his woodworking shop, the yard, the woods, or the farm. He employed a staff headed by Phil Wise to manage his and Rosalynn's correspondence, appointmnets, travel, and to coordinate their activies with the Secret Servce and other government agencies. Carter often talked by telephone with his former staff members about serious mistakes they thought that the Reagan administration was making. Carter enjoyed the freedom that release from presidential responsibilities gave him to improve his furniture-making skills, pursue a writing career, spend more time with Rosalynn, and keep abreast of national and international events. "We are really enjoying this life," he recorded in his diary on April 12.[12]

After Carter spent the morning of March 20 visiting with Emory University president Jim Laney in Atlanta, he declined Laney's offer of a substantial financial contribution if he would build his presidential library and museum on property owned by Emory, but he did consider a future relationship with that institution. Carter did not want his library and museum to be "captured" by a single institution but to be available to all of Georgia's academic institutions as well as the general public. He realized, however, that an association with Emory in Atlanta would help facilitate his goals.[13]

His attention was jerked back to Washington when a deranged gunman gravely wounded President Reagan outside the Washington Hilton Hotel on March 30. Carter was relieved, however, that the Secret Service, law enforcement, and the constitutional system worked well to handle the crisis. He called Nancy Reagan to express his concern for her and prayers for the wounded president. The press, which had been as tough on Reagan as on Carter, softened its reporting about the president after he nearly lost his life. Editorials and news stories became noticeably less critical, and Reagan's approval rate in opinion polls soared to around 73%.[14] Not until later did journalists and investigative sources reveal that the would-be assassin, John Hinckley, Jr., had also stalked President Carter at least twice during the previous fall with intent to kill him.

Carter increasingly began to make public appearances. On May 8, he went to the Harry S. Truman Presidential Library and Museum in Independence to accept the eighth annual Harry S. Truman Public Service Award. Smiling broadly, he felt indeed honored by the warm reception and the award named for his own presidential hero.[15] Although the ceremony in Missouri was one of the first occasions since he had left office that Carter was greeted with respect, he did not shy away from other occasions where he remained the center of controversy.

Carter's next speech revisited his troubled relationship with Jewish Americans. He accepted an invitation to help the New York Board of Rabbis celebrate its one hundredth anniversary at the Waldorf Astoria Hotel in New York City. The world "seems to have gone mad," he told them on May 17, "and deep religious conviction that should bind people together in love— seems often to be part of the madness and murder." He addressed the rabbis as leaders of faith, righteousness, and peace. Justice and human rights, he said, "underlie our nation's enduring relationship with the State of Israel." It was his hope that both countries would resolve "to carry on the struggle for freedom, justice, and peace."[16] Despite his words to the rabbis, Carter's reputation among Jewish Americans did not improve.

Among the first barrage of books that would either condemn or praise the former president, Joseph Califano, the disillusioned former secretary of health, education, and welfare, published *Governing America*, a comparative study of the two presidents whom he had served. In Califano's estimation, Carter, unlike Lyndon Johnson, had never mastered the ability to govern. He portrayed Carter as insecure, duplicitous, and consumed with animosity toward the Washington press corps. Failing to mention the severe and gross upbraiding that Johnson had at least once given him, Califano contended that Carter had reprimanded Andrew Young before the entire cabinet for calling the United Kingdom racist, arguing that Cuban troops in Angola were a stabilizing force, and alleging that there were political prisoners in the United States. Referring to the phony evangelist in Sinclair Lewis's novel *Elmer Gantry*, Califano continued, "there is some Elmer Gantry in this born-again president."[17]

James Fallows, the once-critical former speech writer who had come to admire the Carters, wrote a perceptive review of the Califano book. He agreed with Califano that Carter misunderstood human motivations and erroneously believed that he "could win support in Congress or among reporters or within his staff by sending them memoranda saying 'I need your help.'" Otherwise, Fallows thought Califano dead wrong in accusing Carter of being timid in his commitment to civil rights. Califano was also remiss, Fallows continued, by failing to appreciate Carter's "fundamental integrity and intelligence." Carter understood that grand programs launched in Washington usually looked quite different to the people they were supposed to affect. Fallows reminded Califano that his "human decency . . . made it inconceivable for Carter to humiliate his employees as Lyndon Johnson was said to do."[18]

Jimmy and Rosalynn were becoming accustomed to criticisms such as Califano's as they put the presidency behind them, although Rosalynn still found it difficult to hear disparaging remarks that she thought unfair. Jimmy "is at peace," Rosalynn said in an interview with an Americus newspaper reporter, "totally immersed in his book [memoir] and his woodworking shop." Neither of them missed their life in the White House, she continued, but she admitted that Amy disliked living in Plains and missed her classmates in

Washington. Referring to the new administration, Rosalynn added, bitterly, "I sincerely believe . . . that the country will sorely miss [Jimmy], and soon." She was working on her own memoir, but other demands on her time slowed her progress.[19]

As the weather warmed, Jimmy and Rosalynn vacationed and fished at Wayne Harpster's Spruce Creek home and later in Montana. They entertained foreign dignitaries in Plains and traveled internationally as private citizens to China and Japan. When Anwar and Jehan Sadat visited them in Plains early in August, despite Carter's inability to provide them with a helicopter, he did arrange a chauffeured limousine for their use. Jimmy presented Anwar with a glass laurel wreath sculpture commemorating the peace agreement at Camp David. The laurel wreath, Carter said, would turn away evil and "substitute peace for war." "This is what you mean to us, President Sadat, and to the world." The next day, as they were leaving, Sadat declared to a reporter that "Jimmy Carter has left his fingerprints on the history of our age."[20]

After the Sadats' visit, Jimmy, Rosalynn, and Amy made their first trip to China in late August 1981. As the author of the normalization of relations with that country, Carter received an elaborate red carpet treatment. Greeted by Vice Chairman Deng Xiaoping, Carter renewed his relationship with the Chinese leader who had made normalization possible. At a banquet in their honor, Premier Zhao Ziyang mentioned the healthy status of Sino-US relations and toasted further development of friendly economic and cultural exchanges between the two nations.[21]

From China, the Carters went to Japan where he addressed leading business people. Carter had accepted "an embarrassingly generous offer" to make a speech, serve on a panel, and give television interviews.[22] In his public speeches, he warned of another oil crisis, condemned Khomeini as unpredictable and weak, and again pleaded for human rights. He wished that all world leaders would honor the rights of their countries' citizens and work for peace. His most emotional experience as president, he said publicly, was when he attended the memorial service for the eight men who died in the Iranian desert. Privately, he told one of his biographers that their deaths resulted from bad luck, not his poor judgment, and he prayed for their forgiveness.[23]

The visits to China and Japan energized the Carters and helped them to understand that former presidents have power and privileges not available to ordinary citizens. Since Carter was only fifty-seven and Rosalynn fifty-four, they had the time, energy, and commitment to continue their quest for peace and human compassion. President Reagan may have hoped Carter would truly retire when he and Nancy sent birthday wishes in October, but Carter gave no thought to leaving his active life of public involvement. When Begin visited the Carters in Plains in mid-September, kissed Rosalynn's hand, and once again promised to adhere to the Camp David Accords, Carter smiled but told Begin how concerned he was with the continuing bloodshed between Israelis and Palestinians and how much he wanted peace and tranquility for Israel and its neighbors.[24]

Carter's hopes for peace in the Middle East were set back shockingly on October 6, 1981, when fundamentalist Egyptian army soldiers, enraged by the peace treaty with Israel, assassinated Anwar Sadat. In Egypt that day, Sadat and other officials, as well as thousands of Egyptians, celebrated the eighth anniversary of Egypt's victory over Israel in 1973, the victory that had set the stage for Sadat's visit to Jerusalem. Sadat, dressed in his splendid field marshal's uniform, sat in the stands next to Vice President Hosni Mubarak reviewing the elaborate military parade. Diplomats and dignitaries, including the ambassadors from the United States and Israel, sat near them honoring the man and the nation that had led the way for peace in the Middle East. Jehan, along with the Sadat children and grandchildren, sat in a glassed-in box high above the stands. Fireworks, a marching band, and the exotic Camel Corps gave the military parade a festive appearance. Parachutists dropped to the ground near the stands. Tanks, personnel carriers, and Mirage jets expelling trails of colored smoke entertained the crowd.

A truck carrying troops abruptly stopped directly in front of Sadat. Several young soldiers leaped out carrying grenades and assault rifles. Sadat, thinking they intended to pay him tribute, stood up and saluted. Instead of a salute, he received multiple bullets from Lieutenant Khalid al-Islambouli's automatic rifle. When the carnage ended, Sadat and eleven others lay dead, and Islambouli shouted, "I have killed the Pharaoh!" Egypt had turned against Sadat.[25]

Horrified and broken-hearted by the violent death of their friend, the Carters feared that the death of Sadat at the hands of Muslim radicals might jeopardize the peace agreement with Israel. "Words are not enough," Jimmy told reporters who gathered on the lawn in front of Miss Lillian's house on Main Street, "to pay tribute to a man like him." "I have never had a more personal and closer friend than Anwar Sadat." Flanked by Chip and Amy, and casually dressed in a blue sport shirt and khaki trousers, his face laden with grief, Carter remarked that their families had been close and that he and

Anwar had "shared great events and achievement and we've shared tragedies as well." Carter hoped that the leaders of the United States would "continue the courageous effort toward peace for which President Sadat gave his life."[26]

Elsewhere in the world, the response to Sadat's death discouraged Carter. In the Soviet Union the assassination was reported without comment, but in the Libyan capital of Tripoli, crowds sang in the streets and waved pictures of their "Brotherly Leader" Muammar al-Gaddafi, Sadat's most vocal Arab foe. Muslims in Palestine and Lebanon celebrated, and the spokesman for the PLO wanted to "shake the hand of him who pulled the trigger." Syrians danced in the streets of Damascus, chanting, "The traitor is dead." Moderate Arab governments, however, remained restrained, and Pope John Paul II included a special prayer for Sadat in a telegram to Cairo in which he condemned "this vile, violent act."[27]

The Carters called Jehan, tried to comfort her, and told her that they would come to the funeral. They made plans to travel by commercial airline as private citizens, because they wanted to go as personal friends, not government officials. Both President Reagan and Vice President Bush were advised by their security force not to make such a dangerous trip. Reagan decided that he would send his Secretary of State Al Haig and other officials from his administration, but it would be a greater honor to ask the former US presidents to go. When President Reagan invited the Carters to join the other living presidents to represent the United States, they decided to do so, although Carter said he was "aggravated" by having to accept it. Rosalynn was the only former First Lady to go, but she had a special relationship with Jehan that the others did not.[28]

Jimmy and Rosalynn, Richard Nixon, and Gerald Ford all arrived at Andrews Air Force Base within a minute of each other on the afternoon of October 8. Nixon, who had had longer to recover from the loss of the presidency, suggested to the uneasy group, who seemed confused about protocol, that the most recent president should be considered senior, and the others could follow accordingly. Carter thus led Ford followed by Nixon, and then Rosalynn to the helicopter waiting to whisk them to the South Lawn of the White House. Ford attempted to lighten the atmosphere on the helicopter by suggesting that during the ensuing long flight to Cairo they should refer to each other as Dick, Jimmy, and Jerry. At the White House, the vice president and his wife, George and Barbara Bush, welcomed them to the Blue Room for coffee and canapés. Four presidents and two first ladies appeared together at the White House in what was decidedly not a spirit of brotherly love. Reagan, in his inimitable jovial way, thanked the visitors for standing in for him at the funeral, and said that, since they were all navy men, he would wish them "bon voyage" as they boarded Marine One for the flight back to Andrews Air Force Base.[29]

The somber group, lead by the most recently retired president and followed by his predecessors in the order in which they had served, and finally by Roasalynn, boarded the airplane that would take them on a most unusual trip. Once aloft, Rosalynn walked through the single aisle, pleasantly greeting all of the others. Nixon was especially friendly. He complimented her and engaged her in conversation about his wife Pat, Sadat, and peace. Carter talked with Nixon about China. Because three former presidents and one former first lady were traveling to a very dangerous place, Secret Service agents dominated the trip with individual preparations for security. The agents had stored bullet proof vests for each person to wear in the funeral procession. In the course of the long flight, the lingering hostility between Carter and Ford seemed to abate, creating the possibility that the two men could put the past behind them and become friends.[30] When the group arrived in Cairo on the night of October 9, armored limousines flown in from Washington took them to their well-guarded hotel. President Hosni Mubarak greeted them, and the Carters departed for a thirty-minute visit with Jehan Sadat at her home in Giza. Jimmy and Rosalynn felt that the brief time with Jehan and her family fulfilled their purpose for going. Jehan and Sadat's son Gamal embraced Carter and wept on his shoulder. At a dinner that night hosted by US Ambassador Alfred Atherton, Jr., at the El Salam Hotel, each of the three former presidents spoke extemporaneously. Carter's remarks "had a religious flavor, Ford's an earnest one, and Nixon's a more rambling, discursive tone."[31]

The next day, the three former US presidents, wearing bullet proof vests, marched in the funeral procession, along with Prince Charles of the United Kingdom, King Baudouin of Belgium, Grand Duke Jean of Luxembourg, Chancellor Helmut Schmidt of West Germany, President Francois Mitterrand and former President Valery Giscard d'Estaing of France, Menachem Begin, and representatives from the Soviet Union and several African nations. The men wore black suits on a very hot, dusty day. Giscard, who had lost an election in France, called out to Carter: "Jimmy, Are you working in Washington now?" Carter replied, "No, I have an office in Atlanta." In the middle of numerous guards who spoke several languages, a US Secret Service agent standing near the US presidents notified the driver of an armed vehicle, saying, "if anyone goes down, bring it over to the left."[32] They paused under the tent marking the site where Sadat had been assassi- nated only four days earlier, where blood stains were still visible; the tomb was directly across from it. Heavily armed Egyptian guards formed a spooky escort as the mourners walked the half mile to the tomb.[33]

Carter and Begin did not speak. Rulers of Islamic countries who had disliked Sadat justified their appearance, for, as Jehan wrote, "Islam says that any quarrels we might have with one another in this life are settled by death." Rosalynn joined Farah Pahlavi, the former empress of Iran; Jeane Kirkpatrick, the US Ambassador to the UN; and Jehan Sadat in the reviewing stand. Rosalynn marveled at Jehan's composure and determination to be strong when she returned to the scene of her husband's murder. "She sat in his *chair*," Rosalynn emphasized, referring to the fact that Jehan occupied the very seat in which her husband had been assassinated.[34] The mourning women comprised an odd assortment whose fates had driven them apart but brought them together for a funeral that, in different ways, saddened each of them.[35] After greeting the family, the Americans went to the airport and did not attend the interment, which was restricted to Muslims only, and at which there were major security risks for the dignitaries. Nixon had made his own plans for a private visit in the Middle East following his time in Egypt. During the long flight home, the old feud between Carter and Ford virtually evaporated. They discovered that they agreed on many national issues, and they decided that bipartisan support by former presidents might serve their post-presidential world well.

In Cairo, a monument was later erected on the assassination site, bearing the epitaph Sadat had written before his courageous visit to Jerusalem in case he was murdered by the Israelis: "Do not think of those who have been killed in God's way as dead. They are alive with the Lord, well provided for."[36]Shortly after returning home, the Carters attended a reunion with former members of their administration at a Maryland mansion. Carter bluntly referred to the current occupant of the White House as "an aberration on the polit- ical scene." But he told his former colleagues: "I'm not here to criticize my successors. I try to be generous," at which Rosalynn piped up: "Jimmy, don't be too generous." Angry because Reagan and the new Congress had repealed the Mental Health Systems Act, she was ready to go on the attack. Reagan had also begun shipping enormous amounts of military hardware to Iran, which raised suspicions about a possible deal his campaign had cut with the Iranians the previous October.[37] By the end of the year, Jimmy and Rosalynn had found their places in their new world. He accepted an honorary degree from their alma mater, Georgia Southwestern University, using the occasion to announce that he would soon become a distinguished professor at Emory. In addition to his Atlanta office at the Federal Building, Carter occupied the top floor of the Woodruff Library on the Emory campus. He had business offices in Miss Lillian's house in Plains, and he used his home office for his writing and personal businessJohn and Betty Pope had persuaded them to invest jointly in building a cabin adjacent to a trout stream on twenty wooded acres in North Georgia. Carter made some of the furniture for it, and it provided them a retreat reminiscent of Camp David. Jimmy congratulated Hamilton Jordan upon his impending marriage, but he had too many commitments to attend the wedding in Pennsylvania. Ham would continue to advise and help him, but it had become necessary for Jordan to seek a new life of his own.[38]

As private citizens who would no longer seek public office, Jimmy and Rosalynn did not need political advice from Ham Jordan or others who had once served them well. With offices in Atlanta, they would live at their home in Plains. Like his father, Jimmy would rise an hour before daylight, but not to tend to the farm. He would build furniture, and they would walk the fields and woods hunting for arrowheads, fish in the local creeks and ponds, and teach Sunday School classes at Maranatha Baptist church. They sent Amy, who had trouble adjusting to Plains, to a boarding school in Atlanta. Dignitaries came to visit them in Plains, but the Carters did not dwell on their past. Mindful of their "profound connection to the millions of others with whom we share the earth," they intended to do all they could to help those who were unfortunate and "to help the United States fulfill its destiny as a democracy worthy of its founders."[39]

THIRTY SIX

The Carter Center

Adjusting to their new place in the world, and accepting the fact that their presidency was finished, Jimmy and Rosalynn settled into a comfortable, but restless, life in Plains. They wrote their memoirs, Jimmy focusing intently on his with the help of Steve Hochman, and Rosalynn, struggling with interruptions, taking more time.[1] To write, Jimmy sat at the desk that had once belonged to his father, a daily reminder of Mr. Earl's expectations for his first-born son. Jimmy's first published article about fly-fishing reflected his and Rosalynn's love of the sport. Poking fun at himself, he reminded one reporter of his recent experience when he had let a large brown trout get away. His Baptist upbringing, he confessed, "had not prepared me for such ignominious defeat, and I used a few choice words which disturbed the tranquility of the now quiet, gurgling stream."[2]

The incident of the escaped trout and resulting expletives had transpired at Turnip Town Creek, near Ellijay, Georgia, where Jimmy and Rosalynn, with the Popes, had built a log cabin. With a view of waterfalls and rapids, the isolated mountain cabin provided them with a secluded place to read, write, relax, and fish. Jimmy set up his easel there and resurrected his long-forgotten interest in painting. Rosalynn retained her appreciation for art but did not resume painting.[3]

Writing did not come easily for Rosalynn, and she refused to take the time to sit for her official portrait until she finished her book. Two years later, after completing *First Lady from Plains*, she sat for the portrait.[4] Since returning to Plains, however, she had remained sensitive to the needs of the mentally challenged. There was no way "I could feel that I could just desert them because my husband was no longer president," she said.[5] Before they had left the White House, she and Jimmy had searched for a way to establish a nongovernmental institution dedicated to peace and the preservation of human rights.

All the time they were fishing, painting, and writing, the Carters were consulting, studying, and planning to build what became known as the Carter

Center. The idea had not come to Carter out of the blue suddenly in the night, as Rosalynn wrote in her memoir, but was the result of many months of study and planning that they had begun shortly after he lost his bid for reelection. On February 25, 1982, Hamilton Jordan sent him a memorandum about how to pursue that dream. Comparable to the seventy-page memorandum of November 4, 1972, in which he had outlined the plan for Carter to campaign for the presidency, Jordan, who was teaching at Emory and still advising Carter, created a blueprint to found a peacekeeping center.[6]

Jimmy's idea was as outrageous as his 1972 plan to run for president had been: he intended to build an institution similar to the UN in its peace-keeping and humanitarian aspects in downtown Atlanta. Carter invited his primary advisers to meet with him and Rosalynn at Sapelo Island, Georgia, from July 16 through July 18, 1982, to complete plans for the institution as well as discuss plans for his presidential library. Following the traditional pattern for presidential libraries, the Carters would plan and design it, raise the money to build it, and then gift it to the National Archives to staff and maintain.

The Carter Center, however, would be a private institution established and maintained by the Carters themselves. The building complex they envisioned would resemble their beloved Camp David. Before he had left the White House, Carter had consulted with Charlie Kirbo and Warren Christopher, visited numerous benevolent foundations, and had contacted experts at Harvard and George Mason universities. When he and Rosalynn came to the meeting on Sapelo Island, they knew what kind of institution they intended to establish. Each of them would become a co-chair of an institution that had no chairman.

To help them plan the center, Carter had asked several professionals from Emory to attend the meeting. They included Kenneth Stein, an as-sistant professor of history whose research focused on the Middle East; Ellen Mickiewicz, an authority on diplomatic relations between the United States and the Soviet Union; Dean of the Candler School of Theology Jim Waits; and President Jim Laney. From his administration, Carter chose Cy Vance, Warren Christopher, Zbig Brzezinski, Sol Linovitz, Andrew Young, Hamilton Jordan, and Jody Powell to advise them. The fact that Carter asked Vance for help, and Vance agreed to give it, was an indication that they were aligned in their world views and personal lives; they were committed to di-plomacy rather than war, peace, human rights, Christian faith, and respect for intelligent and helpful wives.

At Sapelo Island, Jimmy and Rosalynn were very much in charge. The focus, Carter informed the group, would be on mediation of conflicts around the world, but there would also be research on nuclear arms, world hunger, energy, the environment, ethics in government, public health, democracy, and freedom.[7]

Warren Christopher, an experienced humanitarian who had advised the Hoover Institution on War, Revolution, and Peace at Stanford University, gave the Carters detailed advice on how to build their center.

In time, Carter's thinking evolved into the seven principles upon which they founded the center: (1) It would "not duplicate or compete with effective work being done by others, such as the United Nations agencies," or the United States government, or other organizations or universities; (2) It would be nonpartisan; (3) It would be an action agency, not only a think tank; (4) The Carters would "not permit the prospect of potential failure to deter" them; (5) Carter would not intrude into a politically sensitive area without first getting permission from the White House; (6) The generic name "Global 2000" would be used for efforts to improve health and agricultural services in developing countries in order to allow native "village chiefs or heads of state" to "be able to claim credit" for successes; and (7) Carter would prepare detailed reports on the Center's projects for his family, staff, the US government, and the UN.[8] Only the first two principles were in place at the conclusion of the Sapelo Island meeting; the others evolved after the Center got underway.

Three months earlier, the Carters had identified the site in Atlanta where they planned to build both the center and the library. Charlie Kirbo had asked the state for a thirty-acre tract of land that was about halfway between Emory University and downtown Atlanta.[9] The site was atop a hill overlooking Georgia's capital city from which Union generals had watched the city burn during the Civil War. In Decatur, where an old, established neighborhood was adjacent to the Atlanta site where the buildings were to be erected, angry citizens did not want ancient trees and stately homes to give way to a major highway that would serve the complex. The mayors of Atlanta, former Ambassador Andrew Young and his successor Maynard Jackson, favored the parkway. John Lewis, civil rights leader, former Carter presidential advisor, and Atlanta City Council member, opposed the highway because it would destroy part of a historic Black neighborhood. Although Carter claimed that he had no part in the controversy, his people attended the public hearings and introduced arguments in favor of his acquisition of that land. Carter got his way. The journalist who covered the debate said that "If you made Carter mad, he would cut your dick off."[10]

Rising above the fray, Carter concentrated on his duties at Emory University when the academic year began on September 1, 1982. On September 15, he delivered his first major address as University Distinguished Professor. Talking about human rights, he quoted several of his presidential addresses. "Silence is the enemy of human freedom," he said. The United States should be in the forefront of bringing freedom and human rights to the oppressed everywhere. "America did not invent human rights," he repeated; "human rights invented America."[11]

Cramped and restless in temporary quarters, Carter pushed hard to raise the money for his permanent library and for the center.[12] He asked Coca-Cola CEO Robert Woodruff, a major benefactor of Emory University, to donate $10 million from the various funds and foundations he controlled, promising that the center would be closely associated with Emory. Furthermore, he told Woodruff that "Georgia and the South will be greatly enriched by this national resource."[13] Woodruff gave him $5 million, and Carter proceeded to approach foreign governments, philanthropists, and large foundations, which would pledge more than half of the $26 million he needed. He visited Houston, Dallas, Aspen, and Los Angeles, where he gathered $10 million more at fundraising dinners. Former cabinet members who headed lucrative businesses pitched in, and soon Carter had most of the money he needed.[14]

In the meantime, he gained national and international attention with the publication in November 1982 of *Keeping Faith: Memoirs of a President*. Well researched from the memoranda he had brought with him from the White House, as well as from his extensive daily diary, it was a detailed, historically correct account of his presidential years. The assistance of historian Steve Hochman also provided context, making the book an insightful portrayal of the late 1970s. One perceptive reviewer, Bill Shipp, found it "accurate and penetrating," but a book that also revealed Carter to be "one of the most complex and contradictory political personalities of our time." Carter, in Shipp's judgement, was a gifted, introspective writer who revealed a psyche that was "sterling" but occasionally "tarnished by flecks of meanness."[15]

Carter was proud of his book, an instant best seller, which celebrated his accomplishments but also divulged some regrets he had about having failed to win reelection. Carter sent President Reagan an inscribed copy; Reagan thanked him but offered no indication that he planned to read the book.[16] Nevertheless, during the first months after it was published, *Keeping*

Faith: Memoirs of a President attracted crowds at the author's signings at bookstores across the nation and led to numerous television and newspaper interviews.

Perhaps related to the international prominence that his memoir created, the University of Tel Aviv invited him to come to Israel and accept an honorary degree on March 11, 1983. He and Rosalynn decided to take a three-week-long research trip in the Middle East where they would explore possibilities for peace in the region, raise money for the Carter Center, and again try to persuade Israel to treat the Palestinians justly. In late February and early March, they traveled to Egypt, Israel, Jordan, Saudi Arabia, and Syria, where they met heads of state, other politicians, citizens, and Palestinian leaders. Typically, Carter did his homework before embarking upon the trip. He studied a memorandum by William Quandt, who had served him on the NSC, entitled "Prospects for Peace in the Middle East," and he studied the Koran and the Torah, the sacred literature of the Muslims and the Jews.[17]

Traveling in a private jet that had been loaned to them by Christopher and Patsy Hemmeter, wealthy real estate developers who promoted tourism in Hawaii and casinos in New Orleans and Colorado, the Carters flew first to Egypt, a stop that was especially poignant and meaningful for them. The highlight of their eight days in Egypt was their visit with Jehan Sadat and her large family at her home in Mit Abu al-Kum, a small town northwest of Cairo which had been Sadat's boyhood home. After lunch, the Carters and their entourage walked through the town's dusty streets and through adjacent orange groves and cotton fields. Wherever they went, crowds of local people shouted greetings and gratitude for his bringing peace to Egypt. Later, after a traditional Egyptian meal, Jehan quietly read to Carter a note that her husband had written shortly before his death: "Jimmy Carter is my very best friend on earth. He is the most honorable man I know. Brilliant and deeply religious, he has all the marvelous attributes that made him adept in dealing with the scoundrels who run the world." Moved to silence, Jimmy could do nothing more than bow his head, for he felt the same about Sadat, whose picture he displayed on his desk at home, next to that of Rosalynn.[18] Regaining his composure, Carter engaged Jehan in a lively conversation about politics. He complained that Begin had failed to live up to the conditions of the Camp David Accords, and he repeated his argument that the Palestinians should have a voice in their own future.[19]

For the remainder of their time in Egypt, the Carters mixed pleasure with politics. They visited Sadat's grave and made a courtesy call on President

Reagan's special envoy to the Middle East, Philip Habib. They also toured Cairo's museums, saw the pyramids, cruised up the Nile River, and walked in fertile fields. After worshipping at a Coptic Orthodox Christian church, he learned from the frantic priests that Sadat had arrested their leader Pope Shenouda III for inciting Christian-Muslim disturbances. Since Shenouda had been imprisoned illegally, Carter began a letter-writing campaign to President Hosni Mubarak that finally resulted in the Coptic's release. In meetings with PLO officials in Cairo, Carter advised that they should curb terrorism if they wanted to win their rights, but he learned that they and Mubarak considered the members of the PLO to be not terrorists but the freedom fighters of the Arab world.[20] At every public place they visited, they were greeted with adulation and praise as peacemakers and friends of Egypt.

From Cairo, Jimmy and Rosalynn flew to Jerusalem, where they found themselves in a very different world. After participating in a moving memorial service at the Yad Vashem shrine for Jews who had perished in the Holocaust, Carter went to visit Prime Minister Begin in a nondescript office in the Knesset building. Begin was coldly courteous and uninterested in hearing Carter tell him again how he had not honored the Camp David Accords. Begin had very little to say and seemed relieved when Carter left. Carter privately called the Israeli leader "a psycho."[21]

As Jimmy and Rosalynn moved into the Palestinian areas of Jerusalem and the West Bank, students threw rocks at their limousine and demonstrated so violently that the police cancelled some of their visits. At the West Bank town of Bethlehem, however, the friendly Mayor Elias Freij, a Palestinian Christian, introduced Carter at a town hall meeting. The Palestinians in attendance were pleased to hear the former US president appeal for their rights, but some Arabs and Jews did not like what he said. Arab youths rolled a burning tire into Bethlehem's Manger Square, and Jewish settlers fired submachine guns and pistols at stone-throwing Palestinians. Carter criticized the Israeli military for shooting demonstrators without cause, demolishing Palestinian housing, and jailing Arabs without a trial. He contended that Israel was holding 9,000 Palestinians in prison, most of them prisoners of conscience, and he argued against settling Soviet Jews in Jerusalem because it sparked Palestinian protests. Under heavy guard of Israeli soldiers, Carter reached Gaza where he conferred with Palestinian leaders in private homes or humble buildings where they were not likely to attract attention.[22]

On March 11, Carter proceeded to Tel Aviv to receive an honorary doctorate from the university. Following the same outline he had used many times when campaigning for reelection, he praised Israel but asked for it to give Palestinians their rights. Addressing the assembled dignitaries and students, he said: "God has ordered and ordained the existence of the State of Israel as a permanent homeland of the Jews. This is my deep religious belief." However, he also pleaded for the Palestinians' right to control their own affairs. He delivered the same message he had done many times before, and he got the same response, namely no results. Carter later complained to a journalist that Begin's view of the Camp David Accords was too narrow.[23]

The Carters' next stop, in Amman, Jordan, on March 13, was more pleasant. In a cordial meeting with King Hussein and his American-born queen, Carter urged the king to participate in peace talks that President Reagan had suggested would not include the PLO. Hussein flatly refused, but later, in a private conversation, he thanked Carter for his work and encouraged him to continue. Carter left Jordan hoping that Hussein might be an important player in some future general peace agreement in the Middle East.[24]

Arriving in Saudi Arabia on March 15, the Carters were disappointed to learn that King Fahd was not in Riyadh, but camped two hundred kilometers to the north in the desert. It was Fahd's way of visiting with tribal leaders and sometimes providing medical care and rudimentary education to those who would not have it otherwise. Carter wanted to see him. After an evening of elegant entertainment with the royal family, Jimmy and Rosalynn boarded a helicopter the next day for the long journey over the desert. Upon arrival, Rosalynn was whisked away to visit with Saudi women while Carter met with the king. Both she and Jimmy respected the Saudi tradition of treating women as less than equal with men, but Rosalynn could expect to receive respect and engage in interesting conversations about family and food with the Saudi women.

The king treated Carter like a visiting head of state. Carter noted that the king's tent had Persian carpets on the floor, comfortable places to sit, electricity, air conditioning, and any other comforts that the king desired. Fahd was eager to tell the former president about how he was modernizing Saudi Arabia with improvements in education, housing, women's rights, and transportation. He wanted Carter to understand that he was guided by the high moral standards of the Koran, and he resented the negative image that Western nations had of Saudi Arabia. Thankful for Carter's having sold AWACs to Saudi Arabia in 1978, King Fahd praised Carter for trying to make Israel accept UN Resolution 242 and treat the Palestinians justly. The King gave Carter $1 million to help build and launch the Carter Center, and it was with some pride that he counted himself among its founders. With money and hope that one Arab nation would work for peace in the Middle East, Carter returned to Riyadh and departed from there for Syria.[25]

In the Syrian capital Damascus, Jimmy and Rosalynn walked down the very street where the Apostle Paul was said to have miraculously regained his eyesight after he converted from Judaism to Christianity. During a four-hour discussion with President Hafez al-Assad, however, Carter's religious belief had no impact upon their political discussions. Assad, an adherent of the Alawite sect of Shia Islam, was inflexible in his distrust of Israel and unlikely to loosen his ties with the Soviet Union.[26] Assad felt strongly that US policy toward Syria was determined by Israel, an implacable enemy of her Arab neighbors, while Assad's support of Iran disturbed both the United States and other Arab nations, suggesting that Syria would be a serious impediment to pan-Arab unity. In the streets of Damascus, the Carters were harassed and taunted by Iranian demonstrators. When he left Syria, Carter, more optimistic than his dealings with Assad warranted, felt slightly encouraged that Assad might be a catalyst for peace if he were included in future peace talks, and if he got from them all he wished for Syria.[27]

The Carters' final stop, in Beirut, Lebanon, was only about fifty miles from Damascus. Flying into a war zone, from the plane they could see the stark contrast between the beautiful Mediterranean coastline and war-ravaged Beirut. When their plane landed, heavily armed US Marines, who were part of a peacekeeping force, quickly supplemented the Secret Service agents in protecting the Carters. Tom Benedict, head of Carter's security detail, handed out bullet proof vests to everyone in the delegation. An armed limousine, escorted by five US Marine Humvees, transported them through the streets as quickly as possible to the hilltop palace of President Amin Gemayel. Elected president the previous September after his brother and predecessor had been assassinated, Gemayel wanted his country to be unified, free of the Palestinians, and no longer a battleground between Jews and Arabs, but he had virtually no power and no chance to reach a peaceful agreement with Israel. Carter realized that when foreign troops pulled out of Lebanon, the country would likely disintegrate into a civil war. Leaving the palace empty-handed, he and Rosalynn quickly began their dangerous trip back to the airport. The Secret Service agents put Jimmy and Rosalynn into an ordinary car while they placed Ken Stein and Carter's secretary Faye Dill in the official limousine to serve as decoys in case of an attack. The Americans gave a sigh of relief when their plane safely exited Lebanese air space.[28]

The Carters returned to Washington, where he reported to Secretary of State George P. Shultz, who showed very little interest in what he had to say. Carter then gave a blunt presentation to the Council on Foreign Relations in New York City. "Israel," he told the Council members, "is the problem toward peace."[29] When Carter offered to brief Reagan, the president allowed him to visit in the Oval Office for thirty minutes on March 17. Reagan's cool but polite indifference to his report disgusted Carter. The same day, Carter declined to attend the hanging of his portrait on the state floor of the White House, requesting that it be done without ceremony.[30]

In the following weeks, Carter began to speak out more freely against the Reagan administration, which ignored him and began to dismantle some of his work. He thought that Reagan did not understand the Middle East, that his economic policies would create a huge deficit, and that his military spending would be a "bottomless pit." Although Carter remained confident that US democracy was in good shape, he believed that Reagan was making mistake after mistake, particularly kowtowing to powerful lobbies and not recognizing the importance of the normalization of relations with China. Carter especially hoped the new administration would honor the Camp David Accords.[31] Invigorated by his three-week trip to the Middle East, Carter proceeded to build the Carter Center with a vengeance. Having won favor with the Japanese by condemning Reagan's demand that Japan change its defense policies, Carter, along with former President Gerald Ford, found himself serving as an honorary advisor to the United States-Japan Foundation, which offered educational grants to promote studies on how to improve relations between the United States and Japan. As a result, Carter became acquainted with Ryoichi Sasakawa, the shipping tycoon who had created the foundation. With Christopher Hemmeter and Emory president James Laney, Carter flew to Japan to meet Sasakawa, who favored organizations that promoted world peace. After learning about Carter's work, Sasakawa contributed $1.7 million to Carter Center programs.[32]

Closer to home, Carter cultivated the friendship of Atlanta's communication mogul, Ted Turner, who owned Cable News Network (CNN). The two men were natural friends, both being sports fans, outdoorsmen, and promoters of Atlanta. Turner not only contributed substantial money to the Carter Center himself, but persuaded many of his wealthy friends to do likewise. His television network provided Carter and the Carter Center extensive national and international publicity.[33]

Carter also gained important support from former President Gerald Ford. In the summer of 1983, the two former presidents held their First Presidential Library Conference on Public Policy at Ford's Library in Ann Arbor, Michigan. They discussed their disappointment with a slow Congress and an antagonistic, sensationalist press that had hindered their presidencies. The solution, Carter thought, would be to use the media and educational institutions to create an informed, educated, and thoughtful electorate. Only an educated public, Carter declared, would make a strong democratic government possible.[34]

That June, Jimmy and Rosalynn learned that his sister Ruth had been diagnosed with terminal pancreatic cancer. Overwhelmed with grief, they found the thought of losing Ruth to be almost unbearable. The same disease had taken Mr. Earl's life when he was in his late fifties, only a few years older than Ruth. Ruth placed her faith in God and hoped to be healed by the divine intervention she had preached to thousands of her disciples. Nevertheless, her health continued to decline, and Jimmy, Rosalynn, Billy, and Miss Lillian traveled to Fayetteville, North Carolina, for an emotional visit with her. Unable to do anything other than pray and comfort her, Carter returned to Atlanta and Plains where he kept busy with his development of the Carter Center and other activities.[35]

More bad news came to the Carters in June when stories about the strange fate of Jimmy's 1980 debate briefing book became public. The Carter people only learned of the theft of his book and its use by the Reagan campaign to prepare nearly three years after the debate when a newly published book about the Reagan presidency mentioned it. Robert Strauss, Carter's 1980 campaign manager, called for an investigation. The FBI, the Justice Department, and a House subcommittee probed the matter. David Stockman, then serving as the director of the Office of Management and Budget, former Reagan National Security Advisor Richard V. Allen, and conservative newspaper columnist George F. Will all admitted to the House investigating committee that they had seen the Carter briefing book material. James A. Baker, Reagan's former chief of staff, and David Gergen, a former Reagan adviser, also admitted to having seen the material. No one seemed to know, or be willing to confess, who had stolen it or if, indeed, it had been stolen.

In a major, hostile confrontation with the wily and evasive William Casey, who had since become Reagan's director of the CIA, Baker accused Casey of the misdeed. Although Casey had earlier casually commented that he had seen the material, he vigorously denied any involvement but began to distance himself from the chief of staff, communicating with him only by curt notes. Baker, who thought the material was of no value to the Reagan campaign, found himself dismayed to be caught up in the possibly criminal affair. The House Subcommittee accused Casey of lying when he denied knowing anything about the book, but they could not prove it. Reagan claimed that he knew nothing about it, and no one was prosecuted.[36]

Carter fumed about the stolen briefing book, which may have contributed to his loss of the election, but he left the investigation to the Justice Department, because he was more interested in his current peacekeeping efforts than returning to old battles.

Rosalynn found it difficult to hide her intense dislike for the Reagan administration, but she too focused on new opportunities to promote the work that she and Jimmy were doing. In August 1983, she joined the Gannett Company, Inc., Board of Directors. A giant conglomerate that included more than eighty daily newspapers, six television stations, and thirteen radio stations, it paid the former First Lady a beginning salary of $17,500. The company's vice president for corporate communications, Walter Wurfel, who had served as a member of the White House Press Office, had recommended her. One of three women on a fourteen-member board, Rosalynn, at age fifty-six, found herself gainfully employed by the very media that had so irritated her husband while in office.[37]

Although they had known for months that Ruth's death was inevitable, Jimmy and Rosalynn were shattered when she died at the age of fifty-four on September 26, 1983. It was Ruth who had brought Rosalynn and Jimmy together, and Jimmy credited his sister with being the catalyst for his "born again" experience. Upon the occasion of her death, he said that his sister was "one of God's special people" who had prepared herself for the premature end of her life. Her impact upon thousands, he said, was "very great," but he regretted that his presidency had focused so much media attention upon her.[38]

A little over a month later, on October 30, Miss Lillian died. Jimmy, Billy, and Gloria were at her bedside in the Sumter County Hospital. She was eighty-five, primarily the victim of breast cancer that had metastasized into pancreatic and other forms of cancer. Billy, Jimmy, and Chip transported the dark hardwood cherry casket containing her body to her beloved Pond House. Placed in a small bedroom filled with the flowers that poured in from celebrities and common people alike, the open casket allowed family and visitors to pay their respects to the revered "Miss Lillian." Stores in Plains closed on November 1 during the hour of her funeral. There was a public graveside service at Lebanon Cemetery where she was buried beside Mr. Earl. Devastated by his mother's death, Jimmy later wrote, "What will we do now?"[39]

Four days after his mother's funeral, Carter was at work at the Carter Center. He had directed Professor Kenneth Stein to organize a group to consult with him about the Middle East. Stein did his work well, and on the morning of November 6, Gerald Ford and an assemblage of experts from ten nations arrived at the Woodruff Medical Center Auditorium on the Emory campus. Fearing for the safety of the group assembled to discuss Jewish-Arab relations, Carter had called for tight security. There were sharpshooters on the roof of the auditorium, sixty police officers from the City of Atlanta, several explosive-sniffing dogs, and teams of Secret Service agents. The participants also included Cy Vance and Zbig Brzezinski, as well as political advisors from Harvard University, the Hoover Institute, the Soviet Union, Egypt, Saudi Arabia, and Jordan. Israel declined to participate. Both Ford and Carter urged that Reagan not retaliate militarily against the recent attack on the marines in Beirut in which 241 had died. The group took on the atmosphere of an emergency UN meeting.[40]

Carter dominated the meeting. He expounded upon the Camp David Accords and the need for all parties who had agreed to them to keep their promises. He emphasized the need for Israel to respect the rights of Palestinians and to find a peaceful resolution to the dilemma of how they could co-exist with Israel. The Carter administration's former Assistant Secretary of State for Near East Affairs, Hal Saunders, urged the United States to recognize the PLO as the legitimate national representative of the Palestinian people. Although there was no chance that the Reagan administration or Israel would agree with that, Carter, as well as other participants and media analysts, called the meeting a success.[41] Indeed, the Carter Center had staged an international peace conference comparable to what might occur at the UN or in the highest diplomatic circle of the United States.

As Carter continued his own private diplomacy, he opened himself to the inevitable criticism that the 1799 Logan Act prohibited private citizens from conducting foreign policy, but Carter saw himself as a law-abiding citizen whose forays into international diplomacy were advisory and thus legal. Unwilling to trust Reagan with national security, Carter met secretly with former Soviet Ambassador Anatoly Dobrynin in Washington on January 30, 1984. He told the seasoned Russian diplomat that he was concerned that Reagan's arms buildup would jeopardize SALT II agreements and negatively impact US-Soviet relations. Reagan's talk of peace, Carter warned Dobrynin, was no more than campaign rhetoric and that there would be no nuclear arms control agreement as long as Reagan was president. Dobrynin, who had never liked Carter, reported in his memoir that Carter was a "poor prophet."[42]

Although public speaking fees did not represent much of his income, Carter occasionally accepted pay for speeches, as in the early months of 1984 when he spoke to young business executives in Australia and to students and others at Southern Methodist University in Dallas. In both speeches, he talked about his presidency, the Camp David Accords, the continuing need for diligence in diplomacy, and fishing. He faulted the Reagan administration for not being aggressive enough in supporting UN Resolution 242, which required Israel to withdraw from territories it had taken in the 1967 war. His increasing defense of the PLO and judgmental statements about the intransigence of Israel identified him as one willing to fight injustice no matter the victims, no matter the perpetrators.[43]

Moving back into the public eye independently of her husband, Rosalynn embarked upon a career similar to her work as First Lady. After her autobiography, *First Lady from Plains*, was published early in 1984, she went to Washington to promote it. In various interviews, she confessed that she missed being in power and even missed the criticisms and hate mail. She regretted not taking a more active part on the capital's cocktail circuit, where she might have given political insiders a chance to understand her husband better.[44]

Political involvement remained Rosalynn's life's blood, and often she would be more frank than her husband. When some friends suggested she should run for the Senate, she quickly rejected the idea. Nevertheless, she continued, "I love politics.... I'll do anything to help get rid of Ronald Reagan." At a symposium on first ladies in April at the Gerald Ford Museum in Grand Rapids, Michigan, she remarked that while she had used her position to promote her own projects, she had also assisted and usually defended her husband's presidency. Sounding like a Southern lady, she said that she had always tried to please the men in her life. Both her father and her husband loved her so much that both of them thought that she could do anything. She believed that her biting criticism of President Reagan counted as her service to the nation. Reagan, Rosalynn said, would be remembered for war and losing lives unnecessarily in Lebanon, whereas Jimmy would be remembered for peace, human rights, and compassion. If Jimmy had taken her advice and bombed Tehran, she still maintained, he would have been reelected.[45]

After the publication of her autobiography, which sold more copies than Jimmy's presidential memoir, Rosalynn became emboldened and was in high demand for interviews and speeches. When Reagan was nominated for a second term in August 1984, she did not hesitate to give him a tongue lashing for dismantling so many of Carter's programs. In a candid newspaper interview, she declared that the women's movement had made a difference in US society and admonished Reagan, declaring that the country needed affirmative action and active women's organizations. When the Democrats, after nominating Walter Mondale for the presidency in July 1984, accepted his choice of Congresswoman Geraldine Ferraro, a liberal advocate for women's rights from New York, for vice president, Rosalynn defended the Democratic ticket and argued that she did not think Geraldine Ferraro would damage it in the South.[46]

Carter thought that he could serve Mondale best by working quietly away from media attention. When Mondale, who wanted his help with the South, asked Carter to approach George Wallace for his support, Carter wrote Wallace, flattered him on the way he had managed Alabama, and assured the Alabamian that Mondale stood for the same Southern principles that he did. The approach worked, and Wallace endorsed Mondale. Although Carter backed Mondale unreservedly in both the Georgia presidential primary in March and the general election in November, he admitted that he was "not good at giving advice on how to run against Ronald Reagan."[47]

The national Democratic leaders had faced a dilemma about what to do with Carter when their national convention had met in San Francisco July 16–19. Hoping that he would not attend, they feared more negative publicity if they banned him. Hence, Chairman Charles T. Manatt put him in a slot early in the convention schedule when there would be a minimum of television coverage. Speaking at 8:30 p.m. on the first day of the convention, Carter began parodying Reagan's winning line four years earlier, "There you go again." "Here I go again," Carter said, before moving into his favorite topics of arms control and human rights. Waxing eloquent in words of his own choosing, he hinted that Reagan's policies might lead to a nuclear holocaust. Referring to the dropping of the atomic bomb on Hiroshima, he warned the bored Democrats that "The survivors of the next world war, if any, would merely scratch for existence in the poisoned ruins of a civilization that has committed suicide."[48] The convention virtually ignored him, and in the November election the voters did too when they rejected Mondale and reelected Reagan by a landslide.

Removing themselves as much as possible from national politics throughout the summer and fall, Jimmy and Rosalynn chased their dream "to do something positive." The Carter Center hosted a symposium on arms control negotiation in May and another one on September 11 concerning the US interest in world resources. The first one as a major project comparable to a Middle East peace conference, and the second one in Michigan was a prelude for a higher level consultation in 1985.[49]

Throughout the summer, the Carters dealt with personal property issues and continued to plan for their center. In June they gave their home on Woodland Drive to the National Park Service, on the condition that they could live in it for the remainder of their lives, and with the understanding that it would boost the tourist industry in Plains. A month later, when the Exxon Corporation contributed $250,000, he had raised the money he needed for the library and the center. As Carter proceeded with plans to build the complex, debate erupted again over the road leading to it. This time, Carter did not win. Instead of a presidential parkway extending from the downtown interstates and overpasses all the way to Ponce De Leon Avenue in Decatur, there would be a two-lane road with stoplights. The access route to the Carter Center and the presidential library would not be grand, but plans for construction continued.[50]

In addition to their work for the Carter Center, on Labor Day, 1984, Jimmy and Rosalynn Carter volunteered to help build houses for Habitat for Humanity. Along with friends from Atlanta and South Georgia, they boarded a Trailways bus in Americus to begin a twenty-four hour ride to New York City. Their destination was a dilapidated six-story tenement house at 742 East Street, which they would renovate to provide decent housing for the working poor. It was one of many similar work projects initiated by Habitat for Humanity (Habitat), an eight-year-old nonprofit organization based in Americus. Two years earlier Carter had attended a meeting of Habitat volunteers at the First Presbyterian Church in Americus. For more than a year, the organization's founder Millard Fuller had been prodding the Carters to volunteer for a Habitat project.

Fuller, an ambitious man with a law degree, had such a knack for salesmanship that he and his wife Linda had become millionaires in their late twenties. Discontented with their affluent but spiritually empty lifestyle, they rid themselves of all the accoutrements of wealth, became itinerant Christian missionaries, and eventually found themselves at Koinonia Farms near Plains. After helping build a house for a poor illiterate tenant farmer, they discovered their milieu. They called for a meeting of Christians from all over the United States at Koinonia Farms on August 26, 1976. Habitat for Humanity was born that day as primarily a Christian organization dedicated to building decent houses for poor people who were willing to help construct them.

Carter at first had ignored Fuller, but Fuller pestered him for money and led him to understand that supporting Habitat, which was headquartered in his own backyard, was commensurate with the type of Christian service he and Rosalynn favored.[51] Carter later said that he considered Millard Fuller and the founder of Koinonia Farms, Clarence Jordan, among the four greatest people he had known. The other two were Anwar Sadat and Nelson Mandela. The Carters made generous contributions and allowed their names to be used for fundraising. Then, on that Labor Day Weekend in 1984, for the first time they went to work building.[52]

Before boarding the bus for their building adventure, Carter grinned and said that he would get the chance to test his new electric saw. He and Rosalynn did not sit together but instead mingled with other passengers. After arriving in New York, Jimmy and Rosalynn spent the next five days working beside the others rebuilding that dilapidated apartment building on the Lower East Side of Manhattan. Donning carpenter's gear, they hammered nails, planed rough boards, operated skill saws, and held boards and studs in place, often under dangerous conditions. When offered a room with a double bed, they rejected it and gave it to a young, newly married couple. The Carters slept in bunk beds and lived exactly like the other volunteers.[53]

Celebrated by the City of New York as well as prominent Christian churches, Jimmy and Rosalynn gave interviews about Habitat and inspired others to participate. Speaking at one church, Carter announced that Habitat would work on a project in Nicaragua the following year. Carter wanted people in Nicaragua to know that he and other Christians did not hate them. Nicaragua's president, a young Sandinista party leader Daniel Ortega, was a Communist sympathizer who was not the sort of national leader Carter might have wanted for Nicaragua, but Ortega, who was in New York City attending a UN meeting, dropped by the Habitat construction site. Carter had met him at the White House five years earlier and believed it might be possible to work with him.[54]

Before leaving New York, Carter decided to take a Christian stand against pornography. He and forty of his fellow Christians sang hymns as they marched through the pornography district on 42nd Street in Manhattan. He posed, with an unusually large grin, beneath a marquee that advertised "the best porn in town."[55]

Although the Carters thereafter contributed only one week of their time per year to building houses for the poor, the fact that they gave their name and money-raising skills to Habitat for Humanity catapulted it into one of the largest and most successful charitable organizations in the country. When Carter had announced that the next year he wanted to build houses in Nicaragua, he pushed Habitat into becoming a major international organization. By the end of 1986, Habitat operated in 171 US communities and 17 foreign countries.[56]

After a brief return to Atlanta where they supervised the work of the Carter Center, and a short fishing trip in late September to the Catskill Mountains in upstate New York, Jimmy declared that he would not slow down. On his sixtieth birthday, he asked anyone who wished to give him a birthday present to write a check to Habitat for Humanity.[57]

A day later, on October 2, 1984, Andrew Young led the groundbreaking ceremony for the library. James Laney, the president of Emory University, joined the Carters and others who wielded ceremonial shovels. A detailed model revealed that the finished complex would be a series of connected circular buildings nestled on the hillside. Carter's four-year-old grandson, James Earl Carter IV, stole the show as his grandfather watched him adoringly.[58]

Two weeks later, Rosalynn, excited about the library and center, resumed her public appearances. With the gentle ferocity for which she had become famous, she took the Southern Baptists to task at a mid-October church conference in Louisville, Kentucky, where she accepted the Convention's Distinguished Christian Woman Award. Shocking the audience by not delivering a meek, mealy mouthed thank-you speech, she took her stand for the equality of women in the nation and in her church. About 650 people attended that conference at the Galt House. Entitled "The Changing Role of Women in Church and Society," it was sponsored by the local Southern Baptist Seminary, an institution known for its conservatism. Rosalynn spared no words in repudiating the four-month-old prohibition of ordination for women. Concluding with a statement many Baptists may not have wanted to hear, she declared: "We're all one in Jesus Christ—men and women."[59]

Black people and White people were one, too, in Jesus Christ, both Carters believed. When famed African-American educator Benjamin Mays, who had headed Morehouse College, the Atlanta school that had trained Martin

Luther King, Jr., died in March 1984, Jimmy spoke at his funeral and quoted from the Beatitudes. Carter never met Martin Luther King, Jr., but he did know his father quite well. When Daddy King died in November, Carter listened quietly as Vice President George H. W. Bush spoke. When it came his turn, Jimmy said he felt as if he had "lost two fathers."[60]

Carter had just returned from Michigan where on November 15, 1984, he and former President Gerald Ford had hosted a symposium at the Ford Library. Much more modest than the one they had held in Atlanta, the subject was new weapons technology and their relationship to Soviet-US diplomacy. Ford's National Security Adviser, General Brent Scowcroft and Reagan's Assistant Secretary of State Richard Burt attended as did Brzezinski and others from the Carter administration. The Reagan people may have been keeping an eye on Carter, but the sponsors intended it to be a nonpartisan event.[61]

In Atlanta, Carter tended his duties at the Carter Center in a very professional way, especially when he hosted its first healthcare symposium, November 26–28, but his heart seemed to be with Habitat. In Texas to raise money for the Carter Center, he and Rosalynn had taken the opportunity to help Habitat, attending a board meeting in Amarillo, Texas, on October 11, where they discussed how they could expand the program globally, use the Carter name for a media blitz, and increase contributions. Carter committed his generous honoraria from speeches to the cause and promised to raise $10 million.[62]

Religion, the library, and the center, building houses, and international politics drove the Carters' lives for most of the following year. Both of them delivered speeches at Emory and elsewhere. On March 13, 1985, Carter received the World Methodist Peace Prize, the first American to do so. When awarding it, Bishop William R. Cannon, who had served Carter as an unofficial envoy during his presidency, cited Carter's efforts in Panama, the Middle East, and SALT II. He added, too, that Carter deserved the award for his work building houses for the poor.[63] Still, Habitat occupied only one week each year in Jimmy and Rosalynn's lives.

Carter asked former President Ford to join him in sponsoring a conference on international security at the Carter Center in April 1985. They invited fifty of the world's best-known thinkers on the subject, including Henry Kissinger, Anatoly Dobrynin, Robert McFarlane, Cy Vance, Harold Brown, James Schlesinger, Howard Baker, and others from both major US political parties. Representatives from China, Egypt, East and West Germany, the

United Kingdom, Japan, Pakistan, and the Soviet Union, notably Anatoly Dobrynin, attended. Twenty academic experts were also there to advise the participants and possibly learn from them. Carter argued that there had been no progress in arms control talks with the Soviet Union since he had left office. He criticized Reagan for his "Star Wars" strategic missile defense program and doubted that the Soviet Union would pursue such a program of its own.[64]

After the conference adjourned, Carter sent both President Reagan and Vice President Bush a long, written report on the participants, their recommendations, and the international journalists who were present. Reagan did not reply. Bush responded with a gracious appreciation of Carter's efforts to "provide a clear sounding board for informed public opinion." Politely, he reminded Carter that the current administration shared the same goals for arms control and hoped they "may soon be achieved."[65]

One Atlanta journalist, who believed that Carter was mean and duplicitous, dismissed the conference as the "Jimmy and Jerry Show." Despite the participation of such seasoned diplomats as Cyrus Vance, Henry Kissinger, Anatoly Dobrynin, and others, he contended that it accomplished nothing.[66] Jimmy and Rosalynn, however, felt that it was a major discussion by people who knew the world and a positive launching of one phase of their Carter Center.

While their parents hosted an international peace conference in Atlanta, Amy and Chip went to Washington to demonstrate against apartheid in South Africa. Amy was arrested in front of that country's embassy, but Chip was not. When interviewed, Amy said that she was "proud to be my father's daughter." Her father was equally proud of her. The next year Amy was arrested again, this time in the office of the IBM Corporation in Providence, Rhode Island, where she had joined others in protesting that company's continued links with South Africa.[67] Amy, age seventeen, had decided to attend Brown University in Providence. An academically distinguished school with historical Southern Baptist connections, it seemed to be a good fit for her and for her parents, but Amy was too liberal for Brown.[68]

Continuing his own push for justice and understanding, Carter published *The Blood of Abraham: Insights into the Middle East* in April 1985. After presenting a brief objective history of the region, he attempted to show that the major world religions—Christianity, Islam, and Judaism—shared a common heritage and common founder, Abraham. Recalling his 1983 visit to the area, he placed his personal experience in context with the history of the region and used the book to advocate for justice for the Palestinians and peace among the disputing parties. His most informed reviewer, Bernard Lewis, writing in the *New York Times*, valued the book for its insights into a major international and interfaith conflict. He praised Carter's skill with language but thought he took Syria's President Hafez al-Assad's assurances at face value and overlooked evidence of Assad's cruelty when he killed some 20,000 people associated with the underground organization called the Muslim Brotherhood. Lewis correctly assessed the book as not a scholarly account but a popular effort to be fair to both sides. It did, however, reveal the author's political animosities, especially his criticisms of his successor.[69]

As he had done with his memoir, Carter sent a copy of his new book to President Reagan, who did not read it but replied on July 8 with his thanks and offered a short summary of what he was doing in the Oval Office. Reagan's secretary had attached a letter from Robert C. McFarlane to the book before delivering it to the president in which he reported that the book had gotten poor reviews, was sour on Israel, sweet on the Arabs, opinionated on the plight of the Palestinians, and irritated with Reagan.[70]

Although honored in their home town if not at the White House, life in Plains had slowed down considerably since Jimmy and Rosalynn had lived at 1600 Pennsylvania Avenue. Although tourists still visited the remote Southwestern Georgia town, the huge crowds were gone, but there was plenty of memorabilia for sale and Jimmy and Rosalynn themselves were helping build a bed and breakfast hotel that had rooms representing the decades of their public career. The Carters could be seen riding their bikes, attending their church, dining at one of the few restaurants in town, or autographing their books. When the town decided to celebrate its centennial on May 17–19, 1985, Jimmy and Rosalynn joined the fun. They observed the crowning of the Peanut Queen, clog dancers on Main Street, and they mixed comfortably with the crowd. Carter entered a five-mile race, and he publicized the fact that his good friend Willie Nelson would soon arrive and give a free concert on the softball field.

After Willie arrived, the crowds picked up as Carter and country music fans listened to Willie and Jimmy sing "On the Road Again." On May 18, when Willie had moved his concert to the auditorium at Plains High School, Jimmy and Rosalynn walked onto the stage with him and joined in singing "Amazing Grace" and "Georgia on My Mind." Willie carefully adjusted the microphone so that only his voice could be heard, but the jubilant crowd stood up and joined in the singing with such enthusiasm that the Carters' voices would have been drowned out anyway.[71]

In late July 1985, Jimmy and Rosalynn boarded a Trailways bus again bound for New York City. Joining thirty-two other volunteers, they talked, visited, joked, slept, and bonded as a happy group on their way to build more houses for the poor. After a stop in Washington for a sunrise treat of coffee and donuts, they headed up Interstate 95 for the Big Apple. As the hour for a Sunday morning worship service approached, Carter asked the driver to take the next exit and get directions to the nearest church. A series of coincidences placed them at a Lutheran church where the service had ended, but the congregation was celebrating the birthday of an eighty-year-old member. To their amazement, the former president and First Lady of the United States walked in with more than thirty others. After determining that the guest was not an impersonator, the young minister E. Walter Cleckley, Jr., and his wife, welcomed the group, repeated the worship service for them, and later visited them at their work site in New York.[72]

History gave Carter a kind nod before the end of 1985 when a young freelance writer Tim Wells published *444 Days: The Hostages Remember*. Consisting of interviews with the former hostages, it gave the personal stories of the men and women who had captured the attention of the world during Carter's last year in office. Rather than confirming the conventional view that the United States had been an impotent giant during that long ordeal, the book suggested that Carter's handling of the hostage crisis had had a dramatic negative impact on the Khomeini regime. Carter's economic embargo had devastated Iran, created internal strife, and weakened its ability to fight the war with Iraq. Most of the freed Americans gave Carter the credit for saving their lives and helping them reintegrate into US society. Greater damage, they contended, had been done to Iran than to the United States.[73]

As 1986 began, the building of the Carter Center and the presidential library continued to progress, and Jimmy and Rosalynn continued their frenetic pace. In January, after being appalled by hearing what Julius Nyerere, former president of Tanzania, said about poor farming techniques in his country, Carter decided to help. He, Andrew Young, Japanese philanthropist Ryolchi Sasakawa, and renowned US agronomist Norman Borlaug toured four African countries for a week. Borlaug, who had received the Nobel Peace Prize in 1970 for his research into plant genetics, had become known as father of the Green Revolution. Carter's group hoped to find ways to teach African farmers how to produce, within a decade, enough food products to feed the people of their continent. Carter met with African heads of state to stimulate their interest and to ask for their help. They were eager to do so and called for native volunteers to do the necessary work in accord with the advisors whom Carter sent to teach them. As a result of this visit, the Carter Center created Project Africa, a program designed to end hunger on that continent.[74]

In addition to Africa and the Middle East, the third part of the world in which the Carter Center took a major interest was Latin America. From February 3 to February 13, 1986, he and Rosalynn, along with Robert Pastor, who had served as a Latin American expert on Carter's NSC staff, and a young assistant named Eric Bord visited several Central American countries. In Costa Rica, Carter met with President-elect Oscar Arias Sanchez, who briefed him about efforts of a half dozen Latin American countries to mediate internal conflicts in Nicaragua and El Salvador for about five years.

In Nicaragua, Carter met with Daniel Ortega, who volunteered to drive him through heavy dust in his open jeep out to a remote Habitat for Humanity site. Once there, Carter embraced the volunteers, laid a few bricks, and attended dedications of completed houses. "Through Christ, peace is possible," Carter told the workers, but he carefully avoided political conversation.[75] An elaborate banquet that Ortega later provided for the former US president, his wife, and their advisers, suggested that he did not view Carter's mission as only religious. He also showed that he reserved for himself the wealth, elegant lifestyle, and power typical of a dictator. Carter bided his time trying to get to know the ambitious Nicaraguan better, because he had already judged him to be someone with whom he might be able to negotiate. Despite his denials to the press, Carter was moving into position to mediate the confrontation between the Sandinistas and the Contras. When he met Violeta Barrios de Chamorro, the owner of an anti-Sandinista newspaper whose journalist husband had been assassinated by unknown gunmen in 1978, he told her that he supported the peace process that had originated in Costa Rica.[76]

In El Salvador, angry mobs who blamed Carter for the civil war that had begun when he was president, became so threatening that the Secret Service begged the Carters to stay at the US ambassador's home rather than a hotel and to cut their visit short. They did both, and Carter left the country believing that there was no hope for him to accomplish anything there.

In Mexico City, Jimmy and Rosalynn did not have to face an angry mob, but they had to deal with being snubbed by Reagan's US ambassador and former Hollywood actor John Gavin. Pretending that his mother was ill, Gavin canceled a reception that had been planned to entertain the Carters, leaving Jimmy and Rosalynn adrift on their own in Mexico City. Carter, who did not believe Gavin, wished his mother a speedy recovery, and Gavin later insulted the Carters even more by admitting that his excuse had been a lie. Carter joked about the snub and took his small group to dinner at a restaurant where he shocked his companions by personally paying the bill.[77]

Returning to Atlanta, Carter planned to go directly to New York to consult with Secretary General Javier Perez de Cuellar at the UN. He planned to volunteer to become the UN mediator of the war in Nicaragua. Rosalynn tried to talk him out of it, but an aide overheard him say, "But Rosie, it is my duty to keep at it until peace is achieved."[78]

Jimmy won the argument with "Rosie," made the trip to New York, and emerged with Perez's official approval and eager to mediate a resolution to the Nicaraguan conflict. Rosalynn may have understood better than he did that there would likely be a long and very rocky road ahead, because she too had witnessed the talks with both the Sandinistas and the Contras. Always optimistic, back in Atlanta Jimmy taught a religion class at Emory about conflict resolution, but he had not resolved his own conflict with Reagan.[79]

The debate, and veiled animosity, between Carter and Reagan continued to fill the newspapers. Carter accused Reagan of distorting facts about his defense buildup, which Reagan denied. Carter retorted that some of the president's "statements are almost more than a human being can bear."[80] However, Carter did help Reagan get the Senate votes he needed to support his sale of missiles and delivery of AWACS to the Saudis.[81] Otherwise, the disagreements between the current and previous presidents were irreconcilable. After Reagan bombed Tripoli, Libya, a stronghold of terrorists, on April 14, 1986, Carter said that his action would kill many innocent people and escalate terrorism. A news story that the bombing had killed Gaddafi's infant daughter particularly infuriated Carter. If someone killed his Amy, Carter responded, he would retaliate. The story about Gaddafi's daughter proved to be false, Libya did not retaliate, and Carter and Reagan continued to promote very different avenues to peace.[82]

Nevertheless, Carter continued to emphasize that the Carter Center was nonpartisan, and the Carters made decisions that enhanced the its human rights and healthcare missions. Carter joined forces with philanthropist and art patron Dominique de Menil to create the Carter-Menil Human Rights Foundation to promote protection of human rights throughout the world.

She and her Franco-American husband had fled Nazi-occupied Paris in 1941, and as heiress to the Schlumberger oil-equipment fortune, whose company housed one of its international headquarters in her home town of Houston, Texas, she was eager to use her wealth to help those who suffered. The Carter-Menil Foundation announced that it would award an annual "100,000 prize to an individual or group that exemplifies human rights leadership."[83]

In June, the Carters chose Dr. William Foege, former chief of the Centers for Disease Control (CDC) in Atlanta, to become the director of the Carter Center. A former medical missionary, who was credited with having rid the world of smallpox through his work at the CDC, he was the perfect choice to guide the center in reaching its global goals. Foege, boasted Carter, wanted to alleviate the suffering of others and would help the Carter Center become "one of the forces in the world . . . for peace."[84]

Happy with their center, Jimmy and Rosalynn celebrated their fortieth wedding anniversary on July 6, 1986, by building houses for the poor in Chicago. The disgraced Watergate operative from the Nixon era, Chuck Colson, who had served time in prison and had emerged as a devout Christian, was among their crew. After spending time with him, Rosalynn was convinced that his religious conversion was sincere.[85]

The death of Admiral Rickover on July 9 struck Carter with the same force as had the death of his father Mr. Earl thirty-three years before. The two men had been much alike, and Carter frequently credited both of them for having influenced him to become a hardworking perfectionist. At an ecumenical service for Rickover in Washington, Carter declared that the Admiral was "second only to my father," and that "Hyman Rickover made my life." At Mrs. Rickover's request, he read from John Milton's "Sonnet on His Blindness." The last line, "They also serve who only stand and wait," seemed relevant, Carter thought, to both his and Rickover's lives. Rickover was buried privately in Arlington National Cemetery.[86]

In Atlanta, the elegant, inauspicious interlocked circular buildings that were to house the Carter Center and the Carter Presidential Library edged toward their final form. Nestled in trees next to lakes and a perfectly designed Japanese garden, the center and the library were monuments to what the Carters had done and to what they were doing and would continue to do. According to the custom, the owner of a new library invited the current president to dedicate it. Accordingly, Jimmy and Rosalynn sent dedication invitations to the Reagans, the Fords, and the Nixons. Ford and Nixon sent regrets. Reagan's staff recommended that he and Nancy attend, "although

Jimmy Carter has been extremely petty and unfairly critical." The occasion would allow "Ronald Reagan's magnanimous character" to "rise above the petty activities of one of his critics." It would also be "another reminder of President Reagan's graciousness to a political foe."[87]

Carter could be gracious too as the occasion required, but in his public speeches he remained unrelentingly critical of both political and religious conservatives, especially the Southern Baptist Convention and narrow-minded fundamentalist preachers. On September 11 at Meredith College, a well-respected women's school with Baptist roots in Raleigh, North Carolina, he declared that television evangelist Jerry Falwell could "go to hell." Falwell had led the rightwing Moral Majority that had opposed Carter in the 1980 election. Carter did not need Falwell or anyone else, he said, to "define for me what is a Christian." "In a very Christian's way, as far as I'm concerned, he can go to hell," he said with a big grin. The students cheered as Carter went on to say that there is "a growing danger that the fundamentalists . . . are closing their grasp on the institutions of the Southern Baptist Convention." Although Carter may have preferred to avoid questions about Reagan, the audience would not let him, and again he criticized his successor's approach to the presidency.[88]

Some of Reagan's aides found it more difficult to overlook Carter's criticisms than did their boss. Pat Buchanan, Reagan's chief speechwriter, dug deeply into Carter's past to find some gems Reagan might use when he dedicated "the Great Man's Library." Referring to Carter's youthful experience entering the Chalk River atomic reactor in Canada where he got "the maximum amount of radiation that was permissible at that time," Buchanan suggested that the effect of that radiation on Carter's brain possibly explained his current activities. Joining the fun, Reagan added a note that "Maybe my speech at his library should be an apology for correcting his mistakes."[89] Although Reagan and his speechwriters may have enjoyed their private humor, the final speech would be sophisticated, respectful, and presidential.

On October 1, 1986, Carter's sixty-second birthday, the Carter Presidential Library and Museum and the Carter Center of Emory University formally opened their doors. Nestled near the top of a hill overlooking Atlanta, the complex was an architectural expression of its namesake's personality. As one approached it, the buildings lay downhill and inconspicuous. Once inside, however, they were elegant, beautifully appointed, replete with busy work areas and sweeping panoramic views of Atlanta. The complex contained an efficiency apartment for the Carters, offices for each of them, a conference room, and a generous selection of their collected artworks. With its chandeliers and brass railings, it mimicked on a much smaller scale the residence and meeting rooms in the White House. A spacious, glassed-in lobby that afforded views of the landscaping in both directions, opened to a colonnade and entry into the museum.

Above the museum, with its separate entrance, the library rested as if detached from the center. They were two different institutions, with the center being the personal fiefdom of the Carters and the presidential library soon to become the property and responsibility of the National Archives. Initially, the library contained 26,000,000 pages of documents, but there was plenty of room for expansion. A small lake, well stocked with fish, lay between the center and the library, and downhill from it a tranquil Japanese Garden chosen by Rosalynn completed the complex. The grounds were well planted with flowers, trees, and shrubs, that when mature would almost obscure the buildings.

An excellent team was already at work. Dr. William Foege moved into the director's office with a small staff. Norman Borlaug, the Nobel Peace Prize winner who became renowned for his greening of America concept, was ready to help them with their agricultural pursuits; Robert Pastor, who had served them in the White House as adviser on Latin American affairs, had assumed the same role with the center. Ellen Mickiewicz provided vital information from her study of the Soviet Union, and Kenneth Stein became the expert on Middle Eastern affairs, especially the Palestinian issue.[90] Steve Hochman, who had assisted Carter with his presidential memoir, remained as special assistant to the president and liaison with Emory University. Other assistants, receptionists, secretaries, and janitors filled the well-staffed building.

On that warm October day, the buildings were spanking new and the landscaping immature, but the promise of growing into a magnificently environmentally beautiful facility was evident. For the dedication ceremony, carpenters had built a wooden platform on the edge of the lake, where the water level was low enough for the red Georgia clay to be clearly visible. When the Reagans arrived at 10:55 a.m., the Carters met them for coffee and a private tour of the museum and the center offices. The program began an hour later with the presentation of the colors, the singing of the national anthem, an invocation, and a few words of welcome by Atlanta Mayor Andrew Young. Five thousand spectators listened attentively under the hot Georgia sun as Carter's former Deputy Secretary of State Warren Christopher made a few remarks and then officially presented the library to the National Archives of the United States.[91]

In his fifteen-minute speech, President Reagan rose to the occasion with elegance, compassion, knowledge, and presidential class so different from the behind-the-scenes talk among his staff. "Our differences arise from goodwill," he said. "We are all Americans." He mentioned the purpose of the Carter Center and said it was the story of a family and the "story of the South." "Because men and women like Jimmy Carter stood up in church to protest the exclusion of Black people," the country has "a new South." The dedication was in fact "a celebration of the South—the new South that Jimmy Carter helped to build." Reagan praised the former president for his commitment to the values of the nation, the values of perseverance, and his faith. He credited him with the freeing of the hostages. Looking down at Carter, he said, "You gave of yourself to this country, gracing the White House with your passion and intellect and commitment."[92]

Carter, after the ceremony, turned to Reagan and said, "As I listened to you speak a few minutes ago, I understood more clearly than I ever have before in my life why you won in November 1980 and I lost." Rosalynn, neatly dressed in a simple red and white and blue outfit, but no match for Hollywood-showy Nancy, looked and listened expressionlessly. Later, after cutting the ribbon for the Japanese Garden, she remarked that the opening of the Carter Center represented a victory for Andrew Young too, because it embodied his battle for justice and equality through his work in the civil rights movement, as United States Ambassador to the UN, and as Mayor of Atlanta. A presidential limousine quickly transported the Reagans to the airport, and they were home in the White House by 2:50 p.m. One of his aides observed that Reagan, the veteran actor, had been performing a role at his best, for he was not sincere.[93]

Carter did not want the library to be a monument to himself. For a number of years after he created it, his indifferent attitude frustrated the archivists and researchers there who might have benefitted from his influence raising money and advertising the research center. The Carter Center dominated the complex, for within its walls resided the institution that Jimmy and Rosalynn intended to nurture. The library stood aside, almost like an afterthought, intimately associated with the presidency that they had put behind them.

In order to accomplish the future work that the Carters envisioned for the center, they had to raise a lot of money. They did it through their personal contributions, such as their annual auctions of furniture Carter had made and other presidential artifacts, and appeals to large private donors and to the public. Corporations such as DuPont, Merck, GlaxoSmithKline, Pfizer, and BASF, donated money and medicines, pesticides, cloth filters, and other products needed where volunteers worked to stamp out rare diseases. As the center succeeded and prospered, other foundations contributed, notably the Bill and Melinda Gates Foundation. From a modest beginning, Jimmy and Rosalynn created a center that would be their legacy long beyond their lifetimes.[94]

THIRTY SEVEN

Humanitarians Adrift

Only a few days after the library and Carter Center had been officially opened, a Nicaraguan soldier shot down a US plane that was carrying arms to the Contra guerrillas fighting against the Sandinista regime. Not only did that shot crash the plane, it also became the first shot in uncovering the complicated Iran-Contra scandal that would rock President Ronald Reagan's administration. The ensuing investigations led back to October 20, 1980, when Reagan's campaign representatives had met in a Paris hotel to negotiate a secret deal with Iranian officials to hold the US hostages in Iran until after the election. The intention was to prevent Carter from achieving an "October Surprise" and ensure the election victory for Reagan. For Reagan, the scandal became the worst crisis of his presidency; for Carter it became a possibly significant revelation about his lost election.[1]

Carter had received better news on September 1, 1986 when he learned that the Soviets had released dissident Soviet physicist Yuri Orlov from his Siberian exile. As president, Carter had pressed the Soviet Union to free Orlov whose only crime had been that he had monitored Soviet compliance with the Helsinki Accords of 1975. Now, without warning, the Soviets had suddenly told Orlov that he and his wife Irina were free to leave for the United States.

Coincidentally, the same day that he was released, Carter announced that Orlov would share the inaugural Carter-Menil Human Rights Prize with a Guatemalan human rights group. Shortly after their arrival on October 5, Orlov and his wife were whisked off to meet President Reagan. The next day Orlov telephoned Carter to say: "I'm very proud of you. You are the first President to place human rights at the top of the agenda as part of American policy." On December 10 in Houston, Carter proudly awarded the Carter-Menil Prize in person to Orlov and the Guatemalan rights advocates, praising them as true "heroes."[2]

Amy became a hero too when she joined demonstrations protesting apartheid in South Africa, illegal activities by the CIA in Central America, and the use of riot police to disperse the demonstrators. She was nineteen, a freshman at Brown University, when she joined other students at the University of Massachusetts at Amherst on November 24 to protest CIA recruiting practices. The university limited on-campus recruitment to law-abiding organizations, and the protesters argued that the CIA was not a law-abiding agency. One of her fellow protestors, Abbie Hoffman, had gained fame and notoriety from his protests outside the Democratic National Convention in Chicago in 1968. An avowed anarchist and an ultra-extreme advocate of equality and justice, Hoffman had been in and out of prison for the past twenty years. He and Amy, and more than fifty others, were arrested, released, and ordered to stand trial the following spring on misdemeanor charges of trespassing and disorderly conduct. Uncertain about how her parents might react, she told reporters that they were "kind of neutral" about her political activism. Whatever Jimmy and Rosalynn said to her in private remained private, but publicly they supported and defended her as she awaited trial.[3]

Meanwhile, Amy's cat Misty Malarky Ying Yang also spent time in the public eye. In his feline retirement, Misty posed for the 1987 Purina Cat Chow Celebrity Cat Calendar, which allowed him to contribute $5,000 to Habitat for Humanity.[4]

As the calendar turned to 1987, challenges abounded. President Reagan, shortly after hearing about the downed US plane carrying weapons to the Contras, appointed a special commission to investigate. Chaired by former Republican senator John Tower of Texas, and including Carter's former secretary of state Edmund Muskie and Ford's former national security adviser Brent Scowcroft, it appeared to be neutral and well qualified to undertake the investigation. When Attorney General Edwin Meese alleged that Marine Lieutenant Colonel Oliver North had diverted funds from US arms' sale to Iran to the US-backed rebels in Nicaragua, Reagan fired North, and North's boss, NSC Adviser John Poindexter, was forced to resign. When asked about these events in interviews, Carter remarked that as president he had kept such tight control over the CIA and the NSC that they could not have committed such illegal activities. At a public speech in Akron, Ohio, on February 28, Carter said that there was no way to undo the damage that had been done in what the press was calling "Irangate." "Reagan," he told his audience, "should have called in North and Poindexter immediately and found out exactly what happened. Had he done that the crisis could have been minimized."[5] Apart from that criticism of Reagan, however, Carter declined to make any public statement about the investigation.[6]

Two weeks later, Jimmy and Rosalynn departed for a sixteen-day trip to Algeria, Egypt, Syria, Jordan, and Israel. They expected to be in Israel on March 29 to celebrate the eighth anniversary of the signing of the Israeli-Egyptian peace treaty that grew out of the Camp David Accords. The main purpose of the trip would be to try once again to persuade Arab nations to hold a comprehensive Middle East peace conference hosted by King Hussein of Jordan.

Carter was also on a secret mission for President Reagan. At the small Georgia airport from which he left on March 15, reporters asked him if he was carrying a letter from Reagan to President Hafez al-Assad of Syria about US hostages in Lebanon. Terrorist groups, believed primarily to be Hezbollah, a militant Islamic group in Lebanon, but also groups in Iran and Syria, had taken more than one hundred foreigners as hostages, most of whom were Americans. When pressed further, Carter would say no more than that he would try to get information about the hostages. Five days later, however, Reagan's National Security Adviser Frank C. Carlucci requested a Special Air Missions Aircraft to fly to Georgia as soon as Carter returned home and bring him back to Washington to brief Secretary of State George P. Schultz about his trip.[7]

At their first stop in Algeria, Carter refused to say whether or not he would ask the Algerians for their help again on behalf of the foreign hostages held in Lebanon. Among those greeting the Carters was John Limbert, a former hostage of the Iranians, who was serving as a political officer in the US Embassy in Algiers. During their two days there, when not touring through the city's dusty streets and taking in its vistas overlooking the Mediterranean Sea, the Carters laid a wreath beneath the Martyrs Monument commemorating the Algerian War of Independence, attended a banquet in their honor, learned about improving relations between the United States and Algeria, and explored the possibility of how the United States might support Algeria's efforts to improve its poultry and dairy industries. Before going on to Cairo, Carter talked with President Chadli Bendjedid, whom he likely thanked again for his help with the Iran captives, but he publicly denied that they discussed the US hostages in Lebanon.[8]

In Cairo, during a meeting with President Hosni Mubarak, Carter criticized Reagan for his weak policy toward Egypt and Begin for not honoring his Camp David promises and for not trying to draw Jordan into peace discussions. When asked by a UPI reporter, he revealed that at his next stop in Syria he would discuss prospects for peace and "the fate of foreign hostages" in Lebanon.[9]

Carter's discussion with Assad in Damascus had no impact on the release of any hostages; except for several who were executed by their captors and a few who managed to escape, they remained in captivity until 1991. Carter, however, came away from his conversations with Assad and Mubarak believing that they were willing to permit King Hussein of Jordan to arrange an international Middle East peace conference.

At Hebron on the West Bank, Carter told friendly Palestinian audiences and leaders that the PLO should have a role in any peace discussions and that he thought the Arab world was ready for peace. Reagan was badly mistaken, he said, by not having the United States take a leadership role in mediating peace for the region.[10]

Pursuing his own brand of private shuttle diplomacy, Carter placed flowers on the grave of the first Israeli prime minister David Ben-Gurion in the Negev Desert. He told reporters that the PLO should have a role in peace talks and that Israel needed peace and economic independence more than it needed weapons. He accepted an honorary academic degree from Haifa University where he was celebrated for making decisions favorable to Israel. Living in seclusion on the outskirts of Jerusalem, Begin, who had been badly broken by his wife's death in 1982 and had resigned as prime minister the following year, refused to receive Jimmy and Rosalyn at his apartment. He spoke to Jimmy on the telephone only long enough to ask about Rosalynn, then said goodbye. Carter forgave him, because when Begin died five years later, he recalled that his "Brilliance, convictions," and courage to take political and personal risks made the Camp David Accords possible.[11]

Shortly after returning to the United States on April 3, Carter went to Washington and briefed Secretary of State George P. Shultz on his trip, but the Reagan administration never admitted to having asked for his help.[12] Neither Carter's secret mission regarding the hostages nor his public one to jumpstart a Middle East peace conference had any tangible results.

The trial of Amy, Abbie Hoffman, and thirteen of their fellow protesters on April 15 at Northampton, Massachusetts, attracted more media attention than the Carters' trip to the Middle East. Acting as his own defense attorney, Hoffman called many famous witnesses and argued his case on the grounds of traditional American civil disobedience. The judge allowed testimony from Daniel Ellsberg, who had stolen and published the so-called Pentagon Papers that revealed the government's illegal activities in Vietnam; President Johnson's former attorney general Ramsey Clark; and former Contra leader Edgar Chamorro, who described decades of the CIA's covert activities in

Nicaragua. The star witness, Amy Carter, declared that "Every time a person sacrifices themselves for a larger injustice, it aids in the cycle of change." When she said that the sight of police officers in riot gear caused her to decide to get arrested, the audience gave her a standing ovation. She, Hoffman, and the others were acquitted on all charges.[13] Later, as the defendants celebrated by dousing one another with champagne, Amy declared, "I don't know what is in the future, but I am sure I am going to be involved in this sort of thing for the rest of my life."[14]

Upon hearing of his daughter's acquittal, Carter announced that he was a proud father.[15] Back at Brown University, however, cynics noted that Amy was "as adept in filling a police rap sheet as in majoring in women's studies." The following summer the university dismissed her because of her low grades. The next year she enrolled in the Memphis College of Art, a small private school where students could study art and design. She became an artist like her father, but much better.[16]

Meanwhile, in Plains, Jimmy and Rosalynn fell into one of the worse disagreements of their marriage. Attempting to write a book together, they discovered that they could not do it. Rosalynn angrily told Jimmy that maybe they should just get a divorce, but she calmed down and they never seriously considered such a drastic solution. Entitled *Everything to Gain, or How to Live the Rest of Your Life*, the book was filled with advice about living healthy lives, memories of their White House years, and confessions of how painful the loss of the election had been. Rosalynn suffered more than Jimmy from the 1980 defeat. Their memories were often not the same, and he accused her of thinking that anything she wrote "was sacred . . . like she just came down off Mount Sinai with it." They resolved the conflict by putting an "R" at the top of chapters that were primarily hers and a "J" at those that were his. They also agreed not to write a book together again, since it was not worth the money they received or the strain it had put on their marriage.[17]

Putting the dispute behind them, Jimmy and Rosalynn set off again in June on a long international trip to advance Carter Center projects for peace to the Middle East. After a ninety-minute meeting with Prime Minister Margaret Thatcher at 10 Downing Street in London on June 12, Carter failed to convince her to take a leading role in a Middle East peace conference. Traveling in a private jet provided by Agha Hasan Abedi, the wealthy Pakistani banker who had founded the Bank of Credit and Commerce International and was willing to dispense $250,000 to Carter for humanitarian projects in Thailand, they met with Thai prime minister Prem Tinsulanonda. He had hoped Carter could use his influence with Russia and China to get Vietnam to withdraw from Cambodia, but Carter could not. From Thailand, the Carters flew to Beijing, where on June 29 Deng Xiaoping welcomed them. They promised the Chinese officials that the Carter Center would aid the training for handicapped people and would support manufacturing artificial limbs, a promise they kept.

The centerpiece of their journey was a meeting with Soviet general secretary Mikhail Gorbachev in the Kremlin on July 1. Noting that Gorbachev had grown up on a farm in south Russia much as he had in South Georgia, Carter told the former Soviet leader, "Two farmers can't be antagonistic toward each other."[18] Agreeing, Gorbachev planned to have several more meetings with the Carters. Rosalynn took notes as the two men discussed Middle East peace and cultural exchanges. Whether or not Gorbachev anticipated a major collapse of the Soviet Union from within, which occurred four years later, he seemed unusually interested in joining the West to bring peace to the Middle East. In his exuberant way, Carter described Gorbachev as "the most striking, interesting and innovative leader on earth." He managed to get the Soviet leader to promise, as Thatcher and Deng had done, to send an official representative to the Middle East peace consultation that was to be held the following November at the Carter Center.[19]

Leaving Moscow on July 3, the Carters returned to the United Kingdom and celebrated American Independence Day at Newcastle-upon-Tyne, a sister city of Atlanta in the north east of England. Riding in the Lord Mayor's carriage through the center of the city, Jimmy and Rosalynn waved and smiled at the thousands who lined the streets to cheer for them.[20]

Relaxing at home, Jimmy and Rosalynn spent most of the rest of the year fishing, hiking, reading, writing, and relaxing. They spent a week during the summer helping to build Habitat houses in Charlotte, North Carolina, but their primary work was operating the Carter Center, which conducted conferences on a variety of topics including international trade, global health, and the future of the Persian Gulf. On November 16–17, Carter convened "A Middle East Consultation: Ten Years after Sadat's Visit to Jerusalem: A Look to the Future." Co-chaired by Carter, William Hyland, editor of *Foreign Affairs*, and Sir Brian Urquhart, a former under-secretary general of the UN, it was the international peace conference Carter had been seeking. As promised, Thatcher, Deng, and Gorbachev all sent delegates. The five permanent members of the UN were represented, and it was attended by a large group of statesman, scholars, and diplomats. Despite such a distinguished assemblage, the group did little more than recognize that the United States would have to play an important role in resolving differences in the region. Although the conference might have become the first step for a long series of conferences to consider how to promote peace in the Middle East, it did not, and peace among the Arab nations and Israel remained as elusive as ever.[21]

In October 1987, Rosalynn scored another triumph for human rights when the Georgia University System Board of Regents approved the establishment of the Rosalynn Carter Institute for Human Development at Georgia Southwestern University. The institute would focus on mental health and caregiving. Many years later, as Rosalynn realized that the greatest need was the type of caregiving delivered by unpaid family members, she changed the name to the Rosalynn Carter Institute for Caregivers. Her work with her institute did not lessen her role as co-chair of the Carter Center, and the month after the institute was created, she sponsored the Third Annual Rosalynn Carter Symposium on Mental Health Policy, which focused on "Mental Illness in Children and Adolescents."[22]

Adding another health initiative, the Carters sent a center representative to Ghana to help in the battle against guinea worm, one of the more deadly diseases in Africa.[23] It was a modest beginning of what would evolve into one of the major goals of the center. In December, Carter accepted the prestigious Albert Schweitzer Prize for Humanitarianism.[24]

No matter how many awards they accumulated or where they went, for the Carters, all roads led to Plains. When Congress passed a law on December 23, 1987, to establish the Jimmy Carter National Historic Site in Plains, it recognized the historical importance of the tiny town. The site included their home and future gravesites on Woodland Drive, his boyhood home and farm in Archery, the Plains High School, and the Plains Depot, but it fell short of including Rosalynn's childhood home, which was of equal significance in preserving their history.

More important to Rosalynn was her work with the center. She hosted a symposium on Women and the Constitution at the Carter Center in February 1988. Such notables as Sandra Day O'Connor, the first woman appointed to the Supreme Court; former Texas Congresswoman Barbara Jordan; Geraldine Ferraro, former vice-presidential candidate; and Coretta Scott King delivered speeches. On another occasion, when she and Jimmy were discussing their post-presidential lives at a public meeting in the Cyprus Room of the Carter Center, she interrupted him, urging him to discuss other things than his personal hobbies. He protested that it would "look like I was puffing myself up." "But, Jimmy," she cajoled, "you have to; otherwise, people would think you spend all your time making furniture."[25]

Carter made furniture, but he also helped special friends who needed special care. When Pakistani billionaire banker Agha Hasan Abedi suffered two heart attacks one after another in February 1988, Carter helped him get a heart transplant in London by arranging for a US surgeon to care for him there. Abedi had co-sponsored Global 2000 with a gift of $17 million to its agricultural projects and donated $500,000 to the Carter Center. Although Abedi's international bank, which employed more than 14,000 people, later proved to be what the New York Times called "an elaborate Ponzi scheme," the Carters did not know that. Rosalynn thought he was a "very special friend" who made possible their Global 2000 programs in Africa, Asia, Bangladesh, Pakistan, and China, which taught farmers how to increase their production and established health programs.[26]

In the United States, Rosalynn appeared before the House Select Committee on Aging, where she asked for an increase in federal spending to combat mental illness among children, the elderly, and the homeless.[27] On April 21–23, Carter sponsored a three-day conference on "Theology, Politics, and Peace" at the Carter Center. In his opening remarks, he sharply criticized Pope John Paul II for failing to denounce human rights violations in Chile, El Salvador, and Nicaragua. He admitted that religion was often a source of conflict, but he said that those committed to monotheistic religion should always fight for social justice and peace. Some of his fellow Baptists, Carter continued, grinning, had attacked his work as "communistic."[28]

In June, Rosalynn connected with her Soviet counterpart in the loosely organized East-West human rights association to plan ways to implement the Universal Declaration of Human Rights. As honorary president of the group, she joined Fyodor Burlatsky, who chaired the Soviet Union Commission on Humanitarian Problems and Human Rights, to plan for sessions first in Moscow and the following year in Atlanta.[29]

No longer writing with Rosalynn, in July Carter published a summer read, An Outdoor Journal, an autobiographical account of many of his adventures as a fisherman, hiker, and mountain climber. Over the years, he and Rosalynn had been skiing in Vail, Colorado, trekked the foothills of the Himalayas to about 20,000 feet, and climbed Mount Kilimanjaro on the Kenya-Tanzania border. He presented himself in the book as an all-American guy who reveled in his outdoor experiences. The reviewer for the New York Times wondered why the man in this book was turned out of office and vilified, for he had all the characteristics that most people admired.[30]

When the Democratic National Convention met at the Omni Hotel in Atlanta, July 18–21, 1988, Carter played a much larger role than he had at the San Francisco convention four years earlier. Less than enthusiastic about the party's choice of Michael Dukakis, who had run a poor primary campaign, Carter nevertheless remained loyal to the party. Addressing the convention on the first night, Carter jokingly announced that he himself would not run again for the presidency, grinning broadly as the crowd laughed and clapped. He praised Dukakis, but he implied that his former secretary of state Edmund Muskie would have made a great president. It was time to look to the future, Carter emphasized, and time to bring back the Democrats. He condemned Reagan's wasteful military spending. Becoming profoundly optimistic, Carter concluded: "We Democrats do not fear change. We welcome it. Change means hope. Change means life. Above all, change means opportunity."[31] Carter referred to the Republican presidential candidate, Vice President George H. W. Bush, as sissy-like and "effeminate," but he knew that Bush's clinging to Reagan's coattails assured him the victory.

Carter spent little time on the campaign, partly because he knew that Bush would win and partly to focus on his brother who had been diagnosed with pancreatic cancer. Jimmy was devastated to learn that Billy suffered with the same disease that had already taken the lives of his father and oldest sister.[32] Jimmy had arranged for Billy to be treated at Walter Reed Army Medical Center in Washington, but there was no cure, and Billy died in his sleep on September 26, 1988. Shortly before his death, Billy told his minister, Dan Arial, that "I want to be remembered as a man who loved his wife, family, and as a good man."[33]

Someone placed a large sign on Main Street in Plains that temporarily covered up the one that designated the town as the home of the Thirty-Ninth President. The new one read: "Plains, Ga., home of Billy Carter—we love you." It was a very hot, sultry afternoon that September day when the Carters buried Billy in the plot with his parents at Lebanon Cemetery. A crowd of about 500 attended. Dan Arial, the pastor at Maranatha Baptist Church, presided, but country music star Tom T. Hall gave the eulogy. Reverend Will Campbell, well known for his liberal and humanitarian stand on social issues as well as country-style demeanor, read a special meditation on love that the family had requested. Before delivering a moving eulogy, Tom T. Hall said that Billy was not wearing a tie and that the family requested that the gentlemen remove their ties. They did so, quietly holding them in their hands in the sweltering heat. "Of all God's creatures," Hall said, "there was only one Billy Carter. His wit and charm made his name a household word around the world." Jimmy and Rosalynn looked sadly on, crippled with grief and perhaps feeling how their love for their brother transcended the wild ride he had sometimes taken them on.[34]

President Reagan sent a sympathy message to Billy's widow Sybil. "Nancy and I were saddened to learn of the death of your husband," the telegram read. "Billy Carter will be remembered . . . for his great good nature," and "you and your family know that the American people are keeping you in our prayers."[35] Two years later, Jimmy celebrated his brother's life: "I am proud of how Billy dealt first with his alcoholism and then his cancer. Sometimes when we're faced with great illness, our true character comes out. . . . [Billy] was triumphant over tragedy."[36]

When Bush won the 1988 presidential election, Carter said that he hoped he would heal the wounds from the campaign and be a better president than Reagan had been.[37] Paying more attention to the hostages still held in Lebanon, Carter had written the Ayatollah Khomeini on October 30, 1988, asking for his help to get them released. As a postscript, he added: "as a matter of personal interest, I request that you help in the release from prison a U.S. citizen by the name of David Rabhan, who has been imprisoned in Iran for more than eight years."[38] The Ayatollah did not answer, but Carter tenaciously continued to correspond with the imprisoned Rabhan in Iran and with his family in the United States.

During November and December, Jimmy and Rosalynn held conferences for representatives from Habitat for Humanity and members of a Soviet peace group. The latter came to discuss the Soviet Peace Fund, a private organization that wanted to launch a joint venture with the United States to promote reconciliation between the superpowers and world peace. Although not always personally present, the Carters or experts who represented them discussed a wide range of topics, from US international economic competitiveness to the importance of junior colleges in improving education in the United States. They searched for answers to problems from human rights in Caribbean countries to governance in African countries.[39]

At the end of their work days in Atlanta, Jimmy and Rosalynn went home to Plains where they rested and worked from their home offices. They traveled extensively, sometimes embarking on dangerous and exotic adventures. In August 1988, for example, Jack, Judy, Chip, and several of their older grandchildren accompanied them to Tanzania where they planned a nine-day trip to climb Mount Kilimanjaro. Well equipped with guides and guards, as they progressed, more and more members of their group turned back. Finally, on August 8, 1988, they carved the date in the cave that the lead group, including Jimmy and Rosalynn, had reached at 17,000 feet. At that point they decided to turn back, but Jimmy always believed that he and Rosalynn could have reached the summit if they had left the others and continued the climb. Wherever they went, whether walking through their own fields and woods or in some exotic foreign location, they were also avid birdwatchers.[40]

Rosalynn went alone in January 1989 to Moscow, where she was the co-leader with Fyodor Burlatsky of a two-day executive council meeting of the East-West Human Rights Conference. Burlatsky saluted Carter for her country's raising the human rights issue in foreign policy negotiations between the two superpowers even though it had frequently been a source of confrontation between them. The council included representatives from thirteen European and North American countries. Its purpose was to promote religious freedom and human rights around the world. Its members were pleased to learn that more than half of the 400 or more prisoners who had been jailed in the Soviet Union for religious reasons had been released as a result of their inquiries. Yet, Rosalynn did not think they could achieve all of their goals until human rights were guaranteed in Soviet law. Responding to an encouraging speech Soviet leader Mikhail Gorbachev had recently delivered at the UN, she joined the other council members in approving the convening of a human rights conference in Moscow in 1991.[41]

When she returned to the United States on January 20, Rosalynn immediately traveled to Lander University in Greenwood, South Carolina, where she held a news conference before addressing about 200 people at an afternoon workshop on "Women in Leadership." When asked at the press conference what advice she would give the new First Lady, she replied that Barbara Bush should do whatever she wanted but it should be something important. In her evening lecture, attended by about 700 people, she told those present that opportunities for women "are wonderful," but they would need to balance careers with "traditional women's responsibilities." During her long career, Rosalynn had achieved both, but she was scarcely a typical American woman, nor was she married to an ordinary American man.[42]

Jimmy hoped that with a new president in office, the Iranians would release David Rabhan from prison. Rabhan had been the pilot during Carter's

1970 gubernatorial race who suggested that he make the famous remark that the day for racial discrimination in Georgia was over. Rabhan had gone to Iran in 1979 to work under a contract issued by the shah, but had later been arrested and accused of being a spy; before going to Iran he had been indicted in Missouri on six counts of securities violations. He had been involved in building homes for the aged and pre-school learning centers. Unable to make his payments, he had shifted funds from one account to another and thus gotten himself into trouble. Some said he went to Iran to escape prosecution in the United States. Carter did not know the details, or whether Rabhan was guilty, but he hoped that when he got out of an Iranian prison and came home, he would not have to face a US prison.[43]

In the spring of 1989, Carter noted the tenth anniversary of the Camp David Accords with numerous public comments on the current unpleasant situation in the Middle East, but he paid more attention to trouble that erupted in Panama, on May 9, 1989.[44] Although military dictator Manuel Noriega had allowed an international team headed by Carter and Ford to monitor the election through which Guillermo Endara became head of the government, he refused to relinquish power. Using troops to seize control of the government, Noriega continued his dictatorial rule. Noriega, who claimed he had once admired Carter, now saw him as a trickster who could not be trusted.

After returning from Panama, where he had observed and condemned the usurped election, Carter went to the White House to confer with President Bush. Carter thought that sending US troops to Panama might backfire and advised Bush against it. Rejecting Carter's advice, as well as the opposition of both the OAS and the UN General Assembly, on December 21, Bush sent 27,000 troops to invade Panama and arrest the dictator. In the ensuing battle to find and capture Noriega, twenty-five Americans died, while more than 1,000 Panamanians, including many civilians, were killed. Bush brought Noriega to the United States to stand trial for drug trafficking and racketeering. Convicted by a Miami court in 1992, he was sentenced to forty years in prison.[45]

During the same months Carter had worked to guarantee a free election and prevent bloodshed in Panama, he and Rosalynn had been also trying to help the poor and sick in the United States and Africa. They built Habitat houses in Milwaukee for one week in June, and perhaps they got a chuckle from a cartoon published in an Atlanta newspaper that depicted Reagan, wearing trunks and a tank top, sitting beside a swimming pool, singing

"Jimmy Builds Homes, And I don't care."[46] Most of their attention, however, was focused on Africa.

On an African trip from July 25 through August 2, the Carters met with leaders of famine-stricken and civil war–torn Sudan and Ethiopia. After winning the trust of warring factions in Sudan, Carter got them to agree to several cease fires that allowed food deliveries to the starving population. In Addis Ababa, the Carters visited Ethiopian president Mengistu Haile Mariam and his wife for a private dinner at their home. According to Jimmy, he and Rosalynn agreed later that Mengistu's wife "was one of the most beautiful women we had ever met, with the aura of one of King Solomon's princesses."[47] Whether she participated in the discussion went unrecorded, but Mengistu agreed to negotiate an end to the long civil war. Likewise, representatives from the rebelling Eritrean People's Liberation Front (ELF) accepted Carter's suggestion that they set up negotiating committees. ELF had been fighting a secessionist war in Ethiopian's northern province of Eritrea for twenty-eight years, which had killed more than a million people. Both sides agreed to send representatives to Atlanta in September 1989.[48]

The full-scale peace talks between of the Eritrean People's Liberation Front (EPLF), the armed Marxist-Leninist organization which wanted independence for Eritria from Ethiopia, and the government of the People's Republic of Ethiopia (PDRE) was one of the most important events ever held at the Carter Center. Jimmy and Rosalynn had been working for more than a year to bring it about. Al-Amin Mohamed Saiyed represented the EPLF negotiating team, and Ashagre Yigletu headed the Ethiopian government's team. The US mediators were Jimmy Carter, Rosalynn Carter, Conflict Resolution Fellow Dayle E. Powell, and African Studies Fellow Richard Joseph, but it was Jimmy and Rosalynn who were trusted by the disputing powers. The conference concluded with an agreement that would eventually set Eritrea free as an independent nation. After more time and conferences, Eritrea won its de facto independence on May 24, 1991, and de jure nationhood on May 24, 1993, but Carter was justifiably "pleased with the significant progress we have made," he said in concluding remarks on September 19, as they continued "to strive for a peaceful solution to this conflict that has caused so much pain and suffering."[49]

During their Africa trip, the Carters had also inspected the progress of Global 2000 projects in Ghana, Nigeria, and Zambia and had launched a separate agriculture program in Zimbabwe. In Ghana and Nigeria, they toured villages that had recently achieved a significant drop in cases of Guinea worm disease, with help from the Carter Center's eradication program. There was no cure for the horrible disease caused when guinea worms entered the body through polluted water and then emerged from the skin. The local people had been surprised to learn that it came from the water they drank. Since it could be easily prevented by protecting the people against contaminated drinking water, Carter persuaded the DuPont chemical company to provide thousands of simple strainers to be delivered to those countries where the disease was rampant. When Jimmy and Rosalynn arrived to inspect the progress that had been made, the village chiefs thanked them profusely.[50]

Carter's interest in Nicaragua had grown since his first visit there to build houses in 1985, and he had become more determined to help the war- and poverty-ravaged country. Since 1982 the Contras, who had been well-armed by the Reagan administration, had been fighting a brutal war against the government, in which 35,000 people had died. After George H. W. Bush was inaugurated president on January 20, 1989, he and his secretary of state quickly reversed Reagan's policy of aiding the Contras and agreed that the Carter Center could be involved in the peace effort in Nicaragua. The OAS helped to negotiate a ceasefire, and the UN declared the chaos in Nicaragua to be an international security threat, justifying its willingness to monitor elections in a sovereign nation.[51]

Carter already knew Nicaraguan president Daniel Ortega. Backed by the influence of the UN and the OAS, Jimmy met with Ortega in Managua in September of 1989 and coaxed him to allow a free election to take place in February 1990. He argued that, if Ortega did so, it would boost the ties between the United States and Nicaragua, ties that had been broken since Reagan had taken office and thus cost Nicaragua economic and humanitarian support. Carter rejoiced that 30,000 Miskito Indian rebels had been allowed to return home from exile in Honduras, and he succeeded in persuading Ortega to allow the free election to be held.[52]

Returning home, Carter visited President Bush in the Oval Office, said that he would return to monitor the elections in Nicaragua, and asked for his help. Bush committed $9 million to help finance the anti-Sandinista candidate Violeta Chamorro whose victory would represent a triumph of democracy over Marxism. Jimmy kept Rosalynn informed, as he had done in the White House, even though she was busy in her own meeting with the Board of Directors of the Rosalynn Carter Institute.[53] The Carters enjoyed a good relationship with President Bush, so unlike the snubs they had received from the previous administration. Rosalynn told an Atlanta audience in October that Bush "has leaned over backwards to help us."[54]

Feeling more comfortable in Washington, Jimmy and Rosalynn attended a reunion with their White House staff and friends on November 5. Carter worked the crowd of 2,000 guests, shaking hands and joking. He "kissed the willing" and even admitted that newspaper editors were beginning to endorse him "thirteen years too late." Laughing about the news reports that Reagan had earned $1 million for a single speech, Carter asked the group to let him know if they heard of a similar offer. "I believe that idealism and practicality go together," he said flashing a mischievous grin at Rosalynn. Hodding Carter III, the former State Department spokesperson who had become disillusioned with Carter when Vance had resigned, said Carter was "like a blind dog in the butcher shop, whirling around, taking a bite in every direction."[55]

Carter and many members of his administration could also appreciate the work of the Miller Center. Some thirty scholars had gathered at the University of Virginia's Miller Center of Public Affairs to assess the Carter presidency. They refuted the image of him as a detail man who did not understand how Washington worked. Had Carter not understood international and national politics, they argued, he could not have negotiated the Camp David Accords or the Panama Canal treaties. They accumulated a huge volume of primary information about the history and legacy of the Carter administration.[56]

Continuing the work she had undertaken in the White House, Rosalynn hosted a symposium on mental health and how untreated mental problems often accounted for physical ills in the elderly. On November 14, Jimmy hosted a forum on the upcoming elections in Nicaragua where members of the ruling Sandinista National Liberation Front came face to face with representatives of the opposing group hoping to defeat them in the election. Later that month, the Carter Center announced that the second Carter-Menil Human Rights Award would be shared by Palestinian and Israeli groups, both of which sought justice in the Middle East.[57]

Throughout December 1989 and into the new year, Carter closely observed developments in Nicaragua that might influence the scheduled February 1990 elections. He wrote to Ortega complaining that the Sandinistas were using newspaper stories to smear the opposition and urged him to put an end to it. He wrote to Gorbachev to ask that the Soviet Union and those it influenced not send "covert or illegal assistance to Nicaragua in order to subvert the legitimacy of the scheduled elections."[58] Although neither leader apparently replied, Carter thought he was creating an environment where free elections might take place.

During Carter's preparations for the Nicaraguan election, in December 1989, his sister Gloria Spann, who lived with her husband Walter in Plains, was diagnosed with pancreatic cancer. She had actively supported his and Rosalynn's campaigns and public careers, and as a child had taken a lot of teasing from her older brother "Hotshot." The prospect of knowing Gloria would die was unsettling enough, but the fact that every member of his immediate family had died of the same disease for which there was no cure must have made Jimmy and Rosalynn apprehensive about his own health.[59]

Perhaps more driven in his work for peace, Carter delivered a scorching annual State of Human Rights address on December 10 at the Carter Center. Speaking after the presentation of the Carter-Menil Award to the Palestinian and Israeli groups, he accused the superpowers of violating human rights by not stepping up to end civil wars and by continuing to sell weapons to warring countries. Many poverty-stricken countries spent money on armaments that had been urged upon them by the United States or the Soviet Union, he said. If that waste were cut by only half, he asserted, there would be $500 billion available for food, health, education, and other necessities. He specifically condemned the United States' "reputation as a prime champion of armed violence, both on our own streets and through the use of military force in other nations." War, Carter declared, is "the greatest human rights crime."[60]

Carter had been working for several months to guarantee that there would be a free election in Nicaragua on February 25, 1990. He persuaded the Nicaraguans who opposed Ortega's government to release the fund that President Bush had sent them to be used to establish safe polling places with objective workers and observers. With himself and Rosalynn at the helm, he assembled a Carter Center team that would monitor the election. To give his team the power and authority of the US government, which he did with the full approval of President George H. W. Bush and Secretary of State James A. Baker III, he recruited eight Representatives and Senators to join his delegation. They joined groups from the UN, the OAS, and a number of former Latin American presidents and prime ministers to comprise the the Council of Freely Elected Heads of Government, headed jointly by Carter and a former Argentine president.[61]

Carter may have owed his chance to take such an important role in the election to James Baker. A staunch Republican, Baker had participated in the opposition to Carter's election both in 1976 and 1980, but he knew that Carter had such a strong interest in Central America that he might be of use to the Bush administration. Shortly after Bush took office, Baker flew to Atlanta to take part in a public appearance at the Carter Center and to talk privately with Carter. Since Carter understood how close Baker was to Bush, he knew that the president was recognizing his work and willing to help.[62]

Since the Iran-Contra trials were happening in the United States at the same time, there was more than usual interest in that Central American country where the Contras had possibly benefitted from former President Reagan's largesse. On Election Day, Jimmy, Rosalynn, and Bob Pastor, all of whom feared that the election might be rigged, met with the campaign chairmen of both candidates and were reassured that they both wanted a fair election. In a surprising upset, Violeta Chamorro, the national opposition candidate, won the election. Using his own experience of loss in 1980, Carter persuaded the shocked and speechless Ortega to accept the outcome. Buying time, Carter asked the victorious Chamorro to delay her victory speech until Ortega had time to concede, perhaps saving the country from civil war. In Washington, many Republicans were chagrinned that Carter seemed in more control of US foreign policy than the State Department.[63]

Secretary of State Baker, however, interpreted Carter's victory as his own. When Carter called him at 4:15 a.m. Washington time to tell him the good news and jokingly advise him not to gloat over it, Baker dutifully asked for the details that he could report poker-faced while disguising his own pleasure with the outcome. When Baker called President Bush fifteen minutes later, Baker's deputy noted that "They were like sky high." Jimmy and Baker formed a unique partnership in which they proved that former political opponents could overcome past differences and work together to achieve a mutual goal.[64]

After the Nicaraguan election, Jimmy and Rosalynn went home to Plains to rest and to visit Gloria. They were with her, her husband, and several close friends when she died on March 3, 1990. She was sixty-three. Famous for being one of the first female members of Harley-Davidson's 100,000 Mile Club and the Most Outstanding Female Motorcyclist in 1978, the funeral procession to her Methodist graveside service in Lebanon Cemetery was led by sixty bikers, and eight more served as pall bearers. In all, more than 300 people attended. Gloria's husband Walter pulled his long hair back into a pony tail and wore a black leather jacket. Jimmy, dressed in a business suit, stood out from the crowd. One biker tried to comfort the former president and First Lady by telling them, "I know she's in biker heaven." Carter issued a simple public statement, saying that "Our family is grieved and saddened."[65] In time, her grave marker informed those who passed by that "She rides in Harley Heaven."

President Bush sent his condolences on March 6, and in a separate communication the same day, he personally thanked Carter "for the pivotal role you and the other observers played in ensuring that the [Nicaraguan election] process was free and fair." Both President Bush and Secretary of State James Baker shared Carter's belief in the use of moral judgment in diplomacy. The peaceful transition of power in Nicaragua was just short of a miracle, and Bush told Jimmy: "[you] should be proud of your accomplishment."[66]

THIRTY EIGHT

Navigating Troubled Waters

The death of his last sibling signaled to Carter that his own time might be running out, and he still had not succeeded in bringing peace, including justice for the Palestinians, to the Middle East. Not only was that peace his own dream, it was also the dream for which Anwar Sadat had given his life. For a peace conference to be successful, Carter had concluded that PLO Chairman Yasser Arafat must be included. The Carters therefore set off in mid-March for Egypt, Syria, Jordan, and Israel as private citizens with the purpose of drawing Arafat into the peace process. In Egypt, Carter easily got a commitment from Hosni Mubarak that he would talk with Assad of Syria and soon stage an international peace conference. Carter's planned meeting with Arafat in Tunis was aborted, allegedly because of a conflict in Arafat's schedule.[1]

The warm welcome the Carters had received in Egypt was not replicated Israel. In Jerusalem, Carter announced that Assad was ready to talk peace, but some Israelis, who remembered that Assad had attacked the Golan Heights, did not trust the Syrian. Carter hoped to negotiate with Israel about the Golan Heights, which Israel had held since 1967, but he met with a hostile rebuttal. Not backing down, he condemned Israel's settlement policy, alleged that Israelis shot demonstrators without cause, demolished their houses, and jailed Arabs without trials. In fact, he thought the Palestinians were rebelling in response to the abuse the Israelis heaped upon them. Speaking bluntly to the press and privately to Prime Minister Yitzhak Shamir, he condemned Israel's deportation of Palestinians, which sometimes resulted in dividing families if they could not prove legal residency in areas Israel had occupied since 1967. He did get a promise from Shmuel Goren, who administered the occupied territories, that the deportation policy would be changed and that women and children who had already been deported would be allowed to return home and join their families. Happy to have achieved that commitment, Carter announced Goren's new policy on national television just before returning to the United States.[2]

Bush welcomed Carter to the Oval Office for a thirty-minute session to brief him and Secretary of State James Baker on his trip. Before Carter arrived, National Security Adviser Brent Scowcroft, who had read Carter's letter gave Bush a brief summary of it. Scowcroft told the president that "the former President has a good deal to say about the human rights of Christians in Israel and Palestinians in the Occupied Territories. What is largely absent . . . are policy prescriptions." Carter did recommend, Scowcroft continued, that the United States should try to stop Israeli settlements in East Jerusalem, press for release of hostages, nurture the peace process, and improve human rights. Bush thanked Carter and treated him with respect during their Oval Office meeting, but in his report, Scowcroft had told the president that Carter's trip was of no help to the administration.[3]

Ken Stein, director of the Carter Center's Middle East program, had not accompanied the Carters on the trip, but he warned Carter that his blunt confrontation with Israel might ruin his chances of negotiating between Israel and the Arabs. He suggested that Carter should apologize to Israel and to Jewish Americans, but Carter did not take Stein's advice.[4] Carter continued to defend Palestinian rights and to press for a meeting with Arafat. "I consider the Palestinians to be human, and I think their rights ought to be defended," he told an Atlanta newspaper.[5]

On April 4, 1990, Carter finally met Arafat in Paris at the Hotel de Crillon. The meeting was arranged by Mary King, who, along with her husband Peter Bourne, had advised the Carters since their gubernatorial years and had developed a friendship with Arafat. She traveled with Arafat and his entourage on his plane from Tunis to Paris. Carter showed up at the hotel with only Mary King and Rosalynn as his assistants, whereas Arafat had several more advisers. French president Francois Mitterrand joined them at the hotel. Arafat at first dominated the conversation; he told them that a peace process could not take place unless the United States, France, and the major powers assumed a fundamental role in it. Though he agreed to hold talks with Israel if Israeli leaders would talk with him. Carter urged Arafat to revise the PLO National Charter, which would require a two-thirds vote, to rid it of references to the illegality of Israel and the necessity of armed struggle. Arafat refused, arguing that the hostility toward the Palestinians remained too great and that the charter was no more than a historical document anyway. When Arafat spoke of having been betrayed by the Reagan administration, Rosalynn interjected that they knew too well about Reagan's betrayals.

In a private meeting after their discussions, Rosalynn described for Arafat how Israeli troops dumped garbage in front of a Palestinian orphanage on the West Bank when the Carters had been there. The story moved Rosalynn and the two men to tears and established a bond between the Palestinian leader and the Carters that Jimmy hoped might lead to Arafat's participation in a successful peace conference. Despite more accusations of anti-Semitism, Carter did not waiver in his commitment to human rights for Palestinians, as well as for Jewish dissidents in the Soviet Union and elsewhere.[6]

Six months later, via sealed letter, Carter asked Arafat for a personal favor, namely to help get his friend David Rabhan freed from the notorious Evin Prison in Iran. In 1979, because of his friendship with Carter, Rabhan had been falsely accused of working for the CIA and arrested. Arafat granted the favor, asked God for success, and pressed former Iranian Premier Mehdi Bazargan for help. On September 15, 1990, Rabhan walked away from the prison with two suitcases stuffed with pen and ink drawings he had made of prisoners and prison life. Carter went with Rabhan's sister to the Atlanta airport to greet him, later invited him to the Carter Center, and displayed his prison art there.[7]

Throughout the spring and summer of 1990, Jimmy and Rosalynn built houses for Habitat, monitored elections, traveled for fun and on missions for international peace, and watched the Carter Center grow into a larger and more effective institution than they had imagined possible. They continued to set aside one week per year to lead what was dubbed the Jimmy Carter Work Project for Habitat for Humanity. In June they were joined by 2,000 volunteers to help build more than one hundred houses in Tijuana, Mexico, and five more across the border in San Diego.[8] They monitored elections in Santo Domingo, Dominican Republic, the results of which they reported to President Bush. Tired of monitoring elections, and perhaps of being unappreciated for doing so, Carter told Bush that it would be his and Rosalynn's preference "to get out of the election monitoring business—except perhaps when Fidel Castro decides to permit them in Cuba."[9]

And yet the Carters were soon off to Haiti and points in the Horn of Africa to monitor elections and resolve disputes. On the July 4 in Philadelphia, Carter became the second person, after Polish president Lech Walesa, to receive the Liberty Medal, awarded by the National Constitution Center of the United States to recognize an individual's leadership in pursuit of freedom. President Bush congratulated Carter on the award and thanked him sincerely for his work through the Carter Center.[10] Three days later, when Jimmy and

Rosalynn celebrated their forty-fourth wedding anniversary, they could reflect on a life they would never have anticipated. Rosalynn said that she liked her current life better than life in the White House.

Since no challenge seemed insurmountable to him, Carter joined others in Oslo for the avowed purpose of stamping out hate. Led by Elie Wiesel, the Nobel peace laureate who had chaired Carter's Committee on the Holocaust Museum, the group included Nelson Mandela of South Africa, Czech president Vaclav Havel, French president Francois Mitterrand, and Carter.[11]

Hate abounded, however, and the real chance that the United States would get into another war posed a new challenge to peacemakers. When President George H. W. Bush faced the challenge of how to handle the invasion of oil-rich Kuwait by Iraq's Saddam Hussein, Carter seized the chance to condemn war, push for international mediation, and, ironically, give Bush the chance to use the updated military weaponry that Carter had developed during his last year in office. Events leading to the war had begun the previous August when 10,000 Iraqi troops had invaded Kuwait. Bush joined other world leaders in condemning the invasion and threatened to use force to chase the Iraqis out of Kuwait. In a speech he delivered in Iowa, Carter reminded Americans that the crisis in the Gulf should emphasize the country's need to revive energy programs that would make the United States independent of foreign petroleum. Furthermore, Carter said that "military action to force Iraqi President Saddam Hussein out of Kuwait 'would be a tragedy,' " but "if Saddam refuses to give in to international pressure it may be the only alternative."[12]

Two months later, as Bush continued a military build-up in the Gulf, Carter again protested. While on a duck hunting trip in Arkansas, Carter told a journalist that "President Bush is too impatient in his handling of the Persian Gulf crisis, which could have adverse consequences."[13] In December, Carter became optimistic that war would be averted. Following a ceremony at New York University when he and Dominique de Menil presented the Carter-Menil Human Rights Prize to humanitarian groups from Guatemala and Sri Lanka, Carter praised Saddam Hussein for promising to release foreign nationals he held hostage, and he noted that Secretary James Baker would now accept Iraq's withdrawal from Kuwait with no other demands. He supported the UN resolution demanding that Saddam leave Kuwait by January 15.[14]

What Carter did not reveal to the journalists, however, was that he had undertaken his own diplomatic effort to prevent a war between Iraq and the United States. On November 19, Carter had risked being accused of treason when, without Bush's prior knowledge, he had written to members of the UN Security Council, arguing that the human and economic costs would be too great if the United States went to war in Kuwait against Iraq. Carter sent a dozen more letters to other heads of state asking them to pressure the four members of the Security Council that were part of the coalition Bush had put together to defeat Saddam to drop out and refuse to support military action. When they learned what Carter had done, Bush and National Security Adviser Brent Scowcroft were outraged that a former president would ask the UN Security Council to vote against his own country. Scowcroft thought Carter was guilty of treason, but Bush decided to let the matter drop.[15]

Carter's desperate effort to stop the Gulf War before it started was linked to his hope for peace in the Middle East and his dream of justice for the Palestinians. In the looming war, the United States would be attacking an Arab nation for the first time in its history, and Carter had built such a good diplomatic, and sometimes financial, rapport with Egypt, Saudi Arabia, Algeria, and others that he did not want it destroyed by the launching of American missiles into a country where they all had an interest. Carter, who favored an international peace conference to resolve the Gulf conflict without war, believed that Palestinian grievances with Israel were connected with Iraq's invasion of Kuwait. If Saddam Hussein would ask for such a conference and insist that Israeli abuse of Palestinians be one of the items on the agenda, the United States should go along with him, Carter said. Bush flatly denied that there was a connection. Secretary of State Baker cynically remarked that Iraq did not invade Kuwait to liberate Palestine but for its own aggrandizement.[16]

Iraq did not withdraw from Kuwait by January 15, 1991, and two days later, President Bush, backed by a coalition of thirty-five mostly Arab nations, sent US troops into battle. The war lasted only one month, one week, and four days, thanks in part to the sophisticated weaponry that the United States had developed during the last year of the Carter presidency. The dead included seventy-nine Americans and more than 100,000 Iraqis. The Kuwaiti monarchy was restored, Saddam Hussein retained power, and the UN imposed economic sanctions against Iraq.

Shortly before the Gulf War ended, in friendly letters to "Jerry," "Dick," "Ron," and "Jimmy," Bush invited the living former presidents to the White House to attend his presentation of the Medal of Freedom to British prime minister Margaret Thatcher. After the ceremony, the former presidents and their spouses were to remain for a small informal dinner with Margaret, which Bush thought she would enjoy. Opposed to the war and disillusioned with the hawkish Thatcher, Carter formally responded that he and Rosalynn were unable to be in Washington on that date.[17]

In Atlanta the Carters nurtured the Carter Center until it grew into an organization with 120 employees and an annual budget of $16 million. Among its health initiatives, the center fought river blindness in Uganda, a parasitic disease caused by the bite of a tiny blackfly that bred rapidly in moving water and posed a threat to more than 120 million people living in Central and East Africa. When scientists discovered that the dreaded disease was easily treated by a single annual tablet of Mectizan, Carter persuaded the Merck pharmaceutical company to donate the needed tablets. Another organization funded by the World Bank delivered them to areas where the blackfly bred. Carter also persuaded the World Bank, together with the World Health Organization, to contribute $125 million to the river blindness program. Separately, John and Becky Moores, who had made a fortune from computer software he invented, contributed $25 million to Carter Center projects.[18]

A scandal broke when an Atlanta newspaper reviewed the donors of the $26 million for building the Carter Center and the library. Major contributors included a Japanese gambling czar and a Pakistani financier whose bank laundered drug money, though both had also helped the sick and handicapped in Africa, Asia, and China. Ryoichi Sasakawa, aged ninety-two, had been imprisoned by the US Army as a war criminal for three years after World War II, but in post-war Japan he had become a financially powerful shipping tycoon who gave much of his wealth to groups who wanted to improve Japanese-American relations. Agha Hasan Abedi, sixty-seven, the president of the Bank of Credit and Commerce International, had contributed many millions to Global 2000 and often transported Carter in his private jet. The investigative journalists, however, were unable to prove that Carter knew of the improper conduct of those men whom he and Rosalynn had praised for being so generous.[19]

Confident of his innocence, Carter did not miss a speech, a symposium, or a trip. He and Rosalynn went to China to dedicate the Beijing Artificial Limb Factory, which Global 2000 had sponsored to help China develop a modern prosthetic manufacturing facility. He asked Chinese officials to release dissidents whom they had jailed in June 1989 for participating in a student pro-democracy movement, but was ignored. From China he went to Tanzania to attend a three-day conference focused on improving African agriculture. The Carters planned, or already had in operation, agricultural projects in Ghana, Tanzania, Sudan, Zambia, Benin, and Togo. During the spring and summer of 1991, he and Rosalynn built Habitat houses, worked on projects to improve both physical and mental health, and sought to resolve conflicts in remote or impoverished parts of the world.[20]

Wherever they went, whether to resolve a dispute or provide medical and agricultural assistance, Jimmy and Rosalynn took advantage of the leisure and educational opportunities at their destinations. They learned about many cultures, jogged, fished, hiked mountains, watched birds, and enjoyed the hospitality of US ambassadors and UN installations. If in a city where museums and concerts were available, they often attended.[21]

The grandest appearance of the living presidents took place in November 1991 in Simi Valley, California, where they gathered for the dedication of the Ronald Reagan Library. The Nixons, Fords, Carters, Reagans, Bushes, and Lady Bird Johnson convened in a very large Spanish-style building atop a beautiful hilltop overlooking the Pacific Ocean. Actor Charlton Heston delivered the keynote address. Quoting Southern novelist William Faulkner's Nobel Prize acceptance speech, he said; "I have a dream, I refuse to accept the end of man. I believe he will endure, he will prevail, man is immortal not because alone among God's creatures, he has a voice, but because he has the soul, a spirit, capable of compassion and sacrifice and endurance." Each president said a few words, Nixon taking care to subtly deny any progress Carter may have made as president. Carter rose to the occasion noting the importance of the continuum of the office of the president where rivals became colleagues in history. He said they had gathered to "honor the great leader of a nation," then made references to Abraham Lincoln, the environment, and human rights in language that could be interpreted as critical of Reagan. Addressing the crowd, President George H. W. Bush turned to Jimmy and Rosalynn to tell them, "America applauds your lifelong commitment, sir, to peace, to human rights, to healing others."[22]

Back in Georgia, the Carters fell into a whirlwind of activities that, Jimmy thought, countered Reagan's legacy. Carter and Nelson Mandela joined Dominique de Menil in her hometown of Houston to present the Carter-Menil award, in memory of six Jesuit priests who had been murdered in El Salvador, to the Human Rights Institute of the University of Central America. Concerned about Georgia's poor, Carter launched the Atlanta Project to help city blocks of deprived citizens learn to help themselves. Different from Habitat for Humanity, which built houses for individuals, the Atlanta Project was designed to create cluster communities where the residents would have enough civic pride to help each other and raise the living standard of the entire community.[23]

The New Year, 1992, began on a high note. Carter and former Soviet Minister of Foreign Affairs Eduard A. Shevardnadze presided at a three-day conference at the Carter Center that discussed how to end conflicts in Afghanistan, Angola, Burma, Cambodia, Cyprus, Korea, Liberia, and Sudan. It was the first meeting of the International Negotiating Network (INN). Others who attended included Desmond Tutu, Elie Wiesel, Andrew Young, representatives from the UN, and Cy Vance. Carter was in his element, simultaneously resolving conflicts, raising money for the Atlanta Project, making speeches, and warning that the United States had not learned anything from the Gulf War.[24]

As the 1992 presidential election approached, however, the ugly history and remaining unanswered questions about the 1980 election again surfaced. The US House of Representatives voted to investigate the 1980 election to determine if the Reagan campaign had been involved in a conspiracy to have the Iranian militants hold the hostages until after the election. The most difficult issue for Carter about the Iran-Contra scandal that had tarnished Reagan's presidency was that President Bush was the vice presidential candidate in 1980 who was accused of having had a seminal role in the conspiracy. In sharp contrast with Reagan, Bush had been unusually friendly to Carter, and he also supported some of the Carter Center initiatives. The House investigation would inevitably continue into the 1992 presidential race and possibly impact Bush's chances for reelection.[25]

Riding an growing wave of popularity, Carter approached the 1992 election with more enthusiasm than he had shown for US elections since he left the White House. He conferred with former Senator Paul Tsongas of Massachusetts who visited him in Plains, but he did not endorse anyone for the Democratic nomination. Arkansas Governor Bill Clinton's campaign kept a healthy distance from Carter, whom they thought might do them more harm than good. When Clinton won the nomination, Carter endorsed him. Clinton, he said, was "an honest, decent, competent, idealistic, practical man" who did not deserve to have his character questioned. Although both Clinton and Carter were from the South, their roots and life experiences were quite different, and there were few reasons for camaraderie between them other than that they were both Southern-born Democrats.[26]

Allegedly eschewing politics, Carter continued to use his access to President Bush to promote his humanitarian projects. He asked for Bush's help to speed up the Atlanta Project. The idea was to use methods adopted from Habitat for Humanity to improve life in rundown parts of Atlanta. Carter got President Bush to cut through the red tape for government assistance, enlisted hundreds of volunteers, and identified about twenty "clusters" where the improvements were needed. Ultimately, the project did not achieve its unrealistic expectations.[27]

The ongoing conflict between the United States and the Soviet Union that had dominated Carter's presidency took a strange new turn after the collapse of the Soviet Union in 1989 and the emergence of Mikhail Gorbachev as a more enlightened leader. Rosalynn commented about what a better world it might have been if Gorbachev had been in power at the same time Jimmy was. Carter credited Gorbachev with the fall of the Berlin Wall in 1989 and the subsequent liberation of the Soviet republics. "The demand of millions of people for increased freedom and human rights ultimately prevailed," he recorded in his diary.[28] In retirement, the Carters and the Gorbachevs became acquaintances, but Raisa Gorbachev showed no interest in socializing with her country's former enemy. When Emory University invited Gorbachev to deliver its commencement address in May 1992 and to consider an offer to join its faculty, he came alone. In his address, the former Soviet leader took a politically neutral stance: he advised the graduating class to focus on the environment, a pet interest of Carter's and one that was unlikely to provoke hostile debate. While in Atlanta, Gorbachev visited Carter and toured the Carter Center, which he thought might become a model for an institution he could create in Russia. He did not accept an appointment to the Emory faculty, and there was little opportunity for the relationship between the two men to develop.[29]

Once again, family and religion became matters of concern to the Carters, in May 1992. When their forty-six-year-old eldest son, Jack, divorced his first wife Judy, Jimmy and Rosalynn both regretted the divorce and seemed sympathetic with Judy whose Langford family had been political and personal friends of theirs since their earliest days in politics. Jack later married Elizabeth Sawyer, a Cleveland banker, whom he had met in Chicago. Jack had earlier graduated from Georgia Tech with a degree in nuclear physics, then attended law school at the University of Georgia and married Judy Langford of Calhoun, Georgia. They moved to Chicago where Jack managed a grain elevator and had less involvement in the presidential campaigns than did the other Carter family members. After his marriage to Elizabeth, they moved to Bermuda and Las Vegas, where Jack expressed a personal interest in politics.

Rosalynn was surprised and delighted when he began to show interest in politics and search for a place from which he might campaign for the Senate.[30]

Remembering the beginning of his own political career, in 1992 Carter published a captivating account of how he had first broken into conservative Georgia politics. *Turning Point: A Candidate, A State, and a Nation Come of Age*, an autobiographical account of his contested 1962 race for a Georgia senate seat, was very good history. With the advantage of thirty years of experience in regional and national politics, Carter not only told a riveting personal tale, but also discussed frankly the hard, early lessons that he had learned about politics and racism in the South at a time when the Civil Rights movement was beginning to change the region and the nation in dramatic ways.

When the US Supreme Court had decided the case of *Baker v. Carr* in March 1962, the "one man, one vote" ruling, it opened the way to demolish the closed county unit system that had protected racial segregation in the South. Carter won the senate seat after a long contest, much of the way paved by a diligent investigative journalist, John Pennington, who exposed the dishonesty and corruption of his opponent. From that beginning, Carter had launched his career, to the governorship and ultimately the White House. Although primarily autobiographical, the book revealed Carter's ability to produce a solid work of history that transcended his personal story.[31]

Having been accepted back into the national Democratic Party, Carter addressed its convention on July 15 in New York City. Introduced by Andrew Young and placed between two prominent African-American speakers, Carter was supposed to attract Black voters. Carter, however, focused his remarks not on domestic racial relations but on international affairs, telling his fellow Democrats that the world "cries out for peaceful resolution of conflict." He warned that the increasing gap between the rich and the poor was detrimental to democracy and tranquility. Concluding, he praised Clinton as "a man of honesty and integrity."[32]

Shortly after leaving the convention in New York City, Bill and Hillary Clinton and vice presidential candidate Al Gore and his wife Tipper met Jimmy and Rosalynn at Manuel's Tavern near the Carter Center. For the cameras and the journalists, they donned work clothes and visited a few Habitat construction sites in Atlanta, hoping that the popularity of the Carters as Habitat workers might help the Clinton and Gore win Southern votes.[33] The Carters, however, rarely commented on the campaign.

Leaving the campaigning to more popular Democrats, Carter focused on the emerging Atlanta Project, chaired sessions on African crops and diseases, and then went to Africa with Rosalynn. In September, after meeting rebel leader Charles Taylor on a Firestone rubber plantation thirty miles east of Monrovia, Liberia, they convinced him to release 500 West African peace-keeping soldiers. The following month they led a team of sixty-seven to Georgetown, Guyana, to observe the elections there.[34]

At home they relaxed, enjoyed Bill Clinton's victory over George H. W. Bush, and looked forward to having another Democrat, another Southerner, in the White House. They attended Atlanta Braves games, where Jimmy usually threw out the first ball. They planned a celebrity ski vacation at Crested Butte, Colorado, to raise money for the Atlanta Project by charging $2,500 per participant and auctioning furniture that Carter had made. Ironically, that resort had been built by their old Georgia Republican adversary, Bo Callaway, who had since fallen into disfavor because of questionable financial deals involving the resort. Carter appeared on the popular television program *Larry King Live*, where he cracked jokes about Amy's arrests for good causes but said nothing new about his own activities. He had arrived as a public celebrity and senior statesman.[35]

Rosalynn, who loved the trips to Africa and elsewhere, was caught up in the missionary spirit of providing food, healthcare, shelter, and freedom to the millions of people in need. She occasionally campaigned for a favorite politician, such as Wyche Fowler of Georgia who won a seat in the House of Representatives. She teamed up with First Lady Betty Bumpers of Arkansas to promote the inoculation of children by age two. She directed her own institute, which she thought would become a model for "the entire country." The most dramatic and prophetic speech she delivered, however, was at the Eighth Annual Rosalynn Carter Symposium on Mental Health Policy at the Carter Center. It was November 19, 1992, and mass murders by deranged individuals, though not unknown in the country, were not yet commonplace. "Superman will die—killed by a super lunatic, an escapee from [an] insane asylum," she said. The nation had been fighting myths, misconceptions, and stereotypes about mental illnesses for decades, she continued. She wanted to change public attitudes, change public policy, ensure national healthcare reform, and create a healthier, safer country.[36]

If Clinton won, the Carters anticipated a brighter time under a Democratic administration. During the campaign, however, the disturbing topic of the October Surprise during the 1980 presidential election was resurrected.

Since Bush had allegedly played a major role in it, investigative journalists wanted to learn the truth. If it could be proved that Bush had participated in cutting that deal with the Iranians to hold the hostages until after the election, it might hurt his chances for reelection in 1992. Carter was in a quandary, torn between his friendship and appreciation for President Bush and outrage upon learning what had really happened twelve years earlier.

In 1991, when Carter first heard the evidence about what had happened in Paris on October 20, 1980, he said it was "nauseating." A decade on, though, he had forgiven his enemies and moved on with his life. Removing himself from the investigations because, he said, he did not want to embarrass President Bush, he later annotated his published diary with the comment that he would "let the reader decide how much credence" to give to Gary Sick's book exposing the October Surprise. Unlike Reagan, Bush had befriended Carter and supported Carter Center projects. Since there was no way to change the outcome of the 1980 election or the lives of the hostages, any damage that had been done could not be undone. When questioned by historians at a professional history conference in 1994, Carter repeated that he did not want to embarrass Presidents Reagan and Bush, but he added that "Congress didn't want to delve too deeply into it . . . and he would not be surprised if Bill Casey had information."[37]

The mounting evidence, scholarship, and journalistic investigations proved that the Republicans' October Surprise did take place. Carter, however, was more interested in peace in the Middle East and human rights around the world than revisiting his presidency or a controversy surrounding his 1980 defeat.[38]

THIRTY NINE

Servant of Peace

With the election over, and a Democrat again installed in the White House, Jimmy and Rosalynn wasted no time on past sins and missed opportunities. Despite his appearance at the Democratic National Convention, the Carters were still outsiders in their own party. At Clinton's inauguration, their seats were far to the back, and speakers paid tribute to almost all of the other prominent guests except the Carters. Stoic as usual, Carter took it in stride, but anger again welled up in Rosalynn. "It was rude beyond belief," she complained. "Not even Reagan would have done a thing like that."[1]

On the day of Clinton's inauguration, both Carter and Democratic Senator Sam Nunn urged the new president to halt the verbal threats against Iraq that had begun with George H. W. Bush during the Gulf War. That war, however, was long over, and the question of what if any action should be taken against Saddam Hussein, the Iraqi dictator, would have to be settled by Bush's successors. Carter, the mediator of peace wherever conflict might exist in the world, intended to speak out and offer his services.[2] How Clinton would respond to him remained to be seen.

The next day, in a more jovial mood, Carter autographed copies of his book *Turning Point* in a Washington bookstore. Although the speed with which he dealt with the crowds who bought copies and lined up for the autograph often deterred much conversation, one young lady did manage to speak her mind. "Mr. President, if you're still lusting in your heart, I'm available," she told him. The whole crowd burst into laughter as Jimmy turned beet red.[3]

Rosalynn, had she been there, likely would have enjoyed the moment, but she was busy with other matters. She joined Betty Ford to appear before the Senate Labor and Human Relations Committee to seek insurance coverage for mental illness and substance abuse. They helped to persuade Congress to pass the Mental Health Parity Act, but despite Rosalynn's many speeches in which she explained the law and the importance of enforcing it, most businesses found ways to work around it. Rosalynn also worked to get children inoculated before age two, to get grant money for her institute, and to assist Jimmy. She went with him to Crested Butte, Colorado, where he auctioned off his handcrafted chess set and earned $61,000 for the Carter Center. They shared the $25,000 Spark M. Matsunaga Medal of Peace awarded by the United States Peace Institute, and they hosted UN talks on human rights abuses at the Carter Center.[4]

United in their stand on the Southern Baptist Convention, they joined about 5,000 moderate Baptists in Birmingham, Alabama, to declare their support for the Cooperative Baptist Fellowship, which had been formed three years earlier as a more moderate alternative to the Southern Baptist Convention. Addressing the group, Carter spoke against intolerance and conformity with the mores of the conservative South that dominated the Southern Baptist Convention. Tolerance and racial and gender equality, he and Rosalynn believed, were more commensurate with the teachings of Jesus. He thought that religious fundamentalism was a threat to human rights, and he felt that threat in his own Baptist church, he said.[5]

Carter got the chance to put his faith into action when he met Arafat in Sana, Yemen. Carter was there giving a speech on human rights, democracy, and guinea worm disease when Arafat asked him to meet secretly at the Taj Sheba Hotel. Arafat told Carter that secret meetings in Oslo had produced an agreement to establish a Palestinian homeland. Israeli Minister of Foreign Affairs Shimon Peres and Prime Minister Yitzhak Rabin were supportive of a Declaration of Principles that would provide interim self-government in Gaza and the West Bank. Arafat wanted to bring his friend Carter into the loop, but he also wanted his help in persuading Clinton and the US State Department not to reject the agreement.

While the Clinton administration had known about the meetings, President Clinton was taken by surprise when informed that an agreement had been reached. He quickly offered to host a signing at the White House. By the time Carter reached home, the Oslo agreement had captured the world's attention. Carter did as promised, and he accepted Clinton's invitation to attend the historic signing on the South Lawn of the White House on September 13.[6]

After Arafat arrived at Andrews Air Force base the day before the ceremony, he went to the Westin Hotel to meet Jimmy Carter. He had insisted upon seeing Carter before President Clinton or Secretary of State Warren Christopher. Following hugs, Arafat explained that he had been to Egypt, Syria, Tunis, and Oman and had found no one opposed to the declaration. Carter said he owed Arafat a debt of gratitude, and he praised the Clinton administration for dealing directly with the PLO. Carter asked Arafat how Palestine would be governed, but he did not get a clear answer.

At the ceremony the next day, 3,000 white plastic chairs provided seating for members of Congress, the cabinet, and other dignitaries, including former presidents Ford, George H. W. Bush, and Carter and former secretaries of state. Rosalynn sat in the front row between Bush and Carter. When Israeli Foreign Minister Shimon Peres and PLO leader Mahmoud Abbas signed the declaration of Palestinian self-government in Gaza and the West Bank, one observer saw a tear roll down Carter's cheek.[7]

Arafat and Rabin won the Nobel Peace Prize that year. Futhermore, in a special ceremony in Oslo on May 18, 1994, Carter and Dominique de Menil presented their Human Rights Foundation award for world peace to the Institute for Applied Social Sciences in Norway to recognize Norway's role in the Israel/PLO agreement.[8]

Jimmy and Rosalynn slept the night of September 17 at the White House in the Queen's bedroom, which had once been the room used by Miss Lillian. George Bush, without Barbara, also passed the night in the White House, but Jerry Ford took lodging elsewhere. Carter and Bush had talked with President Clinton late into the night, discussing Haiti, Latin America, the famine in Sudan, and the Israeli-Palestinian pact. Bush especially urged the president to support the North American Free Trade Agreement (NAFTA), which was then being debated in Congress. Both of the Democrats agreed that a free trade agreement for North America would be to the advantage of the United States.[9]

The Carters' next association with top level politicians was at their funerals. At Tip O'Neill's funeral in early January at the Evangelist Church in Cambridge, Massachusetts, Carter was snubbed by the family. Although he and the former Speaker came from different backgrounds and arrived in Washington by radically different routes, they both believed that politics should serve the needs of the people and they had made peace with each other. When Jimmy and Rosalynn attended former President Richard Nixon's funeral at the Nixon Presidential Library in Yorba Linda, California, on April 27, they got equal treatment with the Clintons, Bushes, Reagans, and Fords.

On May 11, 1994, Rosalynn joined other first ladies to attend a gala event celebrating the opening of the First Ladies' garden at the United States Botanic Garden in Washington. Elegantly dressed in pastel gowns, each was escorted to the stage. The announcer seemed to linger over Rosalynn's name a few seconds longer than the others and apparently admired her as a person and for her post-presidential work. When the five gathered around a table in the shade of a tent later, however, the photographer captured a scene that revealed what they thought of each other. Nancy Reagan was looking off to the left side, apparently indifferent to the rest of the group. Two Democrats, Hillary Clinton and Lady Bird Johnson, were chatting with each other. Two Republicans, Betty Ford and Barbara Bush, were engaged in conversation with Ford's back turned to Rosalynn. Rosalynn was sitting there quite alone, beautifully dressed in a black and white ensemble, smiling, keeping her own counsel, and, despite whatever private thoughts she might have had, being a very proper lady and First Lady who represented her husband and her nation quite well.[10]

The next month, June 1994, in Atlanta, Jimmy modestly accepted a special honor. The State of Georgia unveiled his statue in the northwest corner of the Georgia State Capitol grounds. Paid for by a small group of Carter's friends, commissioned by Charlie Kirbo, and sculpted by Georgia native Frederick E. Hart, the life-sized bronze statue depicted Carter wearing a work shirt with sleeves pushed up and khaki pants. The sculptor gave him a serious expression, not the usual grin. The inscription on the tall granite marker behind the statue duly identified Carter as the thirty-ninth president of the United States, but it was the words on the four low granite benches in front that took the full measure of the man: State Senator, Governor, Naval Officer, Man of Faith, Farmer, Conservationist, Global Citizen, Humanitarian, Peacemaker, Teacher, Author, Poet, and Founder, the Carter Center. At the unveiling ceremony, Carter said he was "grateful and proud to be recognized by my friends," but also "embarrassed." He was thankful that he had had the opportunity to do things that were fulfilling, and he was pleased that the statue was in the form of a working man. "It's that image that put me in the White House and the governor's office," he said. A week later he received the National Freedom Award from the National Civil Rights Museum in Memphis.[11]

Far more important to Jimmy and Rosalynn than the growing list of honors they received was the opportunity to serve as international diplomats for peace. Those opportunities came quickly in North Korea, Haiti, and Bosnia during the last seven months of 1994. In early June, they began preparing for an unprecedented four-day trip to North Korea, a country that had signed the Nuclear Non-Proliferation Treaty in 1985, a treaty for which Carter had pushed hard during his presidency, but was now violating that commitment. President Clinton, concerned about North Korea's nuclear progress, was considering sending massive military reinforcements to South Korea, a step that some US generals said might provoke war. The North Korean government invited Carter to visit and attempt to resolve the dispute. Carter called President Clinton on June 1, 1994, and later sent him a letter saying that he intended to accept the invitation. Clinton gave his approval.

Carter was convinced that the only person in North Korea who could change the course of events was President Kim Il Sung, and he planned to deal with him directly.[12] National Security Adviser Anthony Lake, who had once served as Carter's Director of Policy Planning, told his former boss that his role was to offer the North Koreans a way out, not to make new policy, and not to claim that he spoke for the United States. Carter was not likely to take his former underling's advice, and he pelted the exasperated Lake with numerous questions about sanctions, Kim Il Sung's health, and whether Lake's briefers knew as much as they should.[13]

Jimmy and Rosalynn arrived in Seoul on June 13. Marion Creekmore, a career diplomat who had become the Carter Center's Director of Programs was his only adviser on the trip. Nancy Konigsmark, the Carters' scheduler, and the usual team of Secret Service agents accompanied them. Secretary of State Warren Christopher called to tell Carter that North Korea was about to eject the International Atomic Energy Agency (IAEA) inspectors from his country. In Seoul, the Carters called upon Ambassador James T. Laney and General Gary Luck, commander of US forces on the Korean peninsula. General Luck predicted that the United States could win a war with North Korea but the cost in lives, money, and trauma to both countries would make it a pyrrhic victory.

Clinton, nevertheless, called his war council together in Washington on June 16 to discuss preparation for a massive buildup of troops in South Korea. Senior advisors for former President Bush pressured Clinton to take decisive action. Clinton's Defense Secretary William Perry and his Chairman of the Joint Chiefs of Staff John Shalikashvili both favored sending reinforcements. Most members of the Republic of Korea (ROK) government sided with Clinton and his advisers, not Carter. In fact, they thought Carter's mission ill-timed and more helpful to the North Koreans, who were stalling on the nuclear issue.[14]

No one had ever crossed the Demilitarized Zone (DMZ) and back. It was the most heavily guarded border in the world and had separated North from South Korea since the Korean War Armistice in 1953. The Carters planned to cross at the truce village of Panmunjom. Before crossing, Jimmy, who was carrying a large briefcase filled with documents, and Rosalynn paused with Ambassador Laney, who shook their hands and wished them well as they paused in the protective cusdoy of US Army Colonel Forrest Chilton, secretary of the UN Military Assistance Commission at Panmunjom. It was an awesome and perhaps frightening moment, for scores of heavily armed troops lined both sides of the border. Secret Service agents, backed by less obtrusive military guards, stood ready to protect the lives of the Carters if some unfortunate event should occur. .

Colonel Chilton addressed his North Korean counterpart, who stood about twenty feet away on the other side of the DMZ, and formally requested the safe delivery of the distinguished Americans into his care. Rosalynn asked Nancy to raise her camera and get a photograph of them as they took their first step over the border. While doing so, Nancy twisted to her left ankle and accidentally placed a foot across the line. Instantly, a female Secret Service agent lifted her under her armpits and pulled her back on the southern side, advising her to look straight ahead and keep very quiet, which she did. The North Korean guards ignored the incident, and moments later the Americans walked across the border, with heavy military guards barely out of sight behind them. Rosalynn later loved to retell the story and laugh at Nancy's mishap.[15]

Safely on the other side, where their own guards were joined by those provided by the North Korean government, they boarded vehicles with their Korean hosts. Jimmy rode with Vice Foreign Minister Song Ho Kyong, and Rosalynn rode with Nancy Konigsmark, her interpreter, a body guard, and a Korean official. They traveled along a four-lane highway with very few other vehicles in sight. Cabbage, corn, and rice grew in the lush fields that bordered their route. Occasional clusters of concrete houses interrupted the mostly rural countryside. After a two-hour drive, they entered Pyongyang where row after row of concrete apartment houses, beautiful public buildings, water fountains, flowers, and the Taedong River greeted them. Their guest house was massive, modern, well staffed, and undoubtedly bugged. The food and service were lavish and included silver chopsticks, three wine glasses, and a small bowl of kimchi. Rosalynn thought the ginseng liquor in one of the three glasses was "strong and good."[16]

At 82, Kim Il Sung was vigorous and active and appeared younger than his years. He had been in power for fifty years, knew his nation well, and liked to hunt and fish. Mrs. Kim was physically strong too, a hunter who had killed wild boars at long range with a rifle. Friendly and gracious, she assured

Rosalynn that their soldiers worked for peace, not war When Carter asked Kim to allow United States and North Korean teams to search for and recover the remains of US soldiers from the Korean War, Kim said he would include the request in future negotiations. His wife broke in and told him he should do it. As Rosalynn beamed, Kim said, "OK. It's done. It's done."[17]

In Pyongyang, on June 15, Carter, with Rosalynn at his side taking notes, met with North Korean Foreign Minister Kim Yong Nam, who informed him that the IAEA inspectors would be expelled, the latest action in the fifteen-month standoff over North Korea's nuclear program, unless a deal could be worked out in a third round of talks. Carter took him seriously and dispatched Creekmore back to Panmunjom to send a message to the White House for approval of a third round of high-level talks. Creekmore, however, was not to send the message until Carter had met with the aged Kim Il Sung again the next morning.[18]

Carter explained his unofficial role to Kim Il Sung and then elaborated on the United States' concerns about North Korea's nuclear program. Carter found his host to be well informed about the program but unaware that the IAEA inspectors were about to be dismissed. Carter proposed that Kim freeze his nuclear program and guarantee "total transparency." Kim agreed to do so during a third round of talks and to stop permanently his efforts to develop nuclear weapons if his aging reactors could be replaced with newer, safer ones for peaceful purposes. Kim asked Carter for a guarantee that the United States would not launch a nuclear attack on his country.

Carter sent for Creekmore to return to Pyongyang without contacting Washington, for he believed that he had gotten all that was needed from the North Korean leader. Although he knew that he would later have to defend his conversation with Kim to skeptical US diplomats, he was eager to inform the Clinton administration about what he had done.[19] In the evening, North Korea time, Carter, amazed at what he had accomplished, called the White House and spoke with Robert Gallucci, the specialist on Korea who was then meeting with the war council. Fifteen minutes later, Gallucci shocked the council with the news that Kim Il Sung had agreed to freeze his nuclear program and to resume talks and that Carter believed the agreement was good enough to avoid the rush to sanctions that the United States and others in the UN were considering. Carter further dumbfounded the administration officials huddled in the Cabinet Room with the statement that he was about to go on CNN national news to announce the deal.[20]

What the Clinton people did not know was that Carter had taken CNN reporters with him. When the Clinton advisors viewed the television news, their dismay turned to fury. There was Carter publicly repudiating the sanctions strategy under discussion at the UN. National Security Adviser Tonny Lake angrily called Carter to remind him that he was not supposed to make policy or speak for the administration. Carter ignored Lake's call, postponing until a later time a furious argument over the spent fuel cooling ponds, and Lake refused to suspend the drive for sanctions. Nevertheless, Carter's public appearance, paid off, for he had managed to get more concessions from North Korea. In the Cabinet Room, Vice President Al Gore tried to calm the gathered group by asking if they could make "lemonade out of this lemon." Finally, Clinton seized the opportunity that Carter had offered him and announced that the United States would return to the negotiating table.[21]

In the meantime, the Carters pushed ahead with their unique brand of personal diplomacy. Kim invited them to join him and his wife for a long boat ride on the Taedong River to view a five-mile-long system of dams and barrages he had built at the river's mouth to hold back the Yellow Sea. As the two couples got better acquainted, Kim confessed that he was friendly toward Christianity. Mrs. Kim sometimes interrupted her conversation with Rosalynn to pick her up physically and place her in the spot she needed to be for photographs. The men talked about hunting and fishing, but Carter brought the discussion back to serious business.

Carter insisted that the nuclear freeze had to include a ban on reprocessing while the two nations talked and that Kim should invite South Korean president Kim Young Sam for a summit meeting. Kim agreed to implement the North-South denuclearization accord of 1992, draw forces back from the DMZ, and reduce the number of troops on the border. In return, Carter said that the sanctions activity had been stopped. North Korea would receive oil supplies and could construct light water reactors to replace the graphite ones. Discussions with the United States would begin, and the United States would promise not to launch a nuclear attack on their country.[22]

Mission accomplished, the Carters and their entourage headed back to the DMZ. Jimmy and Rosalynn rode together, and much of the talk with their hosts was about families and children. At the Panmunjom truce village, the Carters and the other members of their group shook hands with the North Koreans and said their goodbyes. A North Korean military officer took his place beside Carter and walked with him to the borderline. In very firm language he told his US counterpart that he was returning President Carter and his entourage to the custody of the US military on the other side. News networks from around the world recorded the historic moment, and soon the Carter party disappeared into the South Korean reception area. Carter briefed South Korean president Kim Young-sam, but Ambassador Laney gave him the disturbing news that the White House was in a furor over what he had done. In a long telephone conversation with Vice President Al Gore from Laney's residence, Carter attempted to clarify and explain what he had done, but the tension between him and the White House did not go away.

After returning home, Carter received a cool reception at the White House. After being made to wait for fifteen minutes for an appointment with Tony Lake, he received a polite but cold welcome from Lake and several others but neither the president nor the vice president greeted him. Tony Lake, who had had reservations about the trip, accepted the fact that Carter had rendered some good to the administration: Kim Il Sung had agreed to everything on the list of demands and requests that Clinton sent to him via Carter.[23]

Clinton and his administration were chagrinned that Carter had done something they could not, but many of them also recognized that Carter had been able to solve a conflict that no one else could. The secret of Carter's success, some believed, was his willingness to meet face-to-face with people, including unsavory dictators, understand their personalities, treat them as human beings, and enter into dialogue with them. Carter admitted that it was a mistake during his televised announcement to give the impression that he spoke for Clinton. Republican Senator John McCain described Carter as an "Innocent abroad," but most grumbling professional diplomats recognized Carter as a serious player in their game. Clinton's State Department spokesman Nicholas Burns admitted, "everyone in this government, from the president on down, has great respect for him."[24]

Several Republicans refused to give Carter any credit. Jeane Kirkpatrick, former US Ambassador to the UN, accused Carter of undermining the policy of the United States with "the liberal illusion that by treating an adversary as a friend we can make him a friend." Caspar W. Weinberger, Reagan's secretary of defense, said Carter should stick to building low cost houses, for he had probably done more damage in four days in North Korea than he had done in four years in the White House. Furthermore, according to Weinberger, Carter had violated the Logan Act which prohibits private citizens from making foreign policy.[25]

Less than three weeks after the Carters had returned home, President Kim Il Sung died suddenly from a heart attack. The looming question was of how his son, Kim Jong Il, might rule. The middle-aged son had remained out of sight during their visit, but Kim did reveal that he had turned the military over to his heir. In a closed society where children were indoctrinated from an early age and taught to resist outside interference, Kim Jong Il might have already been groomed to be his father's successor. Jimmy and Rosalynn expressed their sympathy to the family and people of North Korea over the death of their Great Leader. They hoped that his son and other officials would honor his memory "by maintaining the commitment toward peace that President Kim Il-sung made 2.5 weeks ago." Kim Jong Il did so, promising in a letter to Carter to abide by his father's commitments.[26]

Jimmy and Rosalynn had engineered a stunning accomplishment in both diplomatic and humanitarian terms. To get North Korea to abandon its nuclear program and return the remains of US soldiers who had died on its soil during the Korean War was beyond the imagination of the diplomats who had unsuccessfully attempted to resolve the latter issue for four decades. Their modus operandi was untraditional and also the secret of their success at conflict resolution through the Carter Center. A former president and his wife, both private citizens, approached the North Korean dictator and his wife as fellow human beings who deserved respect, related to them on a personal level, and found the common ground needed to discuss serious issues.

Returning to Georgia, Jimmy and Rosalynn moved quickly on to building houses and operating the Carter Center. They went to Albany, Georgia, to help build a new home for the Carter family's former nanny, Annie Mae Rhodes, 77, whose house had been destroyed in a flood. Annie Mae had taken care of Jimmy when he was a child, and he always remembered that it was Annie Mae who held his father in her arms when he died. Once she was settled into her new home, the Carters turned their attention back to the Carter Center. They agreed to merge it with Emory University, the idea being that a university home would provide highly trained personnel and other resources that would enhance the center's mission. The Carter Center, Jimmy and Rosalynn insisted, was still not to become a think tank, but an organization that actively worked in the world to provide healthcare, promote democracy, and resolve disputes.[27]

In mid-September, Carter put his conflict resolving skills to a serious test in Haiti. A military coup led by General Raoul Cedras had ousted President Jean-Bertrand Aristide in 1991 only seven months after he had won the country's first ever democratic election. Carter had overseen the election that placed the young priest in office. Although not the candidate Carter had wanted to win, the priest from the slums, who spouted anti-US rhetoric and liberation theology, lasted only seven months before the military junta forced him into exile and began murdering many people who continued to claim loyalty to him.[28]

While remaining de facto ruler as commander of the country's armed forces, Cedras approved the Haitian parliament's appointment of former Supreme Court Justice Emile Jonassaint to serve at the titular head of the government. Educated in the United States, Cedras had been trained by both US and Spanish military instructors. He was also a covert intelligence source who had sent information about the leftist Aristide to the CIA. However, he did not bring stability to Haiti. During three years of turmoil, 3,000 people had died in political violence. The United States and various human rights groups blamed the army and paramilitary groups for those atrocities. The ousted President Aristide promised reconciliation instead of revenge if new elections were held.

In September 1994, President Clinton warned the military junta that, if it did not give up power voluntarily, the United States would invade Haiti, force the military rulers out, and reestablish a democratic government. Jonassaint, the junta's aged puppet, facing the destruction of his regime, pleaded for the god of battle to "Fetch me Jimmy Carter." Carter, unmoved by pagan gods but hopeful that he could stop the carnage and prevent US military action, asked Clinton for the chance to go to Haiti and try to resolve the differences before US military forces intervened. General Cedras's wife, Yannick Prosper Cedras, fearing for the lives of her family, called Carter, who responded to her more warmly than he did to the gods of war.[29]

An exasperated Clinton, who wanted to send the troops and end the junta rule quickly, agreed to allow Carter to go, but he was wary of Carter and also had to buck opposition within his administration. Since Carter's trip to North Korea had ended satisfactorily, Clinton told retired chairman of the Joint Chiefs of Staff General Colin Powell, maybe it was worth the risk of allowing Carter another peace mission. Clinton's aides told him that presidents do not approve such missions; they order them. Nevertheless, Clinton approved Carter's choice of General Powell, who thought he might have some influence with Cedras, and Georgia Senator Sam Nunn, chairman of the Senate Armed Services Committee, who disapproved of the proposed military attack on Haiti, to join the mission.[30]

The unusual trio of envoys flew to Port-au-Prince on September 17, while Clinton stationed warships on the horizon and planned an invasion for the next day, because he did not believe that their mission would succeed. When it appeared on the September 18 that the mission had failed, Clinton announced that the US invasion force was on its way and that the trio must leave the country within thirty minutes. On an unsecure phone that allowed the Haitians to listen, Carter asked for a little more time because he said they were close to reaching an agreement. Rosalynn, who had been monitoring the activity from Plains, said she was not worried, because she knew that "Bill Clinton would not attack with Jimmy in the country."[31]

Rosalynn did more than monitor the time Jimmy was in Haiti. She knew that Mrs. Cedras had called Carter for help, and she suggested that Jimmy get her help in persuading her husband to cede power to Aristide. He did so, commenting upon Mrs. Cedras's extraordinary beauty so effusively that some thought he was flirting with her. In reality, she was a powerful influence on her husband and the best way to get to him. Whether the flattery, the deal, or the nearness of the US military jets brought the real pressure, Cedras ceded, and the crisis passed.[32]

Carter's former speechwriter, Hendrik Hertzberg, who thought Carter was a "saint," expressed it best when he said that the "bottom line was that there was no bloodshed." Capable of unsaintly behavior and disregard for his reputation, Carter was willing to do whatever he thought necessary to prevent war. Because of his "bullheadedness and perhaps overweening arrogance" as well as "qualities of perseverance and self-confidence," Carter, according to Hertzberg, was able to get the agreement. He had kept "the Pentagon, the State Department, and the White House on hold while he goes ahead and changes their policies for them—all for their own good, of course."[33] Father Ted Hesburgh, who knew Carter's flaws as well as his accomplishments, agreed with Hertzberg that "Jimmy Carter is a Saint."[34]

Bill Clinton would not have nominated Carter for sainthood, but he was shocked by the former president's ability to succeed with negotiations in Haiti. Carter persuaded the dictators to commit to leaving no later than October 15, after which the exiled President Jean-Bertrand Aristide would return. General Raoul Cedras and his family would be exiled to Panama by the United States and under its protection. The United States would protect his property in Haiti, and 1,500 US peacekeepers would enter the country immediately. The United States would seek to have the UN lift the economic boycott on Haiti as soon as possible. When informed by the Secret Service that he was not to speak with the media as he left the country, Carter used expletives that he later requested be deleted from the record. From their home in Plains, Jimmy and Rosalynn monitored the fulfilment of promises the United States made to Cedras. When the State Department did not carry out the necessary preparations to transport Cedras to his new home in Panama on schedule, they became angry, and Rosalynn declared that the White House had "messed up." Eventually the United States did as it had promised.[35]

Shortly after their return to the United States, Jimmy and Rosalynn held a town meeting at the Carter Center. Rosalynn took the lead, bubbling with enthusiasm about the success of their projects in Africa, where diseases diminished as crop production increased and women sometimes gained improved status. Jimmy, smiling broadly, finally asked if he could have the microphone to talk about Haiti.

Talk he did. Carter had wanted to remain in Haiti after the agreement, but Clinton would not allow that. Carter told of his conversation with Rosalynn and her suggestion that he talk to Cedras's wife. He found Mrs. Cedras "impressive, powerful . . . slim and very attractive." At first he thought that she would not relent, he said, looking mischievously at Rosalynn, "for I have known for fifty years what it's like to be involved with a strong woman." Yannick told Carter that she had heard that a "U.S. Delta force was coming to kill her family, and 'We decided we were ready to die.'" After listening to Carter and Colin Powell, she changed her mind and urged her husband to accept their offer of a comfortable exile in Panama.

The story about Mrs. Cedras appealed to journalists who wanted to know what Rosalynn thought. "Jimmy sees good in everybody," she answered, "and sometimes he sees more than is there." Rosalynn may well have been a better judge of human nature than her husband, because she was cautious, skeptical, and practical in her analysis of others. Carter, drawing upon his religious viewpoint that had once gotten him into trouble in his *Playboy* interview, recounted that all people are sinners, but all can be redeemed.[36]

Clinton's State Department cared little about Carter's religion or Mrs. Cedras's beauty; it resented Carter's private diplomacy and welcomed Carter's invitation to Secretary Warren Christopher to go to Plains to try to reach an accord with him. The arrival of Christopher's limousine at One Woodland Drive in Plains had an eerie resemblance to those days when limousines arrived on the grounds of Carter's White House. Carter claimed that he had White House approval for his trips to North Korea and Haiti despite "vehement opposition" from the State Department. Christopher, who had served as Carter's Deputy Secretary of State, downplayed his opposition to the trip after Carter succeeded. William Safire, a devout Republican and Jewish journalist for the *New York Times* who hated Clinton and Carter equally, viciously criticized Clinton for submitting to Carter, referring to the president as "Jimmy Clinton."[37]

Carter, with his ability to range over many topics at once, raised the issue of the civil war in Somalia with Clinton. Since Africa, and especially the Horn, had occupied so much of his attention during his presidency and was often the scene of gross humanitarian abuses, Carter wanted to help. The civil war had begun there before Clinton's election. Bush had organized a coalition under the auspices of the UN to send 34,000 troops to Somalia on a humanitarian mission to stop the carnage and feed thousands of starving people. Two-thirds of the troops were Americans. In addition, Bush had spent more than $10 million on aid for the starving Africans. During his overnight talk with Clinton the previous September, Carter had tried to persuade the president to "get off the military option" and stop emphasizing the killing rampage of General Mohamed Farah Aidid—the former diplomat and warlord who commanded rebel troops in the south Somalia and was accused of genocide. The political solution Carter sought could only be achieved if someone could communicate with Aidid, who was on the run from UN and US troops.

Carter invited a delegation representing Aidid to Atlanta, and he made a quick trip to East Africa to consult with neighboring heads of state. He learned that Aidid would accept the findings of an independent UN commission's investigations of his killing Pakistani troops in Mogadishu, a battle that had escalated until nineteen Americans and thousands of civilians and native military men had been killed. Passing the information on to Clinton and UN Secretary General Boutros Boutros-Ghali, Carter convinced them to allow him to help. Carter knew that Aidid stayed in a different house every night, where he watched CNN news. Carter had CNN install a satellite in front of his house in Plains, which would allow him to send a prearranged private communication to Aidid. Aidid agreed to board a US plane for a negotiating conference in Addis Ababa. Although the negotiations broke down, and Aidid was killed three years later, US troops and UN humanitarian workers were able to withdraw from Somalia safely.[38]

During the fall of 1994, the Carters enjoyed a respite from international peace negotiations. As in past years, they built houses, gave speeches, and participated in religious events. On his seventieth birthday, Carter attended a celebration in his honor at the State Department in Washington. Besides a letter of commendation from Bill and Hillary Clinton, the highlight was receiving the J. William Fulbright Prize for International Understanding. Carter explained that recent tensions between himself and the Clinton administration had stemmed from "miscommunications, most of which were my fault."

At a separate gala in Atlanta, actor Kirk Douglas noted that Carter's life demonstrated a natural continuity from presidency to post-presidency. He might have added that that continuity had begun much earlier with the instruction Carter had received at Mr. Earl's knee and its reinforcement by Miss Lillian, Rosalynn, Miss Julia Coleman, Admiral Rickover, and Anwar Sadat.[39]

Rosalynn attributed her work for peace and humanitarian concerns to Jimmy and especially to her mother. When she published *Helping Yourself Help Others: A Book for Caregivers,* with Susan K. Golant, in October 1994, she dedicated it to her mother. Based upon research done by the Rosalynn Carter Institute, the book discusses the needs of those who work as caregivers and gives advice on how they can care for themselves. It also listed the numerous organizations to which caregivers can go for help. Partly a memoir of her mother's and her own experiences as caregivers, it offered a useful guide for all caregivers.[40] Rosalynn sent Nancy Reagan a copy of her book with a note that she hoped Nancy would find information, or at least encouragement, in it that would be helpful in dealing with former President Reagan's progressing Alzheimer disease. "My heart goes out to you and President Reagan," she wrote.[41] Apparently Nancy did not reply.

Rosalynn could be both powerful and mischievous. She used her connection with some members of Congress to secure the National Park Service's acquisition of Carter's boyhood farm and fifteen adjacent acres. At a seminar on first ladies in Washington, she joked about the time she and Jimmy had sat down together to think about one good thing they did that was popular. They couldn't think of any, she laughed. She admitted that it was a good thing Jimmy did not listen to her advice about waiting until his second term to push the Panama Canal treaties, because if he had, he would have been a "do nothing president." She dropped in to visit Ted and Vicki Kennedy on election night, where they discussed her book on caregivers and he promised to stay in touch with her about mental health issues when Congress reconvened.[42]

During the last month of the year, Rosalynn and Jimmy negotiated with Clinton for permission to go to Bosnia as private mediators in a bloody civil war that had been going on for thirty-two months, with antecedents that stretched back into the Carter presidency. In May 1980 Marshal Josep Broz Tito had died. He had stood up against Stalin and Hitler and kept a number of diverse ethnic groups together in the country Yugoslavia; after his death it splintered into the republics of Croatia, Slovenia, Kosovo, and Serbia.[43]

From 1992 through 1995, warring factions fell into what the West viewed as civil war and labeled the Bosnian War. Radovan Karadzic, rebel leader of the Bosnian Serbs and a radical Greek Orthodox Christian, had started a campaign for ethnic purity that resulted in the massacre of many thousands of Muslims in Serbia and surrounding areas. A psychiatrist by profession, who had received part of his training at Columbia University, Karadzic helped to organize the Serb Democratic Party in Bosnia and Herzegovina in 1989. Dedicated to unifying Serbs across Yugoslavia, it failed and was rejected by Serbs, who refused to support its constitution and parliament. Nevertheless, Karadzic was elected president of Republika Srpska, one of the two entities of Bosnia and Herzegovina. The Greek Orthodox Church declared him "one of the most prominent sons of our Lord Jesus Christ working for peace."[44] When Karadzic set up his headquarters in Pale, Bosnia-Herzegovina, about twenty miles from Sarajevo, and began fighting the government, including ethnic cleansing by exterminating Muslims, he earned his nickname as the Butcher of Bosnia.[45]

Karadzic met his match in Slobodan Milosevic and Alija Izetbegovic. President of the Republic of Serbia, Milosevic led the Socialist Party of Serbia and engineered constitutional reforms intended to prevent the marginalization of Serbs. Born in 1941 in German-occupied Serbia, he was the son of an orthodox theologian who committed suicide in 1962. A lawyer by trade, and a Communist politician, he seemed equally capable of genocide as Karadzic. Alija Izetbegovic, the first president of the Republic of Bosnia and Herzegovina, had a distinguished pedigree, a law degree, and a fierce passion to promote and defend an Islamic revival in his country.

By the time Clinton became president, the UN had appointed a Contact Group consisting of representatives from the United States, the United Kingdom, France, West Germany, and Russia to try to stop the killing and unravel the tangled mess. The Contact Group had been ineffective, which led the Serbian Ambassador to the United States, Milan Milutinovic, to visit Carter in Plains in June 1994. Delivering a message from President

Milosevic, Milutinovic invited the internationally recognized peacemaker to come to Belgrade and resolve the bloody dispute. Carter at first rejected the invitation, believing that the UN and the United States were already pursuing viable avenues to peace. When the Bosnian situation took more violent forms, he reconsidered, informed Clinton of the invitation, and became increasingly interested in stopping the war and the genocide.[46]

The debate in Washington was furious, as many of Carter's fellow Democrats and some former members of his administration, at their wits' end about how to handle the Bosnian War, still smarted from Carter's recent triumphs in North Korea and Haiti. National Security Advisor Tony Lake feared Carter would undertake more than what would be acceptable for US national security. Secretary of State Warren Christopher, who had been instrumental in achieving both the Camp David Accords and the release of the hostages during Carter's presidency, was as defensive of his State Department's turf as Cyrus Vance had once been of his. The debate ended with the announcement by a senior official at the White House that, if Carter's trip "eases tensions and helps create the climate for negotiations and a cease-fire, we won't quibble."[47]

Karadzic had motivated Carter with a special request to come to the ravaged country. If Carter would come, Karadzic promised to guarantee free passage for UN relief convoys, release captured peacekeepers, and reopen the Sarajevo airport for humanitarian flights.[48]

With White House approval, Jimmy and Rosalynn boarded a commercial flight from Atlanta to Frankfurt, Germany. From there, on December 18, 1994, they transferred to a US Air Force military plane for their flight to Zagreb, Croatia. Aware that Karadzic was trying to use them for his own purposes and that they again would face the wrath of those who condemned them for consulting with dictators, they, especially Jimmy, had high hopes for success.

On arrival in Zagreb, after a brief meeting with the president of Croatia at an impressive palace that had once been Tito's summer home, they met with the prime minister of Bosnia, the US ambassador, and a UN representative. The ambassador, according to Rosalynn, "was negative about our visit." But Jimmy had been encouraged because his conversation with Karadzic had led to some humanitarian convoys being allowed into the city.

From Zagreb, the Carters flew the short distance to Sarajevo. Having been warned that there might be sniper fire at the airport, they donned flak jackets and helmets as they settled in for the hour and fifteen minute flight that took a circuitous route over the Adriatic Sea. Upon arrival, a UN armored vehicle shielded them as they walked to the terminal. They went first by armored vehicle to the UN Protective Forces headquarters, where they met their host, British Lieutenant General Michael Rose, who briefed them before embassy personnel escorted them to an armored US car that took them through the hazardous "sniper's alley." After safely arriving, they were greeted by Bosnian president Alija Izetbegovic. At first hostile, he expressed the hope they would not "be hit while you are here" and doubted that they could negotiate a cease fire. Carter stood up to him, explaining that he had no new offer but came to support the Contact Group plan. Izetbegovic relented and promised to see them again the next day after they had met with Karadzic. He doubted that Karadzic would accept the Contact Group plan, because he would want more than half of the land for the Serbs.[49]

Jimmy and Rosalynn passed the night at UN headquarters where they were served excellent food and French wine. They slept on cots, but the room was cozy, heated, and adjacent to a bathroom with hot water. Early the next morning they set out for the headquarters of Karadzic in Pale, about nine miles away. Traveling in armored vehicles with a UN escort, the Carters saw graves everywhere where there had once been beautifully manicured parks. Their drivers took a scenic rural route in order to avoid mined roads; the nine-mile trip took an hour.[50]

Upon their arrival at Pale, Karadzic, who had invited them, and his wife Liliana, greeted them enthusiastically. General Ratko Mladic and the Serbian Orthodox Archbishop were also among the group of greeters. They went immediately into a meeting with officials who showed them maps and told them the history of the conflict. Afterward, Jimmy and Rosalynn and Karadzic and his wife went to a private room for further discussion. After small talk about their families, Jimmy and Karadzic shared drafts that each had made of a possible agreement. The group broke for a hefty lunch of soup, trout, lamb, potatoes, sour cabbage, and dessert.

In the afternoon, after much discussion, Jimmy got Karadzic to agree to negotiations based upon the Contact Group plan. Jimmy notified the White House, then signed the agreement and held a press conference with the reporters who had been freezing outside. "We heard they had some choice words for us!," Rosalynn reported. Since the agreement did not specifically mention acceptance of the Contact Group plan, it would inevitably be rejected in Sarajevo. But Carter knew it was the first step toward an agreement. Typing furiously on his laptop, Carter tenaciously tried

Jimmy and Rosalynn Carter singing with
Willie Nelson at the Omni Coliseum in Atlanta,
December 12, 1982.
Source: Rick Diamond/Getty Images.

The Carters and
the Reagans on
the Carter Center
grounds, Atlanta,
when President
Reagan dedicated
the Jimmy Carter
Presidential Library,
October 1, 1986.
Source: Reagan Library.

Jimmy and Rosalynn Carter
riding in the Lord Mayor's
parade in Newcastle, England,
April 7, 1987.
Source: PA Images via Getty Images.

President Carter
and North Korean
President Kim Il Sung
in Pyongyang, North
Korea, June 16, 1994.
Source: The Carter Center.

Jimmy Carter (center) with Rosalynn behind him, Bosnian Serb leader Radovan Karadzic (left), and Bosnian Serb Commander Ratko Mladic (right), in Pale, Bosnia, sign a declaration proposing a four-month cease fire in the Bosnian War, after seven hours of negotiations, December 19, 1994.

Source: AP Photo/ Sava Radovanovic.

Rosalynn Carter joins Colin Powell, Jimmy Carter, and Sam Nunn on a trip to Haiti to assess progress in preparing for elections, February 3, 1995. Carter, Powell, and Nunn had convinced the country's military leaders to step down in September 1994.

Source: The Carter Center.

President Carter with Archbishop Desmond Tutu of South Africa meeting with other African leaders in Cairo to address crises in the Great Lakes Region of Africa, November 27, 1995.
Source: The Carter Center.

Former President Jimmy Carter, former Secretary of State James Baker, and former Costa Rica President Oscar Arias Sanchez lead a Carter Center delegation to monitor a national election in Nicaragua, November 1996.
Source: The Carter Center.

Bill Clinton, Rosalynn Carter, and Jimmy Carter, at the Carter Center after President Clinton had awarded the Carters the Presidential Medal of Freedom, August 9, 1999.
Source: Clinton Library.

Jimmy Carter holding a news conference in Plains on October 11, 2002, to tell his friends and neighbors that he has just won the Nobel Peace Prize.
Source: AP Photo/ John Bazemore.

Jimmy Carter showing his Nobel Peace Prize in Oslo, Norway, December 20, 2002.
Source: The Carter Center.

Jimmy Carter's Nobel Peace Prize Medal on display at the Jimmy Carter Museum, Atlanta, November 30, 2009.
Source: AP Photo/ John Bazemore.

Rosalynn Carter christens SSN-23 *Jimmy Carter*
at Groton, Connecticut, on June 5, 2004, splashing
champagne on Carter the husband as well as Carter the
submarine.
Source Still Picture Branch, National Archives.

Jimmy Carter in the control
room of his namesake
submarine, August 11, 2005.
Source: Still Picture Branch, National
Archives.

Jimmy and Rosalynn Carter observing poll closing procedures in Monrovia, Liberia, October 11, 2005.

Source: The Carter Center.

Fusheni Nazeed, a local health worker in Tingali, Ghana, demonstrates for the Carters how trachoma can be prevented with simple environmental changes, February 8, 2007.

Source: The Carter Center.

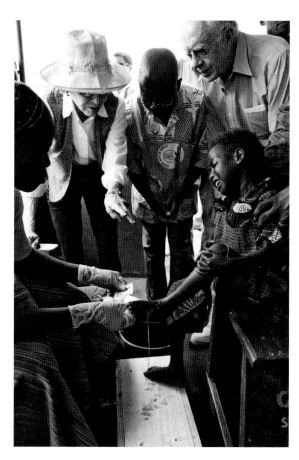

Jimmy and Rosalynn Carter in Savelugu, Ghana, watching a guinea worm health worker dress a child's painful guinea worm wound, February 8, 2007.
Source: The Carter Center.

Jimmy and Rosalynn Carter in Nigeria working for disease prevention, February 15, 2007.
Source: The Carter Center.

Rosalynn Carter testifying before the US House of Representatives subcommittee on the Wellstone Domenici Mental Health Parity and Addiction Equity Act, July 10, 2007.
Source: The Carter Center.

Jimmy and Rosalynn Carter in Bhaktapur, Nepal, examining polling center information while waiting for polls to open, April 10, 2008.
Source: The Carter Center.

Jimmy Carter joined Willie Nelson to play harmonica and sing "Georgia on My Mind," Chastain Park Amphitheater, Atlanta, July 27, 2008.
Source: Rick Diamond/ Getty Images.

Jimmy Carter with his daughter Amy before the Willie Nelson and B. B. King concert at the Chastain Park Amphitheater, Atlanta, July 27, 2008.
Source: Rick Diamond/ Getty Images.

Jimmy Carter talks with voters in Juba, South Sudan, most of whom voted to create South Sudan as a separate nation from Sudan, January 9, 2011.
Source: The Carter Center.

Health and Human Services Secretary Kathleen Sebelius (left) joins Rosalynn Carter and David Wellstone at the Carter Center to celebrate Congressional approval of the Mental Health Parity Act, November 8, 2013.
Source: The Carter Center.

Jimmy Carter greets a Nepalese boy in Kathmandu, Nepal, during his visit to monitor Nepal's November 2013 constituent assembly elections, November 18, 2013.

Source: The Carter Center.

Jimmy Carter teaching his Sunday School class at Maranatha Baptist Church Plains, March 3, 2017.

Source: Library of Congress, LC-DIG-highsm – 42729.

Jimmy and Rosalynn Carter at a news conference in Nashville, Tennessee, where they planned to build Habitat Houses despite an injury to his face from a fall, October 7, 2019.
Source: AP Photo/ Mark Humphrey.

Jimmy and Rosalynn Carter meet with Democratic candidate Pete Buttigieg and his husband Chasten Buttigieg at the Buffalo Café in Plains, March 1, 2020.
Source: AP Photo/Matt Rourke.

Jimmy and Rosalynn walking along West Church Street in Plains after having supper with a friend, August 2, 2018.

Source: Matt McClain/The Washington Post via Getty Images.

The Carter Center, Atlanta, Georgia.
Source: The Carter Center.

to convince each side that it would be better off with this agreement than none. He would not give up. He listened, proved to be fair and unbiased, and stayed focused on the main issue, a style he had perfected at Camp David.[51]

In Sarajevo, Vice President Ejup Ganic predictably refused to accept the document. Loud and tough, he was rude and hostile toward the Carters. Carter argued with him and declared it was the best he could get. After a private meeting with President Izetbegovic, Jimmy got him to sign an agreement to take back to Karadzic. They left immediately for Pale, where Jimmy had a private meeting with Karadzic. Jimmy emerged with an agreement to a cease fire that would commence on December 23, 1994. It called for lifting all restrictions on relief convoys, protection of human rights, and the exchange of all detainees. It would remain in effect for four months or longer if both sides agreed. After rushing back to Sarajevo, Carter succeeded in getting President Izetbegovic to agree to the changes and to sign the document. Catching the last possible flight out of Sarajevo, he and Rosalynn stopped in Belgrade where Slobodan Milosevic, pleased with their success, greeted them.[52]

They spent the night in Frankfurt, and the next day returned to Atlanta. Jimmy said that the people in Sarajevo had not had a good Christmas in a long time and that he hoped this one would be peaceful for them. On board their flight, they donned glasses and both hovered over their laptops to type and correct notes they had taken on that unusual adventure.[53]

After Christmas, Carter offered to return to any of the world hot spots that he had helped to cool down, but the Clinton administration took charge of Bosnia. "I've got plenty of other things to do other places [than Bosnia]," Carter said. He planned to return to Haiti and talked with both sides of a major league baseball strike.[54]

Resumption of hostilities in the Bosnian War in 1995 prompted NATO and other world powers, especially the United States and Russia, to pressure the three sides to attend a peace conference in Dayton, Ohio. Milosevic, Karadzic, and Izetbegovic all attended. US Secretary of State Warren Christopher and negotiator Richard Holbrooke led the conference. Representatives from NATO, Russia, the United Kingdom, France, Germany, other European nations also participated. The fragile agreement to promote peace and stability in Bosnia and Herzegovina and to establish regional balance in the former Yugoslavia was signed in Paris in December 1995 and became known as the Dayton Accords.

The Carters were not given credit for the cease fire they had negotiated a year earlier, nor were they invited to participate. Holbrooke, however, recognized the work Carter had done earlier, chose the site of an US Air Force base near Dayton, Ohio, and conducted a conference that closely imitated the one Carter had held at Camp David.[55]

The three Balkan disputants from the war-torn area were eventually arrested and charged with war crimes. Milosevic died in prison, and Izebegovic served five years before being released in poor health to die shortly thereafter. Karadzic, who was considered the most notorious architect of the genocidal massacre of thousands of Muslims, escaped capture for a dozen years before he was caught, convicted by the International Criminal Tribunal for the Former Yugoslavia, and sentenced to forty years in prison. After a fourteen-year pursuit, General Ratko Mladic, commander of the Bosnia Serb forces, was also caught, tried in the International Court of Justice at the Hague, found guilty of genocide, and sentenced to life in prison. The Balkans healed and became peaceful democratic countries.[56]

Carter's role in Somalia, North Korea, Haiti, and the Bosnian War fell through the cracks of history. Peace was not as glamorous as war, and Carter was the servant of peace. For a civilian, a former president, to play such a huge role as a US peacemaker, was unique in the history of the nation.

FORTY

Tyrants, Books, and Mr. Earl

During the months that the Carters were resolving conflicts in North Korea, Haiti, and Bosnia, he was also writing. Having always appreciated poetry, especially the work of Dylan Thomas, he began to write it himself and published *Always a Reckoning and Other Poems* in the winter of 1994–1995. Carter had been writing poetry since he was in high school, and he wrote some verses for Rosalynn during their courtship and first years of marriage. He started writing seriously in 1990: "I write like an engineer," he said. "I try to be as simple and succinct and clear as possible." He avoided long sentences and complex words. "I write poetry because of the choice of words, the interrelationship among words, how they tie in with some very private thoughts of mine, between words and my inner thoughts, it's an intriguing exercise in the use of language and words," he explained.[1]

Carter's autobiographical, collected poems revolve around the theme of human rights, especially the rights of vulnerable children, African Americans, and Africans. In sparse language, he wrote passionately about the people, places, and politics that had molded his life. Beneath the differences that divided people, the antagonisms that might cause war, the misunderstanding and accidents that separated people from each other, he found a strain of common humanity that gave him hope that a world filled with love, tolerance, and justice might be possible. In "Life on a Killer Submarine," a deeply emotional poem, Carter contrasted the power of natural sounds of living creatures beneath the sea with that of powerful submarines patrolling the waters in search of their enemies. If the crews of those competitive underwater war vessels could hear "the same whale's song," then they might share a common solitude and avoid the wrong move that would destroy the peace they yearned to keep.[2]

Jimmy dedicated his poems to his father, his mother, Rosalynn, Rachel Clark, and ten more individuals or groups. His parents, his wife, and the African-American woman who reared him he remembered as the most important people in his life. It is likely no coincidence that Mr. Earl ranks first on his list. Earl, he said, was "a man who relished discipline, who reached out to his son with love, always tempered with restraint." Jimmy expressed that relationship in the title poem, "Always a Reckoning." His father believed that rewards should be earned by work done, but Jimmy's pony Lady did little more than provide him with rides. If Jimmy had not ridden Lady for some time, his father would ask him when he had last ridden, a subtle reminder that Lady, like Jimmy and others in the household, should earn her keep.

After *Always a Reckoning* was published, Carter perfected a concise standardized technique for autographing the volume's title page that enabled him to sign many copies quickly. A helper would open the book to the title page, hand it to Carter, and he would quickly sign "JCarter." At Emory University, he signed 500 copies in two hours. When someone asked if he had writer's cramp, he joked, "Naw, this is how I make a living. It beats picking cotton."[3]

Carter often brought out a book in time for Christmas sales, and in some years he earned significant amounts from his writings. His stories were usually autobiographical with an inspiring message. In September 1995, he published a children's book, *The Little Baby Snoogle-Fleejer*. Based upon the story he used to tell his children when they were young, it is the tale of a crippled boy, his impoverished mother, and a sea monster. When the monster, the baby Snoogle-Fleejer, came out of the sea, the boy's playmates all abandoned him because he could not run away with them. The friendly monster offers to swim and play with the boy and even give him a ride under the water. When the boy's mother needed surgery that she could not afford, the monster went to the bottom of the sea, brought up a mouthful of gold coins from a shipwreck, and gave them to his human friend. The mother was no longer poor, got the surgery she needed, and, when the boy's friends saw him riding on the head of the Snoogle-Fleejer, he became a hero. Amy illustrated the book with large, colorful drawings of the characters. At first, when Jimmy saw her illustrations, he was startled by the way she envisioned his story, but soon he came to love them.[4]

Although Jimmy liked to spend the early hours of the morning writing, both he and Rosalynn were happy to change their schedule to travel internationally. They went to Africa, March 19–28, 1995, visiting Nigeria, Sudan, Kenya, and Ghana. Their mission was primarily to discuss health, but they dealt with political issues and human rights as well. In Nigeria, they hoped to stop the government's plan to levy a tariff on forty tons of DuPont Precision Fabric cloth filters that were needed to eradicate the guinea worm. But Carter also planned to seek the freedom of his old friend, former President

Olusegun Obasanjo, who had been imprisoned for his criticism of government corruption and human rights abuses. Although General Sani Abacha, a tyrant who controlled the government, refused to make any commitment on either issue to the Carters they were enthusiastically welcomed as they traveled through the Nigerian countryside.

The people cheered, danced, waved, and screamed as the Carters' motorcade made its way through a particularly disease-ridden village. One of them waved a sign that said, "Guinea worm you better go away. President Carter is coming!" The village chiefs gave Jimmy a parcel of land on which he could build a "castle," and they crowned and robed both Jimmy and Rosalynn as honorary chiefs.

General Abacha's wife was more humane than her husband; she agreed to have a water tank installed that would guarantee pure drinking water. Touched by the sincere efforts of the Carters to stamp out guinea worm disease, the general relented and permitted the filters to come into his country. As a personal gift to Carter, Abacha also allowed Obasanjo to return to his farm home under house arrest. And the people in the village of Elugu Ogi in Ebonyi State abandoned their belief that, if Carter Center workers treated their ponds, the gods who protected the spirits of their ancestors there would be destroyed.[5]

In Sudan, a bloody civil war that had been raging for twelve years prevented health workers from getting into areas where the water was infested with guinea worms. The Sudanese government in the north, headed by President Omar Hassan al-Bashir, battled the south's Black Christian and animist rebels led by John Garang. Garang, who had been to Plains and had attended Carter's Sunday School class, approved Carter's request to approach Bashir seeking to stop the shooting long enough for a medical team to enter the afflicted areas safely and combat guinea worm disease. Bashir at first did not want to make the military sacrifice, but when Carter accused him of being insensitive to the humanitarian needs of the people in the south, he relented. The warring factions agreed to a two-month truce, sufficient time to allow health workers safe passage into the areas where they needed to work.[6]

Carter sent his son Chip to monitor the truce he had negotiated the previous month. John Garang's Sudan People's Liberation Army, made up of Dinka tribesmen, was found to be fighting another South Sudan independence movement as much as it fought the government, but the truce remained in place long enough for the Carter Center group to make significant progress combatting the guinea worms.[7]

Back home in Georgia, on April 12, 1995, the fiftieth anniversary of Franklin D. Roosevelt's death, Carter went to his Little White House in Warm Springs, to accept the Four Freedoms Award. Paying tribute to Eleanor Roosevelt, Carter said that she "showed a moral and spiritual courage that too often is unrecognized." "We rich Americans," he continued, "these days have a hard time connecting with the legacy of Franklin Roosevelt. But he transformed . . . the life of our nation." Referencing the four freedoms—from want, of speech, from fear, and of worship—he proclaimed that those freedoms "are still vivid in our lives, and for that we will be eternally grateful."[8]

After returning to Atlanta, the Carters hosted a conference of eight of the sixteen living Nobel literature laureates beginning on Monday, April 24. They talked about the need for privacy, and some of them argued that television "stupefies people." Octavio Paz, from Mexico, thought that recent violence in the United States, particularly the April 19, 1995, bombing of a federal building in Oklahoma City in which 168 people died, did not spell the doom of the country or make it comparable to Nazi Germany. Instead, he said: "In a country that was founded on the 'tension between freedom and equality,' the old notion of the melting pot has resulted in a new . . . multicultural civilization that is both a contradiction and affirmation of democratic ideals."[9] Agreeing, the next month the Carters built Habitat houses in Georgia and in California, and he and Rosalynn prepared to attend an African peace conference in Egypt.[10]

Since peacekeeping organizations such as the UN, were not making any progress bringing calm to Rwanda and Burundi, the Carters went there to try to help. For the remainder of 1995, they immersed themselves in understanding that ethnic conflict in Africa. Hundreds of innocent civilians, as well as combatants, were dying every day. In Rwanda, the Carters persuaded African leaders to attend a summit the following month. That peace conference convened in Cairo, Egypt, on November 27, when the leaders of Rwanda, Burundi, Uganda, Tanzania, and Zaire, who had refused to meet with the UN or other would-be peacemakers, met with Carter and Archbishop Desmond Tutu. Carter got them to stop the fighting, to provide relief for the refugees, and to edge toward peace. During the harmonious meeting, the African leaders agreed to close refugee camps and to halt cross-border raids. After they adjourned, 1.8 million Rwandan refugees were able go home.[11] Since most of them, who were of a different ethnicity against which the Tutsis had fought, feared for their lives if they returned to their country, under the control of the Tutsis, Carter met with the same African leaders again the following March in Tunisia, where he urged Rwandan refugees living in camps on the borders of Zaire, Burundi, and Tanzania, to return to their homes, which he said were safe despite the Tutsi ethnic group being in control of the country.[12]

Peace and democracy in the Middle East, however, continued to elude Carter. When Israeli prime minister Yitzhak Rabin had been assassinated the previous September by an extremist who opposed his attempts to make peace with Palestinians and his Arab neighbors, Carter had hailed Rabin as a hero for peace.[13] In January 1996, when the Israeli government allowed Palestinians in the occupied territories to conduct a free election for the first time ever, he and Rosalynn led a team of forty observers to Palestine. Palestinians in the West Bank, the Gaza Strip, and East Jerusalem went to the polls to choose their president and an eighty-eight-member parliament. In addition to Carter's group, the historic event attracted 300 European Union observers and about 350 election watchers from other countries.

Carter tried to keep the election honest. He reprimanded one Israeli officer for ordering his men to videotape Palestinian voters at polling stations. He appeared unannounced at some other polling places, and he reassured one Palestinian journalist that Prime Minister Shimon Peres had authorized him to report that there would be no retribution for those who voted. Riled up and looking "steely," when Israeli soldiers intimidated the voters, he and Rosalynn threatened to call General Uzi Dayan to stop them. When voting had ended, Carter declared the free election to be a success; Yasser Arafat was elected president of Palestine.[14]

After returning to Georgia, Carter grabbed the headlines by participating in the start of the 1996 Olympic Games in Atlanta. He joined 950 other Georgians to take a turn running with the torch as it approached Georgia's capital city. His impressive display of his jogging ability became lost in the publicity that reminded Americans of the former president's controversial decision to keep their elite athletes away from the 1980 Moscow Games, a bitter memory for many.[15]

Unbowed, Carter used interviews and op-ed pieces to keep his opinions before the public. Inferring that the Republican Party condoned hate and religious discrimination, he wrote an op-ed piece arguing that "It's fundamentally Christian to reject politics of hate." One should not force others to worship in ways they disliked, he wrote, nor should those who were different be treated as second-class citizens. He condemned gay bashing, noted that homosexuality had never been mentioned by Jesus, and argued that no one, even silently, should condone the persecution of homosexuals.[16] Perhaps suggesting that Democratic candidates would make better presidents, he used the occasion of former Secretary of State Edmund Muskie's funeral to comment that Muskie had served the country well and had been imminently qualified to be president.[17]

Rosalynn, like Jimmy, kept her opinions public. Upon accepting the award for being Georgia's Woman of the Year in 1996, she reaffirmed her commitment to improved mental health care. Shortly thereafter she announced that her work had born fruit, because the Senate adopted legislation that would require medical insurers to cover mental health disorders.[18] On July 7, she and Jimmy celebrated their golden wedding anniversary, which he said was "one of the rarest honors left in American life."[19] Later that month, they built Habitat homes in Hungary, where he was again thanked for returning the Holy Crown of St. Stephen to them in 1977.[20]

Feeling alienated from the Democratic Party, Carter announced that he would not attend its late August convention in Chicago. His decision, he said, imitated Harry Truman's decision to attend only one convention after he left office. Bill Clinton would be nominated for reelection virtually by acclamation, and the relationship between Clinton and Carter had steadily cooled. One Clinton State Department official who thought Carter meddled more than he helped, grumbled that "Carter was a major pain in the ass."[21]

Unperturbed by the negative attitude of national Democrats toward him, Carter drew strength from his religion and from the financial success of his writing. In late October, he published *Living Faith*, a collection of his Sunday School lessons. Interspersed with his conservative interpretation of Scripture, numerous autobiographical asides piqued readers' interest. He revealed his grief over his son Jack's divorce and his difficulty refraining from chastising Jack for it. He sometimes illustrated his Bible lessons with stories about his mother, and he made frequent references to his father.[22]

Jimmy and Rosalynn liked to bring members of their large family together on a major trip every year after Christmas. With four married children and numerous grandchildren, as well as their own surviving siblings, nieces, nephews, and cousins, there were plenty of Carters and Smiths to gather. On New Year's Eve 1996, they chartered a Disney cruise ship to visit Harry Truman's semi-secret presidential retreat at the US Naval Base in Key West, Florida, which had been preserved as a museum. It was where Harry, Jimmy's favorite president, had relaxed, sipping bourbon, smoking cigars, and playing poker. The visiting Carter clan did none of those things, but they were allowed to dine at the very table where Harry and his wife Bess once sat.[23]

As 1997 began, Jimmy watched *Living Faith* climb toward the top of the *New York Times* best seller list, but he and Rosalynn gave priority to a visit to parts of South America where people suffered from schistosomiasis, a preventable disease caused by water-borne parasitic worms and popularly called "snail fever." Although it had never received the same level of publicity as guinea worm disease, the Carter Center went to work to control it. They received more publicity when, back in Atlanta, Rosalynn teamed with actors Joanne Woodward, Rod Steiger, and Kathy Cronkite to make a video that tried to dispel the stigma of mental illness, and both Carters announced that they would participate in a Habitat for Humanity house-building summer blitz in impoverished Appalachia.[24]

In Atlanta in late February, Carter attended a conference on his presidency staged by scholars from across the country at the Carter Center. At one session, he and Rosalynn answered questions posed by scholars instead of journalists. Obviously enjoying themselves, the Carters shied away from nothing. When asked if he thought his emphasis on human rights abuses in the Soviet Union helped lead to its collapse in 1991, Carter jumped momentarily from his chair, then thought that maybe it had helped, although the collapse was mostly from within. Since Deng Xiaoping, who had helped him engineer the normalization of relations with China, had just died, one scholar asked for Carter's impression of the Chinese leader. With characteristic hyperbole, Carter remembered him as a "great Leader" despite a poor record on human rights. Rosalynn interrupted to comment that Deng really wasn't that great. Grinning broadly as he submitted to Rosalynn's higher authority, Jimmy corrected himself with a notation that China still had a long way to go. When asked what he thought about the numerous accounts of his presidency, he replied, seriously, that he thought he was doing a pretty good job of telling his own story.[25]

The Carters' work went on, driven in part by the controversial quest for peace in the Middle East. At Carter's invitation, Yasser Arafat came to Plains in early March to give a speech at Carter's old high school. In his speech, Arafat praised Carter profusely and promised to follow in his footsteps to bring peace to the Middle East and justice for the Palestinians. Carter, who agreed with his visitor, criticized Israel's newly elected prime minister Benjamin Netanyahu for moving the peace process backward.[26]

That year, Rosalynn turned seventy, which was Gannett's mandatory retirement age. She had few regrets about leaving the board of the news giant, as she had a heavy work load otherwise, she said. A strike at Gannett's Detroit News and Knight-Ridder's Detroit Free Press made her uncomfortable, for labor union officials asked her to support the strikers. She declined to take sides and was relieved to vacate the board position she had held since 1983.[27]

The Carters returned to Sudan to review the progress they were making to eradicate guinea worm disease, staged a Latin American peace conference in Atlanta, and built Habitat houses in Kentucky. Carter gave the commencement address at Duke University to his grandson Jason's graduating class. Jason appeared to be interested in a career similar to that of his grandfather, but first he headed for a stint in the Peace Corps. Carter, for his part, joined former President George H. W. Bush and President Bill Clinton to clean up slums in Philadelphia, and to demonstrate presidential unity in the United States' battle against poverty.[28]

In July, the Carters began another long trip around the world to support democracy in an African country and in China. China presented a vast, region for the Carters to work in to promote peace and democracy. On their way there, they stopped in Monrovia to monitor an election that attracted a large peaceful turnout. Although a former warlord won, Carter was content because he believed that the Liberian election had been democratic and honest. In Beijing, they met Senator Sam Nunn, Carter's Democratic friend from Georgia, and Mike Oksenberg, the Clinton administration's expert on China. It was the Carters' fifth trip there, but this time they were motivated by a new hope and urgency. With the approval of the Clinton administration they wanted to learn about current affairs, discuss Chinese domination of Tibet, discover if there was religious freedom in China, and ascertain Chinese attitudes toward both Koreas.

What excited Jimmy and Rosalynn most, however, was the opportunity to explore the possibilities for an expanded relationship for the Carter Center in village elections. The center would offer help in those elections, some of which had been democratic, and Carter hoped that from that grassroots level he might transform China into a democratic nation. Chinese Communist Party leaders, however, put a stop to the Center's involvement in Chinese elections. After returning to Atlanta, he reported to the US State department on his trip and published articles urging Americans not to demonize China, but to try to understand that country and share cultural exchanges with it.[29]

China was a promising frontier for the Carter Center, but Africa was the continent where they had worked for more than a decade. On July 25 Jimmy and Rosalynn returned there to attend the International Conference on Guinea Worm in Addis Ababa, Ethiopia, joining agronomist Norman Borlaug and representatives from fourteen African countries to assess their Global 2000 program in Ethiopia and eleven other nations. Three years earlier they had viewed test plots that accounted for progress in agriculture, health, and economics. This trip was cut short, however. On their first night Jimmy awakened with a severe pain in his left knee, which could not be treated successfully in Ethiopia. After Carter returned to Atlanta, doctors at the Emory University Hospital speculated that the malady had been caused by an insect bite, treated it with antibiotics, and soon gave Jimmy a clean bill of health.[30]

Although now over seventy, Jimmy remained healthy and busy. For the remainder of the year, he and Rosalynn enjoyed giving and receiving honors related to their pet interests in mental health and human rights. At a twenty-year reunion of the Carter-Mondale crew at Manuel's Tavern near the Carter Center, Robert Strauss announced what everyone already knew: "Jimmy Carter is a different sort of animal than most," for it would never have occurred to him to install a taping system in the White House or to do anything short of looking ahead to the next task. Carter jokingly advised his old friends to reminisce only about the good times and not to mention the 1980 election.[31]

Rosalynn accepted a large grant from the Robert Wood Johnson Foundation of Princeton University to promote her work for caregivers at the Rosalynn Carter Institute. The National Mental Health Association honored her for her work to get the Mental Health Systems Act of 1980 passed and for her continuing work as chair of the Carter Center's Mental Health Task Force. She presented her own award to Ronald Sunderland in September, who had established a team to care for AIDS victims.[32]

The Carters traveled to College Station, Texas, to participate in the dedication of the George H. W. Bush Presidential Library.[33] The huge gathering in a cow pasture in front of the splendid new Bush Library included four presidents and six first ladies, as well as members of presidential families going as far back as Eisenhower. Lady Bird Johnson represented her late husband, and Nancy Reagan represented her husband Ronald, who was too ill with Alzheimer's disease to attend. Carter praised Bush profusely, joked about himself, and even poked fun at Rosalynn for keeping track of his royalties.

Rosalynn was seated next to Nancy Reagan when Nancy began her speech with a not-so-subtle cut at the Carters. Rosalynn stared ahead carefully showing no emotion. "When Ronnie recaptured the spirit of America," she said, implying that the Carters had lost it, the numerous Democrats on the stage and in the audience could not have missed the stinging barb.[34]

The Carters went home from Texas and attended a Bob Dylan concert in Atlanta. They had loved Dylan since their governor's years when they had invited him to visit the family at the mansion. Then they jetted off to Jamaica, where they observed what Jimmy thought was a fair election. In a continuing debate with the Southern Baptist Convention, which was scheduled to meet in Salt Lake City in early December, Carter defended the Mormons as being part of the Christian community, a status that the Baptists vigorously denied. They ended the year with their typical Christmas family celebrations. Carter had announced in October that he would write a novel about the American Revolution, and in between trips he often disappeared into his home office to work on it.[35]

Looking back on his genealogy, Carter invited all who considered themselves descendants of Wiley Carter to help him celebrate the two-hundredth anniversary of his great-great grandfather's birth. Some 800 responded, and they all called Jimmy cousin, even though most had never met him. "A lot of them were Republicans, unfortunately," Carter joked. He told about one ancestor in particular who had married a second time after his first wife had died. When asked where he wanted to be buried, he said between the wives but "tilted toward the second one."[36]

Thinking of his family genealogy and his own aging, Carter wrote his fourteenth book, *The Virtues of Aging*, which was published the following October. The book offered advice on how to make aging a positive experience. In late 1997, he published *Sources of Strength*, another compilation of his Sunday School lessons and another best seller.[37] Through the retelling of his story, Carter came to terms with his life and with his loss of the presidency in 1980. Remembering Mr. Earl became an increasingly noticeable theme in his writings. He discovered that he was like his father—committed to helping those in need, but also stern, demanding, and unforgiving of imperfection in those close to him or who served him. As it is for many authors, writing for Carter is a cathartic experience.[38]

On a popular night talk show, Carter said that "I don't fear death," but "I want to live as long as I can." There were constant reminders that death was inevitable. His "Cousin Beedie," Hugh Carter, died that year, a great personal loss to Jimmy. He joined President Clinton and former Presidents Ford and Bush to attend the Muslim rites for King Hussein of Jordan. In an interview at the Carter Center, Jimmy said that he expected Rosalynn to survive him and to continue to operate the Carter Center. She evaded the issue, claiming that "Jimmy was a little bit ahead of his time," and said that now that they were in their seventies, she "just want[ed] to stay home more."[39]

Staying home was not on their immediate agenda, nor was the possibility of staying out of contemporary politics. At the beginning of 1998, President Clinton was publicly accused of an improper sexual relationship with Monica Lewinsky, a White House intern, and of lying under oath. The House of Representatives eventually voted for impeachment proceedings, and Carter, like other former presidents, was pressed for comment. He was "deeply embarrassed" by the Lewinsky affair, he said, but he did not think Clinton would resign or be impeached. He and former President Ford agreed that Clinton should be censured, a stand that annoyed Clinton, but such censure was not likely to happen either. Clinton was not convicted, and Carter was relieved to be able to move on to other topics.[40]

A few months after news of the Lewinsky affair broke, Congress announced that the navy would build another nuclear powered submarine and name her for Carter. While holding up a model of the *Seawolf*-class vessel, Carter declared, "I don't see anything incompatible between serving in the military forces of the United States and preserving peace on earth." Referring to the recent renaming of National Airport in Washington as Ronald Reagan National Airport, he quipped that "If I had a choice between a submarine and an airport, I would choose a submarine."

The 353-foot submarine *Jimmy Carter*, SNN 23, was soon under construction. It was decided, too, that when she was launched, Rosalynn would christen her. Admiral Jay L. Johnson, chief of naval operations, described the vessel as "the fastest, quietest, most heavily armed and most technologically advanced submarine in the world." Reflecting Carter's claim, he said she would send a "stealthy and powerful message to those who might disturb the peace."[41]

In 1999, while the submarine was still being built, Jimmy and Rosalynn again traveled the world to promote peace and to fight disease. In Nigeria in February, they helped to monitor elections that Jimmy hoped would restore democracy in that country. Nigeria's large oil reserves were of great interest to Western observers, and those who were touched by humane issues deplored the extensive poverty in that country. To Jimmy's relief, retired

General Olusegun Obasanjo, who had been imprisoned by the military dictator, emerged victorious as the first president of the new Fourth Nigerian Republic.[42]

Three months later, Jimmy and Rosalynn observed elections in Indonesia, where Carter declared that the world wanted free elections. He thought Election Day was "a festival of democracy" and happily declared that those elections were free.[43]

Despite Carter's poor relationship with President Clinton, he and Rosalynn had become so well-known for their work that Clinton likely felt pressured to award them the Presidential Medal of Freedom, the highest honor the president could give to those who had served the country and their profession with extraordinary success. Rather than the typical White House ceremony, Clinton went to the Carter Center to give them the award. At the ceremony, Clinton declared that Jimmy and Rosalynn Carter "have done more good things for more people in more places than any other couple on the face of the earth." His words rang true and sincere as he hung the medals around their necks. After citing a long litany of what each individually and both as a couple had accomplished during and after the Carter presidency, Clinton expressed admiration for their extraordinary partnership. They had "remained strong for more than fifty years," he said, and many people viewed their partnership as a journey "of love and faith." Referring to Carter's quotation of Scripture in his 1977 inaugural address, Clinton continued: "By doing justice, by loving mercy, by walking humbly with their God, Jimmy and Rosalynn Carter are still living their faith," and "it will be hard for any future historian to chronicle all the good work they have done."[44] As Clinton walked away, a Reuters photographer captured his expression that was somehow both a smile and a frown.[45]

Overcome with emotion, Carter claimed to be "almost speechless." He talked about himself, praised Clinton, and said that he and Rosalynn hoped that Bill and Hillary would have a good life themselves when they left the White House. Then turning to Rosalynn, Jimmy said: "it's now my pleasure to introduce someone whom I love and respect and cherish, and honor: my wife, Rosalynn." She responded with thanks and a brief explanation that they had always done the things they "wanted to do and the things that we enjoyed doing." She thanked the American people and their many friends for giving them the opportunity, and Jimmy wrapped it up by saying that the occasion was "one of the most beautiful events of my life."[46]

Jimmy and Rosalynn celebrated his seventy-fifth birthday on October 1, 1999, at a black tie affair in the Rylander Theater in Americus, where the highlight was the singing of the Naval Hymn by the Naval Academy Glee Club, and Carter cut a birthday cake large enough to serve the crowd of 1,000. Following the celebration, Carter traveled around the country autographing copies of *Living Faith*, *The Virtues of Aging*, and *Sources of Strength*.

Still energetic at seventy-five, Carter went to Europe to raise money for the Carter Center and to Africa to monitor elections. With guinea worm disease virtually conquered, he announced that his center would combat trachoma, a disease that had blinded six million people in Mali alone. Grants from the Lions Clubs International Foundation and the Conrad N. Hilton Foundation would help the Carter Center, he said, expand treatment and prevention of the disease to more African and Latin American nations. Spread by flies, the malady could be controlled with improved sanitation conditions.[47]

Unable, or unwilling, to avoid contemporary politics, Carter anxiously awaited the end of 1999, when the United States was to turn the Panama Canal over to Panama. Asked by former Congressman David Bowen, who had supported the controversial treaties, when the ceremony would take place, Carter replied that the "Clinton White House is treating this as a hot potato—a potentially negative issue." He did not know if he would be invited, or even if a ceremony would take place.[48]

Even Secretary of State Madeleine Albright found something more pressing to do than to go to Panama. Clinton, who had no intention of going, asked Carter to head the delegation, which thrilled him and Rosalynn, but also revived criticism of the former president, who still often was accused of "giving away our canal." In Panama City, the people and politicians gave Carter an enthusiastic welcome. Some referred to him as "Uncle Jimmy," and others talked about erecting his statue in a public square. At the ceremony in Panama in mid-December, Carter happily told the Panamanians, "It is yours."[49]

During the course of the new year, Jimmy and Rosalynn observed elections and defended their Christian faith. They went to Guyana, Venezuela, Mexico, Peru, and Bangladesh to observe democratic elections. Carter thought that his religious beliefs were compatible with his commitment to peace, basic human rights, and protecting the environment. His and Rosalynn's faith helped them accept the death of her mother, Miss Allie, at age ninety-four, but that loss could not help but make them aware of how much time had passed since she had cheered them through the election of 1976.[50]

Although the Carters remained steadfast in their belief in the Biblical story of the life, death, and resurrection of Jesus and his mission as the Prince of Peace, they finally decided to make a formal break with the Southern Baptist Convention. At its annual convention, the members had decided that women could not be ordained. In his withdrawal letter to the group meeting in Corpus Christi, Texas, Carter wrote that, after sixty-five years, "I can no longer be associated with the Southern Baptist Convention." He and Rosalynn, as well as their fellow church members, he continued, had "been trying to identify other traditional Baptists who share such beliefs as separation of church and state, servanthood of pastors, priesthood of believers, a free religious press, and equality of women."[51] They had already identified with the more moderate Cooperative Baptist Fellowship.[52]

Reviewing his youth in Archery, Carter wrote what became his magnum opus. *An Hour Before Daylight: Memories of a Rural Boyhood* is Carter's personal account of life on his boyhood farm during the hour before sunrise, as well as an intimate portrait of life in the South during the last years of the Jim Crow era. As a presidential memoir and an unusually well written and accurate portrayal of an important era in US history, the book was a masterpiece, and Simon and Schuster paid him $2 million for it.[53]

Quickly rising and remaining at number one on the *New York Times* best seller list for several months in 2000, *An Hour Before Daylight* was an open window to the heart and soul of its author. It revealed an intimate self-portrait of Carter, the writer, memoirist, historian, humanist, politician, and especially son. The title referred to the bell that Jack Clark rang an hour before daylight to summon everyone, white and black, to work. It was also the story of the waning days of the Jim Crow era in the South before the awakening of the region and the nation to a new era in racial justice. Furthermore, it documented the years before Carter left for the Naval Academy and the new experiences that eventually led him to the White House and a radical awakening from the social structure of his childhood.

Carter realized that, except for his parents, the people who influenced him most were Black playmates, neighbors, and nannies. As a child he was unaware of the indignities heaped upon Bishop Johnson and other African Americans in Archery, but in retrospect he compared injustices, racial or otherwise, in the United States as well as in emerging nations to the society of his childhood. Despite his own extraordinary attachment to the land, he was not sad if his children or grandchildren would not take it over, because "after all, the land belonged to the Indians before to us."[54]

The person who looms largest in the book, as throughout Carter's life, is Mr. Earl. A strict Baptist who required Jimmy to attend church, put a penny in the collection plate, read, and pray, Earl was human enough to smoke cigarettes, sip bourbon, and possibly have a fling with a young widow. He demanded that his son "Hot" not smoke and impressed upon him the importance of punctuality, tolerance, and financial tightness. Perfection and success were not rewarded because they were expected, but failure would instantly be punished.[55]

Joan Ryan, the reviewer for the *San Francisco Chronicle*, stated it best with the title of her review: "A light Passes, Father to Son." When Carter "starts talking about his father . . . suddenly this 76-year-old man, one of the most admired men in the world, is a boy in Georgia again," she wrote. "Carter's story becomes the most universal and most intimate of stories: the story of fathers and sons." He wondered why the father who "taught him to work hard and love the land" did not want him to stay home in Plains and take over the farm from him.[56]

Jimmy did come back to Plains, take over the farm and, with Rosalynn, use it to relaunch himself many times into the world. Jimmy embraced his father's legacy and passed it to his sons. Referring to his volume of poems, *Always a Reckoning and Other Poems*, he explained that "it wasn't until I bared my inner thoughts in poetry that I was able to face the complicated relationship that I had with my father—and to realize that how similar my attitude was toward my own sons."[57]

FORTY ONE

The Nobel Prize

Carter's foray into sentimentality was short-lived. Still disillusioned with President Clinton's foreign policy, he believed that the administration had not pressured Israel into upholding its agreements in the Camp David Accords. On national television, Carter bemoaned the fact that he could do no more than pray for a resolution to the problems in the Middle East. His displeasure with Clinton melded into outrage when the outgoing president granted a large number of pardons on his last day in office. Carter accused Clinton of selling pardons, disgraceful behavior that was unsuitable for the presidency.[1]

Clinton did redeem himself somewhat in the eyes of the Carters when he pardoned Patty Hearst before he left office. Hearst had been kidnapped in the 1970s by a domestic terrorist group who called themselves the Symbionese Liberation Army, participated in an armed bank robbery, and sentenced to prison. Early in 1979, President Carter had commuted her sentence to time served, and later he had asked Clinton to pardon her. Since Clinton had not done it, Carter asked him again after the Medal of Freedom Ceremony. When Clinton again did not respond, Rosalynn wrote to him, reminding him that since Patty's parole she had married, reared a family, and lived an exemplary life. "For her sake," Rosalynn pleaded, "and especially for the sake of her daughters, I hope you can find it in your heart to pardon her." Clinton found it in his heart and listed her name among the 140 whom he pardoned on his last day in office.[2]

Carter's hope to have another Democrat, and one more acceptable to him and Rosalynn, in the White House was dashed when the presidential election of 2000 was finally resolved. The Democratic candidate Vice President Al Gore won a majority of popular votes but victory in the all-important Electoral College depended on the outcome in Florida, where the extreme closeness of the tally and questions about its accuracy led to a tedious and highly controversial recount in a state where Republican candidate George W. Bush's brother Jeb was governor. Carter urged patience while the recount took place in Florida, but his hopes were dashed when, after the recount, the Supreme Court took up the case and declared George W. Bush to be the winner. Carter maintained that Gore had won and that the Florida recount and the Supreme Court decision were politically motivated miscarriages of justice. "We have a long way to go," he complained, "in meeting the standards of most democracies on earth."[3]

From the beginning of George W. Bush's presidency, Carter severely criticized the "bogus" president's foreign and domestic policies. He deplored Bush's proposals to reduce the number of US peacekeepers on the long Egyptian-Israeli border and to open the Alaska National Wildlife Reserve to drilling for oil. Carter and former President Jerry Ford recommended thirteen ways to reform national elections, but when Carter presented their proposals, Bush received them with a stony noncommittal response. Carter, not trusting Bush to do so, reminded Israel of its obligation to withdraw from the Gaza Strip and the West Bank, but Israel also ignored him.[4]

The Virginia Military Institution's award of the Jonathan Daniels medal for public service did not improve Carter's mood.[5] During a four-day visit to China with Rosalynn in early September 2001, Carter again unabashedly criticized Bush's election. Addressing an international symposium on rural China that was held in Beijing, he noted that he came there after an unpleasant election in the United States "in which no one will ever know who received the most votes." He did not, he said, expect Bush to take any action based upon the suggestions for electoral reform that he and Ford had submitted to him.

Getting off the topic of Bush, he reviewed his own long relationship with China and a recent visit that he and Rosalynn had made there. He was proud that the Carter Center had encouraged the use of secret ballots and citizens' nominations in 30,000 of China's 930,000 villages. A small example, Carter admitted, but he found the fact that both Chinese and foreign observers attended his talk indicated a "deep interest in the future of the direct elections in the country." From that meager beginning he hoped the process would move to a higher level, but that "is a decision to be made in China," he concluded.[6]

Jimmy and Rosalynn pressed China to expand its twenty-year experiment with village elections, and during their visit, they observed one in Jiangsu Province, near Shanghai. Despite irregularities, interference by party officials, and a less free process than they wanted, they hoped village elections would be the first step toward democracy in China. Those who were less hopeful believed that the Communist Party allowed the relatively small number of low-level elections only to ease tensions in the countryside. Although only one party was represented at the election the Carters observed, Jimmy declared it "a small step forward for democracy."[7]

Shortly after Jimmy and Rosalynn returned to the United States, their lives, like the lives of countless others around the world, were jolted by the Islamic terrorist attacks on New York City and Washington, DC. On September 11, 2001, the terrorists flew two of their hijacked passenger planes into the twin towers of New York's World Trade Center, destroying them and killing about 3,000 people. They also attacked the Pentagon in the nation's capital, causing 125 casualties but failing to destroy the building. In the immediate confusion, no one knew how many more attacks were planned or where they might occur. A fourth plane, whose passengers overpowered the hijackers and took charge of it, crashed into a field in Pennsylvania, killing everyone on board.

The Carters were en route from Plains to the Carter Center when they heard the news. Since they were traveling by road, the Secret Service decided it would be safest to speed them on to their destination. Massive trucks and additional guards quickly surrounded the complex, turning it into a well-guarded fortress. Inside, Jimmy and Rosalynn, along with some journalists who had joined them, watched the incredible sights on television. There was no hysteria, according to Rosalynn, but there were tears as they watched the smoke rising over New York City, the crumbling towers, and hundreds of people running and screaming in the streets. Jimmy called the center's staff together to try to comfort and reassure them. He said that despite this terrible tragedy, the country was strong; it had been through difficult situations in the past and had always overcome them, as it would overcome this deadly challenge.[8]

Remembering his own crisis when terrorists overran the US Embassy in Tehran and took dozens of US diplomats hostage, Carter quickly declared his sympathy for President Bush. Carter thought the United States must take "punitive action," but he urged the country not to proceed with the same kind of hatred that had motivated the terrorists. He strongly believed, he said, "our nation will survive, as it always has," and he promised to put past differences between himself and Bush aside and "support him as he makes decisions as difficult as any President has ever faced."[9]

Like most Americans after 9/11, the Carters tried to find comfort in their routines. He brought out a book in time for the Christmas trade entitled *Christmas in Plains: Memories*. Among the usual reminiscences, he told a story reinforcing the book's theme of his close, life-defining relationship with his father: when he was ten and Mr. Earl asked him to go hunt for a Christmas tree, he "almost fainted with excitement."[10]

Rosalynn addressed the National Press Club in Washington in early December. She reminded the audience that her husband often said that "politics is the art of self-delusion." Once the laughter subsided she shared her perspectives of her and Jimmy's accomplishments in the White House, emphasizing her tireless work for a viable mental health bill. She did not want the First Lady to be a paid position, she said, because "if you were paid you would have to have a job description, and I liked being able to do what I wanted to do." After the laughter diminished, she went home for Christmas in Plains.[11] The Carter family was little different from any other large family with its marriages, divorces, deaths, births, scandals, successes, and failures. During the winter months of 2002, Jimmy and Rosalynn managed their personal resources, tended to personal health, read, wrote, relaxed, traveled, and hosted conferences.[12]

In March, when spring arrived in South Georgia, Jimmy and Rosalynn again departed for Sudan and South Africa. The cease fire that Carter had brokered in 1995 in the Sudanese civil war had dissolved, making it impossible once again to get personnel and supplies in place to fight guinea worm disease. Sudan still had 45,849 cases of the disease, whereas Nigeria had only 5,344, and Ethiopia only ten. Despite the lack of progress in Sudan, Juba University in Khartoum awarded Carter an honorary degree.[13]

While on the continent, the Carters attended an African National Congress meeting in South Africa. Many of the African attendees responded coldly when he urged aggressive steps to stop the spread of AIDS. Local officials, however, blasted him for trying to turn South Africa's people into guinea pigs for the US pharmaceutical industry. President Thabo Mbeki himself thought the medicine for AIDS was poisonous. Carter would not give up and planned to return to South Africa the next month with reinforcements.[14]

Jimmy and Rosalynn returned to Africa in April accompanied by Bill Gates, Senior, and his wife Mimi. Gates, the father of Microsoft founder Bill Gates, sponsored the trip and planned to fund some of Carter's programs. The couples spent two days each in South Africa and Nigeria, with shorter visits to Namibia, Angola, and Kenya, where they focused on stopping the spread of AIDS. At one refueling stop, Gates reckoned that the trip was a "detour to Hell." They visited a clinic operated by a Japanese woman who treated AIDS victims. Carter compared her to Mother Teresa, and Gates said to let him know how much money she needed. In Africa, according to Gates, Carter was no longer the man who had been "considered a prude as President, sometimes mocked for talking like a preacher and once pilloried for acknowledging to an interviewer that he may have lusted in his heart."

Trying to draw on religion to help Nigerians prevent AIDS transmission, Carter, according to Gates, "assured Nigerian Christians that Jesus Christ would have wanted adulterers to use condoms." Carter delivered the Sunday morning sermon where President Obasanjo invited Abuja citizens to worship. He talked about Christ and sex. After the sermon, the church musicians and choir presented "a snappy Bob Marley reggae," and the congregation began to dance. Gates added that "Christianity would be more successful in the United States if there were more toe-tapping, hip-swinging music." Obasanjo himself led "a stately bump and grind up the aisle toward the exit. Rosalynn Carter follow[ed] behind, her hips gently swaying."[15]

In an unexpected turn of events, Cuban dictator Fidel Castro, who had seen Carter at the funeral of Canadian prime minister Pierre Trudeau, had asked him to come to Cuba. Castro hoped to convince Carter of "the moral, ethical, ideological, political and human fortitude of our revolution." Carter did not agree with the Cuban dictator, but he saw the opportunity to support Cuba's peaceful opposition leaders who hoped for a referendum that would return basic freedoms to Cuba. No sitting or former president had gone to Cuba since the Cuban Revolution of 1953. Some Americans, including former President Clinton, thought Castro had duped Carter before with the Mariel boatlift, and the Cuban dictator might be planning something underhanded again.[16]

Jimmy and Rosalynn would travel to Cuba as co-chairs of the Carter Center. They chose Robert Pastor, who had long advised them about Latin American affairs, to accompany them; Chip Carter was to join them, but notably the chief executive officer for Bell South Telecommunications and the chair of Fuqua Companies completed the entourage. The fame and success of Jimmy and Rosalynn as citizen diplomats for peace and human rights was balanced with expert advice from businessmen who might bridge the wide divide between Cuba and the United States.[17]

Carter, who some said liked to tilt at windmills, arrived in Havana with Rosalynn and the other members of their party by private jet in on May 13, 2002. They were there, he said in Spanish, "as friends of the people." They hoped to get to know citizens from all walks of life, and they avoided any indication that theirs was a political mission. Heavily guarded for their trip to the Santa Isabel Hotel, they rode in a Soviet-made limousine that had been a gift from Leonid Brezhnev to Castro. Castro gave them complete freedom to go wherever they wished and say anything they wanted to say. Carter opted to give a speech in Spanish at the University of Havana, broadcast live on television, where a welcoming band played both the US and Cuban national anthems. Carter praised Castro for his courage to try to change his country's relationship with the United States. He reviewed the history of Cuba, extended the hand of friendship, and offered a vision for the future. He envisioned a time when the two countries would be integrated in a democratic hemisphere with complete exchanges of cultural events, trade, and commitment to human rights.[18]

Carter contended that US public opinion agreed with him that the economic embargo should be lifted. President Bush did not agree. If Castro had tolerated Carter's discussions about human rights and cultural exchanges in the hope that the former president might influence the current one, he would soon be disappointed. Before leaving the island, Jimmy and Rosalynn attended a baseball game and talked about the things the people of both countries shared in common. Carter also met with Castro's political opponents and some religious leaders, but by the time he left for Atlanta, he was certain that Castro intended to keep complete control of Cuban politics and diplomacy.[19] Historic as Carter's visit was, it did not change anything; change would have to wait until another Democrat was elected in 2008. But Carter had done his best.

From Cuba, the Carters went to South Africa to spend a week with Habitat for Humanity building houses. After their return to the United States, Rosalynn went her own way. In June, she applauded the Supreme Court's ruling banning executions of people with intellectual disabilities. Unwilling to give up her battle against the death penalty, she declared at a Washington gathering that the death penalty was "a tragic violation of human rights." She noted that Blacks who may not have had a fair trial, mentally ill people, and sometimes children under age eighteen were executed. Speaking forcefully in her soft accent, she declared that "The United States is the only country in the industrialized world that still executes anyone, and executing children puts us in the company of Somalia—only Somalia."[20] The next month, at a World Congress on Mental Health in London, she remarked that the 9/11 terrorist attack the previous year proved that anyone could suffer from mental illness at any time.[21]

604 JIMMY AND ROSALYNN CARTER

Carter accepted an invitation from President Hugo Chavez to go to Venezuela to observe chaotic elections there. Anti-government forces were marching on the presidential palace, and Chavez hoped to legitimize his election and stop the violence. The anti-government forces did not trust Carter, whom they thought to be biased in favor of Chavez, and their leaders refused to talk with him. This unusual outcome left Carter with no choice but to leave the country with no talks scheduled between the opposing sides.[22]

Of much greater concern to Carter was the continuing quest for peace in the Middle East, now complicated by President George W. Bush's policies that Carter believed exacerbated the situation. Carter had already offered his own advice in an op-ed in the *New York Times*. He deplored Prime Minister Ariel Sharon's plan to establish settlements in occupied territories and to deny Palestinians a political existence. Nevertheless, he maintained that the situation was not hopeless. UN Resolution 242 still called for Israel to surrender the occupied territories, and the US government could bring about a solution. It should press for the right of displaced Palestinians to return to their homeland, he said, with fair compensation. He recommended that the United States cut off the $10 million aid per day to Israel as a way to stop it from building the settlements. Jewish Americans, other pro-Israel groups, and the Bush administration immediately condemned Carter for his suggestion.[23]

In September, Carter wrote a long critical opinion piece for the *Washington Post*, placing the need for "a just peace" in the context of changes taking place in Bush's America. Although Bush, Carter said, had some "quick and well-advised reactions" to the tragedy of September 11, 2001, many conservatives were using that event to release their pent-up ambitions "under the cover of the proclaimed war against terrorism." The United States was no longer respected, Carter charged. It had ignored abuses of nations that supported "our anti-terrorism effort" and had been misled about the presence of weapons of mass destruction in Iraq. He deplored the prospect of a unilateral war with Iraq, called for UN inspections of Iraqi weapons stockpiles and production facilities, and begged for the "well-founded American commitments to peace, justice, human rights, the environment and international cooperation" to prevail.[24] Carter was angry, revealing a controlled explosion of the famous Carter temper, but he was helpless to do more than write op-eds and get deeper and deeper into criticizing the sitting president.

Then, quite unexpectedly on the morning of October 11, 2002, in the middle of his growing foreign policy frustrations, Carter received news of a prestigious and long overdue recognition of his dogged pursuit of world peace, his unwavering defense of democracy and human rights, and his resolute pursuit of social justice. At 4:01 a.m., about one hour before Jimmy's normal rising time, the telephone rang in the Carters' modest ranch-style house at 205 Woodland Drive in Plains. Rosalynn at first thought it was one of the children or a hoaxer, but when she answered and realized the call was from Oslo, she asked Alejandro, the Secret Service man on duty, to wake Jimmy and tell him directly. The message was that Carter was to call Geir Lundestad, secretary of the Norwegian Nobel Committee, at 4:30 a.m. A native of Nicaragua, Alejandro was so excited that he spoke to Carter in Spanish, which, fortunately, Jimmy understood. He called Lundestad at the exact appointed time and learned that in thirty minutes, 11:00 a.m. Oslo time, the committee would announce that Carter had won the Nobel Peace Prize for 2002. In the announcement, the committee noted the long standing worthiness of its honoree and that Carter had been deserving since 1978, because his mediation of the Camp David Accords was "in itself a great enough achievement to qualify for the Nobel Peace Prize."[25]

Eight hours later, Carter held a news conference on Main Street in Plains. The award, he told his friends and neighbors, quoting from the citation, was for his "decades of untiring effort to find peaceful solutions to international conflicts, to advance democracy and human rights, and to promote economic and social development." Carter did not tell his audience that the succeeding paragraphs cited specifically his mediation of the Camp David Accords, the work of the Carter Center, and his unrelenting efforts to end the abuse of power by ruling governments.[26]

Carter joked that he did not mind the early call. While admitting that he was grateful for the award, he shifted much of the praise to the Carter Center, which he saw as a useful tool for his continuing work for peace and justice. The "Nobel Prize itself, you know," Carter said, "encourages people to think about peace and human rights." Becoming emotional, he pointed out that the committee did not mention Rosalynn. The prize, he emphasized, was not his alone; Rosalynn "has helped, questioned, cajoled and ultimately molded this country's thirty-ninth president."

Among the many immediate telephone congratulations that poured in, one came from President Bush. Jimmy and Rosalynn quickly contacted their children to tell them the good news.[27] The Naval Academy gave Carter a distinguished alumnus award, and his former Chief of Staff, Jack Watson, noted that Carter was "the only man in American history who used the United

States presidency as a stepping stone to greatness." The international response to Carter's winning the Peace Prize reflected the global nature of his reputation, which was better in Asia, Africa, and Latin America than in the United States. China refrained from congratulations, but Russia's Gorbachev hailed the committee's choice.[28]

Inevitably, some controversy arose about the timing of the Nobel committee's decision. Gunnar Berge, the chairman of the Nobel committee, said that the award "should be interpreted as a criticism of the line that the current administration has taken."[29] Critics argued that the prize was not so much for Carter as it was a condemnation of Bush. In Carter's defense, journalist Elizabeth Kurylo, who had followed Carter for a decade or more, penned an editorial in the *Atlanta Journal and Constitution*, in which she described him as "stubborn, tenacious, at times impatient" in his relentless pursuit of democracy, peace, and human rights. He was willing to risk his reputation and risk failing, she wrote, for in his mind real failure would be if he did not try. He thought he was doing God's work. "Say what you will about Jimmy Carter, he is serious about his work and would keep doing it even if the secret club in Oslo had never seen fit to honor him."[30]

On Sunday morning, two days after the Nobel prize news, Carter, having chosen to stay in Plains rather than go to Atlanta, walked into the sanctuary of the Maranatha Baptist Church, and the members of the congregation gave him a standing ovation. Although the minister had approved it in advance, Jimmy was embarrassed. "No, no, no, no applause in the church," he instructed them. He then delivered a forty-minute Sunday School lesson about social justice and the growing chasm between the rich and the poor. He would leave soon, Carter said, to monitor an election in Jamaica and would take the same message to the voters there.[31]

Upon the arrival of the Carter Center delegation in Kingston, where they joined fifty-nine other international observers, Carter expressed disgust with Jamaica's "garrison politics" that defied the basic tenets of democracy and tainted the entire country's image. Epithets and gunfire occasionally could be heard in the streets prior to the election. The voters had to decide on the tight contest between Prime Minister P. J. Patterson of the People's National Party and former Prime Minister Edward Seaga of the Jamaica Labor Party. On Tuesday, October 15, the day before Election Day, Jimmy and Rosalynn arose early to go to the mountains and bird watch before the others arose for breakfast. Then they participated in day-long meetings with leaders of both parties before adjourning to a reception at the home of US Ambassador Sue McCourt Cobb, followed by a late dinner at a downtown hotel.

On Election Day, Jimmy and his entourage got an early start, traveling in a small motorcade that would visit forty polling places. Casually dressed in scuffed-up jogging shoes, khaki trousers, and a white T-shirt that identified him as an "International Observer," he was hardly recognizable as the former president of the United States. At every opportunity he reminded voters that they could restore their faith in democracy and put an end to the violence that so often wracked their country. At the end of the day, Prime Minister P. J. Patterson was reelected for a fourth consecutive term, and Carter, who thought the outcome of the election represented the will of the people, recommended to him a tough law-and-order agenda that they both hoped would end the crime and chaos that had dogged the campaign.[32]

Shortly after his return to Atlanta, Carter dutifully sent President Bush a detailed report on the Jamaican election, but Bush did not respond. On the day of the election, Carter had told an Australian reporter that Bush was being insensitive to human rights, that he had abandoned "the pursuit of Middle East peace," and that he was "treating the Palestinians unfairly by being 'in bed' with Israel."[33] The more Carter criticized Bush publicly, the more Bush ignored him, and the tensions between the two became more intense as Carter repeatedly said that Bush was not the legitimately elected president.

Although the Nobel award ceremony in Oslo would not occur until early December, Carter began writing his Nobel lecture in late October. He gave an outline of what he wanted to say to former speech writers Rick Hertzberg and Nesmith Achsah, as well as his assistant Steve Hochman. "I've striven to exalt our nation while outlining some disagreements with present (and transient?) policies," he wrote. He advised them that he wanted his main points to be the Middle East and the work of the Carter Center.[34]

Others whose help Carter requested included Gerald Rafshoon, former White House communications director, who advised him: "Don't be afraid to let the preacher in you overtake the engineer . . . speak from your heart with emotion . . . add some poetry and elegance." Steve Hochman corrected errors, questioned sources, and asked specifically that he omit interpretations of the Samaritans that would offend Jewish listeners. Other old colleagues and friends, including his long-time Latin American and Caribbean affairs advisor Bob Pastor, sent recommendations through Steve.[35]

As always, Jimmy valued Rosalynn's opinion above all others. On one draft she wrote that he should expand on the disparity between the rich and poor as the root causes of the world's unresolved problems. The next day, October 31, he sent her a revised draft. He added: "I'd like your suggestions, and your love, affection, and approbation! Jimmy." Rosalynn replied: "Very good! I have no suggestions." Nevertheless, she made a good many marks on a later draft.[36]

In every interview and every draft of the proposed Nobel speech, Jimmy said the prize was shared by Rosalynn, and he praised her work for the mentally ill. He and Rosalynn joined other Nobel winners at a reception hosted by President Bush at the White House. All three declined to talk about their conversation during a private meeting before the reception. During the brief reception in the Oval Office, Bush merely commented that Carter had spent "a lot of quality time here."[37] Their bitter disagreements about the Iraq War and other major policy issues remained unspoken for the occasion, at least in public.

Neither the tension between Carter and Bush, nor the controversy that in the eyes of some tarnished the prize, could detract from the glory of the ceremony in Oslo and the significance of being a Nobel Peace Prize laureate. Carter invited sixty people to attend as his guests. They included his children and grandchildren, Aunt Sissy, Hamilton Jordan, Stuart Eizenstat, Robert Pastor, William Chase of Emory, William Foege, and the staff of the Carter Center. He unhesitatingly picked Jessye Norman, the renowned African-American diva from Augusta, Georgia, and his country music friend Willie Nelson, among others, to be the musicians.

On December 10, 2002, Carter and his entourage assembled in Oslo City Hall. Jessye Norman sang "He's Got the Whole World in His Hands" right before Carter stepped up to receive the award. Berge mentioned only Carter's excellent qualifications for the award and made no veiled or direct reference to the current Bush administration. In his last sentence, however, he cast an unnecessary slur upon the Carter presidency: "Jimmy Carter will probably not go down in American history as the most effective president. But he is certainly the best ex-president the country ever had."[38] Refusing to allow that statement, which both he and Rosalynn loathed, to mar the occasion, Carter accepted the elaborately decorated Nobel certificate and the handsome gold peace medal inscribed "Pro pace et fraternitate gentium" (For peace and fraternity among peoples), then turned and handed them to Rosalynn. Jessye Norman sang "Then Shall the Eyes of the Blind Open" and "He Shall Feed

His Flock" from Handel's *Messiah*. Jimmy, in semi-formal dress, flashing his trademark smile, and appearing relaxed, went to the podium and delivered his lecture. After brief and proper salutations, he expressed his "deep sense of gratitude" to Rosalynn, his colleagues at the Carter Center, and all who sought to end "violence and suffering throughout the world."

In a passionate and well-rehearsed speech, Carter reviewed previous winners and made special reference to "two of my friends, Anwar Sadat and Yitzhak Rabin, who gave their lives for the cause of peace in the Middle East." He praised the work of the UN and at the Camp David summit and the Oslo meetings that attempted to get the Israelis, Egyptians, and Palestinians to endorse UN Resolution 242, the only rational plan for peace in the Middle East. Furthermore, he pleaded, the crisis in Iraq need not be solved by the ongoing US invasion, but by the UN, which could discuss whether the Iraqis had weapons of mass destruction. After announcing that he worshipped Jesus Christ, the Prince of Peace, he said that he was "convinced that Christians, Muslims, Buddhists, Hindus, Jews, and others can embrace each other in a common effort to alleviate human suffering and to espouse peace."

The growing chasm between the rich and the poor, he said, was the root cause of most of the world's evils, including starvation, war, and "unnecessary illnesses that range from Guinea worm to HIV/AIDS." War is always an evil, he concluded, but "We can choose to work together for peace. We can make these changes—and we must."[39]

The next day, Jimmy and Rosalynn were honored with a gala concert at the Oslo Spektrum. Willie Nelson performed for his old friend, and actors Jessica Lange and Anthony Hopkins emceed a tribute to the Carters. After the gala, Jimmy and Rosalynn returned to their rooms but later emerged on the balcony at the Grand Hotel in Oslo. Below was a choir, a parade, and protesters. Rosalynn glowed, resplendent in a purple wool suit. Beside her, Jimmy struggled to remain humble at the zenith of his quest for peace in the world.[40]

Back home in Atlanta on December 12, Jimmy went to his office, handed the Nobel medal over to an archivist to plan a display in the museum, released to a researcher the papers telling the story of how he had crafted his lecture, and went back to his usual work. He announced that $1 million of the $1.3 million prize would go to the Carter Center and the rest to the Rosalynn Carter Caregiving Institute.[41]

Carter was probably not surprised that the leaders of the Southern Baptist Convention paid little or no attention to his winning the Nobel Prize. They had also been silent when Martin Luther King, Jr., had won it. One of them wrote that "Carter is a prophet without honor" among the Southern Baptists. He thought that "King and Carter took Jesus too literally" for their fellow Baptists. Carter's break with the Southern Baptist Convention, as well as his and Rosalynn's stand for racial equality, made it inevitable that most of his former fellow churchmen would not celebrate or note the international honor and acclaim that had been bestowed on him.[42] Not mentioning the prize, Jimmy said that in "a hundred years or so, if people still remember my name," he hoped "they would associate" it with "peace and human rights."[43]

FORTY TWO

Tuned to the World

During the Christmas 2002 and New Year's holidays, Carter, remembering his father, told an interviewer for *Wine Report Magazine* that, "As a child, I helped my daddy make wine." Using local muscadine grapes, he made both red and white wines, producing about one hundred bottles every three years. On one occasion, to raise money for the Carter Center, he auctioned two of his bottles of wine at Crested Butte, Colorado, for the astronomical sum of $163,000. Most of the brew, however, he used for gifts or occasional personal consumption. "Rosalynn and I don't like to go out to celebrate New Year's Eve or her birthday or my birthday," he told one interviewer. "We tend to stay at home and almost invariably share a drink of wine or Champagne."[1]

Almost three weeks after celebrating the beginning of the New Year, Carter embarked upon a trip to Venezuela to fish and to mediate a violent dispute between Hugo Chavez's dictatorial regime and those who wanted a free election and a democratic form of government. Before going to Caracas, Carter stopped in the southern part of the country where he fished for the rare peacock bass in the Orinoco River. Although the Carter Center had been working in Venezuela for a decade, the future of peaceful, democratic elections remained in doubt because President Hugo Chavez was no democrat. Carter had left the country empty handed the previous year, but on January 20, 2003, he met with Chavez as well as his adversaries. Because Venezuela was a major oil exporter, an unstable government in Venezuela might impact the economy of the United States. Since Chavez had declared that he trusted Carter, Jimmy might have a chance to resolve the dilemma.

After talking with leaders of both sides, Carter presented them with a two-part peace plan: (1) an amendment to their constitution that would shorten the president's term from six to four years and thus initiate an election in about eighteen months; and (2) a binding referendum determining if Chavez should be removed from office for which both sides should wait until August 19, the halfway point of Chavez's presidential term. The workers went back to work, and Carter and his team returned to Atlanta, leaving the Venezuelans to debate his plan.[2]

The media and the public, however, were more interested in what Carter had to say about President Bush's war with Iraq than his efforts in Venezuela. Adamantly insisting that Bush and British prime minister Tony Blair had not made a convincing case, Carter feared that thousands of innocent people would die in an unnecessary war. A preemptive war, Carter wrote in an op-ed piece for the *New York Times* on March 9, was not justified. He believed that the majority of Europeans agreed with him that if Bush and Blair pursued such a war, it would be the United States that posed the "greatest danger to world peace."[3]

But Bush ignored Carter and led a coalition of nations that invaded Iraq on March 20, 2003, claiming that Iraq was a rogue nation harboring terrorists and possessing weapons of mass destruction. Iraqi casualties began to mount from the beginning of the invasion. After Saddam Hussein was captured on December 13, 2003, both Carter and former Vice President Al Gore urged the US government to exercise restraint in dealing with him; three years later he was executed by Iraqis who had taken control of the government. No weapons of mass destruction were found, and the war dragged on until December 18, 2011, long after Bush had left office.

The war might have been ended much sooner, according to comic actor John Irving Bloom, if Bush had asked Carter to resolved the conflict. Carter, Bloom wrote, was the "obvious man in the world to be in Baghdad," because he understood "raving lunatic political parties that all hate one another." Only Carter, Bloom contended, could convince them to "go to the ballot box," and "to shake hands when they do it." Carter did not care about oil deals, he wrote, but Bush did.[4]

Rosalynn also abhorred the Iraq war and said so, but she devoted her time to other humanitarian concerns. She led a symposium at the Carter Center on how to provide the best possible mental health benefits in the workplace. She wrote op-ed pieces calling for the states of Kentucky and Nevada to end juvenile executions. Since terrorist attacks were becoming more common, Rosalynn visited Capitol Hill to speak in favor of a bill that would require officials and first responders to be trained to help people deal with fears triggered by them. She joined Betty Bumpers, the former first lady of Arkansas, to found Every Child by Two, an organization they hoped would educate young parents on the importance of having their children vaccinated. By early summer she joined Jimmy to help build Habitat houses in LaGrange and Valdosta, Georgia, and Anniston, Alabama.[5]

Unfortunately, the Atlanta Project, begun in 1992, did not become another Habitat for Humanity; it never lived up to expectations. Some areas of the city did benefit from the efforts of a community to rebuild a block together, but in general, the project did not provide enough help to be effective in a large metropolis. Carter reluctantly admitted that the project was difficult and challenging, but he continued to maintain that it had had long-term positive consequences for Atlanta.[6]

Having done their best, Jimmy and Rosalynn took time for elaborate, adventuresome, and sometimes exotic vacations. In late June 2003, they flew to Colorado where they spent three days fishing in and floating down the Gunnison River in the Black Canyon of the Gunnison National Park. Because the water level was lower than usual, their outfitter Hank Hotze, his crew, and the Secret Service agents had an unusually challenging job protecting the flotilla of blue rafts that filled the river. When a twenty-four-inch trout struck Rosalynn's line, she gripped her rod and reel so tightly with both hands that she almost went into the water. Hotze quickly rowed their boat downriver after the speeding fish, but it got away. Hotze nevertheless was impressed by Rosalynn's angling skills. "Her cast is like Tiger Woods's golf swing," he said. "It's so effortless. She puts it wherever she wants. And when she corrects something, she corrects it with such touch. That woman is tuned to the world."[7] Elaborating on both Carters, Holtz said: "He's tough. That guy is a kick in the butt. So is she."[8]

For the remainder of the summer, the Carters conducted symposia at the Carter Center or traveled widely to give lectures or appear on television programs. In early September, they were in Tokyo where Jimmy delivered the Sixth U Thant Distinguished Lecture at the United Nations University. He discussed the role of the UN in making peace, preserving history, curing disease, ending hunger, and addressing poverty around the world. He particularly emphasized the Carter Center's agricultural development efforts in Africa, which had been supported since the 1980s by Yohei Sasakawa, president of the Nippon Foundation, who had helped to arrange the Carters' trip to Japan.[9]

While in Asia, on September 8 they stopped in Beijing where Chinese President Hu Jintao met them at the Great Hall of the People. After reviewing the relationship of the United States and China since Carter as president had normalized it, they expressed their shared desire to continue to be on good terms politically and culturally. The next day, in a speech at Beijing University, Carter reviewed his personal history with China from the time in 1949 when he had been a young submarine officer involved in naval exercises off the Chinese coast through his presidential conversations with Deng Xiaoping. He assured his audience that "Democracy is not a scary thing" and talked about the importance of Chinese village elections. Later the Carters met with local officials to discuss the Carter Center's effort to bring democracy to isolated villages.[10]

Jimmy and Rosalynn returned from Asia in time to proudly celebrate the twenty-fifth anniversary of the Camp David Accords on September 17. Good faith, courage, and strong support from the United States, he said in a National Public Radio broadcast, made the accords possible and durable; the fact that they had been negotiated and remained in effect a quarter-century later demonstrated that the problems in the Middle East could be solved. Carter cautioned, however, that the United States had to "take a balanced position between Israel and the Palestinians or other adversaries of Israel."[11] Israel, however, tested his resolve, especially when it constructed a fence between itself and the Palestinians. He fell back on his faith, saying that his prayer and his expectation was that the deadlock between the Israelis and Palestinians would be resolved in his lifetime.[12]

A week later, Carter published an op-ed piece in the *Washington* Post arguing that only the Israelis could choose to make permanent peace with the Palestinians. That same day, both he and Rosalynn spoke passionately at the Carter Center warning Americans that they were jeopardizing human rights by excessively emphasizing national security. Carter condemned Bush's Patriot Act which profiled Muslims as possible terrorists, and he rejected Bush's decision to hold suspected terrorists as prisoners in Guantanamo Bay without bringing them to trial.[13]

On November 11–12, 2003, Jimmy and Rosalynn hosted a conference on "Human Rights Defenders on the Frontlines of Freedom." The UN acting high commissioner on human rights, Bertrand Ramcharan, joined them along with human rights defenders from forty-one countries. In the opening address, Carter severely condemned what President Bush had done by going to war against Iraq, holding prisoners in chains and cages without allowing them a fair trial, and generally lowering the US standard for human rights. The conference culminated with the issuance of the Atlanta Declaration, in which the participants expressed their "alarm at the direction and implications of what has come to be known as the 'war against terrorism.'" There was little expectation, however, that the declaration's numerous recommendations for change would have any immediate impact on US foreign policy.[14]

Carter hoped to spread his views about war, human rights, and the necessity for international cooperation through the medium of his recently published first adult novel. In *The Hornet's Nest: A Novel of the Revolutionary War*, he attempted to capture the drama of the American Revolutionary War in the South. Better history than literature, according to some reviewers, the book tells the story of his Georgia ancestors and other real people from that era. The central characters—two brothers and their wives—were drawn into the conflict on the patriot side. They are surrounded by a cast of dozens, similar to a Russian novel, consisting of both decent people and cowards on both sides of the battle for independence. In no way reticent about sex, bodily functions, or the use of salty language, Carter describes how war involved and changed the lives of ordinary people. The book is also Carter's attempt to demonstrate in fiction how the goals and accomplishments of the American Revolution remained relevant to contemporary events. "It will be good for us to remember the original concept of our country that we have to relate intimately with other nations," he explained in an interview.[15]

Showing an unexpected entrepreneurial talent, Carter made a lot of money from his writing a well as his speeches, teaching, pension, and investments. He also knew how to raise millions of dollars to support the work of the Carter Center, making a point of getting to know the millionaires and billionaires, like Bill and Melinda Gates, who were inclined to support the kinds of charities he liked. The Carters often traveled on private jets provided by their benefactors, but they also bought tickets on commercial airlines and attempted to live like common people.

Refusing to give up hope for peace between Israel and the Palestinians, Carter and Conflict Resolution Program Director Matthew Hodes of the Carter Center attended the Geneva Initiative Public Commitment Event in Switzerland on December 1. It was an odd gathering of Palestinian and Swiss officials, as well as Israeli Foreign Minister Silvan Shalom. There Carter and other Nobel Peace laureates proposed the establishment of an independent Palestinian state, building upon a plan that representatives of Israel and the PLO had signed in Jordan on October 12. Carter addressed the Geneva assemblage with an urgent suggestion of how the Israelis and Palestinians might make peace with each other. He urged the Palestinians to forego violence against Israeli citizens in return for Israel's commitment to consider the Geneva initiative. Despite some desperate speeches by Arafat and other Arabs that they respected Judaism, Israel would have none of it.[16]

Numerous former presidents, prime ministers, and foreign ministers supported Carter's plan. They included Russia's Mikhail Gorbachev, South Africa's F. W. de Klerk, Mexico's Ernesto Zedillo, and US President. Bill Clinton. Israeli Prime Minister Ariel Sharon, however, furiously rejected it. Despite some positive analysts, the Jewish media in the United States and Israel ridiculed it; thousands of Palestinians living in the Gaza Strip rejected it too, for they would be geographically separated from the new Palestinian state on the West Bank.[17]

The defeat in Geneva did not dampen Carter's spirit or drive to pursue peace and democracy anyplace in the world. On December 17 he and Rosalynn, accompanied by some staff members from the Carter Center's Americas Program, traveled to Bolivia where they met with President Carlos Diego Mesa and other officials. Their purpose, Carter said, was to learn about the current political situation in Bolivia and how citizen participation in Bolivian elections might be improved. Since that country was becoming more democratic, he promised that the Carter Center would assist Bolivia in its "time for hope, for tolerance, and for a new spirit of cooperation to emerge."[18]

Several weeks following the family Christmas holiday, Carter traveled to Caracas to meet with the National Elections Council, which had already assembled there to determine if a recall election could be conducted properly. Despite strong anti-US sentiment, the supporters of Chavez welcomed Carter and believed that he would assure a fair recall election. In his soothing Georgia accent, Carter asked both sides to remain calm and to trust the National Elections Council. After three days, January 25–27, Carter returned to Atlanta, convinced that there would be a fair recall election later that year.[19]

From February 2 through 6, Jimmy and Rosalynn traveled with a Carter Center team to West Africa. Their visits to Togo, Mali, and Ghana were intended to draw the world's attention to the need to eradicate the remaining 1% of Guinea worm disease in the world. In Ghana they met with the World Health Organization's Dr. Lee Jong-wook and Deputy Executive Director of UNICEF Kul C. Gautam for a visit to the remote village of Dashei, where the horrific disease had ravaged many of its people. There, the Carter Center, the World Health Organization, and UNICEF presented a united front, urging people to help eradicate Guinea worm disease nationwide. The village chief, resplendent in blue robes, gave Jimmy and Rosalynn a grand welcome. After Carter departed, the chief said, "If, after my friend comes, I die, I know I will be entering heaven."[20] While in Ghana, the Carters also observed the progress their team had made in its fight against elephantiasis, schistosomiasis, and malnutrition.[21]

After returning to the United States, Jimmy held his annual winter weekend auction in Crested Butte, Colorado, on February 28 to raise money for the Carter Center. The two most important items were a self-portrait Carter had painted, believed to be the first such presidential effort, and another of his paintings entitled "Peace," showing him flanked by Begin and Sadat. From Crested Butte, Carter went to Snowbird, Utah, to auction more of his wares. "Peace" brought $125,000, and a baseball signed by both Carter and Castro brought $175,000. A photograph of five presidents and six first ladies, signed by all of them, sold for $72,500.[22]

Feeling good about the work of the Carter Center but unhappy about the Bush administration, Carter had delivered a Sunday sermon at St. Olaf College in Northfield, Minnesota, on February 22, in which he criticized the US government for not doing what it could to bring improved health, freedom, and peace to emerging countries of the world.[23] When marketing *The Hornet's Nest*, Carter continued to criticize the Iraq War. A lesson to be learned from his novel, Carter told one reporter, was that those who ordered troops into battle should know the horrors that warfare would inflict upon innocent people as well as upon the combatants. "Wars," he said, cause people "to degenerate from their natural inclination towards benevolence and kindness . . . into an intense hatred" that justifies "death or even sometimes murder."[24]

Turning from futile peacemaking to world health, both Carters accepted an invitation to the fifty-seventh Assembly of the World Health Organization in Geneva. Jimmy addressed his theme of the dichotomy between the rich and poor retarding healthcare for poor people and for poor nations. Rosalynn emphasized her argument that there should be no stigma attached to mental illness and that insurance companies should provide coverage for the mentally ill.[25]

In June, the month after they returned home, *USS Jimmy Carter SSN-23* was ready to be deployed. Preparing to christen the powerful new atomic submarine, Rosalyn studied films of previous christenings.[26] *USS Jimmy Carter* was the third and final *Seawolf*-type submarine. Nine years in the making, she cost $3.2 billion. Jimmy, Rosalynn, and other distinguished guests gathered in Groton, Connecticut, on June 5 where James R. Schlesinger, Carter's former secretary of energy, gave the keynote address. He described Carter "as a man of solid principles who would not cave to the pressures of political or public relations." Schlesinger said what Carter wanted him to say: "This powerful instrument of war will be part of a deterrent that maintains the peace that Jimmy Carter has devoted so much of his life to preserve." Both he and Carter thought the new submarine would be a symbol to terrorists that the United States maintained military domination of the world.[27]

After Jimmy introduced her, Rosalynn grabbed the neck of the Korbel bottle with both hands, aimed carefully, and shattered it against the *Jimmy Carter*. The crowd of 4,500 navy personnel, submarine workers, and family members, cheered. Some of them chuckled when they realized that Rosalynn had smashed the bottle with such force that enough champagne had splattered on Jimmy that he needed a towel to wipe it off.[28]

Back home in Plains the next day, a Sunday, the Carters learned of Ronald Reagan's death in California. When teaching his Sunday School class that morning, Carter said that it was a "sad day for the country." He noted also that he probably knew better than anyone "what a formidable communicator and campaigner" Reagan was, for it "was because of him that I was retired from my last job." The humor fell flat, and Carter became serious again about the passing of the ninety-three-year-old former president who had suffered with Alzheimer's disease for a decade. "I want to express my admiration for him and his wife and associate myself with the grief that America feels," he said. Jimmy and Rosalynn attended the state funeral in Washington, and at the interment in California, he must have been pleased when Ronald Reagan, Jr., remarked that it was Carter, not his father, who had successfully negotiated the release of the hostages from Iran.[29]

Later that month, Carter delivered the eulogy at young Mattie Stepanek's funeral. Carter had met Mattie through the Make-A-Wish Foundation, which granted a wish to terminally ill children. Mattie had suffered with muscular dystrophy for all thirteen years of his life, and he wrote several volumes of inspirational poems. His appearance on the Oprah Winfrey show and his friendship with Carter made him famous. Thousands attended his funeral in Silver Spring, Maryland, where they heard Jimmy talk about how the boy's faith "includes all human beings who believe in peace and justice and humility and service and compassion and love."[30]

Less than two weeks later, Jimmy and Rosalynn arrived, via Alaska, on the Kamchatka Peninsula in the far east of Russia for six days of fishing. Although they had hoped to keep the trip strictly private, both US and Russian journalists reported it. Extremely isolated as they wanted to be, they were 125 miles from the nearest house, though Jimmy was surprised to learn that they were closer to New York than Moscow. Joined by ten close friends, their Secret Service agents, and professional guides, they rafted down the Zhupanova River, which was known for its varieties of salmon, observing the abundant wildlife and testing their fishing skills.[31]

Ten days after leaving Kamchatka, Jimmy and Rosalynn traveled to Boston to attend the Democratic National Convention. Senator John Kerry had already won the nomination, and Carter had agreed to deliver a major speech. Entitled "We Need Leadership: Do Not Underestimate Us Americans," the speech angrily condemned Bush as much as it praised Kerry. "Our dominant international challenge is to restore the greatness of America—based on telling the truth, a commitment to peace, and respect for civil liberties at home and basic human rights around the world," he proclaimed. He lamented that the United States had alienated its allies and brought the Middle East peace process to a halt. What was needed, he concluded, was "leadership." A Boston newspaper criticized Carter for his "all-out vilification of George W. Bush." The *Kansas City Star* reported that "Jimmy Carter is mad as hell and told us he's not going to take it anymore."[32]

Carter's famous temper, as well as his demand for perfection, had distorted his relationship with his eldest son Jack. During the ten years that he and his wife Elizabeth lived in Bermuda, the Carters had not taken time to visit them, and both Jimmy and Rosalynn had been disappointed with the divorce.[33] When Jack announced that he and his wife Elizabeth were moving to Las Vegas from which he hoped to go into politics, his parents took a serious interest in him and his possible new career.

Carter's primary activities, however, involved the Carter Center. When Guyana's president Bharrat Jagdeo invited him to mediate a dispute between the government and its political opponents, Carter answered the call on August 11. Interior Minister Ronald Gajraj had been accused of operating a hit squad that, in the past two years, had murdered forty people. The controversy also had a racial overtone because about 30.1 % of the 770,000 people in Guyana were Blacks of African descent who supported the opposition, and the rest were of East Indian, Ameridian, or mixed descent who supported the government. Carter helped establish a three-member commission that would begin to discuss the issues in about three weeks.[34]

Only three days later, Carter headed the Carter Center's team that joined monitors from the OAS to observe the presidential recall referendum in neighboring Venezuela, "believed to be the first presidential recall vote in the world." President Hugo Chavez won a crushing victory to remain in power.

Although Carter disliked Chavez's tyrannical approach to government, he reported that the election was honest and that the losers should accept the results in good faith.[35]

Content with the settlement in Venezuela, Carter welcomed his friend Willie Nelson to Plains in early September to tape a television special and to give a free concert. About 3,000 people crowded into the town to hear Willie sing such favorites as "Whiskey River" and "Whiskey For My Men, Beer For My Horses." Willie and Jimmy agreed that they had a lot in common. "We both grew up in cotton fields and shoed horses," Carter said. Performing on the stage at Plains High School, which had been turned into a museum, Willie began to sing "Amazing Grace." Jimmy and Rosalynn joined him, one on either side of the country music star. Nelson quietly moved the microphone away as all of them burst into "Georgia on My Mind." The Country Music Television special, "Homecoming in Plains," was scheduled to air the following December.[36]

As much as the Carters loved their hometown, the outside world and its problems kept calling them away. Rosalynn left on September 13 for Auckland, New Zealand, to open the World Conference on Mental Health the next day. As honorary chair, she held the unusual status of being a high profile person who had worked more than thirty years to help people with mental illness. Presenters from the Netherlands, Australia, and the United States shared the results of their latest research with the attendees who represented the Mental Health Foundation of New Zealand, the Carter Center, the Clifford Beers Foundation, and the World Health Organization. Rosalynn told one interviewer that the continuing threat of terrorism was traumatizing people, especially children. "I don't think I've ever been more frightened than I am today about what's happening in the world," she said. In the United States, she said, mental health workers were working with local homeland security groups to help people cope with the devastating, long-term psychological impact of terrorism.[37]

While Rosalynn worked in New Zealand, Jimmy hoped that the upcoming presidential election in the United States would be honest. He was disturbed because the country had not undertaken any reforms that might prevent the controversy that had impacted the election in 2000. In an op-ed for the *Washington Post,* he argued that the work he and former President Gerald Ford had done after that ill-fated election had resulted in the Help America Vote Act of 2002, but it was not being enforced. They had recommended that there be a nonpartisan electoral commission and uniformity in voting procedures, but with George W. Bush looking for reelection, nothing had been done to correct the problems of 2000. Carter wrote that "It is unconscionable to perpetuate fraudulent or biased electoral practices in any nation. It is especially objectionable among us Americans, who have prided ourselves on setting a global example for pure democracy."[38]

For Jimmy's eightieth birthday, which would take place a month and a few days before the election, Rosalynn planned a grand celebration at the Carter Center. Since it was also the birthday of the famous pianist Roger Williams, they invited him to play a specially built and designed white Steinway concert grand piano decorated with painted autumn leaves. Williams played it for more than thirteen hours to set a new record for himself. After the program, the piano was auctioned off to raise money for the center. Jimmy and Rosalynn appeared periodically during the performance to greet guests, chat informally with Williams and others, and enjoy the music. Both appeared happy, hale, and vigorous, much younger than their actual years. At Jimmy's request, Williams played "Wind Beneath My Wings," "Unchained Melody," "Autumn Leaves," and music from *Phantom of the Opera*. Although Carter did not request them, Williams also played "Happy Birthday" and "Hail to the Chief." During the late afternoon, Jimmy and Rosalynn danced to "Margie." The music went on until after 11:00 p.m.[39]

Soon after turning eighty, Carter set off for a trip to South Padre Island, Texas, with Rosalynn to look for a Least Bittern, a bird that had eluded them on an earlier trip. With the help of Bob Hinckle, chief of outdoor education for Cleveland, Ohio, Metroparks, they found and added it to the list of more than 1,100 species they had already recorded.[40]

Although birdwatching gave the Carters relief from the politics of their day, they still expressed their opinions freely and often. In an interview with Chris Matthews of MSNBC's *Hardball*, Carter complained that "there has been a melding . . . in this country of the Republican Party and the Christian Right-wing." He condemned Bush for not working for peace in the Middle East and not supporting fair treatment for gays. Announcing that he and Rosalynn would soon be helping to build houses in Mexico, he slyly added that he hoped President Bush would soon find more time for volunteer work than for war.[41]

Carter wrote more op-ed pieces condemning the Iraq War, but he said that, despite his disagreement with Bush, he would support the administration when Bush got reelected. His reason, he told journalist Cokie Roberts on *National Public Radio*, was because he believed the constitution remained "the foundation on which we can survive a very unpleasant election, . . . a deeply grieved loss," or an "exhilarating victory." Regardless of the outcome of an election, he declared, "we all feel that we're still part of a team."[42]

After Bush was reelected as expected in a landslide victory over John Kerry, Carter removed himself from national politics and resumed his support of PLO leader Arafat's goal to establish a separate Palestinian state. Arafat died, aged seventy-five, in November in a French hospital, the absence of a cause of death raising the suspicion that he might have been murdered. Carter praised him as "a powerful human symbol and forceful advocate" who united Palestinians. Although it had been frustrating to deal with him, Carter wrote for the *New York Times*, he had concluded the Oslo agreement of 1993, for which he had justifiably won the Nobel Peace Prize. Arafat's peace efforts, Carter complained, had been abandoned by Bush and Prime Minister Ariel Sharon, resulting in suicide bombings and continued strife in the Middle East.[43]

Egypt hosted a Muslim service for Arafat, as it had done for the shah of Iran. It would have been difficult for Arab leaders to travel to Israeli-controlled Palestinian territory for the funeral, but Cairo was a safe haven for them. Egypt's top Muslim clerics offered special prayers for the dead. After the funeral, Arafat's coffin was flown to Ramallah in the West Bank, where he was buried following Muslim custom before sunset.[44] Carter did not attend the funeral.

On November 18, he and Rosalynn joined President and Mrs. Bush, and the other living presidents and first ladies for the dedication of the William Jefferson Clinton Presidential Library in Little Rock, Arkansas. When the Carters arrived on the dais on that cold, rainy day, they discovered that no one had taken care to shelter the guests from the rain or to dump the rainwater from their chairs. Carter held his own umbrella and smiled broadly as he emptied Rosalynn's chair of accumulated water and held it for her to sit down. Then seating himself, he smiled waiting his turn to speak. In his speech, Carter joked about having made "some mistakes in 1980 during the Mariel boat lift, and the presence of Cuban refugees in Arkansas," which may have cost Clinton his bid for reelection as governor. "For that, I apologize," Carter said, smiling broadly. In a later interview, he conceded that he admired Clinton as "one of the consummate politicians in the world," who "did a superb job as president, except for his personal problems."[45]

Early in December, just in time for the Christmas buying season, Carter published his nineteenth book, *Sharing Good Times*, a memoir of the many vacations he and Rosalynn had taken to enjoy their passions for fishing and other types of outdoor adventures. At age eighty-one, he announced that he had no unachieved ambitions, but he did hope to "become a better artist in the next few years."[46]

FORTY THREE

Endangered Values and Apartheid
in Palestine

If he had no unachieved ambitions, Carter was nevertheless ready to continue his work. On January 6, 2005, he, along with many other international observers, was in Jerusalem preparing to monitor the election to replace Yasser Arafat as president of the Palestinian National Authority.[1] Upon his arrival Carter had gone to see Prime Minister Ariel Sharon whom he praised for Israel's 1982 withdrawal from Sinai and the evacuation of the Yamit and Rafah settlements as part of the Camp David Accords. Then, taking a harder line, Carter asked about the eight Palestinians who had been killed earlier in the week by Israeli rockets launched at the Lebanese village of Beit Lahia. Sharon's bureau chief Dov Weissglas, who also attended the meeting, explained that the Israeli rockets were only in retaliation for others fired by the Palestinians and that five of the dead Palestinians were terrorists. He was sorry about the three civilians who were killed. Sharon, also getting tough, told Carter that he did not expect PLO chairman Mahmoud Abbas to stop the terrorist organizations threatening Israel. If the Palestinian terror attacks continued until disengagement from Gaza, Sharon warned, "Israel's response will be harsher than ever."[2]

Despite many irregularities and Israeli efforts to block Palestinians from voting, Carter and his fellow observers were able to work out enough compromises to enable the election to proceed in a fair manner. To no one's surprise, Mahmoud Abbas, the pragmatic chairman of the PLO who had frequently clashed with Arafat in a power struggle, won in a landslide, receiving 62% of the vote. Considered the candidate most likely to be able to negotiate a settlement with Israel, Abbas was the favorite of both Carter and President Bush. Abbas immediately called for an end to violence, but his reference to Israel as the Zionist enemy suggested that his overtures for peace would not likely be accepted by Prime Minister Sharon. Nevertheless, the stage was set for an election the following year to choose members of the Palestinian parliament.

Returning to the United States, Carter reported to President Bush on January 12 that the Palestinian people lived under the total political and military domination of Israel and that he was particularly disturbed by the twenty-foot-high concrete wall that Israel was building to separate the Palestinians from their Israeli neighbors. Nevertheless, except for some problems around Jerusalem, he thought, the election had gone well.[3]

In a public statement, Carter declared that he had "great hope" for a resolution of the Palestinian issue. As the president of the Palestinian Authority, Abbas promised to seek peace with Israel, but Sharon had recently formed a national unity government and declined to make any concession to the Palestinians except a promise to remove twenty-one Jewish settlements from the Gaza Strip and four from the West Bank. Carter, hoping to coax Sharon into serious negotiations with Abbas, favored continuing the United States aid to Israel of $10 million per day as both he and former President George H. W. Bush had. He did not want "to endanger Israel or hurt Israel," Carter said, but real withdrawal "from both Gaza and the West Bank is in Israel's best interest."[4]

On January 20, 2005, Jimmy and Rosalynn attended George W. Bush's second inauguration at the US Capitol, and five days later Carter addressed the OAS in Washington, only a few blocks from the White House. Referring to the violence that so often wracked Latin America, he explained, "When people live in grinding poverty, . . . see no hope, . . . are not receiving the rights and benefits of citizenship, they will eventually make their grievances known, and it may be in radical and destructive ways." The United States, Carter said, should set a good example for its neighbors to the south, and the governments of the hemisphere should "make the Democratic Charter . . . a living document." That document, The Inter-American Democratic Charter, affirmed that democracy should be the common form of government in all the American countries. If they did so, the OAS, he concluded, would emerge stronger and be able to advance the cause of human rights and democracy that he and Rosalynn so dearly cherished.[5]

Because of their ages, on March 22, Jimmy and Rosalynn stepped down from their positions as co-chairs of the Carter Center, but they retained permanent seats on the Board of Trustees. With their strong approval, the board elected John Moores, the wealthy former owner of the San Diego Padres professional baseball team and a major Carter Center benefactor, as the center's new chairman. Observers could detect no change in the Carters' activities, however, for they continued to do the same things they had always done since leaving the White House a quarter-century earlier.[6]

When Pope John Paul II died on April 2, Carter volunteered to head a delegation to the funeral, but President Bush rejected his offer, opting to attend himself along with First Lady Laura Bush, former presidents George H. W. Bush and Bill Clinton, and Secretary of State Condoleezza Rice. Carter politely approved the president's choice of delegates, and he ignored the numerous news stories about the funeral that failed to mention the fact that the Carters had hosted John Paul at the White House in 1979, the first time a pope had visited there. Having disagreed with John Paul about Latin America, where the Pope had tried to stamp out liberation theology, Carter phrased his comments about the Pope's death carefully. John Paul's early years, Carter said, had been shaped by his experience under the brutal Nazi occupation of Poland during World War II, which impelled him to lead a life dedicated to "peace and human rights."[7]

During the spring and summer, the Carters continued to pursue their senior citizen lives with happy events and serious projects. They rejoiced at the news that the United States had ended the death penalty for persons under age eighteen, which had been one of Rosalynn's major goals. They visited with their good friend Jehan Sadat when she came to give a guest lecture at Emory University. Still disturbed by the questionable outcome of the presidential election in 2000 and hoping to apply some of his experience as observer of a great many elections in foreign countries, Carter co-chaired with former Republican secretary of state James Baker the private bipartisan Commission on Federal Election Reform that included nineteen other former political leaders from both major parties.[8] Meanwhile, Rosalynn expanded her mental health appeal to assist children with special needs and hosted a forum to study how the state might better deliver Medicaid services to those who needed them.

When June arrived, she and Jimmy took off for Michigan and Canada to put on their work clothes, build houses, and enjoy one of their favorite weeks of the year. The annual Jimmy and Rosalynn Carter Work Project had become so popular that thousands of volunteers joined them to build more than two hundred Habitat homes in Benton Harbor, Michigan, and in Windsor, Ontario. Then, on July 27, Carter preached a message of love and peace to 13,000 Baptists from around the world who gathered at the Baptist World Congress in Birmingham, England.[9]

Having attended the official commissioning of USS *Jimmy Carter* (SSN-23) at the Naval Submarine Base in Groton, Connecticut, the previous February, Jimmy and Rosalynn returned to Groton on August 12 for an overnight trip aboard the powerful new submarine to King's Bay Naval Submarine Base at St. Mary's, Georgia. The most heavily armed submarine ever built, and with unique listening abilities, the $3.5 billion submarine had a special section in its middle that could house hundreds of commandoes for special operations as well as launch underwater drones and other secret capabilities.[10] The *Jimmy Carter* carried a crew of 151, most of them young and some not particularly enamored with the aged former president for whom their submarine was named. Rosalynn watched through the periscope as the vessel slipped beneath the water while Carter explored the vessel. Family and friends awaited their arrival in Georgia. Once there, Jimmy stood on the narrow bridge "secured by a red harness as the vessel came into the St. Mary's River and tied up to a dock."[11]

When Carter stepped onto the dock at King's Bay, a red carpet rolled out before him, and sailors in white dress uniforms lined either side to salute the former commander-in-chief. Jimmy himself, dressed in white and wearing a souvenir baseball cap bearing the name of the submarine, appeared almost as physically fit as the young men who honored him. In his dockside remarks, Carter quipped that he would not refer to politics, but many in the audience knew that as president, he, with the help of Senator Sam Nunn, had negotiated the legislation that had resulted in the construction of the huge submarine base at King's Bay. Designed to be the home of the Trident-missile carrying submarines, the base's value had diminished after Carter had negotiated an arms reduction treaty with the Soviet Union. On the day that Jimmy and Rosalynn arrived there, it was only a stopover for the massive SSN-23 on her way to her homeport in Bangor, Washington.[12]

Despite having long ago relinquished his power as commander-in-chief, Carter still considered it his responsibility as a citizen to offer the government constructive criticism. Having completed his work with the Commission of Federal Election Reform the previous summer, he and Baker held a news conference at the US Capitol on September 20 to recommend eighty-seven election reforms. Topping their list were photo IDs, verifiable paper trails for electronic voting machines, impartial administration of elections, increased availability and security for absentee ballots, and vote by mail. In early October, Carter told a group at American University that he was certain that

Al Gore had won the 2000 election and that the Supreme Court was "highly partisan" and should not have been involved.[13]

As the year drifted toward Thanksgiving and Christmas with no perceived changes in the Bush administration's foreign policy, Carter's temper exploded when he learned that the president had set up secret prisons where the CIA tortured terror suspects. He accused Bush of "degrading moral standards" that had supported "decades of US foreign policy."[14] Fueled by that anger, and filled with his own feelings of patriotism and his Christian ethics, Carter published, in time for the Christmas trade, a devastating book entitled *Our Endangered Values: America's Moral Crisis.*

In interviews promoting the book, Carter voiced his dismay that under the current administration the country he had served so long had fallen so far. There was a moral crisis in the United States, he repeated time and again. The Republicans needed to explain why US troops were in Iraq, because, he thought, it was "ill-advised and unjust and unnecessary."[15] Bush, Carter charged, was willingly presiding over a government closely allied with conservative religious leaders. Such a relationship, he declared, was "anathema to me and unprecedented."[16] The country needed to return to its firm belief in the separation of church and state, which was a "basic value . . . established under Thomas Jefferson," who had wanted "to build a wall between the two."[17]

Our Endangered Values quickly rose to the top of the *New York Times* best seller list. Carter responded to all criticism, even offering to take phone calls on the *Larry King Show* from conservative Christians. Recalling Mr. Earl, he told a reporter for *USA Today* that "My father was a stern but loving disciplinarian who expected me, even as a child, to do my share of the chores and field work." Mr. Earl was "also a Bible teacher in our local Baptist church," who believed that Christians had an obligation to share their faith with others. "Our country's values are ultimately the same as those of all major religions," Carter continued. The United States had always been in the forefront of avoiding torture of the helpless and should be a proper steward of the earth.[18]

Leaving the book to speak for itself as an attack on the president and the Southern Baptist Convention, Jimmy and Rosalynn journeyed to Liberia to observe an election there on November 23. The Carter Center had been involved in Liberia since 1985, and the Carters had made several visits to attempt to help that country embrace a democratic government. Visiting a rubber plantation on one occasion, Jimmy had been outraged to learn how native Liberians were treated as virtual slaves, laboring to produce the rubber that went to tire manufacturers in the United States. By late 2005, Liberia's despotic president, the notorious warlord Charles Taylor, who had presided over civil wars in which more than 200,000 people had died, had resigned and fled to Nigeria. When the country prepared for a free election, Jimmy and Rosalynn joined their colleagues from the Carter Center and representatives from the UN and other international groups to monitor the voting. Jimmy and Rosalynn visited forty-eight polling places in the Monrovia area on Election Day. The winner, Ellen Johnson Sirleaf, a Harvard-trained economist, became the first woman to be elected president of an African nation. Nicknamed Liberia's "Black Iron Lady," she would work with the Carters to improve her country.[19]

The Carters were back in Georgia for Christmas and the New Year, but no sooner were the holidays over than they, accompanied by Chip, Jeff, and Amy, headed for Israel. Arriving on Saturday, January 7, 2006, they prepared to monitor elections in the West Bank and Gaza for the third time. Carter led a team of eighty from the United States under the auspices of the National Democratic Institute. In addition, there were 440 observers from other parts of the world. After meeting with of all the delegations, Jimmy and Rosalynn had extensive discussions with their long-time friend Ehud Olmert, who was acting Israeli prime minister because Arial Sharon was seriously ill. Olmert made it clear that he would follow Sharon's policies, saying, Carter reported, that he would resume peace talks with Palestinian president Mahmoud Abbas "only if radical Palestinian groups are completely disarmed (a hopeless prospect)".[20]

On Monday, the day before the election, Jimmy and Rosalynn spent the entire day meeting with and addressing various groups and individuals who might influence the election and help to make it fair.[21] On Election Day, January 9, they visited twenty-five polling places "in East Jerusalem and its outskirts, Hebron, Ramallah, and Jericho."[22] Hamas (considered a terrorist organization by Israel) won control of the Palestinian parliament in an "orderly and peaceful" election, a surprise victory that left everyone, including Hamas's leaders, in suspense about what might happen. Carter's colleague Carl Bildt, the former Swedish prime minister, thought Hamas's victory might strengthen the hope for a two-state solution. Carter had seen others make the trek from terror to power, and he hoped that Hamas would do the same: "My prayer is the Hamas leaders, now serving in positions of unprecedented authority, will lead the Palestinian people on a peaceful, non-violent path toward a two-state solution."[23]

There were many obstacles, however, in the path of the new Palestinian legislators. To begin with, the PLO was broke. President Abbas promised to serve the three remaining years of his term, but he explained to Carter that he did not have funds to meet the February payrolls for teachers, nurses, or social workers. The Palestinian political party Fatah refused to join a government with Hamas, and many of the newly elected Palestinian legislators would have to get permits from Israel to travel from their base in Gaza through Israeli territory in order to reach the Palestinian capital Ramallah, in the West Bank. The Israeli prime minister's office informed Carter that no Hamas party member would be given a pass, which would make it impossible to implement the election and possibly provoke more violence. Carter passed that information on to the US Consul General, who promised to relay it to the White House and State Department, thus leaving the fate of the Palestinians in the hands of a US government that had little interest in helping them. Carter's hope that Hamas would no longer be labeled a terrorist organization was in vain. Hamas steadfastly refused to recognize Israel's right to exist, and, despite winning the election, remained a pariah to much of the world.[24]

Biding their time while hoping for a breakthrough in Palestine, the Carters led full personal and professional lives. He carved, built, and painted objects to auction at Crested Butte. They sometimes went skiing, a sport they had taken up in their sixties. On February 7, 2006, they attended Coretta Scott King's funeral at the Martin Luther King, Jr., National Historical Park in Atlanta, where Carter again criticized President Bush, who was present, and argued that the FBI's earlier surveillance of Martin Luther King, Jr., had violated his civil rights."[25] In the spring they went to Nevada to help raise money for their son Jack's US Senate campaign, which helped him to win the Democratic nomination. At the end of July, they led a fifty-eight-member Carter Center delegation to observe the Democratic Republic of Congo's first multi-party presidential and legislative elections in forty years. The annual Jimmy and Rosalynn Carter Work Project occurred in October at a small village near Mumbai, India, and they also visited Habitat projects in Chennai, India, and a small fishing village in southern Thailand.

In November the Carters returned to Nicaragua for the fourth time to observe that country's presidential and legislative elections. Carter thought those elections, as well is the ones he had observed in Arica, were fair. Disappointed that Daniel Ortega won in Nicaragua, Carter urged him to reach out to the United States for aid and advice. They were also disappointed that Jack lost to the incumbent Republican candidate in Nevada.[26]

Despite all they did, the Carters remained driven to try to bring peace to the Middle East. Angered by a disturbing report from a Palestinian doctor who explained how the tall, concrete wall Israel had erected between itself and the Palestinians prevented people who desperately needed medical help from getting it, Carter wrote an impassioned book-length of the need and promise for a peace process in the Middle East. Released late in 2006, *Palestine Peace Not Apartheid* stirred anew the old hornet's nest of Carter's condemnation of Israeli policy toward the Palestinians. As if the title, especially the use of the word "apartheid" were not red flag enough to arouse tempers, the picture on the dustjacket carried an emotional wallop. A photograph of the face of a very pensive and troubled Jimmy was juxtaposed with an aerial view of hundreds of demonstrators waving protest signs at the hated wall looming above them. On the back of the dustjacket, Carter's words leaped from the page like the warning of an Old Testament Prophet: "The spilled blood in the Holy Land still cries out to God—an anguished cry for peace."[27]

Carter intended that the title not include any punctuation and be provocative enough to cause people to "read the book and find out the facts." Using graphic language, he described in detail how bulldozers destroyed Palestinian homes, making way for the concrete wall secured with razor wire, trenches, and electronic devices.

Zbigniew Brzezinski defended his former boss, explaining that Carter used the word "apartheid" to describe the Palestinians as repressed, not as a way to bash the Israelis.[28]

Nevertheless, the word brought a flood of protests from many Jewish Americans and others who accused Carter of anti-Semitism. Alan Dershowitz, a Jewish professor at Harvard Law School and a specialist on constitutional law, launched a major counterattack in an opinion piece in the *New York Sun* entitled "The World According to Carter." The use of the word apartheid, Dershowitz contended, suggested an analogy to the hated policies of South Africa. Carter's work, in his opinion, was outrageous, shallow, superficial, and ahistorical. "It's obvious that Mr. Carter just doesn't like Israel or Israelis," he wrote. "What would motivate a decent man like Jimmy Carter to write such an indecent book?" The Carter Center might be a force for peace, he concluded, "if Jimmy Carter were as generous in spirit to the Israelis as he is to the Palestinians."[29]

Carter responded to Dershowitz during a long television interview with Larry King. Carter denied that he had "alleged in the book or otherwise that Israel, as a nation, was guilty of apartheid." But, he observed, the Israeli government had different policies for the occupied territories from those it applied to itself. The "deprivation of basic human rights among Palestinians is really horrendous," Carter declared. The purpose of his book was to "bring permanent peace to Israel" and "good faith negotiations between the Palestinians for land swaps." In that regard, Israel was not solely at fault, he said, because Palestinian leadership was incompetent and corrupt.[30]

Carter did make one grave error in his book. He asserted that the Palestinians would "end suicide bombings and other acts of terrorism" when Israel accepted international laws and peace with Palestine. It implied that Carter approved the use of terrorism to bring pressure upon Israel, a strategy which was totally unacceptable to him. When called to his attention, he apologized for it, said it was "improper and stupid," and asked his publisher to delete it in future editions of the book.[31] Although Carter took the severe criticism in stride, it grated upon him to be called a liar, bigot, coward, plagiarist, and anti-Semite. In his defense, he reminded his critics of his pro-Israel history and speeches, and he fell back on memories of Mr. Earl to justify himself: "I was taught by my father every Sunday about the special status of the Jewish people," he said.[32]

The controversy may have helped sales, for the book sold more than 300,000 copies, but it caused some defections at the Carter Center. Kenneth W. Stein, who had been associated with the Carter Center for twenty-three years but was off payroll with the honorary title of "Fellow," quit what was actually an honorary post. He had long disagreed with Carter about the Palestinians and used the book as his excuse to exit. But he did not leave quietly. In his two-page letter of resignation, Stein charged that the book was filled with factual errors, "superficialities," and likely plagiarized passages.[33] Agreeing with him, fourteen unpaid Jewish businessmen who served as advisors to the Carter Center also quit. Others, however, who had been traditionally close to Carter, continued to believe firmly in the compassion and goodness of their chief.[34]

The controversy about *Palestinian Peace Not Apartheid* obscured its intrinsic value. Carter was a good writer who had mastered the art of presenting a complex argument in clear and simple terms. He did his writing himself, but he had a professional historian and others, including Rosalynn, check his work for accuracy and literary style. Well-documented with maps, an historical chronology, an appendix that includes every relevant UN resolution from 1967 through 1980, and other historical documents, the book is a treasure trove of accessible information.

The controversial book could not divert Jimmy's attention entirely away from the reality of death that always hovered nearby. His beloved Aunt Sissy Dolvin died at age ninety-four on December 2. An effervescent personality, she loved people and the political game and had been a major campaigner for him in all of his races. Whether prompted by her death, the furor over his book, or the inquisitive media aggravating an eighty-two-year-old famous person about his final resting place, he announced that he wanted to be buried in his front yard in Plains. Although eligible for burial in Arlington National Cemetery, he preferred to be buried at his and Rosalynn's home in Plains. Rosalynn, however, preferred a site at the Carter Center, although she later relented and agreed with Jimmy.[35]

In another regard, Rosalynn achieved equality with men when the Baptists ordained her a deacon on December 20 at the Maranatha Baptist Church. Although she had been reared a Methodist, after nearly a decade of marriage she had joined the Baptist church with Jimmy, but she had never quite accepted some of its conservative rules. At her ordination, the pastor said that she did not like the limelight, but millions of people had "seen her leadership and compassion." Rosalynn was the second woman to be elected deacon by the Maranatha congregation. The first, ordained three years earlier, was Sue Askerzada, a graduate of the Mercer School of Theology, who assisted her husband at religious services.[36]

The day after Christmas, Carter was about to leave for Panama when he heard of the death of his good friend former President Gerald Ford. Carter was committed by prior agreement to deliver a eulogy, but seeing that he had time before the funeral, he continued to Panama where he toured the canal's Miraflores Locks with President Martin Torrijos, the son of the man who had negotiated the canal treaties with him three decades earlier. Carter watched a video of the recently approved project to widen the canal for larger ships and quipped that he hoped to be alive in 2014, aged ninety, when the work was scheduled to be completed. Carter thought it was "a very nice project," and he smiled when Torrijos said "it is always an honor to have Ex-President Carter visit. . . . We consider him part of the Panamanians family." Carter's own family soon joined him in Panama for another of the traditional post-Christmas vacations to which he and Rosalynn continued to treat their children, in-laws, and grandchildren. Twenty-three of them arrived at a hotel on the Isla Cebaco of Panama's Pacific coast, where they celebrated the New Year. Jimmy and Rosalynn then returned to the United States in time for Ford's funeral.[37]

Carter and Ford had agreed that upon the death of one, the other would give a eulogy. After a state funeral in Washington, DC, Ford's casket arrived at the Grace Episcopal Church in Grand Rapids, Michigan, on January 3, 2007, for the final service. Carter delivered an impassioned message. He reminded the mourners that in his inaugural address he had thanked Ford for all he had done to "heal our land." As president, he had sought Ford's advice, notified him in advance of the peace agreement between Israel and Egypt, and agreed to pressure the Soviet Union to comply with provisions regarding dissidents in the Helsinki Accords, which Ford had negotiated. Carter mentioned how close their families had become, and how much alike their wives were, but he thought it equally important that he and Ford shared "a common commitment to our religious faith."[38]

The death of Ford seemed to bring Carter and Bill Clinton a bit closer. A few days later in January they met in Atlanta to announce the creation of a New Baptist Convention, a group which ultimately became known as the Covenant Baptist Fellowship. Their purpose was to form a loose association of Baptists, of all races and genders, to resist the conservative policies of the Southern Baptist Convention. While providing a home for non-fundamentalists and social liberals, the new group, still clinging to the label Baptist, heard more epithets than praise from their conservative brothers and sisters. It would take another year for it to become fully organized, and in the meantime, it attracted very little attention outside Baptist circles, because more people seemed interested in continuing the debate about *Palestine Peace Not Apartheid*.[39]

Former Vice President Walter Mondale rarely entered the public debate about the Carter/Mondale administration, but he tired of the discussions about Carter's book and what he considered the unfair criticism of Carter. In an interview on national television, he described his and Carter's four years in office quite simply and accurately: "We told the truth, we obeyed the law, and we kept the peace." When asked if his comment might be interpreted as a criticism of the current Bush administration, he admitted that it could be. But he preferred to stick to the four years he knew best: "We were true to that oath of office and we did everything we could to enhance American power based on our principles and tried to avoid war. And we accomplished that and I feel good about it."[40]

Carter felt good about it too, but he remained embroiled in the current political fray. He stuck to his guns about his use of the world "apartheid," and he hoped Congress would use its "maximum authority," including the power of the purse, to stop the war in Iraq. But the war went on, and the arguments for and against the book continued.[41]

At Brandeis University on January 27, 2007, before a packed, mostly Jewish, audience, Carter delivered a carefully prepared speech that he hoped would defuse the book controversy once and for all. After defending at some length his presidential record on Israel, Jewish immigration from the Soviet Union, and the establishment of a national Holocaust memorial, Carter turned to the current situation in the Holy Land, saying that he understood Israel's fears for its security and existence. He knew, too, that only a minority of Israelis persecuted Palestinians. Nevertheless, the settlements and walls made the lives of the Palestinians intolerable. Israel, he believed, would "never find peace until it is willing to withdraw from its neighbors' land and accept the school's namesake Louis Brandeis's philosophy of justice and righteousness."[42]

Following his speech, Carter received a standing ovation and answered fifteen pre-selected questions. Then, his principal critic Alan Dershowitz addressed the audience, declaring that he and Carter were both "pro-Israel and pro-Palestine." If Carter's book had contained the information Carter gave in his speech, the professor said, then there would have been no controversy.[43]

Carter's disappointment with continuing failure in the Middle East, and the hurt inflicted by critics of his book, did not lessen his commitment to eradicating diseases in Africa. In February, he and Rosalynn embarked upon a sixteen-day, four-country tour of Africa to spotlight their fight against diseases and to inspect progress the Carter Center had made. The successful completion of a $25 million challenge grant from the Bill and Melinda Gates Foundation had enabled the center to eliminate nearly all of the remaining 25,000 known cases of Guinea worm disease, most of them in Ghana and Sudan. In Tingoli village in northern Ghana, natives dressed them in traditional garb and cheered as they walked through a crowd of grateful Africans with their Secret Service agents close by.[44]

In Sudan, Carter met International Lions Club president Jimmy Ross, who was helping him persuade local community leaders to assist in his ten-year quest to eliminate river blindness and trachoma. At Addis Ababa, Ethiopia, on February 13, the Carters attended the opening of the Ethiopia Public

Health Training Initiative Replication Conference, which highlighted the success of the Carter Center in training health professionals in that country. They also distributed three million mosquito nets in Afeta, Ethiopia, to help millions of people protect themselves from being bitten by malaria-carrying mosquitoes. In Nigeria, Carter asked President Olusegun Obasanjo to assist Carter Center workers in distributing drugs to combat schistosomiasis, a parasitic disease that impaired growth in children.[45]

Back home in Georgia, Carter paid particular attention to his own health and how he might help people suffering from pancreatic cancer. Since his father, mother, two sisters, and brother had all succumbed to that disease, medical researchers wanted to study him and his family to attempt to learn more about it. Such a high incidence in one family was extremely rare, so rare in fact that researchers found only one other such family, and that family was in Japan. Carter assisted the researchers by submitting to experimental procedures and frequent physical examinations. They discovered that Jimmy did not have a gene that indicated that the disease was hereditary. The only known lifestyle factor that differentiated him from every other member of his family was that all of them smoked cigarettes but he did not.[46]

Fascinated by scientific progress, whether in medicine or energy, Carter was ahead of his time in searching for alternate sources of energy. He was pleased when President Bush proposed an energy plan similar to the one that he had advocated as president. Far from the White House, Carter, in late February, dug the first shovel of earth to welcome a biofuel plant to southwestern Georgia. He committed 10% of the harvest from his family farm to the plant that would produce fuel from soybeans, peanuts, and cotton.[47]

Carter's favorite topic, however, remained justice for the Palestinians. Addressing a large crowd at the University of California at Irvine, he urged Jewish and Muslim leaders to travel to Palestine to discover for themselves what was happening. "The main problem with college students," he told them, "is indifference and the lack of deep commitment to change things around the world they deplore." College students could and should "play a crucial role in this debate," he said, because they had nothing to lose. He regretted that his own role was diminished, because neither side seemed interested in accepting his invitation to mediate.[48] A few months later, he complained about the Bush administration to a Canadian journalist, declaring that he was "amazed and almost nauseated to see the encroachment of Israel on Palestinian rights and the persecution that is taking place."[49]

Avoiding domestic political debate as another presidential election approached, Carter joined an international group of Nobel Peace laureates who called themselves The Elders. His first contact with them came in July when he delivered the keynote address at the annual Human Rights Forum in Dublin, Ireland. Both Carter and Ireland's president Mary Robinson, who was also a passionate advocate for human rights, became members of The Elders on that occasion. Organized by famed South African leader Nelson Mandela and funded by billionaire businessman Richard Branson, they were so called because of their collective wisdom and experience battling for freedom and equality. The group included Archbishop Desmond Tutu, Kofi Annan, Mandela's wife Graca Machel, Aung San Suu Kyi, and others. The primary leaders were Carter, Mandela, and Annan. Carter cherished the group because it had complete freedom from political involvement, was well funded, and was, he thought, in position to accomplish much good.[50]

Rosalynn witnessed positive results from her own work. In June an Italian Construction Company donated $54 million to a mental health facility in Ethiopia—Ethiopian First Lady Azeb Mesfin, who was in charge of the facility, served on the board of Women Leaders in Mental Health that was sponsored by the Carter Center.[51] Rosalynn went to Washington in July to testify before the House Education and Labor Committee in favor of the Paul Wellstone Mental Health and Education Equity Act. She argued that if insurance paid for such illnesses, it would remove the stigma from people who suffered mental illness. She applauded those who worked to pass mental health parity laws, for she knew how difficult their task was. But, she continued, "the benefits to our nation will be enormous." On March 7, 2008, the House of Representatives passed the act, pushing Congressional legislation promoting equality for those suffering mental illness a giant step forward.[52]

As tireless as Rosalynn in his fight for human rights, Carter joined The Elders a short time later for a trip to Sudan. They visited a town in northern Darfur, where there were many refugees, among the 2.5 million displaced by an ongoing civil war that had seen 20,000 killed. African rebels had taken up arms against the Arab dominated Sudanese government four years earlier, and the government had responding by unleashing a militia of Arab nomads on them. When no refugees came out to meet him, Carter attempted to walk into the town. Sudanese police blocked him, and he got into a shouting match with them, screaming, "You don't have the power to stop me!" His Secret Service guards, and his colleagues Richard Branson and Graca Machel, convinced him to get back into the car and leave. Before doing so, he agreed to a compromise to meet tribal representatives at another location, but they never showed up. The mission, headed by Archbishop Desmond Tutu and Carter, failed to persuade either side in the Darfur conflict to make peace.[53]

Moving quickly from one undertaking, especially a failed one, to the next, Carter began a marketing tour to promote his new book, *Beyond the White House*. A memoir of his life and work since 1981, it did not attract the attention that the controversial book about Palestine had.[54] In the new memoir, as in others, Carter reevaluated his life, concluding that it had been full and that the influence of his father loomed larger and larger with every look backward. Despite their fame, at home Jimmy and Rosalynn lived simply—an aging couple who had achieved financial success, but for whom the realities of family, health, changing times, joys and sorrows might have been little different from any other elderly couple in any small US town.

FORTY FOUR

"Cootie Man" among The Elders

Carter's active membership in The Elders provided him a new high profile vehicle to fight for international peace, justice, and democracy, but it did not replace his and Rosalynn's work through the Carter Center. Neither did the Carters desist from commenting on or participating in US domestic politics. Senior statespersons in their eighties, Jimmy and Rosalynn maintained a punishing pace.

Rosalynn wrote an op-ed piece for a prominent online medical journal discussing how longevity was leading to new problems of dementia and mental illness. "This blessing of long life," she wrote, "presents us with a new set of formidable challenges: soaring rates of dementia and untreated mental health problems among the elderly, a growing burden of chronic illnesses that affects our communities, disturbing problems of elder abuse, and an unparalleled demand for the services of both professional and family caregivers." Referring to events in her own life, Rosalynn emphasized the importance of caregivers taking care of themselves and reaching out to others who could help them. "I have had a unique opportunity to address the caregiving crisis," she said. At the Rosalynn Carter Institute for Caregiving, "Our hope is to play a key role in developing better supports for both family and professional caregivers."[1]

Jimmy continued his unrelenting quest to reform the Baptist church, to resolve schisms within Christianity, and to teach tolerance and understanding of non-Christian religions. On January 29, 2008, he led a large meeting of liberal and moderate Baptists in the Celebration of a New Baptist Covenant. Standing beside Republican Georgia Governor Sonny Perdue, he sang, smiled, and surveyed the thousands of Baptists holding hands in the huge exhibit hall in Atlanta. Some 20,000 people, including African Americans, Whites, Asians, and Latinos attended the three-day meeting. In his opening address, Carter optimistically declared that he believed that Baptists could "work together in a spirit of harmony and cooperation." Animosity among Christians, he said, was "a cancer metastasizing in the body of Christ."[2]

Closing the meeting, he told the audience: "We can disagree on the death penalty, we can disagree on homosexuality, we can disagree on the status of women and still bind our hearts together in a common, united, generous, friendly, loving commitment."[3]

Carter's call for a "united," "loving" commitment was not likely to affect the 2008 presidential election. Carter liked the personable and eloquent African-American candidate, Barack Obama, whose campaign, he said, "has been extraordinary and titillating for me and my family." Carter compared Obama's speeches to those of the late Martin Luther King, Jr., and he believed that, if nominated, Obama could carry some of the Southern states. Carter's public stance, however, was to remain neutral, especially since former First Lady and current New York Senator Hillary Clinton was also a contender for the nomination.[4]

Since they were not key players in the presidential election, Jimmy and Rosalynn embarked upon ambitious trips to Africa, Nepal, and the Middle East. Traveling on Carter Center Chairman John Moores's private jet, they arrived in Accra, Ghana, on March 30, where they met other members of the Carter Center team to analyze progress in eradicating guinea worm disease. Despite the successful reduction of cases of the disease, they warned "our Ghanaian friends against over-confidence and complacency, and emphasized the need for the scheduled renovation of a water system in Tamale-Savelugu districts by August 2008."

In Abuja, Nigeria, the Carters attended a special ceremony honoring Ethiopia, Cote d'Ivoire, Burkina Faso, and Togo for joining eleven other countries in ending the transmission of Guinea worm disease. Although there had been an outbreak of about one hundred cases in the past two years, they had been contained, and Jimmy believed that there would be no more cases in 2008.[5]

Not only guinea worm, but Nigeria's rampant political corruption motivated Carter to discuss the pressing need of reform with President Umaru Musa Yar'Adua. At a breakfast meeting, the Carters told the Nigerian leader that they looked forward to working with him to help reform his country's electoral process as well as cure and prevent diseases.[6]

Only three days after returning to Atlanta, the Carters left for Nepal with a team of Carter Center election observers to help monitor the April 10 election of an assembly that would write a new constitution for the country. Jimmy and Rosalynn met Carter's co-leader of the Center's international election observation delegation, Dr. Surakiart Sathirathai, deputy prime minister of Thailand. Most of the sixty observers from twenty-one nations, along with several thousand Nepali workers, had already been deployed to remote areas. In a complicated series of elections, voters would choose a 601-member legislative body that would produce a constitution transforming the 240-year-old Hindu kingdom into a republic. In preparation for the election, the Carters met with US Ambassador Nancy Powell, leaders of the observers from all of the represented countries, and Nepali Chief of the Army Staff General Rookmangud Katawal.

On Election Day, the Maoists, who were especially eager to get rid of the king, won the majority of assembly seats. Carter concluded that the Nepali election had been the most "transformational" of the seventy that the Carter Center had observed. It ended a dozen years of conflict, and it began a total change of a government from a monarchy to a democratic republic. It also gave a voice in the new government to large numbers of previously marginalized people, including many women, who would likely enjoy higher social status than they had ever known.[7]

Feeling gratified, he, Rosalynn, and their son Jeff flew to Tel Aviv, where they would begin another controversial mission in Israel, where the sporadic violence by and against the Palestinians continued unabated. Archbishop Desmond Tutu had appealed to the Israelis and the Palestinians to stop attacking one another, and, on behalf of The Elders, he asked Carter, Kofi Annan, and Mary Robinson to try to find a way to restore peace to the Holy Land.

The US State Department had advised Carter against meeting with Hamas leader Khaled Mashal in Syria because it would undercut its policy of isolating that militant group. But Carter insisted that all responsible parties, including Hamas, must be involved in the discussions. Defying the objections of the US and Israeli governments, as well as US and Israeli advice, he met with Mashal to discuss how to lift the Israeli siege of the Gaza Strip and to ask that Hamas swap the one Israeli soldier it held in Gaza for dozens of Palestinian prisoners in Israeli hands. Mashal was unreceptive to a prisoner swap, and he refused to consider declaring a unilateral thirty-day cease fire. Hamas had done that twice before, he told Carter, and Israel had taken advantage of both.[8]

When neither Israel nor Hamas budged, Rosalynn granted an interview with the *Jerusalem Post* that she hoped might ease Israeli fears. Recognizing the emotional damage caused by Hamas's "criminal acts of terrorism" and rocket attacks on Israel, she told the interviewer that she thought "her husband's self-appointed shuttle between Israel and Arab capitals might help end the attacks even if only as part of a temporary ceasefire." Jimmy, she noted, had pressed Khaled Mashal to stop firing rockets. She also recalled how she had initiated the first Friendship Force cultural exchange in 1978 that sent 425 Israelis to Hartford, Connecticut, for a week and an equal number of Americans, including her son Chip, to Israel.[9]

The debate over Carter's role intensified as editorialists and politicians began to accuse him of doing more harm than good. Israel's ambassador to the UN called him "a bigot" for meeting with the militant Hamas leader, and the *Wall Street Journal* condemned him as senile for laying a wreath at the grave of Yasser Arafat. Carter claimed that he was not in Israel to negotiate but to try to stop the fighting and get opposing parties to talk.[10]

Kofi Annan defended Carter for talking with Hamas. Speaking at his Global Humanitarian Forum in Geneva on April 22, the former UN secretary general said that those who wanted peace in the Middle East should "take advantage of whatever openings President Carter has been able to obtain to move the process forward." "He's the only president who's been able to broker an enduring peace agreement between Israel and Egypt," Annan continued, "and for that we are very grateful." Annan rejected the Bush administration's criticism of Carter and urged Bush instead to become more active in the region.[11]

Carter took the now familiar condemnations of his interference in diplomacy and talking with controversial leaders in stride, and he used every available occasion to express his views. Speaking on May 26 at the annual Hay Literature Festival in Hay-on-Wye, Wales, which Bill Clinton once described as the "Woodstock of the mind," Carter found a friendly European audience. Although he was there to promote his latest book, a loving memoir of his mother Miss Lillian, he did not shy away from his emphatic criticism of Israel. "One of the greatest human rights crimes on Earth," Carter told his audience of about one hundred invited guests, "is the imprisonment and starvation of 1.6 million people within Gaza." Britain and the European Union should be doing what he was doing, he said, namely encouraging the formation of a Palestinian unity government that included both Hamas and Fatah. There should be a prisoner exchange and a cease fire in the West Bank. Carter found it "regrettable that Gaza's elected government Hamas was holding one Israeli prisoner but that paled into insignificance compared with the 11,600 prisoners held by Israel." The "most substantial obstacle to peace is the [Israeli] people who want Palestinian Land." Nevertheless, he believed the conflict between Israel and Palestine was not hopeless. With only 150 or more nuclear weapons, Israel would be in no place to challenge Iran's future nuclear capacity and thus should pursue a path of negotiation. He thought that both the United States and Israel should make friends with Iran.[12]

Carter may have been taking advantage of the European venue to rebut his many hostile US critics. For a US audience, British journalist Bronwen Maddox wrote in the *Times* of London, Carter's recent trip to Israel and his book accusing the Israelis of "apartheid" put him "beyond the pale." Even Obama, a smooth politician, although he might have agreed with Carter, had condemned Carter's discussion with Hamas despite Carter's support of his campaign, out of fear that "the pro-Israel Lobby's loathing of Carter [might] transfer to him." Carter's fate, Maddox thought, might be to be "adored abroad and shorn of influence at home." In defense of him, Maddox argued that Carter's two decades of experience working to resolve conflicts, the establishment of the Carter Center, and his Nobel Prize entitled him to be heard when he pointed out that shunning Hamas had not worked and it was time for Americans to consider all sides in the conflict if there was to be reasonable chance for a resolution.[13]

Much of what Carter said and did that stirred so much controversy might have been attributed to the advice that his mother had given him. "My mother's advice to me," he said in an interview, was "to do what you think is right and what you think is exciting and gratifying to you, and not worry if you make a mistake and fail, and not worry if anybody criticizes you. Just go ahead and do it." He added that his mother would have approved of his conversation with Hamas. Miss Lillian, he said, "liked controversy herself," and she would "have added a little bit of spice or titillation to the fact that we were reaching out to people who were scorned."[14] Jimmy made those comments when talking about his new book, *A Remarkable Mother*, a laudatory tribute to Miss Lillian, who, he said, had taught him about human rights and who had molded his life and career.

Again putting his belief into action, he and Rosalynn picked up their hammers, donned their work clothes, and traveled first to the upper Ninth Ward in New Orleans to help rebuild houses that had been badly damaged or destroyed by hurricane Katrina. Working for five days on the Gulf Coast, they chose Biloxi and Pascagoula, Mississippi, as their host cities. Thousands of volunteers joined them from May 11 through 16. Jimmy told a reporter that it was more important for people to have a home than freedom of speech, and if those devastated by poverty or natural disasters did not get help, they would not have been "treated decently, in the greatest democracy in the world."[15]

After returning to Plains, two events brought memories of two of the important people in the Carters' lives. At the opening of the Billy Carter Service Station Museum, Jimmy said that he hoped that the museum would reveal all the facets of Billy's life, not just the image of him as a beer-guzzling redneck.[16] When Hamilton Jordan died at age sixty-three on May 20, both Jimmy and Rosalynn were deeply saddened. He had been a part of their lives and campaigns since 1966, and some gave him credit for Jimmy's victories. "Hamilton was my closest political adviser, a trusted confidant and my friend," Jimmy said. "His judgment, insight, and wisdom were excelled only by his compassion and love of our country."[17]

Although their own national political career were far behind them, Jimmy and Rosalynn still could find no peace when they attended the Democratic National Convention in Denver, Colorado, August 25–28, 2008. One among many speakers on the first day, Carter praised Barack Obama, called for party unity, and seemed happy that the Bushes would soon be vacating the White House. Carter's appearance at the convention, however, was a red flag for many Jewish voters. One of them commented that seeing him there made anyone who cared about Israel uncomfortable. Fearing that Carter might do the party more harm than good, one speaker assured the delegates that Obama disagreed with Carter about Israel, and the appearance of other speakers who were popular with the Jewish community helped marginalize him. Obama remained politely distant from his Democratic predecessor.[18]

Sidelined to the outskirts of contemporary US politics, Carter found fulfillment through the Carter Center and The Elders. On October 8, 2008, he was one of The Elders who arrived in Cyprus to boost reunification talks. Accompanied by Archbishop Desmond Tutu and former Algerian foreign minister Lakhdar Brahimi, for two days they met with leaders from the island's Turkish Cypriot and Greek Cypriot communities. They made it clear that they were not there to negotiate or represent any political system, but simply to help the disputants come to the table to try to resolve their issues. Their purpose was to call international attention to the flagging negotiations in Cyprus and thus put pressure upon both sides to reach an agreement. From their meeting with young people who would be voting for the first time, as well as with UN Special Adviser Alexander Downer and Head of the UN Mission in Cyprus Taye-Brook Zerihoun, Carter hoped that the island's voters would take "essential steps on the path to peace." However, the reunification efforts remained stalled.[19]

When Robert Mugabe refused to allow The Elders into Zimbabwe where hundreds of people were dying from a cholera epidemic and there was virtually no medical help available, they boarded a UN helicopter for Msayleh, Lebanon.[20] Arriving on December 7, Jimmy and Rosalynn received the support they needed from the UN for their five-day visit. After a very busy round of visits with President Michel Suleiman, Prime Minister Fouad al-Sanyurah, and rival Christian leaders Michel Awn and Samir Ja'ja, Carter emphasized that he was there to help find a way to end Israel's occupation of Lebanese territory and violation of that country's sovereignty. He repeated his call on Israel to withdraw "without delay"; recommended that Syria and Lebanon establish diplomatic ties and clearly mark the border between their countries; and offered to send monitors to parliamentary elections the next spring in which the Hezbollah-led opposition hoped to topple the governing coalition.

From Lebanon, the Carters went to Damascus, Syria, to discuss Middle East peace prospects with Syrian President Bashar al-Assad and exiled leaders of Hamas. Carter hoped to persuade Hamas to free Gilad Shalit, an Israeli soldier whom they had held prisoner in Gaza for more than two years. Although he was unable to gain Shalit's freedom, Carter did succeed in obtaining a letter from him to his parents, and he may have paved the way for his exchange for Palestinian prisoners three years later.[21]

On January 5, 2009, the *Christian Science Monitor* ran a feature article praising Carter for his accomplishments and urging his critics to cease picking on him.[22] But Carter invited criticism. Early in the new year, he declared Israel's recent assault on Gaza to be unnecessary and faulted Israel for refusing to increase humanitarian supplies to the impoverished Gaza Strip, an action that he contended was fully supported by the Bush administration.

On a more positive note, Carter went to China in January to celebrate the thirtieth anniversary of his normalization of relations with that country. He declared that he thought that the incoming Obama presidency would expand common interests between the United States and China and help to maintain peace and stability in the world.[23]

As a magnanimous gesture of unity on the eve of the transfer of power at the White House, outgoing President George W. Bush agreed to President-elect Barack Obama's request that he invite former presidents George H. W. Bush, Bill Clinton, and Jimmy Carter to the White House for lunch with

Obama and President Bush. No one revealed what they said during their closed door discussions, but when they posed in the Oval Office, standing together for a group photograph, there was a noticeable space between Carter and Bill Clinton. Carter stood alone at the end of the line. Although Carter and others dismissed the pose as coincidental, they were unable to convince Carter's detractors that there was not a continuing rift between him and the former presidents. Peggy Noonan, noted for her clever use of words and Republican proclivities, wrote: "Did you notice how they all leaned away from Jimmy Carter, the official Cootieman of former presidents?"[24]

On January 20, the day of Obama's inauguration, Carter released a new book about Israel and Palestine that was not inflammatory and easily overlooked. Entitled *We Can Have Peace in the Holy Land: A Plan That Will Work*, the book outlined a practical two-state plan, but neither the Israelis nor the Palestinians was likely to agree with it. Carter thought that Barack Obama made an excellent choice in former Democratic Senator George Mitchell to try to mediate the dispute between Arabs and Israelis, but he also suggested that Hamas had been justifiably provoked into lobbing rockets into Israel after Israel had reduced its food supply. Carter thought Israel needed to urgently accept some agreement, for, if it did not, he predicted that the Israelis would face eventual disaster when the Arab population grew to outnumber them.[25]

Failing to broker peace among religious antagonists in the Middle East, Carter worked harder to get Baptists in the United States to reconcile among themselves. On January 31, he addressed the Sixteenth Street Baptist Church in Birmingham, Alabama, where an infamous hate-crime bombing in 1963 had killed four young Black girls attending church that Sunday. Twelve hundred people packed the church to hear Carter's call for racial reconciliation and cooperation through the Covenant Baptist Fellowship. Almost three months later, on April 24, he joined African-American poet Maya Angelou at the Southeast regional meeting of the New Baptist Covenant at Wake Forest University in Winston-Salem, North Carolina. On that occasion, Carter told the audience that the Covenant Fellowship would provide the catalyst needed to get all Baptists to unite. Despite Carter's optimism, the Baptists were equally as intransigent as the Palestinians and Israelis.[26]

The thirtieth anniversary of the Camp David Accords on March 30, 2009, found many critics questioning the long-term effectiveness of the Israeli-Egyptian agreement. In Egypt, despite celebrations of the treaty, most analysts argued that "after three decades of official peace, the notion of cooperation with Israel—given its rough treatment of the Palestinian population—remains broadly unpopular on the Egyptian street."[27] In Israel, outgoing Prime Minister Ehud Olmert delivered an impassioned farewell speech arguing, like Carter, that the future of Israel rested upon a two-state solution to the Palestinian question. "As a people," Olmert said, "we cannot miss the historic opportunity to realize the vision of two states for two people with massive international support." Prime Minister Designate Benjamin Netanyahu, however, would take the opposite approach, exacerbating the hostility between the Israelis and the Palestinians.[28] Carter, like a voice crying in the wilderness, gave interview after interview in which he defended the accords, truthfully pointing out that the agreement was still in effect, and optimistically predicting, as he entitled his book, *We Can Have Peace in the Holy Land.*[29]

With no peace or acceptable peace plan yet in sight for the Holy Land, life went on for the Carters in their other pursuits for peace, democracy, and basic human rights. During the winter and spring of 2009, Carter auctioned enough personal artifacts and other items to raise $817,590 for the Carter Center—someone paid $80,000 for a fly fishing trip with the Carters. Carter planned to donate $1 million of his own money to the $9 million plan to update and renovate the museum attached to his presidential library. He and Rosalynn cheered New Mexico's legislative action to outlaw the death penalty. In late April, the Carters went to Lima, Peru, to participate in a Carter Center regional conference on the right of access to information. In addition to Peru, they visited Ecuador, Bolivia, and Brazil to meet the presidents of each of those countries and assess Carter Center projects in them.[30]

In May, Carter found some vindication in returning to Washington to testify on energy security before the Senate Foreign Relations Committee. Chaired by Senator John Kerry, the committee welcomed the former president who had fought so hard for an energy program and independence from foreign oil. Since most of his efforts had been checked by subsequent presidents, it was a remarkable moment when President Obama recognized him as an authority on the topic. His central message to the committee was the same one he had been delivering since he had established a Department of Energy and, with the help of Tip O'Neill, finessed complicated energy legislation through Congress. National security, he repeated, depended upon freedom from dependence on foreign oil.[31]

Energized by a Democrat in the White House after eight years of Republican control, Carter again plunged into the Middle East cauldron.

He was particularly pleased by President Obama's speech in Cairo on June 4, promising "A New Beginning" in US relations with the Muslim world. Three days later in Lebanon, Jimmy and Rosalynn joined fifty observers from twenty countries to monitor the country's first free and fair elections since 1972. After visiting 28 polling places with Rosalynn, Jimmy reported that "There were many minor infractions of electoral procedures, but in general it was a good election with the results accepted peacefully by both sides." He attributed the victory of a pro-western coalition primarily to local factors, "but a friendlier attitude toward Obama and America may have helped."[32]

From Lebanon, Carter drove to Damascus, where he met with the Syrian foreign affairs minister and later with President Assad. "They were somewhat peeved at U.S. 'intervention' in the Lebanese election," Carter found, but "eager to have friendly relations with the U.S., believe recent diplomatic meetings were wasted opportunities, look forward to Senator George Mitchell's visit this week, want to help with Iraq border crossing security and the overall Middle East peace process."[33]

After a long walk through the old city of Damascus, following in the footsteps of St. Paul, Carter met with Khaled Mashal and other Hamas leaders, again asking them to accept previous peace agreements and to release Israeli Corporal Shalit. "As in previous meetings," Carter reported, "my impression was that they were frank and honest with me, listening carefully, quickly accepting or rejecting my suggestions, and being flexible when possible. I left written proposals for them to consider."[34]

Driving from Damascus through the West Bank to East Jerusalem, Carter met Corporal Shalit's father, Noam Shalit, who gave him a letter to his son. The next morning, Saturday June 13, at Ramallah in the West Bank, the administrative capital of the Palestinian National Authority, Carter conferred with various Palestinian officials and urged them to put an end to their internal divisions and stop persecuting their rivals. After a private Palestinian communications company awarded him the Palestine International Award for Excellence and Creativity, Carter spoke to a large audience that included Prime Minister Salam Fayyad, declaring, "I have been in love with the Palestinian people for many years." At age eighty-five, he pledged his "assistance, as long as I live, to win your freedom, your independence, your sovereignty and a good life."[35]

Carter thought that Israel's Prime Minister Benjamin Netanyahu might be persuaded to come to terms with the Palestinians, but he was very wrong. On Sunday, June 12, Carter met Israeli president Shimon Peres in Jerusalem.

"We disagreed on a number of issues," Carter reported, "but had a pleasant discussion." Much more disagreeable was Netanyahu's televised speech, which Carter watched later that day. "I . . . was appalled by his introduction of numerous obstacles to peace, some of them insurmountable," Carter recalled." The next morning Carter had a long session with the Knesset's Foreign Affairs and Defense Committee, which he found "very challenging and exciting." "Grilled," he said, for more than an hour with "negative and aggressive questions," he found them respectful and attentive to his responses. "This was one of the high points of the trip," he reported.[36] The low point of Carter's trip came the following day, the last of his trip before he headed home. During a brief visit to Hamas in Gaza with a UN escort, Carter delivered the letter that Noam Shalit had written to his son and learned that he was alive and well. But Carter found his visit to Gaza to be "a heart breaking, infuriating, and embarrassing experience." "The devastation," he reported, "was horrific in what had been an area of small businesses and workshops. They had been first bombed and then the rubble leveled by huge bulldozer. All the agricultural areas along the borders with Israel were empty because the Israelis still fired on anyone who entered, assuming that they might launch a missile or mortar round."[37]

In the middle of his visit to Gaza, Carter was warned that his life was in imminent danger and that he should leave immediately, but he continued with his planned activities. Hamas and Carter's security detail had learned that insurgents from the Army of Islam, a group of Palestinian terrorists, had planted two bombs along the route Carter would travel. Both were removed, foiling the assassination plot.[38]

Leaving behind the deadlock between the Israelis and the Arabs for the time being, Carter returned home and announced a new human rights initiative on July 15. Cleverly entitled "Losing my religion for equality," its focus would be to bring justice and equality to women and girls who had been discriminated against for too long in virtually every country in the world. Twisted interpretations of Scripture had relegated them to subservient roles, Carter said. He had made the "painful and difficult" decision to sever his ties with the Southern Baptist Convention when it voted to prohibit women from being ordained. The view that women are inferior appeared in many faiths, he explained, a reality that would make his new human rights push global in scope. The Elders would challenge this injustice, for the prejudice against women was contrary to the Universal Declaration of Human Rights, the teachings of Jesus Christ, Paul, Moses, the prophets, Muhammad, and other founders of religious groups. He planned to write a book on the subject as well as deliver many speeches at numerous conferences.[39]

The death of Senator Ted Kennedy in late August recalled the long and troubled relationship between the Kennedys and the Carters. Jimmy and Rosalynn joined three other presidents and first ladies at the funeral mass on August 29 in the Basilica of Our Lady of Perpetual Help in Boston. What must have gone through their minds as they sat there can only be guessed, for in recent years Kennedy had worked with Rosalynn to get legislation passed that she had long advocated. Although Kennedy had been a bitter rival within the Democratic Party, he shared many of the same goals with the Carters. Both men wanted improved healthcare, insurance coverage of mental illnesses, human rights at home and abroad, and diplomatic solutions to international crises. Carter as president and former president, and Kennedy as a long-time senator, accomplished many of their goals, but their rivalry had impeded Carter's reelection and had lessened Kennedy's chance to become president.[40]

Two weeks later, Carter's former press secretary, Jody Powell, died of a heart attack. A close adviser and friend since the earliest days of Carter's entry into politics, Jody had been something of a surrogate son, a traveling companion, an irreverent commentator at times, and a splendid press secretary. The inventor of the "killer rabbit" story, Jody could be late for appointments with his boss and get by with mistakes and failures that no other person could. Jimmy's grief over the loss of his "son" was profound but private.[41]

Jimmy revealed none of his private pain when he and Rosalynn celebrated his eighty-fifth birthday on October 1, 2009, with a grand opening of the completely renovated Jimmy Carter Museum. Among the many dignitaries with their speeches that reminisced about them and praised their accomplishments, the Carters waited patiently until the time came for Rosalynn to introduce Jimmy. She said that she had been married to that man for sixty-three years, that there had never been a dull moment, and that she loved him. Jimmy, the man who had heard himself introduced thousands of times as president and former president, grinned broadly, looked down from the podium at Rosalynn and said that that was the best introduction he had ever had.[42]

Jimmy and Rosalynn were both equally enthusiastic about the new Obama administration. When President Obama received the Nobel Peace Prize in the first year of his presidency, Jimmy thought that he unquestionably deserved it, because Obama had said the right things in his inaugural address to restore the traditional values of the United States and set his country again at the forefront of international leadership. By promoting "peace instead of animosity and hatred," Carter said, Obama had "opened up avenues of communication . . . to . . . a dozen nations . . . with whom we had no relationships in the past."[43]

On November 4, the Iranians staged their customary anti-US rally to mark the anniversary of their taking the US hostages, but they also demonstrated against their own President Mahmoud Ahmadinejad, accusing him of human rights violations and voting fraud.

Carter paid little attention to the Iranians, for he and Rosalynn were preparing a trip to Vietnam to participate in a massive Habitat for Humanity project. They were to build 300 houses bordering the Mekong River, including some post-disaster work in Sichuan, China, which had suffered a major earthquake the previous year. Carter had long wanted to put the troubled memories of the Vietnam War to rest and establish good relations with the Vietnamese people. At Rosalynn's suggestion, they invited US veterans who had fought in the war to go back to Vietnam with them to help build houses.[44]

When the Carter's grandson, Jason, announced in early December that he was running for the Georgia State Senate, Jimmy and Rosalynn could not help but recall Jimmy's own difficult campaign so long ago in 1962. After graduating from Duke University and spending time in the Peace Corps in South Africa, Jason had attended the University of Georgia Law School but he hoped to have a political career following in the footsteps of his grandfather. His famous grandparents campaigned for him, but their influence cut both ways. Later in the month when Jimmy wrote an open letter apologizing for any words or deeds of his that might have upset the Jewish community, he had to deny that he had done so because his grandson was running for office from a district with a large Jewish population. Whether the intercession of his grandparents helped or hurt, Jason won the election easily.[45]

Resuming their own busy public lives, in March 2010 Jimmy and Rosalynn went to Seoul, South Korea, where Jimmy accepted an honorary degree from Korea University. During their four-day stay, he urged South Korea to talk directly with North Korea, arguing that while North Korea's reaction was unpredictable, there was "no harm in making a major effort, including unrestrained direct talks." He also urged North Korea's leader Kim Jong-Il to honor his late father's 1994 promise to give up nuclear weapons, but said that

North Korea would not back down on that issue unless the United States met basic demands such as direct talks leading to a framework for an agreement.

While in South Korea, Rosalynn spoke about caregiving and her hope to establish a branch of her institute there.[46] At home, Rosalynn, with Ssan K. Golant and Kathryn E. Cade, published a new book, *Within Our Reach: Ending the Mental Health Crisis*, in which they reviewed the steps that had been taken toward the necessary legislation to provide insurance coverage for mental illnesses. Describing herself as an "accidental activist," Rosalynn traced her career and progress in caring for the mentally ill. Optimistically, she described new research into the causes and treatments of mental illnesses. To promote sales of the book, she gave numerous television interviews and made other appearances where she signed copies for purchasers.[47]

Jimmy remained entangled in international projects and disputes. In the spring of 2010, he went again to Sudan, this time without Rosalynn. Representing both the Carter Center and The Elders, he led a delegation of sixty international observers from over twenty countries to monitor that country's presidential election. Incumbent President Omar al-Bashir was reelected, but Carter and other observers found that the election fell short of the standards set by the Declaration of Principles of International Election Observation that had been adopted by the UN in 2005. Carter thought the election would lead to the secession of southern Sudan where political oppression, human rights abuses, and arrests of domestic observers who disapproved President Bashir were prevalent. In an op-ed piece in the *Los Angeles Times*, Carter said that although the elections had been relatively peaceful, it was "imperative that the U.S. and the international community remain deeply involved in Sudan." That was the "only hope for a long-suffering and courageous people," he continued, "including those in Darfur, who have had at last a partial taste of freedom, peace and democracy."[48] Peace in Sudan, as elsewhere, Carter argued, was necessary to prevent disease, particularly in southern Sudan where most of the remaining cases of guinea worm disease still occurred.[49]

The Carters continued to supervise the work of the Carter Center, but as they aged, they reduced their personal involvement in it activities. They remained home when the center sent eight observers to Guinea to monitor its June 27 elections. In its twenty-eighth year, the center proudly announced that it had helped to improve the lives of people in more than seventy countries by advancing democracy, improving healthcare, and increasing crop production; Jimmy and Rosalynn knew that they deserved much of the credit. The center had observed eighty elections in thirty countries, and as Rosalynn said, it had become a much larger and more effective institution than she and Jimmy had imagined when they first organized it in 1982.[50]

Global events gave them the opportunity to reinforce their message and work. When on May 31, 2010, Israel raided ships in international waters bearing supplies to Gaza, creating a new Middle East crisis, Carter joined the rest of the world in near universal condemnation of that action. Defending his legacy, he also reminded any who would listen that he had through "enormous determination and willpower" achieved an "historic treaty between Egypt and Israel," an accord that "essentially has held."[51]

In August, with Rosalynn's knowledge, Jimmy went on a semi-secret mission to North Korea to try to secure the release of a US prisoner, thirty-year-old Aijalon Mahli Gomes, a devout Christian who had strayed across the border into North Korea from China, where he was a teaching missionary. He had been arrested, tried for illegally the country, and sentenced to eight years of hard labor. In despair, Gomes had attempted suicide, because all efforts to free him had failed. The North Koreans offered to release Gomes if Carter personally would come to take him home. Despite his very bad knees, eighty-five-year-old Jimmy agreed to go.

Upon arrival in Pyongyang, Carter was greeted with flowers and the respect due a head of state. During his two-day stay, he met with Kim Yong Nam, president of the Presidium of the Supreme People's Assembly, who expressed his government's willingness to denuclearize the Korean Peninsula and to resume six-party talks, information that Carter could take back to the US President Obama. Since Supreme Leader Kim Jong-Il was in China at the time, Carter did not speak with him. The talks with Kim Yong Nam were secret, but when they ended, Gomes boarded a plane with Carter on August 27, bound for his home in Boston. Carter, who apparently had reduced his exercise routine, appeared heavier than usual as he and a very thin Gomes stood with arms around each other's backs and surrounded by guards preparing to leave Pyongyang. Carter stayed with the elated teacher until they deplaned in Boston, where Gomes gave his rescuer a warm hug as Carter waved to his grateful family. Carter noticeably stumbled as he left the plane only long enough to deliver Gomes to his family. Jimmy knew that he needed to have both knees replaced, but he thought his mission to save Gomes was more urgent.[52]

Carter later explained that North Korean officials had had a hidden agenda in inviting him to Pyongyang to obtain Gomes's release. They "wanted me to come," he said, "in the hope that I might help resurrect the agreements on de-nuclearization and peace." Talks about those agreements, which had begun during the Clinton administration, had been abandoned by Bush, but there was reasonable hope that President Obama would resume them.[53]

Publication of his *White House Diary* in the late summer of 2010 brought Carter again into the limelight on the major television programs and in na-tional newspapers. Although the published diary represented only a small part of the nine hundred pages he had recorded while president, it revealed much about Carter that was generally unknown. He wrote candidly about his political enemies and pulled no punches when recording how much he disliked Menachem Begin, Helmut Schmidt, Frank Church, and others whom he referred to as "asses."

Jimmy's love for Rosalynn always showed through in the pages of his diary, but the famous Carter temper, impatience, and frustration with Congress are all there as well. He blamed the "irresponsible and abusive" Ted Kennedy for the stalemate that blocked passage of comprehensive healthcare reform. He thought the hostage rescue effort should have worked, and the fact that it did not is what cost him the 1980 election. He wrote that he was sorry to have alienated the Jewish community, but he thought the Jewish criticism of him was unfair. He regretted his poor relationship with the media.

In his interviews promoting the published *Diary* he often repeated his mantra: "We never fired a bullet. We never dropped a bomb. We never launched a missile."[54] A consistent supporter of strong US military forces as president, he was most proud of the peace and freedom that he believed those forces had helped maintain during his four years in office. Carter felt that the United States, as a superpower, should be the champion of peace. But peace and democracy must arise from the grassroots, he said, referring specifically to the Carter Center's efforts to bring democracy to isolated Chinese villages.

In early September, Jimmy and Rosalynn went to China to attend the 2010 China Conference for International Sister Cities and the Fourth China Zhejiang International Peace and Culture Festival. Invited by the Chinese People's Association for Friendship with Foreign Countries, they met with Premier Wen Jiabao on September 6. Both men celebrated the thirty-one years of progress in their countries' relationship and cultural exchanges as they vowed to continue on that path. In carefully chosen words, Carter said: "I am full of confidence in the prospects of US-China relations. The Carter Center and I are willing to make continued efforts in enhancing mu-tual understanding and friendship between the two peoples." He sincerely, if naively, believed that, if the center could advance grassroots election procedures, it could lead China eventually to embrace democracy.[55]

The arrival of democracy in China would not take place, but Carter felt vindicated in Washington when President Obama put the solar panels back on the White House roof. Carter was also filled with new hopes for bringing peace to the Middle East as well as stamping out the last guinea worm, working with The Elders.

FORTY FIVE

Journey into Eternity

On October 1, 2010, Carter turned eighty-six. Even though far older than the age at which most people retire, two weeks later he returned with The Elders to Gaza, the West Bank, Egypt, Syria, Jordan, and Israel "to encourage," as he said, "a just and secure peace for Israel and its neighbors based on international law."[1]

"Peace is not an item on Israel's agenda," a Qatari newspaper declared on October 17 when Israel announced that it would build more settlements in East Jerusalem in open defiance of any plan to reach a settlement with the Palestinians.[2] But peace was on Jimmy Carter's agenda when he joined three of the sixteen Elders for a trip to the troubled Middle East, October 15–23. Former president of Ireland Mary Robinson, former Foreign Minister of Algeria and UN envoy Lakhdar Brahimi, and the founder of the Self-Employed Women's Association of India Ela Bhatt comprised the determined and fearless group who were ready to confront those who opposed peace and comfort those who longed and worked for it. Arab leaders welcomed The Elders, but the Israelis did not.

Traveling with guards and aides, Carter first went to Gaza, where he again witnessed horrible scenes of destruction and mistreatment. Some 40,000 children, he learned, were denied access to schools because Israel would not allow needed building materials to be shipped into Gaza. A few children attended school rooms set up in shipping containers but most had no access to classrooms at all. Carter heard similar accounts of Palestinian despair in East Jerusalem. Everywhere the four Elders went it seemed that they found no hope that the Israelis and Palestinians would sit down together and come to a peaceful settlement of their differences.[3]

When the Speaker of the Knesset, Reuven Rivlin, told Carter that Israelis believed he was "supporting Hamas and encouraging terror," Carter responded that he and his fellow Elders were there only to listen, to meet with people representing all sides of the conflict, and to bring peace. His words had no impact upon the Israeli speaker.[4] Israel had already resumed building apartments for settlers on the West Bank, which the UN's Middle East envoy declared "alarming" and in violation of international law.[5] Nowhere on their trip, Carter reported, did The Elders find any evidence that current peace talks would succeed.[6]

On weekends when he was at home in Plains, Carter taught a Sunday School class at Maranatha Baptist Church, where hundreds of people from across the nation and sometimes from around the world came to hear him. Using his interpretation of Scripture, as well as his worldview, Carter consistently urged his listeners to emulate Christ, condemn warmongering leaders, and recognize that all people of whatever nationality or disposition are equal in the eyes of God and should be treated that way by their fellow human beings.

When pressed after one of his Sunday morning lessons, he answered the question of what happens after we die: "I don't really know. Saint Paul said that it would be a transformation in our basic character, like the difference between a planted peanut seed and a plant that produces peanuts or corn or wheat."[7] Despite his faith, Carter was not ready to find out what life after death might be like; he would not give up his hope for Palestinian reconciliation with Israel, nor his determination to eradicate the very last guinea worm, or his firm belief that peace with Russia, China, and North Korea was possible.

Christmas 2010 came and went in its traditional manner in Plains, and the New Year found Jimmy and Rosalynn prepared to commence the first of five major international trips he had planned for 2011. Eager to finally exterminate an old foe of the last quarter of a century, Carter vowed, "I'm still determined to outlive the last guinea worm."[8] Dr. John Hardman traveled with them to Khartoum, where they joined others from the Carter Center as well as an international group that included Kofi Annan. Before guinea worm disease could be totally conquered, Carter knew, the long, bloody Sudanese civil war had to be ended. Thus, the main purpose of the Carters' trip was to monitor a referendum among South Sudanese to determine whether their region would remain part of Sudan or become a new independent country. Hoping for peace in South Sudan, the Carters conferred with Sudanese president Omar al-Bashir and other officials in Khartoum and then flew with their group of monitors to Juba in South Sudan on January 9 to observe the week-long referendum.[9]

During the next seven days, Jimmy and Rosalynn visited many of the 618 polling places observing long lines of men separated from long lines of

women. The women voted first, because "they had work to do." There were
no paper ballots or voice votes; one upheld hand meant independence, and
two clasped hands indicated unity. The poll managers had to be trusted, and
watched, to make a fair count.[10]

When the referendum ended on January 16, South Sudan emerged as an
independent nation. Four million people, including more than 90% of eligible voters in the South and 40% of South Sudanese living in the North,
had participated. In Juba, now the new capital of South Sudan, cars draped
with black, red, and green flags, honked their horns as they bumped along
the potholed dirt tracks that passed for roads.[11] Although thirty-three people
had been killed in a clash on the North-South border, Carter declared that
those deaths were not an impediment to nationhood, nor did they nullify
the "orderly, pleasant, and productive" voting process. He urged both sides,
however, to address practical and political issues swiftly before the July date
for international recognition of South Sudan's independence. With the war
ended, teams from the Carter Center could visit people in rural areas and
complete the fight against the guinea worm. Carter expected that the "Carter
Center will remain involved in both countries in promoting peace, democracy, and better health and education."[12]

After returning home on January 16, Carter found himself much in demand to appear on panels and grant interviews, and as usual, he was forthright in expressing his opinions. He criticized President Barack Obama's
approach to Israeli-Palestinian peace negotiations for not being tough
enough, but he was optimistic about Egypt, saying that he was not worried
about the growing political power of the Sunni Islamist Muslim Brotherhood
there.[13] Carter also talked about meeting the Pope, the rights of women, and
the fact that, in his view, the United States was "a warmonger," complaining
that United States had initiated armed conflict in thirty countries since the
end of his presidency.[14]

In a joint interview for *Rolling Stone* magazine, Jimmy and Rosalynn talked
about how they worked together and often disagreed. Neither of them, they
revealed, had understood how emotional the issue of the Palestinians was
for Jewish Americans. More serious that the Palestinian issue, Jimmy had
especially offended many Jews with his stigmatizing Israel as guilty of apartheid. Carter explained that he had posted an open letter during his grandson
Jason's campaign the previous year pleading for forgiveness for anything he
had done to offend them. Rosalynn did not think Jimmy needed to ask for
forgiveness. She explained that Jimmy did not want any people, including

the Palestinians, to be oppressed. When Jimmy commented that he had not anticipated his role in the Democratic National Convention being minimized, Rosalynn "curtly" interrupted that she had.[15]

The drama of history continued to surround Jimmy and Rosalynn when, in March 2011, Raul Castro, brother of Fidel Castro and his successor as president of Cuba, invited them to visit the island nation. With the approval of Secretary of State Hillary Clinton, they spent a few days there, March 28–30, where Jimmy was officially supposed to study Cuban economic conditions and opportunities for Carter Center projects, but he was unofficially on a sensitive mission to ask Castro to set free his US prisoner Alan Gross, possibly in exchange for five Cuban spies. Gross, a Jewish-American contractor, had been working for the US Agency for International Development on a humanitarian project to provide hardware for Cuba's tiny Jewish population so that they could access the internet. Cuba's Communist regime had interpreted such access as a spying activity, and in December 2009, Gross had been sentenced to fifteen years in prison for crimes against the state. Jimmy and Rosalynn visited him in a military hospital where he was currently confined because of a recent serious illness. Gross told them that he received better treatment than other prisoners and had "adequate communication with his wife and family." Carter opened himself to severe condemnation in the United States by publicly recommending the release of the Cuban spies, but Castro refused to free Gross.[16]

Otherwise, Carter thought his and Rosalynn's visit to Cuba was a success. The Cubans knew, he reported, that "as President, I lifted all travel restraints and made strides toward normalizing diplomatic relations." Cuban foreign policy officers, with whom Carter talked, acknowledged the progress that the Obama administration was making toward achieving the goals Carter had set more than thirty years earlier. At a meeting with President Raul Castro and his brother Fidel, the Carters discovered that Fidel, although confined to his home with knee and shoulder injuries, was "vigorous" and "alert." At the airport, accompanied by President Raoul Castro, Carter gave a television interview in which he called for "the release of Alan Gross . . . and the establishment of full relations between our two countries."[17]

Less than a month later, Carter joined three other Elders for a trip to the Korean Peninsula, April 22–29, "to learn about the humanitarian food crisis" in North Korea and to analyze the differences between the two Koreas. Accompanied by former Finnish president Martti Ahtisaari, Mary Robinson, and former Norwegian prime minister Gro Brundtland, he hoped to revive the six-party talks that had been initiated by Bill Clinton, abandoned by George W. Bush, but now favorably considered by Barack Obama. If the stalled talks resumed, Carter thought they might reduce tensions between the United States and North Korea and "help the parties address key issues, including denuclearization."

After a stop in Beijing for a briefing about food shortages in North Korea, Carter and his colleagues flew to Pyongyang, where they were lodged in an "ornate guest house." They visited the enormous memorial to the nation's founder, Kim Il Sung, and then got down to the business of discussing with government officials the horrifying hunger suffered by North Korean children. They did not meet the "Great Leader" Kim Jon Il, but as they were departing for South Korea, he sent them a message thanking them for their efforts for peace and humanitarianism and expressing his willingness to participate in an "inter-Korean dialogue, including a summit meeting with President Lee of South Korea."[18] Clearly, Kim Jon Il intended for them to take the message to Seoul.

In Seoul, The Elders delivered Kim's message about resumption of talks to South Korean and US officials, but their discussions centered on North Korea's "dire need for food aid and their unprecedented willingness for donors to monitor delivery." In his role as a totally detached humanitarian, Carter felt free to criticize the United States for refusing to send humanitarian aid to North Korea. Declaring food to be a basic human right, he called upon all nations to do their part to relieve North Korea's plight. Carter's critics, including some in South Korea, were legion, but in July, with the help of the Obama administration, the Koreas returned to the conference table.[19]

The summer of 2011 gave both Carters the opportunity to spend more time at home, which Rosalynn welcomed. Jimmy finally had one knee replaced in June and the other one in August.[20] While he stayed home to recuperate, Rosalynn traveled to Palm Springs, California, to eulogize former First Lady Betty Ford, who had died on July 8. "She was just Betty, as gracious as always," Rosalynn said in her speech. "Millions of women are in her debt today," because of breast cancer detection. She noted that Betty Ford had shown the Carters that there was life after the White House and continuing opportunities for service.[21]

The Fords, however, had had little impact on how Carter treated his sons. In his relationship with his children, Jimmy had mellowed somewhat as he aged, but he was still his father's son. Only one of his four grown children did not experience divorce, and none of them, despite their successful careers, could live up to his expectations. Rosalynn was the glue that held the family together. For her children and her husband, she was ever present with solace, encouragement, rewards, and the kind of unconditional love that only a mother possesses. While maintaining an increasingly public career, she nurtured all four of the children when they were young, and when they were older, she took time from her busy public life for them. Forgiving, helpful, and comforting when they needed it, she guarded their privacy and cheered them along their diverse life paths.

The relationship between Jimmy and Rosalynn, so often written and speculated about, was solidly grounded in their small-town Southern values. They traveled the world but never left Plains. Strong individuals with tempers that sometimes flared in public, they shared a common upbringing, Christian faith, devotion to family, and ambition to succeed at everything they tried. They bonded professionally and personally in a manner unusual for their generation, and sometimes against great odds, to make their unusual way in the world. Jimmy teased her unmercifully, but teasing in his culture signified caring and loving. She criticized him, sometimes joking, sometimes serious, but always constructively, and she was quick to defend him on the campaign trail, in the White House, and during their post-presidential careers. Always putting each other first, Rosalynn and Jimmy slipped into a symbiotic relationship and became a powerful couple who raised their caring and nurturing of family and neighbors to the national and international levels.

Jimmy himself, in an interview he granted for a British newspaper in September 2011, described his sixty-five-year-long marriage to Rosalynn as a love affair, admitting that he would never have become president without her help. Despite the trials and tribulations of their long marriage, their fishbowl existence, and the interminable gossip and questions, Carter said, the "love at first sight" that he had experienced that day when he had first seen young Rosalynn standing on the steps of the Methodist Church in Plains remained as real as it had been sixty-six and a half years earlier.[22]

Carter's international trips became less frequent as age slowed him down, but from October 2 through October 6 he traveled with other members of the Carter Center to the Netherlands, Belgium, United Kingdom, and Norway. In his element when much of the discussion with leaders of those four countries related to progress toward peace in the Middle East, Carter believed that the center's "almost unique commitment to maintain communications with all the involved parties" meant its views were "sought avidly by key political leaders, news media, and the general public." At every stop during the four-day trip, whether a private dinner or an interview with the media, Carter emphasized the "Center's extensive health programs" and clarified its peace plans.[23]

At home in Plains, Carter continued his familiar routine of working on books and shorter pieces almost every morning in his study, taking vacations, teaching Sunday School classes at the Maranatha Baptist Church, and maintaining a keen interest in current political events—and a willingness to comment on them. Not until December 6–15 did he and Rosalynn embark upon another major international trip, when they visited Beijing, Guangzhou, and Hong Kong "to cement ties with the people and leaders of China, to explore future projects of The Carter Center . . . in the region," and to seek financial support for such projects. After participating in "a scholarly forum in Beijing to discuss China's involvement in Africa," the Carters met with Vice President Xi Jinping in the Great Hall of the People to discuss ping pong diplomacy and the history of improved US relations with China since Nixon's visit in 1972. Jimmy pointed out with some pride that more than 160,000 Chinese students were studying in US universities and that US businesses had made numerous investments in China. In Guangzhou, they observed the production of many electronic items that often found their way to the United States. Carter particularly enjoyed his visit to Hong Kong, because he remembered that his Uncle Tom Gordy had sent him gifts from there when he was a boy. Impressed "with the enormous vitality of the Chinese economy," the Carters left for home having "received enough contributions from private sources, mostly speaking fees, to finance our China programs for several years."[24]

Although Carter's international travels in 2021 were reduced from those of the previous year, they were ambitious for an eighty-seven-year-old man. As soon as he finished his traditional post-Christmas vacation with the family, Carter prepared to go to Egypt with a Carter Center delegation to monitor parliamentary elections on January 10–11, 2012. He returned there on May 23–24 with Carter Center observers, to monitor the first round of elections for a new president, which ultimately failed to remove the military from power, as Carter had wished. On May 27–28, Carter and Lakhdar Brahimi, representing The Elders, went to Sudan and South Sudan to urge the presidents of those two nations to resume their stalled peace negotiations. In Khartoum, they also attempted to dissuade Sudanese president Omar al-Bashir, whom many believed to be guilty of genocide in Darfur, from committing more bloody deeds. Bashir, however, remained in power and continued to abuse his people until he was overthrown in 2019 and charged with war crimes.[25]

It was the looming presidential election in the United States, however, that concerned Carter most, although he was in no position to influence it. He thought his country was abandoning its role as champion of human rights, and he found little comfort in the field of Republican candidates. When his fellow Georgian, Newt Gingrich, who had risen to prominence as Speaker of the House of Representatives during the George W. Bush administration, was mentioned as the Republican nominee, Carter dismissed him as a racist. When multi-millionaire George Romney seemed to be leading in the battle, Carter was pleased that his grandson, James Earl Carter IV, a Democratic opposition researcher, discovered a secret meeting at which Romney had disparaged nearly half of Americans who thought they deserved government aid. The evidence Carter sent to *Mother Jones* magazine rocked the Romney campaign.[26]

Carter favored Obama's reelection although his relationship with Obama had never been close and he disagreed with some of the president's policies. Obama's decision to use drones in the ongoing war against terrorism irked Carter, who saw the technology as a gross violation of human rights: "It means you assassinate people without bringing charges, without finding them guilty, and in the process inadvertently causing collateral damage—the killing of completely innocent people who might be in the neighborhood." Carter, however, blamed Congress, not Obama, for the continuing imprisonment of 165 alleged terrorists at Guantanamo Bay, at least half of whom, he thought, were innocent. He was also seriously disturbed by the uncontrolled use of wiretapping that had begun during the George W. Bush presidency.[27]

Despite his complaints, on July 20, Carter accepted the Democratic National Party's invitation to deliver a speech at its convention, which was scheduled to meet in Charlotte, North Carolina, the following September when Obama would be nominated for reelection. Carter did not attend the convention, but he recorded a speech that was shown simultaneously on a large screen in the arena and on national television during prime time on opening night. Carter, who had been lauded a month earlier by party chairman Antonio Villaraigosa for his humanitarianism and championship of democracy, praised Obama for his success in bringing about healthcare reform, drawing down the troops in Iraq, and promoting pro-middle class economic policies. Carter made clear that he and Rosalynn would vote for Obama's reelection.[28]

Although frequently labeled the best ex-president in US history, Carter was no longer influential in US politics. Through his work at the Carter Center, Habitat for Humanity, and The Elders, Carter kept doing the same sort of things he had been doing since 1962, but the political and social climate, opportunities for service, and levels of resistance to his projects had changed with the times.[29]

The story of the Iranian hostage rescue flared anew in October 2012 with the release of a popular movie, *Argo*, starring Ben Affleck. Primarily an overly dramatized account of how the CIA had rescued the six US diplomats who had taken refuge in the Canadian embassy, it played down the role of Ken Taylor, the Canadian ambassador to Iran at the time. Carter, who had assisted with the movie and generally liked it, gave the Canadians more credit than was evident in the film.[30]

While admitting that his time was running out, Carter did not announce a plan for retirement. He spoke often about his new project to promote justice and equality for women and girls around the world and about his work with The Elders. In November 2012 he joined two of his fellow Elders on another Middle East trip to talk to Arab and Israeli leaders about finding a road to peace, again without achieving any tangible results. In December, he and Rosalynn returned to China to pursue Carter Center projects there and to help further strengthen US-Chinese relations.

Jimmy agreed with Rosalynn that they had learned to give each other space to develop their individual interests. But they also shared similar passions, not only in their work, but in their mutual love of fly fishing. In 2013 the Carters found the strength and energy to pursue that passion in two distant places: Argentina in the spring for rainbow trout and Mongolia's Eg River in the fall for taimen, the largest fish in the salmon family.[31]

Traveling for very different purposes than fishing, Jimmy and Rosalynn visited Nepal and Myanmar between March 28 and April 6 to support both nations' transitions to democracy and promote peace and economic development through the Carter Center. They also took some time out for bird watching in Nepal and sightseeing in both countries. Jimmy returned to Nepal in November to help the Carter Center observe elections for a new Constituent Assembly, which it was hoped would accomplish what the assembly elected five years earlier had failed to do—write a constitution and establish an effective government. Although Jimmy was pleased by the record turnout of voters and found the elections to be well organized and peaceful, he was somewhat disconcerted when the defeated Maoists suddenly denounced the elections as fraudulent, leaving matters up in the air as he returned home.[32] Nevertheless, two years later, Nepal succeeded in writing a constitution.

Jimmy's travels in 2013 also took him to Bogotá, Colombia, in January and again with Rosalynn in July to learn about peace talks between the government and the terrorist guerilla group FARC, to discuss improvements in human rights, and to inquire about drug control policies.[33] On April 10, Jimmy braved Jewish protesters in New York City to accept the Benjamin N. Cardozo Law School peace award at Yeshiva University. His old nemesis Alan Dershowitz sided with the protesters, saying of Carter: "He's never met a terrorist he didn't love, and never met an Israeli whom he did."[34]

Jimmy continued to find better understanding and acceptance of his views among The Elders. In July, he was part of a delegation of Elders that went to Washington, DC, and London for meetings with US and British foreign policy officials "to explain the work of The Elders and The Carter Center, to offer our assistance when needed, and to learn as much as possible about the policies of the two governments regarding Syria, Egypt, Israel-Palestine, Sudan, and North Korea." Pleased with their reception in both capitals, they hoped to make a similar visit to Russia sometime in the future.[35]

In October 2013, Jimmy and Rosalynn built Habitat houses in Denver, Colorado. Then in November, Rosalynn achieved the goal for which she had so long fought: parity for mental illness insurance. President Obama successfully managed passage of the Affordable Care Act in Congress, which required health insurance companies to grant parity for mental and physical illness coverage. Secretary of Health and Human Services Kathleen Sebelius made a special trip to Atlanta to make the announcement to Rosalynn and the world at the Carter Center. An Associated Press photographer captured the moment when Rosalynn, tearfully and triumphantly, hugged the secretary who brought the long-awaited news.[36]

Euphoric moments for people approaching ninety years of age inevitably were interspersed with sad ones. Jimmy mourned the fact that the United Sates no longer had a "functioning democracy," and in early December 2013, he mourned the death of Nelson Mandela, whose "passion for freedom and justice created new hope for generations of oppressed people worldwide."[37] A few weeks into the new year of 2014, Jimmy and Rosalynn attended the funeral for Joan Mondale in Minneapolis. Carter praised her for her effective championship of the arts, but his speech and her death attracted very little public attention.[38]

Carter's international trips during 2014 were made principally to pro-mote and support the various programs of the Carter Center and The Elders. In January, he and Rosalynn went to Dubai and Sudan with Dr. Hardman of the Carter Center to discuss regional issues ranging from river blind-ness and guinea worm to the need for democratic reforms in Sudan and easing of tensions with South Sudan. In March, Jimmy traveled to Panama to discuss preparations for its May presidential election, and the following month, he was in Paris talking with French officials about the goals of The Elders and the Carter Center as well as climate change. He also met there with Palestinian leaders, whom he encouraged to persist in their peace talks with Israel despite lack of progress to date. In June, Carter visited Sweden and Norway to explain Carter Center programs around the world to various government officials and diplomats and garner support for them. Finally, in early September Jimmy and Rosalynn returned to China once more to foster good relations and discuss the role of the Carter Center there. Despite "every event" being "pleasant," Carter confessed that he felt his age when he had to make so many speeches.[39]

In the spring of 2014 Carter brought out his new book, *A Call to Action: Women, Religion, Violence and Power*, which explained why his newest program to combat human rights abuses dealt with improving the situation of women. He noted that the World Health Organization had re-ported that one in three women around the world experienced physical or sexual violence at some time in her lifetime. Carter held a conference at the Carter Center on that topic, declared himself to be a feminist, and reaped praise from female participants who said that he had been a better president than almost anyone ever admitted.[40]

When Lawrence Wright's book about the Camp David Accords, *Thirteen Days in September*, was adapted as a play, the Carters attended the grand opening in Washington on April 3. Wright told an interviewer that he had gotten the idea from Gerald Rafshoon, who told him that "when a born-again Christian, an orthodox Jew and a pious Muslim go behind closed doors for 13 days and emerge with the only durable treaty in the Middle East," it is drama. Wright added that Carter was "despised by a number of American Jews. But I don't know any president who gave Israel anything greater than peace with Egypt." He revealed, too, that he had Rosalynn Carter's diary as a source for his book. "She was always Carter's closest adviser . . . Camp David was her idea . . . she's the unacknowledged author of the Camp David Accords."[41]

An Israeli reviewer of the book and of the play was not so enthusiastic. The problem with the book, he thought, was that Sadat and Begin were caricatures while Carter was humanized." The theme of the book, he wrote, was that Begin was bad and Sadat was good. Because the Carters were so close to the Sadats, he contended, anti-Semitism played a role, and the play was not "grounded too well in history."[42]

Unperturbed by such criticisms, Carter gave the keynote address at the annual convention of the Islamic Society of North America in August. Referring to how Muslims worshipped the same god as did Christians and Jews, he emphasized that most Muslims were peace-loving people who condemned the attacks and violence of the radical few.[43]

On October 1, 2014, Jimmy and Rosalynn celebrated his ninetieth birthday at the Carter Center in Atlanta. He had already experienced birthday celebrations at various stops on his recent trip to China. At the site of the famous terracotta warriors near Xian on September 6, Jimmy reported, "there were tens of thousands of tourists present, including many Americans who sang the 'happy birthday' song."[44] In Plains on Sunday September 28, his hometown friends celebrated his birthday after church with an old-fashioned ice cream party at Maxine Reese Park. Two days later at the Carter Center celebration, Jimmy reflected briefly on his life and the current state of the American nation. He believed that the country "is still searching for what it ought to be, and what it can be, and I'm not sure we're making much progress right at this moment."[45]

Carter himself was still searching for many things, but particularly for peace in the Holy Land. In late April 2015, he joined five other Elders in Moscow for discussions with Russian president Vladimir Putin and other top officials about issues ranging from the crisis in Ukraine to the crisis in Syria. Then he and fellow Elder Gro Brundtland went to Jerusalem "to explore latest developments among the Israelis and Palestinians." Israeli prime minister Benjamin Netanyahu and president Reuven Rivlin refused to meet with them, and their planned meetings with Hamas leaders in Gaza were canceled due to security threats there.[46] They were able to confer with Palestinian officials in Ramallah and go to an Israeli village adjacent to Gaza, where the residents strongly supported peaceful relations with their Arab neighbors. Nevertheless, as on his other recent trips to the Holy Land, Carter "met no one who believed there was any viability in the overall peace process."[47]

On May 8, 2015, Carter went to Guyana in South America to help with the Carter Center's monitoring of that nation's presidential and parliamentary elections. But when a head cold that he had contracted in the Middle East worsened, he reluctantly agreed to return to Atlanta for medical care.[48]

Carter's lack of effectiveness in defending the Palestinians, as well as his birthday, prompted him to contemplate the end of his active life. He knew, he said, that change would come when he could no longer travel around the world, but he would keep busy in Plains. "And we're obviously prepared, I'd say in a religious way and psychological way, for inevitable death."[49]

In a reflective mood, Carter published *A Full Life: Reflections at Ninety* in July 2015. Beginning with his childhood and continuing through the most recent house he and Rosalynn had helped build for Habitat for Humanity, he told his story and illustrated it with his own paintings. For those readers unfamiliar with his earlier works, it was an excellent account of Carter and his world. For others, it was a good summary of all he had done penned by a man who had few regrets about how he had lived his life. As in his earlier writings, Mr. Earl loomed large in his memory, the father whose world he wanted to share, and the father whose embrace he craved, the father after whom he patterned his dealings with his own sons, and the father who remained forever alive in him. He might also have added, although he did not, that throughout his political and business careers, as well as his spiritual journey, he was like Mr. Earl.[50]

Carter's recording of *A Full Life* won for him the Grammy Award for the Spoken Word, his second Grammy, the first being for *Our Endangered Values* in 2007. In the round of interviews promoting the new book, Carter made clear that he and Rosalynn were still healthy and active.

He remained as politically outspoken as ever. Refusing to recant his earlier comments about his presidential successors and their policies, Carter approached the presidential election of 2016 with the same candor. He and Rosalynn liked Senator Bernie Sanders of Vermont, but they remained neutral for the Democratic nomination. Sanders, who campaigned passionately for honesty in government and advancement in human rights, wanted a better minimum wage, universal healthcare, aid for education, and increased taxes on the wealthy. Former First Lady, Senator, and Secretary of State Hillary Clinton fought a hard campaign against him, promising to maintain Obama's status quo. Carter thought she would win the nomination because of her vast financial resources, and when she did, he supported her.[51]

The emergence of billionaire Donald Trump, a real estate mogul and popular television personality, as the Republican nominee, however, provoked a bitter reaction from Carter, confirming in his mind that the United States was no longer a democracy. Unlimited money, including foreign money, he asserted, poured into US political and judicial campaigns. A disillusioned former president, Carter declared that the country had disintegrated into an oligarchy where bribes determined who got the nominations and who won the presidency. Congressmen were easily bought, he charged, and the corruption affected governors as well.[52]

As deeply felt as they were, his political concerns were soon eclipsed by others. Carter's luck with his health evaporated that August when he was diagnosed with a rare melanoma of the brain. The people of Plains placed hundreds of signs along the streets reading "Jimmy Carter for Cancer Survivor." When 700 people from all over the country showed up to hear him teach his Sunday School class after he announced his illness, Carter advised them to ask God for strength no matter how heavy the burden. As for himself, he said he was "perfectly at ease with whatever comes." He did want guinea worm to be entirely gone before he died, for eradicating that, he said, would be his greatest legacy.[53]

Rosalynn was worried, but despite occasional displays of emotion, she declared that her Christian faith, as well as Jimmy's, sustained her. Thousands of people from Plains to Palestine marched and displayed posters showing their love and support. In Palestine, one man held up a painted sign: "Palestinians stand with our President Jimmy Carter. You've always stood with Palestine. We love you. Get well. Free Palestine."[54]

After several months of immunology treatment at Emory University Hospital, Carter recovered. Four months after he had revealed his illness, brain scans showed no signs of the cancer.[55] Carter received an unexpected pleasure when a ten-year-old boy from Glen Cove, New York, who had also been cured of cancer, came to see him. Under the auspices of the Make-A-Wish Foundation, Carter Beckhard-Suozzi showed up at the Carter Center, having asked to meet Carter because they had the same name, had defeated cancer, and liked to help people. As the boy approached Carter in his office at the center, the former president opened his arms wide and hugged him. Jimmy asked the "handsome little man" how he was feeling. "Good," came the reply, and Jimmy told him that he felt good too.[56]

Quickly putting discussion of his health behind him, Carter contributed passionate arguments for the recognition of Palestine and restoration of Palestinian human rights to both the *New York Times* and the *Wall Street Journal*. Although he stepped back from his leadership role with The Elders, he did not retreat from his interest in their work. Appalled by a Republican presidential campaign in the fall of 2016 that encouraged a resurgence of racism, Carter urged Baptist faith leaders to combat it. Speaking at a meeting hosted by the New Baptist Covenant in Atlanta, he thundered that for white Americans, keeping quiet was essentially accepting "discrimination and animosity and hatred and division." He also criticized Republican candidate Donald Trump's son for making remarks that seemed to make light of the Holocaust.[57]

After Trump won the election, Jimmy and Rosalynn attended his inauguration on January 20, 2017. At first Carter wanted to give him a fair chance and let the system work, but less than a year into his term, it became clear to Carter that Trump was indifferent to human rights, insulting to allies, and favorable to large corporations. Most of his appointments were unacceptable to Carter, and his ethics and truthfulness seemed nonexistent. Carter was particularly irked to discover that the United States no longer led the world as an advocate for human rights. Disillusioned, Carter declared that the president was a disaster. Rosalynn thought Trump's worst characteristic was that he did not tell the truth. Both Carters nevertheless optimistically believed that the country would right itself again in a future election, for their faith in the United States, they said, especially its people, had not been destroyed.[58]

In the meantime, the Carters continued to build houses. They had planned in 2016 to lead a Habitat crew to construct thousands of houses in Nepal, which had been devastated by an earthquake, but because of unrest in that country and dangerous travel conditions, Habitat cancelled the trip. Therefore, the Carters joined country music stars Garth Brooks and his wife Trisha Yearwood, with whom they had become friends, at a construction project in Memphis, Tennessee, in August. Their Habitat Work Project for the following summer took place in Edmonton and Winnipeg, Canada. While working at the Edmonton site, Carter was overcome by heat and taken to a hospital. Suffering only from dehydration, he quickly recovered and advised his fellow workers to drink plenty of water and continue to work. Although the medics first feared that Carter might be suffering a heart attack, Rosalynn later said that she could have told them that Jimmy had a good heart.[59]

When Rosalynn celebrated her nineteenth birthday on August 18, 2017, she reminisced that when she had turned fifty, on her first birthday in the White House, she thought that was really bad. She recalled how the next year her staff had given her a ride in a blimp to help her celebrate, and in the forty years following she had learned that you could have a full life after fifty. She laughingly welcomed Jimmy's birthday gift of a robotic vacuum cleaner, but she was more grateful for a cocktail party and musical celebration in Plains, where the ticket sales would benefit two local charities.[60]

Jimmy continued to participate in events and activities consistent with his values. He joined four other former presidents at College Station, Texas, in the fall of 2017 to raise money for hurricane victims. He leased thirteen acres of his farmland in Plains to a power company to install 3,500 solar panels. He assisted in their installation and was pleased to announce that they would produce enough energy for 200 of the 215 houses in Plains.[61]

Early in 2018, Rosalynn was stricken with an illness that necessitated complicated abdominal surgery. Jimmy prayed through the night, Rosalynn survived, and soon they were planning new projects to help the needy.

Before he had spent that night waiting anxiously to learn whether or not his wife would live, Jimmy had completed a manuscript for *Faith: A Journey for All*, in which he argued that all people, no matter their religious beliefs, needed faith. He gave credit to his father for teaching him the importance of the separation of religion and politics, the necessity to tell the truth, and the virtues of compassion and self-reliance. Other influences from Karl Barth to Paul Tillich, from Miss Lillian to Rosalynn, and from Billy Carter to Anwar Sadat, had also informed and inspired him.[62] For his recorded version of the book, Carter won his third Grammy for the Spoken Word. Although he did not go to Los Angeles to accept the award, one journalist commented that "God will be Center Stage at the 2019 Grammys."[63]

Jimmy and Rosalynn spent more time in their modest home on Woodland Drive in Plains, cooking their own food and doing many of the domestic chores themselves. They went to Atlanta at least once a month to attend to Carter Center business. In September 2018, they joined a Habitat crew in Mishawaka, Indiana. She was ninety-one, and he was almost ninety-four. Wearing a red bandana around his neck and sporting a belt with a silver buckle engraved with his initials, Jimmy and Rosalynn ate the same meals in the mess tent with the other volunteers. Observing his fellow workers, Jimmy commented that he believed the United States was "oriented toward equality and harmony." Despite the divisiveness of the Trump administration, he had "great confidence in the future of my country." At home, Jimmy and Rosalynn sometimes walked down Church Street in Plains, hand in hand, looking like any other elderly couple. "I am happy," she said.[64]

Undeterred by age, Jimmy and Rosalynn often used walkers and sat down in chairs quickly upon reaching their destinations. On February 4, 2019, they gathered at Koinonia Farm with other friends of Millard Fuller to mark the tenth anniversary of his death and to share remembrances of the man who had prompted their many years of work with Habitat for Humanity. Standing at the graveside, Jimmy remembered how Fuller had twisted his arm to get him to join the movement to build houses for the working poor.[65]

In the spring of that year, they celebrated the fortieth anniversary of his administration's normalization of relations with China. The goals of "mutual respect, the pursuit of peace, prosperity, and progress" bound the two countries together, Carter said, reminding the leaders of both countries that they should be "committed to world peace . . . [and] engender that commitment in the people of their countries."[66]

Also that spring, the Tribeca Film Festival in New York City announced that the following year, on April 15, 2020, they would show a documentary entitled "Jimmy Carter: Rock and Roll President." Garth Brooks, one of Carter's favorite musicians, commented that Carter's "love for music makes all kind of sense to me, because music is the voice of the heart. Music is the voice of the soul." At his home in South Georgia in February 2020, Carter previewed the film and confirmed that it "accurately captures my love for all music and the importance music has played in my personal and professional life." He hoped, he added, that "music can serve to bring us together as a nation."[67]

At the end of mental health month on May 31, 2019, Rosalynn went on a live television broadcast to make a pitch for additional aid to improve mental health. "We are at the beginning of a global mental health revolution," she declared. She retraced her long history of advocating improved care for the mentally ill and respect for those who suffered. Her interest began, Rosalynn said, "in front of a cotton mill in Atlanta" in 1966, when an elderly woman told her that she had no time to sleep because she needed help to care for her mentally ill daughter. Rosalynn bemoaned the fact that ten years after Congress passed the Mental Health Parity and Addiction Equity Act, thirty-two of the fifty states were evading the law. The Carter Center, she said, had partnered with the Kennedy Forum, the Well Being Trust, and other organizations to call for compliance with the law. "We need," Rosalynn concluded, "a chorus of authentic, united voices . . . to push for urgent action, funding, legislation, and beneficial policies."[68] Hers was a powerful statement by a ninety-two-year old woman who had devoted more than half of her life to a cause for which she continued to fight.

Recently tenured after thirty-seven years of service as University Distinguished Professor at Emory University, Jimmy continued to offer occasional seminars there and to give advice to young graduates. During the summer of 2019, he advised the students to prepare to live in a rapidly changing world, one with serious problems related to "global warming and climate change." Especially, he said, they should be prepared to be "more flexible in dealing with other people."[69] At his 38th annual town hall meeting in September 2019, he acknowledged his new tenured status as well as a greeting card with multiple signatures wishing him well for his upcoming 95th birthday. He called for the US to become a superpower "for promoting peace, championing human rights, advancing environmental polices that address climate change, and welcoming everybody as equals to the United States."[70]

The publicity Carter received from his and Rosalynn's seventy-third wedding anniversary on July 7, 2019, their participation in Habitat projects, and journalists' requests for his comments on the approaching presidential election, afforded him the opportunity to give the country some fatherly advice. He favored a Democratic candidate in 2020, he said, who would pledge to make the United States "the world's leading champion for peace, human rights and equality." He warned his fellow countrymen against the perils of perpetual warfare. He believed that China had risen as a major economic and geopolitical competitor with the United States because in the four decades since he had normalized US-Chinese relations, China had spent trillions of dollars on education, infrastructure, and business development, whereas the United States had spent corresponding amounts on military activities. "I just want to keep the world at peace," he concluded."[71]

With the same determination to serve humankind, Carter dealt with life-threatening falls, from which he got up and hobbled back to work. In mid-October 2019, he tripped and fell in his home, suffering a fourteen-inch gash on his forehead and a bad bruise on his right cheekbone. Despite that, he and Rosalynn went to Nashville a short time later to participate in a Habitat project. After a welcoming gala, featuring country music stars Garth Brooks and Trisha Yearwood at the Grand Ole Opry's famous Ryman Auditorium, the Carters joined 1,500 volunteers in building twenty-one houses in five days. Sweating and hammering away, Carter had a large bandage covering the gash on his forehead.[72]

More frequently at home because of his age, Jimmy conducted his last seminar at Emory, "Religion and Public Health," in October, and he taught his last Sunday School class on November 3, 2019. On that Sunday, he began as usual in a folksy manner by asking some visitors where they were from, he would then read a passage of Scripture and explain how it related to love, forgiveness, tolerance, peace, justice, and equality. If individuals would embrace those values in their personal lives, he believed, they would be able to establish more caring communities, political systems, and nations.[73] That fall and winter, Carter approved the use of his comments in a book to be published in the summer of 2020. Entitled *Simple Faith Bible: Following Jesus into a Life of Peace, Compassion, & Wholeness*, it comprised his reflections interspersed with relevant passages from the New Revised Version of the Bible.

In November 2019, Carter underwent more serious brain surgery at Emory University Hospital to relieve pressure caused by bleeding that had resulted from a fall. After spending two weeks in the hospital he went home to Plains and rested there during the Christmas holiday. All members of his and Rosalynn's family gathered in Plains and attended Maranatha Baptist Church that season. The large extended family consisted of four children, their spouses, and Jimmy and Rosalynn's grandchildren and great-grandchildren. They assembled themselves on the pews of the church, with Jimmy and Rosalynn down front and center, for a family photograph.[74]

As the presidential election year of 2020 progressed, Carter continued to denounce the policies of President Donald Trump and pleaded for Americans to vote Democratic. He also condemned Trump's Middle East proposal that would allow Israel to annex a large part of the occupied Palestinian territories and thus undercut "prospects for a just peace between Israelis and Palestinians." Horrified when Trump announced that he would withdraw US support from the World Health Organization, which had assisted the Carter Center with many of its projects in Africa, Carter declared it the only international organization that could provide the desperately needed leadership to control the deadly coronavirus that was beginning to grip the world. And when it appeared that the Republican administration then in power might end the use of mail-in ballots, Carter leaped to defend voting by mail, citing the findings of the nonpartisan 2005 Commission on Federal Election Reform he had co-chaired with former Republican Secretary of State James A. Baker III. The commission had concluded that "where safeguards for ballot integrity are in place . . . there was little evidence of voter fraud." On May 6, 2020, Carter issued a public statement: "I urge political leaders across the country to take immediate steps to expand vote-by-mail and other measures that can help protect the core of American democracy—the right of our citizens to vote."[75]

When the world suddenly changed with the onset of the coronavirus pandemic in March 2020, the danger of becoming infected with the deadly disease, as well as age and injuries, forced Carter into retirement. The release of the documentary, "Jimmy Carter: The Rock and Roll President," was postponed for nine months. Like millions of other Americans, Jimmy and Rosalynn donned face masks when in the presence of other people and retreated to the safety of their home. They appeared once on their front porch, smiling, Jimmy holding a guitar that had been made for him from one of the trees he had grown. Carter instructed contributors to the Carter Center to give their money to local organizations who needed help during the pandemic crisis. As the death rate rose to more than 200,000, and US leaders seemed to be making no progress containing the epidemic, Carter urged citizens to vote by mail in the upcoming presidential election. Leaning on their walkers and surrounded by several African-American children in their home, the Carters announced that they were raising half a million dollars to rebuild and repair all substandard houses in Plains. They issued statements of condolence upon the deaths of Congressman John Lewis, a Georgia hero of the Civil Rights movement; Bill Gates, Sr., whose philanthropy had aided many of their charitable projects; and United States Supreme Court Justice Ruth Bader Ginsburg. The death of Ginsburg, one of the leading liberals on the Court, was particularly sad for the Carters because Jimmy had appointed her to the United States Court of Appeals, from which Bill Clinton had elevated her to the Supreme Court thirteen years later.[76]

On October 1, 2020, Jimmy's ninety-sixth birthday, he and Rosalynn celebrated at their home on Woodland Drive in Plains. Mentally alert, Jimmy was as lively and as interested in those people around him as he had always been. When he looked out of his living room window and saw a National Park Employee wearing a red, white, and blue hat come to wish him a happy birthday, he invited her inside to thank her. With Rosalynn standing nearby by, bracing herself on her walker and beaming, the young woman with eyes smiling above her mask, appeared to be overjoyed by their meeting.

Later that day, Jimmy and Rosalynn, neatly dressed and wearing their face masks, took their places in chairs placed side by side just inside the opened gates to their compound. Flanked by Secret Service agents, aides, a few unnamed friends and relatives, they raised their hands and waved as more than two hundred well-wishers drove by. Organized by the Maranatha Baptist Church and the National Park Service, the procession included many hometown folks and descendants of those who had once seen Jimmy and Rosalynn off to Washington in 1977 and later welcomed them back in 1981 at the Plains Railroad Depot. Carter's age showed on his face and body, but his clear blue eyes twinkled as he held his arm high to express his gratitude to those who came to greet him that day. He and Rosalynn sat there and continued to wave at their friends and neighbors until the last vehicle had passed by.

It had been a long time since that cold January day in 1975 when Jimmy and his brother Billy had loaded his and Rosalynn's personal items in a rented truck outside the Governor's Mansion in Atlanta. Jimmy and Rosalynn had moved up to pinnacles of power and service for the country, the world, and their hometown. In this celebration of their lives and Carter's ninety-sixth birthday, the hundreds driving past their gate and waving—and millions more around the globe—acknowledged that the Carters had helped to transform the world into a better place than it had been when they first found it.

A month and few days after Jimmy's birthday, the Carters happily witnessed the election of a Democratic friend as the next president of the United States. Senator Joe Biden of Delaware and his wife Dr. Jill Biden had been friends and supporters of the Carters since they had first gone to Washington in 1977. Because the Carters were unable to go to Washington to attend the inauguration on January 20, 2021, the Bidens went to Plains and visited them in their home.

The Bidens knew that whatever the Carters had accomplished, they had done it together as a powerful, dedicated husband-wife team. On July 7, 2021, Jimmy and Rosalynn's seventy-fifth wedding anniversary, they became celebrities again for having been the longest married and living presidential couple. His voice weakened with age, Jimmy said the secret of such success was to marry the right woman, never go to bed angry, and pray and read the Bible together. Rosalynn did not contradict him, but she chirped up to add "and space."

Jimmy and Rosalynn's determination to continue to do as much as they could for as long as they could, despite being hampered by advanced age and the isolating impact of the coronavirus pandemic, was reduced to issuing statements condemning domestic and international violations of human rights and praising those people who continued to work for creating what Rosalynn had called "a more caring world." Rosalynn, celebrating her ninety-fourth birthday on August 18, 2021, donned her protective facemask, and with some help from a caregiver, went out into a public place in Plains and helped distribute food to hungry people who lined up to accept it.

Carter's greatness as president rested in the fact that he had kept the nation out of war, used the power of his office to save and improve lives, and defended democracy and human rights in many corners of the world. He had been that rare thing, a non-celebrity president who had appealed to people's better instincts in a troubled and often immoral world and had faced the challenges of his time honestly and courageously. Rosalynn's greatness as First Lady was that she had been truly an equal partner with the president, a partner of extraordinary intelligence, drive, and commitment to peace. She had also maintained her independence, promoting projects of her own, especially her tireless effort to improve mental health care and, in other ways too, to create a more caring society.

Jimmy and Rosalynn's legacy, as they wished, was peace and human rights. The last guinea worm was not dead, peace remained elusive in the Middle East, and democracy and human rights were under attack in the United States, but the Carters had set an example, risen above the din of politics and the many national and international obstacles over which they had no control, and created a model for those who would follow them. Their flourishing Carter Center, located inconspicuously on the John Lewis Freedom Parkway in Atlanta, buzzed with staff and volunteers on site as well as thousands of workers and volunteers scattered over the globe fulfilling its mission to "wage peace, fight disease, build hope."

Notes

Chapter 1

1. *Washington Post*, 13 Dec. 1974.
2. E. Stanly Godbold, Jr., *Jimmy and Rosalynn Carter: The Georgia Years, 1924–1974*, 265–71; W. Carl Biven, *Jimmy Carter's Economy: Policy in an Age of Limits*, 16.
3. Carter interview with Chris Matthews, MSNBC, 14 Oct. 2018.
4. Hamilton Jordan, Miller Center Interview, 17, JCL. See also Peter N. Carroll, *It Seemed Like Nothing Happened: America in the 1970s*, 145; Elizabeth Drew, *American Journal: The Events of 1976*, 102–104; and Laurence H. Shoup, *The Carter Presidency and Beyond: Power and Politics in the 1980s*, 11–17.
5. Peter G. Bourne, *Carter: A Comprehensive Biography from Plains to Post-Presidency*, 259.
6. *Atlanta Journal and Constitution*, 25 Dec. 1974; John M Reardon to Madeline F. McBean, 27 Dec. 1974, Clough File, box 19, Jimmy Carter Library (JCL); *Americus Times-Recorder*, 2 Jan. 1975.
7. Newsweek Collection, Robert W. Woodruff Library, Manuscript, Archives, and Rare Book Library, Emory University (Emory); Walter T. Ridder to JC, 4, 19 Nov. 1974, Record Group (RG) 1-1-5, JC, box 60, Georgia Department of Archives and History (GDAH), RG 1-1-45, JC, box 13, GDAH.
8. *New York Times Magazine*, 14 Dec. 1974.
9. Godbold, *Jimmy and Rosalynn*, 82–83.
10. *New York Times* and *Atlanta Constitution*, both 16 Dec. 1974.
11. Brzezinski to Carter, 17 Dec. 1974, Brzezinski File, JCL; Godbold, *Jimmy and Rosalynn Carter*, 252–53.
12. Dean Rusk to Jimmy Carter (JC), 20 Dec. 1974, JC to Dean Rusk, 27 Dec., 1974, both in RG 1-1-5, JC, box 2, GDAH; Carter to Morris B. Abram, 21 Dec. 1974, Morris B. Abram Papers, box 4, Emory.
13. Letters and Governor's Schedule in RG 1-1-5, JC, box 74, RG 1-1-5, JC, boxes 55 & 63, GDAH.
14. *Chicago Daily News*, 17 Dec. 1974; *The Red Wing (Minnesota) Republican Eagle*, 17 Dec. 1974.
15. *New York Times*, 15 Dec. 1974; and articles reprinted in *Carter News*, vol. 1, no. 3, Feb. 1975, submitted to the Federal Election Commission, copy in Gerald Rafshoon File, Donated, Carter News, box 7, JCL.
16. J. Paul Austin to Zbigniew Brzezinski, 2 Jan. 1975, Brzezinski to Carter, 7 Jan, 1975, both in Brzezinski Donated Material, Trilateral File, box 7, JCL.

17. Earl Black and Merle Black, *The Vital South: How Presidents Are Elected*, 248–49; Tip O'Neill, *Man of the House: The Life and Political Memoirs of Speaker Tip O'Neill*, 300–301.
18. Carter Family Papers, Rosalynn Carter (RSC) Projects & Events, box 123, JCL; Campaign Trip File, 20 Jan. 1975, Clough File, box 25, JCL; Memorandum, Stu Eizenstat to Governor Carter, et al., 21 Jan. 1975, Pre-Presidential: 76 Campaign, Issues, Eizenstat, box 8, JCL; Bourne, *Carter*, 261–62.
19. Campaign Trip File, Feb. 1975, Clough File, box 25, JCL; JC to the President and Congress, 7 Feb., 13, 16 March 1975, White House Central File (WHCF), Name File, Gerald R. Ford Presidential Library (GFL).
20. Stuart Eizenstat, Interview, Ethnic Groups in American Foreign Policy, 11 May 1977, Oral History Collection, Columbia University Library; *New York Times*, 2 Feb. 1975.
21. Martin Schram, *Running for President: A Journal of the Carter Campaign*, 7–9.
22. David Harris, *The Crisis: The President, the Prophet, and the Shah—1979 and the Coming of Militant Islam*, 54; Jules Witcover, *Marathon: The Pursuit of the Presidency, 1972–1976*, 194–98, 157, 162–63.
23. Clough File, Campaign Trip, box 25, JCL; Zbig to Jimmy, 30 Jan. 1975, Brzezinski File, box 5, JCL; Memorandum, Tim Kraft to Hamilton Jordan, 16 Jan. 1975, Kraft Papers, box 1, JCL.
24. Hamilton Jordan, Miller Center Interview, 8, JCL.
25. Memorandum, Eizenstat to JC, RE Defense Posture for Princeton Speech, Pre-Presidential: 76 Campaign, Issues-Eizenstat, box 8, JCL; Briefing with Carter, Eizenstat, Henry Owen, and others at the Brookings Institute on 28 Jan. 1975, referenced in Memorandum, Eizenstat to Management Committee, 11 March 1975, Pre-Presidential: 76 Campaign, Issues-Eizenstat, box 16, JCL.
26. JC to Mrs. Jules Lederer, 4 March 1975, Clough File, Campaign Trip File, boxes 3, 25, and 26, JCL; Pre-Presidential: 76 Campaign, Eizenstat-Issues, box 16, JCL.
27. Paul R. Wieck, "Long Shot: Jimmy Carter of Georgia," *The New Republic*, 12 April 1975, pp. 16–19.
28. Witcover, *Marathon*, 143–44; Carter Speech, 2 April 1975, Speech Writers File, Nesmith, box 1, JCL.
29. 11 April 1975, Speech Writers File, Nesmith, box 1, JCL.
30. Bourne, *Carter*, 262–63; RSC, *First Lady from Plains*, 112–16 (quotation on 116).
31. RSC, *First Lady from Plains*, 117–19.
32. Clough File, Campaign Trip 1976, box 28, JCL; *Americus Times-Recorder*, 12 May 1975; Bourne, *Carter*, 264–65.
33. Witcover, *Marathon*, 148–54.
34. Clipping from the *New Hampshire Times*, 14 May 1975, Pre-Presidential: 76 Campaign, N. Sterrett, box 97, JCL; Carter News, June 1975, Rafshoon Donated, box 7, JCL.
35. *Americus Times-Recorder*, 8, 22 May 1975.
36. Memorandum, Rick Hutchenson to Governor Carter, with attachments and notes, 5 May 1975; Memorandum, Eizenstat to JC, Supplement to Foreign Correspondents

in Tokyo Speech, 9 May 1975; Speech and attachments, all in Pre-Presidential: 76 Campaign, Issues-Eizenstat, box 17, JCL.

37. *Americus Times-Recorder*, 21 May 1975; *New York Times*, 29 May 1975; Bourne, *Carter*, 267–69.
38. Carter Family Papers, RSC, Special Projects and Events, box 135, JCL.
39. Clough File, 76 Campaign file, boxes 17, 28, JCL; *Americus Times-Recorder*, 2 June, 2 July 1975; Sam Nunn to Stuart Eizenstat, 9 June 1975, Pre-Presidential: 76 campaign, Issues-Eizenstat, box 23, JCL; Memorandum, Ham Jordan to JC, [Summer 1975], Pre-Presidential: 76 campaign, Jordan, box 199; Brzezinski to JC, 17 June 1975, Brzezinski File, box 2, JCL; McBean to John M. Reardon, 10 July 1975, Clough File, box 19, JCL.
40. Speech and handwritten letter, 11 July 1975, Helen Mills Collection, box 1, JCL.
41. *New York Times*, 13, 27 July 1975; *Americus Times-Recorder*, 13, 15, 23 July 1975; Memorandum, Charles H. Kirbo to JC, 21 July, 1975, Clough File, box 13, JCL.
42. Bourne, Carter, 270–75; Author interview with Jay E. Hakes, 8 Aug. 2000.
43. *Americus Times-Recorder*, 25 July, 2 Aug., 1975; Jordan quoted in Patrick Anderson, *Electing Jimmy Carter: The Campaign of 1976*, 12.
44. *New York Times*, 27 July 1975; Zbig to JC, Brzezinski File, box 8, JCL, emphasis is Brzezinski's; RSC, *First Lady*, 120–25; Anderson, *Electing Jimmy Carter*, 13–14.
45. *Atlanta Constitution*, 4 Aug. 1975.
46. Quoted in *Atlanta Constitution*, 4 Aug. 1965; Godbold, *Jimmy and Rosalynn Carter*, 115–19; Witcover, *Marathon*, 53–55.
47. Witcover, *Marathon*, 198; Bourne, *Carter*, 277.
48. Memorandum, Tim Kraft to Jeff Carter, 8 Aug. 1975, Memorandum, Tim Kraft to Hamilton Jordan, 28 Aug 1975, Memorandum, Tim Kraft to RSC, 28 Aug. 1975, all in Tim Kraft Papers, box 1, JCL; Bourne, *Carter*, 277.
49. *Americus Times-Recorder*, 28, 29 Aug. 1975: Memorandum, Kissinger to Minister for Foreign Affairs of Israel, 1 Sept. 1975, National Security Administration, Brzezinski Collection, Geographic File, box 13, JCL.
50. JC to Lance, handwritten, 30 Aug., To Kirbo, 9 Sept., To Sybil, 6 Oct. 1975, To Lipshutz, 12 Oct., all 1975, all in Clough File, boxes 5, 13, 14, JCL.
51. Carter Family Papers, RSC Carter, Projects and Events, box 118, JCL; *Americus Times-Recorder*, 25 Sept. 1975; Speech at Bethune-Cookman College, Oct. 1975, Speechwriter File, Nesmith, box 1, JCL.
52. *Americus Times-Recorder*, 27 Sept., 9 Oct. 1975.
53. RSC Carter, interview with David W. Guth, 26 Sept. 1975, Guth Collection, JCL.
54. *Americus Times-Recorder*, 14, 16, 17, 20, 27 Oct. 1975; *New York Times*, 15 Oct. 1975; JC to Tim Kraft, 28 Oct. 1975, with attached memoranda, Tim Kraft Papers, box 1, JCL; Carter quotes in *New York Times*, 26 Oct. 1975; Bourne, *Carter*, 279–80.
55. Witcover, *Marathon*, 201–202, 206–207; Bourne, *Carter*, 279–80.
56. Rudy Hayes, *Americus Times-Recorder*, 30 Oct. 1975.
57. Jimmy Carter, *Why Not the Best?*, 14–17, 19–25, 28–30, 138.
58. Speeches, Tim Kraft Papers, box 1, JCL; *Americus Times-Recorder*, 4, 5, 8 Nov. 1975.

59. *New York Times*, 2, 3 Nov. 1975.
60. Morris B. Abram, *The Day Is Short: An Autobiography*, 244–48.
61. Author interview with Jimmy Carter, 12 Oct. 1994.
62. *Americus Times-Recorder*, 11 Nov. 1975.
63. Letters and note, 3, 12, 15 Nov. 1975, all in Clough, box 4, JCL.
64. Carter on "Face the Nation," Rafshoon Donated, box 9, JCL, and Wanda M. Phelan File, box 1, GFL; Rod Goodwin to JC, 28 Nov. 1975, and JC to Goodwin, 8 Dec. 1975, Clough File, box 9, JCL: Wanda M. Phelan File, box 9, GFL; A. J. Reichley File, box 5, GFL.
65. Mary McGrory, "A Rare Helpmate on the Hustings," *Newsday*, 15 Dec. 1975.
66. *Americus Times-Recorder*, 17, 18, 20, 21 Nov. 1975; *New York Times*, 17, 19 Nov. 1975; *Atlanta Journal and Constitution*, 27 Nov. 1975; Carter Notes in Clough File, boxes 5, 10, 19, JCL; Carroll, *It Seemed Like Nothing Happened*, 168–69.
67. Barbara J. Keys, *Reclaiming American Virtue: The Human Rights Revolution of the 1970s*, 240; Gerald Rafshoon File, Donated, 16 Dec. 1975, box 8, JCL; Anderson, *Electing Jimmy Carter*, 76.
68. Quoted in *Americus-Times Recorder*, 2 Jan. 1976. *See also Americus Times-Recorder*, 19 Dec. 1975; *New York Times*, 26 Dec. 1975; Carter interview with David W. Guth, 26 Dec.1975, Guth Collection, JCL; JC to Milton Katz, 28 Dec. 1975, To Brzezinski, 28 Dec. 1975, both in Clough File, box 4, JCL; Jody Powell to Stuart Eizenstat, 1975, Pre-Presidential: 76 Campaign, Issues-Eizenstat, box 17, JCL; and Witcover, *Marathon*, 92.

Chapter 2

1. Penny Girard, "A First Lady in Waiting," *W*, 9–16 Jan. 1976.
2. Stephen Graubard, *Command of Office: How War, Secrecy, and Deception Transformed the Presidency from Theodore Roosevelt to George W. Bush*, 427–28. Like most commentators, Graubard did not mention or grasp the importance of Rosalynn.
3. Speech Notes, Feb. 1976, Jack Carter Donated Collection, box 2, JCL.
4. Carter comments in *Americus Times-Recorder*, 17 Feb. 2016.
5. Peter G. Bourne, *Jimmy Carter: A Comprehensive Biography from Plains to the Post-Presidency*, 278–81; Betty Glad, *Jimmy Carter in the Search of the Great White House*, 239; *Washington Post*, 25 Jan. 1976; *Time*, 2 Feb. 1976, p. 17.
6. Amber Roessner, *Jimmy Carter and the Birth of the Marathon Media Campaign*, 73–74, 42–43.
7. Roesner, *Carter and Birth of Marathon Media*, 51; Jules Witcover, *Marathon: The Pursuit of the Presidency, 1972–1976*, 212–14; Rosalynn Carter, *First Lady from Plains*, 128; Judith Stein, *Pivotal Decade: How the United States Traded Factories for Finance in the Seventies*, 142–43.
8. Memorandum, Eizenstat to Carter, 27 Jan. 1976, Pre-presidential file: 76 Campaign, Issues, Eizenstat, box 17, JCL; Elizabeth Drew, *American Journal: The Events of 1976*, 92.

9. Kay Mills, *This Little Light of Mine: The Life of Fannie Lou Hamer*, 231–35, 297; Bourne, *Carter*, 281–83; *Americus Times-Recorder*, 26 Jan. 1976; Bill Minor editorial, (*Jackson, MS*) *Clarion-Ledger*, 21 Aug. 2015.

10. *Americus Times-Recorder*, 30 Jan. 1976; Bourne, *Carter*, 284–86.

11. Ibid.

12. Transcript in Ronald H. Nessen Files, box 68, GFL; Curtis Wilkie, *Dixie: A Personal Odyssey through Events that Shaped the Modern South*, 217–18.

13. Genelle Jennings, *Into the Jaws of Politics: The Charge of the Peanut Brigade*, 7–55; Leila Barrett, National Park Service Interview, 2–4, JCL; Hal Gulliver, *A Friendly Tongue*, 122–26.

14. *Americus Times-Recorder*, 21 Jan., 14, 16, 19 Feb., 3 March 1976; "Spend Valentine's Day with Carter," 14 Feb. 1976, a flyer in Rafshoon File Donated, JCL; Richard Reeves, "Pop Stars," 16 Feb. 1976, in *Newsweek* Collection, box 4, Emory; Morris Dees, *A Season for Justice*, 195.

15. *Americus Times-Recorder*, 19 Feb. 1976; March 1976 *Newsweek Collection*, box 4, Emory; Bourne, *Carter*, 287–90; Memorandum, Eizenstat to Carter, 2 March 1976, Pre-Presidential papers: 76 Campaign, Issues, Eizenstat, box 16, JCL.

16. Bourne, *Carter*, 314–15; Witcover, *Marathon*, 225–26; *Atlanta Constitution*, 8 Feb. 1976; Daniel K. Williams, *The Election of the Evangelical: Jimmy Carter, Gerald Ford, and the Presidential Contest of 1976*, 140–41.

17. *New Republic*, 14 Feb. 1976, pp. 14, 16.

18. Witcover, *Marathon*, 320; Robert Shrum, *No Excuses: Concessions of a Serial Campaigner*, 62–64.

19. Robert Shrum, "No Private Smiles: A Disquieting Look at the Carter Campaign," *New Times,* 27 April 1976, pp. 23–42.

20. Witcover, *Marathon*, 319–26; Shrum, *No Concessions*, 61–69; Bourne, *Carter*, 317–19.

21. Leila Barrett, National Park Service Interview, 5–8, JCL (Rosalynn's quotation on 8); Witcover, *Marathon*, 225–37; Bourne, *Carter*, 290–91; RSC, *First Lady*, 128–29; Glad, *Carter*, 239–42.

22. *Americus Times-Recorder*, 25 Feb., 3 March 1976; Handwritten letter, signature illegible, to Powell 4 Jan. 1976, in Pre-Presidential File: 76 campaign, Issues, Eizenstat, box 92, JCL.

23. Witcover, *Marathon*, 234–39; RSC, *First Lady*, 129.

24. Bourne, *Carter*, 291–92.

25. Williams, *Election of the Evangelical*, 151–52; Witcover, *Marathon*, 240–51.

26. Bourne, *Carter*, 292–99; RSC, *First Lady*, 129–30; Glad, *Carter*, 242–44; Gulliver, *A Friendly Tongue*, 133 (beat Wallace quotation).

27. *Atlanta Constitution*, 7, 9 March 1976; Glad, *Carter*, 244–45; *Americus Times-Recorder*, 5 March 1976.

28. *Americus Times-Recorder*, 24 Jan. 1976.

29. Quoted in Witcover, *Marathon*, 258.

30. Earl Black and Merl Black, *The Vital South: How Presidents are Elected*, 248–54.

31. Witcover, *Marathon*, 259–61; RSC, *First Lady*, 130; Bourne, *Carter*, 299–302.

32. Glad, *Carter*, 285; Kandy Stroud, *How Jimmy Won: The Victory Campaign from Plains to the White House*, 290.

33. John D. Marks to Theodore Sorensen,11 Jan. 1976, Declassified Document NLC-9-3-1-17l, JCL; Brzezinski to Steve Clark, with Attachments, 15 March 1976, Pre-presidential File, 76 Campaign, Issues-Eizenstat, box 17, JCL; *Americus Times-Recorder*, 20 Jan. 1976; *New York Times*, 11 March 1976; Copies of Code of Ethics and Campaign Issues Reference Book in Staff Secretary, Handwriting File, box 260, JCL.

34. Address to Chicago Council on Foreign Relations, 15 March 1976, Pre-Presidential file: 76 Campaign, Issues, Eizenstat, box 17, JCL, and President Ford Committee for Reelection, box H24, GFL. See also Carter to David C. Prince, 2 Jan. 1976, Clough File, box 19, JCL; Position Paper: Jimmy Carter on Soviet Jewry, 22 Jan. 1976, Staff Secretary File, box 260, JCL; *Christian Science Monitor*, 30 Jan. 1975; and Brzezinski to Carter, 31 July, 1975, 76 Campaign File, Noel Sterrett Papers, box 96, JCL.

35. Witcover, *Marathon*, 261–62; Bourne, *Carter*, 303–304; Glad, *Carter*, 245–46.

36. Memorandum, Jordan to Carter, N.D., but after the Florida Campaign, Jordan File, box 199, JCL. See also *Americus Times-Recorder*, 2 Feb., 13 March 1976; Bourne, *Carter*, 307–308; Glad, *Carter*, 246–47; Hal Gulliver, *Atlanta Constitution*, 26 March 1976.

37. Quoted in Gary Scott Smith, *Faith and the Presidency: From George Washington to George W. Bush*, 295. See also Leo P. Ribuffo, "God and Jimmy Carter," in M. L. Bradbury and Gilbert, *Transforming Faith: The Sacred and Secular in Modern American History*, 142; Martin Schram, *Running for President: A Journal of the Carter Campaign*, 111–15.

38. Quoted in Bourne, *Carter*, 306.

39. Witcover, *Marathon*, 270–72; *Atlanta Constitution*, 28 March 1976; *Americus Times-Recorder*, 17, 24, 1976.

40. Witcover, *Marathon*, 263–64; Hamilton Jordan, Miller Center Interview, 73, JCL.

41. *Atlanta Constitution*, 28 March 1976; *Washington Star*, 14 March 1976.

42. Quoted in Marshall Frady, *Southerners: A Journalist's Odyssey*, 344. See also Witcover, *Marathon*, 276, 284–85, 286–88; RSC, *First Lady*, 131; and Bourne, *Carter*, 308–309.

43. Leila Barrett, National Park Service Interview, 7, 10, JCL.

44. Witcover, *Marathon*, 295, 302–303; Bourne, *Carter*, 310–12.

45. Quoted in Bourne, *Carter*, 313.

46. Quoted in *Americus Times-Recorder*, 8, 26 April 1976. See also Wilkie, *Dixie*, 223.

47. Witcover, *Marathon*, 305–308; Bourne, *Carter*, 313–17.

48. Quoted in *St. Louis Post Dispatch*, 11 April 1976. See also *Atlanta Constitution*, 13 April 1976.

49. Copy of Murphy article in Ron Nessen Papers, box 32, GFL; Witcover, *Marathon*, 311–19; Bourne, *Carter*, 315; Dan Cohen, *Undefeated: The Life of Hubert H. Humphrey*, 452–59; Williams, *Election of the Evangelical*, 122–23.

Chapter 3

1. *Atlanta Constitution*, 24, 25 Feb. 1976.

2. Jules Witcover, *Marathon: The Pursuit of the Presidency, 1972–1976*, 327–28.

3. Quoted in Anderson, *Electing Jimmy Carter*, 24–25. See also Rosalynn Carter, *First Lady from Plains*, 133–34, and Peter G. Bourne, *Carter: A Comprehensive Biography from Plains to the Post-Presidency*, 323.

4. Bourne, *Carter*, 324–26 (quotations on 325, 326); Patrick Anderson, *Electing Jimmy Carter: The Campaign of 1976*, 31–33, 171–75.

5. James C. Cobb, *The South and America since World War II*, 141–43.

6. *Americus Times-Recorder*, 3 May 1976; Dean Rusk to Carter, 4 May 1976, Clough File, box 20, JCL.

7. Memo, Eizenstat to Carter, 3 May 1976, RE: Religious Issue, Pre-Presidential: 76 Campaign, Issues, Eizenstat, box 27, JCL; Eizenstat's emphasis.

8. Bill Moyers interview with Carter, PBS, 6 May 1976, transcript in Speechwriter File, Nesmith, box 1, JCL. See also Wesley G. Pippert, *The Spiritual Journey of Jimmy Carter in His Own Words*, dustjacket, 42, 56, 58; Leo P. Ribuffo, "God and Jimmy Carter," in M. L. Bradbury and James B. Gilbert, editors, *Transforming Faith: The Sacred and Secular in Modern American History*, 142; Daniel K. Williams, *The Election of the Evangelical: Jimmy Carter, Gerald Ford, and the Presidential Contest of 1976*, 202–207.

9. Quoted in Douglass Cater, "How Different IS the South?", *Washington Post Outlooks*, 10 Oct. 1976. See also Carter to Jody Powell, 4 Jan. 1977, Powell File, box 5, JCL, and JC, *Why Not the Best?*, cited in Pippert, *Spiritual Journey*, 37.

10. E. Stanly Godbold, Jr., *Jimmy and Rosalynn Carter: The Georgia Years, 1924–1974*, 191–92, 258; Gaddis Smith, *Morality, Reason, and Power: American Diplomacy in the Carter Years*, 19.

11. Ribuffo, "God and Jimmy Carter," 142–43.

12. RSC interview in *Americus Times-Recorder*, 20 May 1976.

13. *Atlanta Constitution*, 7, 8, 1976; Memo, Eizenstat to Carter, with attached correspondence by Richard Holbrooke, 8 May 1976, Pre-Presidential papers: 76 Campaign, Issues, Eizenstat, box 17, JCL; Carter to Holbrooke, 9 May 1976, Clough File, box 11, JCL.

14. Copies of speech in Staff Secretary, Handwriting File, box 260, and Speechwriter, Nesmith, box 1, JCL; *New York Times*, 14 May, 1976.

15. *New York Times*, 14, 17 May 1976; Rod Goodwin to Carter, 23 May 1976, Clough File, box 9, JCL; *Atlanta Constitution*, 28 May 1976.

16. Michael A. Poling, Director of Opposition Research, to Dick Cheney, 31 May 1976, with attachments, Richard Cheney Files, box 16, GFL; Poling to A. J. Reichley, 29 June 1976, A. J. Reichley Files, box 1, GFL; Gerald Ford address to the Southern Baptist Convention in Norfolk, VA, 15 June 1976, A. J. Reichley Files, box 5, GFL; Patrick J. Buchanan on Richard Milhous Carter, in *New York Daily News* and *Chicago Tribune*, 3 June 1976, copy in Ron Nessen papers, box 32, GFL.

17. Carter speech, 6 June 1976, WHCF, box PL-1, JCL.

18. Meg Greenfield, "Carter and the Once Born," *Newsweek*, August 1976; Statement by Governor Carter on Middle East, Wanda Phelan Files, box 1, GFL; Ribicoff speech in Pre-Presidential papers: 76 Campaign, Issues, Eizenstat, box 22, JCL; *Atlanta Constitution*, 6, 8 June 1976. See also Richard E. Cohen, "The Carter-Ribicoff Connection," *National Journal*, 7 Aug.19767, p. 1122.

19. Charles W. Yost, "Arab Views of the Arab-Israeli Conflict," Pre-Presidential: 76 Campaign Issues, Eizenstat, box 25, JCL.

20. Witcover, *Marathon*, 347–50; Glad, *Carter*, 258; Anderson, *Electing Jimmy Carter*, 36; Bourne, *Carter*, 326–27.

21. Quoted in Witcover, *Marathon*, 351. See also Leila Barret National Park Service Interview, 13, JCL, and RSC, *First Lady*, 134–35.

22. Memo, Hamilton Jordan to Staff, 9 June 1976, Tim Kraft Donated Papers, box 1, JCL; Laura Kalman, *Right Star Rising: A New Politics, 1974–1980*, 152–160; Leila Barret, National Park Service Interview, 13, JCL; RSC, *First Lady*, 134–35; Witcover, *Marathon*, 351.

23. *New York Times*, 11 June 1976.

24. Lauren Blanton, National Park Service Interview, 19, 33, 39, 40, JCL; *Americus Times-Recorder*, 12, 13, 14 June 1976.

25. Anderson, *Electing Jimmy Carter*, 39–40.

26. Witcover, *Marathon*, 357–58; Betty Glad, *Jimmy Carter in Search of the Great White House,* 261–70; copy of "A New Beginning" in Helen Mills Collection, box 1, JCL.

27. Memo, Brzezinski to Carter, 22 June 1976, RE Proposed statement on Cyprus, Pre-Presidential: 76 Campaign, Issues, Eizenstat, box 8, JCL; Carter's address "Relations between the World's Democracies," 23 June 1976, Staff Secretary File, box 260, JCL; Rod Goodwin to Carter, 25 June 1976, Carter to Governor John West, 27 June 1976, and others, all in Clough File, boxes 9, 24, 17, 12, and 1, JCL; *Americus Times-Recorder*, 26 June 1976.

28. *Newsweek*, "Nominee in Waiting," 21 June 1976.

29. Memo, Hamilton Jordan to Carter, June 1976, Re Advice on selection of a VP, Jordan File, box 199, JCL; Witcover, *Marathon*, 259–60, 361–62; Bourne, *Carter*, 330–31; *Raleigh News and Observer*, 15 May 1992.

30. Bill Shipp, "Beware the Slow-talking Lawyer," *Atlanta Constitution*, 5 July 1976 (quotations); *Los Angeles Times*, 1 July, 1976; *Washington Post*, 5 July 1976; *New York Times, 14 July 1976*.

31. Witcover, *Marathon*, 363.

32. Ibid., 364–66; RSC, *First Lady*, 135; Bourne, *Carter*, 331–33; *Americus Times-Recorder*, 6, 9, 13 July 1976; Finlay Lewis, *Mondale: Portrait of an American Politician*, 1–6.

Chapter 4

1. Stephen Graubard, *Command of Office: How War, Secrecy and Deception Transformed the Presidency, from Theodore Roosevelt to George W. Bush*, 429; Jules Witcover,

Marathon: The Pursuit of the Presidency, 1974–1976, 353–55, 358; Richard Reeves, *Convention*, 3.

2. Reeves, *Convention*, 16; Peter G. Bourne, *Jimmy Carter: A Comprehensive Biography from Plains to the Post-Presidency*, 333.

3. Reeves, *Convention*, 19–21.

4. Rosalynn Carter, *First Lady from Plains*, 136–37; *New York Times*, 12 July, 1976.

5. Mary Beth Rogers, *Barbara Jordan: American Hero*, 264–69 (quotations on 165 and 269); Witcover, *Marathon*, 366; Betty Glad, *Jimmy Carter in Search of the Great White House*, 275–76; Memorandum, Hamilton Jordan to Carter, July 1976, details the schedule at the convention, 76 Campaign, Jordan file, box 199, JCL.

6. Glad, *Carter*, 276–77 (quotations on 277); Carter to Rodino, 31 August 1976, Rodino to Carter, enclosing speech, 25 August 1976, both in Clough File, box 20, JCL; Leo Ribuffo, "God and Jimmy Carter," in M. L. Bradbury and James B. Gilbert, editors, *Transforming Faith: The Sacred and the Secular in Modern History*, 143.

7. Quoted in Witcover, *Marathon*, 341.

8. Reeves, *Convention*, 127, 131–32, 165–66.

9. Ibid., 127,131–32, 165–66; Larry J. Sabato, *The Kennedy Half Century: The Presidency, An Assassination, and Lasting Legacy of John F. Kennedy*, 324.

10. Reeves, *Convention*, 177–79; Witcover, *Marathon*, 366–67; RSC, *First Lady*, 137; Bourne, *Carter*, 334; Glad, *Carter*, 277–79.

11. Bert to Jimmy, 14 July 1976, Carter Family Papers, RSC Gubernatorial Special Projects and Events, box 123, JCL; Maddox comments, 15 July 1976, in PCFR, box H30, GFL.

12. Quoted in Glad, *Carter*, 278. See also Memorandum, Orin Kramer to Issues Staff, 6 Aug. 1976, Pre-Presidential: 76 Campaign, Issues, Eizenstat, box 25, JCL; *Americus Times-Recorder*, 15 July 1976.

13. Carter quoted in *The Washington Star*, 21 Jan. 1976, cited in PFCR, box H28, GFL; Rabbi Harold H. Gordon to Carter, 16 July 1976, Pre-Presidential: 76 Campaign, Issues, Eizenstat, box 8, JCL; William Safire article, *New York Times*, 22 July, 1976.

14. Author interview with Rod Goodwin, 15 July 1994.

15. Witcover, *Marathon*, 368; Glad, *Carter*, 279.

16. Reeves, *Convention*, 207–208.

17. Witcover, *Marathon*, 369; Bourne, *Carter*, 335–36; Glad, *Carter*, 279–80; Stuart E. Eizenstat, *President Carter: The White House Years*, 53.

18. Witcover, *Marathon*, 370; Bourne, *Carter*, 336; Reeves, *Convention*, 213–14.

19. Reeves, *Convention*, 212–13, 215–16.

20. *Americus Times-Recorder*, 15 July 1976, p. 3 (quotations from both Ford and Reagan).

21. Miss Lillian quote in *Washington Post*, 16 Jan. 1976; Kirbo in *New York Times*, 2 Feb. 1976; author interview with Rick Allen, Atlanta, GA, 17 May 1994.

22. Witcover, *Marathon*, 373–80; Patrick Anderson, *Electing Jimmy Carter: The Campaign of 1976*, 79.

23. Witcover, *Marathon*, 396–406, 413.

24. Ibid., 402, 411, 418, 470. See also David McCullough, *The Path Between the Seas: The Creation of the Panama Canal, 1870–1914*.

25. Witcover, *Marathon*, 499–502, 509–10; Mary Beth Durkin, Interview with David Hume Kennerly, 25 July 2008, "Betty Ford: The Real Deal," MacNeill Lehrer Productions.

26. Witcover, *Marathon*, 513–18; Anderson, *Electing Jimmy Carter*, 47–48.

27. Hamilton Jordan, *A Boy from Georgia: Coming of Age in the Segregated South*, ix-x, 13, 15, 34–35, 121, 131–41, 159–67, 175–76, 182, 206–209; Edward A. Hatfield, et al., "Hamilton Jordan (1944–2008), *New Georgia Encyclopedia*; Witcover, *Marathon*, 517–18; Eizenstat, *Carter*, 71–72.

28. Witcover, *Marathon*, 517, 529.

29. Bourne, *Carter*, 338; Anderson, *Electing Jimmy Carter*, 69–70.

30. Bourne, *Carter*, 338; Anderson, *Electing Jimmy Carter*, 70.

31. Bourne, *Carter*, 338–40; Anderson, *Electing Jimmy Carter*, 70–75; Glad, *Carter*, 356, 373.

32. John L. Helgerson, *Getting to Know the President: Intelligence Briefings of Presidential Candidates, 1952–2004*, 87–91; Jon Meacham, *Destiny and Power: The American Odyssey of George Herbert Walker Bush*, 202–203.

33. Christopher Andrew, *For the President's Eyes Only*, 426;

34. John Robert Greene, *The Presidency of Gerald R. Ford*, 102–103, 112–16, 161; Bourne, *Carter*, 339; Glad, *Carter*, 373.

35. Martin Gilbert, *Shcharansky: Hero of Our Time*, 133.

36. Anderson, *Electing Jimmy Carter*, 75–77, 102; Dan Ariel, *The Carpenter's Apprentice*: The Spiritual Biography of Jimmy Carter, 72–73.

37. Witcover, *Marathon*, 518–23; Bourne, *Carter*, 339; Finlay Lewis, *Mondale: Portrait of an American Politician*, 24.

38. Witcover, *Marathon*, 525–26; Bourne, *Carter*, 351.

39. Quoted in Witcover, *Marathon*, 526. See also Bourne, *Carter*, 339–41.

40. *Atlanta Constitution*, 25 Aug., 1976; Criticism of JC by Leading Democrats, L. W. Seidman Files, box 320, GFL; Bourne, *Carter*, 341; Witcover, *Marathon*, 525–26.

41. *Atlanta Constitution*, 21 June, 1 July 1976; Carter and Blacks, Background books, 1–7, PFCR, GFL; *Los Angeles Times*, 5 July 1976; Carter to Christopher Edley, 6 July 1976, Morris Abram Papers, Emory University; Martin Luther King, Sr., Remarks, Pre-Presidential: 76 Campaign, Issues, Eizenstat, box 2, JCL.

42. Eizenstat, *Carter*, 575.

43. Jack Guthman to Morris B. Abram, 23 Sept. 1976, Abram Papers, box 8, Emory University. See also Abram to Harriet Zimmerman, 2 Sept. 1976, Abram to Mr. and Mrs. R. Horowitz, 2 Aug. 1976, Abram to Carter, 29 June 1976, and similar letters and documents, all in Abram Papers, box 8, Emory University. See also Eli N. Evans, *The Lonely Days were Sundays: Reflections of a Jewish Southerner*, 111–12.

44. Rabbi Mayer Abramowitz to Carter, 7 July 1976, Clough File, box 1, JCL.

45. "Carter and the Once Born," *Newsweek*, August 1976, Pre-Presidential: 76 Campaign, Harriet Zimmerman File, box 310, JCL.

46. *Today Show*, NBC TV, 6 Aug. 1976, Transcript in Pre-Presidential: 76 Campaign, Issues, Eizenstat, box 22, JCL.

47. *New York Daily News*, 31 Aug. 1976; Speech to New York Board of Rabbis, 31 Aug. 1976, *Los Angeles Times*, 23 July 1976, and other clippings in Pre-Presidential: 76 Campaign, Harriet Zimmerman Papers, box 310, JCL; Campaign Flyer, Nov. 1976, Powell Donated File, box 34, JCL.

48. Carter's speech, 8 Sept. 1976, Pre-Presidential: 76 Campaign, Harriet Zimmerman Papers, box 309, JCL.

49. Christian Philip Peterson, "The Carter Administration and the Promotion of Human Rights in the Soviet Union, 1977–1981," *Diplomatic History* 38, No. 3 (2014), 632.

50. Carter to Lance, 25 July 1976, Clough File, box 13, JCL.

51. Mary Finch Hoyt, The *East Wing: A Memoir,* 91, 122–27; RSC, *First Lady,* 138–39.

52. Witcover, *Marathon*, 527; Glad, *Carter*, 285–86; Paul F. Boller, Jr., *Presidential Anecdotes*, 342.

53. Douglass Cater, "'How Different is the South?,'" *Washington Post Outlooks*, 10 Oct. 1976.

54. *Washington Post*, 19 July 1976.

55. *(Nashville) Tennessean*, 10 Oct. 1976.

56. AP story, 4 Oct. 1976, copy in PFCR, box H23, GFL; Carter to Rabbi Emmanuel Feldman, 21 Aug. 1976, Clough File, box 8, JCL; Graham to Carter, 26 July 1976, Carter to Graham, 26 Aug. 1976, both in Clough File, box 9, JCL.

57. Eppie Lederer to Carter, 27 July 1976, with attached correspondence between Carter and Hesburgh, Clough File, box 13, JCL.

58. *Americus Times-Recorder*, 26 July 1976; *Mideast Review*, 28 July 1976, copy in PFCR, box H29, GFL.

59. O'Neill to Carter, 24 June, 1976, Carter to O'Neill, 30 July 1976, both in Clough File, box 17, Vance to Carter, 31 July 1976, Clough File, box 23, JCL.

60. Memorandum, 31 July 1976, Carter et al. meeting with Eizenstat, Re Campaign Issues, Rafshoon Donated, box 7, JCL; *Chicago Daily News*, 31 July, 1 Aug. 1976.

Chapter 5

1. Memorandum, 1 Sept. 1976, Rita Thompson to Members of the Peanut Brigade, Helen Mills File, box 1, JCL.

2. Jules Witcover, *Marathon: The Pursuit of the Presidency 1972–1976*, 545–46; Peter G. Bourne, *Jimmy Carter: A Comprehensive Biography from Plains to the Post-Presidency*, 341–42; Betty Glad, *Jimmy Carter in Search of the Great White House*, 380; *Americus Times-Recorder*, 7 Sept. 1976; Patrick Anderson, *Electing Jimmy Carter: The Campaign of 1976*, 101; William E. Leuchtenburg, *In the Shadow of FDR: From Harry Truman to Ronald Reagan*, 177–79.

3. Jimmy Carter News Summary, 17 Sept.1976, Ron Nessen Papers, 1974–77, GFL; Witcover, *Marathon*, 546–52, 559–60; Glad, *Carter*, 381–82.

4. *New York Times*, 1 Sept 1976; Rockefeller to Carter, 1 Sept. 1976, Clough File, box 19, JCL.

5. *Atlanta Constitution*, 10 Sept. 1976.

6. (*Plainfield, NY*) *National Courier*, 17 Sept. 1976; *Washington Post*, 21 Sept. 1976.

7. Amber Roessner, *Jimmy Carter and the Birth of the Marathon Media Campaign*, 151, 158–59; *Atlanta Constitution*, 29 Sept. 1976.

8. Daniel K. Williams, *The Election of the Evangelical: Jimmy Carter, Gerald Ford, and the Presidential Contest of 1976*, 291; Witcover, *Marathon*, 564; Anderson, *Electing Jimmy Carter*, 111; Robert Scheer, "Interview: Jimmy Carter," *Playboy Magazine*, November 1976.

9. Bourne, *Carter*, 348.

10. Golson remark that Carter knew the tape was running is in Witcover, *Marathon*, 569, n1; Jonathan Alter, *His Very Best: Jimmy Carter, A Life*, 266.

11. Witcover, *Marathon*, 561–67; Bourne, *Carter*, 345–48; Glad, *Carter*, 383–84.

12. Kandy Stroud, *How Jimmy Won: The Victory Campaign from Plains to the White House*, 354–55; see also Paul F. Boller, *Presidential Anecdotes*, 342–43, and Williams, *Election of the Evangelical*, 294–99.

13. Witcover, *Marathon*, 567–68.

14. Ibid., 568–70; Glad, *Carter*, 384.

15. Memorandum, 27 Sept. 1976, Jack Valenti to Carter, Clough File, box 23, JCL; Norman Vincent Peale to Carter, 4 Oct. 1976, Clough File, box 18, JCL; *Oklahoma Journal*, 30 Oct. 1976; Bob Woodward, *Shadow: Five Presidents and the Legacy of Watergate*, 55–58.

16. *San Francisco Chronicle*, 16 Sept. 1976; *Atlanta Journal*, 22 Sept. 1976, both in PFCR, box H23, GFL; Rosalynn Carter, *First Lady from Plains*, 139–40; Jonathan Alter, *His Very Best: Jimmy Carter, A Life*, 269.

17. Ray Cromley, "Rosalynn Carter a powerful influence," 14 Aug. 1976, unidentified clipping, VF, Box Carter, R., JCL.

18. Memorandum, Mary Hoyt to RSC, Madeline MacBean, & Jane Fenderson, 16 Aug. 1976, Hoyt Papers, box 1, JCL; *Detroit Free Press*, 8 Sept. 1976, in PFCR, box H23, GFL; *Women's Wear Daily*, 8 Sept. 1976, copy in Charles McCall File, box 66, GFL; Speeches, some in Rosalynn's handwriting, dated 2, 6, 13 Sept. and 15 Oct, 1976 in First Lady Press Office File, box 1, JCL; James S. Gordon to RSC, 1 Oct. 1976, First Lady Projects, Mental Health, box 6, JCL; *Washington Post*, 4 Oct. 1976.

19. 15 Oct. 1976, UPI Story, PFCR, box H21, GFL; Carter to Helen Rafshoon, 18 Oct. 1976, Clough File, box 19, JCL.

20. Undated clipping from *Wall Street Journal* [Nov.1976] includes Jordan remark, Richard Cheney File, box 16, GFL; UPI story, 30 Oct. 1976, PFCR, box H23, GFL, quotes Rosalynn.

21. *U.S. News and World Report*, 18 Oct., 1976, p. 24; *New York Daily News*, 30 Oct. 1976, and many more similar news stories in PFCR, box H23, GFL.

22. *Ford Newsletter*, 22 Sept. 1976, copy in William J. Usery Collection, Special Collections, Georgia State University Library, Atlanta (GSU).

23. Witcover, *Marathon*, 573; Bourne, *Carter*, 348–49; RSC, *First Lady*, 139; Glad, *Carter*, 385.

24. Pat Anderson to Jody Powell and Hamilton Jordan, Sept. 1976, with attachments, Jack Valenti to Carter, 2 Sept. 1976, Ted Sorensen to Stu Eizenstat, 15 Sept. 1976, all in Pre-Presidential: 76 Campaign, Issues, Eizenstat, box 8, JCL; Marvin L. Stone to Carter, 4 Sept. 1976, Clough File, box 22, JCL.

25. Witcover, *Marathon*, 577–78; Bourne, *Carter*, 349–50.; *New York Times*, 12 Dec. 2008.

26. *Time*, 4 Oct. 1976, p. 14; Witcover, *Marathon*, 578–79; Bourne, *Carter, 350; The Presidential Campaign 1976*, Vol. 3, 63–91.

27. Witcover, *Marathon*, 580–82; Bourne, *Carter*, 350; Anderson, *Electing Jimmy Carter*, 115–16.

28. *Atlanta Constitution*, 24 Sept. 1976.

29. Carter to Chuck Robb, 29 Sept. 1976, Clough File, box 19, JCL.

30. DNC Analysis of Energy, Sept. 1976, Congressional Liaison, Boudeaux, box 98, JCL; Carter handwritten draft of speech about nuclear weapons, Pre-Presidential: 76 Campaign, Issues, Eizenstat, box 2, JCL; *New York Times*, 26 Sept. 1976; Memorandum, Richard Holbrooke to Carter, Aug.1976, Pre-Presidential: 76 Campaign, Issues, Eizenstat, box 17, JCL; Excerpts from interview by William Lowther, Wanda M. Phelan Files, box 1, GFL; Memorandum, Anne Burnsdale to Dave Gergen, 7 Oct. 1976, David Gergen Files, box 8, GFL; Jack H. Watson, Jr., to George Ball, with copies to Ted Sorensen, Cyrus Vance, and Paul Warnke, and their position papers attached, Plains File, box 42, JCL; Carter speech at Notre Dame University, 9 Oct. 1976, Wanda M. Phelan Files, box 2, GFL.

31. Memorandum, Zbigniew Brzezinski to Stuart Eizenstat, 27 Sept., RE Foreign Policy Debate, Richard N. Gardner to Stuart Eizenstat, 29 Sept. 1976, both in Pre-Presidential: 76 Campaign, Issues, Eizenstat, box 8, JCL; Bourne, *Carter*, 351–53; Witcover, *Marathon*, 594–600; RSC, *First Lady*, 139; Gaddis Smith, *Morality, Reason and Power: American Diplomacy in the Carter Years*, 31; Roessner, *Jimmy Carter and the Birth of the Marathon Media Campaign*, 178–81.

32. Witcover, *Marathon*, 600–608: Bourne, *Carter*, 353; *The Presidential Campaign 1976*, Vol. 3, 92–118.

33. Jay Carlson for Dick Holbrooke, 7 Oct. 1976, Richard N. Gardner to Carter, 7 Oct. 1976, Pre-Presidential: 76 Campaign, Issues, Eizenstat, box 8, JCL; Andrew Young to Carter, 16 Oct. 1976, Clough File, box 24, JCL.

34. Author interview with Goodwin, 15 July 1994.

35. Rod Goodwin to Jimmy, 16 Oct., 1976, Clough File, box 20, JCL.

36. Bourne, *Carter*, 353; Witcover, *Marathon*, 612–16.

37. Witcover, *Marathon*, 616–24; Bourne, *Carter*, 354; Scott Kaufman, *Ambition, Pragmatism, and Party: A Political Biography of Gerald R. Ford*, 288–300; *The Presidential Campaign 1976*, Vol. 3, 119–53.

38. Anderson, *Electing Jimmy Carter*, 131; RSC Speeches, 23, 31 Oct., Nov. 1976 in First Lady Press Office File, box 1, JCL.

39. Dominic Sandbrook, *Eugene McCarthy: The Rise and Fall of Postwar American Liberalism*, 271–75; Dominic Sandbrook, *Mad as Hell: The Crisis of the 1970s and the Rise of the Populist Right*, 210.

40. Clennon King to Bruce Edwards, with copy to Carter, 24 Oct. 1976, Clough File, box 13, JCL.

41. Witcover, *Marathon*, 625–35; Glad, *Carter*, 396–98; Dan Arial, *Carpenter's Apprentice: The Spiritual Biography of Jimmy Carter*, 100–101; Curtis Wilkie, *Dixie: A Personal Odyssey through Events that Shaped the Modern South*, 231–33.

42. RSC, Carter, *First Lady*, 141; *Time Magazine*, 15 Nov. 1976, pp. 13–16.

43. *Time Magazine*, 15 Nov. 1976, p. 13; Gerald Pomper, *The Election of 1976: Reports and Interpretations*, 54–65; Herbert B. Asher, *Presidential Elections and American Politics: Voters, Candidates, and Campaigns since 1952*, 172–80; John Robert Greene, *The Presidency of Gerald R. Ford*, 175–87.

44. https://en.wikipedia.org/wiki/1976_United_States_presidential_election; Williams, *Election of the Evangelical*, 334–46.

45. Roessner, *Carter and the Birth of the Marathon Media Campaign*, 197–98.

46. Bourne, *Carter*, 356; RSC, *First Lady*, 141–42; *Americus Times-Recorder*, 2 Nov. 1976.

47. NBC News, 3 Nov. 1976; Carters' quotes in *Americus Times-Recorder*, 17 Feb. 2016; Witcover, *Marathon*, 643–44; Bourne, *Carter*, 356; Stephen Graubaud, *Command of Office: How War, Secrecy, and Deception Transformed the Presidency*, 431; Speeches, Speechwriter File, Nesmith, box 1, JCL.

48. RSC, *First Lady*, 142; Glad, *Carter*, 399–400.

49. Quoted in Sandbrook, *Mad as Hell*, 217.

Chapter 6

1. John Robert Greene, *Betty Ford: Candor and Courage in the White House*, 98–99; Ford to Carter, 3 Nov. 1976, WHCF-Subject, box 6, Gerald Ford Library (GFL); *Atlanta Constitution*, 4 Nov.1976. President Woodrow Wilson was born in Virginia and grew up in Georgia and South Carolina, but he had moved to New Jersey long before he went into politics. President Lyndon Johnson was a native of Texas, but he had moved to Washington and claimed to be southwestern long before he became president. Carter was the first native of the Deep South, living in the Deep South, since Zachary Taylor in 1848 to be elected President.

2. *Americus Times-Recorder*, 5 Nov., 1976; UPI News story, 5 Nov., 1976, copy in Charles McCall Files, box 83, GFL; Carl M. Brauer, *Presidential Transitions: Eisenhower Through Reagan*, 196–98.

3. *Americus Times-Recorder*, 6 Nov. 1976.

4. Letters in Clough File, boxes 1, 4, 10, 11, 12, 13, 16, 18, 19, 21, 23, 24, JCL.

5. Asadollah Alam, *The Shah and I: The Confidential Diary of Iran's Royal Court, 1969–77*, 500, 524.

6. John D. Rockefeller III to Carter, 4 Nov. 1976, Carter to John D. Rockefeller, 17 Nov. 1976, "David" to "Jimmy," 4 Nov. 1976, all in Clough File, box 19, JCL.

7. *The Atlanta Constitution*, 8 Nov.1976;http://www.ontheissues.org/Celeb/Jimmy_Carter_Energy_+_Oil.htm.

8. Paul Zuckerman to Governor and Mrs. Carter, 10 Nov.1976, Clough File, box 24, JCL.

9. http://www.notablebiographies.com/Ro-Sc/Sakharov-Andrei.html; Richard Lourie, *Sakharov: A Biography*, 243–76.

10. Sakharov to Carter, telegram, 3 Nov. 1976, Staff Secretary, Handwriting File, box 2, JCL; Andrei Sakharov, *Memoirs*, 462.

11. Memorandum, Jack Valenti to Carter, 3 Nov. 1976, Tim Kraft File, box 3, JCL; Anna Elisa Trimble to Carter, 11 Nov. 1976, WHCF, Box PP-10, JCL.

12. Peter G. Bourne, *Jimmy Carter: A Comprehensive Biography from Plains to the Post-Presidency*, 358 (quotation), see also 361.

13. Ibid., 360–62.

14. *New York Times*, 8 Nov. 1976; *Americus Times-Recorder*, 15 Nov. 1976; Religious News Service, 15 Nov. 1976, Baptist History File, Jimmy Carter, Southern Baptist History Archives, Nashville, TN.

15. *Time Magazine*, 15 Nov. 1976, pp. 22–23; Memorandum, Jack Watson, David Aaron, and Tony Lake to the President-Elect, 11 Nov. 1976, Re Foreign Policy Issues, Declassified Document NLC-126-1-3-1-7, JCL; Memorandum, David Aaron to President-Elect, 26 Nov. 1976, RE CIA Briefing, Declassified Document NLC-17-116-9-4-2, JCL; Memorandum, David Aaron to President-Elect, 27 Nov. 1976, RE Meeting with Averell Harriman, Declassified Document, NLC-7-66-7-9-6, JCL; Anatoly Dobrynin, *In Confidence: Moscow's Ambassador to America's Six Cold War Presidents*, 428–29.

16. *Americus Times-Recorder*, 15 Jan. 1977; Clare Crawford and Joyce Leviton, "The Leap from Plains to Pennsylvania Avenue: How Rosalynn Will Do It," *Up Front*, 15 Nov. 1976, p. 23, VF, box Carter, Rosalynn, JCL; Helen Thomas, AP Story, *Atlanta Journal and Constitution*, 19 Nov. 1976.

17. Lillian Hellman, "Plain Speaking with Mrs. Carter," *Rolling Stone*, 43, 45 (quotations).

18. Gail Sheehy, "Rosalynn Carter: The Indispensable Half," *Atlanta Journal and Constitution*, 27 Nov. 1976; Jimmy Carter, Invitation from DNC to a country supper at the Pond House, 2 Oct. 1976, Clough File, box 22, JCL.

19. Crawford and Leviton, "Leap from Plains," 23.

20. Quoted in Hellman, "Plain Speaking," 43.

21. Multiple letters, 14–24 Nov. 1976, in Clough File, boxes 4, 9, 11, JCL; Theodore M. Hesburgh, *God, Country, Notre Dame*, 269–74.

22. Carter note on his letter to Leslie Huffman, 30 Nov. 1976, Clough File, box 11, JCL.

23. *New Times*, 26 Nov. 1976, clipping in Jordan File, box 1, folder: Appointments Procedure O/A 10,628, JCL.

24. Memorandum, Eizenstat to Carter, 30 Nov. 1976, RE: Message from Rabin, Staff Secretary, Handwriting File, box 2, JCL.

25. Memorandum, Ribicoff to Carter and Mondale, Nov. 1976, RE: Personal and Private Background Notes on the Middle East, Staff Secretary, Handwriting File, box 2, JCL.

26. Bourne, *Carter*, 364-65.

27. Book of Campaign Promises, Nov. 1976, Press File, Granum, box 80, JCL.

28. *Atlanta Constitution*, 21 Nov. 1976; Press Guidance for Meeting with Governor Carter, 22 Nov. 1976, Michael Raoul-Doall Papers, box 32, GFL.

29. Jimmy Carter, *Keeping Faith: Memoirs of a President*, 24; Rosalynn Carter, *First Lady from Plains*, 143–44.

30. Barbara Walters to Carter, 1 Dec. 1976, Clough File, box 23, JCL.

31. *New York Times*, 2 Dec. 1976, in Charles McCall File, box 83, GFL.

32. Memorandum, Peter Bourne to Rosalynn Carter, 6 Dec. 1976, Bourne File, box 28, JCL.

33. *The Atlanta Constitution*, 11 Dec. 1976.

34. JC, *Keeping Faith*, 22–23.

35. *Americus Times-Recorder*, 19 Dec. 1976.

36. *Atlanta Constitution*, 2 Dec. 1976; National Park Service (NPS) interview with Jimmy and Rosalynn Carter, 11 May 1988, JCL.

37. *New York Times*, 16 Nov. 1976; Joel Havemann, "Carter is Taking Pains in Picking His Plums," *National Journal*, 20 Nov. 1976, pp. 1650–51; Unidentified newspaper clipping, 20 Nov. 1976, Charles McCall File, box 83, GFL; Appointments Procedure, 26 Nov. 1976, Jordan File, box 1, JCL.

38. *The American Spectator*, 17 Nov. 2006; Christopher Andrew, *For the President's Eyes Only: Secret Intelligence and the American Presidency from Washington to Bush*, 428; Jon Meacham, *Destiny and Power: The American Odyssey of George Herbert Walker Bush*, 202–204.

39. Bourne, *Carter*, 366.

40. *Atlanta Constitution*, 21 Dec. 1976; Bourne, *Carter*, 367.

41. Frederick Allen, *Atlanta Rising: The Invention of an International City, 1946–1996*, 213–14.

42. Rogers, *Barbara Jordan*, 276–80, 142. An embittered Jordan retired the following year after serving six years in Congress, her brief, historic, and glorious year in national politics ironically terminated by the end of Carter's first year in office. Returning to Texas, she taught at the University of Texas's LBJ School of Public Affairs, did not endorse any candidate for president in 1980, and succumbed to her disease at age fifty-nine in January 1996. See Rogers, *Jordan*, ix, 295, 305–06.

43. After a furious debate, because Bell belonged to all-White country clubs and opposed busing to bring about integration, Thurmond succeeded, and Bell was confirmed on January 26, 1977. See Allen, *Atlanta Rising*, 195–96; Carter, *Public Papers of the Presidents of the United States*, 1977, Vol. I, 19–20.

44. Bourne, *Carter*, 367; *Americus Times-Recorder*, 20 Dec. 1976.

45. JC, *Keeping Faith*, 51; Author interview with Vance, 14 July 1992.

46. *Atlanta Constitution*, 21 Dec. 1976; *New York Times*, 24 Dec. 1976.

47. Brzezinski, Miller Center Interview, 58–67, JCL; Brzezinski, NARA Exit Interview, 20 Feb. 1981, JCL; JC, *Keeping Faith*, 51–54.

48. Bergland, Miller Center Interview, 36, 44, JCL.

49. Memorandum, Bundy to Brown, 27 Dec., 1976, Brown to Bundy, 8 Jan. 1977, WHCF, box JL-1, JCL; JC, *Keeping Faith*, 55; Frederick Allen, *Secret Formula*, 359, 363–64, 372, 378; Andrew Krepinevich and Barry Watts, *The Last Warrior: Andrew Marshall and the Shaping of Modern American Defense Strategy*, 129.

50. *New York Times*, 15, 16, 17, 21, 22, 24 Dec. 1976; Memorandum, Carter to Cabinet Designees, 22 Dec. 1976, Minorities folder, WHCF, box FG-96, JCL; Talent Group [late 1976], Jordan File, boxes 4, 10, JCL: Janet M. Martin, *The Presidency and Women: Promise, Performance, and Illusion*, 204–208.

51. Bourne, *Carter*, 370–71; JC, *Keeping Faith*, 67–68; Lee H. Hamilton, *Congress, Presidents, and American Politics*, 116; John A. Farrell, *Tip O'Neill and the Democratic Century*, 448–52; Author interview with O'Neill, 25 Oct. 1990.

52. *New York Times*, 19 Dec. 1976.

53. Bourne, *Carter*, 367.

54. *Time Magazine*, 3 Jan. 1977.

55. The multiple drafts of the speech are in Staff Secretary, Handwriting File, box 2, JCL; *Americus Times-Recorder*, 3 Jan. 1977; Bourne, *Carter*, 365.

56. Carter to Graham, 7 Jan. 1977, Shlomo Goren to Carter, 10 Nov., 1976, Carter to Goren, 10 Jan. 1977, all in Clough File, box 9, JCL; Mother Teresa to Carter, 21 Dec. 1976, Carter to Mother Teresa, 10 Jan. 1977, both in Clough File, box 16, JCL.

57. *Americus Times-Recorder*, 4 Jan. 1977; *New York Times*, 18, 19 Jan. 1977.

58. *The Atlanta Constitution*, 17 Jan. 1977; *Americus Times-Recorder*, 20 Jan. 1977.

59. *Americus Times-Recorder*, 20 Jan. 1977.

60. *USA Today*, 20 Jan. 2009.

61. *Washington Star-News*, 19 Jan. 1977; Presidential Daily Diary, box PD-1, JCL.

62. William Booth, "Betty Ford's Tabled Resolution," *Smithsonian Magazine*, June 2008; Image: B2843-09A, GFL; David Hume Kennerly Interview with Mary Beth Durkin, Producer, "Betty Ford: The Real Deal," PBS Documentary, 25 July, 2008.

Chapter 7

1. Pool Report, 20 Jan. 1977, Joe Albright of the Cox Newspapers, Presidential Daily Diary (PDD), box PD-1, JCL.

2. Tip O'Neill, *Man of the House: The Life and Political Memoirs of Speaker Tip O'Neill*, 269; D. Jason Bergren, "'I Had a Different Way of Governing': The Living Faith of President Carter," *Journal of Church and State* 47, No. 1 (Winter 2005), 44; Signed copy of the oath, 20 Jan. 1977, White House Counsel, Lipshutz, box 5, JCL; *New York Times*, 21 Jan. 1977; Jimmy Carter, *White House Diary*, 9–10.

3. Jerry Rafshoon to Carter, Carter to Rafshoon, Inauguration Memorandum, Jan. 1977, Staff Secretary, Handwriting File, box 2, JCL; JC, Miller Center Interview, 6, JCL; JC, *Public Papers of the Presidents of the United States, 1977, Book I*, 1–4; Jimmy Carter, *Keeping Faith: Memoirs of a President*, 19–21; Samuel Moyn, *Human Rights and the Uses of History*, 69–70.

4. Senator William Proxmire to Carter, 20 Dec. 1976, Carter to Proxmire, 4 Jan. 1977, Clough File, box 19, JCL; Peter G. Bourne, *Jimmy Carter: A Comprehensive Biography from Plains to the Post-Presidency*, 365; Stephen M. Bauer, *At Ease in the White House: The Uninhibited Memoirs of a Presidential Social Aide*, 213–14; Kai Bird, *The Outlier: The Unfinished Presidency of Jimmy Carter*, 152–53.

5. Betty Glad, *Jimmy Carter in Search of the Great White House*, 409–10.

6. Bauer, *At Ease in the White House*, 220; JC, *White House Diary*, 10; *Atlanta Journal and Constitution*, 26 Sept. 1999; Addition to Pool Report, 20 Jan. 1977, PDD, box PD-1, JCL; "The Carter Presidency," *Atlanta Magazine*, January 1977, pp. 28, 36, 38, 45.

7. JC, *Keeping Faith*, 23–24; JC, *White House Diary*, 10; Bourne, *Carter*, 365–66; PDD, 20 Jan. 1977, box PD-1, JCL; Helen Thomas, *Front Row at the White House: My Life and Times*, 326.

8. *Atlanta Journal-Constitution*, 1 March 1981; RSC comment to Gil Troy, Historical Press Conference, 20 Feb 1997, Carter Center, Atlanta, Author's notes; *Christian Science Monitor*, 21 Jan. 1977; JC, *White House Diary*, 10; William E. Leuchtenburg, *The American President: From Teddy Roosevelt to Bill Clinton*, 560.

9. Rosalynn Carter, *First Lady from Plains*, 143–49.

10. Bauer, *At Ease in the White House*, 215; Pool Report, Inaugural Parties, Sally Quinn, 20 Jan. 1977, PDD, box PD-1, JCL; JC, *Keeping Faith*, 24–25; RSC, *First Lady*, 148.

11. Bauer, *At Ease in the White House*, 218–20; RSC, *First Lady*, 151–53; JC, *White House Diary*, 11.

12. Carter to Rosey Grier, 28 Jan. 1977, Grier to Carter, 21 Jan. 1977, both in WHCF, box JL-1, JCL.

13. Bourne, *Carter*, 366; *Public Papers, 1977, I*, 5–6; *Washington Post*, 21 Jan. 1977; Proclamation, 21 Jan. 1977, Jody Powell File, box 69, JCL.

14. "Ma" to "Hot," n.d., Staff Secretary, Handwriting File, box 4, JCL.

15. Helen Thomas interview with Rosalynn Carter in *Atlanta Constitution*, 13 March 1977; Memorandum, JC to Treasury Secretary Michael Blumenthal, 25 Feb. 1977, WHCF, box PP-5, JCL.

16. *Americus Times-Recorder*, 4 Jan., 4 Feb. 1977; *New York Times*, 4 Feb. 1977; JC, *Keeping Faith*, 30; JC, *White House Diary*, 25; Douglas Brinkley, *The Unfinished Presidency: Jimmy Carter's Journey beyond the White House*, 255–56.

17. John P. Burke, *Honest Broker?: The National Security Advisor and Presidential Decision Making*, 158, 324–27, 332–35; John Prados, *Keepers of the Keys: A History of the National Security Council from Truman to Bush*, 381.

18. Minutes of Cabinet Meeting, 24 January 1977, VF, JCL; Ted Sorensen, *Counselor: A Life at the Edge of History*, 487–503.

19. Memorandum, Brzezinski to Carter, 22 Jan. 1977, Declassified Document NLC-1-1-6-6-7, JCL.

20. Brzezinski, Miller Center Interview, 21-22, 26-27, 52; 80-82; Brzezinski, Exit Interview, 3–7, both in JCL; Madeleine Albright, *Memo to the President Elect*, 19; JC, *Keeping Faith*, 54; Erwin C. Hargrove, *Jimmy Carter as President: Leadership and the Politics of the Public Good*, 111–15; Timothy P. Maga, *The World of Jimmy Carter: U.S. Foreign Policy, 1977–1981*, 3.

21. JC, *Public Papers, 1977, I*, 8; JC, *White House Diary*, 12–13.

22. Carter to Schlesinger, 15 March 1977, Staff Secretary, Handwriting File, box 12, JCL; JC, *White House Diary*, 29.

23. *Atlanta Journal and Constitution*, 22 Nov. 1992; RSC, *First Lady*, 155; JC, *White House Diary*, 13.

24. Secretary Vance Evening Report with Carter's annotations, 31 Jan. 1977, Plains File, box 37, JCL; Elliot E. Slotnick and Jay E. Hakes, "Carter and the Judicial Recruitment Process," in Steven A. Shull and Lance T. LeLoup, *The Presidency: Studies in Public Policy*, 95–113.

25. Carter note to Tim Kraft, 23 Jan. 1977, Jack Watson memorandum to Carter, 23 Jan. 1977, Carter notes to Jordan, Eizenstat, Lipshutz, Brzezinski, Vance, all in Staff Secretary, Handwriting File, box 4; JCL; David Rubenstein, Miller Center Interview, JCL, 8–9; *New York Times*, 23, 27 Jan. 1977; Albright, *Memo to the President Elect*, 101.

26. Memorandum for the Record, Discussion with Dr. Brzezinski, 29 Jan. 1977, Brzezinski Collection, Donated, box 21, JCL.

27. Carter comment at Historical Press Conference, Carter Center, 20 Feb. 1997, Author's notes.

28. Rosalynn Carter to Jan Williams, 18 Feb., 1977, WHCF; First Lady Social Office, Subject File, box 13, JCL; *Washington Star*, 31 Jan. 1977; JC, *Keeping Faith*, 56; JC, *White House Diary*, 32.

29. News clipping, 8 Feb. 1977, White House Administration, Hugh Carter, box 101, JCL; Scott Kaufman, *Rosalynn Carter: Equal Partner in the White House*, 35–36; Carl Sferrazzo Anthony, *First Ladies, Vol.II: The Saga of the Presidents' Wives and Their Power, 1961–1990*, 282–85; Mary Finch Hoyt, *East Wing: A Memoir*, 108–10; Bauer, *At Ease in the White House*, 226.

30. Memorandum, Brzezinski to Mrs. Carter, 27 Jan. 1977, and Press Release, 15 Feb. 1977, both in First Lady Press Office, State Dinners, box 20, JCL.

31. *Washington Star*, 31 Jan. 1977.

32. Presidential Directive/NSC 9, Army Special Operations Field Office in Berlin, 30 March 1977, VF, Presidential Directives, JCL; *New York Times*, 2, 10 March 1977. Dale R. Herspring, *The Pentagon and the Presidency: Civil-Military Relations from FDR to George W. Bush*, 15–20, 237–41, gives a negative interpretation of Carter as commander in chief.

33. Presidential Review Memorandum/NSC-17, 26 Jan. 1977, and Memorandum of Conversation with Harold Brown, 26 Jan. 1977, both in Brzezinski Collection, Donated, box 21, JCL; Memorandum, Cyrus Vance to Carter, Re Your Visit to NATO, 6 Jan. 1977, Declassified Document NLC-23-28-7-29-8, JCL.

34. Memoranda for the Record, Discussions with Brzezinski, 29 Jan. 1977, Brzezinski Collection, Donated, JCL; Memorandum, Jack Watson to Carter, 30 Jan. 1977, Staff Secretary, Handwriting File, box 5, JCL; JC, *White House Diary*, 17; Kristina Spohr, *The Global Chancellor: Helmut Schmidt & the Reshaping of the International Order*, 5, 30–32.

35. David Rubenstein, quoting Frank Moore, Miller Center Interview, 76, JCL, 76.

36. Memorandum, Carter to Hugh Carter, 15 March 1977, Staff Secretary, Handwriting File, box 13, JCL; Hugh Carter to Jimmy Carter, 23 March 1977, WHCF, box WH-9, JCL; Memorandum, Carter to Secretary of Defense, 30 March 1977, WHCF, box PQ-1, JCL; Lipshutz to Carter, 7 March 1977, Staff Secretary, Handwriting File, box 11, JCL; Eric Alterman and Kevin Mattson, *The Cause: The Fight for American Liberalism from Franklin Roosevelt to Barack Obama*, 297.

37. JC, Miller Center Interview, 8, JCL; Stephen Graubard, *Command of Office: How War, Secrecy and Deception Transformed the Presidency, from Theodore Roosevelt to George W. Bush*, 431–32.

38. O'Neill, *Man of the House*, 283; Bourne, *Carter*, 370, 375 (Lance quotation); JC, *Keeping Faith*, 67–71; Charles O. Jones, *The Trusteeship Presidency: Jimmy Carter and the United States Congress*, 79–98; Carter interview in Brian Till, *Conversations with Power: What Great Presidents and Prime Ministers Can Teach Us about Leadership*, 181.

39. Erwin C. Hargrove, *Jimmy Carter as President: Leadership and the Politics of the Public Good*, 17, 19–28; Memorandum, Frank Moore to Carter, with attached article from *Washington Star*, 21 Feb. 1977, Staff Secretary, Handwriting file, box 9, JCL; Author interview with Tip O'Neill, 25 Oct. 1990.

40. Bourne, *Carter*, 369; JC, *Keeping Faith*, 72–73; Robert Shogan, *Promises to Keep: Carter's First 100 Days*, 91–93.

41. Bourne, *Carter*, 372.

42. Richard Reeves, *Convention*, 100–101; JC, *Keeping Faith*, 73; O'Neill, *Man of the House*, 323–24.

43. Memorandum, Frank Moore to Carter Re Letter from Javits and Cranston, 2 Feb. 1977, WHCF, box HE-10, JCL.

44. Memorandum, Brzezinski to Carter, 4 Feb 1977, Declassified NLC-15-65-5-1-8, JCL.

45. Ibid.; Memorandum, Brzezinski to Carter, Re Middle East Evening Report, 10 Feb. 1977, Declassified Document NLC-15-20-1-2-0, JCL.

46. Memorandum, BQ [Bill Quandt] to Carter, with Carter comment, [Feb. 1977], NSA Brzezinski File, Geographic Files, box 14, JCL.

47. Memorandum for the Record, 2 Feb. 1977, in Cabinet Feb. 1, NSA, Brzezinski File, box 50, JCL.

48. Tony Lake, "A Human Rights Strategy for the United States," 2 Feb. 1977, NSA, Brzezinski Collection, Subject File, box 29, JCL; Bourne, *Carter*, 383–90; JC, *White House Diary*, 20.

49. Julian E. Zelizer, "Conservatives, Carter, and the Politics of National Security," in Bruce J. Schulman and Julian E. Zelizer, editors, *Rightward Bound: Making America Conservative in the 1970s*, 271.

50. Andrew Young, *An Easy Burden: The Civil Rights Movement and the Transformation of America*, 117, 169, 287.

51. Memorandum, Carter to Bob Lipshutz, 2 Feb. 1977, WHCF, box PR-70, JCL.

Chapter 8

1. Rosalynn's comment in *Americus Times-Recorder*, 20 April 1977; Jerry Rafshoon to Carter, 7 Feb. 1977, Staff Secretary, Handwriting File, box 6, JCL; Betty Glad, *Jimmy Carter in Search of the Great White House*, 410; Carter, *Public Papers*, 1977, Vol. I, 69–77: William E. Leuchtenburg, *The American President: From Teddy Roosevelt to Bill Clinton*, 561.

2. *Baptist Press*, 7, 9, 15, Feb (quotation in 15 Feb. issue), 4 April, 13 May, copies in Baptist History File, Jimmy Carter, Southern Baptist History Library and Archives, Nashville, TN; Unidentified clipping, 25 May 1977, VF, Fitzpatrick, Mary, JCL.

3. Memorandum, Robert Shultze to White House Staff for Carter, 7 Feb. 1977, Jody Powell File, box 42, JCL; *New York Times*, 6 Feb. 1977; Minutes of Cabinet Meeting, 7 Feb.,1977, in Patricia Harris Papers, box 51, Library of Congress; Carter to Richard Harden, 7 Feb. 1977, WHCF, box WH-1, JCL; Memorandum, H. S. Knight to Carter, Re Secret Service Armored Car program, 14 Feb.1977, WHCF, box WH-9, JCL; Minutes of Cabinet Meeting, 11 April 1977, VF, JCL.

4. Memorandum, Jimmy Carter to Hugh Carter, Jr., 11 Feb. 1977, Staff Secretary, Handwriting File, box 9, JCL; Memorandum, Jim Fallows to Carter, 27 Feb.1977, Staff Secretary, Handwriting File, box 10, JCL.

5. Carter, *Public Papers*, 1977, Vol. I, 149–54 (quotation on 154).

6. Rosalynn Carter, *First Lady from Plains*, 221–24; Menus for State Dinners during the Carter Administration, Feb. 14, 1977, JCL; *New York Times*, 15 Feb. 1977.

7. Carter, *Public Papers*, 1977, Vol. I, 208–13, 353–60, 467–69; Stephen M. Bauer, *At Ease in the White House: The Uninhibited Memoirs of a Presidential Aide*, 227.

8. Memorandum, Gary Sick to Brzezinski, 12 Feb. 1977, with Carter 7 Feb. letter attached, Declassified Document, NLC-15-20-1-2-0, JCL; Ryan Irwin, "Human Rights and the 1970s," *Diplomatic History*, 40, no. 4 (2016), 791–96; David Farber, *Taken Hostage: The American Hostage Crisis and America's First Encounter with Radical Islam*, 80–82.

9. Christopher Andrew, *For the President's Eyes Only: Intelligence and the American Presidency from Washington to Bush*, 426–30.

10. Andrew, *For the President's Eyes Only*, 426–433; *Washington Times*, 20 Aug. 2004; Jimmy Carter, *White House Diary*, 16–17; Duane R. Clarridge, *A Spy for All Seasons: My Life in the CIA*, 164; Rhodri Jeffreys-Jones, *The CIA and American Democracy*, 216–18; Stansfield Turner, *Burn before Reading: Presidents, CIA Directors, and Secret Intelligence*, 159–60; Tim Weiner, *Legacy of Ashes: The History of the CIA*, 358–61: Richard H. Immerman, *The Hidden Hand: A Brief History of the CIA*, 115–17; David Priess, *The President's Book of Secrets: The Untold Story of Intelligence Briefings to America's Presidents from Kennedy to Obama*, 110–13, 121–28.

11. *National Journal*, 36, no. 41 (October 9, 2004), 3080.

12. Stansfield Turner, *Secrecy and Democracy: The CIA in Transition*, 197–205; Author interview with Carter, 12 Oct. 1994; Author interview with Turner, 6 April 1992; Andrew, *For the President's Eyes Only*, 430–34; *New York Times*, 18 Jan. 2018.

13. News clipping, VF, Vance, Cyrus-Water Projects, JCL; Memorandum, Vice President Mondale to Carter, 10 Feb.1977, Staff Secretary, Handwriting, box 9, JCL; Memorandum, Brzezinski to Carter, Re Soviet Negotiating Deceptions in SALT I, [March 1977], Brzezinski Collection, box 36, JCL; Jody Powell to JC, 18 Feb. 1977, WHCF, box PU-1, JCL; *New York Times*, 15 March 1977.

14. Julia E. Sweig, *Cuba: What Everyone Needs to Know*, 93–94; Memorandum, Brzezinski to Carter, Weekly National Security Report #3, 5 March 1977, Brzezinski Collection,

box 41, JCL; *New York Times*, 12 Feb. 1977; State Department Report, 14 Feb. 1977, Declassified Document NLC-1-18-73-1, JCL.

15. Carter, *Public Papers*, 1977, Vol. I, 77–78, 101, 102, 126, 143,151, 155, 167, 181, 197, and more.
16. Carter to Congressman John Cavanaugh, 7 March 1977, WHCF, box PP-5, JCL.
17. Indira Gandhi to Carter, 22 March 1977, Carter to Gandhi, 30 March 1977, Speechwriters, Hertzberg, box 38, JCL; JC, *White House Diary*, 18.
18. Memorandum, Brzezinski to Carter, 25 March 1977, National Security Report #6, Brzezinski Collection, box 41, JCL.
19. Janet M. Martin, *The Presidency and Women: Promise, Performance, and Illusion*, 203–04, 210, 214, 219–22.
20. Carter to Jody, Ham, Stu, et al. 15 Feb. 1977, Richard Harden Papers, box 3, JCL; Memorandum, Carter to Cabinet Officers and Agency Heads, 15 Feb. 1977, WHCF, box FG-95, JCL: *Americus Times-Recorder*, 19 Feb. 1977.
21. Memorandum, Carter to Heads of Executive Departments, 1 March 1977, WHCF, box FG-9, JCL; Note, Harold Brown to Carter, 2 March 1977, Carter unsent memorandum to Heads, 2 March 1977, Carter to Bert Lance et al., 3 March 1977, all in Staff Secretary, Handwriting File, box 11, JCL; Gaddis Smith, *Morality, Reason & Power: American Diplomacy in the Carter Years*, 45.
22. W. Dale Nelson, *The President Is at Camp David*, 130–31; Kai Bird, *The Outlier: The Unfinished Presidency of Jimmy Carter*, 163–64.
23. Minutes of Fifth Cabinet Meeting, 21 Feb. 1977, Staff Secretary, Handwriting file, box 10, JCL; *New York Times*, 18 Feb. 1977.
24. *Newsweek*, 21 Feb., 1977.
25. Carter Speech, 19 March 1977, Staff Secretary, Handwriting File, box 13, JCL.
26. Presidential Review Memorandum/NSC-10,18 Feb. 1977 PRM/NSC 11, 22 Feb. 1977, VF, Presidential Review Memoranda, JCL; Reports of Cabinet Members, Cabinet Meeting Minutes, 21 Feb. 1977, Staff Secretary, Handwriting File, box 10,JCL; Note, Brzezinski to Carter, 23 Feb. 1977, William B. Quandt to Brzezinski, 22 Feb. 1977, both in VF, Middle East, JCL; Memorandum of Conversation of Carter with Waldheim, 25 Fb. 1977, NSA- Brzezinski Material, Subject file, box 34-35,JCL; Memorandum, Bob Lipshutz to Carter, Re Human Rights Treaties, 26 Feb., 1977, Staff Secretary, Handwriting file, box 10, JCL; Weekly National Security Report 3, 26 Feb.1977, Brzezinski Collection, box 41, JCL; D. Jason Bergren, "'I Had a Different Way of Governing,' The Living Faith of President Carter," *Journal of Church and State*, 55.
27. Memorandum, Tim Kraft to Carter, 28 Feb. 1977, re *Atlanta Journal and Constitution* story 13 Dec. 1974, Staff Secretary, Handwriting file, box 10, JCL; JC, *White House Diary*, 32; *New York Times*, 12 March 1977.
28. JC, *White House Diary*, 15–29; Carter, *Public Papers*, 1977, Vol. I, 92–100.
29. Cecil Andrus, Miller Center Interview, 47–50, JCL; Carter, *Public Papers*, Vol. I, 1977, 207–208; George C. Edwards III, "Exclusive Interview: President Jimmy Carter," *Presidential Studies Quarterly*, 38, no. 1, (2008), 13; Jules Witcover, *Party of the People: A History of the Democrats*, 604.

30. Bourne, *Carter*, 373; Bergren, "'I Had a Different Way of Governing,'" 52; Byrd to Carter, cited in *New York Times*, 12 March 1977; Jimmy Carter, *Keeping Faith: Memoirs of a President*, 78–79; JC, *White House Diary*, 23.

31. Note, Carter to Cecil Andrew, 7 March 1977, Staff Secretary, Handwriting File, box 11, JCL.

32. Carter to Brzezinski and Fallows, 9 March 1977, Staff Secretary, Handwriting File, box 11, JCL.

33. Carter, *Public Papers*, 1977, Vol. I, 44–561.

34. *Americus Times-Recorder*, 18 March, 1977; *New York Times*, 18 March 1977; William R. Gruver to Charles Kirbo, 18 March 1977, with Carter note, Staff Secretary, Handwriting File, box 14, JCL.

35. Avital Schransky to Rosalynn Carter, 11 Feb. 1977, WHCF-Name File, Box Schransky, Anatoli & Avital, JCL; *New York Times*, 17 Feb. 1977.

36. Carter, *Public Papers*, 1977, Vol. I, 185–87; Federal Records, President's Commission on Mental Health, RG 220, JCL; Rosalynn Carter to Muriel Humphrey, 18 Feb. 1977, First Lady Project: Mental Health, box 6, JCL; Mondale to Carter, 22 Feb. 1977, Staff Secretary, Handwriting, box 10, JCL; Memorandum, Thomas E. Bryant to Rosalynn Carter, 3 Feb. 1977, Peter Bourne File, box 28, JCL; S. Kaufman, *Rosalynn Carter: Equal Partner in the White House*, 38.

37. Carter to Brezhnev, 26 Jan. 1977, Brezhnev to Carter, 4 Feb. 1977, Carter to Brezhnev, 14 Feb. 1977, all in Plains File, box 17, JCL.

38. Brezhnev to Carter, 25 Feb., Carter to Brezhnev, 4 March, Brezhnev to Carter, 15 March, Carter to Brezhnev, 24 March, 1977, all in Plains File, box 17, JCL; JC, *White House Diary*, 20; Smith, *Morality, Reason & Power*, 40–41.

39. Martin Gilbert, *Shcharansky: Hero of Our Time*, 187–88; Robert M. Gates, *From the Shadows: The Ultimate Insider's Story of Five Presidents and How They Won the Cold War,* 90–96, 178–79 (quotation on 95).

40. Richard Lourie, *Sakharov: A Biography*, 286–87; Andrei Sakharov, *Memoirs*, 462–66; Friedbert Pfluger, "Human Rights Unbound: Carter's Human Rights Policy Reassessed," *Presidential Studies Quarterly* 19, no. 4 (1989), 705–16.

41. Gal Beckerman, *When They Come for Us, We'll Be Gone: The Epic Struggle to Save Soviet Jewry*, 111–12, 344–46; Stuart E. Eizenstat, *President Carter: The White House Years*, 195–97; Sakharov, *Memoirs*, 464–66.

42. Carter, *Public Papers*, 1977, Vol. I, 327; Kathryn Sikkink, *Mixed Signals: U.S. Human Rights Policy and Latin America*, 122, 130–33 (quotation on 125); Barbara J. Keys, *Reclaiming American Virtue: The Human Rights Revolution of the 1970s*, 259–64; H. R. Brands, *American Dreams*, 201. The Mississippi Carters were unrelated to the Georgia Carters.

43. Dan Kurzman, *Soldier of Peace: The Life of Yitzhak Rabin*, 19–20, 34–51; Memorandum, Brzezinski to Carter, 10 March 1977, NSA, Brzezinski Material, Country File, box 34, JCL; JC, *White House Diary*, 31, 33 (quotation on 33; Glad, *Carter*, 411.

44. Laura Kalman, *Right Star Rising: A New Politics, 1970–1980*, 286–89; Eizenstat, *Carter*, 423–26; William B. Quandt, *Camp David: Peacemaking and Politics*, 43–49;

Rory Miller, *Inglorious Disarray: Europe, Israel and the Palestinians since 1967*, 69, 168; Kenneth W. Stein, *Heroic Diplomacy: Sadat, Kissinger, Carter, Begin, and the Quest for Arab-Israeli Peace*, 191-99.

45. Memorandum, Brzezinski to Carter, 29 March 1977, Declassified Document NLC-1-3-69-1, JCL.

46. Carter, *Public Papers*, 1977, Vol. I, 149-54 (quotation on 154).

47. Lawrence Wright, *Thirteen Days in September: Carter, Begin, and Sadat at Camp David*, 10-14; Jehan Sadat, *A Woman of Egypt*, 72-96; Raphael Israeli, *Man of Defiance: A Political Biography of Anwar Sadat*, 31-32.

48. Wright, *Thirteen Days*, 10-14.

49. Wright, *Thirteen Days*, 26-30, 38-39; Yossi Beilin, *Israel: A Concise Political History*, 42-43; *Wall Street Journal*, 4 Feb. 1991; Michael B. Oren, *Power, Faith, and Fantasy: America in the Middle East, 1776 to the Present*, 539-41; Quandt, *Camp David*, 39-40, 137-43; Ian Black and Benn Morris, *Israel's Secret Wars: A History of Israel's Intelligence Services*, 324-27.

50. Donnie Radcliffe, "A Different Kind of Tea," *Washington Post*, 5 April 1977; Jurate Kazickas AP story, 5 April 1977, clipping in Mary Hoyt File, box 4, JCL; Sadat, *A Woman of Egypt*, 401-02.

51. Memorandum, Fallows to Carter, 31 March 1977, WHCF, box CO-23, JCL; JC, *White House Diary*, 38-39; Carter, *Public Papers*, 1977, Vol. I, 567-70; JC notes on his meeting with Egyptian foreign minister Ismail Fahmy, Brezezinski to Carter, both 4 April 1977, both in Staff Secretary, Handwriting File, box 15, JCL.

52. *New York Times*, 4 and 5 April 1977; Quandt, *Camp David*, 50-53: Cyrus Vance, *Hard Choices: Critical Years in America's Foreign Policy*, 173-75.

Chapter 9

1. Raymond L. Garthoff, *Détente and Confrontation: American-Soviet Relations from Nixon to Reagan*, 584-90; Memorandum, Brzezinski to Carter, 1 April 1977, Weekly National Security Report, # 7, Brzezinski Collection, box 41, JCL.

2. Brezhnev to Carter, 4 April 1977, Plains File, box 17, JCL.

3. Carter to Brezhnev, 9 June 1977, Plains File, box 17, JCL.

4. Memorandum, Brzezinski to Carter, Re King Hussein interview with *Le Monde*, 23 April 1977, WHCF, box CO-40, JCL.

5. Jimmy Carter, *White House Diary*, 43; Carter, *Public Papers*, 1977, Vol. I, 710-11, 720-23; Note, "Nell" to Carter, Re Mrs. Carter's phone call to King Hussein, 27 April 1977, WHCF, box CO-40, JCL; *New York Times*, 27 April 1977; Memorandum, Brzezinski to Carter, 29 April 1977, Weekly National Security Report # 11, Brzezinski Collection, box 41, JCL.

6. Leo Ribuffo, "God and Jimmy Carter," in M. L. Bradbury and James B. Gilbert, editors, *Transforming Faith: the Sacred and the Secular in Modern American History*, 151-52.

7. Carter to the Rev. John F. Steinbruck, 12 May 1977, Staff Secretary, Handwriting File, box 24, JCL; news clippings in White House Counsel: Lipshutz, box 12, JCL.

8. Memorandum, Brzezinski to Carter, 13 May 1977, NSC Weekly Report # 12, Brzezinski Collection, box 41, JCL.

9. *New York Times*, 3 April 1977; Memorandum, Carter to Heads of Departments and Agencies, 5 April 1977, Staff Secretary, Handwriting File, box 15, JCL; *Americus Times-Recorder*, 11, 13, 20 May 1977.

10. Carter, *Public Papers*, 1977, Vol. I, 611–16; Peter G. Bourne, *Jimmy Carter: A Comprehensive Biography from Plains to the Post-Presidency*, 391; Memorandum, Brzezinski to Hamilton Jordan et al., 16 May 1977, Congressional Liaison- Bourdeaux, box 105, JCL.

11. Quoted in William E. Leuchtenburg, *The American President: From Teddy Roosevelt to Bill Clinton*, 566–67. See also *Business Week*, 22 May 2006, p. 63; Memorandum, Charles Warren et al. to Carter, 8 April 1977, Staff Secretary, Handwriting File, box 19, JCL; Bourne, *Carter*, 376; and Carl W. Biven, *Jimmy Carter's Economy: Policy in an Age of Limits*, 156–59; JC, *White House Diary*, 41–42, 55.

12. Dominic Sandbrook, *Mad as Hell: The Crisis of the 1970s and the Rise of the Populist Right*, 226–29.

13. "National Energy Plan," Carter, Public Papers, 1977, Vol. I, 663–88; Christopher Andrew, For the *President's Eyes Only: Secret Intelligence and the American Presidency from Washington to Bush*, 432; Memorandum, Eizenstat to Carter, Re CIA Study of Oil Reserves with Carter comment, 16 April, 1977, Staff Secretary, Handwriting File, box 18, JCL; Jay Hakes, *Energy Crises: Nixon, Ford, Carter and Hard Choices in the 1970s*, 215–18.

14. Memorandum, Frank Moore to Carter, 26 April 1977, Staff Secretary, Handwriting File, box 20, JCL; Bourne, *Carter*, 376–77; Jimmy Carter, *Keeping Faith: Memoirs of a President*, 94–99; Glad, *Jimmy Carter in Search of the Great White House*, 421–22; Paul Clancy and Shirley Elder, *Tip: A Biography of Thomas P. O'Neill, Speaker of the House*, 175; Hakes, *Energy Crises*, 228–29.

15. Jimmy Carter, "Open Letter on the National Energy Plan," Executive Office of the President: US Government Printing Office, 1977.

16. Quoted in Rosalynn Carter, *First Lady from Plains*, 167; Scott Wansbrough to Stanly Godbold, 14 May 2016, private collection.

17. David Aaron, Exit Interview, 6, JCL; RSC, *First Lady*, 165; see also Bourne, *Carter*, 381–82.

18. Carter notes, 3 May 1977, Staff Secretary, Handwriting File, boxes 22, 23, JCL; Carter to Vance and Brzezinski, 1 April 1977, copies to (Republican) Senator Howard Baker and Congressman John J. Rhodes, NSA, Brzezinski Material, Subject file, box 49, JCL.

19. Presidential Directives, 5 May 1977, VF, JCL; Bob Carr et al. to Carter, 8 June 1977, Office of Congressional Liaison, Moore, box 17, JCL; *New York Times*, 20 May 1977; Bourne, *Carter*, 394–95; JC, *White House Diary*, 55; Carter to Senator John Stennis, 2 June 1977, WHCF, box ND-7, JCL.

20. Carter, *Public Papers*, 1977, Vol. I, 809–36, (quotation on 813); JC, *White House Diary*, 46–49; Stein, *Pivotal Decade*, 161.

21. https://www.express.co.uk/new/royal/1273552/royal-news-queen-mother.

22. JC, *White House Diary*, 49; Philomena Jurey, *A Basement Seat to History: Tales of Covering Presidents Nixon, Ford, Carter, and Reagan for the Voice of America*, 140–41.
23. JC, *White House Diary*, 49; *New York Times*, 11 May 1977.
24. White House Press Secretary Pool Report, Air Force One, 10 May 1977, DPS-Eisenstat, box 238, JCL; *New York Times*, 11 May 1977; Bourne, *Carter*, 397; JC, *White House Diary*, 50.
25. JC, *White House Diary*, 46; Carter to Hafiz al-Asad, 6 June 1977, NSA, Foreign Leaders, box 18, JCL; Jurey, *A Basement Seat to History*, 141.
26. Carter, *Public Papers*, 1977, Vol. I, 841–46, 881–82; JC, *White House Diary*, 51–52.
27. Pahlavi to Carter, 27 April 1977, 8 June 1977, both in Plains File, box 23, JCL; *New York Times*, 13, 15 May 1977; Author interview with Senator Abraham Ribicoff, 4 March 1994.
28. *Americus Times-Recorder*, 18 May 1977.
29. Memorandum, Hamilton Jordan to President Carter, June 1977, secret, and Mark Siegel, "Jewish Identify, Zionism and Israel," both in Jordan File, box 34, JCL; *New York Times*, 1 June 1977.
30. "A Chronology of the History of the Canal," Carter notes to advisers, 1977, George D. Moffett Donated Collection, box 6, JCL.
31. Memorandum, Vance to Carter, Re Negotiations with Pakistan, Memo, Brzezinski to Carter, both 8 April 1977, both in NSA Staff North/South, box 95, JCL; Memorandum, Brzezinski to Carter, 26 May 1977, NSC Weekly Report # 14, Brzezinski Collection, box 41, JCL.
32. Quoted in *Atlanta Constitution*, 26 May 1977. See also JC, *White House Diary*, 52; William Michael Schmidli, "Institutionalizing Human Rights in U.S. Foreign Policy: U.S.-Argentine Relations, 1976–1980," *Diplomatic History* 15, No. 2 (April 2011): 353, 375–76.
33. Nesmith to Fallows, May 1977, Speechwriter File: Nesmith, box 4, JCL.
34. Laurence Lerner, "Squaring Off in Washington: Tip O'Neill vs. Jimmy Carter," *New York Magazine*, 16 May 1977; Carter to O'Neill, 22 May 1977, 1 June 1977, both in Staff Secretary, Handwriting File, boxes 26, 29, JCL.
35. Bourne, *Carter*, 385; H. W. Brands, *The Devil We Knew: Americans and the Cold War*, 142–46.
36. Carter, *Public Papers*, 1977, Vol. I, 991–93, 1006–1009.
37. Memorandum, Brzezinski to Carter, May 1977, Maps and other documents about Africa, Re PRC review of Situation in Horn of Africa, NSA-Staff-Horn/Special, boxes 1, 3, JCL; Nancy Mitchell, *Jimmy Carter in Africa: Race and the Cold War*, 214–25.
38. JC note on Mondale memorandum, 10 May 1977, NSA, Brzezinski, Geographic, box 14, JCL.
39. CIA document, May 1977, declassified item NLC-20-10-4-195-8, JCL.
40. Andrew, *President's Eyes Only*, 432–34.
41. Memorandum, Eizenstat to Carter, 26 April 1977, Powell File, box 41, JCL; Robert Shogun, *Promises to Keep: Carter's First 100 Days*, 276–85; JC, *White House Diary*, 38.
42. Memorandum, Brzezinski to Carter, April 29, 1977, with Carter notes, Re Weekly National Security Report # 11, box 41, Brzezinski Collection, JCL.

43. Al McDonald, Miller Center Interview, 85, JCL.

44. Willie Nelson, *It's a Long Story: My Life*, 249–51; Nelson does not identify Chip in his narrative, but other sources and interviews make it clear that Chip was the night visitor. See Kate Andersen Brower, *The Residence: Inside the Private World of The White House*, 98.

45. Carter to Howard Bucknell II, March 1977, WHCF, box PP-83, JCL.

46. Memorandum, Brzezinski to Carter, April 29, 1977, with Carter notes, Re Weekly National Security Report # 11, box 41, Brzezinski Collection, JCL.

47. Carter note on Memorandum, Brzezinski to Carter, 13 May 1977, NSC Weekly Report # 12, Brzezinski Collection, box 41, JCL.

Chapter 10

1. Kathy Cade, White House Exit Interview, JCL; Mary Anne Borrelli, *The Politics of the President's Wife*, 124–28; Sarah McClendon, *Mr. President, Mr. President! My Fifty Years of Covering the White House*, 184; David Rothkopf, *Running the World: The Inside Story of the National Security Council and the Architects of American Power*, 171.

2. Rosalynn Carter Comments, Historical Press Conference, 20 Feb. 1997, Carter Center, Atlanta, Georgia; *Americus Times-Recorder*, 11, 15 Jan. 1977; Paul F. Boller, Jr., *Presidential Wives: An Anecdotal History*, 433–34, 442–48.

3. Trude B. Feldman interview, *Star-Ledger*, 17 Feb. 1977.

4. Quoted in Feldman, *Star-Ledger*, 17 Feb. 1977. See also Emily Walker Cook, "Women White House Advisers in the Carter Administration: Presidential Stalwarts or Feminist Advocates?" PhD dissertation, Vanderbilt University, 1995, pp. 165, 167, 175–77; and Rosalynn Carter, *First Lady from Plains*, 166.

5. Author interview with Mary Hoyt, 27 March 2003. See also Stuart E. Eizenstat, *President Carter: The White House Years*, 106, 114–115.

6. Ann Anderson, White House Exit Interview, JCL; *The Atlanta Journal-Constitution*, 21 Feb. 2005.

7. Interview, *US News and World Report*, 21 March 1977. See also Betty Boyd Caroli, *First Ladies*, 304–306.

8. *New York Times*, 9 March 1977; *Americus Times-Recorder*, 9 March 1977.

9. Press Release from Embassy of Sri Lanka, 2 April 1977, and Memorandum, Fallows to Mrs. Carter, 2 April 1977, RE Human Rights Talk, both in First Lady Press Office, box 2, JCL.

10. Kaufman, *Rosalynn Carter: Equal Partner in the White House*, 40, 46; Gerald N. Grob, "Public Policy and Mental Illness: Jimmy Carter's Presidential Commission on Mental Health," *The Millbank Quarterly* 83, No. 3 (2005), 432.

11. Quoted in Kandy Stroud, "Rosalynn's Agenda in the White House," *New York Times Magazine*, 20 March 1977, (all quotations).

12. Grob, "Public Policy and Mental Illness," 432.

13. "Draft Report on Ethnic and Minorities," First Lady Project, Mental Health, box 6, JCL; Grob, "Public Policy and Mental Illness," 432; *New York Times*, 18 Nov. 1977.

14. *Americus Times-Recorder*, 19 April 1977; Records of President's Commission on Mental Health, RG 220, JCL.

15. Records of President's Commission on Mental Health, RG 220, JCL: *Americus-Times Recorder*, 20 April 1977; *New York Times*, 22 April 1977.

16. *New York Times*, 25 May, 1977; First Lady Press Office Release, 29 April 1977, JCL; Scott Kaufman, *Rosalynn Carter: Equal Partner in the White House*, 42.

17. *Americus Times-Recorder*, 4 May 1977; Kathy B. Smith, "The First Lady Represents America: Rosalynn Carter in South America," *Presidential Studies Quarterly*, 27, no. 3 (Summer 1997), 545; Carl Sferrazza Anthony, *First Ladies, Vol. II: The Saga of the Presidents' Wives and Their Power, 1961–1990*, 273–74; Minutes of the Cabinet Meeting, 23 May 1977, VF, JCL.; National Park Service Interview with Rosalynn Carter, III, 250, JCL.

18. Mary Finch Hoyt, *East Wing: A Memoir*, 145–47; Handwritten notes, Re Venezuela, 7 May 1977, First Lady Press Office, Foreign Trips, box 24, JCL; Kaufman, *Rosalynn Carter*, 63–64; Rick Harden to Carter, 25 May 1977, Staff Secretary, Handwriting File, box 29, JCL; Smith, "The First Lady Represents America," 540–49; RSC, *First Lady*, 185–91; Kati Marton, *Hidden Power: Presidential Marriages that Shaped Our Recent History*, 230–31.

19. Kaufman, *Rosalynn Carter*, 63.

20. Memorandum, Brzezinski to Carter, Re Letter from Mother of Peace Corps Volunteer, 25 May 1977, with attached letter from Mrs. Charlotte Jensen, Carter to Mrs. Jensen, 26 May 1977, both in Staff Secretary, Handwriting File, box 29, JCL.

21. Smith, "The First Lady Represents America," 540–49; Kaufman, *Rosalynn Carter*, 65; Photograph of Rosalynn and Gay Vance on the plane, 11 July 1977, inscribed "For Gay Vance, I enjoyed being with you ---Rosalynn Carter," WHCF-Name File, Vance, Cy, JCL; Telegram, 28 Dec. 1977, Rosalynn's hairdresser, Hoyt File, box 6, JCL; RSC, *First Lady*, 187–91.

22. First Lady Press Office News Release, 26 May 1977, Hoyt File, box 4, JCL; Jimmy Carter, National Park Service Interview, III, 252–53, JCL.

23. Quoted in Carters, National Park Service Interview, IV, 48–49, JCL.

24. Quoted in Jimmy Carter, *White House Diary*, 58. See also Memorandum, Tim Kraft to Carter, 26–31 May, Your Visit to St. Simon's, Georgia, and Trip to Cape Canaveral, FL, Staff Secretary, Handwriting File, box 29, JCL; *New York Times*, 28 May 1977; Carter, *Public Papers*, 1977, Vol. 1, 1035–41; Carter to Rickover, 1 June 1977, WHCF, box ND 35, JCL; and Patrick Tyler, *Running Critical: The Silent War, Rickover, and General Dynamics*, 158–59.

25. JC, *White House Diary*, 59–60.

26. *Americus Times-Recorder*, 1 June 1977; RSC Carter arrival statement, 30 May, 1977, Foreign Media Review, 26 May-1 June,1977, both in First Lady Press Office, Foreign Trips, box 24, JCL; RSC, *First Lady*, 191–92.

27. *New York Times*, 31 May 1977; Smith, "The First Lady Represents America," 545; Kaufman, *Rosalynn Carter*, 64–66; RSC, *First Lady*, 192–94; Peter Bourne, *Jimmy Carter: A Comprehensive Biography from Plains to the Post-Presidency*, 388–89.

28. *Americus Times-Review*, 1 June 1977; Foreign Media Review, 26 May–1 June, 1977, Arrival Statement in Costa Rica, both in Foreign Trips, First Lady Press Office, boxes 24, 25, JCL.

29. *New York Times*, 1 June 1977; Kaufman, *Rosalynn Carter*, 67–-68; RSC, *First Lady*, 196–97.

30. *New York Times*, 2 June 1977; Foreign Media Review, 26 May–1 June, 1977, First Lady Press Office, Foreign Trips, box 25, JCL; RSC, *First Lady*, 198–201; JC, *White House Diary*, 61.

31. *Americus Times-Recorder*, 3 June 1977; *Washington Post*, 3 June 1977; Andrew Cockburn and Leslie Cockburn, *Dangerous Liaison: The Inside Story of the U.S.-Israeli Covert Relationship*, 193; Foreign Media Review, 26 May–1 June, 1977, First Lady Press Office, Foreign Trips, box 24, JCL; *Atlanta Journal and Constitution*, 5 June 1977; Kaufman, *Rosalynn Carter*, 68–69; RSC, *First Lady*, 198–99.

32. Smith, "The First Lady Represents America," 545.

33. Rosalynn Carter interview on flight from Quito to Lima, 3 June 1977, First Lady Press Office, Foreign Trips, box 24, JCL.

34. *Americus Times-Recorder*, 4 June 1977; RSC, *First Lady*, 202–203.

35. *Atlanta Journal and Constitution*, 5 June 1977.

36. Marin Canas editorial in telegram from Brasilia, 3 June 1977, First Lady Press Office, Foreign Trips, box 24, JCL.

37. JC, *White House Diary*, 61.

38. *New York Times*, 6 June 1977; similar stories in *Washington Post*, *Los Angeles Times*, and *Atlanta Constitution*; Kaufman, *Rosalynn Carter*, 70–71.

39. U.S. Information Agency interview with Rosalynn, June 1977, First Lady Press Office, Foreign Trips, box 24, JCL; *New York Times*, *Washington Post*, *Atlanta Constitution*, *Los Angeles Times*, all on 7 June 1977; *Americus Times-Recorder*, 8 June 1977; Telegram, 3 June 1977, Brasilia Embassy to Secretary of State, First Lady Press Office, Foreign Trips, box 24, JCL.

40. RSC, *First Lady*, 207. See also *Americus Times-Recorder*, 8, 9 June 1977; Kaufman, *Rosalynn Carter*, 72.

41. Memorandum Embassy Brasilia, 11 June 1977, Declassified document NLC-1-2-6-5-7, JCL.

42. Cable, Embassy Notes for our government from Torrijos, 9 June 1977, Declassified Document NLC-1-2-8-56-9, JCL.

43. *Americus Times-Recorder*, 10 June 1977; *New York Times*, 11 June 1977; Declassified Document NLC-1-2-6-5-7, JCL; RSC, *First Lady*, 208-209; Bourne, *Carter*, 399.

44. RSC, *First Lady*, 209–10; Kaufman, *Rosalynn Carter*, 75.

45. *Americus Times-Recorder*, 11 June 1977; Mrs. Carter's visit to Venezuela, 10–12 June 1977, First Lady Press Office, Foreign Trips, box 25, JCL; RSC, *First Lady*, 210–12.

46. JC, *White House Diary*, 64; *New York Times*, 12 June 1977; Arrival Statement, 12 June 1977, First Lady Press Office, Foreign Trips, box 24, JCL; Kaufman, *Rosalynn Carter*, 73–74; Hoyt, *East Wing*, 145–51.

47. Carter to Senator Harrison Williams, Carter to Senator Robert Byrd, both 20 June 1977, Carter to Richard Nixon, 29 June 1977, all in WHCF, box PP-2, JCL; Anthony,

First Ladies, Vol. II, 274; Cadell Memorandum, 30 July 1977, with attached note, Powell File, box 42, JCL; Margaret Truman, *First Ladies*, 147–49.

48. Anthony, *First Ladies, Vol. II*, 274–75; Zbigniew Brzezinski, *Power and Principle: Memoirs of the National Security Adviser*, 32; Betty Glad, *An Outsider in the White House: Jimmy Carter, His Advisors, and the Making of American Foreign Policy*, 11; Doreen Mattingly, *A Feminist in the White House: Midge Costanza, the Carter Years, and America's Culture Wars*, 9–10.

Chapter 11

1. *Americus Times-Recorder*, 20, 22 June 1977; Douglas J. Bennet to Senator Malcolm Wallop, 18 Aug. 1977, WHCF, box PP-4, JCL; Rosalynn Carter, *First Lady from Plains*, 272–81.

2. Records of the President's Commission on Mental Health, 22 June, 11 July 1977, RG 220, JCL; Scott Kaufman, *Rosalynn Carter: Equal Partner in the White House*, 41–42.

3. RSC, *First Lady*, 305; Memorandum, Mary Hoyt to Rosalynn 11 July 1977, First Lady Press Office, box 3, JCL.

4. Proclamation, 16 June 1977, in Speechwriters, Hertzberg File, box 38, JCL.

5. Jimmy Carter, *White House Diary*, 64, 67; *New York Times*, 27 June 1977; Minutes of meeting with Jewish Leaders, 6 July 1977, DPS-Eizenstat, box 235, JCL; Author interview with Carter, 12 Oct. 1994.

6. Peter G. Bourne, *Jimmy Carter: A Comprehensive Biography from Plains to the Post-Presidency*, 400; *Washington Star*, 21 June 1977; Declassified document NLC-7-68-4-2-4, JCL; Frank Gervasi, *The Life and Times of Menachem Begin: Rebel to Statesman*, 26.

7. Memorandum, Eizenstat to Brzezinski, 27 June 1977, DPS-Eizenstat, box 235, JCL.

8. Telegram, 17 July 1977, Declassified document NLC-13-12-6-1-7, JCL.

9. Note, Susan to Carter, Re Rosalynn, 18 July 1977, Clough File, box 40, JCL; Aaron David Miller, *The Much Too Promised Land: America's Elusive Search for Arab-Israeli Peace*, 166.

10. Lawrence Wright, *Thirteen Days in September: Carter, Begin, and Sadat at Camp David*, 34–35.

11. Ibid., 36–37.

12. Ibid., 35–38.

13. Quoted in JC, *White House Diary*, 71. See also Carter, PDD, 19 July 1977, JCL.

14. Wright, *Thirteen Days*, 34–35.

15. JC, *White House Diary*, 71; Carter's notes on conversation with Begin, 20 July 1977, Staff Secretary, Handwriting File, box 39, JCL; Stuart E. Eizenstat, *President Carter: The White House Years*, 456–60; Burton I. Kaufman, *The Arab Middle East and the United States*, 105.

16. Yehuda Avner, "The Day Jimmy Carter Was Reduced to Silence," (19 July 1977), *Jerusalem Post*, 12 Sept. 2003, copy in Staff Secretary, Handwriting File, box 39, JCL; Gervasi, *The Life and Times of Menachem Begin*, 308–309.

17. Carter, PDD, 19 July 1977, JCL.

18. Record of conversation with Rosalynn, 20 Jan. 1977, Hoyt Papers, box 2, JCL.

19. Carter, *Public Papers, 1977, Vol. II*, 1287–92, 1295–96.

20. PDD, 19, 20 July 1977, with appendices, JCL; Author interview with Rosalynn Carter, 12 Oct. 1994; Daniel Gordis, *Menachem Begin: The Battle for Israel's Soul*, 143; Cyrus Vance, *Hard Choices: Critical Years in America's Foreign Policy*, 181–84 (quotation on 181).

21. Handwritten note, record of conversation between Jimmy and Rosalynn, 20 July 1977, Hoyt Papers, box 2, JCL.

22. Memorandum, James M. Wall to Carter, 22 July 1977, Staff Secretary, Handwriting File, box 40, JCL.

23. Memorandum, Costanza to Carter, 13 July 1977, Carter Notes for Cabinet meeting, 5 June 1977, both in Staff Secretary, Handwriting File, boxes 29, 30, JCL; *New York Times*, 6 June 1977; Congressman Edward P. Beard to Carter, 6 June 1977, WHCF, box IT-10, JCL; *Americus Times-Recorder*, 8 June 1977; Hugh Carter to Carter, 10 June 1977, Staff Secretary, Handwriting File, box 30, JCL; Bartlett C. Jones, *Flawed Triumphs: Andy Young at the United Nations*, 13, 112, 139.

24. *Americus Times-Recorder*, 1, 5 July 1977; Lauren Blanton, National Parks Service Interview, 32, JCL.

25. Memorandum, Caddell to Carter, 22 July 1977, Major Issues in Current Mail, Staff Secretary, Handwriting File, box 40, JCL; *Atlanta Constitution*, 21 July 1977; *Americus Times-Recorder*, 23 April 1977; *New York Times*, 22 July 1977.

26. Author interview with Cyrus Vance, 14 July 1992.

27. Adam Clymer, *Drawing the Line at the Big Ditch: The Panama Canal Treaties and the Rise of the Right*, 40; *New York Times*, 22, 24, 25 July 1977; *Americus Times-Recorder*, 22 July 1977; Tom Offenburger to Young, White House, and State Department, 27 July 1977, WHCF, box IT-10, JCL; Author interview with Cyrus Vance, 1 May 1992, p. 9, Stennis Oral History Project, Mississippi State University.

28. Quoted in JC, *White House Diary* (30 July–2 Aug. 1977), 74–75. See also *Atlanta Constitution*, 27 July 1976; *Americus Times-Recorder*, 27 July 1977; Carter to O'Neill, 28 July 1977, WHCF, box CO-31, JCL; Carter to Hubert Humphrey, 28 July 1977, WHCF, box ND-5, JCL.

29. Jay E. Hakes, "Conflict or Consensus? The Roots of Jimmy Carter's Energy Policies," in Robert F. Lifset, editor, *American Energy Policy in the 1970s*, 50–51; Carter notes for Cabinet Meeting on 1 Aug. 1977, 29 July 1977, Staff Secretary, Handwriting File, box 41, JCL; *New York Times*, 29 July 1977; Patrick H. Caddell to Rosalynn Carter, 30 July 1977, Hoyt Papers, box 4, JCL; Mary Hoyt to Rosalynn, 29 July 1977, Hoyt Papers, box 1, JCL; JC, *White House Diary*, 76–78; Eizenstat, *Carter*, 145–46; Bruce J. Schulman, *The Seventies: The Great Shift in American Culture, Society, and Politics*, 126–27.

30. Memorandum, Brzezinski to Carter, 29 July 1977, NSC Weekly Report # 23, Brzezinski Collection, box 41, JCL.

31. Carter to Dr. Richard D. Mudd, 24 July 1977, Mudd to Carter, 31 July 1977, WHCF, box JL-2, JCL.

32. Presidential Review Memorandum/NSC-28, 1 Aug. 1977, Re Human Rights, Declassified Document NLC-28-10-10-2-7, JCL; Carter to Senator Dennis DeConcini, 3 Aug. 1977, White House Counsel: Lipshutz, box 19; Central Intelligence Agency Directorate of Intelligence, 5 Aug. 1977, Declassified Material NLC-28-10-11-1-7, all in JCL; Scott Kaufman, *Plans Unraveled: The Foreign Policy of the Carter Administration*, 30; Kathryn Sikkink, *Evidence for Hope: Making Human Rights Work in the 21st Century*, 28.

33. Lucy Komisar, "Documented Complicity: Newly Released Files Set the Record Straight on U.S. support for Pinochet," Progressive.org, 9/06/99 13:42:15–21; Robert Stephen Littlefield, "An Analysis of the Persuasion and Coercion Used by the Carter Administration to Promote Human Rights in Argentina, Brazil, and Chile," PhD dissertation, University of Minnesota, 1983, 49–50; David F. Schmitz, *The United States and Right-Wing Dictatorships*, 166–71; Kathryn Sikkink, *Mixed Signals: U.S. Human Rights Policy and Latin America*, 125–27.

34. *Atlanta Constitution*, 3 Aug. 1977; *Americus Times-Recorder*, 5, 6 Aug. 1977.

35. JC, *White House Diary*, 78–80.

36. Memorandum, Senator Frank Church to Carter, Vance, Brzezinski, 12 Aug. 1977, Declassified Document NLC-34-5-9-1-9, JCL.

37. Gal Beckerman, *When They Come for Us, We'll Be Gone: The Epic Struggle to Save Soviet Jewry*, 366–71, 464–66.

Chapter 12

1. David McCullough, *The Path between the Seas: The Creation of the Panama Canal 1870-1914*, is an excellent source for the history of the canal, and it is the account that convinced Carter that "we cheated the Panamanians out of their canal." Jimmy Carter, *White House Diary*, 86. See also Jimmy Carter, *Keeping Faith: Memoirs of a President*, 152–59.

2. Background Notes: Panama, Department of State, Sept. 1977, George G. Moffett Donated Collection, box 6, JCL.

3. Peter G. Bourne, *Jimmy Carter: A Comprehensive Biography from Plains to the Post-Presidency*, 38–82; Gaddis Smith, *Morality, Reason, and Power: American Diplomacy in the Carter Years*, 111–25; JC, *White House Diary*, 84.

4. Robert Beckel, Miller Center Interview, 3, JCL; Wallace Irwin, Jr., *Panama: A Great Decision Approaches*, 4, 12; Carter handwritten notes, 12 Aug. 1977, Re Panama, Staff Secretary, Handwriting File, box 43, JCL; Scott Kaufman, *Rosalynn Carter: Equal Partner in the White House*, 77–78; Rosalynn Carter, *First Lady from Plains*, 165.

5. Adam Clymer, *Drawing the Line at the Big Ditch: The Panama Canal Treaties and the Rise of the Right*, 75–76; Memorandum, Jordan to Carter, Re Status report on Panama Canal, 24 Aug. 1977, Jordan Papers, box 36, JCL; Landon Butler to Governor Harriman, 25 Aug. 1977, WHCF, box F0–17, JCL; Brzezinski to Carter, NSC Weekly Report # 25, 26 Aug. 1977, with Carter notes, Brzezinski File, box 41, JCL; Memorandum, Harold Brown to Carter, Re Military Utilization of the Panama

Canal, 29 Aug. 1977, Mondale Donated Papers, box 206, JCL; Memorandum, Jordan to Carter, Re People and Institutional Leaders, 30 Aug. 1977, Landon Butler Papers, box 149, JCL; Barry Goldwater to Carter, 26 Aug. 1977, and Memorandum, Brown to Carter, 26 Aug. 1977, both in WHCF, box FO-16, JCL; *The Fritz Hollings Report*, Sept. 1977, WHCF, box FO-16, JCL; John Dumbrell, *The Carter Presidency: A Re-evaluation*, 41; Robert A. Strong, *Working in the World: Jimmy Carter and the Making of American Foreign Policy*, 165.

6. Brzezinski Exit Interview, 8, JCL.

7. Memorandum of Conversation, Carter to Torrijos, 24 Aug. 1977, Jordan File, box 36, JCL; Memorandum, Peter Tarnoff to Brzezinski, 1 Sept.1977, WHCF, box FO-16, JCL.

8. Janelle Conaway, "Savvy Navigator of a Turbulent Canal," *Americas*, 51, no. 1, (Feb. 1999), 1–16; Bourne, *Carter*, 391–93; JC, *White House Diary*, 90–93; Carter, *Public Papers, Vol. II, 1977*, 1542–44.

9. PDD, 7 Sept. 1977, JCL; Rosalynn notes to 24 heads of state, Sept. 1977, First Lady's Social Office, Subject File, box 6, JCL; Memorandum, Jordan to Carter, 7 Sept. 1977, Jordan File, box 36, JCL; *New York Times*, 7 Sept. 1977; Rosalynn's note, 13 Sept. 1977, First Lady's Social Office, Subject File, box 6, JCL; Lady Bird to Carters, 15 Sept. 1977, WHCF, box SO-1, JCL; Carter to Hollings, 19 Sept. 1977, WHCF, box FO-16, JCL.

10. Bourne, *Carter*, 393; JC, *White House Diary*, 80; Carter's notes on his conversations with Kissinger, Skowcroft, and others, 15 Aug. 1977, Plains File, box 3, JCL; Memorandum, Frank Moore and Dan Tate to Carter, 23 Aug. 1977, Staff Secretary, Handwriting File, box 45, JCL.

11. *New York Times*, 7, 12 Aug. 1977; Carter handwritten notes on Panama Canal, 12 Aug. 1977, Staff Secretary, Handwriting File, box 43, JCL.

12. Memorandum, Senate: Assessments of Panama, 6 Aug. 1977, Jordan Papers, box 36, JCL: Senator Jesse Helms to Carter, 12 Aug. 1977, WHCF, box FO-16, JCL; JC, *White House Diary*, 83–87.

13. Note, Jordan to Carter, 19 Sept. 1977, Re Canal and fireside chat, Mondale Donated Papers, box 205, JCL; Harold Brown Speech, 27 Sept. 1977, Staff Secretary, Handwriting File, box 52, JCL; *New York Times*, 27 Sept. 1977, 12, 16 Oct. 1977; "An Analysis of Public Attitudes toward the Panama Canal Treaties," Oct. 1977, Powell Donated Papers, box 18, JCL; Memorandum, Jordan to Rosalynn, Report on Panama Canal treaty, 30 Nov. 1977, WHCF, First Lady's Social Office, Subject File, box 6, JCL; McCullough to Carter, with Carter note, 21 Oct. 1977, Staff Secretary, Handwriting File, box 71, JCL; Warren Christopher, *Chances of a Lifetime: A Memoir*, 81–88.

14. JC, *White House Diary*, 66; Memorandum, Brown to Carter, 16 Sept. 1977, Staff Secretary, Handwriting File, box 50, JCL; Bourne, *Carter*, 394–96; JC, *Keeping Faith*, 163, 171; Author interview with Cyrus Vance, 1 May 1992, pp. 8–9, Stennis Oral History Collection, Mississippi State University.

15. Telegram, Torrijos to Senators, 4 Dec. 1977, NSA Daily Press, CIA, box 6, JCL.

16. JC, *White House Diary*, 95.

17. Memorandum, Hamilton Jordan to Carter, N.D., Re Bakke Case, Jordan File, box 33, JCL; "Resolution on the Bakke Decision," N.D., White House Counsel: McKenna, Box 120, JCL.

18. Dumbrell, *The Carter Presidency*, 93–94, 106–107; Walter Mondale, *The Good Fight: A Life in Liberal Politics*, 177–80; Bourne, *Carter*, 425–26; Griffin Bell, *Taking Care of the Law*, 30–32; Laura Kalman, *Right Star Rising: A New Politics, 1974–1980*, 193–98.

19. Bourne, *Carter*, 372; Burton I. Kaufman and Scott Kaufman, *The Presidency of James Earl Carter, Jr.*, 75–77.

20. Author interview with Ribicoff, 14 March 1994, Stennis Oral History Collection, Mississippi State University; Ribicoff, "Reminiscences," 243, Oral History Project, Columbia University, (used by permission).

21. Clark Clifford, *Counsel to the President: A Memoir*, 628–32; JC, *White House Diary*, 87–88; *New York Times*, 9 Sept. 1977; Memorandum, Greg Schneiders to Carter, 13 Sept. 1977, Staff Secretary, Handwriting File, box 44, JCL; Lance Hearings recording, 15 Sept. 1977, White House Staff: Press, Edwards, box 9, JCL.

22. Author interview with Carter, 12 Oct. 1994; Lance to Carter, 21 Sept., Carter to Lance, 24 Sept. 1977, Jordan File, box 35, JCL; Ted Kennedy to Carter, 22 Sept. 1977, WHCF, box SO-2, JCL; *New York Times*, 22 Sept. 1977, ("tears" quotation); Bourne, *Carter*, 412–15; JC, *White House Diary*, 88; Memorandum, Bob Lipshutz to Carter, Re Bert Lance, 18 Aug. 1977, and Carter Statement re Bert Lance, both in Staff Secretary, Handwriting File, box 44, JCL; *Time*, 22 Aug. 1977, p. 19; JC, *Keeping Faith*, 135; Stuart E. Eizenstat, *President Carter: The White House Years*, 130; LaBelle Lance, *This Too Shall Pass*, 11–22, 153–58; Bert Lance, *The Truth of the Matter: My Life In and Out of Politics*, 148–50.

23. Eizenstat, *Carter*, 130–33; Tip O'Neill, *Man of the House: The Life and Political Memoirs of Speaker Tip O'Neill*, 310; Author interview with O'Neill, 25 Oct. 1990; Richard E. Neustadt, *Presidential Power and the Modern Presidents: The Politics of Leadership from Roosevelt to Reagan*, 249–53; Bill Shipp, *The Ape-Slayer and Other Snapshots*, 144–45.

24. Memorandum of Conversation, Carter and Gromyko, 23 Sept. 1977, NSA-Brzezinski Material, Subject File, boxes 34–35, JCL; *New York Times*, 20 Sept. 1977; Anatoly Dobrynin, *In Confidence: Moscow's Ambassador to Six Cold War Presidents*, 399–400; Volker Skierka, *Fidel Castro: A Biography*, 209–11.

25. Gal Beckerman, *When They Come for Us, We'll Be Gone: The Epic Struggle to Save Soviet Jewry*, 311–12, 364–65, 385, 388, 398, 402–403; JC, *White House Diary*, 105; Martin Gilbert, *Shcharansky: Hero of Our Time*, 200, 224, 248.

26. JC, *White House Diary*, 111.

27. President's Commission on Mental Health, RG 220, box 25, JCL, published in *Journal of Contemporary Psychotherapy*, 9, no. 2, (Winter 1978), 183–86; RSC, *First Lady*, 277.

28. Memorandum, Richard Harden to Mary Hoyt, Re Speech in Vancouver, 16 Aug. 1977, Richard Harden File, box 14, JCL; *Americus Times-Recorder*, 26 Aug. 1977; Thomas E. Bryant to Carter, 1 Sept. 1977, Staff Secretary, Handwriting File, box 44, JCL; RSC, *First Lady*, 169, 173.

29. Carter Birthday, 1 Oct.1977, notes in Hoyt File, box 1, JCL; Memorandum, Les Francis to Frank Moore, Re Analysis of Senate and House votes, 5 Oct. 1977, Jordan File, box 33, JCL.

30. Sasha Polakow-Suransky, *The Unspoken Alliance: Israel's Secret Relationship with Apartheid South Africa*, 104; Memorandum, Lipshutz and Eizenstat to Carter, 23 Sept. 1977, with Carter notes, Staff Secretary, Handwriting File, box 45, JCL; Presidential Message to Begin, 24 Sept. 1977, Declassified document NLC-1-3-7-33-4, JCL; Dumbrell, *The Carter Presidency*, 116–17.

31. JC, *White House Diary*, 111.

32. *New York Times*, 4, 5 Oct. 1977; JC, *White House Diary*, 111–17 (quotation on 114); Terrence Cardinal Cook to Carter, 5 Oct. 1977, WHCF, box JL-2, JCL; Joint Statement, 5 Oct. 1977, DPS-Eizenstat, box 235, JCL.

33. "Meeting with Senators," 6 Oct. 1977, Staff Secretary, Handwriting File, box 53, JCL; Author interview with Ribicoff, 4 March 1994, Stennis Oral History Collection, Mississippi State University; *New York Times*, 7 Oct. 1977; JC, *White House Diary*, 115–16.

34. Brzezinski to Carter, 14 Oct. 1977, NSC Weekly Report # 32, Brzezinski Donated Material, box 41, JCL; Aron Belmar to Carter, 21 Oct. 1977, WHCF, box RM-1, JCL; *New York Times*, 6 Nov. 1977.

35. JC, *White House Diary*, 118–120.

36. Carter note to Harold & Zbig, 18 Oct.1977, Staff Secretary, Handwriting File, box 227, JCL.

37. Firouz to Carter, 23 pp., 18 Oct. 1977, WHCF, box CO-31, JCL.

38. Memorandum, Brzezinski to Turner, RE Political Intelligence and Analysis, Nov. 1977, NSA Staff Special File, box 1, JCL.

39. *Washington Times*, 11 Feb. 2006; *Wall Street Journal*, 19 Jan. 2007.

40. United States Intelligence Activities, 5 Dec. 1977, with Carter's notes, White House Counsel: Lipshutz, box 22, JCL.

41. K. Neill Foster, *Dam Break in Georgia: Sadness and Joy at Toccoa Falls*, 9–10.

42. JC, *White House Diary*, 131–32.

43. Ibid., 133–34.

44. *New York Times*, 16 Nov. 1977.

45. JC, *White House Diary*, 135–37; RSC, *First Lady*, 306; JC, *Keeping Faith*, 433–37; PDD, 15–16 November 1977, JCL; Farah Pahlavi, *An Enduring Love: My Life with the Shah*, 270–72; Ray Takeyh, *The Last Shah: America, Iran, and the Fall of the Pahlavi Dynasty*, 195.

46. Andrew Scott Cooper, *The Fall of Heaven: The Pahlavis and the Final Days of Imperial Iran*, 263: David Harris, *The Crisis: The President, the Prophet, and the Shah—1979 and the Coming of Militant Islam*, 71–72 (quotation on 72); Kenneth M. Pollack, *The Persian Puzzle: The Conflict between Iran and America*, 123–24.

47. Memorandum, Patricia M. Derian to Mr. Atherton, 5 Dec. 1977, with Carter note, with attached Department of State, Human Rights Policy Review, 25 Oct. 1977, Staff Secretary, Handwriting File, box 67, JCL; Pollack, *The Persian Puzzle*, 120–22, 131; Smith, *Morality, Reason and Power*, 51.

48. O'Neill, *Man of the House*, 319.

49. JC, *White House Diary*, 137.

50. Aaron David Miller, *The Much Too Promised Land: America's Elusive Search for Arab-Israeli Peace*, 168–72; Bourne, *Carter*, 401–403.

Chapter 13

1. Frank Gervasi, *The Life and Times of Menachem Begin: Rebel to Statesman*, 52–56; Carter to Sadat, 12 Nov. 1977, WHCF, box CO-23, JCL.

2. Begin to Carter, 17 Nov. 1977, Powell File, box 39, JCL; Robert A. Strong, *Working in the World: Jimmy Carter and the Making of American Foreign Policy*, 186.

3. *New York Times*, 18 Nov. 1977; Burton I. Kaufman, *The Arab Middle East and the United States*, 106–107.

4. Patrick Tyler, *A World of Trouble: The White House and the Middle East—from the Cold War to the War on Terror*, 176–78.

5. Jimmy Carter, *White House Diary*, 139–40.

6. Quoted in Kaufman, *The Arab Middle East*, 106–107.

7. Jimmy Carter, *Keeping Faith: Memoirs of a President*, 297; JC, *White House Diary*, 138–39.

8. JC, *White House Diary*, 151; JC, *Keeping Faith*, 298–300.

9. Brezhnev to Carter, 30 June 1977, Carter to Brezhnev, 4 Nov. 1977, Brezhnev to Carter, 15 Nov., 16 Dec. 1977, all in Plains File, box 17, JCL.

10. JC, *White House Diary*, 138–39. See also Kaufman, *The Arab Middle East*, 106.

11. Carter to Harold Brown, with attachments, 21 Dec. 1977, Staff Secretary, Handwriting File, box 65, JCL.

12. Memorandum, Califano to Carter, with Carter's comment, Re Meeting on Elementary and Secondary Education, 5 Dec., 1977, Staff Secretary, Handwriting File, box 62, JCL.

13. "Rosalynn Carter and Margaret Mead: A Meeting of the Minds," *Redbook Magazine* (October 1977), pp. 123, 204–209; Draft of Op-ed piece, 31 Oct. 1977, with Carter's comments, Hoyt Papers, box 3, JCL.

14. Mary Beth Durkin, Producer, Yellowbrickroad Productions, email to Stanly Godbold, 1 Sept. 2016.

15. Kathy Cade, White House Exit Interview, JCL; Marjorie J. Spruill, "Gender and America's Right Turn," in Bruce J. Schulman and Julian E. Zelizer, *Rightward Bound: Making American Conservative in the 1970s*, 84–88.

16. *Americus Times-Recorder*, 7, 19 Nov. (quotation) 1977; *New York Times*, 8 Nov. 1977; National Women's Conference, First Lady Office, Projects, Cade, box 29, JCL; Marjorie J. Spruill, *Divided We Stand: The Battle Over Women's Rights and Family Values that Polarized American Politics*, 217–18.

17. Scott Kaufman, *Rosalynn Carter: Equal Partner in the White House*, 76–77; Suzanne Braun Levine and Mary Thom, *Bella Abzug*, 195, 213–15.

18. Memorandum, Kathy to Rosalynn, Re Dedication, 2 Dec. 1977, First Lady Office, Projects, Cade, box 18, JCL; *Americus Times-Recorder*, 6, 7 Dec. 1977 (quotation).

19. Farmers' Statement, 1 Dec. 1977, WHCF, box AG-2, JCL.

20. *Americus Times-Recorder*, 10 Dec. 1977.

21. Note, Carter to Bergland and Powell, 15 Dec. 1977, Staff Secretary, Handwriting File, box 64, JCL.

22. Memorandum, Mondale to Carter, RE Human Rights, 7 Dec. 1977, Mondale Papers Donated, box 205, JCL; Douglas J. Bennett, Jr. to Senator Alan Cranston, 12 Dec. 1977, Re Bolivia, WHCF, box JL-8, JCL.

23. *New York Times*, 25 Dec. 1977, copy in Staff Secretary, Handwriting File, box 67, JCL.

24. Dec. 15, 1977, Notes for comments at lighting of Christmas tree, Staff Secretary, Handwriting File, box 64, JCL.

25. Letters dated 8 July, 29 Sept., 14, 17, 30 Nov. 1977 between Allen and the Carters, Jimmy R. Allen Papers, AR 661, box 1, folder 13, Carter, Jimmy, Southern Baptist Historical Library and Archives, Nashville, TN.

26. *Americus Times-Recorder*, 13, 25 Aug. 1977; *New York Times*, 14 Aug. 1977.

27. Charlie Schultz to Carter, 5 Dec. 1977, Staff Secretary, Handwriting File, box 62, JCL; Memorandum, Eizenstat and Rubenstein to Carter, 4 Dec. 1977, Staff Secretary, Handwriting File, box 62, JCL; Memorandum, Patricia Harris to Carter, 30 Dec. 1977, Harris Papers, box 2, Library of Congress; Memorandum, Brzezinski to Carter, 12 Jan. 12, 1978, NSC Report for 1977, Brzezinski Donated Collection, box 3, JCL; John Major, *Prize Possession: The United States and the Panama Canal, 1903–1979*, 345–57.

28. ABC News, 26 Jan. 2007.

29. JC, *White House Diary*, 147; Frank Moore, Miller Center Interview, 82, JCL.

30. No date, Jordan File, box 33, JCL.

31. JC, *White House Diary*, 152.

32. Lauren Blanton, National Park Service Interview, 27–32, JCL.

33. *Americus Times-Recorder*, 21, 22, 23, 24 Dec. 1977; *New York Times*, 24, 25 Dec. 1977; Memorandum, Eizenstat to Kraft, 12 Dec. 1977, Carter to Harold Israel, 27 Dec. 1977, WHCF, box AG-2, JCL.

34. JC, *White House Diary*, 154; Minutes of Cabinet Meeting, 5 Dec. 1977, VF, JCL.

35. *New York Times* and *Los Angeles Times*, both 29 Dec. 1977.

36. Program of the Official Visit, 29–31 Dec. 1977, Staff Secretary, Handwriting File, box 66, JCL; White House Memorandum, 30 Dec. 1977, Declassified document NLC-1-48-43-1, JCL; JC, *White House Diary*, 154.

37. *Americus Times-Recorder*, 30 Dec. 1977; JC, *White House Diary*, 155; *New York Times*, 30 Dec. 1977.

38. Carter, *Public Papers, 1977, II*, 2205.

39. "Mrs. Carter's Day," Pool Report, 30 Dec. 1977, First Lady Press Office, Foreign Trips, box 26, JCL.

40. *Washington Post*, 31 Dec. 1977.

41. JC, *White House Diary*, 155.

42. Telegram, Warsaw Embassy to Secretary of State, Jan. 1978, Re Carter's visit to Poland, Declassified Document NLC-23-29-4-20-9, JCL.

43. Pool Report # 3, 30 Dec. 1977, First Lady Press Office, Foreign Trips, box 26, JCL.

44. Telegram, U.S. Embassy in Tehran to Mary Hoyt, Re Mrs. Carter's Interview, 31 Dec. 1977, Hoyt Papers, box 6, JCL.

45. JC, *White House Diary*, 156; Pool Report No. 9, 31 Dec. 1977, First Lady Press Office, Foreign Trips, box 26, JCL; JC, *Keeping Faith*, 300, 437; Carter, *Public Papers, II*, 1977, 2217–22 (toast on 2221); Strong, *Working in the World*, 58–62 (quotations from the British ambassador and the shah); Farah Pahlavi, *An Enduring Love: My Life with the Shah*, 272–73; William Shawcross, *The Shah's Last Ride*, 129–31.

46. Memorandum of Conversation, 1 Jan. 1978, King Hussein of Jordan, Court Minister Sharaf, General Amar Khamash; Carter, Vance, Brzezinski, Ambassador Tomas Pickering, Assistant Secretary of State Atherton, Gary Sick (note taker) at Saadabad Palace, 8:20–8:50 a.m., Brzezinski Collection, box 36, JCL.

47. Pool Report, 1 Jan. 1978, Wilkie/Boston Globe, First Lady Press Office, Foreign Trips, box 26, JCL; *New York Times*, 1 Jan. 1978.

48. Kenneth M. Pollack, *The Persian Puzzle: The Conflict between Iran and America*, 121.

49. Carter, *Public Papers, 1978, Vol. I*, 2–15.

50. Interview with Indian Press, 2 Jan. 1978, First Lady Press Office, Foreign Trips, box 26, JCL.

51. *New York Daily News*, 4 Jan. 1978, Hoyt Papers, box 1, JCL; *The Times of India*, 4 Nov. 2010; Pool Report # 23, 4 Jan. 1978, Hoyt Papers, box 1, JCL; JC, *White House Diary*, 159; Carter Notes for Cabinet meeting, 6 Jan. 1978, Staff Secretary, Handwriting File, box 66, JCL.

52. Carter, *Public Papers, 1978, Vol. I*, 18–18.

53. *New York Times*, 3 Jan. 1978, Carter interview; JC, *White House Diary*, 160; Minutes of Cabinet Meeting, 9 Jan. 1978, VF, JCL.

54. Pool Report # 23, 4 Jan. 1978, Hoyt Papers, box 1, JCL; *New York Daily News*, 4 Jan. 1978; *Washington Star*, 11 Jan. 1978; Rosalynn Carter Speech, Sumter County Chamber of Commerce, 7 Feb. 1978, First Lady Office, Special Projects, Cade, box 29, JCL.

55. JC, *White House Diary*, 160–61; Carter, *Public Papers, 1978, Vol. I*, 18–19; Dennis Ross, *Doomed to Succeed: The U.S.-Israel Relationship from Truman to Obama*, 152–53.

56. JC, *Keeping Faith*, 303; Carter, *Public Papers, 1978, Vol. I*, 19–20; Carter to Sadat, 4 Jan. 1978, WHCF, box CO-24, JCL.

57. Pool Report # 23, 4 Jan. 1978, Hoyt Papers, box 1, JCL; Helen Thomas, UPI story, 6 Jan. 1978, Hoyt Papers, box 1, JCL.

58. Carter, *Public Papers, 1978, Vol. I*, p. 25; PDD, 4 Jan. 1978, JCL; Burton I. Kaufman and Scott Kaufman, *Presidency of James Earl Carter, Jr.*, 59.

59. Carter, *Public Papers, 1978, Vol. I*, pp. 27–32; Helen Thomas, UPI story, 6 Jan. 1978, with attached telegram, Hoyt Papers, box 6, JCL.

60. O'Neill interview, Unidentified news magazine, 28 Feb. 28, 1978, VF, O'Neill, Tip, JC; Carter, *Public Papers, 1978, Vol. I*, 32–39; JC, *Keeping Faith*, 303–304; PDD, 6 Jan. 1978, JCL. See also Tip O'Neill, *Man of the House: The Life and Political Memoirs of Speaker Tip O'Neill*, 311.

61. Memorandum, Jordan to Carter, [Jan. 1978], Jordan File, box 33, JCL.

62. Faye Lind Jensen, "An Awesome Responsibility: Rosalynn Carter as First Lady," *Presidential Studies Quarterly*, 20, no. 4 (Fall 1990), 769.

63. Carter, *Public Papers, 1978, Vol. I*, 281–84.

64. *US News and World Report*, Jan. 1978, p. 17.

65. *New York Times*, 12 Dec. 1977; JC, *White House Diary*, 159; PDD, 6 Jan. 1978, JCL.

Chapter 14

1. Katalin Kadar Lynn, "The Return of the Crown of St. Stephen and Its Subsequent Impact on the Carter Administration," *East European Quarterly* 34, no. 2 (Summer 2000), 181; Patrick J. Kelleher, *The Holy Crown of Hungary*, 19, 107–108; Endre Toth and Karoly Szelenyi, *The Holy Crown of Hungary*.

2. Tibor Glant, "Contested Gesture: Jimmy Carter and the Return of the Holy Crown to Hungary, 1977–1981," a lecture based upon his book, *The American Adventures of the Holy Crown, 1945–1978*, read at the annual conference of the Society for Historians of American Foreign Relations in Princeton, NJ, June 24–26, 1999; Lynn, "The Return of the Crown," 196.

3. Lynn, "The Return of the Crown," 187–90; Glant, "Contested Gesture," 1999; Carter to President Pal Losonczi, Hungary, 6 Jan. 1978, Staff Secretary, Handwriting File, box 66, JCL; J. Brooks Flippen, *Jimmy Carter, The Politics of Family, and the Rise of the Religious Right*, 111, 197.

4. "The Crown of St. Stephen," 23 Dec. 1977, NSA, Brzezinski Material, Country File, boxes 18–33, JCL.

5. Glant, "Contested Gesture," 1999; The crown rested, as Carter wished, in the National Museum until it was moved to a secure and honored spot beneath the dome of the parliament building in 2000. In the meantime, Carter had lost the election of 1980 and Hungary had gained independence from the Soviet Union in 1991. On March 18, 1998, in a ceremony at the Carter Library and Museum in Atlanta, Arpad Goncz, the president of the Republic of Hungary, presented a special replica of the crown to Jimmy Carter. He accepted it "of behalf of the people of the United States . . . [as] a generous and gracious gesture of the abiding faith and trust that exists between our two countries." "The Crown of St. Stephen," http://www.jimmycarterlibrary.gov/museum/crown.phtml.

6. *Emory Magazine* 88, no. 1 (Spring 2012), 8.

7. Rosalynn Carter, *First Lady from Plains*, 218–19.

8. *Washington Post*, 10 Jan. 1978; *Atlanta Constitution*, 27 Feb. 1978.

9. The Humphrey Program is funded by the US Department of State and administered by the Institute of International Education. The Rollins School of Public Health at Emory University, which Carter supported in his post-presidency, is a major host university for many of the fellows.

10. *New York Times*, 12 Jan. 1978.

11. Memorandum, Brzezinski to Carter, Weekly Report, Far East, 8 Jan. 1978, NSA Staff Material, Armacost, box 1, JCL; Jimmy Carter, *White House Diary*, 167.

12. Drafts of speech with comments, 18, 19 Jan. 1978, Staff Secretary, Handwriting File, box 69, JCL.

13. Carter, *Public Papers, 1978, Vol. I*, 90–123 (quotations on 94, 95–96, 103); *New York Times* and *Americus Times-Recorder*, both 18, 20 Jan. 1978; Robert C. Wood, *Whatever Possessed the President?*, 131–32.

14. Carter, *Public Papers, 1978, Vol. I*, 155–58.

15. JC, *White House Diary*, 164–65.

16. Brezhnev to Carter, 5, 12, 14 Jan., 27 Feb. 1978, Plains File, box 17, JCL.

17. Carter to Brezhnev, 25 Jan. 1978, Plains File, box 17, JCL; Wayne S. Smith, *The Closest of Enemies: A Personal and Diplomatic Account of U.S.-Cuban Relations since 1957*, 122–27; Gerard H. Clarfield and William M. Wiecek, *Nuclear America: Military and Civilian Nuclear Power in the United States, 1940–1980*, 406–10.

18. PDD, 16 Jan. 1978; *New York Times*, 12 Jan. 1978; *Washington Post*, 14 Jan. 1978.

19. Carter Notes, 18 Jan. 1978, Staff Secretary, Handwriting File, box 70, JCL; JC, *White House Diary*, 171; Stuart E. Eizenstat, *President Carter: The White House Years*, 567.

20. Outline for Panama Speech with Carter comments, 25 Jan. 1978, Staff Secretary, Handwriting file, box 70, JCL; Ham to Carter, with Carter's notes, 31 Jan. 1978, Staff Secretary, Handwriting file, box 71, JCL; Carter, *Public Papers, 1978, Vol. I*, 258–63.

21. Note, Carter to Jordan, 2 Feb. 1978, Panama Canal Calls, Jordan File, box 50, JCL; JC, *White House Diary*, 176–77.

22. Memorandum, Brzezinski to Carter, 9 Feb. 1978, NSC Weekly Report # 46, Brzezinski Donated Material, box 41, JCL.

23. Carter to Hodges, 3 Feb. 1978, White House Staff, Jordan File, box 50, JCL.

24. Long to Carter, 28 Feb. 1978, Staff Secretary, Handwriting File, box 76, JCL.

25. Handwritten note to Harold and Zbig, 14 March 1978, Staff Secretary, Handwriting File, box 76, JCL.

26. 14 March 1978, "Personal," Carter to Stennis, WHCF, box FO-18, JCL; Jimmy Carter, *Keeping Faith: Memoirs of a President*, 171.

27. *New York Times*, 17 March 1978; JC, *White House Diary*, 178; Carter, *Public Papers, 1978, Vol. I*, 516–17.

28. Jeff Broadwater interview with Talmadge, 10 April 1992, pp. 14–15, Stennis Oral History Collection, Mississippi State University.

29. *New York Times*, 17 March 1978; many letters, 22 March 1978, Carter to individual Senators, WHCF, box FO-19, JCL; Sen. Edward Zorinsky to Carter, 23 March 1978, WHCF, President, box PP-3, JCL.

30. JC, *White House Diary*, 189–90; Eizenstat, *Carter*, 571.

31. JC, *White House Diary*, 188–89; Carter to Torrijos, 18 April 1978, Jordan File, box 50, JCL; Carter, *Public Papers, 1978, Vol. I*, 758; Peter N. Carroll, *It Seemed Like Nothing Happened: America in the 1970s*, 255.

32. Telegram, Carter to Hayakawa and others, 19 Aug. 1977, WHCF, box FO-16, JCL; Janelle Conaway, "Savvy Navigator of a Turbulent Canal," *Americas* 51, no. 1 (Feb. 1999), 8; Kai Bird, *The Outlier: The Unfinished Presidency of Jimmy Carter*, 243–47; Jonathan Alter, *His Very Best: Jimmy Carter, A Life*, 382–84.

33. *Chicago Tribune*, 27 April 1978; Eric Alterman and Kevin Mattson, *The Cause: The Fight for American Liberalism from Franklin Roosevelt to Barack Obama*, 299–300: Burton I. Kaufman and Scott Kaufman, *The Presidency of James Earl Carter, Jr.*, 53.

34. Carter note on Floor Statement by Senator Thomas J. McIntyre, 1 March 1978, Staff Secretary, Handwriting File, box 75, JCL; Nancy Reagan Smith and Mary C. Ryan, editors, *Modern First Ladies: Their Documentary Legacy*, 145; Scott Kaufman, *Rosalynn Carter: Equal Partner in the White House*, 77–78; JC, *White House Diary*, 177, 188–89.

35. Memorandum, Stu Eizenstat to Carter, 23 June 1978, Re Urban policy, with Carter notes, Staff Secretary, Handwriting File, box 70, JCL; *Washington Post*, 19 Feb. 1978.

36. Memorandum, Griffin Smith to Mary Hoyt, 31 Jan. 1978, Speechwriters File, Subject, box 3, JCL; Rosalynn Carter Speech, 4 Feb. 1978, First Lady Office, Projects, Cade, box 29, JCL; *New York Times*, 14 Feb. 1978; *Atlanta Constitution*, 16 Feb. 1978.

37. *Americus Times-Recorder*, 25 Jan. 1978; Inscription, 28 Jan. 1978, WHCF, box TR-16, JCL.

38. *US News and World Report*, 13 March, 1978, p. 74; Helen Thomas, *Thanks for the Memories, Mr. President*, 123.

39. Minutes of Cabinet Meeting, 13 May 1978, copy in Patricia Harris Papers, box 51, Library of Congress; Author interview with Rosalynn Carter, 12 Oct. 1994; Margaret Truman, *First Ladies*, 148–49; Gil Troy, *Affairs of State: The Rise and Rejection of the Presidential Couple since World War II*, 254; Helen Thomas, *Front Row at the White House: My Life and Times*, 268.

40. Christopher Andrew, *For the President's Eyes Only: Secret Intelligence from Washington to Bush*, 36; Draft of speech with Carter handwritten corrections, 17 March 1978, Hertzberg File, box 39, and Staff Secretary, Handwriting File, box 77, JCL; Carter, *Public Papers, 1978, Vol. I*, 529–35.

41. Carter, *Public Papers, 1978, Vol. I*, 534–35, 537; JC, *White House Diary*, 179.

42. Carter, *Public Papers, 1978, Vol. I*, 534–35, 537; JC, *White House Diary*, 179.

43. *New York Times*, 4 April 1978; Memorandum of conversation, 7 May 1978, Carter and Schmidt, Plains File, box 1, JCL; JC, *White House Diary*, 173, 179.

44. Carter to Obasanjo, draft letter, Jan. 1978, Carter to Tito, Jan. 1978, both in NSA Staff, Horn/Special, box 1, JCL; JC, *White House Diary*, 181; Carter, *Public Papers, 1978, Vol. I*, 610–11; Stan Grant, *Jimmy Carter's Odyssey to Black Africa-Part One*, 24–25: Jasper Ridley, *Tito: A Biography*, 410.

45. Carter, *Public Papers, 1978, Vol. I*, 613–16.

46. Ibid., 617–27.

47. Ibid., 500–502, 627–40; JC, *White House Diary*, 181–82.

48. Stan Grant, *Jimmy Carter's Odyssey to Black Africa—Part One*, 28.

49. Levi A. Nwachuku and Godfrey N. Uzoigwe, *Troubled Journey: Nigeria since the Civil War*, 111–26; *US News and World Report*, 3 April 1978, p. 21; see also Scott Kaufman, *Ambition, Pragmatism, and Party: A Political Biography of Gerald R. Ford*, 307–308, and Stan Grant, *Jimmy Carter's Odyssey to Black Africa*, 30–31, 47–49.

50. *Nigerian Tribune, 31* March 1978, with photograph of the plane; *New Nigerian,* 3 April 1978; PDD, 31 May 1978, JCL; Carter, *Public Papers, 1978, Vol. I,* 643–45.

51. Ibid., 647.

52. Nancy Mitchell, *Jimmy Carter in Africa: Race and the Cold War,* 420–24; Grant, *Jimmy Carter's Odyssey to Black Africa,* 69–72.

53. JC, *White House Diary,* 182; *New Nigerian,* 1, 3, 4, 17 April, 1978; *Nigerian Chronicle,* 1, 3, 4, 8, 1978, articles by Chinwoko Mbadiuju, Nigerian National Archives.

54. PDD, 2 April 1978; Carter, *Public Papers, 1978, Vol. I,* 654–66.

55. *US News and World Report,* 3 April 1978, p. 28; Chinwoko Mbadiuju quoted in *Daily Times Nigeria,* 8 April 1978, p. 5.

56. *Americus Times-Recorder,* 3 April 1978, p. 3.

57. *Afriscope,* April 1978, pp. 6–11.

58. PDD, 3 April 1978, JCL; Carter notes for speech, 3 April 1978, Plains File, box 2, JCL; Carter, *Presidential Papers, 1978, Vol. I,* 671–78.

Chapter 15

1. Brzezinski to Carter, 6 Jan. 1978, NSC weekly Report # 41, Brzezinski Donated Material, box 41, JCL; Memorandum, Edward Sanders and Roger Lewis to Robert J. Lipshutz and Hamilton Jordan, 11 Jan. 1978, White House Counsel, Lipshutz, box 6, JCL.

2. East Room Speech, 17 Jan. 1978, First Lady Press Office, box 4, JCL.

3. *Americus Times-Recorder,* 25 Jan. 1978.

4. Presidential Commission on World Hunger, 20 Jan. 1978, box 14, JCL; Memorandum, Peter Bourne to Carter, 20 Jan. 1978, Re first meeting, DPS, Eizenstat, box 140, JCL.

5. Bernard S. White to Carter, 26 Jan. 1978, Public Liaison, Constanza, box 55, JCL.

6. Memorandum, Brzezinski and Frank Moore to Carter, 22 March 1978, Re Middle East Arms Package, Staff Secretary, Handwriting File, box 77, JCL.

7. Carter, *Public Papers, 1978, Vol. I,* 279–81, 291; Memorandum of Conversation, 4 Feb. 1978, President's Meeting with Sadat at Camp David, Brzezinski Collection, box 36, JCL; Aaron David Miller, *The Much Too Promised Land: America's Elusive Search for Arab-Israeli Peace,* 164–65; William B. Quandt, *Camp David: Peacemaking and Politics,* 172–76.

8. Jimmy Carter, *White House Diary,* 169–70.

9. Author interview with Ribicoff, 14 March 1994; "The Reminiscences of Abraham A. Ribicoff," 285–89, Oral History Collection, Columbia University.

10. *Washington Star,* 8, 9 March 1978; Douglas J. Benet to Congressman Clarence D. Long, 10 March 1978, WHCF, box FO-30, JCL; *New York Times,* 10 March 1978; Howard Simons, *Jewish Times: Voices of the American Jewish Experience,* 368–69.

11. JC, *White House Diary,* 175–76; *New York Times,* 10 March 1978; Jimmy Carter, *Keeping Faith: Memoirs of a President,* 310.

12. JC, *White House Diary,* 179, 168, 192; JC, *Keeping Faith,* 310–311; Carter, *Public Papers, 1978, Vol. I,* 794; Ibid., *Vol. II,* 1239.

13. Memorandum of Conversation, Carter, Begin, and large group, 21 March 1978, Brzezinski Collection, box 36, and Staff Secretary, Handwriting File, box 77, JCL; JC, *White House Diary*, 180.

14. *US News & World Report*, 3 April 1978, p. 24; Carter, *Public Papers, 1978, Vol. I*, 544–45, 547–48, 550–53.

15. Jimmy Carter, *White House Diary*, 183; Carter, *Public Papers, 1978, Vol. I*, 710.

16. JC, *White House Diary*, 203, 208–210; Walter Mondale, *The Good Fight: A Life in Liberal Politics*, 192–94.

17. Memorandum, Mondale to Carter, 5 April 1978, Mondale, Donated Material, box 205, JCL; Lipshutz speech at the Temple, 8 April 1978, and many others, DPS, Eizenstat, box 235, JCL.

18. Memorandum of Conversation between Carter and David Rockefeller, Chairman of the Board, Chase Manhattan Bank, 20 April 1978, NSA, Brzezinski File, Subject, box 36–38, JCL.

19. Sadat to Carter, handwritten note, 24 April 1978, NSA, Brzezinski Collection, box 13, JCL.

20. Miller, *The Much Too Promised Land*, 170, 172; Joshua Muravchik, *Making David into Goliath: How the World Turned against Israel*, 130–33.

21. Sylvia Beck to Lipshutz, 26 April 1978, Public Liaison, Constanza, box 55, JCL; *Chicago Tribune*, 1 May 1978.

22. Press Release, Office of First Lady Press Secretary, 24 April 1978, First Lady Office, Mental Health Project, box 7, JCL; Gerald N. Grob, "Public Policy and Mental Illness: Jimmy Carter's Presidential Commission on Mental Health," *Millbank Quarterly* 83, no. 3 (2005), 440–47. Carter signed the bill into law on 7 October 1980, but when his successor, Ronald Reagan, was inaugurated on 21 January 1981, he reversed the policy.

23. Doreen Mattingly, *A Feminist in the White House: Midge Costanza, the Carter Years, and America's Culture Wars*, 105, 144–45; Memorandum, Costanza to Carter, 25 April 1978, Re National Advisory Committee for Women, with Carter's comments, Clough File, box 45, JCL; Memorandum, Brzezinski to Carter, 11 April 1978, Re Costa Rican president, Staff Secretary, Handwriting File, box 80, JCL: Memorandum, Stu, Jody, Anne Wexler to Carter, 24 April 1978, Re Bella Abzug, Staff Secretary, Handwriting File, box 82, JCL; Carter, *Public Papers, 1978, Vol. I*, 680–81, 883; Marjorie J. Spruill, *Divided We Stand: The Battle over Women's Rights and Family Values that Polarized American Politics*, 124–25.

24. Minutes of the Cabinet Meeting No. 47, 14 April 1978, Declassified Document NLC-5-2-5-6-3, JCL.

25. Ruth Douglas Currie, *Kwajalein Atoll, the Marshall Islands and American Policy in the Pacific*, 132–36; Carter, *Public Papers, 1978, Vol. I*, 885–86; Timothy P. Maga, *The World of Jimmy Carter: U.S. Foreign Policy, 1977–1981*, 77–79, 81, 83, 85–86.

26. Andrew Cockburn and Leslie Cockburn, *Dangerous Liaison: The Inside Story of the U.S.-Israeli Covert Relationship*, 194; James M. Perry, "American Jews and Jimmy Carter," *Wall Street Journal*, 2 March 1978; Memorandum, Edward Sanders to Carter

and Mondale, 6 March 1978, Staff Secretary, Handwriting File, box 75, JCL; JC, *White House Diary*, 194–95.

27. JC, *White House Diary*, 193; Stuart E. Eizenstat, *Imperfect Justice: Looted Assets, Slave Labor, and the Unfinished Business of WWII*, 16–19; Carter, *Public Papers, 1978, Vol. I*, 812–14; Edward T. Linenthal, *Preserving Memory: The Struggle to Create America's Holocaust Museum*, 11, 15, 19–23, 41. The result of the committee's work became the Holocaust Memorial Museum in Washington, which opened in 1993.

28. "Jerusalem: Some Aspects of a Complex Problem," May 1978, research paper prepared by National Foreign Assessment Center, Declassified Document NLC-4-36-1-8-9, JCL.

29. Harriman to Carter, 16 May 1978, WHCF, Name File, box Harriman, JCL, emphasis in original; Dan Fleshler, *Transforming America's Israel Lobby*, 13.

30. Folder of Jewish Hate mail, 17 May 1978, Jordan File, box 47, JCL.

31. Secret-Sensitive, 17 May 1978, Declassification Document NLC-1-6-3-24-5, JCL.

32. Carter to Ribicoff, 25 May 1978, WHCF, Name File, A. Ribicoff, JCL; Author interview with Abraham Ribicoff, 14 March 1994; JC, *White House Diary*, 195; Carter, *Public Papers, 1978, Vol. I*, 896–97.

33. Memorandum of Conversation, 31 May 1978, Carter and Prime Minister Ecevit, NSA, Staff Horn/special, box 2, JCL; Carter, *Public Papers, 1978, Vol. I*, 1018–19; Minutes of Cabinet Meeting, 5 June, 10 July 1978, VF, JCL.

34. *New York Times*, 14 May 1978; First Lady Project: Mental Health, 26 May 26, First Lady Press Office, box 5, JCL.

35. *Americus Times-Recorder*, 22 Feb. 1978; Carter, *Public Papers, 198, Vol. I*, 313–14, 316, 331, 333, 366, 379, 419–20, 508; Straight Wire, 6 March 1978, Carter go Governors, White House Counsel, Lipshutz, box 9, JCL; Memorandum, 13 March 1978, Jack Watson to Carter, Re Strike Report, Staff Secretary, Handwriting File, box 76, JCL.

36. Carter, *Public Papers, 1978, Vol. I*, 824–26; *New York Times*, 4 May 1978.

37. *Washington Post*, 19, 22 May 1978; Scott Kaufman, *Rosalynn Carter: Equal Partner in the White House*, 98–99.

38. JC, *White House Diary*, 196.

39. Declassified Document NLC-31-39-2-5-8, JCL. Orlov was released from Siberia in 1986. He received the Carter-Menil Human Rights prize of $100,000, and the next year he began work as a scientist at Cornell University.

40. JC, *White House Diary*, 197–98.

41. Peter W. Rodman, *Presidential Command: Power, Leadership, and the Making of Foreign Policy from Richard Nixon to George W. Bush*, 121–23.

42. Carter to the Shah, 2 June 1978, Plains File, box 23, JCL.

43. JC, *White House Diary*, 198–99; *New York Times*, 8 June 1978; multiple drafts of the speech are in Staff Secretary, Handwriting file, boxes 89 and 90, JCL; JC, *Keeping Faith*, 229–30; PDD, June 7, 1978, JCL.

44. Pool Report # 1, 7 June 1978, Press File, Granum, box 100, JCL.

45. Alexander Solzhenitsyn, *A World Split Apart*. For similar speeches, see *Warning to the West*. Solzhenitsyn returned to Russia in 1994 after the collapse of the Soviet Union.

46. Carter comments at Desai working dinner, 13 June 1978, Plains File, box 2; Telegram, Gov. Edmund G. Brown, Jr., to Carter, WHCF, box BE-9; Rosalynn to Lenore Hershey, 15 June 1978, First Lady, Subject File, box 18, all JCL; Joseph Pearce, *Solzhenitsyn: A Soul in Exile*, 236.

47. First draft of speech has some corrections in Carter's handwriting, transcript in First Lady Press Office, box 5, JCL.

48. JC, *White House Diary*, 202 (quotation); Sally Quinn's articles in *Washington Post*, 25 June and *Boston Evening Globe*, 27 June 1978.

49. Rosalynn Carter to Aliza Begin, 20 June 1978, Declassified Document NLC-28-11-8-2-9, JCL; Memorandum, Joyce Starr to Lipshutz and Eizenstat, 20 June 1978, RE Trial of Ida Nudel, with attached letters of A. Begin, R. Carter, and memoranda that suggest the administration will send letters of concern, Public Liaison, Costanza, box 53, JCL. Nudal was sentenced to four years of hard labor, released and lived haphazardly in Russia until she finally got her visa to travel to Israel in 1991, after the collapse of the Soviet Union.

50. Rosalynn Carter to Joe Califano, 17 June 1978, First Lady Office, Projects, Cade, box 18, JCL.

51. JC, *White House Diary*, 203.

52. JC, Carter to Fallows, 27 June 1978, Fallows to Carter, 21 June 1978, Clough File, box 45, JCL.

53. Carter to General Charles Graham, 24 June 1978, WHCF, box ND-50, and others in WHCF, box PR-3, JCL.

54. CIA National Foreign Assessment Report on Human Rights Review, 4 May 1978, Declassified Document NLC-31-39-2-01-2, JCL; Carter to Dubs, 25 May 1978,WHCF, box FO-5, JCL; Carter, *Public Papers, 1978, Vol. I*, 1022–23.

55. "Inside Hitler's Death Tunnels," *Telegraph Magazine*, 5 June 1993; Mary Kathryn Barbier, *Spies, Lies, and Citizenship: The Hunt for Nazi Criminals*, vii-viii; Author interview with Scott McMurry.

56. Carter to Brezhnev, 2 Sept. 1978, Brezhnev to Carter 14 Sept. 1978, Plains File, box 17, JCL.

Chapter 16

1. First Lady Press Office, August 1978, box 5, JCL.

2. Jimmy Carter, *Talking Peace: A Vision for the Next Generation*, 9. 12.

3. Rosalynn Carter, *First Lady from Plains*, 226; Scott Kaufman, *Rosalynn Carter: Equal Partner in the White House*, 79.

4. *Los Angeles Times*, 2 July 1978; Memorandum, Ham, Stu, Bob, Mark Siegel to Carter, 6 July 1978, Re Jewish Leaders, DPS, Eizenstat, box 235, JCL; Mondale to Carter, 4 July 1978, Re Trip to Israel and Egypt, Mondale Donated Material, box 205, JCL; Memorandum, Harold Brown to Carter, 7 July 1978, Re Actions July 1–7, (quotation), Staff Secretary, Handwriting File, box 94, JCL.

5. Memorandum, Dan Tate to Frank Moore, 12 July, 1978, Re Stennis and SALT, with Carter note, Staff Secretary, box 95, JCL; Multiple letters to Carter, 12, 13 July 1978, Re Andrew Young, WHCF, box IT-10, JCL; *Americus Times-Recorder*, 14 July 1978; *US News and World Report*, 24 July 1978, p. 56; Martin Schram, "Andy Young is Running Out of Chances to be Quiet," *Newsday*, 16 July 1978; William Raspberry, "Was Young Really So Far Off Base?," *Washington Post*, 17 July 1978.

6. Author interview with Cyrus Vance, 14 July 1992, Stennis Oral History Collection, Mississippi State University; Memorandum of Conversation, 7 July 1978, Carter and Schmidt, Plains File, box 1, JCL.

7. Carter, *Public Papers, 1978, Vol. II*, 1286.

8. Jimmy Carter, *White House Diary*, 206; Carter, *Public Papers, 1978, Vol. I*, 719–20; Carter, *Public Papers, 1978, Vol. II*, 1284–89; Pool Report, 14 July 1978, Hoyt File, box 1, JCL; Carter, "Notes from Trip Germany," July 1978, Plains File, box 1, JCL.

9. Carter to General Blanchard, 17 July 1978, Carter to General William Evans, 2 Nov. 1978, Robert D. Linder to Harold Brown, 2 Nov. 1978, all in WHCF, box ND-8, JCL; Carter to Schmidt, 17 July, 1978, Plains File, box 1, JCL; Carter, *Public Papers, 1978, Vol. II*, 1290–91 (quotations).

10. Carter, *Public Papers, 1978, Vol. II*, 1289–1315; JC, *White House Diary*, 205–206.

11. Carter, *Public Papers, 1978, Vol. II*, 1322; Bourne to Carter, 20 July 1978, White House Counsel, Lipshutz, box 5, JCL; *Washington Star*, 20 July 1978; *New York Times*, 21 July 1978; 1980 Campaign Papers, Tony Dolan Files, box 858, Ronald Reagan Presidential Library (RRL). Bourne was reprimanded by the Georgia State Medical Board and hired the next year by the United Nations.

12. JC, *White House Diary*, 208.

13. Ibid., 209; Betty Glad, *Jimmy Carter in Search of the Great White House*, 424; Author interview with Muskie, 3 April 1992, Stennis Oral History Collection, Mississippi State University. For a friendly roast of the Speaker by the president five months earlier, see Carter, *Public Papers, 1978, Vol. I*, 286–88.

14. *Congress and the Nation*, Vol. V., 1977–1980, pp. 162, 1030; *Congressional Quarterly*, 25 July 1978—Senate, 2250 (quotation about the Beards); Andrew Borowiec, *Cyprus: A Troubled Island*, 131, 178 (Carter quotation); Robert Beckel, Miller Center Interview, 30, JCL; Christopher Hitchens, *Hostage to History: Cyprus, from the Ottomans to Kissinger*, 134; Scott Kaufman, *Plans Unraveled: The Foreign Policy of the Carter Administration*, 57–59, 148–49.

15. *Congressional Record*, 25 July 1978 – Senate, 22557; Carter to McGovern, with attachments, 3 Aug. 1978, WHCF, box FG-7, JCL; *New York Times*, 26 July 1978; Carter to Ribicoff, 28 July 1978, WHCF, Name File, A. Ribicoff, JCL; Carter to 57 Senators who voted to lift the embargo, 4 April 1978, Staff Secretary, Handwriting File, box 98, JCL.

16. Doreen Mattingly, *A Feminist in the White House: Midge Costanza, the Carter Years, and America's Culture Wars*, 105,183–89; Emily Walker Cook, "Women White House Advisers in the Carter Administration: Presidential Stalwarts or Feminist Advocates?" PhD dissertation, Vanderbilt University, 1995, 183–85; *Atlanta Journal and Constitution*, 30 July 1978; Costanza to Carter, 2 Aug. 1978, White House

Counsel, Lipshutz, box 11, JCL; Janet M. Martin, *The Presidency and Women: Promise, Performance, and Illusion*, 220–32, 245–48.

17. Carter to Begin, 3 Aug. 1978, VF, box Begin, JCL.

18. Pool Report, 4 Aug. 1978, White House Press File, Edwards, box 9, JCL.

19. Carter's remarks, 5 Aug. 1978, Staff Secretary, Handwriting File, box 98, JCL; JC, *White House Diary*, 212; Carter, *Public Papers, 1978, Vol. II*, 1383–84.

20. Remarks of Admiral Rickover, 5 Aug. 1978, Staff Secretary, Handwriting File, box 98, JCL.

21. Mary Hoyt notes, First Lady Press Office, box 41, JCL.

22. Carter, *Public Papers, 1978, Vol. II*, 1392–93; PDD, 11 Aug. 1978, JCL; Memorandum, Lipshutz to Carter, 16 Aug. 1978, Re Pope Paul VI, Staff Secretary, Handwriting File, box 100, JCL.

23. White House Press Secretary News Release, VF, box Carter, R., JCL; First Lady Press Office, Foreign Trips, box 26, JCL; Phil Wise to Carter, 12 Aug. 1978, Staff Secretary, Handwriting File, box 99, JCL; Memo, Brzezinski to Carter, 21 Aug. 1978, Declassified Document NLC-1-7-6-21-4, JCL; Scott Kaufman, *Rosalynn Carter: Equal Partner in the White House*, 78–9; JC, *White House Diary*, 213–14.

24. Ibid., 212; William B. Quandt, *Camp David: Peacemaking and Politics*, 201–205.

25. Declassified Document, NLC-15-70-10-7-0, JCL.

26. Carter, *Public Papers, 1978, Vol. II*, 1393.

27. Carter, *Public Papers, 1978, Vol. I*, 435–38, 444–49; PDD, 14, 15 Aug. 1978, JCL; Martin, *The Presidency and Women*, 216.

28. Carter, *Public Papers, 1978, Vol. II*, 1436–37; Addresses, notes, talking points, 16 Aug. 1978, Declassified Document NLC-126-14-4-1-1; JC, *White House Diary*, 214; Griffin Bell, *Taking Care of the Law*, 103–105.

29. Carter, *Public Papers, 1978, Vol. II*, 1281–82.

30. Louis Harris Poll, 18 Aug. 1978, DPS, Eizenstat, box 253, JCL.

31. JC, *White House Diary*, 214.

32. Ibid., 214–15.

33. Memo, Frank Moore and Time Kraft to Carter, Re 1978 Elections, Staff Secretary, Handwriting File, box 100, JCL.

34. Presidential Review Memorandum/NSC-42, 43, 24 Aug.1978, VF, box Presidential Review Memoranda/NSC, JCL; Carter to Senator Riegle and ninety-nine more, 31 Aug. 1978, Jordan, box 44, JCL.

35. PDD, 18–30 Aug. 1978, JCL; *Americus Times-Recorder*, 18, 21 Aug. 1978; Pool Report, White House Press File, Granum, box 105, JCL; *U.S. News and World Report*, 28 Aug. 1978; JC, *White House Diary*, 214–15.

Chapter 17

1. Carter, *Public Papers, 1978, Vol. II*, 1489–90.

2. H. R. Brands, *American Dreams: The United States since 1945*, 201–202.

3. Jimmy Carter, *Keeping Faith: Memoirs of a President*, 319–22; George C. Edwards III, "Exclusive Interview: President Jimmy Carter," *Presidential Studies Quarterly* 28, no. 2 (March 2008), 8.

4. JC, *Public Papers, 1978, II*, 1496–97; Roy E. Licklider, *Political Power and the Arab Oil Weapon: The Experience of Five Industrial Nations*, 206–210, 261–63, 267–71.

5. Ed Sanders to Carter, with attached memorandum, 4 Sept. 1978, Staff Secretary, Handwriting File, box 101, JCL; *Americus Times-Recorder*, 4 Sept. 1978; JC, *Keeping Faith*, 322–24; Philomena Jurey, *A Basement Seat to History: Tales of Covering Presidents Nixon, Ford, Carter, and Reagan for the Voice of America*, 162, 166.

6. Jehan Sadat, *A Woman of Egypt*, 388.

7. Christoher Andrew, *For the President's Eyes Only: Secret Intelligence and the American Presidency from Washington to Bush*, 437–38; Memorandum, Situation Room to Brzezinski, 5 Sept. 1978, Declassified Document NLC-1-7-7-2-0, JCL.

8. A. Denis Clift, *With Presidents to the Summit*, 163–69; Lawrence Wright, *Thirteen Days in September: Carter, Begin, and Sadat at Camp David*, 51; Carter, handwritten "Framework," 5 Sept. 1978, and Carter, "notes made at Camp David before Begin and Sadat arrive, 5 Sept. 1978, both in Plains File box 28, JCL; Jimmy Carter, *White House Diary*, 216; JC, *Keeping Faith*, 326–27.

9. Wright, *Thirteen Days*, 51–53; Peter G. Bourne, *Jimmy Carter: A Comprehensive Biography from Plains to the Post-Presidency*, 405–406.

10. Jurey, *A Basement Seat to History*, 164–65; JC, *White House Diary*, 216–17; Rosalynn Carter, *First Lady from Plains*, 243–44; JC, *Keeping Faith*, 328–29.

11. Wright, *Thirteen Days*, 53; Carl Sferrazza Anthony, *First Ladies*, Vol. II: *The Saga of the Presidents' Wives and Their Power, 1961–1990*, 300; Author interview with Rosalynn Carter, 12 Oct. 1994; RSC, *First Lady*, 239–40, 243; Clift, *With Presidents to the Summit*, 167.

12. Wright, *Thirteen Days*, 55; JC, *Keeping Faith*, 326; Moshe Dayan, *Breakthrough: A Personal Account of the Egypt-Israel Peace Negotiations*, 59–64.

13. Secret Chronology of Camp David Memcons, 5–16 Sept. 1978, Declassified Document NLC-128-9-5-3-2, JCL; JC, *White House Diary*, 219–20; JC, *Keeping Faith*, 332–37.

14. JC, *Keeping Faith*, 322–24; RSC, *First Lady*, 235–37.

15. Quoted in Wright, *Thirteen Days*, 53–54; Carter, Notes taken at Mtg Begin-Sadat, 7 Sept. 1978, Plains File, box 28, JCL; RSC, *First Lady*, 245–46.

16. Sadat, *A Woman of Egypt*, 389; RSC, *First Lady*, 244; quote from Rosalynn's unpublished diary in Jonathan Alter, *His Very Best: Jimmy Carter, A Life*, 397.

17. Zbigniew Brzezinski, *Power and Principle: Memoirs of the National Security Advisor*, 256; Eric Alterman and Kevin Mattson, *The Cause: The Fight for American Liberalism from Franklin Roosevelt to Barack Obama*, 301; JC, *White House Diary*, 221–22; Declassified Document NLC-128-9-5-3-2, JCL; Bourne, *Carter*, 406.

18. A. Denis Clift, *With Presidents to the Summit*, 159; JC, *White House Diary*, 222–27; Brzezinski Exit Interview, 14–18, JCL; Declassified Document NLC-128-9-5-3-2, JCL.

19. William P. Quandt, *Camp David: Peacemaking and Politics*, 223–25; Michael Giorgione, *Inside Camp David: The Private World of the Presidential Retreat*, 134–35; Author interview with Ribicoff, 14 March 1994.

20. Anthony, *First Ladies*, 300; *New York Times*, 8 Sept. 1978; RSC, *First Lady*, 246–47.

21. Wright, *Thirteen Days*, 117–20, 135; RSC, *First Lady*, 251–52; JC, *Keeping Faith*, 369.

22. JC, *White House Diary*, 228, 234–35; Declassified Document NLC-128-9-5-5-3-2, JCL.

23. For details of the battle and its significance for the South, see Richard M. McMurry, *Atlanta 1864: Last Chance for the Confederacy* and *The Fourth Battle of Winchester: Toward a New Civil War Paradigm*.

24. JC, *White House Diary*, 229–30; JC, *Keeping Faith*, 372 (quotation); Bourne, *Carter*, 408; Wright, *Thirteen Days*, 170–73; RSC, *First Lady*, 253; Jody Powell, *The Other Side of the Story*, 76–77.

25. Moshe Dayan, *Breakthrough: A Personal Account of the Egypt-Israel Peace Negotiations*, 172–74; JC, *White House Diary*, 231–36; Wright, *Thirteen Days*, 179; Brzezinski, *Power and Principle*, 264–65; Memorandum, Tom Thornton to Brzezinski, 11 Sept. 1978, Re Afghanistan, Declassified Document NLC-6-1-1-7-6, JCL.

26. Andrew, *For President's Eyes Only*, 437; Wright, *Thirteen Days*, 207–210 (quotations); RSC, *First Lady*, 260; JC, *Keeping Faith*, 388–89; Brzezinski, *Power and Principle*, 265.

27. Memorandum, Brzezinski to Carter, 13 Sept. 1978, Declassified Document NLC-1-7-8-24-9, JCL.

28. Sept. 14, 1978, Bureau of Intelligence and Research Analysis Report, Declassified Documents NLC-6-54-2-16-7 and NLC-25-34-3-2-2, JCL.

29. *Jerusalem Post*, 7 Nov. 2014; Wright, *Thirteen Days*, 232.

30. JC, *White House Diary*, 237–38; JC, *Keeping Faith*, 391–92; Bourne, *Carter*, 410; Wright, *Thirteen Days*, 232–34; RSC, *First Lady*, 262–64; Quandt, *Camp David*, 238–40.

31. Sadat, *A Woman of Egypt*, 391.

32. Carter to Sadat, Carter to Begin, 15 Sept. 1978, Plains File, box 28, JCL.

33. Declassified Document NLC-128-9-5-3-2, JCL; RSC, *First Lady*, 262; JC, *Keeping Faith*, 393–94.

34. JC, *White House Diary*, 238–41; Richard H. Curtiss, *Stealth PACs: How Israel's American Lobby Took Control of U.S. Middle East Policy*, 31–32.

35. Wright, *Thirteen Days*, 235–36.

36. JC, *White House Diary*, 241–43; Carter remarks, 13 Nov. 2013, Symposium, CIA and Camp David, JCL; Review of "Back Door Channels: The Price of Peace," a PBS documentary on Camp David, *Variety*, 15 Nov. 2010; Yossi Beilin, *Israel: A Concise Political History*, 44; Wright, *Thirteen Days*, 237–38, 257–62; JC, *Keeping Faith*, 397–401; Seth Anziska, *Preventing Palestine: A Political History from Camp David to Oslo*, 119–27; Yossi Melman and Dan Raviv, *Friends in Deed: Inside the U.S.-Israel Alliance*, 182–83.

37. Wright, *Thirteen Days*, 262; Sadat, *A Woman of Egypt*, 392; RSC, *First Lady*, 267; JC, *Keeping Faith*, 401; Daniel Gordis, *Menachem Begin: The Battle for Israel's Soul*, 162–79; W. Dale Nelson, *The President Is at Camp David*, 124.

38. Bourne, *Carter*, 411; Wright, *Thirteen Days*, 262–63; RSC, *First Lady*, 267–69; *New York Times*, 3 Dec. 2001.

39. Wright, *Thirteen Days*, 264; Carter, *Public Papers, Vol. II, 1978*, 1519–28; Jeremy Pressman, "Explaining the Carter Administration's Israeli-Palestinian Solution," *Diplomatic History* 37, no. 5 (2013), 1146–47; Brzezinski quoted in Nelson, *The President Is at Camp David*, 124; Michael B. Oren, *Power, Faith, and Fantasy: America in the Middle East 1776 to the Present*, 538–45.
40. Raphael Israeli, *Man of Defiance: A Political Biography of Anwar Sadat*, 244.
41. Wright, *Thirteen Days*, 265–66 (quotations); Jurey, *A Basement Seat to History*, 172–74.
42. Carter, Address to Joint session of Congress, 18 Sept. 1978, Staff Secretary, Handwriting File, box 101, JCL; JC, *Keeping Faith*, 405; Carter, *Public Papers, Vol. II, 1978*, 1533–37; Burton I. Kaufman and Scott Kaufman, *Presidency of James Earl Carter, Jr.*, 149–53; Quandt, *Camp David*, 251–58.
43. JC, *White House Diary*, 245–46.
44. Wright, *Thirteen Days*, 266–69; Situation Room to Brzezinski, 18 Sept. 1978, Noon Notes, Declassified Document NLC-1-7-8-42-9, JCL; JC, *Keeping Faith*, 405-407; Carter to Begin, 27 Sept. 1978, Carter, *Public Papers, 1978, Vol. II*, 1651.
45. Memorandum, Mondale to Carter, 20 Sept. 1978, Re meeting with Sadat on Sept. 18, Mondale Donated Material, box 205, JCL.
46. Sadat, *Woman of Egypt*, 393.
47. Martin I. Elzy, "Camp David Accords Set Model for Lasting Peace, Piece by Piece," *The Austin (TX) American-Statesman*, 17 Sept. 2003.
48. Laura Kalman, *Right Star Rising: A New Politics, 1974–1980*, 301–304 (Red Sea quotation).
49. JC, *White House Diary*, 246–47; Carter note citing Kissinger, 18 Sept. 1978, Staff Secretary, Handwriting file, box 101, JCL.
50. Robert A. Strong, *Working in the World: Jimmy Carter and the Making of American Foreign Policy*, 187, 201–207; John Dumbrell, *The Carter Presidency: A Re-evaluation*, 12–13, 212; Betty Glad, *Jimmy Carter and the Search for the Great White House*, 431–34; Burton I. Kaufman, *The Arab Middle East and the United States*, 113–14; Author interview with Cyrus Vance, 1 May 1992, 13–15, Stennis Oral History Collection, Mississippi State University.
51. Rostropovich to President and Mrs. Carter, 19 Sept. 1978, WHCF, President, box PP-3, JCL.
52. *Americus Times-Recorder*, 20 Sept. 1978; George to Mr. President, 20 Sept. 1978, WHCF, President, box PP-6, JCL: Memorandum, Edward Sanders to Carter, 2 Sept. 1978, WHCF, box FO-44, JCL; Kurt Waldheim to Carter, 25 Sept. 1978, WHCF, box Fo-44, JCL; Beilin, *Israel: A Concise Political History*, 44.

Chapter 18

1. Raphael Israeli, *Man of Defiance: A Political Biography of Anwar Sadat*, 244-45; Lawrence Wright, *Thirteen Days in September: Carter, Begin, and Sadat at Camp

David, 268; Jimmy Carter, *White House Diary*, 256; Carter, *Public Papers, 1978, Vol. II*, 1877; *New York Times*, 11 Oct., 1998.

2. H. H. Sanders to Secretary of State, 22 Sept. 1978, with Carter note, Declassified Document NLC-SAFE B-13-72-4-7, JCL.

3. Carter to the Shah, 28 Sept. 1978, Plains File, box 23, JCL; Ian Black and Benny Morris, *Israel's Secret Wars: A History of Israel's Intelligences*, 327.

4. Carter to Brezhnev, Hot Line Message, 5 Oct. 1978, Brezhnev to Carter, 6 Oct. 1978, Plains File, box 17, JCL; Jimmy Carter, *Keeping Faith: Memoirs of a President*, 406–407.

5. JC, *White House Diary*, 248–49; Brezhnev to Carter, 17 Nov. 1978, Carter to Brezhnev, 21 Nov. 1978, via telegram from Brzezinski to Ambassador Toon, Plains File, box 17, JCL.

6. Minutes of the Cabinet Meeting, 25 Sept. 1978, Staff Secretary, Handwriting File, box 103, JCL; Omnibus Judgeship Bill, 9 Oct. 1978, and "Carter Administration Selection of Judges," both in White House Counsel: Lipshutz, box 29, JCL.

7. *Congress and the Nation, Vol. 5, 1977–1980*, 725–27.

8. JC, *White House Diary*, 251–52, 258; Carter, *Public Papers, 1978, Vol. II*, 1761–66, 1784–85; *Congress and the Nation, Vol. 5, 1977–1980*, 831–33; *Washington Post*, 26 April 2007; "Carter Administration Selectin of Judges," 10 Nov. 1978, White House Counsel: Lipshutz, box 9, JCL (quotation).

9. *The Atlanta Journal*, 31 Oct. 1978; JC, *White House Diary*, 258; *Congress and the Nation, Vol. 5, 1977–1980*, 798–800.

10. Rosalynn Carter handwritten notes, 19 Sept. 1978, First Lady Press Office, Trips, box 14, JCL.

11. Eleanor Randolph, "President's One-Woman Brain Trust," *Chicago Tribune Magazine*, 17 Sept. 1978.

12. Tim Kraft to Carter, Re Campaign Phone Calls, 1 Nov. 1978, Staff Secretary, Handwriting File, box 108, JCL.

13. Carter, *Public Papers, 1978, Vol. II*, 1849, 1853, passim; CIA, "Human Rights Performance: January 1977–July 1978," Sept. 1978, Brzezinski Collection, box 42, JCL.

14. Carter, *Public Papers, 1978, Vol. II*, 1856, 1872–75, 1916–20, 1978, 2104–11, and passim.; *Congress and the Nation, Vol. V, 1977–1980*, 958, 960, 963–73.

15. JC, *White House Diary*, 249–51, 255–56, 267; Carter, *Public Papers, 1978, Vol. II*, 1684–94;

16. Speech, 1 Oct. 1978, Staff Secretary, Handwriting File, box 104, JCL.

17. Telegram, Dept. of State to American Embassy in Tripoli, 1 Oct 1978, Staff Secretary, Handwriting File, box 104, JCL; Lipshutz to Carter, 5 Dec. 1978, Staff Secretary, Handwriting File, box 111, JCL.

18. Interview with Miss Lillian, *Louisville Courier Journal*, 26 Nov. 1978.

19. Carter, *Public Papers, 1978, Vol. II*, 1785; Carter to Millie O'Neill, 28 Oct. 1978, Staff Secretary, Handwriting File, box 108, JCL.

20. JC, *White House Diary*, 256–58, 260–67; Carter. *Public Papers, 1978, Vol. II*, 1697, 2099.

21. Memorandum, Situation Room for Brzezinski, 7 Nov. 1978, Declassification Document NLC-1-8-4-36-9, JCL.
22. Iran Chronology, Brzezinski Collection, box 11, JCL.
23. Author interview with Stansfield Turner, 6 April 1992, Stennis Oral History Collection, Mississippi State University; Memorandum, Jordan to Carter, 28 Nov. 1978, with Carter notes, Jordan File, box 34, JCL.
24. Christopher Andrew, *President's Eyes Only: Secret Intelligence and the American Presidency from Washington to Bush*, 438–41; Statement by Cyrus Vance, 14 Nov.1978, Brzezinski Collection, box 11, JCL; Jordan to Carter, 28 Nov. 1978, Jordan File, box 34, JCL; Carter notes on his meeting with Zahedi, 21 Nov. 1978, Staff Secretary, Handwriting file, box 109, JCL.
25. Vance to Carter, 30 Nov. 1978, Plains File, box 39, JCL; Situation Room to Brzezinski, 30 Nov. 1978, NSA, Brzezinski, Subject, box 29, JCL; *Americus Times-Recorder*, 6 Dec. 1978; Prince Mozaffar Firouz to Carter, 6 Dec. 1978, WHCF, box CO-31, JCL; Evacuation Plans, 2 Dec. 1978, Declassified Document NLC-6-29-3-1-0, JCL.
26. Memorandum, Jerry Rafshoon and others to Carter, with Carter notes, 22 Nov. 1978, Re speech, and Memorandum, Rafshoon to Carter, 22 Nov. 1978, Re *Sports Illustrated*, both in Staff Secretary, Handwriting File, box 110, JCL.
27. Speech, 6 Dec. 1978, Powell File, box 63, JCL.
28. *Washington Post*, 14 Nov. 1978; *New York Times*, 29 Nov. 1978; Surrender of power to VP, 22 Dec. 1978, White House Counsel, Lipshutz, box 42, JCL; *Washington Star*, 23 Dec. 1978.
29. *Americus Times-Recorder*, 22, 26 Dec. 1978; JC, *White House Diary*, 266-68; Wright, *Thirteen Days*, 269.

Chapter 19

1. Carter to Brezhnev, 14 Dec. 1978, Plains File, box 17, JCL.
2. Quoted in Brian Hilton, "Maximum Flexibility for Peaceful Change: Jimmy Carter, Taiwan, and the Recognition of the People's Republic of China," *Diplomatic History* 33, no. 4 (September 2009), 595; Anatoly Dobrynin, *In Confidence: Moscow's Ambassador to America's Six Cold War Presidents*, 409–10; Zbigniew Brzezinski, *Power and Principle: Memoirs of the National Security Advisor*, 232.
3. Ezra F. Vogel, "Deng is the Leader to Celebrate," *New York Times*, 4 Oct. 2009; Hilton, "Maximum Flexibility for Peaceful Change," 601–603; Alan I. Marcus and Amy Sue Bix, *The Future is Now: Science and Technology Policy in America since 1950*, 167–70; Ezra R. Vogel, *Deng Xiaoping and the Transformation of China*, 4.
4. Vogel, *Deng Xiaoping*, 334–35; Memorandum, 1978, State 5/78, for Brzezinski, Re Taiwan and US Normalization Policy, Declassified Document NLC-4-38-5-2-9, JCL; Breck Walker, "Friends, but not Allies—Cyrus Vance and the Normalization of Relations with China," *Diplomatic History* 33, No. 4 (September 2009), 580–90; Hilton, "Maximum Flexibility for Peaceful Change," 604–606; Patrick Tyler, "The (Ab)normalization of U.S.-Chinese Relations: Cabinet Warfare," *Foreign Affairs*,

78, no. 5 (September–October 1999), 93–95; Zbigniew Brzezinski, *Power and Principle: Memoirs of the National Security Adviser, 1977–1981*, 211.

5. Warren Christopher, *Chances of a Lifetime: A Memoir*, 90; Steven Hurst, *The Carter Administration and Vietnam*, 82–83; Michael Schaller, *The United States and China in the Twentieth Century*, 203–13; Patrick Tyler, *A Great Wall: Six Presidents and China, An Investigative History*, 276–77.

6. Jimmy Carter, *White House Diary*, 193; Brzezinski, *Power and Principle*, 206.

7. Ibid., 209.

8. Quoted in Vogel, *Deng Xiaoping*, 320.

9. Brzezinski, *Power and Principle*, 213.

10. Ibid., 218–19.

11. Ibid., 219–21; JC, *White House Diary*, 196.

12. Brzezinski, *Power and Principle*, 230–33.

13. Brzezinski, Miller Center Interview, 73–74, JCL.

14. Tyler, "The (Ab)normalization of U.S.-Chinese Relations," 97–101; Daniel J. Sargent, *A Superpower Transformed: The Remaking of American Foreign Relations in the 1970s*, 270–71.

15. Robert J. Spitzer, "President, Congress and Foreign Policy," in David Gray Adler and Larry N. George, *The Constitution and the Conduct of American Foreign Policy*, 88; Tyler, "The (Ab)normalization of U.S.-Chinese Relations," 109; Memorandum, Griffin Bell to Carter, Re Taiwan Mutual Defense Treaty, with Carter comment, 6 June 1979, White House Counsel: Lipshutz, box 7, JCL.

16. Walker, "Friends, but not Allies," 591–93; Hilton, "Maximum Flexibility for Peaceful Change," 596–97; Enrico Fardella, "The Sino-American Normalization: A Reassessment," *Diplomatic History* 33, no. 4 (September 2009), 545; Randall Balmer, *Redeemer: The Life of Jimmy Carter*, 89 (Bob Jones quotation).

17. Nixon to Carter, 20 Dec. 1978, Carter to Nixon, 22 Dec. 1978, both in Plains File, box 39, JCL.

18. *China Post*, 5 Feb. 2007; Jean A. Garrison, "Explaining Change in the Carter Administration's China Policy: Foreign Policy Adviser Manipulation of the Policy Agenda," *Asian Affairs: An American Review* 29, no. 2 (Summer 2002), 83; Carter, *Public Papers, 1979, Vol. I*, 165–66, 640–41; Dale R. Herspring, *The Pentagon and the Presidency: Civil-Military Relations from FDR to George W. Bush*, 419–20: JC, *White House Diary*, 279–80.

19. Memorandum, Brzezinski to Carter, Jan. 1979, Brzezinski Donated Material, Geographical File, box 9, JCL.

20. *Newsweek*, 12 Feb. 1979, 22: Vogel, *Deng Xiaoping*, 336–38.

21. Carter, *Public Papers, 1979, Vol. I*, 189–91.

22. JC, *White House Diary*, 283–84.

23. Memorandum of Conversation, 29 Jan. 1979, National Security Affairs, Staff Material Office, Outside the System File, box 47, China, "ZB's Notes, reviewed by P," JCL; *The Foreign Relations of the United States*, 13, 766–70.

24. Menus for State Dinners during the Carter Administration, Jan. 29-31, 1979, JCL.

25. John Roderick recalls Deng's Humor, AP Online, 22 Aug., 2004; Carter, *Public Papers, 1979, Vol. I*, 192–95.

26. Guest List, WHCF, box PR-30, JCL; *Newsweek*, 12 Feb. 1979, pp. 22 ff.

27. *Time*, 31 March 1979; Henry Kissinger, "The Philosopher and the Pragmatist," *Newsweek*, 3 March 1997, p. 42; Jimmy Carter, *Faith: A Journey for All*, 109–10.

28. Carter, *Public Papers, 1979, Vol. I*, 189–95.

29. JC, *White House Diary*, 285; Carter, *Public Papers, 1979, Vol. I*, 195.

30. Memorandum of Conversation, 30 Jan. 1979, National Security Affairs, Staff Material, Office, Outside the System File, box 47, China: President's Meeting with Vice Premier Deng: 1–2, Top Secret, published in *The Foreign Relations of the United States, 1977–1980*, 13, 772–82.

31. JC, *White House Diary*, 285.

32. Vogel, *Deng Xiaoping*, 342.

33. JC, *White House Diary*, 285-86; Carter, *Public Papers, 1979, Vol. I*, 200–12.

34. Carter, *Public Papers, 1979, Vol. I*, 209–13; *Newsweek*, 12 Feb. 1979; Vogel, *Deng Xiaoping*, 343–45.

35. Carter to Brezhnev, 7 Feb. 1979, Brezhnev to Carter, 15 Feb. 1979, both in Plains File, box 17, JCL.

36. Remarks by Jimmy and Rosalynn Carter, 20 Feb. 1997, Historical Press Conference, Carter Center, Atlanta; Peter G. Bourne, *Jimmy Carter: A Comprehensive Biography from Plains to the Post-Presidency*, 440: Vogel, *Deng Xiaoping*, 339–41.

Chapter 20

1. Memorandum, Vance to Carter, 2 Jan. 1979, Plains File, box 39, JCL; Christopher Andrews, *For the President's Eyes Only: Secret Intelligence and the American Presidency from Washington to Bush*, 441.

2. Sullivan to Vance, 2 Jan. 1979, Plains File, box 23, JCL.

3. *New York Times*, 3 Jan. 1979; Memorandum, Mondale to Carter, 19 Feb. 1979, Re O'Neill, Staff Secretary, Handwriting File, box 119, JCL.

4. Memorandum, Edward Sanders to Carter, 3 Jan. 1979, NSA, Brzezinski, Country, box 36, JCL.

5. Mutual Defense Treaty Fact sheet, 5 Jan. 1979, WHCF, box CO-17, JCL; Opinion Poll, 5 Jan., 1979, 5 Jan. 1979, Staff Secretary, Handwriting File, box 114, JCL.

6. *New York Times*, 7 Jan. 1979, "Carter Arrives in Guadeloupe."

7. Carter, *Public Papers, 1979, Vol. I*, 17–20.

8. *New York Times*, 7 Jan. 1979, "Rationale for Guadeloupe."

9. Helmut Schmidt, *Men and Powers: A Political Retrospective*, 72, 123–24, 189–91, 212–13. 264.

10. JC, *White House Diary*, 173–75 (quotations on 275).

11. Carter, *Public Papers, 1979, Vol. I*, 19–20; Robert M. Gates, *From the Shadows: The Ultimate Insider's Story of Five Presidents and How They Won the Cold War*, 111–12.

12. Rosalynn Carter, *First Lady from Plains*, 307–308; Andrew Scott Cooper, *The Fall of Heaven: The Pahlavis and the Last Days of Imperial Iran*, 477–78; Minutes of Cabinet Meeting, 20 Nov. 1978, VF, JCL.

13. Abbas Milani, *The Shah*, 401–402; Mohammad Reza Pahlavi, *Answer to History*, 171.

14. *Atlanta Journal and Constitution*, 14 Jan. 1979; Alfred King, II, to Carter, 14 Jan. 1979, Staff Secretary, Handwriting File, box 114, JCL.

15. Iran Chronology, Brzezinski Collection, box 11, JCL; Carter notes, 4, 5 Jan., 1979, Plains File, box 23, JCL.

16. *Washington Star*, 20 Jan. 1979; *Atlanta Journal and Constitution*, 21 Jan. 1979; Author interview with Edmund Muskie, 3 April 1992, Stennis Oral History Collection, Mississippi State University.

17. *Atlanta Constitution*, 16 Jan. 1979.

18. Carter notes for Cabinet meeting, 15 Jan. 1979, Staff Secretary, Handwriting File, box 114, JCL; *Atlanta Constitution*, 15 Jan. 1979; Lipshutz to Carter, 16 Jan. 1979, White House Counsel: Lipshutz, box 1, JCL; John Dumbrell, *The Carter Presidency: A Reevaluation*, 70; Suzanne Braun Levine and Mary Thom, *Bella Abzug*, 221, 226 (Bella quotation); Marjorie J. Spruill, *Divided We Stand: The Battle Over Women's Rights and Family Values that Polarized American Politics*, 270–77.

19. Mark Siegel, Memorandum for the Record, 23 Jan. 1979, Vertical File, Middle East, JCL.

20. First Lady's comments, 19 Jan. 1979, Staff Secretary, Handwriting File, box 116, JCL.

21. Peter G. Bourne, *Carter: A Comprehensive Biography from Plains to the Post-Presidency*, 435–36.

22. Carter, *Public Papers, 1979, Vol. I*, 103–109.

23. Author interview with Stansfield Turner, 6 April 1992, Stennis Oral History Collection, Mississippi State University.

24. Sandra Mackey, *The Iranians: Persia, Islam, and the Soul of a Nation*, 277–78;

25. Carter Notes, 1 Feb. 1979, Staff Secretary, Handwriting File, box 117, JCL; Andrews, *President's Eyes Only*, 441–42; Iran Chronology, Brzezinski Collection, box 11, JCL; Shaul Bakhash, *The Reign of the Ayatollahs: Iran and the Islamic Revolution*, ix.

26. State Sketch, Declassified Document NLC-25-34-3-47-3, JCL.

27. CIA Biography of Bazargan, Declassified Document NLC-25-34-3-56-4, JCL.

28. Notes from the Director, No. 39, 7 Feb. 1979, Declassified Document NLC-6-59-3-0-7, JCL.

29. Kenneth M. Pollack, *The Persian Puzzle: The Conflict between Iran and America*, 136–37; Author interview with Turner, 6 April 1992, Stennis Oral History Collection, Mississippi State University.

30. Carter, *Public Papers, 1979, Vol. I*, 269, 295; Afghanistan, VF, JCL; *Redwood City (CA) Tribune*, 19 Feb., 1979; Press Release, 20 Feb. 1979, Staff Secretary, Handwriting File, box 120, JCL; Anatoly Dobrynin, *In Confidence: Moscow's Ambassador to Six American Cold War Presidents*, 435; Stuart E. Eizenstat, *President Carter: The White House Years*, 636–39; Nancy Mitchell, *Jimmy Carter in Africa: Race and the Cold War*, 510–13.

31. Pollack, *The Persian Puzzle*, 153; Stansfield Turner, *Secrecy and Democracy: The CIA in Transition*, 129–30.
32. Robert Wright, *Our Man in Tehran*, 87; Robin Wright, *In the Name of God: The Khomeini Decade*, 60–64, 75; Memorandum, Charles Duncan to Carter, 16 Feb. 1979, Staff Secretary Handwriting File, box 120, JCL; Jimmy Carter, *Keeping Faith: Memoirs of a President*, 453; Gordon A. Craig and Francis L. Loewenheim, editors, *The Diplomats, 1939–1979*, 651, 653.
33. Carter, *Public Papers, 1979, Vol. I*, 275.
34. Ibid., 272–92 (quotations on 278–79).
35. *New York Times*, 16 Feb. 1979.
36. *Washington Post*, 8 March 1979.
37. *New York Times*, 28 Feb., 1979, other stories on 16, 22, 26 Feb. 1979; Carter's notes from his diary, 22, 23, 24, 27, 1979, Staff Secretary, Handwriting File, box 234, JCL; Carter, *Public Papers, 1979, Vol. I*, 255–64, 348.
38. *New York Times*, 3 Feb. 1979.
39. Scott Kaufman, *Rosalynn Carter: Equal Partner in the White House*, 46; Transcript, ABC News Now Time Tunnel, 7 Feb., 2007; *Americus Times-Recorder*, 7 Feb. 1979; *Washington Post*, 8 Feb. 1979.
40. Carter, *Public Papers, 1979, Vol. I*, 300–306; *New York Times*, 20 Feb., 1979; Memorandum, Brzezinski and Jerry Rafshoon to Carter, 12 Feb. 1979, Staff Secretary, Handwriting File, box 119, JCL; Department of State Bulletin, March 1979, No. 57; Carter's Remarks, 24 Feb. 1979, Staff Secretary, Handwriting File, box 121, JCL.
41. Note, Carter to Califano, 27 March 1979, Staff Secretary, Handwriting File, box 124, JCL; Jordan to Califano, 10 April 1979, Jordan File, box 33, JCL; JC, *White House Diary*, 308; Frank Moore to Speaker O'Neill, 8 March 1979, WHCF, Name File, Tip O'Neill, JCL.
42. *Washington Star*, 6 April 1979, with Rosalynn's comment, Staff Secretary, Handwriting File, box 126, JCL.
43. Memorandum, Cade to Rosalynn Carter, Re Hearing on the Mental Health Systems Act, 24 May 1979, with Carter comment, Staff Secretary, Handwriting File, box 233, JCL; Rosalynn note to Jimmy on Memorandum, Tom Bryant to Rosalynn Carter, RE Mental Health Matters, 29 March 1979, Staff Secretary, Handwriting File, box 125, JCL; Kaufmann, *Rosalynn Carter*, 47; Dumbrell, *Carter Presidency*, 33.
44. Bourne, *Jimmy Carter*, 432–35.
45. JC, *White House Diary*, 311–12, 316, 323, 325–26; Jack Nelson interview with Rosalynn, *Los Angeles Times*, 6 April 1979.
46. Emily Walker Cook, "Women White House Advisers in the Carter Administration: Presidential Stalwarts or Feminist Advocates?," PhD dissertation, 186, 194, 198; *Atlanta Constitution*, 27 April 1979; *New York Times*, 27 April 1979; Speech in First Lady Office Projects, Cade, box 29, with attached letter from Rosalynn dated 6 Oct 1977, JCL; RSC, *First Lady*, 286–88; Dumbrell, *Carter Presidency*, 75–76.
47. Carter, *Public Papers, 1979, Vol. II*, 1876–77, *1977, Vol. I*, 955.
48. Theodore M. Hesburgh, *God, Country, Notre Dame*, 143–53, 274–78; Ellen Weiss and Mel Friedman, *Jimmy Carter, Champion of Peace*, 115.

Chapter 21

1. Peter G. Bourne, *Jimmy Carter: A Comprehensive Biography from Plains to the Post-Presidency*, 437; Jimmy Carter, *Keeping Faith: Memoirs of a President*, 413.
2. Carter notes on lunch with Stu, Ed, Bob, Ros, Fritz, 1 March 1979, Staff Secretary, Handwriting File, box 121, JCL.
3. Jimmy Carter, *White House Diary*, 297–298; JC, *Keeping Faith*, 413–15, quoting Diary for 2 March 1979; Carter, *Public Papers, 1979, Vol. I*, 372, 374–75.
4. JC, *White House Diary*, 298.
5. JC, *White House Diary*, 298–99; Carter, *Public Papers, 1979, Vol. I*, 374–75.
6. Rosalynn to Gay Vance, 5 March 1979, WHCF, Name File, Vance, JCL.
7. JC, *White House Diary*, 299.
8. Ibid.
9. Carter, *Public Papers, 1979, Vol. I*, 382.
10. JC, *Keeping Faith*, 416.
11. JC, *White House Diary*, 299.
12. Carter, *Public Papers, 1979, Vol. I*, 383; JC, *White House Diary*, 298–99; JC, *Keeping Faith*, 415–17.
13. JC, *White House Diary*, 299–300.
14. Department of State Document, 7–14 March 1979, copy in First Lady Press Office, State Dinners, box 23, JCL; *New York Times*, 9 March 1979. See also Robert A. Strong, *Working in the World: Jimmy Carter and the Making of American Foreign Policy*, 196–97.
15. Carter, *Public Papers, 1979, Vol. I*, 407–12.
16. Jehan Sadat, *A Woman of Egypt*, 402–403; JC, *White House Diary*, 299–300; JC, *Keeping Faith*, 417–19; Carter, *Public Papers, 1979, Vol. I*, 402 (quotation), 405–15.
17. Department of State Document, 7–14 March 1979, First Lady Press Office, State Dinners, box 23, JCL; JC, *White House Diary*, 301–303; Sadat, *Woman of Egypt*, 303.
18. Carter, *Public Papers, 1979, Vol. I*, 426.
19. Carter speech to Knesset with notes, 12 March 1979, Staff Secretary, Handwriting File, box 122, JCL; Carter's Personal Notes from Mid East Trip, 8–13 March 1979, Plains File, box 28, JCL; Carter, *Public Papers, 1979, Vol. I*, 415–30; Carter, *White House Diary*, 302–303; Strong, *Working in the World*, 197–200; Philomena Jurey, *A Basement Seat to History: Tales of Covering Presidents Nixon, Ford, Carter, and Reagan for Voice of America*, 177–80; William B. Quandt, *Camp David: Peacemaking and Politics*, 23; William B. Quandt, *Peace Process: American Diplomacy and the Arab-Israeli Conflict since 1967*, 315–21; Cyrus Vance, *Hard Choices: Critical Years in America's Foreign Policy*, 243–45.
20. Pool Report, 11 March 1979, First Lady Press Office, box 8, JCL.
21. JC, *White House Diary*, 303; JC, *Keeping Faith*, 425.
22. Carter, *Public Papers, 1979, Vol. I*, 429.
23. JC, *Keeping Faith*, 424.
24. Carter, *Public Papers, 1979, Vol. I*, 430.
25. Susan Clough to Carter, 13 March 1979, Plains File, box 28, JCL.

26. Sadat, *Woman of Egypt*, 404; O'Neill quoted in JC, *White House Diary*, 303–304.

27. Bourne, *Carter*, 439; Jack Watson, Miller Center Interview, 105, JCL; Author interview with Cyrus Vance, 1 May 1992, pp. 14–15, Stennis Oral History Collection, Mississippi State University.

28. Dennis Ross, *Doomed to Succeed: The U.S.-Israel Relationship from Truman to Obama*, 148, 177.

29. Department of State Publication 8971, Near Eastern and South Asian Series 89, March 1979, JCL; Carter, *Public Papers, 1979, Vol. I*, 430–32; Quandt, *Peace Process*, 321.

30. JC, *White House Diary*, 304; JC, *Keeping Faith*, 426.

31. Memorandum, Harold Brown to Carter, 16 March 1979, Staff Secretary, Handwriting File, box 123, JCL; JC, *White House Diary*, 304–306; Carter to Speaker O'Neill, 9 April 1979, WHCF, box CO-24, JCL; Lawrence Wright, *Thirteen Days in September: Carter, Begin, and Sadat at Camp David*, 271–74; Carter, *Public Papers, 1979, Vol. I*, 495–527. Carter requested supplemental appropriations in the amount of $1,470,000,000 for fiscal year 1979 for foreign assistance in support of the peace treaty between Egypt and Israel, Special International Assistance Act of 1979, 96th Congress, 1st session, H. doc. 92.

32. Memorandum, Gretchen Poston to the Carters, 24 March 1979, First Lady Press Office, State Dinners, box 23, JCL.

33. Hugh Sidey, *Portraits of the Presidents: Power and Personality in the Oval Office*, 135.

34. Daniel Gordis, *Menachem Begin: The Battle for Israel's Soul*, 179.

35. Avital Shcharansky to Mr. President, April 1979, WHCF, box CO-60, JCL.

36. JC, *White House Diary*, 307–308; Jurey, *A Basement Seat to History*, 180–81: Quandt, *Peace Process*, 329–30; Jody Powell, *The Other Side of the Story*, 55; Lawrence H. Shoup, *The Carter Presidency and Beyond: Power and Politics in the 1980s*, 120–22.

37. Sidey, *Portraits of the Presidents*, 135.

38. Sadat, *A Woman of Egypt*, 405, 409; JC, *Keeping Faith*, 427–28; *Washington Post*, 3 April 1979.

39. Memorandum, Edward Sanders to Carter, Re Sanders trips, 7 May 1979, Staff Secretary, Handwriting File, box 130, JCL.

40. *Washington Post*, 26 April 1979; JC, *White House Diary*, 311, 315 (quotation, emphasis added); PDD, 24 April 1979, JCL; Carter, *Public Papers, 1979, Vol. I*, 687–90; Kathryn J. McGarr, *The Whole Damn Deal: Robert Strauss and the Art of Politics*, 249–51, 255–58.

Chapter 22

1. PDD, 1 April, 1979, JCL; Jimmy Carter, *White House Diary*, 309–11; Alan I. Marcus and Amy Sue Bix, *The Future is Now: Science and Technology Policy in America since 1950*, 163–66; *New York Times*, 17 April 1979.

2. Memorandum, Rafshoon and Hertzberg to Carter, with Carter notes, 1 April 1979, Staff Secretary, Handwriting File, box 125, JCL; Carter, *Public Papers, 1979, Vol. I*, 609–14.

3. PDD, 5 April 1979, JCL.

4. *Atlanta Journal and Constitution*, 29 Oct. 1995; Carter's successor, Ronald Reagan, took the solar panels down in 1986, and they were placed in various museums in the United States, China, and at the Jimmy Carter Presidential Library and Museum in Atlanta.

5. David Biello, "Where Did the Carter White House's Solar Panels Go?," *Scientific American*, 6 Aug. 2010; Carter, *Public Papers, 1979, Vol. I*, 1097–1107; PDD, 20 June 1979, JCL.

6. JC, *White House Diary*, 312–13; PDD, 9, 11 April, 1979, JCL; Carter to O'Neill, 20 March 1979, Clough File, box 46, JCL.

7. JC, *White House Diary*, 312; Memorandum, Vance to Carter, 20 April 1979, Declassified Document NLC-7-21-6-2-3, JCL.

8. Memorandum, Carter to Top Administration Officials, with attachments, 28 April 1979, Staff Secretary, Handwriting File, box 128, JCL; Carter to O'Neill, 10 March 1979, Clough File, box 46, JCL; Carter, *Public Papers, 1979, Vol. I*, 386–89; PDD, 20 April 1979, JCL.

9. JC Notes, telephone calls while at Camp David, 4/7/79–4/8/79, Staff Secretary, Handwriting File, box 126, JCL; JC, *Keeping Faith*, 238–39; Christopher Andrew, *For the President's Eyes Only: Secret Intelligence and the American Presidency from Washington to Bush*, 443; Dale R. Herspring, *The Pentagon and the Presidency: Civil-Military Relations from FDR to George W. Bush*, 419.

10. JC, *White House Diary*, 313; PDD, 20 April 1979, JCL.

11. Carter Interview, *Atlanta Journal and Constitution*, 29 Oct. 1995; Author interview with Carter, 12 Oct. 1994; Jody Powell, *The Other Side of the Story*, 104–107; Amber Roessner, *Jimmy Carter and the Birth of the Marathon Media Campaign*, 201–202.

12. JC, *White House Diary*, 311, 314, 32, 322; PDD, 24 April 1979, JCL; Memorandum, Ed Sanders to Jordan and Wise, Re Iranian Jews, with Carter note, 14 May 1979, Staff Secretary, Handwriting File, box 130, JCL.

13. Fallows to Carter, with Carter note to Jody, 4 April 1979, Clough File, box 45, JCL; Lynn Darling, "'Passionless Presidency' and the Insider's Dilemma," *Washington Post*, 25 April 1979 (contains Fallows confession and self-defense); Robert A. Strong, *Working in the World: Jimmy Carter and the Making of American Foreign Policy*, 121.

14. *New York Times*, 22 April 1979. With the passage of time, and the goodwill of both Fallows and the Carters, forgiveness prevailed as they reestablished a decent relationship. Fallows progressed to a long, distinguished, and liberal career in journalism.

15. *Washington Post*, 25 April 1979; Susan S. Clough to Jim Fallows, 31 May 1979, Fallows to Clough, 3 May 1979, both in WHCF, Box RE-4, JCL; Frank Moore, Miller Center Interview, 83, JCL.

16. *New York Times*, 17 April 1979; Carter, *Public Papers, 1979, Vol. I*, 558–59 (quotation on 558).

17. Memorandum, Vance to Carter, 20 April 1979, Declassified Document NLC-7-21-6-2-3, JCL; JC, *White House Diary*, 315-17; John Dumbrell, *The Carter Presidency: A Re-evaluation*, 127.

18. Agenda for Meeting with First Lady, 3 May 1979, WHCF, First Lady Social, Subject box 35, JCL; Remarks to the Medical Society 7 May 1979, First Lady Press Office, Project Mental Health, box 18, JCL.
19. Hugh Sidey, "Second Most Powerful Person," *Time*, 7 May 1979.
20. B. Drummond Ayers, Jr., "The Importance of Being Rosalynn," *New York Times Magazine*, 3 June 1979, pp. 39–49.
21. Richard Gardner to Carter, 11 May 1979, WHCF, box PP-3, JCL; *New York Times*, 11 May 1979.
22. JC, *White House Diary*, 319; Carter to Willie Nelson, 23 May 1979, WHCF, box PP-81, JCL; Author interview with Jimmy and Rosalynn Carter, 12 JC, Oct. 1994; Willie Nelson, *It's a Long Story: My Life*, 250–51.
23. JC, *White House Diary*, 97, 320–21; Memorandum, Brzezinski to Carter, NSC Weekly Reports # 96 and # 97, 12, 15 May 1979, Brzezinski Collection, box 42, JCL.
24. Speech in Staff Secretary, Handwriting File, box 132, JCL; Carter, *Public Papers, 1979, Vol. I*, 908–13.

Chapter 23

1. Jimmy Carter, *Keeping Faith: Memoirs of a President*, 239–40.
2. Carter, *Public Papers, 1979, Vol. I*, 693–99 (quotations on 694 and 699).
3. Memorandum, Brzezinski to Carter, NSC Weekly Report # 98, 15 May 1979, Brzezinski Collection, box 42, JCL; Anatoly Dobrynin, *In Confidence: Moscow's Ambassador to America's Six Cold War Presidents*, 428–29.
4. Jimmy Carter, *White House Diary*, 321–22.
5. *Washington Star*, 29 May 1979; John Prados, *Keepers of the Keys: A History of the National Security Council from Truman to Bush*, 300–308.
6. JC, *White House Diary*, 318–19.
7. Carter, *Public Papers, 1979, Vol. I*, 832–36 (quotations on 834, 833); *New York Times*, 11 May 1979.
8. *New York Times*, 11 May 1979.
9. JC, *White House Diary*, 326.
10. *New York Times*, 15 June 1979. See also JC, *White House Diary*, 326.
11. *New York Times*, 15 June 1979.
12. JC, *White House Diary*, 318, 319, 324.
13. Memorandum, Sanders to Carter, 6 June 1979, WHCF, box HU-3, and Brzezinski Collection, box 19, JCL. See also Carter, *Public Papers, 1979, Vol. I*, 626–28.
14. Carter, *Public Papers, 1979, Vol. I*, 1038–39; Handwritten memorandum, Carter to "Top Administration Officials, 28 April 1979, with "Salt II: The Reasons Why" (U. S. Department of State, Bureau of Public Affairs, Washington, D.C., May 1979) attached, Staff Secretary, Handwriting File, box 128, JCL. See also Lloyd Jensen, "Negotiating Strategic Arms Control, 1969–1979," *Journal of Conflict Resolution* 28, no. 3 (September 1984), 535–59.
15. *New York Times*, 15, 17, 18, 1979.

16. *New York Times*, 18 June 1979.
17. Carter, *Public Papers 1979, I*, 1047–48; *New York Times*, 15 June 1979.
18. *New York Times*, 16 June 1979.
19. JC, *White House Diary*, 326; *Americus Times-Recorder*, 15 June 1979; JC, *Keeping Faith*, 244.
20. JC, *Keeping Faith*, 244–45.
21. Ibid., 244.
22. *New York Times*, 16 June 1979.
23. Ibid.
24. *New York Times*, 17 June 1979.
25. Ibid.
26. JC, *Keeping Faith*, 246–47.
27. Ibid., 247–48.
28. Ibid., 248–49.
29. JC, *White House Diary*, 328; JC, *Keeping Faith*, 250–51.
30. Carter, *Public Papers, 1979, Vol. I*, 1048.
31. JC, *White House Diary*, 328; JC, *Keeping Faith*, 251.
32. JC, Keeping Faith, 251–53 (quotation on 252).
33. JC, *White House Diary*, 329.
34. JC, *Keeping Faith*, 254–56; see also *New York Times*, 18 June 1979.
35. JC, *Keeping Faith*, 257.
36. Ibid., 257–58.
37. Ibid., 258–59.
38. JC, *Keeping Faith*, 259–60; JC, *White House Diary*, 331.
39. JC, *White House Diary*, 330–31; see also Betty Glad, *Jimmy Carter in Search of the Great White House*, 435.
40. JC, *White House Diary*, 331; JC, *Keeping Faith*, 260–62; Andrei Gromyko, *Memoirs*, 288–96 ("kiss" on 291); Carter, *Public Papers, 1979, Vol. I*, 1051–87; Stuart E. Eizenstat, *President Carter: The White House Years*, 114; Philomeno Jurey, *A Basement Seat to History: Tales of Covering Presidents Nixon, Ford, Carter, and Reagan for Voice of America*, 184–85; Warren I. Cohen, *America in the Age of Soviet Power, 1945–1991*, 212; Raymond L. Garthoff, *Détente and Confrontation: American-Soviet Relations from Nixon to Reagan*, 735–37.
41. *New York Times*, 18 June 1979.
42. Ibid., 19 June, 1979; Carter, *Public Papers, 1979, Vol. I*, 1087–92.
43. JC, *White House Diary*, 332.
44. *New York Times*, 24 June 1979.
45. *National Journal*, "White House Wheels Turning for 80 Race," 10 March 1979; *New York Times*, 11 March 1979; JC, *White House Diary*, 334.
46. *New York Times*, 25 June 1979.
47. JC, *White House Diary*, 334; *New York Times*, 24, 25 1979.
48. JC, *White House Diary*, 334–35.
49. Ibid., 335.
50. Ibid.

51. Carter, *Public Papers, 1979, Vol. II*, 1187–1200.
52. *Washington Post*, 30 June 1979.
53. JC, *White House Diary*, 337–38.
54. *Washington Post*, 30 June 1979.
55. *New York Times*, 3 July 1979; Carter, *Public Papers, 1979, Vol. II*, 1202–11.

Chapter 24

1. Jefferson Cowie, *Stayin' Alive: The 1970s and the Last Days of the Working Class*, 302; Daniel Horowitz, *Jimmy Carter and the Energy Crisis of the 1970s: The "Crisis of Confidence" Speech of July 15, 1979*, 16–19.
2. Stuart E. Eizenstat, *President Carter: The White House Years*, 662–64, 667.
3. Kevin Mattson, *"What the Heck Are You Up To, Mr. President?": Jimmy Carter, America's "Malaise," and the Speech that Should Have Changed the Country*, 21–25; Elizabeth Drew, "A Reporter at Large," *New Yorker*, 27 Aug. 1979, 50–53; Joe Klein, *Politics Lost: How American Democracy Was Trivialized by People Who Think You're Stupid*, 46–54; Jonathan Alter, *His Very Best: Jimmy Carter, A Life*, 459–61.
4. Mattson, *What the Heck*, 47; Drew, "Reporter at Large," 50–53; Eizenstat, *Carter*, 667.
5. Drew, "Reporter at Large," 50–53; Eizenstat, *Carter*, 668 (Mondale quotation); Walter Mondale, *The Good Fight: A Life in Liberal Politics*, 234–35.
6. Eizenstat, *Carter*, 664.
7. Jay Hakes, *Energy Crises: Nixon, Ford, Carter, and Hard Choices in the 1970s*, 279–83.
8. Carter, *Public Papers, 1979, Vol. I*, 610–11; *Vol. II*, 1226–27.
9. J. William Holland, "The Great Gamble: Jimmy Carter and the 1979 Energy Crisis," *Prologue: Quarterly of the National Archives* 22, no. 1 (Spring 1990), 63–67; Mattson, *What the Heck*, 16, 17, 25–28, 67.
10. Mattson, *What the Heck*, 67–68; Jimmy Carter, *White House Diary*, 318.
11. Mattson, *What the Heck*, 68, 70, 77–78, 80–81.
12. JC, *White House Diary*, 342.
13. Mattson, *What the Heck*, 81–82; Peter G. Bourne, *Jimmy Carter: A Comprehensive Biography from Plains to the Post-Presidency*, 442–43; Author interview with Jimmy and Rosalynn Carter, 12 Oct. 1994; Eizenstat, *Carter*, 701–707; Jonathan Alter, *His Very Best: Jimmy Carter, A Life*, 461–62.
14. Ibid., 98–99, 106–107, 114–15, 128.
15. Mattson, *What the Heck*, 129–32; Jimmy Carter, *Keeping Faith: Memoirs of a President*, 115–116; Eizenstat, *Carter*, 675; Hakes, *Energy Crises*, 283–91.
16. Eizenstat, *Carter*, 675–76; Leo P. Ribuffo, "'Malaise' Revisited: Jimmy Carter and the Crisis of Confidence," in John Patrick Diggins, *The Liberal Persuasion: Arthur Schlesinger, Jr., and the Challenge of the American Past*, 165–66.
17. Patrick Caddell, "Of Crisis and Opportunity," Powell File, box 40, JCL; Drew, "A Reporter at Large," 53–60; Holland, "The Great Gamble," 71; Mattson, *What the Heck*, 4; Laura Kalman, *Right Star Rising: A New Politics,1974–1980*, 327–29; Eizenstat, *Carter*, 677; Eizenstat, Miller Center Interview, 80–81, JCL.

18. Mondale, *The Good Fight*, 236–37; Eizenstat, *Carter*, 682–83; Memorandum, Jordan to Carter, 3 July 1979, Jordan Papers, box 37, JCL; Mattson, *What the Heck*, 5–6; Bourne, *Carter*, 443–44; Rosalynn Carter, *First Lady from Plains*, 302–303; W. Dale Nelson, *The President is at Camp David*, 125.

19. William H. Cable, Miller Center Interview, 9, JCL; Bourne, *Carter*, 446; Kalman, *Right Star Rising*, 329–30: Eizenstat, Miller Center Interview, 81, JCL; Joseph A. Califano, Jr., *Inside a Public and Private Life*, 334; Chris Matthews, *Hardball: How Politics is Played by One Who Knows the Game*, 98–103.

20. Griffin Bell, Miller Center Interview, 58, JCL; Bob Bergland, Miller Center Interview, 32, 58–62, JCL.

21. JC, *White House Diary*, 340–41; JC, *Keeping Faith*, 116–17.

22. Hamilton Jordan, Miller Center Interview, 64, JCL.

23. Carter, Miller Center Interview, 54, JCL.

24. E. Stanly Godbold, Jr., *Jimmy and Rosalynn Carter: The Georgia Years, 1924–1974*, 242–43; Memorandum, Jack Watson to Carter, 6 July 1979, Re Governors, Staff Secretary, Handwriting File, box 237, JCL.

25. Mattson, *What the Heck*, 140, 137–38; David Barber, *The Presidential Character: Predicting Performance in the White House*, 434.

26. Gordon Stewart, Op-Ed piece, *New York Times*, 14 July 2009; JC, *Keeping Faith*, 118.

27. Mattson, *What the Heck*, 135; *Washington Post National Weekly Edition*, 27 July–2 Aug. 2009, 38; Ribuffo, " 'Malaise' Revisited,"125.

28. Mattson, *What the Heck*, 135–37; *Washington Post National Weekly Edition*, 27 July–2 Aug. 2009; Eizenstat, *Carter*, 683–88.

29. Mattson, *What the Heck*, 140–41.

30. Mattson, *What the Heck*, 141–44; JC, *White House Diary*, 343; Reinhold Niebuhr, *Moral Man and Immoral Society*.

31. Carter notes on telephone call, 6 July 1979, Staff Secretary, Handwriting File, box 137, JCL.

32. JC, *White House Diary*, 341–42; Telegram, Gary Sick to Carter, 10 July 1979, Declassified Document NLC-16-127-6-39-6, JCL.

33. Memorandum, Tim Kraft to First Lady, 7 July 1979, Re Call sheets; Memorandum, Kraft to Carter, 21 July 1979, Re Call sheets, with Carter notes, Tim Kraft Papers, box 2, JCL.

34. JC, *White House Diary*, 342.

35. JC, *White House Diary*, 343; Drew, "Reporter at Large," 71; Kalman, *Right Star Rising*, 326–27.

36. Memorandum, Caddell to Carter, 12 July 1979, Handwriting File, box 138, JCL; JC, *White House Diary*, 343.

37. Memorandum, Tim Kraft to Hamilton Jordan, 13 July 1979, Tim Kraft Donated Material, box 2, JCL; Note, Ham to Rosalynn, n.d., Jordan File, box 34, JCL; Daniel Horowitz, *Jimmy Carter and the Energy Crisis of the 1970s*, 91–94.

38. Master copy of speech 14 July 1979, Staff Secretary, Handwriting File, box 138.

39. Mattson, *What the Heck*, 155 (quotation); *Washington Post National Weekly Edition*, 27 July–2 Aug. 2009, p. 38; Author interview with Gordon Stewart, 22 Feb. 1997; Eizenstat, *Carter*, 689.
40. PDD, 15 July 1979, JCL.
41. Draft of Speech, handwritten, Staff Secretary, Handwriting File, box 139, JCL; Carter, *Public Papers, 1979, Vol. II*, 1235–41; Mattson, *What the Heck*, 7; RSC, *First Lady*, 303.
42. RSC, *First Lady*, 303; PDD, 15 July 1979, JCL.
43. Handwritten note, Carter to Caddell, 16 July 1979, Staff Secretary, Handwriting File, box 139, JCL.
44. Kevin Mattson, National Public Radio, 12 July 2009; Mattson, *What the Heck*, 156–59.
45. PDD, 15 July 1979, JCL; Bourne, *Carter*, 445.
46. Carter, *Public Papers, 1979, Vol. II*, 1241–47.
47. Daniel Horowitz, *The Anxieties of Affluence: Critiques of American Consumer Culture, 1939–1979*, 244 (quotation); Mattson, *What the Heck*, 159–62; Folder containing many letters re the speech, 15 July 1979, Staff Secretary, Handwriting File, box 139, JCL; Eizenstat, *Carter*, 691–93; Horowitz, *Jimmy Carter and the Energy Crisis of the 1970s*, 120–51; Richard V. Pierard and Robert D. Linder, *Civil Religion and the Presidency*, 255.
48. Clark Clifford, *Counsel to the President: A Memoir*, 634–36.
49. E. Stanly Godbold, Jr., "Kennedy, Carter Shared a Similar Vision," *Atlanta Journal and Constitution*, 30 Aug. 2009; *New York Times*, 2 Aug. 2009.
50. Oliver Howard to Carter, 17 July 1979, Staff Offices, Cabinet Secretary, Watson, box 32, JCL.
51. Memoranda, Jordan to Carter and Powell to Carter, 15 July 1979, Jordan File, box 33, JCL; Author interview with Vance, 14 July 1992, p. 7, John C. Stennis Oral History Project, Mississippi State University; JC, *White House Diary*, 344–45.
52. Eizenstat, *Carter*, 696–701. See also J. William Holland, "The Great Gamble: Jimmy Carter and the 1979 Energy Crisis," *Prologue: Quarterly of the National Archives* 22, no. 1 (Spring 1990), 63–79.
53. Jordan to Carter, "Eyes Only," 16 July 1979, Jordan File, box 34, JCL.
54. Jordan to Carter, 17 July 1979, Jordan File, box 34, JCL.
55. David F. Schmitz, *The United States and Right-Wing Dictatorships*, 182–92; Morris H. Morley, *Washington, Somoza, and the Sandinistas: State and Regime in U.S. Policy toward Nicaragua, 1969–1981*, 116–19; Derek N. Buckaloo, "Carter's Nicaragua and Other Democratic Quagmires," in Bruce J. Schulman and Julian E. Zelizer, editors, *Rightward Bound: Making America Conservative in the 1970s*, 248–62: Malcolm Byrne, *Iran-Contra: Reagan's Scandal and the Unchecked Abuse of Presidential Power*, 16–17.
56. Carter to Califano, 19 July 1979, WHCF, Name File, Califano, JCL; Califano to Carter, Carter to Califano, Blumenthal to Carter, all 19 July 1979, all in Staff Secretary, Handwriting File, box 139, JCL; Joshua Seitz, *Building the Great Society: Inside Lyndon Johnson's White House*, 317.

57. Carter to Schlesinger, 20 July 1979, Staff Secretary, Handwriting File, box 140, JCL; JC, *White House Diary*, 346–47; PDD, 19 July 1979, JCL; White House News Summary, 21 July 1979, Richard Harden File, box 20, JCL.

58. Jerry Rafshoon to Carter, Carter to Rafshoon, Inauguration Memorandum, Jan. 1977, Staff Secretary, Handwriting File, box 2, JCL; Carter, Miller Center Interview, 6, JCL; *New York Times*, 11 Sept. 2004; Carter to Adams, 20 July 1979, Staff Secretary, Handwriting File, box 140, JCL.

59. Griffin B. Bell, *Taking Care of the Law*, 41–43; Griffin B. Bell Interview, 16 Aug. 1979, Record Group Biographical Questionnaire, GDAH; Carter to Bell, 3 Aug. 1979, Staff Secretary, Handwriting File, box 141, JCL; Carl M. Brauer, *Presidential Transitions: Eisenhower through Reagan*, 197.

60. Paul A. Volcker, *Keeping at It: The Quest for Sound Money and Good Government*, 103–104; JC, *White House Diary*, 346–48; Bourne, *Carter*, 448–49 (Lance quotation on 448); W. Carl Biven, *Jimmy Carter's Economy: Policy in an Age of Limits*, 237–40; and William L. Silber, *Volcker: The Triumph of Persistence*, 145–46, 267.

61. *Arkansas Gazette*, 23 July 1979; *Fort Worth Star-Telegram*, 24 July 1979; *New York Times*, 24 July 1979; *Los Angeles* Times, 27 July 1979.

Chapter 25

1. Jules Witcover, *Party of the People: A History of the Democrats*, 606–608; Edward M. Kennedy, *True Compass: A Memoir*, 357–67; Eric Alterman and Kevin Mattson, *The Cause: The Fight for American Liberalism from Franklin Roosevelt to Barack Obama*, 309; Stuart E. Eizenstat, *President Carter: The White House Years*, 837–38: Barbara A. Perry, *Edward M. Kennedy: An Oral History*, 200–19.

2. Nixon to Carter, 23 July 1979, Carter to Nixon, 27 July 1979, Clough File, box 46, JCL.

3. Jimmy Carter, *White House Diary*, 347–48; Carter to Ribicoff, 17 July 1979, WHCF, Name File, A. Ribicoff, JCL; Gerard H. Clarfield and William M. Wiecek, *Nuclear America: Military and Civilian Nuclear Power in the United States, 1940-1980*, 427–28, 435–36.

4. JC, *White House Diary*, 347–48; Carter to Ribicoff, 17 July 1979, WHCF, Name File, A. Ribicoff, JCL; Clarfield and Wiecek, *Nuclear America*, 427–28, 435–36.

5. Andrew Cockburn and Leslie Cockburn, *Dangerous Liaison: The Inside Story of the U.S.-Israeli Covert Relationship*, 313; Sasha Polakow-Suransky, *The Unspoken Alliance: Israel's Secret Relationship with Apartheid South Africa*, 176.

6. Author interview with Cyrus Vance, 1 May 1991, pp. 22–24, (quotations), Stennis Oral History Project, Mississippi State University; JC, *White House Diary*, 351; Author interview with Jimmy Carter, 12 Oct. 1994; *Americus Times-Recorder*, 15 Aug. 1979; Andrew J. DeRoche, *Andrew Young: Civil Rights Ambassador*, 111–14; Bartlett C. Jones, *Flawed Triumphs: Andy Young at the United Nations*, 132–33.

7. Carter comments at swearing in ceremony for Donald McHenry, 22 Sept. 1979, Staff Secretary, Handwriting File, box 148, JCL; PDD, 15 Aug. 1979, JCL; Author interview with Jimmy Carter, 12 Oct. 1994; JC, *White House Diary*, 352; DeRoche, *Andrew*

Young, 71-72; *Memphis Commercial Appeal*, 22 Jan. 2002; Gaddis Smith, *Morality, Reason and Power: American Diplomacy in the Carter Years*, 140–45; Herman E. Talmadge, *Talmadge: A Political Legacy, A Politician's Life*, 218.

8. Young Resigns, Memoranda, President Carter, 5/1/79–9/24/79, Powell File, box 40, JCL; Carter to Young, 15 Aug., 1979, Staff Secretary, Handwriting File, box 142, JCL; *Atlanta Journal and Constitution*, 15 Aug., 1993; *Washington Post*, 16, 17 Aug. 1979; *Washington Star, Atlanta Constitution, New York Times*, all 16 Aug. 1979.

9. *New York Times*, 2 Nov. 1979; JC, *White House Diary*, 349–50.

10. Zia-ul-Haq to Carter, 9 Aug. 1979, NSA Staff Material/North-South, Thornton/Country, box 96, JCL.

11. Rosalynn's schedule, 8–10 Aug.1979, First Lady Press Office, Foreign Trips, box 24, JCL; *Washington Post*, 16 Aug. 1979.

12. Interview with Dennis Brown by Richard McMurry, 11–18 Sept. 1997, author's private collection.

13. Memorandum, Lloyd Cutler to Carter, Re Jordan Investigation, 25 Sept. 1979, Staff Secretary, Handwriting File, box 148, JCL; Cynthia LeJeune Nobles, *The Delta Queen Cookbook: The History and Recipes of the Legendary Steamboat*, 105–107; *Washington Post*, 21 Aug. 1979; *New York Times*, 22 Aug. 1970; JC, *White House Diary*, 352–53; Telegram, Moore to Carter, 17 Aug. 1979, Staff Secretary, Handwriting File, box 143, JCL; *Atlanta Constitution*, 23 Aug. 1979; Susan Clough to Sarah MacClendon, enclosing copy of MacClendon's article annotated by Carter, 28 Sept. 1979, WHCF, box PP-1, JCL.

14. *Americus Times-Recorder*, 3 Sept. 1979; PDD, 30, 31 Aug., 1, 2, 3, Sept. 1979, JCL; JC, *White House Diary*, 353–54.

15. Pool Report # 10, Marty Tolchin, *New York Times*, 1 Sept. 1979, Press Office, Granum File, box 20, JCL.

16. First Lady Press Office, Trips, 4 Sept. 1979, box 15, and Projects, Cade, 5 Sept. 1979, box 18, JCL; Margaret Shannon, "The First Lady Fights Back," *Atlanta Journal and Constitution Magazine*, 2 Sept. 1979.

17. JC, *White House Diary*, 355–56 (quotations on 356, 362, 365, 367).

18. *Atlanta Constitution*, 11 Sept. 1979.

19. Quoted in Adam Clymer, *Edward M. Kennedy: A Biography*, 285.

20. JC, *White House Diary*, 355; W. Dale Nelson, *The President Is at Camp David*, 132.

21. Memorandum, Brzezinski to Jordan, 18 Sept. 1979, Declassified Document NLC-24-45-7-1-8, JCL; *New York Times*, 18 Sept. 1979; JC, *White House Diary*, 393.

22. JC, *White House Diary*, 355; Executive Order 12148, 20 July 1979.

23. *New York Times*, 31 Aug. 1979.

24. Author interview with Stansfield Turner, 6 April 1992, Stennis Oral History Project, Mississippi State University; Robert A. Strong, *Working in the World: Jimmy Carter and the Making of Foreign Policy*, 227–32.

25. JC, *White House Diary*, 356.

26. Clark Clifford, *Counsel to the President: A Memoir*, 638.

27. Ibid., 638–39; Christopher Andrew, *For the President's Eyes Only: Secret Intelligence and the American Presidency from Washington to Bush*, 446.

28. Carter, *Public Papers, 1979, Vol. II*, 1802–1806; Teleprompter Notes, 28 Sept. 1979, White House Press File, Anne Edwards, box 5, JCL.

29. JC, *White House Diary*, 358–59.

30. Quoted in Andrew, *President's Eyes Only*, 447.

31. Brzezinski to Turner, 20 Sept. 1979, Re Afghanistan, VF, Afghanistan, JCL.

32. Memorandum, Thomas Thornton to Brzezinski, 17 Sept. 1979, Declassified Document NLC-24-91-1-77, JCL; Memorandum, Thomas Thornton to Brzezinski, 24 Sept. 1979, VF, Afghanistan, JCL.

33. Carter to O'Neill, 1 Oct. 1979, Clough File, box 46, JCL.

34. JC, *White House Diary*, 364, 366.

35. First Lady Office Projects, Cade, box 29, JCL; *Washington Post*, 2 Oct. 1979; Rosalynn to Millie and Tip O'Neill, 2 Oct. 1979, WHCF, Name File, Tip O'Neill, JCL; Hoyt Collection, box 1, JCL.

36. Pool Report, 6 Oct. 1979, and Press Statement, 6 Oct. 1979, both in Powell File, box 69, JCL.

37. JC, *White House Diary*, 360; Eizenstat, *Carter*, 604.

38. JC, *White House Diary*, 360–61.

39. Ibid., 361; Carter's notes for speech, 6 Oct. 1979, Staff Secretary, Handwriting File, box 150, JCL.

40. *New York Times*, 3 Oct. 1979.

41. Carter, *Public Papers, 1979, Vol. II*, 1816; Memorandum, Powell to Carter, 2 Oct. 1979, Powell File, box 40, JCL.

42. JC, *White House Diary*, 461–62.

43. Memoranda, Paul Watson Irwin to Rosalynn Carter, 16 Oct. 1979, Gretchen Poston to Rosalynn Carter, 12 Oct. 1979, both in First Lady Press File, box 10, JCL.

44. Eizenstat to Carter, 18 Oct.1979, Staff Secretary, Handwriting File, box 152, JCL.

45. *Ashland (OR) Daily Tidings*, 20 Oct. 1979; *New York Daily News*, *New York Times*, 21 Oct. 1979; video in George H. W. Bush and other presidential libraries; Larry J. Sabato, *The Kennedy Half Century: The Presidency, An Assassination, and Lasting Legacy of John F. Kennedy*, 330 (Carter quotation).

46. Draft of Kennedy Library remarks, 16 Oct. 1979, Staff Secretary, Handwriting File, box 152, JCL.

47. Memorandum, Rick Hertzberg to Carter, with Carter note, 7 Oct. 1979, Speech Writers File, Hertzberg, box 1, JCL.

48. Carter, *Public Papers, 1979, Vol. II*, 1979–82 (quotation on 1982); Carter's Speech, 20 Oct. 1979, White House Press Office, Granum, box 108, JCL; JC, *White House Diary*, 363.

49. JFK Library.Org/1979 Dedication Remarks by President Carter; Carter, *Public Papers, 1979, Vol. II*, 1979–82.

50. Pamela Harriman to Carter, 20 Oct. 1979, WHCF, Name, Harriman, JCL; Memorandum, Hedley Donovan to Carter, 22 Oct. 1979, Donovan File, box 2, JCL.

51. JFK Library.org 1979 Dedication Remarks by Senator Kennedy.

52. *New York Times*, 20 Oct. 1979; *Boston Herald American*, *New York Daily News*, *Washington Star*, all 21 Oct. 1979; *Boston Globe*, 22 Oct. 1979; Clymer, *Edward*

M. Kennedy, 290–91: Timothy Stanley, *Kennedy vs. Carter: The 1980 Battle for the Democratic Party's Soul*, 94–96.

53. *Boston Globe*, 26 Oct. 1979; Kandy Stroud, "The Steel Magnolia," *Cosmopolitan*, Oct. 1979, 291–93, 332–34.

54. Memorandum, Jordan to Donovan, 24 Oct. 1979, Re Country Music Stars, Staff Secretary, Handwriting File, box 241, JCL; Benjamin Mayes to Carter, with Carter note, 25 Oct. 1979, Staff Secretary, Handwriting File, box 153, JCL (quotations).

55. PDD, 1–31 Oct. 1979, JCL; Kristina Spohr, *The Global Chancellor: Helmut Schmidt & the Reshaping of the International Order*, 5, 91–92.

56. Andrew Scott Cooper, *The Fall of Heaven: The Pahlavis and the Final Days of Imperial Iran*, 234–35; Jimmy Carter, *Keeping Faith: Memoirs of a President*, 452–54.

57. Abbas Milani, *The Shah*, 383, 386–87; Eizenstat, *Carter*, 761; David Farber, *Taken Hostage: The Iran Hostage Crisis and America's First Encounter with Radical Islam*, 100–101.

58. Kai Bird, *The Chairman: John J. McCloy and the Making of the American Establishment*, 641, 644–45 (quotation); Pierre Salinger, *America Held Hostage: The Secret Negotiations*, 17–20; Roham Alvandi, *Nixon, Kissinger, and the Shah*, 170–75.

59. David Harris, *The Crisis: The President, the Prophet, and the Shah—1979 and the Coming of Militant Islam*, 193; Carter, Miller Center Interview, 36–37, JCL; Milani, *The Shah*, 419–22; Peter G. Bourne, *Jimmy Carter: A Comprehensive Biography from Plains to the Post-Presidency*, 455, quoting Steven Gillon, *The Democrats' Dilemma: Walter F. Mondale and the Liberal Legacy*, 271 (Carter quotation); Memorandum, Brzezinski to Carter, 20 Oct. 1979, Re the Shah, with attachments, Plains File, box 23, JCL; JC, *White House Diary*, 364; JC, *Keeping Faith*, 454–56; Hamilton Jordan, *Crisis: The Last Year of the Carter Presidency*, 31–32; Robert D. McFadden, et al., *No Hiding Place: Inside Report on the Hostage Crisis*, 149–64; Nelson, *The President is at Camp David*, 128. David Rockefeller, *Memoirs*, 356–75, denies having had a role in Carter's final decision to admit the Shah, but Salinger's *America Held Hostage*, 19–21, provides evidence that seriously incriminates Rockefeller.

60. Eizenstat, *Carter*, 761–63; Mark Bowden, *Guests of the Ayatollah: The First Battle in America's War with Militant Islam*, 19; Hamilton Jordan, Miller Center Interview, 80–82, JCL; David Crist, *The Twilight War: The Secret History of America's Thirty-Year Conflict with Iran*, 27–28; Farber, *Taken Hostage*, 124–26; Tim Wells, *444 Days: The Hostages Remember*, 26–27.

61. Telegram, Embassy Tehran to Secretary of State, Oct. 1979, Declassified Documents NLC-4-4-2-7-4 and NLC-4-40-2-8-3, both in JCL; Robin Wright, *In the Name of God: The Khomeini Decade*, 75–76; Timothy P. Maga, *The World of Jimmy Carter: U.S. Foreign Policy, 1977–1981*, 146–47.

62. Polakow-Suransky, *The Unspoken Alliance*, 111–13, 134, 136–42.

63. Interview with Howard K. Smith, 1 Nov. 1979, Powell Donated Material, box 29, JCL.

64. Carter, Miller Center Interview, 37, JCL; Shaul Bakhash, *The Reign of the Ayatollohs: Iran and the Islamic Revolution*, 70; Brzezinski to Mohamed Benhahi, 7 Nov. 1979, WHCF, box FG-29, JCL; Cooper, *The Fall of Heaven*, 449–50.

65. Eizenstat, *Carter*, 764–65; *New York Times*, 1 Nov. 1979.

66. Iran Briefing Book, 2 Nov. 1979, clipping from the *Iran Times*, White House Counsel, Cutler, box 85, JCL.

Chapter 26

1. Quoted in "Islam in Iran," Declassified Document NLC-25-43-7-2-8, JCL.

2. Jimmy Carter, *White House Diary*, 367; David Newson obituary, *New York Times*, 5 April 2008; Ervand Abrahamian, *A History of Modern Iran*, 168,

3. PDD, 4 Nov. 1979, JCL.

4. Telegram, 4 Nov. 1979, Embassy and State to White House Situation Room, Declassified Document NLC-16-67-1-2-8, JCL.

5. Ibid.

6. Timothy Naftali, *Blind Spot: The Secret History of American Counterterrorism*, 99–115.

7. Gary Sick, *All Fall Down: America's Tragic Encounter with Iran*, 228–31; William J. Daugherty, *In the Shadow of the Ayatollah: A CIA Hostage in Iran*, 122; "The Hostage Crisis in Iran," Plains File, box 24, JCL; Peter G. Bourne, *Jimmy Carter: A Comprehensive Biography from Plains to the Post-Presidency*, 452; Christopher Andrew, *For the President's Eyes Only: Secret Intelligence and the American Presidency from Washington to Bush*, 450; PDD, 4 Nov. 1979, JCL; David Crist, *The Twilight War: The Secret History of America's Thirty Year Conflict with Iran*, 29; Robin Wright, *In the Name of God: The Khomeini Decade*, 58–59, 66–69: Daniel J. Sargent, *A Superpower Transformed: A Remaking of American Foreign Relations in the 1970s, 288*.

8. JC, *White House Diary*, 368; Executive Order Blocking Iranian Government Property, 5 Nov. 1979, Staff Office-Cutler, box 89, JCL.

9. Handwritten notes on the meeting, Al M. McDonald Collection, box 11, JCL.

10. Tim Wells, *444 Days: The Hostages Remember*, 33–47.

11. Brzezinski to Carter, Declassified Document NLC-16-128-2-37-1, JCL.

12. Memorandum, "Special Coordination Committee Meeting," 5 Nov. 1979, JCL; Farah Pahlavi, *An Enduring Love: My Life with the Shah*, 329–38.

13. William Shawcross, *The Shah's Last Ride*, 278.

14. PDD, 6 Nov. 1979, JCL.

15. Carter to Quainton, 6 Nov. 1979, box JL-10, JCL.

16. JC, *White House Diary*, 374–75; Daugherty, *In the Shadow of the Ayatollah*, 126–29; Stansfield Turner, *Terrorism and Democracy*, 90–94.

17. PDD, 6 Nov. 1979, JCL.

18. Week by Week Chronology of Iranian Crisis, 4–10 Nov. 1979, White House Press File, Granum, box 65, JCL; Bourne, *Carter*, 455; JC, *White House Diary*, 368; Sargent, *A Superpower Transformed*, 288.

19. Ian Black and Benny Morris, *Israel's Secret Wars: A History of Israel's Intelligence Services*, 330–31.

20. "The Hostage Crisis in Iran," 4 Nov. 1979, Plains File, box 24, JCL; S. Res. 292, H. Res. 493, copies in White House Counsel: Cutler, box 89, JCL; PDD, 6 Nov. 1979, JCL.

21. Carter, *Public Papers, 1979, Vol. II*, 2090–91; PDD, 7 Nov. 1979, JCL.

22. Thailand Trip, 2–6 Nov. 1979, Projects, Cade, First Lady Office, box 6, JCL; First Lady Press Office, Foreign Trips, box 27, JCL; Edna Langford and Linda Maddox, *Rosalynn: Friend and First Lady*, 14–16; Katai Marton, *Hidden Power: Presidential Marriages that Shaped Our Recent History*, 217–18.

23. PDD, 7 Nov. 1979; Handwritten notes on Leadership Breakfast, 7 Nov. 1979, Al M. McDonald Collection, box 11, JCL; JC, *White House Diary*, 368; President Carter's Notes/Instructions Re Iran (Handwritten), Plains File, box 23, JCL.

24. "The Revolutionary Council Takes Charge, An Intelligence Memorandum," Nov. 1979, Declassified Document NLC-6-29-6-26, JCL; Ray Takeyh, "The Ayatollah and the U. S. Embassy," *The Weekly Standard*, 2 Feb. 2015, p. 18; Kathryn Koob, *Guest of the Revolution*, 113.

25. "Hostage Crisis in Iran: 1979–81," Plains File, box 24, JCL; Jimmy Carter, *Keeping Faith: Memoirs of a President*, 459–60; Memorandum, Anne Wexler to Jordan and Powell, 7 Nov. 1979, Wexler File, box 30, JCL; PDD, 8 Nov. 1979, JCL.

26. PDD, 8 Nov. 1979, JCL; Carter, *Public Papers, 1979, Vol. II*, 2095–97; Memorandum, Bob Beckel to Ham Jordan, RE Congressional Reaction Iran, 8 Nov. 1979, Staff Secretary, Handwriting File, box 155, JCL.

27. President Carter's Personal Notes—November 1979, Staff Secretary, Handwriting file, box 234, JCL.

28. Kathy Cade, White House Exit Interview, JCL; Rosalynn Carter, *First Lady from Plains*, 295–98; *Washington Post*, 10 Nov. 1979; *New York Times*, 10, 11 Nov. 1979; PDD, 9 Nov. 1979, JCL.

29. Speech, First Lady Press Office, Foreign Trips, box 27, JCL; *Americus Times-Recorder*, 8 Nov. 1979; Report of Mrs. Rosalynn Carter on Cambodian Relief, 8–10 Nov. 1979, First Lady Press Office, Projects, Cade, box 6, JCL; JC, *White House Diary*, 369.

30. Robert M. Gates, *From the Shadows: The Ultimate Insider's Story of Five Presidents and How They Won the Cold War*, 114.

31. "The Events of 1979–1980, JCL, referencing State Department cable 5771 to U.S. Embassy Moscow, "Brezhnev Message to President on Nuclear False Alarm," 14 November 1979, Secret, and Brigadier General Carl Smith, USAF, Military Assistant to the Secretary of Defense to William Odom, Military Assistant to the Assistant to the President for National Security Affairs, "Proposed Oral Message Response," 16 November 1979, FOIA release.

32. Pool Report, 9 Nov. 1979, Powell File, box 62, JCL; Hostage Families, 9 Nov. 1979, WHCF, box 32, JCL; *New York Times*, 16 Nov. 1979; JC, *Keeping Faith*, 460; Carter, *Public Paper, 1979, Vol. II*, 2102–2103.

33. JC, *White House Diary*, 369.

34. Langford and Maddox, *Rosalynn: Friend and First Lady*, 16–17; JC, *White House Diary*, 369; Talking Points, 12 Dec. 1979, RSC meeting with Waldheim, Speech, 12 Dec. 1979, Re Presidential Action 13 Nov. 1979, and Kathy Cade to RSC, 30 Nov. 1979, all in First Lady Office, Projects, Cade, box 6, JCL.

35. Speech, 12 Dec. 1979, First Lady Press Office, box 62, JCL.

36. Elizabeth Drew, *Portrait of an Election: The 1980 Presidential Campaign*, 32–35; JC, *White House Diary*, 367 (quotation); *Time Magazine*, 7 Sept. 2009, p. 36;

E. Stanly Godbold, Jr., "Kennedy, Carter Share a Similar Vision," *Atlanta Journal and Constitution*, 30 Aug. 2009, A13; Bourne, *Carter*, 456; Larry J. Sabato, *The Kennedy Half Century: The Presidency, An Assassination, and Lasting Legacy of John F. Kennedy*, 328; Robert Shogan, *Bad News: Where the Press Goes Wrong in the Making of the President*, 94–97; Barbara A. Perry, *Edward M. Kennedy: An Oral History*, 213–14, 231.

37. James Lewis Hicklin III to Lillian Carter, 10 Dec. 1979, Staff Secretary, Handwriting File, box 161, JCL; Leadership Breakfast, 5 Nov. 1979, Al M. McDonald Collection, box 11, JCL; Memorandum, Richard Harden to Carter, Re Miss Lillian's Political Activities, 5 Nov. 1979, and Memorandum, Jack Watson and Arnie Miller to Carter, Re Secretary of Commerce, 5 Nov. 1979, both in Staff Secretary, Handwriting File, box 155, JCL.
38. Rosalynn's New Hampshire Speech, 29 Nov. 1979, with Carter comment, Staff Secretary, Handwriting File, box 157, JCL; *Newsweek*, 5 Nov. 1979 (quotations); *US News and World Report*, 5 Nov. 1979.
39. David Blumenthal and James A. Morone, *The Heart of Power: Health and Politics in the Oval Office*, 263–64.
40. Handwritten note, Rosalynn to Strauss, 20 Nov. 1979, attached editorial from *Chicago Sun-Times*, 13 Nov. 1979, Clough File, box 37, JCL.
41. Author interview with Rosalynn Carter, 12 Oct. 1994.
42. *Meet the Press* transcript, 5 Nov. 1979, Powell Donated Collection, box 29, JCL.
43. Memorandum, Stu Eizenstat to Ham Jordan, Re Actions Toward Iran, 9 Nov. 1979, Chief of Staff Papers, Jordan, box 34, JCL; Bourne, *Carter*, 455–568; Carter, *Public Papers, 1979, Vol. II*, 2109–11.
44. JC Handwritten notes on meeting with Cabinet (re Iran), Sunday, 11 Nov. 1979, Staff Secretary, Handwriting File, box 156, JCL; Carter, *Public Papers, 1979, Vol. II*, 2109–11.
45. PDD, 12 Nov. 1979, JCL.
46. Memorandum, Vance to Carter, 13 Nov. 1979, Re Rhodesia, NSA Brzezinski Material, box 50, JCL; Carter, *Public Papers 1979, Vol. II*, 2120–21; Memorandum, David Aaron to Phil Wise, Re Cuban Political Prisoners, 8 Nov. 1979, NSA, Brzezinski-Country, box 14, JCL.
47. Huber Matos to Carter, 15 Nov. 1979, NSA, Brzezinski File-Country, box 14, JCL.
48. Carter, *Public Papers, 1979, Vol. II*, 2118–20; JC, *White House Diary*, 370; Shawcross, *The Shah's Last Ride*, 278–81.
49. Carter, Handwritten Notes with Instructions Re Iran, 7 Nov. 1979, Plains File, box 23, JCL; JC, *Keeping Faith*, 459–62; "Hostage Crisis in Iran: 1979–81," Plains File, box 24, JCL; Press Release, 14 Nov. 1979, Powell File, box 62, JCL; Telegram, Carter to the Pope, 14 Nov. 1979, Declassified Document NLC-15-55-8-24-1, JCL; Carter *Public Papers, 1979, Vol. II*, 2109–11.
50. Carter, Handwritten Speech, 13 Nov. 1979, and Draft of Speech for AFL-CIO, 14 Nov. 1979, both in Staff Secretary, Handwriting File, box 156, JCL; Carter, *Public Papers, 1979, Vol. II*, 2122–26.

51. Khomeini speech excerpts, 20 Nov. 1979, Declassified Document NLC-6-30-1-8-3, JCL; JC, *White House Diary*, 371.
52. JC, *White House Diary*, 371.
53. Tehran Domestic Service, 21 Nov. 1979, Iran Briefing Book, White House Counsel: Cutler, box 85, JCL; *Washington Post*, 22 Nov. 1979.
54. Reports, 21–24 Nov. 1979, White House Counsel: Cutler, box 85, JCL.
55. Carter, *Public Papers, 1979, Vol. II*, 2150; *New York Times*, 23, 28 1979.
56. Sargent, *A Superpower Transformed*, 288; *New York Times*, 23 Nov. 1979; Bruce Riedel, *Avoiding Armageddon: America, India, and Pakistan to the Brink and Back*, 85–86; PDD, 30 Nov. 1979, JCL.
57. Telegram, Laingen to Vance, 22 Nov. 1979, Jordan File, box 34, JCL; Bruce L. Laingen, *Yellow Ribbon: The Secret Journal of Bruce Laingen*, 19–34.
58. *Washington Post*, 23 Nov. 1979.
59. Wells, *444 Days: The Hostages Remember*, 165; Telegram, Vance to All Diplomatic Posts, 20 Nov. 1979, Jordan File, box 34, JCL; Iran Briefing Book, 18 Nov. 1979, White House Counsel: Cutler, box 85, JCL; Notes on Senior Staff Meetings, 19 Nov. 1979, White House Press File, Jenkins, box 5, JCL; Vernon Jordan comment, Powell File, box 62, JCL; Telegram, Newson to Vance, 21 Nov. 1979, Declassified Document NLC-16-70-5-52-5, JCL; Hamilton Jordan, Miller Center Interview, 86, JCL; Hamilton Jordan, *Crisis: The Last Year of the Carter Presidency*, 63. Mohammad Reza Pahlavi, the Shah of Iran, *Answer to History*, 161.
60. JC, *White House Diary*, 371; Memorandum, Jordan to Carter, 22 Nov. 1979, Jordan File, box 34, JCL.
61. Paris AFP, 22, 23 Nov. 1979, Iran Briefing Book, White House Counsel: Cutler, box 85, JCL; *New York Times*, 23 Nov. 1979.
62. JC, *White House Diary*, 372.
63. Ibid.
64. Don McLeod, AP story, tape, 20 Nov. 1979, box PD-66, JCL.
65. Barry Gewen, *The Inevitability of Tragedy: Henry Kissinger and His World*, 351.
66. Memorandum, Paul B. Henze to Brzezinski, RE Popular Concern about Iran, 21 Nov 1979, NSA, Staff-Horn (Special), box 4, JCL.
67. JC, *White House Diary*, 373.
68. Carter personal notes, 20 Nov.1979, Staff Secretary, Handwriting File, box 234, JCL.
69. Carter's personal notes, 27 Nov. 1979, Staff Secretary, Handwriting File, box 234, JCL; JC, *White House Diary*, 373.
70. Memorandum, Rick Hertzberg to Brzezinski, Re Iran/Muslims, Mrs. Carter, 28 Nov. 1979, Speechwriters File, Subject, box 13, JCL.
71. Memorandum, Brzezinski to Carter, Re Iran, 27 Nov. 1979, Declassified Document NLC-15-79-7-3-9, JCL.
72. JC, *White House Diary*, 373–75.
73. *New York Times*, 5 Dec. 1979.
74. Handwritten notes on phone calls, 25 Nov. 1979, Clough File, box 37, JCL; Rosalynn's notes on phone calls, 27, 28 Nov. 1979, Clough File, box 52, JCL.
75. PDD, 30 Nov. 1979, JCL; RSC, *First Lady*, 312–13.

76. *Washington Post*, 1 Dec. 1979.
77. *New York Times*, 25 Nov. 1979; Stuart E. Eizenstat, *Imperfect Justice: Looted Assets, Slave Labor, and the Unfinished Business of World War II*, 19–20.

Chapter 27

1. "Special Analysis" by CIA, 1 Dec. 1979, Declassified Document NLC-23-65-2-9-4, JCL; Carter, *Public Papers 1979, Vol. II*, 2192–94.
2. Memorandum, Dictated by Ambassador Dobrynin, 4 Dec. 1979, with Carter comments, Plains File, box 23, JCL; Jimmy Carter, *White House Diary*, 376.
3. Carter Notes on NSC meeting, 4 Dec. 1979, Plains File, box 23, JCL: Minutes of National Security Council Meeting, 4 Dec. 1979, Vertical File, Pakistan, JCL; Carter Interview, Visions, November 1984, Miscellaneous Interviews, JCL; JC, *White House Diary*, 376; Stansfield Turner, *Terrorism and Democracy*, 19–20.
4. Stuart E. Eizenstat, *President Carter: The White House Years*, 637; William J. Daugherty, *Executive Secrets: Covert Action & the Presidency*, 188–89: The Brzezinski Interview with *Le Nouvel Observateur* (Paris), pp. 15–21 Jan. 1998, translation in David N. Gibbs, "Afghanistan: The Soviet Invasion in Retrospect," *International Politics* 37, no. 2 (2000); David Rothkopf, *Running the World: The Inside Story of the National Security Council and the Architects of American Power*, 186, 204.
5. Cong. Rec., 96th Cong., 1st session, vol. 125, pt. 26, 4 Dec. 1979; Edward F. Kelly to Carter, 4 Dec. 1979, WHCF, box CO-33, JCL.
6. President's Remarks, 5 Dec. 1979, Powell File, box 61, JCL; PDD, 5 Dec. 1979, JCL.
7. Carter, *Public Papers, 1979, Vol. II*, 2205; PDD, 7 Dec. 1979, JCL.
8. Telegram, Secretary of State to Embassies, 6 Dec. 1979, Declassified Document NLC-16-74-7-5-1, JCL.
9. Telegram, "Bureau of Intelligence and Research Analysis," 6 Dec. 1979, with Carter comment, Declassified Document NLC-23-65-2-11-1, JCL; Peter G. Bourne, *Jimmy Carter: A Comprehensive Biography from Plains to the Post-Presidency*, 456; JC, *White House Diary*, 375; ABC News, 9 Dec. 1979, Iran Briefing Book, White House Counsel: Cutler, box 86, JCL; *New York Times*, 8 Feb. 1979; Memorandum, Brzezinski to Director of Central Intelligence, 10 Dec. 1979, VF, Afghanistan, JCL.
10. JC, *White House Diary*, 373, 375, 380; PDD, 1, 4, 15, 1979, JCL; Carter, *Public Papers 1979, Vol. II*, 2191, 2251; Jordan, *Crisis*, 75–97; Pahlavi, Mohammad Reza, *Answer to History*, 27, 33, 161.
11. "The Iran Hostage Crisis: A Chronology of Daily Developments," Report for Committee on Foreign Affairs, 97th Cong., 1st session, 12 Dec. 1979, p. 58.
12. Ibid., 13 Dec. 1979, pp. 59–60 (quotation on page 60).
13. *New York Times*, 17 Nov. 1979; "Week by Week in Iran," 2–29 Dec. 1979, Plains File, box 24, JCL; *The London Observer*, 15 Feb. 2009; John Dumbrell, *The Carter Presidency: A Re-evaluation*, 168–69; Carter, *Public Papers, 1979, Vol. II*, 2287; Cyrus Vance, *Hard Choices: Critical Years in America's Foreign Policy*, 378–79.

14. Memorandum, Central Intelligence Agency, National Foreign Assessment Center, 7 Dec. 1979, to Carter, with Carter note, Declassified Document NLC-8-18-6-8-0, JCL.

15. Interview with Shirley Hufstedler in Kenneth W. Thompson, *The Carter Presidency: Fourteen Intimate Perspectives on Jimmy Carter*, 22, 30–31.

16. Carter Remarks Re Thatcher, 17 Dec. 1979, Plains File, box 2, JCL; Carter to Vance, 18 Dec. 1979, WHCF, box PR-7, JCL; Christmas greetings, 18 Dec. 1979, WHCF, box PR-7, JCL; JC, *White House Diary*, 379.

17. Mother Teresa to Carter, 17 Nov. 1979, Susan Clough for Carter to Teresa, 19 Dec. 1979, WHCF, box MA-9, JCL; Bureau of Intelligence and Research Analysis, 19 Dec. 1979, Declassified Document NLC-SAFE 17 D-24-15-10-9, JCL.

18. JC, *White House Diary*, 382; PDD, 24–27 Dec. 1979, JCL; Rosalynn Carter, *First Lady from Plains*, 314.

19. Report for Committee on Foreign Affairs, 97th Cong., 1st sess., 25 Dec. 1979, p. 70.

20. Brzezinski Report on Soviet Invasion of Afghanistan, ca. 1 Dec. 1979, Plains File, box 1, JCL; Carter, *Public Papers 1979, Vol. II*, 2195–96; Barnett R. Rubin, *The Search for Peace in Afghanistan: From Buffer State to Failed State*, 28–30; Bruce Reidel, *What We Won: America's Secret War in Afghanistan*, 21–34.

21. RSC, *First Lady*, 314–15.

22. Nsarchive2.gwuedu/carterbrezhnev/docs/Temple.edu-Brzezinski   Memoranda; Douglas Frantz and Catherine Collins, "fallout from U.S. Policy in Pakistan *Washington Post*, 11 Nov. 2007.

23. Carter, *Public Papers, 1979, Vol. II*, 2109, 2133, 2285–86.

24. Memoranda of Conversation, 28 Dec. 1979, Vertical File, Afghanistan, JCL; PDD, 28 Dec. 1979, JCL; Margaret Thatcher, *The Downing Street Years*, 86–88.

25. Carter to Brezhnev, 21 Dec. 1979, Plains File, box 17, JCL; *Washington Post*, 11 Nov. 2007, includes quotation from Brzezinski's letter to Carter, 24 Dec. 1979; Christopher Andrew, *For the President's Eyes Only: Secret Intelligence and the American Presidency from Washington to Bush*, 447; Memorandum of Conversation, Carter with Zia, 28 Dec. 1979, NSA Staff Material/North-South, Thornton, Country, box 96, JCL; PDD, 29 Dec. 1979, JCL; Bourne, *Carter*, 456–57; Riedel, *What We Won*, 99. Rodric Braithwaite, *Afgantsy: The Russians in Afghanistan 1979–89*, 112–14, contends that the Russians never intended to push on to the Indian Ocean.

26. Madeleine Albright, *The Mighty and the Almighty: Reflections on America, God, and World Affairs*, 41–42.

27. Rubin, *The Search for Peace in Afghanistan*, 51; Husain Haqqani, *Magnificent Delusions: Pakistan, the United States, and an Epic History of Misunderstanding, 221*. 241–55.

28. *Malaysia New Strait Times*, 8 Feb., 2007; Andrew, *President's Eyes Only*, 48; JC, *White House Diary*, 379.

29. Powell to Carter, 28 Dec. 1979, with Carter notes, Staff Secretary, Handwriting File, box 161, JCL.

30. RSC, *First Lady*, 315–16; Bob Bergland, Miller Center Interview, 102, JCL.

31. *The London Independent*, 17 Sept. 2001; Carter message to Brezhnev in *Foreign Relations of US, 1977-80*, Vol. 7, 248; see also Charles Gati, *Zbig: The Strategy and Statecraft of Zbigniew Brzezinski*, 80.

32. *Foreign Relations of US, 1977–80*, Vol.7, 248.

33. Ibid., Vol. I, 133.

34. Carter interview with Frank Reynolds, Oval Office, 31 Dec. 1979, Powell Donated Material, box 29, JCL.

35. Jimmy Carter, *White House Diary*, 383.

36. Ibid., 387–88.

37. Carter to Byrd, 3 Jan. 1980, Clough File, box 45, JCL; JC, *White House Diary*, 387; Carter, *Public Papers, 1980–81, Vol. I*, 11–12; Bourne, *Carter*, 457; Zbigniew Brzezinski, *Power and Principle: Memoirs of the National Security Advisor*, 432.

38. Brian J. Auten, *Carter's Conversion: The Hardening of American Defense Policy*, 2, 23, 305, 309; Bourne, *Carter*, 457.

39. Peter G. Boyle, *American-Soviet Relations from the Russian Revolution to the Fall of Communism*, 193.

40. JC, *White House Diary*, 387–88; Carter, *Public Papers, 1980-81, Vol. I*, 21–24; *Atlanta Journal and Constitution*, 5 Jan. 1980; Memorandum, Carter to Secretary of Commerce, 7 Jan. 1980, WHCF, box AG-4, JCL.

41. Rosalynn's List, 2 Jan. 1979, Clough File, box 53, JCL.

42. Press Release, Speech and other Memoranda, 3 Jan. 1980, First Lady Press File, box 11, JCL.

43. Ibid.; *New York Times*, 4 Jan. 1980; JC, *White House Diary*, 388.

44. Rosalynn to Miss Lillian, 4 Jan. 1980, with attached newspaper clipping, WHCF, First Lady's Social Office, box 14, JCL.

45. "The Afghan Insurgents and Pakistan: Problems for Islamabad and Moscow," Foreign Assessment Center, CIA, Jan. 1980, Declassified Document NLC-12-1-5-2-0, JCL; *New York Times*, 4 Jan. 1980; JC, *White House Diary*, 388; Carter comments at staff meeting, 8 Jan. 1980, Notes, Al M. McDonald Collection, box 12, JCL; Chronology Afghanistan, Vertical File, JCL; Carter, *Public Papers, 1980-81, Vol. I*, 34–35.

46. Memorandum, Vance to Carter, 11 Jan.1980, NSA Staff, North/South, box 95, JCL.

47. Quoted in *Atlanta Constitution*, 7 Jan. 1980; see also *Atlanta Journal and Constitution*, 13 Jan. 1980.

48. *New York Times*, 7, 8, Jan. 1980; JC, *White House Diary*, 389.

49. Carter quotes in notes on staff meetings, 8, 10 Jan. 1980, White House Press File, Jenkins, box 5, JCL.

50. Bergland, Miller Center Interview, 99, 101–102, JCL.

51. Carter notes from his diary, 8 Jan. 1980, Staff Secretary, Handwriting File, box 234, JCL; JC, *White House Diary*, 390.

52. *Atlanta Constitution*, 16 Jan. 1980, and Hal Gulliver story in the same paper; RSC, *First Lady*, 317.

53. Memorandum and Speech, 8 Jan. 1980, First Lady Press Office, box 16, JCL; and Pamela Harriman to Mrs. Carter, 9 Jan.1980, WHCF, Name File, box Harriman, JCL.

54. Carter comments in Staff Meeting, Notes, 14 Jan. 1980, White House Press, Jenkins, box 5, JCL.

55. PDD, 14, 15, 1980, JCL;

56. Carter comments in Notes on Senior Staff Meeting, 16 Jan. 1980, White House Press, Jenkins, box 5, JCL, emphasis in original.

57. *Foreign Relations of US, 1977–80*, Vol. VI, *259*.

58. *New York Times*, 21 Jan. 1980; *Americus Times-Recorder*, 18 Jan. 1980; Carter Interview on *Meet the Press, US Department of State, Bureau of Public Affairs*, Jan. 1980; Chronology Afghanistan, Vertical File, JCL; Carter, *Public Papers, 1980–81, Vol. I*, 107–14.

59. Carter to Gandhi, 22 Jan. 1980, Staff Secretary, Presidential Files, box 147, JCL.

60. JC, *White House Diary*, 394–95; Bourne, *Carter*, 457.

61. *Washington Post*, 25 Jan. 1980.

62. Carter, *Public Papers, 1980-81, Vol. I*, 114–188, 194–200; Current Policy No. 131, *U.S. Department of State, Bureau of Public Affairs*, Feb. 1980; *Atlanta Constitution*, 22 Jan.1980; *New York Times*, 22 Jan. 1980; Carter comments on Notes, 23 Jan. 1980, White House Press, Jenkins, box 5, JCL; Memorandum, Al McDonald, Rick Hertzberg, Gordon Stewart to Carter, with Carter notes, Jan. 1980, Re State of the Union working draft, Staff Secretary, Handwriting File, box 162, JCL; Bourne, *Carter*, 457–58; Robert W. Love, Jr., *History of the U.S. Navy, 1942–1991*, Vol. 2, 698–99.

63. *Foreign Relations of the United States, 1970–80, Vol. I*, 134; see also *Vol. 18*, 45.

64. Daniel J. Sargent, *A Superpower Transformed: The Remaking of American Foreign Relations in the 1970s*, 261–62, 289; David Crist, *The Twilight War: The Secret History of America's Thirty-Year Conflict with Iran*, 33–34, 47–48; Thomas G. Paterson, *Meeting the Communist Threat: Truman to Reagan*, 144; Dennis Ross, *Doomed to Succeed: The U.S.-Israel Relationship from Truman to Obama*, 148–49.

65. *Washington Post*, 25, 30 Jan. 1980.

66. Memorandum, Frank Moore to Carter, 26 Jan. 1980, Weekly Legislative Report, Staff Secretary, Handwriting File, box 167, JCL; *New York Times*, 24, 25 Jan. 1980; *Atlanta Constitution*, 24 Jan. 1980; Memorandum of Conversation, Helmut Schmidt, 24 Jan. 1980, Plains File, box 1, JCL; JC, *White House Diary*, 394–95.

Chapter 28

1. Carter comments, 24 Jan. 1980, White House Press File, Granum, box 80, JCL; *Washington Post*, 9 Dec. 1979.

2. Carter Personal Notes, Jan. 1980, Staff Secretary, Handwriting File, box 234, JCL; *New York Times*, 26 Jan. 1980; Carter, *Public Papers, 1980–81, Vol. I*, 200–202, 207–12; PDD, 24 Jan. 1980, JCL. *Washington Post*, 25 Jan. 1980; Donnie Radcliffe and Elisabeth Bumiller, "Friends, Romans and Country Music," *Washington Post*, 25 Jan. 1980.

3. *New York Times*, 29 Jan., 1980; Memorandum, Brzezinski to Carter, 29 Jan. 1980, Plains File, box 2, JCL; Jimmy Carter, *White House Diary*, 395.

4. Tim Wells, *444 Days: The Hostages Remember*, 219–226.

5. Robert Wright, *Our Man in Tehran*, 301–304; Wells, *444 Days: The Hostages Remember*, 232–39; Stansfield Turner, *Burn before Reading: Presidents, CIA Agents, and Secret Intelligence*, 173–76; Carter, *Public Papers, 1980–81, Vol. I*, 255–56; Christopher Andrew, *For the President's Eyes Only: Secret Intelligence and the American Presidency from Washington to Bush*, 450–51; Malcolm McConnel, "Escape with the Master of Disguise," *Reader's Digest*, April 1998, 124–31; JC, *White House Diary*, 396; Bruce L. Laingen, *Yellow Ribbon: The Secret Journal of Bruce Laingen*, 63–64; Arthur Milnes, *Jimmy and Rosalynn Carter: A Canadian Tribute*, 27–29. A recent popular movie, called *Argo* and starring Ben Affleck, overdramatized the event and gave too much credit to the CIA, though both Carter and the Canadian ambassador claimed that Canada deserved most of the credit for the escape. See Antonio Mendez and Matt Baglio, *Argo: How the Cia and Hollywood Pulled off the Most Audacious Rescue in History* (2012).
6. Carter to Hughes, 26 Feb. 1980, Powell File, box 40, JCL.
7. *New York Times, Atlanta Constitution*, 31 Jan. 1980; JC, *White House Diary*, 396; Carter, *Public Papers,1980–81, Vol. I*, photo six pages before 501.
8. Carter, *Public Papers, 1980–81, Vol. I*, 239–54.
9. Ibid., 256–57.
10. *Washington Post*, 2 Feb. 1980.
11. Chronology of Events in Afghanistan, February, VF, JCL; *New York Times*, 3 Feb. 1980.
12. FBIS Foreign Broadcast Information Service, 1 Feb. 1980, with Carter note, Staff Secretary, Handwriting File, box 170, JCL.
13. *New York Times*, 31 Jan., 5, 8 Feb. 1980; *Atlanta Constitution*, 31 Jan. 1980; Kennedy to Carter, 31 Jan. 1980, Staff Secretary, Handwriting File, box 168, JCL; *Atlanta Constitution*, 6 Feb. 1980; Carter comment, Senior Staff Meeting, 11 Feb., 1980, White House Press, Jenkins, box 3, JCL; Rosalynn Carter, *First Lady from Plains*, 315–17.
14. Memorandum, Chief of Iran Task Force to Hamilton Jordan, 6 Feb. 1980, and Memorandum, Jordan to Carter, 6 Feb. 1980, both in Jordan File, box 34, JCL; *New York Times*, 7, 13 Feb. 1980.
15. Carter notes on national prayer breakfast, 7 Feb. 1980, Staff Secretary, Handwriting File, box 169, JCL; identical letters, Carter to Christian Bourquet and Hector Villalon, 8 Feb.1980, Clough File, boxes, 45, 46, JCL; Memorandum, Carter to Jordan, 15 Feb. 1980, Jordan File, box 34, JCL; JC, *White House Diary*, 399: Hamilton Jordan, *Crisis: The Last Year of the Carter Presidency*, 190 ("crazy" quotation); Farah Pahlavi, *An Enduring Love: My Life with the Shah*, 361, 368; Memorandum, Jordan to Carter, 13 Jan. 1980, Re Hostages, both in Chief of Staff, Jordan, box 34, JCL; Jordan and Saunders to Carter, 8 Jan. 1980, and RSC, *First Lady*, 319; Gary Sick, *All Fall Down: America's Tragic Encounter with Iran*, 301; Jordan to Bourguet and Villalon, 30 Jan. 1980, Jordan File, box 34, JCL.
16. Carter note to Eizenstat, 11 Feb. 1980, Staff Secretary, Handwriting File, box 170, JCL.
17. JC, *White House Diary*, 400.
18. Senior Staff Meeting Notes, 18 Feb. 1980, White House Press File, Jenkins, box 5, JCL.
19. *Atlanta Constitution*, 18 Feb. 1930; UPI Telegram, 21 Feb. 1980, Re Rosalynn interview, First Lady Press Office, box 41, JCL; *Washington Post*, 26 Feb. 1980.

20. Remarks of Dr. Brzezinski, 4 March 1980, NSA, Brzezinski Material, Schecter/ Friendly, box 1, JCL; Carter, *Public Papers, 1980–81, Vol. I,* 377.

21. Peter G. Bourne, *Jimmy Carter: A Comprehensive Biography from Plains to the Post-presidency,* 459.

22. Memorandum, 3 March 1980, Tim Kraft to Rosalynn, Jordan, and Strauss, Tim Kraft Donated Material, box 1, JCL.

23. Memorandum, 4 March 1980, Landrum Bolling to Rosalynn Carter, with Carter comments, Clough File, box 45, JCL.

24. Andrew Cockburn and Leslie Cockburn, *Dangerous Liaison: The Inside Story of the Israeli-U.S. Convert Relationship,* 313–14.

25. Al Moses Comments, Senior Staff Meeting, 18 March 1980, Al McDonald Donated Material, box 13, JCL.

26. Kahn to Carter, 19 March 1980, Staff Secretary, Handwriting File, box 176, JCL.

27. Bourne, *Carter,* 458.

28. Rowland Evans and Robert Novak, "Rosalynn's the Most Powerful First Lady since Abigail Adams," *The Star,* 18 March 1980, copy in Hoyt Papers, box 1, JCL.

29. JC, *White House Diary,* 407–14; Piero Gleijeses, *Visions of Freedom: Havana, Washington, Pretoria, and the Struggle for Southern Africa, 1976–1991,* 139–50.

30. President's Personal Notes, 18 March 1980, Plains File, box 32; *New York Times,* 18 March 1980; Carter, *Public Papers, 1980–81, Vol. I,* 503.

31. JC, *White House Diary,* 411; Shaul Bakhash, *The Reign of the Ayatollahs: Iran and the Islamic Revolution,* 116–17; Chronology of Iran Crisis, 23 March 1980, White House Press, Granum, box 75, JCL; Jimmy Carter, *Keeping Faith: Memoirs of a President,* 501; Pahlavi, *An Enduring Love,* 364–65.

32. *New York Times,* 25, 26 March 1980; *Washington Star,* 26 March 1980; Ham Jordan's Notes, 26 March 1980, White House Counsel, Cutler, box 93, JCL; Pahlavi, *An Enduring Love,* 368–69.

33. JC, *White House Diary,* 412; Robert Shogan, *Bad News: Where the Press Goes Wrong in the Making of the President,* 92.

34. *New York Times,* 24 March 1980; "The Baron Report," 25 March, 1980, Speechwriters, Subject, box 1, JCL; Leo Ribuffo, "I'll Whip His Ass: Jimmy Carter, Edward Kennedy, and the Perennial Crisis of American Liberalism," a paper read to a meeting of the Organization of American Historians, privately owned; Leo Ribuffo, *Right, Center, Left: Essays in American History,* 242; E. Stanly Godbold, Jr., *Jimmy and Rosalynn Carter: The Georgia Years, 1924–1974,* 262; David Blumenthal and James A. Morone, *The Heart of Power: Health and Politics in the Oval Office,* 272–78; Timothy Stanley, *Kennedy vs. Carter: The 1980 Battle for the Democratic Party's Soul,* 43–55.

35. Memorandum, 4 March 19804, Gary Sick to Brzezinski, RE Iran, and Memorandum of Conversation, Bourguet and Henry Precht, 6 March 1980, both in Jordan File, box 34, JCL; Memorandum, 8 March 1980, Vance to Carter, JCL; *Washington Post,* 21 March 1980.

36. Carter, *Public Papers, 1980–81, Vol. I,* 517–60, 568–75 (quotation on 574).

NOTES TO PAGES 399–403   757

37. Ibid., 5–6.
38. JC, *White House Diary*, 400.
39. Government Documents Relating to Olympic Boycott, 37–41.
40. *Washington Post,* 26 Feb. 1980.
41. Carter, *Public Papers, 1980-81, Vol. I*, 517–21; see also Roy L. Morrison Government Documents Relating to Olympic Boycott" (Educational Resources Informationa Center, Jan. 1, 1982 A digital library provided by the US Department of Education), 12, 38, and *Politico Magazine*, 9 Feb. 2014, p. 8.
42. Morrison,Government Documents Relating to Olympic Boycott, 13–14, 42.
43. JC, *White House Diary*, 411–13; Carter, *Public Papers, 1980-81, Vol. I*, 576–77.
44. *Washington Post*, 28, 30 March 1980; Unidentified Clipping, 3 April 1980, White House Press File, Jenkins, box 1, JCL.
45. *Washington Post*, 28 March 1980.
46. Bahman Bakhtiari, "Parliamentary Elections in Iran," *Iranian Studies* 26, no. 3–4 (Summer–Autumn, 1993), 375–88.
47. Carter, *Public Papers, 1980–81, Vol. I*, 611–15; *New York Times*, 2, 4 April 1980; Iran Chronology File, 6 April 1980, White House Press File, Granum, box 75, JCL; Announcements of Decisions on Iran, 5 April 1980, copies in Jordan, box 34, and Clough File, box 23, JCL; Memorandum, Carter to Secretary of the Treasury, 7 April 19080, WHCF, box CO-32, JCL; 3–29 April 1980, Afghanistan, VF, JCL; Memorandum, Paul B. Henze to Brzezinski, 11 April 1980, Re Iran and the Soviets, NSA Staff, Horn Special, box 4, JCL.
48. *Washington Post*, 28 March 1980.
49. JC, *White House Diary*, 415; *Washington Post*, 28 March 1980.
50. *New York Times*, 8 April 1980; 1980 Campaign Papers, Series XXI: Correspondence Unit Constituent Files, box 690, Ronald Reagan Library (RRL); News Release, 10 April 1980, 1980 Campaign Papers, Press Section, box 549, RRL; Nicholas Evan Sarantakes, *Dropping the Torch: Jimmy Carter, The Olympic Boycott, and the Cold War*, 12–21.
51. Memorandum, Carter to Eizenstat, et al., Re Farmer-Held Grain Reserves, 9 April 1980, Staff Secretary, Handwriting File, box 180, JCL; JC, *White House Diary*, 415.
52. *Washington Post*, 8 April 1980; Carter to Henry Precht, 8 April 1980, Staff Secretary, Handwriting File, box 179, JCL; JC, *White House Diary*, 416.
53. Carter, *Public Papers, 1980–81, Vol. I*, 617–24; JC, *White House Diary*, 416; JC, *Keeping Faith*, 495.
54. RSC, *First Lady*, 319.
55. "The Iran Hostage Crisis: A Chronology of Daily Developments," Report for Committee on Foreign Affairs, 97th Congress, 1st session, 152.
56. JC, *White House Diary*, 416.
57. ABC News Transcript, Bob Sirkin reporting, April 10, 1980.
58. Ibid.
59. RSC, *First Lady*, 323–25.

Chapter 29

1. National Security Council Meeting, 11 April 1980, Plains File, box 30, JCL; Jimmy Carter, *Keeping Faith: Memoirs of a President*, 506; Robert A. Strong, *Working in the World: Jimmy Carter and the Making of American Foreign Policy*, 242–46.
2. National Security Council Meeting, 15 April 1980, Plains File, box 30, JCL; JC, *Keeping Faith*, 507.
3. Author interview with Cyrus Vance, 1 May 1992, pp. 9–10, Stennis Oral History Collection, Mississippi State University; Strong, *Working in the World*, 247 (Carter quotation); Cyrus Vance, *Hard Choices: Critical Years in America's Foreign Policy*, 406–409.
4. Carter, *Public Papers, 1980–81, Vol. I*, 679–80, 686–93; Jimmy Carter, *White House Diary*, 417–18; Jimmy Carter, *Keeping Faith: Memoirs of a President*, 495.
5. Carter, *Public Papers, 1980–81, Vol. I*, 686–93.
6. Ibid., 694–95.
7. Charlie A. Beckwith, *Delta Force: The Army's Elite Counterterrorist Unit*, 1–5; JC, *Keeping Faith*, 507–10; Mark Bowden, *Guests of the Ayatollah: The First Battle in America's Battle with Militant Islam*, 411–13; Hamilton Jordan, *Crisis: The Last Year of the Carter Presidency*, 255–64.
8. Christopher Andrew, *For the President's Eyes Only: Secret Intelligence and the American Presidency from Washington to Bush*, 451.
9. Beckwith, *Delta Force*, 6–10; James H. Kyle, *The Guts to Try*, 223–24; Stansfield Turner, *Terrorism and Democracy: The CIA in Transition*, 107–14; William L. Waugh, Jr., "The Structure of Decision-Making in the Iranian Hostage Rescue Attempt and its Implications for Conflict Management," *Conflict Quarterly* (Spring 1990), 31–32.
10. Carter, *Public Papers, 1980–81, Vol. I*, 704–14.
11. Rafshoon to Carter, Eyes Only, 18 April 1980, Clough File, box 34, JCL.
12. Carter, *Public Papers, 1980–81, Vol. I*, 704–16; PDD, 16 April 1980, JCL; Excerpts from Carter news conference, 17 April 1980, *US Department of State Bulletin*, in Vance, Cyrus, VF, JCL; Author interview with Cyrus Vance, 1 May 1992, Stennis Oral History Collection, Mississippi State University.
13. Volker Skierka, *Fidel Castro: A Biography*, 226–29; Wayne S. Smith, *The Closest of Enemies: A Personal and Diplomatic Account of U.S.-Cuban Relations since 1957*, 206–16; Interview with Shirley Hufstedler in Kenneth W. Thompson, *The Carter Presidency: Fourteen Intimate Perspectives of Jimmy Carter*, 28–29; *New York Times*, 15 April 1980; Carter, *Public Papers, 1980–81, Vol. I*, 684–85.
14. CIA National Foreign Assessment Center, 18 April 1980, Declassified Document NLC-6-31-3-11-6, JCL.
15. Carter, *Public Papers, 1980–81, Vol. I*, 723–71.
16. PDD, 21 April 1980, JCL; JC, *White House Diary*, 419–20.
17. *Foreign Relations of the US, Vol. I*, 144.
18. Vance to Carter, 21 April 1980, Staff Secretary, Handwriting File, box 183, JCL; PDD, 21 April 1980, JCL; Author interview with Cyrus Vance, 1 May 1992, pp. 9–10, John

C. Stennis Project, Mississippi State University; JC, *White House Diary*, 425 (loy- alty quotation); JC, *Keeping Faith*, 510–11, 513; Zbigniew Brzezinski, *Power and Principle: Memoirs of the National Security Advisor*, 36–44; Interview with Cyrus Vance, in Thompson, *The Carter Presidency*, 138–41; Vance, *Hard Choices*, 410–13.

19. JC, *White House Diary*, 420.
20. Mirta Ojito, "You Are Going to El Norte," *New York Times Magazine*, 23 April 2000, 68–73, 78.
21. Author interview with Scott Singletary, an enlisted man on *Nimitz*, 7 June 2006; *Lexington Herald*, 2 July 1980; *United States Ship Nimitz CVN-68 Yearbook*, "Operation Evening Light," April 1980, pp. 378–79.
22. Beckwith, *Delta Force*, 295.
23. PDD, 24, 25 April 1980, JCL.
24. Mark Bowden, "The Desert One Debacle," *Atlantic*, May 2006, 9–11.
25. Ibid., 8–9, 11–14.
26. Ibid., 15–19; JC, *White House Diary*, 421.
27. Bowden, "Desert One Debacle," 19.
28. Harold Brown's statement to the Pentagon, 25 April 1980, White House Administration, Hugh Carter, box 37, JCL; Kyle, *The Guts to Try*, 330–31; Gerald Rafshoon, "Profiles in Courage, the Jimmy Carter Edition," www.bloomberg.com/news/2012-05-10; *Roanoke (VA) Times*, 5 April 2005; Interview with Army General James B. Vaught, *Newsday*, 24 April 2005; PDD, 24 April 1980, JCL; News Release, 25 April 1980, Powell File, box 62, JCL; "Hardball" MSNBC transcript, 25 April 2005, Chris Matthews; JC, *White House Diary*, 421–22; JC, *Keeping Faith*, 514–18; *Atlanta Journal and Constitution*, 27 Nov. 1983; Bowden, *Guests of the Ayatollah*, 556–57; William J. Daugherty, *In the Shadow of the Ayatollah: A CIA Hostage in Iran*, 188; Eric L. Haney, *Inside Delta Force*, 190–203; Dale R. Herspring, *The Pentagon and the Presidency: Civil-Military Relations from FDR to George W. Bush*, 253–58, 420; Turner, *Terrorism and Democracy*, 115–25.
29. Memorandum, 25 April 1980, Brad Woodward to Linda Peek, Re Reaction to the Rescue, Congressional Liaison File, Pinson, box 279, JCL; Andrew, *President's Eyes Only*, 453; Carl Sferrazza Anthony, *First Ladies, Vol. II: The Saga of the Presidents' Wives and Their Power, 1961–1990*, 308–309; Rosalynn Carter, *First Lady from Plains*, 325–27 (quotation on 327).
30. Carter, *Public Papers, 1980–81, Vol. I*, 772–73; *New York Times*, 25 April 1980.
31. JC, *White House Diary*, 422.
32. MSNBC transcript, Iran Chronology, White House Press File, Granum, box 75, JCL.
33. Ricky Sickmann, *Iranian Hostage: A Personal Diary of 444 Days in Captivity*, 92–106, 308, passim; *New York Times*, 10 Feb. 2002.
34. Tim Wells, *444 Days: The Hostages Remember*, 327–29 (quotation on 329).
35. *Washington Post*, 21 Dec. 2018.
36. Comments to families, Powell File, box 26, JCL; *Tehran Times*, 26 April 1980; *New York Times*, 27 April 1980; Bruce L. Laingen, *Yellow Ribbon: The Secret Journal of Bruce Laingen*, 119.

37. JC, *White House Diary*, 423; Andrew, *President's Eyes Only*, 453; Beckwith, *Delta Force*, 194, 316; Herspring, *The Pentagon and the Presidency*, 262; Kyle, *The Guts to Try*, 355.

38. Eric L. Haney, *Inside Delta Force*, 202.

39. JC, *White House Diary*, 422–23; Carter, *Public Papers, 1980–81, Vol. I*, 779–80; Warren Christopher, *Chances of a Lifetime: A Memoir*, 105–106.

40. *Foreign Relations of the U.S., Vol. I*, 144.

41. *Washington Post*, 21 Dec. 2018.

42. *Washington Post*, 29 April 1980.

43. Author interview with Edmund Muskie, 3 April 1992, Stennis Collection, Mississippi State University.

44. Author interview with Jimmy Carter, 12 Oct. 1994; Staff Meeting Notes, 28 April 1980, Al McDonald Donated Material, box 13, JCL; E. Stanly Godbold, Jr., "A 'Serious Moment' April 21 1980: The Day the Secretary of State Resigned," paper delivered at the Organization of American Historians, Atlanta, April 1994; Zbigniew Brzezinski, Miller Center Interview, 70–73, JCL; Hamilton Jordan, Miller Center Interview, 52, JCL.

45. Carter to Vance, 28 April 1980, WHCF, box ND-8, JCL; *New York Times*, 28 April 1980; Carter, *Public Papers, 1980–81, Vol. I*, 781; Jordan, *Crisis*, 281–84.

46. JC, *White House Diary*, 423; Author interview with Edmund Muskie, 3 April 1992, Stennis Collection, Mississippi State University Library.

47. Ann Blackman, *Seasons of Her Life: A Biography of Madeleine Korbel Albright*, 171–72, 177–78; Author interview with Muskie, 3 April 1992; Timothy P. Maga, *The World of Jimmy Carter: U.S. Foreign Policy, 1977-1981*, 153–54.

48. Carter, *Public Papers, 1980–81, Vol. I*, 782–85; *New York Times*, 28 April 1980.

49. Granum Notes, Powell File, 28 April 1980, box 62, JCL; PDD, 28 April 1980, JCL; Carter, *Public Papers, 1980–81, Vol. I*, 786–87.

50. Carter, *Public Papers, 1980–81, Vol. I*, 791–801; Draft of Speech, 29 April 1980, Staff Secretary, Handwriting File, box 183, JCL.

51. PDD, 28 April 1980, JCL.

52. JC, *White House Diary*, 424; Memorandum, 29 April 1980, Frank Moore to Carter, Staff Secretary Handwriting File, box 183, JCL; Author interview with Jimmy Carter, 12 Oct. 1994; Maga, *The World of Jimmy Carter*, 4–6, 140, 154–56; *Washington Post*, 8 May 1980.

53. Author interview with Scott Singletary, 14 June 2006; *Virginia Pilot*, 16 May 1980; *Lexington Herald*, 2 July 1980; JC, *White House Diary*, 423; Carter, *Public Papers, 1980–81, Vol. II*, 969–73 (quotations). Bluebeard-5 is on display at the Wrightstown Gate of Joint Base McGuire-Dix-Lakenhurst in New Jersey, and one of the wrecked helicopters is at the Naval Museum in Pensacola, Florida.

Chapter 30

1. Nelson to Carter, with Carter note, 1 May 1980, Staff Secretary, Handwriting File, box 183, JCL.

2. Leo Ribuffo, "'I'll Whip His Ass: Jimmy Carter, Edward Kennedy, and the Latest Crisis of American Liberalism,'" unpublished Paper, 28–31, JCL; Jon Ward, *Camelot's End: Kennedy vs. Carter*, 125–26; Chris Matthews, *Hardball: How Politics is Played by One Who Knows the Game*, 199–200.

3. Katai Marton, *Hidden Power: Presidential Marriages that Shaped Our Recent History*, 241 (quotation, "you can just go to hell"); Carl Sferrazza Anthony, *First Ladies, Vol. II: The Saga of the Presidents' Wives and their Power, 1961–1990*, 308–309.

4. Scott Kaufman, *Rosalynn Carter: Equal Partner in the White House*, 137.

5. Memorandum, 2 May 1980, Brzezinski to Carter, NSC weekly Report # 139, Re his trip to Algeria, Brzezinski File, box 42, JCL.

6. *New York Times*, 5 May, 1980; Declassified Document NLC-23-12-1-14-7, JCL; Jimmy Carter, *White House Diary*, 425; Carter, *Public Papers, 1980–81, Vol. I*, 827; Jasper Ridley, *Tito: A Biography*, 21, 413.

7. *Christian Science Monitor*, 5 Aug. 2005.

8. Carter, *Public Papers, 1980–81, Vol. I*, 864–65; Speech, 9 May 1980, Program, Arlington National Cemetery, Staff Secretary, Handwriting File, box 185, JCL.

9. JC, *White House Diary*, 427; Jimmy Carter, *Keeping Faith: Memoirs of a President*, 521–22; James H. Kyle, *The Guts to Try*, 361–62.

10. *The Miami Herald*, 3 Oct. 2010; *Atlanta Journal and Constitution*, 10 April 2005; JC, *White House Diary*, 424–25; David W. Engstrom, *The Carter Administration and the Mariel Boatlift*, 45, 53–54: Julia E. Sweig, *Cuba: What Everyone Needs to Know*, 96–98.

11. Mirta Ojito, "You are Going to El Norte," *New York Times Magazine*, 23 April 2000, 68–73, 78; Mirta Ojito, *Finding Manana: A Memoir of a Cuban Exodus*, 5, 46, 49, 199, 205; JC, *White House Diary*, 427.

12. Profile of Cuban Refugees, 7 July 1980, Declassified Document NLC-24-18-6-1-9, JCL; *Atlanta Journal and Constitution*, 10 April 2005; *Washington Post*, 17 Nov. 2015; *New York Times*, 8 June 1980; JC, *White House Diary*, 427–28, 433–34; Carter, *Public Papers, 1980–81, Vol. I*, 819–20, 849–50; Carol Felsenthal, *Clinton in Exile: A President Out of the White House*, 63–64; Engstrom, *The Carter Administration and the Mariel Boatlift*, 73, 75, 79–80.

13. Carter, *Public Papers, 1980–81, Vol. I*, 861–64; Swearing in Ceremony, 13 May 1980, WHCF, box PR-32, JCL; Carter Notes for East Room, Staff Secretary, Handwriting File, box 184, JCL.

14. Memoranda, Muskie to Carter, 19, 20 May 1980, Plains File, box 40, JCL; JC, *White House Diary*, 429.

15. Press Release, 11 May 1980, First Lady Office, Projects, Cade, box 29, JCL; Carter, *Public Papers, 1980–81, Vol. II*, 1514–18.

16. *The Star-Ledger*, 22 May 1980; JC, *White House Diary*, 417, 432.

17. Folder: Jewish Leaders, 17 May 1980, Jordan File, box 48, JCL.

18. Carter, *Public Papers, 1980–81, Vol. I*, 950–61 (quotation on 954).

19. PDD, 28, 29 May 1980, JCL; *Christian Science Monitor*, 29 May 1980; *Dayton Daily News*, 3 July 2016.

20. Carter, *Public Papers, 1980–81, Vol. II*, 1024–25; PDD, 3 June 1980, JCL; *Americus Times-Recorder*, 24 June 2020.

21. PDD, 5 June 1980, JCL.

22. Carter, *Public Papers, 1980-81, Vol. II*, 1037-41; *Washington Post*, 8, 11 June 1980.

23. Memorandum, Frank Moore and Bill Cable to Ham Jordan, 5 June, 1980, Jordan File, box 78, JCL; JC, *White House Diary*, 434-35 (Carter quotation); Adam Clymer, *Edward M. Kennedy: A Biography*, 312-13.

24. Carter, *Public Papers, 1980-81, Vol. II*, 969, 1665, 1275.

25. Statement by Robert B. Pirie, Jr., 4 June 1980, 1980 Campaign Papers, Tony Dolon Files, box 860k RRL; Memorandum, Patricia Bario to Carter, 12 June 1980, Re Jewish Editors, Staff Secretary, Handwriting File, box 191, JCL.

26. *New York Times*, 12, 13 June 1980; JC, *White House Diary*, 436-37.

27. JC, *White House Diary*, 437; PDD, 4, 6, 12, 18 June 1980, JCL.

28. *Atlanta Constitution*, 20 July 1980; Staff Meeting Minutes, 21 July, 1980, Al McDonald Papers, box 14, JCL; *New York Times*, 21, 23, 25 July, 1980; JC, *White House Diary*, 438-39; Carter, *Public Papers, 1980-81, Vol. II*, 1406-1407, 1420, 1439, 1443, 1466; Final Report of the Office of Professional Responsibility, 1 Aug. 1980, Robert M. Kimmitt File, Legal: Billy Carter, RRL; *Star Ledger*, 17 Aug. 1980; Gil Troy, *Affairs of State: The Rise and Rejection of the Presidential Couple since World War II*, 268.

29. PDD, 1, 5, 6, 10 June 1980, JCL; *Washington Post*, 30 May 1980.

30. Carter, *Public Papers, 1980-81, Vol. II*, 1056-60; PDD, 19, 20 June 1980, JCL.

31. *Washington Post*, 22 June 1980.

32. Ibid.

33. PDD, 21 June 1980, JCL; Carter notes on conversation with Schmidt, 21 June 1980, Staff Secretary, Handwriting File, box 193, JCL; JC, *White House Diary*, 439-40 (quotations); JC, *Keeping Faith*, 535-38.

34. PDD, 21, 22 June 1980, JCL.

35. Carter, *Public Papers,1980-81, Vol. II*,1164-68; JC, *White House Diary*, 440-42; *Atlanta Journal and Constitution*, 22 June 1980; First Lady Press Office, Trips, box 24, JCL; Notes, 22-26 June 1980, Staff Secretary, Handwriting File, box 193, JCL.

36. *Washington Post*, 24 June 1980; PDD, 24 June 1980, JCL.

37. Carter, *Public Papers, 1980-81, Vol. II*, 1211-13.

38. Ibid., 1220-22.

39. Ibid.; PDD, 25 June 1980, JCL.

40. Memorandum, Brzezinski to Carter, 27 June 1980, Daily Report, NSA, Brzezinski Material, box 29, JCL; JC, *White House Diary*, 442-43; Carter, *Public Papers, 1980-81, Vol. II*, 1208-36.

41. Ibid., 1231-32.

42. PDD, 26 June 1980, JCL.

43. Ibid., 1, 2 July 1980.

44. JC, *White House Diary*, 443-44; Memorandum, Caddell to Powell, 25 June 1980, Powell Donated Materia, box 20, JCL; Memorandum, Kraft to Jimmy and Rosalynn Carter, 26 June 1980, Kraft Donated Material, box 1, JCL; Welty to Carter, 27 June 1980, Staff Secretary, Handwriting File box 193, JCL; Memorandum, Charles Goodwin to Media Liaison Stat, 25 June 1980 RE Medals, WHCF, box RE-3, JCL; Notes, Jenkins, Senior Staff Meeting, 30 June 1980, White House Press File, box 5, JCL (Carter quotation).

Chapter 31

1. *Washington Post*, 2, 3, 4 July 1980; PDD, 4 July 1980, JCL; Jimmy Carter, *White House Diary*, 444–45.
2. JC, *White House Diary*, 445; PDD, 5, 6 July 1980, JCL.
3. JC, *White House Diary*, 445–46; PDD, 8, 9 July 1980, JCL.
4. JC, *White House Diary*, 444–47; *Atlanta Constitution*, 30 Jan. 2004.
5. PDD, 17 July 1980, JCL; *Washington Post*, 18 July 1980.
6. Carter, *Public Papers, 1980–81, Vol. II*, 1349–60; *Washington Post*, 18 July 1980.
7. Carter, *Public Documents 1980–81, Vol. II*, 1360–62; *Washington Post*, 18 July 1980.
8. JC, *White House Diary*, 447–48.
9. Memorandum, Mondale to Carter, 16 July 1980, Staff Secretary, Handwriting File, box 195, JCL.
10. Carter comments on first draft of speech, 30 July 1980, Staff Secretary, Handwriting File, box 199, JCL; Draft of speech, with notes, in Staff Secretary, Handwriting File, box 199, JCL.
11. Memorandum, Jordan to Carter, July 1980, Clough File, box 37, JCL.
12. *Washington Post*, 22 July 1980.
13. Cynthia Helmel, "On the Road with Rosalynn," *Atlanta Journal and Constitution*, 12 July 1980.
14. Minutes of PRC Meeting on Iran with Carter notes, 1 Aug, 1980, Declassified Document NLC-128-10-9-28-0, JCL.
15. JC, *White House Diary*, 449–50; Memorandum, Secretary of Interior to Carter, 17 July, 1980, Re Presidential Alaska calls, with Carter's annotations, Staff Secretary, Handwriting File, box 196, JCL; Carter, *Public Papers, 198–81, II*, 1386–88 (quotation on 1386).
16. JC, *White House Diary, 449-50*; Carter, *Public Papers, 1980–81, Vol. II*, 1408–11.
17. JC, *White House Diary*, 449–50; Carter to Byrd, handwritten note, 23 July 1980, Clough File, box 45, JCL.
18. *Washington Post*, 16 July 2020; PDD, 5 Aug. 1980, JCL.
19. JC, *White House Diary*, 449–50.
20. JC, *White House Diary*, 450; Walter Mondale, *The Good Fight: A Life in Liberal Politics*, 223.
21. *New York Times*, 28 July 1980; *Star Ledger*, 27 July 1980; Jimmy Carter, *Keeping Faith: Memoirs of a President*, 544.
22. Press Statement, 11 July 1980, Carter to Farah, and Rosalynn to Farah, 29 July 1980, all in WHCF, box CO-32, folder CO 71, and Plains File, box 23, JCL.
23. Jehan Sadat, *A Woman of Egypt*, 432; *Tupelo (MS) Daily Journal*, 30 July 1980; David Harris, *The Crisis: The President, the Prophet, and the Shah–1979 and the Coming of Militant Islam*, 370–71 (Nixon quotation on 370); Farah Pahlavi, *An Enduring Love: My Life with the Shah*, 386–88; Roham Alvandi, *Nixon, Kissinger, and the Shah*, 1–2.
24. JC, *White House Diary*, 451–53 (quotation on 452).
25. *Washington Post*, 11 June 1980.

26. Walter Shapiro, "John Anderson: The Nice Guy Syndrome," *The Atlantic*, Feb. 1980.

27. Carter, *Public Papers, 1980–81, Vol. II*, 1439.

28. JC, *White House Diary*, 453–54.

29. JC, *White House Diary*, 454–55; PDD, 7 Aug. 1980, JCL.

30. *60 Minutes* Transcript, 10 Aug. 1980, Powell Donated Papers, box 28, JCL.

31. Adam Clymer, *Edward M. Kennedy: A Biography*, 316–18; Timothy Stanley, *Kennedy vs. Carter: The 1980 Battle for the Democratic Party's Soul*, 166–67.

32. *Atlanta Constitution*, 14 Aug. 1980; Laura T. McCarty, *Coretta Scott King: A Biography*, 64–65.

33. Carter, *Public Papers, 1980–81, Vol. II*, 1532–40 (quotations on 1533–34, 1540).

34. *Time*, 25 Aug. 1980, p. 20.

35. Kai Bird, *The Outlier: The Unfinished Presidency of Jimmy Carter*, 547–48; Hugh Sidey, "The First Lady is First-Rate," *Miami Herald*, 25 Aug. 1980; Rosalynn Carter, *First Lady from Plains*, 332–33; Kathryn J. McGarr, *The Whole Damn Deal: Robert Strauss and the Art of Politics*, 258–65; Theodore H. White, *America in Search of Itself: The Making of the President 1956–1980*, 341–42.

36. Clymer, *Edward R. Kennedy*, 318; JC, *White House Diary*, 457–58; Robert Shrum, *No Excuses: Concessions of a Serial Campaigner*, 116, 120, 122, 127–29; Peter G. Bourne, *Jimmy Carter: A Comprehensive Biography from Plains to the Post-Presidency*, 462; Stanley, *Kennedy vs. Carter*, 166–69; Stuart E. Eizenstat, *President Carter: The White House Years*, 861–62; Edward M. Kennedy, *True Compass: A Memoir*, 381; Jon Ward, *Camelot's End: Kennedy vs. Carter*, 253–73; Larry J. Sabato, *The Kennedy Half Century: The Presidency, Assassination, and Lasting Legacy of John F. Kennedy*, 333–34; John Norris, *Mary McGrory: The First Queen of Journalism*, 189.

37. Vance to Carter, Carter to Vance, both 20 Aug. 1980, Staff Secretary, Handwriting File, box 200, JCL; Bert Lance, Miller Center Interview, 51–52, JCL.

38. Tom Wicker, "The Ordeal of Jimmy Carter," *New York Times*, 3 Aug. 1980.

39. Author interview with Frederick Allen, 17 May 1994, private collection.

40. Reagan Campaign Notes, 14 Aug. 1980, 1980 Campaign Papers, Tony Dolan Files, box 860, RRL.

41. Eizenstat, *Carter*, 867–69; James H. Broussard, *Ronald Reagan: Champion of Conservative America*, 96–102.

42. O'Neill to Carter, 19 Aug. 1980, Carter to O'Neill, 20 Aug. 1980, C-Track File Number 76709, JCL.

43. Memorandum, Frank Moore to Carter, 19 Aug. 1980, Re Senate vote, Staff Secretary, Handwriting File, box 200, JCL; JC, *White House Diary*, 458–59 (quotation on 459); Carter, *Public Papers, 1980–81, Vol. II*, 1548.

44. *Congressional Quarterly Weekly Report*, Alaska Lands Bill, 23 Aug. 1980.

45. Eizenstat, *Carter*, 243–45, 273.

46. Reagan Speech at Charleston Navy Yard, 20 Aug. 1980, 1980 Campaign Papers, Press Section, box 547, RRL.

47. Draft of Speech with Carter emendations, 21 Aug. 1980, Staff Secretary, Handwriting File, box 200, JCL.

48. Surrogate Attacks, 21 Aug. 1980, 1980 Campaign Papers, Tony Dolan Files, box 865, RRL.

49. Carter to Lipshutz, 21 Aug. 1980, Staff Secretary, Handwriting File, box 201, and WHCF, box FG 8, JCL; Memorandum, Al McDonald to Carter, 8 Aug. 1980, Re American Legion speech, Clough File, box 38, JCL; Brown News Conference, 22 Aug. 1980, 1980 Campaign Files, Tony Dolan Files, box 980, RRL.

50. Memorandum, Eizenstat to Carter, 28 Aug. 1980, Re Interview with Trude Feldman, Staff Secretary, Handwriting File, box 202, JCL.

51. JC, *White House Diary*, 459–61.

Chapter 32

1. Richard Primuth, "Ronald Reagan's Use of Race in the 1976 and 1980 Presidential Elections," *Georgia Historical Quarterly* 100, no. 1 (Spring 2016), 37, 45; Earl Black and Merle Black, *The Vital South: How Presidents are Elected*, 307–11; Earl Black and Merle Black, *The Rise of Southern Republicans*, 211–17.

2. PDD, 1 Sept. 1980, JCL; *Atlanta Constitution*, 2 Sept. 1980; (Florence, AL) *Daily Times*, 4 Sept. 2010.

3. *Atlanta Constitution*, 1 Sept. 1980; Jimmy Carter, *Keeping Faith: Memoirs of a President*, 556.

4. *New York Times*, 2 Sept. 1980.

5. Carter, *Public Papers, 1980–81, Vol. II*, 1601–05; JC, *Keeping Faith*, 556–57; *Americus Times-Recorder*, 1 Sept. 1980.

6. Carter, *Public Papers, 1908–81, Vol. II*, 1605; George Weigel, *The Final Revolution: The Resistance Church and the Collapse of Communism*, 137–41.

7. Memorandum, Anthony R. Dolan to Ed Meese, 2 Sept. 1980 (Carter quotation), 1980 Campaign Papers, Tony Dolan File, box 876, RRL; Carter, *Public Papers, 1980–81, Vol. II*, 1640; Jimmy Carter, *White House Diary*, 462.

8. JC, *White House Diary*, 462 (quotation); Carter, *Public Papers, 1980–81, Vol. II*, 1610–25.

9. Don Campbell article, Gannett News Service, 2 Sept. 1980, copy in Al McDonald File, box 5, JCL.

10. *New York Times*, 5 Sept. 1980; Notes on Staff Meeting, 8 Sept. 1980, White House Press, Jenkins, box 5, JCL; Memorandum, Moses to Carter, 5 Sept. 1980, Re Meeting with Jewish Organization, Staff Secretary, Handwriting File, box 204, JCL; Morris Abram, Op-Ed, 15 Oct. 1980, and Abram to Charles Kirbo, 30 Nov. 1976, both in Morris Abram Papers, box 8, Special Collections, Woodruff Library, Emory University.

11. William Casey Statement, 5 Sept. 1980, 1980 Campaign Papers, Tony Dolan Files, box 859, RRL; Memorandum, Cutler and Moses to Carter, Re Your Personal Notes, 8 Sept. 1980, White House Counsel, Cutler, box 59, JCL; *New York Times*, 8 Sept. 1980.

12. Gary Sick, *October Surprise: America's Hostages in Iran and the Election of Ronald Reagan*, 84; H. R. Brands, *Reagan: The Life*, 231–37; Jonathan Alter, *His Very Best: Jimmy Carter, A Life*, 608–609.

13. Andrew J. DeRoche, "Standing Firm for Principles: Jimmy Carter and Zimbabwe," *Diplomatic History* 43, no. 4 (Fall 1999): 657; Piero Gleijeses, "A Test of Wills: Jimmy Carter, South Africa, and the Independence of Namibia," *Diplomatic History* 34, No. 5 (November 2010): 853–91; Scott Kaufman, *Plans Unraveled: The Foreign Policy of the Carter Administration*, 60–61.

14. First Lady Press Office, speeches and schedules, boxes 18 and 19; JCL; PDD, 1 Sept. 1980, JCL; *Americus Times-Recorder*, 12 Sept. 1980; Mrs. Ribicoff to Mrs. Carter, 12 Sept. 1980, WHCF, Name File, Ribicoff, JCL; Invitation to Kirbo Farm 15 Sept. 1980, WHCF, Name, Kibo, JCL; Note, Clough to Carter, re Mrs. Daley, 17 Sept. 1980, Staff Secretary, Handwriting File, box 205, JCL.

15. Byrd to Carter, 10 Sept. 1980, Clough File, box 456, JCL.

16. H. Brandt Ayres to Carter, 12 Sept. 1980, Staff Secretary, Handwriting File, box 206, JCL.

17. Carter to Hugh Sidey, 12 Sept. 1980, Staff Secretary, Handwriting File, box 205, JCL.

18. Eizenstat to Congressman Parren J. Mitchell, 16 Sept. 1980, WHCF, box BEW-26, JCL; *Columbus (GA) Ledger*, 16 Sept. 1980; *Atlanta Constitution*, 17 Sept. 1980.

19. *Atlanta Constitution*, 17, 18 Sept., 7, 10 Oct. 1980; Carter Speech at Ebenezer Baptist Church, 16 Sept. 1980, Staff Secretary, Handwriting File, box 205, JCL.

20. Statement of the Reagan-Bush "Truth Squad," 14 Oct. 1980, 1980 Campaign Papers, Press Section, box 563, RRL; The Truth Squad, Sept. 1980, 1980 Campaign Papers, Political Operations, box 417, RRL; Biographical Profiles of R-B "Truth Team," Oct. 1980, Political Operations, Jerry Carmen, Truth Squad, 1980 Campaign Papers, box 417, RRL; Memorandum, Anthony R. Dolan to Ed Meese, Oct. 1980, 1980 Campaign Papers, Tony Dolan Files, box 867, RRL ("brawlers" quotation).

21. Bureau of Intelligence and Research, 10 Sept. 1980, Declassified Document NLC-SAFE-17-E-30-27-2-7, JCL; JC, *White House Diary*, 466–67; Craig Shirley, *Rendezvous with Destiny: Ronald Reagan and the Campaign That Changed America*, 528–29.

22. JC, *White House Diary*, 466; Gordon A. Craig and Francis L. Loewenheim, *The Diplomats, 1939–1979*, 655–660; Duane R. Clarridge, *A Spy for All Seasons: My Life in the CIA*, 196–97; Robert Kagan, *A Twilight Struggle: American Power and Nicaragua, 1977–1990*, 43, 51–53, 110–11, 127; Morris H. Morley, *Washington, Somoza, and the Sandinistas: State and Regime in U.S. Policy toward Nicaragua, 1969–1981*, 308–18; William M. LeoGrande, *Our Own Backyard: The United States in Central America, 1977–1992*, 16–117, 29–32; Stansfield Turner, *Secrecy and Democracy: The CIA in Transition*, 87–89: Tim Weiner, *Legacy of Ashes: The History of the CIA*, 380; Bob Woodward, *Veil: The Secret Wars of the CIA 1981–1987*, 6–7, 67–68.

23. JC, *White House Diary*, 467.

24. JC, *White House Diary*, 468–69; JC, *Keeping Faith*, 561; Richard V. Pierard and Robert D. Linder, *Civil Religion and the Presidency*, 244–45; Leo P. Ribuffo, *The Old Christian Right: The Protestant Far Right from the Great Depression to the Cold War*, 262–63; Gary Scott Smith, *Faith and the Presidency: From George Washington to George W. Bush*, 298.

25. Various Notes, 1 Oct. 1980, Staff Secretary, Handwriting File, box 212, JCL.

26. Carter, *Public Papers, 1980–81, Vol. III*, 2013.

27. JC, *White House Diary*, 470.

28. Carter, *Public Papers, 1980–81, Vol. III*, 2057–65 (quotations); PDD, 3 Oct. 1980, JCL.

29. JC, *White House Diary*, 470.

30. Schedule, 3 Oct. 1980, Staff Secretary, Handwriting File, box 208, JCL; Note, 3 Oct. 1980, Carter to Rick Hertzberg, Staff Secretary, Handwriting File, box 208, JCL; *New York Times*, 8 Oct. 1980; Carter, *Public Papers, 1980–81, Vol. III*, 2095–2105 (Rosalynn quotation on 2100).

31. *Americus Times-Recorder*, 9 Oct. 1980; *Atlanta Constitution*, 10 Oct. 1980; *New York Times*, 11 Oct. 1980; JC, *White House Diary*, 471.

32. Draft of Speech for Nashville Town Meeting, 10 Oct. 1980, Staff Secretary, Handwriting File, box 209, JCL; *Murfreesboro Post*, 1 Jan. 2012. Six months later, Hinckley severely wounded President Ronald Reagan in an assassination attempt on 30 March 1981 in Washington, DC.

33. Dolan to Larry Seidler, Re Incumbency Abuse, 5 Oct. 1980 ("played well" quotation), Dolan to Ed Meese, 15 Oct. 1980, and others, all in 1980 Campaign Papers, Dolan File, box 868, RRL; Opinion Survey, 15 Oct. 1980, WHCF, box PR-76, JCL.

34. JC, *White House Diary*, 476.

35. PDD, 15, 19, 20 October 1980, JCL; Clymer, *Edward M. Kennedy: A Biography*, 319.

36. Iran Working Group, 21 Oct. 1980, Re Algeria, Declassified Document NLC-43-61-6-1-0, JCL.

37. Shirley, *Rendezvous with Destiny*, 449, 496, 508, 521–22; Jules Witcover, *Party of the People: A History of the Democrats*, 613–14; Carter, *Public Papers, 1980–81, Vol. III*, 2013, 2168–69 (quotation), 2320; Elizabeth Drew, *Portrait of an Election: The 1980 Presidential Campaign*, 310; Burton I. Kaufman and Scott Kaufman, *The Presidency of James Earl Carter, Jr.*, 239–41.

38. Memorandum, Anthony R. Dolan to Robert Garrick, Oct. 1980, Re Next Two weeks, 1980 Campaign Papers, Tony Dolan Files, box 876, RRL; Betty Glad, *An Outsider in the White House: Jimmy Carter, His Advisers, and the Making of American Foreign Policy*, 272; Barbara Honegger, *October Surprise*, 52.

39. Peter G. Bourne, *Jimmy Carter: A Comprehensive Biography from Plains to the Post-Presidency*, 469–70; Author interview with Edmund Muskie, 3 April 1992, John C. Stennis Oral History Collection, Mississippi State University; Brands, *Reagan*, 234–35.

40. Proposed Carter Tactics for Debate and Campaign Advertising, 21 Oct. 1980, apparently a page from the briefing book, 1980 Campaign Papers, Ed Meese File, box 140, RRL; Memorandum, Wayne Valis to Ed Meese, 21 Oct. 1980, p. 3 of briefing book (quotation), RRL. A copy of the briefing book is in 1980 Campaign Papers, White House Staff Member and Office Files, Roberts, John G. Files 1982–86, box 7, RRL. See also Michael Kelly, *Things Worth Fighting For: Collected Writings*, 70, and Stuart E. Eizenstat, *President Carter: The White House Years*, 878–80; Shirley, *Rendezvous with Destiny*, 515–16, 529, 610; Alter, *His Very Best*, 588–89.

41. *Unauthorized Transfers of Nonpublic Information during the 1980 Presidential Election*, Report of the Subcommittee on Human Resources of the Committee on Post Office and Civil Service, 17 May 1984, 98th Cong., Second Session.
42. Malcolm Byrne, *Iran-Contra: Reagan's Scandal and the Unchecked Abuse of Presidential Power*, 35, 40–41.
43. Author interview with Stansfield Turner, 6 April 1992, pp. 21–27, John C. Stennis Oral History Project, Mississippi State University; Mike Evans, "An October Surprise," *Jerusalem Post*, 25 July 2019.
44. The most detailed, scholarly account of the October Surprise is Kai Bird, *The Outlier: The Unfinished Presidency of Jimmy Carter*, 551–63, 625. Other important sources include the following:

Robert Parry, a controversial investigative journalist who publicized the Iran-Contra scandal of the Reagan administration, gives the most detailed account of the emergence and likelihood of the conspiracy. He offers proof that Bush was not in Washington where he said he was that night of the Paris meeting in "Keeping a Curious Bush Secret," *The Smirking Chimp*, 13 Aug. 2011.

Gary Sick, *October Surprise: America's Hostages in Iran and the Election of Ronald Reagan*, explored the idea in his 1991 book, and a number of people involved appeared on the Phil Donahue television show on May 16, 1991, to confirm or deny that the Republican campaign had made the deal with the Iranians.

Former Secretary of State Cyrus Vance "put a lot of credence on whatever Gary said." Author interview with Cyrus Vance, 1 May 1992, p. 16, Stennis Oral History Project, Mississippi State University.

Ari Ben-Menashe, *Profits of War: Inside the Secret U.S.-Israeli Arms Network*, 12. Ben-Menashe was a former Israeli military intelligence officer who had worked with the Likud Party, which agreed with their leader Begin that Carter was too friendly with the Arabs and could not be trusted. He notes how details of the meeting were revealed by a French arms dealer, a French investigative reporter, Iran's ex-President Bani-Sadr, and a classified report from the Russian government. He, like virtually everyone on either side of the debate, had a personal, political, vengeful, or hidden agenda that might have tainted his testimony. Yet his testimony, the subject of many subsequent investigations, became as hard to disprove as to prove. The most detailed investigation of Ben-Menache, which tends to support his veracity, is in Seymour M. Hersh, *The Samson Option: Israel's Nuclear Arsenal and American Foreign Policy*, 260–63, 271–83, 309–10, 322–24.

Ian Black and Benny Morris, *Israel's Secret Wars: A History of Israel's Intelligence Services*, 183, sheds light on the cooperation of Iranian and Israeli Secret services and Israeli intelligence operations.

Author interview with Martin Franks, 3 April 1992, in which Franks suggests there were some in the Carter campaign who suspected "Republican activities vis-à-vis the Iranians," especially after the quick transference of Carter's debate book to the Reagan campaign. Martin Franks is related to David D. Newsom, the undersecretary for political affairs who opposed the admission of the shah in to the country for medical care.

H. R. Brands, *American Dreams: The United States since 1945*, 219, notes the accusations against the Reagan campaign. His biography of Reagan, *Reagan: The Life*, is more detailed and explicit, but still slightly tentative.

Barbara Honegger, an insider in the Reagan campaign who became an elite investigative journalist, used the same evidence to state categorically that the Republican secret dealings with Iran before the election happened. Entitled *October Surprise*, her book was published before Sick's and others, and before the 1992 election.

Stansfield Turner, Carter's Director of the CIA, said his "personal opinion is that [William] Casey tried to make a deal. Whether he made one or not, I don't know; I can't back that up, but sense there is just a lot of smoke there." He found it interesting that Reagan did not criticize Carter before October 20, possibly for fear that Carter would get the hostages out. On October 20, the same day "there was supposedly a deal made in Paris," Reagan gave a speech excoriating Carter's handling of the hostage situation, "which you can attribute to the possibility that he knew the hostages weren't going to get out." Furthermore, Turner suggested, in light of the Iran-Contra scandal of the Reagan administration, that "one person" "who would have been one of the few people who knew that there was a deal, and that he could be blackmailed if he didn't continue playing the game. That was Ronald Reagan." Author interview with Stansfield Turner, 6 April 1992, pp. 31–33, John C. Stennis Oral History Project, Mississippi State University. See also Turner, *Terrorism and Democracy*, 152–53.

Sarah McClendon, *Mr. President, Mr. President! My Fifty Years of Covering the White House*, 186, heard from two people who knew the pilot who flew some of the principals to Paris and who revealed to them that the meeting did take place.

Robert M. Gates, *Duty: Memoirs of a Secretary at War*, 177–78, alludes to the episode but is not specific. See also David MacMichael, " 'October Surprise': Gates May Have Inadvertently Bolstered Allegations," New York Times News Service, reprinted in Memphis *Commercial Appeal*, 22 Oct. 1991, from the *Los Angeles Daily News*. MacMichael was a former estimates officer with the CIA's National intelligence Council and Director of the Association of National Security Alumni.

Additional information about the October Surprise and documentation will be in a subsequent chapter dealing with the presidential election of 1992, when the story first became public.

45. Kathryn Koob, *Guest of the Revolution*, 178.
46. Memorandum, Dolan to Ed Meese, Oct. 1980, 1980 Campaign Papers, Tony Dolan Files, Memoranda box 867, RRL.
47. Reagan to Schmidt, 11 Oct. 1980, 1980 Campaign Papers, Press Section, box 547, RRL; Reagan Statement on Human Rights, 17 Oct. 1980, Remarks of Ambassador George Bush, 19 Oct. 1980, both in 1980 Campaign Papers, Press Section, boxes 563 and 553 respectively, RRL.
48. *Washington Star*, 20 Oct. 1980, *Washington Post*, 21 Oct.1980, both in 1980 Campaign Papers, Tony Dolan Files, box 903, RRL.
49. *Ladies Home Journal*, Oct. 1980, copy in VF, box Carter, R., JCL.
50. "Head to Head on the Issues," *US News and World Report*, 6 Oct. 1980; Debate Material in AL Moses Papers, box 1, JCL.

51. *New York Times*, Oct. 1980, copy in Moses Papers, box 18, JCL.

52. Stephen F. Hayward, "Make Mine Malaise," *Washington Times*, 20 July 2009.

53. Speech draft, 22 Oct. 1980, Sarah Weddington Papers, box 18, JCL; JC, *White House Diary*, 474.

54. JC, *White House Diary*, 475.

55. Memorandum, Max Hugel to Bill Casey, and others, 23 Oct. 1980, Re hostages, 1980 Campaign Papers, 1965–68, Series X: Citizens Operations (Max Hugel), box 299, RRL; *Atlanta Constitution*, 24 Oct. 1980; Memorandum, Charlie Schultz to Carter, 23 Oct. 1980, Staff Secretary, Handwriting File, box 211, JCL; *New York Times*, 24 Oct. 1980; Rosalynn's speech notes for Oct., First Lady Press Office, boxes 19, 32, JCL.

Chapter 33

1. *Atlanta Constitution*, 28 Dec. 1980; National Public Radio Interview with Sam Popkin, San Diego, 30 Sept. 2004.

2. Herbert B. Asher, *Presidential Elections and American Politics: Voters, Candidates, and Campaigns since 1952*, 181.

3. Walter Shapiro, "John Anderson: The Nice Guy Syndrome," *The Atlantic*, Feb. 1980.

4. Jimmy Carter, *White House Diary*, 466.

5. Ibid., 480; *Washington Post*, 4 Dec. 2017.

6. Richard Nixon, "Possible Debate Questions," 27 Oct. 1980, 1980 Campaign Papers, Tony Dolan Files: Unsorted Drafts, Memoranda and Research Papers, box 878, RRL.

7. JC, *White House Diary*, 476.

8. Copy of Speech, 27 Oct. 1980, First Lady Press Office, box 19, JCL. After his release in 1986, Anatoly Shcharansky emigrated to Israel, where he adopted the Hebrew name Natan and simplified his last name to Sharansky. See JC, *White House Diary*, 105, and Presidential Directive/NSC on Human Rights, with Carter's annotations, Nov. 1980, VF, box '80 Campaign, JCL.

9. Lee Linder, "First Lady Attends Soviet Jewry Conference and Sees Play," AP News Release 27 Oct. 1980; "Avital Sharansky to First Lady," Jewish Telegraphic Agency, 31 Oct. 1980.

10. PDD, 27, 28 Oct. 1980, JCL.

11. Philip Jenkins, *Decade of Nightmares: The End of the Sixties and the Making of Eighties America*, 98–107; Rhodri Jeffreys-Jones, *The CIA and American Democracy*, 227–30; JC, *White House Diary*, 476–77; Carter, *Public Papers, 1980–81, Vol. III*, 2476–2502; Asher, *Presidential Elections*, 185–90; Rosalynn Carter, *First Lady from Plains*, 337–38; Jimmy Carter, *Keeping Faith: Memoirs of a President*, 564–65: Peter G. Bourne, *Jimmy Carter: A Comprehensive Biography from Plains to the Post-Presidency*, 471; W. Carl Biven, *Jimmy Carter's Economy: Policy in an Age of Limits*, 12–13; Burton I. Kaufman and Scott Kaufman, *The Presidency of James Earl Carter, Jr.*, 243.

12. PDD, 29, 30, 31 Oct. 1980, JCL.

13. Carter, *Public Papers, 1980–81, Vol. III*, 2650; *Atlanta Constitution, New York Times*, 3 Nov. 1980; JC, *Keeping Faith*, 567.

14. Carter Notes, 3 Nov. 1980, Senior Staff Meeting, Alonzo M. McDonald Collection, box 15 ("we do not know"); Pool Report, 3 Nov. 1980, unsigned, WHCF, box POR-82, JCL ("good relations").

15. Ibid., pp. 1, 2, 3 Nov. 1980, JCL; JC, *White House Diary*, 477–79.

16. Jordan interview in the *Atlanta Constitution*, 28 Dec. 1980; Hamilton Jordan, *Crisis: The Last Year of the Carter Presidency*, 360.

17. Rosalynn's Remarks, 2 Nov. 1089, First Lady Press Office, box 19, JCL; RSC, *First Lady*, 339–40.

18. News clipping, 3 Nov. 1980, Staff Secretary, Handwriting File, box 212, JCL.

19. Senior Staff Meeting Notes, 4 Nov. 1980, Al McDonald Collection, box 15, JCL; JC, *White House Diary*, 478–79; Carter, *Public Papers, 1980–81, Vol. III*, 2677–82.

20. RSC, *First Lady*, 338–39; JC, *Keeping Faith*, 568; Stuart E. Eizenstat, *President Carter: The White House Years*, 889–90.

21. RSC, *First Lady*, 340–41; *New York Times*, 19 Nov. 1980 (Rosalynn quotation); *Americus Times-Recorder*, 4 Nov. 1980; Carter, *Public Papers, 1980–81, Vol. III*, 2683–85; Scott Kaufman, *Rosalynn Carter: Equal Partner in the White House*, 142; Bush quote in Jon Meacham, *Destiny and Power: The American Odyssey of George Herbert Walker Bush*, 260.

22. Jerry Parr to Mr. President, 1 Dec. 1980, Carter to Parr, 3 Dec. 1980, both in Clough File, box 46, JCL; Carter, *Public Papers, 1980–81, Vol. III*, 2685.

23. JC, *White House Diary*, 479; Carl Sferrazza Anthony, *First Ladies, Vol. II: The Saga of the Presidents' Wives and Their Power*, 18; RSC, *First Lady*, 341–42.

24. PDD, 4 Nov. 1980, JCL (Carter quotation); "Goodbye Mr. President," *Atlanta Constitution*, 28 Dec. 1980 (Jordan quotation); RSC, *First Lady*, 342.

25. Speechwriters, Hertzberg, box 21, JCL; Carter, *Public Papers, 1980–81, Vol. III*, 2687–88; RSC, *First Lady*, 342–43.

26. Telegram, Carter to Reagan, 4 Nov. 1980, WHCF, box PL-5, JCL; JC, *White House Diary*, 480.

27. Eizenstat, *Carter*, 891–92; Douglas Brinkley, *The Unfinished Presidency: Jimmy Carter's Journey beyond the White House*, 1–2 (Carter quotation).

28. *Atlanta Constitution*, 5 Nov. 1980; Hanes Walton, Jr., *The Native Son Presidential Candidate: The Carter Vote in Georgia*, 90, 99; *New York Times*, 12 Nov. 2000; Gregory P. Domin, *Jimmy Carter, Public Opinion, and the Search for Values, 1977–1981*, 87–91; Kenneth S. Baer, *Reinventing Democrats: The Politics of Liberalism from Reagan to Clinton*, 22–35; Morris B. Abram, *The Day Is Short: An Autobiography*, 251–69; Author interview with Tip O'Neill, 25 Oct. 1990 ("sad" quotation); Author interview with Jimmy and Rosalynn Carter, 12 Oct. 1994 ("deserved" quotation); Theodore H. White, *America in Search of Itself: The Making of the President, 1956–1980*, 413–15.

29. JC, *Keeping Faith*, 572.

30. Senior Staff Meeting, Instructions from the President, 5 and 6 Nov. 1980, McDonald Papers, box 15, JCL ("*full cooperation*," emphasis is Carter's); Carter, *Public Papers, 1980–81, Vol. III*, 2698; JC, *White House Diary*, 481.

31. PDD, 5 Nov. 1980, JCL.

32. JC, *White House Diary*, 481; JC, *Keeping Faith*, 573–74.

33. Brzezinski to Carter, 5 Nov. 1980, Staff Secretary, Handwriting File, box 212, JCL.

34. Telegram, Sadat to Carter, 5 Nov. 1980, NSA, Brzezinski Material, Country File, boxes 18–33, JCL.

35. Popes to Carters, 6 Nov. 1980, WHCF, box PP-10, JCL.

36. JC, *White House Diary*, 481.

37. PDD, 7–10 Nov. 1980, JCL; JC, *White House Diary*, 482–83.

38. Woodruff to Carter, 8 Nov. 1980, Robert W. Woodruff Papers, box 15, Emory University; *New York Times*, 7, 10 Nov. 1980; JC, *White House Diary*, 504.

39. Form Letter, 14 Nov. 1980, WHCF, box PP-10, JCL; Carter to Jimmy Allen, 13 Nov. 1980, WHCF, Name File, Southern Baptist Convention, JCL.

40. David Paul Kuhn, *The Neglected Voter: White Men and the Democratic Dilemma*, 73, 82, 104–107; Alexander P. Lamis, *The Two-Party South*, 211–14; Jason Sokol, *There Goes My Everything: White Southerners in the Age of Civil Rights, 1945–1975*, 280; Hedrick Smith, *The Power Game: How Washington Works*, 673; JC, *White House Diary*, 485; Daniel K. Williams, *God's Own Party: The Making of the Christian Right*, 184–85, 188–94.

41. Begin to Carter, 6 Nov. 1980, Carter to Begin, 7 Nov. 1980, both in Plains File, box 23, JCL; Lawrence Wright, *Thirteen Days in September: Carter, Begin, and Sadat at Camp David*, 268; Yossi Melvin and Dan Raviv, *Friends in Deed: Inside the U.S.-Israel Alliance*, 188–89.

42. Carter, *Public Papers, 1980–81, Vol. III*, 2719–20; JC, *White House Diary*, 484, 505; JC, *Keeping Faith*, 575–76.

43. JC, *White House Diary*, 485; Dan Fleshler, *Transforming America's Israel Lobby*, 102–106.

44. RSC, *First Lady*, 343–44.

45. Memoranda, Mary Hoyt to Rosalyn, 14 and 17 Nov. 1980, both in Hoyt Papers, box 3, JCL; *Americus Times-Recorder*, 19 Nov. 1980.

Chapter 34

1. Reuters article by Jonathan Sharp, 5 Nov. 1980, in 1980 Campaign Papers, Series Materials from Unknown Office, box 575, RRL. Other similar reports in the same location suggest that the arrival of Reagan and departure of Carter was of no importance to the Iranians. See also Interview with Bruce Laingen, 9 Jan. 1993, Foreign Affairs Oral History Project, Library of Congress; Shaul Bakhash, *The Reign of the Ayatollahs: Iran and the Islamic Revolution*, 150.

2. Carter's notes for the State Department event, 18 Nov. 1980, and his personal note to Vance, both in Staff Secretary, Handwriting File, box 213, JCL; Carter note to Cy with notes, 19 Nov. 1980, WHCF, Name, Vance, C., JCL; Carter, *Public Papers, 1980–81, Vol. III*, 2732–33; Jimmy Carter, *White House Diary*, 486.

3. JC, *White House Diary*, 486; Carter, *Public Papers, 1980–81, Vol. III*, 2733–36.

4. Ibid., 2734–35.

5. Ibid., 2736–39; JC, *White House Diary*, 486 (Carter quotation); Carter "pain in the ass" quote in Rosalynn Carter, *First Lady from Plains*, 344–45.

6. Carter notes on meeting with Reagan, 20 Nov. 1980, Declassified Document NLC-2732–33, JCL; JC, *White House Diary*, 486.

   Jimmy Carter, *Keeping Faith: Memoirs of a President*, 577–78.

7. Mary Finch Hoyt, *East Wing: A Memoir*, 204; Hoyt's notes on Nancy Reagan's visit, 20 Nov. 1980, Hoyt Papers, box 1, JCL. Mrs. Reagan did return on December 13 when the Carters were at Camp David and met with Rex Scouten and her decorator (note in Hoyt Papers, box 3, JCL).

8. Allison Leland to Mary Hoyt, 24 Nov. 1980, with attachments, Hoyt Papers, box 3, JCL.

9. Daily Schedule, 2 Dec. 1980, WHCF, box PF-32, JCL; *New York Times*, 3 Dec. 1980 (quotation); Cecil Andrus, Miller Center Interview, 67–77, JCL; Carter, *Public Papers, 1980–81, Vol. III*, 2756–62; JC, *White House Diary*, 483, 490; JC, *Keeping Faith*, 581–83.

10. JC, *White House Diary*, 493–94.

11. AP News Release, 12 Dec. 1980; Carter to Penne Laingen, 17 Dec. 1980, Clough File, box 45, JCL.

12. JC, *White House Diary*, 495–96. Ten years after Carter's prediction, the Soviet Union collapsed and the Cold War ended in 1991. See also Stuart E. Eizenstat, *President Carter: The White House Years*, 657.

13. JC, *White House Diary*, 497.

14. Carter's comments, 18 Dec. 1980, Staff Secretary, Handwriting File, box 216, JCL; JC, *White House Diary*, 494; PDD, 18 Dec. 1980, JCL.

15. *Americus Times-Recorder*, 24, 25 Dec. 1980; *Atlanta Constitution*, 26 Dec. 1980 (quotation); JC, *White House Diary*, 498–99; Grant Hayter-Menzies, *Lillian Carter: A Compassionate Life*, 198.

16. *Atlanta Journal and Constitution*, 27 Dec. 1980; *New York Times*, 27 Dec. 1980.

17. *New York Times*, 28 Dec. 1980; Handwritten draft of speech, with comments, 31 Dec. 1980, Staff Secretary, Handwriting File, box 217, JCL; JC, *White House Diary*, 508.

18. JC, *White House Diary*, 503.

19. *New York Times*, 3 Jan. 1981; *Washington Star*, 3 Jan. 1981; JC, *White House Diary*, 503-504.

20. *New York Times*, 5 Jan. 1981 (quotation); JC, *White House Diary*, 504.

21. Bob Bergland, Miller Center Interview, 45, JCL ("barbs"); *Atlanta Constitution*, 5 Jan. 1981; UPI News Release, 12 Dec. 1981, Clough File, box 46, JCL; Carter comments, Staff Meeting, 15 Dec. 1980, White House Press, Jenkins, box 5, JCL.

22. *Washington Post*, 12 Dec. 1980, copy in VF, Box Carter, R., JCL.

23. John Paul II to Carter, 12 Dec. 1980, Plains File, box 23, JCL.

24. Telegram for President's Eyes Only, 9 Jan. 1981, Declassified Document NLC-16-128-7-27-7, JCL; Foreign Affairs Oral History Project, Interview with Bruce Laingen, 9 Jan. 1993, Library of Congress; Carter, *Public Papers, 1980–81, Vol. III*, 2264.

25. JC, *White House Diary*, 505–508.

26. JC, *White House Diary*, 506; JC, *Keeping Faith*, 593–94.

27. Carter, *Public Papers, 1980–81, Vol. III*, 2891–92; *New York Times* and *Atlanta Constitution*, 15 Jan. 1981; JC, *White House Diary*, 507.

28. Carter, *Public Papers, 1980–81, Vol. III*, 2892–93.

29. RSC, *First Lady*, 345–46.

30. Carter, *Public Papers, 1980–81, Vol. III*, 2893–2912, 2916.

31. VF, Presidential Directives, JCL.

32. JC, *White House Diary*, 508–10.

33. Carter, *Public Papers, 1980–81, Vol. III*, 2922–30 (quotation on 2924); JC, *White House Diary*, 509.

34. Memorandum, Rick Hertzberg to Jack Watson, 20 Nov. 1980, Powell File, box 47, JCL.

35. Carter, *Public Papers, 1980–81, Vol. III*, 2931–97 (quotation on 2997).

36. JC, White House Diary, 508–11.

37. RSC, *First Lady*, 346; *New York Times*, 16, 18, 19 Jan. 1981; Carter's Statement Re Hostages, 18 Jan. 1981, Plains File, box 14, JCL.

38. Begin to Carter, 19 Jan.1981, Plains File, box 23, JCL.

39. Warren Christopher, *Chances of a Lifetime: A Memoir*, 116–20; Robert B. Owen, "The Final Negotiation and Release in Algiers," in Warren Christopher, et al., *American Hostages in Iran: The Conduct of a Crisis*, 297–324, 411; *Washington Post*, 25 Jan. 1981.

40. Carter, *Public Papers, 1980–81, Vol. III*, 3026–43; Eizenstat, *Carter*, 809–10; Bob Woodward, *Shadow: Five Presidents and the Legacy of Watergate*, 85.

41. Staff writers, "Sands in the Hourglass: The Story of the Hostage Release," *Washington Post*, 25 Jan. 1981.

42. Tim Wells, *444 Days: The Hostages Remember*, 418–23.

43. *Time Magazine*, 26 Jan. 1981, p. 13.

44. The note cards, dated 19 Jan. 1981, are in Plains File, box 24, JCL.

45. Telegram, Intelligence and NSA to Carter, 19 Jan. 1981, and others, Plains File, box 24, JCL; JC, *White House Diary*, 510; Will Bunch, *Tear Down This Myth: How the Reagan Legacy Has Distorted Our Politics and Haunts Our Future*, 14–15.

46. Robin Wright, *In the Name of God: The Khomeini Decade*, 95; Wells, *444 Days*, 426–29.

47. Interview with L. Bruce Laingen, 9 Jan. 1993, Foreign Affairs Oral History Project; Mark Bowden, *Guests of the Ayatollah: The First Battle in America's War with Militant Islam*, 584–89; David Harris, *The Crisis: The President, the Prophet, and the Shah— 1979 and the Coming of Militant Islam*, 424; Bruce L. Laingen, *Yellow Ribbon: The Secret Journal of Bruce Laingen*, 271; Wells, *444 Days*, 429–31.

48. JC, *White House Diary*, 512. It was not clear to Carter whether the hostages were all on the same plane or divided into groups and on two planes. Most accounts suggest that the hostages were all on the same plane, which meant that the other two planes would serve as decoys in case hostile Iranian aircraft chased or tried to attack them.

49. Wells, *444 Days*, 431.

50. RSC, *First Lady*, 351; JC, *White House Diary*, 513; Christopher, *Chances of a Lifetime*, 120–21; Gary Sick, *All Fall Down: America's Tragic Encounter with Iran*, 402.

51. JC, *White House Diary*, 513; RSC, *First Lady*, 351–52.

52. "The Hostage Crisis in Iran: 1979–81," Plains File, box 24, JCL; Michael Reagan interview, 8 June 2004, Fox News; Trudeau to Carter, 20 Jan.1981, Plains File, box 23, JCL; RSC, *First Lady*, 350–51.

53. *Atlanta Constitution*, 21 Jan. 1981; *Austin (Texas) American-Statesman*, 19 July 2004 (Secret Service Agent); JC, *White House Diary*, 513–14; *New York Times*, 21 Jan. 1981; "Declaration of Algiers, 21 Jan. 1981, WHCF, box CO-32, JCL; Hamilton Jordan, *Crisis: The Last Year of the Carter Presidency*, 402–403.

54. *Atlanta Constitution*, 21 Jan., 1981; JC, *White House Diary*, 514; Christopher, *Chances of a Lifetime*, 122–23.

55. *Life Magazine*, 21 Jan. 1981, VF, box Hostages, JCL (Carter quotation).

56. Draft for speech in Speechwriters, Hertzberg, box 21, JCL; *New York Times* interview with Mary Hoyt and article by Terrence Smith, 21 Jan. 1981.

57. Hayter-Menzies, *Lillian Carter*, 200 (Lillian quotation).

58. *Atlanta Constitution*, 21 Jan. 1981; Wells, *444 Days*, 436–37.

59. JC, *White House Diary*, 514–15.

60. Author interview with Gary Sick, 23 March 1992, p. 5, Stennis Oral History Collection, Mississippi State University; JC, *White House Diary*, 515; Jordan, *Crisis*, 408–409.

61. UPI Story, 21 Jan. 1981, "Carter Meets Hostages."

62. Laingen, *Yellow Ribbon*, 278.

63. Carter remarks, 21 Jan. 1981, VF, Hostages, JCL; JC, *White House Diary*, 515–17.

64. UPI Story, 21 Jan. 1981, "Carter Meets Hostages"; Laingen, *Yellow Ribbon*, 278–79.

65. Kathryn Koob, *Guest of the Revolution*, 211–18 (quotation on 218); Douglas Brinkley, *The Unfinished Presidency: Jimmy Carter's Journey beyond the White House*, 41–42; William J. Daugherty, *In the Shadow of the Ayatollah: A CIA Hostage in Iran*, 216–18.

66. *Americus Times-Recorder*, 22 Jan. 1981; *New York Times*, 22 Jan. 1981, 6 June 2016 (Shaefer quotation); JC, *White House Diary*, 516–17; Wells, *444 Days*, 442–44 (quotation on 443).

67. Carter to Reagan, 21 Jan. 1981, Plains File, box 24, JCL.

68. National Park Service, III, interview with Carter, 293, JCL; Author interview with Gary Sick, 23 March 1992, p. 6; Hamilton Jordan, *Crisis*, 417 ("freedom" quotation).

69. JC, *White House Diary*, 517; Hamilton Jordan, *Crisis*, 418–19.

70. "Outline of Presidential Decision" Memorandum on Iranian Agreements, 23 Jan. 1981, and Memorandum, Frank Hodsoll to David Gergen, Re Iranian Hostage Return, 23 Jan. 1981, both in 1980 Campaign Papers, White House Staff Members and Offices Files, Hodsoll, Francis, box 2, RRL.

Chapter 35

1. Carter interview, *Americus Times-Recorder*, 22 Jan. 1981; Jordan interview, *Atlanta Constitution*, 22 Jan. 1981.

2. Clark Clifford, *Counsel to the President: A Memoir*, 618; Author interview with Cyrus Vance, 1 May 1992, pp. 25–26, Stennis Oral History Collection, Mississippi State University. For a good analysis of the rhetoric of Carter's human rights policy versus the reality of it, see David P. Forsythe, *Human Rights and World Politics*, 93–110.

3. Gaddis Smith, *Morality, Reason, and Power: American Diplomacy in the Carter Years*, 3, 34–35.

4. Quoted in Eizenstat, *President Carter: The White House Years*, 894.

5. *New York Times*, 27, 28 (quotation) Jan. 1981; Jimmy Carter, *White House Diary*, 521.

6. Jimmy Carter, National Park Service Interview, III, 311, JCL; JC, *White House Diary*, 520.

7. *New York Times*, 19 Feb. 1981.

8. *Atlanta Constitution*, 12 Feb. 1981; *Americus Times-Recorder*, 12 Feb., 7 March 1981; JC, *White House Diary*, 521.

9. Frederick Allen report, *Atlanta Constitution*, 14 March 1981; *New York Times*, 15 March 1981.

10. JC, *White House Diary*, 524.

11. *New York Times*, 14, 18 March, 17 July 1981; JC, *White House Diary*, 523.

12. JC, *White House Diary*, 520–22, 525.

13. Ibid., 523–24.

14. *Americus Times-Recorder*, 31 March 1981; Author interview with Tip O'Neill, 25 Oct. 1990.

15. Author interview with Jimmy Carter, 12 Oct. 1994, Plains.

16. Speech and Notes for Speech, 17 May 1981, Clough File, boxes 57 & 59, JCL; Peter G. Bourne, *Jimmy Carter: A Comprehensive Biography from Plains to the Post-Presidency*, 476.

17. *Austin (Texas) American-Statesman, Atlanta Constitution*, 3 May 1981; *Washington Post*, 4 May, 1981. See also Randall B. Woods, *Prisoners of Hope: Lyndon B. Johnson, the Great Society, and the Limits of Liberalism*, 255–56, and Joseph Califano, *Governing America: An Insider's Report from the White House and the Cabinet*.

18. James Fallows, "On Political Books," *The Washington Monthly*, July/August 1981, p. 53.

19. *Americus Times-Recorder*, 9, 11 June, 1981.

20. Speech welcoming Sadat, 9 Aug. 1981, Clough File, box 59, JCL: *Americus Times-Recorder*, 10 Aug. 1981; VF, Sadat, JCL; JC, *White House Diary*, 524.

21. Premier Zhao Ziyang Toast, 25 Aug. 1981, Clough File, box 57, JCL; Bourne, *Carter*, 477.

22. JC, *White House Diary*, 522 (quotation), 523; *Atlanta Constitution*, 2, 24 July 1981; Memorandum, Phil Wise to Carter, RE Japan visit, 15 July,1981, Clough File, box 58, JCL; *New York Times*, 27 July 1981.

23. Douglas Brinkley, *The Unfinished Presidency: Jimmy Carter's Journey beyond the White House*, 42; Carter lecture in Osaka, 4 Sept. 1981, Clough File, box 58, JCL; *New York Times*, 5 Sept. 1981; Carter to Ziyang and to Deng Xiaoping, 10 Sept. 1981, Clough File, box 57, JCL.

24. *Atlanta Constitution* and *New York Times*, 16 Sept. 1981; Telegram, Reagan to Carter, 30 Sept. 1981, WHORM, Subject, RRL.

25. Lawrence Wright, *Thirteen Days in September: Carter, Begin, and Sadat at Camp David*, 275–78; Jehan Sadat, *A Woman of Egypt*, 17–21. Islambouli and three others were executed by firing squad in April 1982.

26. *Washington Post*, 7 Oct. 1981; *Americus Times-Recorder*, 7 Oct. 1981.

27. *Americus Times-Recorder*, 7 Oct. 1981.

28. Mark K. Updegrove, *Second Acts: Presidential Lives and Legacies after the White House*, 131; *The Washington Post*, 8 Oct. 1981.

29. Nancy Gibbs and Michael Duffy, *The Presidents Club: Inside the World's Most Exclusive Fraternity*, 337–42; Updegrove, *Second Acts*, 132–34.

30. *New York Times*, 9 Oct. 1981; *Atlanta Constitution*, 17 Oct. 1981; *Washington Post*, 19 Oct. 1981; Gibbs and Duffy, *Presidents Club*, 337–38.

31. Haynes Johnson, "Nixon's Redemption," *Washington Post*, 13 Oct. 1981; Gibbs and Duffy, *Presidents Club*, 345.

32. Haynes Johnson, "International Elite Trade Small Talk under Close Guard, *Washington Post*, 11 Oct, 1981.

33. Gibbs and Duffy, *Presidents Club*, 345–46.

34. Johnson, "Nixon's Redemption," *Washington Post*, 13 Oct. 1981, emphasis added.

35. Jehan Sadat, *Woman of Egypt*, 30–31.

36. *Atlanta Constitution*, 17 Oct. 1981; Wright, *Thirteen Days*, 279 (monument quotation); Gibbs and Duffy, *Presidents Club*, 346–51; Updegrove, *Second Acts*, 131–36.

37. *Atlanta Constitution*, 17, 18 1981; Bourne, *Carter*, 473.

38. Bourne, *Carter*, 476.

39. JC, *White House Diary*, 537; Scott Kaufman, *Rosalynn Carter: Equal Partner in the White House*, 144.

Chapter 36

1. Steven H. Hochman, "With Jimmy Carter in Georgia: A Memoir of his Post-Presidential Years," in Richard Norton Smith and Timothy Walch, editors, *Farewell to the Chief: Former Presidents in American Public Life*, 123–29.

2. *New York Times*, 7 Jan. 1982; *Atlanta Journal and Constitution*, 8 Jan. 1982 (quotation).

3. Lynn Burnett McGill, "Shared Simplicity: The Jimmy Carters and the John Popes at Home in the Mountains," *Southern Homes/Atlanta*, 1983; *New York Times*, 11 Feb. 1982.

4. Scott Kaufman, *Rosalynn Carter: Equal Partner in the White House*, 145–46; *Atlanta Constitution*, 18 Jan. 1982; *New York Times*, 14 Jan. 1982.

5. Carter Interview, National Park Service, II, 267–70, JCL.

6. Douglas Brinkley, *The Unfinished Presidency: Jimmy Carter's Journey beyond the White House*, 77–78; see also E. Stanly Godbold, Jr., *Jimmy and Rosalynn Carter: The Georgia Years, 1924–1974*, 255.

7. Carter Center Timeline and History, 1982; Brinkley, *The Unfinished Presidency*, 89–91.

8. Jimmy Carter, *Beyond the White House: Waging Peace, Fighting Disease, Building Hope*, 7–8.

9. Peter G. Bourne, *Jimmy Carter: A Comprehensive Biography from Plains to the Post-Presidency*, 479.

10. Author interview with Frederick Allen, 17 May 1994; *Atlanta Constitution*, 22 April, 15 July 1982; *New York Times*, 22 April 1982; Jonathan Alter, *His Very Best: Jimmy Carter, A Life*, 626–27.

11. Carter Speech at Emory, 15 Sept. 1982, VF, box Carter, Jimmy, JCL; Carter Center Timeline, 1981, 1982.

12. *Campus Report*, 13 Sept. 1982, VF, Carter, Jimmy, JCL; Bourne, *Jimmy Carter*, 479–80.

13. Carter to Woodruff, 10 Sept. 1982, Robert W. Woodruff Collection, Woodruff Library, Emory University.

14. Bourne, *Carter*, 480–81; Brinkley, *Unfinished Presidency*, 77–78.

15. Bill Shipp, Review, *Atlanta Journal and Constitution*, 14 Nov. 1982.

16. Reagan to Carter, 24 Dec. 1982, WHORM, ID # 1167668, RRL.

17. Brinkley, *Unfinished Presidency*, 102.

18. Ibid., 104–106.

19. *Atlanta Constitution*, 23 Feb., 4 March 1983; *New York Times*, 2, 3 March 1983.

20. Brinkley, *Unfinished Presidency*, 104–106,

21. Jimmy Carter, *The Blood of Abraham: Insights into the Middle East*, 50–51; Jonathan Alter, *His Very Best: Jimmy Carter, A Life*, 404 ('psycho" quotation).

22. UPI Story, 9 March 1983; *New York Times*, 9, 10 March 1983; *San Francisco Examiner*, 8 March 1983; *Peninsula Times Tribune*, 10 March 1983, all in VF, Carter, Jimmy, JCL; JC, *Blood of Abraham*, 117.

23. *New York Times*, 11 March 1983.

24. Brinkley, *Unfinished Presidency*, 108–109.

25. JC, *Blood of Abraham*, 179–90.

26. Brinkley, *Unfinished Presidency*, 112–14.

27. JC, *Blood of Abraham*, 82–84.

28. Brinkley, *Unfinished Presidency*, 114–15; JC, *Blood of Abraham*, 105.

29. Brinkley, *Unfinished Presidency*, 116.

30. *San Francisco Sunday Examiner & Chronicle*, 13 March 1983; *New York Times*, 14 March 1983; News Release, 17 March, First Lady's Press Office, box 13304, RRL; Memorandum, William P. Clark to William K. Sadlier, 17 March 1983, WHORM, Subject, ID 134724, RRL.

31. JC, Interview, *Penthouse*, April 1983, 116 ff.

32. Brinkley, *Unfinished Presidency*, 11–17.

33. Ibid., 95–98.

34. Thomas M. DeFrank, *Write It When I'm Gone: Remarkable Off-the-Record Conversations with Gerald R. Ford*, 79–80, 113; News Release, *Kettering Review*, Summer 1983; *Newsletter*, Domestic Policy Association, Anne Arbor, MI; *New York Times* and *Washington Post*, 10 Feb. 1983, all in Domestic Policy Association Conference Papers, Gerald Ford Library; Scott Kaufman, *Ambition, Pragmatism, and Party: A Political Biography of Gerald R. Ford*, 320–23.

35. *Americus Times-Recorder*, 13 May 1983; *Atlanta Constitution*, 2 June 1983; *New York Times*, 14 June 1983.

36. *Atlanta Constitution*, 23 June 1983, 24 May 1984; *Star-Ledger*, 1 July 1983, 24 Feb. 1984; *New York Times*, 10 July 1983; Peter Baker and Susan Glasser, *The Man Who Ran Washington: The Life and Times of James A. Baker III*, 126–27, 201–206.

37. *Atlanta Constitution*, 8 May, 1, 22 Aug. 1982; *Washington Post*, 24 Aug. 1983.

38. *Atlanta Constitution*, 26, 29 Sept. 1983 (quotation on 29).

39. *Washington Post*, 31 Oct. 1983; *Americus Times-Recorder*, 31 Oct., 2 Nov. 1983; Jimmy Carter, *Always a Reckoning and Other Poems*, 19.

40. Brinkley, *Unfinished Presidency*, 118–20.

41. Ibid.; *Atlanta Constitution*, 6, 7, 10 Nov. 1983; Timeline of the Carter Center, 1983, www.cartercenter.org.

42. William Safire, *Atlanta Constitution*, 30 Jan. 1984; Anatoly Dobrynin, *In Confidence: Moscow's Ambassador to America's Six Cold War Presidents*, 547.

43. *Atlanta Journal and Constitution*, 5 Feb. 1984; *Harper's Magazine*, Winter 1983–84; SMU Speech, VF, box Carter, Jimmy, JCL.

44. *New York Times*, 13 March, 1984.

45. *Atlanta Constitution*, 13, 20, 16 April 1984.

46. Becky King, "Rosalynn: A Candid Interview, *Atlanta Women's News*, September 1984; *Atlanta Journal and Constitution*, 17 June 1984.

47. Brinkley, *Unfinished Presidency*, 120.

48. Quoted in Brinkley, *Unfinished Presidency*, 130.

49. Steve Hochman to Stanly Godbold, 17 Feb. 2022.

50. *Atlanta Constitution*, 4, 26 June, 25 July, 2 Sept., 1984.

51. Brinkley, *Unfinished Presidency,* 144–50.

52. Dan Ariel Interview, National Park Service, 7, JCL; Bourne, *Carter*, 479; Millard Fuller and Linda Fuller, *The Excitement Is Building*, 41–47; JC, "Opening Remarks for the Clarence Jordan Symposium," in Kirk Lyman-Barner and Cori Lyman-Barner, editors, *Fruits of the Cotton Patch: The Clarence Jordan Symposium 2012*, xiii–xvi.

53. Bourne, *Carter*, 483–84.

54. Brinkley, *Unfinished Presidency*, 155.

55. *Atlanta Journal and Constitution*, 9, 17 Sept. 1984; *The Christian Index*, 13 Sept. 1984.

56. JC, *Beyond the White House*, 257–58; David Rubel, *If I Had a Hammer: Building Homes and Hope with Habitat for Humanity*, v–xi, 11–17.

57. Brinkley, *Unfinished Presidency*, 156.

58. *Atlanta Constitution*, 1, 3 Oct. 1984; https://www.cartercenter.org/about/history/chro nology_1981.html.

59. *Louisville Courier-Journal*, 16 Oct. 1984.

60. *Atlanta Constitution*, 13 April, 16 Nov. 1984.

61. *Gerald Ford Library Newsletter*, 14 Nov. 1985.

62. Brinkley, *Unfinished Presidency*, 156–57; Carter Center Timeline, 1984.

63. *Atlanta Constitution*, 21–23 Jan., 5 Feb. 1985; *New York Times*, 17 March 1985; Program, Emory ceremony for Peace Award, 13 March 1985, Dolvin Donated Material, box 3, JCL.

64. *Atlanta Constitution*, 7 April 1985.

65. Carter to Vice President George Bush, 17 April 1985, Bush to Carter, 2 May 1985, George H. W. Bush Library, WHORM, Office of the VP, # 368845VP; Carter to Reagan, Sven F. Kraemer Files, OA 91202, RRL.

66. Frederick Allen, *Atlanta Journal*, 14 April 1985.

67. *New York Times*, 9 April 1985, 20 March 1986.

68. *Atlanta Constitution*, 20 April 1985; *New York Times*, 22 April 1985.

69. Bernard Lewis, *New York Times*, 22 April 1985. See also *Atlanta Journal and Constitution*, 5 May 1985.

70. Reagan to Carter, 8 July 1985, with attachment, WHORM, ID # 302962, RRL.

71. "Remember When Willie Nelson Sang 'Amazing Grace' with Jimmy and Rosalynn Carter?," www.wideopencountry.com/category/music/, 9 Oct. 2020; Brinkley, *Unfinished Presidency*, 173; *Rolling Stone*, 8 Feb. 2011.

72. Brinkley, *Unfinished Presidency*, 159–60.

73. U.S. Rep. Wyche Fowler, review, *Atlanta Journal and Constitution*, 17 Nov. 1985; *Duke University Libraries Magazine*, Fall 2009, pp. 12–17.

74. *Atlanta Constitution*, 30 Jan. 1986; Bourne, *Carter*, 490–91.

75. *Atlanta Journal*, 25 Feb. 1986; Brinkley, *Unfinished Presidency*, 199–202.

76. Ibid., 202–206.

77. Ibid.

78. Ibid.

79. *Atlanta Journal and Constitution*, 9 Feb. 1986; *Atlanta Journal*, 25 Feb. 1986.

80. *Atlanta Constitution*, 2 March 1986.

81. Memorandum, James R. Stark to John M. Poindexter, 20 March 1986, WHORM, ID # 410781, RRL; Reagan to Carter, 5 July 1986, WHORM, ID # 406065, RRL.

82. *The Atlanta Constitution*, 16 April 1986.

83. Carter Center Annual Report 1982–1988, p. 2.

84. *Atlanta Journal and Constitution*, 21 Sept. 1986 (quotation); Brinkley, *Unfinished Presidency*, 255; *Atlanta Constitution*, 12 May, 14 June, 1986.

85. *Atlanta Constitution*, 17 July 1986.

86. *Atlanta Constitution*, 9 July 1986; *New York Times*, 15 July 1986.

87. Memorandum, Frederick Ryan, Jr., to Donald T. Regan, 11 July 1986, Re Dedication of Carter Presidential Library, Carters to Reagans, 23 May 1986, Reagan to Carter, 6 Aug. 1986, WHORM, ID # 404476, Subject File TR170, RRL.

88. *Atlanta Constitution*, 21 Sept. 1986; *Lincoln Journal*, 12 Sept. 1986 (quotations).

89. Memorandum, Pat Buchanan to Reagan, 17 Sept. 1986, with attachments, WHORM ID #614529PC, Subject TR 170, RRL.

90. Brinkley, *Unfinished Presidency*, 162–63, 210; Burton I. Kaufman, *The Post-Presidency from Washington to Clinton*, 455–57, 464–67.

91. Memorandum, Donald T. Regan to The President, RE Carter Library Dedication Service, 1 Oct. 1986, WHORM # 4039855, TR 170, RRL; *New York Times*, 2 Oct. 1986.

92. Peter M. Robinson Files, box 10937, RRL.

93. *New York Times*, *Atlanta Constitution*, *Americus Times-Recorder*, 2 Oct. 1986 (quotations); Memorandum, Regan to President, WHORM #40639855m RRL; Leonard Bernardo and Jennifer Weiss, *Citizen-in-Chief: The Second Lives of American Presidents*, 101–102; Brinkley, *Unfinished Presidency*, 220.

94. JC, *Beyond the White House*, 9–13.

Chapter 37

1. Malcolm Byrne, *Iran-Contra: Reagan's Scandal and the Unchecked Abuse of Presidential Power*, dustjacket blurb.

2. *Atlanta Journal and Constitution*, 5 Oct. 1986; *Atlanta Constitution*, 7 Oct. 1986 (quotation); Timeline of the Carter Center, 1986, www.cartercenter.org; *Washington Post*, 6, 7 Oct. 1986.

3. *Atlanta Constitution*, 25, 26 Nov. (quotation on 26), 1986; Douglas Brinkley, *The Unfinished Presidency: Jimmy Carter's Journey beyond the White House*, 207–209; AP News, 27 Nov. 1986; *Harvard Crimson*, 26 Nov. 1986.

4. 1986 Cat Calendar, VF, Carter, Jimmy, JCL; Jimmy Carter, National Park Service Interview, IV, 93–94, JCL.

5. Sylvia Lewis, "Meeting an Honest Man," *Akron (Ohio) Jewish News*, 1 March 87, VF, box Carter, Jimmy, JCL.

6. *Atlanta Constitution*, 17, Jan., 15 Feb. 1987; Will Bunch, *Tear Down this Myth: How the Reagan Legacy Has Distorted Our Politics and Haunts Our Future*, 77.

7. *Atlanta Constitution*, 16 March 1987; Memorandum, Frank C. Carlucci to Chief of Staff, RE SAM Aircraft Request, 20 March 1987, ID # 447216, F0008, WHORM, RRL.

8. *Atlanta Constitution*, 18 March 1987.

9. Ibid., 20, 22 March 1987.

10. *Star Ledger*, 29 March 1987; *Atlanta Constitution*, 29 March 1987.

11. Ibid., 8 March 1992.

12. *Atlanta Constitution*, 16, 18,20, 29, 31 March 1987; Leonard Bernardo and Jennifer Weiss, *Citizen-in-Chief: The Second Lives of the American Presidents*, 152–53; *Time*, 20 April 1987, p. 38; Lawrence Wright, *Thirteen Days in September: Carter, Begin, and Sadat at Camp David*, 282;.

13. *New York Times*, 14, 16 April 1987; *Atlanta Constitution*, 5, 9, 11, 15, 16 April 1987.

14. AP News, 16 April 1987.

15. *Atlanta Constitution*, 15 (quotation), 16, 17 April 1987.

16. Ibid., 5 April (quotation), 21 July 1987.

17. *New York Times*, 18 May 1987; *Austin (TX) American-Statesman*, 26 May 1987.

18. AP News, 1 July 1987.

19. Brinkley, Unfinished Presidency, 242-45.

20. *(New Castle) Evening Chronicle*, 1977, 1987.

21. *Carter Center News*, Spring 1988.

22. Ibid.

23. *Americus Times-Recorder*, 14 Oct., 11 Nov. 1987; Carter Center In-House Newsletter, Nov. 1987, VF, Carter, Billy et al., JCL; *Campus Report*, 9 Nov. 1987.

24. *Atlanta Constitution*, 13, 17 Dec. 1987.

25. *Americus Times-Recorder*, 13 Feb. 1988; Author interview with Bert Nason, January 1988.

26. Jonathan Beaty and S. C. Gwynne, *The Outlaw Bank: A Wild Ride into the Secret Heart of BCCI*, 11, 61, 195–96; *Americus Times-Recorder*, 2, 7, 20 March 1988; Rosalynn

Carter, National Park Service Interview, IV, 9–10, JCL (quotation); *Atlanta Journal and Constitution*, 17 Aug. 1991, 2 Oct. 1992; *Los Angeles Times*, 30 July 1991; *New York Times*, 6 Aug. 1995.

27. *Americus Times-Recorder*, 3 March 1988.

28. *Atlanta Constitution*, 22 (Carter quotation), 23 April 1988.

29. *Atlanta Constitution*, 10, 28 June 1988.

30. *New York Times*, 3 July 1988; Peter G. Bourne, *Jimmy Carter: A Comprehensive Biography from Plains to the Post-Presidency*, 498.

31. *Atlanta Constitution*, 18, 19 July, 1988 (quotations); Bernardo and Weiss, *Citizen-in-Chief*, 217–19; Brinkley, *Unfinished Presidency*, 246–51.

32. *Atlanta Constitution*, 17 Dec; *Johns Hopkins Magazine*, December 1987, VF, box Carter, Jimmy, JCL.

33. *Star-Ledger*, 26 Sept. 1988 (Carter statement); *Americus Times-Recorder*, 27 Sept. 1988 (Billy quotation).

34. *Americus Times-Recorder*, 27 Sept. 1988 (quotations); *New York Times*, 26 Sept. 1988.

35. Telegram, Reagan to Mrs. Sybil Carter, 26 Sept. 1988, WHORM #588607, RRL.

36. *Atlanta Constitution*, 12 Jan. 1990.

37. *Delaware Gazette*, 11 Nov. 1988; Brinkley, *Unfinished Presidency*, 250–51; Mark K. Updegrove, *Second Acts: Presidential Lives and Legacies after the White House*, 160–61.

38. Carter to Khomeini, 30 Oct, 1988, in David Rabhan, *Conscious Coma: Ten Years in an Iranian Prison*, 309.

39. *Carter Center News*, Fall 1988.

40. Jimmy Carter, *Sharing Good Times*, 114–20; *Atlanta Journal and Constitution*, 19, 20 Nov., 3 Dec. 1988; *Birdwatching*, August 2012, p. 29.

41. *Los Angeles Times*, 17 Jan. 1989; *Americus Times-Recorder*, 14 Jan. 1989; *Atlanta Journal and Constitution*, 17 Jan. 1989.

42. *Americus Times-Recorder*, 20 Jan. 1989.

43. Carter to Attorney General Richard Thornburgh, 29 Jan. 1989, attached to letter from Carter to Bush, WHORM, Subject, CO 071, Case # 109781, GBL; Jimmy Carter, National Park Service Interview, IV, 55–56, JCL.

44. *Americus Times-Recorder*, 24 March 1989; *Atlanta Constitution*, 24 March 1989.

45. Manuel Noriega, *The Memoirs of Manuel Noriega, America's Prisoner*, 145–48; *Atlanta Constitution*, 9, 10 May, 1989; *New York Times*, 9, 11 May 1989; *Americus Times-Recorder*, 12 May 1989; Bourne, *Carter*, 492–93; Jimmy Carter, *Beyond the White House: Waging Peace, Fighting Disease, Building Hope*, 91–95.

46. *Atlanta Journal and Constitution*, 13 June 1989.

47. JC, *Beyond the White House*, 216.

48. Bourne, *Carter*, 491; *Atlanta Constitution*, 4 June 1989.

49. *Carter Center News*, Fall 1989; Carter Center Timeline, 1989.

50. *Atlanta Journal and Constitution*, 23 July 1989; *Atlanta Constitution*, 18 Aug. 1989; *Americus Times-Recorder*, 29 July, 13, 16 Sept. 1989; JC, *Beyond the White House*, 158–84,

51. JC, *Beyond the White House*, 96.

52. Ibid., 91–97.

53. *Atlanta Constitution*, 17, 22 Sept. 1989; *New York Times*, 21 Sept. 1989; *Americus Times-Recorder*, 21 Sept. 1989; Bruce Nichols, "Religious Conciliation between the Sandinistas and the East Coast Indians of Nicaragua," in Douglas Johnston and Cynthia Sampson, editors, *Religion, the Missing Dimension of Statecraft*, 79–80.

54. *Americus Times-Recorder*, 23 Oct. 1989; *Atlanta Journal and Constitution*, 26 Oct. 1989 (quotation).

55. *Washington Post*, 6 Nov. 1989 (quotations).

56. *Atlanta Journal and Constitution*, 5 Nov. 1989. Copies of the Miller Center interviews are available among the Oral Histories in the Carter Library, and they became the major source for several early positive assessments of the Carter administration, including Charles O. Jones, *The Trusteeship Presidency: Jimmy Carter and the United States Congress*, Erwin C. Hargrove, *Jimmy Carter as President: Leadership and the Politics of the Public Good*, and Robert A. Strong, *Working in the World: Jimmy Carter and the Making of American Foreign Policy*.

57. *Atlanta Constitution*, 17 Nov. 1989; *Americus Times-Recorder*, 13, 16, 20 Nov. 1989; Carter Center Timeline, 1989, www.cartercenter.org.

58. *Atlanta Constitution*, 30 Nov. 1989; Carter to Bush, 22 Nov., 6 Dec. 1989, Bush to Carter, 12 Jan. 1990, GBL, WHORM 103786.

59. *Atlanta Journal and Constitution*, 1 Dec. 1989.

60. *Americus Times-Recorder*, 11 Dec. 1989.

61. *Americus Times-Recorder*, 8 Feb. 1990; *Carter Center Newsletter*, Spring 1990.

62. Peter Baker and Susan Glasser, *The Man Who Ran Washington: The Life and Times of James A. Baker III*, 334.

63. Julian E. Zelizer, *Jimmy Carter*, 135; Brinkley, *Unfinished Presidency*, 288–311; Bourne, *Carter*, 494.; JC, *Beyond the White House*, 97–99; "How Nicaragua's Sandinista Revolution Was Resurrected—and Betrayed," *Daily Beast*, 19 July 2019. Ortega and his wife Rosario Murillo regained power in 2009 and reinstated an often violent dictatorship that caused thousands of Nicaraguans to flee the country.

64. Baker and Glasser, *The Man Who Ran Washington*, 373.

65. *Americus Times-Recorder*, 3 March 1990; *Atlanta Journal and Constitution*, 7 March 1990 (quotations).

66. Bush to Carter, 6 March 1990, WHORM Subject File, ME 001 = 03, 121494, GBL; Bush to Carter, 6 March 1990, WHORM, Subject File CO 114, Item 124419, GBL.

Chapter 38

1. *New York Times*, 20 March 1990; *Austin American-Statesman*, 15, 20 March 1990; *Atlanta Constitution*, 17, 18, 25 March 1990; *Americus Times-Recorder*, 24, 26 March 1990; Douglas Brinkley, *The Unfinished Presidency: Jimmy Carter's Journey beyond the White House*, 3318–20.

2. *Star Ledger*, 20 March 1990; *Atlanta Constitution*, 25 March 1990; Elizabeth Kurylo, "Carter Defends Palestinian Rights Despite Criticism from U.S. Jews," *Atlanta Journal*

and Constitution, 31 March 1990; Brinkley, *The Unfinished Presidency,* 321–22; Memorandum, Brent Scowcroft to Bush, 27 March 1990, WHORM, #133776, GBL.

3. Memorandum, Brent Scowcroft to Bush, 27 March 1990, WHORM, #133776, GBL; *Atlanta Constitution,* 28 March 1990.

4. Brinkley, *Unfinished Presidency,* 323.

5. *Atlanta Constitution,* 28 March 1990.

6. Brinkley, *The Unfinished Presidency,* 323–29; *Austin American-Statesman,* 15 Sept. 1990; *Atlanta Journal and Constitution,* 5 April 1990; Peter G. Bourne, *Jimmy Carter: A Comprehensive Biography from Plains to the Post-Presidency,* 492–93.

7. David Rabhan, *Conscious Coma: Ten Years in an Iranian Prison,* 274–323; Brinkley, *Unfinished Presidency,* 337–39.

8. *Habitat World,* April and June 1990; *Atlanta Constitution,* 20 April 1990.

9. *Americus Times-Recorder,* 15, 17 May 1990; Memorandum, Carter to President George Bush and Secretary of State James Baker, 21 May, 1990, WHORM, CO-942, #144449SS, GBL.

10. *Americus Times-Recorder,* 25 April, 15 May, 5 July 1990; Bush to Carter, WHORM, Subject File, ME 001, #156475, GBL.

11. *Atlanta Journal and Constitution,* 26 Aug. 1990.

12. *Americus Times-Recorder,* 26 Sept. 1990.

13. Ibid., 28 Nov. 1990.

14. Ibid., 11 Dec. 1990.

15. Ibid., 13 Feb. 1991; George Bush and Brent Scowcroft, *A World Transformed,* 413–14; Bartholomew Sparrow, *The Strategist: Brent Scowcroft and the Call of National Security,* 403–404.

16. *The Atlanta Journal and Constitution,* 12 Jan. 1991.

17. Weapons stories, *Wall Street Journal,* 22 Jan. 1991; Bush to others, 20 Feb. 1991, WHORM, MA020, #201398 and 215926, GBL; Carter to Bush, 22 Feb. 1991, GBL; Brinkley, *Unfinished Presidency,* 342.

18. Mary Ellis Barrett, "How Jimmy Will Save the World," *USA Weekend,* 15–17 March, 1991; *Americus Times-Recorder,* 5 March 1991; *Atlanta Journal and Constitution,* 19 March 1991; Brinkley, *Unfinished Presidency,* 261–63; Paige Parvin, "2020 Vision," *Emory Magazine* (Autumn 2012), 24–33.

19. *Atlanta Journal and Constitution,* 21 March 1991; James Ring Adams and Douglas Frantz, *A Full Service Bank: How BCCI Stole Billions around the World,* 7–8.

20. *Atlanta Journal and Constitution,* 15 April, 11 May, 16, 17 June 1991; *Atlanta Constitution,* 19 April 1991; *Americus Times-Recorder,* 13 June 1991; *Los Angeles Times,* 9 July, 1991.

21. Jimmy Carter, *Sharing Good Times,* 79–166.

22. "Opening Ceremonies at the Ronald Reagan Presidential Library," YouTube, Reagan Foundation, October 4, 2012; *Americus Times-Recorder,* 4, 5 Nov. 1991; *New York Times,* 5 Nov. 1991.

23. *Atlanta Journal and Constitution,* 7, 8, 22, 27 Dec. 1991; Bourne, *Carter,* 500.

24. *Atlanta Constitution,* 7 Jan. 1992.

25. *Americus Times-Recorder,* 6 Feb. 1992.

26. *Atlanta Constitution*, 12 April 1992; Brinkley, *Unfinished Presidency*, 351–54.
27. Memoranda, Carter meeting with Bush Cabinet members, 15, 16 April 1992, Bush Presidential Records, National Service, Carter Meeting, 20 April 1992, GBL; Memorandum, C. Gregg Petersmeyer to Cabinet Secretary, Re Carter Meeting, 15 April 1992, GBL; Brinkley, *Unfinished Presidency*, 356–63.
28. JC, *White House Diary*, 496.
29. *Atlanta Constitution*, 11, 12 May 1992.
30. Ibid., 14, 23 May 1992.
31. E. Stanly Godbold, Jr., *Jimmy and Rosalynn Carter: The Georgia Years, 1924–1974*, pp. 92–101.
32. *Atlanta Constitution*, 15 July 1992.
33. *Family Circle*, 21 July 1992.
34. *Atlanta Constitution*, 16 July, 1992; Bush Presidential Records, National Service, J. R. George Papers, OaId 9813, GBL; *Atlanta Constitution*, 23 Aug., 12 Sept. 1992.
35. *Americus Times-Recorder*, 7 Oct., 5 Nov., 10 Dec. 1992.
36. Rosalynn Carter Remarks, 19 Nov. 1992, Beyond Boundaries Display, Jimmy Carter Library and Museum, 1996.
37. Author's notes on Carter's speech at the Atlanta Hilton, 14 March 1994. See also Jimmy Carter, *White House Diary*, 480.
38. Kai Bird, *The Outlier: The Unfinished Presidency of Jimmy Carter*, 551–63, 625, is a convincing, scholarly account of the October Surprise. Other sources alleging that the October Surprise took place are listed and analyzed in a footnote in Chapter 32. More accounts proliferated during the 1992 campaign. The primary and secondary sources argued both sides of the question, but the preponderance of evidence suggests that the Surprise did take place.

    Leading articles that argue that the Surprise did happen include the following: Sandy Grady, "Laying to Rest the Ghost of the 'October Surprise,'" *Atlanta Journal and Constitution*, 7 Aug. 1991; Craig Unger, "October Surprise," *Esquire*, October 1991, p. 98; Eizenstat article in *Atlanta Journal and Constitution*, 9 May 1991; Jody Powell, "The White House Years: The Press and the Presidency," April 1992, Conversations at the Carter Center, Atlanta Public Television, WPBA; Gary Sick article in *The Washington Post National Weekly Edition*, 3–9 Feb. 1992, p. 35; Robert Parry, "The Original October Surprise," adapted from Parry's *Secrecy and Privilege: Rise of the Bush Dynasty from Watergate to Iraq*, October 2006, https://www.scoop.co.nz/stories/HL0610/S00412.htm, pp. 4–23; Andrew E. Busch, "The Election of 1980," in Scott Kaufman, editor, *A Companion to Gerald R. Ford and Jimmy Carter*, 470–90.

    Unpublished letters and documents that support the contention that the Surprise did take place include: Memorandum, Casey to Staff, 27 Oct. 1980, Campaign Papers 1965–80: Ed Meese files, box 148, Notes on 9 July Meeting, 1980, Campaign Papers, 1965–80, Series III: Ed Meese Files: Campaign Files, box 103, both in RRL. Records and Files in George H. W. Bush Presidential Library include: Bush to Moorehead Kennedy, 9 May 1991, George H. W. Bush Presidential Records, Counsel's Office, White House: Gray, C. Boyden Files; Confidential Miscellaneous Files, CFO 1826,

Secret Service Logs; DCI's Iran Testimony for HPSCI and SSCI, 21 November 1986, George H. W. Bush Presidential Records, Counsel's Office, White House, Von Lembke Files, OIC Iran-Contra Files, CFO 594; William Casey File; Memorandum from Daniel Finn, RE October Surprise, 3 Dec. 1991, Bush Presidential Records, Counsel's Office, Jane Rehnquist Files, 45587, October Surprise Memoranda; and others.

The Interview with L. Bruce Laingen, 9 Jan. 1993, Library of Congress, discusses the possibility of the Republican intervention, but Laingen was not convinced that it happened.

Biographies and books that attempt to exonerate Bush, but are inconclusive, include: John Robert Greene, *The Presidency of George H. W. Bush*, 25–25, 157–58; Jeffrey A. Engel, *When the World Seemed New: George H. W. Bush and the End of the Cold War* (2017); and Jon Meacham, *Destiny and Power: The American Odyssey of George Herbert Walker Bush* (2015). Books that attempt to prove that the deal with the Iranians did happen include: Barbara Olson, *The Final Days: The Last, Desperate Abuses of Power by the Clinton White House*, 171; and Will Bunch, *Tear Down This Myth: How the Reagan Legacy Has Distorted Our Politics and Haunts Our Future*, 77.

Robert Parry published multiple works proving that the Republicans were guilty: *The October Surprise X-Files: The Hidden Origins of the Reagan-Bush Era* (1996), *Secrecy and Privilege: Rise of the Bush Dynasty from Watergate to Iraq* (2004), and *America's Stolen Narrative* (2012), all published under his own label, The Media Consortium, which he dedicated to the promotion of independent journalism. His *Trick or Treason: The October Surprise Mystery*, 23–24, 68–69, 110–14, 160–61, 166, 182–85, 242–44, contains the essence of his argument.

Two journalists, Edwin M. Yoder and Mark Hosenball, both writing for *Washington Post* during the 1992 campaign were convinced that President Bush had participated in the deal that was cut in a Paris hotel room in October 1980. Yoder repeated the evidence provided by Gary Sick and Robert Parry and concluded that it was comparable to the Watergate scandal that forced President Nixon to resign. Hosenball concluded that the facts of the case were sufficient to prove that the story was not just another conspiracy. Both articles were reprinted in the *Atlanta Constitution*, 23 April 1991.

Chapter 39

1. Scott Kaufman, *Rosalynn Carter: Equal Partner in the White House*, 149; Douglas Brinkley, *The Unfinished Presidency: Jimmy Carter's Journey beyond the White House*, 370–71 (quotation); Carol Felsenthal, *Clinton in Exile: A President Out of the White House*, 64; Hamilton Jordan, *No Such Thing as a Bad Day*, 199–200.
2. *Atlanta Constitution*, 21 Jan. 1993; John Robert Greene, *The Presidency of George H. W. Bush*, 159–61.
3. *Newsweek*, 23 Jan. 1993.
4. Kaufman, *Rosalynn Carter*, 151–54; Carter Museum Display, "Beyond Boundaries," May 1996; *Atlanta Constitution*, 4, 5, 9, 27 Jan. 1993; *Americus Times-Recorder*, 17

April 1993; Rosalynn Carter, "No Time to Waver," *Memphis Commercial Appeal*, 15 Aug. 1993.

5. *Baptist Press News*, 20 Oct. 2000; *Americus Times-Recorder*, 14 May 1993; Peter G. Bourne, *Jimmy Carter: A Comprehensive Biography from Plains to the Post-Presidency*, 496–97; David T. Morgan, *New Crusades, New Holy Land: Conflict in the Southern Baptist Convention, 1969–1991*, 106, 171–77.

6. Seth Anziska, *Preventing Palestine: A Political History from Camp David to Oslo, 283;* Brinkley, *Unfinished Presidency*, 376–79.

7. Brinkley, *Unfinished Presidency*, 378–81.

8. *Atlanta Journal and Constitution*, 13 Sept. 1993; *Americus Times-Recorder*, 27 Oct. 1993; Carter Center Newsletter, Summer 1994.

9. *Atlanta Journal and Constitution*, 15 Sept. 1993.

10. Lindsay Kimble, "The Story Behind the Photo: Nancy Reagan's Sit-Down with Five Other First Ladies," People.com, 7 March 2016, Photo: by Barbara Kinney in The William J. Clinton Presidential Library.

11. *Atlanta Constitution*, 4, 8 (quotation) June, 1994; Memphis *Commercial Appeal*, 15 June 1994; *Wanderlust Atlanta*, September 2020.

12. Marion Creekmore, Jr., *A Moment of Crisis: Jimmy Carter, the Power of a Peacemaker, and North Korea's Nuclear Ambitions*, 25–27; Leon V. Sigal, "Jimmy Carter Makes a Deal," *Bulletin of the Atomic Scientists*, 54, no 1 (January 1998); Felsenthal, *Clinton in Exile*, 65; Don Oberdorfer, *The Two Koreas: A Contemporary History*, 317–18.

13. Sigal, "Jimmy Carter Makes a Deal," 5.

14. Ibid., 6–7; Oberdorfer, *The Two Koreas*, 322–23.

15. Creekmore, *A Moment of Crisis*, 128–30; Rosalynn Carter's "Report on our Trip to North Korea" June 1994, Beyond Boundaries Display, May 1996, JCL Museum.

16. RSC, "Report on our Trip to North Korea," June 1994, JCL Museum.

17. Carter interview, *Atlanta Journal and Constitution*, 3 July 1994; RSC, "North Korea," May 1996, JCL Museum; Kaufman, *Rosalynn Carter*, 158–59; Brinkley, *Unfinished Presidency*, 406.

18. *Americus Times-Recorder*, 18 June 1994; Sigal, "Carter Makes a Deal," 8.

19. Sigal, "Carter Makes a Deal," 8–9; Leon U. Sigal, *Disarming Strangers: Nuclear Diplomacy with North Korea*, 150–62.

20. Sigal, "Carter Makes a Deal," 10–11; Creekmore, *A Moment of Crisis*, 174–76; Oberdorfer, *Two Koreas*, 327–29.

21. Sigal, "Carter Makes a Deal," 12–13; Oberdorfer, *Two Koreas*, 330–32; Sigal, *Disarming Strangers*, 162–67.

22. RSC, "Report on Our Trip to North Korea," June 1994, JCL Museum; Creekmore, *A Moment of Crisis*, 92–96; Sigal, "Carter Makes a Deal," 14; *China Post*, 6 Aug, 2009; Bourne, *Carter*, 503–04; Jimmy Carter, *Beyond the White House*, 23–36; Oberdorfer, *Two Koreas*, 332–33. The deal collapsed in 2002 when North Korea tested a nuclear weapon and President George W. Bush adopted a hard line toward the Communist country. The deal Carter had negotiated was revived under President Barack Obama in 2008 and disintegrated again in 2016 after the election of Donald Trump.

23. *New York Times*, 19 June 1994; *U.S. News and World Report*, 27 June 1994, 8-9, 48; *Americus Times-Recorder*, 20 June 1994; Creekmore, *A Moment of Crisis*, 199-201, 221-22.

24. Sam Nunn's comments in *Atlanta Journal and Constitution*, 18 June, 1995; Carter interview in *Atlanta Journal and Constitution*, 3 July 1994.

25. Kirkpatrick in *Boston Herald*, 2 July 1994; Weinberger in *Forbes*, 8 July 1994.

26. RSC, "Our Trip to North Korea," June 1994, JCL Museum; *Atlanta Journal and Constitution*, 10 July 1994 (quotation); Author's notes on town meeting, Carter Center, 20 Sept. 1994.

27. *Atlanta Journal-Constitution*, 28 Aug. 1994; Jimmy Carter, *Faith: A Journey for All*, 71-73.

28. Bob Shacochis, *The Immaculate Invasion*, 9.

29. Kathleen Marie Whitney, "Sin, Fraph, and the CIA: U.S. Covert Action in Haiti," *Southwestern Journal of Law and Trade in the Americas*, 3, no. 2 (1996), 321; Bourne, *Carter*, 505; Kaufman, *Rosalynn Carter*, 159; *Americus Times-Recorder*, 10 Sept. 1994; Shacochis, *Immaculate Invasion*, 53 (quotation).

30. David Halberstam, *War in a Time of Peace: Bush, Clinton, and the Generals*, 280.

31. *Americus Times-Recorder*, 19 Sept. 1994; *Memphis Commercial Appeal*, 20 Sept. 1994; *Atlanta Constitution*, 19 Sept. 1994; Author interview with Rosalynn Carter, 12 Oct. 1994; Shacochis, *Immaculate Invasion*, 72-77; Halberstam, *War in Time of Peace*, 281-81.

32. Kaufman, *Rosalynn Carter*, 160; Shacochis, *Immaculate Invasion*, 75; Bourne, *Carter*, 505; JC, *Beyond the White House*, 46-52; Brinkley, *Unfinished Presidency*, 420-31.

33. Hendrik Hertzberg, *Politics: Observations & Arguments, 1966-2004*, 49 (quotation); Hendrik Hertzberg, "Jimmy Carter, 1977-1981," in Robert A. Wilson, editor, *Character above All*, 173.

34. Quoted in Ellen Weiss and Mel Friedman, *Jimmy Carter: Champion of Peace*, 114-15.

35. *Atlanta Constitution*, 19 Sept. 1994; Author interview with Carters, 12 Oct. 1994 (Rosalynn quotation); JC, *Beyond the White House*, 52-53.

36. *Time*, 3 Oct. 1994, 36 (Rosalynn's quotations); Michael Kelly, "Letter from Washington: It All Codepends," *New Yorker*, 3 Oct. 1994, p. 81.

37. *Memphis Commercial Appeal*, 24 Sept. 1994.

38. Kelly, "Letter from Washington: It All Codepends," 83-84; Greene, *George H. W. Bush*, 239-41; Bourne, *Carter*, 508; Leonardo Bernardo and Jennifer Weiss, *Citizen-in-Chief: The Second Lives of American Presidents*, 164.

39. Transcript, Office of Public Information, The Carter Center; *Fulbright Association Newsletter*, 17, no. 2 (1994); *Starkville, MS, Daily News*, 2 Oct. 1994; Bourne, *Carter*, 508.

40. Rosalynn Carter, *Helping Yourself Help Others: A Book for Caregivers*, New York: Times Books, 1994.

41. Rosalynn Carter to Nancy Reagan, 23 Nov. 1994, Beyond Borders JCL Museum Display, May 1996.

42. *Atlanta Constitution*, 12 Oct. 1994; *Americus Times-Recorder*, 20, 26 Oct. 1994; *Atlanta Journal and Constitution*, 23, 27 Oct. 1994; Ted Kennedy to Rosalynn Carter, 10 Nov. 1994, Beyond Borders, JCL Museum Display, May 1996.

43. JC, Beyond the *White House*, 64.

44. Mitja Velikonja, *Religious Separation and Political Intolerance in Bosnia-Herzegovina*, 265; James Bamford, *Body of Secrets: Anatomy of the Ultra-Secret National Security Agency from the Cold War through the Dawn of a New Century*, 445–46.

45. JC, *Beyond the White House*, 64.

46. Ibid., 62–73.

47. Unidentified clipping of article by Kevin Fedarko in VF, Bosnia, JCL.

48. *Americus Times-Recorder*, 15 Dec. 1994; Kaufman, *Rosalynn Carter*, 159.

49. RSC, "Report on Trip to Bosnia-Herzegovina," 18–20 Dec.1994, Carter Museum Display, JCL; *Atlanta Constitution*, 19 Dec. 1994.

50. RSC, "Report," 3–5; JC, *Beyond the White House*, 67; *Atlanta Constitution*, 18 Dec. 1994.

51. RSC, Carter, "Report on Trip to Bosnia-Herzegovina," 6; *Roanoke Times and World News*, 21 Dec. 1994.

52. RSC, "Report on Trip to Bosnia-Herzegovina," 6–7; Brinkley, *Unfinished Presidency*, 445–50.

53. Atlanta Constitution, 22 Dec. 1994; JC, *Beyond the White House*, 62–73.

54. *Americus Times-Recorder*, 18 Jan. 1995 (quotation); *Atlanta Constitution*, 1 Feb. 1995.

55. George Packer, *Our Man: Richard Holbrooke and the End of the American Century*, 316, 367–86.

56. JC, *Beyond the White House*, 62–73; *The Wall Street Journal*, 24 Nov. 2017; Brinkley, *Unfinished Presidency*, 453; Author's notes on Balkan visit and interview with Peter Bastjancic.

Chapter 40

1. Author interview with Carter, 12 Oct. 1994.

2. Jimmy Carter, *Always a Reckoning and Other Poems*, 125–26.

3. Douglas Brinkley, *The Unfinished Presidency: Jimmy Carter's Journey beyond the White House*, 439.

4. *Time*, 25 Sept. 1995, 78.

5. Brinkley, *Unfinished Presidency*, 458–60; Jimmy Carter, *Beyond the White House*, 178–84; Jimmy Carter, *A Full Life: Reflections at Ninety*, 211.

6. *U.S. and World Report*, 10 April 1995; *Time*, 10 April 1995, p. 46; *Starkville (MS) Daily News*, 29 March 1995; Jimmy Carter to Stanly Godbold, 7 April 1995.

7. Author interview with Steve Hochman, 30 April 2022.

8. Transcript of speech, Office of Public Information, Carter Center.

9. *Memphis Commercial Appeal*, 29 April 1995; see also *Atlanta Constitution*, 24 April 1995.

10. *Atlanta Constitution*, 21 May, 24 April, 11 Aug., 1995; *Americus Times-Recorder*, 9 May, 1995; *New York Times*, 17 Sept. 1995; *Atlanta Journal and Constitution*, 23 July 1995; *The Economist*, 15 July 1995; JC, *Beyond the White House*, 95–99.

11. *Atlanta Constitution*, 10, 20 Nov. 1995; *Atlanta Journal and Constitution*, 30 Nov. 1995; Carter interview on PBS "The News Hour," 4 Dec. 1995; Timeline for Carter Center, 28 Nov.–2 Dec. 1995, www.cartercenter.org.

12. *Atlanta Journal and Constitution*, 19 March 1996.

13. *New York Time*, 12 Sept. 1995; *Atlanta Constitution*, 6 Nov. 1995.

14. AP Story, 20 Jan. 1996; *Atlanta Journal and Constitution*, 20, 21 Jan., 1996; *Atlanta Constitution*, 22 Jan. 1996.

15. *Atlanta Journal and Constitution*, 15 Feb., 24 March 1996.

16. Carter commentary, 23 Feb. 1996, *Los Angeles Times; Atlanta Journal and Constitution*, 15 Feb. 1996.

17. *Atlanta Constitution*, 19 March 1996; News Release from Carter Center, 26 March, 1996.

18. *Americus Times-Recorder*, 12 March 1996; *Carter Center News*, 28 May 1996; July Interview with RSC, Office of Public Information, The Carter Center, 8 Aug. 1996.

19. *Atlanta Journal and Constitution*, 6 July 1996.

20. *Americus Times-Recorder*, 27 July 1996; *Atlanta Constitution*, 1 Aug. 1996.

21. Leonardo Bernardo and Jennifer Weiss, *Citizen-in-Chief: The Second Lives of American Presidents*, 222.

22. Review in *Christian Century*, 19–27 March, 1997.

23. *Atlanta Constitution*, 3 Jan. 1997; Author's notes of Truman White House.

24. *New York Times*, 19 Jan. 1997; *Atlanta Constitution*, 6 Feb. 1997; *Americus Times-Recorder*, 8 Feb. 1997; JC, *Beyond the White House*, 197.

25. Questions posed by E. Stanly Godbold, Jr., Author's notes on Carters' comments at Historical Press Conference, Carter Center, Feb. 20–22, 1997. See also Gary D. Fink and Hugh Davis Graham, editors, *The Carter Presidency: Policy Choices in the Post-New Deal Era* (1998).

26. *Atlanta Constitution* and *Americus Times-Recorder*, both 6 March 1997.

27. *Atlanta Constitution*, 7 March 1997.

28. *Americus Times-Recorder*, 21, 28 April, 18 May 1997.

29. *Atlanta Journal and Constitution*, 19 July 1997; Trip Report: Visit to China, by Jimmy Carter, 23–29 July, 1997, Office of Public Information, the Carter Center, 14 August 1997: author interview with Steve Hochman, 23 April 2022..

30. Carter Speech, 26 Aug. 1997 "Global 2000 Workshop," Carter Trip Report on Africa, 21 Aug.—2 Sept. 1997, both in Office of Public Information, Carter Center, 18 Sept. 1997; *Atlanta Constitution*, 18 Aug. 1997. See also Gregg Easterbrook, "Forgotten Benefactor of Humanity," *The Atlantic Monthly*, January 1997, 75–82, and *The Carter Center Report*, Summer 1996.

31. *Atlanta Journal and Constitution*, 16 Oct. 1997.

32. *Americus Times-Recorder*, 17 Sept, 31 Oct., 1997.

33. *Atlanta Constitution*, 25 Sept. 1997, 7 Nov. 1997.

34. *Atlanta Constitution*, 7 Nov. 1997; Author's notes on the inauguration ceremony.

35. *Greenwood, SC, Index Journal*, 21 Nov., 1977; *Atlanta Journal and Constitution*, 6 Oct. 1997; *Atlanta Constitution*, 2 Dec. 1997; *Americus Times-Recorder*, 18 Dec., 1977;

Carter Trip Report on Jamaica, 18 Dec. 1997, Office of Public Information, Carter Center, 14 Jan. 1998.

36. *The Oxford American*, Carter comment on his book, Jan.–Feb. 1998, 23–24; *Atlanta Constitution*, 22 Jan. 1998; Greenwood, SC, *Index Journal*, 5 Jan. 1998; *Starkville, MS, Daily News*, 3 May 1998 (quotation).

37. Jimmy Carter, *Sources of Strength: Meditations on Scripture For a Living Faith*.

38. See Timothy D. Wilson, *Redirect: Changing the Stories We Live By* (2011).

39. *Memphis Commercial Appeal*, 9 March 1999; *New York Times*, 28 June 1999; *Larry King Live*, 26 Oct. 1998; *Hardball with Chris Matthews*, 12 Nov. 1998, transcript; Author's notes on Carter Center interview (quotations).

40. *Columbus (GA) Ledger-Enquirer*, 24 Sept. 1998 (quotation); Carol Felsenthal, *Clinton in Exile: A President Out of the White House*, 65–66; Bob Woodward, *Shadow: Five Presidents and the Legacy of Watergate*, 497–99.

41. *Starkville (MS) Daily News*, 28 April 1998 (quotations).

42. *Atlanta Journal and Constitution*, 28 Feb. 1999.

43. *Jakarta Post*, 5 April 1999; *New York Times*, 28 June 1999.

44. Weekly Compilation of Presidential Documents, 8/16/99, vol. 35, issue 32, p. 1605, Item Number 2317432; *Chicago Tribune*, 10 Aug. 1999.

45. *Chicago Tribune*, 10 Aug. 1999.

46. White House Press Secretary Release, 9 Aug. 1999; *Carter Center Update*, March 2000.

47. *Greenwood, SC, Index Journal*, 21 Sept. 1999; *Americus Times-Recorder*, 3 Oct. 1999; Cox News Service, 20 Oct. 1999; *Indian Ocean Newsletter*, 27 Nov. 1999.

48. Carter to Bowen, 28 June 1999, David R. Bowen File, Congressional and Political Research Center, Mitchell Memorial Library, Mississippi State University.

49. *Memphis Commercial Appeal*, 11, 15 Dec. 1999 (quotation); Author interview with Panamanian guide, 13 Feb. 2020. As of February 2020, the Panamanians have not erected the statue of Carter, which they still propose to do.

50. *Atlanta Journal and Constitution*, 7 April, 18 May 2000.

51. Carter to "My Fellow Baptists," 17 Oct. 2000, Author's collection.

52. *Memphis Commercial Appeal*, 29 Oct. 2000; *Daily Telegraph*, 24 Oct. 2000; Transcript, NBC News interview with Katie Couric, 27 Oct. 2000.

53. *The (London) Financial Times*, 29 April 2000.

54. Carter Interview, *USA Today*, 11 Jan. 2001.

55. Review in *Boston Globe*, 22 Jan. 2001.

56. Joan Ryan, "A Light Passes, Father to Son," *San Francisco Chronicle*, 4 Feb. 2001.

57. Carter Interview, *Horizons*, Summer 2001, p. 3.

Chapter 41

1. Barbara Olson, *The Final Days: The Last, Desperate Abuses of Power by the Clinton White House*, 169, 171, 193–94.

2. Rosalynn Carter to Clinton, 10 Jan. 2001, AP Story; *Boston Globe*, 3 March 2001; Jeffrey Toobin, *American Heiress: The Wild Saga of the Kidnapping, Crimes and Trial of Patty Hearst*, 337–38.

3. Carter interview, *Larry King Live*, 9 Jan. 2001; *Washington Times*, 26 Feb. 2001; *Atlanta Journal and Constitution*, 27 March 2001 (quotation).

4. *Jerusalem Post*, 24 April 2001; *The Hindu*, 5 Aug. 2001; *Greenwood (SC) Index Journal*, 1 Aug. 2001.

5. *VMI Alumni Review*, 77, no. 3 (spring 2001), and 96, no. 2 (219), 32; *Atlanta Journal and Constitution*, 30 March 2001.

6. Carter speech, 3 Sept. 2001, Carter Center.org/news/documents/doc547, 13 Jan. 2008.

7. *Atlanta Journal and Constitution*, 6 Sept. 2001 (quotation); *South China Morning Post*, 9 Sept. 2001.

8. Rosalynn Carter interview, Cox News Service, 9 Sept. 2002.

9. *Atlanta Journal and Constitution*, 14 Sept. ("survive"), 20 Oct. 2001; *New York Times*, 28 Sept. 2001 ("support him").

10. Quoted in *USA Today*, 29 Nov. 2001.

11. Rosalynn Carter speech, 5 Dec. 2001, Carter Center-Op-eds/Speeches Archive:2001-2005 .

12. Jimmy Carter, *Beyond the White House*, 185–92.

13. *New York Times*, 10 March 2002.

14. *New Orleans Times-Picayune*, 12 March 2002.

15. Karen DeYoung, "AIDS Warriors: Carter, Gates Sr. Find Hell and Hope in a Continent's Plague," *Washington Post*, 14 April 2002.

16. *San Diego Union-Tribune*, 12 April 2002.

17. *Atlanta Journal and Constitution*, 19 April 2002.

18. CNN.com, 14 May 2002; *Washington Post*, 24 May 2002.

19. *Starkville (MS) Daily News*, 13 May 2002; *Memphis Commercial Appeal*, 14 May 2002; *New York Times*, 15 May 2002; Carter interview, CNN "Daybreak," 16 May 2002; *Time*, 27 May 2002, p. 8; JC, *Beyond the White House*, 81–89.

20. Ascribe, Inc., 20 June 2002; Cox News Service, 12 Aug. 2002 (quotation).

21. Cox News Service, 9 Sept. 2002.

22. *Washington Post*, 10 July 2002; AP story, 7 July 2002; *The London Financial Times Limited*, 9 July 2002; UPI story, 9 July 2002.

23. Carter, "America Can Persuade Israel to Make a Just Peace," *New York Times*, 21 April 2002.

24. *Washington Post*, 5 Sept. 2002. See also *USA Today*, 1 July 2002.

25. Irwin Abrams, "The Nobel Peace Prize and Jimmy Carter," *Antioch Review*, Vol. 62, No. 2 (Spring 2004), 355.

26. Ibid., 359–60.

27. CNN.com/US, 11 Oct. 2002; *New York Times*, 11 Oct. 2002; Rosalynn Carter interview, *Atlanta Journal and Constitution*, 12 Oct. 2002; *Atlanta Journal and Constitution*, 13 Oct. 2002 (quotation); *Carter Center Update*, Winter 2002; Mark K. Updegrove, *Second Acts: Presidential Lives and Legacies after the White House*, 174–75.

28. *Agene France Press*, 12 Oct. 2002; *Baltimore Sun*, 12 Oct. 2002; *CanWest Global Communications Corp.*, 12 Oct. 2002 (Watson quotation).

29. *Atlanta Journal and Constitution*, 24 Sept. 2002.

30. Abrams, "The Nobel Prize and Jimmy Carter," *The Antioch Review* 62, no. 2 (Spring 2004), 360; Elizabeth Kurylo, editorial, *Atlanta Journal and Constitution*, 13 Oct. 2002; Adriana Bosch, Director, *Jimmy Carter, The American Experience*, WGBH Education Foundation, 2002.

31. Cox News Service, 13 Oct. 2002.

32. *The Miami Herald*, 17 Oct. 2002; *Atlanta Journal and Constitution*, 17 Oct. 2002.

33. *Agence France Press*, 18 Oct. 2002; Carter interview about Bush, *The Australian*, 16 Oct. 2002; Trip Report, Jamaica, 14–18 Oct. 2002, 11/05/2002, Report, 542166, 542166[1], Subject files PP, WHORM, George W. Bush Library (GWBL), Dallas, Texas.

34. First Nobel Outline, 25 Oct. 2002; Carter to Rick, Steve, and Achsah, 30 Oct. 2002, VF, Nobel Speech, JCL.

35. Rafshoon to Carter, 8 Nov. 2002, Hochman comments on draft dated 4 Nov. 2002, and others, VF, Nobel Speech, JCL.

36. Draft dated 30 Oct. 2002 with Rosalynn's comments; Jimmy to Rosalynn, attached to draft dated 31 Oct. 2002, with her response, Nobel Speech, VF, JCL.

37. *Atlanta Journal and Constitution*, 19 Nov. 20, 2002; Carter interview, *Larry King Live*, CNN, 15 Nov. 2002.

38. Abrams, "The Nobel Prize and Jimmy Carter," 362.

39. Jimmy Carter, *The Nobel Peace Prize Lecture*, New York: Simon & Schuster, 2002, 5, 6, 12, 16–17, 20.

40. *Atlanta Constitution*, 11 Dec. 2002.

41. Author, who was that researcher, interview with archivists, Author's private collection.

42. Robert Marus, "Carter Accepts Peace Prize," 10 Dec. 2002, and EthicsDaily.com E-newsletter, Baptist History File, Carter Biography, Southern Baptist History Library and Archives, Nashville, TN.

43. Carter Interview, National Park Service III, 260, JCL.

Chapter 42

1. *The Wine Report*, Jan. 2003; *Bon Appetit*, Feb. 2003.

2. Carter Center Timeline 2003; *Memphis Commercial Appeal*, 21 Jan. 2003; *Atlanta Journal and Constitution*, 20, 21 Jan. 2003; *Washington Post*, 22 Jan. 2003; CNN.com./ World, 21 Jan., 2003; Jimmy Carter, *Beyond the White House*, 121–26; Jimmy Carter, *Sharing Good Times*, 151.

3. *New York Times*, 9 March 2003 .

4. John Bloom, "Where's Jimbo? Where's Jimmy Carter?," UPI story, 29 May 2003.

5. *Kentucky Herald-Leader*, 11 Feb. 2003; *Las Vegas Sun*, 23 April 2003; *Atlanta Journal and Constitution*, 12 Feb., 2003; *Albuquerque Journal*, 24 April 2003; Ascribe Newswire, 5 May 2003; AP story, 5 June 2003.

6. *Atlanta Journal-Constitution*, 2 June 2003; JC, *Beyond the White House*, 235–45. For a good overview of the Atlanta Project, see Kaye Minchew, *Jimmy Carter: Citizen of the South*, 153-55.

7. *Rocky Mountain News*, 27 June 2003. The witnesses use the words "raft" and "boat" interchangeably, but apparently the flotilla consisted of rafts of different sizes and weights with the Carters assigned to the one that was safest.

8. Ibid.

9. *Kyodo News Service*, 15 Feb. 2003; *New York Times*, 13 July 2003; *Dallas Morning News*, 5, 6, 9 Sept. 2003; Jimmy Carter, "Sixth U Thant Distinguished Lecture, United Nations University, Tokyo, Japan, Carter Center Op-eds/Speeches, Archive, 2001-2005.

10. President Carter Delivers Speech to Beijing (Peking) University, 9 Sept 2003, Carter Center Op-eds/Speeches Archive 2001–2005. *Financial Times Information Global News Wire*, 8 Sept. 2003; Carter Center Timeline 2003.

11. National Public Radio, 17 Sept. 2003.

12. "Camp David Accords: Jimmy Carter Reflects twenty-Five Years Later," 17 Sept. 2003, Carter Center Op-eds/Speeches Archive 2001–2005.

13. *Chattanooga Times Free Press*, 24 Sept., 2003; Jimmy Carter, "The Choice for Israelis," *Washington Post*, 23 Dec. 2003.

14. "Remarks by former U.S. President Jimmy Carter at the conference "Human Rights Defenders on the Frontlines of Freedom," Nov. 11–12, 2003, Atlanta, Ga., Carter Center, Op-Ed Speeches.

15. *Greenwood (SC) Index-Journal*, 14 Nov. 2003 (quotation); *Sunday Times of London*, 13 April 2003; *Columbia (SC) State*, 23 Nov. 2003; *The Dallas Morning News*, 16 Nov. 2003.

16. Jimmy Carter, "Geneva Initiative Public Commitment Event: Remarks by Former U.S. President Jimmy Carter, 1 Dec. 2003, www.cartercenter.org/news/documents/doc1556.html; *BBC Worldwide Monitoring*, 29 Oct. 2003.

17. *Newsday*, 1 Dec. 2003; *The London Independent*, 2 Dec. 2003; Carter Center.

18. Jimmy Carter, "Speech to the Joint Session of Congress of Bolivia," 18 Dec. 2003, Carter Center Op-eds/Speeches Archive, 2001–2005.

19. Associated Press Online, 26 Jan. 2004; Xinhua General News Service, 27 Jan. 2004; *Atlanta Journal and Constitution*, 27 Jan. 2004; Carter Center Timeline 2004.

20. *Atlanta Journal and Constitution*, 28 Jan., 4 Feb. 2004 (quotation); *Ascribe*, 23 Jan. 2004; BBC Monitoring Latin America, 28 Jan. 2004; BBC Monitoring Africa, 3 Feb. 2004; Carter Center Timeline, 2004, www.cartercenter.org.

21. *Atlanta Journal and Constitution*, 4 Feb. 2004; Carter Center Timeline 2004.

22. Ascribe Newswire, 30 Jan. 2004; *Washington Post*, 22 Feb. 2004; *Atlanta Journal and Constitution*, 21 Feb., 11 March 2004.

23. Minneapolis *Star Tribune*, 22 Feb. 2004.

24. Andrew Buncombe in Atlanta, "Carter Savages Blair and Bush: 'Their War Was Based on Lies,'" *London Independent*, 22 March 2004.

25. *Winston-Salem Journal*, 10 May 2004; *Atlanta Journal and Constitution*, 13 May 2004; *Africa News*, 18 May 2004; Remrks of President Crtr at the World Health Assembly, May 19, 2004, Carter Center Op-eds/Speeches Archive, 2001–2005.

26. AP State and Local Wire, 28 March, 2004; *Cleveland Plain Dealer*, 15 April 2004.

27. *Hartford Courant*, 6 June 2004; *Seattle Post-Intelligencer*, 5 June 2004 (quotations).

28. *Greenwood (SC) Index Journal*, 6 June 2004; *Seattle Post-Intelligencer*, 5 June 2004.

29. AP story, 6 June 2004 (quotations).

30. "Eulogy for Mattie Sink," 9 28 June 2004, Carter Center Op-eds/Speeches Archive, 2001-2005.

31. www.mosnews.com/news/2004/o7/12/carter.shtml; *Tass*, 16 July 2004; JC, *Sharing Good Times*, 151.

32. Jimmy Carter Address Democratic National Convention, July 27, 2004, Carter Center Op'eds/Speeches Archive, 2001-2005; *Boston Herald*, 31 July 2004; *Kansas City Star*, 3 Aug. 2004.

33. Jonathan Alter, *His Very Best: Jimmy Carter, A Life*, 208, 215, 621.

34. AP Worldstream, 11 Aug. 2004; www.accessnorthga.com/news/, 13 Aug. 2004; author interview with Steve Hochman, 25 April 2022..

35. *Las Vegas Review-Journal*, 16 Aug. 2004; *New York Times*, 17 Aug. 2004; *Atlanta Constitution*, 13, 16, 27 Aug. 2004; Carter Center Timeline, 15 Aug. 2004 (quotation); *Dallas Morning News*, 15 Aug. 2004.

36. *Atlanta Journal and Constitution*, 11 Sept. 2004; *Star Tribune*, 11 Sept. 2004.

37. AP Press Online, 15 Sept. 2004 (quotation); *Ascribe*, 14 Sept. 2004.

38. Jimmy Carter, "Still Seeking a Fair Florida Vote," *Washington Post*, 27 Sept. 2004.

39. Author's notes on the event; *Atlanta Journal and Constitution*, 29 Oct. 2004.

40. *National Wildlife*, Oct./Nov. 2004.

41. MSNBC, 18 Oct. 2004; *Atlanta Constitution*, 25 Oct. 2004.

42. NPR, 22 Oct. 2004.

43. *New York Times*, 12 Nov. 2004.

44. *Dallas Morning News*, 12 Nov. 2004.

45. Carter's Remarks at the Dedication of the Clinton Presidential Library, 18 Nov. 2004, Carter Center Op-eds/Speeches Archives, 2001–2005; Author's notes on the event; Carter interview, *Charlie Rose Show*, 9 Dec. 2004 (quotation).

46. *Atlanta Constitution*, 23 Nov., 5 Dec. (quotation), 23 Dec. 2004.

Chapter 43

1. President Carter's Trip Report on the Palestinian Presidential Election, 12 Jan. 2005, Carter Center Trip Reports 2005.

2. *Jerusalem Post*, 7 Jan. 2005.

3. CNN News, 10 Jan. 2005; Trip Report, 12 Jan. 2005, Carter Center: Jimmy Crter Trip Reports Archives, 2001–2005; *Atlanta Journal and Constitution*, 12 Jan. 2005; *Carter Center News*, Spring 2005, 6–7.

4. *Atlanta Journal and Constitution*, 12 Jan. 2005; Joshua Muravchik, *Making David into Goliath: How the World Turned against Israel*, 219.

5. Carter Keynote Speech to OAS, 25 Jan. 2005, Carter Center Op-eds?Speeches Archive, 2001–2005; the *Atlanta Journal and Constitution*, 26 Jan. 2005.

6. Carter Center Timeline 2005.

7. *American Spectator* and *Atlanta Journal and Constitution*, 6 April 2005.

8. Jimmy Carter, *Beyond the White House*, 252–54; Peter Baker and Susan Glasser, *The Man Who Ran Washington: The Life and Times of James A. Baker, III*, 580.

9. Carter Center Timeline 2005; Global News Wire, 15 May, 2005; BBC Monitoring International Reports, 1 June 2005; *Carter Center Update*, Winter 2005; *Birmingham Post and Mail*, 28 Jan. 2005.

10. Program for the Coimmssioning of the *USS Jimmy Carter*, 19 Feb. 2005, VF, *USS Jimmy Carter*, JCL; *New York Times*, 13 Feb. 2005.

11. Atlanta Journal and Constitution, 13 Aug.2005.

12. W. Frederick Zimmerman, *SSN-23 Jimmy Carter U.S. Navy Submarine*, 20; *Atlanta Journal and Constitution*, 13 Aug. 2005; US Navy photo by 1st class Jennifer Spinner, ID 050812-N-1433S-016.

13. *Congressional Quarterly*, 19 Sept. 2005; *Raw Story*, 22 Sept. 2005; *Atlanta Journal and Constitution*, 6 Oct. 2005 (quotation); *Washington Post*, 10 Sept. 2005; "Building Confidence in U.S. Elections: Report of the Commission on Federal Election Reform," September 2005, compiled by Center for Democracy and Election Management, American University.

14. *Agence France Presse*, 2 Nov. 2005.

15. CBS News, 3 Nov., 2005.

16. NPR, 4 Nov. 2005.

17. *Charlie Rose Show*, Transcript, 9 Nov. 2005. See also *Atlanta Journal and Constitution*, 4 Nov. 2005.

18. *USA Today*, 12 Dec. 2005.

19. JC, *Beyond the White House*, 137–45; Jimmy Carter, "There's Hope In Liberia's History," *New York Times*, 13 July 2003; *Atlanta Journal and Constitution*, 12, 24 Nov. 2005; *Africa News*, 8 Nov. 2005.

20. "Palestinian Elections: Trip Report by Former U.S. President Jimmy Carter," Carter Center Online Trips 2006.

21. Ibid.

22. Ibid.

23. *Toronto Star*, 27 Jan. 2005.

24. "Palestinian Elections," Carter Center Online Trips 2006; *(Columbia, SC) State*, 25 Jan. 2006; *Atlanta Journal and Constitution*, 28 Jan. 2006; *New York Times*, 29 Jan. 2006.

25. *Larry King Live*, CNN, 5 Feb. 2006; *USA Today*, 8 Feb. 2006; *Atlanta Journal and Constitution*, 8 Feb. 2006.

26. *Atlanta Journal and Constitution*, 26 Feb., 10, 25 May, 6, 7 July, 18 Oct., 7 Nov. 2006; *London Observer*, 1 March 2006; *New York Times*, 5 March 2006; *Nevada Frontrunner*, 3 May 2006; Carter speech, 2 March 2006.

27. Jimmy Carter, *Palestine Peace Not Apartheid*, First Edition, 2006, hardcover, front and back of dustjacket.
28. JC, *Beyond the White House*, 230–31; NPR, 12 Nov. 2006; Randall Balmer, *Redeemer: The Life of Jimmy Carter*, 171–72; John J. Mearsheimer and Stephen M. Walt, *The Israel Lobby and U.S. Foreign Policy*, 9, 173, 193–95.
29. *New York Sun*, 22 Nov. 2006; Balmer, *Redeemer*, 172.
30. *Larry King Live*, CNN, 27 Nov. 2007; Sasha Polakow-Suransky, *The Unspoken Alliance: Israel's Secret Relationship with Apartheid South Africa*, 233–35.
31. *Atlanta Journal and Constitution*, 28 Jan. 2007.
32. Ibid.; Leonard Bernardo and Jennifer Weiss, *Citizen-in-Chief: The Second Lives of the American Presidents*, 170–73.
33. *New York Times*, 7 Dec. 2006; *New York Post*, 10 Dec. 2006.
34. *Bristol (VA) Herald Courier*, 12 Jan. 2007.
35. *Atlanta Journal and Constitution*, 4 Dec. 2006; *(Columbia, SC) State*, 4 Dec. 2006.
36. *Americus Times-Recorder*, 19 Dec. 2006.
37. AP Worldstream, 28, 29 Dec. 2006.
38. *Congressional Quarterly*, 3 Jan. 2007; Carter Speech, Jan. 3 2007, in Carter Center Op-eds/Speeches Archive, 2006–2009; Thomas W. DeFrank, *Write It When I'm Gone: Remarkable Off-the-Record Conversations with Gerald R. Ford*, 140–42, 147–48.
39. *Atlanta Journal and Constitution*, 10 Jan. 2007; *Wall Street Journal*, 2 Feb. 2007.
40. Interview with Wolfe Blitzer, CNN, 19 Jan. 2007.
41. Keren Batiyov review in *Pittsburg Tribune Review*, 19 Jan. 2007.
42. "Remarks by Former U.S. President Jimmy Carter at Brandeis University," 23 Jan. 2007, Carter Center Ops/eds Speeches Archive, 2006–2007; Dan Fleshler, *Transforming America's Israel Lobby*, 187–88.
43. *Boston Globe*, 24 Jan. 2007.
44. JC, *Beyond the White House*, 148.
45. *Africa News*, 6, 13 Feb., 18 May, 2007; *New York Times*, 18 Feb. 2007; *Carter Center News*, Spring 2007.
46. JC, *Beyond the White House*, 149–50.
47. *Atlanta Journal and Constitution*, 25 Feb. 2007; *Waste News*, 5 March 2007.
48. *Los Angeles Times*, 4 May 2007.
49. *Memphis Commercial Appeal*, 4 Sept. 2007; *(Canada) Globe and Mail*, 21 Sept. 2007 (quotation); Carter speech, 26 Sept. 2007, Carter Center Op-eds/ Speeches Archive, 2006–2009.
50. *Irish Times*, 19 July 2007; *Africa News*, 19 July 2007; Carter speech , June 17, 2007, in Carter Center Op-eds/Speeches Archive, 2006–2009.
51. *Africa News*, 20 June 2007; JC, *Beyond the White House*, 215–20.
52. Rosalynn Carter speech, 10 July 2007; *The Washington Times*, 18 July 2007; Congressional Documents and Publications, 7 March 2008.
53. *Africa News*, 1 Oct. 2007; *Bellsouth News*, 4 Oct. 2007; *Washington Post*, 4 Oct. 2007.
54. Carter interview, *Good Morning America*, 8 Oct. 2007; Cox News Service, 24 Oct. 2007; *Xinhua General News Service*, 21 Nov. 2007; Carter Center Timeline, 20–24 Nov. 2007.

Chapter 44

1. Rosalynn Carter, "Addressing the Caregiving Crisis," *Preventing Chronic Disease* 5, no. 1 (7 Jan. 2008).
2. *(Greenwood, SC) Index Journal*, 31 Jan. 2008.
3. New Baptist Covenant Celebration, 29 Jan. 2008, http://www.newbaptistcelebration. org/; *Los Angeles Times*, 1 Feb. 2008; *Atlanta Journal and Constitution*, 26 Jan. 2008; *Washington Post*, 26 Jan. 2008; *New York Times*, 27 Jan. 2008; AP Wire, 2 Feb. 2008 (quotations).
4. *Wall Street Journal*, 30 Jan. 2008.
5. Trip Report by Former U.S. President Jimmy Carter to Accra, Ghana, and Abuja, Nigeria: March 30–April 3, 2008, Carter Center 2008.
6. *Africa News*, 4 April 2008.
7. Trip Report by Former U.S. President Jimmy Carter to Nepal: April 6–14, 2008, Carter Center Trips 2008; BBC Monitoring Carter in Nepal, 8 April 2008; *Carter Center Update*, Summer 2008; *Hindustan Times*, 10 April 2008; *Washington Times*, 11 April 2008.
8. *Washington Post*, 11 April 2008; *Wall Street Journal*, 15 April 2008; *Atlanta Journal and Constitution*, 20 April 2008; Carter Center Timeline, 13–21 April 2008.
9. *Jerusalem Post*, 22 April 2008.
10. Mortimer B. Zuckerman, "The Damage of Jimmy Carter," *U.S. News & World Report*, 28 April–5 May, 2008, 72; AP Wire, 23 April 2008; *Wall Street Journal*, 25 April 2008.
11. *Agence France Presse*, 22 April 2008.
12. Shahid Naqvi, "Mr. President's Rocky Road to Peace," *Birmingham Post*, 26 May 2008 (quotations); *London Independent*, 26 May 2008.
13. Bronwen Maddox, "Carter is Right to Say the Unsayable," *Times (London)*, 28 May 2008.
14. "Miss Lillian's Remarkable Life Now Guides Jimmy Carter's," *USA Today*, 24 April 2008, 4D.
15. *Times-Picayune*, 14 May 2008.
16. *(Bristol, VA) Herald Courier*, 15 May 2008; Carter interview on *Today Show*, 28 April 2008; *(Greenwood, SC) Index Journal*, 8 May 2008 (quotations).
17. *(Greenwood, SC) Index Journal*, 21 May 2008.
18. *Jerusalem Post*, 22 Aug. 2008.
19. BBC Monitoring Europe, 8 Oct. 2008.
20. *Africa News*, 24 Nov. 2008; *Atlanta Journal and Constitution*, 2 Dec. 2008; *New York Times*, 23 Nov. 2008.
21. BBC Worldwide Monitoring, 13 Dec. 2008, 28 Oct. 2011.
22. Walter Rogers, "Stop Picking on Jimmy Carter," *Christian Science Monitor*, 5 Jan. 2009.
23. *Agence France Presse*, 8 Jan. 2009; *Xinhu (New China News Agency)*, 14 Jan. 2009; States News Service, 13 Jan. 2009; Carter Center Timeline 2009.
24. Peggy Noonan editorial, *Wall Street Journal*, 10–11 Jan. 2009; Carter Center Timeline, 2009, www.cartercenter.org; *Daily News (New York)*, 8 Jan. 2009; *USA Today*, 8 Jan. 2009.

25. AP Worldstream, 15, 27 Jan. 2009; *Charlie Rose Show*, 27 Jan. 2009; CTV (Canada), 28 Jan. 2009.

26. AP Worldstream, 1 Feb. 2009; Targeted News Service, 12 March 2009.

27. Adam Morrow and Khaled Moussa Al-Omani, "Camp David Accord Unacceptable to Many," IPS (Latin America), 30 March 2009.

28. "Remarks by Israeli Prime Minister Ehud Olmert, in an Address to the Special Knesset Session Marking the 30th Anniversary of the Peace Treaty with Egypt (The Israeli Knesset, Jerusalem, March 30, 2009), Federal News Service 31 March 2009.

29. *Daily News (New York)*, 15 Feb. 2009; *Jerusalem Post*, 13 March 2009; *San Francisco Chronicle*, 8 Feb. 2009: *Saint Louis Post-Dispatch (Missouri)*, 4 Feb. 2009; Interview with Former President Jimmy Carter, Meredith Vieira, *Today*, 26 Jan. 2009.

30. Carter Center Timeline, 27 April–4 May 2009; States News Service, 8 Feb., 13 April, 1, 5 May, 2009.

31. *Congressional Quarterly*, 13 May 2009; *Washington Post*, 13 May 2009.

32. *Carter Center Reports-Middle East*, 2009.

33. Ibid.

34. Ibid.

35. Ibid.

36. Ibid.

37. Ibid.

38. Ibid.; Trip Report by Former U.S. President Jimmy Carter to Lebanon, Syria, Israel, West Bank, and Gaza—June 2–17, 2009, Carter Center.

39. Jimmy Carter, "Losing my Religion for Equality," 15 July 2009, Carter Center copy; *Christian Science Monitor*, 25 Aug. 2009; Joshua Muravchik, *Making David into Goliath: How the World Turned against Israel*, 221.

40. *(London) Sunday Times*, 30 Aug. 2009; E. Stanly Godbold, Jr., "Kennedy, Carter, Shared a Similar Vision," *Atlanta Journal and Constitution*, 30 Aug. 2009.

41. *Atlanta Journal and Constitution*, 15 Sept. 2009.

42. ABC News Transcript, 1 Oct. 2009; Author's notes.

43. Carter interview, *Today Show*, 15 Oct. 2009.

44. *Wall Street Journal*, 4 Nov. 2009; CNN News, 14 Nov. 2009.

45. *Starkville (MS) Daily News*, 24 Dec. 2009; CNN News, 24 Dec. 2009.

46. *U.S. Federal News*, 20 March 2010; *Agence France Presse*, 23 March 2010.

47. States News Service, 13 April 2010; *Atlanta Journal and Constitution*, 16 May 2010; *Jerusalem Post*, 3 March 2010; *Toronto Sun*, 3 April 2010; Carter Center Timeline, 29 April 2010.

48. AP Story, 8 April 2010; *(Canada) Globe and Mail*, 27 April 2010; Carter Op-Ed in *Los Angeles Times*, 28 April 2010; Carter Center Timeline 2010.

49. *New York Times*, 29, 30 April 2010.

50. *Atlanta Journal and Constitution*, 24 May 2010.

51. *Korea Times*, 8 June 2010.

52. *New York Times*, 23 Aug. 2010; *Christian Science Monitor*, 25 Aug. 2010; *Xinhua General News Service*, 26 Aug. 2010.

53. *Guardian*, 17 Sept. 2010.

54. Jimmy Carter, *White House Diary*, passim; *New York Times*, 17 Sept. 2010; *Washington Post*, 17, 28 Sept. 2010 (quotations); *(Chattanooga, TN) Times Free Press*, 19 Sept. 2010; *Los Angeles Times*, 21 Sept. 2010; Gary Wills, "The Strange Success of Jimmy Carter," *New York Review of Books*, 28 Oct. 2010, pp. 23–24.

55. Liu Dongkai, "Premier Wen Jiabao Meets with Former US President Carter in Beijing on 6 September" China News Agency, BBC Worldwide Monitoring, 6 Sept. 2010 (quotations); Carter Center Timeline, 4–10 September 2010.

Chapter 45

1. BBC Monitoring Middle East, 17, 21, 23 Oct. 2010.

2. BBC Monitoring Middle East, 17 Oct. 2010.

3. Jimmy Carter, Trip Report: Visit by the Elders to Gaza, Egypt, Syria, Jordan, Israel, and the West Bank, Oct. 15–23, 2010, Carter Center Trip Reports 2010.

4. BBC Monitoring Middle East, 21 Oct. 2010.

5. *New Zealand Herald*, 22 Oct. 2010.

6. Carter Trip Report Middle East 2010.

7. Manuel Roig-Franzi, "The Book of Jimmy: In Print or in Person, Former President Preaches Policy," *Washington Post*, 18 Oct. 2010.

8. *Korea Times*, 5 Jan. 2011 (quotation); *Africa News*, 30 Oct. 2010; *Atlanta Now*, Mar–April 2017, p. 19.

9. Trip Report by Former U.S. President Jimmy Carter to Sudan, Jan. 5–16, 2011, Carter Center Trips 2011; *Africa News*, 7 Jan. 2011.

10. Trip Report, Sudan 2011.

11. Stephen White, "Birth of A Nation; Clooney Joy as 4M Vote Over Sudan Breakaway, *Mirror*, 10 Jan. 2011.

12. Ibid.; *(Thailand) Nation*, 14 Jan. 2011; *Washington Post*, 16 Jan. 2011.

13. Martin I. Elzy to Stanly Godbold, 17 Feb. 2011, Author's private collection.

14. Mark K. Updegrove, *Destiny of Democracy: The Civil Rights Summit at the LBJ Presidential Library*, 72–86.

15. Nicholas Dawidoff, "The Riddle of Jimmy Carter," *Rolling Stone*, 3 Feb. 2011.

16. Trip Report by Former U.S. President Jimmy Carter to Cuba, March 28–30, 2011 (quotation), Carter Center Trips 2011. *Chattanooga Times Free Press*, 30 March 2011; *Nation*, 25 April 2011; *Jerusalem Post*, 1 April 2011; *Wall Street Journal*, 4 April 2011.

17. Trip Report, Cuba, March 28–30, 2011; Mary Anastasia O'Grady, "Jimmy Carter Lobbies for Cuban Spies," *Wall Street Journal*, 4 April 2011; *Washington Times*, 7 April 2011.

18. Trip Report by Former U.S. President Jimmy Carter to the Korean Peninsula, April 22–19, 2011, Carter Center Trip Reports 2011; msnbc.com, 25 April 2011.

19. Trip Report, Korean Peninsula, April 22–29, 2011 (quotation); *Christian Science Monitor*, 26 April, 2011; *New York Times*, 29 April 2011; *Wall Street Journal*, 4, 26 April 2011; *Washington Times*, 8 June 2011.

20. Rosalynn Carter to Jeannie Godbold, 31 Aug. 2011, Author's Collection.

21. *New Zealand Herald*, 7 July 2011; *USA Today*, 13 July 2011 (quotation); *Washington Post*, 15 July 2011.

22. *Observer*, 11 Sept. 2011.

23. Trip Report by Former U.S. President Jimmy Carter to the Netherlands, Belgium, United Kingdom, and Norway, October 2–6, 2011, Carter Center Trip Reports 2011.

24. Trip Report by Former U.S. President Jimmy Carter to Beijing, Guangzhou, Shenzhen, and Hong Kong, China, Dec. 6–15, 2011, Carter Center Trips 2011.

25. *International Herald Tribune*, 13 Jan. 2012; *Christian Science Monitor*, 24 April 2012; BBC Monitoring Khartoum, 28 May 2012; *Africa News*, 11, 19 Jan., 27 June, 6 July 2012; Carter Center Timeline, 23–24 May 2012.

26. *Atlanta Journal and Constitution*, 12 Jan. 2012; *New York Times*, 25 June 2012; NBC News, 18 Sept. 2012; *(Columbus, MS) Dispatch*, 19 Sept. 2012; *Huffington Post*, 23 Feb. 2013.

27. *Australian*, 5 July 2012; *New York Times*, 4 July 2012.

28. Nick Wing, Politics, *Huffington Post*, 4 Sept. 2012.

29. *New York Times*, 10 April 2013; *Washington Post*, 7 May 2013; ABC News interview, 7 Dec. 2013 (quotation); Carter to Author, 6 May 2014.

30. *Investor's Business Daily*, 22 Feb. 2013.

31. *Washington Post*, 3 May 2013.

32. Carter Center Trip Reports Nepal & Myanmar April 2013 and Nepal November 2013.

33. Carter Center Trip Reports Colombia January 2013 and Colombia July 2013.

34. *USA Today*, 10 April 2013.

35. Carter Center Trip Reports Washington and London July 2013.

36. *New York Times*, 8 Nov. 2013; *Epoch Times*, 21–27 Nov. 2013.

37. *Atlanta Journal and Constitution*, 4 Feb. 2014*; New York Times*, Blogs, 21 Oct. 2015 (quotation).

38. *Atlanta Journal and Constitution*, 4 Feb. 2014.

39. Carter Center Trip Reports China 2014.

40. *Africa News*, 28 March 2014; Women in the World Conference, 2 April 2014, Carter Center, Atlanta; Carter Center Timeline, 24 March 2014.

41. *Toronto Star*, 1 Nov. 2014.

42. *Jerusalem Post*, 7 Nov. 2014.

43. *Christian Science Monitor*, 29 Aug. 2014.

44. Carter Center Trip Reports China 2014.

45. Carter Center Jimmy Carter 90th Birthday Remarks.

46. http://legalinsurrection.com/2015/04/israeli-pm; BBC Monitoring Europe, 27 April 2015.

47. Carter Center Trip Reports Moscow, Palestine 2015.

48. Carter Center Trip Reports Guyana 2015.

49. *AARP Bulletin*, June 2105.

50. Jimmy Carter, *A Full Life: Reflections at Ninety*, 10–14; David Holahan, Review of *A Full Life*, *Christian Science Monitor*, 7 July 2015.

51. *Australian*, 13 July 2015.

52. *Huffington Post*, 3 Aug. 2015.

53. *Guardian*, 21 Aug. 2015; *(Tupelo, MS) Daily Journal*, 24 Aug. 2015; *Washington Post*, 21, 22 Aug. 2015 (quotation).

54. *Addicting Info: The Knowledge You Crave*, 19 Aug. 2015. addictingfo.com.

55. *(Starkville, MS) Daily News*, 7 Dec. 2015, 16 May 2016; *New York Times*, 23 May, 28 Nov. 2016.

56. Katie Kindelan, "10-Year-Old Cancer Survivor Granted Wish to Meet Namesake President Jimmy Carter," *ABC News*, 13 July 2016.

57. *St. Louis Post-Dispatch*, 16 Sept. 2016 (quotation); *Wall Street Journal*, 9 Dec. 2016; *Carter Center News*, Spring 2016.

58. *ArmenPress News Agency*, 27 March 2018; PressTV, 25 July 2018; *Washington Post*, 17 Aug. 2018.

59. *Atlanta Journal-Constitution*, 10 July 2017; *New York Times*, 13 July 2017; *Habitat: The Magazine of Habitat for Humanity*, Sept. 2017, p. 5.

60. *Atlanta Journal-Constitution*, 13 August 2017.

61. *Sierra*, Sept.–Oct. 2017.

62. *Atlanta Journal-Constitution*, 19 Feb. 2018; Jimmy Carter, *Faith: A Journey for All*, 15, 116.

63. Nicole Darrah, "Jimmy Carter wins third Grammy award for audiobook on his faith," https://foxnews.com/entertainment/jimmy-carter-wins-third-grammy-award.print (quotation); Success World News, 11 Feb. 2019.

64. *Time*, 24 Sept. 2018 (Carter quotation); *Washington Post*, 17 Aug. 2018 (Rosalynn quotation); *Habitat: The Magazine of Habitat for Humanity*, December 2018, 26–30.

65. https://fullecenter.org/carters-family-friends-gather-at-koinoia-frm-to-remember-millard-fuller, 28 Feb. 2019.

66. "President Carter Marks 40th Anniversary of U.S.-Cia Relations," *Carter Center News*, Spring 2019, 4–5.

67. *Rolling Stone*, 17 Feb. 2020.

68. Rosalynn Carter and Bill Jallah, "We Are at the Beginning of a Global Mental Health Revolution," CNN Live TV, 31 May 2019.

69. "Conversations with Claire," *Emory Magazine*, 94, no. 3 (Summer 2019), p. 8.

70. Steve Hochman to Stanly Godbold, 29 April 2022.

71. *Starkville Daily News*, 18 Sept. 2019.

72. *USA Today*, 21 Oct. 2019; *Habitat: The Magazine of Habitat for Humanity*, Fall 2019, p. 3.

73. *(Columbus, MS) Dispatch*, 11 Nov. 2019; Carter's schedule supplied by Steve Hochman to author in emails dated 29 April and 2 May 2022

74. *(Columbus, MS) Dispatch*, 30 Dec. 2019.

75. Carter Center Press Releases, 6 May 2020, Carter Center News and Events 2020.

76. *Chattanooga Times Free Press*, 4 Nov. 2019; *Wall Street Journal*, 6, 11–12 April 2020; Carter Center Press Releases, 18, 30 July, 18 Sept. 2020.

Bibliography

Manuscript Collections

Americus, Georgia:
Lake Blackshear Regional Library
  Special Collections

Ann Arbor, Michigan:
Gerald R. Ford Presidential Library
  David Gergen File
  Charles McCall File
  President Ford Committee for Reelection File
  A. J. Reichley File

Atlanta, Georgia:
Jimmy Carter Presidential Library and Museum
  Zbigniew Brzezinski Donated Materials
  Carter Family Papers
  CIA Declassified Documents
  Susan Clough File
  Emily Gordon Dolvin File
  Donated Historical Papers
  Federal Records
  Mary Finch Hoyt Papers
  Hamilton Jordan File
  National Security Affairs
  Gerald Rafshoon Collection
  Jody Powell File
  Pre-Presidential File, 1962-1974

Speechwriters File
Staff Secretary File
Vertical File
White House Central File
White House Staff File
Robert W. Woodruff Library, Manuscript,
  Archives, and Rare
  Book Library. Emory University
Morris B. Abram Papers
Ralph McGill Papers
Charles M. Rafshoon Collection
  Robert W. Woodruff Papers

Nashville, Tennessee
Southern Baptist Historical Library and
  Archives
  Southern Baptist History Collection

New York City, New York
Columbia University Library Oral
  Histories

Starkville, Mississippi
Mississippi State University Library
  David Bowen Papers
  John C. Stennis Oral History Collection

Oral Histories

Jimmy Carter Presidential Library
and Museum
Carter Library Oral Histories
  Miller Center Oral Histories
  Miscellaneous Interviews
Rosalynn Carter, 1974
  National Archives and Records
  Administration Interviews
  National Park Service Interview

Library of Congress, Washington, DC
Interview with L. Bruce Laingen, The
  Association for Diplomatic Studies and

Training Foreign Affairs Oral History
  Project, January 9, 1993

Harry S. Truman National Historic Site,
Independence, Missouri
Oral History Interview with Jimmy and
  Rosalyn[n] Carter
  October 1991, Plains, Georgia
Presidential Studies Quarterly Vol. 38, No.
  1, 1–13
  George C. Edwards III, "Exclusive
  Interview: President Jimmy Carter"

Interviews

Rick Allen
Peter Bastjancic
Carl Biven
Jimmy Carter
Rosalynn Carter
Morris W. H. Collins, Jr.
Juanita Edmundson
Dan Edwards
Marty Franks
Rod Goodwin
Jay Hakes
O. M. Harrelson

Steven Hochman
Mary Finch Hoyt
Howard Jones
Billie Larson
Jackie Lassiter
Edmund Muskie
Thomas "Tip" O'Neill
Abraham Ribicoff
John Van Dyke Saunders
Julia Vissotto Saunders
Gary Sick
Scott Singletary

"Miss Allie" Smith
Rear Admiral James
R. Stark (ret.)
Gordon C. Steward
India Thompson
Stansfield Turner
Cyrus Vance
Brenda Wall
Mary Whitehead
Annette Wise

Public Documents and Printed Collections

The Foreign Relations of the United States, 1977–1980. Vols. 2 & 13. Washington, DC: Department of State, Government Printing Office, 2013.
The Presidential Campaign 1976. 3 vols. Compiled by the Committee On House Administration, U.S. House of Representatives. Washington: U.S. Government Printing Office, 1978, 1979.
Public Papers of the Presidents: Richard M. Nixon, 1973. Washington, DC: Government Printing Office, 1975.
Public Papers of the Presidents: Jimmy Carter, 1977–1981. 9 vols. Washington, DC: Government Printing Office, 1977–1981.

Videos

Affleck, Ben. Director. *Argo*. Warner Bro., Burbank, California, 2013.
Bosch, Adriana. Director. *Jimmy Carter*. American Experience Series. Boston: WGBH, 2002.
———. *Citizen Carter*. Discovery Education, Santa Conica, California, 1991.
———. "We the People: The President and the Constitution." Anthony Potter Productions: Commission on the Bicentennial of The Trust for the Bicentennial of the United States Constitution, Greenwich, Connecticut, 1991.
Carter, Lillian. *Press Conference with Miss Lillian Carter*. Special Collections, Mississippi State University Library, Starkville, Mississippi.
Durkin, Mary Beth. Producer. *Betty Ford: The Real Deal*. MacNeill Lehrer Productions, Arlington County, Virginia, 2008.
Goldberg, Alan. Producer. *Jimmy Carter: To the White House and Beyond*. New York: A & E Network, 1995.
Strauss, Robert. *An American Profile: Robert Strauss, Ambassador-Designate to the Soviet Union*. Washington, DC: C-Span, 1991.

Wharton, Mary. Director. *Jimmy Carter: Rock and Roll President*. New York: Trebeca Films, 2020.

Unpublished Materials

Barnes, Paula Curlee. "Educating the Conscience: Betty Bumpers and Peace Links, a Study of Feminist Peace Work." Ph.D. dissertation, University of Arkansas, 1996.

Cloonan, Kevin A. "Jimmy Carter and the MX Debate: Passions that Move American Strategy." PhD dissertation, Claremont Graduate School, 1997.

Cook, Emily Walker. "Women White House Advisers in the Carter Administration: Presidential Stalwarts or Feminist Advocates?" PhD dissertation, Vanderbilt University, 1995.

Damico, John Kelly. "From Civil Rights to Human Rights: The Career of Patricia M. Derian." PhD dissertation, Mississippi State University, 1999.

DELETEGlant, Tibor. "Contested Gesture: Jimmy Carter and the Return of the Holy Crown to Hungary, 1977–1978." Lecture based upon his 1977 book *The American Adventures of the Holy Crown, 1945–1978*, presented at the annual conference of the Society for Historians of American Foreign Relations in Princeton, NJ, June 24–26, 1999.

Kramer, Scott. "Struggles of an Outsider: The 1979 Energy Crisis and President Carter's Call for Confidence." B.A. thesis, Princeton University, 1992.

Lindley, William Giles. "Jimmy Carter's Sermon to the Heathen: A Narrative Analysis of the Playboy Interview." M.Sc. Thesis, University of Southern Mississippi, Hattieburg.1993.

Littlefield, Robert Stephen. "An Analysis of the Persuasion and Coercion Used by the Carter Administration to Promote Human Rights in Argentina, Brazil, and Chile." PhD dissertation, University of Minnesota, 1983.

Lucella, Mel. "Cyrus Vance's World View: The Relevance of the Motivated Tactician Perspective." Ph.D. dissertation, The Union Institute, New York City, 1996.

Motter, Russell D. "Jimmy Carter's Presidential Style: Energy Policy as a Case Study." M.A. thesis, University of Hawaii, 1992.

Ribuffo, Leo P. " 'I'll Whip His Ass': Jimmy Carter, Edward Kennedy, and the Latest Crisis of American Liberalism." Unpublished paper, Jimmy Carter Library, Atlanta, Georgia. N.D.

Ruechel, Frank A. "The Articulation and Synthesis of Jimmy Carter's Human Rights Policy." Ph.D. dissertation, Georgia State University, 1991.

Stansfield, Burns F. "Faith and Politics in the Presidency of Jimmy Carter." M.Div. Senior Paper, Harvard Divinity School, 1988.

Newspapers and Magazines

Atlanta Constitution
Atlanta Journal
Atlanta Journal and Constitution

Atlanta Journal and Constitution Magazine
Atlanta Magazine
Augusta Chronicle (GA)
Austin American-Statesman (TX)
The Boston Globe Magazine
Columbus Ledger-Enquirer (GA)
Executive Intelligence Review
Georgia Crop Improvement News, 1959–1966
Georgia Tech Whistle
Good Housekeeping
Georgia Life
Georgia Magazine
Gwinnett Daily News (County, GA)
Harper's Magazine
The Humanist
Hustler
Ideal Magazine
Index Journal (Greenwood, SC)
Jackson Clarion-Ledger (MS)
London Independent
McCall's Magazine
Memphis Commercial Appeal (TN)
National Inquirer
New Orleans Times-Picayune (LA)
Newsweek
New York Daily News
New Yorker
New York Magazine
New York Times
Plains Echoes
Playboy
Pleasant Daily Tribune (TX)
Redbook Magazine
Rolling Stone
Savannah Evening Press (GA)
The Scottish Rite Journal
Seattle Post-Intelligencer (WA)
Southern Voice (Atlanta)
Sumter Republican (Americus, GA)
The Daily News (Starkville, MS)
The State (SC)
Time Magazine
Valdosta Daily Times (GA)
The Wall Street Journal
The Washington Post
The Washington Star
Watson's Magazine
Weekly Sumter Republican

Books and Pamphlets

Abernethy, Glynn, Dilys M. Hill, and Phil Williams. Editors. *The Carter Years: The President and Policy Making*. New York: St. Martin's Press, 1984.

Abrahamian, Ervand. *A History of Modern Iran*. New York: Cambridge University Press, 2008.

Abram, Morris B. *The Day Is Short: An Autobiography*. New York: Harcourt, Brace, Jovanovich, 1982.

Abramson, Rudy. *The Life of W. Averell Harriman, 1891–1986*. New York: William Morrow and Co., 1992.

Adams, Bruce, and Kathryn Kavanagh-Baran. *Promise and Performance: Carter Builds a New Administration*. Lexington, MA: D. C. Heath and Co., 1979.

Adams, James Ring, and Douglas Frantz. *A Full Service Bank: How BCCI Stole Billions around the World*. New York: Pocket Books, 1992.

Adelman, Kenneth L. *The Great Universal Embrace: Arms Summitry—A Skeptic's Account*. New York: Simon & Schuster, 1989.

Adler, Bill. Editor. *The Wit and Wisdom of Jimmy Carter*. Secaucus, NJ: Citadel Press, 1977.

Adler, David Gray, and Larry N. George. Editors. *The Constitution and the Conduct of American Foreign Policy*. Lawrence: University of Kansas Press, 1996.

Alam, Asadollah. *The Shah and I: The Confidential Diary of Iran's Royal Court, 1969–77*. Edited and translated by Alinaghi Alikhani. New York: St. Martin's Press, 1991.

Albright, Madeleine. *Madam Secretary: A Memoir*. New York: Miramax Books, 2003.

———. *Memo to the President Elect*. New York: HarperCollins, 2008.

———. *The Mighty and the Almighty: Reflections on America, God, and World Affairs*. With Bill Woodward. Introduction by President Bill Clinton. New York: HarperCollins, 2006.

Alexander, Edward. Editor. *With Friends Like These. The Jewish Critics of Israel*. New York: Shapolsky Publishers, Inc., 1993.

Allen, Frederick. *Atlanta Rising: The Invention of an International City, 1946–1996*. Marietta, GA: Longstreet Press, 1996.

———. *Secret Formula*. New York: HarperCollins, 1994.

Allen, Gary. *Jimmy Carter—Jimmy Carter*. Concord, MA; Concord Press, 1976.

Alsop, Joseph W. *I've Seen the Best of It: Memoirs*. With Adam Platt. New York: Norton, 1992.

Alter, Jonathan. *His Very Best: Jimmy Carter, A Life*. New York: Simon & Schuster, 2020.

Alterman, Eric, and Kevin Mattson. *The Cause: The Fight for American Liberalism from Franklin Roosevelt to Barack Obama*. New York: Viking, 2012.

Alvandi, Roham. *Nixon, Kissinger, and the Shah*. New York: Oxford University Press, 2014.

Anderson, Jack. *Peace, War, and Politics: An Eyewitness Account*. New York: Forge, 1999.

Anderson, Patrick. *Electing Jimmy Carter: The Campaign of 1976*. Baton Rouge: Louisiana State University Press, 1994.

Anderson, William. *The Wild Man from Sugar Creek: The Political Career of Eugene Talmadge*. Baton Rouge: Louisiana State University Press, 1975.

Andrew, Christopher. *For the President's Eyes Only: Secret Intelligence and the American Presidency from Washington to Bush*. New York: HarperCollins, 1995.

Andrus, Cecil. *Cecil Andrus: Politics Western Style*. With Joel Connelly. Seattle, WA: Sasquatch Books, 1998.

Angelo, Bonnie. *First Mothers: The Women Who Shaped the Presidents*. New York: HarperCollins, 2001.

Anthony, Carl Sferrazza. *First Ladies, Vol. II: The Saga of the Presidents' Wives and Their Power, 1961–1990*. New York: William Morrow and Co., 1991.

Anziska, Seth. *Preventing Palestine: A Political History from Camp David to Oslo*. Princeton, NJ: Princeton University Press, 2018.

Arial, Dan. *The Carpenter's Apprentice: The Spiritual Biography of Jimmy Carter*. With Cheryl Heckler-Feltz. Grand Rapids, MI: Zondervan Publishing House, 1996.

Asher, Herbert B. *Presidential Elections and American Politics: Voters, Candidates, and Campaigns since 1952*. Fourth Edition. Chicago: The Dorsey Press, 1988.

Ashmore, Harry. *Civil Rights and Wrongs*. New York: Pantheon Books, 1994.

Austin, Curtis J. *Up Against the Wall: Violence in the Making and Unmaking of The Black Panther Party*. Fayetteville: University of Arkansas Press, 2006.

Auten, Brian J. *Carter's Conversion: The Hardening of American Defense Policy*. Columbia: University of Missouri Press, 2008.

Baer, Kenneth S. *Reinventing Democrats: The Politics of Liberalism from Reagan to Clinton*. Lawrence: University Press of Kansas, 2000.

Bahcheli, Tozun. *Greek-Turkish Relations since 1955*. London: Westview Press, 1990.

Baker, James A., III. *"Work Hard, Study . . . and Keep Out of Politics": Adventures and Lessons from an Unexpected Public Life*. New York: G. P. Putnam's Sons, 2006.

Baker, James Thomas. *A Southern Baptist in the White House*. Philadelphia, PA: Westminster Press, 1977.

Baker, Peter, and Susan Glasser. *The Man Who Ran Washington: The Life and Times of James A. Baker III*. New York: Doubleday, 2020.

Bakhash, Shaul. *The Reign of the Ayatollahs: Iran and the Islamic Revolution*. New York: Basic Books, Inc., 1984.

Balmer, Randall. *Redeemer: The Life of Jimmy Carter*. New York: Basic Books, 2014.

Bamford, James. *Body of Secrets: Anatomy of the Ultra-Secret National Security Agency from the Cold War through the Dawn of a New Century*. New York: Doubleday, 2001.

Bani-Sadr, Abol Hassan. *My Turn to Speak: Iran, the Revolution and Secret Deals with the U.S.* Washington: Brassey's, Inc., 1991.

Barber, James David. *The Presidential Character: Predicting Performance in the White House*. Fourth Edition. Englewood Cliffs, NJ: Prentice-Hall, 1972.

Barbier, Mary Kathryn. *Spies, Lies, and Citizenship: The Hunt for Nazi Criminals*. Potomac Books: University of Nebraska Press, 2017.

Barnes, Fred. *Rebel-in-Chief: Inside the Bold and Controversial Presidency of George W. Bush*. New York: Crown Forum, 2006.

Bar-On, Mordechai. *In Pursuit of Peace: A History of the Israeli Peace Movement*. Washington, DC: US Institute Of Peace, 1996.

Barron, John. *Operation Solo: The FBI's Man in the Kremlin*. Washington, DC: Regnery Publishing Inc., 1996.

Bartley, Numan V. *Jimmy Carter and the Politics of the South*. St. Louis, MO: Forum Press, 1979.

———. *The New South, 1945–1980*. Baton Rouge: Louisiana State University Press, 1995.

Bass, Jack. *Taming the Storm*. New York: Anchor Books, 1993.

Bass, Jack, and Walter DeVries. *The Transformation of Southern Politics: Social Change and Political Consequence since 1945*. New York: Basic Books, Inc., 1976.

Bauer, Stephen M. *At Ease in the White House: The Uninhibited Memoirs of a Presidential Social Aide*. With Frances Spatz Leighton. New York: Carol Publishing Group, 1991.

Beaty, Jonathan, and S. C. Gwynne. *The Outlaw Bank: A Wild Ride into the Secret Heart of BCCI*. New York: Random House, 1993.

Becker, Elizabeth. *When the War Was Over: Cambodia and the Khmer Rouge Revolution*. New York: Public Affairs, 1998.

Beckerman, Gal. *When They Come for Us, We'll Be Gone: The Epic Struggle to Save Soviet Jewry*. Boston: Houghton Mifflin Harcourt, 2010.

Beckwith, Charles A. *Delta Force: The Army's Elite Counterterrorist Unit*. New York: Avon Books, 1983.

Beilin, Yossi. *Israel: A Concise Political History*. New York: St. Martin's Press, 1993.

Bell, Coral. *President Carter and Foreign Policy: The Costs of Virtue?* Canberra Studies in World Affairs No. 1. Canberra: Department of International Relations, Australian National University, 1980.

Bell, Griffin. *Taking Care of the Law*. With Ronald J. Ostrow. New York: William Morrow and Co., 1982.

Ben-Menashe, Ari. *Profits of War: Inside the Secret U.S.-Israeli Arms Network*. New York: Sheridan Square Press, 1992.

Benson, Harry. *First Families: An Intimate Portrait from the Kennedys to the Clintons*. Boston: Little, Brown, and Co., 1997.

Bergen, Peter L. *The Longest War: The Enduring Conflict between America and Al-Qaeda*. New York: Free Press, 2011.

Berkowitz, Edward D. *Something Happened: A Political and Cultural Overview of the Seventies*. New York: Columbia University Press, 2006.

Bernardo, Leonard, and Jennifer Weiss. *Citizen-in-Chief: The Second Lives of the American Presidents*. New York: William Morrow, 2009.

Bernstein, Carl, and Marco Politi. *His Holiness: John Paul II and the History of Our Time*. New York: Penguin Books, 1997.

Bill, James A. *The Eagle and the Lion*. New Haven: Yale University Press, 1988.

Bird, Kai. *The Chairman: John J. McCloy and the Making of the American Establishment*. New York: Simon & Schuster, 1992.

———. *The Outlier: The Unfinished Presidency of Jimmy Carter*. New York: Crown, 2021.

Bissell, Richard M., Jr. *Reflections of a Cold Warrior*. With Jonathan E. Lewis and Frances T. Pudlo. New Haven: Yale University Press, 1996.

Bisnow, Mark. *Diary of a Dark Horse: The 1980 Anderson Presidential Campaign*. Carbondale: Southern Illinois Press, 1983.

Biven, W. Carl. *Jimmy Carter's Economy: Policy in an Age of Limits*. Chapel Hill: University; of North Carolina Press, 2002.

Black, Earl. *Southern Governors and Civil Rights*. Cambridge, MA: Harvard University Press, 1976.

Black, Earl, and Merle Black. *Politics and Society in the South*. Cambridge, MA: Harvard University Press, 1987.

———. *The Rise of Southern Republicans*. Cambridge, MA: The Belknap Press of Harvard University, 2002.

———. *The Vital South: How Presidents are Elected*. Cambridge, MA: Harvard University Press, 1992.

Black, Ian, and Benny Morris. *Israel's Secret Wars: A History of Israel's Intelligence Services*. New York: Grove/Atlantic, Inc., 1992.

Blackman, Ann. *Seasons of Her Life: A Biography of Madeleine Korbel Albright*. New York: Scribner, 1998.

Blount, Roy. *Crackers: This Whole Many-Angled Thing of Jimmy, More Carters, Ominous Little Animals, Sad Singing Women, My Daddy, and Me*. New York: Ballantine Books, 1982.

Blumenthal, David, and James A. Morone. *The Heart of Power: Health and Politics in the Oval Office*. Berkeley: University of California Press, 2009.

Boller, Paul F., Jr. *Presidential Anecdotes*. New York: Oxford University Press, 1981.

———. *Presidential Wives: An Anecdotal History*. New York: Oxford University Press, 1988.

Borns, Steven. Photographer and Editor. *People of Plains, Georgia*. New York: McGraw-Hill Book Co., 1978.

Borstelmann, Thomas. *The 1970s: A New Global History from Civil Rights to Economic Inequality*. Princeton, NJ: Princeton University Press, 2012.

Borowiec, Andrew. *Cyprus: A Troubled Island*. Westport, CT: Greenwood Press, 2000.

Borrelli, Mary Anne. *The Politics of the President's Wife*. College Station: Texas A&M Press, 2011.

Bourne, Peter G. *Jimmy Carter: A Comprehensive Biography from Plains to the Post-Presidency*. New York: Simon & Schuster, Inc. 1997.

Bowden, Mark. *Guests of the Ayatollah: The First Battle in America's War with Militant Islam*. New York: Grove Press, 2006.

Boyle, Peter G. *American-Soviet Relations from the Russian Revolution to the Fall of Communism*. New York: Routledge, 1993.

Bradbury, M. L., and James B. Gilbert. Editors. *Transforming Faith: The Sacred and Secular in Modern American History*. Westport, CT: Greenwood Press, 1989.

Braithwaite, Rodric. *Afgantsy: The Russians in Afghanistan 1979–89*. New York: Oxford University Press, 2011.

Brands, H. W. *American Dreams: The United States since 1945*. New York: The Penguin Press, 2010.

———. *The Devil We Knew: Americans and the Cold War*. New York: Oxford University Press, 1994.

———. *Reagan: The Life*. New York: Doubleday, 2015.

Branch, Taylor B. *At Canaan's Edge: America in the King Years, 1965–1968*. New York: Simon & Schuster, 2006.

———. *Parting the Waters: America in the King Years, 1954–1963*. New York: Simon & Schuster, 1988. 19

———. *Pillar of Fire: America in the King Years, 1963–1965*. New York: Simon & Schuster, 1998.

Brauer, Carl M. *Presidential Transitions: Eisenhower through Reagan*. New York: Oxford University Press, 1986.

Brinkley, Douglas. *The Unfinished Presidency: Jimmy Carter's Journey beyond the White House*. New York: Viking, 1998.

Broussard, James H. *Ronald Reagan: Champion of Conservative America*. New York: Routledge, 2015.

Brower, Kate Anderson. *The Residence: Inside the Private World of the White House*. New York: HarperCollins, 2015.

Brown, Charles C. *Niebuhr and His Age: Reinhold Niebuhr's Prophetic Role in the Twentieth Century*. Philadelphia, PA: Trinity, 1992.

Brown, Harold. *Thinking about National Security: Defense and Foreign Policy in a Dangerous World*. Boulder, CO: Westview Press, 1983.

Bryant, James C. *A Gift for Giving: The Story of Lamar Rich Plunkett.* Macon, GA: Mercer University Press, 1993.

Brzezinski, Zbigniew. *Power and Principle: Memoirs of the National Security Advisor.* New York: Farrar, Strauss, Giroux, 1983.

Buckaloo, Derek N. "Carter's Nicaragua and Other Democratic Quagmires." In Schulman and Zelizer. Editors. *Rightward Bound: Making America Conservative in the 1970s.* Cambridge, MA: Harvard University Press, 2008, 246–264.

Busch, Andrew E. "The Election of 1980." In Scott Kaufman. Editor. *A Companion to Gerald R. Ford and Jimmy Carter.* Chichester, UK: John Wiley & Sons, Inc., 2016, 470–490.

Bumpers, Dale. *The Best Lawyer in a One-Lawyer Town: A Memoir.* New York: Random House, 2003.

Bunch, Will. *Tear Down this Myth: How the Reagan Legacy Has Distorted Our Politics and Haunts Our Future.* New York: Free Press, 2009.

Burke, John P. *Honest Broker?: The National Security Advisor and Presidential Decision Making.* College Station: Texas A&M University Press, 2009.

Burns, Michael. Editor. *Miller Williams and the Poetry of the Particular.* Columbia: University of Missouri Press, 1991.

Bush, George, and Brent Scowcroft. *A World Transformed.* New York: Alfred A. Knopf, 1998.

Byrne, Malcolm. *Iran-Contra: Reagan's Scandal and the Unchecked Abuse of Presidential Power.* Lawrence: University Press of Kansas, 2014.

Califano, Joseph A., Jr. *Governing America: An Insider's Report from the White House and the Cabinet.* New York: Simon & Schuster, 1981.

———. *Inside a Public and Private Life.* New York: Public Affairs, 2004.

Cannon, Carl N. *The Pursuit of Happiness in Times of War.* New York: Roman & Littlefield, 2004.

Carlson, Jody. *George C. Wallace and the Politics of Powerlessness: The Wallace Campaigns for the Presidency, 1964–1976.* New Brunswick, NJ: Rutgers University Press, 1996.

Carney, Col. John T., Jr., and Benjamin F. Schemmer. *No Room for Error: The Covert Operations of America's Special Tactics from Iran to Afghanistan.* New York: Ballentine Books, 2003.

Caroli, Betty Boyd. *First Ladies.* New York: Oxford University Press, 1995.

Carroll, Peter N. *It Seemed Like Nothing Happened: America in the 1970s.* New Brunswick, NJ: Rutgers University Press, 1982.

Carter, Billy, and Sybil Carter. *Billy: Billy Carter's Reflections on His Struggle with Fame, Alcoholism and Cancer.* With Ken Estes. Newport, RI: Edgehill Publications, 1989.

Carter, Dan T. *The Politics of Rage: George Wallace, The Origins of the New Conservatism, and the Transformation of American Politics.* New York: Simon & Schuster, 1995.

Carter, Hugh Alton. *Cousin Beedie and Cousin Hot: My Life with the Carter Family of Plains, Georgia.* As Told to Frances Spatz Leighton. Englewood Cliffs, NJ: Prentice-Hall, 1978.

Carter, Jason. *Power Lines: Two Years on South Africa's Borders.* Introduction by Jimmy Carter. Washington, DC: National Geographic, 2002.

Carter, Jeff. *Ancestors of Jimmy and Rosalynn Carter.* Foreword by President Jimmy Carter. Jefferson, NC: McFarland & Company, 2012.

Carter, Jimmy. *Christmas in Plains: Memories.* Boston: Houghton Mifflin, 1985.

———. *Addresses of James Earl Carter, Governor of Georgia, 1971–1975*. Compiled by Frank Daniel. Atlanta: Georgia Department of Archives and History, 1975.

———. *Always a Reckoning and Other Poems*. New York: Times Books, 1995.

———. *Beyond the White House: Waging Peace, Fighting Disease, Building Hope*. New York: Simon & Schuster, 2007.

———. *The Blood of Abraham: Insights Into the Middle East*. Boston: Houghton Mifflin, 1985.

———. *A Call to Action: Women, Religion, Violence, and Power*. New York: Simon & Schuster, 2014.

———. *The Craftsmanship of Jimmy Carter*. Macon, GA: Mercer University Press, 2018.

———. *Faith: A Journey for All*. New York: Simon & Schuster, 2018.

———. *A Full Life: Reflections at Ninety*. New York: Simon & Schuster, 2015.

———. *A Government as Good as Its People*. New York: Simon & Schuster, 1977.

———. *The Hornet's Nest: A Novel of the Revolutionary War*. New York: Simon & Schuster, 2003.

———. *An Hour Before Daylight: Memories of a Rural Boyhood*. New York: Simon & Schuster, 2001.

———. *Keeping Faith: Memoirs of a President*. New York: Bantam Books, 1982.

———. *The Little Baby Snoogle-Fleejer*. Illustrated by Amy Carter. New York: Times Books, 1995.

———. *Living Faith*. New York: Times Books, 1996.

———. *Negotiation: The Alternative to Hostility*. Macon, GA: Mercer University Press, 1984.

———. *The Nobel Peace Prize Lecture* New York: Simon & Schuster, 2002.

———. *Our Endangered Values: America's Moral Crisis*. New York: Simon & Schuster, 2005.

———. *An Outdoor Journal: Adventures and Reflections*. New York: Bantam Books, 1988.

———. *Palestine Peace Not Apartheid*. New York: Simon & Schuster, 2006.

———. *The Personal Beliefs of Jimmy Carter*. New York: Three Rivers Press, 2002.

———. *Public Papers of the Presidents of the United States*. 9 vols. Washington, DC: United States Government Printing Office, 1977–1982.

———. "Reflections." In *Simple Faith Bible: Following Jesus Into a Life of Peace, Compassion & Wholeness*. New Revised Standard Version. Grand Rapids, MI: Zondervan, 2020.

———. *A Remarkable Mother*. New York: Simon & Schuster, 2008.

———. *Sharing Good Times*. New York: Simon & Schuster, 2004.

———. *Simple Faith Bible: Reflections from Jimmy Carter*. Grand Rapids, MI: Zondervan, 2020.

———. *Sources of Strength: Meditations on Scripture For a Living Faith*. New York: Times Books, 1997.

———. *The Spiritual Journey of Jimmy Carter*. New York: Macmillan, 1978.

———. *Talking Peace: A Vision for the Next Generation*. New York: Dutton Children's Books, 1993.

———. *Through the Year with Jimmy Carter: 366 Daily Meditations from the 39th President*. Grand Rapids, MI: Zondervan, 2011.

———. *Turning Point: A Candidate, A State, and a Nation Come of Age*. New York: Times Books, 1992.

———. *The Virtues of Aging*. New York: The Ballantine Publishing Co., 1998.

———. *We Can Have Peace in the Holy Land: : A Plan That Will Work*. New York: Simon & Schuster, 2009.

———. *White House Diary*. New York: Farrar, Straus and Giroux, 2010.

———. *Why Not the Best?* Nashville, TN: Broadman Press, 1975.

Carter, Jimmy, and Rosalynn Carter. *Everything to Gain: How To Make the Most of the Rest of Your Life*. New York: Random House, 1987.

Carter, Lillian. *Miss Lillian and Friends: The Plains, Georgia, Family Philosophy and Recipe Book*. As Told to Beth Tartan and Rudy Hayes. New York: A and W Publishers, Inc., 1977.

Carter, Lillian, and Gloria Carter Spann. *Away from Home: Letters to My Family*. New York: Warner Books, 1977.

Carter, Rosalynn. *First Lady from Plains*. Boston: Houghton Mifflin, 1984.

———. *Helping Yourself Help Others: A Book for Caregivers*. With Susan K. Golant. New York: Times Books, 1994.

———. *Helping Someone with Mental Illness*. With Susan K. Golant. New York: Times Books, 1998.

Carter, Rosalynn, Kathryn E. Cade, and Susan K. Golant. *Within Our Reach: Ending the Mental Health Crisis*. New York: Rodale Press, 2010.

Chace, James. *Acheson: The Secretary of State Who Created the American World*. New York: Simon & Schuster, 1998.

Chafe, William H., Raymond Gavins, and Robert Korstad. *Remembering Jim Crow: African Americans Tell about Life in the Segregated South*. New York: The New Press, 2001.

Christopher, Warren. *Chances of a Lifetime: A Memoir*. New York: Scribners, 2001.

Christopher, Warren, et al. Editors. *American Hostages in Iran: The Conduct of a Crisis*. New Haven, CT: Yale University Press, 1985.

Clancy, Paul, and Shirley Elder. *Tip: A Biography of Thomas P. O'Neill, Speaker of the House*. New York: Macmillan, 1980.

Clarfield, Gerard H., and William M. Wiecek. *Nuclear America: Military and Civilian Nuclear Power in the United States, 1940–1980*. New York: Harper and Row, 1984.

Clark, Henry B. *Serenity, Courage, and Wisdom: The Enduring Legacy of Reinhold Niebuhr*. Cleveland, OH: The Pilgrim Press, 1994.

Clarridge, Duane R. *A Spy for All Seasons: My Life in the CIA*. With Digby Diehl. New York: Scribner, 1997.

Cleland, Max. *Strong in the Broken Places*. Marietta, GA: Longstreet, 2001.

Clifford, Clark. *Counsel to the President: A Memoir*. With Richard Holbrooke. New York: Random House, 1991.

Clift, A. Denis. *With Presidents to the Summit*. Fairfax, VA: George Mason University Press, 1993.

Clymer, Adam. *Drawing the Line at the Big Ditch: The Panama Canal Treaties and the Rise of the Right*. Lawrence: University Press of Kansas, 2008.

———. *Edward M. Kennedy: A Biography*. New York: HarperCollins, 1999.

Cobb, James C. *The South and America since World War II*. New York: Oxford University Press, 2011.

Cockburn, Andrew, and Leslie Cockburn. *Dangerous Liaison: The Inside Story of the U.S.-Israeli Covert Relationship*. New York: HarperCollins, 1991.

Cohen, Dan. *Undefeated: The Life of Hubert H. Humphrey*. Minneapolis, MN: Learner Publications Company, 1978.

Cohen, Michael J. *Truman and Israel*. Berkeley: University of California Press, 1990.

Cohen, Naomi. *Jews in Christian America: The Pursuit of Religious Equality*. New York: Oxford University Press, 1992.

Cohen, Warren I. *America in the Age of Soviet Power, 1945–1991*. New York: Cambridge University Press, 1993.

Collins, Tom. *The Search for Jimmy Carter*. Waco, TX: Word Books, 1976.

Columbus, Theodore A. *The United States, Greece, and Turkey: The Troubled Triangle*. New York: Praeger Publishers, 1983.

Cooper, Andrew Scott. *The Fall of Heaven: The Pahlavis and the Final Days of Imperial Iran*. New York: Henry Hold and Company, 2016.

Cowie, Jefferson. *Stayin' Alive: The 1970s and the Last Days of the Working Class*. New York: The New Press, 2010.

Cox, Jack F. *History of Sumter County, Georgia*. Roswell, GA: W. H. Wolfe Associates for the Sumter County Historic Preservation Society, 1983.

Craig, Gordon A., and Francis L. Loewenheim. *The Diplomats, 1939–1979*. Princeton, NJ: Princeton University Press, 1994.

Creekmore, Marion, Jr. *A Moment of Crisis: Jimmy Carter, The Power of a Peacemaker, and North Korea's Nuclear Ambitions*. New York: Public Affairs, 2006.

———. Compiler. *The Carter Presidency under Pressure: Articles by Dom Bonafede, Richard E. Cohen and William J. Lanouette*. Washington, DC: Government Research Corp., 1979.

Crist, David. *The Twilight War: The Secret History of America's Thirty-Year Conflict with Iran*. New York: Penguin, 2012.

Cuddihy, John Murray. *No Offense: Civil Religion and Protestant Taste*. New York: Seabury Press, 1978.

Currie, Ruth Douglas. *Kwajalein Atoll, the Marshall Islands and American Policy in the Pacific*. Jefferson, NC: McFarland & Company, Inc., 2016.

Curtiss, Richard H. *Stealth PACs: How Israel's American Lobby Took Control of U.S. Middle East Policy*. Washington, DC: American Educational Trust, 1990.

Dallek, Robert. *Flawed Giant: Lyndon Johnson and His Times, 1961–1973*. New York: Oxford University Press, 1998.

———. *Hail to the Chief: The Making and Unmaking of American Presidents*. New York: Hyperion, 1996.

———. *Lone Star Rising: Lyndon Johnson and His Times, 1908–1960*. New York: Oxford University Press, 1991.

Daugherty, William J. *Executive Secrets: Covert Action & the Presidency*. Lexington: The University Press of Kentucky, 2004.

———. *In the Shadow of the Ayatollah: A CIA Hostage in Iran*. Annapolis, MD: Naval Institute Press, 2001.

Davis, Harold E. *Henry Grady's New South: Atlanta, A Brave and Beautiful City*. Tuscaloosa: University of Alabama Press, 1990.

Dawsey, Cyrus B., and James M. Dawsey. Editors. *The Confederados: Old South Immigrants in Brazil*. Tuscaloosa: The University of Alabama Press, 1995.

Dayan, Moshe. *Breakthrough: A Personal Account of the Egypt-Israel Peace Negotiations*. New York: Alfred A. Knopf, 1981.

Dees, Morris. *A Season for Justice: The Life and Times of Civil Rights Lawyer Morris Dees*. With Steve Fiffer. New York: Charles Scribner's Sons, 1991.

DeFrank, Thomas W. *Write It When I'm Gone: Remarkable Off-the-Record Conversations with Gerald R. Ford*. New York: G. P. Putnam's Sons, 2007.

DeRoche, Andrew J. *Andrew Young: Civil Rights Ambassador*. Washington, DC: Scholarly Resources Books, 2003.

Diggins, John Patrick. *The Liberal Persuasion: Arthur Schlesinger, Jr., and the Challenge of the American Past*. Princeton, NJ: Princeton University Press, 1997.

Dobrynin, Anatoly. *In Confidence: Moscow's Ambassador to America's Six Cold War Presidents*. New York: Random House, 1995.

Domin, Gregory Paul. *Jimmy Carter, Public Opinion, and the Search for Values, 1977–1981*. Macon, GA: Mercer University Press, 2003.

Drew, Elizabeth. *American Journal: The Events of 1976*. New York: Random House, 1977.

———. *Portrait of an Election: The 1980 Presidential Campaign*. New York: Simon & Schuster, 1981.

Dumbrell, John. *American Foreign Policy: Carter to Clinton*. London: MacMillan Press, 1997.

———. *The Carter Presidency: A Re-evaluation*. Manchester and New York: Manchester University Press, 1993.

Dunbar, Anthony. Editor. *Here We Stand: Voices of Southern Dissent*. Foreword by Jimmy Carter. Montgomery, AL: New South Books, 2004.

Edwards, George C. III. *Presidential Influence in Congress*. San Francisco: W. H. Freeman Co., 1980.

Eizenstat, Stuart E. *Imperfect Justice: Looted Assets, Slave Labor, and the Unfinished Business of World War II*. Foreword by Elie Wiesel. New York: Public Affairs, 2003.

———. *President Carter: The White House Years*. Foreword By Madeleine Albright. New York: Thomas Dunne Books, 2018.

Engel, Jeffrey A. *When the World Seemed New: George H. W. Bush and the End of the Cold War*. Boston: Houghton Mifflin Harcourt, 2017.

Engstrom, David W. *The Carter Administration and the Mariel Boatlift*. New York: Rowman & Littlefield Publishers, Inc., 1997.

Escott, Paul D., and David R. Goldfield. Editors. *Major Problems in the American South, Vol. II: The New South*. Lexington, MA: D. C. Heath and Co, 1990.

Evans, Eli N. *The Lonely Days Were Sundays: Reflections of a Jewish Southerner*. Jackson, MS: University Press of Mississippi, 1993.

———. *The Provincials: A Personal History of Jews in the South*. New York: Atheneum, 1973.

Farber, David. *Taken Hostage: The Iran Hostage Crisis and America's First Encounter with Radical Islam*. Princeton, NJ: Princeton University Press, 2005.

Farrell, John A. *Tip O'Neill and the Democratic Century*. Boston: Little, Brown and Company, 2001.

Felsenthal, Carol. *Clinton in Exile: A President Out of the White House*. New York: William Morrow, 2008.

Fink, Gary M. *Prelude to the Presidency: The Political Character and Legislative Leadership Style of Governor Jimmy Carter*. Westport, CT: Greenwood Press, 1980.

Fink, Gary M., and Hugh Davis Graham. Editors. *The Carter Presidency: Policy Choices in the Post-New Deal Era*. Lawrence: University of Kansas Press, 1998.

Fleshler, Dan. *Transforming America's Israel Lobby*. Washington, DC: Potomac Books, 2009.

Flippen, J. Brooks. *Jimmy Carter, the Politics of Family, and the Rise of the Religious Right*. Athens: University of Georgia Press, 2011.

Ford, Betty. *The Times of My Life*. New York: Harper and Row, 1978.

Foster, K. Neill. *Dam Break in Georgia: Sadness and Joy at Toccoa Falls*. With Eric Mills. Introduction by Rosalynn Carter. Camp Hill, PA: Horizon House Publishers, 1978.

Forsythe, David P. *Human Rights and World Politics*. Lincoln: University of Nebraska Press, 1983.

Fowler, James W. *Stages of Faith: The Psychology of Human Development and the Quest for Meaning*. New York: HarperCollins, 1995.

Fox, Richard W. *Reinhold Niebuhr: A Biography*. New York: Harper and Row, 1985.

Frady, Marshall. *Southerners: A Journalist's Odyssey*. New York: New American Library, 1980.

Fuller, Millard, and Linda Fuller. *The Excitement Is Building*. Dallas: Word Publishing, 1990.

Gaillard, Frye. *Prophet from Plains: Jimmy Carter and His Legacy*. Foreword by David C. Carter. Athens, GA: University of Georgia Press, 2007.

Garrow, David J. *The FBI and Martin Luther King, Jr.: From "Solo" to Memphis*. New York: W. W. Norton and Company, 1981.

Garthoff, Raymond L. *Détente and Confrontation: American-Soviet Relations from Nixon to Reagan*. Washington, DC: The Brookings Institution, 1985.

Gates, Robert M. *From the Shadows: The Ultimate Insider's Story of Five Presidents and How They Won the Cold War*. New York: Simon & Schuster, 1996.

———. *Duty: Memoirs of a Secretary at War*. New York: Alfred A. Knopf, 2014.

Gati, Charles. Editor. *Zbig: The Strategy and Statecraft of Zbigniew Brzezinski*. Foreword by President Jimmy Carter. Baltimore, MD: The Johns Hopkins University Press, 2013.

Gelfand, H. Michael. *Sea Change at Annapolis: The United States Naval Academy, 1949–2000*. Chapel Hill: University of North Carolina Press, 2006.

Gervasi, Frank. *The Life and Times of Menachem Begin: Rebel to Statesman*. New York: G. P. Putnam's Sons, 1979.

Gewen, Barry. *The Inevitability of Tragedy: Henry Kissinger and His World*. New York: W. W. Norton and Company, 2020.

Gibbons, Tony. *The Complete Encyclopedia of Battleships*. London, UK: Salamander Books, Ltd., 1983.

———. *Battlecruisers: A Technical Directory of all the World's Capital Ships from 1860 to the Present Day*. London, UK: Salamander Books, Ltd., 1983.

Gibbs, Nancy, and Michael Duffy. *The Presidents Club: Inside the World's Most Exclusive Fraternity*. New York: Simon & Schuster, 2012.

Gibson, Dot Rees, and Dianne Chavers Barfield. *Plains, Ga.—Carter Country, U.S.A.* Waycross, GA: Dot Gibson Publications, 1977.

Gilbert, Martin. *Shcharansky: Hero of Our Time*. New York: Viking, 1986.

Gilkey, Langdon. *On Niebuhr: A Theological Study*. Chicago, IL: University of Chicago Press, 2001.

Gillon, Steven M. *The Democrats' Dilemma: Walter F. Mondale and the Liberal Legacy*. New York: Columbia University Press, 1992.

Giorgione, Michael. *Inside Camp David: The Private World of the Presidential Retreat*. Boston; Little, Brown and Company, 2017.

DELETE_Glad, Betty. *Jimmy Carter in Search of the Great White House*. New York: W. W. Norton and Co., 1980.

———. *An Outsider in the White House: Jimmy Carter, His Advisors, and the Making of American Foreign Policy*. Ithaca, NY: Cornell University Press, 2009.

Gleijeses, Piero. *Visions of Freedom: Havana, Washington, Pretoria, and the Struggle for Southern Africa, 1976–1991*. Chapel Hill: University of North Carolina Press, 2013.

Godbold, E. Stanly, Jr. *Jimmy and Rosalynn Carter: The Georgia Years, 1924–1974*. New York: Oxford University Press, 2010.

Goldman, Sheldon. *Picking Federal Judges: Lower Court Selection from Roosevelt through Reagan*. New Haven, CT: Yale University Press, 1997.

Goodwin, Doris Kearns. *Leadership in Turbulent Times*. New York: Simon & Schuster, 2018.

Goolsby, Iva P., et al. Compilers. *Randolph County, Georgia: A Compilation of Facts, Recollections, and Family Histories*. N. P., 1977.

Gordis, Daniel. *Menachem Begin: The Battle for Israel's Soul*. New York: Schocken Books, 2014.

Gould, Lewis L. Editor. *American First Ladies: Their Lives and Their Legacy*. Hamden, CT: Garland Publishing Co., 1996.

Grant, Donald L. *The Way It Was in the South: The Black Experience in Georgia*. Edited with an Introduction by Jonathan Grant. New York: Carol Publishing Group, 1993.

Grant, Stan. *Jimmy Carter's Odyssey to Black Africa*—Part One. Miami, FL: Courier Press, 1980.

Grantham, Dewey W. *The Regional Imagination: The South and Recent American History*. Nashville, TN: Vanderbilt University Press, 1979.

Graubard, Stephen. *Command of Office: How War, Secrecy and Deception Transformed the Presidency, from Theodore Roosevelt to George W. Bush*. New York: Basic Books, 2004.

Gray, Macy Bishop. *Through the Years, A Brief Informal Record of Georgia Southwestern College*. Americus, GA: Americus Printing Co., 1957.

Greene, John Robert. *Betty Ford: Candor and Courage in the White House*. Lawrence: University Press of Kansas, 2004.

———. *The Presidency of George H. W. Bush*. Revised and Expanded Edition. Lawrence: University Press of Kansas, 2015.

———. *The Presidency of Gerald R. Ford*. Lawrence: University of Kansas Press, 1995.

Gromyko, Andrei. *Memoirs*. New York: Doubleday, 1989.

A Guide to the United States Naval Academy. Works Projects Administration in Maryland. New York, 1941.

Gulliver, Hal. *A Friendly Tongue*. Macon, GA: Mercer University Press, 1984.

Halberstam, David. *War in a Time of Peace: Bush, Clinton, and the Generals*. New York: Scribner, 2001.

Hamilton, Lee H. *Congress, Presidents, and American Politics*. Bloomington: Indiana University Press, 2016.

Haney, Eric L. *Inside Delta Force*. New York: Bantam Dell, 2002.

Hakes, Jay. "Conflict or Consensus? The Roots of Jimmy Carter's Energy Policies." In Robert F. Lifset. Editor. *American Energy Policy in the 1970s*. Norman: University of Oklahoma Press, 2014, 47–57.

———. *Energy Crises: Nixon, Ford, Carter and Hard Choices in the 1970s*. Norman: University of Oklahoma Press, 2021.

Haqqani, Husain. *Magnificent Delusions: Pakistan, the United States, and an Epic History of Misunderstanding*. New York: Public Affairs, 2013.

Hargrove, Erwin C. *Jimmy Carter as President: Leadership and the Politics of the Public Good*. Baton Rouge, LA: Louisiana State University Press, 1988.

Harris, David. *The Crisis: The President, the Prophet, and the Shah—1979 and the Coming of Militant Islam*. New York: Little Brown and Co., 2004.

Hart, Gary Warren. *Right from the Start: A Chronicle of the McGovern Campaign.* New York: Quadrangle Books, 1973.

Hatfield, Edward A., et al., "Hamilton Jordan (1944–2008). In *New Georgia Encyclopedia.* The University System of Georgia/Georgia Library Learning Online, 2004.

Haugabook, Allene T. *Remembering Plains.* N. P., 1996.

Hayter-Menzies, Grant. *Lillian Carter: A Compassionate Life.* Jefferson, NC: MacFarland and Co., Inc., 2015.

Hefley, James, and Marti Hefley. *The Church That Produced a President: The Remarkable Spiritual Roots of Jimmy Carter.* New York: Wyden Books, 1977.

Helgerson, John L. *Getting to Know the President: Intelligence Briefings of Presidential Candidates, 1952–2004.* Second Edition. Washington, DC: Center for the Study of Intelligence, 2012.

Henderson, Harold P., and Gary L. Roberts. Editors. *Georgia Governors in an Age of Change: From Ellis Arnall to George Busbee.* Athens: University of Georgia Press, 1988.

Hersh, Seymour M. *The Sampson Option: Israel's Nuclear Arsenal and American Foreign Policy.* New York: Vintage Books, 1993.

Herspring, Dale R. *The Pentagon and the Presidency: Civil-Military Relations from FDR to George W. Bush.* Lawrence: University Press of Kansas, 2005.

Hertzberg, Hendrik. "Jimmy Carter, 1977–1981." In Robert A. Wilson. Editor. *Character above All.* New York: Simon & Schuster, 1995, 172–201.

———. *Politics: Observations & Arguments, 1966–2004.* New York: Penguin Press, 2004.

Hesburgh, Theodore M. *God, Country, Notre Dame.* New York: Fawcett Columbine, 1990.

History of Plains, Georgia. Compiled by Plains Historical Preservation Trust, Inc. Fernandina Beach, FL: Wolfe Publishing, 2003.

Hitchens, Christopher. *Hostage to History: Cyprus, from the Ottomans to Kissinger.* New York: Noonday Press of Farrar, Straus and Giroux, 1984.

Hochman, Steven H. "With Jimmy Carter in Georgia: A Memoir of His Post-Presidential Years." In Richard Norton Smith and Timothy Walch. Editors. *Farewell to the Chief: Former Presidents in American Public Life.* Worland, WY: High Plains Publishing Co., Inc., 1990, 123–134.

Hollings, Ernest F. *Making Government Work.* With Kirk Victor. Columbia: University of South Carolina Press, 2008.

Honegger, Barbara. *October Surprise.* New York: Tudor Publishing Co., 1989.

Horowitz, Daniel. *The Anxieties of Affluence: Critiques of American Consumer Culture, 1939–1979.* Amherst: University of Massachusetts Press, 2004.

———. *Jimmy Carter and the Energy Crisis of the 1970s: The "Crisis of Confidence" Speech of July 15, 1979.* Boston: Bedford/St. Martin's, 2005.

Hoyt, Mary Finch. *East Wing: A Memoir.* Bloomington, Ind.:Xlibris Corp., 2001.

Hurst, Steven. *The Carter Administration and Vietnam.* London: Macmillan Press Ltd., 1996.

Hurwitz, Harry, and Yisrael Medad. Editors. *Peace in the Making: The Menachem Begin-Anwar El-Sadat Personal Correspondence.* New York and Jerusalem: Gefen Publishing House, 2011.

Hutchinson, Duane. *Jimmy Carter's Hometown: People of Plains.* Lincoln, NE: Foundation Books, 2003.

Hyatt, Richard. *The Carters of Plains.* Huntsville, AL: Strode Publishers, 1977.

Immerman, Richard H. *The Hidden Hand: A Brief History of the CIA.* Malden, MA: Wiley Blackwell, 2014.

Irwin, Wallace, Jr. Editor. *Panama: A Great Decision Approaches*. New York: Foreign Policy Association, 1977.

Israeli, Raphael. *Man of Defiance: A Political Biography of Anwar Sadat*. Totowa, NJ: Barnes and Noble, 1985.

Jacobs, Meg. *Panic at the Pump: The Energy Crisis and the Transformation of American Politics in the 1970s*. New York: Hill & Wang, 2016.

Jacoway, Elizabeth, et al. Editors. *The Adaptable South: Essays in Honor of George Brown Tindall*. Baton Rouge: Louisiana State University Press, 1991.

Jeffreys-Jones, Rhodri. *The CIA and American Democracy*. New Haven, CT: Yale University Press, 1989.

———. *Cloak and Dagger: A History of American Secret Intelligence*. New Haven, CT: Yale University Press, 2002.

Jenkins, Philip. *Decade of Nightmares: The End of the Sixties and the Making of Eighties America*. New York: Oxford University Press, 2006.

Jennings, Genelle. *Into the Jaws of Politics: The Charge of The Peanut Brigade*. Huntsville, AL: Strode Publishers, 1979.

Jones, Bartlett C. *Flawed Triumphs: Andy Young at the United Nations*. Lanham, MD: University Press of America, Inc., 1996.

Jones, Charles O. *The Trusteeship Presidency: Jimmy Carter and the United States Congress*. Baton Rouge, LA: Louisiana State University Press, 1988.

Johnston, Douglas, and Cynthia Sampson. Editors. *Religion, the Missing Dimension of Statecraft*. Foreword by Jimmy Carter. New York: Oxford University Press, 1994.

Jordan, Hamilton. *A Boy from Georgia: Coming of Age in the Segregated South*. Edited by Kathleen Jordan. Foreword by President Jimmy Carter. Athens: University of Georgia Press, 2015.

———. *Crisis: The Last Year of the Carter Presidency*. New York: Putnam, 1982.

———. *No Such Thing as a Bad Day: A Memoir*. Foreword by Jimmy Carter. Marietta, GA: Longstreet Press, 2000.

Jordan, Vernon, Jr. *Vernon Can Read: A Memoir*. New York: Public Affairs, 2001.

Jurey, Philomena. *A Basement Seat to History: Tales of Covering Presidents Nixon, Ford, Carter, and Reagan for the Voice of America*. Washington, DC: Linus Press, 1995.

Kagan, Robert. *A Twilight Struggle: American Power and Nicaragua, 1977–1990*. New York: The Free Press, 1996.

Kalman, Laura. *Right Star Rising: A New Politics, 1974–1980*. New York: W. W. Norton & Co., 2010.

Kaufman, Burton I. *The Presidency of James Earl Carter*. Lawrence: University Press of Kansas, 1993.

———. *The Arab Middle East and the United States*. New York: Twayne Publishers, 1996.

———. *The Post-Presidency from Washington to Clinton*. Lawrence: University Press of Kansas, 2012.

Kaufman, Burton I., and Scott Kaufman. *The Presidency of James Earl Carter, Jr.* Second Edition, Revised. Lawrence: University Press of Kansas, 2006.

Kaufman, Jonathan. *Broken Alliance: The Turbulent Times between Blacks and Jews in America*. New York: Charles Scribner's Sons, 1988.

Kaufman, Robert G. *Henry M. Jackson: A Life in Politics*. Seattle: University of Washington Press, 2000.

Kaufman, Scott. *Ambition, Pragmatism, and Party: A Political Biography of Gerald R. Ford*. Lawrence: University Press of Kansas, 2017.

————. Editor. *A Companion to Gerald R. Ford and Jimmy Carter*. Chichester, UK: John Wiley & Sons, Inc., 2016.

————. *Plans Unraveled: The Foreign Policy of the Carter Administration*. DeKalb: Northern Illinois University Press, 2008.

————. *Rosalynn Carter: Equal Partner in the White House*. Lawrence: University Press of Kansas, 2007.

Kelleher, Patrick K. *The Holy Crown of Hungary*. Rome: American Academy in Rome, 1951.

Kelly, Michael. *Things Worth Fighting For: Collected Writings*. New York: Penguin Press, 2004.

Kennedy, Edward M. *True Compass: A Memoir*. New York: Twelve, 2009.

Keys, Barbara J. *Reclaiming American Virtue: The Human Rights Revolution of the 1970s*. Cambridge, MA: Harvard University Press, 2014.

King, Martin Luther, Sr. *Daddy King: An Autobiography*. With Clayton Riley. Foreword by Benjamin E. Mays. Introduction by Andrew J. Young. New York: William Morrow and Company, Inc. 1980.

Klein, Joe. *Politics Lost: How American Democracy Was Trivialized by People Who Think You're Stupid*. New York; Doubleday, 2006.

K'Meyer, Tracy Elaine. *Interracialism and Christian Community in the Postwar South: The Study of Koinonia Farm*. Charlottesville: University Press of Virginia, 1997.

Koob, Kathryn. *Guest of the Revolution*. Nashville, TN: Thomas Nelson, Inc., 1982.

Kornbluh, Peter, and Malcolm Byrne. Editors. *The Iran-Contra Scandal: The Declassified History*. A National Security Archive Documents Reader. New York: The New Press, 1993.

Kotkin, Stephen. *Armageddon Averted: The Soviet Collapse, 1970–2000*. New York: Oxford University Press, 2002.

Krepinevich, Andrew, and Barry Watts. *The Last Warrior: Andrew Marshall and the Shaping of Modern American Defense Strategy*. New York: Basic Books, 2015.

Kucharsky, David. *The Man From Plains: The Mind and Spirit of Jimmy Carter*. New York: Harper & Row, 1976.

Kuhn, David Paul. *The Neglected Voter: White Men and the Democratic Dilemma*. New York: Palgrave Macmillan, 2007.

Kurzman, Dan. *Soldier of Peace: The Life of Yitzhak Rabin, 1922–1995*. New York: HarperCollins, 1998.

Kyle, James H. *The Guts to Try*. New York: Ballantine Books, 1995.

Laingen, Bruce L. *Yellow Ribbon: The Secret Journal of Bruce Laingen*. New York: Brassey's, 1992.

Lamis, Alexander P. *The Two-Party South*. Second Edition. New York: Oxford University Press, 1990.

Lance, Bert. *The Truth of the Matter: My Life in and Out of Politics*. With Bill Gilbert. New York: Summit Books, 1991.

Lance, LaBelle. *This Too Shall Pass*. With Gary Sledge. New York: Bantam Books, 1978.

Langford, Edna, and Linda Maddox. *Rosalynn: Friend and First Lady*. Foreword by Rosalynn Carter. Old Tappan, NJ: Fleming H. Revell Company, 1980.

Lazo, Caroline. *Jimmy Carter: On the Road to Peace*. Parsippany, NJ: Dillon Press, 1996.

Lea, James F. Editor. *Contemporary Southern Politics*. Baton Rouge: Louisiana State University Press, 1988.

Lee, Dallas. *The Cotton Patch Evidence*. New York: Harper and Row, 1971.

LeoGrande, William M. *Our Own Backyard: The United States in Central America, 1977–1992*. Chapel Hill: University of North Carolina Press, 1998.

Lesher, Stephen. *George Wallace: American Populist*. New York: Addison-Wesley, 1993.

Leuchtenburg, William E. *The American President: From Teddy Roosevelt to Bill Clinton*. New York: Oxford University Press, 2015.

———. *In the Shadow of FDR: From Harry Truman to Ronald Reagan*. Ithaca, NY: Cornell University Press, 1983.

———. *The White House Looks South*. Baton Rouge: Louisiana State University Press, 2005.

Levine, Suzanne Braun, and Mary Thom. *Bella Abzug*. New York: Farrar, Straus and Giroux, 2007.

Lewis, Finlay. *Mondale: Portrait of an American Politician*. New York: Harper and Row, 1980.

Licklider, Roy E. *Political Power and the Arab Oil Weapon: The Experience of Five Industrial Nations*. Berkeley: University of California Press, 1988.

Lifset, Robert. Editor. *American Energy Policy in the 1970s*. Norman: University of Oklahoma Press, 2014.

Linenthal, Edward T. *Preserving Memory: The Struggle to Create America's Holocaust Museum*. New York: Penguin Books, 1995.

Lourie, Richard. *Sakharov: A Biography*. Hanover, NH: University Press of New England, 2002.

Love, Robert W. Jr. *History of the U.S. Navy. Vols. I & II*. Harrisburg, PA: Stackpole, 1991.

Lyman-Barner, Kirk, and Cori Lyman-Barner. Editors. *Fruits of the Cotton Patch: The Clarence Jordan Symposium 2012, Vol. II*. Eugene, Oregon: Cascade Books, 2014.

Mackey, Sandra. *The Iranians: Persia, Islam, and the Soul of a Nation*. With W. Scott Harrop. New York: Dutton, 1996.

Maddox, Robert L. *Preacher in the White House*. Nashville, TN: Broadman Press, 1984.

Maga, Timonthy P. *The World of Jimmy Carter: U.S. Foreign Policy, 1977–1981*. West Haven, CT; University of New Haven Press, 1994.

Major, John. *Prize Possession: The United States and the Panama Canal, 1903–1979*. New York: Cambridge University Press, 1993.

Marcus, Alan I., and Amy Sue Bix. *The Future is Now: Science and Technology Policy in America since 1950*. New York: Humanity Books, 2007.

Martin, Harold H. *A Good Man . . . A Great Dream: D. W. Brooks of Gold Kist*. Atlanta, GA: Gold Kist Inc., 1982.

Martin, Janet M. *The Presidency and Women: Promise, Performance, and Illusion*. College Station: Texas A&M Press, 2003.

Marton, Katai. *Hidden Power: Presidential Marriages that Shaped Our Recent History*. New York: Pantheon Books, 2001.

Mason, Jim. *No Holding Back: The 1980 John B. Anderson Presidential Campaign*. Lanham, MD: University Press of America, Inc., 2011.

Matthews, Chris. *Hardball: How Politics is Played by One Who Knows the Game*. Revised and Updated. New York: Touchstone, 1988.

Mattingly, Doreen. *A Feminist in the White House: Midge Costanza, the Carter Years, and America's Culture Wars*. New York: Oxford University Press, 2016.

Mattson, Kevin. *"What the Heck Are You Up To, Mr. President?": Jimmy Carter, America's "Malaise," and the Speech That Should Have Changed the Country*. New York: Bloomsbury, 2009.

May, Rollo. *The Courage to Create*. New York: W. W. Norton & Co., 1975.

Mazlish, Bruce, and Edwin Diamond. *Jimmy Carter: An Interpretative Biography*. New York: Simon & Schuster, 1979.

McCarty, Laura T. *Coretta Scott King: A Biography*. Westport, CT: Greenwood Press, 2009.

McClendon, Sarah. *Mr. President, Mr. President! My Fifty Years of Covering the White House*. Santa Monica, CA: General Publishing Group, Inc., 1996.

McCullough, David. *The Path Between the Seas: The Creation of the Panama Canal, 1870–1914*. New York: Simon & Schuster, 1977.

McFadden, Robert D., Joseph B. Treaster, and Maurice Caroll. *No Hiding Place: Inside Report on the Hostage Crisis*. New York: Times Books, 1981.

McGarr, Kathryn J. *The Whole Damn Deal: Robert Strauss and the Art of Politics*. New York: BBS Publications, 2011.

McLellan, David. *Unto Caesar: The Political Relevance of Christianity*. Notre Dame, IN: Notre Dame University Press, 1992.

McMath, Robert C., Jr. "Jimmy Carter: A Southerner in the White House?" In Jacoway, Elizabeth, Dan T. Carter. Lester C. Lamon, and Robert C. McMath Jr. Editors. *The Adaptable South: Essays in Honor of George Brown Tindall*. Baton Rouge: Louisiana State University Press, 1991, 237–263.

McMorrow, Fred. *Jimmy: The Candidacy of Carter*. New York: Whirlwind Book Company, 1976.

McMurry, Richard M. *Atlanta 1864: Last Chance for the Confederacy*. Lincoln: University of Nebraska Press, 2000.

———. *The Fourth Battle of Winchester: Toward a New Civil War Paradigm*. Kent, Ohio: Kent State University Press, 2002.

Meacham, Jon. *Destiny and Power: The American Odyssey of George Herbert Walker Bush*. New York: Random House, 2015.

Mearsheimer, John J., and Stephen M. Walt. *The Israel Lobby and U.S. Foreign Policy*. New York: Farrar, Straus and Giroux, 2007.

Melman, Yossi, and Dan Rviv. *Friends in Deed: Inside the U.S.-Israel Alliance*. New York: Hyperion, 1994.

Mendez, Antonio, and Matt Baglio. *Argo: How the CIA and Hollywood Pulled off the Most Audacious Rescue in History*. New York: Viking, 2012.

Michael, Deanna L. *Jimmy Carter as Educational Policymaker*. Albany: State University of New York Press, 2005.

Milani, Abbas. *The Shah*. New York: McMillan, 2011.

Miller, Aaron David. *The Much Too Promised Land: America's Elusive Search for Arab-Israeli Peace*. New York: Bantam Books, 2008.

Miller, Rory. *Inglorious Disarray: Europe, Israel and the Palestinians since 1967*. New York: Columbia University Press, 2011.

Miller, William Lee. *Yankee from Georgia: The Emergence of Jimmy Carter*. New York: Times Books, 1978.

Mills, Kay. *This Little Light of Mine: The Life of Fannie Lou Hamer*. New York: Dutton, 1993.

Milnes, Arthur. Editor. *Jimmy and Rosalynn Carter: A Canadian Tribute*. Kingston, ON, Canada: Queens University, 2011.

Minchew, Kaye Lanning. *Jimmy Carter: Citizen of the South*. Athens: University of Georgia Press, 2021.

Mitchell, Nancy. *Jimmy Carter in Africa: Race and the Cold War*. Stanford, CA; Stanford University Press, 2016.

Mondale, Walter. *The Good Fight: A Life in Liberal Politics.* With David Hage. New York: Scribner, 2010.

Morgan, David T. *New Crusades, New Holy Land: Conflict in the Southern Baptist Convention, 1969–1991.* Tuscaloosa: University of Alabama Press, 1996.

Morley, Morris H. *Washington, Somoza, and the Sandinistas: State and Regime in U.S. Policy toward Nicaragua, 1969–1981.* New York: Cambridge University Press, 1994.

Morris, Kenneth E. *Jimmy Carter: American Moralist.* Athens: University of Georgia Press, 1996.

Moyn, Samuel. *Human Rights and the Uses of History.* New York: Verso, 2014.

Muravchik, Joshua. *Making David into Goliath: How the World Turned against Israel.* New York: Encounter Books, 2014.

———. *The Uncertain Crusade: Jimmy Carter and the Dilemmas of Human Rights Policy.* Lanham, MD: Hamilton Press, 1986.

Murray, Robert K., and Tim H. Blessing. *Greatness in the White House: Rating the Presidents.* Second, Updated Edition. University Park: Pennsylvania State University Press, 1994.

Naftali, Timothy. *Blind Spot: The Secret History of American Counterterrorism.* New York: Basic Books, 2005.

Niebuhr, Reinhold. *Moral Man and Immoral Society: A Study in Ethics and Politics.* New York: Charles Scribner's Sons, 1932..

Nelson, W. Dale. *The President Is at Camp David.* Foreword by David Eisenhower. Syracuse, NY: Syracuse University Press, 1995.

Nelson, Willie. *It's a Long Story: My Life.* With David Ritz. New York: Little, Brown and Company, 2015.

Neustadt, Richard E. *Presidential Power and the Modern Presidents: The Politics of Leadership from Roosevelt to Reagan.* New York: The Free Press, 1990.

Nichols, Bruce. "Religious Conciliation between the Sandinistas and the East Coast Indians of Nicaragua." In Douglas Johnston and Cynthia Sampson. Editors. *Religion, the Missing Dimension of Statecraft.* Foreword by Jimmy Carter. New York: Oxford University Press, 1994, 64–87.

Nobles, Cynthia LeJeune. *The Delta Queen Cookbook: The History Of the Legendary Steamboat.* Baton Rouge: Louisiana State University Press, 2012.

Noriega, Manuel. *The Memoirs of Manuel Noriega, America's Prisoner.* With Peter Eisner. New York: Random House, 1997.

Norris, John. *Mary McGrory: The First Queen of Journalism.* New York: Viking, 2015.

Norton, Howard. *Rosalynn: A Portrait.* Plainfield, NJ: Logos International, 1977.

Norton, Howard, and Bob Slosser. *The Miracle of Jimmy Carter.* Plainfield, NJ: Logos International, 1976.

Notaker, Hallvard, Giles Scott-Smith, and David J. Snyder. Editors. *Reasserting America in the 1970s: U.S. Public Diplomacy and the Rebuilding of America's Image Abroad.* Manchester, UK: Manchester University Press, 1016.

Nwachuku, Levi A., and Godfrey N. Uzoigwe. Editors. *Troubled Journey: Nigeria since the Civil War.* Lanham, MD: United Press of America, 2004.

Oberdorfer, Don. *The Two Koreas: A Contemporary History.* Reading, MA: Addison-Wesley, 1997.

O'Brien, William Patrick. *Special History Study: Jimmy Carter National Historic Site and Preservation District, Georgia.* N. P., 1991.

Ojito, Mirta. *Finding Manana: A Memoir of A Cuban Exodus*. New York: Penguin Press, 2005.

Olson, Barbara. *The Final Days: The Last, Desperate Abuses of Power by the Clinton White House*. Washington, DC: Regnery Publishing, Inc., 2001.

O'Neill, Tip. *All Politics Is Local, and Other Rules of the Game*. With Gary Hymel. Holbrook, MA: Bob Adams, Inc., 1994.

———. *Man of the House: The Life and Political Memoirs of Speaker Tip O'Neill*. With William Novak. New York: Random House, 1987.

Oren, Michael B. *Power, Faith, and Fantasy: America in the Middle East 1776 to the Present*. New York: W. W. Norton and Co., 2007.

Owen, Robert B. "The Final Negotiation and Release in Algiers." In Warren Christopher, et al. Editors. *American Hostages in Iran: The Conduct of a Crisis*. New Haven, CT: Yale University Press, 1985, 297–324.

Packer, George. *Our Man: Richard Holbrooke and the End of the American Century*. New York: Alfred A. Knopf, 2019.

Pahlavi, Farah. *An Enduring Love: My Life with the Shah*. New York: Miramax Books, 2004.

Pahlavi, Mohammad Reza, the Shah of Iran. *Answer to History*. New York: Stein and Day, 1980.

Parry, Robert. *America's Stolen Narrative*. Arlington, VA: The Media Consortium, Inc., 2012.

———. *The October Surprise X-Files; The Hidden Origins of the Reagan-Bush Era*. Arlington, VA; The Media Consortium, 1996.

———. *Secrecy and Privilege: Rise of the Bush Dynasty from Watergate to Iraq*. Arlington, VA: The Media Consortium, Inc., 2004.

———. *Trick or Treason: The October Surprise Mystery*. New York: Sheridan Square Press, 1993.

Parry, Robert, Sam Parry, and Nat Parry. *Neck Deep: The Disastrous Presidency of George W. Bush*. Arlington, VA; The Media Consortium, Inc., 2007.

Pastor, Robert A. "The Carter Administration and Latin America: A Text of Principle." In John D. Martz. Editor. *United States Policy in Latin America: A Quarter Century of Crisis and Challenge*, Lincoln: University of Nebraska Press, 1988, 61–97.

Paterson, Thomas G. *Meeting the Communist Threat: Truman to Reagan*. New York: Oxford University Press, 1988.

Patterson, James T. *Restless Giant: The United States from Watergate to Bush v. Gore*. New York: Oxford University Press, 2005.

Pearce, Joseph. *Solzhenitsyn: A Soul in Exile*. Grand Rapids, MI: Baker Books, 1999.

Pendergrast, Mark. *For God, Country, and Coca-Cola: The Unauthorized History of the Great American Soft Drink and the Company that Makes It*. New York: Macmillan Publishing Co., 1993.

Perry, Barbara A. *Edward M. Kennedy: An Oral History*. New York: Oxford University Press, 2019.

Pierard, Richard V., and Robert D. Linder. *Civil Religion and the Presidency*. Grand Rapids, MI: Academic Books, 1988.

Pippert, Wesley G. Compiler. *The Spiritual Journey of Jimmy Carter*. New York: Macmillan, 1978.

Poinsett, Alex. *Walking with Presidents: Louis Martin and the Rise of Black Political Power*. New York: Rowan and Littlefield, 1997.

Polakow-Suransky, Sasha. *The Unspoken Alliance: Israel's Secret Relationship with Apartheid South Africa*. New York: Pantheon Books, 2010.

Pollack, Kenneth M. *The Persian Puzzle: The Conflict between Iran and America*. New York: Random House, 2004.

Polmer, Norman, and Thomas B. Allan. *Rickover: Controversy and Genius*. New York: Simon & Schuster, 1982.

Polmer, Norman, and K. J. Moore. *Cold War Submarines: U.S. and Soviet Design and Construction*. Washington, DC: Brassey's, Inc. 2002.

Pomper, Gerald. *The Election of 1976: Reports and Interpretations*. With Colleagues. New York: David McKay Company, Inc., 1977.

Powell, Jody. *The Other Side of the Story*. New York: William Morrow and Company, 1984.

Prados, John. *Keepers of the Keys: A History of the National Security Council from Truman to Bush*. New York: William Morrow and Company, 1991.

———. *Presidents' Secret Wars: CIA and Pentagon Covert Operations from World War II through the Persian Gulf*. Revised and Expanded Edition. Chicago: Elephant Paperbacks, 1996.

Priess, David. *The President's Book of Secrets: The Untold Story of Intelligence Briefings to America's Presidents from Kennedy to Obama*. New York: Public Affairs, 2016.

Quandt, William B. *Camp David: Peacemaking and Politics*. Washington, DC: The Brookings Institute, 1986.

———. *Peace Process: American Diplomacy and the Arab-Israeli Conflict since 1967*. Washington, DC: Brookings Institution, 1993.

Rabhan, David. *Conscious Coma: Ten Years in an Iranian Prison*. Foreword by President Jimmy Carter. Mexico Beach, FL: Dream Catcher Publishing, Inc., 2004.

Radcliffe, Donnie. *Simply Barbara Bush: A Portrait of America's Candid First Lady*. New York: Warner Books, 1989.

Reeves, Richard. *Convention*. New York: Harcourt Brace Jovanovich, 1977.

Reston, James. *Deadline: A Memoir*. New York: Random House, 1991.

Reidel, Bruce. *Avoiding Armageddon: America, India, and Pakistan to the Brink and Back*. Washington, DC: Brookings Institution Press, 2013.

———. *What We Won: America's Secret War in Afghanistan, 1979–89*. Washington, DC: Brookings Institution Press, 2014.

Ribuffo, Leo P. "God and Jimmy Carter." In Leo P. Ribuffo, *Right, Center, Left: Essays in American History*. New Brunswick, NJ: Rutgers University Press, 1992, 214–248.

———. "'Malaise' Revisited: Jimmy Carter and the Crisis of Confidence." In John Patrick Diggins. Editor. *The Liberal Persuasion: Arthur Schlesinger, Jr., and the Challenge of the American Past*. Princeton, NJ: Princeton University Press, 1997, 164–184.

———. *The Old Christian Right: The Protestant Far Right from the Great Depression to the Cold War*. Philadelphia: Temple University Press, 1983.

Ridley, Jasper. *Tito: A Biography*. London: Constable and Co. Limited, 1994.

Rivers, Charles. Editor. *Anwar Sadat: The Life and Legacy of The Egyptian President*. Lexington, KY: Charles Rivers Editors, 2016.

Rockefeller, David. *Memoirs*. New York: Random House, 2002.

Rodman, Peter W. *Presidential Command: Power, Leadership, and the Making of Foreign Policy from Richard Nixon to George W. Bush*. Introduction by Henry A. Kissinger. New York: Alfred A. Knopf, 2009.

Roessner, Amber. *Jimmy Carter and the Birth of the Marathon Media Campaign*. Baton Rouge: Louisiana State University Press, 2020.

Rogers, Mary Beth. *Barbara Jordan: American Hero*. New York: Bantam Books, 1998.

Ross, Dennis. *Doomed to Succeed: The U.S.-Israel Relationship From Truman to Obama*. New York: Farrar, Straus and Giroux, 2015.

Ross, Jerilyn. *Triumph Over Fear*. Foreword by Rosalynn Carter. New York: Bantam Books, 1994.

Rothkopf, David. *Running the World: The Inside Story of the National Security Council and the Architects of American Power*. New York: Public Affairs, 2004.

Rowan, Bobby. *Georgia's Modern Day Legislature: A Personal History of Georgia's Politics, 1962-1998*. Pine Mountain, GA: Main Street Printers, 1999.

Rozell, Mark J. *The Press and the Carter Presidency*. Boulder, CO: Westview Press, 1989.

Rubel, David. *IF I Had a Hammer: Building Homes and Hope with Habitat for Humanity*. Foreword by Jimmy Carter. Somerville, MA: Candlewick Press, 2009.

Rubenzer, Steven J., and Thomas R. Faschingbauer. *Personality, Character, & Leadership in the White House: Psychologists Assess the Presidents*. Washington, DC: Brassey's, Inc. 2004.

Rubin, Barnett. R. *The Search for Peace in Afghanistan: From Buffer State to Failed State*. New Haven, CT: Yale University Press, 1995.

Rusk, Dean. *As I Saw It*. As Told to Richard Rusk. New York: W. W. Norton, 1990.

Sabato, Larry J. *The Kennedy Half Century: The Presidency, Assassination, and Lasting Legacy of John F. Kennedy*. New York: Bloomsbury, 2013.

Sadat, Anwar el-. *In Search of Identity: An Autobiography*. New York: Harper & Row, Publishers, 1977.

Sadat, Jehan. *My Hope for Peace*. New York: Free Press, 2009.

———. *A Woman of Egypt*. New York: Simon & Schuster, 1987.

Sakharov, Andrei. *Memoirs*. New York: Alfred A. Knopf, 1990.

Salinger, Pierre. *America Held Hostage: The Secret Negotiations*. New York: Doubleday and Company, 1981.

Sandbrook, Dominic. *Eugene McCarthy: The Rise and Fall of Postwar American Liberalism*. New York: Anchor Books, 2005.

———. *Mad as Hell: The Crisis of the 1970s and the Rise of the Populist Right*. New York: Alfred A. Knopf, 2011.

Sarantakes, Nicholas Evan. *Dropping the Torch: Jimmy Carter, The Olympic Boycott, and the Cold War*. New York: Cambridge University Press, 2011.

Sargent, Daniel J. *A Superpower Transformed: The Remaking of American Foreign Relations in the 1970s*. New York: Oxford University Press, 2015.

Schaller, Michael. *The United States and China in the Twentieth Century*. Second Edition. New York: Oxford University Press, 1990.

Scheer, Robert. *Playing President*. New York: Akashic Books, 2006.

Schmidt, Helmut. *Men and Powers: A Political Retrospective*. New York: Random House, 1989.

Schmitz, David F. *The United States and Right-Wing Dictatorships*. New York: Cambridge University Press, 2006.

Schneller, Robert J., Jr. *Breaking the Color Barrier: The US Naval Academy's First Black Midshipmen and the Struggle for Racial Equality*. New York: New York University Press, 2005.

Schram, Martin. *Running for President: A Journal of the Carter Campaign*. New York: Penguin Books, 1976.

Schulman, Bruce J. *The Seventies: The Great Shift in American Culture, Society, and Politics.* New York: The Free Press, 2001.

Schulman, Bruce J., and Julian E. Zelizer. Editors. *Rightward Bound: Making America Conservative in the 1970s.* Cambridge, MA: Harvard University Press, 2008.

Shacochis, Bob. *The Immaculate Invasion.* New York: Viking, 1999.

Shawcross, William. *The Shah's Last Ride.* New York: Simon & Schuster, 1988.

Shipp, Bill. *The Ape-Slayer and Other Snapshots.* Macon, GA: Mercer University Press, 1997.

Shirley, Craig. *Rendezvous with Destiny: Ronald Reagan and the Campaign That Changed America.* Wilmington, DE: Intercollegiate Studies Institute, 2009.

Shogan, Robert. *Bad News: Where the Press Goes Wrong in the Making Of the President.* Chicago: Ivan R. Dee, 2001.

———. *Promises to Keep: Carter's First 100 Days.* New York: Thomas Y. Crowell Company, 1977.

Short, Bob. *Everything is Pickrick: The Life of Lester Maddox.* Macon, GA: Mercer University Press, 1999.

Shoup, Lawrence H. *The Carter Presidency and Beyond: Power and Politics in the 1980s.* Palo, CA: Ramparts Press, 1980.

Shrum, Robert. *No Excuses: Concessions of a Serial Campaigner.* New York: Simon & Schuster, 2007.

Shull, Steven A., and Lance T. LeLoup. *The Presidency: Studies in Public Policy.* Brunswick, OH: King's Court Communications Inc., 1979.

Sick, Gary. *October Surprise: America's Hostages in Iran and the Election of Ronald Reagan.* New York: Times Books, 1991.

———. *All Fall Down: America's Tragic Encounter with Iran.* New York: Penguin Books, 1985.

Sickman, Rocky. *Iranian Hostage: A Personal Diary of 444 Days in Captivity.* Topeka, KA: Crawford Press, 1982.

Sidey, Hugh. *Portraits of the Presidents: Power and Personality in the Oval Office.* New York: Time Books, 2000.

Sigal, Leon U. *Disarming Strangers: Nuclear Diplomacy with North Korea.* Princeton, NJ: Princeton University Press, 1998.

Sikkink, Kathryn. *Evidence for Hope: Making Human Rights Work in the 21st Century.* Princeton, NJ: Princeton University Press, 2017.

———. *Mixed Signals: U.S. Human Rights Policy and Latin America.* Ithaca, NY: Cornell University Press, 2004.

Silber, William L. *Volcker: The Triumph of Persistence.* New York: Bloomsburg Press, 2012.

Simmons, Dawn Langley. *Rosalynn Carter: Her Life and Work.* New York: Frederick Fell Publishers, Inc., 1979.

Simons, Howard. *Jewish Times: Voices of the American Jewish Experience.* Boston: Houghton Mifflin Harcourt, 1988.

Simpson, T. McNin, III. "Jimmy Carter and the Transformation of Southern Politics, 1953–1987." In James F. Lea. Editor. *Contemporary Southern Politics.* Baton Rouge: Louisiana State University Press, 1988.

Skierka, Volker. *Fidel Castro: A Biography.* Malden, MA: Polity Press, 2004.

Slotnick, Elliot E., and Jay E. Hakes, "Carter and the Judicial Recruitment Process." In Steven A. Shull and Lance T. LeLoup. Editors. *The Presidency: Studies in Public Policy.* Brunswick, OH: King's Court Communications Inc., 1979, 95–113.

Smith, Gaddis. *Morality, Reason, and Power: American Diplomacy in the Carter Years.* New York: Hill and Wang, 1986.

Smith, Gary Scott. *Faith and the Presidency: From George Washington to George W. Bush.* New York: Oxford University Press, 2006.

Smith, Hedrick. *The Power Game: How Washington Works.* New York: Random House, 1988.

Smith, Nancy Keagan, and Mary C. Ryan. Editors. *Modern First Ladies: Their Documentary Legacy.* Washington, DC: National Archives Trust Fund Board, 1990.

Smith, Wayne S. *The Closest of Enemies: A Personal and Diplomatic Account of U.S.-Cuban Relations since 1957.* New York: W. W. Norton, 1987.

Sokol, Jason. *There Goes My Everything: White Southerners in the Age of Civil Rights, 1945–1975.* New York: Alfred A. Knopf, 2006.

Solzhenitsyn, Alexander. *Warning to the West.* New York: Farrar, Strauss and Giroux, 1975.

———. *A World Split Apart.* New York: HarperCollins, 1978.

Sorensen, Ted. *Counselor: A Life at the Edge of History.* New York: HarperCollins, 2008.

Sparrow, Bartholomew. *The Strategist: Brent Scowcroft and the Call of National Security.* New York: Public Affairs, 2015.

Spiegel, Steven L. *The Other Arab-Israeli Conflict: Making America's Middle East Policy, from Truman to Reagan.* Chicago: University of Chicago Press, 1985.

Spirz, Bob. *Dylan: A Biography.* New York: W. W. Norton, 1989.

Spitzer, Robert J. "President, Congress and Foreign Policy." In David Gray Adler and Larry N. George. Editors. *The Constitution and the Conduct of American Foreign Policy.* Lawrence: University of Kansas Press, 1996. Pp. 85–113.

Spohr, Kristina. *The Global Chancellor: Helmut Schmidt & The Reshaping of the International Order.* New York: Oxford University Press, 2016.

Spruill, Marjorie J. *Divided We Stand: The Battle over Women's Rights and Family Values that Polarized American Politics.* New York: Bloomsbury, 2017.

———. "Gender and America's Right Turn." In Bruce J. Schulman and Julian E. Zelizer. Editors. *Rightward Bound: Making American Conservative in the 1970s.* Cambridge, MA: Harvard University Press, 2008, 71–89.

Stanley, Timothy. *Kennedy vs. Carter: The 1980 Battle for the Democratic Party's Soul.* Lawrence: University Press of Kansas, 2010.

Stapleton, Ruth Carter. *Brother Billy.* New York: Harper and Row, 1978.

———. *The Gift of Inner Healing.* Waco, TX: Word Books, 1976.

Stein, Judith. *Pivotal Decade: How the United States Traded Factories for Finance in the Seventies.* New Haven, CT: Yale University Press, 2010.

Stein, Kenneth W. *Heroic Diplomacy: Sadat, Kissinger, Carter, Begin, and the Quest for Arab-Israeli Peace.* New York: Routledge, 1999.

Strong, Robert A. *Working in the World: Jimmy Carter and the Making of American Foreign Policy.* Baton Rouge: Louisiana State University Press, 2000.

Stroud, Kandy. *How Jimmy Won: The Victory Campaign from Plains to the White House.* New York: William Morrow, 1977.

Sweig, Julia E. *Cuba: What Everyone Needs to Know.* New York: Oxford University Press, 2009.

Takeyh, Ray. *The Last Shah: America, Iran, and the Fall of the Pahlavi Dynasty.* New Haven: Yale University Press, 2021.

Tall, Jeffrey. *Submarines & Deep-Sea Vehicles.* San Diego, CA: Thunder Bay Press, 2002.

Talmadge, Herman E. *Talmadge: A Political Legacy, A Politician's Life.* With Mark Royden Winchell. Atlanta, GA: Peachtree Publishers, Ltd., 1987.

Teel, Leonard Ray. *Ralph Emerson McGill: Voice of the Southern Conscience.* Knoxville, TN: University of Tennessee Press, 2001.

Thatcher, Margaret. *The Downing Street Years.* New York: HarperCollins, 1993.

Thomas, Dylan. *The Collected Poems of Dylan Thomas, 1934–1952.* New York: New Directions Publishing Corporation, 1957.

Thomas, Helen. *Front Row at the White House: My Life and Times.* New York: Simon & Schuster, 1999.

———. *Thanks for the Memories, Mr. President.* New York: Scribner, 2002.

Thomas, Kenneth H., Jr. *The Rock House: McDuffie County, Georgia.* Atlanta, GA: N. P., 1974.

Thompson, Hunter S. *Fear and Loathing on the Campaign Trail—'72.* New York: Warner Books, Inc., 1985.

———. *The Great Shark Hunt.* New York: Ballentine Books, 1979.

Thompson, Kenneth W. Editor. *The Carter Presidency: Fourteen Intimate Perspectives of Jimmy Carter.* Lanham, MD: University Press of America, 1990.

Till, Brian. *Conversations with Power: What Great Presidents and Prime Ministers Can Teach Us about Leadership.* New York: Palgrave Macmillan, 2011.

Toobin, Jeffrey. *American Heiress: The Wild Saga of the Kidnapping, Crimes and Trial of Patty Hearst.* New York: Doubleday, 2016.

Toth, Endre, and Karoly Szelenyi. *The Holy Crown of Hungary.* Budapest: Kossuth Publishing, 1996.

Troy, Gil. *Affairs of State: The Rise and Rejection of the Presidential Couple since World War II.* New York: Free Press, 1997.

Truman, Margaret. *First Ladies.* New York: Random House, 1995.

Tuck, Stephen G. N. *Beyond Atlanta: The Struggle for Racial Equality in Georgia, 1940–1980.* Athens: University of Georgia Press, 2001.

Turner, Stansfield. *Burn Before Reading: Presidents, CIA Directors, and Secret Intelligence.* New York: Hyperion 2005.

———. *Secrecy and Democracy: The CIA in Transition.* Boston: Houghton Mifflin Co., 1985.

———. *Terrorism and Democracy.* Boston: Houghton Mifflin Co., 1991.

Tyler, Patrick. *A Great Wall: Six Presidents and China, An Investigative History.* New York: Public Affairs, 1999.

———. *Running Critical: The Silent War, Rickover, and General Dynamics.* New York: Harper and Row, 1986.

———. *A World of Trouble: The White House and the Middle East—from the Cold War to the War on Terror.* New York: Farrar Straus Giroux, 2011.

Updegrove, Mark K. *Destiny of Democracy: The Civil Rights Summit at the LBJ Presidential Library.* Austin: Tower Books, 2015.

———. *The Last Republicans: Inside the Extraordinary Relationship Between George H. W. Bush and George W. Bush.* New York: HarperCollins, 2017.

———. *Second Acts: Presidential Lives and Legacies after the White House.* Guilford, CT: The Lyons Press, 2006.

Vance, Cyrus. *Hard Choices: Critical Years in America's Foreign Policy.* New York: Simon & Schuster, 1983.

Velikonja, Mitja. *Religious Separation and Political Intolerance in Bosnia-Herzegovina.* College Station: Texas A&M University, 2003.

Vogel, Ezra F. *Deng Xiaoping and the Transformation of China.* Cambridge, MA: Belknap Press of Harvard University, 2011.

Volcker, Paul A. *Keeping at It: The Quest for Sound Money and Good Government.* With Christine Harper. Public Affairs: New York, 2018.

Wallace, Robert B., Jr. *Dress Her in White and Gold: A Biography of Georgia Tech and the Men Who Led Her.* Atlanta, GA: Georgia Tech Foundation, Inc., 1969.

Walters, Beth. Compiler. *A History of Plains, Georgia, 1885–1985.* Americus, GA: Gammage Print Shop, N.D.

Walton, Hanes, Jr. *The Native Son Presidential Candidate: The Carter Vote in Georgia.* New York: Praeger, 1992.

Ward, Jon. *Camelot's End: Kennedy vs. Carter and the Fight that Broke the Democratic Party.* New York: Twelve Hachette Book Group, 2019.

Watson, Robert P., and Anthony J. Eksterowicz. Editors. *The Presidential Companion: Readings on the First Ladies.* Second Edition. Columbia: University of South Carolina Press, 2006.

Weigel, George. *The Final Revolution: The Resistance Church and the Collapse of Communism.* New York: Oxford University Press, 1992.

Weiner, Tim. *Legacy of Ashes: The History of the CIA.* New York: Doubleday, 2007.

Weiss, Ellen, and Mel Friedman. *Jimmy Carter: Champion of Peace.* New York: Alladin Paperbacks, 2003.

Weisberg, Jacob. *Ronald Reagan.* New York: Henry Holt and Company, 2016.

Wells, Della Wager. *The First Hundred Years: A Centennial History of King and Spalding.* N. P., N. D.

———. *George Waldo Woodruff: A Life of Quiet Achievement.* Macon, GA: Mercer University Press, 1987.

Wells, Tim. *444 Days: The Hostages Remember.* New York: Harcourt Brace Jovanovich, 1985.

White, Theodore H. *America in Search of Itself: The Making of the President 1956–1980.* New York: Harper and Row, 1982.

Wilkie, Curtis. *Dixie: A Personal Odyssey through Events that Shaped the Modern South.* New York: Scribner's 2001.

Williams, Daniel K. *The Election of the Evangelical: Jimmy Carter, Gerald Ford, and the Presidential Contest of 1976.* Lawrence: University Press of Kansas, 2020.

———. *God's Own Party: The Making of the Christian Right.* New York: Oxford University Press, 2010.

Williford, William Bailey. *Americus through the Years.* Atlanta, GA: Cherokee Publishing Co., 1975.

Witcover, Jules. *Marathon: The Pursuit of the Presidency, 1972–1976.* New York: The Viking Press, 1977.

———. *Party of the People: A History of the Democrats.* New York: Random House, 2003.

Wood, Robert C. *Whatever Possessed the President?* Amherst: University of Massachusetts Press, 1993.

Woods, Randall B. *Prisoners of Hope: Lyndon B. Johnson, the Great Society, and the Limits of Liberalism.* New York: Basic Books, 2016.

Woodward, Bob. *The Agenda: Inside the Clinton White House.* New York: Simon & Schuster, 1994.

————. *Shadow: Five Presidents and the Legacy of Watergate*. New York: Simon & Schuster, 1999.

————. *Veil: The Secret Wars of the CIA 1981–1987*. New York: Pocket Books, 1987.

Woodward, C. Vann. *The Burden of Southern History*. Third Edition. Baton Rouge, LA: Louisiana State University Press, 1993.

Wooten, James T. *Dasher: The Roots and the Rising of Jimmy Carter*. New York: Summit Books, 1978.

Wright, Lawrence. *Thirteen Days in September: Carter, Begin, and Sadat at Camp David*. New York: Knopf, 2014.

Wright, Robert. *Our Man in Tehran*. New York: Other Press, 2010.

Wright, Robin. *In the Name of God: The Khomeini Decade*. New York: Simon & Schuster, 1989.

Young, Andrew. *An Easy Burden: The Civil Rights Movement and the Transformation of America*. New York: Harper- Collins, 1996.

Zeitz, Joshua. *Building the Great Society: Inside Lyndon Johnson's White House*. New York: Viking, 2018.

Zelizer, Julian E, "Conservatives, Carter, and the Politics of National Security." In Schulman and Julian E. Zelizer. Editors. *Rightward Bound: Making America Conservative in the 1970s*. Cambridge, MA: Harvard University Press, 2008, 265–287.

————. *Jimmy Carter*. New York: Times Books, 2010.

Zimmerman, W. Frederick. *SSN-23 Jimmy Carter U.S. Navy Submarine*. Ann Arbor, MI: Nimble Books LLC, 2007.

Articles

Abrams, Irwin. "The Nobel Prize and Jimmy Carter." *The Antioch Review* 62, No. 2 (Spring 2004): 355–362.

Allen, Henry. "Just Plains Folk." *The Washington Post/Potomac* (August 15, 1976).Bakhtiari, Bahman. "Parliamentary Elections in Iran." *Iranian Studies* 26, No. 3/4 (Summer–Autumn, 1993): 375–388.

Battelle, Phyllis. "Jimmy and Rosalynn: Living Well is the Best Revenge." *Woman's Day* (June 16, 1987).

Bergren, D. Jason. "'I Had a Different Way of Governing': The Living Faith of President Carter." *Journal of Church & State* 47, No. 1 (Winter 2005): 43-61.

Biello, David. "Where Did the Carter White House's Solar Panels Go?" *Scientific American* (6 August 2010). https://www.scientificamerican.com/article/carter-white-house-solar-panel-array/.

Bonafede, Dom. "No One Tries to Roll Over Jordan in the White House." *National Journal* (April 16, 1977): 580-584.

————. "Charles Kirbo—The President's One-Man 'Kitchen Cabinet.'" *National Journal* (July 22, 1978. 1152–1156.

Boney, F. N. "Georgia's First President: The Emergence Of Jimmy Carter." *Georgia Historical Quarterly* 72 (Spring 1988). 119–126.

Bourne. Peter G. "Jimmy Carter: A Profile." *The Yale Review* 72 (Autumn 1982):. 126–140.

Bowden, Mark. "Among the Hostage-Takers: The Iranian Students Twenty-Five Years Later." *The AtlanticMonthly* (December 2004): 76–96.

————. "The Desert One Debacle." *The AtlanticMonthly* (May 2006): 62–77.

Brill, Steven. "Jimmy Carter's Pathetic Lies." *Harper's Magazine* (March 1976): 77–88.

Brinkley, Douglas. "A Time for Reckoning: Jimmy Carter and the Cult of Kinfolk." *Presidential Studies Quarterly* (December 1999: 778–798.

———. "Bringing the Green Revolution to Africa: Jimmy Carter, Norman Borlaug, and the Global 2000 Campaign." *World Policy Journal* 13, No. 1 (Spring 1996). 53–63.

———. "Jimmy Carter's Modest Quest for Global Peace." *Journal of Foreign Affairs* 74, No. 6 (November–December 1995): 90–100.

———. "The Rising stock of Jimmy Carter." *Diplomatic History* 20, No. 4 (Fall 1996): 505–529.

Brooks, Jennifer E. "Winning the Peace: Georgia Veterans and the Struggle to Define the Political Legacy of World War II." *Journal of Southern History* 66, No. 3 (August 2000): 563–604.

Brzezinski, Zbigniew. "White House Diary, 1980." *Orbis* 32, No. 1 (Winter 1988): 32–48.

Callaghan, Karen J., and Simo Virtanen. "Revised Models of The 'Rally Phenomenon': The Case of the Carter Presidency." *Journal of Politics* 55, No.3 (August 1993): 756–764.

Carter, Jimmy. "The Challenge of Education for Health in America's Schools." *The Journal of School Health* 60, No. 4 (April 1990): 129

———. "The Geneva Initiative: A Promising Foundation for Peace." *Israel Journal of Politics, Economics, and Culture*, 2, No. 9 (2004): 9–11.

———. "The Greatest Human Rights Crime: War." *Emory International Review* 17, No. 1 (Spring 1990): 16.

———. "Human Rights: The Real Cost of War." *Security Dialogue 1992*, Vol. 23(4): 21–24.

———. "The Middle East Consultation: A Look to the Future." *Middle East Journal* 42, No. 2 (Spring 1988): 187–192.

———. "The Third World Is Not a Hopeless Place." *New Age Journal* 7, No. 2 (March 2001): 52.

———. "The United States and the Advancement of Human Rights Around the World." *Emory Law Journal* 40 (Summer 1991): 723–730.

Chambers, John Whiteclay, II. "Jimmy Carter's Public Policy Ex-Presidency." *Political Science Quarterly* 13, No. 3 Fall 1998): 405–461.

Chancey, Andrew S. "'A Demonstration Plot for the Kingdom Of God': The Establishment and Early Years of Koinonia Farm." *The Georgia Historical Quarterly* 75, No. 2 (Summer 1991): 321–353.

Chanley, Virginia A; "The First Lady as Presidential Advisor, Policy Advocate, and Surrogate: Rosalynn Carter and the Political Role of the First Lady." *White House Studies* 1, No. 4 (Fall 2001): 549–564.

Cobb, Charles, et al. "Jimmy Carter's Roots." *National Enquirer* (March 15, 1977): 47–48.

Cogan, Charles G. "Desert One and Its Disorders." *The Journal of Military History* 67, No. 1 (January 2003): 2012–2016.

Cohen, David B., and Chris J. Dolan. "Debunking the Myth: Carter, Congress, and the Politics of Airline Deregulation." *White House Studies* 1, No. 2 (Spring 2001): 197–204.

Conaway, Janelle. "Savvy Navigator of a Turbulent Canal." *Americas* 51, No. 1 (Feb. 1999): 16.

Coombs, Orde. "The Hand that Rocked Carter's Cradle." *New York* (June 14, 1976: 40–43.

Darling, Lynn. "'Passionless Presidency' and the Insider's Dilemma: James Fallows Defends His 'Honorable Criticism.'" *The Washington Post* (April 25, 1979).

DeRoche, Andrew J. "Standing Firm for Principles: Jimmy Carter and Zimbabwe." *Diplomatic History* 23, No. 4 (Fall 1999): 657–685.

Drew, Elizabeth. "A Reporter at Large: In Search of a Definition." *New Yorker* (August 27, 1979): 45–73.

Driemen, John. "Jimmy and Rosalyn." *Good Housekeeping* (January 1992): 100–101, 170, 172–173.

Edwards, George C. III. "Exclusive Interview: President Jimmy Carter." *Presidential Studies Quarterly* 28, No.2 (March 2008): 1-13.

Elowitz, Paul H. "Three Days in Plains." *Journal of Psychohistory* (Fall 1977): 175–199.

DELETEElzy, Martin I. "Camp David Accords Set Model for Lasting Peace, Piece by Piece." *The Austin (TX) American- Statesman* (September 17, 2003).

Fardella, Enrico. "The Sino-American Normalization: A Reassessment." *Diplomatic History* 33, No 4 (September 2009): 545–578.

Fallows, James. "The Passionless Presidency." *The Atlantic Monthly* (May and June1979): 33–48, 75–81.

Fontham, Elizabeth T. H., and Pelayo Corres. "Epidemiology Of Pancreatic Cancer." *Surgical Clinics of North America* 69 (June 1989). 551–567.

Foot, M. R. D. "Britain—Intelligence Services." *The Economist* (March 15, 1980): 54.

Forsythe, David P. "US Foreign Policy and Human Rights." *Journal of Human Rights* 1, No. 4 (December 2002): 501–521.

Garrison, Jean A. "Explaining Change in the Carter Administration's China Policy: Foreign Policy Adviser Manipulation of the Policy Agenda." *Asian Affairs: An American Review* 29, No. 2 (Summer 2002): 67–82.

Gaughan, Anthony. "Woodrow Wilson and the Rise of Militant Interventionism in the South." *Journal of Southern History* 55, No. 4 (November 1999): 771–808.

Gleijeses, Piero. "A Test of Wills: Jimmy Carter, South Africa, and the Independence of Nambia." *Diplomatic History* 34, no. 5 (November 2010): 853–892.

Godbold, E. Stanly, Jr. "Dusty Corners of the Mind: Jimmy Carter's Poetry." *Studies in the Literary Imagination* (Spring 1997):. 107–117.

Gorman, Siobhan, and Sydney J. Freedberg, Jr. "Carter and Turner on Intelligence Reform." *National Journal* 36, No. 41 (October 9, 2004): 3080–3082.

Green, Joshua. "Better Luck This Time." *The Atlantic* (July/August 2009): 78–86.

Grob, Gerald N. "Public Policy and Mental Illness: Jimmy Carter's Presidential Commission on Mental Health." *The Millbank Quarterly* 83, No. 3 (2005): 425–456.

Hall, Arthur L., and Peter G. Bourne. "Indigenous Therapists in a Southern Black Urban Community." *Archives of General Psychiatry* 28 (January 1973): 137–142.

Hellman, Lillian. "Plain Speaking with Mrs. Carter." *Rolling Stone* (November 18, 1976).

Hilton, Brian. "'Maximum Flexibility for Peaceful Change': Jimmy Carter, Taiwan, and the Recognition of the People's Republic of China." *Diplomatic History* 33, No. 4 (September 2009): 595–613.

Holifield, E. Brooks. "The Three Strands of Jimmy Carter's Religion." *The New Republic* (June 5, 1976): 15–17.

Holland, J. William. "The Great Gamble: Jimmy Carter and the 1979 Energy Crisis." *Prologue: Quarterly of the National Archives* 22, No. 1 (Spring 1990): 63–79.

Jensen, Faye Lind. "An Awesome Responsibility: Rosalynn Carter as First Lady." *Presidential Studies Quarterly* 20, No. 4 (Fall 1990): 769–775.

Jensen, Lloyd. "Negotiating Strategic Arms Control, 1969–1979." *Journal of Conflict Resolution* 28, No. 3 (September 1984): 535–559.

Jones, Blake W. "'How Does a Born-Again Christian Deal with a Born-Again Moslem?' The Religious Dimension of the Iranian Hostage Crisis." *Diplomatic History* 39, No. 3 (2015): 423–451.

Kaufman, Victor S. "The Bureau of Human Rights during the Carter Administration." *The Historian* 61, No. 1 (Fall 1998): 51–65.

Lisby, Gregory C. "Trying to Define What May Be Indefinable: The Georgia Literature Commission, 1953–1973." *The Georgia Historical Quarterly* 84, No. 1 (Spring 2000): 72–97.

Lynn, Katalin Kadar. "The Return of the Crown of St. Stephen and Its Subsequent Impact on the Carter Administration." *East European Quarterly* 34, No. 2 (Summer 2000). 181–209.

McDonald, Darren J. "Blessed are the Policy Makers: Jimmy Carter's Faith-Based Approach to the Arab-Israeli Conflict." *Diplomatic History* 39, No. 3 (2015): 452–476.

Methvin, Eugene H. "Guess Who Spells Disaster for Education?" *Reader's Digest* 124, No. 745 (May 1984): 89–94, 43.

Murphy, Reg. "The New Jimmy Carter." *The New Republic* (February 14, 1976): 14–17.

Mantzikow. Ioanis. "U. S. Foreign Policymaking toward Ethiopia and Somalia, 1974–1980." *African Journal of Political Science and International Relations* 4, No.6 (June 2010): 241–248.

Meroney, John. "'There's an Awakening in Our Country': A Q&A with Jimmy Carter." *The Atlantic* (July 13, 2015): https://www.theatalntic.com/politics/archive/2015/07/jimmy-carter-QA/398279

O'Conner, Charles S. "The Politics of Industrialization and Interracialism in Sumter County, Georgia: Koinonia Farm in the 1950s." *The Georgia Historical Quarterly* 89, No. 4 (Winter 2005): 505–527.

Osborne, John. "Carter Talk." *New Republic* (September 25, 1976): 15–20.

Peterson, Christian Philip. "The Carter Administration and The Promotion of Human Rights in the Soviet Union, 1977–1981." *Diplomatic History* 38, No. 3 (2014): 628–656.

Pfluger, Friedbert. "Human Rights Unbound: Carter's Human Rights Policy Reassessed." *Presidential Studies Quarterly* 19, No. 4 (Fall 1989): 705–717.

Pressman, Jeremy. "Explaining the Carter Administration's Israeli-Palestinian Solution." *Diplomatic History* 37, No. 5 (2013): 1117–1147.

Price, Reynolds. "Family Stories: The Carters of Plains." *Time* (January 3, 1977): 26, 29.

Primuth, Richard. "Ronald Reagan's Use of Race in the 1976 and 1980 Presidential Elections." *Georgia Historical Quarterly* 100, No. 1 (2016): 36–66.

Randolph, Eleanor. "The Carter Complex." *Esquire* (November 1977): 166–184.

Raymond, John, Jack Wilkinson, Selby McCash, Erv Cuevas, and Prentice Palmer. "Jimmy Carter: A Midterm Report." *Georgia* 16, No. 7 (February 1973).

Ruechel, Frank A. "Politics and Morality Revisited: Jimmy Carter and Reinhold Niebuhr." *Atlanta History* 37, No. 3 (Winter 1994): 19–39.

Rosati, Jerel A. "Jimmy Carter, a Man Before His Time? The Emergence and Collapse of the First Post-Cold War Presidency." *Presidential Studies Quarterly* 23, No. 3 (Summer 1993): 459–476.

Rozell, Mark J. "Carter Rehabilitated: What Caused the 39th President's Press Transformation?" *Presidential Studies Quarterly* 23, No. 3 (Spring 1993): 317–330.

Safran, Clair. "The Women in Jimmy Carter's Life." *Redbook Magazine* (October 1976): 82, 84, 92, 94.

Sanders, Randy. "'The Sad Duty of Politics': Jimmy Carter and the Issue of Race in His 1970 Gubernatorial Campaign." *The Georgia Historical Quarterly* 76, No. 3 (Fall 1992): 612–638.

Scheer, Robert. "Interview: Jimmy Carter." *Playboy Magazine* Vol. 6, No. 1 (November 1976): 132.

Schmidli, William Michael. "Institutionalizing Human Rights in U.S. Foreign Policy: U.S.-Argentine Relations, 1976–1980." *Diplomatic History* 35, No.2 (April 2011): 351–377.

Schmitz, David E., and Vanessa Walker. "Jimmy Carter and The Foreign Policy of Human Rights: The Development of A Post-Cold War Foreign Policy." *Journal of Diplomatic History* 28, No. 1 (January 2004: 1131–1143.

Shaffer, Martin B. "An Aerial Photograph of Presidential Leadership: President Carter's National Energy Plan Revisited." *Presidential Studies Quarterly* 25, No. 2 (Spring 1995): 286–299.

Shannon, Margaret. "A President in the Family." *The Atlanta Journal and Constitution Magazine* (January 16, 1977): 8–9, 19–23.

Simpson, T. McNin, III. "Restyling Georgia Courts." *Judicature* 59, No. 6 (January 1976): 282–287.

Sigal, Leon V. "Jimmy Carter Makes a Deal. (President Carter Defuses Conflict between U.S. and North Korea)." *Bulletin of the Atomic Scientists* 54, No. 1 (January 1998): 40–46.

Smith, Kathy B. "The First Lady Represents America: Rosalynn Carter in South America." *Presidential Studies Quarterly* 27, No. 3 (Summer 1997): 540–567.

Spann, Willie Carter. "The Other Carter." With Burton H. Wolfe. *Hustler* (May 1977): 49–52.

Stein, Kenneth W. "My Problem with Jimmy Carter." *The Middle East Quarterly* 14, No. 2 (Spring 2007): 1–8.

Stevens, Simon. "From the Viewpoint of a Southern Governor: The Carter Administration and Apartheid, 1977–81." *Diplomatic History* 36, No. 5 (November 2012): 843–880.

Stohl, Michael, David Carleton, and Steven E. Johnson. "Human Rights and U.S. Foreign Assistance from Nixon to Carter." *Journal of Peace Research* 21, No. 3 (September 1984: 215–226Strong, Robert A. "Recapturing Leadership: The Carter Administration and the Crisis of Confidence." *Presidential Studies Quarterly* 16, No. 4 (Fall 1986): 636–650.

Terry, Janice J. "The Carter Administration and the Palestinians." *Arab Studies Quarterly* 12, No. 1/2 (Winter/Spring 1990): 153–166.

Thompson, Hunter S. "Jimmy Carter and the Great Leap of Faith: An Endorsement with Fear and Loathing." *Rolling Stone* 214 (June 3, 1976): 54–60.

Tyler, Patrick. "The (Ab)Normalization of U.S.-Chinese Relations: Cabinet Warfare." *Foreign Affairs* 78, No. 5 (September–October, 1999: 93–123.

Walker, Breck. "'Friends, but not Allies'–Cyrus Vance and the Normalization of Relations with China." *Diplomatic History* 33, No. 4 (September 2009): 579–613.

Wall, James M. "Jimmy Carter: Doing Work that Speaks for Itself." *The Christian Century* 107, No.17 (November 1990): 515-516.

———. Jimmy Carter: Finding a Commonality of Concern. *The Christian Century* 107, No. 18 (December 1990): 555-556.

Waugh, William L., Jr. "The Structure of Decision-Making in the Iranian Hostage Rescue Attempt and Its Implications for Conflict Management." *Conflict Quarterly* (Spring 1990): 26–40.

Wested, Odd Arne. "Secrets of the Second World War: The Russian Archives and the Reinterpretation of Cold War History." *Diplomatic History* 2, No. 2 (Spring 1997): 259–271.

Whitney, Kathleen Marie. "Sin, FRAPH, and the CIA: U.S. Covert Action in Haiti." *Southwestern Journal of Law and Trade in the Americas* 3, No. 2 (1996): 303–332.

Wilkie, Curtis. "Blessed is the Peacemaker: The Resurrection of Jimmy Carter." *The Boston Globe Magazine* (August 12, 1990).

Williams, Miller. "A Conversation with Jimmy Carter." *Image: LA Journal of the Arts and Religion* 24 (Fall 1999): 61.

Wills, Brian S. "Georgia History in Pictures: D. W. Brooks: Gold Kist's Goodwill Ambassador." *The Georgia Historical Quarterly* 74, No. 3 (Fall 1990: 487–502.

Wills, Garry. "The Underestimation of Jimmy Carter." *Notre Dame Magazine* (Summer 1985): 18–21.

———. "The Plains Truth: An Inquiry into the Shaping of Jimmy Carter." *Atlantic* (June 1976): 49–54.

Woodward, C. Vann. "The Best?" *New York Review of Books* (April 3, 1980).

Index

For the benefit of digital users, indexed terms that span two pages (e.g., 52–53) may, on occasion, appear on only one of those pages.

concern of Jewish Americans, Israelis,
12, 88–89
Gallup poll of voters, 70
Jones's negative comments, 73
Quinn's positive assurances to voters, 38
Bosnian War, 578–79, 581–82. *See also*
Izetbegovic, Alija; Karadzic,
Radovan
Boston Globe newspaper, 395
Bourne, Peter, 17, 552
advisory role to Carter, 61–62
resignation from cabinet, 239–40
role in tackling world hunger, 222–23
Boutros-Ghali, Boutros, 248–49, 576
boycott of 1980 Olympic Games, 384–85,
387, 392–93, 398–400
boycott of the Olympic Games, 384–85
Brahimi, Lakhdar, 644–45, 656, 662–63
Brandeis, Louis, 635
Brands, H. R., 768–69n.44
Branson, Richard, 637
Brazil, travels/meetings, 218
Brezhnev, Leonid, 114, 126
condemnation of plans for a neutron
bomb, 209
distrust of Middle East peace deal, 189
heated exchange with Carter, 381
human rights and, 135
letter exchange with Carter, 129–30,
135–36, 209
pre-SALT II summit research
on, 312–13
refusal to support Camp David
agreement, 263
briefing book (of J. Carter), theft of,
456, 514–15
Brill, Steven, 32
Brookings Institute, 11
Brooks, D. W., 222–23
Brooks, Garth, 670, 672, 673
Brown, Harold, 63–64, 99, 216–17, 359,
404, 481–82, 522–23
Brown, Jerry, 37, 42, 55, 66–67
*Brown v. Topeka, Kansas Board of
Education*, 310
Brundtland, Gro, 659–60, 667
Bryant, Thomas E., 128–29, 150, 151–
52, 181

Brzezinski, Muska, 273
Brzezinski, Zbigniew, 9, 10, 17, 25–26
address to World Jewish Congress, 395
advice to Carter on Afghanistan,
375, 379
advice to Carter on Pakistan, 380
announcement of Camp David
summit, 243
appearance on *Meet the Press*, 274
attendance at Ford Library and Museum
symposium, 522
comparison to Vance, 231
complaints about the CIA, 268
conversation with Dobrynin, 271
in entourage to Venezuela, 217
inappropriate comments on SALT
II, 274
knowledge of planned Russian invasion
of Afghanistan, 347
letter to Carter about the Soviets, 110
meeting with Special Coordinating
Committee on storming of U.S.
embassy in Tehran, 357–58, 359
post-China visit with Carter, 274
receipt of Presidential Medal of
Freedom, 481–82
role as national security advisor, 98–
99, 110
role at Camp David Arab-Israeli peace
conference, 248, 258–59
role in hostage rescue plan, 404
secret visit to Peking, 273
strained relationship with
Vance, 274–75
trip to Algeria, 355–56
warning about selling bombers to Saudi
Arabia, 223
warnings on challenges in foreign
policy, 123
warnings on India's ruling Congress
Party, 123–24
weekly briefings for Rosalynn, 112, 113
witness to Presidential Proclamation
483, 108–9
Bumpers, Betty, 561, 612
Bumpers, Dale, 14
Bunau-Varilla, Philippe, 173
Bundy, McGeorge, 90, 99